PASTON LETTERS AND PAPERS OF THE FIFTEENTH CENTURY

Part III

Early English Text Society

S.S. 22

2005

PASTON LETTERS AND PAPERS OF THE FIFTEENTH CENTURY

EDITED BY

RICHARD BEADLE

AND

COLIN RICHMOND

PART III

Published for

THE EARLY ENGLISH TEXT SOCIETY

by the

OXFORD UNIVERSITY PRESS

2005

OXFORD
UNIVERSITY PRESS

Great Clarendon Street, Oxford OX2 6DP

Oxford University Press is a department of the University of Oxford.
It furthers the University's objective of excellence in research, scholarship,
and education by publishing worldwide in

Oxford New York

Auckland Cape Town Dar es Salaam Hong Kong Karachi
Kuala Lumpur Madrid Melbourne Mexico City Nairobi
New Delhi Shanghai Taipei Toronto

With offices in

Argentina Austria Brazil Chile Czech Republic France Greece
Guatemala Hungary Italy Japan Poland Portugal Singapore
South Korea Switzerland Thailand Turkey Ukraine Vietnam

Oxford is a registered trade mark of Oxford University Press
in the UK and in certain other countries

Published in the United States
by Oxford University Press Inc., New York

First published 2005

British Library Cataloguing in Publication Data
Data available

Library of Congress Cataloging in Publication Data
Data available

ISBN 0-19-722423-7 978-0-19-722423-6

1 3 5 7 9 10 8 6 4 2

Typeset by Anne Joshua, Oxford
Printed in Great Britain
on acid-free paper by
Print Wright Ltd., Ipswich

PREFACE

THIS CONTINUATION of Norman Davis's edition of *Paston Letters and Papers of the Fifteenth Century* has been undertaken at the invitation of the Council of the Early English Text Society, and we are indebted to the Honorary Director, Professor J. A. Burrow, and to the Editorial Secretary, Dr Helen Leith Spencer, for continued advice and practical assistance. Other members of the Council who have lent help at various stages include Dr A. I. Doyle, Professor Douglas Gray, Mr R. F. S. Hamer, Professor Anne Hudson and Professor M. B. Parkes. We are particularly indebted to Dr Alison Truelove, who worked for a year under the Society's auspices as a research assistant on the project. Her contribution is reflected especially in the selection and organisation of the glossary, in the compilation of the index, and in the collation of many of the texts with the original manuscripts.

The opportunity to consult Norman Davis's papers and to make use of his photostats of many of the manuscripts (the photography of which was originally funded by the Leverhulme Trust) came through the generosity of the University of Otago, on behalf of the Norman Davis Estate. Particular thanks are due to Professor A. G. Fox, of the University of Otago, whose attention to these materials while they were still in New Zealand significantly assisted our work.

Many colleagues in the field of fifteenth-century studies have given of their time and expertise to assist us. Dr Anthony Smith has been a constant source of advice, and his unrivalled knowledge of Sir John Fastolf's estate business and litigation could not have been more generously placed at our disposal. We also acknowledge with gratitude the help we have received on specific points from Dr Helen Castor, Dr Alison Hanham, Dr G. L. Harriss, Dr Rosemary Horrox, Professor Jonathon Rose, Paul and Elizabeth Rutledge and Dr Daniel Wakelin. Acknowledgement of the crucial importance of the late Roger Virgoe's work in relation to the letters will be found in a number of places below.

We are indebted to the following for permission to publish the texts contained in manuscripts in their keeping: the British Library Board, the President and Fellows of Magdalen College, Oxford, and the authorities at the Bodleian Library, Oxford, the Folger Shakespeare Library, Washington D. C., the Gloucestershire Record Office, Gloucester, the Houghton Library, Harvard University, Cambridge MA., the library of the University of Illinois,

Urbana-Champaign IL., the Norfolk Record Office, Norwich, the Northamptonshire Record Office, Northampton, Pembroke College, Cambridge, and Lord Walpole of Wolterton, Mannington Hall, Norwich. We wish to thank for their courteous assistance the staffs of all the aforementioned libraries and archives, and to mention especially Dr Robin Darwall-Smith, archivist of Magdalen College, Oxford, for his unfailing patience and good humour in the face of repeated and extended calls upon his time.

Writing shortly after the publication of Part I of this edition, Norman Davis recalled James Gairdner's reflection upon the nature of the task confronting an editor of the Paston Letters:

> An almost perfect edition, no doubt, might conceivably be produced with considerable labour and expense if anyone could be induced to devote the necessary time and energy to the task of collating all the letters with the long-lost originals, now that they have been so completely recovered, and supplying all the missing passages. But so great a work, even if the editor succeeded after all in including all the stray Paston Letters of the period, would hardly justify, even in a younger and less occupied man than myself, the sacrifices that it would involve.

'I have often, in moments of faint-heartedness,' added Davis, 'thought he was right. But in fact he was not, as soon became evident when his texts began to be used as sources of detailed linguistic information' ('On editing the Paston Letters', 1973, p. 140). Following where Davis led has given us some awareness of the sacrifices involved in seeking to establish a trustworthy text of these writings. His editorial method, concentrating in the first instance on the handwriting and language of each document in isolation, and then in relation to other work by its writer or scribe together with its date, reaped rewards (and difficulties) that Gairdner was in no position to anticipate. In Part III we have sought to bring Davis's work to a degree of completion that we hope he would have found acceptable. The avenues for further enquiry presented by the letters and papers in all three parts of this edition are virtually limitless, and we offer this continuation of Norman Davis's work not as a conclusion, but as a new point of departure for the study of the Pastons and their world.

Richard Beadle
Cambridge

Colin Richmond
Woodbridge

CONTENTS

CONTENTS

LIST OF ILLUSTRATIONS

PLATES (*at end*)

INTRODUCTION

In 1971, shortly after the publication of Part I of his edition of *Paston Letters and Papers of the Fifteenth Century*, Norman Davis gave a conference paper entitled 'On Editing the Paston Letters', which included an informal but important account of the origin and gestation of his work. Since the paper is not well known and the publication in which it appeared not widely available, the passage may be quoted at length here:[1]

A lot of what needs to be done is work for a drudge, who can take comfort from the thought that he is as likely to be as harmless as a lexicographer. Not quite all of it is, for the most important single task is to get to know the characters, their concerns, and their handwritings if possible; and I have found that this takes long years and cannot be rushed. It is really work not for one drudge but for a team, which should include linguists, palaeographers and historians of various special talents. Here, in order to explain the form in which the first part has appeared, I hope I may be allowed a brief chapter of autobiography. Something like twenty years ago I suggested to the Clarendon Press that a new edition of the letters would be useful to students of medieval English. The Delegates of the Press—who had not at that time thought of an edition—fairly enough took the view that this would be too narrow an approach, and that historians were the right sort of people to do it. The late Bruce McFarlane of Magdalen, who knew more about fifteenth-century England than anyone else of his generation, was commissioned to prepare an edition, and recruited historians to help him. I suggested to him that it might expedite matters if I, as the drudge, made the transcription, and perhaps a glossary, while he and the historians wrote the commentary. But he could not believe that this would work; and I dropped the idea of an edition altogether until C. T. Onions, then Director of the Early English Text Society, suggested to me that whatever the historians might do the Paston Letters ought to be edited with the interests of English scholars in mind, and that the E.E.T.S. should be prepared to publish such an edition. I thought he was right; but this meant working out how so intricate a body of material could be satisfactorily fitted into a programme that was committed to a very various series of texts at the rate of two modest-sized volumes a year. Gairdner had of course, rightly from his point of view, attempted to begin at the beginning and go on in chronological order to the end. I thought that this was not necessarily the best order for readers interested in the language and expression of individual writers, especially members of a single family many of whose letters were to each other. By an accident of preservation it happens that the material falls into three main types—letters written by members of the Paston family and their wives; letters written to them by employees and friends; and miscellaneous other documents

[1] 'On Editing the Paston Letters', *English Studies Today* (1973), pp. 135–48 (146–8).

related to their affairs. It happens also that the first two of these classes are of very roughly equal bulk, the third much smaller. It seemed sensible, therefore, to divide the papers into these three sections—from the family, to the family, and the rest—and to include this third section in the final volume which would contain notes, glosses and the essential indexes and concordances. I must leave it to others to judge how satisfactory this arrangement is—it is necessarily provisional until the indexes make the material properly accessible. To me it seems to have the advantage of giving the family writings the prominence they deserve, and showing each author in action in a continuous series . . . so that his linguistic habits, stylistic development, and general interests can be taken in without the shuffling that a general chronological arrangement entails. But the disadvantages are obvious too.

The plan was devised, then, largely to suit the needs of E.E.T.S. But by the time that Part I, the 400 odd family letters and papers, was coming towards completion the E.E.T.S. queue was long and we did not know quite what to do with what would have to be at least two volumes of Part I alone. Meanwhile the historians' project had come to nothing. I do not know why—other interests somehow competed, the team dissolved; McFarlane died grievously before his time, leaving nothing whatever towards an edition of the Paston Letters. The Clarendon Press generously took up my old suggestion as a *pis aller* and E.E.T.S. was relieved of its problem.

Some of these remarks elaborate a little on information that Davis had already given in the Preface and the first section of the Introduction to Part I, but they are worth reprinting here since they also contain the clearest statement we have of his view that Parts I and II of the edition should be regarded as provisional until the ancillary material, 'the essential indexes and concordances' that he envisaged for inclusion in Part III had appeared. Davis died on 2 December 1989, and his British Academy obituarist wrote with feeling of the scholarly community's disappointment that the 'magisterial and definitive achievement' represented by Parts I and II of *Paston Letters and Papers of the Fifteenth Century* had not been followed by the fulfilment of the project in the shape of Part III.[1] Moreover, Parts I and II of the edition were by this time out of print, and had even become notoriously difficult to obtain *d'occasion*. In 1992 the Council of the Early English Text Society, of which Davis had been Honorary Director, resolved upon a project that was intended to lead towards a reissue of his work as part of the series for which it had originally been destined, together with a third volume which would serve to complete the project along the lines he had envisaged.

The form in which Part III now appears reflects certain changes in circumstance which have rendered some aspects of Davis's original plan obsolete, while making provision for other kinds of material that he did not envisage.[2] It is probably fair to say that recent studies of the Paston and Fastolf papers by Colin Richmond, Roger Virgoe, Anthony Smith, Helen Castor and others have, in the elucidation of circumstantial and prosopographical detail,

[1] Douglas Gray, 'Norman Davis 1913–1989', *Proceedings of the British Academy*, lxxx (1993), 261–73 (272).

[2] Part I, p. xxiii.

gone far beyond the 'notes on persons and events' that Davis might have had in mind to include in Part III. Likewise, where Davis had envisaged 'some discussion of the language', it is now difficult to see how, in the space available in an introduction, this could usefully be pursued beyond his own extensive series of studies in this field (some of them written after the publication of Parts I and II), given the very large number of writers represented in the collection.[1] On the other hand, the need for 'the text of some associated papers which are outside the classes covered in Parts I and II, a glossary, and indexes' is still plainly evident, and we feel sure that to this list Davis would have subjoined further notes of additions and corrections of the kind that he included in Part II.

Before proceeding with Part III it was naturally necessary to consult Davis's own papers—most generously placed at our disposal by the University of Otago—for further indications of how he intended to proceed, and for any work-in-progress that might have survived. It was disappointing that nothing was to be found towards the selection, transcription or editing of texts that might be included in Part III, and no material directly relevant to the compilation of a glossary.[2] Invaluable, however, have been a set of index cards bearing entries for persons, places etc. not incorporated in the Select Index which had been included, as a result of a change of plan, at the end of Part II.[3] The entries on these cards have been merged with the Select Index (which has accordingly been removed from Part II), and into this body of material have been inserted entries for the texts now appearing in Part III, so that there now exists a consolidated index covering the documents printed in all three parts of the edition.

As well as a conventional index and a glossary Davis also envisaged other forms of ancillary material for Part III, but he was not specific about their precise nature. We have interpreted his intentions in two ways, of which one reflects with some probability what he is likely to have had in mind, while the second may go beyond his original plan. In the first place we have included a concordance of this edition with the previous editions that possess independent textual authority: those of Fenn (1787–1823) and Gairdner (1900–1 and 1904). It is ordered according to the numbering of the documents in Gairdner's 'new and complete Library edition' of 1904, and includes manuscript references for the documents.[4] It is thus possible to see the number

[1] See the Select Bibliography below for recent studies of the letters, and for a listing of Davis's publications on their language.

[2] Two sheets in Davis's hand bear a list of some thirty-five Gairdner (1900–1) numbers headed 'Texts to be given in Part III', but it must date from an early stage in the planning of the project, since a number of items on it appear in Part II.

[3] Part II, p. v.

[4] The prototype for this listing will be found in H. S. Bennett, *The Pastons and their England* (Cambridge, 1922; 2nd. edn. 1932, reprinted with corrections 1968) Appendix IV, pp. 265–76; cf. Part II, p. vi. Gairdner's edition of 1904 also exists in a modern reduced photographic reprint (Gloucester: Alan Sutton, 1983), though with the accidental omission of some material (e.g. letters no. 258 and 259).

given to each document in the present edition alongside references to where they are printed, wholly or in part (p), or given in abstract (a), in the editions of Fenn and Gairdner. The same information also appears in the Headnotes to the documents printed in Parts I–III.

The second long listing of the letters and papers given in this edition may or may not have formed part of Davis's original plan. Davis was no less conscious than users of Parts I and II that his arrangement of most of the letters by author and recipient was made at the expense of the historical sweep, drama, and general convenience of reference that many readers had become accustomed to through the use of Gairdner's chronologically arranged editions. In order to offset this disadvantage we have included what we term a Working Chronology of the letters and papers. The heading is chosen advisedly. Any attempt to order these materials chronologically must make large allowance for the fact that a significant number of the documents are, and are likely to remain for the foreseeable future, datable only with varying degrees of probability or approximation. Internal evidence for their dates may be open to different interpretations, and new external information from other sources of record is constantly being brought to bear. Fresh discovery of a firm date for a particular letter may go on to fix, alter or unsettle the dates assigned to other documents, and so on. Consequently, any chronology of the collection will inevitably possess many uncertain and temporary features, and it will soon pass into obsolescence. A great many features of Gairdner's chronological arrangement (and, it should be added, his information about the attribution of many letters) were thus superseded as a result of Davis's different angle of editorial approach. The issue is now thrown into particular relief by the fact that some of the datings offered by Davis in Parts I and II have themselves been revised in the light of new external information, or by renewed scrutiny of the existing evidence. Redated documents in the Working Chronology are marked with an asterisk, and the dates offered by Davis have been shown in square brackets, since they still appear in their places in Parts I and II. Evidence for the new dates according to which the papers concerned are now placed is discussed separately, in the list of Additions and Corrections to Parts I and II.

For reasons explained above, the selection and arrangement of the letters and papers given in Part III have been carried out *ab initio*, though the numbering of the documents themselves continues uninterrupted from the sequence of Related Documents which Davis placed in the latter section of Part II. First, there are a number of Paston documents which Davis would have included in Parts I or II, had they come to his attention in time, though a few of them, such as the agreements between John Paston II and Bishop Wainfleet (nos. 947–8) he might himself have been reserving for Part III. Most of these Paston papers have not been printed until now, and they are placed in a separate section at the beginning of the sequence in Part III, headed

Additional Letters and Papers of the Paston Family. The ordering by writer follows the arrangement favoured by Davis for Parts I and II. Among the most important of these are the documents relating to the family's struggle to acquire and retain possession of the manor of East Beckham, an episode whose importance has only been fully grasped since Davis's time.[1] A number of them are from among the papers deposited at the Norfolk Record Office by W. Ketton-Cremer of Felbrigg Hall not long before the publication of Part II of Davis's edition in 1976. As has been observed, the manner in which the East Beckham documents eluded Davis replicated in miniature Gairdner's frustrating experience in attempting to trace a larger body of Paston papers a century before:

> Gairdner suspected that other manuscripts might also be recovered, and asked George Frere, then head of the Frere family, whether they might be at his house, Roydon Hall near Diss. He tells with much feeling how Frere replied that nothing was known of them, how he eventually went on with his edition, and how after he had sent the third volume to press Frere sent a message that a number of letters had come to light.[2]

So it was that Davis wrote to Colin Richmond in August 1977:

> I did not know about the Ketton Cremer papers, and am of course most grateful to you for telling me about them. It would have been more convenient if I had heard years ago, naturally; but much better late than never. I am a little surprised that Ketton Cremer didn't tell me, because we had some correspondence when I was working on my little selection [published in 1958] and he was very amiable in other matters; perhaps it didn't strike him that they might be relevant.[3]

Also of primary importance among the additional Paston family papers are three unpublished late letters of William Paston II, now in the Northamptonshire Record Office (nos. 943–5). These are especially significant since they did not form part of the great mass of papers that passed out of the possession of the family and into the hands of the Norfolk antiquaries during the eighteenth century.[4] Like the two letters now at Belvoir Castle, also from William II (nos. 108–9), they are rare survivals of Paston missives archived by their recipient, and, as explained below, they also happen to differ in appearance from the rest of the collection, having been written on long narrow strips of paper carried as rolls, rather than on the normal rectangular sheet. The business affairs of William II and his mother Agnes are represented by a hitherto unpublished estate paper in the Bodleian (no. 941), and those of Margaret Paston by a document formerly in the Phillipps collection, now in

[1] Richmond, *First Phase*, Chapter 3, pp. 64–116.

[2] Part I, p. xxviii.

[3] Colin Richmond, 'The Lithuanian Fragments: Homage to Lithuania', *Journal of Historical Sociology*, 14 (2001), 361–73 (367).

[4] Part I, pp. xxv–xxvii; see also D. Stoker, '"Innumerable Letters of Good Consequence in History": the Discovery and First Publication of the Paston Letters', *The Library*, 6th ser., xvii (1995), 107–155.

the Norfolk Record Office (no. 946). John Paston III's concerns are further reflected in two legal documents, one now in the United States (no. 949) and another that has lain unnoticed amongst the Stowe Charters in the British Library (no. 950). A short letter from John Paston I to one of his estate servants (no. 940, showing him in a more favourable light than he usually appears) must have come to Davis's attention in the Fastolf archives at Magdalen after Parts I and II had been published, since a photocopy of the manuscript was found among his papers.

We have found that the larger body of documents printed in Part III, many of them also for the first time (nos. 951–1051), consists of letters and papers best described as relating chiefly to Sir John Fastolf and his wide circle of associates. This section is so headed, and the documents within it placed as far as possible in a chronological ordering. Fastolf was a close neighbour and distant relative of the Pastons,[1] and many of these papers shed light on how their fortunes became intertwined. The convergence of Paston and Fastolf concerns is evident even in the earliest letters preserved among the Fastolf estate papers at Magdalen (see nos. 951–2 of 1422–5), and William Paston I appears to have been active as a legal agent for Fastolf from at least as early as 1426.[2] Margaret Mautby's marriage to John Paston I in 1440 brought the Pastons into kinship with Fastolf (see no. 955, which perhaps bears upon the making of this match), and the growing importance of John I in the conduct of Fastolf's business affairs and litigation is evident from 1450.[3]

Many of the letters dating from after 1450 are among the Fastolf papers now collected in BL Additional MS 39848, from which Davis extracted those addressed to John Paston I for inclusion in Part II. Others of the same period are scattered among the predominantly Paston papers in BL Additional MSS 27443–4, 34888 and 43488–9. In many cases these letters have hitherto been given only in abstract by Gairdner, or printed in part (sometimes without notice of the fact) by Fenn, and reprinted in the same partial form by Gairdner. An important group of documents bearing on Fastolf's relations with his stepson Stephen Scrope are among the Castle Combe manuscripts given to the British Museum in 1870 by the geologist and political economist George Poulett Scrope (BL Additional MSS 28205–13 and Additional Charters 18207–556).[4] Other Fastolf letters are found among the various classes of estate documents in the archives of Magdalen College, Oxford.

[1] See Part I, p. lv, n. 10, referring to what is now no. 996, lines 119 and 128, and Part II, p. xxv.

[2] See CUL Add. 6968 (Sandford's Geneaology of the Paston Family), p. 12, which gives a copy of a document of that date appointing William Paston I (among others) as an attorney to act on Fastolf's behalf in pursuing the executors of Henry V and Thomas, Duke of Exeter for sums said to be owing to him for military sevice. BL Additional Charter 18266 is a Castle Combe *inspeximus* of 1433 witnessed by Fastolf, Willam Paston I, Stephen Scrope, Henry Inglose and others.

[3] See for example nos. 457 and 985 (line 41).

[4] See *Oxford D.N.B.*, *s.n.* He adopted the surname Scrope when he married the daughter of the last male representative of the Scrope family in 1821, and made use of the manuscripts in compiling his privately published *History of the Manor and Ancient Barony of Castle Combe* (1852).

Gairdner noted or gave in abstract a few of these (from the Hickling papers), but others from the Fastolf, Titchwell, Lovel and Guton Hall classes are printed here for the first time. These documents, along with many others relating to Fastolf's business affairs, were originally kept either in Norfolk, in the tower (still extant) of his castle at Caister, or at his London mansion, Fastolf Place, which stood by the Thames in Southwark. Fastolf's personal secretary William Worcester arranged for them to be removed to Oxford, where, by about 1481, William Wainfleet had built the muniment tower at Magdalen, where the College's archives are still stored.[1] A few Fastolf letters that became detached from these larger bodies of material are now in institutional or private ownership. No. 991 is also at Magdalen, having been bought in the saleroom by K. B. McFarlane and taken into the archives with his papers,[2] while nos. 957 and 1018 are isolated acquisitions by the Bodleian and the British Library respectively. No. 1030 is a letter written by Worcester on Fastolf's business and preserved by its recipients, unearthed in the Gloucestershire Record Office by McFarlane. The circumstances under which no. 1025 came to be preserved at Mannington Hall, Norwich, are described in its Headnote. Two Fastolf letters are now in the United States, no. 1002, in the library of the University of Illinois, Urbana-Champaign, and no. 1009, in the Folger Shakespeare Library, Washington D.C.

Though many of Fastolf's estate papers and many documents relating to the protracted struggle over his will remain to be published, the present volume completes the task of making his correspondence and that of his household fully available for the first time in print. Nonetheless, various aspects of the archival history of the Paston and Fastolf letters remain to be elucidated, since among the papers printed here are a handful of letters which appear *prima facie* to have no immediate or direct connection with either the family or their patron. An example is the well-known letter purportedly written by William, Duke of Suffolk to his son on 30 April 1450, the date he left England bound for exile, and, as it turned out, assassination (no. 980). This is not of course the original missive, but a copy in a professional-looking contemporary hand, subsequently endorsed by the sixteenth-century annotator who commented on many of the family's own letters. How Suffolk's letter became part of their archive is not clear. The circumstances of the preservation of no. 1022, the memorandum from the Yorkist lords to Henry VI on the eve of the first Battle of St Albans in 1455, are possibly a clue. It is a copy by William Worcester, in his best handwriting, sent in the manner of a letter to John Paston I, who accordingly filed it. Examples of other significant letters whose Paston or Fastolf connection (if they exist) are not immediately apparent are nos. 963 (from John Northwood to Viscount Beaumont, 28 May

[1] Richmond, *Fastolf's Will*, pp. 270–1.

[2] Sotheby's sale of 22 May 1950, lot 213A. See K. B. McFarlane, *Letters to Friends 1940–1966*, ed. G. L. Harriss (Oxford, 1997), p. 77.

1448) and 971 (from William Tailboys to Viscount Beaumont, probably 20 August 1449). It is possible that they were gathered into the collection by antiquarians and others who circulated such manuscripts among themselves: no. 979, for instance, is a copy of a Fastolf letter by Blomefield, which he let go (to Sir Andrew Fountain of Narford), and it remains untraced. On the other hand, the notable letter from Robert Wenyngton to Thomas Daniel describing sea battles in the Channel in the spring of 1449 (no. 968) does appear to have a Fastolf connection, since it probably has some bearing on the recovery of a loan made by Fastolf to Daniel which was still outstanding in 1455.

A small handful of documents known to Fenn and Gairdner (noted below in the Concordance of earlier editions and original sources) also remain untraced. Like the crucial but missing 'Remembraunce of the wurshypfull Kyn and Auncetrye of Paston'[1] they are probably still in existence somewhere, and it is of course possible and perhaps not unlikely that other Paston and Fastolf papers unknown to previous editors or to us may yet come to light.

[1] Part I, pp. xli–ii.

LIST OF AUTHORS WHOSE NAMES OR IDENTITIES ARE KNOWN

LIST OF IDENTIFIABLE WRITERS OF PAPERS NOT AUTOGRAPH, AND OF COPIES

BARKER, William:	for Sir John Fastolf, 962, 966, 967, 978, 997, 1003, 1004
BOKKYNG, John:	for Sir John Fastolf, 985, (with Worcester) 987, 1002, 1007, 1019, 1021
CALLE, Richard:	for Piers, 1041
DENYS, Thomas:	for the Earl of Oxford, 999, 1000
SPIRLENG, Geoffrey:	for Thomas Howes, 961, 964, 965
WAYTE, William:	copy of letter by J. Bokkyng, 1001
WORCESTER, William:	for Sir John Fastolf, 955, 956, 960, 981, 982, 983, 986, (with Bokkyng) 987, 988, 989, 990, 991, 993, 994, 995, 996, 1005, 1006, 1009, 1011, 1015, 1017, 1027, 1034
	copy of memorandum by the Duke of York and others, 1022
	draft of declaration by Robert Inglose, 1043

ADDITIONS AND CORRECTIONS TO PARTS I AND II

Part I

p. 19, no. 11. No. 931, of 18 September 1425, can now be identified as the indenture referred to in line 2 of this document, which must therefore be of the same date.

p. 40, no. 27. The negotiations for a match between Elizabeth Paston and John Clopton reflected in this document must have taken place after the death of William Paston I (in August 1444) and before that of John's father William, which is said to have occurred in April 1446. No. 493, a letter from John Clopton to John Paston I mentioning the same matter (see lines 5–16 thereof) must therefore be of similar date. Later in the same letter Clopton also mentions a meeting with 'Crane' (line 20), in all likelihood Robert Crane, who is now known to have died by November 1445, which would serve to date no. 493 to 19 March 1445 (Richmond, *Endings*, pp. 220–1, nn. 171, 173–4).

p. 69, no. 45. The abduction of Jane Boys is now known to have taken place on 8 June 1451, and the episode has been dealt with in detail by Roger Virgoe, 'The Ravishment of Jane Boys', in *East Anglian Society and the Political Community of Late Medieval England: Selected Papers of Roger Virgoe*, ed. C. Barron *et al.* (Norwich, 1997), pp. 151–8. Castor, *Blood and Roses*, p. 316, n. 21, takes this letter to have been written shortly after the event, on 18 July 1451. Virgoe (p.153) followed Davis in placing it a year later, after Edmund Witchingham had brought an appeal against Robert Langstrother in the King's Bench, on 10 May 1452. In this case the exact date of the letter should be corrected to 16 July for the Sunday before the feast of St Margaret in 1452.

p. 114, no. 65. The date of this document may be given more precisely as 1463, after 25 March. Lines 16–18 refer to the forcible entry of William Yelverton and William Jenney at Cotton in early September 1462, ('Mighelmes a yere passed'), for which see below, the note on the redating of no. 644, Part II, p. 247. This draft must therefore date from some time after the beginning of the new year on 25 March 1463, (see Castor, *Blood and Roses*, p. 322, n. 22).

p. 116, no. 66. This letter is now datable to late September or early October 1462. The second paragraph is devoted to John Paston I's response to the forcible entry at Cotton by William Yelverton and William Jenney, now known to have taken place on 3 September 1462 (see below, the note on the redating of no. 644, Part II, p. 247). John Paston the younger (i.e. John III) and Richard Calle are here instructed to ride to Cotton to collect rents, which they did, arriving on 8 October (see Calle's no. 647, now redated to 13 October 1462, lines 1–2, and Castor, *Blood and Roses*, p. 322, n. 22).

p. 131, no. 73. The date is more likely to be 21 February 1465, the day before the feast of St Peter's Chair, rather than two days before Sts Peter and Paul on 29 June. See Castor, *Blood and Roses*, p. 323, n. 38, who points out the closeness in tone to no. 72 of 15 January, and (in lines 68–9) Paston's intention to expedite a case 'befor Estern'.

p. 167, no. 92. The date must be before 8 June 1467, when George Neville, Archbishop of York, was dismissed from the Chancellorship (Richmond, *Fastolf's Will*, p. 180, n. 55, and cf. below on the redating of Part II, no 741).

p. 204, no. 120. Davis's dating of this letter to 18 March 1466 was based on the belief that the Earl of Kent referred to in line 25 was Edmund, Lord Grey of Ruthin, created 30 May 1465. As Richmond has shown (*Fastolf's Will*, pp. 150–1), the Earl of Kent in question is more likely to have been William Neville, Lord Fauconberg (created November 1461, died January 1463); the letter should therefore be dated 18 March 1463. Edward IV's journey northwards in March 1463 is reflected in the last paragraph. John Paston II, who was with him at Stamford, had already written to his father on 13 March for funds towards his horsing and harnessing (no. 232, lines 5–11), and Clement here appeals to John I on behalf his nephew in similar terms.

p. 241, no. 140. 18 May 1452 is a more probable date for this letter (Castor, *Blood and Roses*, p. 316, nn. 20, 22). 'Charlys and his felashep' (line 16) refers to Charles Nowell, whose riotous behaviour preoccupied John Paston in 1452 (nos. 40, 43–44), and the allusion to Bradeston (line 13) relates to the second occupation of that manor, by Nowell and his associates in February 1452, rather than to the first (of 1450) by Thomas Daniel. Margaret's reminder about a girdle for Margery (lines 18–19) follows on naturally from the initial request for one conveyed on Margaret's behalf in John Osbern's letter to John I of 14 May 1452 (no. 487, lines 32–4).

p. 243, no. 142. Dr Helen Castor has pointed out that 1452 is a more likely year than 1451 for this letter (*Blood and Roses*, p. 316, n. 25). The arrest of Roger Church of Burlingham (lines 12–14) would presumably have been after his offences against the bishop's men and others, described by Paston in nos. 40–41 and related documents of April 1452. For the initial request for a girdle for Margery and a first reminder (cf. lines 24–5), see the preceding note on the redating of no.140 to May 1452. The Tuesday next before this St. Thomas's day (the Translation of St Thomas of Canterbury) in 1452 was 4 July.

p. 245, no. 143. Dr Helen Castor observes (pers. comm.) that Gairdner's dating of this letter to 16 April 1451, on the ground that John Paston I was almost thirty ('vp-on the age of xxx wynter', line 9) in that year, seems more likely than Davis's suggestion of 21 April 1452, by which time he was six months past his thirtieth birthday. John I was himself at Norwich on 23 April 1452 (see nos. 42 and 43), which renders Margaret's writing to him from there two days earlier somewhat less plausible. During April 1452 John I was much preoccupied with the activities of Charles Nowell and his associates, who had been responsible for an assault on him, also in Norwich, on 3 April of that year. Given the prominence of St George's day in the civic calendar at Norwich it is perhaps less surprising than it might otherwise be that Margaret dates her letter in relation to it, rather than by Palm Sunday (18 April in 1451).

p. 246, no. 144. This letter may now be securely dated to 5 November 1451 by reference to the death of 'Gerrardys wyff' (line 20). She was Katherine, widow of John

Gerard, citizen and alderman of Norwich, whose will dated 27 August 1451 was proved on 8 November 1451 (Richmond, *Endings*, p. 106, n. 74, *ex inf.* Roger Virgoe).

p. 252, no. 149. The murders at Tunsted mentioned in lines 13–15, committed by three men associated with Henry Inglose *fils*, occurred on 6 November 1455, according to P. R. O. KB 9/281/11. Margaret must therefore have been writing on 12 November of that year (Richmond, *Endings*, p. 202, n. 100).

p. 275, no. 166. The date is a year later, 2 December 1462. Pampyng's imprisonment at Ipswich in the aftermath of the entry by Yelverton and Jenney at Cotton took place on 5 September 1462; see below, the note on the redating of no. 644, Part II, p. 247.

p. 283, no. 172. Davis understandably dated this letter to 1463, by reference to the Duke of Suffolk's expected attendance at an election of knights of the shire to be held in Norwich (lines 21–7), 1463 being the only year during Edward IV's reign in which such an election is known to have taken place in January. Notwithstanding, there are, as Dr Helen Castor suggests (pers. comm.), reasons for thinking that the letter belongs a year earlier, on 20 January 1462. The reference to the murder involving Thomas Gurney and his man (lines 30–1) serves to place no.172 in the same year as no. 677, which may be convincingly redated to 1462, before 20 January (see below, on Part II, p. 287, no. 677, and cf. no. 677 lines 1–5). There was in the event no election in January 1462, though there had been serious disorder in Norwich on 28 December 1461, sparked by rumours of an election, which the sheriff had denied (see no. 167, postscript, and no. 653, lines 1–14, both of 29 December 1461). If no. 172 is of 20 January 1461, then the Monday next on which the Duke of Suffolk was due in Norwich would have been 25 January. This would fit with lines 29–34 of no. 169, from Margaret to John I on 27 January 1462, alluding to Suffolk's presence in Norwich on the Monday two days previously.

p. 350, no. 208. The date is now known to be 28 October 1469. This is Margaret's response to no. 328, from John III, with his request that she send John II some of the family silver to help fund action to retain East Beckham (lines 10–17), redated as below to 1469. See Richmond, *Fastolf's Will*, p. 225, n. 26, and Castor, *Blood and Roses*, p. 327, n. 22.

p. 356, no. 210. The date is more likely to be November 1466, during a period when financial negotiations with the Duchess of Suffolk over Hellesdon were taking place (Richmond, *Fastolf's Will*, p. 178, n. 49). These are said to be 'in my lord Chaunceleres hande', i.e. George Neville, Archbishop of York, who was dismissed from the Chancellorship on 8 June 1467. See no. 92 (also to be dated before the dismissal in 1467, as proposed above) lines 3, 26–7, and no. 741 (redated as below to 28 July 1467) lines 2, 4–7.

p. 357, no. 211. For a suggestion that this letter is more likely to have been addressed to John Paston III rather than John II, see Castor, *Blood and Roses*, p. 328, n. 18. Margaret here reminds the younger John to send spices and malmsey (lines 21–2), the first having been the subject of an enquiry in her letter to him of 5 November 1471 (no. 209, lines 54–8) and the second a request relayed to John III by Edmond II in a letter of 18 November (no. 394, lines 37–8). To judge by no. 212 of 29 November, addressed explicitly to John III, Margaret was at this time extremely unhappy with her eldest son over his financial situation, but no trace of anxiety or reproach appears in no. 211, which one might expect if it were in fact to John II.

p. 360, no. 213. Redated to 1470, 1 December: see Part II, p. xxv.

p. 366, no. 217. The date of this letter is 19 October 1470, during the Readeption; see Richmond, *Fastolf's Will*, p. 241, n. 101, and Castor, *Blood and Roses*, p. 328, n. 38. The Duke of Norfolk's men are still in occupation at Caister, where they remained until December 1470, and Margaret's remarks about the constableship of Norwich Castle (lines 19–24) are made in response to John III's news about the same matter in his letter to her of 12 October 1470 (no. 345, lines 16–18).

p. 367, no. 218. Redated to 1470, 22 November: see Part II, p. xxv.

p. 368, no. 219. Redated to 1470, 23 November: see Part II, p. xxv.

p. 394, no. 234. Dr Helen Castor (*Blood and Roses*, p. 324, n. 16) notes that this letter would be more aptly placed in March 1465, a year later than Davis has it. The rift between John Paston I and his eldest son, that led to John II's banishment from the household, appears to have occurred in December 1464: see no. 178, lines 37–8, assuming that the St Thomas's Mass there referred to was either the feast of St Thomas the Apostle (21 December) or St Thomas of Canterbury (29 December). John I's anger at his son was at its most intense during January and February 1465 (see no. 72, and no. 73, redated as above to 21 February 1465). John II returned home on 4 May 1465 (no. 179, line 23).

p. 411, no. 247. The person to whom this letter was to be passed by Roger Townshend may be identified as Sir Robert Wingfield, and its date confirmed as 12 February 1470. See a previous reference to the financial transaction referred to in lines 6–7 in no. 338 of 23 January 1470, lines 57–9.

p. 428, no. 254. Another copy of the text contained in this document is Norwich, Norfolk Record Office, Phillipps MS. 539.

p. 485, no. 292. The date is more likely to be 13 June 1474, rather than 1475. John II's reference to the Bishop of Lincoln's appointment to the Chancellorship (lines 6–7) sounds as if it were recent news, and Thomas Rotherham had been instituted in the office on 24 May of that year. The tone of his remarks suggests that Edmond II's intention at this point is to join his eldest brother in the garrison at Calais ('come hyddre and. . .lyve lyke a jentylman', lines 1–2), rather than to embark upon active military service of the kind Davis envisaged when he related the letter to Edward IV's campaign in France in 1475. (See Richmond, *Endings*, pp. 30–1, n. 35).

p.536, no. 328. Gairdner and Davis were uncertain of the year, but it must certainly be 1469. Lines 21–3, 'neythyr the kyng nor the lordys can as yet undyrstand no serteynté whedyr they shall go to-gydyr a-yen by the werre or not', probably refer to the conflict between Edward IV and the Earl of Warwick during July and August of that year; and the concern to raise money to retain East Beckham (lines 10–12) connects this letter with others of October 1469, notably no. 245 (lines 5–7) and no. 335 (lines 30–3), See Richmond, *Endings*, p. 135, n. 22, followed by Castor, *Blood and Roses*, p. 327, n. 15. Margaret's reply is no. 208, redated as above to 1469, 28 October.

p. 537, no. 329. Davis was uncertain of the year, but it is much more likely to be 1467 rather than 1468. John III's remarks about a dispute involving his older brother and Hugh at Fenne (lines 13–17) connect this letter directly with no. 749, which may be firmly redated to 24 March 1467: see the note on the latter below, and Castor, *Blood and Roses*, p. 325, n. 25. No. 236 is probably John II's reply to this letter, and John III's no. 327 follows not long after it.

Part II

p. xxxiii. Add to this list: SPIRLENG, Geoffrey: for Sir John Fastolf, 547.

p. 4, no. 425. The agreement delivering seisin of the manor of Walshams in Walsham is BL Stowe Charter 214, of 5 January 1439, which serves to date this letter to 5 February of that year (see line 11; Richmond, *Fastolf's Will*, pp. 11–12, n. 15).

p. 6, no. 426. The date of Alianor Chambre's marriage given in the headnote is incorrect. It had occurred by 1422, perhaps as early as 1418 (Richmond, *First Phase*, pp. 125–6, nn. 41, 42).

p. 7, no. 428. The date of the original must be before September 1441, by which time Joan Mariot had died (Richmond, *First Phase*, p. 94, n. 122).

p. 8, no. 429. Richmond (*First Phase*, p. 93, n. 117) proposes that this letter be dated 30 May 1437, after the case of novel disseisin in respect of East Beckham had begun in the autumn of 1436, but before the false inquisition of 1437.

p. 9, no. 430. This original of this letter is definitely to be dated 7 December 1442 (Richmond, *First Phase*, p. 100, n. 146).

p. 10, no. 431. The year for this letter, which was written shortly after the death of Joan Mariot, is 1441 (Richmond, *First Phase*, pp. 94–6, nn. 122, 128).

p. 38, no. 453. There are reasons for thinking that this letter (together with no. 454, also hitherto placed in 1450) belongs rather in 1448, the year of Lord Moleyns's occupation of the Pastons' property at Gresham. No. 453 is addressed to John Paston I at Winchester, where it appears he was in the summer of 1448, petitioning Bishop William Wainfleet for the recovery of Gresham: see no 873, of 13 June 1448, where Moleyns, writing to Wainfleet, refers to 'the dayely sute to your lordschyp as of Pastun as for the mater betwyx hym and me' (lines 3–4). Had James Gresham been writing to Paston on 3 July 1450, this would have been the day when various violent and outrageous events ensued upon the entry of Jack Cade's rebels into London, a significant episode which he might be expected to mention. (See Castor, *Blood and Roses*, p. 313, n. 18). If the year is 1448, the particular date would be 5 July.

p. 39, no. 454. This letter followed not long after the same writer's no. 453, as redated above, and is probably therefore of 10 July 1448. In the Headnote to no. 453 Davis notices the reference to Cardinal Kemp in the address of no. 454, but it is not clear how his appointment to the Chancellorship on 31 January 1450 might bear upon the date of the letter. Indeed, if the letter post-dated the appointment it might be expected that the address would style him 'my lord Chancellor'.

p. 84, no. 490. The year is probably 1450. Gairdner's main reason for not placing this letter near no. 452—that the Earl of Oxford could not have been at Wivenhoe in Essex four days after being at Winch in Norfolk—is unconvincing (G. 97/124, n. 1): the journey between the two is a matter of 70 miles or so. See further Colin Richmond, 'The Murder of Thomas Denys', *Common Knowledge*, ii (1993), p. 87, n. 10.

p. 89, no. 493. The date of this letter is probably 19 March 1445; see above, on Part I, p. 40, no. 27.

p. 99, no. 504. The date is likely to be 19 August 1456, when York spent the summer at Sandal (P. A. Johnson, *Richard Duke of York 1411–1460* (Oxford, 1988), p. 175). The letter appears to be a follow-up to no. 505, being concerned with the Earl of Warwick's purchase of the manors of Walcotes and Boules in Little Snoring, negotiations for which commenced in 1455; see next.

p. 100, no. 505. A date of 23 August 1455 is indicated by a declaration made by George Heath, former holder of the manors of Walcotes and Boules in Little Snoring, on 20 July 1455. For the background, references and further details of the suggested dating see C. Richmond, 'Sir John Fastolf and the Land Market', *East Anglia's History: Studies in honour of Norman Scarfe*, ed. C. Harper-Bill *et al.*, (Woodbridge, 2002), pp. 108–10, nn. 8–12.

p. 140, no. 547. The year is 1455, when Fastolf and Hickling Priory agreed to go to arbitration over their rent dispute, first between the common lawyers John Paston and John Fyncheham, failing which the case would be referred to the Archbishop of Canterbury and the Bishop of Norwich (lines 4–9). These arrangements are set out in Magdalen College, Hickling 152, dated in that year: see A. R. Smith, 'Sir John Fastolf's Dispute with Hickling Priory', *St George's Chapel, Windsor in the Late Middle Ages*, ed. E. Scarff & C. Richmond (Windsor, 2001), p. 76, nn. 42, 43. This letter is in the hand of Geoffrey Spirleng (see nos 603, 961).

p. 150, no. 554. See above, on the redating of no. 547 to 2 May 1455. Smith ('Sir John Fastolf's Dispute with Hickling Priory', p. 68, n. 44), places this letter in the same year, indicating that Fastolf subsequently decided not to pursue arbitration, but to return his dispute with Hickling to the court of Common Pleas (lines 28–31).

p. 157, no. 560. The references to Fastolf's attorney Raulyns and the development in Fastolf's litigation with Hickling Priory (lines 2–5) serve to place this letter soon after nos. 547 and 554, redated as above to 1455 (see Smith, as cited there, p. 68, nn. 44, 45).

p. 177, no. 576. The writ referred to in the Headnote was not one of *pone* (to remove an action from a county court to a royal court at Westminster), but a writ of trespass, in the opening formula of which the word *pone* happens to occur. (*Ex inf.* Professor J. Rose).

p. 179, no. 578. Following Gairdner, Davis regarded this letter as being certainly of 24 June 1459. However, Barker's statement that at the time he wrote Fastolf was in good health, 'as freshe as ever he was this ij yere' (line 17), conflicts with William Worcester's account of Fastolf's last illness (in BL, Sloane 4, f. 38v), where it is said that he endured a hectic fever that began on 1 June, and culminated with his death on 5 November 1459. The earlier attribution of the letter to 1459 arose from Barker's remarks in the first paragraph about the provision of a new incumbent to the parsonage of Rendlesham, about which there was to be an enquiry the following day. Gairdner's researches in the register of the bishop of Norwich revealed that the John Clerk mentioned by Barker was instituted to the living of Rendlesham on 20 June 1459 (G. 379, n. 1), and he therefore concluded that Barker wrote a few days later in ignorance of the fact. Were that the case (as Dr Alison Hanham points out, 'The Curious Letters of Friar Brackley'), the enquiry to which Barker alludes would have been going forward after the recorded date of the appointment. These difficulties over Fastolf's illness and the Rendlesham living may both be removed by placing the letter a year earlier, on 24 June 1458. At this time Fastolf had recovered from an illness that had seriously affected him exactly two years previously during the summer of 1456 (see no. 553, lines 7–10), and he was evidently well enough to travel to London in November of 1458 (G. 351, n. 1). John Clerk's predecessor in the living at Rendlesham was John Sybton, with whom Fastolf had been in dispute in 1450–1 (see Index, *sub* Shipton).

p. 184, no. 582. As Dr Alison Hanham has observed, ('The Curious Letters of Friar Brackley'), Brackley wrote this letter from the priory at Walsingham, not, as Gairdner and Davis read it, 'Walsham' (line 50; Brackley abbreviated the name Walsham differently, as shown in line 35). The date is somewhat later in 1459 than October. The Prior mentioned in line 9 was Thomas Hunt, and the priest Sir John Tattershall (line 7) was his chaplain. That no pious formula was attached to Fastolf's name in line 40 is not a decisive obstacle in placing the letter in the immediate aftermath of his death. Brackley says that he is writing on a Wednesday night ('feria quarta in nocte', line 50), and in lines 23–5 he lists the names of commissioners lately charged with seeking out supporters of the Yorkist lords in Norfolk. Their names were enrolled on 21 December 1459 (*Cal. Pat. Rolls 1452–61*, p. 588), a Friday. It seems reasonable to assume that news of their appointment reached Brackley shortly before that date, and that he hastened to tell John Paston I, probably on Wednesday 19 December 1459.

p. 201, no. 602. Richmond, *Fastolf's Will*, p. 74, n. 73, proposes late 1459 for this letter, rather than 1460, making clear that the 'Midsummer' mentioned (line 10) would be that of the year of Fastolf's death.

p. 208, no. 608. Davis followed Gairdner in placing this letter in the year after Fastolf's death, but as Dr Alison Hanham has suggested ('The Curious Letters of Friar Brackley'), it is more likely to be later, perhaps not long before the death of Brackley himself, which probably occurred early in 1466 (see no. 693, Headnote). Here, Brackley speaks of having been seriously ill, and sometimes near death, for two years, and both the handwriting and the epistolary style differ from those of his letters datable to 1459–60. The reference to the dispute over Fastolf's will, which served for Gairdner and Davis to place the letter in 1460, could have been made at any time before John Paston I's death in May 1466. It may date from 1464, or perhaps more likely 1465.

p. 211, no. 610. This letter is related to no. 612 (which it probably preceded by a short time), redated below to late November–December 1459 by reference to the Parliament sitting at Coventry at the time. The Duke of Exeter's concern with Fastolf Place in Southwark, and his support for Worcester and Yelverton (see lines 20–8) also link this letter with William Paston II's no. 86 (see lines 18–21 thereof), datable to 12 November 1459.

p. 212, no. 611. As Dr Alison Hanham has pointed out ('The Curious Letters of Friar Brackley'), this letter should be placed before rather than after no. 609, since it appears that Brackley is unsure whether Paston will be in London at the time of the Parliament, which was summoned to meet on 7 October 1460 ('si contingat vt sitis Londiniis hoc termino in principio parliamenti', lines 2–3). By the time of no. 609 Paston had been elected a knight of the shire for Norfolk.

p. 214, no. 612. Davis, following Gairdner, placed this letter together with no. 610 in 1460, believing the reference to Parliament in lines 22–3 to relate to the sitting in

October of that year. The fact that it is the King *and Queen* who are said to be raising money means, however, that Brackley must have been writing before the summer of 1460, and the reference must therefore be to the Parliament that sat at Coventry from 20 November to 20 December 1459 (see Richmond, *Fastolf's Will*, p. 82). The letter is likely to date from mid-December 1459. Towards the end (lines 29–30) Brackley anticipates the arrival in Norfolk of William Yelverton, and undertakes to report on his attitude. This is the subject of his letter to William Paston II (no. 705) from Walsingham, describing his encounter there with Yelverton, probably around 17–18 December; see above, on no. 582, and below, on no. 705.

p. 216, no. 613. Dr Rosemary Horrox (pers. comm.) points out that the writer's 'xij day of Octobre' (line 41) is probably a slip of the pen for 'vij day'. The King is said to be 'at Eltham and at Grenewych . . . bydyng the parlement' (lines 17–18), and the session began on 7 October, which a writer in London would have known. Richard Duke of York is expected at Fastolf Place in the near future (lines 4–5), and he arrived in London on 10 October.

p. 227, no. 623. Fenn, Gairdner and Davis were perhaps too ready to assume that this letter was addressed to John Paston I. It is more likely (especially in the light of the last sentence) to have been destined for John III at some time in the period prior to his marriage in 1477, and it may date from Wingfield's known period of administrative activity in Suffolk in the mid-1470s: see Richmond, *Endings*, pp. 225–6.

p. 247, no. 644. The date should be amended to 5 September 1462. This is the first in a series of letters and related documents to be redated to 1462, all of them concerned directly or indirectly with John Paston I's dispute with William Yelverton and William Jenney over possession of the manors of Cotton and Nacton, part of the Fastolf inheritance. From records of proceedings in the King's Bench (noted by Roger Virgoe, for references to which see Richmond, *Endings*, pp. 199–200, n. 93) it is now known that Yelverton and Jenney took forcible possession of Cotton on Friday 3 September 1462. From this letter it appears that Paston immediately dispatched Pampyng to enquire into their actions, whereupon he was imprisoned, at Jenney's instance, on Sunday 5 September. For other papers now redated in the light of this discovery see nos. 65, 66, 166, 645, 647, 648, 650, 651, 703, 731 and 737. Calle's accounts for receipts from Paston manors for 1461 on the dorse (printed on p. 249) are numbered 'xij' in the top left-hand corner (one of Davis's extremely rare oversights). They comprise the foreign receipts, which would stand last in the accounts. Calle also used the dorses of no. 645 (accounts for Matlask, numbered 'vj') and no. 703 (manors numbered 'j–v' and 'ix', see p. 328) for the same purpose. The dorses of other letters of this period presumably carried accounts for the manors that would have been numbered 'vij', 'viij', 'x' and 'xj' in the sequence, but these have not survived. See C. Richmond, 'Landlord and Tenant: the Paston Evidence', *Enterprise and Individuals in Fifteenth-Century England*, ed. J. Kermode (Stroud, 1991), pp. 25–42 (25).

p. 249, no. 645. The date should be amended to 23 September 1462, in the light of the redating of the Cotton episode from 1461 to 1462. See above, on no. 644, and likewise for the placing of Calle's notes on the receipts from the manor of Matlask on the dorse.

p. 253, no. 647. The year should be amended to 1462, this being another letter relating to the forcible occupation of Cotton by Yelverton and Jenney, which had begun on 3 September 1462; see above, the note on no. 644.

p. 255, no. 648. This is a further letter relating to the situation at Cotton in the autumn of 1462, and the year should therefore be amended accordingly; see above, the note on no. 644.

p. 257, no. 650. This letter may now be firmly dated to 1462 by the reference to the trouble at Cotton, which began in September of that year; see above, the note on no. 644.

p. 258, no. 651. The redating of Calle's no. 650 to 1462 (see above) serves to place this letter likewise a year later.

p. 259, no. 652. There can be little or no doubt that the writer was Robert Cutler. Davis followed Gairdner in placing this letter in 1461, but noted that the suspicions regarding Howes expressed in lines 10–15 were rather stronger than might be expected at that date: 'Estrangement can be seen in 1464 (Margaret Paston's no. 177), but is not apparent in Howes's no. 662 of early 1462'. 1463 is undoubtedly a more plausible year. Writing in December, Cutler says that the date for the opening of the probate hearing on Fastolf's will has been set for the Conversion of St Paul, 25 January (lines 33–4). The abstracts of the depositions given by Gairdner from Phillipps MS. 9309 (now Bodleian, Top. Norf. c. 4) begin in 1464 (G. 565), and in the course of these hearings Howes's defection becomes clear.

p.263, no. 655. This letter appears to have followed very soon upon no. 582, redated above by reference to the enrolment of Heydon as a commissioner on 21 December 1459, to which Brackley here recurs (lines 6–7, 'commissionarius J. Heydon, vester ac meus capitalis inimicus'). If, as seems probable, no. 582 was written on Wednesday 19 December 1459, then this letter may have followed on the Friday ('feria sexta', line 33) of the same week. Also, if John Paston I took Brackley's advice to remove himself promptly to London (lines 10–12), it may explain Margaret Paston's keen disappointment at his absence from home at Christmas 1459 (see no. 154, probably of 24 December 1459, lines 19–21).

p. 269, no. 659. Davis followed Gairdner in assuming that the 'Perys of Legh' to whom this letter refers was the same 'Piers', formerly a servant of John Berney, who was imprisoned *c.* 1460–2, and accordingly dated the letter to about that time. Information since brought to light from King's Bench records by Roger Virgoe (see Richmond, *Endings*, p. 138, n. 27) identifies Perys of Legh as Peter Lye, keeper of the bishop of Norwich's prison in Lynn. It was this man who was involved, with others, in a feud with the Earl of Oxford's servants during 1447–9, including violent incidents on 24 December 1447 (the episode described in no. 659) and 18 March 1448, followed by litigation during 1449 (KB 27/754 rot. 53, rot 111d; KB 27/755 rot. 60. We are indebted to Dr Anthony Smith for confirming and extending these references). No. 659 was therefore probably written in late December 1447, or early January 1448. It may be noted that Douebiggyng's apparently jocular reference in the address to Paston's uncertain tenure of Gresham thus precedes the date given for Lord Moleyns's entry at the manor, on 17 February 1448 (see no. 36, lines 5–7).

p. 281, no. 671. As Davis points out, this letter is unlikely to date from before 1462, and it must be before John Paston I's death in May 1466. Dr Helen Castor has suggested that the likeliest year for Russe to write to Paston strongly urging him to come down from London to Norfolk (lines 20–7) would be 1464 (*Blood and Roses*,

p. 323, n. 34). Paston was certainly in London in June of that year (see nos. 177 and 685). In 1464, hearings on the probate of Fastolf's will, involving the production of hostile local witnesses by Yelverton and Worcester, were in train, and the defection of Thomas Howes was becoming clear (see G. 565). For the supportive attitude of Edward Wydwell (bailiff of Yarmouth) and his brother Hugh at Fenne towards Paston's interests at about this time (lines 5–7) see no. 652, redated as above to December 1463, lines 16–18.

p. 287, no. 677. This letter is likely to have been written in 1462, and before 20 January of that year, rather than in January 1463 (Castor, *Blood and Roses*, p. 322, n. 18). Davis's dating of no. 677 to 1463 rested on his belief that no. 172 was of 19 January of that year, but for its likely redating to 20 January 1462 see above, the note on Part I, p. 283. Lines 23–5 of no. 677 refer to the letting of land at Boyton, a matter about which Richard Calle had recently written to John Paston I, reminding him about it in no. 653, of 29 December 1461 (see lines 23–30). Also, Playter's concern that Paston had not been in communication with Margaret (lines 13–16) appears to reflect no. 168, from Margaret to her husband on 7 January 1462, lines 3–9, where she says she has not heard from him since before Christmas. In addition, the reference to 'tho that were werst avysed at the last shire' (lines 7–8) would appear to refer to the recent trouble at the shire meeting at Norwich on 28 December 1461, as reported in nos. 167 and 653 (both of 29 December 1461).

p. 292, no. 680. See above on no. 652, also firmly attributable to Robert Cutler, and redated after this letter, to December of 1463.

p. 326, no. 703. The date is 1462, not long before 24 August. Calle's accounts on the dorse form part of the sequence including those on the dorses of nos. 644 and 645, both now known to be of September 1462, and here he must have taken up another letter of the previous month for his work. See above, on no. 644, and Richmond, *Endings*, p. 200, n. 93.

p. 332, no. 705. See above, on the redatings of nos. 582 and 612. 'Our Ladyes place' whence Brackley wrote was the Augustinian priory at Walsingham that housed the famous Marian shrine (as in no. 582), and the letter goes on to describe the meeting with Yelverton that he anticipated in no. 612. No. 582 is probably of 19 December 1459, and this letter was evidently written a day or two before that. According to lines 90–3, William Paston II had spoken to a servant of the Prior's chaplain in London about coming to Walsingham at this time, and when Brackley wrote he had been in Norfolk with John I and his family (lines 98–100). No. 582 is probably the letter Brackley says means to write to John I in the near future (lines 100–1).

p. 347, no. 720. Davis's dating of this letter to 7 February 1465 would place it during a known period of severe estrangement between John Paston I and his eldest son, from December 1464 to May 1465, and it would appear most unlikely that they would be found together in London at this time: see nos 72, 73 (redated as above to 21 February 1465), 178 and 234 (redated as above to March 1465). It is more likely to have been written in 1466: see Castor, *Blood and Roses*, p. 325, n. 35. (Davis's exclusion of 1466 as a year when John I and John II were in London together was by reference to no. 742, for the redating of which to 1465, see below).

p. 349, no. 722. This letter is more likely to date from the earlier part of August 1465, since it evidently preceded and perhaps prompted Margaret Paston's interview with the Bishop of Norwich about the presentation to the living of Drayton, as related in no. 190 (lines 27–31), datable to 18 August 1465 (Richmond, *Fastolf's Will*, p. 142, n. 132).

p. 354, no. 727. Worcester's complaint in lines 38–40 about the attitude of the new Abbot of St Benet's (who succeeded in 1470) points to this letter having been written in about 1471, as explained in the Headnote to no. 1049 below. Cf. Castor, *Blood and Roses*, p. 328, n. 43, Richmond, *Fastolf's Will*, p. 179, n. 50.

p. 355, n. 3. Davis found Worcester's 'I wold he [Russe] had ben at Irland for one Day ys sake' unintelligible as it stands, and took Irland and Day to be personal names. Dr Alison Hanham observes that *at* + a place name of this kind is however attested as a Middle English idiom (O.E.D. *s.v.* At prep. 2), and that Ireland was probably intended, conceivably with some reference to the slighting 'Hibernicus' nickname that Friar Brackley had applied to Worcester.

p. 356, no. 728. Davis linked this letter with Osbern's to John Paston II, no. 767, dated 10 May 1472, giving his valuation of the wood at Sporle, but it appears that the felling described here by Calle did not proceed until late 1474. References in John Paston's letters of 1473 indicate that felling and sale had still not taken place by November of that year (see no. 274, lines 41–82, no. 276, lines 3–7, no. 281, lines 40–1, and no. 282, lines 22–31). Margaret Paston eventually wrote to John II about money forthcoming from wood sales at Sporle in the summer of 1475 (no. 224, lines 30–1, no. 225, lines 12–14). See further, Richmond, *Fastolf's Will*, p. 264, nn. 22–4.

p. 357, no. 729. See above, on the redating of no. 728 to November 1474. This letter belongs about a year later (Richmond, *Fastolf's Will*, p. 264, n. 22).

p. 358, no. 730. The year in which this letter was written remains unknown. The writer died in 1479, and Davis inclined to place it sometime before Margaret Paston took up long term residence at Mautby in 1474. Richmond (*First Phase*, p. 130, n. 67), noting the appearance of Alan Roos in the accounts for Salle Kirkhall in 1445–6, albeit not as Edward Mautby's receiver (see line 7), would place it nearer 1450 than 1470.

p. 369, no. 737. This is one of a number of letters to be redated to 1462 in the light of the discovery that this was the year in which Yelverton and Jenny occupied Cotton (on 3 September): see above, on no. 644. Calle's addressee is John Paston III (who called himself John Paston the Younger, or junior) rather than John Paston II, and it was John III who had been at Cotton with Calle earlier in October. The phrase 'crastino Annemarum, weche schalbe on Tuesday next comyng' (lines 11–12) is ambiguous, but Calle must have meant that All Saints' Day was Tuesday (as it was in 1462), rather than the day after. See Castor, *Blood and Roses*, p. 322, nn. 22, 24.

p. 371, no. 738. The date is not in doubt, but Calle's addressee is John Paston III ('the yonger'), not John II (see above, on no. 737, and Castor, *Blood and Roses*, p. 322, n. 22). It is much more likely to have been John II who was involved in a scuffle with Debenham in London at this time (see lines 17–19), and John II's concern with shipping during the summer of 1462 is also attested in no. 233.

p. 373, no. 741. This letter should be redated to 28 July 1467. Gairdner and Davis assumed from the allusion to the Duke of Suffolk's entry at Hellesdon (lines 3–4) that it was written shortly after the first occasion on which Suffolk entered, in July

1465. Mention of George Neville ('the Byshop of York', line 2) and the discussion with him about a loan of 100 marks to the Duchess of Suffolk (lines 4–7), serve however to associate this letter with the negotiations for the eventual sale of Hellesdon to the Suffolks in 1467. The matter is referred to in William Paston II's no. 92 to John II, which was written before Neville was dismissed from the Chancellorship on 8 June 1467 (see lines 3, 26–7); here, in Wykes's letter, he is referred to by his ecclesiastical title again. In neither of those letters is there any mention of John Paston I (d. May 1466), who, were he alive, would surely be part of the picture. Also relevant to the establishment of the year is no. 744, redated as below to 1467 by reference to Magdalen College, FP 88 (1), an indenture for the sale of Hellesdon dated 1 July of that year.

p. 374, no. 742. See above, on the redating of Wykes's no. 720 to 1465. This letter, by contrast, does appear to belong to the period of severe estrangement between John Paston I and his eldest son, from December 1464 to May 1465 (see lines 17–19). In line 20 Wykes mentions the marriage of the son of the Earl of Arundel to the Queen's sister (Margaret Woodville). The date given for their betrothal is October 1464 (*Complete Peerage*, i. p. 374) which strengthens the case for this letter belonging to 1465 rather than 1466.

p. 376, no. 744. As Davis observes, the endorsement would permit a date of 1467 for this letter, and it now appears that this is the likely year. The background to lines 55–64 is the negotiations for the sale of Hellesdon to the Duke and dowager Duchess of Suffolk by executors of Fastolf opposed to the Pastons (Yelverton, Worcester and others), as set out in indentures of 1 July and (probably) 28 September 1467 (Magdalen College, FP 88 (1) and (2)). See Richmond, *Fastolf's Will*, p. 148, n. 155.

p. 384, no. 749. Gairdner and Davis attribute this letter to 1468, but the reference to 'my lorde Chauncellers avyse' (lines 36–7) serves to place it a year earlier, whilst Archbishop George Neville, who had concerned himself in the matter of Fastolf's will, was still Chancellor. Neville was dismissed on 8 June 1467, and was succeeded on 20 June by Robert Stillington, Bishop of Bath and Wells, who is not known to have been active in the dispute. The letter was therefore most likely written on the Tuesday in Easter week earlier in that year, 24 March 1467. Fenne's involvement with John Paston I at this time is also alluded to in no. 329 (see lines 13–17 thereof, and above), which must also belong in this year. See Castor, *Blood and Roses*, p. 325, n. 25.

p. 411, no 772. Davis rightly inclined to place this letter towards the end of the 1470s and perhaps in the notable plague year of 1479. The suggestion that 1479 is likely to be the exact year may be strengthened by reference to the request in John Paston II's letter to his mother dated 29 October 1479, that Pecock send him money (no. 315, lines 14–16). He was also pressing Pecock for funds by other means at this time (see lines 1–3) and this seems to be Pecock's response. There is perhaps less of a contradiction between this letter and the Vicar of Paston's of 3 November 1479 (no. 783) than Davis surmised: Pecock may have believed he had earlier set the minds of the tenants at Paston at rest (see line 8), and was unaware of Harry Waryns's activities since then, especially if the vicar's letter to Margaret was unknown to him, or had yet to arrive.

p. 474, no. 835. The date of Sir Henry Grey's death is in fact given at the end of his inquisition *post mortem* (but overlooked by Davis) as 4 February 1496; the letter may therefore be dated to 14 September 1495.

p. 480, no. 841. The information that Fenn had previously printed this letter should be added to the Headnote: F. v, p. 422.

p. 581, no. 911. The negotiations for John Paston II's sale of Hellesdon to the Duke and dowager Duchess of Suffolk took place in the late summer of 1467 (see the notes on nos. 741 and 744 above); this statement seems likely to date from about the same time.

A WORKING CHRONOLOGY OF THE LETTERS AND PAPERS

Items printed in Parts I and II that have since been redated or reattributed are marked with an asterisk, and the date previously assigned or the previous attribution is shown within square brackets. The placing of some documents depends upon the detailed discussion of the date in the Headnote.

1420–1430

951. From Henry Notyngham to Sir Henry Barton, 1422 or 1423, 14 April
952. From Henry Notyngham to Sir Henry Barton, 1424 or 1425, 5 May
1. From William Paston I to John Staynford, 1425
422. From Nicholas, Prior of Bromholm, to William Paston I, 1425, 5 July
931. William Paston I: Indenture of agreement with William Joye, 1425, 18 September
*11. William Paston I: Inventory, [not after 1444] 1425, 18 September
2. From William Paston I to an unidentified lawyer in Rome, 1425, 5 November
3. From William Paston I probably to Master John Urry, 1425, November
868. From John Paston or Wortes to the Lawyers of the Temple, 1426, 23 January
423. From Elizabeth Rothenhale to William Paston I, about 1426, 26 January
4. From William Paston I to William Worstede, John Longham and Piers Shelton, 1426, 1 March
870. Petitions by Juliane Herberd against William Paston I, about 1426 and 1437
867. Petition by Walter Aslak against William Paston I, 1426
5. William Paston I: Memorandum to Arbitrators, 1426–7
953. From Sir John Fastolf to John Fastolf of Oulton and John Kirteling, probably 1429, 31 October
954. From Sir John Fastolf to Stephen Scrope, probably 1429–33, 5 July

1430–1439

6. From William Paston I to the Vicar of the Abbot of Cluny, probably 1430, April
7. William Paston I: Recipe, probably 1430
424. From Robert Lord Willoughby to William Paston I, 1431, 8 January
869. Petition by William Dallyng against William Paston I, probably 1433

8. From William Paston I to an unidentified lord, 1436

932. William Paston I: Petition on behalf of Joan and John Mariot concerning East Beckham, 1436, probably October

*429. From Joan Maryot to William Paston I, [probably 1442] 1437, 30 May

955. From Sir John Fastolf to Henry Inglose and John Berney, perhaps 1436–40

*425. From John Gyn to William Paston I, [about 1436] 1439, 5 February

933. William Paston I: Petition to the Earl of Suffolk or his arbiter concerning East Beckham, perhaps 1439

9. From William Paston I to John Berney, 1439–40

438. From John Gyn to William Paston I, probably before 1440

1440–1444

13. From Agnes Paston to William Paston I, probably 1440, 20 April

934. From Henry, Cardinal Beaufort to Lord Bardolf, probably 1440, 31 May

439. From Robert Repps to John Paston I, 1440, 1 November

*428. From Joan Maryot to William Paston I, [probably 1442] before September 1441

124. From Margaret Paston to John Paston I, about 1441

935. William Paston I: Petition of Joan Mariot to King Henry VI for custody of East Beckham, 1441, 22 February–10 April

*431. From John Maryot to William Paston I, [1443] 1441, 9 September

10. From William Paston I to Philip Berney, probably 1441, 22 October

125. From Margaret Paston to John Paston I, probably 1441, 14 December

936. William Paston I: Petition to King Henry VI concerning East Beckham, 1442, March

426. From Alianor Chambre to William Paston I, about 1442, November

*430. From Thomas West to William Paston I, [probably] 1442, 7 December

440. From the Duke of Norfolk to John Paston I, probably before July 1443

871. Deposition against John Hauteyn by James Gresham and others, 1443, not before 8 September

427. From Rauf, parson of Cressingham, to William Paston I, not after 1443, 20 September

126. From Margaret Paston to John Paston I, probably 1443, 28 September

432. From James Gresham to William Paston I, probably 1444, 28 January

956. From Sir John Fastolf probably to Sir William ap Thomas, 1444, probably May or June

127. From Margaret Paston to John Paston I, 1444, 8 July

433. From William Wotton to William Paston I, not after 1444

872. Report by William Burgeys of advice by William Paston I, not after 1444

12. William Paston I: Testament and Last Will, 1444, 10 and 21 January

937. John Paston I: Memorandum concerning East Beckham, probably late 1444 or 1445
874. Petition by John Hauteyn to the Archbishop of Canterbury, 1444–9
441. From an unidentified person to John Paston I, late 1444

1445–1448

35. From John Paston I to John Damme, probably soon after 1444
437. John Paston I: Petition to the Commons, 1445, probably early
442. Probably from John Osbern to John Paston I, perhaps about 1445
14. From Agnes Paston to Edmond Paston I, 1445, 4 February
938. Declaration at Cromer concerning East Beckham, 1445, 17 March
939. Declaration at Beckham concerning East Beckham, 1445, 17 March
*27. Agnes Paston: Draft indenture of marriage settlement, [perhaps about 1454] August 1444–April 1446
*493. From John Clopton to John Paston I, [perhaps about 1454] 1445, 19 March
434. From Sir Roger Chamberlain to Agnes Paston, perhaps about 1445, 15 September
15. Agnes Paston: Indenture of lease, 1446, 30 October
16. Agnes Paston: Indenture of lease, 1446, 10 November
957. From Sir John Fastolf to John Lynford, perhaps about 1445–6
958. From William Wangford and William Jenney to Sir John Fastolf, 1445 or 1446, 6 February
79. From Edmond Paston I to John Paston I, perhaps 1447, 5 July
707. From an unidentified person probably to Margaret Paston, perhaps about 1447
959. From Thomas Pirys to Sir John Fastolf, 1447, 15 October
960. From Sir John Fastolf to Thomas Howes and John Green, 1447, 21 October
961. From Thomas Howes to Sir John Fastolf, 1447, 26 October
704. From John Downyng to Edmond Paston I, 1447–8, November
704A. Accounts of Edmond Paston I
17. Agnes Paston: Indenture of lease, 1447, 29 November
*659. From John Douebiggyng to John Paston I, [1460–2, December–January] 1447, late December
128. From Margaret Paston to John Paston I, 1448, April
962. From Sir John Fastolf to Howes, Cole and Shipdam, 1448, 12 May
129. From Margaret Paston to John Paston I, 1448, 19 May
963. From John Northwood to Viscount Beaumont, 1448, 28 May
130. From Margaret Paston to John Paston I, 1448
873. From Lord Moleyns to William Wainfleet, Bishop of Winchester, 1448, 13 June
*453. From James Gresham to John Paston I, [1450] probably 1448, 5 July
*454. From James Gresham to John Paston I, [1450] probably 1448, 10 July

443. From James Gloys to John Paston I, 1448, 22 November

444. From John Damme to John Paston I, 1448, 30 November

964. From Thomas Howes and Geoffrey Spirleng to Sir John Fastolf, 1448, late December

1449

965. From Howes, Shipdam and Spirleng to Sir John Fastolf, 1449, 12 January

966. From Sir John Fastolf to Howes, Cole and Shipdam, 1449, probably January–February

967. From Sir John Fastolf to Thomas Howes, early 1449

131. From Margaret Paston to John Paston I, 1449, 15 February

132. From Margaret Paston to John Paston I, 1449, 28 February

445. From James Gresham to John Paston I, 1449, 10 March

80. Edmond Paston I: Nuncupative Will, 1449, 21 March

875. From Lord Moleyns to the tenants of Gresham, 1449, 24 March

133. From Margaret Paston to John Paston I, 1449, 2 April

134. From Margaret Paston to John Paston I, perhaps 1449

135. From Margaret Paston to John Paston I, probably 1449, 9 May

968. From Robert Wenyngton to Thomas Daniel, 1449, 25 May

969. From John Crop to William Worcester, 1449, mid-May

970. From John Crop to William Worcester, 1449, 2 June

446. From Elisabeth Clere to John Paston I, not after 1449, 29 June

448. From Sir John Fastolf to John Paston I, previously misdated 1449, 10 July; see no. 530/1025 of 1455, 10 July

36. John Paston I: Petition to King Henry VI, 1449, before 16 July

971. From William Tailboys to Viscount Beaumont, probably 1449, 20 August

447. From James Gresham to John Paston I, 1449, 16 October

972. From the Earl of Warwick to Sir Thomas Tuddenham, probably 1449, 2 November

973. From Sir William Willy to Thomas Howes, probably 1449, December

974. From Thomas Howes to Sir William Willy, probably 1449, December

37. From Paston I to an unidentified person in London, about 1449

876. James Gloys: Memorandum on Oxnead, not after 1449

18. From Agnes Paston to John Paston I, not after 1449

975. From Thomas Hakeborn to Sir John Fastolf, probably 1449–50

1450

976. From Thomas Huntley to Henry Fylongley, probably 1450

977. From John Austell to Henry Fylongley, probably 1450, 14 January

19. From Agnes Paston to John Paston I, probably 1450, 18 February

38. John Paston I: Petition to the Chancellor, 1450
978. From Sir John Fastolf to Howes, Cole and Shipdam, 1450, 7 March
20. From Agnes Paston to John Paston I, probably 1450, 11 March
136. From Margaret Paston to John Paston I, 1450, 12 March
979. From Sir John Fastolf to Howes, Cole and Shipdam, 1450, 16 April
449. From Lord Scales to John Paston I, 1450, 22 April
980. From William Duke of Suffolk to his son John, nominally 1450, 30 April
450. From William Lomnor to John Paston I, 1450, 5 May
451. From John Crane to John Paston I, 1450, 6 May
981. From Sir John Fastolf to Thomas Howes, 1450, 7 May
452. From Thomas Denys to John Paston I, 1450, 13 May
*490. From the Earl of Oxford to John Paston I, [not after 1453] probably 1450, 17 May
982. From Sir John Fastolf to Thomas Howes, 1450, 27 May
983. From Sir John Fastolf to Thomas Howes, 1450, 8 August
455. From James Gresham to John Paston I, 1450, 19 August
456. From the Earl of Oxford to John Paston I, perhaps 1450, 21 August
456A. Copies of Letters from the Earl of Oxford to Sir Miles Stapleton and Thomas Brews
984. From the Earl of Oxford to the Duke of Norfolk, probably 1450, 21 August
39. From John Paston I to James Gresham, 1450, 4 September
985. Memoranda of Sir John Fastolf's affairs, 1450, September
986. From Sir John Fastolf to Howes, Grene and Shipdam, 1450, 7 September
987. From Sir John Fastolf to Berney, Howes and Shipdam, 1450, 7–14 September
457. From Sir John Fastolf to John Paston I, 1450, 14 September
988. From Sir John Fastolf to Thomas Howes, 1450, 15 September
458. From King Henry VI to John Paston I, 1450, 18 September
470. From the Vicar of Sporle to John Paston I, about 1450, 29 September
459. From Thomas Denys to John Paston I, 1450, 4 October
460. From William Wayte to John Paston I, 1450, 6 October
460A. Copy of letter from the Duke of York to King Henry VI
461. From James Gresham to John Paston I, 1450, October
462. From James Gresham to John Paston I, 1450, October–November
463. Probably from William Yelverton to John Paston I, 1450, about October
989. From Sir John Fastolf to Howes and Barker, 1450, 15 and 18 October
464. From the Duke of Norfolk to John Paston I, probably 1450, 16 October
465. From the Earl of Oxford to John Paston I, probably 1450, 18 October
466. From the Duke of Norfolk to John Paston I, probably 1450, 22 October
467. From John Damme and James Gresham to John Paston I, 1450, 11 November
990. From Sir John Fastolf to Thomas Howes, 1450, 11 November

877. From William Yelverton to Sir John Fastolf, 1450, November
878. From William Yelverton to John Bokkyng, 1450, November
991. From Sir John Fastolf to Howes, Bokkyng and Shipdam, 1450, 23 November
992. From Thomas Playter to Sir John Fastolf, probably 1450, September–December
993. From Sir John Fastolf to Howes, Jenney and Bokkyng, 1450, 2 December
994. From Sir John Fastolf to Thomas Howes and John Bokkyng, 1450, 4 December
995. From Sir John Fastolf to Thomas Howes and John Bokkyng, 1450, 5 December
996. From Sir John Fastolf to Thomas Howes, 1450, 20 December
468. From the Earl of Oxford to John Paston I, 1450, 23 December
997. From Sir John Fastolf to John Berney and Thomas Howes, 1450, 27 December
469. From Robert, Prior of Bromholm to John Paston I, perhaps about 1450
708. From Thomas Gnatyshale to Margaret Paston, perhaps about 1450
709. From Thomas Gnatyshale to Margaret Paston, perhaps about 1450
710. From Thomas Gnatyshale to Margaret Paston, perhaps about 1450
879. From Lord Scales to Thomas Gnatyshale, perhaps 1448–51
*730. From Edward Mautby to Margaret Paston, [probably not after 1473] perhaps about 1450, 24 November

1451

998. From Sir John Fastolf, probably to Thomas Howes, 1450, December, or 1451, early January
880. John Paston I: Memorandum on prosecutions 1451
881. Petition to Parliament by the town of Swaffham, 1451
999. From the Earl of Oxford to John Jermyn, 1451, 2 January
1000. From the Earl of Oxford to Sir John Fastolf, 1451, 2 January
1001. From John Bokkyng to William Wayte, 1451, 2 January
471. From William Wayte to John Paston I, 1451, 3 January
1002. From Sir John Fastolf to Berney, Howes and others, 1451, 3 January
1003. From Sir John Fastolf to John Berney and Thomas Howes, 1451, 7 January
472. From William Wayte to John Paston I, 1451, 9 January
1004. From Sir John Fastolf to Thomas Howes and John Bokkyng, 1451, 12 January
1005. From Sir John Fastolf to Thomas Howes and John Berney, 1451, 28 January
473. From James Gloys to John Paston I, 1451, 1 March
474. From James Gloys to John Paston I, 1451, 2 March
137. From Margaret Paston to John Paston I, 1451, 3 March
475. From Thomas Denys to John Paston I, 1451, 4 March
138. From Margaret Paston to John Paston I, 1451, 15 March

139. From Margaret Paston to John Paston I, 1451, 30 March
1006. From Sir John Fastolf to Thomas Howes, 1451, 13 April
*143. From Margaret Paston to John Paston I, [probably 1452, 21 April] 1451, 16 April
1007. From Sir John Fastolf to Thomas Howes, 1451, 21 April
476. From the Earl of Oxford to John Paston I, not after 1451, 30 April
477. From Debenham, Tymperley and White to John Paston I, 1451, 2 May
478. From William Lomnor to John Paston I, 1451, about May
1008. From Thomas Howes to Sir John Fastolf, 1451, 9 May
21. From Agnes Paston to John Paston I, probably 1451, 12 May
22. From Agnes Paston to John Paston I, probably 1451
479. From John Osbern to John Paston I, 1451, 27 May
480. From James Gresham to John Paston I, 1451, probably June
481. From John Berney of Witchingham to John Paston I, 1451, 20 June
1009. From Sir John Fastolf to Thomas Howes, 1451, 24 June
141. From Margaret Paston to John Paston I, 1451, 1 July
*45. From John Paston I to Richard Southwell, [perhaps 1452, 20 July] 1451, 18 July
1010. From Walter Lyhert, Bishop of Norwich, to Sir John Fastolf, probably 1451, 18 August
1011. From Sir John Fastolf to Thomas Howes, 1451, 23 September
*144. From Margaret Paston to John Paston I, [probably 1452] 1451, 5 November
23. From Agnes Paston to John Paston I, probably 1451, 8 November
24. From Agnes Paston to John Paston I, probably 1451, 21 November
482. From Lord Willoughby to John Paston I, not after 1451, 16 December
483. From Richard Southwell to John Paston I, 1451, 18 December
1012. Stephen Scrope, first schedule of grievances against Sir John Fastolf, about 1450–1
1013. Stephen Scrope, rejoinders to Sir John Fastolf's replies to his schedule of grievances, August 1451–July 1452

1452–1453

1014. From Lord Scales to Sir John Fastolf, probably 1452, 8 January
484. From the Duke of York to John Paston I, 1452, 9 February
485. From Osbern Mundford to John Paston I, 1452, 9 February
486. From John Clopton to John Paston I, 1452, 1 April
40. John Paston I: Petition to the Lords, 1452
41. John Paston I: Petition to the Chancellor, 1452
42. From John Paston I probably to the Sheriff of Norfolk, 1452, 23 April
43. From John Paston I probably to the Sheriff of Norfolk, 1452, 23 April

44. From John Paston I probably to the Sheriff of Norfolk, 1452
882. From John Clopton to the King and Council, 1452, May
487. From John Osbern to John Paston I, 1452, 14 May
*140. From Margaret Paston to John Paston I, probably [1451, 3 June] 1452, 18 May
81. From William Paston II to John Paston I, 1452, 16 June
*142. From Margaret Paston to John Paston I, probably [1451, 6 July] 1452, 4 July
25. From Agnes Paston to John Paston I, probably 1452, 16 November
46. John Paston I: Memorandum, 1452, late
47. From John Paston I to John Norwode, not before 1453
488. From William Cotyng to John Paston I, 1449–53, April
489. From Edmund Witchingham to John Paston I, perhaps 1450–3, October
145. From Margaret Paston to John Paston I, perhaps 1453, 30 January
146. From Margaret Paston to John Paston I, 1453, 20 April
435. From William Reynolds to Agnes Paston, 1453, 26 April
26. From Agnes Paston to John Paston I, 1453, 6 July
147. From Margaret Paston to John Paston I, 1453, 6 July
148. From Margaret Paston to John Paston I, perhaps 1453, 15 October

1454

150. From Margaret Paston to John Paston I, perhaps 1454, 29 January
151. From Margaret Paston to John Paston I, perhaps 1454, 1 February
491. From Thomas Denys to John Paston I, 1454, 20 March
491A. Copy of petition by Walter Ingham, 1454
492. From Thomas Denys to John Paston I, 1454, 8 April
48. John Paston I: Petition, probably 1454
49. From John Paston I to the Earl of Oxford, 1454, 31 March
494. From Thomas Denys to John Paston I, 1454, 3 May
495. From Lord Scales to John Paston I, not after 1454, 17 May
496. From William Worcester to John Paston I, 1454, 8 June
497. From R. Dollay to John Paston I, 1454, 29 June
498. From William Worcester to John Paston I, 1454, 5 July
499. From Lord Grey to John Paston I, 1454, 11 July
1015. From Sir John Fastolf to Thomas Howes, 1454, 12 July
50. From John Paston I to Lord Grey, 1454, 15 July
1016. From Sir John Fastolf to Thomas Howes, 1454, 20 July
82. William Paston II: Memorandum on French Grammar, probably 1450–4
83. From William Paston II to John Paston I, 1454, July
506. From William Worcester to John Paston I, perhaps 1454, 2 September
507. From Thomas Howes to John Paston I, perhaps 1454, 2 September
84. From William Paston II to John Paston I, 1454, 6 September

1017. From Sir John Fastolf to Richard Waller, 1454, 30 October
1018. From Sir John Fastolf to Henry Frowyk, probably 1454, 30 October
508. From John Russe to John Paston I, 1454, October–November
1019. Memoranda of Sir John Fastolf's legal counsellors, 1454, November
1020. From William Barker to Sir John Fastolf, probably 1454, 3 November
509. From Sir John Fastolf to John Paston I, 1454, 11 November
*149. From Margaret Paston to John Paston I, [probably 1453] 1454, 12 November
510. From Thomas Howes to John Paston I, 1454, 13 November
511. From Thomas Howes to John Paston I, 1454, 18 November
500. From Elisabeth Clere to John Paston I, probably before 1460, 25 May
501. From the Countess of Oxford, to John Paston I, not after 1454, 7 August
502. From the Countess of Oxford to John Paston I, not after 1461, 1 February
503. From the Countess of Oxford to John Paston I, not after 1466, 13 August

1455

51. From John Paston I to the Duke of Norfolk, probably 1455
512. From Edmund Clere to John Paston I, 1455, 9 January
513. From Sir John Fastolf to Henry Fylongley and John Paston I, 1455, 24 January
514. From Sir John Fastolf to John Paston I, 1455, 7 February
515. From Lord Cromwell to John Paston I, not after 1455, 10 February
516. From Thomas Howes to John Paston I, 1455, probably March
517. From the Abbot of St. Benet's to John Paston I, 1455, 17 March
518. From Sir John Fastolf to John Paston I, 1455, 29 March
1021. From Sir John Fastolf to the Duke of Norfolk, 1455, 2 April
*547. From Sir John Fastolf to John Paston I, [1456] 1455, 2 May
520. From Sir John Fastolf to John Paston I, 1455, 3 May
519. From Richard Calle to John Paston I, probably 1455, 8 May
521. From Thomas Cannon to John Paston I, 1455, 16 May
1022. From the Duke of York to King Henry VI, nominally 1455, 21 May
522. From John Crane to John Paston I, 1455, 25 May
1023. Relation of the first Battle of St Albans, 1455, 25–9 May
523. From Sir John Fastolf to John Paston I, 1455, 28 May
1024. From William Barker to William Worcester, 1455, early June
524. From the Duchess of Norfolk to John Paston I, 1455, 8 June
525. From Sir John Fastolf to John Paston I, 1455, 11 June
526. From Sir John Fastolf to John Paston I, 1455, 22 June
*554. From Sir John Fastolf to John Paston I, probably [1456] 1455, 24 June
527. From John Jenney to John Paston I, 1455, 24 June
528. From John Jenney to John Paston I, 1455, 25 June
711. From Alice Crane to Margaret Paston, perhaps about 1455, 29 June

529. From William Worcester to John Paston I, 1455, 7 July
530. From Sir John Fastolf to John Paston I, 1455, 10 July
1025. (530 bis). From Sir John Fastolf to John Paston I, 1455, 10 July
1026. From Henry Windsor to John Bokkyng and William Worcester, 1455, 19 July
532. From James Gloys to John Paston I, probably 1455, 25 July
52. From John Paston I to James Gloys, probably 1455, 25 July
533. From John Chedworth, Bishop of Lincoln to John Paston I, 1455, 26 July
*560. From Sir John Fastolf to John Paston I, probably [1456] 1455, 31 July
*505. From the Earl of Warwick to John Paston I, probably [1454] 1455, 23 August
534. From James Gresham to John Paston I, 1455, 28 October
1027. From Sir John Fastolf to Nicholas Molyneux, 1455, 30 October
535. From William Worcester to John Paston I and John Bokkyng, 1455, 13 November
536. From Sir John Fastolf to John Paston I, 1455, 11 December
1028. From Thomas Hert to William Worcester, probably 1455, 30 December
531. From Sir John Fastolf to John Paston I, perhaps 1455–6

1456

537. From William Worcester to John Paston I, probably 1456, 6 January
538. From Sir John Fastolf to John Paston I, for Lady Whytyngham, 1456, 25 January
539. From Sir John Fastolf to John Paston I, 1456, 26 January
540. From William Worcester to John Paston I and others, 1456, 27 January
541. From Sir John Fastolf to John Paston I, 1456, 5 February
1029. From John Bokkyng to Sir John Fastolf, 1456, 9 February
542. From Sir John Fastolf to John Paston I, 1456, 12 February
543. From Hugh at Fenne to John Paston I, probably 1456, 1 March
1030. From William Worcester to Sir John Fastolf's servants at Oxenton, 1456, 16 March
544. From James Gresham to John Paston I, perhaps 1456, 24 March
1031. From Archbishop Thomas Bourchier to Sir John Fastolf, 1456, 27 March
545. From Dame Alice Ogard to John Paston I, 1456, 30 March
546. From Hugh at Fenne to John Paston I, perhaps 1456, 25 April
548. From John Bokkyng to John Paston I, 1456, 8 May
549. From John Bokkyng to John Paston I, 1456, 15 May
550. From Henry Windsor to John Paston I, perhaps 1456, 16 May
551. From John Russe to John Paston I, 1456, 1 June
552. From John Bokkyng to John Paston I, 1456, 7 June
553. From Sir John Fastolf to John Paston I, probably 1456, 18 June
555. From Sir John Fastolf to John Paston I, probably 1456, 24 June

556. From John Dory to John Paston I, perhaps 1456
557. From Friar John Brackley to John Paston I, probably 1456, 29 June
558. From William Worcester to John Paston I, perhaps 1456
559. From William Worcester to John Paston I, about 1456
561. From Lord Scales to John Paston I, 1456, 11 August
*504. From the Duke of York to John Paston I, probably [1454] 1456, 19 August
562. From Thomas Bourchier, Archbishop of Canterbury, to John Paston I, 1456, 7 September
563. From Lord Scales to John Paston I, about 1456, 20 September
564. From Thomas Howes to John Paston I, probably 1456, 6 October
565. From John Bokkyng to John Paston I, 1456, 8 October
566. From William Worcester to John Paston I, perhaps 1456, 12 October
567. From James Gresham to John Paston I, 1456, 16 October
568. From Sir John Fastolf to John Paston I, probably 1456, 10 November
569. From Sir John Fastolf to John Paston I, probably 1456, 15 November
570. From Sir John Fastolf to John Paston I or William Barker, probably 1456, 18 November
1033. From Sir Richard Byngham to Sir John Fastolf, perhaps 1456–7

1457–1458

571. From William Worcester to John Paston I, 1457, 20 April
572. From William Worcester to John Paston I, 1457, 1 May
1032. From Henry Fylongley to Sir John Fastolf, probably 1457, 17 July
573. From Thomas Playter to John Paston I, probably 1457, 20 July
1034. From Sir John Fastolf to William Yelverton, 1457, 29 October
1035. From Sir John Fastolf to Stephen Scrope, 1457, 30 October
28. Agnes Paston: Memorandum of 'errands', 1458, 28 January
883. From William Worcester to Sir John Fastolf, 1458, 1 February
884. From William Worcester to Sir John Fastolf, 1458, probably early March
1036. From John Bokkyng to Sir John Fastolf, 1458, 15 March
53. From John Paston I and Thomas Howes to Sir John Fastolf, 1458, 24 May
712. From John Jernyngan to Margaret Paston, 1458, 1 June
*578. From William Barker to John Paston I, [1459] 1458, 24 June
85. From William Paston II to Margaret Paston, probably 1458, 10 August
574. From Henry Windsor to John Paston I, probably 1458, 27 August
575. From Richard Southwell to John Paston I, about 1458, 6 October
576. From William Worcester to John Paston I, probably 1458

1459

121. From Elizabeth Poynings (*née* Paston) to Agnes Paston, 1459, 3 January

577. From Sir John Fastolf to John Paston I, 1459, 13 April
579. From Sir John Fastolf to John Paston I, 1459, 3 July
580. From William Jenney to John Paston I, probably 1459, 22 August
581. From Friar John Brackley to John Paston I, not after 1459
152. From Margaret Paston to John Paston I, about 1459, September
583. From Friar John Brackley to John Paston I, 1459, October–November
54. John Paston I: Nuncupative Will of Sir John Fastolf, nominally 1459, 3 November
887. Statement by William Wainfleet, Bishop of Winchester, about Fastolf's executors, 1459, November
86. From William Paston II to John Paston I, 1459, 12 November
*610. From Friar John Brackley to John Paston I, probably [1460, October] 1459, November
885. Declaration by Robert FitzRawff about Fastolf's will, 1459, 26 November
886. Petition to Parliament by Sir Philip Wentworth, 1459, November–December
584. From John Bokkyng to John Paston I and others, 1459, 7 December
*612. From Friar John Brackley to John Paston I, [1460, October] 1459, mid-December
*705. From Friar John Brackley to William Paston II, [1460, before Easter] 1459, mid-December
*582. From Friar John Brackley to John Paston I, 1459, [probably October] 19 December
*655. From Friar John Brackley to John Paston I, [perhaps 1461] 1459, probably 21 December
153. From Margaret Paston to John Paston I, probably 1459, 24 December
*602. From John Davy to John Paston I, probably [1460] late 1459
87. William Paston II: Inventory, probably 1459–60
585. From Sir John Fastolf to John Paston I, 1454–9
586. From Sir John Fastolf to John Paston I, 1454–9, 19 September
587. From Sir John Fastolf to John Paston I and William Yelverton, 1455–9, 20 March
588. From Sir John Fastolf to John Paston I, 1455–9, 13 June
589. From Sir John Fastolf to John Paston I, 1455–9, August
590. From John Bokkyng to John Paston I, 1455–9, 2 April
591. From the Earl of Warwick to John Paston I, perhaps about 1459, 1 March
592. From Lord Scales to John Paston I, not after 1459, 18 July
593. From Lord Scales to John Paston I, not after 1459, 3 August
594. From Lord Scales to John Paston I, not after 1459, 31 August
595. From Lord Scales to John Paston I, not after 1459, 9 October
596. From Lord Scales to John Paston I, not after 1459, 16 October
597. From Lord Scales to John Paston I, not after 1459, 9 November

598. From Lord Scales to John Paston I, not after 1460, 13 April
599. From William Yelverton to John Paston I, not after 1459, 4 October
600. From Elisabeth Clere to John Paston I, not after 1460, Easter
601. From an unidentified person to John Paston I and William Yelverton, not after 1460

1460

436. From Robert Williamson to Agnes Paston, probably 1460–4
706. From Peter Marham to William Paston II, perhaps 1460–70
721. From William Cotyng to Margaret Paston, 1460–5, 31 July
603. From Geoffrey Sperlyng to John Paston I, 1460, 6 January
888. From William Worcester to John Berney, 1460, January
88. From William Paston II to John Paston I, 1460, 28 January
604. From William Worcester probably to a member of Fastolf's household, 1460, 7 February
605. From Friar John Brackley to John Paston I, perhaps about 1460
606. From Friar John Brackley to John Paston I, probably 1460, early
940. From John Paston I to Richard Charles, 1460, 9 April
1037. From Hugh at Fenne to William Worcester, 1460, 9 April
89. From William Paston II to John Paston I, 1460, 2 May
889. From the Abbot of Langley to Master John Stokes, 1460, 8 May
607. From Osbern Mundford to John Paston I, before June 1460
55. From John Paston I to Margaret Paston, 1460, 19 June
890. From King Henry VI to John Nedham and Thomas Littleton, about 1460, 26 July
56. From John Paston I to Margaret Paston, 1460, 28 July
1038. From Lord Beauchamp to Thomas Howes, probably 1460, 28 August
*611. From Friar John Brackley to John Paston I, 1460, early October
609. From Friar John Brackley to John Paston I, 1460, October
57. John Paston I: Petition to King Henry VI, 1460, 7 October
*613. From Christopher Hansson to John Paston I, 1460, [12] 7 October
614. From Richard Calle to John Paston I, perhaps about 1460, 17 October
615. From Thomas Playter to John Paston I, 1460, October
616. From Thomas Playter to John Paston I, 1460, probably 21 October
154. From Margaret Paston to John Paston I, 1460, 21 October
617. From Friar John Brackley to John Paston I, 1460, 24 October
155. From Margaret Paston to John Paston I, 1460, 29 October
618. From Richard Calle to John Paston I, perhaps 1460, 11 November
156. From Margaret Paston to John Paston I, 1460, 25 November
157. From Margaret Paston to John Paston I, 1460, 1 December

619. From Geoffrey Boleyn to John Paston I, probably 1460, 5 December
620. From William Jenney to John Paston I, not after 1460, 13 December
621. From John Radclyff to John Paston I, not after 1460, 17 December
622. From the Earl of Oxford to John Paston I, not after 1460, 28 December
713. From Robert Spany to Margaret Paston, probably 1460
1039. Stephen Scrope, second schedule of grievances against Sir John Fastolf, late 1460 or early 1461

1461

114. From Clement Paston to John Paston I, 1461, 23 January
624. From John, Prior of Bromholm, to John Paston I, 1461, 31 January
158. From Margaret Paston to John Paston I, probably 1461, 1 March
317. From John Paston III perhaps to Thomas Playter, 1461, March
90. From William Paston II to John Paston I, 1461, 4 April
625. From Thomas Playter to John Paston I, 1461, 18 April
626. From Thomas Denys to John Paston I, 1461, probably April–May
627. From John Smyth to John Paston I, 1461, 10 May
628. From Thomas Playter to John Paston I, 1461, early May
629. From Thomas Denys to John Paston I, 1461, May
630. From the Earl of Oxford to John Paston I, probably 1461, 31 May
631. From Thomas Playter to John Paston I, 1461, June
632. From Richard Calle to John Paston I, 1461, 5 June
633. From William Pryce to John Paston I, 1461, 18 June
634. From Robert Lethum to John Paston I, probably 1461, 19 June
635. From James Gresham to John Paston I, 1461, 21 June
716. From Thomas Denys to Margaret Paston, 1461, 21 or 28 June
115. From Clement Paston to John Paston I, 1461, 26 June
159. From Margaret Paston to John Paston I, 1461, perhaps 2 July
717. From Richard Calle to Margaret Paston, probably 1461, 3 July
636. From William Lomnor to John Paston I, 1461, 6 July
160. From Margaret Paston to John Paston I, 1461, 9 July
637. From John Berney of Witchingham to John Paston I and William Rokewode, 1461, 10 July
58. From John Paston I to Margaret Paston, 1461, 12 July
161. From Margaret Paston to John Paston I, 1461, 15 July
638. From John Berney of Witchingham to John Paston I and William Rokewode, 1461, 16 July
639. From John Berney of Witchingham to John Paston I, 1461, 17 July
162. From Margaret Paston to John Paston I, 1461, 18 July
642. From the Earl of Oxford to John Paston I, not after 1461, 25 July

640. Grant from King Edward IV to John Paston I, 1461, 27 July
641. From Thomas Playter to John Paston I, 1461, probably July–August
59. From John Paston I to Margaret Paston, 1461, 1 August
231. From John Paston II to John Paston I, 1461, 23 August
643. From John Russe to John Paston I, 1461, 23 August
116. From Clement Paston to John Paston I, 1461, 25 August
646A. Copy of letter from Lord Hungerford and Robert Whityngham to Margaret of Anjou, 1461, 30 August
646. From Henry Windsor to John Paston I, 1461, 4 October
117. From Clement Paston to John Paston I, 1461, 11 October
163. From Margaret Paston to John Paston I, 1461, 2 November
649. From Richard Calle to John Paston I, 1461, 5 November
318. From John Paston III to John Paston I, probably 1461, 10 November
164. From Margaret Paston to John Paston I, 1461, 16 November
165. From Margaret Paston to John Paston I, probably 1461, 20 November
29. From Agnes Paston to John Paston I, 1461, 1 December
167. From Margaret Paston to John Paston I, 1461, 29 December
653. From Richard Calle to John Paston I, 1461, 29 December
654. From Thomas Playter to John Paston I, 1461, December
714. From Piers to Margaret Paston, probably 1461
715. From Piers to Margaret Paston, about 1461
1041. From Piers to Sir Robert Rokesby, probably 1461
60. John Paston I: Petition to the Chancellor, 1461–2
61. John Paston I: Statement of Fastolf's intention, after 1459, before May 1466
1040. Stephen Scrope, bill of charges against the estate of Sir John Fastolf, late 1461 or early 1462
656. From Joan Keteryche, Abbess of Denny to John Paston I, about 1461–2, 31 January
657. From Elizabeth Mundford to John Paston I, after 1460, before 1467, February
658. From an unidentified person to John Paston I, probably not after 1461

1462

168. From Margaret Paston to John Paston I, 1462, 7 January
*677. From Thomas Playter to John Paston I, [1463, January] probably 1462, before 20 January
660. From John Felbrigg to John Paston I, probably 1462, 19 January
*172. From Margaret Paston to John Paston I, [1463, probably 19 January] probably 1462, 20 January
169. From Margaret Paston to John Paston I, 1462, 27 January
661. From Richard Calle to John Paston I, probably 1462, 1 February

662. From Thomas Howes to John Paston I, 1462, February
62. From John Paston I, perhaps to Thomas Howes, perhaps 1462, 9 February
63. From John Paston I, perhaps to the Sheriff of Norfolk, 1462, March
170. From Margaret Paston to John Paston I, 1462, March
232. From John Paston II to John Paston I 1462, 13 March
*120. From Clement Paston to John Paston I, [1466] 1462, 18 March
663. From James Gresham to John Paston I, 1462, 24 March
664. From John Wykes, usher, to John Paston I, 1462, 25 March
665. From William Lomnor to John Paston I, perhaps 1462, 11 April
666. From John Russe to John Paston I, 1462, before 14 April
718. From William Barker to Margaret Paston, 1462, May
667. From William Barker to John Paston I, 1462, 4 May
171. From Margaret Paston to John Paston I, 1462, 18 May
233. John Paston II to John Paston I, 1462, probably May–June
64. John Paston I: Inventory and indenture, 1462, 6 June
668. From John Daubeney to John Paston I, 1462, 3 July
669. From Richard Calle to John Paston I, probably 1462, 5 July
*738. From Richard Calle to John Paston [II] III, 1462, about July
670. From Richard Calle to John Paston I, 1462, about July
91. From William Paston II to John Paston I, 1462, about 20 July
673. From Thomas Playter to John Paston I, 1462, July
674. From Thomas Playter to John Paston I, 1462, July
*703. From James Gresham to John Paston I, [not after 1466] perhaps 1462, early August
672. From the Duke of Norfolk to John Paston I, 1462–3, 31 August
*644. From John Pampyng to John Paston I, [1461] 1462, 5 September
675. From John Russe to John Paston I, 1462, September
676. From John Russe to John Paston I, 1462, September–October
*645. From James Gloys to John Paston I, [1461, 24] 1462, 23 September
*66. From John Paston I to Pampyng, Calle and Wykes, [about 1463] 1462, September–early October
*647. From Richard Calle to John Paston I, [1461] 1462, 13 October
*648. From William Naunton to John Paston I, [1461] 1462, October
*737. From Richard Calle to John Paston [II] III, [1461] 1462, late October
319. From John Paston III to John Paston I, 1462, 1 November
*650. From Richard Calle to John Paston I, [probably 1461] 1462, 20 November
*166. From Margaret Paston to John Paston I, [1461, 3] 1462, 2 December
320. From John Paston III to John Paston II, 1462, 11 December
*651. From Sir John Heveningham to John Paston I, [1461] 1462, 12 December

1463–1464

678. From Richard Calle to John Paston I, 1463, February
*65. John Paston I: Petition to the Duke of Norfolk, [1462–3] 1463, after 25 March
891. Declaration by Ralph Lampet about Fastolf's will, 1463, 19 March
892. Declaration by Sir Roger Chamberlain about Fastolf's will, 1463, 6 April
173. From Margaret Paston to John Paston I, 1463, before 10 April
*680. [Probably] From Robert Cutler to John Paston I, 1463, May
679. From Thomas Playter to John Paston I, 1463, early July
739. From the Abbot of Langley to John Paston II, 1463, 4 September
174. From Margaret Paston to John Paston I, probably 1463, 13 November
175. From Margaret Paston to John Paston II, 1463, 15 November
*652. [Probably] From Robert Cutler to John Paston I, [perhaps 1461] probably 1463, December
719. From John Pampyng to Margaret Paston, probably 1463
67. John Paston I: Petition to Robert Welles and others, probably 1463–5
681. From James Gresham to John Paston I, 1464, 26 January
682. From Henry Berry to John Paston I, probably 1464, 28 January
118. From Clement Paston to John Paston I, 1464, 15 February
683. From Richard Calle to John Paston I, 1464, 27 February
684. From John Pampyng to John Paston I, 1464, 29 February
321. From John Paston III to John Paston I, 1464, 1 March
119. From Clement Paston to John Paston I, 1464, 18 April
68. John Paston I: Inventory, probably 1464, not later than April
69. John Paston I: Memorandum, 1464, April
70. John Paston I: Petition to King Edward IV, 1464
894. From John Russe to Master Rothewell, about 1464
176. From Margaret Paston to John Paston I, 1464, 6 May
322. From John Paston III to John Paston I, probably 1464, 2 June
177. From Margaret Paston to John Paston I, 1464, 8 June
685. From Richard Calle to John Paston I, 1464, 28 June
*671. From John Russe to John Paston I, [not before 1462] perhaps 1464, 15 July
686. Licence from King Edward IV to John Paston I, 1464, 10 September
893. From Sir Walter Blount to the Prior of Norwich, 1464, 27 November
687. John Paston I: Copies of writs concerning his outlawry, 1464, August–November
694. From an unidentified person, initial 'T,' to John Paston I, perhaps 1464, not after 1465, 3 December

1465

71. From John Paston I to Margaret Paston, 1465, 14 January

72. From John Paston I to Margaret Paston, Daubeney and Calle, 1465, 15 January
*742. From John Wykes to John Paston II, [1466] probably 1465, 17 February
*73. From John Paston I to Margaret Paston, John Daubeney and Richard Calle, 1465, [27 June] 21 February
*234. John Paston II to John Paston I, probably [1464] 1465, 5 March
178. From Margaret Paston to John Paston I, 1465, 8 April
179. From Margaret Paston to John Paston I, 1465, 3 May
688. From John Russe to John Paston I, 1465, 6 May
180. From Margaret Paston to John Paston I, 1465, 10 May
181. From Margaret Paston to John Paston I, 1465, 13 May
182. From Margaret Paston to John Paston I, 1465, 20 May
183. From Margaret Paston to John Paston I, 1465, 27 May
695. From William Calthorp to John Paston I, not after 1465, May
184. From Margaret Paston to John Paston I, 1465, 11 June
740. From Richard Calle to John Paston II, 1465, 15 June
689. From John Rising to John Paston I, 1465, 18 June
185. From Margaret Paston to John Paston I, 1465, 24 June
186. From Margaret Paston to John Paston III, 1465, probably 30 June
697. From Roger Taverham to John Paston I, not after 1465, June
698. From Roger Taverham to John Paston I, 1461–6
187. From Margaret Paston to John Paston II, 1465, perhaps 6 July
*608. From Friar John Brackley to John Paston I, [1460] probably 1465, 6 July
690. From Richard Calle to John Paston I, 1465, 10 July
188. From Margaret Paston to John Paston I, 1465, 12 July
74. From John Paston I to Margaret Paston, 1465, 13 July
1042. From John Eastgate to an unidentified servant of John Paston I, probably 1465, before August
*722. From John Daubeney to Margaret Paston, 1465, probably [September] early August
75. From John Paston I to Margaret Paston, Gresham and Calle, 1465, 7 August
76. From John Paston I to Margaret Paston, 1465, 7 August
189. From Margaret Paston to John Paston I, 1465, 7 August
190. From Margaret Paston to John Paston I, 1465, 18 August
191. From Margaret Paston to John Paston I, 1465, probably August
323. From John Paston III to Margaret Paston, 1465, 14 September
77. From John Paston I to Margaret Paston, 1465, 20 September
192. From Margaret Paston to John Paston I, 1465, 27 September
193. From Margaret Paston to John Paston I, 1465, 27 September
235. John Paston II to John Paston I, 1465, 27 September
696. From B.D.M.S. to John Paston I, not after 1465, late September

324. From John Paston III to John Paston I, 1465, 3 October
784. From the Duke of Norfolk to John Paston III, 1465, 12 October
194. From Margaret Paston to John Paston I, 1465, 17 October
195. Margaret Paston: Inventory of goods stolen, 1465, soon after 17 October
196. From Margaret Paston to John Paston I, 1465, 27 October
30. From Agnes Paston to John Paston I, perhaps 1465, 29 October
691. From John Wyndham to John Paston I, probably 1465, 10 November
692. From J. Payn to John Paston I, 1465
78. John Paston I: Draft message from the King to Sir William Yelverton, 1465
898. From Ralph Lampet to John Daubeney, perhaps about 1465
899. From William Worcester to an unidentified person, not before 1465

1466

*720. From John Wykes to Margaret Paston, [1465] probably 1466, 7 February
895. Declarations about Fastolf's will:
A. by Thomas Neve, 1466, 6 April
B. by Robert FitzRawff, probably 1466
1043. Declaration by Robert Inglose concerning Fastolf's will, probably 1466
197. From Margaret Paston perhaps to John Berney, before May 1466
723. From Sir John Heveningham to Margaret Paston, not after 1466, 7 May
693. From Friar John Mowth to John Paston I, 1466, 12 May
896. From King Edward IV to the Bailiffs of Yarmouth and others, 1466, 26 and 27 July
743. From the Earl of Oxford to John Paston II, probably 1466, 31 July
31. Agnes Paston: Draft will, 1466, 16 September
32. Agnes Paston: Part of Draft Will, probably 1466
33. Agnes Paston: Part of Draft Will, probably 1466
900. Inquisition *post mortem* on John Paston I, 1466, October
198. From Margaret Paston to John Paston II, 1466, 29 October
*258. From John Paston II to John Paston III, [1470] 1466, 15 November
910. From Thomas Grene to William Yelverton, not before 1466, 22 December
897. Statement in the name of King Edward IV, probably 1466
699. From Thomas Shotbolt to John Paston I, 1459–66
700. From Richard Southwell to John Paston I, not after 1466
701. From Richard Southwell to John Paston I, not after 1466
702. From James Arblaster to John Paston I, not after 1466
724. From Elisabeth Clere to Margaret Paston, 1466 or soon after
725. From John Russe to Margaret Paston, 1466 or soon after
906. Claim by Fastolf's executors against John Paston I's executors, not before 1466
919. Sermon by James Gloys, perhaps 1466, not after 1473

1467–1468

325. From John Paston III to John Paston II, 1467, 27 January
745. From Thomas Daverse to John Paston II, 1467, 29 January
326. From John Paston III to John Paston II, 1467, 7 February
726. From John Herlyng to Margaret Paston, not before Lent 1467
*329. From John Paston III to John Paston II, [probably 1468] 1467, March
236. From John Paston II to John Paston III, 1467, probably March
*749. From Hugh at Fenne to John Paston II, [1468, 12 April] 1467, 24 March
327. From John Paston III to John Paston II, 1467, April
746. From Richard Calle to John Paston II, 1467, 3 April
237. John Paston II: Indenture of Wager, 1467, 1 May
*92. From William Paston II to John Paston II, 1467, before 8 June
927. From Queen Elizabeth to the Earl of Oxford, 1467, 25 June
747. From James Gresham to Simon Damme, for John Paston II, probably 1467, 2 July
199. From Margaret Paston to John Paston II, 1467, 11 July
901. Declarations by Thomas Howes about Fastolf's will, 1467, 21 July
*741. From John Wykes to John Paston II, [1465, 30 July] 1467, 28 July
748. From John Daubeney to John Paston II, 1467, 8 August
*911. Declaration by Thomas Bourchier, Archbishop of Canterbury, probably [1469] 1467, about September–November
*744. From James Gloys to John Paston II, [probably 1466] 1467, 10 November
122. From Elizabeth Poynings (*née* Paston) to John Paston II, probably 1467, 15 December
122A. Copy of writ to Sir Robert Fynys, enclosed with no. 122
750. From King Edward IV to John Paston II, 1468, 18 April
330. From John Paston III to Margaret Paston, 1468, 8 July
751. From William Ebesham to John Paston II, 1468, July–October
902. From Thomas Howes to Thomas Bourchier, Archbishop of Canterbury, 1468, 10 October
752. From an unidentified person to John Paston II, 1468, 28 October
753. From Cecily Daune to John Paston II, 1463–8, 3 November
238. From John Paston II to John Paston III, 1468, 9 November

1469

754. From the Earl of Oxford to John Paston II, probably 1469, 7 January
903. From William Cotyng to John Cook for Richard Calle, 1469, 9 January
757. From King Edward IV to John Paston II, 1469, 18 January
200. From Margaret Paston to John Paston II, 1469, 12 March
239. From John Paston II to John Paston III, 1469, 17 March

755. From William Ebesham to John Paston II, 1469, Spring
201. From Margaret Paston to John Paston II, 1469, 3 April
93. From William Paston II to Margaret Paston, probably 1469, 7 April
331. From John Paston III to John Paston II, 1469, 7 April
904. From Lord Scales to a member of the Duke of Norfolk's council, 1469, 10 April
905. From Lord Scales to an unidentified person, 1469, 10 April
332. From John Paston III to John Paston II, 1469, May
759. From Richard Calle to John Paston II, 1469, 22 May
760. From Jakys Hawte to John Paston II, 1469, 22 May
240. From John Paston II to John Paston III, 1469, early June
333. From John Paston III to John Paston II, 1469, June
761. From Richard Calle to John Paston II, 1469, 3 July
1044. From John Aubry to Sir Henry Spelman, 1469, 6 July
762. From the Earl of Oxford to John Paston II, 1469, 18 July
763. From King Edward IV to John Paston II, 1469, 23 July
202. From Margaret Paston to John Paston II, 1469, 31 August
764. From Robert Browne to John Paston II, 1469, before September
861. From Richard Calle to Margery Paston, 1469
1045. From John Bokkyng to Robert Kyrton, probably 1469, 5 September
241. From John Paston II to Walter Writtle, 1469, early September
242. From John Paston II to Walter Writtle, 1469, 10 September
203. From Margaret Paston to John Paston II, 1469, 10 or 11 September
204. From Margaret Paston to John Paston II, 1469, 12 September
243. From John Paston II to Margaret Paston, 1469, 15 September
907. From Walter Writtle to Sir John Heveningham and others, 1469, September
908. From Walter Writtle to Thomas Wingfield, 1469, September
785. From Walter Writtle to John Paston III, 1469, September
244. From John Paston II to John Paston III, 1469, 18 September
334. From John Paston III to John Paston II, 1469, about 25 September
786. From the Duke of Norfolk to John Paston III, 1469, 26 September
909. Statement by the Duke of Norfolk on the Surrender of Caister, 1469, 26 September
205. From Margaret Paston to John Paston II, 1469, 22–30 September
335. From John Paston III to John Paston II, 1469, 5 October
245. From John Paston II to Margaret Paston, 1469, October
*328. From John Paston III to Margaret Paston, [perhaps 1467] 1469, about October
*208. From Margaret Paston to John Paston II, [1470] 1469, 28 October
336. From John Paston III to John Paston II, 1469, after September
246. John Paston II: Indenture of sale 1469, 6 November

337. From John Paston III to John Paston II, 1469, December
756. From John Strange to John Paston II, 1467–9
758. From George Nevill, Archbishop of York, to John Paston II, about 1468–9, 7 May

1470

338. From John Paston III to John Paston II, 1470, 23 January
*247. From John Paston II to Roger Townshend, for [another] Sir Robert Wingfield, [perhaps about] 1470, 12 February
248. From John Paston II to John Paston III, 1470, about 20 February
249. From John Paston II to the Bishop of Winchester, 1470, February–July
339. From John Paston III to John Paston II, 1470, 1 March
1046. Memorandum from William Worcester to William Wainfleet, Bishop of Winchester, 1470, 1 March
787. From an unidentified person to John Paston III, 1470, 27 March
340. From John Paston III to John Paston II, 1470, 14 May
912. From William Worcester to William Wainfleet, Bishop of Winchester, 1470, 17 May
341. From John Paston III to John Paston II, 1470, 25 May
913. From William Worcester to a servant of Wainfleet, 1470, June
342. From John Paston III to John Paston II, 1470, 22 June
343. From John Paston III to John Paston II, 1470, 25 June
250. John Paston II: Indenture pledging plate, 1470, 3 July
206. From Margaret Paston to John Paston III, probably 1470, 6 July
251. John Paston II: Indenture pledging plate, 1470, 8 July
252. John Paston II: Indenture of agreement on Fastolf estate, 1470, 14 July
253. John Paston II: Indenture of release and quitclaim of Fastolf manors, 1470, 14 July
254. John Paston II: Indenture of agreement concerning Fastolf manors, 1470, 14 July
914. Statement about the transfer of Fastolf's foundation to Oxford, probably 1470
255. From John Paston II to Lord Beauchamp, 1470, July
765. From John Pampyng to John Paston II, 1470, 15 July
207. From Margaret Paston to John Paston II, 1470, 15 July
256. From John Paston II to John Paston III, 1470, 5 August
257. John Paston II: Indenture pledging plate, 1470, 7 August
94. William Paston II: Indenture pledging plate, 1470, 15 August
344. John Paston III: Declaration concerning the Fastolf estate, 1470, 27 August
345. From John Paston III to Margaret Paston, 1470, 12 October
*217. From Margaret Paston to John Paston III, [perhaps 1472, 23 October] 1470, 19 October

210. From Margaret Paston to John Paston II, perhaps 1470, 15 November

*218. From Margaret Paston to John Paston III, [1472] 1470, 22 November

*219. From Margaret Paston to John Paston III, [1472] 1470, 23 November

*213. From Margaret Paston to John Paston III, [probably 1471] 1470, 1 December

259. John Paston II: Inventory, probably 1470

851. Bill of expenses of John Wykes, perhaps 1470–1

*623. From John Wingfield to John Paston [I] III, [not after 1465, perhaps about 1461] perhaps about 1470–5

1471

260. John Paston II: Declaration concerning the Fastolf estate, 1471, 12 February

1047. From the Earl of Oxford to Thomas Vere, 1471, 14 March

1048. From the Earl of Oxford to Henry Spelman and others, 1471, 19 March

766. From James Gresham to John Paston II, 1471, early April

915. Probably from the Earl of Oxford to the Countess, 1471

261. From John Paston II to Margaret Paston, 1471, 18 April

346. From John Paston III to Margaret Paston, 1471, 30 April

916. Memorandum on the Battle of Tewkesbury, 1471, May

347. From John Paston III to Margaret Paston, 1471, 5 July

262. John Paston II: Schedule to release of lands, 1471, 12 July

348. From John Paston III to Margaret Paston, 1471, 22 July

263. From John Paston II to John Paston III, 1471, 15 September

264. From John Paston II to John Paston III, 1471, 28 September

265. John Paston II: Inventory of papers, after 1470

788. From R.L. to John Paston III, 1471, 21 October

349. From John Paston III to Margaret Paston, 1471, 28 October

209. From Margaret Paston to John Paston III, 1471, 5 November

394. From Edmond Paston II to John Paston III, 1471, 18 November

*211. From Margaret Paston to John Paston [II] III, 1471, 20 November

212. From Margaret Paston to John Paston III, 1471, 29 November

917. Bill of expenses, 1471, November

350. From John Paston III to John Paston II, 1471

*727. From William Worcester to Margaret Paston, probably [1468] 1471

1472

351. John Paston III: Verses, probably after 1471

214. From Margaret Paston to John Paston II, about 1472

1049. Petition of William Worcester to James Goldwell, Bishop of Norwich, probably 1472

266. From John Paston II to Margaret Paston, 1472, 8 January

215. From Margaret Paston to John Paston III, 1472, 5 February
267. From John Paston II to John Paston III, 1472, 17 February
268. From John Paston II to John Paston III, 1472, 30 April
767. From John Osbern to John Paston II, 1472, 10 May
395. From Edmond Paston II to John Paston III, probably 1472, 16 May
216. From Margaret Paston to John Paston II, 1472, 5 June
352. From John Paston III to John Paston II, 1472, 5 June
353. From John Paston III to John Paston II, 1472, 8 July
354. From John Paston III to John Paston II, 1472, 21 September
354A. John Paston III: Letter in the name of James Arblaster to the Bailiff of Maldon, 1472, 20 September
355. From John Paston III to John Paston II, 1472, 16 October
269. From John Paston II to John Paston III, 1472, 4 November
270. From John Paston II to John Paston III, 1472, 8 November
271. From John Paston II to Margaret Paston or John Paston III, 1472, 22 November
356. From John Paston III to John Paston II, 1472, 24 November
357. From John Paston III to John Paston II, 1472, late November
358. From John Paston III to John Paston II, 1472, 18 December
359. From John Paston III to the Duke of Norfolk, 1472, late
768. From John Kendale to John Paston II, probably not after 1472

1473–1474

918. Memorandum by John Wykes, not before 1473
771. From the Tenants of Sporle to John Paston II, perhaps 1473
220. From Margaret Paston probably to James Gloys, probably 1473, 18 January
272. From John Paston II to John Paston III, 1473, 3 February
360. From John Paston III to John Paston II, 1473, 8 March
361. From John Paston III to John Paston II, 1473, 26 March
273. From John Paston II to John Paston III, 1473, 2 April
274. From John Paston II to John Paston III, 1473, 12 April
275. From John Paston II to John Paston III, 1473, 16 April
276. From John Paston II to John Paston III, 1473, 18 May
947. Agreement between William Wainfleet, Bishop of Winchester, and John Paston II concerning Fastolf's estate, 1473, 1 June
277. From John Paston II to John Paston III, 1473, 3 June
278. From John Paston II to Edmond Paston II, 1473, 5 July
279. From John Paston II to Margaret Paston, 1473, 30 July
769. From Martin Rondelle to John Paston II, 1473, 28 August
731. From Thomas Hert to Margaret Paston, not after 1473, September

770. From Lord Hastings to John Paston II, 1473, 16 September

280. From John Paston II to John Paston III, 1473, late

281. From John Paston II to John Paston III, 1473, 6 November

282. From John Paston II to John Paston III, 1473, 22 November

283. From John Paston II to John Paston III, 1473, 25 November

732. Margaret Paston (?): Inventory, not after 1473

284. From John Paston II to Margaret Paston, 1474, 20 February

*292. From John Paston II to Edmond Paston II, [1475] 1474, 13 June

362. From John Paston III to 'Mistress Annes', 1474, 22 July

363. From John Paston III to John Paston II, 1474, 25 July

1050. From William Worcester to William Wainfleet, Bishop of Winchester, 1474, 21 August

95. William Paston II: Indenture pledging plate, 1474, 24 October

96. From William Paston II to John Paston II, perhaps 1474–5

97. William Paston II: Part of draft deed, perhaps 1474–5

285. From John Paston II to Margaret Paston, 1474, probably November

286. From John Paston II to Margaret Paston, 1474, 20 November

287. From John Paston II to John Paston III, 1474, 20 November

*728. From Richard Calle to Margaret Paston, probably [1472] 1474, 27 November

948. Agreement between William Wainfleet, Bishop of Winchester, and John Paston II concerning Fastolf's college 1474, 29 November

288. From John Paston II to John Paston III, 1474, 11 December

1475–1476

289. From John Paston II to John Paston III, 1475, 17 January

221. From Margaret Paston, to John Paston II, 1475, 28 January

222. From Margaret Paston to John Paston III, 1475, 28 January

290. From John Paston II to John Paston III or others, 1475, 5 February

291. From John Paston II to Margaret Paston, 1475, 22 February

223. From Margaret Paston to John Paston III, 1475, 5 March

364. From John Paston III to Margaret Paston, probably 1475, 29 March

396. Edmond Paston II: Indenture for military service, 1475, 7 April

224. From Margaret Paston to John Paston II, 1475, 23 May

225. From Margaret Paston to John Paston II, 1475, 9 August

293. From John Paston II to Margaret Paston, 1475, 11 September

365. From John Paston III to John Paston II, 1475, 10 October

366. From John Paston III to John Paston II, 1475, 23 October

*729. From Richard Calle to Margaret Paston, [perhaps 1473] probably 1475, about October

294. John Paston II: Petition to King Edward IV, 1475

295. From John Paston II to Margaret Paston, 1476, 17 January
367. From John Paston III to Margaret Paston, 1476, 21 January
368. From John Paston III to John Paston II, 1476, 23 January
296. From John Paston II to John Paston III, 1476, 27 January
369. From John Paston III to John Paston II, 1476, 3 February
370. From John Paston III to Lord Hastings, 1476, 2 March
297. From John Paston II to John Paston III or Margaret Paston, 1476, 12 March
298. From John Paston II to Margaret Paston or John Paston III, 1476, 21 March
371. From John Paston III to Margaret Paston, 1476, probably late March
372. From John Paston III to John Paston II, 1476, 6 May
299. From John Paston II to Margaret Paston or John Paston III, 1476, 27 May
949. John Paston III: Attestation concerning a forced entry at Bixley Trowse, 1476, 16 June
300. John Paston II to John Paston III, 1476, 30 June
301. From John Paston II to Margaret Paston, probably 1476, 30 August
373. From John Paston III to an unknown lady, probably 1476

1477–1478

789. From Dame Elizabeth Brews to John Paston III, 1476–7
790. From Dame Elizabeth Brews to John Paston III, probably 1477
791. From Dame Elizabeth Brews to John Paston III, 1477, about 9 February
415. From Margery Brews to John Paston III, 1477, February
416. From Margery Brews to John Paston III, 1477, February
792. From Thomas Kela to John Paston III, 1477, February
302. From John Paston II to John Paston III, 1477, 14 February
374. From John Paston III to Margaret Paston, 1477, 8 March
773. From Sir Thomas Brews to John Paston II, 1477, 8 March
303. From John Paston II to John Paston III, 1477, 9 March
375. From John Paston III to John Paston II, 1477, 9 March
376. John Paston III: Memorandum of marriage terms, 1477
304. From John Paston II to Margaret Paston, 1477, 28 March
377. John Paston III: Memorandum on marriage negotiations, 1477
305. From John Paston II to John Paston III, 1477, 14 April
306. From John Paston II to John Paston III, 1477, probably April
774. From John Pympe to John Paston II, 1477, 16 May
775. From John Pympe to John Paston II, 1477, perhaps May
776. From John Pympe to John Paston II, 1477
226. From Margaret Paston to Dame Elizabeth Brews, 1477, 11 June
307. From John Paston II to John Paston III, 1477, 23 June
378. From John Paston III to Margaret Paston, 1477, probably 28 June

308. From John Paston II to Margaret Paston, 1477, 7 August
227. From Margaret Paston to John Paston II, 1477, 11 August
777. From Edmond Bedyngfeld to John Paston II, 1477, 17 August
98. William Paston II: Memorandum on rent collection, 1477, 22 August
309. John Paston II: Copy of will, nominally 1477, 31 October
778. From William Pecock to John Paston II, 1477, 19 November
779. From William Pecock to John Paston II, 1477, 30 November
379. From John Paston III to John Paston II, 1478, 21 January
380. From John Paston III to Margaret Paston, 1478, 3 February
780. From William Worcester to John Paston II, probably 1478, 1 March
781. From Constance Reynyforth to John Paston II, 1478, 21 March
310. From John Paston II to John Paston III and Osbern Berney, 1478, 5 May
311. From John Paston II to Margaret Paston, 1478, 13 May
402. From Walter Paston to Margaret Paston, before 1479, 19 May
782. From J. Whetley to John Paston II, 1478, 20 May
228. From Margaret Paston to John Paston II, 1478, 27 May
99. William Paston II: Memorandum on the benefice of Oxnead, 1478, 31 July
312. From John Paston II to John Paston III, 1478, 25 August
100. From William Paston II to Nicholas Goldewell, 1478, 9 October
101. From William Paston II to William Pope, 1478, 17 October
406. From William Paston III to John Paston III, probably 1478, 7 November

1479

102. William Paston II: Memorandum on Marlingford Manor, 1479, 18 January
733. From William Pickenham to Margaret Paston, probably 1479, 2 February
407. From William Paston III to John Paston III, probably 1479, 23 February
103 William Paston II: Memorandum to Richard Lee, 1479, March
734. From Edmund Alyard to Margaret Paston, 1479, 4 March
313. From John Paston II to Margaret Paston, 1479, about May–June
941. William Paston II: Declaration concerning the manor of Huntingfield in Bacton, 1479, 21 May
403. From Walter Paston to John Paston II, 1479, 22 May
404. From Walter Paston to John Paston III, 1479, 30 June
104. William Paston II: Indenture depositing plate, 1479, 7 July
105. From William Paston II to Thomas Lynsted, 1479, 11 July
106. From William Paston II to Harry Waryns, 1479, 19 July
405. Walter Paston: Copy of Will nominally 1479, 18 August
942. William Paston II: Indenture recording delivery of plate, 1479, 19 August
920. Declaration by Marlingford tenants, 1479, 26 August
314. John Paston II: Memoranda, 1479, August

397. From Edmond Paston II to John Paston III, 1479, 21 August
315. From John Paston II to Margaret Paston, 1479, 29 October
783. From the Vicar of Paston to John Paston II, 1479, 3 November
*772. From William Pecock to John Paston II, [not after] probably 1479, 4 November
381. From John Paston III to John Paston II, 1479, 6 November
107. From William Paston II to Robert Walsche, 1479, 22 November
793. From William Lomnor to John Paston III, 1479, 28 November
110. William Paston II: Memoranda on Knapton, probably 1479–80
921. From Jullye to his father, 1479, November
735. From the Vicar of Paston to Margaret Paston, 1479, about December
316. John Paston II: Inventory of Books, not after 1479
382. John Paston III: Account, 1479, after 25 November
383. From John Paston III to Margaret Paston, 1479, November
108. From William Paston II to Richard Roos, probably 1479, 28 November
384. From John Paston III to Margaret Paston, 1479, December
109. From William Paston II to Richard Roos, probably 1479, 19 December
34. Agnes Paston: Extract from Will, not after 1479

1480–1485

923. William Paston II: Inventory of plate, perhaps after 1479
946. Margaret Paston: Enquiries on behalf of tenants at Flegghall, to an unidentified lawyer, after 1479
385. John Paston III: Memorandum of complaints against William Paston II, after 1479
408. From William Paston III to Edmond Paston II, after 1480, 22 February
111. From William Paston II to John Kyng, 1480, 24 February
229. Margaret Paston: Indenture of lease, 1480, 1 August
922. From George, servant to William Paston II, to John King, perhaps about 1480, 17 December
808. From the Duchess of Norfolk to John Paston III, 1480–6, 2 October
112. William Paston II: Memorandum to the Duchess of Norfolk, about 1480
809. From John, Prior of Bromholm, to John Paston III, 1480–6, 14 October
398. From Edmond Paston II to William Paston III, perhaps after 1480, January
399. From Edmond Paston II to Margaret Paston, 1481, 27 January
924. Agreement with the Priory of St. Faith, 1481, August
417. From Margery Paston (*née* Brews) to John Paston III, perhaps 1481, 1 November
418. From Margery Paston (*née* Brews) to John Paston III, perhaps 1481, 4 November
230. Margaret Paston: copy of Will, nominally 1482, 4 February

794. From T. Cryne to John Paston III, 1482, 10 April
795. From Lord Hastings to John Paston III, probably 1483, 26 April
796. From Sir Ralph Hastings to John Paston III, probably 1483, 9 May
797. From Robert Browne to John Paston III, probably after 1479 not after June 1482
798. From the Duchess of Suffolk to John Paston III, probably after 1479, not after 1483
799. From the Duke of Norfolk to John Paston III, 1483, 10 October
800. From Sir George Browne to John Paston III, not after 1483
736. From J. Burton to Margaret Paston, probably after 1466, before 1484
386. From John Paston III to Margaret Paston, between 1482 and 1484
387. John Paston III: Bill of complaint against William Paston II, 1484
1051. From the Duke of Suffolk to Thomas Jeffrey, 1484, 1 May
950. Indenture of loan between John Paston III and Henry Colet, 1485, 12 February
801. From the Duke of Norfolk to John Paston III, 1485, about 12 August
388. John Paston III: Draft letter from Elizabeth Browne (*née* Paston), 1485, before 23 September
802. From the Countess of Surrey to John Paston III, probably 1485, 3 October
803. From the Duke of Suffolk to John Paston III, 1485, 20 October
925. Declaration by William Barker and Margaret Worcester, perhaps about 1485

1486–1489

393. From John Paston III to an unknown knight, after 1485
419. From Margery Paston (*née* Brews) to John Paston III, 1486, 21 January
805. From the Countess of Oxford to John Paston III, 1486, 19 May
804. From King Henry VII to John Paston III, 1486, 12 August
806. From Lord FitzWalter to John Paston III, 1486, 19 September
854. From the Earl of Oxford to Edmond Paston II, 1486–9, 7 April
926. From John Bonewell, Prior of Norwich, to two unidentified persons, 1486–7
807. From the Earl of Oxford to John Paston III, 1487, 24 January
409. From William Paston III to John Paston III, 1487, 7 March
810. From T. Balkey to John Paston III, probably 1487, 29 April
811. From Sir Edmond Bedyngfeld to John Paston III, 1487, 16 May
811A. Copy of letter probably from the Earl of Oxford to Sir Edmond Bedyngfeld, 1487.
123. Elizabeth Browne (*née* Paston): Will, 1487, 18 May
812. From Robert Clere to John Paston III, not before 1487, 24 October
410. From William Paston III to the Bailiff of Mautby, 1487
855. From Thomas Andrew to William Paston III, 1488 or 1494, 1 December
856. From Thomas Andrew to William Paston III, 1488 or 1494, 16 December

400. From Edmond Paston II to John Paston III, June 1487–February 1493
389. From John Paston III to Margery Paston (*née* Brews), 1487–95
390. From John Paston III to Lord FitzWalter, 1487–95
813. From Lady Fitzhugh to John Paston III, probably 1488, 23 February
814. From Lord FitzWalter to John Paston III, about 1488, 7 April
411. From William Paston III to John Paston III, 1488, 13 May
815. From Dame Elizabeth Brews to John Paston III, about 1488
816. From T. Grigges to John Paston III, 1489, 2 February
420. From Margery Paston (*née* Brews) to John Paston III, 1489, 10 February
817. From the Earl of Oxford to John Paston III, perhaps 1489, 12 March
818. From the Earl of Oxford to John Paston III, 1489, 30 April
412. From William Paston III to John Paston III, 1489, April
819. From the Earl of Oxford to John Paston III, 1489, 6 May
413. From William Paston III to John Paston III, 1489, 6–10 May

1490–1499

821. From John Sherwood, Bishop of Durham, to John Paston III, 1490, 27 January
822. From the Earl of Oxford to John Paston III, probably 1491, 27 March
824. From the Earl of Oxford to John Paston III, 1491, 10 April
823. From the Earl of Oxford to John Paston III, probably about 1491, 31 July
826. From the Earl of Oxford to John Paston III, about 1491, 20 October
827. From the Earl of Oxford to John Paston III, about 1491, October
828. From the Earl of Oxford to John Paston III, about 1491, 28 October
401. Edmond Paston II: Claim for allowances, between 1489 and 1492
830. From Sir Henry Heydon to John Paston III, 1488–92, 4 March
414. From William Paston III to John Paston III, 1492, 18 February
829. From Roger Lestrange to John Paston III, probably 1492, 16 April
943. From William Paston II to Thomas Carey, 1492, 9 November
944. From William Paston II to Thomas Carey, 1493, 10 September
825. From the Bailiffs of Yarmouth to John Paston III, perhaps about 1491–4, September
831. From T. Lyng to John Paston III, 1494, November
832. From Lord FitzWalter to John Paston III, 1488–94, March–April
945. From William Paston II to Thomas Carey, 1495, 5 January
833. From the Bailiffs of Yarmouth to John Paston III, 1495, 11 July
834. From Robert Crowmer to John Paston III, 1495, 12 July
*835. From the Duchess of Norfolk to John Paston III, 1495[-6], 14 September
421. From William Paston IV to John Paston III, perhaps about 1495
820. From Dame Elizabeth Brews to John Paston III, not before June 1487 or after 1495

836. From the Duchess of Norfolk to John Paston III, perhaps 1496, 28 February
113. William Paston II: Will, 1496, 7 September
837. From the Countess of Oxford to John Paston III, 1494–8, 15 January
838. From the Earl of Oxford to John Paston III, 1499, 20 August

1500–1520

839. From King Henry VII to John Paston III, 1500, 20 March
840. From Robert Whynbergh to John Paston III, about 1500
841. From Sir John Kendal to John Paston III, not after 1500, 1 June
391. From John Paston III to Richard Croft, probably about 1500
392. From John Paston III to William Paston III and Richard Lightfoote, probably 1503, after April
849. From the Earl of Oxford to John Paston III, not after 1503, 15 September
850. From the Earl of Oxford to John Paston III, not after 1503, 22 September
845. From Richard Calle to John Paston III, not after 1503, November
846. From the Countess of Richmond probably to John Paston III, 1497–1503, 10 February
843. From the Earl of Surrey to John Paston III, 1489–1503, 25 September
858. From John Wryght to William Paston III, not after 1503, 24 November
859. From John Breton to William Paston III, not after 1503
853. From Lumen Haryson to John Paston III, not after 1504, March-April
842. From the Earl of Surrey to John Paston III, not before 1490 or after 1504, 24 April
844. From the Earl of Surrey to John Paston III, 1489–1504, 6 July
928. Award by John Yaxlee and James Hobart, 1503, 6 February
848. From the Earl of Oxford to John Paston III, 1503–4, 26 June
847. From the Countess of Richmond to John Paston III, not after 1504, 10 April
862. From William Barons, Bishop-elect of London to William Paston IV, 1504, 6 September
929. Will of Margaret Paston, widow of Edmond Paston II, 1504, 24 November
863. William Paston IV: Receipt by Thomas Bradbury, 1504, 10 December
860. From an unidentified servant of the Earl of Oxford to William Paston III, not after 1504
852. From Robert Crowmer probably to John Paston III, not after 1504
857. From William Barnard to William Paston III, not after 1504, 30 April
930. Will of Agnes Paston, widow of John Paston III, 1510, 31 May
864. From the Earl of Surrey to William Paston IV, not after 1513, 4 December
865. From John Eston to William Paston IV, 1518, 18 April
866. From William Ocley to William Paston IV, not after 1520, 3 September

CONCORDANCE OF EARLIER EDITIONS AND ORIGINAL SOURCES

Abbreviations used in the Table

(a)	abstract
Add.	Additional MS(S)
BL	London, British Library
Blomefield	Francis Blomefield, *An Essay towards a Topographical History of the County of Norfolk*, second edn., 11 vols, London 1805–10
Bodl.	Oxford, Bodleian Library
Ch.	Charter(s)
CUL	Cambridge, University Library
Folger	Washington DC, Folger Shakespeare Library
FP	Fastolf Papers (Magdalen College, Oxford)
Gloucs. RO	Gloucester, Gloucestershire Record Office
Magd. Coll.	Oxford, Magdalen College, Archives
(n)	note
NRO	Norwich, Norfolk Record Office
Nthtn. RO	Northampton, Northamptonshire Record Office
(p)	part
PCC	Prerogative Court of Canterbury
Pemb. Coll.	Cambridge, Pembroke College
Pierpont ML	New York, Pierpont Morgan Library
PRO	London, Public Record Office (now National Archives)

Fenn	Gairdner 1901	Gairdner 1904	This edition	Original
	1	1		BL Add. 27443, f. 74
	I	2		BL Add. 34889, f. 141
	II	3		BL Add. 34889, f. 142
	2(a)	4(a)		BL Add. Ch. 17225
	3(a)	5(a)		BL Add. Ch. 17243
	4	6	5	BL Add. 27443, ff. 75–7
	III	7	1	BL Add. 34889, f. 213
	IV	8	422	BL Add. 34888, f. 1

Fenn	Gairdner 1901	Gairdner 1904	This edition	Original
	959(a)	9(a)		Bodl. Ch. Norfolk a. 8, no. 730
			931	NRO Phillipps 532
	5	10	2, 3	BL Add. 27443, f. 78v
	6	11	868	BL Add. 27443, f. 79
			867	PRO S.C. 8/135/6715
	7	12	4	BL Add. 27443, f. 80
			870A	PRO, S.C. 8/169/8449–50
	8(a)	13(a)		BL Add. 27443, ff. 81, 82
	960(a)	14(a)		Bodl. Ch. Norfolk a. 8, no. 731
	9(a)	15(a)	423	BL Add. 27443, f. 83
	10(a)	16(a)		BL Add. 27443, f. 84
	11(a)	17(a)	427	BL Add. 27443, f. 85
	12(a)	18(a)		BL Add. 27443, f. 86
			954	BL Add. 28212, f. 23
	13(a)	19(a)		BL Add. Ch. 17226
	14	20	6, 7	BL Add. 27443, f. 87v
	15(a)	21(a)		BL Add. 27443, f. 89
	16(a)	22(a)	424	BL Add. Ch. 17227
	17(a)	23(a)		BL Add. Ch. 14313
	18	24		BL Add. Ch. 17228
iii. 14	19	25	869	BL Add. 34888, f. 3
	20(a)	26(a)		BL Add. 39848, f. 1
	21(a)	27(a)		BL Add. Ch. 17237
	22(n)	28(n)		BL Add. Ch. 17229–31
	V	29	438	BL Add. 34888, f. 4
	VI	30	8	BL Add. 34889, f. 140
			870B–D	PRO S.C. 336/14868A–C
i. 36	23(n)	31(n)		Untraced; mentioned by Fenn
			932	NRO WKC 1/43/11
	24(a)	32(a)		BL Add. Ch. 17232
	961	33		BL Add. 27446, f. 113
			933	NRO WKC 1/43/10
i. 2	25	34	13	BL Add. 43488, f. 4
	26(a)	35(a)	9	BL Add. 27443, f. 88
			934	NRO WKC 1/43/21
i. 4	27	36	439	BL Add. 43488, f. 5
	28(a)	37(a)	872	BL Add. 27443, f. 90
iii. 18	29	38	124	BL Add. 34888, f. 7
	VII	39	955	Pemb. Coll. LC. II. 230, f. 3
			935	NRO WKC 1/43/20
	30(a)	40(a)		BL Add. Ch. 14598
			10	BL Add. 45099, f. 2
			428	BL Add. 45099, f. 1, ij
			429	BL Add. 45099, f. 1, iij

Fenn	Gairdner 1901	Gairdner 1904	This edition	Original
			430	BL Add. 45099, f. 1, iiij
	31(a)	41(a)		BL Add. Ch. 17233
	32(n)	42(n)		*Rotuli Parliamentorum*, v. 59
			936	NRO WKC 1/43/20 dorse
	962(a)	43(a)		Bodl. Ch. Norfolk a. 8, no. 740
	33(a)	44(a)		BL Add. Ch. 17234
	34(a)	45(a)	426	BL Add. 27443, f. 91
	35	46	871	BL Add. 27443, f. 93
iii. 20	36	47	126	BL Add. 34888, f. 8
	963(a)	48(a)		PRO Chancery Roll, Lanc. 22H.VI, Y.2c, 29
	964	49	11	Bodl. Douce Ch. 18
	VIII	50	876	BL Add. 34888, f. 19
iii. 26(p)	37(p)	51(p)	432	BL Add. 34888, f. 9
iii. 28	38	52	425	BL Add. 52410
	39(a)	53(a)		BL Add. Ch. 14571
	40(a)	54(a)	431	BL Add. 27443, f. 94
	41(a)	55(a)	433	BL Add. 27443, f. 95
	42	56	441	BL Add. 27443, f. 96
			956	Magd. Coll. FP 40
	IX	57		BL Add. 34888, f. 10
i. 10	43	58	440	BL Add. 43488, f. 6
	965	59	57	Bodl. Tanner 95, f. 82
iii. 16	44	60	808	BL Add. 34888, f. 12
			35	BL Add. 45099, f. 2
	45	61	482	BL Add. 27443, f. 97
			937	NRO WKC 1/43/4
iii. 32	46	62	14	BL Add. 34888, f. 13
			938	BL Add. Ch. 14525
			939	Bodl. Douce Ch. a.1, f. 92
iii. 36	47	63	874	BL Add. 34888, f. 14
iii. 38	48	64	434	BL Add. 34888, f. 15
			437	PRO S.C. 8/198/9884
i. 16	49	65		BL Add. 43488, f. 8
			957	Bodl. Eng. lett. c.291, f. 95
i. 20	50	66	599	BL Add. 43488, f. 9
	51(a)	67(a)	15	BL Add. Ch. 14819
			16	BL Add. Ch. 19336
	52	68		BL Add. 27443, f. 98
	53	69	79	BL Add. 27443, f. 99
	54(a)	70(a)		BL Add. Ch. 17235
			959	BL Add. Ch. 18239
	966.1(a)	71.1(a)	960	Magd. Coll. Hickling 130
	966.2(a)	71.2(a)	961	Magd. Coll. Hickling 140

Fenn	Gairdner 1901	Gairdner 1904	This edition	Original
	967.1(a)	72.1(a)	958	Magd. Coll. Hickling 71
	967.2(a)	72.2(a)	952	Magd. Coll. Hickling 74
	967.3(a)	72.3(a)	951	Magd. Coll. Hickling 75
	967.4(a)	72.4(a)	1010	Magd. Coll. Hickling 89
	967.5(a)	72.5(a)	1014	Magd. Coll. Hickling 104
	55(a)	73(a)	17	BL Add. Ch. 17236
	X	74	445	BL Add. 34889, f. 178
iii. 54	56	75	128	BL Add. 34888, f. 18
	57	76	879	BL Add. 27443, f. 100
			962	Magd. Coll. FP 26
	59(a)	77(a)	129	BL Add. 39848, f. 2
i. 12	60	78	963	BL Add. 43488, f. 7
i. 190	61	79	873	BL Add. 43491, f. 5
	XI	80	442	BL Add. 34889, f. 143
	XII	81	443	BL Add. 34888, f. 57
			964	Magd. Coll. Titchwell 41
			965	Magd. Coll. Titchwell 158
iii. 408	62	82	151	BL Add. 34888, f. 23
			966	Magd. Coll. Add. 99, f. 23
			967	Magd. Coll. Titchwell 170
	992(a)	83(a)	132	BL Add. 34888, f. 24
iii. 80	63	84	469	BL Add. 34888, f. 28
	64	85	80	BL Add. 27443, f. 101
i. 192	65	86	875	BL Add. 43488, f. 52
	66	87	133	BL Add. 27443, f. 102
iii. 314	67	88	130	BL Add. 34888, f. 29
	XIII	89	488	BL Add. 34889, f. 164
i. 208	68	90	968	BL Add. 43491, f. 7
			969	Magd. Coll. Add. 99, f. 21
			970	Magd. Coll. Add. 99, f. 22
	69	91	81	BL Add. 27443, f. 103
	XIV	92	448	See G. 968/298 and this ed. 530/1025
iii. 202	70	93	18	BL Add. 34888, f. 33
iii. 204	71	94	446	BL Add. 34888, f. 34
	XV	95	444	BL Add. 34888, f. 32
	993(a)	96(a)	447	BL Add. 34888, f. 30
	72	97	953	BL Add. 28212, f. 21
i. 184	73	98	972	BL Add. 43488, f. 22
	74(a)	99(a)		BL Add. 27443, f. 104
			973	Magd. Coll. Titchwell 208/1
			974	Magd. Coll. Titchwell 208/2
			975	Magd. Coll. Add. 99, f. 18
			976	Magd. Coll. Add. 99, f. 16

Fenn	Gairdner 1901	Gairdner 1904	This edition	Original
			977	Magd. Coll. Add. 99, f. 7
	75	100	971	BL Add. 34888, f. 35
			82	NRO MS Walter Rye 38, ff. 64–6
iii. 62	76	101		BL Add. 34888, ff. 36–9
	77	102	36	BL Add. Ch. 17240
	78	103	131	BL Add. 27443, f. 105
	79(a)	104(a)	978	BL Add. 39848, f. 3
iii. 304	80	105	20	BL Add. 34888, f. 40
i. 28(p)	81(p)	106(p)	136	BL Add. 43488, f. 11
	82(a)	107(a)	979	BL Add. 39848, f. 4
	83	108	449	Bodl. Douce 393, f. 100
iii. 364	84	109	596	BL Add. 34888, f. 41
	85	110	598	Bodl. Douce 393, f. 99
	XXII	111	592	Pemb. Coll. LC. II. 230, f. 6
	86	112	593	Bodl. Douce 393, f. 101
	87	113	594	Bodl. Douce 393, f. 102
	88(a)	114(a)	600	BL Add. 27443, f. 106
	89	115	595	Bodl. Douce 393, f. 103
	90	116	597	BL Add. 27443, f. 107
i. 32	91	117	980	BL Add. 43488, f. 12
	XVI	118	476	BL Add. 34888, f. 164
	92(a)	119(a)		BL Add. 27443, f. 108
i. 38	93	120	450	BL Add. 43488, f. 13
i. 44	94	121	451	BL Add. 43488, f. 14
	95(a)	122(a)	981	BL Add. 39848, f. 5
i. 162	96	123	452	BL Add. 43488, f. 43
iii. 160	97	124	490	BL Add. 34888, f. 42
i. 52(p)	98(p)	125(p)	982	BL Add. 43488, f. 15
i. 54	99	126	692	BL Add. 43491, f. 1
	XVII	127	453	BL Add. 34888, f. 73
	100	128	454	BL Add. 27443, f. 109
	101(a)	129(a)	703	BL Add. 27443, f. 110
	102(a)	130(a)	983	BL Add. 39848, f. 6
iii. 86	103	131	455	BL Add. 34888, f. 43
	104	132	456	Bodl. Douce 393, f. 88
	105	133	456A	BL Add. 27443, f. 111
	106	134	984	BL Add. 27443, f. 112
	107	135	38	BL Add. Ch. 17239
	108	136	39	BL Add. 27443, f. 113
	109(a)	137(a)	986	BL Add. 39848, f. 7
	110(a)	138(a)	988	BL Add. 39848, f. 8
iii. 362	111	139	458	BL Add. 34888, f. 44
	112(a)	140(a)	470	BL Add. 27443, f. 114
	XVIII	141	459	BL Add. 34888, f. 45

Fenn	Gairdner 1901	Gairdner 1904	This edition	Original
iii. 154	113	142	460	BL Add. 34888, ff. 47–8
i. 64	114	143	460A	BL Add. 43488, f. 17
iii. 92(p)	115(p)	144(p)	989	BL Add. 34888, f. 49
	116	145	463	BL Add. 27443, f. 115
iii. 94	117	146	461	BL Add. 34888, f. 50
	118	147	462	BL Add. 27443, f. 116
	119	148	464	Bodl. Douce 393, f. 93
i. 98	120	149	465	BL Add. 43488, f. 26
	121	150	466	Bodl. Douce 393, f. 94a
iii. 100	122	151	467	BL Add. 34888, f. 51
	XIX	152	618	BL Add. 34889, f. 160
	123(a)	153(a)	990	BL Add. 39848, f. 9
iii. 50	124	154	877	BL Add. 34888, f. 52
	125	155	878	BL Add. 27443, f. 117
	126(a)	156(a)	991	Magd. Coll. Fastolf Additional 2
	127(a)	157(a)		BL Add. Ch. 17238
			992	Magd. Coll. FP 37
	128(a)	158(a)	993	BL Add. 39848, f. 10
	129(a)	159(a)	985	BL Add. 39848, f. 11
iii. 102(p)	130(p)	160(p)	994	BL Add. 34888, f. 53
	131(a)	161(a)	995	BL Add. 39848, f. 12
	132	162	996	BL Add. 27443, f. 118
	XX	163	468	BL Add. 34888, f. 168
	133(a)	164(a)	997	BL Add. 39848, f. 13
	XXI	165	134	BL Add. 34889, f. 150
	137	166	998	BL Add. 27443, f. 121
iii. 106	138	167	999	BL Add. 34888, f. 61
	139	168	1000	BL Add. 27443, f. 122
iii. 134	140	169	1001	BL Add. 34888, f. 62
	XXIII	170	471	BL Add. 34888, f. 63
			1002	Urbana, Univ. of Illinois 4122
	141(a)	171(a)	1003	BL Add. 39848, f. 14
	XXIV	172	472	BL Add. 34889, f. 230
	142(a)	173(a)	1004	BL Add. 39848, f. 15
	143(a)	174(a)	1005	BL Add. 39848, f. 16
	144	175	880	BL Add. 27444, f. 1
	145	176		BL Add. 27444, f. 2
	XXV	177	605	BL Add. 34889, f. 158
	146	178	473	BL Add. 27444, f. 3
	147	179	474	BL Add. 27444, f. 4
iii. 288	148	180	137	BL Add. 34888, f. 64
	XXVI	181	475	BL Add. 34889, f. 169
	XXVII	182	138	BL Add. 34888, f. 55
iii. 238	149	183	148	BL Add. 34888, f. 65

Fenn	Gairdner 1901	Gairdner 1904	This edition	Original
	150	184	139	BL Add. 27444, f. 5
	151	185	881	BL Add. 27444, f. 6
	152(a)	186(a)	1006	BL Add. 39848, f. 17
iii. 84(p)	153(p)	187(p)	143	BL Add. 34888, f. 66
	154(a)	188(a)	1007	BL Add. 39848, f. 18
	155	189	477	BL Add. 27444, f. 7
	156	190	478	BL Add. 27444, f. 8
iii. 144	157	191	723	BL Add. 34888, f. 67
iii. 116	158	192	1008	BL Add. 34888, ff. 68v–69r
iii. 308	159	193	479	BL Add. 34888, f. 70
			1009	Washington Folger X.d.274
	160	194	22	BL Add. 27444, f. 9
	161	195	21	BL Add. 27444, f. 10
iii. 44	162	196	24	BL Add. 34888, f. 71
iii. 424	163	197	140	BL Add. 34888, f. 72
	164	198	480	BL Add. 27444, f. 11
	165	199	481	BL Add. 27444, f. 12
iii. 133n	166(n)	200(n)		Untraced; mentioned by Fenn
iii. 124	167	201	141	BL Add. 34888, f. 74
	168(a)	202(a)	1016	BL Add. 39848, f. 19
	169(a)	203(a)	987	BL Add. 39848, f. 20
	170(a)	204(a)	457	BL Add. 39848, f. 21
iii. 132(p)	171(p)	205(p)	1011	BL Add. 34888, f. 75
iii. 366	172	206	483	BL Add. 34888, f. 78
	XXVIII	207	23	BL Add. 34888, f. 76
			1012	BL Add. 28209, f. 21
			1013	BL Add. 28212, f. 22
			484	Pierpont ML, Thane Collection
	XXIX	208	485	BL Add. 34888, f. 79
	XXX	209	486	BL Add. 34888, f. 60
iii. 248	173	210		BL Add. 34888, f. 82
	174	211	42A–C	BL Add. 27444, ff. 15r, 14, 13
	175	212	43	BL Add. 27444, f. 15v
	176	213	44	BL Add. 27444, f. 16
	177	214	882	BL Add. 27444, f. 17
	XXXI	215	487	BL Add. 34888, f. 83
iv. 14	178	216	142	BL Add. 34888, f. 84
	179	217	40	BL Add. 27444, f. 18
	180	218	41	BL Add. Ch. 17241
	181	219	46	BL Add. 27444, f. 19
	XXXII	220	489	BL Add. 33597, f. 1
iii. 168(p)	182(p)	221(p)	144	BL Add. 34888, f. 85
iii. 162	183	222	25	BL Add. 34888, f. 86
	184	223		BL Add. Ch. 17242

Fenn	Gairdner 1901	Gairdner 1904	This edition	Original
iii. 324	185	224	150	BL Add. 34888, f. 87
	186	225	47	BL Add. 27444, f. 20
i. 68(p)	187(p)	226(p)	146	BL Add. 43488, f. 18
iii. 182	188	227	26	BL Add. 34888, f. 88
iii. 186	189	228	147	BL Add. 34888, f. 89
	190	229	152	BL Add. 27444, f. 21
iii. 108	191	230		BL Add. 34888, f. 90
	XXXIII	231	435	BL Add. 34889, f. 225
	192	232	501	BL Add. 27444, f. 22
	193	233	502	BL Add. 27444, f. 23
	194	234	503	Bodl. Douce 393, f. 82
	195	235		BL Egerton 914
iii. 170	196	236	145	BL Add. 34888, f. 91
iii. 188	197	237	19	BL Add. 34888, f. 92
	198	238	491A	BL Add. 27444, f. 24
iii. 174	199	239	491	BL Add. 34888, f. 93
	200	240	49	BL Add. 27444, f. 25
	201	241	48	BL Add. Ch. 16545
iii. 192	202	242	493	BL Add. 34888, f. 97
iii. 196	203	243	27	BL Add. 34888, f. 98
	XXXIV	244	492	BL Add. 34888, f. 94
	204	245	494	BL Add. 27444, f. 26
iii. 200	205	246	495	BL Add. 34888, f. 99
i. 76(p)	206(p)	247(p)	496	BL Add. 43488, f. 20
iii. 210	207	248	497	BL Add. 34888, f. 100
i. 140	208	249	498	BL Add. 43488, f. 37
iii. 214	209	250	499	BL Add. 34888, f. 101
	XXXV	251	1015	BL Add. 34888, f. 102
iii. 216	210	252	50	BL Add. 34888, f. 104
	XXXVI	253	573	BL Add. 34889, f. 217
i. 72	211	254	83	BL Add. 43488, f. 19
	LXXIX	255	85	BL Add. 33597, f. 5
i. 92	212	256	504	BL Add. 43488, f. 24
i. 88	213	257	505	BL Add. 43488, f. 23
iii. 318	214	258	506	BL Add. 34888, f. 105
iii. 320	215	259	507	BL Add. 34888, f. 106
iii. 220	216	260	84	BL Add. 34888, f. 107
	217(a)	261(a)	586	BL Add. 39848, f. 22
iii. 376	218	262	575	BL Add. 34888, f. 108
	219	263	508	BL Add. 27444, f. 27
	220(a)	264(a)	1017	BL Add. 39848, f. 23
			1018	BL Add. 29747, f. 2
	221	265	1020	BL Add. 27444, f. 28
iii. 224	222	266	509	BL Add. 34888, f. 109

Fenn	Gairdner 1901	Gairdner 1904	This edition	Original
iii. 230	223	267	510	BL Add. 34888, f. 110
			1019	Magd. Coll. Misc. 367
	224	268	511	BL Add. 27444, f. 29
	225	269	585	BL Add. 27444, f. 30
i. 80	226	270	512	BL Add. 43488, f. 21
	227(a)	271(a)	513	BL Add. 39848, f. 24
iii. 232	228	272	514	BL Add. 34888, f. 111
	229	273	516	BL Add. 27444, f. 31
iii. 236	230	274	517	BL Add. 34888, f. 112
	231(a)	275(a)	587	BL Add. 39848, f. 25
	232	276	518	BL Add. 27444, f. 32
	233	277	51	BL Add. 27444, f. 33
iii. 338	234	278	1021	BL Add. 34888, f. 113
	235(a)	279(a)	520	BL Add. 39848, f. 26
	236(a)	280(a)	519	BL Add. 27444, f. 34
	237(a)	281(a)	521	BL Add. 39848, f. 27
iii. 178	238	282	1022	BL Add. 34888, f. 114
	239	283		PRO Chancery Misc. 37, III, 4–11
	240	284	1023	BL Add. 39848, f. 28
i. 100	241	285	522	BL Add. 43488, f. 27
	242(a)	286(a)	523	BL Add. 39848, f. 29
i. 104(p)	243(p)	287(p)	1024	BL Add. 43488, f. 28
i. 96	244	288	524	BL Add. 43488, f. 25
	245(a)	289(a)	525	BL Add. 39848, f. 30
	246	290	531	BL Add. 27444, f. 35
iii. 432	247	291	633	BL Add. 34888, f. 115
	248(a)	292(a)		BL Add. 39848, f. 31
	XXXVII	293	526	BL Add. 34889, f. 171
iii. 240	249	294	527	BL Add. 34888, f. 116
iii. 380	250	295	528	BL Add. 34888, f. 117
iii. 146	251	296	711	BL Add. 34888, f. 118
iii. 128	252	297	529	BL Add. 34888, f. 119
	968/XIV	298/92	530	Bodl. Top. Norf. b. 3, f. 68v and Palmer, *Yermouthe*, p. 61 (copies)
			1025	Mannington Hall, Walpole Archive (original)
i. 108	253	299	1026	BL Add. 43488, f. 29
iv. 32	254	300	532	BL Add. 34888, f. 120
	255	301	52	BL Add. 27444, f. 36
ii. 246	256	302	533	BL Add. 34888, f. 121
i. 114(p)	257(p)	303(p)	534	BL Add. 43491, f. 2
	258(a)	304(a)	1027	BL Add. 39848, f. 32
	259	305	535	BL Add. 27444, f. 37
iii. 252	260	306	156	BL Add. 34888, f. 122

Fenn	Gairdner 1901	Gairdner 1904	This edition	Original
	261(a)	307(a)	536	BL Add. 39848, f. 33
			1028	Magd. Coll. FP 61
	262	308	1033	BL Add. 28212, f. 26
iii. 260	263	309		BL Add. 34888, ff. 123v-4r, 27444, f. 38
iii. 268	264	310		BL Add. 34888, ff. 125–6, 27444, ff. 39–41
iii. 261n.1	265(n)	311(n)		Untraced; mentioned by Fenn
	266(a)	312(a)	588	BL Add. 39848, f. 34
ii. 290	969	313	515	BL Add. 43490, f. 41
iii. 256	267	314	537	BL Add. 34888, f. 127
	268	315	558	BL Add. 27444, f. 42
	269	316	559	BL Add. 27444, f. 43
	270–1(a)	317–8(a)	538	BL Add. 39848, ff. 35–6
	272	319	539	Untraced; *olim* W.A. Tyssen Amherst
	273	320	540	BL Add. 27444, f. 44
i. 120	274	321	541	BL Add. 43488, f. 31
	275	322	1029	BL Add. 39848, f. 37
	276(a)	323(a)	542	BL Add. 39848, f. 38
iii. 332	277	324	543	BL Add. 34888, f. 128
			1030	Gloucs. RO D1367/M13
	278	325	544	BL Add. 27444, f. 45
i. 124	279	326	1031	BL Add. 43488, f. 32
iii. 290	280	327	545	BL Add. 34888, f. 129
	XXXVIII	328	546	BL Add. 34889, f. 173
	XXXIX	329	547	BL Add. 35251, f. 24
	281	330	548	BL Add. 27444, f. 46
i. 130	282	331	549	BL Add. 43488, f. 34
iii. 278	283	332	550	BL Add. 34888, f. 130
	284	333	551	BL Add. 27444, f. 47
i. 134(p)	285(p)	334(p)	552	BL Add. 43488, f. 35
	286(a)	335(a)	553	BL Add. 39848, f. 39
	287(a)	336(a)	554	BL Add. 39848, f. 40
	288(a)	337(a)	555	BL Add. 39848, f. 41
	289	338	557	BL Add. 27444, f. 48
	996	339	581	BL Add. 34889, f. 154
i. 166	290	340	1032	BL Add. 43488, f. 45
	291	341	560	BL Add. 27444, f. 50
i. 138	292	342	561	BL Add. 43488, f. 36
	293	343	563	BL Add. 27444, f. 51
iii. 276	294	344	562	BL Add. 34888, f. 131
	295	345	565	BL Add. 27444, f. 52
	296	346	566	BL Add. 27444, f. 53

Fenn	Gairdner 1901	Gairdner 1904	This edition	Original
	297	347	564	BL Add. 27444, f. 54
i. 24(p)	298(p)	348(p)	567	BL Add. 43488 f. 10
	299(a)	349(a)	568	BL Add. 39848, f. 42
	300(a)	350(a)	569	BL Add. 39848, f. 43
i. 164(p)	301(p)	351(p)	570	BL Add. 43488, f. 44
	302	352		BL Add. Ch. 17244
	XL	353	556	BL Add. 34889, f. 170
	303	354	590	BL Add. 27444, f. 55
iii. 294	304	355	571	BL Add. 34888, f. 132
iii. 298	305	356	572	BL Add. 34888, f. 133
	306	357	589	BL Add. 27444, f. 56
	307(a)	358(a)		BL Add. Ch. 17245
	308(a)	359(a)	1034	BL Add. 39848, f. 44
iii. 42	309	360	1035	BL Add. 34888, f. 134
i. 146	310	361		BL Add. 43488, f. 39
i. 142	311	362	28	BL Add. 43491, f. 3
iii. 40	312	363	30	BL Add. 34888, f. 135
i. 150(p)	313(p)	364(p)	883	BL Add. 43488, f. 40
	314(a)	365(a)	884	BL Add. 39848, f. 45
i. 154	315	366	1036	BL Add. 43488, f. 41
	XLI	367	695	BL Add. 34889, f. 163
	316	368	53	BL Add. 39848, f. 46
i. 156	317	369	712	BL Add. 43488, f. 42
i. 170(p)	318(p)	370(p)	574	BL Add. 43488, f. 46
	319(a)	371(a)		BL Add. 27444, f. 57
	320	372	576	BL Add. 39848, f. 47
	321(a)	373(a)		BL Add. Ch. 17246
iii. 328	322	374	121	BL Add. 34888, f. 136
			591	Pierpont ML, Thane Collection
iii. 336	323	375	234	BL Add. 34888, f. 137
	324(a)	376(a)	577	BL Add. 39848, f. 48
i. 174	325	377	176	BL Add. 43488, f. 47
	326	378	607	BL Add. 27444, f. 58
	327	379	578	BL Add. 27444, f. 59
	328(a)	380(a)	579	BL Add. 39848, f. 49
i. 128	329	381		BL Add. 43488, f. 33
i. 194	330	382		BL Add. 43488, f. 53
iii. 342	331	383	583	BL Add. 34888, f. 139
iv. 38	970	384	580	BL Add. 34888, f. 138
	332	385		BL Add. 27444, ff. 60–6, 39849
	333	386	54	BL Add. 22927
	334	387		Untraced; *olim* A. Fountaine of Narford
	335	388		BL Add. Ch. 17247

Fenn	Gairdner 1901	Gairdner 1904	This edition	Original
	336	389		Untraced; see *Archæologia* xxi (1827), 232
	337	390	61	BL Add. 27444, f. 67
iii. 352	338	391	86	BL Add. 34888, f. 140
	971	392	885	Bodl. Ch. Norfolk a. 8, no. 725
iii. 358	339	393	887	BL Add. 34888, f. 141
	340(a)	394(a)	713	BL Add. 27444, f. 68
iii. 346	341	395	582	BL Add. 34888, f. 142
i. 178	342	396	584	BL Add. 43488, f. 48
	343	397	886	BL Add. 27444, f. 69
	344(a)	398(a)	603	BL Add. 27444, f. 70
i. 182(p)	345(p)	399(p)	888	BL Add. 43488, f. 49
i. 186(p)	346(p)	400(p)	88	BL Add. 43491, f. 4
	347	401	604	BL Add. 27444, f. 71
	348	402	665	BL Add. 27444, f. 72
	349	403	705	BL Add. 27444, f. 73
	XLII	404	606	BL Add. 34888, f. 161
	XLIII	405	1037	BL Add. 34888, f. 143
			940	Magd. Coll. Guton Hall 178/3
	350	406	89	BL Add. 27444, f. 74
iii. 398	351	407	889	BL Add. 34888, f. 146
	352	408	55	BL Add. 27444, f. 75
	XLIV	409	608	BL Add. 34888, f. 147
iii. 244	353	410		BL Add. 34888, f. 149
	972(a)	411(a)	890	BL Add. 27446, ff. 114–5
iv. 36	973	412	56	BL Add. 34888, f. 150
	974(a)	413(a)		Magd. Coll. Southwark 50a
	354	414	601	BL Add. 27444, f. 76
iii. 382	355	415	609	BL Add. 34888, f. 151
	997	416	611	BL Add. 34888, f. 152
	XLV	417	610	BL Add. 34888, f. 158
	356	418	612	BL Add. 27444, f. 77
i. 198	357	419	613	BL Add. 43491, f. 6
	358(a)	420(a)	614	BL Add. 27444, f. 78
	359	421	615	BL Add. 27444, f. 79
	360	422	616	BL Add. 27444, ff. 80–1
iv. 194	361	423	154	BL Add. 34888, f. 155
	362	424	714	BL Add. 27444, f. 82
			715	BL Add. 34888, f. 163
iii. 432	363	425	1041	BL Add. 34888, f. 156
iii. 386(p)	364	426	617	BL Add. 34888, f. 157
	365	427	155	BL Add. 27444, f. 83
	366	428	619	BL Add. 27444, f. 84
			1039	BL Add. Ch. 18238

Fenn	Gairdner 1901	Gairdner 1904	This edition	Original
	XLVIII	429	655	BL Add. 34889, f. 156
i. 202	367	430	114	BL Add. 43488, f. 55
iii. 404	368	431	624	BL Add. 34888, f. 172
iii. 412	369	432	158	BL Add. 34888, f. 173
iv. 78	370	433	602	BL Add. 34888, f. 174
	371	434	699	BL Add. 27444, f. 85
	XLVI	435	127	BL Add. 34889, f. 199
iii. 392(p)	372(p)	436(p)	919	BL Add. 34888, f. 171
	XLVII	437	642	BL Add. 34888, f. 166
iii. 138	373	438	622	BL Add. 34888, f. 169
iii. 140	374	439	623	BL Add. 34888, f. 170
	375	440	45	BL Add. 27444, f. 86
	376(a)	441(a)		BL Add. 27444, f. 87
	377(a)	442(a)		BL Add. 27444, f. 88
	378(a)	443(a)	620	BL Add. 27444, f. 89
	379(a)	444(a)	736	BL Add. 27444, f. 90
	380(a)	445(a)	721	BL Add. 27444, f. 91
	381(a)	446(a)	658	BL Add. 27444, f. 92
	382(a)	447(a)	500	BL Add. 27444, f. 93
	383(a)	448(a)	918	BL Add. 27444, f. 94
i. 226	384	449	317	BL Add. 43489, f. 6
i. 216	385	450	90	BL Add. 43489, f. 4
i. 222	386	451	625	BL Add. 43489, f. 5
iv. 2	387	452	628	BL Add. 34888, f. 177
	388	453	627	BL Add. 27444, f. 95
	XLIX	454	626	BL Add. 34888, f. 175
iv. 10	389	455	629	BL Add. 34888, f. 178
	390	456	630	Bodl. Douce 393, f. 85
i. 230	391	457	631	BL Add. 43489, f. 7
iv. 6	392	458	632	BL Add. 34888, f. 179
	393	459	634	BL Add. 27444, f. 96
i. 232	394	460	635	BL Add. 43489, f. 8
	395	461	115	BL Add. 27444, f. 97
	396	462	159	BL Add. 27444, f. 98
iv. 18	397	463	716	BL Add. 34888, f. 180
	398	464	717	BL Add. 27444, f. 99
	399	465	636	BL Add. 27444, f. 100
	400	466	160	BL Add. 27444, f. 101
i. 236	401	467	637	BL Add. 43489, f. 9
iv. 240	402	468	58	BL Add. 34888, f. 184
iv. 24	403	469	161	BL Add. 34888, f. 185
i. 238	404	470	638	BL Add. 43489, f. 10
iv. 28	405	471	639	BL Add. 34888, f. 186
iv. 30	406	472	162	BL Add. 34888, f. 187

Fenn	Gairdner 1901	Gairdner 1904	This edition	Original
	407	473	640	PRO C.66/494, Pat. Roll 1Ed.IV, III m.2, 13
	L	474	641	BL Add. 34888, f. 181
	408	475	59	BL Add. 27444, f. 102
iv. 42	409	476	643	BL Add. 34888, f. 188
iv. 46	410	477	231	BL Add. 34888, ff. 189v–90r
iv. 52	411	478	116	BL Add. 34888, f. 191
iv. 96	412	479	1038	BL Add. 34888, f. 192
i. 246	413	480	646A	BL Add. 43491, f. 8
	414	481	644	BL Add. 27444, f. 103
iv. 58	415	482	645	BL Add. 34888, f. 193
i. 240	416	483	646	BL Add. 43489, f. 11
	417	484	117	CUL Add. 6968, pp. 19–20
	418	485	647	BL Add. 27444, f. 104
iii. 414	419	486	648	BL Add. 34888, f. 194
	420	487	737	BL Add. 27444, f. 105
iv. 232	421	488	163	BL Add. 34888, f. 195
	422	489	165	BL Add. 27444, f. 106
iv. 252	423	490	697	BL Add. 34888, f. 196
iv. 258	424	491	698	BL Add. 34888, f. 197
	425(a)	492(a)	650	BL Add. 27444, f. 107
	426	493	29	BL Add. 27444, f. 108
	427	494	651	BL Add. 27444, f. 109
iv. 64	428	495	652	BL Add. 34888, f. 198
iv. 106(p)	429(p)	496(p)	166	BL Add. 34888, f. 199
	134	497	167	BL Add. 27443, f. 119
iii. 150	135	498	653	BL Add. 34888, f. 54
	136	499	649	BL Add. 27443, f. 120
	430	500	654	BL Add. 27444, f. 110
iv. 104	432	501	710	BL Add. 34888, f. 200
iv. 108	433	502	657	BL Add. 34888, f. 201
iii. 48	434	503	436	BL Add. 34888, f. 202
	435	504	168	BL Add. 27444, f. 111
	436	505	169	BL Add. 27444, f. 112
v. 328	437	506	659	BL Add. 27444, f. 113
			656	Bodl. Gough Camb. 3, f. 227
	438	507	661	BL Add. 27444, f. 114
	439	508	62	BL Add. 27444, f. 115
iv. 68	440	509	662	BL Add. 34888, f. 203
ii. 288	441	510	170	BL Add. 43490, f. 40
iv. 126	442	511	232	BL Add. 34888, f. 204
i. 250(p)	443(p)	512(p)	63	BL Add. 43489, f. 13
iv. 76	444	513	663	BL Add. 34888, f. 205
i. 252	445	514	664	BL Add. 43489, f. 14

Fenn	Gairdner 1901	Gairdner 1904	This edition	Original
iv. 112	446	515	666	BL Add. 34888, f. 206
	447	516	667	BL Add. 27444, f. 116
	448	517	171	BL Add. 27444, f. 117
iv. 100	449	518	233	BL Add. 34888, f. 207
	450(n)	519(n)	64	BL Add. 39848, ff. 50–3
	451(n)	520(n)		Bodl. Norfolk Ch. a. 8, no. 722
iv. 138	452	521	668	BL Add. 34888, f. 208
iv. 144	453	522	738	BL Add. 34888, f. 209
iii. 430	454	523	670	BL Add. 34888, f. 210
	455(a)	524(a)	669	BL Add. 27444, f. 118
iv. 120	456	525	671	BL Add. 34888, f. 211
	457	526	91	BL Add. 27444, f. 119
iv. 124(p)	458(p)	527(p)	673	BL Add. 34888, f. 212
i. 270	459	528	674	BL Add. 43489, f. 19
i. 260	460	529	675	BL Add. 43489, f. 16
	461	530	60	BL Add. 27444, ff. 120–1
i. 262	462	531	676	BL Add. 43489, f. 17
i. 266	463	532	319	BL Add. 43489, f. 18
i. 272	464	533	320	BL Add. 43489, f. 20
	LI	534	65	BL Add. 34889, f. 182
	LIII	535	71	BL Add. 34889, f. 183
iv. 150	465	536	172	BL Add. 34888, f. 213
iv. 153(a)	466(a)	537(a)	677	BL Add. 34888, f. 214
	467	538	678	BL Add. 27444, ff. 122–3
	975	539	173	BL Add. 27446, f. 116
	468(a)	540(a)	66	BL Add. 27444, f. 124
	469	541	891	Bodl. Tanner 106, f. 35b
	470(a)	542(a)	898	BL Add. 27444, f. 125
	471(a)	543(a)	892	BL Add. 39848, f. 55
iv. 188	472	544	135	BL Add. 34888, f. 215
	473	545	679	BL Add. 27444, f. 126
iv. 130	474	546	719	BL Add. 34888, f. 216
	475(a)	547(a)		BL Add. Ch. 14514
iv. 250	476	548	672	BL Add. 34888, f. 217
iv. 146	477	549	739	BL Add. 34888, f. 218
iv. 128(p)	478(p)	550(p)	680	BL Add. 34888, f. 219
iv. 88	479	551	174	BL Add. 34888, f. 220
iv. 168	480	552	175	BL Add. 34888, f. 221
	LII	553	157	BL Add. 34889, f. 198
	481(a)	554(a)		BL Add. 27444, f. 127
iv. 156	482	555	681	BL Add. 34889, f. 1
i. 278	483	556	682	BL Add. 43489, f. 21
	LV	557	118	BL Add. 34889, f. 2
iv. 72	484	558	683	BL Add. 34889, f. 5

Fenn	Gairdner 1901	Gairdner 1904	This edition	Original
iv. 158	485	559	684	BL Add. 34889, f. 6
i. 284	486	560	321	BL Add. 43489, f. 22
	487(a)	561(a)	69	BL Add. 27444, ff. 129
	976	562	68	BL Add. 27446, f. 117
	977	563	87	BL Add. 27446, f. 118
	LVI	564	19	BL Add. 34889, f. 7
	488(a)	565(a)		Bodl. Top. Norf. c.4
	489(a)	566(a)		Bodl. Ch. Norfolk a. 8, no. 734
iv. 176	490	567	177	BL Add. 34889, f. 8
	491	568	685	BL Add. 27444, f. 130
	492.1	569.1	70A	Bodl. Ch. Norfolk a. 8, no. 727
	492.2	569.2	70B	Bodl. Ch. Norfolk a. 8, no. 726
	492.3	569.3	70C	BL Add. 27444, f. 131
	LVIII	570	894	BL Add. 33597, ff. 6–7
iv. 182	493	571	686	BL Add. 34889, ff. 12–13
	494(a)	572(a)	687	BL Add. 27444, ff. 132–6
	LVII	573	893	Pemb. Coll. LC. II. 230, f. 4
iii. 418	496	574	694	BL Add. 34889, f. 14
	LIX	575	72	BL Add. 34889, ff. 15–16
iv. 134	497	576	720	BL Add. 34889, f. 25
	498	577	899	BL Add. 27444, f. 137
	499	578	178	BL Add. 27444, f. 138
	500	579	179	BL Add. 27444, f. 139
			1040	BL Add. 28209, f. 22
	501	580	688	BL Add. 27444, f. 140
	502	581	180	BL Add. 27444, f. 141
iv. 164	503	582	181	BL Add. 34889, f. 26
iv. 200	504	583	182	BL Add. 34889, f. 27
iv. 206	505	584	183	BL Add. 34889, f. 28
	506	585	184	BL Add. 27444, f. 142
	LX	586	322	BL Add. 34889, ff. 190v-191r
	507	587	740	BL Add. 27444, f. 143
	508	588	689	BL Add. 27444, f. 144
	509(a)	589(a)		Bodl. Top. Norf. c. 4
	510	590	185	BL Add. 27444, f. 145
	LXI	591	73	BL Add. 34889, f. 9
	511	592	187	BL Add. 27444, f. 146
iv. 212	512	593	690	BL Add. 34889, f. 29
iv. 218	513	594	188	BL Add. 34889, f. 30
	514	595	74	BL Add. 34889, f. 147
	515	596	191	BL Add. 34889, f. 148
	516	597	197	BL Add. 34889, f. 149
	517	598	741	BL Add. 34889, f. 150
	518	599	189	BL Add. 27445, f. 1

Fenn	Gairdner 1901	Gairdner 1904	This edition	Original
	519	600	76	BL Add. 27445, f. 2
	520	601	75	BL Add. 27445, f. 3
	521	602	1042	BL Add. 27445, f. 4
	522	603		BL Add. 27445, f. 5
iii. 370(p)	523(p)	604(p)	190	BL Add. 34889, f. 31
	524(n)	605(n)		
	525(a)	606(a)		BL Add. 27450 (1)
iv. 224	526	607	323	BL Add. 34889, f. 32
	527	608	722	BL Add. 27445, f. 6
iv. 90(p)	528(p)	609(p)	77	BL Add. 34889, f. 33
	529	610	192	BL Add. 27445, f. 8
	530	611	193	BL Add. 27445, f. 9
	LXII	612	235	Pemb. Coll. LC. II. 230, f. 5
iv. 80	531	613	324	BL Add. 34889, f. 34
iv. 62	532	614	784	BL Add. 34889, f. 35
	978	615	195	Bodl. Ch. Norfolk a. 8, nos 738–9
	533	616	194	BL Add. 27445, f. 10
iv. 226(p)	534(p)	617(p)	196	BL Add. 34889, ff. 36v–37r
	535	618	78	BL Add. 27445, f. 11
iv. 240	536	619	691	BL Add. 34889, f. 40
	LXIII	620	149	BL Add. 33597, f. 2
	537(n)	621(n)		
	LXIV	622		BL Add. 34889, f. 38
			67	Magd. Coll. FP 74
	LXV	623	186	BL Add. 34889, f. 208
	LXVI	624	621	BL Add. 34889, f. 223
iv. 242	538	625	660	BL Add. 34889, f. 41
iv. 246	539	626	742	BL Add. 34889, f. 42
	540	627	120	BL Add. 27445, f. 12
			895A	Magd. Coll. FP 83
			895B	Magd. Coll. FP 75
			1043	Magd. Coll. FP 76
i. 256	541	628	693	BL Add. 43489, f. 15
	LXVII	629	210	BL Add. 34889, f. 99
	542	630	164	BL Add. 27445, f. 13
iv. 262	543	631	696	BL Add. 34889, f. 43
	544(a)	632(a)	700	BL Add. 27445, f. 15
	545(a)	633(a)	318	BL Add. 27445, f. 14
	546(a)	634(a)	708	BL Add. 27445, f. 16
	547(a)	635(a)	709	BL Add. 27445, f. 17
	548(a)	636(a)	702	BL Add. 27445, f. 18
	549	637		Untraced; copy in Blomefield, vi. 483
	979	638	906	Magd. Coll. FP 87(3)
	550(a)	639(a)		BL Add. 27450(2)

Fenn	Gairdner 1901	Gairdner 1904	This edition	Original
	551(n)	640(n)	901B	Magd. Coll. Norf. and Suff. 34
	552	641	896	CUL Add. 6968, pp. 23–4
	553	642		BL Add. 27445, f. 19
	554	643	897	CUL Add. 6968 pp. 22–3
	555	644	31	BL Add. 27445, f. 20
	556	645	32	BL Add. 27445, f. 7
	557	646	34	CUL Add. 6968, pp. 11–12
iii. 15(n)	558(p)	647(p)	33	BL Add. 34889, ff. 44v-45r
	559(a)	648(a)	900A	BL Add. Roll 17258
			900B	Bodl. Don. 3. 93
iv. 272	560	649	198	BL Add. 34889, f. 46
	561(a)	650(a)	744	BL Add. 27445, f. 21
	562(a)	651(a)	910	BL Add. 27445, f. 22
iv. 264	563(a)	652(a)	313	BL Add. 34889, f. 47
	564(a)	653(a)	730	BL Add. 27445, f. 23
	565(a)	654(a)	724	BL Add. 27445, f. 24
	566	655	280	BL Add. 27445, f. 25
	LXVIII	656	725	BL Add. 34889, f. 226
iv. 286	567	657	756	BL Add. 34889, f. 50
	LXIX	658		BL Add. 34889, f. 51
	LXX	659	325	BL Add. 33597, f. 3
iv. 172	568	660	745	BL Add. 34889, f. 55
iv. 276	569	661	326	BL Add. 34889, f. 56
iv. 326	570	662	236	BL Add. 34889, f. 57
	571	663	746	BL Add. 27445, f. 26
	LXXI	664	92	BL Add. 33597, f. 8
	572(p)	665(p)	236(p)	CUL Add. 6968, p. 20(p)
iv. 330	573	666	327	BL Add. 34889, f. 58
	574(a)	667(a)	237	BL Add. 34898, f. 56
	LXXII	668		BL Add. 34889, f. 59
	LXXIII	669		BL Add. 34889, f. 61
	575	670	747	BL Add. 27445, f. 27
iv. 294	576	671	199	BL Add. 34889, f. 63
	980	672	901A	Magd. Coll. FP 89
	LXXIV	673	328	BL Add. 34889, f. 196
	LXXV	674	255	BL Add. 35251, f. 25
	577(n)	675(n)		Magd. Coll. Norf. and Suff. 47
	578(a)	676(a)		BL Add. 27445, f. 28
	579(n)	677(n)		Magd. Coll. Norf. and Suff. 12
	580(a)	678(a)	726	BL Add. 27445, f. 29
	LIV	679	753	BL Add. 34889, f. 166
	581(a)	680(a)		Bodl. Ch. Appendix no. 43
iv. 280	582	681	727	BL Add. 34889, f. 64; missing
iv. 290(p)	583(p)	682(p)	749	BL Add. 34889, f. 65

Fenn	Gairdner 1901	Gairdner 1904	This edition	Original
	584	683	750	CUL Add. 6968, p. 21
ii. 2	585	684	330	BL Add. 43491, f. 11
	586(a)	685(a)		BL Add. Ch. 17248
ii. 26	587	686	762	BL Add. 43489, f. 33
ii. 294	588	687	362	BL Add. 43490, f. 43
iv. 298	589	688	902	BL Add. 34889, f. 66 + Norwich, A. Hamond
	590(a)	689(a)	901B	Magd. Coll. Norf. and Suff. 34
	591	690	752	BL Add. 27445, f. 30
iv. 302	592	691	238	BL Add. 34889, ff. 67v–68r
iv. 266	593	692	122	BL Add. 34889, f. 69
	594(a)	693(a)	122A	BL Add. 27444, f. 31
iv. 100	595	694	800	BL Add. 34889, f. 72
ii. 10(p)	596.1(p)	695.1(p)	751	BL Add. 43491, f. 12
	597	696	754	BL Add. 27445, f. 32
ii. 10	596.2	695.2	755	BL Add. 43491, f. 13
	598(a)	697(a)	903	BL Add. 27445, f. 33
	599	698	757	CUL Add. 6968, p. 21
	LXXVI	699	247	BL Add. 34889, f. 186
	LXXVII	700	329	BL Add. 33597, f. 4
	LXXX	701	200	BL Add. 34889, ff. 202v–203r
	LXXXI	702	911	BL Add. 34889, f. 127
iv. 308	600	703	239	BL Add. 34889, f. 73
iv. 312	601	704	201	BL Add. 34889, f. 74
iv. 318	602	705	331	BL Add. 34889, f. 75
iv. 322	603	706	904	BL Add. 34889, f. 76
iv. 324	604	707	905	BL Add. 34889, f. 76
	605(a)	708(a)		BL Add. Ch. 18249
ii. 34	606	709	758	BL Add. 43489, f. 35
iv. 344	607	710	332	BL Add. 34889, f. 77
	LXXVIII	711	764	BL Add. 34889, f. 70
	608(a)	712(a)	759	BL Add. 27445, f. 34
iv. 350	609	713	861	BL Add. 34889, ff. 78–9
ii. 16	610	714	760	BL Add. 43489, f. 29
ii. 22(p)	611(p)	715(p)	240	BL Add. 43489, f. 31
iv. 334	612	716	333	BL Add. 34889, ff. 80v–81r
	613(a)	717(a)	761	BL Add. 27445, f. 35
ii. 18	614	718	1044	BL Add. 43489, f. 30
	615	719		BL Add. 43489, f. 37
			763	Pierpont ML, Thane Collection
iv. 366	616	720	202	BL Add. 34889, f. 82
			1045	Magd. Coll. FP 94
iv. 358	617	721	203	BL Add. 34889, ff. 83r–84v
iv. 370	618	722	241	BL Add. 34889, f. 85

Fenn	Gairdner 1901	Gairdner 1904	This edition	Original
iv. 372	619	723	242	BL Add. 34889, ff. 86v-87r
iv. 382	620	724	204	BL Add. 34889, f. 88
iv. 386	621	725	243	BL Add. 34889, ff. 89v-90r
iv. 404	622	726	907	BL Add. 34889, ff. 91–2
	623	727	908	BL Add. 27445, f. 36
	624	728	785	BL Add. 27445, f. 36
iv. 394	625	729	244	BL Add. 34889, f. 93
ii. 24	626	730	786	BL Add. 43489, f. 32
	627	731	909	London, College of Arms MS; missing
iv. 410	628	732	334	BL Add. 34889, f. 94
iv. 396	629	733	205	BL Add. 34889, ff. 95v-96r
	630(n)	734(n)	259	BL Add. 39848, f. 50
iv. 412	631	735	335	BL Add. 34889, f. 97
i. 292(p)	632(p)	736(p)	245	BL Add. 43491, f. 10
	633(a)	737(a)	336	BL Add. 27445, f. 37
	634(a)	738(a)	246	BL Add. Ch. 14526
	635(a)	739(a)		Magd. Coll. Norf. and Suff. 40
iv. 416(p)	636(p)	740(p)	337	BL Add. 34889, f. 98
	LXXXII	741	339	BL Add. 34889, ff. 192v-93r
			1046	Magd. Coll. FP 96
ii. 28(p)	637(p)	742(p)	248	BL Add. 43491, f. 14
ii. 36	638	743	787	BL Add. 43489, f. 36
	639(a)	744(a)	913	Magd. Coll. Titchwell 120
	640(a)	745(a)	912	Magd. Coll. Titchwell 199
iv. 428	641	746	342	BL Add. 34889, f. 101
iv. 434	642	747	343	BL Add. 34889, f. 102
	643(a)	748(a)	250	BL Add. 27445, f. 38
	644(a)	749(a)	251	BL Add. Ch. 17249
	645.1(a)	750.1(a)	254	Magd. Coll. Norf. and Suff. 11; also in NRO Phillipps MS 539
	645.2(a)	750.2(a)		Magd. Coll. Norf. and Suff. 17
	645.3(n)	750.3(n)	253	Magd. Coll. Norf. and Suff. 28
	645.4(n)	750.4(n)	252	Magd. Coll. Norf. and Suff. 29; also 36, 51 and Folger Z.c.24(2)
	646	751	765	BL Add. 27445, f. 39
	647	752	207	BL Add. 27445, f. 40
ii. 46(p)	648(p)	753(p)	256	BL Add. 43491, f. 15
	649(a)	754(a)	257	BL Add. Ch. 17250
	650(a)	755(a)		Magd. Coll. Caldecote 85
	651.1(a)	756.1(a)		BL Add. 27445, f. 41
	651.2(a)	756.2(a)	94	BL Add. 27445, f. 44
	651.3(a)	756.3(a)		BL Add. 27445, f. 42
	652(a)	757(a)	344	Magd. Coll. Norf. and Suff. 4

Fenn	Gairdner 1901	Gairdner 1904	This edition	Original
iv. 438	653	758		Untraced; *olim* B. P. Fountaine of Narford
ii. 50	654	759	345	BL Add. 43489, f. 40
iv. 448	655	760		BL Add. 34889, f. 104
	LXXXIII	761	208	BL Add. 34889, f. 206
iv. 450	656	762	258	BL Add. 34889, ff. 105v–106r
	657(a)	763(a)		Magd. Coll. Norf. and Suff. 49
	658(a)	764(a)		Magd. Coll. Norf. and Suff. 64
	659(a)	765(a)		Magd. Coll. Norf. and Suff. 48
iv. 288	660	766	206	BL Add. 34889, f. 107
			914	Magd. Coll. FP 100(2)
	661(a)	767(a)	260	Magd. Coll. Norf. and Suff. 50
	662(a)	768(a)		Bodl. Ch. Norfolk a. 8, no. 732
ii. 54	663	769	1047	BL Add. 43489, f. 41
ii. 58	664	770	1048	BL Add. 43489, f. 42
ii. 60	665(p)	771(p)	766	BL Add. 43489, f. 43
	666(a)	772(a)	766	BL Add. 27445, f. 43
	667(a)	773(a)		Magd. Coll. Norf. and Suff. 30
ii. 62	668	774	261	BL Add. 43489, f. 44
ii. 68	669	775	915	BL Add. 43489, f. 45
v. 2	670	776	346	BL Add. 27445, f. 45
	671	777	916	BL Add. 39848, f. 57
iv. 116	672	778	347	BL Add. 34889, f. 111
	673(a)	779(a)	262	Magd. Coll. Norf. and Suff. 5
v. 6	674	780	348	BL Add. 27445, f. 46
ii. 72(p)	675(p)	781(p)	263	BL Add. 43491, f. 16
ii. 80(p)	676(p)	782(p)	264	BL Add. 43489, f. 47
	677	783	788	BL Add. 34889, f. 112
	678	784	349	BL Add. 27445, f. 47
	679	785	265	BL Add. 27445, f. 48
	680(a)	786(a)	772	BL Add. 27445, f. 49
	681	787	209A	BL Add. 27445, f. 50
v. 10			209B	BL Add. 34889, f. 113
	682	788	917	BL Add. 27445, f. 51
	LXXXV	789	394	BL Add. 34889, f. 130 + 27445, f. 52
	684(a)	790(a)	211	BL Add. 27445, f. 53
	685	791	212	BL Add. 27445, f. 54
	LXXXVI	792	213	BL Add. 34889, f. 211
	686	793	350	BL Add. 27445, f. 55
	LXXXIV	794	214	BL Add. 34889, f. 116
			1049	Magd. Coll. FP 84
ii. 86(p)	687(p)	795(p)	266	BL Add. 43491, f. 17
iv. 420(p)	688(p)	796(p)	338	BL Add. 34889, f. 120
iv. 424	689	797	215	BL Add. 34889, f. 121

Fenn	Gairdner 1901	Gairdner 1904	This edition	Original
ii. 90	690	798	267	BL Add. 43489, f. 49
	691(a)	799(a)		Magd. Coll. Norf. and Suff. 38
i. 288	692	800	268	BL Add. 43491, f. 9
	693	801	340	BL Add. 27445, f. 56
	694	802	341	BL Add. 27445, f. 57
	695	803	216	BL Add. 27445, f. 58
ii. 92(p)	696(p)	804(p)	352	BL Add. 43489, f. 50
v. 16	697	805	353	BL Add. 27445, f. 59
	698(a)	806(a)	249	BL Add. 39848, f. 58
	699(a)	807(a)		Magd. Coll. Norf. and Suff. 63
ii. 98	700	808	354A	BL Add. 43489, f. 51
ii. 102	701	809	354	BL Add. 43489, f. 52
v. 24	702	810	355	BL Add. 27445, f. 60
	LXXXVII	811	217	BL Add. 34889, f. 108
ii. 112	703	812	269	BL Add. 43491, f. 18
ii. 118(p)	704(p)	813(p)	270	BL Add. 43491, f. 19
	705	814	218	BL Add. 27445, f. 61
v. 28	706	815	271	BL Add. 27445, f. 62
	707	816	219	BL Add. 27445, f. 63
v. 36	708	817	356	BL Add. 27445, f. 64
	709(a)	818(a)		Magd. Coll. Southwark 17a
	710	819	767	BL Add. 27445, f. 65
	711	820	728	BL Add. 27445, f. 66
v. 40	712	821	357	BL Add. 27445, f. 67
	713(a)	822(a)		Magd. Coll. Norf. and Suff. 75
ii. 42(p)	714(p)	823(p)	358	BL Add. 43489, f. 38
v. 44	715	824	359	BL Add. 27445, f. 68
v. 152	716	825	220	BL Add. 27445, f. 69
ii. 120(p)	717(p)	826(p)	272	BL Add. 43489, f. 55
	718(n)	827(n)		See Blomefield, xi. 208
	719(a)	828(a)	360	BL Add. 39848, f. 59
v. 46	720	829	361	BL Add. 27445, f. 70
ii. 122	721	830	273	BL Add. 43490, f. 4
v. 50	722	831	274	BL Add. 27445, f. 71
ii. 130	723	832	275	BL Add. 43490, f. 6
ii. 136(p)	724(p)	833(p)	276	BL Add. 43490, f. 7
			947	Magd. Coll. FP 99
ii. 138	725	834	277	BL Add. 43490, f. 8
	726(a)	835(a)		Magd. Coll. Norf. and Suff. 67
ii. 146	727	836	278	BL Add. 43490, f. 9
	LXXXVIII	837	279	BL Add. 34889, f. 125
	728	838	769	BL Add. 27445, f. 72
ii. 152	729	839	770	BL Add. 43490, f. 10
	730(n)	840(n)		PRO Close Roll 13Ed.IV, m.5

Fenn	Gairdner 1901	Gairdner 1904	This edition	Original
ii. 126(p)	731(p)	841(p)	281	BL Add. 43490, f. 5
v. 54	732	842	282	BL Add. 27445, f. 73
v. 62	733	843	283	BL Add. 27445, f. 74
	734	844	771	BL Add. 27445, f. 75
	735(n)	845(n)		*Early Chancery Proc.*, i. xc
ii. 154	736	846	284	BL Add. 43490, f. 11
ii. 296	737	847	795	BL Add. 43490, f. 44
	LXXXIX	848	796	BL Add. 34889, f. 122
	738(a)	849(a)		BL Add. Ch. 14973
v. 66	739	850	363	BL Add. 27445, f. 76
			1050	Magd. Coll. Guton Hall 290
	740(a)	851(a)	95.1	BL Add. 27445, f. 77
			95.2	BL Add. 27451, f. 1
	741(a)	852(a)	783	BL Add. 27445, f. 78
	742(a)	853(a)	735	BL Add. 27445, f. 79
	743	854	96	BL Add. 27445, f. 80
	744(a)	855(a)	97	BL Add. 27445, f. 81
v. 72	745	856	285	BL Add. 27445, f. 82
v. 78	746	857	286	BL Add. 27445, f. 83
ii. 164	747	858	287	BL Add. 43490, f. 13
	748(a)	859(a)	948	Magd. Coll. Norf. and Suff. 33
ii. 170(p)	749(p)	860(p)	288	BL Add. 43490, f. 14
ii. 174	750	861	289	BL Add. 43490, f. 15
v. 82	751	862	222	BL Add. 27445, f. 84
v. 86	752	863	221	BL Add. 27445, f. 85
v. 92	753	864	290	BL Add. 27445, f. 86
v. 96	754	865	291	BL Add. 27445, f. 87
ii. 178	755	866	223	BL Add. 43490, f. 15v
v. 102	756	867	701	BL Add. 27445, f. 88
iv. 444	757	868	364	BL Add. 34889, f. 129
			396	Pierpont ML, Thane Collection
	XC	869	93	BL Add. 34889, f. 215
iii. 426	58	870	395	BL Add. 34888, f. 22
v. 104	758	871	224	BL Add. 27445, f. 89
	759.1(a)	872.1(a)		Magd. Coll. Norf. and Suff. 13
	759.2(a)	872.2(a)		Magd. Coll. Norf. and Suff. 32
v. 110	760	873	292	BL Add. 27445, f. 90
ii. 180(p)	761(p)	874(p)	225	BL Add. 43490, f. 16
v. 112	762	875	293	BL Add. 27445, f. 91
v. 116	763	876	365	BL Add. 27445, f. 92
ii. 182	764	877	366	BL Add. 43490, f. 17
v. 134	765	878	371	BL Add. 27445, f. 93
	766	879	294	Bodl. Ch. Norfolk a. 8, no. 728
	767(a)	880(a)	840	BL Add. 27445, f. 94

Fenn	Gairdner 1901	Gairdner 1904	This edition	Original
ii. 186	768	881	295	BL Add. 43490, f. 18
v. 138	769	882	367	BL Add. 27445, f. 95
v. 120	770	883	368	BL Add. 27445, f. 96
ii. 190	771	884	296	BL Add. 43491, f. 20
	772	885	369	BL Add. 27445, f. 97
v. 124	773	886	370	BL Add. 27445, f. 98
	774	887	373	BL Add. 27445, f. 99
v. 130	775	888	297	BL Add. 27445, f. 100
ii. 198	776	889	298	BL Add. 43490, f. 20
v. 140	777	890	372	BL Add. 27445, f. 101
v. 144	778	891	299	BL Add. 27445, f. 102
			949	Harvard, Houghton Eng. 824
v. 148	779	892	300	BL Add. 27445, f. 103
	XCI	893	301	BL Add. 34889, f. 188
	780	894	789	BL Add. 27445, f. 104
	781	895	790	BL Add. 27445, f. 105
ii. 208	782	896	791	BL Add. 43490, f. 22
ii. 210	783	897	415	BL Add. 43490, f. 23
ii. 214	784	898	416	BL Add. 43490, f. 24
ii. 216	785	899	792	BL Add. 43490, f. 25
ii. 204	786	900	302	BL Add. 43490, f. 21
ii. 220	787	901	374	BL Add. 43490, f. 26
ii. 224	788	902	773	BL Add. 43490, f. 27
v. 164	789	903	303	BL Add. 27445, f. 106
v. 166	790	904	375	BL Add. 27445, f. 107
v. 170	791	905	376	BL Add. 27445, f. 108
ii. 226	792	906	774	BL Add. 43491, f. 21
	793	907	775	BL Add. 27445, f. 109
ii. 234	794	908	776	BL Add. 43491, f. 22
v. 180	795	909	306	BL Add. 27445, f. 110
v. 172	796	910	377	BL Add. 27445, f. 111
ii. 238	797	911	304	BL Add. 43491, f. 23
ii. 244	798	912	305	BL Add. 43490, f. 31
v. 184	799	913	226	BL Add. 27445, f. 112
ii. 248	800	914	307	BL Add. 27445, f. 32
v. 188	801	915	378	BL Add. 27445, f. 113
v. 196	802	916	308	BL Add. 27446, f. 1
v. 200	803	917	227	BL Add. 27446, f. 2
ii. 250	804	918	777	BL Add. 43490, f. 33
	805	919	98	BL Add. 27446, f. 3
	806	920	309	BL Add. 27446, f. 4
	807	921	778	BL Add. 27446, f. 5
v. 206	808	922	779	BL Add. 27446, f. 6
ii. 256	809	923	125	BL Add. 43490, f. 34

Fenn	Gairdner 1901	Gairdner 1904	This edition	Original
	810(a)	924(a)		BL Add. 27446, f. 7
v. 208	811	925	379	BL Add. 27446, f. 8
v. 212	812	926	380	BL Add. 27446, f. 9
	XCII	927	780	BL Add. 34889, f. 152
v. 220	813	928	781	BL Add. 27446, f. 10
	814	929	310	BL Add. 27446, f. 11
ii. 260	815	930	311	BL Add. 43490, f. 35
v. 224	816	931	402	BL Add. 27446, f. 12
v. 228	817	932	782	BL Add. 27446, f. 13
ii. 264	818	933	228	BL Add. 43491, f. 24
	819	934	99	BL Add. 27446, f. 14
	820(a)	935(a)		BL Add. 27446, f. 15
ii. 270	821	936	312	BL Add. 43491, f. 25
	822(a)	937(a)	100	BL Add. 27446, f. 16
	823(a)	938(a)	101	BL Add. 27446, f. 17
v. 236	824	939	406	BL Add. 27446, f. 18
	825	940	102	BL Add. 27446, f. 19
v. 238	826	941	733	BL Add. 27446, f. 20
i. 296	827	942	407	BL Add. 43489, f. 25
	828	943	103	BL Add. Ch. 17251; also (p) in Norwich, A. Hamond
v. 242	829	944	734	BL Add. 27446, f. 22
			945	Bodl. Ch. Norf. a.1, f. 6
v. 244	830	945	403	BL Add. 27446, f. 23
v. 248	831	946	404	BL Add. 27446, f. 24
	832(a)	947(a)	104	BL Add. 27446, f. 21
	833(a)	948(a)	105	BL Add. 27446, f. 25
	XCIII	949	106	BL Add. 34889, f. 133
	834	950	405	BL Add. 27446, f. 26
	835	951	942	BL Add. 27451, f. 2
v. 250	836	952	397	BL Add. 27446, f. 27
	837(a)	953(a)	920	BL Add. 27446, f. 28
	838	954	314	BL Add. 27446, f. 29
	839	955	729	BL Add. 27446, f. 30
ii. 276	840	956	315	BL Add. 43490, f. 38
v. 254	841	957	381	BL Add. 27446, f. 32
	842	958	107	BL Add. 27446, f. 31
	843	959	921	BL Add. 27446, f. 33
	844	960	110	BL Add. 27446, f. 34
v. 252	845	961	382	BL Add. 27446, f. 35
ii. 280	846	962	383	BL Add. 43490, f. 39
			108	Belvoir Castle MSS, Letters I, f. 29
v. 262	847	963	793	BL Add. 27446, f. 36
	848(a)	964(a)	107	BL Add. 27446, ff. 37–8

Fenn	Gairdner 1901	Gairdner 1904	This edition	Original
v. 266	849	965	384	BL Add. 27446, f. 39
			109	Belvoir Castle MSS, Letters I, f. 30
	850	966	385	BL Add. 27446, f. 40
			947	NRO, Phillipps 536
v. 272	851	967	37	BL Add. 27446, f. 41
	852	968	923	BL Add. 27451, ff. 4–10
	853(a)	969(a)	408	BL Add. 27446, f. 42
	854	970	111	BL Add. 27446, f. 43
			229	NRO, Bradfer-Lawrence Collection, VI b (iv)
	855	971	922	BL Add. 27446, f. 44
iii. 400	856	972	809	BL Add. 34889, f. 134
	857(a)	973(a)		BL Add. 27446, f. 45
v. 282	858	974	398	BL Add. 27446, f. 46
v. 276	859	975	399	BL Add. 27446, f. 47
	860	976	924	BL Add. Ch. 17252
	981(a)	977(a)	707	BL Add. 27446, f. 119
	861	978	230	BL Add. Ch. 17253
v. 296	862	979	386	BL Add. 27446, f. 48
v. 284	863	980	794	BL Add. 27446, f. 49
	864(a)	981(a)		BL Add. 27446, f. 50
v. 288	865	982	417	BL Add. 27446, f. 51
v. 292	866	983	418	BL Add. 27446, f. 52
	XCIV	984	797	BL Add. 34889, f. 220
	867	985	925	BL Add. Ch. 17256
	868(a)	986(a)	718	BL Add. 27446, f. 53
ii. 300	869	987	316	BL Add. 43491, f. 26
ii. 304	870	988	351	BL Add. 43491, f. 27
	871(a)	989(a)	391	BL Add. 27446, f. 54
	872(a)	990(a)	731	BL Add. 27446, f. 55
	873(a)	991(a)	704	BL Add. 27446, f. 56
v. 302	874	992		Untraced; copy *olim* J. E. Blackett
ii. 292	875	993	798	BL Add. 43490, f. 42
ii. 314	876	994	799	BL Add. 43490, f. 48
	877(a)	995(a)		Bodl. Ch. Norfolk a. 8, no. 733
	878(a)	996(a)		CUL Add. 6968, pp. 24–5
ii. 316	879	997	1051	BL Add. 43490, f. 49
	880	998	387	BL Add. Ch. 17257
ii. 330	881	999	153	BL Add. 43490, f. 52
	882(a)	1000(a)	112	BL Add. 27446, f. 59
			950	BL Stowe Ch. 194
ii. 318	883	1001		BL Add. 43490, f. 50
ii. 334	884	1002	801	BL Add. 43490, f. 53
v. 304	885	1003	388	BL Add. 27446, f. 60

Fenn	Gairdner 1901	Gairdner 1904	This edition	Original
v. 310	886	1004	802	BL Add. 27446, f. 61
	XCV	1005		BL Add. 34889, f. 228
ii. 326	887	1006	803	BL Add. 43490, f. 51
v. 314	888	1007	419	BL Add. 27446, f. 62
ii. 336	889	1008	813	BL Add. 43490, f. 54
ii. 338	890	1009	805	BL Add. 43490, f. 55
	891	1010	804	CUL Add. 6968, p. 18
	XCVI	1011	806	BL Add. 34889, f. 176
	892	1012	807	Bodl. Douce 393, f. 79
v. 316	893	1013	926	BL Add. 27446, f. 63
v. 336	894	1014	811	BL Add. 27446, f. 64
v. 340	895	1015	811A	BL Add. 27446, f. 65
	XCVII	1016		BL Add. 34889, f. 135
	896	1017	820	BL Add. 27446, f. 66
v. 344	897	1018	815	BL Add. 27446, f. 67
v. 346	898	1019	389	BL Add. 27446, f. 68
v. 332	899	1020	927	BL Add. 27446, f. 69
	900	1021	743	Bodl. Douce 393, f. 84
	XCVIII	1022	748	BL Add. 34889, f. 48
	901(a)	1023(a)	812	BL Add. 27446, f. 70
	902	1024	814	BL Add. 27446, f. 71
	903	1025	832	BL Add. 27446, f. 72
v. 366	904	1026	411	BL Add. 27446, f. 73
	XCIX	1027	855	BL Add. 34889, f. 139
v. 324	905	1028	856	BL Add. 27446, f. 74
v. 348	906	1029	816	BL Add. 27446, f. 75
v. 350	907	1030	420	BL Add. 27446, f. 76
ii. 158(p)	908(p)	1031(p)	409	BL Add. 43490, f. 12
	909	1032	817	Bodl. Douce 393, f. 80a
iv. 310	910	1033	410	BL Add. 34889, f. 137
	911	1034	854	Bodl. Douce 393, f. 81
	912	1035	401	Bodl. Douce 393, f. 80b
v. 370	913	1036	412	BL Add. 27446, f. 77
	914	1037	818	Bodl. Douce 393, f. 83
v. 358	915	1038	819	BL Add. 27446, f. 78
v. 360	916	1039	413	BL Add. 27446, f. 79
v. 376	917	1040	821	BL Add. 27446, f. 80
v. 380	918	1041	853	BL Add. 27446, f. 81
v. 382	919	1042	390	BL Add. 27446, f. 82
v. 384	920	1043	842	BL Add. 27446, f. 83
			843	Pierpont ML, Thane Collection
	CI	1044	844	Pemb. Coll. LC. II. 230, f. 7
v. 390	921	1045	822	BL Add. 27446, f. 84
v. 392	922	1046	824	BL Add. 27446, f. 85

Fenn	Gairdner 1901	Gairdner 1904	This edition	Original
v. 396	923	1047	823	BL Add. 27446, f. 86
v. 402	924	1048	825	BL Add. 27446, f. 87
	925	1049	826	Bodl. Ch. Norfolk a. 8, no. 729
v. 404	926	1050	827	BL Add. 27446, f. 88
	927	1051	828	Bodl. Douce 393, f. 90
	928	1052	849	Bodl. Douce 393, f. 89
			850	Pierpont ML, Thane Collection
v. 412	929	1053	414	BL Add. 27446, f. 89
v. 416	930	1054	829	BL Add. 27446, f. 90
			943	Nthtn. RO Fitzwilliam Roll 370/1
	931	1055	857	BL Add. 27446, f. 91
v. 432	933	1056	400	BL Add. 27446, f. 93
	C	1057	830	BL Add. 33597, f. 9
			944	Nthtn. RO Fitzwilliam Roll 370/2
v. 418	935	1058	831	BL Add. 27446, f. 95
			945	Nthtn. RO Fitzwilliam Roll 370/3
v. 426	936	1059	833	BL Add. 27446, f. 96
v. 430	937	1060	834	BL Add. 27446, f. 97
v. 398	932	1061	835	BL Add. 27446, f. 92
v. 410	938	1062	421	BL Add. 27446, f. 98
	941	1063	846	CUL Add. 6968, p. 13
			847	Pierpont ML, Thane Collection
v. 388	934	1064	836	BL Add. 27446, f. 94
	942	1065	838	Bodl. Douce 393, f. 87
	943	1066	839	CUL Add. 6968, p. 26
	944	1067	845	BL Add. 27446, f. 100
	945(a)	1068(a)	852	BL Add. 27446, f. 101
v. 422	946	1069	841	BL Add. 27446, f. 102
v. 408	947	1070	837	BL Add. 27446, f. 103
	939	1071	392	BL Add. 27446, f. 99
	940	1072	848	Bodl. Douce 393, f. 86
iv. 458	948	1073	393	BL Add. 34889, f. 138
v. 438	949	1074	928	BL Add. 27446, f. 104
v. 440	950	1075	862	BL Add. 27446, f. 105
	951	1076	768	BL Add. 27446, f. 106
	952(a)	1077(a)	863	BL Add. 27446, f. 107
	953	1078		BL Add. 27446, f. 108
	954	1079	732	BL Add. Ch. 17255
	CII	1080	851	BL Add. 34889, f. 231
	CIII	1081	810	BL Add. 33597, f. 10
	CIV	1082	860	BL Add. 34889, f. 148
	CV	1083		BL Add. 34889, f. 181
	982	1084		BL Add. 27451, f. 3
	955(a)	1085(a)	858	BL Add. 27446, f. 109

Fenn	Gairdner 1901	Gairdner 1904	This edition	Original
	956(a)	1086(a)	859	BL Add. 27446, f. 110
	957(a)	1087(a)	706	BL Add. 27446, f. 111
	958(a)	1088(a)	866	BL Add. 27446, f. 112
			864	Bodl. Douce 393, f. 104
			865	BL Add. 27446, f. 120
		1016bis		BL pr. bk. IB. 49432, ff. 73r–74r

Wills

Fenn	Gairdner 1901	Gairdner 1904	This edition	Original
	983	1		NRO, Reg. Hyrning, 51b
	984	2	12(p)	PRO, PCC Reg. Luffenham, 29
	985	3		NRO, Episcop. Reg. 16
	986	4		NRO, Archdeaconry Reg., I, 29b
	987	5		NRO, Archdeaconry Reg., I, 76a
	988	6	123	PRO, PCC Reg. Milles, 12
	988	7	113	PRO, PCC Reg. Horne, 12
	988	8(p)	929	NRO, Reg. Rix, 128a–29b
	988	9(a)	930	PRO, PCC Reg. Benet, 29

SELECT BIBLIOGRAPHY

Barron, C. M., 'Who were the Pastons?', *Journal of the Society of Archivists*, iv (1972), 530–5.

Beadle, R., 'Private Letters', *A Companion to Middle English Prose*, ed. A. S. G. Edwards (Woodbridge, 2004), pp. 289–306.

—— 'Sir John Fastolf's French Books', *Medieval Texts in Manuscript Context*, ed. G. Caie & D. Renevey (London, 2007), forthcoming.

Beadle, R., and L. Hellinga, 'William Paston II and Pynson's *Statutes of War* (1492), *The Library*, 7th ser., ii (2001), 107–19.

Beadle, R., and C. Richmond, 'The Expenses of John Paston I, 1457–1458', *Proceedings of the Suffolk Institute of Archaeology and History*, xlii (2006), forthcoming.

Bennett, H. S., *The Pastons and their England* (Cambridge, 1922; 2nd. edn. 1932, reprinted with corrections 1968).

Blomefield, F., *An Essay towards a Topographical History of the County of Norfolk*, first edn., 5 vols. (Kersfield and Lynn, 1739–75); second edn., 11 vols. (London, 1805–10).

Britnell, R. H., 'The Pastons and their Norfolk', *Agricultural History Review*, xxxvi (1988), 132–44.

Bühler, C. F., 'Some New Paston Documents', *R.E.S.* xiv (1938), 129–42.

Castor, H. *The King, the Crown and the Duchy of Lancaster* (Oxford, 2000), pp. 128–55, 'East Anglia in the 1440s: the Paston Evidence'.

—— *Blood and Roses: the Paston Family in the Fifteenth Century* (London, 2004).

Davis, N., 'The Text of Margaret Paston's Letters', *Medium Ævum*, xvii (1949), 12–28.

—— 'A Paston Hand', *R.E.S.* ns iii (1952), 209–21.

—— 'A Scribal Problem in the Paston Letters', *English and Germanic Studies*, iv (1952), 31–64.

—— 'The Letters of William Paston', *Neophilologus*, xxxvii (1953), 36–41.

—— 'The Language of the Pastons', *Proceedings of the British Academy*, xl (1955), 119–44, reprinted with minor revisions and corrections in *Middle English Literature: British Academy Gollancz Lectures*, ed. J. A. Burrow (Oxford, 1989), pp. 45–70.

—— *Paston Letters* (Oxford, 1958). Selected edition.

—— 'Scribal Variation in Late Fifteenth-Century English', in *Mélanges . . . Fernand Mossé in Memoriam* (Paris, 1959), pp. 95–103.

—— 'The *Litera Troili* and English Letters', *R.E.S.*, ns xvi (1965), 233–44.

—— 'Style and Stereotype in Early English Letters', *Leeds Studies in English*, ns i (1967), 7–17.

Davis, N., 'The Epistolary Usages of William Worcester', *Medieval Literature and Civilization: Studies in Memory of G. N. Garmonsway*, ed. D. A. Pearsall and R. A. Waldron, (London, 1969), pp. 249–74.

——'Sheep-farming terms in medieval Norfolk', *Notes & Queries*, ccxiv (1969), 404–5.

——'Margaret Paston's Uses of DO', *Neuphilologische Mitteilungen*, lxxiii (1972), 55–62.

——'On Editing the Paston Letters', *English Studies Today* (1973), 135–48.

——'Language in Letters from Sir John Fastolf's Household', *Mediæval Studies for J. A. W. Bennett*, ed. P. L. Heyworth (Oxford, 1981), pp. 329–46.

——'The Language of Two Brothers in the Fifteenth Century', *Five Hundred Years of Words and Sounds: a Festschrift for Eric Dobson*, ed. E. G. Stanley and D. Gray (Cambridge, 1983), pp. 23–8.

Davis, N., and G. S. Ivy, 'MS Walter Rye 38 and its French Grammar, *Medium Ævum*, xxxi (1962), 110–24.

Davis, V., *William Waynflete*, (Woodbridge, 1993).

Faurot, R. M., 'From Records to Romance: Stevenson's *The Black Arrow* and the Paston Letters', *Studies in English Literature 1500–1900*, v (1965), 677–90.

Fenn, J. *Original Letters, Written during the Reigns of Henry VI. Edward IV. and Richard III.* (London, vols i and ii 1787, vols iii and iv 1789, vol. v 1823).

Gairdner, J., *The Paston Letters 1422–1509 A. D.*, four vols. (Westminster, 1900–1); six vols. (London and Exeter, 1904).

Hanham, A., 'The Curious Letters of Friar Brackley', *Historical Research*, lxxix (2006), forthcoming.

Haskell, A. S., 'The Paston Women on Marriage in Fifteenth-Century England', *Viator*, iv (1973), 459–71.

Haward, W. I., 'Gilbert Debenham: a medieval rascal in real life', *History*, xiii (1928–9), 300–13.

Lester, G. A., *Sir John Paston's 'Grete Boke'* (Cambridge, 1984).

——'The Books of a Fifteenth-Century English Gentleman, Sir John Paston', *Neuphilologische Mitteilungen*, lxxxviii (1987), 200–17.

Lewis, P. S., 'Sir John Fastolf's Lawsuit over Titchwell', *The Historical Journal*, i (1958), 1–20.

Maddern, P., 'Honour among the Pastons: Gender and Integrity in Fifteenth-Century Society', *Journal of Medieval History*, xiv (1988), 357–71.

McFarlane, K. B., *England in the Fifteenth Century: Collected Essays*, ed. G. L. Harriss (London, 1981).

——'The Investment of Sir John Fastolf's Profits of War', *Transactions of the Royal Historical Society*, 5th ser., vii (1957), 91–116; repr. in *England in the Fifteenth Century*, pp. 175–97.

——'William Worcester: A Preliminary Survey', *Studies presented to Sir Hilary Jenkinson*, ed. J. Conway Davies (Oxford, 1957), 196–221; repr. in *England in the Fifteenth Century*, pp. 199–224.

——'William Worcester and a Present of Lampreys', *Medium Ævum*, xxx (1961), 176–80, repr. in *England in the Fifteenth Century*, pp. 225–30.

——*Letters to Friends 1940–1966*, ed. G. L. Harriss (Oxford, 1997).

Pearson, P. C., 'The Paston Letters: Carriage of Mail in the Fifteenth Century', *The London Philatelist*, xcix (1990), 178–83, 189–95, 232–37, 276–79.

Richmond, C., 'The Pastons revisited: Marriage and the Family in Fifteenth-Century England', *B.I.H.R.*, lviii (1985), pp 25–36.

—— 'The Expenses of Thomas Playter of Sotterley, 1459–60', *Proceedings of the Suffolk Institute of Archaeology and History*, xxxv (1981), 41–52.

—— *The Paston Family in the Fifteenth Century: the First Phase* (Cambridge, 1990).

—— 'Landlord and Tenant: the Paston Evidence', *Enterprise and Individuals in Fifteenth-Century England*, ed. J. Kermode (Stroud, 1991), pp. 25–42.

—— 'What a Difference a Manuscript Makes: John Wyndham of Felbrigg (d. 1475)', *Regionalism in Late-Medieval Manuscripts and Texts*, ed. F. Riddy (Cambridge, 1991), pp. 129–41.

—— 'The Murder of Thomas Denys', *Common Knowledge*, ii (1993). 85–98.

—— *The Paston Family in the Fifteenth Century: Fastolf's Will* (Cambridge, 1996).

—— *The Paston Family in the Fifteenth Century: Endings* (Manchester, 2000).

—— 'Elizabeth Clere: Friend of the Pastons', *Medieval Women: Texts and Contexts in Late Medieval Britain*, ed. J. Wogan-Browne *et al.*, (Turnhout, 2000), pp. 251–73.

—— 'The Pastons and London', *Courts and Regions in Medieval Europe*, ed. S. Rees-Jones *et al.*, (York, 2000), pp. 211–26.

—— 'Sir John Fastolf and the Land Market', *East Anglia's History: Studies in honour of Norman Scarfe*, ed. C. Harper-Bill *et al.*, (Woodbridge, 2002), pp. 107–21.

—— 'Once Again: Fastolf's Will', *People, Places and Perspectives: Essays on Later Medieval and Early Tudor England*, ed. K. Dockray & P. Fleming (Stroud, 2005), pp. 115–30.

Robbins, E. C., 'The Cursed Norfolk Justice: A Defence of Sir William Yelverton', *Norfolk Archaeology*, xxvi (1936–8), 1–51.

Rosenthal, J. T., 'Looking for Grandmother: The Pastons and their Counterparts in Late Medieval England', *Medieval Mothering*, ed. J. C. Parsons & B. Wheeler (New York, 1996), pp. 259–77.

—— *Telling Tales: Sources and Narration in Late Medieval England* (University Park, PA., 2003), Chapter 3, 'Margaret Paston: The Lady and the Letters'.

Rowling, M. A., 'New Evidence on the Disseisin of the Pastons from their Norfolk Manor of Gresham, 1448–1451', *Norfolk Archaeology*, xl (1989), 302–8.

Serpell, M., 'Sir John Fenn, his friends and the Paston Letters', *Antiquaries Journal*, lxiii (1983), 95–121.

Scrope, G. Poulett, *History of the Manor and Ancient Barony of Castle Combe, in the County of Wilts.* etc. (Printed for private circulation, 1852).

Smith, A. R., 'Aspects of the Career of Sir John Fastolf (1380–1459)', D.Phil. thesis, University of Oxford, 1982.

—— 'Litigation and Politics: Sir John Fastolf's Defence of his English Property', *Property and Politics: Essays in Later Medieval English History*, ed. T. Pollard (Gloucester, 1984), pp. 59–75.

—— '"The Greatest Man of that Age": The Acquisition of Sir John Fastolf's Estates', *Rulers and Ruled in Late-Medieval England: Essays presented to Gerald Harriss*, ed. R. E. Archer & S. Walker (London, 1995), pp. 137–53.

—— '"My Confessors have exorted me gretely ther too": Sir John Fastolf's Dispute with Hickling Priory', *St George's Chapel, Windsor in the Late Middle Ages*, ed. E. Scarff and C. Richmond (Windsor, 2001), pp. 57–70.

——' "her to they wolle swere uppon a boke": Sir John Fastolf and the estate of Bathampton, Wiltshire', *Much Heaving and Shoving: late-medieval gentry and their concerns. Essays for Colin Richmond*, ed. M. Aston and R. Horrox (n.p., 2005), pp. 55–9.

Stoker, D., ' "Innumerable Letters of Good Consequence in History": the Discovery and First Publication of the Paston Letters', *The Library*, 6th ser., xvii (1995), 107–155.

Virgoe, R., *Private Life in the Fifteenth Century: Illustrated Letters of the Paston Family* (London, 1989).

——'The Will of Hugh atte Fenne, 1476', *Norfolk Record Society*, lvi (1991), 31–57.

——'Hugh atte Fenne and Books at Cambridge', *Transactions of the Cambridge Bibliographical Society*, x (1991), 92–8.

——'The Ravishment of Jane Boys', *East Anglian Society and the Political Community of Late-Medieval England: Selected Papers of Roger Virgoe*, ed. C. Barron *et al.* (Norwich 1997), pp. 151–8.

——'William Tailboys and Lord Cromwell: Crime and Politics in Lancastrian England', *idem*, pp. 287–307.

Whitaker, E. A., 'Reading the Paston Letters Medically', *English Language Notes*, xxxi (1993), 19–27.

William Worcestre, *Itineraries*, ed. J. H. Harvey (Oxford, 1969).

ADDITIONAL ABBREVIATIONS AND SHORT TITLES USED IN PART III

B.I.H.R.
Bulletin of the Institute of Historical Research

Castor, *Blood and Roses*
Helen Castor, *Blood and Roses: the Paston family in the Fifteenth Century* (London, 2004).

Hanham, 'The Curious Letters of Friar Brackley'
Alison Hanham, 'The Curious Letters of Friar Brackley', *Historical Research*, lxxix (2006), forthcoming.

Lewis, 'Sir John Fastolf's Lawsuit over Titchwell'
P. S. Lewis, 'Sir John Fastolf's Lawsuit over Titchwell', *The Historical Journal*, i (1958), 1–20.

McFarlane, *England in the Fifteenth Century*
K. B. McFarlane, *England in the Fifteenth Century: Collected Essays*, ed. G. L. Harriss (London, 1981).

Richmond, *First Phase*
Colin Richmond, *The Paston Family in the Fifteenth Century: The First Phase* (Cambridge, 1990).

Richmond, *Fastolf's Will*
Colin Richmond, *The Paston Family in the Fifteenth Century: Fastolf's Will* (Cambridge, 1996).

Richmond, *Endings*
Colin Richmond, *The Paston Family in the Fifteenth Century: Endings* (Manchester, 2000).

G. P. Scrope, *Castle Combe*
G. Poulett Scrope, *History of the Manor and Ancient Barony of Castle Combe, in the County of Wilts.* etc. Printed for private circulation, 1852.

Smith, 'Aspects of the Career of Sir John Fastolf'
Anthony Robert Smith, 'Aspects of the Career of Sir John Fastolf (1380–1459)' D.Phil. thesis, University of Oxford, 1982.

Smith, 'Fastolf's Dispute with Hickling Priory'
Anthony Smith, '"My Confessors have exorted me gretely ther too": Sir John Fastolf's Dispute with Hickling Priory', *St George's Chapel, Windsor in the Late Middle Ages*, ed. E. Scarff and C. Richmond (Windsor, 2001), pp. 57–70.

Wedgwood, *History of Parliament: Biographies*
J. C. Wedgwood, *History of Parliament. Biographies of Members of the Commons House 1439–1509* (London, 1936)

ADDITIONAL LETTERS AND PAPERS OF THE PASTON FAMILY

WILLIAM PASTON I

931. Indenture of agreement with WILLIAM JOYE
1425, 18 September

Norwich, Norfolk Record Office, Phillipps 532. Parchment, $8\frac{1}{2} \times 7$ in. (indented). Same hand as no. 11, but here with more attention to calligraphic detail.

Dorse: In a rough and hasty hand resembling John Paston I's, 'Joy Indent*ur*e *and* oblygac*i*on molendum'.

Dated. This document is probably the indenture referred to in the inventory printed as no. 11 (see line 2), which is undated, but was assigned by Blomefield to 1424.
Unprinted.

This bille indentyd made þe xviij day of Septembr*e*, the ferde yeer of þe regne of Kyng Henry þe Sexte after þe conquest, wittenesseth þ*at* it is acorded be-twen William Paston and William Joye that þe seid Will*iam* Joye at his owyn costes p*ro*pree shal, in þe yeer next folwyng Michelmesse next comyng, well and sufficiauntly to his p*ro*fyt *and* p*ro*fyt of þe seid Will*iam* Paston, of þe dimise *and* letyng of þe seid Will*iam* Paston, ocupie, eryn, telyn, sedyn, sowen *and* harwyn in seisonable tyme al þe arable londes of þe ⌜seid⌝ Will*iam* Paston in Paston *and* Edyngthorp,[1] which þe seid Will*iam* Joye hath had in ferme be-for þis tyme of þe seid Will*iam* Paston, and all þoo londes which arn fallyn in þe seid Will*iam* Paston hand or by hym purchased in Paston *and* Edithorp, *and* þe cornes þer-of sufficiauntly to jnnyn in þe berons[2] of þe seid Will*iam* Paston in Paston. Wherfore þe seid Will*iam* Paston wille *and* grauntyth to yeve *and* paie to þe seid Will*iam* Joye þe halfendell þe crop of þe fornseid londes *and* all þe issues *and* p*ro*fites þer-of of þe seid yeer, *and* ou*er* that xl s. in monye reserued, *and* sauyng eu*er*more to þe seid Will*iam* Paston þe other halfendell of þe seid crop, *and* all þe issues *and* p*ro*fytes ther-of. And in cas þe seid Will*iam* Joye after þe seid yeer up-on his trouthe and his oth will afferme *and* seie þ*at* þe hires of his heruestmen passen þe su*m*me of xl s., þat þanne þe same William Paston shal paie to þe seid Will*iam* Joye his custages of his seid heruesthires a-boue þe seid xl s., after þe qu*an*tité to þe su*m*me of vj s. viij d. Ferthermore, if þe seid Will*iam* Joye wille in þe

931. [1] *Dotted circumflex over* p *here and in several words (e.g.* crop*) below, not apparently intended as abbreviation.* [2] *Dotted circumflex over* n.

forme afornseid after þe seid yeer seyn *and* affermyn up-on his trouth *and* his oth þ*a*t he lesyth good be þe seid bargayn, þat þanne þe seid Will*iam* Paston shal paie *and* reward to þe ⌜seid⌝ Will*iam* Joye his seid losse after þe qu*an*tyté to þe su*m*me of vj s. viij d. Ou*er*more, þe seid Will*iam* Paston *and* Will*ia*m Joye arn acorded þat þe seid Will*iam* Joye shal be *and* is be-come s*er*u*au*nt to þe seid Will*iam* Paston be an holl yeer next folwyng Michelmesse come twelvemoneth, be which yeer þe seid Will*iam* Joye shal do al ⌜his⌝ trewe *and* diligent seruice to þe seid William Paston in office of husbondrie, in sowyng *and* telyng of his londes, jnnyng of his heruest, maker of his cariages, *and* haue ou*er*syght *and* gou*er*naunce of all his seid husbondrie; *and* to ryde *and* goo on þe erandes of þe seid Will*iam* Paston whan he is desired. For which seruice þe seid Will*iam* Paston shal yeve to þe seid Will*iam* Joye xxvj s. viij d., *and* mete *and* drynk resonable, and a govne of his owyn weryn, and suffre þ*a*t his ploughes *and* harwes shuln telyn þe londes of þe seid Will*iam* Joye, to þe su*m*me of iiij acres; and carye inne his cornes in heruest suych tyme as his ploughes *and* cariage moon best attende þer-to. And þ*a*t nought w*ith*stondyng þese couen*au*ntes, þe seid Will*iam* Joye shall paie to þe seid Will*iam* Paston all his greynes *and* catell þ*a*t he toke w*ith* his ferme be-forn þe date of þis bill. In wittenesse of which thyng þe seid Will*iam* Paston *and* Will*iam* Joye to þis bill haue sette here seales.

932. Petition on behalf of JOAN and JOHN MARIOT concerning East Beckham: draft — 1436, probably October

Norwich, Norfolk Record Office, WKC 1/43/11. $11\frac{3}{4} \times 6\frac{3}{8}$ in. In an unidentified hand, with minor corrections in the hand of William Paston I.

Dorse: Blank.

In 1436 Joan and John Mariot, with the backing of William Paston, were involved in proceedings in Chancery against Edmund Winter, who had occupied the manor of East Beckham on 20 December 1434, and subsequently succeeded in litigation against them. This is a draft of their rejoinder to Winter's response to their initial petition, framed by Paston, and dating from two years and two months after the time of Winter's seizure of the manor. For the general context and further details of the proceedings see Richmond, *First Phase*, pp. 88–91.

Unprinted.

Also,[1] wher the seid Edmond Wynter[2] allegeth all þ*a*t he can ymagyne to put þe court oute of jurisdic*i*on of knowyng of þe matier of þe bille, please it to yow, my lord the Chaunceler, to knowe þ*a*t þe seid Edmond hath no trewe grownded title to þe seid man*er*, ne credible evidence ⌜to entitle hym þ*er*to⌝,[3] for if he hadde swich title or evidence he is so gret a visager *and* so

932. [1] *Added to left in larger script.* [2] for his answer to þe seid bille *canc.* [3] *Interl. by main hand.*

abundaunt of langage he wold prese to blowe it thorgh all þe courtes þe Kyng hath. Also, þe Kyng, atte sute made to hym by þe seid bille, sente þe same bill to yow, my lorde, by S*er* Rauf Botiller, knyght, willyng yow to here *and* knowe the matier *and* to reporte to hym ⟨yo⟩*ur*[4] good conceit þ*er*-jn.

Also, thogh þe matieres of þe bille were determinable atte co*mmon*e lawe, þe seid Edmond hath no cause to compleigne thogh he be put to answer beforn yow in this high court of conscience, for as moch as he is cause why þe ⌜seide compleign*au*ntz⌝[5] may have no remedye by þe lawe. He hath wrongfully[6] by strength ⌜put hem⌝[7] oute of þe seid maner, which was all heer lyflode, *and* his possession ther-of hath ⌜so⌝ wrongfully contynued by ij yeer except ij monethes, *and* yet doth; *and* hath drawe down heer houses, hewen heer wodes *and* destroied heer fysshyng wattres *and* all wasted þe seid maner, *and* vntrewly condempned hem in c marcz and xl li.; *and* hath þe body of þe seid John þe sone in execuc*io*n þ*er*-fore in þe Kynges Bench; *and* hath outelawed þe seid Johane þe moder, *and* therto cursedly w*ith* many forsworn othes slawndred *and* noysed her of mannes deth. For a-nother so gret a forswerer, ne so dampnabil a slawnderer, ne so shameles, vsuell langager, visager *and* contryver of vntrewe, feyned *and* slawnderous tales *and* matieres as he is was never in his dayes of his degree in þat shire.

So þe seid compleign*au*ntz have noo good to lyfe by, ne sewe w*ith* þe lawe, so þei arn wrongfully by craft oppressed by þe seid Edmond. *And* with-oute goode þei may not sewe þe lawe, *and* so withoute remedie but in þe grace *and* myght of oure souereyn lorde.

933. Petition to the EARL OF SUFFOLK or his arbiter concerning East Beckham: draft — Perhaps 1439

Norwich, Norfolk Record Office, WKC 1/43/10. 12 × 5 in. Hand unidentified.

Dorse: Blank.

The seizure of East Beckham, by the agents of Edmund Winter named in the petition, occurred on 20 December 1434, and an initial action of novel disseisin was brought by John Clement and John Rudde in Michaelmas Term 1436. During 1437 Winter succeeded in delaying this action, but John Clement appears to have renewed it by himself after Rudde's death, in a subsequent November, perhaps that of 1438, which would place this petition in 1439. The exact dating however remains uncertain; see Richmond, *First Phase*, pp. 91–2. No addressee is named, but the acccount of the events drawn up by John Paston I shortly after his father's death states that he had 'besechyd my lord of Suff*olk* to examyn þe mat*er*'; see no. 937, lines 31–2.

Unprinted.

[4] *Hole in paper.*
[5] *Added in Paston's hand.*
[6] put þe seid compleign*au*ntz *canc.*
[7] *Added in Paston's hand.*

John Drev, clerk, *and* oþer, sesed in her demesne ⌜as of fee⌝ of þe man*er* of Estbekham, of þe ⌜yeerly⌝ value of xx marcz, sold þe ⌜same⌝ maner to William Mariot of Crowmere, now deed, *and* Johane his wyf, now lyvyng, for cccc l m*a*rcz by hem to þe seid John Drev trewly paied; *and* by force of þe seid sale þ*er*-of enfeffed þe seid William *and* Johane to have *and* to holde to hem *and* to here heires en fee. þe which William of þe seid man*er* enfeffed John Rudde *and* John Clement of Crowmere, to have *and* to holde to hem *and* to her heires for evere to þe oeps of þe seid William *and* Johane. And after, þe seid William[1] dyed; after whos deth þe seid Johane[2] bargeyned *and* sold þe same man*er* to William Paston in certeyn fourme betwen hem accorded, ⌜to have *and* to holde to þe same William Paston *and* to his heires in fee⌝. *And* after þis to seigne, þe Moneday next beforn Cristemesse þe xiij yeer of þe regne of þe Kyng þ*a*t now is, John Griffyn, Rob*er*t Brampton *and* Thom*as* Saxthorp[3] w*ith* force wrongfully put owt þe seid John Rudde *and* John Clement, *and* hem dissesed of þe seid man*er*, *and* gret wast *and* destrucc*i*on dede in þe same man*er*. And after, þe seid John Rudde deyed. And þanne þe seid John Clement þe xviij day of Nouembr*e* last passed, to þe oeps of þe seid Johane *and* William Paston, sewed *and* arained assise of *nouel dissesine* of þe same man*er* ageyn Edmond Hampden esquier, þ*a*t tyme ten*au*nt of þe seid man*er*, as of fre hold, *and* ayen þe seid John Gryffyn, Robert Brampton *and* Thom*as* Saxthorp, to be restored to þe possession of þe seid man*er*, *and* to be satisfied of þe issues *and* p*ro*fitz of þe same, after þe annuell value aboveseid *and* þe rate of þe tyme sith þe seid dissesyne, *and* of þe costages of þe sute of þe seid assise; to þ*a*t intent *and* ende þ*a*t þe seid William Paston may have *and* enioye þe seid man*er* after þe effecte of þe seid bargeyn. And þ*a*t þe seid Johane may have *and* enioye þe price of þe seid man*er* after þe fourme *and* effect of þe same bargeyn, *and* þe seid issues *and* p*ro*fitz *and* costages of þe seid assise, þe which assise hangeth yet vndetermyned. Whervpon þe seid William Paston, touchant his interesse in þese p*re*misses, preyeth to have *and* receyve þ*a*t lawe, good feyth[4] *and* conscience requireth, after þe discrec*i*on *and* reule of his good maister þe justice arbitrour.

934. From HENRY, CARDINAL BEAUFORT to LORD BARDOLF: copy — Probably 1440, 31 May

Norwich, Norfolk Record Office, WKC 1/43/21. $11\frac{1}{2} \times 4\frac{3}{4}$ in. Hand unidentified, same as no. 936.

933. [1] made his testament *and* his wille of þe seid man*er canc.*

[2] on of þe executoures of þe seid testament // accordyng to þe wille // accordyng to þe wille of þe same William *canc.*

[3] *Crescent-shaped flourish over* p, *also in second instance of name below.*

[4] *One word canc. and erased.*

934. *From Henry, Cardinal Beaufort to Lord Bardolf, 31 May 1440*

Dorse: see no. 936.

Rot. Parl. V, p. 59 records an enquiry conducted by Lord Bardolf on 18 May 1440 into a proposed exchange of property lying in Paston and Edingthorpe, between William Paston and the Duchy of Lancaster. The letter authorising the exchange, of which Paston must have obtained this copy, could date from immediately after the enquiry, or possibly from 1441 if the administration moved more slowly. See Richmond, *First Phase*, pp. 4–5 and 97, n. 135.

Unprinted.

Right trusty *and* entierly ⌜we⟨l⟩⌝ belouyd freend, I grete yow right hertili weel. *And* ye be remembred touchyng þe chartre l⟨on⟩d of Willia⟨m⟩ ⟨Pas⟩ton, justice, lying in Paston *and* Edithorp in Gemyngham soken, whiche lond þe seid Paston hath sued to ent*er*chaunge with copiehold lond withinne þe seid tounship⟨e⟩s of Paston *and* of Edithorp, how my l*ett*res patentes in forme of a com⟨mi⟩ssion ⟨wer⟩ directe⟨d⟩ to yow or to your*e* deputé, to Oliuer Groos *and* Richard Gedge, for to enque⟨re⟩ ⟨. . .⟩[1] by wrytyng if ony hurte shuld growe to þe Kyng my sou*er*aygn lord or on-to vs ⟨. . .⟩[2] ⌜of⌝ þe seid feffement by þe seid ent*er*chaunging or not. Vpon þe whiche mat*er*⟨is⟩, wol ye we⟨te⟩ þat I haue seen þe v*er*edit whiche at Shene ye delyu*er*ed to me vpon þe same. And for to eschue in al vise þ⟨at⟩ ⟨n⟩oon hur⟨t⟩ shuld growe to þe Kyng by þe forseid ent*er*chaunging, callyng on-to me Piers Ardern, vndirstiward to my cosyn of Suffolch in the Duché of Lancastr*e*, I charged hym to visite *and* ou*er*see ⟨. . .⟩pely[3] þe seid v*er*dit, and wheder þe commission þat was directid to yow *and* other were duely execut *and* s*er*uet or not. Þe whiche Piers Ardern, by good delib⟨era⟩acion, aduised a⟨t⟩ layser, *and* vnderstandyng h⟨im⟩self vpon þe seid v*er*edit, with al his circumstances, hath certified to me þat þow Pastons entente *and* suyte be executed after þe fourme of his bille þat I haue seen, *and* is enclosed vnder my signet to be take yow with þe v*er*edit w*ith* þe berar her-of,[4] *and* þe whiche bille Paston p*ur*poseth hym at þis tym for to sue ⟨to þe⟩[5] Kyng, it may not hurte his hignesse, ner to þe seid lordship of Gemyngham, neyther to vs of þe feffement be p*re*iudicial or harmfull. And as[5] fer as I can conceyve or vndirstonde after myn oppinyon, me thynketh þe same.

Preyng Our*e* Lord to yiue yow, my right trusty freend, good lyff *and* longe, *and* haue yow eu*er* in his blissid kepyng. Wretyn at Asshier þe last day of Maij.

N*ota* Your*e* trewe frend, H. Cardinal of Engelond.

To my righte trusty and entierly welbeloued frend þe Lord Bardolf, þe Kyng*es* Chamberleyn.

934. *The document is in very poor condition, both torn and stained by damp, with many readings visible only under ultra-violet light.*

[1] *Space for about eight letters.*
[2] *Probably two letters canc.*
[3] *Space for two or three letters.*
[4] of this *canc.*
[5] *No space.*

935. Petition of JOAN MARIOT to KING HENRY VI for custody of East Beckham

1441, between 22 February and 10 April

Norwich, Norfolk Record Office, WKC 1/43/20. $18\frac{3}{4} \times 6$ in. Unidentified clerk's hand.

Dorse: Blank.

Like no. 932, this petition would have been drawn up by William Paston I on Joan Mariot's behalf in the course of their attempts to recover possession of East Beckham. As a result of an inquisition held at Swaffham on 27 July 1437, East Beckham had been taken into the hands of the Crown, and on 11 November of that year it was granted for life to Edmund Hampden, esquire of the body to Henry VI. Hampden vacated his grant on 22 February 1440, and Joan Mariot petitioned for custody from that date. The petition mentions an unresolved action of novel disseisin by John Clement against Edmund Winter, who had seized East Beckham in 1434; this is known to have been determined on 10 April 1441. See *Cal. Pat. Rolls 1436–41*, pp. 99, 245, 386, and Richmond, *First Phase*, pp. 91–3, 97.

Unprinted.

To our*e* sou*er*aign lord the Kyng.

R.H.

Besechith louly a pou*er*e old widwe Johane, þ*at* was the wiff of William Mariot, now deed; that where the seid William and Johane purchasid to hem *and* to here heires in fee the maner of Estbekham in the counté of Norff*olk* of John Drewe, clerk, and other, bi force of whiche purchace the same John Drewe and other of the seid maner enfeffed the seid William and Johane to haue and to holde to hem and to here heires in fee. The whiche William after of the seid maner infeffed John Rudde, now deed, and John Clement in fee, to þ'entente to parfourme therof the will of the seid William and Johane. By vertue of whiche feffement thei were seesed vnto the Moneday nexte before Cristemes the xiij yeer of your regne, þ*at* Edmond Wynter, esquier, and other, to hise oeps, hem therof hanne w*ith* force and armys disseised, and the issuez and p*ro*fitez therof hath receyved and takyn continuelly sithe the seid dissesine, to the value of xl li. The whiche Edmond by too vntrewe, feyned and ymagyned sutes hath made the seid Johane and John Mariot hire soon to be condempned to hym in xl li., and the seid John Mariot the sone in c marc.; and in execucion of the jugement of the seid xl li., hadde the body of the seid John the soon in prison a yeer and more. After whiche tyme, for as moche as the seid John Clement, to þe oeps of the seid Johane, sewed assise of *nouell dissesine* of the seid maner ageyn the seid Edmond and other, whiche hangith yet vndetermined. The same Edmond hath mad to be founden bi an jnquisicion, takyn beforn your*e* eschetour in Norff*olk* bi vertue of hise office the xxvij day of Juyll the xv^{e} yeer of your regne, among other matieris and articules, þ*at* the fader of the seid William was an alien born in Frisland,

and þ*a*t þe seid maner is holdyn of yow, sou*er*aign lord, in chief; bi force of which jnquisicion the seid maner was seesed into your*e* handes, and in your possession remaignyth now; where the fader and moder and alle the auncestres of the seid William were born in Ingelond, trewe liege men and women to yow and to your*e* p*ro*genitourz, and where the seid maner is holdyn of the Erle of Stafford and other, and not of yow in chief.

Please it to your*e* highnesse graciously to considre these matieris, and þ*a*t þe seid Johane hath noughte to susteigne with hire[1] self and hire ij sones and ij doughtres, ne to contente w*ith* the creditoures of hire seid husbond of the dette of ccc marc. and morc, but only that almyghti God and ye, soueraign lord, and your*e* lawe will suffre hir to haue of þe seid maner; ne no good ne hath to sewe the lawe a-geyn the seid Edmond, but of borwyng and of mennys almes. And þ*a*t the seid Edmond Wynter caused the takyng of the seid jnquisicion only to delaye the seid assise, and not to th'entente to forthere ne preferre your*e* righte; and þ*a*t thow it were trewe þ*a*t hire seid husbond was an alien, where the trouthe is the cont*ra*rie, yet for as moche as hir seid husbond hadde never noughte in the seid maner but joynte with hire in the seid fourme, and is deed, lyvyng hir the seid maner of righte by your*e* lawe, is *and* owith to be hire owyn and not yourez, sou*er*aign lord, by the cause beforn reherced. And thervpon of your gret pité and habundaunt grace, and of your*e* almes, to g*ra*unte to þe seid pou*er*e wedowe in helpe of hire susten*au*nce youre lettres patentz of þe kepyng *and* the warde of the seid maner, fro the xxij day of Febr*é* last passid into the ende of iij yeerez thanne nexte comyng, after þ'effecte of þe cedule to þis bille annexed,[2] and she shall alle the dayes of hire liff prey to God for yow.[3]

936. Petition to King Henry VI concerning East Beckham: draft 1442, March

Norwich, Norfolk Record Office, WKC 1/43/21, dorse. $11\frac{1}{2} \times 4\frac{3}{4}$ in. Hand unidentified, same as no. 934.

The date is given by two additions in different hands at the foot of the document: (i) 'hec e*st* ver⟨a⟩ copia bille facie m*arcij* a*nno* r*egni* r*egis* Henr*ici* vj xx^{o}'; (ii) 'Datu*m* litt*erarum* patent*es* facie Will*el*mo Paston de costod*is* man*er*ij de Estbekh*a*m xxij die marcij a*nno* regni reg*is* H*enrici* vj xx^{o}'. See also Richmond, *First Phase*, pp. 4, n. 14, and 97, n. 135.
Unprinted.

To our*e* sou*er*eign lord þe Kyng.

Besecheth lowely yo*ur* pou*er*e s*er*u*au*nt William Paston, þat where John Clement late enfeffed en fee in þe maner of Estbekham in þe counté of

935. [1] *MS.* hise
[2] *A Latin draft of letters patent for the grant is on a slip attached to the main document.*
[3] *At the foot of the document another hand has added* Grunez *(?)* Paston.

Norff⟨*olk*⟩, þe v ⟨. . .⟩[1] wedewe now ded, Johanne, þat was þe wyff of William Maryot of þe same man*er*, was disseised by Edmund Wynter esquyer *and* other, a-yens whom þe seid John Clement ⌜to þe oeps of þe seid Johane⌝ suyd assise of *nouell desseisyn* of þe s⟨ei⟩d maner. Whiche assise hangyng, the same Edmund, to delaye þe same assi*s*e, made to be founde by an jnquisicion take beforn yo*ur* eschetour in Norff*olk*, by vertu of his office, þe xxvij day of Juyll þe xv yeer of yo*ur* regne,[2] þat þe fader of þe seid William Maryot was an alien born in Frisland, and þat þe seid maner is holden of yow, souereign lord in chief. By force of whiche inquisici*o*n þe seid man*er* was seised in-to yo*ur* handis, *and* in yo*ur* possession remaigneth. Now where þe fadir *and* modir *and* ale þe auncestres of þe seid William Maryot wer born in Inglond, trewe liege men w⟨itt⟩en[3] to yow *and* to yo*ur* p*ro*genitours; and wher þe seid man*er* is holden of the Erl of Stafford *and* other, *and* not of yow in chief, in þe whiche assise þe seid Edmund preyed help[4] of yow, souereign lord. *And* ther up-on þe seid John Clement sewed *and* hadde in yo*ur* Chauncerye writtes of *prosedendo in loquela and ad iudici⟨um⟩*,[5] and þ*er* up-on hath by þe seid assi*s*e recouered þe seid maner ageyn þe seid Edmund *and* other. Please ⌜it⌝ to yo*ur* highnesse g*ra*ciously to considere þat ⟨þe⟩[6] seid Johane hadde nought wherwith to do sewe þe seid assi*s*e, but only of borwyng of þe seid besecher. Wherfor *and* for other causes þe seid Joha⟨ne⟩[7] died endetted, *and* yet is to þe seid besecher in c li. *and* more; *and* ther up-on to g*ra*unte to þe same besecher yo*ur* g*ra*cious l*ett*res patentes of yo*ur* gr⟨ete⟩[8] seal, made in dewe fourme after þ'effecte of þe cedule to þis bille annexed, for þe loue of God *and* for charité.

936. *For the condition of the document see no. 934.*

[1] *Edge of page gone, several words lost.*
[2] Amonge other articles *interlined and then canc.*
[3] *Hole in paper; space for two or three letters.*
[4] *Dotted circumflex over* p
[5] *Edge of page gone.*
[6] *Edge of page gone.*
[7] *Edge of page gone.*
[8] *Edge of page gone.*

JOHN PASTON I

937. Memorandum concerning East Beckham: draft

Probably late 1444 or 1445

Norwich, Norfolk Record Office, WKC 1/43/4. Three sheets stitched together to form a roll, $11\frac{3}{8} \times 38\frac{3}{4}$ in. In an unidentified hand, with corrections and additions in the hand of John Paston I.

Dorse: 'The tytle of S*er* John Paston to the manor of Est Bekham', in a late-fifteenth or early sixteenth-century hand.

This was probably drawn up soon after the death of William Paston I, the date of which is given here as 14 August 1444.

Unprinted.

Will*ia*m[1] Mariot purchasyd þe[2] sayd man*er* of Jon Drewe *and* othir, *and* toke estat þ*er*of to hym *and* Jone hys wyfe on fee simple, of trust þ*a*t he had to her*e* þ*a*t sche wold p*er*fou*r*me hys wylle; *and* aftyr, for diu*er*se causes þ*a*t mevyd hy*m*, be þe assent of þe seyd Joone *and* at hyr special request, e⟨nfy⟩ffyd[3] therof on Jon Clement *and* Jon Rudde to p*er*fou*r*me[4] hys wylle; *and* mad hys wyll, that þe sayd man*er* xuld be sold *and* þ*a*t ⟨. . .⟩[5] hys dettys xuld be payd *and* iche of hys sonys to haue xx^{ti} li. of þe sayd mony; *and* mad hys executor*ys* þe sayd Jone *and* Jon Mariot hys son, þ*a*t now p*re*tend to enioy þe sayd man*er* to hys owyn vse. And þe sayd Will*ia*m Mariot died þe v day of Septembr*e* þe xiij ȝer*e* of þis[6] Ky*n*g owr*e* sou*er*eyn lord.

Aftyr ⌜hoos⌝[7] deses þe seyd Joone, be þe assent of þe seyd feffeys, sold þe seyd man*er* to Will*ia*m Paston be word, *and* p*er*myttyd hym to haue þe evydense; *and* þ*a*t he xuld pay no mony tyl sche ⌜be his auise⌝ had mad hym a cler*e* astat, *and* warant hym þe place cler*e* *and* ouȝt of truble. And Jon Paston, þ*a*t p*re*tend to haue þe sayd man*er* be lawe *and* conscience, is sone *and* heyr*e* of [þe] seyd Will*ia*m Paston.

And aft*yr*, on Edmu*n*d Wyntyr *and* othyr, of envye þ*a*t ⌜þei⌝[8] had to þe sayd Will*ia*m Paston *and* Joone Mariot, dissesyd þe seyd Jon Cleme*n*t *and* Jon

937. [1] *One word erased and canc.*

[2] þ *in the form of* y *with* e *superscript, and so throughout, except that* þ *is occasionally written in its normal form. Representative instances are noted below.*

[3] *Hole in paper.*

[4] hyll *canc.*

[5] *Holes in paper; three or four words lost.*

[6] is *superscript.*

[7] *In John Paston I's hand, over* þe *canc.*

[8] *Interl. by Paston, who writes* þ *in its normal form.*

Rud⟨de⟩[9] of þe seyd man*er* on Seynt Thom*as* euyn þe Apostle þe sayd xiij ȝer*e*; aftyr wyche dyssesin, þe seyd Joone compleynyd to þe sayd Paston, seyng þ*a*t be cause sche had sold þe seyd man*er* to hy*m* *and* not to þe seyd Edmu*n*d whan he had desiryd of hir*e* to by it, þ*er*for*e* he disesyd her*e* feffeys, ⌜to the intent to make ⌜þe seyd Will*iam* Paston⌝[10] to leue his bargayn *and* herto acord w*y*t*h* hym as he wold⌝, p*ra*yng hym at hir*e* cost to sewe for her*e* bothens ryth in þe sayd man*er*, ⌜*and* to[11] pay for her þe mony þ*a*t shuld be spent þeron; *and* gr*a*ntyd þ*a*t⌝[12] if it wer*e* recou*er*id, it xuld[13] be set on-ward in p*ar*tye of payme*n*t, *and* if it wer*e* not recou*er*id sche wold content hym a-geyn[14] þeroff.

And[15] aftir, þe ⌜seyd⌝ Jon Clement browth an sis*er* ageyn þe seyd Edmu*n*d Wynt*yr* *and* othyr, *and* þe seyd Edmu*n*d Wynt*yr* be craft delayd þe seyd asis*er* ij ȝer*e* *and* mor*e*, on-to þe tyme þ*a*t the pleyntyffys besechyd my lord of Suff*olk* to examyn þe mat*er*. *And* than be a-cord of bothe p*ar*tys, it was put in my seyd lord [award],[16] *and* he for þe trowth of þe mat*er*,[17] aft*yr* þe examynaciyu*n*, had awarded þ*a*t the seyd Edmu*n*d xuld no leng*er* delay þe seyd Jon Clement, but sufryn þe cu*n*tr*é* to passyn þ*er* vp-on. And þe seyd assis*er* was a-wardyd, *and* fond for þe seyd Jon Cleme*n*t, be fors of þe wyche he had jugement for to recou*er*, whos estat Philyp Berney *and* Rob*er*t Reppys *and* Nich*o*lus Rake *and* othir haue be feffement to þe vse of þe seyd Jon Paston.

Aftyr þe qwyche recou*er*, *and* be-for execusion suyd, þe seyd Joone Mariot deid; *and* at þe day of her*e* deth, in p*re*sens of all her*e* neybo*urs*, sche chargyd þe seyd Jon Mariot her*e* sone þ*a*t the seyd Will*ia*m Paston xuld haue hys bargayn, *and* all þe mony þ*a*t[18] he had payd xuld be trewly a-lowyd hym, and w*y*t*h* þ*a*t comyth ou*yr* her*e* husboundys dettys xuld be payd as for as it wold strech.

Aftyr whos deth, *and* aft*yr* þe seyd recou*er*y*n*g, þe ⌜seyd⌝ Jon Mariot t*ur*nyd all strawnge to þe seyd Will*ia*m Paston, and was familiar w*it*h he*m* þ*a*t beforn tyme wer*e* adu*er*sarijs to hym *and* to þe seyd Paston in þe seyd mater*e*; a*n*d entred in þe seyd man*er*, clamy*n*g þ*a*t his fadyr *and* modyr deyd seysid þ*er*of, and also seyd he wold hauyd *and* kepe it to his owyn vse, a*n*d þ*a*t the seyd Will*ia*m Paston xuld neu*er* haue his bargeyn, cont*ra*ry to all mater*e* beforn rehersyd, the which mat*er* was knolachid, labo*ur*yd *and* pu*r*veyd be his assent.

And þe seyd Will*ia*m Paston, conseyvy*n*g be his word þ*a*t þe seyd Jon

[9] *Edge of page gone.*
[10] *Interl. by Paston, over* hym *canc.*
[11] be *canc.*
[12] *Interl. by Paston, over* leue for no money *and*, *canc.*
[13] *Miswritten and corrected by superimp.*
[14] *Next word added by Paston. Another incomplete clause by the main scribe is canc.:* þe sayd John Clement *and* Jon Rudde browt ass*é* *and* whan þe sayd Edmu*n*d Wyntyr aspyed þ*a*t he cowd not kepe þe sayd man*er* be þe lawe he *and* his counsell.
[15] *Prec. by* Aftir *canc.*
[16] *This or a similar word appears to have been omitted.*
[17] had *canc.*
[18] *Normal* þ.

Mariot was avysyd to do his lab*our* to diseyvyn his owyn fadir and modyr *and* hym, toke a wryt of entr*é*[19] in nature of asis*er*, in þe namez of Rob*er*t Crane, now ded, *and* þe seyd Philyp Berney, Rob*er*t Reppis *and* Nich*ol*us Rake, ageyns þe seyd Jon Mariot, þ*at*[20] pledyd he dishesyd hym not. *And* aft*yr*ward, for maynteinanc*e*,[21] þe seyd Jon enfeffed in þe same man*er* Milys Stapylton, esquier*e*, *and* odyr, as he seyd, *and* sent þe seyd Will*iam* Paston word be his wyfe þ*at* he had mad a feffament to on þ*at* xuld bet*yr* dele w*yth* hym than he cowd. And þe seyd Crane *and* othyr suyd forth þe seyd wryt, not w*yth*standy*ng* þe[22] ⌜seid⌝ feffeme*nt*, on-to þe tyme þ*at*[23] þe inquest was take, þe qwych enquest gaffe her*e* verdyt at large, and þ*er*jn was contenyd in s*u*bsta*u*ns all þe mat*er* a-boue rehersyd; *and* ⌜ou*yr* mor*e*⌝, þ*at* þe seyd Jon ⌜Mariot⌝,[24] p*re*te*n*di*ng*[25] þ*at* his fadyr *and* his modyr deid seysid, wher*e* now þ*yr* of hem deyd sesid, entryd;[26] be þe weche verdyt þe jugys consevyd þ*at* þe seid Jon Mariot had disesyd þe seyd Rob*er*t Crane *and* ⌜his cofeffes⌝,[27] *and* gaffe jugeme*nt* þ*at* they sxuld recuu*er*;[28] þe wech jug*ement* was geff in T*ri*nit*é* terme ⌜þe xxij yer of o*ur* seid souerayn lord,⌝[29] *and* þe sayd deme*n*dant*ys* sued execuci*un*.

And þe[30] seyd Will*iam* Paston deid þe xiiij day of August þe xxij ȝer*e* of owr*e* seyd sou*er*ayn lord.

And þe seyd Jon Mariot suyd a writ of[31] a-teynt ageyns þe seyd Rob*er*t Crane *and* his seid cofeffys, ret*ur*nabl*e* in þe Comown Place, on þe morwyn aftyr Sowlemesday þ*at* was þe t*er*me next aft*yr* þe deth of þe seyd Will*iam* Paston; *and* þ*er*in seyd[32] þ*at* þe seyd v*er*dyte ⌜in the seid writ of entré⌝ was ontrue, in þ*at* that þ*er*in was conteynyd þ*at* his fadyr *and* his modyr died not seysid ⌜of þe seyd man*er*,⌝ for he seyd þ*at* his fadyr *and* modyr wern ⌜þ*er*of⌝[33] joyntly sesid in fee, *and* his fadyr died sesid ⌜and his modir ou*er* lyvyd ⌜*and* was sool sesid þ*er*of⌝[34] be þe survivir, *and* aft*yr* of that estat died seysid. And fro his seyd modir⌝ þe seyd man*er* descend*et*[35] on-to hym as sone *and* heire, *and* he entrid and was of þ*at* estat sesid on-to þe time þ*at* þe seyd Jon Cleme*nt* ⌜be colo*ur* of a writ of *h*ab*ere facias seisin*am⌝ dissehyd hym. And aft*yr* þe seyd writ a-batyd be þe deth of þe seyd Rob*er*t Crane, pletyd on þe morw aft*yr* Sowlemesse ⌜day⌝ last pasid, þe qwyche ateynt was all cont*ra*rie to þ*at* that his fad*yr* *and* mod*yr* wrouȝth in her*e* lyve, *and* cont*ra*rie to all accyo*u*ns take in his modyrs lyve.

And þe viij day of Nouembr*e* next folwyng þe seyd Sowlemesday, þ*at* was

[19] *Next two words inserted by Paston in blank space left by main scribe.*
[20] *Normal* þ.
[21] -anc*e* *corrected by Paston.*
[22] *Normal* þ.
[23] all *canc.*
[24] *Interl. by Paston.*
[25] *In Paston's hand, in a blank space left by the main scribe.*
[26] *Next four words in Paston's hand, in blank space left by main hand.*
[27] *Interl. by Paston over several words heavily canc.*
[28] *Remainder of this clause (except the interl., see next note) in Paston's hand.*
[29] *Interl. by main scribe over* last paste *in Paston's hand, canc.*
[30] *Normal* þ.
[31] ateynt *canc.*
[32] *and canc.*
[33] *Interl. in Paston's hand.*
[34] *Interl. in Paston's hand over and* held it *canc.*
[35] t *superscript.*

but v days aft*yr* þe seyd ateynt abatyd, browt anothir accyon of a-nodyr kynd ⌜called⌝[36] a *cui in vita* a-geyn a straunge p*er*son, on Simon Gu*n*nor*e*, ret*ur*nable at þe xv day of Seynt Martyn; for þe wyche Simo*n*d an aturné aperyd, *and* be assent suffryd þe seyd Jon Mariot to recou*er* þe next day folwyng.

The wyche Simon Gunnore neu*er* had ryth ner tytille in þe seyd maner*e*, but as ten*au*nt t*er*me of yeris of þe lees of the ⌜seid⌝ Will*ia*m Paston, mad to hym be dede indendyth be þe assent of hem þ*a*t wer*e* infeffyd þ*er*-in. And also, as it fortunyd, þe seyd Simon was neu*er* w*y*t*h*jn þe shir*e* of Norff*olk* a-twyx þe day that þe seyd a-teynt batyd, wer*e*jn þe seyd Jon Mariot supposid þe seyd Philyp Berney *and* Reppys to be ten*au*ntis, and þe day that þe seyd John recou*er*yd a-geyn, þe seyd Simon as ten*au*nt.[37] And so it is but a feynyd recou*eré*, for þe seid Simond is and alwey hath be of couyne and counseyl w*y*t*h* þe seyd Jon Mariot; and if he wold haue pleted[38] it, he and eu*er*y man þ*a*t auys[39] swech accyon myth have be browth ageyn, myth haue had sufficient mat*er* lawfulli *and* truly to have barrid þe seyd John, if he had wold.

And þe mater*e* and pledyng jn þe *cui in vita* is cont*ra*rie to þe seid a-teynt browth be hym self,[40] and þe mater*e* of iche of hem cont*ra*ry to odyr, and p*ro*vyth ⌜odyr⌝ ontreuly brouȝt and feynyd.

And yet hanggy*n*g, þe seyd atteynt, þ*a*t *and* þe mat*er* þ*er*of, wer*e* mayntenyd and vesagid as thow it had be trew as þe gospell, and many men wer*e* wrongfully hurt þ*er*-by.

And not w*y*t*h*standyng þe seyd recou*eré*, a-geyns ⌜þe seid⌝ Simond, the ⌜seid⌝ feffeys of the seyd Jon Paston haue good ryth *and* titill to þe seyd maner, bothe be entr*é* and accion. And[41] þe seyd Jon Paston, be cawse þ*a*t the seyd Jon Mariot *and* his counsell haue so sklau*n*drid þe p*ar*té of the seid Jon ⌜Paston⌝, þ*a*t is trowth, to be on-trew, and colo*ur*yd her owyn p*ar*té be sotyll menys, that makit su*m* p*er*sones to be-leve þ*a*t herd neu*er* bothe p*ar*tis, that troweth wer*e* ontrowth ⌜in þis mat*er*⌝,[42] tarijth *and* abydyth tyme þ*a*t his p*ar*té may be knowe swech as it js.

And as for þe bargayn *and* comenaunt*ys* a-twix þe seyd John Paston *and* Mariot, first þe seyd Joone, in þe comunycac*io*n þ*er*of, g*ra*ntid it to þe seid ⌜Will*ia*m⌝[43] Paston c s. w*y*t*h*jn þe valew þ*er*of or þ*a*t ony man wold geff þ*er*for*e*, *and* that sche xuld make hym a cler*e* estat *and* bryng ⌜to hym⌝ þe evidens. And ⌜aft*yr*⌝, the seid Edmu*n*d ⌜Wyntir diseysid the seid John Cleme*n*t that was feffid þ*er*in; and aftir that disseson þe seid Joone Mariot⌝ come ageyn to þe seid Paston, p*ra*yng hym to abyde be his bargayn and to do

[36] *Interl. in Paston's hand.*
[37] *Final* t *flourished as if for pl. abbrev.*
[38] *Partly superimp. on another word.*
[39] *Partly superimp. on another word.*
[40] ad *canc.*
[41] *In Paston's hand, superimp. on a different word by main scribe.*
[42] *Interl. in Paston's hand.*
[43] *Over* John *canc.*

his p*ar*t to saue his rigth *and* her*ys* at her*e* cost, and he xuld have it xl li. w*y*t*h*jn þe prise, wer*e*of þ*er* is wrytyng and seelys. And sey*n*g also to þe seid Paston that þe seid Edmu*n*d Wynt*yr* had nowthir rith ner titell þ*er*in, ⌜but he dede it to make hym to leve his bargayn, and for odir causis, as it is be-for*e* rehersid in þe iij article of þis bill⌝.[44]

And aft*yr* for þe mor*e* certeynt*é* of the very pryse of the seid man*er*, it was acordyd be-twix þe seid Will*ia*m Paston *and* ⌜þe seyd⌝[45] John Mariot, þe Tuesday next be-for*e* Kandylmesse day þe xxj yeer*e* of þe Kyng that now is, be writyng vndyr þe seid John Mariot hand, ⌜þ*a*t þe seid Will*ia*m Paston⌝ xul hauc it for asmyche as it wer*e* worth in xx^{ti} yeer*e*, a-bate þ*er*of þe seid xl li. and alle odyr mony spent vp-on þe ple for the recou*er*e of þe seid man*er*, and all mony deliu*er*d to þe seid Jone Mariot *and* John Mariot,[46] and xxiiij li. ⌜xv s. vij d.⌝,[47] þe qwyche þe seid Jone *and* John owth to diu*er*s p*er*sones, þe qwyche thei had[48] borwyd,[49] and[50] whom þe seid Will*ia*m Paston hath content at[51] her*e* request.

And the seyd man*er* is not worth ⌜clerli be yer⌝ xvj mark. And thow it wer*e*, þ*a*t drawyth in xx yeer ccc xx marke. And the seid Will*ia*m Paston hath deliu*er*d to þe seid Joone and John in mony, w*y*t*h* þe seid xxiiij li. ⌜xv s. vij d.⌝ wyche þei[52] haue ete, dru*n*kyn *and* spent, ciiij li. viij s. iiij d.[53]

And the exspencys the qwyche þe[54] seid Will*ia*m Paston hath spent vp-on the seid pleys, *and* in odyr plez be ⌜her⌝ assent,[55] in p*ur*sute and diffence of ix or x accyou*n*s þ*a*t wer*e* sewyd atwix the seid Edmu*n*d Wyntir *and* hem and þe seid John Cleme*n*t ⌜in þe live of þe seyd Joone⌝,[56] of the wyche ij wer*e* speciall assis*e*[57] that indurid ij yeer *and* half, and in jche of hem wer*e* viij speciall sesciou*n*s of the justic*e* of thoo assis*e*, Lynne *and* Hengh*a*m in the seid count*é* of Norff*olk*, and ⌜in⌝ tweyn of the seid accyou*n*s the seid Joone *and* John wer*e* condempnyd in an c mark. *and* xl li., wer*e*of the seid Will*ia*m Paston dischargid hem, drawith to þe su*m*me of lxxj li. vij s. j d.[58]

The wiche su*m*mys, w*y*t*h* the seid xl li. pardonyd of the price, is ccxv li. xv s. v d.; the wyche ccxv li. xv s. v d. js mor*e* than the seid man*er* is worth in xx^{ti} yer, valuyd at xvj mark. be yer*e*, be v mark. *and* odde mony. The qwyche þe seid Mariot xuld owyn to þe seid John Paston, sauy*n*g that þe seid Will*ia*m Paston had of odyr st*ra*nge p*er*sones for diu*er*s causis certeyn mony toward the helpy*n*g of the seid plez, wer*e*of the seid John Mariot hath veri knowlach *and* wryty*n*g vnd*er* bill endendyd. And þe seid John Paston is *and* alwey hath he redy to rekken *and* to pay if owth þ*a*t he owe, so that þe seid John Mariot at his cost wol cler*e* þe seid man*er* acordy*n*g to his comenaunt, sawy*n*g to þe

[44] *Last seven words in Paston's hand.* [45] *Interl. in Paston's hand.*
[46] to leve by duryng þe ple *canc.* [47] *Over and* odde mony *canc.*
[48] also *canc.* [49] to leue by *canc.* [50] whov *canc.*
[51] ye seid J *canc.* [52] ei *supercript, and so below.* [53] *Sum spaced to right.*
[54] þ *in normal form.* [55] befor*e* disses of the seid Jone *canc.*
[56] *Interl. in Paston's hand.* [57] and *canc. and subpuncted.*
[58] the qwyche su*m*mys *canc.*

seid John Paston of that mony þ*a*t he xuld owe, if he owe ony, as myche as xal content certeyn ⌜odyr⌝[59] p*er*sonys þ*a*t in the lif of the seid Joone labo*ur*yd in þe seid accyou*n*s for her auayll, not takyng her reward be cause of the pou*er*té of the seid Joone, but g*ra*untyd her to abyde til þe ple wer*e* det*er*mynyd to þe end. The wiche reward*ys* the seid Joone in her lif g*ra*ntyd to pay, and þei drawy*n*g be estymaciu*n* to þe su*m*me of xx li., as the seid John Paston kan rekkyn be p*ar*cell, sauy*n*g also to þe seid John his resonabl*e* recompens aft*yr* conscience deniyd for the wronfull seutys þ*a*t the seid John Mariot hath take as wele a-geyn hym *and* his fadiris feffeis, and for the issuys *and* p*ro*fitys of the seid man*er* sith it was recou*er*yd be John Cleme*n*t of þe seid Edmu*n*d Wynt*yr*, consid*er*ed that his fadir payd so myche mony owth of his purse ther-for*e*, and so longe for-bore it w*y*t*h*owth ony avayle.

938. Declaration at Cromer concerning East Beckham

1445, 17 March

Add. Charter 14525. Parchment, $10\frac{3}{4} \times 6\frac{1}{2}$ in., two seals attached. Unidentified clerk's hand.

Dorse: Blank

Dated.
Unprinted.

Be it knowe to alle men þat Johane, þat was þe wiff of William Maryot, sumtyme of Crowemer, liggyng on hir dedbed þe day þat she dyed, in þe p*re*sence of S*er* Symond, vicar*e* of þe chirche of Crowemer *and* other, preyd John Clement of Crowemer forseid, for as meche as he was soul seised of þe maner of Estbekham by feoffement of hir housbond, to make astate of þe seid maner to þe seid Johane *and* John Maryot hir sone. And she seid þat she *and* hir seid sone shuld make astate ageyn to hym *and* many oþ*er* þat same day as strong þ*er*-inne as he was to-fore, up-on trust to p*er*fourme hir seid husbond*es* wille *and* heres, and to p*er*fourme þe bargayne whiche she hadde made with William Paston, justice. Wher up-on þe seid John Clement seid he wold be auysed til þe next day, *and* departed.

And þe seid Johane, rehersyng to hir seid sone John Maryot þat hir husbond *and* she were gretly indetted, *and* þat it was hir husbond*es* wille *and* hir also þat þe maner of Bekham shuld be solde *and* his dett*es* payed, she charged hym þat he shuld paye bothe his fader*es* dett*es and* heres of þe mony þat come of þe sale of þe seid maner. And þe seid John hir sone seide hir dettes *and* his faderis was xv^{xx} mark. or more, and he seid ou*er* þe su*m*mes resceyved of William Paston *and* to be alowed hym, þe remen*au*nt of þe mony

[59] *Interl. in Paston's hand.*

þat shuld come of þe sale of þe seid maner shuld not paye þe dettes. And she charged hym þat if þe seid William Paston wolde haue it þat he shuld haue it, as her*e* bargayn was xl li. with-inne þe price þat any man wold gyf þerfore with-owte fraude, and þat noman shuld haue it til he hadde refusid it *and* forsake his bargayn. And if he wolde leve his bargayn *and* not haue þe man*er*, þanne she charged hir sone þat he shuld selle it as ⌜he⌝ myght best, *and* þat þe seid Paston shuld be first payed *and* content. And if þe mony þat come of þe sale, Paston allowid of his dette if he wolde haue þe maner or payed if he wold not haue þe maner, myght not suffice to paye þe dett*es*, þat þanne he shuld selle þe places in Crowemer *and* so content eu*er*y man, as he wold answere atte day of doom.

And William Maryot, an-oþ*er* sone of þe seid Johane, seid he shuld haue by his faderis wille ⌜xl m*arc*.⌝[1] of þe seid sale, and she seid þat first hir husbond*es* dett*es* *and* heris shuld be payed, and ⌜þan⌝ þe remen*au*nt of þe wille shuld be p*er*fourmed as for as þe mony wole stretche. And þe seid Johanne dyed þe same day.

In wittenesse of þese p*re*misses, we, Symond Norman, vicar*e* of Crowemer, John Clement of þe same toun, Thomas Note of þe same toun *and* William Shepherd of Bekham, to þis writyng haue sette our*e* seales.

Youen at Crowemer þe Wednesseday next a-fore Palme Sunday, þe xxiij yeer of þe regne of Kyng Herry þe Sext after þe conquest.

939. Declaration at Beckham concerning East Beckham 1445, 17 March

Bodl. Douce Charters a. 1, f. 92. Parchment, $10\frac{1}{4} \times 3\frac{1}{4}$ in. Unidentified clerk's hand.

Dorse: In a late fifteenth or early sixteenth-century hand, 'testi*mon*iall of Jah. entré *and* of astat to S*er* M. Stapiltun'.

Dated.
Unprinted.

Be it knowe to alle men þat William Maryot, sumtyme of Crowemer*e*, whoes soule God assoile, at Estbekham made a feoffement of þe maner of Estbekham to John Clement of Crowemer*e* *and* John Rudde of Crowemer*e*, *and* seison þanne delyu*er*ed *and* attornement of þe ten*au*ntz, in þe p*re*sence of diu*er*se men yet a-lyve. And afterward þe seid William by suffraunce of his seid feoffes, as þe comune cours is, ocupyed *and* afterward dyed. After whoes deth Edmund Wynter, esquyer, entred, after whiche entré Johanne Maryot, sumtyme wif to þe seid William, come neu*er* atte seid toun of Estbekham

938. [1] *Over* xx li. *canc.*

as for as any ten*au*nt or dweller in þe seid toun of Estbekham or þere abowte covde aspie or knowe. And John Maryot, sone of þe seid Johane, entred first into þe seid maner*e* a-bowte Alhalwetyde or Cristemesse after þe deth of þe seid Johane his moder. And þe seid John Maryot of þe seid maner enfeoffed Miles Stapilton esquyer in þe eende of hervest þanne next folwyng, *and* non erst, at whiche tyme þe seid Miles went to þe see. And o*þer* astate ne feoffement openly knowe were noon made of þe seid maner, til þe seid John Clement entred by þe Kyngg*es* writte *and* made astate to John Damme and other. In wittenesse of this, we, William, vicar*e* of þe chirche of Westbekham, Thomas Note of Crowemere, John Clement of þe same toun, William Shepherd of Bekham, John Chervell, John Redyng of Estbekham, John Note of þe same toun, John Beeston of þe same toun, Thomas Hoddes of þe same toun, John Hawe of þe same toun, William Tournour*e* of the same toun, *and* John of Crosse of þe same toun, haue sette owr seales to þis writyng.

Yoven at Bekham, þe Wednesseday next to-fore Palme Sunday, þe xxiij yeer*e* of þe regne of Kyng Herry þe Sext after þe conquest.

940. To RICHARD CHARLES 1460, 9 April

Oxford, Magdalen College, Guton Hall 178/3. $7\frac{1}{2} \times 3\frac{1}{2}$ in. Hand unidentified.

Dorse: Marks of folding, slits for tape, remains of red wax seal. Address in hand of letter:

*To Rychard Charl*es *be thys lett*er *delyu*er*yd in hast.*

The letter is attached to a set of accounts for Guton Hall, Brandiston, dated 1459–60, where Richard Charles was bailiff.

Printed by Richmond, *Fastolf's Will*, p. 28.

I grete yow welle, letyng yow wete þ*a*t as for*e* þe v[1] combz of ferme ⌜barly⌝[2] that Mychael Frary schuld paye to yow, I haue relecyd ⌜*and* forgefyn⌝ it hym for*e* the req*u*est of Mayst*er* Roberd Popye, concyderyng the hurte that he hathe had wyth fyer*e* thys same yer*e*. Nomor*e* to yow at thys tyme, but Good haue yow in hys kepyng. Wretyn at Norwych, the Weddynnsday nex aftyr*e* Palme Sonday.

Be J. PASTON

940. [1] comb *canc.* [2] *Over* þ*a*t the *canc.*

WILLIAM PASTON II

941. Declaration concerning the manor of Huntingfield in Bacton 1479, 21 May

Bodl. Charters Norfolk a.1, f. 6. Parchment, $11\frac{1}{4} \times 7\frac{1}{4}$ in. Unidentified clerk's hand.

Dorse: Blank.

Dated.
Unprinted.

To alle Crysten men disposid to here the trouthe to whome this p*re*sente wrytyng comyth, Waryn Kyng, Nicholas Burghe, William Barker, John Boule, Henry Lessy, William Pope, William Fayerman, Roberd Hardyng, Richard Rowlande, John Kydeman the elder and John Hornyngtoft sende gretyng. For as muche as it is plesyng to God and merytorye in eu*ery* doughtfull mater*e* to testifye the trouthe, we before named seye and witnesse for trouthe as we wyll answer*e* be-fore God, that in the next day after the Assencion of our*e* lorde God, the yer*e* of the reigne of our*e* sou*er*eyn lorde Kyng Edwarde the iiij^{e} the xix^{te} we be-fore wretyn, wyth many other, at the jnstauns and spe*ci*all laboure*e* and request of Henry Waryns of Paston, gadered and aperyd at the man*er*e of Huntyngfeld in Bakton in the shire of Norfolk. And ther*e* and than Symonde Gunore, be fors of a dede wyth a l*ett*re of attornye to hym made ⌜as he seid⌝ be Agnes Paston, and ther*e* shewed, delyu*er*ed seasson of and jne the halfdele of the forseid man*er*e of Huntyngfeld, other wyse called Sewerdsby, wyth the aporten*au*nce ther*e* to be-longyng only, and of non other*e* man*er*es, londes nor ten*emen*tes in the forseid shir*e*, to William Paston, swyer, and other wyth hym named in the ⌜seyd⌝ dede, be fors of letter*e* of attornye made to vs, the forseid William Barker and John Boule, be ⌜þe⌝[1] seid William Paston and other named in the dede.

941. [1] þ *in form of* y.

942. Indenture recording delivery of plate 1479, 19 August

Add. 27451, f. 2. $5\frac{1}{2} \times 6\frac{3}{4}$ in. Hand unidentified.

Dorse: Marks of folding. In a hand different from but contemporary with the inventory: 'plate of Willia*m* Paston left w*ith* John Russhe the xiiij day of Sept*ember* A^{o} xix^{o}'.

G. 835/951.

This indenture made the xix day of August Anno xix^{o} [witnesseth] that I, Richard Lee, have deliu*er*ed to M*aister* John Russhe thes p*ar*cellis folouyng of plate[1] of silu*er*:
First a bason and an ewer with iij combis in a skochyn.
It*em* a silu*er* potte.
A layer of silu*er*, p*ar*te gilte, with an acorne on the knopp.
A gilte stonding coppe, ponsid, with a[2] cou*er*.
A chasid pece with a[3] cou*er*, p*ar*te[4] gilte.
ij playne pecys.
ij deppe disshis.
x sponys.
A white playn coppe with a starre in the botom, with a cou*er*.
A standing coppe, gilte, with a cou*er*.
A candellstik of silu*er* with a sokette.
A trevett of silu*er*.
A salt of silu*er* with a brokyn cou*er*.
A cou*er* for a playn pece, the knoppe gravid with armys.

RICHARD LEE

943. To THOMAS CAREY 1492, 9 November

Nos. 943–945 consist of three late letters of William Paston II to Thomas Carey, from amongst the muniments of the family of Fitzwilliam of Milton, Northamptonshire. Fitzwilliam Roll 370 consists of five narrow strips of paper of differing lengths, but of similar widths. The roll format is uncharacteristic of the Paston correspondence in general (see Part I, pp. xxxiii-iv). It is evident from the remnants of sealing wax on the exterior of all three, and from an endorsement on one and the address on another, that all three were missives. The letters are here designated in their chronological order, as Fitzwilliam Roll 370/1–3.

Northampton, Northamptonshire Record Office, Fitzwilliam Roll 370/1. Two strips of paper, the first $6 \times 16\frac{1}{4}$ in., itself made up of two strips of

942. [1] and *canc.* [2] *No space.* [3] *No space.* [4] *MS.* aparte.

unequal length ($12\frac{1}{4}$ and 4 in.) pasted together; the second 6 × $33\frac{3}{4}$ in., made up of four shorter strips (3 in., $8\frac{1}{4}$ in., $10\frac{3}{4}$ in., $11\frac{3}{4}$ in.), likewise pasted. In an unidentified hand, different from those of nos. 944 and 945.

Dorse: traces of sealing wax on second strip.

The year is confirmed by the reference to Henry VII's *Statutes of War*, printed by Pynson early in 1492, and issued with the military indentures for the war against France, sealed on 9 May (Rymer, *Foedera*, xii. 478). The text begins abruptly, without the normal epistolary greeting, suggesting that a preceding part of the letter may have been lost.

Partly printed by R. Beadle and L. Hellinga, 'William Paston II and Pynson's *Statutes of War* (1492)', *The Library* 7th ser., ii (2001), 107–19.

I[1] thank you for the labour that ye toke in the matt*er* of S*er* Amys Powlett. He hathe promysed the payment of the money, but I geve no credence therto. Yf ye happen to mete of fortune eyther w*ith* S*er* Amys, Heron, Bevyn or Dauy, handell the matt*er* as ye seme best by your dyscrec*i*on, for they all excepte S*er* Amys wolde the money were payd. It is an vnconcyonable dede to kepe a power house of relygyon from theyr duté by myght of power.

I thank you hartely for the pakthrede that ye sent me. I receyued iiij skeynes of iiij dyu*er*se sort*es*, eche sorte grett*er* threde than oder, but the grettest pakthrede, whiche is made at Skypton, is most metyst aft*er* myn entent. I vse it most for byndyng of my bok*es* but ye haue sent me inough for many yeres.

As for the lett*er* I sent[2] to M*aster* Huddysfeld, your graunc*er*, yf it dyd you any good, or yf ye stode any more in the fauo*ur* of hym for it, I am well pleased. Ye may send hym parte of the tydyng*es* that I send you nowe.

As for the pedegrewes that I sent you, yf they haue do you any good I am glad of it. And I am glad that ye haue spede so well in the recou*er*y of your londe. I spake w*ith* bothe justyse of assyse in your countrey, and I founde theym right good to you.

As for the coppy of the bok*es* of a-compte that ye wolde haue of Knyght the audyto*ur*, it is so that it[3] wolbe[4] nygh Crystm*as* or Knyght be here. He is takyng of my lady the Kyng*es* moders accompt*es* in Deuonshere w*ith* M*aster* Hugh*es*,[5] my lady the Kyng*es* moders receyuo*ur*.

I am sory of the hurte that I fele by your wrytingis done at Chilton, bothe in the game, in the tymb*er*, and in the housen; and I fele by your wryting your entent in that matt*er*. And yf ye shulde opteyne accordyng to your mynde, ye had nede to take wise wayes therin, for ye know well i-nough, the offyce is not in the gyft of one p*er*sone alone, and I wolbe glade to helpe you w*ith* my councell and w*ith* myn aduyse. I wolde aduyse you by a dyscrete way

943. [1] *Upper edge of first strip of paper worn away, leaving lower portions of letters in a line of writing partially visible. Each section of the letter is preceded by a small capitulum mark resembling a superscript* a.

[2] t *superimposed on* d. [3] t *superimposed on* s.

[4] *Two or three letters heavily canc.*

[5] *MS.* Hugh + *a superscript mark or letter, apparently* s.

to breke your mynde to Thom*as* Warren. He is a full fast frende where as he louythe, and his frenshypp can not hurte you. Yf it do you good, so moche the bett*er*, and yf ye make hym of yo*ur* councell he must ned*es* owe you the bett*er* wyll in your matt*er*.

M*aster* S*er* Thomas Burght shalbe here w*ith* in this fortinyght, and entendyth to dwell in this countrey. And yf ye entreate my lady of Wylshere to wryte tweyn lettres for you, one to M*aster* Burgh and a-nother to my lady[6] Bray, shewyng the hurte that is done, and the inconvenyence that woll fall therof yf it be not holpen by suche an offycer as woll take bett*er* hede therto, *and* woll haue a loue and a fauo*ur* to the place. And these lettres wolbe dyscretely dyuysed, and I woll helpe to[7] the delyu*ery* of theym, *and* put therto as good word*es* as I can.

Here is my lady Jane, *and* olde Stephyn dealys full sympelly w*ith* our rent*es* of Warwyk*es* In. And yf she be suffred to do as she begynneth to do, she shall make theym of lytell p*ro*ffyte to vs in shorte space. She callyth her-self lady of the place, *and* saythe the Kyng hathe gyven it her, which is nothyng so.[8]

As for the boke of the Statut*es* of Warre w*ith* the portrature of the Kyng*es* armes and bagys that ye desyred me by your wrytyng to sende you, it is so that Pynson the p*ri*nt*er* that dwellyth w*ith*oute Tempill Barr, and dyd p*ri*nte theym, hathe delyu*er*ed all the book*es* that he made for the kyng vnto S*er* Thom*as* Lovell before the Kyng dep*ar*ted, whiche were delyu*er*ed seyn vnto the capitaignes of his hooste. Neu*er*theles, be cause of your desyre, and for the pleasur that ye woll do to M*aster* Huddysfeld therin, I haue be crafte gotten you one, whiche I sende you by this berer.

As for th'armes and the bagis portraid in the fyrst leffe of the book of the Statut*es* of Warre coude not be coloured, be cause John Pyk myght not tary. But ye may make a paynt*er* to sette saffron colour on it for that that shulde be golde, and other coloures in all plac*es* convenyent, for the valure of a peny.

Th'aungell may be what colour ye list.

The best w*ith* the ram*m*es horne must be whyte and the hornes golde w*ith* saffron.

The harte must be whyte, and the crowne and chayne golde.

The greyhounde whyte, and the[9] coller golde.

The dragon rede.

The pecok made in his propre colour as a pecok shulde be.

The portcolys *and* chaynes all golde; the egill whyte and the crowne and chayne golde; the ij rosys on the portcolys rede.

As for the duble rosys on the borders, one all rede, a-nother the leves w*ith*in the myddys whyte, *and* the vtter levys rede.

The iij scochons be-nethe crowned w*ith* golde.

The mydde scochon, the fylde sabill, iij estryge fedders sylu*er*.

[6] Bry *canc.* [7] *Repeated.*
[8] *End of first strip of paper.* [9] colour *canc.*

The scochon on the ryght honde, the ryght syde of the same scochon sylu*er*, the lefte syde azur, for Lancast*er* colours.

The scochon on the lefte honde, the ryght syde whyte and the left syde grene.

The armes of Englond, the felde rede, iij lyberd*es* golde.

The armes of Fraunce, the felde azure, iij flowrdeluc*es* golde.

All crownes and septers golde.

As for the matt*er* of Shaftysbury, I am full sory for it, and I doubte not but so be ye, for it becomyth vs and all suche as stond in the caas that ye and I do to be sory of it, for many considerac*io*ns, and to be gladde to endevour ourselffe to helpe to the remedy of it; and so haue I bene and woll be to my power possible. Neu*er*theles, and a man haue a sore ⌜or⌝[10] be seke and woll not tell his fesyssyan or surgeon where his greffe is, it woll be hard to helpe hym. And I haue done all that eu*er* I can to knowe of the p*ar*tie the trouthe, to th'entent to remydé the same. And I can not make the p*ar*tie to confesse it by no meanes. Neu*er*theles, yf the man that ye wotte of come to this towne to dwell here as ye wryte to me he woll, than I doubte me that it woll be so openly knowen that it shall passe our powers to help to the remydy; wherof I wolde be sory, be my trouthe.

And as for Robert John, taylour of Watlyng Strete, I fele by your wrytyng that he was in the contré aboute*s* Shaftysbury, and that he shewed my lady Wilshyre that he see the thyng hym-selffe. I haue sent to hym, but I can not speke w*ith* hym at any leysure as yette.

Also I receyued by John Pyk, my ladys s*er*u*au*nt, a pursse wherin I founde ij nobles *and* xl d. in grot*es*, and a pece of golde of ij s. *and* vj d.; and how this money was paid it apperyth aft*er*ward in this bill.

I founde also w*ith*in your seid bill iij letters in-sealed, the fyrst lett*er* to John Kyng, my s*er*u*au*nt, whiche is not here, he is rydden in-to Wales for besynes towchyng the Kyng*es* grace; the ij^{de} lett*er* directed to Lowes Pollerd of the Tempill, a man of your councell that hathe the typett of golde; the iij^{de} lett*er* to Moleyns. And be-cause John Kyng whom ye wrote vnto to solyst your matt*er* was oute of towne in[11] Wales, and also for that ye desyred me that I shulde open your lett*er*s to th'entent to spede the matters conteyned therin, þ*er*for I dyd as ye desyred me, and sent my s*er*u*au*nt*es* to Pollard w*ith* his lett*er*,[12] and to Moleyns w*ith* his[13] lett*er*.

And as for Pollerd*es* answere of hys lett*er*, it nedyth you not to haue any lett*er* from hym, for Moleyns hath spoken w*ith* hym, *and* hathe wrytten you his mynde in all thyng*es*. He denyeth that he receyued any noble of your brother, and so he hath receyued of Moleyns the ij nobles in grot*es* that ye sent me in the pursse. And Molleyns hath agreyd w*ith* hym for the iij^{de} noble,

[10] *Over* and *canc.* [11] Calleis *canc.*
[12] *Final* s *canc.* [13] h *superimposed on another letter.*

and theruppon Pollerd hathe delyu*er*ed your typpett of golde, which I promyse you is right a good *and* a ryche one, and it were pitté it shulde be mysentreated. And syr, as for John Pyke this bryng, he durst not tary for the makyng of a boxe, nor take vppon hym the jup*ar*dy of the caryage w*ith*oute a boxe, whiche I wolde not haue aduysed hym to do, for it coude not ell*es* haue bene caryed w*ith*out hurte, *and* that had bene pytté. And therfore it is left w*ith* Annes Alden to kepe vnto suche tyme as ye woll send for it by suche one as may see to the suer carryage therof. And wryte me the carryars name that ye woll haue it delyu*er*ed vnto, for I know not whiche of theym ar to be trusted. And also wryte me the jentilwomans name that ye woll shall trusse it, for it is so good thyng that I dare not take vppon me to trusse it, nor to medle w*ith*all. Me thynketh M*astr*es Hyde or M*astr*es Robsard were good to do it, yf my lady woll wrytt to theym so to do.

Also as for Molens, I haue delyu*er*ed hym the xl d. and he wryt*es* you an answer of it, *and* of all o*þer* matters &c.

Writte at London this Fryday the ixth day of Noue*m*b*er*. I pray you I may be recomaunde to M*aster* Huddysfeld your vncle.

By your frende WILLIAM PASTON

944. To THOMAS CAREY — 1493, 10 September

Northampton, Northamptonshire Record Office, Fitzwilliam Roll 370/2. See no. 943. Single strip of paper, 6 × 17 in. Hand unidentified, different from those of nos. 943 and 945; subscription autograph.

Dorse: Traces of sealing wax. Address in hand of letter, damaged at edge:

To Master Cary at Chilton by Hungerford in Wiltshire. And in absens to my lady of Wilt⟨shi⟩re and to my brother Spencer knyght her⟨. . .⟩.

The year appears from the reference to 'my nevew Ponynges' and 'the matier beyonde see' (lines 29–30), which alludes to the embassy to Bruges, in July 1493, of William Warham and Sir Edward Poynings, in order to negotiate with Duke Philip the Fair concerning Perkin Warbeck; see I. Arthurson, *The Perkin Warbeck Conspiracy 1491–1499* (Stroud, 1994), pp. 67–8.

Unprinted

M*aster* Cary, I recom*m*aunde me vnto you, and pray you that this bille may recom*m*aunde me vnto my lady, my broder Spencer, and maistresse Margarete your*e* wyfe. And I pray you thanke my lady and my brother Spencer for her s*er*u*au*nt John a Devynshir*e* and her hors, and in the moost humble wyse excuse me to my lady for kepyng of theym, for my myende to kepe theym her*e* so longe hath ben to th'entent that the seid John Devensher shuld haue led furth ageyne the yonge woman that he brought hyder w*ith* hym, whiche I fele nowe can not be yet. And also I haue had suche mat*er*s, that haue letted me aboute suche besynesse, as the King hath com*m*aunded me, *and* of suche matiers as my lady will be glad to her*e* the goode spede of, that I cowde not deliuer hym to myne ease; for God know*eth*, John Devenshir hath be full wery here, *and* called full often to be deliu*er*ed, *and* full ferd is he that he shall be shent whan he cometh home. But my lady is so good lady that I am homely vpon her to kepe both her s*er*u*au*nt and her hors her*e*, how be it it is sore ayenst his wille, for I will that my lady, my broder Spencer, and ye be as homely vpon my s*er*u*au*nt or eny other thynge that I haue that may do hir ladyship, hym, or you good.

Neuirthelesse, whethir I shall haue the leysour or noo ⌜to send this yong woman ageyn w*ith* John a Devynshir I⌝[1] can not tell, but my myend is that John Devynsher*e* shall come toward you eyther on Wednysday or Thursday, or on Friday at the furthest, w*ith*out faile. And I pray you thanke my lady that she will send me her owne hors, *and* shewe her that he hath not sith the tyme he came hyder passed ij myle out of the stable, *and* kept as well[2] as John Devenshir*e* can kepe hym. And I pray you whan John Devensher*e* cometh that he be not rebuked for his long tarying, for than am I shamed for euir, for many a tyme hath he bralled w*ith* me *and* I haue p*ro*mysed hym to save hym w*ith*oute blame.

As for tyding*es*, the King, the Quene, *and* my lady the King*es* moder lye at Northampton, *and* will tary ther*e* till Mighelmas. As for the matier beyonde see, my nevew Ponyng*es* came from the Kyng yesterdaye, and be ye sure ye maye slepe in rest for eny trouble that shall be this yere or the next.

And as for your*e* standard *and* your*e* mayle, William Dame *and* John Devenshir*e* haue be ther*e* diu*er*se tymes, *and* your*e* standard is sold. Ye may haue another standard, but it is moche wers than that, *and* the mayle *and* that standard will cost you w*ith* the mayle xxiij s. iiij d. Neu*er*thelesse, now the werres be done, ye shalle haue harneyse eu*er*y daye better chepe than other. And it were well do ye sent worde whether ye will haue harneys bought w*ith* your*e* money, or ell*es*[3] that ye will that William Dame send your*e* money ageyne; *and* name the p*er*sone by whom ye will haue the money sent. And whan John Devenshir*e* cometh ye shall haue writyng of alle maner thing*es*.

And I pray you that I may here hastely from my lady, my broder Spencer, *and* you. And eny thynge that I may do for you I will be glad, that know Our*e* Lord, whom I beseche to p*re*s*er*ue you. Wryten at London the x daie of Septembr*e*.

Be your*e* frend to his power, W. Paston

I[4] haue sent tyding*es* to M*aster* Enderby, and streytly desyred hym to shew them to M*aster* Huddesfeld in your*e* name, w*ith* other as good wordes to

944. [1] *Interl. in darker ink, similar to that of postscript.* [2] *No space.* [3] *No space.* [4] *Postscript added later, in darker ink.*

your*e* p*ro*ffyte as I can deuyse, that myght cause nowe M*aster* Huddesfeld to bere the bett*er* favour*e* to you.

M*aster* Cary, ye haue so well acquytt you in my matters, that I haue forgeven the quarell that I had to you for your*e* hasty de⟨*par*⟩ting[5] when ye went hense last.

945. To Thomas Carey 1495, 5 January

Northampton, Northamptonshire Record Office, Fitzwilliam Roll 370/3. See no. 943. Two strips of paper, the first 6 × 12 in., the second 6 × $10\frac{1}{2}$ < $10\frac{3}{4}$ in. Hand unidentified, different from those of nos. 943 and 944, subscription autograph.

Dorses: Traces of sealing wax and note in an unidentified contemporary hand on second strip: 'A leter that M*aster* Paston sent Thomas Carey the vth day of January A^{o} x^{o} H. vij^{us}'.

The accuracy of the date given in the endorsement is confirmed by record of the appointment of Richard Pudsey as sheriff for Wiltshire on 5 November 1494 (cf. lines 67–9); see *A List of the Sheriffs for England and Wales from the earliest times to A. D. 1831*, PRO Lists and Indexes Series, IX (1898), p. 153.

Unprinted.

M*aster* Carey, I recom*m*aunde me hartely vnto you, and I pray you this bill may recom*m*aunde me humbly vnto my lady, to my broder Spencer, and to mastres Marget. I haue received yo*ur* letter, beryng date in Ramesbury the ij^{de} day of January, by M*aster* Thom*a*s Lambert, my lorde of Salisburys s*er*u*aunt*.

As for yo*ur* matter to my lorde of Ormond, towching the okes, my lorde was not in towne neu*er* sithen ye wrote to me first in the matter, but I vnderstond he shalbe in towne on Wednysday next, and than shall I handle your matter for your okes w*ith* hym well ynough.

As for the boke of the Just*es*, M*aster* Garter King of Arms was w*ith* me this day, and shewed me asmuch of the said boke as was clene made vp. It woll conteign whan it is fully made vp a vj or vij shet*es* of paper, and in conclusion the King hath com*m*aunded M*aster* Garter that he shall in no wise puplish it nor shew it to no man beffore his g*ra*ce haue sene it and affermed it.

I vnderstonde ye ar this Cristm*a*s w*ith* my lorde of Salisbury, and to his good lordship I besech you that I may be humbly recom*m*aunded as his s*er*u*au*nt to my pore [. . .],[1] and to shew his lordship such tiding*es* as I send you, and to shew hym also how that my lord th'Archbisshop of Yorke and M*aster* Tarnbull his old s*er*u*au*nt and lover be both in good hele, blissed be

[5] *Hole in paper.*

945. [1] *No space, but evidently a word omitted, perh.* power.

Our Lorde; and I am very glad that ye stond so well in the fauo*ur* of his good lordship.

I fele by your wryting that the King*es* grace sent my lord of Salisbury a newe yeres gift, and how my seid lorde sent the Kyng*es* grace by M*aster* Lamberde his s*eruau*nt this berer a-noder gift. I thinke my lorde was in the same case that my lorde of Wynchester *and* oder bisshops wer in, which thought that the King*es* grace mynded neither to haue geven nor taken yeres gift*es*. It was so that the King*es* grace sent my lord of Winchest*er* a new yeres gift, and my lorde of Winchester, not purveid of no yeres gift*es* redy made, sent his grace an c m*ar*kc in a purs. And also he sent a letter to M*aster* Braye to excuse hym to the King, that he was no better purveid of a gift for his grace, trusting that he wolde be better purveid for hym the next yere, w*ith* oder good wordes, that the King was aswell pleased w*ith* the wordes in the lett*er* as w*ith* the money.[2]

And where as ye desyre to know when M*aster* Mody wilbe here w*ith* me, he was not w*ith* me seen afore Cristmas, lyke as I wrote vnto you than, at whiche tyme he had money here for my lady of Wilshire. But he wold not delyu*er* it neyther to M*aster* Moleyns, nor to non oder, till he had a bill assigned both w*ith* the handes of my lady of Wilshire and of my broder Spenc*er* for his discharge. And the good man of the Rose tavern desired me that tyme to wryte to you to be his good help to my lady, that he myght haue receyvid part of that money, and he wold haue geven you a reward for yo*ur* labour, and so I wrote to you. And as I am remembred, ye wrote me an answere ageyn that ye had spoken in the matt*er*, but ye cowd not help it.

I fele by yo*ur* wryting that M*aster* Mody hath dealyd vnkyndly w*ith* you at Chilton. I m*er*veled that he hath so don, for ye haue ben his good frend alway. Neu*er*theles, me thought by you or ye dep*ar*ted that ye thought asmuche by hym yo*ur*self, as me semeth by you he hath shewed you nowe cause. Neu*er*theles, yf ye send me worde what your matt*er* is, and what vnkyndnez he hath shewed you, and I shall handle hym for you at his next comyng as wele as I can.

I haue shewed my lady Reu*er*se of youre kynd mynde toward*es* her, and she recom*ma*unde her vnto[3] my lady, to my broder Spenc*er*, to Mastres M*er*get, *and* to you all, and thanketh you. She hath be very seke, but blissed be J*es*u she is now wele amended. And where as ye wryte that ye be sory of M*aster* Enderbys seknesse, in good fayth so was I as eu*er* I was for any man that eu*er* I was acqueynted w*ith*-all; and so were both many lordes and noble men, and as many as were acqueyntid w*ith* hym. J*es*u haue m*er*cy on his sawle, he discessed on Wednysday was fourtnyght.

I vnderstonde that ye entende to ryde on Thursday next to-ward*es* the west countrey, into Dorsetshire and Deuonsh⟨ire⟩,[4] in whiche journey I think ye

[2] *End of first strip.* [3] you *canc.* [4] *Paper torn.*

shall mete w*ith* M*aster* Pudsey, for he rode thidder to comfort my mastres his awnt, M*aster* Enderbys wyf. I pray you yf it fortune you to mete w*ith* hym, recom*m*aunde me to hym, and tell hym that my lorde Daubeney and M*aster* Awmen*er* and all his good frendes here be in good hele, and wold be glad to here from hym. And also I pray you shew hym suche tyding*es* as I send you now, and tell hym that I sent hym a lett*er* this last weke past. Wheder it cam to his handes or not I can not tell. I vnderstonde that M*aster* Pudsey shalbe on Thursday nexte at Salusbury, at sessi⟨o⟩ns[5] in Whyltshire, where he is shryve.

And Our Lorde p*reser*ue you. Wretten at London the v^{te} day of January.

Be your frend WILLIAM PASTON

M*aster* Cary, I send by this beyng a letter to m⟨y⟩ l⟨or⟩d S⟨alisbury⟩.[6]

[5] *Hole in paper.*

[6] *Lower half of Paston's signature and parts of postscript (to left of subscription) lost owing to damage to paper.*

MARGARET PASTON

946. Enquiries on behalf of tenants at Flegghall, to an unidentified lawyer: draft or copy — After 1479

Norwich, Norfolk Record Office, Phillipps 536. $11\frac{3}{4} \times 5\frac{3}{4}$ in. Hand unidentified.

Dorse: Memoranda concerning the Mautby family, extracted from the document, in two hands, one of about the turn of the fifteenth century and one of the sixteenth century. Though the sheet has been folded small it shows no sign of having been a missive.

Robert Mautby (d. 1418) was Margaret Paston's grandfather, and John Mautby (d. 1433) her father. The manor of Flegghall in Winterton was to be part of her inheritance, but under a settlement of 3 October 1442 it had been granted in succession to her uncles Thomas and Edward Mautby for their lives. The date of Thomas's death is not known, but Edward died seized of the manor in 1479, at which time it reverted to Margaret. The enquiries set out in the letter perhaps date from not long after the manor came into the possession of the Pastons. See Richmond, *First Phase*, pp. 123–30.

Unprinted.

Syr, this is the mat*er* by informacion, how that Rob*er*t Mawby had issu John, Edward *and* Thomas; the qwech seyd Rob*er*t was sesyd of the man*er* of Fleghalle &c, with villains and othyr app*er*tin*ance* ther to be-longgyng, and so seasid gafe and g*ra*unt the seyd man*er* wyth the app*er*tinance to Thomas hys yonggys son for t*er*me of hys lyve &c; the remaindr*e* therof to Edward hys myddlest son for terme of hys lyve &c; the remaindr*e* to John hys oldest son and to the eyrys of hys body lawfully to be begotyn. The seyd Thomas the yong*er* son so beyng seasyd of the seyd man*er*, c*er*tein p*er*sons whech that be claymyd for to be natiue to the seyd man*er* affermyd an accion of trespas a-ȝens the seyd Thomas, lord of the seyd man*er* &c. And villinage was allegg*e* be the seyd Thomas, lord of the seyd man*er*, for t*er*me of lyve and issue take be-twyn them, that is to sey fre *and* noth villeyn, whech was fonde fre *and* non villein, as mor*e* opynly apperyth be the exemplyficacion of the mat*er* of record vndyr the justic*e* seale that ȝe haue seyn be-forn, as I am informyd. Now whedyr the seyd p*er*son[s] that suyd the seyd accion of trespas[1] be infraunchesyd, in someche as Thomas had noth in the man*er* but for t*er*me of

946. [1] *MS.* tr*a*ns

lyve, or noth, a-ȝens John and hys issu; and[2] qwethir John or hys issu may sese them a-ȝen ⌜or noth⌝ ? Mor*e* ou*er*, the seyd Edward *and* Thomas, lordis of the seyd man*er* ⌜for t*er*me of ther lyvys⌝ &c, ben deyd wyth-owte issu of ther bodyys be-gotyn, as I am in-formyd. Now that ȝe wille shew them the law ther jn, whethyr they be infraunchesyd or[3] noth, they trost sor*e* in ȝow.

[2] we *canc.* [3] north *canc.*

JOHN PASTON II

947. Agreement between WILLIAM WAINFLEET, Bishop of Winchester, and JOHN PASTON II concerning Fastolf's estate: draft 1473, 1 June

Oxford, Magdalen College, Fastolf Paper 99. Two sheets stitched together, $16\frac{3}{4} \times 11\frac{1}{2}$ in. and $13 \times 11\frac{1}{2}$ in. Clerk's hand, same as no. 948, but looser and less formal.

Dorse: 'Fastoffe' in a contemporary hand, and later notes of the content.

Dated.
Unprinted.

The last appoyntment and agrem⟨e⟩nt b⟨e⟩twix[1] W., Bisshop of Wynchestr, and S*er* John Paston, knyght.

Me*morandum*, hit is accorded the first day of Juyn the xiijth yere of the Kyng[2] Edward the iiijth betweyn my lord of Wynchestr*e* and S*er* John Paston, knyght, jn man*er* and forme folowyng.

That is to wytte that the said S*er* John and all other*e* by hym or to his vse[3] any thyng haueyng in any man*er*s, lond*es*, tenement*es* or enheritament*es* whi⟨ch⟩ we⟨re⟩[4] of S*er* John Fastolf, knyght, or of any other*e* haueyng theryn astayte atte any tyme to the vse of the said S*er* John Fastolf, except the maners of Castr*e*, with th'app*ur*ten*au*nce, in the counté ⟨of Nor⟩ffo*lk*, and all the londes and[5] tenement*es* called Vaux, Redh*a*m or Bosonis in Castr*e*, the man*er* ⟨called⟩ Spencers in Haryngby, the maners of Haylesdon, Drayton, Tolthorp and ten⟨ement*es* in⟩ the cité of Norwich, and except the manar*e* of Wyntreton called Begvilez, the man*er* of Reppes in Bastwyk, the londes and tenement*es* called[6] Catt*es* in Haryngby, the therde parte of the man*er* of Rounh*a*m, londez and tenement*es* in Yermouth, londes and tenement*es* called Billes in Stokesby with ther*e* membres and app*ur*tenaunce, ⌜and all the londes and tenement*es* in Castr*e*[7] Haryngby, Rowgh*a*m, Wynterton, Som*er*ton, Bastwik, Ornesby, Filby, Maultby, Scrowdby, Martham and Thyrkby, with th'app*ur*tenaunc*es* in the counté aforesaid⌝[8] stonde from this tyme forward feffeez to th'use and behove of

947. [1] *Sheet torn and repaired.* [2] of Kyng *repeated.* [3] h *canc.*
[4] *Hole in MS., with loss of one or two words in this and the following two lines.*
[5] te *canc.* [6] cattes *canc.* [7] he *canc.*
[8] *Copied on a separate slip attached to the main document, and marked for insertion at this point.*

the said Bisshop and of his heirs, and[9] natte to the vse or behofe of the said S*er* John Paston nor ⌜any⌝ of his heirs in any wise.

And that the said Bisshop, and all other*e* by hym or to his vse any thyng haueyng in the said man*er* of Castr*e* and all the londes and tenement*es* called Vaux, Redh*a*m or Bosonis in Castr*e*, the ma⟨n*er*⟩[10] called Spenc*er*s in Haryngby, the man*er* of Haylesdon, except the tenement*es* called Fairechild*es*, and Tolthorp, ⌜Tavernh*a*m, Horstede, Felthorp⌝ and tenement*es* in [the] cité of Norwich; tenement*es* in Over*e* Erleh*a*m and Nether*e*[11] Erlham, the man*er* of Wynt*er*ton called Begviles, the man*er* of Reppes in Bastwik, londes and tenement*es* called Catt*es* in Haryngby, the iij^{de} parte of the man*er* of Rounh*a*m, londes and tenement*es* in Yermouth, londes and tenement*es* called Billes in Stokesby and the londes and tenement*es* in Westflegge and Estflegge, and all man*er* of londes and tenement*es* in Haylesdon, Tolthorp and Norwich,[12] somtymes S*er* John Fastolf, except Fairchildes, with their*e* membres and[13] app*ur*tenaunce, stond frome thys tyme forward feffees to th'use and behofe of the said S*er* John[14] Paston and of his heirs, and notte ⌜to⌝ th'use of the said Bisshop and of his heirs in any wise.

And that all euidenc*es* concernyng sooly the man*er*s, londes and tenement*es* aforesaid which by this accorde shall remayn to the said Bisshop be oonly the propre euidence of the said Bysshop and of his heirs, and that all euidenc*es* concernyng sooly the man*er*s, londes and tenement*es* afore said which by this accorde shall remayn to the said S*er* John Paston be oonly the propre euidenc*es* of the said S*er* John Paston and of his heir*es*.

And that all euidenc*es* concernyng the man*er*s, londes and tenement*es* aforesaid which as welle shall remayn to the said Bisshop as to the said S*er* John Paston be kept indifferently to th'use of bothe parties.

Also, bifore the feste of Estir next co*m*myng, the said Bisshop shall eyther opteyn and make clere the man*er* of Castr*e* to be hadde to the said S*er* John Paston and to his heirs or to suche p*er*sones as the said S*er* John Paston will asign, withoute impediment of John, Duk of Norff*olk* or of any other*e* to his vse theryn enfeffed, or els pay to the said S*er* John Paston c marc. of lawfull money of Englond.

It*em*, hit is agreed that the said Bisshop shall relesse vnto the said S*er* John all man*er* accions, dett*es*, comptes et c*etera* and demaundes.

Me*morandum*, ⌜that hit is agreid⌝ that the[15] iiij^{m} marc. to haue be paid for the bergayn made with S*er* John Fastolf to ⌜be⌝[16] relessed especiall.

It*em*, the said S*er* John shall make a dede of rel*esse* of all man*er* of accions, dettes, compt*es* et c*etera* and demaundes as his dede to be delivred vnto the Maist*er* of the Rolles, as a[17] man indefferently, vnto[18] this vse and intent,[19] that if the said Bisshop shewe a sufficient auctorité from the Pope of

[9] g *canc.* [10] *Edge of page gone.* [11] Herlh*a*m *canc.*
[12] som tyme tymys *canc.* [13] a pp *canc.* [14] Ba *canc.* [15] Rel of *canc.*
[16] R *canc.* [17] *No space.* [18] thys *canc.* [19] and *canc.*

dispensacion to chaunge the makyng of the college atte Castr*e* fro Castr*e* aforesaid to anothere*e* place, and theryn make suer*e* imp*er*petueté vij prestes and vij pore men to syng and pray p*er*petuell for the sowll of S*er* John Fastolf, Millicent his wife, his frendes and benefacto*ur*s, and that hit so be thought by the said Maist*er* of the Rolles to delyu*er*e the said relesse vnto the said Bisshop as the dede of the seid S*er* John Paston, and ells to be delivred ayayn to the said S*er* John Paston.

948. Agreement between WILLIAM WAINFLEET, Bishop of Winchester, and JOHN PASTON II concerning Fastolf's college 1474, 29 November

Oxford, Magdalen College, Norfolk and Suffolk 33. Parchment, 15 × 11½ in. Formal clerk's hand, same as no. 947.

Dorse: Blank.

Dated.
G. 748/859 (abstract).

To all menne to whom this p*re*sent wrytyng shal com, William Wayneflete, Bysshop of Winton, sendethe gretyng. Be it knowen that where Sir John Fastolf, knyght, a litel beforn his dethe, as it was p*re*tended, barganyed and sold all his maners, londez and ten*ementes*, with th'app*ur*ten*aunces*, that he than hadde or any man to his vse in the shirez of Norff*olk*, Suff*olk* and Norwich, to John Paston, esquier, for four*e* thowsand marc., and for to make and founde a collage at Castr*e* by syde Yernemuth, in the said counté of Norff*olk*, of vij prestes and vij poer men, in certayn forme and maner as among other thyngges was conteyned in the said bargayn whych John Fastolf made; the said Bysshop, William Yelverton, knyght, the said John Paston, Thomas Howes, clerk, and William Wircestr*e* his executo*ur*s. And made his wyll, wheryn he specialy remembr*ed* the fundacion of the said college, wich willed and chareged above all thyngys that it sholde be doon as bi his said last wille more plenarly dothe appere. And died. Aftyr whos decesse, grete variancez and debate was betwene the said John Paston and the said William Yeluerton, Thomas Howes and William Worcestr*e* for and vppon the said bargayn and wylle. Which contrauersijs and debates dured all the liffe of the said John Paston, and long aftyr betwyne the said William Yeluerton, Thomas Howes and William Worcestr*e* and John Paston, knyght, son and heyre to John Paston, esquyer. In somuche that the said William Yeluerton, Thomas Howes and William Wyrcestr*e* solde grete parte of the said livelode, and suffered dyvers maners[1] and londes by feyned titles to be recouered, so that neyther the said bargayn ner wyll cowde ner myght be p*er*formed. And all

948. [1] *Superfluous* er *abbrev.*

this tyme was there noon of them that toke vpon them the administracon et c*etera* accordyng to the lawe.

We, the said Bysshop, consideryng the said grete debates and strives, and howe all his said coexecutours were dede or els hadde renunsed the administracion, and howe the said godes wer wasted and the hool lond like to growe to the same; remembryng also the grete trust that the said S*er*e John Fastolf putte jnne vs, and above all thynges wold doo that thyng that myght be to the plesure of God and to the relief of the soule of the said S*er* John Fastolf and his frendys, toke vpon vs the administracion of the said godes, accordyng to the lawe, and co*m*moned with the said John Paston, knyght, to haue a peas and rest for and vpon the p*re*myssez. And thervpon it was aggreed, accorded and couenanted bitwene vs, the said Bysshop, and the said S*er* John Paston, that the said Bisshop beyng executo*ur* of the testament of the said S*er* John Fastolf, knyght, and administrato*ur* of the same, sholde opteyn a dispensacion of our*e* holy fader the Pope, for to alter and translate the said seven prestes and seven poer men that the seid John Paston, esquier, shold haue mortesed at Castr*e*. Therefore, and in stede thereof, to morteys, stabilissh and endowe vij prestes and vij poer scolers in the College of Mary Magdaleyn at Oxenford. Which to p*er*forme the said John Paston, knyght, agreed that we shuld haue alle the maners, londez and ten*emen*t*es* comprised in the bargayn bitwene John Fastolf, knyght, and John Paston, esquier, that is to say, all the maners, londes and ten*emen*t*es* that were the seid John Fastolffes, knyght, in the counté of Norf*olk*, Suff*olk* and in the cité of Norwiche, excepte those manerez, londes and tenementes that were of the same John Fastolf in the hundredez of Estflegge *and* Westflegge, with theyr*e* apporten*aunces*, and excepte also the man*er*s of Heylesdon, Drayton et Tolthorp, with theire app*ur*tenanc*es*, and alle londez and ten*emen*t*es* in Heylesdon, savyng Fayrechild*es*, in Drayton, Tolthorp, Catton, Horsted, Felthorp, Ouer Erlesh*a*m et Nether*e* Erlesh*a*m, with all the londez and ten*emen*t*es* in Norwiche that were the seid ⌜John⌝ Fastolff*es* to vs, our*e* heyrez and executours foreu*er*more.

For the which we, the seid Bisshop, executo*ur* and administrato*ur* afore named, relesse to the seid John Paston, knyght, m^{l}m^{l}m^{l}m^{l} marc. that myght be clamed of hym by the seid bargayne. And also we relesse vnto hym all the good*es* and catall*es* that were the said John Fastolff*es*, knyght, that euer come to the hondez of the said John Paston, esquier, nowe dede, or to the hondez of John Paston, knyght, or to the handys of any other*e* to their*e* vse. And also we discharge hym of the fundacion of the said college at Castr*e*. And forthermore, we, the said Bisshop, executo*ur* and administrato*ur* afore named, willed, graunted and relessed and bi theez p*re*sentez wolle graunt and relesse to the said John Paston, knyght, to his heires and executo*urs* foreu*er*more, all the maners, londes and ten*emen*t*es* that were the said S*er* John Fastolfes in the hundredez of Estflegge and Westflegge in the counté of Norff*olk*, and also the maners of Haylesdon, ⌜excepte⌝ Fairchild*es*, Tolthorp, Catton, Horstede, Felthorp, Ouer Erleh*a*m et Ne[th]*er*[2] Erleh*a*m in the same countie, and ten*ementes* in Norwiche, and all the londes and ten*ementes* in the townes of Haylesdon, except Fayrchildys, in Drayton, Tolthorp, Catton, Horsted, Felthorp, Ou*er* Erleh*a*m and Nether Erleh*a*m and [the] cité of Norwiche.

In witnesse wherof to this our*e* p*re*sent wrytyng and declaracion we, the seid Bysshop and administrat*our* afore named, haue sette to our*e* seale and signe manuell. Yeven the xxix day of Nouembr*e* Anno R. R. E. iiij^{ti} xiiij^{o}.

[2] *MS.* neu*er*.

JOHN PASTON III

949. Attestation concerning a forced entry at Bixley Trowse
1476, 16 June

Cambridge, MA., Harvard University, Houghton Library MS Eng. 824. $14 \times 5\frac{1}{2}$ in. Unidentified clerk's hand.

Dorse: Blank.

Dated.

Printed by K.G. Madison, *Iowa State Journal of Research*, lvi (1981), 167–9.

To alle Cristen peple to whom this p*re*sent writyng shall come to see or here: John Wellys, maire of the cité of Norwich, William London, Will*ia*m Peper, Hamon Claxton, citezens and aldermen of the seid cité, and Rob*er*t Wellys of the same, mercer, due reu*er*ence and gretyng after eu*er*y estate accordyng, in our lord J*es*u euerlastyng.

For als moche as it is meritory to testifie the trouthe in eu*er*y mater, to the honour and laude of hym that is essencall trouth, it is so that the xvj of June the xvj yeer of the reigne of oure sou*er*aign lord Kyng Edward iiijth come one Will*ia*m Wesbiche of the parish of Seynt Petre of Mancroft in Norwich, yoman, seyeng these woordes in effecte.

Maister maire, I pray yow to testefie these woordes in writyng vnder youre seal of office, the whiche I shal seye by-fore you and my maisters here present; that on Cristemas evenys even, the whiche was the Saterday by-fore Cristemas day last passed, I was one of those p*er*sones that was with Nicholas Derby of Shelfangre in the shire of Norff*olk*, esquier, Herry Langcastre of the same town, gentilman, Will*ia*m Walden, late of the same town, yoman, with others dyuers riotous felaship there, whan we entred in to a place, londys and ten*emen*tis in Biskeley Trows, and other townys there abowte, in the whiche John Paston, esquyer, was seased er we come.

And for suernesse of oure p*er*sones, we were defensibly arrayed. I am weel remembred we had v long bowes, v sheef arwes, ij sperys, wherof one of them with-out an hed, j jakke, ij salettys, a trussyng doublet of defense, and another trussyng doublet of defense with-out sleves. What harneys or wepen we had elles I am nat remembred. And these wordes arn true, as I wole answer afore God at my most nede. And so I require yow to witnesse what I seye.

Whervpon I, the maire a-fore named, witnessyng the seid Will*ia*m

Wesbyche thus to haue seid, no thyng added nor mynused that myght chaunge the effecte of the rehersell of the same Will*ia*m Wesbyche, the seal of myne office of mairalté of the seid cité haue do to be appendent; and we, Will*ia*m London, Will*ia*m Peper, Hamon Claxton, and Rob*er*t Wellys a-fore named, oure seales to these p*re*sentz haue set to at Norwich the seid xvj day of June the xvj yeer aforeseid.

950. Indenture of loan between JOHN PASTON III and HENRY COLET 1485, 12 February

Stowe Charter 194. 13½ × 15 in., indented at head, red seal attached displaying animal head (probably a bear's) and collar motif. Formal clerk's hand, signed by Paston.

Dorse: 'S*er* John Paston' in a contemporary or slightly later hand.

Dated. The other part of the indenture is College of Arms MS. 326/91.
Unprinted.

This endenture made the xijth day of Feu*er*er the secunde yere of the regne of Kyng Richard the Third, betwene John Paston esquyer on that oon p*ar*tie, and Henr*é*[1] Colet, citezen[2] and alderman of London on that other p*ar*tie, witnesseth that it is couen*au*nted betwene the seid p*ar*ties, that for asmoche as the seid John hath resceyved before the hande of the seid Henr*é* v^{c} marc. of lawefull money of Engeland, for the suerté wherof and the repayment of the same the seid John is bounde to the seid Henr*é* in an obligacion of estatute of the Staple of Westm*inster*, beryng date the day of the date of these p*re*sentz in vj^{c} marc. sterling*es*, payable in the Fest of Estern next comyng after the date of these p*re*sentz. Neu*er*ethelesse the seid Henr*é* g*ra*unteth by these p*re*sentz, that yf the seid John, betwixt this and the day of the Annunciacion of Our Lady Seint Mary next comyng after the date of these p*re*sentz, by dede endented make or cause to be made, a lawefull and sufficiant estate of and in the maners of Mawdeby, Freton, Wynterton, Waxam and Horsey w*ith*ynne the shires of Norff*olk* and Suff*olk*, with alle their appurten*au*ntz, to S*er* William Knyvet, knyght, John Wymondh*a*m, esquyer, William Gurney, esquyer, Rob*er*t Clere, esquyer, ⌜Edmund Paston, esquyer⌝, Thomas Jenney, gentilman, and Rob*er*t Drury, gentilman, to haue and to holde to them and to their heires for eu*er*e. The whiche estate the seid John g*ra*unteth and delcareth by these p*re*sentz to be to the vse and entent folowyng, that is to wite, that the seid S*er* William Knyvet, John Wymondh*a*m, William Gurney, Robert Clere, ⌜Edmund Paston⌝, Thomas Jenney and Robert Drury shull stonde and reste feoffees, to the vse of the seid Henr*é* till the same Henr*é* be satisfied, paid and contented of the seid v^{c} marc. And after the seid v^{c} marc.

950 [1] *MS.* Henr *with upward curl on* r *throughout.* [2] *MS.* citezem be plenerly paid to the seid Henr*é*, the seid feoffees to stonde and reste feoffees to the vse alonly of the seid John Paston and of his heires. And the seid John shall delyu*er*e or do to be delyu*er*ed to the seid Henr*é* a deede beryng date[3] after the seid feoffament ensealled vnder his seale, conteynyng in the same a like g*ra*unte and declaracion of the seid estate to the vse and entent as is before reherced, w*ith* a due request made to the seid feoffees conteyned in the same, accordyng to the seid vse, as Thomas Jenney shall indifferently devise betwene them; and deliu*er*e also the oon p*ar*t of the seid dede of feoffament endentyd, to remayne with the seid Henr*é* till he be full satisfyed, paid and contented of the seid v^{c} marc. And that the seid feoffees shull suffre the seid Henr*é* to make a lees of the seid maners with their appurten*au*ntz, by dede endented, to the seid John Paston, to haue and to holde to hym and to his assignez the t*er*me of v yeres, w*ith*out int*er*rupcion or defetyng the seid leesse by entré or by accion; the t*er*me therof to begynne at the Septas of the Purificacion of Oure Lady last passed, to endure to the ende and t*er*me of v yeres thanne next folowyng; yeldyng and paying to the seid Henr*é* and to his assignez v^{xx} marc. of good and lawefull money of Engeland yerely at the seid Septas of the Purificacion of Oure Lady; the first payment therof to begynne at the Septas of the Purificacion of Our Lady next now comyng, and so yerely at the seid Septas v^{xx} marc. duryng the seid terme of v yeres. And yf it fortune the seid yerely v^{xx} marc. to be behynde vnpaid in part or in alle at eny of the dayes of payment therof before lymyted, that thanne the seid John Paston shall forfaite to the seid Henr*é* and to his assignez x marc. in the name of peyne, as often as it shall fortune the seid yerely v^{xx} marc. so to be behynde vnpaid; for the whiche peyne it shall be leeffull to the seid Henr*é* and to his assignez in the seid maners to distreyn, and tho distresses to lede, carie awey and kepe in the name of a distres, till he and his seid assignez of the seid yerely peyne be plen*er*ly payed and contented. And yf the seid yerely payment of v^{xx} marc. or eny part of the same be behynde vnpaid by the space of half a yere next after eny of the dayes of payment therof before lymyted, that thanne it shall be leeffull to the seid Henr*é* and to his seid assignez to entre into the seid maners with their appurten*au*ntz and put out the seid John Paston and his seid assignez, the seid leesse notw*ith*stondyng, w*ith*out int*er*rupcion of the seid John Paston and of the seid feoffees or eny of them or of their heires or assignez; and after that entré so made to be suffryd to haue, p*er*seyve and peisibly to enioye the soole issues, reuenuz and p*ro*fitees of the seid maners with their appurten*au*nz, w*ith*out int*er*rupcion or lette of the seid John or of the seid feoffees or of eny of them or of their heires or assignez, till the seid Henr*é* be fully satisfied, paid and contented of the seid v^{c} marc. The whiche leesse the seid Henr*é* g*ra*unteth by these p*re*sentz to make to the seid John in man*er*e and fourme as is before lymytted, as sone after the

[3] *Gap of about 1½ in.*

seid feoffament so made as the seid John Paston will therto require the seid Henr*é*; which couen*au*ntz on the p*ar*tie of the seid John Paston, his heires and his assignez, to be p*er*fo*ur*med as is before lymyted. Yf the seid couen*au*ntz so in man*er*e and fourme as is before exp*re*ssed on their p*ar*tie be well and truly p*er*fourmed, than the seid Henr*é* *gra*unteth by these p*re*sentz that the seid obligacion of statute of the seid Staple be hadde for voide and of noon strengthe ner force. And ou*er*e this, the seid Henr*é* *gra*unteth by these p*re*sentz that as sone as he is plenerly paid and contented of the seid v^{c} marc. to take noon au*a*untage of the seid astate so to be made of the seid maners wi*th* their appurten*au*ntz to his vse, nor of the seid leesse so to be made by dede endented as is before exp*re*ssed, but that the seid feoffees shall make suche astate as the seid John, his heires or assignez shall require them to doo. In witnesse wherof the p*ar*ties aboueseid to these endentures alternatly haue sette to their seales. Yoven the day and yere aboveseid.

JOHN PASTON
Parker

LETTERS AND PAPERS CHIEFLY OF SIR JOHN FASTOLF AND HIS CIRCLE

951. From Henry Notyngham to Sir Henry Barton

1422 or 1423, 14 April

Oxford, Magdalen College, Hickling 75. $11\frac{1}{2} \times 4\frac{1}{4}$ in. Same hand as no. 952, probably autograph.

Dorse: Marks of folding, slits for tape, remains of red wax seal. Address in hand of letter:

À mon tres*hon*uré *S*er*e Herry Barton, sitezeyne* and *aldirman de Londres.*
*P*er *Notyngham.*

Sir Henry Barton (d. 1435) purchased an annual rent payable by Hickling Priory in 1421, which was bought by Sir John Fastolf in 1428. It appears that soon after acquiring the rent, Barton fell into dispute with the Prior of Hickling, John de Hickling, who died in 1424 (see next letter, Headnote). The date of this letter must therefore be either 1422 or 1423. For Barton and Hickling see J. S. Roskell *et al.*, *The History of Parliament. The House of Commons 1386–1421* (Stroud, 1992), ii, pp. 137–8 and further references there, and for Fastolf's continuing dispute with the priory, A. R. Smith, as cited in the Headnote to no. 958.

G. 967[3]/72[3] (abstract).

Worchipfull s*er*e, I recomande me to ȝou, certifynge ȝiff ȝou plese þ*a*t[1] I delyuerd Paston the copye off ȝour dedys, as ȝe were assentyde to comune w*ith* the P*r*iour *and* couent þ*er*off. And afftir þat I bare hem ȝour l*ett*re, *and* reported the credence in the moste godelye wyse I colde to haue sped off ȝour entent. Bot jt wolde ⌜not⌝ be g*ra*untyde for no thynge I colde do. Ande þen desired I to whyt what cause they lafflte fore, *and* they sayden they wolde plese ȝou full fayne, *and* do alle þ*a*t they myght for ȝou, *and* hauen atto*ur*ned to ȝou *and* paide ȝou truly, *and* so well forthe. Bot to sele or bynde hem be ony suche comfermac*i*on, they ansuerde þ*a*t alle theyr councell is full ther-aȝens, *and* þ*er*fore they durre not ensele. Ande þ*er*fore, s*er*e, I paide not the man as ȝe wolde no money.

951. [1] þ *in form of* y, *and so throughout.*

Ande, s*er*e, I gropyde *and* conceyued more off þe[2] P*r*iour *and* off þe elde men off þe hous, be myne examynac*io*n þ*a*t they were full sore bounden be theire couent seall to hym þat haght þat gode afore ȝou, *and* to hys heirs, bot not to hys assignez. *And* þ*er*off, s*er*e, me semez ȝe nede to take gode auyse *and* councell for ȝour owne ese *and* p*ro*fuyte, for truly, þ*er* is litill trist in þat meyné. Ande bot ȝe gete Pastons assent *and* g*ra*unte to helpe thys mat*er*e, I can not se it wille be done, bot ȝiff they be compelled be lawe, as wolde God they myght. Ande þis[3] nede ȝe to co*min*e w*it*h the beste lerned men ȝe con gete. Ande also, s*er*e, I wolde councell ȝou þ*a*t ȝe myght gete Paston to ȝou in p*re*sens off hym þat made ȝour dedez; *and* off som other wele lerned man to whit off hym what defulcultye he fyndez ther jne, *and* ȝiff oght wolde he haue amendyde ther jne, so it were not aȝens ȝou, be wyche ȝe *and* ȝour frendez chull be lerned ȝiff ony p*ri*ué sore to ȝour harmynge or hynderynge be ther jne.

Right dere s*er*e, no more I write ȝou at þis tyme, bot send ȝou ȝour box w*it*h ȝour dedys as ȝe toke hem me. *And* truly *and* o'gode faythe, I haue besyde me for ȝou to haue ȝour entent fullffylde with alle my spritez, *and* eu*er* chall be redy in þat *and* ony thynge ellez þ*a*t lithe in my pouer, be the leue off alle myghty God, wiche haue ȝou eu*er* in hys blisfull kepynge, withe helthe off body *and* saule, as ȝe desyre beste.

Writene at Norwicȝ comynge fro Hiklynge, þe xiiij^{e} day of App*ri*ll.

Ȝour owne man, H. NOTYNGHAM

952. From HENRY NOTYNGHAM to SIR HENRY BARTON 1424 or 1425, 5 May

Oxford, Magdalen College, Hickling 74. $11\frac{3}{4} \times 3\frac{1}{4}$ in. Same hand as no. 951, probably autograph.

Dorse: Marks of folding, slits for tape, trace of red wax. Address in hand of letter:

To my worchypfull Sere *Henry Barton, aldirman off London.*
Per *Notyngham.*

See the Headnote to the previous letter. John de Hickling, the Prior of Hickling here spoken of as 'obstenant', died in 1424 (*VCH Norfolk*, ii (London, 1906), p. 385), and this letter appears to have been written not long afterwards.

G. 967[2]/72[2] (abstract).

Ryght worchipfull s*er*e *and* entier trusty mestre, I recomande me to ȝou, certifynge ȝiff ȝou plese, þat[1] I haue counceld *and* co*min*ed w*it*h Paston off

[2] e *superscript, and so throughout in this word.* [3] i *superscript, and so throughout in this word.*

952. [1] þ *in the form of* y, *and so throughout.*

ȝour mat*ere*, *and* fynde hym more frendlye *and* helplye to p*er*fo*ur*ne ȝour entent *and* my desire þen eu*er* I fonde hym afore. *And* the cause why is, as I suppose, þ*a*t the P*ri*our off Hyklynge þ*a*t wase obstenant in þe[2] mat*ere* is ded, *and* ⌜a⌝ nother made, wiche Paston trustez chall be more esye to styrre þen þe tother wase. *And* he *and* I ben acordite þ*a*t at hys next comynge hom, I hope in Wyssone halydaiez, whe chull be there to-gedir to p*er*fo*ur*ne ȝour entent, Crist forthe it as I wolde. *And* sothely, s*er*e, I chall truly do my deueyr þ*er*to, þ*a*t ȝe chull holde ȝou plesyde. Ande, s*er*e, p*ra*ey ȝou thankez Paston of þe gode comforte he ȝaffe me, *and* hertly besechez hym of gode contenuance.

Dere s*er*e, no more I write ȝou at þis[3] tyme, bot entierly p*ra*ey ȝou let a[4] child off ȝours bere þis other l*ett*re onon to my mestre Jankyn Leuenthorpe þe ȝonger, *and* spyrre redily at my lordez Ine off Dor*e*ham, or off Ratclyff, or some other whom ȝe thynge beste, ȝiff he chall be at þis P*ar*lement; *and* þ*a*t I myght haue a[5] bylle fro ȝou þ*er*off sende to Thomelyn Grys, spicer, off Norwicȝ, to sende ⌜me⌝ als sone as eu*er* ȝe may godely, by some loder þ*a*t comen iche woke to Rossamez Ine at Sent Laurens Lane. Ande, s*er*e, I chall do als myche for ȝou, be the leue off God, wiche haue ȝou eu*er* in hys blisfull kepynge, w*ith* helthe of body *and* saule as ȝe desyre best.

Writen at Lenn in haste, þis Friday laste in þe seconde woke afftir Esterne.

By ȝour owene man, HENRÉ NOTYNGH*A*M

953. From SIR JOHN FASTOLF to JOHN FASTOLF of Oulton and JOHN KIRTELING Probably 1429, 31 October

Add. 28212, f. 21. $11\frac{1}{2} \times 16$ in. Two unidentified hands, the second less professional in appearance than the first; subscription autograph.

Dorse: Marks of folding; the seal noted by G. P. Scrope is gone, but remains of red sealing wax are visible. Address in second hand of letter:

To my ryght trvsty and welbelouede cosin and *frende John Fastolf and* Ser *John Kirtelinge* p*arson of Arkesay*.

Near the head of the sheet another early hand has added: 'Appu*n*ctuament*um* fact*um* p*ro* Steph*an*o Scrope A° xxviij° R. H. vj: ad maritand*um*.'

The date given in the later endorsement (1449) does not reflect the circumstances of the letter, which is concerned mainly with Stephen Scrope's plans to marry Katherine Cobham, the widow of Sir Reginald Cobham the younger, of Hoo, who had died in September 1428 (*Cal. Fine Rolls, 1422–1430*, p. 235). Scrope himself, specified in the letter as its intended carrier, was serving in France in 1428 (G. P. Scrope, *Castle Combe*, p. 266). The arrangements envisaged in the letter were apparently not pursued much further, and Scrope went on to marry Margaret Dorward in 1433 (*Cal. Pat. Rolls, 1429–*

[2] e *superscript, and so in this word throughout.*
[3] i *superscript, and so in this word throughout.*
[4] *No space.*
[5] *No space.*

1436, p. 283). John Kirteling was Fastolf's receiver-general in England at this date, and John Fastolf of Oulton was another member of his council.

Printed by G. P. Scrope, *Castle Combe*, pp. 274–5, and G. 72/97.

Trusty and welbeloved frendz, y grete yow wel. And for as moche as y haue appointed wiþ my sone Steph*en* Scrop*e*, lyke as y sende yow þe appointement writen hereafter in þis lett*er*, þe whiche appointement y woll ye fulfylle be þe avys of my cou*n*sel jn þat at longeth to my party, like as hit ys writen.

Thys ys þe appointement made be-twene S*er* John Fastolf, knight, and Steph*en* Scrop*e*, squier, in þe man*er* as here-after hit ys writen.

Fyrst, for as moche as þe mariage of þe saide Steph*en* Scrop*e* was solde to S*er* William Gascoyng, þe Chefe Justice of Englonde, for v^{c} marke, with þe whiche mariage was deliu*er*d in hande to þe sayde Gascoyng þe man*er* of Wyghton on þe Wolde, in Yorke schyre, with þe ap*er*tenau*n*ce of þe saide man*er*; and whan þe sayde Gascoyng hade hym, he wolde have solde hym agayn, or maried[1] þe saide Steph*en* Scrop*e* þ*er* he schulde haue byn desparieged. Wherfore, at þe request of þe sayde Scrop*e* and hys frendes, þe saide Fastolf boght þe mariage of þe saide Scrop*e* of þe saide S*er* William Gascoyng for v^{c} marke, wherby þe saide Fastolf haþ mariage of þe saide Steph*en* Scrop*e*, or elles to haue þe saide somme of v^{c} marke þat he payde for hym, like as hit ys above sayde.

It*em*, for as moche as þe sayde Steph*en* Scrop*e* ys comyn to þe saide Fastolf, sayinge þat he hath fownde wey to be maried at his lyst, and also for his worschippe and profyt, so þat þe saide Fastolf woll consent þ*er*to, þat ys to say, to Faucon*er*is dogh*ter* of London, þat S*er* Reynalde Cobh*am* had weddid.

It*em*, for as hit ys þe saide Fastolf ys wille to forþ*er* and helpe þe saide Scrop*e* in any wize þ*er* he may be fortherede, þe sayde Fastolf consenteth þat þe sayde Scrop*e* marie hym to þe [sayde] Faucon*er*is doghter, with þat, þ*a*t þe sayde Faucon*er* gyf to þe sayde Fastolf þe saide so*m*me of v^{c} marke, þe whiche he payde for þe saide Scrop*e*.

Item, yf þat þe sayde Steph*en* Scrop*e* pay or do pay þe so*m*me afore-sayde of v^{c} marke sterling, þan þe sayde S*er* John Fastolf and Dame Mylicent his wyf schall make astate of þe sayde man*er* of Wyghton on þe Wolde in Yorke schyre, w*ith* þe ap*er*tenau*n*ce of þe sayde man*er*, to þe saide Steph*en* Scrop*e*, and to þe woman þe whiche schalbe his wyf, and to here eyres of here bodyes begete be-twix hem two.

It*em*, yef þe sayde Steph*en* dye w*ith*oute eyre of his body begeten, þan þe sayde man*er* of Wyghton, after þe descece of þe sayde ___ hys wyfe, schall retourne agayne to þe sayde Fastolf and Dame Mylicent his wyf, and to þe eyres of þe sayde Mylicent.

953. *The condition of the paper has deteriorated since the time of G. P. Scrope and Gairdner, and readings attributable to them are shown in angle brackets.*

[1] hym *canc.*

Item, yf so be þat þe sayde Faucon*er* wilnot pay þe sayde so*m*me of v^{c} marke, bot p*er*auenture wolde gyf ⌜a⌝ lesse so*m*me, þen þe sayde Fastolf wyl deliu*er* to þe mariage of þe saide Scrop*e* c*er*tayn londe, havynge rewarde to þe so*m*me þat þe sayde Faucon*er* wil gyf,[2] hauyng rewarde to þe afferrant of xl pounde worth land *and* v^{c} mark of golde.

Item, if þat þe saide Fauconer wilnot gyf no so*m*me of golde for þe sayde mariage, þe sayde Fastolf wyl take þe mariage of þe childe þat ys eyr*e* to þe forsaide S*er* Reynolde Cobh*a*m; and þat þe sayde Scrop*e* forto conferme þe astat hys moder has made to þe saide Fastolf, yf so be þat þe cou*n*sel of þe saide Fastolf se by þaire avys þat hit be for to do,[3] and þ*a*t þe said mariage may be ⟨as⟩ moche worth to þe said⟨e⟩ Fastolf as v^{c} mark.

Item, ȝe sende me be Raufm⟨an an⟩ answare of þe lett*er*s þat y sende yow, þat I may haue verray knolage how þat hit standys w*ith* me þ*er* in al man*er* of thyng*es*, and þat I haue an answare of eu*er*y article þat y wrote to yow.[4]

It*em*, for as ⟨moche⟩ as þat I am bonden for my lord Scales to my lord Cardnale in v^{c} mark, þe qu⟨ich⟩ so*m*me he kan not fynd no way to pay hit, onlese þen þ*a*t he sel a p*ar*cel of his land, querfore he sendis ower a[5] man of his called Pessemerche, with[6] whom I wil þ*a*t ȝe spek, and se be ȝore avis whech of þe places of my said lord Scales þ*a*t standis most cler to be solde. *And* if þe pl⟨ac⟩e þ*a*t is beside W⟨al⟩syngham stand cler, I haue hit leuer þen þe toþ*er*. And þ*er*fore I pray ⟨ȝo⟩w þat ȝe make apointeme*n*t w⟨it⟩h þe said Pesemerche in þe best wise þat ȝe may, athir of þe ton place or þe toþ*er*; and or ȝe let take hit aft*er* xx ȝere, hauyn⟨ge⟩ rewarde to þe verray val⟨ue⟩ þ*er*of; and as[7] ȝe don, send me worde be þe nexst messager.

It*em*, my lord of Hungerford has writen to me for to haue þe warde of Rob*er*t Monpyns⟨on⟩ is sone, wher-of I am agreed þ*a*t he schal hit, like as I has wretyn to hym in a lett*er*, of þe whe⟨ch⟩ I send ȝow a copé closed here-jn. Wher-fore I pray ȝow to enquere of þe verray valu of þe land þ*a*t Monpynson haldis of me, and sendis me worde jn hast, for my said lord Hungerford sais jn his lett*er* þ*a*t hit is worth bot xl s. a[8] ȝere aboufe þe rentis, as ȝe may se [in] þe lett*er* þ*a*t he sent me, þe qu⟨ich⟩ I send ȝow be my son Scrop*e*. And I pray ȝow to demene ȝow to my said lord as eesely as ⌜ȝe⌝ may in þis mat*er*, *and* al oþ*er* þ*a*t I haue to do with hym, as ȝe may se be þe copé aforesaid. And [Our Lord][9] haue ȝow in his kepyng.

Wretyn at R⟨oa⟩n, þe last day of October.

J. FASTOLFE

[2] *The remaining words of this paragraph added by the second hand, which usually writes* þ *in the form* y.

[3] *Remaining words of this paragraph added by the second hand.*

[4] *Remainder of letter in the second hand.*

[5] *No space.*

[6] quo *canc.*

[7] do *canc.*

[8] *No space.*

[9] *Edge of sheet gone,* o *visible; G. P. Scrope* God, *Gairdner* or.

954. From SIR JOHN FASTOLF to STEPHEN SCROPE
Probably 1429–33, 5 July

Add. 28212, f. 23. $11\frac{1}{2} \times 15\frac{3}{4}$ in. Unidentified formal clerk's hand, including subscription.

Dorse: Marks of folding, and wafer seal showing Fastolf's crested helmet motif. Address in hand of letter:

*To my right welbeloued son Sthephen Scrop*e *at the Bere in Fryday Strete at Lond*on.

Like no. 953 (probably of 1429, see the Headnote), this letter also mentions the matter of a marriage for Scrope, who married in 1433. He was in France in 1428, and a letter addressed to him in London and recommending that he marry seems likely to belong between those two dates.

Printed by G. P. Scrope, *Castle Combe*, pp. 270–1.

Right entierly welbeloued son, I comau*n*de me vnto yow, and late you wete that I haue resceyved youre l*ett*re, and vnderstand ⟨. . .⟩ the mater conteined in it. And as touchyng that the cause of youre goyng in-to Englond was because that my lord of Gloucestre was not ⟨in charge . . . with⟩ yow, ⟨and that⟩ ye wol abyde on hys gode lordeshyp if ye couth do hym such s*er*uice whereby ye might des*er*ue hys good lordeship ⟨. . .⟩ to youre forthyryng, it were to me grete gladnesse. And as touchyng that ye desire of me su*m* lyvelode to abyde on hys lordship ⟨servyce, mesemeth that⟩ if he haue gret desire of youre s*er*uice he wol do to yow that ye shul not nede nothyng of me to susteyne yow in hys s*er*uice. And therefore, seurly I am not aduised as yet to assigne yow eny lyvelode as for that cause. But if it so be that I saw you maried to youre p*ro*fyt, and to the plesance of youre moder and me, then I wol do to you as me oght to do, and as ye shul hold you content, as be reson as I haue seid vn-to yow herebefore.

And as touchyng that y⟨ow⟩ couth not do youre-self but litul p*ro*fit syn Mighelmas was xij moneth that ye haue be here, and that ye suppose to do youre-self there grete p*ro*fyt or oght long, I hold me content that ye assay there as ye haue here. And if ye like not youre ⟨. . .⟩[1] tarré aft*er* that ye haue assaid it, cometh agayne vn-to me, and I wol do vn-to yow as me oght to do be keynd, as wel or bett*er* than eu*er* ⟨I do⟩, so that ye shal fynd me alwey good fad⟨er⟩ vn-to you, as vn-to my feble powere. And as vn-to that ye desire to haue an answere and wetyng of my aduise of thys mat*er* w*ith*yn a xiij dayes, treuly I can not se be my feble wytte in whate wise it might be more p*ro*fitable for you there than it was here, al thyng ⟨considered. Where⟩fore, my son, w*ith*out that ye wist of more p*ro*fyt or of othir thyngs than I know of or may

954. *The upper right-hand area of the sheet is stained and damaged, with some loss of text. Some readings given by G. P. Scrope are no longer visible; these are shown within angle brackets.*

[1] *G.P. Scrope's reading and conjecture seem doubtful:* moch [not to].

p*er*ceyve be youre wrytyng, ye wold not haue partyd hens so sodenly; and therefore I rep*or*te[2] me to youre good discrec*io*n, for it is to me a derk mat*er*.

Also, as touchyng that ye wol do me such s*er*uice as me list to comau*n*de you, youre worship sauued, I thonke you hertly of youre good entent. But I m*er*vaille gretly of tho wordys, for I can not remembre me in no wise that eu*er* I charged yow ne none othir ma*n* w*ith* eny thyng that eu*er* shuld to*ur*ne yow to disworship. And thogh I take aworth whate-eu*er* ye wryte vn-to me, for I must tendre both youre p*er*son and worship, I wold not ye wrote so to none othir ma*n*, for tho wordys be vnfyttyng, but if they be betwene[3] contrarie p*ar*ties, as betwene an Englishma*n* and an Arminake. Nerethelatt*er*, I p*ra*y yow send ⌜me⌝ a more redy declarac*io*n hereaft*er* of tho wordys, and of youre othir mat*er*s, if ye wol that I be in eny wise of youre consaill. For whate-eu*er* that ye mene, or be whos cou*n*saill that ye werk, I wold ye did right well, that wote Godde, that eu*er* haue yow in hys blessyd gou*er*n*au*nce.

Wreten at Cales the v day of Juyll.

Youre fad*er*, JOH*N* FASTOLF

955. From SIR JOHN FASTOLF to HENRY INGLOSE and JOHN BERNEY — Perhaps between 1436 and 1440

Pembroke College, Cambridge, LC.II.230, f. 3. 10 × 4½ in. William Worcester's hand.

Dorse: Remnants of red wax. Address in Worcester's hand:

To my ryght wel belovyd cosyns Herry Inglose and *John Berney, escuiers.*

The early dating of this letter proposed by Richmond, *First Phase*, pp. 207–8, n. 14, would place it after Fastolf had been knighted, which was prior to January 1416, and before Inglose was, by November 1419. It has since been observed, however, that the letter is undoubtedly in the hand of William Worcester, including the stylised subscription, which he sometimes appended in identical manner to other letters that Fastolf himself did not sign; see for example no. 1011 (23 September 1451) and no. 1015 (12 July 1454). That Worcester styled Inglose, as well as Berney, 'escuier' in the address on the dorse must have been an oversight on his part. It is possible that Worcester was in Fastolf's service by 1436, the other *terminus* for the letter being Inglose's death in 1451 (see K. B. McFarlane, *England in the Fifteenth Century*, p. 202, n. 18, and p. 183, n. 31). The 'Mautbye sqwyer' who is mentioned was John Mautby (whose daughter Margaret went on to marry John Paston I), and the implication appears to be that he is deceased at the time of writing, given that Inglose and Berney are being requested to vouch for his ransom by Fastolf. He died in 1433, and in 1434 his daughter's wardship was granted to Sir John Radcliff, Fastolf's brother-in-law. Richmond, *First Phase*, pp. 123–4, suggests that in the aftermath of Mautby's death, Fastolf may have had a hand in arranging that Margaret Mautby should be married to the son of his own legal advisor William Paston, as she eventually was

[2] *The* -er- *abbreviation is clear, but 'report' in the sense 'submit' is evidently intended.*

[3] as *not canc.*

in 1440. Since no other likely context for this letter at present suggests itself, it is therefore tentatively placed at around this time. Whether Fastolf spent time in London during the later 1430s is not clear, but it is certain that he ended his long-term residence in France and returned to England for good at around Michaelmas 1439 (McFarlane, *op. cit.*, p. 178, n. 9).

G. VII/39

Ryght welbelovyd cosyns, I comaund me to yow. And please you to hafe in knoulege that at whych tyme ye were delyu*er*ed out of pryson by the moyen of ij prysonners that y delyu*er*ed yow, whych as ye know well ⌜one⌝ was Burd Vynollys *and* the othyr John[1] de Seint John, dit Dolot. And in lyke wyse I bought anothyr prysonner clepyt John Villers for the delyu*er*aunce of Mautbye sqwyer, whych mater ye knowyth well. And forasmoch as my wrytyng*ys* that makyth menc*i*on of that delyu*er*aunce of the seid Mautbye be not in my warde, y pray you that ye wolle vndre your seelys certyffye me the trouth, how the said Mautbye was delyu*er*ed by my moyen. Y hafe founde a cedule that makyth menc*i*on of that prysonner, of whych y sende you a double, to be bett*er* au*er*tysed of the mater. And therfor as my trust ys yn yow, that ye sende me your gode remembr*a*unce in as goodly haste as ye may. And Our Lord kepe you.

Wryt at London the v day of Noue*m*ber.

JOHN FASTOLF, ch*evalie*r

956. From SIR JOHN FASTOLF probably to SIR WILLIAM AP THOMAS: draft. 1444, probably May or June

Oxford, Magdalen College, Fastolf Paper 40. $10\frac{1}{2} \times 4$ in. William Worcester's hand.

Dorse: Note of receipts from Fastolf's manor of Titchwell, collected by his receiver Nicholas Bokkyng, dated 7 September 22 Henry VI (1444).

It is sufficiently clear from the tone and substance of this draft that it was drawn up by Worcester on behalf of Fastolf (whom he invariably refers to as 'my master', not 'my lord'), rather than on his own account. The unnamed 'my lord' of the letter is Richard, Duke of York, and the two matters mentioned are known to have been of concern to him during the early months of 1444, whilst he was in Normandy. It appears that at this time he wrote instructing Fastolf, one of his leading councillors, to consult with other members of his council, one of whom is referred to here as 'Sir Andreu', undoubtedly Sir Andrew Ogard. The intended recipient of the letter would have to be another member of York's council, and external evidence suggests that this was probably Sir William Ap Thomas. The sensitive matter referred to in the second paragraph was evidently the duke's possible claim to the throne of Castile, based on John of Gaunt's part in the treaty of Bayonne (1388). The

955. [1] Dolot *canc.*

956. *The MS. is damaged along left hand edge, and there are two irregular holes in centre causing further loss of text.*

accounts of York's receiver-general, John Wygemore, for 1444 include '£10 paid for a copy of the articles between John, king of Castile and duke of Lancaster, and John son of Henry late count of Trastamara his adversary, by order of Sir John Fastolf, Sir Andrew Ogard and Sir William Ap Thomas' (BL Egerton Roll 8782, quoted in translation by A. Goodman and D. Morgan, 'The Yorkist claim to the throne of Castile', *Journal of Medieval History* xi (1985), 61–69 (at p. 64)); 40s. was paid to the scribe who copied the document, and a further 14s. for a breakfast at the Mermaid, 'super communicacione istius materie'.

Cardinal Beaufort was understood to be considering how to dispose of Canford after March 1443 (G. L. Harriss, *Cardinal Beaufort* (Oxford, 1988), p. 373), and in 1444 the Duke of York made enquiries about buying it (P. A. Johnson, *Duke Richard of York* (Oxford, 1988), p. 12, citing BL Egerton Roll 8782). If the Cardinal was thinking of giving the manor to Edward Beaufort whilst he was still Earl of Dorset, he would have had to do so before 27 May 1444, the date at which he succeeded to the dukedom of Somerset upon the death of John Beaufort. The 'Waller*e*' whom the recipient of the letter is encouraged to consult was Richard Waller (*D.N.B.*), a long-term associate of Fastolf's (see no. 1017), and master of Cardinal Beaufort's household by 1443–4 (Harriss, pp. 360–1). It appears therefore likely that the draft dates from about May or June 1444.

Unprinted.

⟨We⟩lbelovyd brothyr*e*, I co*m*maund me to you, latyng you wete that[1] on Sonday that last was[2] ther*e* was delyu*er*yd me at Brentwod, on ⟨the⟩ wey to Castreward, ij l*ett*res, whereof I sende you the double,[3] wher*e*-ynne ye mow weel se *and* vndrestand that my lord ⌜ys enfourmyd⌝[4] ⟨that⟩[5] my lord Cardinal of England ys avysyd to syll the maner*e* *and* the lordshyp of Canneford in Dorsetshyr*e*. Wherof my lord wrytith vn-to you ⌜as ye may see by the tenur*e* of my l*ett*re⌝[6] for to[7] purchasse it, yeff the matier be such. And whethyr*e* my lorde C*a*rdynall wyll ⌜syll⌝[8] the ⟨seyd⟩[9] place or no I can not veele, for a was jsett to yeff it to the Erle of Dorset. But for to be acerteynyd of thys matyer*e*,[10] or for to ease h⟨. . .⟩e,[11] I pray you comynyth wyth my brothyr*e* Waller*e*, reco*m*maundyng me vn-to hym, *and* saith I prayd hym on my behalf to say you therevp⟨pon as h⟩e[12] knoueth, for I wote weel he can best sey you of ony man that I know.[13]

Also, I sende you[14] the double ⌜of⌝ the othyr l*ett*re whych[15] my lord send me at thys tyme, whych l*ett*re I wold send to no man in England, but it were

[1] the *canc.* [2] I *canc.* [3] wretyn at *canc.*

[4] *Over* vndrestand, *but evidently to be substituted for* supposith *canc. after* lord.

[5] he *canc.*

[6] to au*er*tise *and* yeff me jn knoulege of my lorde ys wyll whych I suppose it be *canc.*

[7] by *canc.* [8] *Over* by *canc.*

[9] *Hole in paper; part of* s *visible.* [10] fo *canc.*

[11] *Hole in paper; space for five or six letters.* [12] *Hole in paper.*

[13] *The following is evidently a rejected alternative draft of what precedes, prefixed by a capitulum mark, and subsequently stroked out:* But I suppose he ys misenformyd, for as I have (end *canc.*) herd seid, he hath ordeyn it for one of ⌜my lordys⌝ hys nefewys. Neu*er*thelese, I pray you enqueryth thys matier*e* on my behalf of my ryght (well *canc.*) trusty brothyr Waller*e*, reco*m*maundy*n*g me vn-to hym, *and* that I prayd hy*m* hertly to say you in secre wys hou thys matier standith. (And þ*ere* *canc.*) *And* vppon such knoulage as we have, ye *and* I shall wyrke þ*er*evppon, *and* aftyr*e* c⟨. . .⟩s spedefull, *and* the case requyrith, we sholl send my lord worde.

[14] worde *canc.* [15] I *canc.*

my bro*þere* S*er* Andreu or to you, p*r*a*y*ng you to sheu it to my bro*þere* S*er* Andreu; *and* that it lyke hym to be avysyd *þer*evppon, *and* kepe it close tyll we mow speke to-gedyr*e*, for the matier ys str*a*unge, *and* peisith moch, but it be weel demenyd. For as me thynkyth by my symple wyt, it ys no matier for no simple wyttyd men ne folys to dele wyth. And moreou*er*e it lykyd my bro*þere* S*er* Andreu to enserche the cronicles *and* pedegreys conveyng the fourme *and* ordre of such descent*ys* as longith to that matier, whych I suppose he hath bok*ys* redy, *and* I shall seke vpp-on my partie.

957. From Sir John Fastolf to John Lynford
Perhaps about 1445–6

Oxford, Bodleian Library, MS. Eng. lett. C. 291, f. 95. 10 × 5 in. Hand unidentified.

Dorse: Marks of folding, slits for tape, remains of red wax seal. Address in hand of letter:

Vnto my right trusty and weelbe-loued frende John Lynford, my styward of my courtes.

Fastolf bought the manor of Mundham in Sisland in about 1430, and sold it in 1450. His councillor John Lynford, esquire, of Stalham (d. 1457), had been a feoffee of its previous owner (see Smith, 'Aspects of the Career of Sir John Fastolf', p. 7, and p. 27 n. 98; also no. 1005). At what time between these two dates Fastolf wrote to Lynford cannot be precisely determined at present. The letter may date from about the time that long-standing arrears owed by Laurence Clerk in relation to Mundham were mentioned in Oxford, Magdalen College, Norfolk and Suffolk 1, of 1445–6 (with Thomas Westgate as bailiff there). Fastolf Papers 9, 12 and 14 at Magdalen refer to John Westgate as bailiff of Mundham in 1433–6 (*ex inf.* Dr Anthony Smith).

Unprinted.

Right trusty and weelbeloued frende, I com*m*aunde me to yow. And for as Laurence holdyth of me a place in Sislond with c*er*tayn lande *þer*to longyng, as Walt*er* Pye *and* Joh*n* Clerk helde it; whiche place *and* lande by men of my cou*n*seill was graunted to þe said Laurence and to his heires, fyndyng me sufficient suyrté forto paye to me at t*er*mes and dayes of þe manoir vsed xxx s. of rent; and ovirmore, to repaire þe place competently at þe cost*es* of þe said Laurence, and for defaute of payem*en*t *and* repayryng me to entre agayn. S*er*, I pray you to se þe place, for as I am enformed it is not repayred as couuen*au*nt was. Wherfor I praye þat ye wole g*ra*unte þe said place *and* land be þe court rolle[1] be lete vnto[2] one John Westgate, Thom*as* *and* John his sones, *and* to her heires, paying to me yeerly xxxj s.; and to repair*e* þe same place sufficiently at her owne costys be a pety fyne. And also þ*a*t ye wole sese

957. [1] *Partly superimposed on other letters.* [2] on to *canc. and subpuncted.*

alle corne *and* catell ⌜þat⌝ þe saide Laurence hath jn þat place, for wast done ayens his couen*au*nt, vnto þe tyme þat ye here othere fro me.

Trist be your*e* speed. Wrytyn at Castre þe v day of March.

JOHN FASTOLF

958. From WILLIAM WANGFORD and WILLIAM JENNEY to SIR JOHN FASTOLF 1445 or 1446, 6 February

Oxford, Magdalen College, Hickling 71. $11\frac{1}{4} \times 6\frac{3}{8}$ in. Hand unidentified.

Dorse: Marks of folding, slits for tape, trace of seal. Address in hand of letter:

*To our right worshipful maist*er *S*ere *John Fastolf.*

Fastolf's prolonged litigation with Hickling Priory over a claim for rent arrears was precipitated by his entry of their manor at Palling, and the distraint of three horses valued at twelve marks, on 30 October 1444. The priory countered his claim, and Fastolf was obliged to investigate the legal grounds for his right to the rent. This counsel's opinion must date from soon after the entry and distraint. See Smith, 'Fastolf's Dispute with Hickling Priory', pp. 58–9.

G. 967[1]/72[1] (abstract).

Honorable and right w*ur*shipful mayster, we recomaunde vs to ȝou. And like ȝou to wete that we have seyn and ⌜throghly⌝[1] comou*n*d ȝoure mater betwyx ȝou and the Priour of Hikelyng. And, s*er*e, like ȝou to wete that as touchyng the xx li. which shuld be forfet for defaute of payment of the xxv m*a*rc., we kan no*gh*t see that the xx li. kan be made sekyr to ȝou, be cause that the condicyon of the same xx li. strecchyth ⌜but to the⌝[2] heirs of S*er* Hugh Clyfford, and no*gh*t[3] to the assignez; which condicyon was neu*er* broke aȝens the seid heirs,[4] and so there may be no thyng of the forseid annuyté of xx li. growe to ȝou, that bee but assigne &c. And thus the seid xx li. kan no*gh*t be devysed to be made sekyr to ȝou.

Also, s*er*e, like ȝou to wete that as for the xxv marc., it is sekyr to ȝow be ȝoure evydencez and in no wyse ⌜may⌝ be avoyded, as fer as we kan conceyve in the mater, and ȝe may aske the seid annuyté of xxv m*a*rc. and the arr*é* theroffe. And if the Priour of Hikelynge denye ⌜to paye it⌝,[5] ȝe may recou*er*e the annuyté of xxv m*a*rc., w*ith* the arr*é* theroffe, and ȝoure damagez *and* costez, by assise or be a writ of entr*é* in the nat*ur*e of assise in the Co*m*en Place.

And whedir ȝe may distreyne for the annuyté of the xxv m*a*rc. and the arr*é* theroffe ⌜or no*gh*t⌝, we kan no*gh*t knowe the certeynté theroffe, no*gh*t ȝit, be

958. [1] *Over* thrghly *canc.* [2] *Over* to *canc.*
[3] *Previous two words repeated and canc.*
[4] ne *and another partially formed letter canc.* [5] *Over* it *canc.*

cause that there is no distresse gr*a*unted to ȝou be the fyn. But we shal comown w*ith* justicez and s*er*uantes theroffe, and w*ith* Godd*es* gr*a*ce ȝe shal knowe the certeynté hastely. But ȝe may have gode recou*er*er be the lawe as ofte as ⌜the payment of⌝ the seid annuyté of xxv m*a*rc. is denyed ȝou. But as for the xx li., it kan no*gh*t be made sekyr to ȝow because above rehersed.

We wryte no more to ȝou at this tyme, but the blissed Trynyté have ȝou in his blissed kepyng,[6] and sende ȝou gode lyff and longe, to his ples*a*unce.

Wreten at West*minster*, the vj day of Feverer.

Ȝoure s*er*u*au*ntz, WILL*IAM* WANGEFORD *and* WILL*IAM* JENNEY

959. From THOMAS PIRYS to SIR JOHN FASTOLF

1447, 15 October

Add. Charter 18239. $9\frac{3}{8} \times 4\frac{3}{4}$ in. Hand unidentified, perhaps autograph.

Dorse: Marks of folding, four seals originally attached, three remaining. Address in hand of letter:

Suo domin*o*, *d*omin*o* *Joh*ann*i* *Fastolf milit. &c.*

The year is reasonably certain through the letter's connection with an extended enquiry, conducted by Nicholas Bokkyng and William Dorset between 1444 and 1447, into the accounts of John Tudworth, Fastolf's receiver of revenues at Castle Combe and Bathampton (BL Add. 28212, f. 24). At the conclusion, dues which Tudworth had failed to collect at Bathampton were ordered by Fastolf to be brought in, as described in the letter; see Smith, 'Aspects of the Career of Sir John Fastolf', pp. 80–81. The making of the accounts, described as occurring on the eve (being a Sunday) of the feast of St Michael in Monte Tumba, suggests that the year was 1447, and that the letter was written on that day. The writer's name is also given elsewhere as Piers and Perys.

Printed by G. P. Scrope, *Castle Combe*, p. 259.

Ryȝt worschypful and reuerent lord, y reco*m*mande me vn-to yowr*e* hynesse, by-sekyng ȝow of ȝowr*e* grete goodnes that ȝe be good lord vn-to ȝowr*e* tenent John Aleyn &c. And as ȝe send wrytyng to Langeford to ȝowr*e* p*re*ste and bedman Ser*e* Thomas, y to do ȝowr*e* co*m*mandement; truly *and* effectually y haue don my parte in[1] the chyrch of Stypellangford, to ȝowr*e* tenantes Robert Edward, Robert Rose, Ad*a*m Warrock, Wyliam Pet*er* of Bathampton Wyly, that þey haue truly payd to Thomas Shurlok the rentes of ij ȝer*e*, and ther to they wollen swer*e* vppon a boke.

Al-so, as for the billys that Wilia*m* Dorset wrote schal be sende in the lett*er*, as ȝe co*m*mandyd. Furþ*er*more, we haue a-countyd and leyd that Thomas Schurlok hath receywyd ix li. xiij s. iiij d. for ij ȝere,[2] y-contyd in þe chirch of Langeford for-sayd, ⌜by-twixte⌝[3] matens *and* masse the Sonday

[6] Wrete *canc.*

959. [1] þ *canc.* [2] to *subpuncted.* [3] *Added in margin, caret mark after* by.

a-for*e* þe feste of Sente Mycael[4] in Monte Tu*m*ba, to þe whech wrytyng we, al ȝowr*e* tenent*es*, putton to owr*e* selys.

No more vn-to ȝow, but þe Holy[5] Trynité haue how eu*er* in hys blessyd kepyng. Y-wrete at Langeford, the xv day of Octobir.

By ȝowr*e* owyn trew por*e* bedman,[6] S*ER* THOMAS PIRYS, p*re*ste of Stipillang*ford*.

960. From SIR JOHN FASTOLF to THOMAS HOWES and JOHN GREEN 1447, 21 October

Oxford, Magdalen College, Hickling 130. $11\frac{1}{4} \times 5$ in. William Worcester's hand, subscription autograph.

Dorse: Marks of folding, slits for tape, remains of red wax seal. Address in Worcester's hand:

*To my ryght welbelovyd frend Sir Thomas Howys, p*arson *of Castellcomb,* and *to John Grene.*

Howes's reply to this letter is no. 961, dated 26 October 1447.
G. 966[1]/71[1] (abstract).

Trusty and welbelovyd frendys I grete you well. And woll ye wete that as to the plee atwyxt the Pryour of Hykelyng *and* me for the xxv mark*es* &c, the Pryour ys councell have leyd ynne for her plee that ⌜one⌝ Robert Eccles shuld be at thys day lyvyng *and* heyr to John Eccles; and seyn that the seid Rob*er*t most be avouched *and* made pryvie to the Pryour ys plee, be cause John Eccles was one of the feffeez that yafe the seid lond was yeven in to the house. And my councell replyen *and* seyn for my ryght that seth the tyme that the Pryour hath decesed me of[1] my rent of xxv mark., the forseid Rob*er*t Eccles, yff ony such heyr bee, was not possessed ⌜*and* seised⌝ off the rent of xxv mark. by the Pryour, ne none off hys auncestres. Wherfor, the vouche ys not suffis*a*unt. And therfor I pray you that by the avice of John Grene, ye wolle do inquere where the seid Rob*er*t ys, and ghete a suffis*a*unt record *and* wytnesse that he toke no proffitz of the seid rent charge, ne off the lond seth that[2] the Pryour decesed me of my rent.

And so fro that tyme that the Pryour hath decesed me of the rent, the seid Rob*er*t Eccles ne none of hys auncestres was neuer seised of the seid rent in the forme as the Pryour hath allegged. Wherfor I p*ra*y you *and* John Grene to wyrk in thys mater as ye shall thynk best for the sauac*i*on of my ryght. For all

[4] c *over* f *or long* s. [5] *MS.* Loly.
[6] Ser *subpuncted.*

960. [1] the *canc.* [2] he *canc.*

men may of verry ryght vele *and* conceyve that the Pryour gave no maner possession to no man of the seid rent. And I suppose there ys none such Rob*er*t Eccles, heyr to John Eccles, as the Pryour counsell have alegged. And therfor I desyre to have such a notable record of thys mat*er* that it[3] may be a suffis*a*unt wytnesse to me for my aunsuer.

It*em*, ye most jnquere whate othyr surname John Eccles had, for he had a nothyr name, and hys cousyns also, for the seid John Eccles ys clepit Eccles of the toune that he duelled ynne.

Wretyn at London, xxj day of Octob*er*.

J. FASTOLFE

961. From THOMAS HOWES to SIR JOHN FASTOLF 1447, 26 October

Oxford, Magdalen College, Hickling 140. 18 × $11\frac{1}{4}$ in., with additional matter on a separate sheet, $8\frac{3}{4}$ × 11 in., attached to front. Geoffrey Spirleng's hand (see Part II, no. 603).

Dorse: Marks of folding, slits for tape, traces of red wax seal. 'Hyklyng' and 'Fastolf' added later in different fifteenth-century hands. Address in Spirleng's hand:

*To myn right reue*rent *and wurchepfull mayster, S*er *John Fastolf, knyght.*

Dated. On Spirleng, see further R. Beadle, 'Geoffrey Spirleng (*c.* 1426–*c.* 1494): a scribe of the *Canterbury Tales* in his time', *Of the Making of Books: Medieval Manuscripts, their Scribes and Readers. Essays presented to M. B. Parkes*, ed. P. R. Robinson & R. Zim (Aldershot, 1997), pp. 116–46.

G. 966[2]/71[2] (abstract).

Right reu*er*ent and w*ur*chepfull s*er* and mayst*er*, I recomaunde me vn-to you as lowly as any s*er*u*au*nt can do to his right reu*er*ent and w*ur*chepfull mayst*er*. Please you to wete that I and my clerk haue seten in the Registr*é* and s*er*ched for the yssew of John Eccles &c.[1]

*In prim*is, we fynd the test*am*en*t* of Reginald Eccles his fadre and his wyll bothe, and ther*e* he specyfyeth his sone John Eccles. And the seid Reginald was hefded in the Ryflyng tyme, and is beryed in the chauncell of Byllokby, as it sheweth by a note of his testament and wyll whiche I send you, as Wylly*a*m W*ur*cestr*e* can enforme you by a l*ett*re I haue sent hym &c.

It*em*, I send you a lytell note of his wyves testament Agnes, whiche dyed in the yeer after hym &c.

It*em*, wher as ye desire to knowe of one Rob*er*t Eccles whiche the Pri*our*z

[3] be *canc.*

961. [1] *The following three paragraphs are bracketed to the left and marked* De copia testatme*n*tor*um in Spirleng's hand.*

counsell seyn it is cosyn and heyre to John Eccles. It semeth by diu*er*s weyes þ*a*t he had neu*er* yssew, for if he had hadde any yssew, it is lyke þat eyther he shuld a gof hym sum of his meueable godys, or of his maner*es*, lond*es* or ten*ementes*. But he specyfieth neyther in his wyll ner in his test*ame*n*t*, for he maketh a gret wyll of his maner*es* and londys, wher*e* of we send you a copy woord for woord as it is regestred; and he is beryed wyth his fadr*e* in Byllokby. Notwythstandyng this serche, we haue inquired of dyu*er*s men and they sey he had neu*er* yssew. And my clerk spak wyth Lynford of this mat*er*, and he coud weell telle bothe of hym and of his fadr*e*, and seyd that he dwelled in Byllokby, and lyved nat passyng iij yeer aft*er* his fadre, and fell in gret det; and it semeth the same by hys wyll &c.

It*em*, the seid Lynford seyth he wote weell þ*a*t he had neu*er* yssew savyng, q*uo*d he, þ*er* be Eccles in Marth*a*m, but they be born of good gentylmen of olde aunsetr*é*, and no thyng of that kynred of Regnald Eccles, ner of John Eccles, for Regynald Eccles com vp of pou*er*té, as Heydon dooth, and was a s*er*ge*a*unt in lawe; and these o*þer* Eccles com of berthe of gentylmen of an olde stok &c.[2]

It*em*, it semeth verryly that it was the same John Eccles þ*a*t the Prio*ur* of Hykelyng alleggeth, for Jefray Som*er*ton and he wer*e* gret rewlers, and he made Jefrey Som*er*ton his executo*ur*, as he sheweth in his testament, whiche I send yow &c.

It*em*, I send you a note of Thom*as* Bardolf testament of Spykesworth; and of Adam of Stokeneylond; and ⌜the⌝ test*ame*n*t* of Edmund of Seynt Om*er*, þ*a*t dyed A^{o} m^{o} ccc^{mo} nonag*esimo* s*ecun*do; and of[3] Edmund Vfford, A^{o} m^{o} ccc^{mo} lxxiiij^{to}; and a no*þer* test*ame*n*t* of an other Edmund Vfford, of A^{o} m^{o} ccc^{mo} lxxiiij^{to}; and a note of a test*ame*n*t* of Jehane Vfford, þat dyed m^{l} ccc lxxv. And other testament*es* can we non fynde in the bokys at Chapell of Feld ⌜touchyng yo*ur*e ryght⌝. And we shuld a serched the bok*es* in the Paleys, but Mayst*er* Symond seyth he muste sende first to an offic*er* of my lord of Norwich for the keyes, and he hath gr*a*unte vs to haue sight in all hast. And as we fynde we shall sende you answer, by the g*ra*ce of Jh*es*u, to the incres of your*e* right &c.[4]

It*em*, wher*e* as ye write I shuld labo*ur* to the Prio*ur* of Yarmouth to do his p*a*rish preest expresse the faire profer*es* þ*a*t ye, in weye of charité, haue p*ro*fered to Rafman. S*er*, it shall be do in all hast, and thanne shull we send answer*e*.[5]

It*em*, as for the *cap*ias *vtlag*atum[6] a-yens Ric*hard* Elys, I haue out a warant, and it shall be execute in short tyme &c.[7]

It*em*, as for the testament*es* of Bertylmew Antyngh*a*m and of Thom*as*

[2] Non sic *written to left, apparently later.*

[3] an other *canc.*

[4] *This paragraph bracketed to the left and marked* De copi*a* testatmen*torum in Spirleng's hand.*

[5] De Joh*anne* Rafman *to left in Spirleng's hand.*

[6] *MS. vltlag*atum.

[7] De Ric*ardo* Elys *to left in Spirleng's hand.*

Seynt Omer, we can nat fynde them as yet. But we suppose it is nat lyke we shull fynde them here, for yf a[8] man haue lyvelod in ij dyoces or in more than one, than his testament and wyll shall be proued and registred at Caunterbury, as lerned men enforme me &c.[9]

Item, ser, please you to wete, as for the suerté to be made on myn part for arbitracion of Richard Chen. Ser, I haue made suerté. And in as muche as my mayster Inglose hath promysed to send[10] bothe obligacionz vp to London, þerfore I haue delyuered hym myn obligacion to be sent you wyth ynne suche tyme as Dam shall be come to London. For he was here at the shire of Norffolk holden the Monday by fore Seynt Symond and Jude, at whiche tyme were declared straunge tydynges, to blenchyng of one of oure aduersariez, as it sheweth in[11] a bylle closed in thes lettre, whiche is copy of the Kynges lettre &c.[12]

Item, forthermore please you to wete that after the writyng of these jtemz byfore writen, Watkyn Shipdam inquired at Byllokby of the stok and yssue of ⌜John⌝ Eccles ⌜of Byllokby⌝, and ther it is tolde hym pleynly that John Eccles had neuer yssue, as it is rehersed byfore. And in as muche as we were informed that ther wer other Eccles in Martham, we sent thedre Jefray Spirlyng and Robert Bottiler to inquire sadly yf any yong man or chyld were there clepid Robert Eccles. And the self answer þat they brought from Martham the same answer brought W. Shipdam from Byllokby, bothe of the Eccles of Martham and Eccles of Byllokby, whiche were neuer of kynred ner of stok &c, as it sheweth right pleynly in a[13] bylle annexed to this lettre &c.[14]

Item, ser, please you, as for alle other materes to be answered, we shull send you answer by Wyllyam Burgh wyth ynne iiij dayes after this writyng. And all myghty Jhesu haue yow in his blysfull kepyng.

Wretyn at Castre in hast, the Thursday[15] byfore Seynt Symond and Jude, A^{o} xxvj^{to} R. H. vj^{to}.

Youre seruaunt, PARSON OF CASTELCOMBE[16]

Ser, ther was Regnald Eccles, a sergeaunt of lawe or a prentys of court, and com vp in pouerté, as Heydon dooth; which Regnald was hefded in the Ryflyng tyme, and his hed set at Norwich, as Lynford told Spirlyng; whiche had sone John Eccles. And that John Eccles dwelled in Byllokby, and there is beried by his fadre Regnald, as her bothez testamentes and wyllys specyfye. And that John Eccles sold and gaf dyuers of his maneres, londes and tenementes to dyuers men, and specyfieth non yssue. Natwythstandyng the specificacionz of hys wyll and testament, we haue do inquired, and many men can telle her of, and sey pleynly þat John Eccles had neuer yssue &c.

[8] *No space.* [9] De testamenta *to left in Spirleng's hand.*
[10] them *canc.* [11] the last item of this lettre *canc., and the words that follow added later.*
[12] De Ricardo Chen *to left in Spirleng's hand.* [13] *No space.*
[14] De exitu Johannis Eccles *to left in Spirleng's hand.* [15] in *canc.*
[16] *Remainder of text on the separate sheet attached to the main body of the letter.*

Item, ther was one Wyllyam Eccles, whom ⌜dyuers⌝ men ⌜in Martham⌝ knew þat lyuen yet at this day, whiche Wyllyam duelled in Yarmuth, and was a draper, and is beried at Yarmuth; whiche had yssue ⌜Robert⌝[17] Eccles dwellyng in Belton, in a place þat sumtyme was John Spitelynges. And þat Robert had yssue Robert, and þat secund Robert had yssue the thrid Robert, whiche is now lyvyng in Martham, of viij yeer in age, and was warde to the Lord Cobham; whiche wardship one Thomas Chirche of Martham hath boughte of the Lord Cobham, and fyndeth the chyld at this day to[18] scole for that same Thomas Chirche hath wedded the modre of that heyre.

Item, ser, please you to gef credence to this ⌜writyng⌝, for it hath be laboured by Watkyn Shipdam at Byllokby, and by me and my clerk in the Registré, and by Spirlyng at Martham and oþer placez of the iij^de part. And alle folwen vpon one conclusion by cleer[19] informacion of dyuers men, þat John Eccles had neuer yssue, and þat yong heyre þat now lyveth,[20] clepid Robert Eccles, was sone of Robert Eccles, and that secund Robert was sone to the thrid Robert, and that thridde Robert was sone to Wyllyam Eccles, sumtyme of Yarmuth, draper; whiche accordeth to Heydonz plee, yf that Wyllyam Eccles had be clepid John Eccles. But as to that name John Eccles, ther was non suche but John Eccles of Byllokby, whiche had neuer yssue. And by this meane it may weell be conceyued and opynly how he is set in the vntruthe of the mater.

Item, where it is a-bove rehersed that Lynford seyd that thoo Eccles of Martham were gentylmen of old aunsetré, the cause that they be reported gentylmen is this, as we suppose, þat[21] the seid Wyllyam Eccles purchased xx marc. worth of lyvelod in Martham of a man ⌜sumtyme⌝ clepid Martham; and this yong Eccles and the fadre of hym bar armys, as we here sey. What the armys of that stok be we can ⌜nat⌝ telle, but we shull inquyre &c.

962. From Sir John Fastolf to Howes, Cole and Shipdam — 1448, 12 May

Magdalen College, Fastolf Paper 26. $14\frac{1}{4} \times 11\frac{1}{2}$ in. William Barker's hand, subscription autograph.

Dorse: Marks of folding, slits for tape, remains of red sealing wax. Four lines of accounting notes in a later hand. Address in Barker's hand:

To my tristy and weel be-loved frendes Thomas Howys, clerk, William Cole and Watkyn Shipdam, in hast.

[17] *Over* John *canc.* [18] scl *canc.* [19] d *canc.*
[20] w *canc.* [21] they *canc.*

962 *From Sir John Fastolf to Howes, Cole and Shipdam, 12 May 1448*

Dated. John Rafman, prior to his imprisonment described in the letter, had been steward of Fastolf's household at Caister, and his bailiff in Yarmouth; see Smith, 'Aspects of the Career of Sir John Fastolf', pp. 77–80.

Unprinted.

Weel be-loved frendes, I grete yow weel. And where as I have vnderstande by a remembraunce þ*at*[1] John Rafman send me by Will*ia*m Barker*e* my seruaunt, of hese owen hand wrytyng, desyreth to knowe a fynalle hende how it standeth be-twen me and hym, as it sheweth by the seyd bille, where of the tenur*e* is thys: 'Will*ia*m Barker*e*, I p*ra*ye you hertyly to speke vn-to my mayst*er* Fastolf for John Rafman hese p*ri*soner*e*, þ*at* hym wold lyke of hese good grace for to assigne hese atto*ur*nes here to appoynt sum*m*e issew resonable for hys seyd p*ri*soner, of suche money as yo*ur*e audyto*ur*es have leyde vpon hym; the wheche longe hath ben in p*re*son, and may have non ende, to hese vtter destrucc*io*n as in thys werld, for ye shal weel conceyve þ*at* he bett*er* at hese fyrst ⟨. . .⟩[2] in to p*re*son myght have payed x li. than now he may paye x s. Wherefore lyket it hym of good grace and greet bountyvowsnesse for to have m*er*cy *and* pyté vppon hys seyd p*re*soner; and þ*at* hym lyketh to thenke of olde servyse of long contynuaunce to hym don afore in tyme past, for the love of God and in the weye of charyté &c.'

Wheche seyd rem⟨embr⟩aunce I have weel vnderstande; and where þ*at* he compleyneth hym þ*at* he may have non ende to hese vtter[3] destrucc*io*n ⟨. . .⟩ seyth nought weel, as I reporte me to you. For if he had acquit hym justly to me as a good s*er*u*au*nt ought vpon hese acompt, and a payed hese dewtes that was founde vp-on hym by audyto*ur*es assigned, as it was examined be-fore notable men in Yarmouth,[4] he beyng p*re*sent diu*er*se tymes, he had had hese ende at that tyme he was committed ⟨to ward⟩, and at ony tyme seth if he or ony man for hym wold a[5] payed hys verrey dewté, as I have wrete before thys tyme, as I reporte me to you.

And þ*er*e as he seyth he myght better*e* a payed x li. at the tyme he was comitted to ward th⟨. . .⟩ now x s., the default was the gretter in hym self, that he wold nought frelye confesse hys powere of good and ⟨. . .⟩ satyfyed hese dette as ferre hese goodys wolde a streched.

And where he desyreth I shuld have mercye and ⟨pyté vppon⟩ hym, and thenk vpon the old servyse of long contynuaunce don, I wolde it were knowe to alle men wh⟨. . .⟩ dede vn-to me, and what harme I hadde by hym whan he kest an obligac*io*n of iij^{c} mark, as he seyth in hese ⟨. . .⟩ wheche was owyng me by the Duchesse of Bedford; wheche obligac*io*n I delyu*er*ed hym to a receyved the seyd ⟨. . .⟩ thys lande. And also þ*at* he wold brynk to mynde þ*at* I payed for hese fynaunce and raunsom c m*a*rc. and qu⟨it hym⟩ ought of

962. *The right hand edge of the sheet is damaged by damp and wear, carrying away the ends of many lines.*

[1] þ *in form of* y *throughout.*

[2] *One, two or three words lost at edge of sheet, and so in places likewise indicated below.*

[3] *No space.* [4] þ *written for* Y. [5] *No space.*

p*re*son in Fraunce, where alle the mayst*er*es and frendz that ever he hadde wold nought a don it. ⟨. . .⟩ nought the gyse ner costom of men of armes to acquite everye p*re*soner þ*a*t is take, as I reporte me, and ma⟨ny. . .⟩ frendly dedes I dede for hym, wheche he ful sympelye hath thought vpon.

Neverthelesse, thys fauo*ur*e and ⟨. . .⟩ shewe hym at the reu*er*ence of God, noughtwythstandyng he hath geve me but esye cause, I wole that S*er* Thom*a*⟨s Howys⟩, Will*ia*m Cole and Watkyn Shipda*m*, Thom*a*s Hill and Roger Hogges of Jarmouth, my trusty frendes, ou*er*se egally ⟨. . .⟩ hese acom*m*pt*es*, and what verry and cler dewté he oweth me ou*er*e the respytes wheche be desp*er*at and can nought ⟨. . .⟩ verry dewté vp-on the seyd acom*m*pt, shewed by seche menes as he can nought denye. And seche sum*m*e as ⟨. . .⟩ founde dewe to me ou*er*e þ*a*t, I wole he make me payment of it, or fynde me seche sewerté as the seyd S*er* Thom⟨*a*s Howys⟩ and Shipda*m* shal concyder resonable, wyth the advyse of my seyd frendes Thom*a*s Hill *and* Roger Hogges, so as he, S*er* Thom⟨*a*s. . .⟩ wole hald you agreed to content me at a nye day &c.

And thys don, I geve yow, S*er* Thom*a*s Howys, Cole and ⟨Shipd*a*m⟩, ful power be thys my wrytyng, seled and signed wyth my signe manuall, to acquitaunce the seyd Rafman, and discharge hym ought of p*re*son &c. And I p*ra*ye you if nede be recomaunde me to my weel be-loved fader ⟨. . .⟩ P*riour*e of Yarmouth, and shew hym thys lett*re*, and her by he shal seen how I am demened &c.

An⟨d allmyghty God kepe you⟩. Wrete at London in hast, the xij day of Maij A^{o} xxvj^{to} R. H. vj^{ti}.

J. FAS⟨TOLFE⟩

963. From JOHN NORTHWOOD to VISCOUNT BEAUMONT 1448, 28 May

Add. 43488, f. 7. $11\frac{1}{4} \times 8\frac{1}{4}$ in., uneven at foot. In an unidentified hand.

Dorse: Marks of folding, address panel soiled. Address in hand of letter:

To my worshypfull and reuerent Lord John, Vicont Beaumont.

The year is fixed by the mention towards the end of the letter of the death of the sheriff of Warwickshire, Thomas Porter, which took place the day before it was written (*Inq. p. m.* 27 Henry VI, no. 13).

F. i, p. 12. G. 60/78.

Ryȝth worshypfull and my reuerent *and* most spesiall lord, y recomaund me vn-to ȝowr*e* good grace in the most humble and lowly wyse that y canne or may, desyryng to her of ȝowr*e* prosperité and well fare a⟨s to my⟩[1] most syngeler ioy *and* spesiall comfort.

And ȝyf hyt plees ȝowr*e* hygnes, as towchyng the soden aventewr*e* that fell la⟨tly at⟩[2] Couentré: plees hyt ȝowr*e* lordshyp[3] to her*e* that on Corpus *Christ*i even last passed, be-twene viij *and* ix of the clok at a⟨fternoo⟩n,[4] Syr Umfrey Stafford had browth my mayster*e* Syr James of Vrmond towa[r]d hys yn from my lady of Shrewusb⟨ery and r⟩[5]etorned from hym toward hys yn, he met w*ith* Syr Robert Harcowrt comyng frome hys moder*e* toward hys yn, *and* pa⟨ssed Syr⟩ Vmfrey; *and* Richard hys son came sumwhat be-hynde. *And* when they met to-gyder they fell in handes to-gyder, *and* ⟨Syr Robe⟩rt[7] smot hym a grette stroke on the hed w*ith* hys[8] sord. *And* Richard w*ith* hys dagger hastely went toward hyme, *and* as he stombled, on of Harcowrt*us* men smot hym in the bak w*ith* a knyfe. Men wott not ho hytt was reddely. Hys fader herd noys, *and* rode toward hem, *and* hys men ronne befor*e* hym thyder ward. *And* in the goyng downe of hys hors, on, he wotte not ho, be[9]-hynd hym smot hym on the hede w*ith* a nege tole—men know not w*ith* vs w*ith* what wepone—that he fell downe. *And* hys son fell downe be-fore hym as good as dede. And all thys was don, as men sey, in a Pater Noster[10] wyle. And forth w*ith* Syr Vmfrey Stafford men foloed after, *and* slew ij men of Harcowrttus, on Swynerton, *and* Bradshawe, *and* mo ben hurt. Sum ben gonne and sum ben in pryson in the jayll at Couentré.

And be-fore the coroner of Couentré, vp-on the syȝth of the bodyes, ther ben endited, as prynsipall for the deth of Richard Stafford, Syr*e* Robert Harcowrt *and* the ij men that ben dede. And for the ij men of Harcowrt*us* that ben dede ther ben endited ij men of Syr Vmfrey as prynsipall. And as ȝytte ther hath ben no thyng fownden before the Justice of the Pees of Couentré of thys riot, be caws the shreffe of Warwyk shyre is dede, *and* they may not sytt in to the tyme ther be a new shreve. And all thys myschef fell be cawse of a nold debate that was be-twene heme for takyng of a dystres, as hyt is told.

And all myȝthy J*es*u preserve ȝowr*e* hye astat, my spesiall lord, *and* send ȝow long lyve *and* good hele. Wryton at Couentr*é* on Tewusday next after Corpus *Christ*i day, &c.

Be ȝowr*e* own por*e* s*er*uand JOHN NORTHWOOD

963. [1] *Fenn's readings. The paper was 'chafed' in his time, and there are now holes in the MS. here and where his readings are given below.*
[2] *F.* [3] *Abbrev.-like mark over* p. [4] *F.* [5] *F.*
[6] *F.* [7] *F.* [8] a *canc.* [9] s *canc.* [10] wyll *canc.*

964. From THOMAS HOWES and GEOFFREY SPIRLENG to SIR JOHN FASTOLF 1448, late December

Oxford, Magdalen College, Titchwell 41. $11\frac{3}{4} \times 11\frac{1}{4}$ in. Geoffrey Spirleng's hand.

Dorse: Marks of folding, slits for tape, remains of red wax seal. Address in Spirleng's hand:

To oure right *reue*r*ent and right wurchepfull maist*er *S*er *John Fastolf in hast.*

This is the first of a number of letters of 1448–50 concerned wholly or partly with Fastolf's defence of his possession of the manor of Titchwell in north Norfolk. A royal commission sitting nearby at Litcham on 30 October 1448 found grounds to challenge Fastolf's title, and the manor was taken into the hands of the Crown. On 14 December 1448 Sir Edward Hull was granted the farm of the manor, and this letter relating the initial enquiries of Fastolf's servants dates from soon afterwards. These and other particulars of the proceedings that followed are documented in P. S. Lewis, 'Sir John Fastolf's Lawsuit over Titchwell 1448–55', *The Historical Journal,* i (1958), 1–20.

Unprinted.

Right reu*er*ent and our*e* right worchepful maist*er*, we recomaunde vs to you in als louly wise as any seru*au*nt*es* may to ther right w*ur*chepful maist*er*. Please you to wete, that where as ye write vn-to vs to labo*ur*e eff*ect*ualy to get you a copy of the office whiche ⌜was⌝ take ayens you at Lycheham for your*e* manour*e* of Tichewell, we, S*er* Thom*as* and Gefrey Spirlyng, laboured the Sonday byfor*e* Seynt Thomas Ap*ost*le vn-to Norwich, and from Norwich to dyu*er*s[1] townys in the contré, to jnquir*e* aft*er* Dallyng. And, w*yth* labo*ur*, he was spoke wyth at Wesbiche in Mershlond; and p*ro*fered hym, aft*er* the tenur*e* of your*e* l*ett*re, a gret reward to haue had a copy. And he seid, and affermed gret othez ther*e* vpon, that als sone as the office was take by the labo*ur* of Wylly, Heydon dede send for Dallyng, and made hym to swere vp-on a book that he shuld kepe no copy w*yth* in hym, ner note of the seid veredite. W*yth* more, that he shuld neu*er* late you haue knowlege in what forme it was take, ner by whom, to that entent that the seid Heydon and Wylly shuld t*ur*ne and make that veredight in suche forme as them plesed, natwythstandyng it is ensealed w*yth* the seal*es* of the juré that passed thervpon. And therfore the seid Dallyng ⌜seith⌝ he dar nat, bothe for fer and for perel of his othe, non ferther to lete you haue knowlege in no wyse. And forthermor*e*, as fer as we can fele, the seid Dallyng haue be chef solicito*ur* a-yens you in the[2] seid mat*er* at all tymez; and but for hise besynesse, the seid Wylly had neu*er*[3] be so besy as he hath be in the seid mat*er*. And this was the answer*e* we coud gete in any wyse.

It*em*, please you to wete, the Sonday byfor*e* Cristemasse day yong Willy

964. [1] speke w*yth* Dally *canc.* [2] sed *canc.*
[3] *The five preceding words repeated and canc.*

and a yoman of S*er* Edward Hull come rydyng doun to Tichewell, and cleped the ten*aun*t*es* vn-to them, and shewed them[4] the Kyng*es* writyng vnd*er* hise brod seal, rehersyng vn-to them that the Kyng hath sent doun to entr*e* the seid manoyr*e*, and mad*e* S*er* E. Hull his fermo*ur*. And as for all other lond in the seid toun that shuld be your*e* in the seid toun, beside the manoyr*e* lond*es*, they seid pleynly they wold nat entr*e* them, for to tho lond*es* had they no power. And by vertue of this co*m*mission they haue[5] charged your*e* fermo*urz* to avoyde, and they ner non other to occupie the seid manoyr*e* tyl they take it in ferme of them. Vp-on whiche mat*er*, please you to write your*e* comaundement, in what forme we may labour*e* forther her*e* in &c.

It*em*, please your*e* tendernesse to accept this for our*e* excuse, that yt hath be long er we myght send you any answer*e* of your*e* l*ett*rez, for a-bout this tyme of Cristemasse come no man out of these p*ar*tyez to London. And as for the speed of makyng of ⌜oure⌝[6] l*ett*rez, they arn at all tymes redy to send forth yf we myght gete any massanger*es*.

Be yo*ur*e s*er*u*au*nt S*er* Thom*as* Howys[7]

965. From Howes, Shipdam and Spirleng to Sir John Fastolf — 1449, 12 January

Oxford, Magdalen College, Titchwell 158. Two sheets, 14 × 11½ and 17 × 11½ in., stitched together. Geoffrey Spirleng's hand.

Dorse (second sheet): Continuation of text. Marks of folding, slits for tape, trace of red wax seal. Address in Spirleng's hand:

*To our*e *right reu*er*ent and w*ur*chepfull maist*er *S*er *John Fastolf in hast be this delyu*er*ed.*

Dated. The text begins abruptly, and a preceding sheet carrying the responses to the first three 'articles' in a lost letter of Fastolf's, to which this is the reply, is wanting. There is no sign of stitching at the head of the first sheet, however.

Unprinted.

It*em*, as to the[1] iiij^{te} article of your*e* seid l*ett*re, there as ye writen that we sended you neu*er* l*ett*re but one. Please you nat to be displesed ner to take it to gref, we sent you answer*e* by Cornel*ius* as fer as we coud at that tyme; and yf ther koude a be get any massanger*es* to London ward a-yens Cristemasse, your*e* l*ett*rez were redy at all tymes &c.

It*em*, as to the v^{te} article of your*e* seid l*ett*re, there as ye write that we shuld

[4] *Repeated and canc.* [5] di *canc.* [6] *Over* youre *canc.*

[7] *The tops of the letters in another line of writing, now cut away, are visible at the foot of the sheet.*

965. [1] f *canc.*

assay to speke w*y*t*h* the[2] att*ur*nyes of Nich*olas* Dale. S*er*, we, the seid Watkyn and Gefrey, come ridyng doun from Tichewell to Crowmer, and ther*e* we haue vnderstand that one Goodknape of Cleye is his att*ur*ny, and it shal ⌜be⌝[3] laboured vn-to hym in all hast. And as for any evydenc*es* to be serched among*es* Rauf Lampet evidenc*es*, I, S*er* Thom*as*, haue mad*e* all the serche I can, but I can non fynde &c.

It*em*, as to the vj^{te} article of your*e* seid l*ett*re, there as ye write to haue knowlege what yeer Willyam Louel dyed. We can nat sey w*y*t*h*out mor*e* cler serche, savyng, as we vnderstand, he was ⌜slayne⌝[4] at the Batayl of Agyncourt, whiche was the iij^{de} yeer of Herry v^{te}. And what tyme Margery dyed we can nat knowe as yet. And where ye write to haue knowlege whether the seid Marg*er*y was ded whan Roys sold*e* it you, she was dede a[5] gret while by fore. And for to wete what tyme he wedded hir, we fynde þ*a*t he entred the manoyr*e* in A^{o} iij^{o} H. ⌜quinti⌝.[6] And as it ⌜is⌝ nat vnknowe to dyu*er*s olde men and gentylmen of this, that the seid Margery dede make a-syne er thanne Roys solde it to you. And yf it be wel s*er*ched, it must nedyng*es* be be twix the iij^{de} yeer of Kyng H. v^{te} and the[7] ij^{de} yeer of the Kyng that now is at the ferthest, for w*y*t*h*out*e* any fayl a-syne she maad.

It*em*, as to the vij^{de} article of your*e* seid l*ett*re, wher*e* as ye write that Jankyn Cotelr*e* and G. Spirlyng shuld breke vp the lok of the nether almary in your*e* chaumbre to send you certeyn clospys knyt to gedre in a clout, we send you xj of them by Rob*er*t Cotelr*e*, bryng*er* of this l*ett*re.

It*em*, as to the viij^{te} article of your*e* seid l*ett*re, where as ye write that I, S*er* Thom*as*, shuld haue set in x or xj shipmen, and alle Duchemen. S*er*, please you to[8] wete, I trust to God I haue had non suche p*re*vysion as ye write I shuld haue ⌜had⌝, for I haue set in non suche Duchemen, savyng your*e* owen shipmen whiche haue ruled the plaighte here byfor*e*. The rather that Corneli*us* seid and he shuld kepe the plaighte he wold neu*er* to haue do w*y*t*h* hir in wynt*er* seson. And whether it be bett*er* to lete your*e* new ship to ferme or ell*es* to occupye it your*e* self; please you to wete, savyng your*e* bett*er* advyce, one ship wer*e* ynough sufficiauntly, and w*y*t*h* oute that ye bye moche greynes mor*e* thanne ye shal receyue of your*e* manoyrez, your*e* plaighte shal nat at all tymez be imployed. And yf it lyke you to send*e* vs writyng, we shal do our*e* part to lete it to ferme aft*er* the su*m*me of xx marc., yf we can bryng it to, of whiche mat*er* please you to send*e* vs writyng &c.

It*em*, as to ix article of your*e* seid l*ett*re, ther*e* as ye write to vs in gen*er*al, to se a weye and a condyte þ*a*t ye myght haue your*e* dutez, as well of your*e* baylyfz as of alle other accomptaunt*es*; and þ*a*t we shuld applye your*e* accompt*es* and sende you a t*ra*nscript how it stande w*y*t*h* youre officers. Please you to wete, we haue concluded w*y*t*h* alle accomptaunt*es* savyng w*y*t*h* Rob*er*t Broun, and vp-on hym we shal p*ro*cede. And that fynisshed, we shal

[2] ar *canc.* [3] *Over several miswritten letters canc.* [4] *Over* kylled *canc.* [5] *No space.* [6] *Over* v^{ti} *canc.* [7] y *canc.* [8] *No space.*

send*e* you an extrete of alle your*e* creditours in short tyme, yf we haue non impedyment*es* vp-on other of your*e* comaundement*es*.

It*em*, as to the x article of your*e* seid l*ett*re, there as ye write that ij or iij of vs shuld go in to youre evydence hous, þer*e* to fynde a box ful of evidenc*e* longyng to Roys. S*er*, please you to wete, we haue made serche in your*e* seid evydence hous, but we can non fynde of Roys evydencys. Nertheles, bothe we, S*er* Thom*as* and Watkyn, knowen verryly that ther*e* was one dede of Roys lyvelode about a iiij yeer passed a-monge*s* your*e* evydencez, but and it be nat w*yth* you at London jt is right straunge and it be so gon. And as for evydenc*es* of Tichewell, we can nomor*e* fynde than we sent you her*e*byfore, and yf any may be founde in any wyse we shal sende you by the next comer bytwix &c.[9]

It*em*, as to the xj article, ther*e* as ye write to vs to be wysely ruled in gou*er*naunce of your*e* housold. We trust to God we demene it in[10] suche wyse as shal be founde non exces of expens more thanne shal be to your*e* plesur*e*.

It*em*, to the xij article, wher*e* as ye write that all your*e* malt suche as shall be made shuld be ou*er*seen er it come from the kylne. S*er*, and it please you, we haue charged Rob*er*t Broun to ou*er*se it. Nertheles, and it please to write in your*e* next l*ett*re a comaundement to the seid Rob*er*t chargyng hym to ou*er*se it at eu*er*y stepyng, to th'entent he shall be the more diligent for your*e* writyng þanne for our*e* chargyng in your*e* name.

It*em*, to the xiij article of your*e* seid l*ett*re, wher*e* as ye write we shuld be weel advysed that your*e* malt be good that shal be sent you. S*er*, please you to wete, in eschewyng of the lasse damage vn-tyl the tyme we haue a warant from you, we haue take in one John Brig to assaye hym yf he can do bett*er* than the other Ducheman that hath made your*e* malt here byfor*e*, in lyke forme as we write vn-to you lateward by Cornel*ius*. Nertheles, als sone as the new kylne hous is made, they shall inow be occupyed ⌜bothe⌝, and herevpon we, S*er* Thom*as*, Cole, Shipdam and Rob*er*t Broun be fully, wyth oute your*e* bett*er* advyce, accorded; of whiche article please you to send*e* answer at your*e* next writyng &c.

Item,[11] as to the xiiij article of your*e* seid l*ett*re, touchyng these word*es* that we shuld sende you word how your*e* newe ballyfz of Heylesdon doth. S*er*, we trust he shal do weel, as fer as we can fele as yet. And wher*e* as ye write in the same item to send*e* you answer how Bertilmew Hulu*er*, late bayly of Guton, doth and wher*e* his abydyng is. S*er*, we can get hym at non avauntage to attache hym, and his abydyng is in Poryngglond P*ar*ua, iiij mile out of Norwich. And as for Thom*as* Wynt*er*, late one of your*e* warennar*e* at Heylesdon, he is gon, for he occupied nat w*yth* you sythe ye departed from Castr*e*; and one Broun that was w*yth* them at Castr*e* occupieth in his name, and they arn countrolled by the bayllyfz of bothe manoyrez of Heylesdon and D*ra*yton.

[9] *End of first sheet.* [10] sup *canc.* [11] that ye send me wo *canc.*

It*e*m, to the xv article of your*e* seid l*ett*re, wher*e* as ye write that we shuld speke w*yth* my lord Norwich Chaunce*le*r to wete what he hath don to the mat*er* of Hykelyng. S*er*, please you to wete, we sent G. Spirlyng to Lenn to do the massage vp-on your*e* comaundement, and he answered that he had receyued the day afor*e* he come vn-to hym a l*ett*re from you, and all your*e* entent in your*e* seid l*ett*re he wole do his part in labo*ur*yng to my lord Norwich, and as he can vnderstand my lordys entent he wole send you answer by his owen writyng in all hast goodly.

It*e*m, as to the xvj article of your*e* seid l*ett*re, where as ye write that we shuld send you word how Ric*hard* Elys doth, and how the baylyfz of Yarmuth wole acquyte them vn-to you at this tyme of Cristemasse. Please you to wete that I, S*er* Thom*a*s, dede speke w*yth* Thom*a*s Fen[12] of Yarmuth, and demaunded hym how he wold be ruled vn-to you. And he answereth þat and it please you to send*e* doun a *capias vtlag*atum and he wold do hise part that execuc*io*n shal be had, and ell*es* he shal send to his att*ur*ny to London and he wole[13] sewe it on hise owen cost.

It*e*m, as to the xvij article of your*e* seid l*ett*re, to be answered whether S*er* Willyam, the new chauntry preest of Heylesdon, wole haue the p*ar*sonage of Heylesdon, or kepe stylle the chauntry. S*er*, please you to wete that Mayst*er* John Salade, Chauncel⟨*er*⟩[14] w*yth* my lord Norwich, seid vn-to G. Spirlyng that the seid S*er* Willyam wole haue nouther the chauntry ner the p*ar*sonage, for he seith he is worthy to haue a moche bett*er* than eyther of them be. And in this mat*er* the seid Chaunce*le*r wole answer you by his owen l*ett*re, ioyntely w*yth* other mater*es* above specyfied and rehersed.

It*e*m, to the xviij article of the seid l*ett*re, ther*e* as ye write that we shuld nat forgete the greynes of Guton. S*er*, as to that mat*er*, we answered ful pleynly in our*e* l*ett*re to you sent by Corneli*us*, for in trouth the chirche is evel s*er*ued, and yf ye paye all the dutyez that arn specyfied in our*e* seid l*ett*re, thanne ye shul haue lytel or nought in restituc*io*n of the dutez that the p*ar*son aught you that late decessed &c.

It*e*m, as to the xix and last article of your*e* seid l*ett*re, that we shuld restreyne Geneys fee. S*er*, we shall fulfylle your*e* comandement. And as for alle other mat*erz* to you to be answered by⌜side⌝[15] the articlez comp*re*hended in your*e* seid l*ett*re, we answer*e* you vp-on the bac of this l*ett*re.[16]

It*e*m, we sent you a twelmoneth go the wil of the elder Rauf Louel, whos wyf was called Jone, the which was the wyf of Thom*a*s Fastolf by for*e*, as fer as we can fele,[17] which dyed A^{o} d*omi*n*i* m^{o} ccc^{o} lxj^{o}. And now we send you the[18] wil of the last Rauf, fader to Will*iam* Louell, as[19] it sheweth in the v^{te} article in the begyny*n*g of this l*ett*re, which we, the seid Watkyn and G. Spirlyng, found at Tychewell &c.

[12] *Dotted crescent over* n. [13] do *canc.* [14] *Edge of page worn away.*
[15] *Over* seid *canc.* [16] *End of second sheet.* Verte *written at foot, remainder of text on dorse.*
[17] An *canc.* [18] wyf *canc.* [19] we *canc.*

It*em*, we inquired of the ten*aun*t*es* there yf any part of the manoyr*e* wer*e*[20] hold of the Kyng, and of that they coud make seu*er*aunce what was olde of the Kyng and whas nat holde of the Kyng &c. And it wold be serched by your*e* olde ded*es* whiche lond*es* be of purchas, þ*at* we may haue the mor*e* knowlege of it &c.

It*em*, forthermor*e*, we found*e* there an jndent*ur*e of certeyn lees of lond*es* letyn by Nich*olas* Dale vn-to iiij men of that contré ioyntely w*y*t*h* the man*er* of Tichewell. First, an jnclos called Morlees, w*y*t*h* lij acr*e* lond, di. rod ariable, w*y*t*h* ij acr*e* mersh, j acr*e* of medew, cleped Childerhouslond*es*; wherof the seid Shipdam hath inquired xxxviij acr*e* and where they lye, w*y*t*h* the seid ij acr*e* m*er*sh and j acr*e* medew, and of the residue it is to inquir*e* of. And we suppose the seid Childerhouslond*es* wer*e* purchased by the last Rauf Louell. Moreou*er*, we haue found the seid clos cleped Morlees clos cont*eyneth* ij acr*e* planted w*y*t*h* okes, which cam by an eschaunge, as they sey.

It*em*, we[21] found*e* also ther*e* in the seid jndent*ur*e xxx acr*e* of lond, beside medew and m*er*sh, which John Roys purchaced of Thom*as* Perot of Bynham *and* Kat*er*ine his wyf for xl m*a*rc., cleped Herlewyns; of which lond the seid Shipd*am* hath found*e* and buttayled xxviij acr*e* di. rod, w*y*t*h* the seid m*er*sh and medew, and all is holden of the man*er* of Tichewell by ij s. of rent, and wer*e* lete to ferme by the seid Roys for xxvj s. viij d.

It*em*, ye purchaced ther lond*es* and ten*ementes*, medews and m*er*shez, lateward John Tychewell, for xl li., wherof we know the buttayle of the most part, and they arn hold of the man*er* of Tichewell by x s. iiij d. of rent, and ye shal receyue of dyu*er*s ten*aun*t*es* a-yen yerly of rente xij s. ix d. And for all these seu*eral* ten*ement*t*es* and lond*es* which we can fy*n*de ther*e* was p*ro*fered vs but vij m*a*rc., but we wold nat lete them, by cause we trust to bryng them to a bett*er* ferme. But our*e* trust ⌜is⌝ ye shall kepe possession of all the man*er* w*y*t*h* the seid p*ar*ticl*er* purchas.

It*em*, the ten*aun*t*es* of Tichewell sey that Willyam Louell sold the man*er* of Corby and Roys sold the man*er* of Emneth &c.

Nat ell*es*, but of all other mat*er*z to you to be answered and in your*e* comaundement*es* to be obeyed and fulfylled we shall do our*e* diligence to your*e* plesur*e*, by the g*ra*ce of Jh*es*u, whom we beseche[22] all myghty Jh*es*u haue you in his m*er*cyful gou*er*n*au*nce.

Wret*e* in hast at Castr*e* the Sat*er*day aft*er* Epiph*an*ie, A° xxvij° R. H. vj°.

Your*e* seru*aun*t*es*, P*AR*SON OF CASTELCOMB
W. SHIPDAM
G. SPIRLYNG

[20] *Three letters heavily canc.* [21] fynde *canc.* [22] yo b *canc.*

966. From Sir John Fastolf to Howes, Cole and Shipdam 1449, probably January or February

Oxford, Magdalen College, Add. 99 (Lovel Papers), f. 23. $11\frac{1}{4} \times 8\frac{1}{2}$ in. William Barker's hand, subscription autograph.

Dorse: Marks of folding, slits for tape, trace of red wax seal; some later pen-trials. Address in Barker's hand:

*To my ryght trusty and weel loved frendes Thom*as *Howys, clerk, Will*iam *Cole and Wat*er *Shipd*am.

The letter cannot be dated precisely, but is concerned with the initial phase of Fastolf's investigations into the Lovel pedigree, a preliminary to the defence of his possession of the manor of Titchwell, which gathered momentum in the early months of 1449; see the Headnote to no. 964, and further reference there.

Unprinted.

Ryght trusty and welbeloved frendz, I grete ʒow weel, and p*ra*ye ʒow hertyly to tender the mater of Tychwell, for[1] weche[2] I sende to ʒow Rob*er*t, to have a trewe and a good adu*er*tysement of seche materes as I have wrete for &c. And now we have founde here how that Margaret, wheche late was the wyf of Will*iam* Lovelle, and afterward the wyf of John Fastolf of Olton, hadde xiij^{e} m*ar*cs ʒerly ought of the seyd maner of[3] Tichewell for here dower, as it sheweth be a dede wheche I have here &c. And so it is lyke that John Fastolf hath the chef dedes of the seyd maner for to make entré þ*er*inne[4] for nowne payement of the seyd dower to hese wyf, beyng dewe terme of here lyf &c. And so be that mene the dedes have left stylle wyth hym. Wherfore, S*er* Thom*as*, I p*ra*ye to labo*ur*e wysely to Rauf Lampytte to gete owght as many dedes of the seyd place as can be geten &c, for it is wyth owght fayle, by alle lyklynesse as I conceyve, that he is nought wyth ought the dedes &c.

And also, wher they have made ther pe de gree, and make Thom*as* last of the stok, wheche shuld have isseu Margery and Anneys whec⟨he⟩[5] ben wedded on of them to S*er* Edward Hull *and* an other to on Wake, wheche make ther cleyme in the seyd maner be thys tale, as ʒe may seen be the bille þ*a*t we sent ʒow by Rob*er*t Boteler. I thenk it may in no wyse be that þ*er* was seche a Thom*as*, ⌜for than⌝ be[6] alle reson Thom*as* shuld a be possed in the maner, whech was never, as I can fele be no mene. But I knowe weel be owre evydence here þ*a*t Will*iam* Lovell was seised in the Kyng*es* dayes that deed is, and deyed wyth owght isseu, wheche I wold ʒe shuld inq*ui*re wysely of. And also, by the last tayle that iij fofe*es* made to Rauf Lovell and hese wyf was tayled to the heyre male for defaut of isseu, to ret*ur*ne to the ryght heyres of the seyd Rauf. And so be thys wey Wyll*iam* shuld have hadde it in fe symple, as I vnderstand.

966. [1] *No space.* [2] I send ʒow have *canc.* [3] Hykelyng *canc.* [4] þ *in form of* y *and so below.* [5] *Edge of page worn away.* [6] b *superimp. on* f *or long* s.

966. *From Sir J. Fastolf to Howes, Cole and Shipdam, Jan. or Feb. 1449*

I p*ra*ye ȝow comon here ⌜of⌝ saddely to Grene, but than be-fore ȝe must have wysely the pedegré from Rauf downward to whom the tayle was made to &c, and wheder ther were any Thom*as* sethe[7] that Rauf, as they have a-legged, or nought &c. And also, that ȝe wole serche the cort roll sethe Edwardes dayes, how many lordes have be ther, for at ther entré the names of the lordes be[8] put in evyry corte ⌜roll⌝, as the forme is. I p*ra*y ȝow send me alle tho names, and in what kynges tyme þei[9] were.

J. FASTOLFE

967. From SIR JOHN FASTOLF to THOMAS HOWES

Early 1449

Oxford, Magdalen College, Titchwell 170. 11 × 5¼ in. William Barker's hand.

Dorse: Marks of folding, slits for tape, trace of red wax seal. Address in Barker's hand:

To S*er Thom*as *Howys, p*ars*on of Castelcomb*e.

Howes later used the blank spaces on both sides of the sheet for his own rough notes and memoranda, including a sketch of the Lovel arms, and information about members of the Lovel family and Thomas Fastolf. The abrupt opening, the absence of the usual epistolary greeting, and the want of any normal closure or subscription, suggest that this may be a fragment of a longer missive, perhaps cropped in the course of Howes's re-use of the sheet. Alternatively, it may be a postscript or afterthought continuing from another letter. In any event, the presence of Barker's hand and the content leave no doubt that it is from Fastolf. It is closely related to the slightly earlier no. 966, probably of January or February 1449; see Lewis, 'Sir John Fastolf's Lawsuit over Titchwell', p. 10.

Unprinted.

It*em*, s*er*, I p*ra*y you to send me the disent of the heyres of Lovell, from the fyrst Thom*as* the astate shuld be made to of the seyd maner of Tichewell, vn-to William Lovell þ*at*[1] alyened the maner, and to whom it was alyened, and how Roys cam þ*er*by, and what armes they bar*e* &c.

It*em*, to have knowlache of the wyf[2] of the [seyd] Lovell, and hise doughteres þei[3] were, and what armes þei bare &c.

It*em*, to wete the cause why that Margaret, wheche was wyf of Willi*am* Lovell, had here dower of the seyd maner*e* when she was wedded to John Fastolf of Olton, and whos doughter she was, and whether the seyd woman was wedded to Wychyngh*am* be-fore or nought.

It*em*, ther is a maner in Lyncolneshyre cleped Corbye, if ȝe con wete who is lord þer-of &c.

[7] *MS.* shethe. [8] *MS.* but. [9] ei *superscript.*

967. [1] þ *in form of* y, *and so throughout.* [2] f *fourished, perh. signifying pl. inflection.*
[3] ei *superscript, and so in this word below.*

It*em*, to inquire if S*er* Edward Hull ⌜*and* Wake⌝ tale be trewe, as he hath made hese pe de gre,[4] of wheche ȝe have a copye closed in on of the l*ett*re*s* &c.

It*em*, to wete how many alyenaciou*n*s hath be made of Tichewell seth it come ought of Lovell hendes, and to who*m* &c, wyth the knowlache of alle other cyrcu*m*staunces that ȝe shal concýderen be ȝowr*e* wyse discrec*i*on most expedient for the savac*i*on of my ryght &c. And as it is don me to wete, on Bloye of Tichewell can geve ȝow ryght good informac*i*on. I p*ra*ye ȝow if Grene may be ther, that he be there in ony wyse &c, as I may trust vp-on hym &c.

968. From ROBERT WENYNGTON to THOMAS DANIEL

1449, 25 May

Add 43491, f. 7. 12 × 10¼ in. In an unidentified clerk's hand.

Dorse: Marks of folding, slits for tape, remains of red wax seal. Address in hand of letter:

*To my reu*er*end mayster*e *Thom*as *Danyell, Squier for the Kyng*ys *Body, be thys lett*er *delyu*er*d in haste.*

The career of Robert Wennington of Dartmouth is surveyed in Wedgwood, *History of Parliament: Biographies*, pp. 932–3. The royal commission to him to 'do us service in the sea, for the cleansing of the same and rebuking of the robbers and pirates thereof' was dated 3 April 1449. Thomas Daniel was an esquire in the king's household who at this time is mentioned with increasing frequency in East Anglian affairs, becoming well known to Fastolf and the Pastons. On 27 July 1447 he was commissioned 'to go with his *posse* on the sea for the safe keeping thereof, with full power to lead, rule and govern all masters and mariners and others of his company, and to punish the same, and to fight the king's enemies', an appointment which perhaps explains Margaret Paston's reference to Daniel's having been 'made amerel' at about this time (*Cal. Pat. Rolls 1446–52*, p. 270; no. 134, lines 8–10, and Headnote). It was evidently in relation to this expedition that Fastolf lent Daniel £100, a debt that was said to be still outstanding in 1455 (G. 263/309, 264/310). A letter patent dated 8 November 1450 (printed and discussed by C. F. Bühler, *R.E.S.* xiv (1938), 130–2) concerns an attempt to recover Fastolf's loan out of the sale by the Crown of *The George of Prussia*, a ship captured by Daniel and renamed *Danyellis Hulke*. The recovery of the same loan also appears to be the issue about which Lord Scales wrote to Fastolf early in 1452; see no. 1014, and cf. *Cal. Pat. Rolls 1446–52*, p. 437.

F. i, p. 208. G. 68/90.

Most reu*er*end maystere*e*, I reco*m*maund me on-to yowr*e* gracius mays-teschup,[1] ever deseryng to her of yowr*e* wurschupfull astate, the whyche all myghté God mayntayne hyt *and* encr[e]se hyt on-to hys plesans; plesyng yow to knaw of my well fare *and* of all yowr*e* men, at the makyng of thys l*ett*r*e*, we wer*e* in gode hele of body, j-blessyd be God.

[4] *Originally* gresse, *last three letters canc.*

968. [1] *Dotted circumflex over* p, *and so in other instances of final p below.*

Mo over, mayster, I send yowe word by Ravly Pykeryng of all maters, the whyche I be-seche yow yeve[2] hym credens, as he wyll enforme yow of all. So, sur*e*, I be-seche yow in the reu*er*ens of God that ye wyll enforme owr*e* sou*er*ayn[3] lord the Kyng of all maters that I send yow in thys lett*er*, lyke as I have send a lett*er* to my lord Chaunseler *and* to all my lordys by the sayd Pykeryng; the whyche lett*er* I be-seche yow that ye take *and* delyver to my lord *and* all my lordys by yowr*e* awne handys, *and* lete the sayd Pykeryng declar*e* all thyng*ys* as he hath sayn *and* knaw*yth*.

Furst, I send yow word that when ⌜we⌝ went to see we toke ij schyppys of Brast comyng owte of Flaundrys *and* then after*e* ther ys made a[4] grete armyng in Brytayn to mete w*yth* me *and* my felyschyp, that ys to say the grete schyp of Brast, the grete schyp of Morleys, the grete schyp of Vanng, w*yth* other*e* viij schyppis, bargys *and* balynger*ys*, to the nu*m*ber*e* of iij^{ml} men. And so we lay on the see to me[te] w*yth* them.

And then we mette w*yth* a flote of a c grete schyppys of Pruse, Lubycke, Campe, Rastocke, Holond, Selond *and* Flandres, betuxte Garnysé *and* Portlond. And ther I cam a-bord the Admirall *and* bade them stryke in the Kyngys name of Englond, *and* they bade ⌜me⌝ go skyte in the Kyngys[5] name of Englond; *and* then I *and* my feleschyp sayd, but he wyld streke don the sayle, that I wyld over sayle ham, by the grace of God, *and* God wyld send me wynd *and* wether*e*. *And* dey bade do my wurst, by cause I had so fewe schyppys *and* so smale, that they scornyd w*yth* me. And as God wuld, on Fryday last was we had a gode wynd, *and* then we armyd vs to the nu*m*br*e* of ij^{ml} men in my felyschyp, *and* made vs redy for to over sayle them. *And* then they lonchyd a bote *and* sette vppe a sto*n*dert of truesse, *and* com *and* spake w*yth* me; *and* ther ⌜they⌝ were yolded all the hundert schyppys to go w*yth* me in what port that me lust, *and* my felawys. But they faoth w*yth* ⌜me⌝ the day before, and schotte[6] atte vs a j^{ml} govnnys *and* quarell owte of nu*m*ber*e*, *and* have slayn meny of my felyschyp, *and* meymyd all soo. Wher*e*for me thyngkyt that they have forfett bothe schyppe *and* godys at owr*e* sou*er*ayn lord the Kyng*ys* wyll. Besechy*ng* yow that ye do yowr*e* parte in thys mater*e*, for thys I have wrytyn to my lord Chaunseler *and* all my lordys of the Kyng*ys* Counsell. *And* so I have brofte them, all the c schyppys, w*yth* in Wyght, in spyte of them all.

And ye myghte gete leve of owr*e* sou*er*ayn lord the Kyng to com hydder, hyt schall turne yow to grete wurschup *and* profett, to helpe make owr*e* a-poyntement in the Kyng*ys* name, for ye sawe never suche a syght of schyppys take in to Englond thys c wynter*e*; for we by armyd nyght *and* day to kepe them in to the tyme that we have tydeng*ys* of owr*e* souerayn *and* his Counsell. For truly, they have do harme to me *and* to my feleschyp, *and* to yowr*e* schyppys more [than] iij^{ml} li. worth harme, and therfor I am avesyd, *and* all

[2] them *canc.* [3] the *canc.* [4] *No space.*
[5] *No space.* [6] after vs *canc.*

my feleschyp, to drovne them *and* slee them, w*yth* oute that we hast tydyng*ys* from ow*re* sou*er*ayn the Kyng *and* hys Counsell.

And therfor, in the reu*er*ens of God, come ye yow*re* sylf *and* ye schall have a grete avayle *and* wurschup for yow*re* comyng to see a suche syght, for I der well sey that I have her[7] at þ*is* tyme all the chef schyppys of Duche lond, Holond, Selond *and* Flaundrys, *and* now hyt wer*e* tyme for to trete for a fynell pese as for that partyes.

I writ no more to yowe[8] at þ*is* tyme, but all myghty J*es*u have [yowe] in hys kepyng. I-writ in hast[9] w*yth* in Wyght on Soneday at nyght after the[10] Ascenc*io*n of Ow*re* Lord.

By yowr avne s*er*uant ROB*ER*T WENYNGTON

969. From JOHN CROP to WILLIAM WORCESTER

1449, mid-May

Oxford, Magdalen College, Add. 99 (Lovel Papers), f. 21. $8\frac{1}{2} \times 7\frac{3}{8}$ in. Autograph.

Dorse: Marks of folding, slits for tape, trace of red wax. Address autograph:

This lett*re* *be delyu*er*ed to Thom*as* Fissh, p*rayng *you delyu*ere *this said* lettre *to Will*iam *Worcestr*e, *being with Syr John Forstall.*
P*er* *John Crop.*

The approximate date appears from this letter's relation to the one that follows, which it preceded by a short time; see the Headnote, and further reference there.

Unprinted.

Right hertily and welbylouyd, I recomaunde me vn-to yow, c*er*tifying yow that I laboured for yow the Friday aft*er* you*re* ridyng oute of Bristowe, like as y p*ro*mised to yow. First I ded yo*ur* erau*ntes* to Sir Nicoll of Glassinbyry, *and* he comaundid hym to yow. ⌜*And*⌝ as for the mater that ye spake to hym of, he wyll spede hit in all the haste that he may at the tokyn that ye spake to hym of, a tabyll of augrym, els a boke of augrym, els an ast*er*leber*e*. Y wote neu*er* whether it is of this thre ⌜that S*er* John Glassinbury shuld send hym⌝.[1] But neu*er*thelat*er*, he did me grete cher*e* *and* grete cost for ȝour*e* sake. Forsoth, he yaf me and ij other men ⟨. . .⟩[2] at a tayler*e* is house.

And then a-morow aft*er*, I wente to Wellis and spake w*ith* Edmond Wexchaundeler*e*, and he seid me that Syr Thom*as* Louel is fader*e* was a sqwier*e*, *and* Syr Thom*as* Louel had a sone deyed at Bryanston by sides

[7] *No space.* [8] and thys *canc.* [9] at w *canc.* [10] ad *canc.*

969. [1] *In margin, with caret mark in body of text.*
[2] *Five or six words thoroughly erased.*

Bruton. *And* then he seid me if that y wold go to Brianston, that I shulde speke with olde John Rogg*er*, and he wolde tell me moch mor*e* of that awnsatry. And fro Wellis I went to Clifdon, and ther*e* y made a steyno*ur* that went with me to marke oute this armes[3] that was lord of[4] Clifdon, *and* his wif, *and* y wrote the sc*ri*ptur*e* that was vp-on her*e* toumbe. *And* as ye like this, send me word, *and* y wylle laboure to Brianston for mor*e* enqueraunce of this mat*er*is.

And as of other*e* mat*er* to M*ayster* Rauf Hoby, I sought hym the Wennysday in the same wike that ye went, *and* he was out of Brystow. But y wyll nat for-yete non of ȝour*e* erant*es*, *and* as hastyly as I may þey shal be do. Mor*e* ou*er*, the[5] Wennysday ⌜after⌝ that yo*ur* brother resseyuyd yo*ur* lett*er*, I spake w*ith* Mayst*er* Hoby as for ij queyers, as that ⌜lett*er*⌝ made mencion, *and* he seid me his bokes ⌜wer*e*⌝ remevid of his cha*u*mbr*e*, for a lady that lay in his cha*u*mbr*e*, like as he told yow. But he seid me that it shuld be redy ⌜lokid vp⌝ in that wike. Also, he g*ra*unte me the copye of Wallens *De vita* et *doctrina philosoforu*m, also the queier*e* of Oved, *De vetula*, *De remedio moris*, *De arte amande*, *and* of the verse vp-on Boicius.

And then went y the Thursday to Glassinbury ayen to Syr Nicholl, *and* so p*ur*posed me to come by Blandford *and* Bruton, to speke with old John Rogg*er*[6] for mor*e* enqu⟨erau*n*⟩ce[7] of this mat*er*s a-for*e*seid. Then made y my letter*e* *and* sent hit to your*e* ⌜brother⌝ with this scochyn ⟨. . .⟩d[8] in this seid lett*er*. For Silly Loder*e* made hym redy to London ward*es* the Sat*er*day aft*er* *and* no ro⟨. . .⟩d[9] as sone as I have spedde of my other*e* mat*er*s ye shall haue redy awnswer*e* by lett*er* in al⟨l the haste th⟩at y may.

Wryten in grete hast the[10] [day of] May. No mor*e* to yow at this tyme, ⟨but the⟩ Holy Trinité kepe yow. Amen.

And I besech yow hertyly, co*m*maund ⟨me vnto May⟩st*er* Fissh *and* his wif, my good dame, and wite of hym if [I] shal bryng my son*n*e whe⟨n. . .⟩[11] shendith hym at home.

It*em*, yo*ur* brother delyu*er*ed me xx[d].

⟨. . . JOHN CROP⟩[12]

[3] *A coloured drawing of an escutcheon, with* Arma Louell *written on the back is f. 20 of MS. Add. 99.*
[4] his *canc.* [5] wr *canc.* [6] and *canc.*
[7] *A portion of the sheet approx. 2 ins long by ½ in. < 1½ in. wide is torn away from this point to the foot, carrying off parts of the text.*
[8] *One word (?* enclosed*) gone.* [9] *Two or three words gone.*
[10] *Line left incomplete.* [11] *Four or five words gone.*
[12] *Remainder of foot of sheet torn away, but traces of tops of letters of subscription and signature visible.*

970. From John Crop to William Worcester

1449, 2 June

Oxford, Magdalen College, Add. 99 (Lovel Papers), f. 22. $8\frac{1}{2} \times 7\frac{3}{8}$ in. Autograph.

Dorse: Continuation of text. Marks of folding, slits for tape, trace of red wax. Address autograph, partially torn away:

This 〈. . .〉 *Thomas Fissh* 〈. . .〉*ng in London* 〈. . .〉 *praying hym to d*〈*elyu*er〉*e this seid lett*er *to Will*iam 〈*Wor*〉*cestr*e, *beyng w*it*h S*er *John Forstalle.*

The genealogical research described by the writer in this letter and in no. 969, written shortly before it, was commissioned by William Worcester during a visit to Somerset during April or early May 1449 (Magdalen College, Fastolf Paper 42, membr. 2, as cited by Lewis, 'Sir John Fastolf's Lawsuit over Titchwell', p. 12). Whitsun in that year fell on 1 June.

Unprinted.

Right hertly and welbilouyd, I recomaunde me to yow, c*er*tifiyng that I haue bene at Glastynbury with Sir Nicholl, and spake to hym of the evidens*es*[1] that ye desired to haue. And he seid me that he couth gete none, for he hadde enqwerid ther*e*-aft*er* in the Abbey. And then he seid me if ther*e* wer*e* eny inquisicion with in iiij yher*e*, or v yher*e*, or vj yher*e*, that it myght be getyn, els not, for her clerkis kepith it no leng*er*. And then he sende me to Dan Thom*as* Braban, at the tokyn that ye sent hym, a penner *and* an hynkehorn, by S*er* Nicholl. And so y did my erau*nt*e*s* to hym as for this evidens*es*. And, forsoth, he did me gode cher*e* for your*e* sake. And then he spake to Dan Hew Forst*er*, and to the Abbot is kerver*e*, but he wulde not be hasty vp-on this seid mater*es*, by cause it shuld be kepte secrete, and he made me to tary at Glastynbury fro Thorsday in to Monday aft*er*. And ȝit in all this tyme y had no knowlich. And then Dan Thom*as* Braban seid me that he wolde sende me redy worde and knowlich by wrytyng to Bristow with in iij or iiij dayes aft*er*.

And fro thens y went to Wellys, and fro Wellys to Frome, and ther*e* y enquerid of agid men. And one seid me that ther*e* was a Sher*e*thorsday was xxxvij wynt*er*s that the Lorde Lovel made a-sawte a-ȝenst Frome, and that same lord had ij doughtris; that one dought*er* was weddid to S*er* Ric*hard* Stafford, and the other dought*er* was weddid to S*er* Jam*us* of Vrmoth. And the yong Lord Talbot weddid S*er* Jam*us* of Vrmowth is sister, but wher*e* that lord deyed they couth tel me ⸢no⸣ redy trouth. And fro Frome y went to Mellis, and by the wey thiderwardis y met with a baker*e* that dwellid som tyme in Glastynbury, and he tolde that ther*e* was a lorde that was callid Lorde Louel the Rich, and he had ij douȝtris; and that one dought*er* was weddid to a knyght that was callid S*er* Gie the Bryan, and he died in Gloucestr*e* shir*e*, but in whate towne he couth not tell me.

970. [1] *Long* s + er *abbrev. for pl. inflection.*

And in eu*er*y place wher*e* that y laboured for this seid mat*er* y myght not fynde iij men ne ij men yn one tale, but eu*er*y man haue dyu*er*s talis. And so y wote neu*er* after whom to wryte the redy trouth. ⟨There⟩for*e*[2] y taried somdele the leng*er* aft*er* my comyng home for the wrytyng of this seid lett*er*, for to haue redy wordis ⟨. . .⟩yng[3] from Dan Thom*a*s Braban of Glastynbury, and ȝit y had non. Wher*e* for y be-sech yow to holde me excuse⟨d. . .an⟩d[4] y wist wher*e* to haue redy knowlych of this seid mat*er*e y wolde do my p*ar*te ther*e*-to, they y shuld go a c mile.

⟨No mo⟩r*e* to yow[5] at this [tyme], but the Holy Trinité kepe yow body and soule. Wryten at Bristow the Wennysday to-for*e* ⟨. . .⟩.[6]

By yo*ur* owne s*er*uau*n*t JOHN CROP

It*em*, your*e* brother*e* Thom*a*s A⟨. . .w⟩hen[7] y wente to Glastynbury xx^{d} in money. But for soth, y spend mor*e*, for y was oute vjj dayes, that is to ⟨sey fro Thorsda⟩y in to Wennysday aft*er*, for y come home Ascension Eve.[8]

It*em*, ferthermor*e*, I resseyuyd your*e* lett*er* that ye sent me last, the which l*ett*r*e* made mencion to haue knowlych whose doughter*e* was the knyght*es* is wif that I sent yow the armys ⌜of⌝; and that the skucchon shuld be departed in the lift side. And that y axid of my peynt*er*, *and* he seid, weny*n*g to hym, it was wel y-nough, for he had grete hast *and* litel siȝt ther*e* of; wher*e* for*e* it shall be sayed aȝhen, the trowth. Also, to spye of Rogg*er* of Bridport of this mat*er*is a-for*e*seid, and at Castelcarye, Northbarow, Sowthbarowe *and* Blakeford &c. And so y p*ur*posed me at the wrytyng of this to say onys aȝen to haue somwhate bett*er* knowlech, if it may be.

Wryten in hast the morow vp-on Witsonday, for y resseyuyd your*e* lett*er* a Wytsonday at evyn.

P*er* man*us* Joh*ann*i Crop.

971. From WILLIAM TAILBOYS to VISCOUNT BEAUMONT Probably 1449, 20 August

Add. 34888, f. 35. $9\frac{1}{2} \times 9\frac{1}{2}$ in. In an unidentified clerk's hand.

Dorse: Marks of folding, slits for tape, remains of red wax seal. Address in hand of letter:

To my right honorabull and *right wurshipful lord, my lord Viscont Beaumont.*

Roger Virgoe discussed this letter in the context of Tailboys's career in general, and in relation to his feuds with Lords Willoughby, Welles and Cromwell. The indictment of

[2] *A portion of the sheet approx.* $2\frac{1}{4}$ *ins long by* $\frac{1}{2}$ *in.* < $1\frac{1}{4}$ *ins wide is torn away from this point to the foot, carrying away parts of the text.*

[3] *One or two words gone.*

[4] *One or two words gone.*

[5] to yow *repeated.*

[6] *Two or three words gone.*

[7] *Three or four words gone.*

[8] *Remainder of text on dorse.*

Tailboys mentioned in the letter occurred in 1447, and by 18 November 1449 he was in custody in the Fleet prison; see 'William Tailboys and Lord Cromwell: Crime and Politics in Lancastrian England', *East Anglian Society in the Political Community of Late Medieval England* (Norwich, 1997), pp. 287–307 (at pp. 289–90 and 305, n. 35).

F. iii, p. 182. G. 75/100.

Right honorabull and my right wurchipfull lord, I reco*m*aund me vnto yo*ur* gode lordship with all my s*er*uice, eu*er*more des*er*eng to here of yo*ur* p*ro*sp*er*ité and welfare, the which I p*ra*y God encres and co*n*tynue to his plesur, and aft*er* yo*ur* ovne hert*es* desire; thankyng you of the gode lordship þ*a*t ye haue shewid me at all tymes, beseching you alway of gode co*n*tynuance.

Plesid yo*ur* gode lordship to be remembred how afore this tyme Hugh Wythom hath said he wold be in rest *and* peese w*ith* me, *and* not to maligne agayn me oþ*er*wise þan lawe and right wold. That notwithstandyng, vpon Munday last past, he and iij men w*ith* hi*m* come into a s*er*u*au*nt hous of myn in Boston, cald Willia*m* Shirref, and þ*er* as he sete at his werke, stroke him vpon the hede *and* in the body with a dagg*er*, *and* wondet him sore, *and* pulled him out of his hous *and* set him in p*re*son w*ith*out any cause resonabull, or w*ith*out writ or any oþ*er* p*ro*cesse shewid vnto him. And þat, me semes, long*es* not for hi*m* to do; bot as he sais, he is endited. And as yo*ur* gode lordship knawes wele, I and all my s*er*u*au*nt*es* are in like wise. Bot *and* any man shuld haue don hit, it long*es* other to the shirreff or to yo*ur* baliff, as I conceyve. And oþ*er* cause he had non to him, as fer as I kan knawe, but alonly for the malissiousnes þ*a*t he hath vnto me, ne I kan think non oþ*er* bot it is so.

And now, yistre nyght, my lord Welles come to Boston w*ith* iiij^{xx} horses, *and* ⌜in⌝ þe mornyng foloyng toke hym out of p*re*son, sayng afore all peple, 'Fals thefe, þ*o*u shall be hanget, *and* as mony of thy maistre men as may be goten', as yo*ur* s*er*u*au*nt John Abbot kan report vnto yo*ur* gode lordship; *and* hath taken him away with him to Tatessall, what to do w*ith* him I kan not say, bot, as I suppose, to haue him to Lincoln Castell.

Wherfore I besech yo*ur* gode lordship in þis mat*er* to be my gode lord, and at it please yo*ur* gode lordship to write a[1] lett*er* to the kep*er*e of the Castell of Lincoln, þ*a*t it liked him to deliu*er* him out of p*re*son vndre a sufficient seurety had for him; for and thai may kepe him still be þis meyne, þai may take all the s*er*u*au*nt*es* þ*a*t I haue, and so I may do agayn in like wise.

And also, as I am enfo*ur*med, w*ith*out he be had out of p*re*son in hast, it will be right grevewis to hi*m* to heile of his hurt, he is so sore streken. And if þ*er* be any s*er*uice þ*a*t yo*ur*[2] gode lordship will co*m*aund me to do in any cuntré, plesid you to send me word, and it shal be done to my power*e*, w*ith* the g*ra*ce of God, which haue you, my right honorabull and wurshipfull lord, alway in his blessid kepyng.

971. [1] *No space.* [2] þ *written for* y.

Writen at Kyme vpon Wednesday next aft*er* Our*e* Ladi day the Assumpcion.

Also, plese yo*ur* gode lordship to wit, aft*er* þis lett*er* was made, þ*er* come a man fro Tatessall into my fenne which ogh me gode will, and be cause he wold not be holden suspect he speke w*ith* wemen which were mylkand kye, and bad þeme goo to a preest of myn to Dokdike, and bid him fast goo gif me warnyng how þ*a*t my lord Wilughby, my lord Cromwell and my lord Welles p*ur*posid þeme to set a sessions and hang þe said Willia*m* Shirreff, *and* þai myght bryng þ*er* entent abowte. And so as I *and* yo*ur* s*er*ua*u*nt John Abbot stode to-ged*er* þe prest come *and* gaf me warnyng herof, which I trist for my worship yo*ur* gode lordship wold not shuld happen, for it wer*e* to me the grettest shame þ*a*t myght falle. Bot *and* it plese yo*ur*[3] gode lordship to write to all yo*ur* s*er*ua*u*nt*es* in þis[4] cuntré, þat þai will be redy vpon a day warnyng to come when I send þeme word. I trist to God þai shal not hang him agayn the lawe, bot I, w*ith* help of yo*ur* gode lordship, shall be abull to let hit.

By yo*ur* s*er*ua*u*nt WILLIA*M* TAILBOYS

972. From RICHARD, EARL OF WARWICK to SIR THOMAS TUDDENHAM Probably 1449, 2 November

Add. 43488, f. 22. $11\frac{1}{2} \times 8\frac{1}{4}$ in. In an unidentified clerk's hand.

Dorse: Marks of folding, slits for tape, remains of red wax seal. Address in hand of letter:

*To owr*e *ryght trusty and welbelouyd frend Ser Tho*mas *Todenham.*

Gairdner suggested that this letter might date from soon after Richard Neville succeeded to his earldom in 1449, at which time he was in London attending Parliament. Tuddenham's career entered a turbulent period after Cade's rebellion in June 1450, when he lost the keepership of the King's Wardrobe, and his lodgings in London were looted in December of that year (see Wedgwood, *History of Parliament: Biographies*, pp. 880–1).

F. i, p. 184. G. 73/98.

Ryght trusty and welbelouyd frend, we gr*e*te 3ou[1] well, hertely desyryng to her*e* of 3o*ure* welfar*e*, which we p*ra*y God p*re*s*er*ue to 3o*ure* hert*es* desyr*e*. And yf yt please 3ou to her*e* of owr*e* welfar*e*, we wer*e* in goud hele atte þe[2] makyng of þis[3] lettre, p*ra*yng 3ou hertely þ*a*t 3e wyll co*n*sid*er*e owr*e* message, which owr*e* chapleyn Mayst*er* Robert Hoppton shall enforme 3ou of. For*e*, as God knowyth, we haue gr*e*t besynesse dayly, and has had her*e* by for*e* þis tym.

Wherfor*e* we p*ra*y 3ou to co*n*syd*er*e þe p*ur*chas þ*a*t we haue made wyth on

[3] þ *written for y.* [4] sh *canc.*

972. [1] u *superscript, and so in other instances below.* [2] e *superscript, and so in other instances below.* [3] is *superscript, and so in other instances below.*

John Swysshcotte, sq*uire*, of Lyncoln shyre, of lxxx *and* viij lj. by ȝer*e*, wher*e*uppon vs must pay þe last payment þe Moneday nexte aftyr*e* Seynt Martyn[4] day, which *sum*ma ys cccc and lviij lj. Wherfor*e* we p*ra*y ȝou wyth all owr*e* herte þ*a*t ȝe wyll lend vs x lj. or*e* twenty, or*e* what þe seyd Mayst*er* Robert want*es* of hys payment, as we may do for*e* ȝou in tym for*e* to com. And we shall send yt ȝou ageyn afor*e* Newȝer*es*day, wyth þe g*ra*ce of God, as we ar*e* trew knyght. For*e* þ*er* is noma*n* in ȝo*ure* cuntré þ*a*t we myght wryght to for*e* trust so well as vn-to ȝou, for*e* as we be enformyd ȝe be owr*e* well wyller*e*, and so we p*ra*y ȝou of goud co*n*tynuaunce. Wherfor*e* we p*ra*y ȝou þ*a*t ȝe co*n*syd*er*e owr*e* entent of this mony as ȝe wyll[5] þ*a*t we do for*e* ȝou in tym to com, as God knowyth, who haue ȝou in hys kepyng.

Wreten atte London on All Salwyn day wyth-jnne owr*e* loggyng jn þe G*ra*y Frer*es* wyth-jnne Newgate.

RIC*HARD*, ERLE WARWYKE

973. From SIR WILLIAM WILLY to THOMAS HOWES: copy — Probably 1449, December

Oxford, Magdalen College, Titchwell 208/1. $11\frac{1}{2} \times 3\frac{1}{2}$ in., tied to Titchwell 208/2, no. 974. Hand unidentified.

Dorse: Note added in William Worcester's hand: 'Cop*ia* l*itte*re Wylly de man*er*io Tychewell ext*ratum* man*us* Joh*ann*is Fastolf'.

On 14 December 1448 farm of Titchwell had been granted by the Crown to Sir Edward Hull, who went on to sub-let the manor to Sir William Willy shortly afterwards (see no. 964, Headnote, and further reference there). In late December of that year 'yong Wylly' (presumably the writer's son) had appeared at Titchwell and served notice on Fastolf's tenants to quit (no. 964, lines 30–1). This letter speaks of the King having assigned the manor to Hull 'as for the yere passed', and may therefore be placed approximately twelve months later.

Unprinted.

Right wurshipfull s*er*, I comaund me to yow &c. And as I vndrestand be report, ye haue ⌜be⌝ at Tychewell, in the maner*e*, and ther*e* sesed suche good*es* as ben w*ith*in; m*er*ueilyng moche ye wold do so, knowyng that suche ent*er*esse that S*er* Edward Hull had, he had gr*a*unted me.[1] And yf it had touched your*e* p*er*soon, I wold for olde aqueynt*a*unce not so str*a*ungely a demenyd me vnto yow. But, s*er*, as for the yere passed, the Kyng hath assigned it, and I am bounde for the payment, the whiche I am loth to lese. But, s*er*, yf my maist*er* Fastolf haue bett*er* cause to enjoye it than I, he shall not fynde but that I woll do hym s*er*uyce, yf he geve me cause. God hath so

[4] y *written over* e.

[5] þ*a*t weldo for*e* *partly canc. and subpuncted.*

973. [1] *Note to left of first two lines in hand of no. 974:* L*itt*e*re* Will*elm*o Willy, Thom*e* Howys cl*ericus* missus usq*ue* Brancastr*e*.

vesite me, I thanke hym of grace, I may neither goo ner*e* ryde, and yf I myght I wold come to yow. But yf I may haue that right woll, I wold hold me content &c. And I am not so maist*er*les but suche a[2] man shall haue it as shall ocupye it. I pray yow late me haue a bill from yow &c.

974. From Thomas Howes to Sir William Willy: copy Probably 1449, December

Oxford, Magdalen College, Titchwell 208/2. 11½ × 3½ in., tied to Titchwell 208/1, no. 973. Hand unidentified.

Dorse: miscellaneous undated accounts relating to Fastolf's manors.

This is a file copy of Howes's immediate reply to no. 973.
Unprinted.

Respons*io* l*itter*e Will*elm*o Willy, Thome Howys cl*eric*us miss*us* &c.

Worshipfull s*er*, I comaunde me to yow. And this nyght I have receyved a l*ett*re from yow by Burgeys of Tichewell, *and* in p*ar*tye vnderstande the contynew þer-of,[1] wher inne amonges other I conceyve ye thenk myn demenyng ther*e* strangely, *and* other wyse than I aught. S*er*, myn gou*er*-naunce hath not ben so as ye take hit, as I trust ye, or any[2] ⌜other⌝ weel advysed man, the mater take as hit is shal thenk. And there as ye wryte that, and ⌜hit⌝[3] hadde [touched] yo*ur*e p*er*sone, ye wold for olde acqueyntaunce not so straungely a demened yow vn-to me: s*er*, I have vnderstande yo*ur*e vysitac*io*n of sekenesse, of wheche I am ryght sorye, *and* for that cause, if I myght have teryed, fayn I wold have sen yow, in good feyth; but in this cas, as the mater standeth, I aught not. And as for the resydew of yo*ur*e l*ett*re, I trust that the mater shal drawe to suche conclusion as ryght lawe *and* good concyens require. And God kepe yow. In hast this same nyght.

Yo*ur*e S*er* Thomas Howys

To the worshipfull S*er* Will*iam* Willy.

[2] *No space.*

974. [1] þ *in the form of* y. [2] *MS.* or ar any [3] *Over the canc.*

975. From THOMAS HAKEBORN to SIR JOHN FASTOLF
Probably 1449–50

Oxford, Magdalen College, Add. 99 (Lovel Papers), f. 18. $11\frac{1}{2} \times 5\frac{1}{2}$ in. Hand unidentified.

Dorse: Marks of folding, slits for tape, trace of red wax. Address in hand of letter:

To my wurshipful and *reu*er*ent lord S*er *John Fastolf this l*ett*re be delyered.*

The writer is mentioned on several occasions between 1434 and 1454 as one of Fastolf's leading tenants at Castle Combe, where he evidently held some sort of official position (G. P. Scrope, *Castle Combe*, pp. 212 ('officiarius'), 216, 240, 243). His name also appears in the address of no. 1030 of 16 March 1456, which Worcester wished him to deliver locally. There is no explicit connection between the present letter and the matter of the Lovel ancestry and the Titchwell lawsuit, with which all of the other letters and papers in Magdalen Add. 99 are concerned (see no. 964, Headnote, and further reference there). However, William Lord Lovel held a knight's fee at Castle Combe from 1426, and still did so in 1454 (*Castle Combe*, p. 218). Hakeborn may therefore have been involved in enquiries about Lovel's antecedents at the same time as similar investigations were going forward elsewhere during 1449–50.
Unprinted.

Most wurshipful and reu*er*ent lord, I recomawnde me vn-to you in the lowlokest wyse that y can or may, as for a por*e* ten*au*nt*e* and a s*er*aunt*e* of your*es*; at all tymys doyng you to vndurstond, as twechyng to the mat*er* that ye send me for*e*, y trust to God hit be y-do vn-to your*e* entent as hit is ther*e*. And that Thom*a*s Nortyn of Brystow wul record, for hit was y-made be his counsell and his avyse. And Thomas Nortyn wul be with you this weke or the next weke aft*er* the writyng of this l*ett*re, and he wull enforme you, as hit is plesyng to allmyghty God, and to you &c.

I-write at Castelcomb the Monday to-for*e* Seynt Clement is day.

By your*e* por*e* ten*au*nt*e* *and* s*er*vant*e* TH. HAKEBORN

976. From THOMAS HUNTLEY to HENRY FYLONGLEY
Probably 1450

Oxford, Magdalen College, Add. 99 (Lovel Papers), f. 16. $11\frac{1}{2} \times 5$ in. In an unidentified professional-looking hand.

Dorse: Marks of folding, holes for thread, remains of red wax seal. Address in hand of letter:

To my wor⌜*schep*⌝*fful* ser *Fynynglé, beynge w*ith *my lorde of Wylteschere.*

The writer was an elderly relative by marriage of the Lovels, into whose antecedents Fastolf's agents continued to enquire, in connection with the defence of his possession of Titchwell. See the Headnote to no. 964, and Lewis, as cited there, pp. 14–15.
Unprinted.

976. *From Thomas Huntley to Henry Fylongley, probably 1450*

Ryht worschepffull s*er*, I recom*m*maunde ⌜me⌝ to yow, *and* do yow to vndresto*n*de ther was a man of yowris w*ith* me late tyme a-go. *And* he seyde me that ye wolde fayn wete of the byrthe of Thom*as* Louell, *and* how nye kynne he was to the olde Lorde Louell, *and* what wer*e* hys armys. *And*, s*er*, y enformyde hym as wel as y can, *and* her*e* y sende yow his armys. *And* if ther wer*e* any seruyse that y can do to yowr*e* plesau*n*ce, y wolde do hit w*ith* all myn herte. The holy Trenyté kepe yow.

Yowr*e* man T. HUNTLEY

977. From JOHN AUSTELL to HENRY FYLONGLEY
Probably 1450, 14 January

Oxford, Magdalen College, Add. 99 (Lovel Papers), f. 7. $11\frac{1}{2} \times 4\frac{1}{2}$ in. Hand unidentified.

Dorse: Marks of folding, slits for tape, trace of red wax. Address in hand of letter:

Right trusty and entyer belouyd soon Harry Fylungley.

John Austell (d. 1463) occupied various offices in the west country, and was at this time sheriff of Somerset and Dorset; see Wedgwood, *History of Parliament, Biographies*, p. 30. Henry Filongley (Wedgwood, p. 325) was Fastolf's 'nephew' by marriage, keeper of the writs in the court of Common Pleas, and one of his principal counsellors. The letter belongs with several others of early 1450, concerned with Fastolf's investigations into the Lovel family's previous ownership of his manor of Titchwell. See the Headnote to no. 964, and Lewis, as cited there, p. 13.

Unprinted.

Right worshipfull *and* entyer belouyd soone, y me recoumaunde, p*ra*yng God for his endeles mercy you to p*re*serue to his pleser, *and* after your owne hertys desire. S*er*e,[1] y haue receyued a l*ett*re of yourys, willyng me to sende the pedygr*é* of ⌜S*er*e⌝ Thom*as* Lovell to you. So helpe me God *and* holydome, y wote ner*e* wher*e* hit ys be come. Wherfore, this ij dayes y shalle make a serche a-monge all the evidence that y haue, to fynnde ⌜h*i*t⌝.[2] And yf y fynnde h*i*t not, y shalle ryde to my lady Dynh*a*m, that was doughter to the worthi Lord Lovell in Kynge Richard ys daye, and to haue the informac*i*on of hir, and so to sende h*i*t you.

And as towchand S*er*e Thom*as* Lovell of Clevedon, y shalle do enquer*e* and sende you worde. Nertheles, and yf ye speke with S*er*e Edward Hull, or with Wake, that ye luste to enquer*e* of them, for they haue wedded the doughters and heyres of the sayde S*er*e Thomas Lovell. For, sone, so God helpe me *and* holydome, y hadde leuyr then xx nobeles that y wyst where h*i*t

977. [1] *Second* e *superscript, and so in instances of this word below.*
[2] *MS.* h^t *and so below.*

wer*e*, to the pleser bothe of my lord *and* of you, consideryng my p*ro*mysse a-fore; the wiche haue you vnder his p*ro*tecc*io*n.

Wreten at Churchehill the xiiij daye of Januar*é*.

Your fader JOHN AUSTELL

978. From SIR JOHN FASTOLF to HOWES, COLE and SHIPDAM — 1450, 7 March

Add. 39848, f. 3. 12 × 17 in. William Barker's hand, subscription autograph.

Dorse: Marks of folding and slits for tape. Address in Barker's hand:

*To my ryght trusty and weel beloved frendez S*er *Thomas Howys, clerk, Will*iam *Cole and Watkyn Shipdam be this* lett*re delu*ered.

Dated.

G. 79/104 (abstract).

Ryght trusty and weel be-lovyd frendez I gr⟨. . .⟩ inne a bille in the p*ar*lem*en*t of the extorc*io*ns don⟨. . .⟩ anno xvij hederward and every mater in a ⟨. . .⟩ fynde by my bok*es* there and what mynusyng ⟨. . .⟩ bynde me to the Kyng and offer hym that ⌜if⌝ o⟨. . .⟩ ell*es* to make good to the Kyng of as moche as ⟨. . .⟩ as hit is of trought and that I have hit here ⟨. . .⟩ were slowthed and dreve foorth over this p*ar*l⟨. . .⟩ wrongously as weel in the duchie F⟨. . .⟩enh*a*m as ⟨. . .⟩ this same mater*es* lete hem be sent heder also as ⟨. . .⟩ an homage cleymed for the maner of Drayton *and* ⟨. . .⟩ Fyrst[1] how many shep were distreyned at Drayton for ⟨. . .⟩ of kepyng and what the hors and cart were worth that the p*ar*son lost for th⟨. . .⟩.

It*em*, what the mater of travers be-twen the Lady Bardolf and me for Huntyn⟨. . .⟩ as weel at Norwiche as other plac*es* &c.

It*em*, as for Cheveres mater in Blyclyng, what that mater cost and stood me vpon ⟨. . .⟩ handes by replevyn makyng w*ith* what the sewt cost me for the acc*io*n of trespas w⟨. . .⟩[2] and diffendyng[3] the pleynt*es* attained a-yenst my ten*au*nt*es* officeres and me.

It*em*, for Hiklyng, for the amunte that I shuld have there, how longe hit hath be restreyned and not payed and what cost*es* þ*er*⟨in⟩[4] I have boorn in the seute of the same mater &c.

It*em*, of the maner of Tichewell, Bradwell *and* Beyton, what decaye I have hadde in theym, and by how longe tyme they have be ought of my hand*es* &c.

978. *A large part of the top right hand corner of the sheet has been torn off, carrying away much of the second portions of the first eighteen lines.*

[1] *This and the remaining clauses preceded by a capitulum mark.*

[2] *Remainder of text substantially intact from this point.*

[3] *First* d *miswritten.*

[4] *Edge of page gone.* þ *written in form of* y *throughout.*

It*em*, for the homage cleymed of the maner of Heynforth, what I have payed for the respyte of the same &c.

It*em*, to speke w*ith* Nicollas Bokkyng, to wete of hym to whom the c li. for Busshop was payed, that he wryte to me the mater a-longe as hit was of trought, for he payed the seyd money and a-compted þ*er*fore &c.

It*em*, for the vexing of Rob*er*t Blyclyng for Dynn, what hit cost hym, and wat I was disadvayled by in the sale of my corn.

It*em*, that ye[5] sende me alle other materes concernyng the seyd causes as ye wold aunswere, so that I be not sha⟨me⟩d ner reproched in my articles puttyng inne &c.

It*em*, where-as that Broun ocupyeth Castre and Wynt*er*ton, I wold have that hit shal be ocupyed by ij sadde men, for hit is to moche for on to ocupye weel as hit aught to be, and in the same wyse at Heylesdon and Drayton.

It*em*, that ye for-gete not to sende me aunswere what that Lampyt hath don to my mater, and wheder ye fynde hym frendly to me or nought, and ther-after I wole thank hym her*e*-after &c.

It*em*, as to my shippys, þei beeth bothe come in savetee, blyssed be God, who have yow in hese kepyng.

Wrete*n* in hast at Londo*n* the vij day of Marche Anno xxviij^{o} R. H. vj^{ti}.

J. FASTOLFE

979. From SIR JOHN FASTOLF to HOWES, COLE and SHIPDAM 1450, 16 April

Add. 39848, f. 4. $8\frac{1}{4} \times 4\frac{3}{4}$ in. Copy by Blomefield.

Copied on a blank strip taken from a piece of correspondence addressed (on the dorse) to Blomefield. At the head of the text: 'Gave y^{s} original L^{r} of Sr John's to Sr Andr. Fountain'. The original, if it has survived, remains untraced.

To S*er Thomas Howys, parson of Castellcombe, Willia*m *Cole*[1] and *Watkyn Shipdam.*

G. 82/107 (abstract).

S*er* p*ar*son, I pray you spede the aunsuer of my letters; in especiall to sende me yn all haste to the[2] utmost knoulege of all grevaunces, extorc*i*ons *and* damages don to me by John Heydon thys xiij yers, whych my servaunts *and* the mynystrs boks can help. Reme*m*br ye have sent me ye costs of the plees, but I have not p*ar*ticlerly declared how oft I have be*n* distreyned wrongly by ye enforcing of ye s^{d} Heydon, and hou so many other causes doon to me

[5] seye *canc.*

979. [1] *MS.* Coke [2] *No space.*

wrongly that I toke never plee in the maters, because the world was[3] allwey set after his rule. *And* as for I w^{d} have engroced ⌜upp⌝ my byll long ere this tyme, that y^{e}[4] sent upp this matter before thys tyme as I desyred, whych noyeth me in my servaunts gretely. And for in all my maters to do your gode diligence, God have you in hys kepyng.

Wryt at London xvj day of Aprill A^{o} xxviij R. r. H. vj.

J. FASTOLF

Serche ye the accompts of Drayton, Heylysdon, Laxthorp, Guton, Blyklyng, Lody*n*lond, Castr &c theese xiij yers, in *titulo expens*is *et forinsec*es or *partic*ul*o allocaciorum*.[5] *And* I pray you to take my lettres to the best entent, *and* tendryth y^{m} to my p*ro*fytt as my grete trust is in you.

980. From WILLIAM, DUKE OF SUFFOLK to his son JOHN: copy Nominally 1450, 30 April

Add. 43488, f. 12. 11½ × 8 in. In an unidentified clerk's hand.

Dorse: Originally blank. The sixteenth-century hand that annotated many items in the Paston correspondence (see Part I, pp. xxxi–xxxiii) has added 'The Copie of a notable l*ett*re written by the duke of Suff*olk* to his Sonne, yeving hym therein very good counseile.'

London, College of Arms MS 48, containing historical memoranda by William Worcester and others, records that Suffolk set sail into exile from Ipswich on 30 April 1450; see J. Stephenson, ed., *Letters and Papers Illustrative of the Wars of the English in France* (Rolls Series, 1861–4), ii, p. 767. How and when a copy of the letter to his son came into the possession of the Pastons does not appear.

F. i, p. 32. G. 91/117.

My dere and only welbeloued sone, I beseche Oure Lord in heven, þe[1] maker of alle the world, to blesse you and to sende you eu*er* grace to loue hym and to drede hym; to þe which, as ferre as a fader may charge his child, I bothe charge you and prei you to sette alle youre spirites and wittes to do and to knowe his holy lawes and co*m*maundement*es*, by the which ye shall, w*ith* his grete m*er*cy, passe alle þe grete tempestes and troubles of þis wrecched world. And þ*a*t also, wetyngly, ye do no thyng, for love ner drede of any erthely ceature, þ*a*t shuld displese hym. And þ*er*e as any freelté maketh you to falle, besecheth hys m*er*cy soone to calle you to hym ayen w*ith* repentaunce, satisfacc*io*n and contric*io*n ⟨o⟩f[2] ⟨y⟩oure herte never more in will to offende hym.

[3] allwey *canc.*
[4] *Followed by one letter not clearly formed.*
[5] *The abbreviations intended in the preceding words are not all clear.*

980. [1] e *superscript, and so in other instances of this word below.*
[2] *Fenn described the MS. as chafed and illegible in places, and it has continued to deteriorate, with holes here and below. Unless otherwise indicated, the readings given in angle brackets are his.*

Secoundly, next hym aboue alle erthely thyng, to be trewe liege man in hert, in wille, in thought, i⟨n⟩ dede vnto þe Kyng oure alder most high and dradde soue*re*ygne lord, to whom bothe ye and I been so moche bounde too; chargyng you, as fader can and may, rather to die þan to be þe contrarye, or to knowe any thyng þ*a*t were ayenste þe welfare or p*ro*spe*r*ité of his most riall p*er*sone; but þ*a*t as ferre as youre body and lyf may strecche, ye lyve and die to defende it, and to lete his highnesse haue knowlache þ*er*of in alle þe haste ye can.

Thridly, in þe same wyse, I[3] charge you, my dere sone, alwey as ye be bounden by þe co*m*maundement of God, to do, to love, to worshepe youre lady and moder, and also þ*a*t ye obey alwey hyr co*m*maundement*es*, and to beleve hyr councelles and advyses in alle youre werk*es*, þe which dredeth[4] not but shal be best and trewest to you. And yef any other body wold stere you to þe contrarie, to flee þe councell in any wyse, for ye shall fynde it nought and evyll.

Forthe⟨ly . . . ⟩[5] as ferre as fad⟨e⟩r may and can, I charge you in any wyse to flee þe co*m*pany and councel of proude men, of coveitowse men and of flateryng men, the ⟨more esp⟩ecially ⟨and⟩ myghtily to withstonde hem, and not to drawe ne to medle w*ith* hem, w*ith* al youre myght and power; and to drawe to you and ⟨to⟩ youre com⟨pany good an⟩d v*er*tuowse ⟨m⟩en, and suche as ben of good conu*er*sac*i*on and of trouthe, and be them shal ye neu*er* be deseyved ner repente you of. ⟨Moreover never follow⟩ youre owne witte in no wyse, but in alle youre werkes of suche folk*es* as I wryte of above axeth youre advyse a⟨nd counsell;⟩ and doyng thus, w*ith* þe m*er*cy of God, ye shall do right well and[6] lyve in right moche worship and grete hert*es* rest and ease. And I ⟨shall⟩[7] be to you as g⟨o⟩od lord and fader as my hert can thynke.

And last of alle, as hertily and as lovyngly as ever fader blessed his child in erthe, I yeve you þe blessyng of Oure Lord and of me, whiche of his infynite m*er*cy encrece you in alle vertu and good lyvyng; and þ*a*t youre blood may by his grace from kynrede to kynrede multeplye in this erthe to hys s*er*uise in suche wyse as, after þe departyng fro this wrecched world here, ye and thei may glorefye hym et*er*nally among*es* his aungelys in hevyn.

Wreten of myn hand, þe day of my dep*ar*tyng fro this land.

Youre trewe and lovyng fader, SUFFOLK

[3] *One minim canc.*

[4] *Second letter unclear.*

[5] *Fenn printed* Forthe[more] *but there are traces sufficient to suggest that the reading given here is more likely; there was evidently another word between* Forthely *and* as.

[6] le *canc.*

[7] *Fenn read* wyll, *but the lower parts of* sh *and* ll *are sufficiently visible.*

981. From SIR JOHN FASTOLF to THOMAS HOWES

1450, 7 May

Add. 39848, f. 5. $10\frac{3}{4} \times 8\frac{1}{4}$ in. Worcester's hand, subscription autograph.

Dorse: Marks of folding, slits for tape, traces of red wax. Address in Worcester's hand:

*To my welbelovyd frendys S*er *Thomas Howys, p*ars*on of Castellco*m*be beyng at Castr*e *by Iernmuth in haste.*

Dated.

G. 95/122 (abstract)

Trusty and welbelovyd frendys, I grete you well, and p*ra*yng yow to solicit and labour the expedic*i*on of my mater*es* comprysed in my l*ett*res sent to you seth[1] the fest of Pasch last passed to my moost proffyt and avaylle; and that ye send me word of all the dewe debt that Thomas Symmys may owe me, as[2] well for rent*es and* fermys gederyng vpp as for othyr foreyn debt*es* growyng to me by delyu*er*aunce of my wolles and makyng sale of hem, that I am not yhyt payd in Dedh*a*m.

And as to my mater of Rydlyngfeld *and* Hykel*yng*[3] that I hafe oft wryt vnto you for; seth it ys soo the world ys ch*a*unged gretely ouer it was, y pray you and charge you, p*ar*son, labour ye to my frendz Lampet *and* othyr*es* that ye can know may wyrk *and* do in the mater, so as I may com by aco*mpt* of theyr evidens*es*.[4] For know it for certeyn, that how be it the said P*ri*orasse sey that hyr evidens*es* be in the Duc of Suff*olk* kepyng or hys councell, the said Pryorasse hafe a boke wyth-ynne hyr gouu*er*n*an*ce in whych ys copied all theyr evidens*es*, whate-eu*er*e they sey or dissimile. And yff my lord Norwych ch*a*uncell*o*r or Maist*er* Popé lyked to hafe labo*ur*ed effectuelly in thys mater, as they promysed to me *and* seth to yow they wold hafe don, it had be sped long or thys tyme, for and it had be her oune mat*er* they had recuu*er*ed a syght *and* cop*é*[5] of all my mat*er* long or thys tyme. Yff ye hafe not reme*m*bred hem but slakly or not wayted vppon hem when tyme was, it caused he*m* to hafe thys mat*er* in lesse fauo*ur*. And for God ys sake sende me a gode aunsuer of thys.[6]

Item, yff an ordynat boke be made reme*m*bryng the delyu*er*aunce as well as the resseyt of all clothys, garment*es and* stuff that hath be delyu*er*ed in to my wardrobe, or to onye man ys gouu*er*n*au*nce, or sent hedr*e* by endentur*e*, that the said endentur*es* be engrosed in a boke; and as well such stuff as longyth to my wardrobe and ys noo endentur or bill wryt of it, as that stuff that ys wryt.

981. [1] *First letter miswritten.* [2] *No space.* [3] *MS.* Hykel *with barred* l.

[4] *Plural inflection represented by long* s + *the 'er' abbreviation, as occasionally elsewhere in Worcester's hand.*

[5] *Abbr. a dotted cirumflex over* p.

[6] *This sentence apparently added later, perhaps after the rest of the letter had been completed.*

It ys an thyng of grete charge, and I doubt me lest it ys but litill attended as it ought bee. And begynne your boke as ferre tyme as ye can and ought be don.

Item,[7] I hafe grete m*er*veylle that ye, ne none othyr of my s*er*u*au*ntz beyng of long tyme wyth me, hafe not ne can not sende me seuerell and partic*u*ler declarac*i*on, aft*er* the trouth ys or was, of the grete dam*m*ag*es* and hurt*es* don to me in especiall and to dyu*er*s of my ten*au*nt*es* thys x or xij yeer day by meynten*au*nce of myne adu*er*saryes &c, as I hafe sondry tymys wryt vnto you. A declar*aci*on of cost*es and* paym*entes* made in deffendyng certeyn of theym ye sent, but the cruell am*er*cym*entes* and dyu*er*s opp*re*ssions don to me, to my ten*auntes and* to my catell distreynyng how oft, ye sent me not no gode grounde hedr*e*to. I pray you take thys mat*er* somwhate bett*er* to hert. Also, to hafe a l*ett*re fro*m* Nicholas Bokkyng of the c li. payeng, to whom it was payd, I hafe none aunsuer &c, whych causyth me to kepe my bille of damag*es* stille vnput vpp yn youre deffaut; for had ye send me gode declarac*i*on *and* just of theese mater*es* I had put hem vpp in the lyffe tyme of hym that ys passed, whych had be more autentik. Hast ye the aunsuer of all my mater*es* vnaunsuered vtt*er*ly betyme &c.

Allmyghty God kepe you. Wryt at London vij day of Maij A° xxviij° r. r. H. vj .

J. FASTOLFE

982. From SIR JOHN FASTOLF to THOMAS HOWES

1450, 27 May

Add. 43488, f. 15. $10\frac{3}{4} \times 5\frac{3}{4}$ in. Worcester's hand, subscription autograph.

Dorse: Marks of folding, slits for tape, remains of red wax. Address in Worcester's hand:

To my trusty and welbelovyd frende Sir Thomas Howys, parson of Castellcombe.

Dated. Fenn (followed by Gairdner) printed only the postscript beneath Fastolf's signature.

F. i, p. 52. G. 98/125 (part).

Trusty and welbelovyd frende I grete you well. And forasmoch as I hafe late vndrestand that Thomas Fouler hath distreyned my ten*au*nt*es* in Blyclyng by her plowys for certeyn am*er*ciem*entes*[1] by the offic*er*s of South Herpyngh*a*m, and ye knou well that Lumno*ur* delyu*er*ed a wryt of *cerciorare* vnto Heydon to remeoffe the said am*er*ciem*entes*, and as I was enformed he said he wold obbey it, and now hys offic*er*s doth the contrarie; p*ra*yng you to comyn wyth

[7] Oyer *and* determin*er written to left by another hand.*

982. [1] of *canc.*

Thomas Grene and my lerned councell to see whate remedie may be in thys mater, and whethyr Fouler or onye othyr man ought distreyn w*it*h*ynne my lordshyp, ⌜consideryng the lordshyp that they hafe,⌝ and the remedie of it.

Allso, y vndrestand that I bere grete losse[2] to the decrese of cc shepe pasture yerlye, by lak of the ferme of Bryston londz and othyr londz &c, in my bayllye deffaut, and my shyppard gon from my s*er*vice; and y hafe none amendys ne remedie sett vppon it, whych ys in the deffaut of you and myne offic*er*s.

Allso, it ys said I pay for londez *and* pastur*es* to Lumno*ur*, whych parcell of the said londes longyth to me, and yhyt I hafe not all the londes whych I pay for to Lu*m*no*ur*, but ys occupied by Brampton and othyr there about; prayng and chargyng you that thys be remedied as ferre as ys in you, ⌜and as justice woll yefe you councell.⌝ I kepe not that ye shuld owe to moch fauo*ur* because ⌜of⌝ hys children beyng w*it*h you, for I wold that Jankyn Porter hafe that at ys hys, and yn lyke wyse I myne dewteez. As to the v m*arkes* to resseyve I hafe wryt to you myne entent; and that ye wolle I meoffe ⌜*and* councell⌝ Jankyn to owen myne ten*au*nt*es* gode wille as he[3] owght to do.

The p*ar*son of Brandeston was at a court of Blyclyng, and herd my ten*au*nt*es* compleyn of the grete hurt I bere of my pasture by deffaut of gode surveyeng, and the londz of Brystons owt of my hand in myne adu*er*saryes handz. That at may be amended I pray you. I wryte you an article for John Multon, as for recuu*er*e of hys distresse. I pray you labour it effectuelly yff it may be don.

Allmyghty God kepe you. Wryt at London xxvij day of Maij A^{o} xxviij^{o} r.r. H. vj.

J. FASTOLFE[4]

And I pray you sende me word who darre be so hardy to berk ayen you in my ryght, and sey hem on my half that they shall be qwyt as ferre as law and reson wolle. And yff they wolle not dredde ne obbey that, then they shall be quyt by Blacberd or Whyteberd, that is to sey by God or the Devyll. And therfor I charge yow send me word whethyr such as hafe be myne adu*er*saries before thys tyme contynew still yn her wylfullnesse &c.

It*em*, I hyre oft tymys manye str*a*unge rapport*es* of demeny*n*g of the gouu*er*n*au*nce of my place at Castr*e*, *and* othyr plasys, as yn my chatell approwyng, yn my wynys, the kepyng of my wardrobe *and* clothys, the avaylle of my conyes at Haylysdon &c, *and* approweme*n*t of my londys; pr*a*yng you hertly as my full trust ys yn you to help reso*ur* me it, and that ye suffre no vicyouse man at my place of Castr*e* abyde, but woll gouu*er*ned and diligent as ye woll aunsuer to it.

[2] th *canc.* [3] h *altered from* y.

[4] *The following two paragraphs, added to the left of and beneath Fastolf's signature, are the part of the letter printed by Fenn and Gairdner.*

983. From SIR JOHN FASTOLF to THOMAS HOWES 1450, 8 August

Add. 39848, f. 6. $11\frac{1}{2} \times 8$ in. Worcester's hand, subscription autograph.

Dorse: Marks of folding, slits for tape, traces of red wax. Address in Worcester's hand:

To my ryght trusty[1] *frende Sir Thomas Howys, parson of Castellcombe, at Castre.*

Dated.
G. 102/130 (abstract).

Ryght trusty frende I grete you wel, letyng you wete that I hafe sent home certeyn l*ett*res by John Bedford, p*ra*yng yow to tendyr the said l*ett*res as[2] ye shall considre it moste to my p*ro*ffyt and avayle. More-ou*er*e, I sende you home by the berer here-off, Thomas Medew, viij wrytt*es* of grene wex of dyu*er*s p*ro*cesses that I have in Norff*olk* esp*ec*iall, wyth a distr*es* for S*er* John Shypton, whych I pray you by the avice of Thomas Grene and othyr off my trusty frendz ye do that wryt to be s*er*ued, and th'enquest to be labo*ur*ed and certiffied of the trouth. And as to my l*ett*re testi*mo*niall or certific*aci*on that I neide, seled[3] none such[4] quytau*n*ce; ye shall have it when it shall be nedefull to-fore the jur*é*. Ye can enforme hem of the vntrue colour*es and* alleggyng*es* that the said Shypton wold fortifie hys vntrouth, and was p*ro*vyd fals in it; ⌜and let see yhyt yff he can fynde the man that told hy*m* the quyt*a*unce⌝. And as thus avysed, savyng the correcc*io*n of my frendz there, it were moste expedient and p*ro*ffytable that the jur*é* be labo*ur*ed to kepe her day at Westm*inster* to appere, and that ye wolle sende me your avice vtt*er*ly in short tyme.

Item, as to the execuc*io*n of the othyr wrytt*es*, whych som of hem ben *capias*[5] &c: in caase that agreem*en*t ⌜for t*re*spass*es*⌝[6] or paym*entes* of my dewetees can not be had thys vacac*io*n tyme, then lett dewe excuc*io*n be doon as ryght wille. And reme*m*bre ye all the namys specified wythynne the wrytt*es* at the delyu*er*aunce of hem, to th'entent ye may allwey hafe the namys redye of theym whych ye have in p*ro*cesse, and to know how feere they be in p*ro*cesse.

Item, as to the rolle of articles whych that I send you by the forsaid Bedford, I pray you that ye wille desyre Thomas Greene to see and correct hem, and make eu*er*y mater shortyr, and it can be to the vndyrstand of the mater not lessed.[7] And there as it hath ben by negligence of yow there or of

983. [1] and *canc.* [2] it *not canc.* [3] relesse *canc.*
[4] *Sense incomplete;* I have *perh. om. before* seled. [5] *Abbr.* cap *with dotted circumflex.*
[6] *Long* s + *'er' abbreviation for pl. inflection.*
[7] eyer and dete*r*mine*r added to left by another hand.*

my s*er*u*a*untz here, moo of my greu*au*nces *and* extorc*io*ns don to me left out vnreme*m*bred, as I doubt nott there ys, as myne offic*er*s can sey &c, I pray yow doo ye putt and ingroose hem among*es* the othyr. And as for cost*es* *and* da*m*mag*es* made *and* specified in the boke rolle, yff the damag*es* be specified to lytill or to moch my councell there may refo*ur*me it. And som seyn the da*m*mag*es* be to lytill assessed &c. I wold vele your wytt*es* and resons there as ye have owr*es* there, and kepe ye it secrete till[8] my councell advice yow to speke off it.

And as to othyr mater*es* that I reme*m*bre not, I pray yow thynk ye bettyr vppon, for I have so moch to doon[9] here that I may not. And allmyghty God kepe you. Wryt at London the viij day of August A^{o} xxviij^{o} R. R. H. vj.

Item, I pray you reme*m*bre speciallye to Maist*er* Doket and to such as ye shall well considr*e*, for to hafe aco*m*p*t* of the said evidens*es*[10] of Rydlyngfeeld,[11] that I may the bett*er* ground my mater bye. And yff Waryn make hy*m* str*a*unge as he hath don before, sey hym on yo*ur* heede it wolle not be hys p*ro*ffyt.[12]

It*e*m, purvey me at the leest v doseyn ⌜long⌝ bowes wyth shot longyng thertoo, and purveyeth also quarell hedys to be made ther*e*, for the p*ri*ce ys derer heer*e* then ther. And let no langage be had of orden*au*nces makyng.

J. FASTOLFE

984. From the EARL OF OXFORD to the DUKE OF NORFOLK: copy — Probably 1450, 21 August

Add. 27443, f. 112. $11\frac{1}{4} \times 5\frac{5}{8}$ in. Hand unidentified.

Dorse: Blank, but with marks of folding and slits for tape.

For the likely year see no. 456, written at Bury St Edmunds. In 1450 August 21 was a Friday, so Oxford would have had time to travel from Bury to the King's presence at Westminster by the next day, as envisaged in this letter. The original, of which this must be a copy, was carried by Thomas Denys to John Paston I for presentation to the Duke of Norfolk (see no. 456, lines 6–8). No. 456A consists of similar copies, made by Paston's servant John Osbern, of letters addressed by Oxford to Sir Miles Stapleton and Thomas Brews, which Paston had also been requested to deliver.

G. 106/134.

Ryght high and myghty prynce and my right good lord, I recomaunde me vnto youre good lordshep. And for asmouch[1] as I am enformed ⟨that⟩ certeyn notable[2] knyghtis and squyers of this counté dispose thaym self to be wi*th*

[8] I *canc.* [9] to doon *repeated, not canc.* [10] *See n. 6 above.*
[11] *Second* e *superimposed on another letter.* [12] *Remainder added to the left Fastolf's signature.*

984. *Part of the right hand edge of the sheet, approximately 4 in. by 2 in. has been torn off, carrying away parts of the text.*
[1] *Long* s *superimp. on sigma-shaped* s. [2] kny *canc.*

youre lordshep in hasty tyme at Fram⟨yngh*a*m⟩, theer to have comonyng*es* w*ith* youre good lordshep for þe[3] sad rule and gou*er*naunce of this counté, wych standyth ryght ⟨. . .⟩[4] indisposyd, God amend it; for qwych sad rule *and* gou*er*naunce to be had I wold full fayn aben w*ith* your good ⟨lordshep . . .⟩.[5] But for asmouch as þe Kynge hath geve to me straitly in charge to be w*ith* hys highnesse at Westm*inster* on Sat*er*da⟨y . . .⟩[6] dep*ar*te toward London. Therfore ⌜therof⌝ I beseche your*e* good lordship that ye[7] vouchesaf to comon w*ith* þe seyd k⟨nyghtis and squyers⟩ as w*ith* your*e* feytfull s*er*u*a*unt*es*; and I trost to God to se your*e* good lordship at Framyngh*a*m as I shall ⟨. . .⟩.[8] And yf your*e* lordshep seme necessary þ*a*t I now beynge at Westm*inster* shall any thynge labour*e* or desir⟨e for the rule⟩ *and* gou*er*naunce of þe counté forsayd, or for reformac*io*n of such wronge as þe peples hert*es* most agrugge a⟨. . .⟩[9] lyke that I meve to þe Kynge and þe lordes of the Counceyll, so wyll I meve, and non oþ*er*wyse as ⟨. . .⟩.[10] Wheryn I beseche your*e* g*ra*ce to know your*e* entente by the bryng*er* herof. And my s*er*uice is redy to your*e* lords⟨hip . . .⟩[11] m*er*cy, who kepe[12] nobley for hese g*ra*ce.

985. Memoranda of Sir John Fastolf's affairs

1450, September

Add. 39848, f. 11r-v. $5\frac{3}{4} \times 13$ in., mounted back to front, mutilated on verso at head. Mostly in John Bokkyng's hand, signed by Fastolf.

Though these memoranda bear Fastolf's signature, they do not show any sign of having been sent as a letter; they may have been carried by a servant. All but two of the items (see below, notes) are in Bokkyng's hand. The date is indicated by the imminence of the *oyer et terminer* which began at Norwich on 16 September 1450, where Fastolf brought a bill of maintenance against Nicholas Appleyard; cf. no. 987, written sometime between 7 and 14 September 1450, and no. 457, dated 15 September 1450, for similar concerns.

G. 129/159 (abstract).

⟨. . .⟩[1] for Robert Brigh⟨. . .⟩[2] ⟨me⟩ynten*au*nce in the same matier þ*a*t hangith att⟨wix⟩ ⟨. . .⟩[3] and the Priour of Hikelyng.

It*em*,[4] that by the same enqueste John Vlueston and John Andrewe may be enditid for the fals contrivyng, forgynge and fyndyng the offyce of B[e]yton,[5] in lyke wyse as for Bradwell in Suff*olk*, of whiche Brayn shal delyu*er*e copies.

[3] þ *in form of* y *and so below.*
[4] *Two or three words gone.*
[5] *Two or three more words gone.*
[6] *Two or three words gone.*
[7] w *canc.*
[8] *Three or four words gone.*
[9] *Three or four words gone.*
[10] *Three or four words gone.*
[11] *Three or four words gone.*
[12] who kepe *repeated, not canc.; this closing phrase imperfectly copied.*

985. [1] *Fol. 11v; top of sheet torn off. Space for about ten words.*
[2] *Space for end of name and about five words.*
[3] *Space for about three words.*
[4] *Each item preceded by a small capitulum mark.*
[5] *MS.* Boyton.

It*e*m, en caas they sitte in Suff*olk*, to take good hede at Sypton is matier, and at the seid mat*er*es of Vlueston *and* Andrewes.

It*e*m, as to the accion vp-on a bylle ayenst Nicholas Apleyerd of meynten*au*nce: it is lyke and noo dowte of he wyl appere, whereupon the Priour, the Secresteyn and S*er* Henr*é* Inglose must duely be laboured too, to sey and yif enformac*i*on of vtt*er* and open meynten*au*nce, as it apperid opinly at the *nisi prius*, for the seid Aplierd amendid corageously the cost*es* a-noon by v nobles in encres. And also it was hyght hym that the matier atwix Jenney and hym shuld take to non effette, but if he wolle haue doo þ*a*t day for T. and H. as thei myght haue her entent*es* spedde.

It*e*m, to see what p*ro*cesse cometh jnne ayenst Dynne, Prentys, Fowler, Tudenh*a*m, Heydon, Brampton, Willy and suche at þis retorn at Norwiche, for sum comen jn in issews, sum owtlawid &c.

It*e*m, that the obligac*i*on of cc marc. that Bryan Stapilton hathe in kepyng, in whiche my*n* maist*er* is bounden jnne to the Lady Bardolf, that by Inglose entretyng hit may be delyu*er*ed, and thanne they shal haue delyu*er*ance of Clyfton is obligac*i*on.

It*e*m, that the p*ar*son of Castelcombe speke w*ith* John Emond of Tau*er*h*a*m by a secret and good meyane, the whiche hathe c*er*teyn evidenc*es* of on that p*re*tendid hym a title to Dedh*a*m Ou*er*halle, and seithe that he is of the Dedh*a*ms and was born besyde Attilbryghe &c; to enquere of the seid Emond of what kynne the seid p*re*tender is comen of, and hoo was his fader and moder, and wher he was born, and to p*ro*mys the seyd Emond a suffic*ient* reward to see his ded*es* or haue hem, and therto if he wille to make hym baily of Drayton.

It*e*m, that redy worde come alwey atwix Norwiche and þis of the tiding*es* that ar ther.

It*e*m,[6] that the ple of the matier, jugement and all þinge þ*er*-too conc*er*nyng of Margrete Brigge be duerly engroced be Brayne, and Jenny to see it that it may be soo suer þ*a*t non erro*ur* be founden.

It*e*m,[7] to M*aster* Rob*er*t Pop*é* for þe corones off þe p*ar*sonage of Brandeston, þe wich Edmu*n*d Lawes *and* Nich*olas* Red had, þe wich draweth xij mark.

It*e*m, to Sp*er*lyng to deliu*er* þe stiward my book.

It*e*m, to speke w*ith* Blake for the seal of the Meyre of Norwiche vp-on the enditement &c, and that it be hadde agayne or on in bett*er* forme.

It*e*m, that Paston conceyve the crossed l*ett*re, and say ther-jnne to my*n* lady Felbrigge.

It*e*m, to speke to Jenny for Heyh*a*m is wyf and to S*er* Thomas for the same matier.

J. FASTOLFE

[6] *Fol. 11r.*
[7] *This item and the next in a different hand.*

It*em*, to comown sadly w*ith* Paston and Jenney shewyng them the euidenc*es*, and to see what may be doon other by distresse or otherwyse in the mater of Hikelyng.

It*em*, that noo sute, s*er*uice, rent ne other thinge be paied in Castre to the Lord Beaumond, but alwey to the Lady St*er*burghe.

It*em*, that Reppys be spoken w*ith* that he fele my*n* lord Scales and the Priour of Hikelyng iointly, if thei will yet trete as my lord Scales and my*n* maist*er* were agreed at London.

It*em*, to putte Maist*er* Hewe Acton in chois whether he wole haue to purchace the man*er*es of Abethorp or Rees in St*ra*ton.

986. From Sir John Fastolf to Howes, Grene and Shipdam — 1450, 7 September

Add. 39848, f. 7. $11\frac{3}{4} \times 11$ in. Worcester's hand, subscription autograph.

Dorse: Marks of folding, slits for tape and remains of red wax. Address in Worcester's hand:

*To my ryght trusty frendys S*er *Thomas Howys, p*ar*son off Castellco*m*be, Thomas Grene* and *Watkyn Shypdam.*

Dated.
G. 109/137 (abstract).

Ryght trusty frendys, I greete yow well. And forasmoch as I hafe no woord from you of the correcc*i*on, amendem*en*t and engrosyng*es* of the damagys doon[1] vn-to me by dyuers men *and* officers in Norff*olk*, parcell of whych mater*es* I send you home to Castre a rolle by John a Berney s*er*u*au*nt a monthys day passed, therfor I sende to you eftsones my trusty s*er*u*au*nt John Bokkyng, to bryng aunsuer to me whate correcc*i*on *and* amendem*en*t ys made vppon the said materys. And there as all the namys be not p*ar*ticlerly[2] specified in the said articles whych da*m*maged me so wrongyslye in sondry mater*es*, I pray yow doo hem to be engroced, all the grete doers seu*er*elly in eu*er*y article as the trouth ys, so as my councell there can by her[3] enformac*i*on best avice to grounde my said mater*es*, to hafe a recuu*er*e of theym that so offended. And I sende you a rolle of parcell of the namys whych I veele that noyed and damaged me, whych rolle oone Berd, caryour, hath wyth hym, w*yth* othyr l*ett*res thys day to be send yow.

Item, I was oftyn tymes da*m*maged by the Duc of Suff*olk* officers in Lodylond, both by greete and vndewe amerciement*es*, as by distreynyng*es* of my catell as othyr wyse; and yn lyke wyse in othyr sondrye places in Norff*olk* *and* Suff*olk*, both at Cotton and by officers of Cossey, that I can make no

987. [1] *Large letter* a *added to left by another hand.* [2] er *with bar over, significance uncertain.* [3] *Begun as* your *and altered by superimposition.*

menc*i*on in the said rolle of da*m*mag*es*, by asmoch as ⌜myne⌝[4] offic*er*s and theyr reme*m*br*a*unces ys at Castr*e*. Therfor I charge yow to examyn the said greu*au*nces and wrong*es* and make menc*i*on of hem among*es* othyr articles, so that no mater of dam*m*age that ys of subst*a*unce I barre dam*m*age by it be made menc*i*on off.[5]

Item, that as to the l*ett*re that ys left wyth the Bysshop of Norwych concernyng the awaard of[6] Dedh*a*m, I send vnto yow a l*ett*re to speke wyth hym to hafe delyu*er*aunce off the said l*ett*re, as reson and trouth wolle, of whych mater I hafe none aunsuer of your diligence. Wherfor I pray you and charge yow to see and know an aunsuer of your diligence heere-ynne, and whethyr ye hafe resseyved it or not, and yff ye be denyed the delyu*er*é off it. My lord of Caunterburye wenyth that I hafe it yn myne kepyng.

Item, as to the diligence ye shuld doo abowte the mater of Rydlyngfeld that I hafe so offt wryten vn-to yow for, I pray you sende me woord yff ye hafe be there and hafe owt aco*mpt* of the principall evidenc*es* that they be payd theyr part of xxv m*a*rk*es*, and whate frendshyp ye hafe founde more yn that matier.

Item,[7] I pray yow that ye in onye wyse doo comyn to-ghedre my trusty frendys Willia*m* Jenney *and* Thomas Greene and such othyr as ye trust well vntoo, that they may oversee the said articles and mater*es* such as ye can reme*m*bre more; and that they may be made and sett in such termys and ordynat fo*ur*me aftyr the trouth, so as none of myne adu*er*saries can not voyd it ne contrarie it wyth trouth. The said mater*es* ys of grete charge, and shall be shewed to lordes and men of greete autorité and of grete audience, wherfor the said mater*es* most be greetly examyned or it be shewed. Now the mater ys be-gonne ye may the esyer contynew it, and sparyth for no wrytyng whyle ye hafe help ynogh to renewe the said articles and make it well.

It*e*m, I m*er*veylle greetly that ye sende me no word by l*ett*res of your gouu*er*n*au*nce, labo*ur*es and demenyng in that parties, for it ys manye day seth I had l*ett*res from yow. Also, to wete vndre your wrytyng*es* whate approweme*n*t ye myght ordeyn that myght be mooste avayle to me to vtter heere, beyng yn your gouu*er*n*aun*ce there, whych I desyre to know by your l*ett*res, and the prisees. As to all othyr mater*es* necessary for my proffyt to be remembred, I wolle ye gefe credence to my said s*er*u*au*nt for my moste avayle to be consid*er*ed.

And allmyghty God kepe you. Wryt at London the vij day of Septe*m*ber A^{o} ⌜xxix^{o}⌝[8] r. r. H. vj.

J. FASTOLFE

[4] *Over* the *canc.*

[5] *No satisfactory sense can be made of the last nine words, of which* baare *is possibly intended for deletion. Worcester may have either misheard Fastolf's dictation or miscopied his own notes, and then failed to complete a correction.*

[6] *Preceded by a miswritten letter.*

[7] *Large letter* a *added to left by another hand.*

[8] *Over* xxviij^{o} *canc.*

987. From SIR JOHN FASTOLF to BERNEY, HOWES and SHIPDAM 1450, between 7 and 14 September

Add. 39848, f. 20. $11\frac{1}{2} \times 9$ in. Two hands, the first William Worcester's, the second John Bokkyng's; Fastolf's name subscribed by Bokkyng.

Dorse: Marks of folding, slits for tape, wafer seal attached to slip of paper, showing design of a rose. Address in Bokkyng's hand:

*To my trusty and welbeloued frend*es *John a Berney, S*er *Thomas Howys and Walt*er *Shipd*a*m.*

Gairdner dated his abstract of this letter to early September 1451, having overlooked the alteration to the date of no. 457 of 14 September 1450, which it evidently preceded; see the Headnote to no. 457. Since Bokkyng was still in London to write the latter half of the letter, it must post-date no. 986 of 7 September 1450, where he is spoken of as being sent down to Norfolk 'eftsones'. It is probable that Bokkyng was the carrier of no. 457 (see lines 6–9, 15–16 thereof).

G. 169/203 (abstract).

Ryght trusty frendz, I grete yow well, p*ra*yng yow to haste to London Robert Botill*er* wyth all such mater*es* that I have wretyn vnto yow for, as manye as ye can aunsuer. And as for the residue that ye can not fynde there, I shall do serche heere.

It*em*, I have late be enformed that the Thursday aftyr Holy Rode day the oyer *and* termyner shall eftsonys be jnquired vppon in Norwych, and William Yelu*er*ton, justice, as I vndrestand, wolle be there. And I pray yow therfor that ye labour to such as knowen the disposic*io*n of the subst*a*unciall men in Norwych, how they be sett in my mat*er* that I have ayenst Appulȝerd. And yff ye by the avice *and* consid*er*ac*io*n of my cosyn Paston thynk and know verrylye that my seid mat*er* shall hafe forth as ryght and trouth wolle, ayenst the seid Appulȝerd as ayenst onye othyr that I have suffis*a*unt mater and cause whereoff to compleyn, then I woll weell that ye labour it to a[1] gode ende. And yff so bee ye veele by the world that Appulȝerd make such labour to hys kynnesmen and frendz that my mater shall take none ende at that tyme, then doo ye by the avice of my lerned councell and othyr of my frendz yn such wyse as it may moste be to my worshyp and proffyt. I am avysed to sende John Bokkyng or Willia*m* Barker to yow ayenst the seid tyme.

It*em*, I have wryten to yow for th'endenture of Cornelys Florysson and Cornelys Heynsson, whych went awey wyth the wheete and malt that ye[2] delyu*er*ed hem to sende or bryng me to London, be cause I have arrested the shyp heere, and Cornelys Heynesson. And ye most sende me also th'endenture that ye delyu*er*ed ⌜to⌝ the seid shypmen the seid greynys, that my councell may justifie and preffe that the said Cornelys resseyvyd the seid

987. [1] *No space.* [2] toke h *canc.*

greyn, and kepe ye a double of hem wyth yow. But it most be sent in all haste, because my p*ro*cesse ys in the courte.[3]

It*em*, as touching the matier ayenst Applierd and other, as Tudenh*a*m, Heydon, Wymondh*a*m, Willy, Brampton, and Dynne. If thei or ony of hem wille apperen and labo*ur* for ther acquitaile of here jnditement for meynte*n*aunce ayenst me in the Lady Bardolf*es* matier, as it is no*gh*t vnknowe*n* how falsly thei were demened, and in esp*eci*al the seid Applizerd, I p*ra*y yow as my*n* ful triste is jnne yow ye wille labo*ur*e the cont*ra*rie, and doo therjnne as may be moste to my*n* p*ro*fite and worchip. I triste the Meire that now is and hise p*re*dcesso*ur*e that was wille considre how willyng I haue ben at all tymes to the weelfare of the town and of the comowns w*ith*jnne it, and conne sey how Applyȝerd was demened that day; and soo can Will*ia*m Jenney and hise brother, by cause of ther matier atwix hem and Appliȝerd the same day &c. Ye muste take owte a copye of Brayne of the seid enditement *in warda de Mancrofte* in Norwiche. And as I am enformed, the seid Appliȝerd wille seye that th'enqueste made neu*er*e non suche p*re*sentem*en*t. S*er* Thomas, as Bokkyng telleth me, ye wote what wise it was doon, and the bille sente vnder the Maire is signet by a s*er*ieaunt of the toun, Will*ia*m Jenney the same tyme beyng p*re*sent in Seint Petris chirche in market.

It*em*, as for copies of the plee and all þing*es* p*er*teynyng to the same ye haue w*ith* yow þ*er*e, and now I sende yow th'endenture of lees vnder wax of the Lady Sterburghes p*ar*te, and Bardolf*es*, made by Wichingh*a*m and Blake. It*em*, a confirmac*io*n of S*er* Reynold Cobh*a*m and þe seid Lady Sterburgh his wif. It*em*, a l*ett*re testim*on*iall of the P*ri*our and Secresteyn of Norwiche, and a l*ett*re testim*o*niall of Inglose and many other; w*ith* whiche whanne ye haue don sende hem me agayn.

It*em*, that ye p*ur*uey for the stabilshyng of Rob*er*t of Burton, bring*er* of this l*ett*re, jn suche wise as he may be at hise ease at Seint Benett, that he may pray for me &c.

It*em*, that ye recomaunde me to my*n* lord of Ely, my*n* lord of Oxford in cas thei be ther, and to my*n* cousyn Yelu*er*ton and all my*n* other frend*es*; and þ*a*t ye wyte yette of my*n* lord of Norwiche sum tiding*es* of Hikelyng, for there he hathe ben and dyned, as it is tolde me.

It*em*, blessid be God of hise visitac*io*n, I haue ben right soore seeke, and am weel amendid; and triste to Our Lorde to see you hastily, and other of my frend*es*, and soo I pray you to telle them.

S*ER* JOHN FASTOLF

[3] *Worcester's hand ends; remainder in Bokkyng's hand.*

988. From Sir John Fastolf to Thomas Howes
1450, 15 September

Add. 39848, f. 8. 11¾ × 9¼ in. Worcester's hand, subscription autograph.

Dorse: Marks of folding, slits for tape, remains of red wax seal. Address in Worcester's hand:

To my ryght trusty frendys Sir Thomas Howys, parson of Castellcombe beyng at Castre, or at Norwych, at Pokethorp, or at Haylysdon manere.

Dated.

G. 110/138 (abstract).

Ryght trusty frendys I grete you well, letyng yow [wete] that I hafe resseyvyd a l*ett*re by Thomas Fastolf from you touchyng yo*ur* diligence doon abowte the recuu*er*e of [the] l*ett*re wyth the Bysshop of Norwych, and also of the evidencez of Rydlyngfeld, wyth aco*mpt* of a certeyn endenture, whych mater I hafe[1] redye enseled the originall. But I hafe none aunsuer of the labo*ur* that ye do *and* my councell abowte the correcc*i*on of the articles that y sent yow home ij monthys passed. And now it ys soo that my lord of Norfolk ys at Norwych, as I vndrestand, to sytt vppon the oyer and termyner. Wherfor I pray you and charge yow to labo*ur* to my councell, and shew hem my greu*au*nces and extorc*i*ons doon to me yn many wyses, and aftyr theyr avice ye make such diligence foorth to the jur*é* or to such as shall hafe rule yn such causes for the remedie off it as by your wysdoms ye shall best conceyve. And there as I can not remembr*e* all myne extorc*i*ons don to me in Lodylond and by the offic*er*s at Cossey ⌜&c⌝ I pray you reme*m*bre hem in wrytyng as the trouth ys.

It*em*, as to the *venir*e *facias* for the jur*é* of Sybton, there may nought be doon to it till the day of the reto*ur*n of the *venire facias*, whych ys xv^{a} or iij sep*te*manis aft*er* Myghellm*a*sse. And aft*er* that I wolle as ye avice me take owt a *nisi prius* to be had at Bury or Yeppyswych about Cristm*a*sse, and so my frendez ne the jur*é* shall hafe no nede to labo*ur* hem hedr*e*. And as for onye labour to be doon on Moneday next at Bury, it nede not, for the day of reto*ur*n ys not com.

It*em*, I hafe wryt a l*ett*re to John a Berney by the p*ar*son of Estharlyng thys weke, the s*u*bst*a*unce of whych l*ett*re ys that he shuld speke wyth John Waryn, stuard of Lodylond; Brampton, att*ur*ney, that hath be so moch yn eu*er*y fals cause ayenst me; Dynne, Fouler, *and* such othyr*es* as ye can name bett*er* then I; that the said Berney shuld gefe hem such maner langage yn councellyng hem to be ware how they doo *and* labo*ur* ayenst me, for they shall be qwyt yn such wyse as othyr*es* shall be ware by hem, and they amend not &c. I hafe herd late that the said Bernay hath doon greete frendshyp and fauo*ur* vnto my adu*er*sarie that hath be mooste ayenst me, and y m*er*veylle

988. [1] *Letter* a *added to left by another hand.*

that he woold doo soo, for there [ben] othyr*e* men that woold hafe doon for hym and hys allye as[2] well as he, and to theyr worshyp moch more, for it wolle cause hym and Mundford to be yn lasse fauo*ur* of the shyre.[3]

It*em*,[4] forasmoch as I hafe no leyser to wryte vnto you of myne mat*er* touchant the extorc*i*ons &c, now that John Bokkyng ys in that parties he shall and can ⌜to⌝ you *and* to my councell all myne entent concernyng that mater, whych I pray you hertly, slepyth it not, but to wyrk *and* to doo there-ynne as it may be to my worshyp *and* moost p*ro*ffyt.

Allmyghty God kepe yow. Wryt at London xv day of Septe*m*ber A^{o} xxix^{o} R. H. vj.

It*em*,[5] such mater*es* as ye shall nede to labo*ur* or meoffe vnto my lord of Norff*olk* that hys goode lordshyp may help &c, ye, s*er* p[*ar*]son, or John Bernay, or onye othyr of my lerned councell may[6] meoffe vnto hym, and I doubt not but he wolle gefe you audience. And I pray you reco*m*maund me to my lord ys gode gr*a*ce; and ye may sey hy*m* I shall be ther*e* yn short tyme and awayt vppon hys gode lordshyp. Allso, ye woll reco*m*maund me to all my othyr gode lordz *and* maist*er*s [*and*] co*m*missione*r*s yn all my mater*es*, and speke wyth my councell Willia*m* Jenney, Paston *and* Thom*a*s Grene for her avice to be had[7] yn my extorc*i*ons t[o][8] be remedyed. And such mater*es* as most be sped, sende me hasty word &c.

J. FASTOLFE

989. From SIR JOHN FASTOLF to HOWES and BARKER 1450, 15 and 18 October

Add. 34888, f. 49r-v. $11\frac{3}{4} \times 13\frac{1}{4}$ in. Worcester's hand, subscription autograph.

Dorse: Marks of folding, slits for tape, traces of red wax. Address in Worcester's hand:

*To my ryght trusty freende S*er *Thomas Howys, p*ar*son of Castellco*mb*e, beyng at Castr*e, ⌜and⌝ *Willia*m *Barker in haste at Cast*er *Yn by Jermuth.*

Dated. Fenn printed (and Gairdner reprinted) only a short extract from the first section of this long letter, namely the paragraph added at the foot of the recto beneath Fastolf's signature of 15 October. Though a single missive, the letter as a whole was composed in two distinct instalments, the recto on 15 October and the verso on 18 October 1450.

F. iii, p. 92. G. 115/144 (part).

It[1] ys to remembre that, forasmoch as John Heydon and othyrs that bee founde fautye in certeyn mater*es* put ayenst hem in that parties &c, the said

[2] *No space.* [3] And it ys *canc.* [4] *The letters* b C *added to left by another hand.*
[5] *Letter* a *added to left by another hand. The last lines of this paragraph are written partly around Fastolf's previously inserted signature at the foot of the sheet.*
[6] doon it *canc.* [7] till *canc.* [8] t + *a miswritten letter, canc.*

989. [1] *Letter* a *added to left by another hand.*

Heydon hath be wyth my Lord Ch*a*unceller and othyr lordes, to declare hym of hys excuse, that he dyd not but as a lerned man of councell ayenst me; *and* the lordes hafe grete credence to hys resons vnto tyme it be shewed and declared the contrarye. And he desyryth in especiall to declare hym-sylf ayenst me before the lordys, but I excused, and delay it be-cause my evidenses were not heere. And som of my frendes avysen me to delay it till the next session be vppon the oyer and termyner. Neu*er*ethelesse, to be redye, I wolle that ye sende me my articles that I sent yow wyth your correcc*i*ons, as it may be avowed of trouth and of no malice to put no thyng ynne, but as the verray deede was. And also sendyth me the originall evidens*es*[2] *and* copé of the plees concernyng the p*ro*cesse off the said articles by a sure comer betwene; and kepe ye the *vidim*us *and* copé of hem there, for doubt of lesyng or takyng by the wey. And by avyse of my cosyn Paston, I pray yow sendyth me in articles the best resons that ye can to fortiffie myne articles made menc*i*on yn the rolle, for I doubt not but the said Heydon wolle make full myghty colourable resons ayenst myne articles to safe hys worshyp. But my ryght ys so opynly knowen that he shall not avoyd it, by Goddes grace.

It*em*, it ys ryght expedient that there be made speciall moc*i*on to my lord of Norff*olk* [and] to my lord Oxford for sufficiaunt men of worshyp[3] to be named, for one of theym to be shyrevys of Norff*olk and* Suff*olk*; and namelye that they bee such men as be of gode conceyt among*es* the comyns, not covetouse, ne takyng partie ne meede. And as it co*m*myth to my reme*m*-brunce, S*er* William Chambyrleyn, Osbern Mundford, wyth S*er* John Hevenyngh*a*m, were hable, or such othyr well sett men not haldyng the left hand, for vppon thys hangyth the well-fare of the shyre.

It*em*, seth that John Jenney and John Adam be the rathyr put yn the comyssion for her wysdom and gode demenyng yn the shyre, and[4] at inst*a*unce of such as owed hym gode wille here &c, I pray yow meovyth hem to be in my mater*es* and yn my lord Cromewell mater*es* for Saxthorp[5] as ryghtwyse as they may. And that a speciall bille myght be conceyved in my lord Cromewell name, whethyr it shalbe put vpp to-fore the justice of pease or to-fore the co*m*myssioners of oyer *and* te*r*miner, that my said lord Cromewell ryght and myne may be savyd in the said maner off Saxthorp, concernyng the tenure of the said maner; and that Gent Newton *and* othyrs that hafe offended yn the said maner as dryvyng awey my chatell there may make me amendys.

It*em*, forasmoch as John Dynne, Fouler, Brampton *and* such othyr*es* ⌜that⌝ have put me to greete cost*es and* da*m*mag*es*, and my ten*au*nt*es* of Blyclyng yn the Duchee *and* Rychemond fee &c, I woold desyre that ye and my councell woold fynde a dew meene that they were corrected, and makyng me amendys for the greete da*m*mag*es* that I hafe suffred wrongyslye.

[2] *Long* s + *'er' abbreviation for plural inflection.*
[3] s *superimposed on* d.
[4] for *canc.*
[5] *MS.* be

It*em*, that myne articles I sent home by Willia*m* Barker in a long rolle may be sent vpp ayen in all goodly haste corrected as ys beforesaid; and that the said William may spede hym hedre, for there he may not be occupied but yff the oyer and termyner had be contynued and satyn stille.

It*em*, the p*ar*son of Brandeston hath delyu*er*ed in to the audyt a bundell of French papirs and billes whych be of no subst*a*unce, ne make no menc*i*on of the maters that I wroote vn-to yow; willyng that ye serche better, and sende me yff ye onye fynde.

It*em*, as for thoo that ye remembre me to thank hem &c for her gode wille to me ward in the expedic*i*on of my mater*es*, I hafe don it aft*er* your councell; and such as be not my frendys in my ryght, I pray yow sende me wetyng off it.

It*em*, as for Sybeton mater, the wryt ys delyu*er*ed to the att*ur*ney, and a *nisi prius* shall be had betweene thys and Cristmasse or therevppon. Neu*er*thelesse, when ye speke wyth the jur*é* or wyth onye of hem, I pray yow doth enforme hem of the trouth of the mater.

It*em*, as for thoo that offended ayenst me at Flodgatys, as John Swettyng *and* othyrs, whych ye avyse to be respited till I meete wyth S*er* Mylys Stapulton &c: as to that, in caase I speke not wyth hym wythynne short tyme, I pray yow to see an eende there as trouth off the mater ys, and I hald me content.

It*em*, I pray yow, p*ar*son, to ordeyn that my stuff of p*ro*uision for housold be sent hedre as I wroote vnto yow. And there hath be sent[6] to London reede heryng and othyr nouueltee by cart*es* from Jermuth; but and ye had y-had me in reme*m*br*a*unce, ye myght hafe sent me j cade or ij for my ples*a*unce.

It*em*, as to all othyr mater*es* to be sent me aunsuer off that it be doon yn all goodely haaste, as my grete trust ys yn yow.

Wretyn at London the xv day of October Aº xxixº r.r. H. vj.

J. FASTOLFE[7]

It*em*, as for Hygh*a*m place to be sold, as ye avysen me to bye it at the som*me* of c mark or wythynne and res*er*ve yn the said paym*en*t myne oune dewtee, and pay the remenant in wolle to the said Hygh*a*m credyt*our*s &c,[8] as yo*ur* l*ett*re[9] makyth menc*i*on. I hafe vndrestand that Willia*m* Jenney shall be her*e* thys weke, and I shall veele hym how neere it may be sold, for yff the wydow wolle sylle it aft*er* xiiij yeer*e* or xv yeere, that it may be leten, sendyth me vtterly word, for I wolle not melle off it ellys thus avysed. And sende ye me word how mech more yn value yn a stoon shall I syle my wolle, and how [mech] anothyr chapman wolle gefe me for the place when I hafe bought it; but aft*er* xiiij yeer*e* I wold by the place.[10]

6 me *canc.*

7 *The following paragraph was added after Fastolf had signed, and is the part of the letter printed by Fenn and Gairdner.*

8 assone as t *canc.*

9 *Superimposed on another word.*

10 *End of f. 49r.*

It*em*, Jenney-ys Clere hath lete me hafe wetyng that sessions of pese shall be held at Yeppyswych on Twysday vij dayes aft*er* Seint Luke ys day, and William Jenney shall be there. And forasmoch as Hulueston and John Andrew causyd an office to be forged and putt ynne the Chekyr, wherbye my maner of Bradwell was cast yn the Kyng*es* hand, whych office ys seyd that it shuld be take at ⌜Nedam Market xiiij° die Ap*ri*l⌝[11] A° xxvij° r.r. H vj, whych the escheto*ur* dysavowed yn the Kyng*es* Eschequyer. And it ys made menc*i*on yn the office that Nicholas Framysden, Jamys Baynard, John Bacon, Thomas Brygge, John Segillmer, Willia*m* Bunne, John Sparow, John Skylfull, John Goldyngh*am*, John Damett, Richard Martyn, Thomas Sparow, Willia*m* Pylberegh, Thomas Roger. Wherfor I pray yow to be the said day at Yeppyswych, and by avice of Thomas Grene and[12] Jenneys ye may hafe a notable man of my lord of Norff*olk* wyth, and do examyn the said men at Yeppyswych before the comyssioners or apart, whethyr they passed ⌜vppon⌝[13] such an office, and yff they yaffe yn veredit all that mater that ys comp*ri*sed yn the said office. And as I am lerned, the said juree appered not. And whethyr they appered to-fore John Andreu or to-fore one that made hy*m* sylf the escheto*ur* debité, the trouth of the mater ys that the escheto*ur* gafe never autorité ne power to John Andre ne to none othyr to take such an office. And therfo[r] in conclusion of myne entent ys that I wold a certificat, aft*er* that the said jur*é* seid or p*re*sented, in whate termys they p*re*sented, as it ys yn the office or no, or whethyr they appered there or no, for it myght be that they nevyr appered, and yff they appered it myght be for som othyr mater. Had I such a certificat vndr*e* theyr selys, it shuld be an evidence to me to grounde my acc*i*on ayenst Hulueston, John Andreu and othyrs. And y sende you a cop*é* of the said forged office, wyth the endocem*en*t of receyvyng yn the Chekyr and dysavowyng, to ground yo*ur* mat*er* the bett*er*, wyth a cop*é* of the maner of a certificat. I pr*a*y yow labo*ur* ye thys mat*er* diligently to the vtmost, and Willia*m* Barker may help yow as he co*m*myth hedr*e*ward.

It*em*, ye may labo*ur* that the said John Andreu and Hulueston, wyth othyr wyrkers, to be p*re*sented at the oyer t*er*miner in Norff*olk* for theyr vntrouth *and* meyntena*u*nce, causyng[14] falsly my manere of Bradwell to be cast yn the Kyng*es* hand, and takyng offices be-thout autorité &c.

It*em*, the minut that I sende yow may be corrected &c, and labo*ur*ed esyly as the world ys set now yn trouth; and I wold that ye assayd to ghete such anothyr l*ett*re enseled of the men that passed vppon the office Tychewell, how they p*re*sented neu*er*e such office &c.

It*em*, as for S*er* John Sybton *nisi prius*, I am avysed to ghete ⌜S*er*[15] Willia*m*⌝ Falthorp that ys yn Suff*olk* to sit vppon it; but therfor when ye be at Yeppyswych, weete ye off hy*m* whate day he may suerly kepe to sytt ther*e*,

[11] *Over* Todenham x° die Junii *canc.*
[12] *Superimposed on* ye.
[13] *Over* and made *canc.*
[14] fa *not canc.*
[15] John *canc.*

and send me word betyme to warn Sybton attorney, or ell*es* I must gete Willia*m* Yelu*er*ton, justice.

It*em*, ye shall resseyve money of Agnes Fastolf when ye be ther*e* x m*a*rk*es* &c.

Wryt hastly at London xviij day of Octob*er*, thys syde.

It*em*, sendyth me a cop*é* of the said offices I sende you home by Willia*m* Barker. And now at thys tyme or onye othyr tyme where ye nede to hafe help to solicit wyth yow to myne avayle, takyth to you such as may stand yn steede.

J. FASTOLFE

990. From SIR JOHN FASTOLF to THOMAS HOWES
1450, 11 November

Add. 39848, f. 9. 11¾ × 11⅜ in. Worcester's hand, subscription autograph.

Dorse: Marks of folding, slits for tape, remains of wafer seal over red wax. Address in Worcester's hand:

*To my ryght trusty frende Sir Thom*as *Howys, p*arson *of Castellcombe.*

The year may be inferred from the references to William Yelverton's proposed presence at the *oyer et terminer* in Norwich (see nos. 467 and 877–8), and to the escheator's inquisition regarding Titchwell (see P. S. Lewis, 'Sir John Fastolf's Lawsuit over Titchwell', *The Historical Journal* i (1958) 1–20, at pp. 16–17).

G. 123/153 (abstract).

Ryght trusty and welbelovyd frendys, I greete yow well. And y con yow gode thank*es* for the quyt*a*unce of full paym*en*t of Richard Sellyng that ye sent me now by Worcestr*e*, wyth a quyt*a*unce of Faucon*er*e for the p*ur*chasse of Davyngton, and a-nothyr quyt*a*unce of Roys for the p*ur*chasse off Tychewell; p*ra*yng yow to labour eftsones wyth my cosyn Herry St*ur*mer wyff, and that ye wolle pray hyr to serche for an endentur*e* vppon the obligac*io*n of ij m^{l} m*a*rk*es* made by Ric*hard* Sellyng, and gen*er*ally for all maner wrytyng*es* that she can fynde made betwene me *and* the said Sellyng, or the Lady Wyltshyr*e*.

It*em*,[1] where as ye send me word that S*er* Thomas Tuddenh*a*m sent late to John Clere to be at London &c, my desyre ys that ye speke wyth hym before, and that he and hys wyffe be entreted to com to-fore the bayllyffs of Jermuth; and[2] requyryng hem certyfie vndre theyr seale of office, how the said Bysshopp ys wyffe resseyved no peny of the c li. that I was rewled to pay hyr for the wythdrawyng of the appele sewed by the said Bysshop wyff. And as I vndrestand, she had but xl s. or lytill more. And yff ye have othyr selys of credyble p*er*sones of Jermuth, so moch the bettyr, and thys don to be sent in

990. [1] oyer and det*er*min*er* *added by another hand to left.* [2] make *canc.*

haaste, whych shall be a suffis*a*unt record to preffe that thys c li. was wrongysly taken; and that John Clere com not vpp till I sende for hym, and that he com oonlye to me.

It*e*m, there hath be speciall labour made heere that William Ȝeluerton, justice, shuld not com doune at thys M*a*rtysm*a*sse, but notwythstandyng that the Kyng and the lordys hafe avysed and determyned fully that he shall kepe hys day. And the labour that ye wyth my cosyn Paston made late to my lord Norff*olk* was ryght well avysed, yn caase that the justice shuld be countermaunded.

It*e*m, as to all my mater*es* of subst*a*unce lab*our*ed last at the oyer and termyner, and now to be lab*our*ed at thys tyme: I pray yow ryght speciall to applie your laboure*s* in the best maner that ye con, and that ye assay all my frendys there to do for me as ferre as ryght and trouth wolle, for I wold not for v^{c} li. but tho mater*es*[3] be lab*our*ed in such wyse as it may take a worshypfull eende on my syde.

It*e*m, y thank Nicholas Bokkyng for hys gode lab*our* about the enselyng of the certificat of the jur*é* that were named yn the office of Tychewell, and were not to-fore none escheto*ur*, ne gafe no such veredyt as ys wryt yn the said office; and p*ra*yng hym to lab*our* it to be enseled betyme, for taryeng drawyth parell. And it wolle ease myne hert gretely that it may be sped, and be a grete evidense to recuu*er*e my maner ayen.

It*e*m, as [to] a fer[m]o*ur*[4] at my place of Castre: forasmoch as I vndrestand he ys hald of gode rule and gouu*er*n*au*nce, and a lykly man to do s*er*vice and stand yn steede at neede, it ys my wille that he contynew and ferme my place stille.

It*e*m, I sende home ij of my roode hors*es*, both the blac morell and benetgrey, for to be occupied yn the cart and such occupac*io*n as they may doo, desyryng that ye co*m*maund my s*er*u*au*nt*es* that hafe the gouu*er*n*au*nce of that office that they be well kept as it belonghyth to hem. Oft tymys my hors*es* be foundred yn deffaut of kepyng.

It*e*m,[5] as to all othyr maters that ys to sped, I pray yow hertly to tendyr hem in your best maner, co*m*maundyng me vnto my cosyn John Berney.

It*em*, byasmoch as the greete besynesse of myne audyt fallyth now, I pray you to do sende for Willia*m* Cole, and that he wold see and hyre the examyny*ng* and makyng of the acco*mpt*es, yovyng hys gode avice theretoo; and that Geffrey Spyrlyng forbere hym and gefe none occ*asi*on to displese hym.

It*e*m, thank the p*ar*son of Haylysdon for the iij wrytyng*es* of Wyltshyre ys wille and Goney he sent me by Worcestr*e*, but sey I prayd hym to serche aft*er* moo yff he can fynde onye, and sende hem me.

[3] *Repeated and not canc.*

[4] *MS.* ferro*ur*.

[5] *Fastolf's signature appears at this point, and the remainder of the text is to the left of and below his name.*

No more for haaste, but God hafe you in hys kepyng. Wryt at London on Seint M[*a*]rtyn day before noone.

J. Fastolfe

991. From Sir John Fastolf to Howes, Bokkyng and Shipdam 1450, 23 November

Oxford, Magdalen College, Fastolf Additional 2. $11\frac{1}{4} \times 13$ in. Worcester's hand, subscription autograph.

Dorse: Marks of folding, slits for tape. Address in Worcester's hand:

*To my right trusty frend*es *S*er *Thomas parson of Castelcombe, John Bokkyng* and *Watkyn Shipdam.*

Dated.

Blomefield, iv, pp. 388–9, note 9 (part). G. 126/156 (abstract).

Ryght trusty and welbelovyd frendes, I grete yow well, and let you we[te][1] that I hafe late resseyved a l*ett*re be Rob*er*t Bottil*o*r from you, s*er* p*ar*son, and a-nothyr by John Clere, of whych l*ett*res *and* mater*es* comp*ri*sed in yo*ur* l*ett*res I con you gode thank. And where ye, p*ar*son, desyre Willia*m* Jenney *and* John Bokkyng to be yn that parties be-tyme, to make avyse and solicit my mater*es* to be sped at the oyer and t*er*miner, your entent ys s*er*vyd, p*ra*yng theym and you to labour it effectually aft*er* that the trouth ys and as the case shall requyre.

It*em*, I hafe resseyved a l*ett*re of jnstrucc*i*on of the fyrst purchasse of Haylysdon, that I vndrestand Sturmer wyffe shuld take yow. But and she were wellwylled she wold delyu*er*e yow bett*er* matters then thoo, for the trouth ys that he resseyved and kept the chyeff part of evydens*es*[2] atwyxt Sellyng *and* me. Assay ye ferthyr.

It*em*, as to John Clere, I am well content that he ys com, and it shewyth well by hys seyneng and your wrytyng that there hath be moch str*a*unge labo*ur* made to hym by Tasborogh and Swolle; havyng grete m*er*veylle that so neere as ye *and* my frendys were at Jermuth that ye had no wetyng rathyr off it. Neu*er*thelese, byasmoch as the said Tasborogh and Swolle hath so vntrulye don to the said John Clere yn the ward makyng[3] for Alson Westwod, I pray yow to comyn the mat*er* all along to my lerned councell there, and that there myght be founde a grounde to endyte hym at the oyer and t*er*miner. And it shall awake well the said Tasborogh, because that he made John Clere enseele a fals quyt*a*unce to Westwodd wyff, whych the said Clere knew not whate he seled.

It*em*,[4] it comyth to my reme*m*braunce of grete meynten*au*nce and vntrouth doon to me by Appulȝerd of Norwych yn the Lady Bardolf mater, aswell as

991. [1] *MS.* well. [2] *Long* s + *'er' abbrev. for plural inflexion.* [3] to Isabell *canc.* [4] *Letter* a *added to left by another hand.*

by othyrs that ye know well, pr*a*yng yow that ye wolle meoffe my lerned councell to wete whethyr I may hafe onye mat*er* ayenst hym at thys oyer t*er*myner. He hath allwey be ayenst me yn my maters and y offended never ageynst hym. Also there ys a baylly of Hykelyng that meynteynyth the Pryour yn hys wrong ayenst me, and hath proud langage and vnsyttyng of me. I pray you that as a meynteno*ur* he may be put vpp.

It*em*, where-as Willia*m* Barker had a box of the evidens*es* of the ferme off the Lady Bardolf londz, also a dede of Norman feffem*en*t wyth evidens*es* of Saxthorp, my s*er*u*au*nt Bokkyng supposyng they had be broug⌜ht⌝ ayen, and serche hath be made here for the said evidens*es*, and can not be founde; wherfor it pr*o*vyth well that they be left there at Norwych or at Castr*e*. And foryete ye not Norman mat*er*, the meynteno*ur*s *and* forgers of the fals inquest of Beyton Bradwell, and on ⌜of⌝ Wylbie &c. for Tychewell enquest forgyng. Y wryte but shortly, for ye may know by a lytill whate the more menyth.

It*em*, Wyndam escuier hath meoved me to be hys gode frende and excusith hym of the Lady Bardolf*es* mat*er*. I vndrestode he wold hafe ben sworn yn the quest, safe that Bacon squyer chalangod hym. Neu*er*ethelese, as I fynde hym here-aft*er* to me, so wolle I take hy*m*.

It*em*, s*er* p*ar*son, wolle ye wete that the Maist*er* of Seint Gylys wyth my lord Norwych ch*a*uncell*o*r hath be wyth me for the purchasse of Mu*n*dh*a*m maner wyth appurten*au*nce yn Cyselond. And so I am acorded, and hafe pr*o*mysed hym to make astate to such as he wolle name, payeng me ij^c marc there as he and I shall accord; and I shall do seende the new evidens*es* home to yow in haste how ye shall be demened. Sende me word whethyr I hafe made a gode bargeyn. I was not avysed to sylle it except it goth to a goode vse, for it [hath] clere gode and *sesen*[5] wyth avouson. And he wold I shuld hafe do almesse on hem, and relessed hem som money, but ye may sey hym the vntrouth of the Pryour of Hykelyng drawyth awey my deuoc*i*on in such caus*es*. The said Maist*er* seith he wolle telle the Pryo*ur* hys oune when he spekyth wyth hym; and also reme*m*br*e* the Bysshop when he co*m*myth to Norwych, that he shall shew hys evidens*es*.

It*em*, as to the debt that Nicholas Waterman demaundyth of yow, he most sende me a wrytyng of the p*ar*cellys, and my lord shall sende a discharge off it vppon my fee, or vppon a prest I lend late to certeyn of my lord ys councell &c.[6]

It*em*, spekyth wyth Maist*er* Piers Seint Feyth to sende me a l*ett*re or aunsuer whethyr he wolle resseyve the benefice of Tau*er*ham or no; and that I hafe a l*ett*re or suffis*a*unt witnesse as Maist*er* Hue Acton wolle reme*m*br*e* you, for I hafe gr*a*unted hym the pr*e*sentac*i*on to such an honest preest as he wolle name.

[5] *Reading doubtful; MS.* s + er *abbreviation* + e, *with what appears to be a superscript single minim (rather than a tilde). Worcester quite often wrote* s + er *abbreviation for the* -es *inflection at the end of words ending in long* s; hath *or a similar word appears to have been omitted earlier in the sentence.*

[6] *Fastolf's signature appears at this point, and the remainder of the letter is to the left of and beneath it.*

It*e*m, I pray yow foryeete not the bayly of Hykelyng that seid I shuld forge evidence, or ell*es* hafe forged evidence of the xxv m*a*rc yn Hykelyng, off whych he lyeth falsly. And he meynteynyth the Pryo*ur* in hys wrong.

It*e*m, sende me accompt of Mu[*n*]dh*a*m to know the verray value, and yff I made onye mo p*ur*chasse there or no.

It*e*m, sende me word how moch money I resseyvyd of Hopton escuier for Yoksford, and who accomptyth therfor. I vndrestand I sold it for ml^{o} m*a*rc and a hors.

No more for hast, but allmyghty God kepe you. Wryt at London xxiij day off Noue*m*ber A^{o} xxix^{o} r.r. H vj.

J. FASTOLFE

It*e*m, I pray you myne audyt be dewlye attended as ryght wolle to all parties.

992. From THOMAS PLAYTER to SIR JOHN FASTOLF
Probably 1450, September–December

Oxford, Magdalen College, Fastolf Paper 37. 12 × $7\frac{1}{4}$ in. Autograph.

Dorse: Traces of red wax. Address autograph:

To my rygth worchipfull and *my most sp*eci*all maist*er *S*er *John Fastolf, knygth.*

It is evident from what remains of this letter that it originally consisted of a report by Playter of a meeting with Walter Lyhert, Bishop of Norwich, where they discussed two disputes in which Fastolf was especially concerned during 1450. The arbitration mentioned took place on 16 February 1450, and it enabled Fastolf to regain possession of his manor at Dedham (Essex) from the duke of Suffolk, shortly after the latter's fall from power (Smith, 'Aspects of the Career of Sir John Fastolf', p. 126). A later copy of the arbitration itself is Magdalen College 154/8, f. 3v, estate memoranda, *c.* 1471 (Richmond, *Fastolf's Will*, p. 237, n. 89). Letters dated 7 and 15 September 1450 (nos. 986, 988) mention that documentation of Fastolf's concerning the Dedham award was with the Bishop. The aftermath of the recovery of Dedham, involving damage to some of Fastolf's property there by members of Suffolk's affinity, is also mentioned in letters of 4 and 5 December 1450 (nos. 994, 995). It was also at about this time that Fastolf entertained hopes that the Bishop's influence would secure his success in the long-running dispute with the Hickling Priory over rent arrears: see Smith, 'Sir John Fastolf's Dispute with Hickling Priory', pp. 57–70 (at pp. 64–6). In addition, a letter of Fastolf's dated 23 November 1450 (no. 991) mentions 'a baylly of Hykelyng that meynteynyth the Pryour yn hys wrong ayenst me'. It thus appears probable that Playter's letter dates from the latter months of 1450.

Unprinted.

Rygth ⟨worchipfull *and*⟩[1] my most esp*eci*all maist*er*, I recomend me vn-to your good maisterchip. Lyke it you to wete that I have ben wyth my lorde[2]

992. *The bottom left hand corner of the sheet is altogether gone, and an area extending upwards, varying in width from about $\frac{1}{2}$ in. to $1\frac{1}{2}$ in., is also missing. Much damaged by damp, and a number of readings visible only under ultra-violet light.*

[1] *As in the address on the dorse.*

[2] e *over* es *abbrev.*

⟨of Nor⟩wich, ⟨. . .⟩[3] ⟨wi⟩th hys lordchip vpon swyche mat*er*s as was conteyned wyth-in youre letter whyche ye sent vn-to hym. And as for ⟨my lady of⟩ Suff*olk*, he told me that sche meved no thyng to hym as for youre m⟨a⟩ne⟨r⟩ of De⟨d⟩h⟨a⟩m, f⟨o⟩r he was so syke ⟨. . .⟩[4] Oxon*ford* that sche toke no leyser wyth hym to talke of ony swych maters. Neu*er*thelesse, as he told me he ⟨. . .⟩[5] herin⟨ne⟩ nowth ne wyll in swyche man*er* of doyng*es*, wher-for ⌜he⌝ desyred to have a copy ⟨*and*⟩ a sygth of the arby⟨trement⟩ ⟨. . .⟩[6] ⌜was⌝ ⟨made⟩ by my lord[7] of Caunt*er*bury *and* hym,[8] that he mygth be the ryper to comoun wyth here in thys. ⟨. . .⟩[9] to breke to hym ther-of, and so I schewed hym the same arbytrement that Wyll*ia*m ⟨. . .⟩,[10] whyche he made to be copyed for his remembrau*n*ce, *and* was rygth gladde that ch⟨. . .⟩.[11] ⟨. . .⟩[12] as wel as he and he ⌜comendyd⌝[13] hym hartely to you, *and* seyth what he may do for ⟨. . .⟩[14] was rygth wel pleased that ye were amendyd.

And as for Hykelyng mater, I meved ⟨. . .⟩[15] comuanded me, and he seyde they arn so rewled aft*er* Heydon that they woll putte the mat*er* ⟨. . .⟩[16] Heydon. But if it come to hys hand he wole do as trouthe *and* consyens wold, *and* that schuld ⟨. . .⟩.[17] whom I p*ra*y *and* schall ⌜p*ra*y⌝ send you youre hertes desyres, long bodely helthe, *and* plesa*u*ns with the pl⟨. . .⟩[18] ⟨. . .⟩[19] ⟨. . . ien⟩.

⟨. . .⟩[20]

By youre man *and* seruaunt THOMAS PLAYT*ER*

993. From SIR JOHN FASTOLF to HOWES, JENNEY and BOKKYNG — 1450, 2 December

Add. 39848, f. 10. $11\frac{3}{4} \times 9\frac{1}{4}$ in. Worcester's hand, subscription autograph.

Dorse: Marks of folding, slits for tape, wafer seal over remains of red wax. Address in Worcester's hand:

*To my ryght trusty frendys S*er *Thomas parson of Castellcombe, William Jenney and John Bokkyng.*

Dated.

G. 128/158 (abstract).

3 *Space for about ten letters.*
4 *Space for about twenty letters.*
5 *Space for about twenty-two letters.*
6 *Space for about twenty letters.*
7 Sir *canc.*
8 And I *canc.*
9 *Space for about thirty letters.*
10 *Space for about thirty letters.*
11 *Space for two or three letters before edge of page.*
12 *Corner of page gone; space for about thirty-five letters.*
13 *Over* comend *canc.*
14 *Corner of page gone; space for about thirty letters.*
15 *Corner of page gone; space for about thirty letters.*
16 *Corner of page gone; space for about twenty-five letters.*
17 *Corner of page gone; space for about twenty-five letters.*
18 *Two or three letters missing at edge of page.*
19 *Corner of page gone; space for about thirty letters.*
20 *Paper torn; first line of subscription not legible.*

Ryght[1] trusty and welbelovyd frendys I greete you well, and lete you wete that I hafe resseyved a l*ett*re from my trusty[2] s*er*u*au*nt John Bokkyng, and[3] vndrestand well the diligent labour doon by yow and my gode frendys abow[t] the processe of my materys yn that parties, trustyng to you of your conti*nuau*nce. And fyrst, as for the p*ro*cesse ayenst Wymdam in my name touchyng the Ladye Bardolf, for ⌜whych⌝ he daylie lesyth issues as I am lerned, I have gr*a*unted to the said Wymdam to respyte the said mater till the next terme, wythynne whych tyme he offryth to agree wyth me, yff hit can be found *and* p*re*vyd that he was meynteyno*ur* ayenst me yn that mater.[4]

It*em*, for all maner p*er*sones except S*er* Thomas Tuddenh*a*m, Heydon [and] Pykeryng[5] that been endyted at my sewte: in caas they wolle fynde you suffis*a*unt suertee made to me to obbey the orden*au*nce of my lerned councell, and to fullfille such orden*au*nce and awaard as shall wyth ryght be made, I hald me content wyth that yee thynk it mooste for my worshyp and proffyt that y take hem to agreem*en*t. And yff your wysdoms thynkyth that there be certeyn of hem that hafe so[6] grevouselye offended ayenst me that it ys bett*er* for me the rygour or vtmost off the[7] lawe be shewed and doon vnto hem, till I be satisfyed of my cost*es* and da*m*mag*es*, I wolle welle ye procede on thoo. It nede not expresse you the namys ne the causys, for ye have remembr*a*unces wyth yow of hem. And the cause whye I make menc*i*on to you of thys mater ys, byasmoch ye meove me that manye of thoo that been endited appere not, but lesen issues to the Kyng whych may not avayle me, safe oonlye a chastysyng to theym that they enbold hem not to mysdon to me here-afft*er*.

It*em*, Maist*er* John Botewryght hath sent a l*ett*re to me of certeyn grete losse and da*m*magys don by S*er* Thomas Tuddenh*a*m and Heydon to the comyn off Swaffam, benymmyng vj^{c} acres lond of her comyn, whych l*ett*re I shall do it to be remembred as it shall be thought necessarie.

It*em*, where as ye reme*m*bre that I wryte l*ett*res of reco*m*mendac*i*on to my lord Oxford and to my brothyr Ȝelu*er*ton, I hafe wryten vnto my said brothyr Ȝelu*er*ton at thys tyme. But I may not have the leysei*ur* to wryte now, I am so gretely vexed yn my labour *and* spyrit*es* yn thys trouble seson, that at tyme I myght not abyde the syngnyng ne selyng of my l*ett*re that I wold send, and therfor excuse ye me as ye thynk best. And ⌜as⌝[8] for tydyng*es* &c the berer here off can sey yow. I shuld hafe aunsuer John Bokkyng l*ett*re more p*ar*tic*u*ler,[9] but I had send it out at the wrytyng here-off, and therfor that at ys foryeete shall be reme*m*bred at the next wrytyng.

It*em*, I pray you seeyth well to the charg*es* and allowaunces of myne officers accomptant*es*, and that they make lyu*er*eez of money vppon her charg*es* bett*er*

993. [1] *Letter* a *added to left by another hand.* [2] *First* t *over* ser *abbrev.*
[3] vndre *not canc., at end of line.*
[4] *Fastolf's signature appears at this point, and the remainder of the text is written to the left of and below it; see the closing passage below.*
[5] *Underlined.* [6] *Over* ser *abbrev.*
[7] *As n. 1 above.* [8] *Over* ther *canc.* [9] l *barred, possibly representing abbrev.*

then I vele they doo, for and myne audit*our*s had such offic*er*s vndre hem they wold be ryght wroth, but they had moo lyu*er*ees of her charge *and* office then I have. I sey allwey a comyn sawe, shew me the meete but shew me not the man &c.

No more for haste, but Gode hafe you yn hys kepyng. Wryt hastly at London ij^{d} day of December A^{o} xxix r.r. H. vj. And be cause I myght [not] abyde till the wrytyng*es* of the mater*es* that I co*m*maunded Worcestr*e* to wryte, I signed the l*ett*re so neere the begynnyng; but I wolle ye tendyr neu*er*e the lasse my l*ett*re *and* articles for my moost p*ro*ffyt and avayle.

J. FASTOLFE[10]

994. From SIR JOHN FASTOLF to THOMAS HOWES and JOHN BOKKYNG 1450, 4 December

Add. 34888, f. 53. $11\frac{3}{4} \times 8\frac{1}{2}$ in. Worcester's hand, subscription autograph.

Dorse: Marks of folding, remains of red wax. Address in Worcester's hand:

To my ryght trusty frende and *s*eru*au*n*t*es *S*er *Thomas* p*ar*s*on of Castellcombe and John Bokkyng, at Prynce Inne yn Norwych, or at Beklys.*

Dated.

F. iii, p. 102. G. 130/160 (parts).

Ryght[1] trusty and welbelovyd s*er*u*au*nt, I grete yow well, and lete you wete that my lord of Oxford hath late be wyth me, and delyu*er*ed me a l*ett*re from my said lord wyth certeyn credence, whych I have and shall tendyr yn all goodly haste it may; and a-nothyr l*ett*re delyu*er*ed by hym from you to me, whych l*ett*re I have herd radd mater by mater and well vndrestand the contenew off it. And for the expedic*i*ons of my mater*es* comprysed yn the said l*ett*re I con yow ryght goode thank, for the deede shewyth well your gode diligencez. And where as the Lord Scalys woold colour the sheepe *and* catell of S*er* Thomas Tuddenham *and* Heydon to be hys, to th'entent that the Kyng shuld beere no proffyt of the issues that they throw her obstinacie have lost &c: I hafe reme*m*bred the mater yn such wyse to lordes of the Councell and to the Treso*ur*ier, that hit shall not be coloured yn such wyse, for that were an vntrue wey for ony gentleman to colour such a deede.

It*em*,[2] forasmoch as I vndrestond that on Monday next the oyer *and* t*er*miner shall be halden at Beklys, and ye avysen to seende yow a certificat for cause of the forged quyt*a*unce by S*er* John Sypton, whych wrytyng I seende you by the berer here-off; p*ra*yng you that ye solicit to my councell that the

[10] *See n. 4 above.*

994. [1] *Letter* a *added to left by another hand.*
[2] *As n. 1 above. This item printed by Fenn and Gairdner.*

said S*er* John Sypton be endited therevppon, and that ye foryete not Vlueston, Andreus, and tho othyr*es* that forged a fals office to cast my maner of Bradwell ynto the Kyng*es* hand.

It*e*m, I have thys day spoke wyth Symond Baker, and demanded of hym whate men were of councell and causyng that the new mille dam of my maner of Dedh*a*m Ou*er*hall was broken and a trenche maade throw my grounde ayenst my wille by the Duc of Suff*olk* councell, and so lost the water of the seid mille. And the said Simond seid vnto me that S*er* John Squyer was chieff councell, and John Waryn was stuard of Dedh*a*m at that tyme, was yn all the Duc ys mater*es* there of councell also. Wherfor byasmoch as S*er* John Squyer ys decesed, and can hafe no remedie ayenst hym, wherfor I wold ye comyned w*ith* my lerned councell yff the said John Waryn myght be p*re*sented for that cause, byasmoch he was made an offic*er* there and of councell wyth[3] the said Duc. And ou*er*e that there was one John Cole of ⌜Stoke in Suffolk,⌝[4] that dyd arrest my tymbr*e* at Cadywade w*ith* S*er* John Squyer, ⌜to the dam*m*age off xiij li.;⌝ and therfor yn lyke wyse that he myght be endyted of t*re*spasse, for othyr remedie hafe I none, p*ra*yng you to remembr*e*[5] all othyr mater*es* ye thynk best for my worshyp and moste proffyt.

It*e*m, where as onye man hath onye thretyng langage to yow or to onye of my s*er*u*au*nt*es* yn the name of Tuddenh*a*m or Heydon, let me hafe knoulege off it, and it shall be remedied. And reco*m*maund me to my lord off Oxford and my brothyr Ʒelu*er*ton; and I wryte l*ett*res to hem by my lord of Oxford s*er*u*au*nt.

It*em*, the offic*er*s off the Duchee be chaunged, for Blake ys vndrest[ua]rd,[6] whych ys one off the clerk*es* of the Signett; and he labo*ur*yth effectuelly for to remedie the damag*es* of the Duché yn the best wyse.

It*em*,[7] I sende you a cop*é* of Sybeton ple *and* quyt*a*unce forged to grounde your bille by it.[8]

No more for haste, but God kepe you. Wryt at London iiij day of December A^{o} xxix^{o} r.r. H. vj.[9]

It*em*, S*er* John Buk, p*ar*son of Stratford, physshed my stankys at Dedh*a*m and holp brake my damme, destroyed my new mille, and was ayenst me allwey at Dedh*a*m, to the damage off xx li., whych may be endyted allso.

It*em* the seid John Cole hath[10] by force ayenst my wille thys yeer*e* *and* othyr yeer*es* ⌜take⌝ out off my waters at Dedh*a*m, as I am credybly enformed, and S*er* John Bukk, to the no*m*br*e* of xxiiij swannys *and* signett*es*; and I pray you thys be not foryeted at thys oyer *and* te*r*miner in Suff*olk*.

J. FASTOLFE

[3] no*ta* to left in Worcester's hand.
[4] *Over* Manytr*e*.
[5] *MS.* rembembr*e*, *first* b *subpuncted.*
[6] *Miswritten.*
[7] *Fenn and Gairdner printed also the remainder of the letter from this point, with abridgements in the final paragraph.*
[8] It*em* the vn *canc.*
[9] *Fastolf's signature appears at this point. Remainder of text written to left of and beneath it.*
[10] fl *canc.*

995. From Sir John Fastolf to Thomas Howes and John Bokkyng 1450, 5 December

Add. 39848, f. 12. $11\frac{3}{4} \times 9\frac{1}{2}$ in. Worcester's hand, subscription autograph.

Dorse: Marks of folding, slits for tape, wafer seal with rose motif attached on a strip of paper. Address in Worcester's hand:

*To my ryght trusty frendys S*er *Thomas, p*ar*son of Castelc*om*be,* and *John Bokkyng, in haste at Prince ys Inn yn Norwych.*

Dated.
G. 131/161 (abstract).

Ryght[1] trusty frendys I grete you well. And forasmoch as I vndrestand by your l*ett*res that the oyer *and* t*er*miner in Suff*olk* shall be halden at Beklys on Monday next, wherfor I pray you to solicit vnto my lerned councell that S*er* John Sypton may be endyted for forgyng of the fals acquyt*a*unce, and that Bury hys att*ur*ney whych leyd ynto the court and ⌜meynteyned⌝[2] the seyd fals acquyt*a*unce be endyted also, for I wold not for moch goode but he were chastysed by that wey.

It*e*m, I have thys weke comyned wyth my ten*au*nt*es* of Dedh*a*m, who were the chieff councell of brekyng my mylledam, whereby I hafe lost xx li. by yeere. And they seyn that S*er* John Squyer was chieff, but John Waryn was of councell and court halder there; also S*er* John Buk, p*ar*son of Stratton, was off councell and doer also, whych physshyd my stank*es* and waters at Dedh*a*m and destroyed the grete[3] qu*an*tité of physsh to the da*m*mage of xx li. yn pykys, bremys *and* p*er*chys. And one John Cole of Stoke in the same counté hath taken by dyu*er*s tymys in yeer*es* passed moo then xx of my swannes *and* signett*es* beyng yn my ryuers at Dedh*a*m, as I am ryght credyblye enformed. And also the seid John Cole dy[d] arrest my tymbr*e* wrongyslye at Dedh*a*m, whych the grete waters hafe born awey to the value[4] of xx m*ark*es; and therfor that they be p*re*sented for thoo grevouse offens*es* doon to me.

It*e*m[5] the p*ar*son off Cotton that late was duellyng there fast by Cotton, whych falsly enformed Willia*m* Cole and Shypd*a*m myne audito*ur*s that tho off my ten*au*nt*es* in Cotton that plegged owt Herry Holm late my baylly there wer notable and sufficient men to pay me the debt that the said Herry Holm owed vn-to me. And the seid plegg*es* were of no value, the said audito*ur*s gevyng credence to the said p*ar*son toke the said vnsufficient men to be plegge. And the said Herry Holm discharged out of pryson by that p*ar*son fals suggestion, and y yhyt not payd. And the seid Herry decesed and hath none executo*ur* ne mynstro*ur*. Wherfor I wold ye inqueryd of the p*ar*son, my

995. [1] *Letter* a *added to left by another hand.* [2] *Over* forged *canc.*
[3] *One word canc.* [4] v *superimposed on* s.
[5] *Gap of about one inch.*

resseyuo*ur* or of such as ye can com by to enforme you the grounde of thys mater, soo as the trouth ys, that I myght hafe a cause ayenst that p*ar*son off Cotton and such as disseyved me. And aft*er* that Willia*m* Cole enformed me, the seid Herry Holm was arrested and com*m*ytted to John Segbroke of Cotton to kepe, and bryng the said Herry to the yaile at Burye. And the said Segbroke dyd lett the seyd Herry goo bethout licence of the audito*ur*s, wherfor me thynkyth the said Segbroke ought aunsuer to thys mat*er*. Ye may speke wyth Sym off Daale, he can enforme yow moch of thys mat*er*.

It*e*m, I hafe sent you by Rychart Baxst*er* a l*ett*re of testi*m*onial ayenst S*er* John Sybton and the plee to grounde yo*ur* mater by, wyth a l*ett*re missyve of my reme*m*br*au*nces, whych I pray yow effectuelly to tendyr for my moste p*ro*ffyt and avayle.[6]

It*e*m, I wrote before thys to you that the jur*é* in Suff*olk*, whych John Andreu falsly toke and caused my maner of Bradwell to be cast yn to the Kyng*es* hand, myght be examyned yff they p*re*sented onye such office; and that to-fore the co*m*myssioners the said ex*am*inac*i*on myght be made yff it cowde be, or ell*es* apart to-fore worshypfull men of credence, and sett to her selys as the jur*é* named yn the certificat of Tychewell.

It*e*m, I have wryt to you l*ett*res by Maist*er* Hue Acton, and seth by othyrs goers betwene, but I hyre no word of how manye peyr l*ett*res the p*ar*son and ye[7] hafe resseyvyd seth ye rode; also by Wymdam s*er*u*au*nt &c. And yff Ric*hart* Baxst*er* that rode yerstenday com not be-tyme to you to Beclys, sendyth for hy*m* but iiij myle from yow to resseyve hys l*ett*res.

No more, but I pray you tendryth *and* reme*m*bryth all othyr mat*er*s that I can not reme*m*br*e* her*e*; reco*m*maundyng me to [my] ryght trusty frende Willia*m* Jenney, and p*ra*yng hym to tendyr me yn all my mater*es* as I vele well he dooth.

Wryten at London the v day of December A^{o} xxix^{o} r. r. H. vj.

J. FASTOLFE

996. From SIR JOHN FASTOLF to THOMAS HOWES
1450, 20 December

Add. 27443, f. 118r–v. 11$\frac{3}{8}$ × 19 in. Worcester's hand, subscription autograph.

Dorse: Continuation of text. Marks of folding, slits for tape, traces of red wax. Address in Worcester's hand:

To my ryght trusty and welbelovyd frendys, Sir Thomas, parson of Castellcombe.

[6] *Fastolf's signature appears here; remainder of letter to left of and beneath it. Letter* a *added to left and connected to first word of next paragraph by a line.*

[7] e *superimposed on* h.

996. *From Sir John Fastolf to Thomas Howes, 20 December 1450*

Dated. The manuscript is in two pieces, the lower section having been acquired by the British Museum as part of Add. 39848 in 1919, and since reunited with the upper portion.
G. 132/162.

Ryght trusty frendys, I grete you well, and lete you wete that I have resseyved your l*ett*re thys day, whych was wryt xv day of Dece*m*ber; and vndre[stand] well your ryght gode moc*i*ons and causes shewed of jnconvenient*es* that myght falle, yff the shyreve have not a gode vndreshyreff whych were not enclynyng to the partie off T. H. And thereas ye meoffe me to wryte to ij lordys for the said cause, they be both forth to theyr contré, and shall therfor wryte vnto hem vppon the teno*ur* of your l*ett*rez in that at y can or may, as forre as reson and justice wolle, for such an officer as woll not, for no mede, hate, or loffe, execut dewlye hys office to the weele of the contré.

It*em*,[1] the day of thys l*ett*re wrytyng, John Bokkyng ys com to me, and hath exp*re*ssely enformyd me by mouth as by wrytyng*es* the greete labour and diligence whych ye have take vppon yow, seth Martism*a*sse, in especiall, abowte the expedic*i*on of my p*ro*cesse of oyer *and* te*r*miner before the Kyng*es* co*m*myssione*r*s attained; and I vele ryght well by the au*au*ncem*en*t of my processe your faithfull diligence, for whych y can you ryght gode thank, and trustyng vppon your gode contin*ua*nce. And seth the co*m*missioners shall sytt at Lynne aft*er* the Epiphanye, such of my mater*es* as have take none ende, but hang yn processe for deffaut of aunsuer or app*ar*aunce of my partie adu*er*se, I pray you that the said mater*es* may be called vppon of the now, and dew p*ro*cesse had as ferre as justice and gode concience wolle.

It*em*, it ys so, as I vndrestand, that the Lord Scalys woll be at Lynne thys Cristm*a*sse, and at the oyer *and* te*r*miner halden there; and S*er* Thomas Tuddenh*a*m and Heydon wolle appere, of whych I am well content. And it ⌜ys⌝ lyke that grete labour and speciall pursute shall be made to the Lord Scalys, that he wolle meynteyn the said Tuddenh*a*m and Heydon in all he can or may, and thus I have herd sey. Wherfor such p*er*sones as have founde hem soore greved by extorc*i*on, as I have ben, and have p*ro*cesse or wolle hafe p*ro*cesse before the co*m*missioner*es*, they most effectuelly labour to my lord Oxford, and to my brothyr Ȝelu*er*ton, justice, that they wolle as ferre as justice, reson, *and* concience do that justice may [be] egallie myn*i*stred, and not to wythdrawe theyr couragez well sett from the pore peple. For and they hald not the hand well and stedfast yn thys mater from hens forth whyle it shall dure, as they have herebefore, the pore peple and all the grete part of both shyr*es* of Norff*olk* and Suff*olk* be destroyed. For it shewyth well by whate manyfold vndewe menys of extorc*i*on they have lyved yn miserie and grete pouu*er*te by manye yeer*es* contynewed, that the moste part of the comyners have litill or nought to meynteyn theyr menage *and* housold, ne to pay the Kyng*es* taskys, nothyr theyr rent*es* *and* se*r*vises to the lordz they be

996. [1] *Letter* a *added to left by another hand.*

ten*au*nt*es* vntoo, as it shewyth daylie to all the world, whych ys ou*er*e a grete pitie to thynk. And when the said pore peple have be by such jniuries ouerladd and so vndoon, nedz most the gentlemen that have theyr pore lyvelode amonge*s* hem be gretely mi*n*nusshed and hyndered of theyr encrese and levyng.

It*e*m, where as I vndrestand by a l*ett*re sent to me from my welbelovyd frende Maist*er* John Botewryght, that grete extorc*io*n have be don by the offic*er*s off the Duchee in takyng awey cxl acres pasture at Swaffam, whych ys of the Kyng*es* demeynz and of hys enherit*a*unce as of the Duchee of Lancastr*e*. For whych pastur*es*, yff it com not ynne ayen, it woll be grete disherit*a*unce to the Kyng, and[2] fynell destrucc*io*n of the ten*au*nt*es* there, for whych the seid Maistr*e* John desyryth and prayeth of remedie yn the name of all the toune of Swaffam. As to thys, such as wold here the encrese and wellfare of hym, of hys parysshons, and off all thoo so mysdon vntoo, most by the avice of som lerned man to put theyr op*r*essions and greu*au*ncez in wrytyng, well grounded, and as the trouth of the mat*er* ys; and that the said wrytyng or bille may be enseled wyth the seles of such gentlemen that have lyvelode there, and wyth tho men that be cowthest knowen; and that ⌜wrytyng*es*⌝[3] so enseled to be directed to the Kyng,[4] and to the lordz of hys Councell. And then it ys *and* woll be of more credence to the Kyng *and* the lordys then a simple l*ett*re. And thys doon wyth the labour*es* that they may make there in shewyng theyr greu*au*nces to the co*m*missione*rs*; and the seid greu*au*nces shewed also here amonge*s* the Kyng *and* the lordz, it ys verrayly to thynk that they shall be purveyd of a remedie. And foryete not to sende or wryte to Maist*er* Botewryght in goodly haste of thys article, wyth your correcc*io*n to be had where the au*er*tisment*es* of you *and* my frendz that have more p*ar*ticuler knoulege yn such mater*es*.

It*e*m, I have grete m*er*veylle that yong Jenney, whych ys of my lord Cromewell councell, and Rob*er*t Ledam, also off hys councell, *and* hys man, be not spoke w*y*t*h*, there that they doo not attaine an acc*io*n ayenst S*er* Thomas Tudden[ham], Heydon, *and* John Gent, whych have and wold daylye labour to disseisse my Lord Cromewell of[5] a knyghten s*er*vice in Saxthorp, whych ye have ryght suffis*a*unt evidens*es* by an endenture of Kyng Edw*a*rd iij^{d} dayes enseled, as off Kyng Herry dayes the iiij^{the}, that the seid maner ys hald by the iiij^{the} part of a kny*ȝ*t fee of my Lord Cromewell as of the maner of Tateshale. And the seid Tuddenh*a*m *and* Heydon wold aft*er* theyr voulenté have it hald yn meen of the maner of Hetersete, whych suffis*a*unt evidens*es* that ye have specifyeth no thyng soo. And I have lost xx li. yeerly yn approweme*n*t of my chatell, for cause my lord Cromewell, throw neglicence of hys offic*er*s in Norff*olk*, have not meynteyned hys ryght. And there as John Bokkyng seith that John Jenney hath no co*m*maundm*en*t of my

[2] is *canc.* [3] *Over* mater *canc.*
[4] *MS.* kynge*s* [5] hys *canc.*

lord to pursue hys ryght, it shewyth off reson that seth he ys of hys councell in especiall for that shyre, he ought doo hys ryȝt to be savyd, *and* kept of hys dewtee. And thertoo he knouyth well that my said lord hath co*m*maunded hym dyu*er*s tymys to take kepe hys ryȝt be savyd in thys mat*er*. Wherfor I pray you requyre hy*m* on my lord ys behalf[6] to compleyn to justice at thys oyer *and* ⟨terminer⟩ for remedie, and that the bille be made yn my lord ys name. And therto ⟨he may⟩ have co*m*maundme*n*t ryȝt sone of my lord eftsonys, and he wolle sende vnto hy*m* by such as goth dayly in to that contree to Tateshale. And I had send hy*m* hys speciall ⟨com⟩maundm*en*t, had he sent me such word be-tyme whyle he was heere. I pr*a*y you reme*m*br*e* ye so John Jenney and Rob*er*t Ledam as I have no cause to ⟨wri⟩te more, ne to compleyn to my lord of theyr necligence.

Item, s*er* p*ar*son, where it ys soo that my cosyn Boys ys passed to God, whoos soule God assoyle, ye shall fynde amonge*s* my boke*s* of accompte*s* at Castr*e*, or amonge*s* othyr wrytynge*s*, he owed me monney for a ferm he heeld of me, as Watkyn Shypdam ys reme*m*bred; and also I lent hym xl s. whych I shuld have an oblig*aci*on at Castr*e* off, p*ra*ying you to inquire off thys dewteez, and see recuu*er*e may be made off it &c.

It*e*m, I seende a l*ett*re at thys tyme to my cosyn Wychyngh*a*m, to hys modre also, for a mat*er* that touchyth my cosyn Rob*er*t Fitzrauff ys au*au*ncem*en*t, and the partie also; whych l*ett*re I woll ye breke to vndrestand my wrytyng and the subst*a*unce off it the more. And y pray you hertly to speke wyth the partie at Norwych aswell as w*y*t*h* my ryght welbelovyd cosyn S*er* Herry Inglose, and wyth my cosyn Wychyngh*a*m assone as ye goodly may. And meoffe ye the said mat*er* yn such wyse as your discrec*io*n can well considre that the rathyr the said mat*er* may take a gode ende, yff it may be yn ony wyse; yn whych mat*er* ye shall do me ryght singler plesyr, and that thys be not slewthed, for tarye⟨n⟩g drawyth perell &c. I wryte but briefflye, for *pora*[7] *mitte* s*a*pi*e*n*t*er &c.

It*e*m, where as Brome ys not wellwyllyng yn my matere*s*, whych for the wronge*s* takyng and wyth-haldyng my shepe I ought take a acc*io*n ayenst hym; for declarac*io*n in whate wyse he dyd it, John Bele my sheperefe can enforme you best, for he laboured about the recuu*er*e of it. My lady Norff*olk* sent me a[8] l*ett*re viij yere goon, whych I shuld hafe, desyryng that the p*ro*cesse I was purposed[9] take ayenst hym shuld be respited, and all that reson wolld he shuld obbey. I am avysed therfor let som man about my lord ⌜Norff*olk*⌝ and my lady have wetyng, or I begynne. Yhyt I wold ye had declarac*io*n before of the conduyt *and* grounde of thys mat*er*.

It*e*m, where my cosyn Inglose avyse me fully to take a speciall assise on the Pryo*ur* of Hykelyng for my rent, I have abydden vppon my cosyn Paston that

[6] *Lower portion of MS., earlier torn away, begins here; some loss of text at join.*
[7] p *superimposed on* e.
[8] *No space.*
[9] *First* p *doubled.*

he *and* I shuld take one to-ghedyr, and I vele hym no thyng spedie in it. Let me knou how he woll doo thys next t*er*me, for ell*es* am I fully avysed to take myne owt, and to trau*er*se all iij offices for Beyton, Bradwell and Tychewell, wyth the help of my frendz. Not ell*es* at thys tyme, but I pray you comfort all thoo that fynde hem greved to abyde by theyr ryȝt, and that ye woll contynew forth for my worshyp *and* p*ro*ffyt as ferre as ryȝt wolle; whych I trust to God shall bett*er* have hys cours then it hath beforn, who have you in hys kepyng.

Wryt at London, the xx day of Decemb*re* A^{o} xxix^{o} r.r. H. vj.

It*em*, that thys l*ett*re co*m*maund me to my cosyn John a Berney.

J. FASTOLFE[10]

It*em*, I have sende ij l*ett*res to my lord Erle of Oxford, the ton by[11] Robson ys man, a[12] squyer of my lordys. And the grete subst*a*unce of the l*ett*re ys that the issues forfeted may be sent vpp be-tyme to my lord Tresorer, for there shall be none assignem*en*t made, ne may not, till it com yn wrytyng. It be don, had it be sent. Grete sute ys made to pardon it, but the Kyng*es* councell woll not suffre it. The ij^{d} l*ett*re Nicholas Bokkyng beryth for excuse of my cosyn Inglose, be cause grete labo*ur* hath be made to my lord York ayenst my cosyn Inglose and Seggeford, that they shuld endyte the P*ri*our of Walsyng-h*a*m tenauntes yn Salle. Wherevppon my lord York, vnadu*er*tised of the trouth, sent a[13] l*ett*re to my lord Oxford to support the Pryo*ur* ys ten*aun*tes ayenst Seggeford namely &c.

It*em*, I desyre that and John Berney or onye man can mete wyth Dallyng, that fals vndre escheto*ur*, in onye place prouiable, that he may by force brought to Castr*e* bethout da*m*mage of hys bodye, and there to be kept yn hold, that he may confesse the trouth of the fals office he[14] forged off my maner of Tychewell.

It*em*, forasmoch as ye shall have to doon at Lynne for my mater*es* there as for Tychewell and othyr*es*, therfor I wolle that yee doo purvey of gode frendys as be aboute Flegg that passen yn jureez, that they may wayt vppon yow there at Lynne, and othyr such trusty men that ye can ghete to spede my p*ro*cesses,[15] and that ye do hem goode chier and cost vppon ⌜hem⌝ aft*er* that the case shall requyre. I co*m*myt thys mater to be ruled by your wysdom, that it be not forȝeted.[16]

[10] *Foot of f. 118v. Remainder of text on dorse.*
[11] th *canc.*
[12] *No space.*
[13] *No space.*
[14] toke it *canc.*
[15] And I shall *canc.*
[16] *Last letter uncertain, but not* n.

997. From Sir John Fastolf to John Berney and Thomas Howes 1450, 27 December

Add. 39848, f. 13. $11\frac{1}{2} \times 4\frac{1}{2}$ in. William Barker's hand, subscription autograph.

Dorse: Marks of folding, slits for tape, remains of red wax seal. Address in Barker's hand:

To my trusty frendes John a Berney and *to S*er *Thomas Howys, clerk.*

St. John's day in Christmas is 27 December, and the matters referred to in the letter relate it to no. 996 of 20 December 1450 and no. 1003 of 7 January 1451, amongst others, where sessions at Lynn in January 1451 are mentioned as forthcoming.
G. 133/164 (abstract).

Ryght trusty and weel be-lovyd, I grete you weel, and p*ra*ye you that ye take good hede to alle my materes there to be spedde the Tewesday after the twelth, and that no thyng be for-geten at that tyme. And in especyall I p*ra*ye[1] you that ye labo*ur*e the juré that was supposed[2] to a past in the office founde for Tychewell, that they may appere at Lynne and ther make a sertyfycat be-fore my lord of Oxford *and* the justyce Will*iam* Yelu*er*ton, that þei[3] were never p*re*vye ner concentyng to suche an office fyndeng, and vpo*n* that than to grounde myn acc*ion* a-yenst Dallyng, the fals harlotte &c; wheche I wold Berneye, so hit were secretly don, rewarded for his good labo*ur*e, and Dynne also, ye wete what I mene. I p*ra*y yow se wel forth, for *mitte sapient*er &c.

Wrete at London in hast the Seynt Johnes day in Crystemasse. For he cam to Castr*e* and ther seye myn evydence, and than made the office ther-by, *and* for Suff*olk* also the fals offices founde there in lyke wyse &c. I p*ra*ye yow spare hi[t][4] in no wyse for ought þ*a*t may be-falle, but that ye sewe hem to the vtmost &c. I p*ra*ye yow saddely to thenk on this materes, þ*a*t I may have aunswere aye*n* sewerly how ye do*n* in them.

J. Fastolfe

998. From Sir John Fastolf probably to Thomas Howes: fragment 1450, December, or 1451, early January

Add. 27443, f. 121. $11\frac{3}{8} \times 2\frac{1}{4}$ in. William Barker's hand, subscription autograph.

Dorse: Blank, except for a pen-trial in an early hand: 'Amen y Trusty and well'.

997. [1] I p*ra*ye *repeated.* [2] *Letter* a *added to left by another hand.*
[3] þ *is written in the form* y *in this hand;* ei *superscript, but no abbreviation seems intended.*
[4] *Last letter uncertain, apparently* t *superimposed on* s. *Fastolf's signature previously inserted to right of this, the last word of a shortened line.*

The manuscript is a fragment detached from the foot of a letter, and carries only a postscript written to the left of and beneath Fastolf's signature. As Gairdner remarked, Fastolf reminded Howes about the matter mentioned here in no. 1003 of 7 January 1451, and likewise Bokkyng in no. 1004 of 12 January 1451.

G. 137/166.

It*em* that S*er* Herry Ingelose and the meyer be spoke to for here worship, that the man weche that herd Heydon seye the langage vpo*n* wheche he[1] is endyted be sent heder, for that aught not to be kept p*re*vye, but oplyshed, seyng any thyng towchyng or sownyng to treson. And on the other part it is to greet necye to noyse any man w*ith*-ought cause &c. Hit is not here wurship, this mater, if hit be trew, is so longe kept p*re*vye w*ith* theym &c.

J. FASTOLFE

999. From THE EARL OF OXFORD to JOHN JERMYN

1451, 2 January

Add. 34888, f. 61. $11\frac{1}{2} \times 8\frac{3}{4}$ in. Hand of Thomas Denys; see Plate XXVII.

Dorse: Marks of folding, traces of red wax. Address in Denys's hand:

To my ryght trusty and intierly welbel⟨oved⟩[1] *John Jermyn, Shirreve of Norffolk.*

The year is evident from the fact that John Jermyn was sheriff of Norfolk in 1451 (as Gairdner observed), and from the reference to 'this next sessions at Lenn', which took place later in January of that year; cf. nos. 996, 1003.

F. iii, p. 106. G. 138/167.

Right trusty and intierly welbeloued, I grete yow wele. And where late by the Kyng*es* comaundment in the tyme of his Parlement, holden now last at Westm*inster*, I was in p*er*sone at Norwich, holdyng sessions of oir det*er*myner w*ith* Yelu*er*ton, on of the Kyng*es* juges, by greet space and greet attendaunce; which for to a do w*ith* suych diligence in the P*ar*lement tyme I wold a be right lothe, but for the pupplyk wele of all the shire.

It is also not oute of yo*ur* reme[m]braunce[2] what indisposic*i*on the com*m*ons of bothe countes in the ende of somer last passed wer of, and how the Kyng by the hole aduyse of all the greet councell of Inglond, to sese their rumo*ur*, send hider his said comission; and how I have do my part therynne I reporte me to all the world. I here a gruggyng, neu*er*thelesse, that trew fauo*ur* in yo*ur* office to the pople that hath compleyned by many and grete horible billes agayn certeyn p*er*sones shuld not be shewid at this next

998. [1] *No space.*

999. [1] *Obliterated by MS. repair.* [2] *MS.* remenbraunce*;* by *canc.*

sessions at Lenn, ne ferther*e* in the said comission, which if it so were, as God defend, myght cause a latt*er* erro*ur* wurs than the first.

I p*ra*y yow, therfore, that ye wole write to me yo*ur* disposic*i*on, how ye p*ur*pose to be demened, and how I shal take yow for[3] ⌜th'execuc*i*on of the⌝ Kyng*es* comission and the pupplik wele of al the shire. And aftir that that ye write to me, so wole I take yow, latyng yow wete that I were lothe to labo*ur* ferther, but if I wist that the com*m*ons shuld be easid as Goddes law wold. And if ony erro*ur* grow the defaute shal not be founde in me.

I p*ra*y yow more ou*er* to gif credence to the berer her-of. And the Trinité kepe yow.

Wretyn at Wynch the second day of January.

THE ERLE OF OXENFORD

1000. From THE EARL OF OXFORD to SIR JOHN FASTOLF 1451, 2 January

Add. 27443, f. 122. $11\frac{5}{8} \times 8\frac{3}{8}$ in. Hand of Thomas Denys.

Dorse: Marks of folding, remains of red wax seal. Address in Denys's hand:

*To my ryght trust[y] and intierly welbeloued S*er *John Fastolf, knyght.*

In appearance and handwriting this letter closely resembles no. 999, likewise written by Thomas Denys for the Earl of Oxford from Winch on a 2 January, in a year that can be deduced as 1451. It must have been issued at the same time.

G. 139/168.

Right trusty and intierly welbeloued, I grete yow wele, and p*ra*y you to be right sadly aduysed of the contynue of a bille of instrucc*y*on closid her-ynne; and ther-vpon, as I trust yow, to comon w*ith* suych my lord*es* of the Kyng*es* councell as be p*re*sent now at this tyme, in especiall my Lord Chaunceller. And that ye wole send me instruccyon agayn of their avise, and how I shal demene me. And the Trinité p*re*serve yow.

Wretyn at Wynch, the second day of January.

THE ERLE OF OXENFORD

1001. From JOHN BOKKYNG to WILLIAM WAYTE: copy 1451, 2 January

Add. 34888, f. 62. $10\frac{1}{2} \times 4\frac{1}{4}$ in. Wayte's hand.

Dorse: Marks of folding, slits for tape; no address.

The letter is not in Bokkyng's hand, but Wayte's, though in a somewhat more formal style than he used for his own letters. It must be the copy that he said he enclosed for John

[3] the *canc.*

Paston I with no. 472, of 9 January 1451 (see lines 16–17 thereof, and cf. no. 460A for a similar enclosure of Wayte's). For the commission of *oyer et terminer* in Kent mentioned in lines 11–14 see *Cal. Pat. Rolls 1446–52*, p. 435 (14 December 1450).

F. iii, p. 134. G. 140/169.

Rith feithfule welbelouyd bro*þer*[1] Wiliam Wayte, I comaunde me to yow as þe lord may to hes ten*au*nt, prayng you effectualy to recomaunde me to my sing*u*ler*e* gode mayst*er and* your*es*, excusyng me þ*a*t I write not to hym, for I dar not envolde me in the same. And as for tydyng*es* her*e*, I certifye you þ*a*t all is no*ugh*t or will be no*ugh*t. The Kyng borweth hes exp*ense*s[2] for Cristemesse. The Kyng of Aragon, þe Duc of Myleyn, þe Duc of Ostrich, þe Duc of Burgoyn wolde ben assistent to vs to make a conquest, and noþing is answered ner agreed in maner, saue abydyng the grete delibera*c*ion þ*a*t at þe last xal spill all to-geder*e* &c.

The Chief Justice hath waited to ben assauted all this seuenyght nyghtly in hes hous, but noþing come as yett, þe more pité &c. An oyr *and* det*er*miner goth in to Kent, *and* comissione*r*s my lord þe Duc of York, Bouchier, my mayst*er*, þ*a*t will not come þ*er*e *de p*rodi*c*i*o*ni*b*us &c; but Kent praieth hem to hang no men when þei come.

Other tydyng*es* as yett can I non tell you, saue Vlueston is styward of þe Mydill Inne, and Isley of the Inner Inne, be cause thei wold haue officz for excuse for dwellyng this tyme from her wyves &c. S*er* T. T. lost hes p*ri*mer at the Toure Hill *and* sent his man to feche it, *and* a good felaw wyshed hit in Norff*olk*, so he wold fetche hit þ*er*e &c. Men wene þ*a*t Norff*olk* men wer*e* hardier þanne þei be.

God graunte, and at the reu*er*ence of God, help too, þ*a*t an outas *and* clamo*ur* be made vpon the Lord Scalez, preyng hym for well of the cuntré neythir susteyn ner help hym ner Heydon in no wyse; and þ*a*t ye crye vpon my maist*er* and your*es* þ*a*t he obeye not the *ser*c*iorar*e as yett, as ye may se be hes l*ettr*e from my mayst*er*, rudely *and* in hast be me endited, of which I p*ra*y excuse &c. And prey Blake to do Swaffh*a*m men sey sum-what to þe matier. I wote well T. *and* H. wil not come þ*er*e at this tyme, as it is verily reported &c. *Mitte sapienc*er &c. Brayn *and* I shalbe w*ith* you on Sat*er*day nest at evyn, with þe grace of J*es*u, to whom I be-take you.

In hast at London, the ij^{de} day of Januaré.

B[e] J. Bokkyng

1001. [1] þ *written in the form of* y *throughout.* [2] *Long* s + *'er' abbrev. for pl. inflection.*

1002. From Sir John Fastolf to Berney, Howes and others 1451, 3 January

Urbana, Illinois, University of Illinois MS 4122. $11\frac{3}{4} \times 8\frac{1}{2}$ in. John Bokkyng's hand, subscription autograph.

Dorse: Marks of folding and slits for tape. Address in Bokkyng's hand:

*To myn ryght tristy and welbeloued John a Berney, squier, S*er *Thomas Howes, Walt*er *Shipdham and Geffrey Spirlyng d*ed*i*t.

Dated.

Printed by K. Madison, *Iowa State Journal of Research*, lvi (1981), 161–3.

Right trusty and welbeloued frend*es*, I grete yow weel, and c*er*tifie yow I haue receivid yo*ur* l*ett*re and weel[1] vnderstande it. And as for a *pro*c*edendo* to be grauntid vp-on the *c*er*tiorari*, the Chief Juge thinkith it may no*ugh*t be doon by lawe, in as moche as c*er*tein of hem haue apperid in the King*es* Benche and pledid. Wherupon the *c*er*tiorari* now[2] cam downne by vertu[3] of a *c*er*tiorari* be-fore this hadde owte of the Chaunc*er*ye the last t*er*me, to remeve c*er*tein enditement*es* vp-on hem in Norff*olk and* in Norwiche by-fore the justices of the peas; vp-on whiche enditement*es*, whan thei were come jnne in-to the King*es* Benche, c*er*tein of hem apperid, as Heydon, Dynne, Vlueston, Prentys and Brigge, and pledid; vp-on whiche apperaunce the seid *c*er*tiorari* was[4] made owte of coors of þe place and *ex officio* &c. But as for Tudenh*a*m, Brampton, Woode[5] and others þ*a*t apperid no*ugh*t,[6] I shal haue a *pro*c*edendo*, and otherwise I am answerid of þe juge I may no*ugh*t. Neu*er*theles I shal labo*ur* to my*n* lord Chaunceller, if I may ghete on of hym in gen*er*all spede if I may &c.

It*em*, where as the Kyng hadde grauntid *sup*er*sedies* to a come downn for to surcese of all the oyer det*er*myner, that is lettid, for suche shal noon passe as yette, as my*n* lord Chaunceller grauntith &c.

It*em*, cousyn Bereney and p*ar*son, in as moche as the Lord Scales is at Lynne, and as I am enformed wille be there bygge of his men and ten*au*ntes in mentinyng the seid Tudenh*a*m and Heydon, and p*er*auenture speke grete wordis,[7] whiche is noo grete hurte if he doo noo more. Yit c*er*tein of my*n* frend*es* and weelwillers[8] haue councellid me that for suche mat*er*es as I haue there in p*ro*cesse, that I haue good councell and other men of worship to be p*re*sent in my*n* mat*er*es forseid p*ur*suying; as my*n* cousyn Paston, whom I trist moche, I wete weel wil be there, and also my*n* frend*es* Will*ia*m Jenney, John Jenney and Lomno*ur*. And if ye thinke it to be doon, I pray yow, cousyn, be

1002. [1] *No space.* [2] *Large letter* a *by another hand in left margin.* [3] wherof *canc.* [4] gra *canc.* [5] *Repeated with mark or letter resembling* c *above.* [6] w *canc.* [7] as *canc.* [8] w *canc.*

ye there. I suppose the seid Lord Scales wille no*ugh*t be opinly p*ar*ciall, seyng he [is] a commission*er*e and a[9] Knyght of the Gartier &c.

It*em*, I shal sende the *procedendo* by Brayn and Bokkyng, whiche shal be w*ith* Yelu*er*ton on Sat*er*day at nyght next comyng, and also the *procedendo* gen*er*all if I may ghete hit. This *certiorari* hurtith the Kyng gretely but no*ugh*t the p*ar*tyes, saf for tho that exigenc*es* ben awardid ageinste hem, and yet p*ro*cess*es* of outlawery shal p*ro*cede ayenst hem neu*er*the latter. As for all other mat*er*es p*ar*tic*u*ler that ar or may be to my*n* aduaile and p*ro*fite in that p*ar*ties, I pray yow tendirly to solicite hem to my grettest p*ro*fite, as I trist fully ye will &c, bringyng w*ith* yow, S*er* Thomas, all man*er*e euidenc*es* conc*er*nyng my*n* billes at this oyer and det*er*myner &c.

It*em*, as for tendernesse of lordship to be shewid to Tudenham and Heydon by my*n* lord of Norff*olk*, fere yow no*ugh*t ther of in noo wyse &c.

And[10] Our Lord haue yow in kepyng. Writen at London the iij day of Januar*é* A° xxix R. H. Sexti &c.

I haue hadde grete sute and labo*ur* that I shuld entrete w*ith* S*er* Thomas Tudenham and Heydon, and I haue answerid non otherwyse, but in cas thei will appere in p*ro*pre p*er*sone or by attorney, and plede the mat*er*es tried and founden for hem, I agre me. And if thei be founden for me, I wille surcesse of execuc*i*on suynge and put my*n* mat*er*es in comprimys of my*n* lord Chaunceller and other men of conciens, and lerned. And otherwise thei ghete noon agrem*en*t of me, for I haue leu*er*e it were knowen in the contré howe I haue be don too, thanne to be recompensid of all my*n* losses þat I haue hadde by them, for me thinkith it more my*n* worchip, by whiche I sette more than by ought ell*es*; and so I wille the contré knewe &c.

It*em*, my*n* shippe w*ith* stuffe is come this nyght, and hathe be longe hiderward.

J. FASTOLFE

1003. From SIR JOHN FASTOLF to JOHN BERNEY and THOMAS HOWES — 1451, 7 January

Add. 39848, f. 14. 12 × 8½ in. William Barker's hand, subscription autograph.

Dorse: Marks of folding, slits for tape, address panel heavily soiled. Strip of paper and wafer seal still attached. Address in Barker's hand:

To my ryght trusty and weel be-lovyd frendez John a Berney and S*er Thomas Howys, clerk.*

Dated.

G. 141/171 (abstract).

[9] c *canc.*

[10] as for *canc.*

1003. *From Sir John Fastolf to J. Berney and T. Howes, 7 January 1451*

Ryght trusty and weel be-lovyd frendys, I grete you hertly weel, and late you wete þ*a*t[1] I send to you my trusty s*er*u*au*nt John Bokkyng[2] in applying suche materes of myn to be speed at this oyer and t*er*myner at this tyme to be hold; p*ra*yng you to labo*ur* eu*er* for yo*ur*e part in the same to my most worship, p*ro*fyte and advayle, consyderyng at this tyme ther is ought a *certiorare*[3] of the Kyng*es* Benche, as I have wreten to you be fore. And where as a *procedend*o at on tyme was graunted for certeyn wheche hadde not appered in the place and pleted, and now delayed, as the seyd Bokkyng shal enforme you, to whom I p*ra*ye you hertly to yeve ful feyth and credens of that that he shal seye to yow on my behalf. And as for the seyd *procedend*o, I shal don my parte to gete hit if I may be any wyse &c.

It*em*, I have reseyved alle the stuff conteyned in a bille indented beryng date the xxviij^{ti} day of Noue*m*br*e*, made by John Davye of[4] Yarmouth, made and delyu*er*ed to on called Roger Metsharp, mayst*er* of the lytel boot called the *Blythe*; but I m*er*veyle greetly that ye sende not the greet ship w*ith* malt as I am wont to have &c, to wheche at this tyme shewe yo*ur*e good wylle &c.

It*em*, S*er* Thom*as*, I p*ra*ye yow that ye send me heder by the next ship that cometh stuff for this Lenton, as sturgeon, if any come, salt salmon, so hit be of the mase, elys, stokfyshe and suche other stuff conuenyent for thys seson.

It*em*, that ye wole remembre my cosyn Inglose that the man wheche that appeched Heydon be sent vp heder, if he dar stande by his wordes that he hath seyde &c, and send me worde how that he wole don. Alle the endytement*es* that be sent vp on Heydon be not worth on halfpenye &c. Lete this mater be holpen the best wyse that hit may by the good advyse of my cosyn John a Berney, for he can good skyll to examyn suche a mater &c.

And God kepe yow. In hast at London, the Thursday after the twelthe &c, A^{o} xxix^{o} R. H. vj^{ti}.

It*em*,[5] that for Bardolf mater, that alle thoo that were vpon the enquest that they be endyted, what so hit cost, as the seyd Bokkyng shal enforme yow; and that S*er* Herry Inglose and the P*r*io*ur*e be speke w*ith* for the seyd mat*er*, for these materes must be amended, w*ith* the hepe or the croke &c.

J. FASTOLFE

1003. [1] þ *in the form of* y. [2] *MS.* Brokkyng
[3] ought *canc.* [4] Jarmouth *canc.*
[5] *A letter* a *added by another hand in margin to left of this paragraph.*

1004. From Sir John Fastolf to Thomas Howes and John Bokkyng — 1451, 12 January

Add. 39848, f. 15. 11$\frac{1}{2}$ × 5 in. William Barker's hand, subscription autograph.

Dorse: Marks of folding, slits for tape, strip of paper and wafer seal over red sealing wax. Address in Barker's hand:

To my trusty and frendes Thomas Howys, clerk, and John Bokkyng, in hast.

Dated.

G. 142/173 (abstract).

Trusty and weel belovyd frendes, I grete yow weel, and p*ra*ye yow to labo*ur* suche materes as I have a don þ*er*e[1] at this tyme in yo*ur*e most effectuell wyse, as my[2] singeler trust is in yow. And in especyall for-gete not that old shrew Dallyng, for he is sore at my stomak. And as for this *procedendo* ayenst Tud[e]nh*a*m and otheres, I have gete hit ought w*ith* greet labo*ur*e. I lete yow wete I sende hit yow by the p*a*rson, w*ith* a l*ett*re to my broþ*er*e Yelu*er*ton, wheche I p*ra*ye yow delyu*er*e to hym &c. And as to an assise for Hikkelyng, I shal ther on in the begynnyng of this terme, and for Tichewell in lyke wyse &c.

I p*ra*ye yow, Bokkyng, for-gete not to remembre my cosyn Ingelose for the endytement*es* of treson of Heydon, that the man myght be sent vp to p*re*ve the seyd mater. Hit is slept to longe, I am aferde. And I p*ra*ye yow, s*er* p*ar*son, whan ye have leyser, that ye wole sende me heder my ship called the *Blythe* w*ith* malt, as ye have ben a-customed by-fore tyme, as my trust is in yow.

And God kepe yow. In hast at London, the xij day of Janyver A^{o} xxix^{o} R. H. vj^{ti}.

J. Fastolfe

It*em*,[3] that ye make my lord *and* Yelu*er*ton wryte a l*ett*re to Blake of the Kyng*es* hows, thankyng hym of hese frendlynesse to the cuntré shewed &c. And for-yete not that Dallyng be hadde be-for my lord and Yelu*er*ton, and make his confessio*n* be-fore he*m* &c. And lete the greet men that have most materes a-yenst help su*m* what to this *procedendo* sewyng &c.

1004. [1] þ *in form of* y *throughout.*
[2] *Large letter* a *by another hand in left margin.*
[3] *Remainder of text to left of and beneath Fastolf's signature.*

1005. From Sir John Fastolf to Thomas Howes and John Berney — 1451, 28 January

Add. 39848, f. 16. $11\frac{3}{4} \times 15\frac{1}{2}$ in. Worcester's hand, subscription autograph.

Dorse: Marks of folding, slits for tape, traces of red sealing wax. Address in Worcester's hand:

*To my ryght trusty and welbelovyd frendys S*er *Thomas Howys,* parson *off Castellcombe, and John Berney, beyng at Castre, in hast, or at hys place in Pokethorp at Norwych.*

Dated. There are notes in the left margin by Blomefield, who referred to this letter, and gave short extracts from the first paragraph in his *History of Norfolk*, iv. 388, n. 9. An indenture dated 24 January 1451, recording the agreement between Fastolf and Hugh Acton concerning the sale of Mundham, was printed by C. F. Bühler, *R.E.S.*, xiv (1938), 134–5.

G. 143/174 (abstract).

Ryght trusty frendys, I grete you well. And forasmoch as Maist*er* Hue Acton hath be wyth me at London at thys tyme for the new evidences enseled for the maner of Mundh*a*m, whych I have sold hym to the vse of the chyrche of Seint Gylys that he ys Maist*er* off, for twohondred marc st*er*lyng. And my feffeez have enseled to such of hys trusty frendz as he lust name. And I have delyu*er*ed hym the said new evidens*es*, to delyu*er*e hem to yow at hys co*m*myng, to geffe and make astate vnto hym of the said maner of Mu*n*dh*a*m, wyth the appurten*au*nce. But before ye make astate of the said maner ye most[1] resseyve of the seid Maist*er* Hue the said so*m*me of ij^{c} marc ⌜bethout onye delay⌝, except j noble payd me here in arnest, and at such place as ye darre vndretake to be sure caryed *and* kept. But also ye most inquyre of myne audito*ur*s yff I have onye othyr lond in the tounys that be specyfied in the dede of Mu*n*dh*a*m, whych longyth to onye othyr place or maner of myne, for then I myght dam*m*age so moch myne othyr place, and onye such lond were longyng to, except onlye to Mu*n*dh*a*m. And were it nought bought for the vse of the said place of Seint Gylys I wold ⌜not⌝ have sold it yhyt.

It*em*, the said Maist*er* Hue hath comyned wyth me and meoved to by my londz clepyt Rees, but we coude not accord of price, for I wolle not sylle it lesse then aft*er* the value of xx yeere as it makyth clerlye in value now at thys day, or in value at the yer*es* late before I purchased the said place. It lyeth nere to Mundh*a*m, and therfor it ys bett*er* worth to hym by a[2] grete money then to onye othyr, notwythstandyng in acquytyng me to my cosyn S*er* William Chambyrleyn. I wold ye wete of hym before yff he wolle chaunge[3] wyth me for that place asmoch lond in value lyeng off hys in Corton and Newton by my maner*es* in Lodylond. Then I wold well he have Rees, for

1005. [1] *Repeated but not canc.* [2] *No space.*
[3] *Superfluous* au *abbrev. above.*

such a ch*a*unge suffis*a*untlye made, as ye and my councell shall well avyse, for my moste proffyt and avaylle. I have vndrestand well a l*ett*re of you, p*ar*son, wryten vppon the value of the said Rees, but I desyre to see the acco*mpt*e*s* of it wythall.

It*em*, I have vndrestand well by rapport of my s*eruaun*te*s* and othyrwyse of your gode and diligent labour*e* made and doon about the expedic*i*ou[n][4] of my mater*es* pursued before the com*m*issioner*s* of oyer *and* ter*m*iner at Lynne *and* othyr plac*es*, of whych ye do me ryght singler comfort, and con you[5] ryght gode thank, trustyng vppon your gode continu*an*ce. And where as I have vndrestand late that Appulȝerd ys sonne shuld sey to my s*eruaun*te*s* that th'enquest of Mannecrof in Norwych, whych passed ayenst Appulȝerd yn an acc*i*on of meynten*au*nce I toke ayenst hym as tro⟨uth⟩[6] was for the Lady Bardolf*es* [mater], how now the said jnquest wold goo from theyr p*re*sentm*en*t, and that they p*re*sented it neu*er*e. And therfor I pray you to speke wyth my cosyn Inglose for to have hys gode avice, and wyth the Meyr of Norwych; and that the Mayr lyke to sende for the said inquest, and do hem to be sure and stedfast in theyr p*re*sentm*ent*e*s*, for ell it wolle t*ur*ne hem to grete vylenye. And I prey you foryete not thys mat*er* to be thought vppon betyme, and vppon all such othyr mater*es* concernyng thys mater, for ye wote well yo*ur* sylf the Mayr sent it at yo*ur* labour vndre hys signet from Seint Pet*er* ys chyrche in Norwych to th'enquest.

It*em*, as to myne audit, I vndrestand that the bok*es* be almoste made vpp and engroced, but abydyth William Cole ys examinac*i*on and visityng of hem; p*ra*yng you in onye wyse that in all your allouaunce of rep*ar*ac*i*ons or othyr caus*es* that requyrith maundm*en*tes, that ye the audito*ur*s clepe you to wytnesse the work*es* or the deede, or that ell ye see that my lyfelode be not minussed by nedelese allou*au*nces, or make werk*es* where no nede ys. I wold my lyvelode there were aswell approwed and aunsuerd no wors then my wyff*es* londz that lyeth ferre from me, or onye of my surveyors or s*eruaun*te*s* about hem. At the reu*er*ence of God, tendyr ye thys mat*er*, for it ys the subst*a*unce of my wellfare, and of you all. And myne audito*ur*s ought not take str*a*ungelie none mat*er* that ye or my s*eruaun*te*s* meoffe or wryte on my behalf *and* by my co*m*maundm*en*t. And I desyre to have my bok*es* valued in the ende of the rolle, as the old maner ys, and also the greyny*ng* and aunsueryng of my offic*er*s in the margyn vppon eu*er*y title to be set owt. I doubt they can doo it, they I reme*m*br*e* it not, but yhyt it esyth my spiryt*es* to sey my conceyt wyth hem, *and* to be corrected and amended for the bett*er*.

It*em*, I have resseyvyd a[7] l*ett*re from my cosyn John Bernay, and vndrestand well the contenew of it. And where as he ouerseeith to the safegard of my place in myne absence I thank hym hertly, for he puttith me in grete

[4] *One minim short.*

[5] oyere at Lynne *to left in another hand.*

[6] *Edge of page worn away.*

[7] *No space.*

comfort. And where as he wrytith to me that he[8] ⌜doth⌝ respyt and suffer*a*unce of hys entree in the maner of Rokelond Tofft*es* at my request doon ys lyke to p*re*iudice hys title, as to that I were ryȝt loth that he shuld be dam*m*aged in hys ryght. And yff it myght lye in my power I wold gladlye sett it in a gode wey as hys ryȝt were saved, and both parties contented. Neu*er*ethelesse, I kepe not ne wold not but that he doo hys au*au*ntage laufullie to nygh hys ryght yff he have onye, and that he doo by councell, that it p*re*iudice hym not here aft*er*.

It*em*, s*er* p*ar*son, yff there be onye dett*es* to be pursued, that ye sende me the oblig*aci*ons or namys betyme, and demaundyth of myne audit*our*s &c.

It*em*, I wold ye frende you well in Norwych ayenst Est*er* next, that the oyer *and* terminer shall be next haldyn there, for I wolle procede in my mater a-yenst Appulȝerd as ferre as lawe wolle, for there was no mat*er* that greved me so mekylle and it had drawe to a grett*er* value then that dyd, it was so vntrulie wrought. And yff ye ley gode wayt when Dynne co*m*myth home, I shall ordeyn *capias* to be take out to arrest hym for to aunsuer to the p*re*senteme*n*t. Allso, I wold wete whate ys doon to the wrytt*es* for Margyt Brygge &c.

Allmyghty God kepe you. Wryt at London, xxviij day of Januar*é* A° xxix° r. r. H. vj.

J. FASTOLFE

It*em*,[9] as to my greynes *and* malt to be sent hedr*e*, I pray you that it com yn a sure vessell and in gode companye of othyr vessell, wyth a[10] gode wynde, for ye know well that I have had grete losses yn my shypp*es*[11] and greyn late before thys, and therfor ye most the wyselyer demesne thys gouu*er*n*aun*ce from hens forth.

It*em*, in caas that William Hach have take no work yn grete, I wold desyre that he myght com to me thys Marche tyme, for I wold have a ground work made vpp ayenst som*our* in my place where I duelle.

It*em*, I pray you foryete ye not the mat*er* of Appulȝerd, and to comyn wyth the Mayr of Norwych vppon the mat*er* abofe wrytyn whych touchyth Appulȝerd; for there was no cytee in England that I lovyd and trusted moost ⌜vppon⌝, till they dyd so vnkyndly to me and ayenst trouth in the Lady Bardolf*es* mater, where I never gafe hem cause, but had mekylle magree because I held not wyth that partie that wrought ayenst hem, as ye may vndrestand ⟨. . .⟩.[12]

[8] *MS.* the [9] *Remainder of text written to left of and below Fastolf's signature.*
[10] *No space.* [11] *Bar over* pp *apparently for pl. inflection.*
[12] *Tear at foot of page with loss of two or three words.*

1006. From SIR JOHN FASTOLF to THOMAS HOWES
1451, 13 April

Add. 39848, f. 17. 11¾ × 8½ in. Worcester's hand, subscription autograph.

Dorse: Marks of folding, slits for tape, impression of wafer seal. Some pen trials, including 'John Russe' twice. Address in Worcester's hand:

*To my ryght trusty frend S*er *Thomas Howys, par*son *of Castellcombe, at Castr*e *beyng.*

Dated.

G. 152/186 (abstract).

Ryght trusty frende, I grete you well, letyng you wete that I have resseyved a[1] l*ett*re from you iij^{d} day of Aprill last, wyth the last accompt of S*er* John Kyrtelyng and Intewod. And where as I vndrestand that Rob*er*t Norwych wolle not occupie as vndreshyreff, be cause that Jenneys had geve hem langage that was not hys plesu⟨re⟩,[2] and so Aleyn shuld occupie, whych ys not my wellwiller. But I can you gode thank that yee have by labo*ur* made to the shyreff and othyr*es* that ye have purveyd a remedie, and so I pray you to hald yo*ur* hand well in thys mater. And assone as the *venire facias* may be had owt it shall be laboured to be sent you. And y shall hafe Paston ys avice in thys mater, as ye reme*m*bre me.

It*em*, as to fals Dallyng, I veele well hys obstinat wille in hys vntrouth. And they it so be ye can not ghete wrytyng nethyr syght of l*ett*res of hym, I pray you to wryte vnto my trusty frend Nicholas Bokkyng, that as y am crediblie lerned may meoffe and rule hym moost of onye man in Norff*olk*; so thanne that the seid Bokkyng may take a[3] labour for me at thys tyme to speke wyth Dallyng and entreete hym in hys best maner, by all the weyes that he canne, to have wrytyng, or the l*ett*res that were sent to hym by Sharbo*ur*n to forge that office. And y shall reward hym well for hys labo*ur and* cost. He qwyt hym full well in the mater certyfyeng by the jur*é* named in the office, and so I doubt not but he wolle in thys, and ye labo*ur* to hym on my behalf.

It*em*, as to Margyt Bryg, ye most labo*ur* in all that ye can or may for levee of it, be cause that Aleyn *and* hyr att*ur*neys have labo*ur*ed a *cerciorare* and delyu*er*ed it to Brayn for to reto*ur*n vpp the mater; but he woll none certiffye because jugem*en*t ys yovyn, and allso he hath not the bokys in hys kepyng.

It*em*,[4] as to the oyer *and* te*r*miner, it ys seid for certeyn that Heydon, wyth S*er* Thomas Tuddenh*am*, woll be at Norwych and in Norff*olk* wyth all the meyntena*u*nce and felishyp as they can ghete. And Prysot justice shall sytt there also as it ys seid. And ther ye most wyse and secretely wyrk,[5] and make

1006. [1] *No space.* [2] *Edge of page rubbed and faded.* [3] *No space.* [4] *Letter* a *added to left by another hand.* [5] k *flourished as if for* -es *inflection.*

your frendz stedfast to be in theyr mater*es*. And all such as fyndyth hem greved, and have p*ro*cesse attained at thys oyer *and* te*r*miner, to labour in theyr part and to make hem frendys. And y shall labour in the meene tyme here, and sende you word how the world ys sett. Men of the citee of Norwych have gode audience and fauo*ur* among*es* the lordz, and abyden vppon aunsuer of her mater*es*.

It*em*, I hafe delyu*er*ed vpp the shypmen and left the shypp*es*[6] heere, for such caus*es* as y shall and wryte vnto you, for the rayse hath been full costuys, except they came in saufftee.

Allmyghty God kepe you. Wryt at London the xiij day of Aprill A^{o} xxix^{o} R. R. H. vj^{ti}.

J. FASTOLFE

1007. From SIR JOHN FASTOLF to THOMAS HOWES
1451, 21 April

Add. 39848, f. 18. $11\frac{1}{2} \times 9\frac{3}{4}$ in. Hand of John Bokkyng, subscription autograph.

Dorse: Marks of folding, slits for tape, impression of wafer seal. Address in Bokkyng's hand:

*To my weelbeloued frend S*er *Thomas Howys at Castre in Flegge be this delyu*ered *in haste.*

Dated.
G. 154/188 (abstract).

Right trusty and welbeloued frend, I grete yow wele, and lete yow wyte I sende at this tyme to yow ij *venire fac*ias for Beyton in Norff*olk* and Bradwell in Suff*olk*, retornable xv^{ti} Pasche, whiche is a shorte day; but I take hit for spede of my*n* matiers, whiche ye muste delyu*er*e in haste to the shireve by Paston is aduyce, by whom I sende yow them. And ye w*ith* suche helpe must labour*e* effectuelly to the shiref for retornyng of suche panells as will sey for me in my*n* right, and suche as ⌜ar⌝ men of worship and good, that wyllen no*ugh*t be shamed. I dowte no*ugh*t ther hath ben, is, and shalben grete labo*ur* made vn-to the shirefe for the same matier by Wentworthe is parté, wherfore I pray yow entrete the shirefe as weel as ye can by resonable reward*es*, rather þanne faile. For I wolde no*ugh*t but ȝif the matier wente weel, in as moche as thei haue taken w*ith* me as fals an jsseu as can ben ymagyned by H. aduyce, for oolde love, whiche fals jsseu refereth noo þing to the matier conteyned in the office, as it ought of right. For where it is founden by the jnquisi*cions* that I deceasid S*er* Hue Fastolf of the man*er*es &c, whiche mater soo founden I

[6] *Dotted crescent over* pp *apparently for pl. inflection.*

haue t*ra*uesed, leynge for my*n* plee that I neu*er*e diseasid the seid S*er* Hue, whiche of right shuld now be tried, whether ther were dissesyn or noo. But thei haue goon all a nother wey, and seyne in there replicac*io*ns that at the day of takyng of þe seid jnquisic*io*ns I hadde no*ugh*t in the seid man*er*es but iointly w*ith* other men, and rehersen many lord*es* and other men that shuld haue ben enfeffid by me, and diu*er*se other that neu*er*e were enfeffid by me in noo good or londe that I haue. And whi the cause is my*n* cousyn Paston can declare yow, and all the matier alonge conc*er*nyng the same, to whom ye lyke to yife credenc*e* &c. I shal doo write the trau*er*ses, the replicac*io*ns and remicc*iou*ns, and sende hem yow in haste &c.

It*em*, for the names suche as ye sent me for Bradwell, thei be[1] lyke to doo weel, safe Hopton, that hathe maried w*ith* the Lady Wentworthe. And also I am endowte of on Reppes of Heringflete, whiche is Heydon is man &c; wherfore ye must thinke vp-on the best men and frend*es* as welle for Beyton in Norff*olk* as Bradwell in Suff*olk*. This muste be diligently laboured, be cause the retorne is soo shorte a day, xv^{ti} Pasche. And en caas the shirefe take of you a rewarde, entrete ye hym soo that ye may haue a p*ro*mys to retorne a panell of the same men that now shalbe for Bradwelle at the next *venir*e *fac*ias for the same Bradwell vp-on an other trau*er*se; for ye wote weel ther were founden ij offices, on at Nedh*a*m Market and an oþ*er* at Todenh*a*m, whiche bothe we haue be dryven to trau*er*se. And for sparing of money that bothe myght be s*er*ued by on rewarde therfore I meve yow, and the same enqueste and names as shal be for this *venir*e *fac*ias ghete ye graunte to haue hit in suche forme, for bothe ar on matier, in as moche as the same title that is founden in the on office is founden in the other &c.

It*em*,[2] as for the oyer an t*er*myner, I hadde p*ur*posed to haue ben there þis tyme, but I may no*ugh*t. Wherfore I pray[3] yow doo your*e* parte with other of my*n* councell suche as ar in thoo parties, and that ye remembre weel Applierd*es* matier vp-on his enditement as weel as vp-on the bille that I haue ayenste hym, of whiche ye must take a copye of Brayne. I wolde in noo wyse but the matier toke a good wey, for ful opyn meynten*au*nce was ayenst me, and the same Applierd heyued the costys v marc. malic*io*usly and p*ar*cially. I shall sende a man to y*o*u w*ith* other au*er*tisement*es* in haste.

And God haue yow in kepyng. Writen in haste at Horshighdoun, the xxj day of Aprill Anno xxix R. H. vj^{ti}.

J. FASTOLFE

1007. [1] *No space.*
[2] *Letter* a *added to left by another hand.*
[3] d *canc.*

1008. From Thomas Howes to Sir John Fastolf
1451, 9 May

Add. 34888, ff. 68v–69r. 11 × 16 in., folded in half and mounted sideways at the fold. Two unidentified hands.

Dorse: Marks of folding, slits for tape, traces of red wax. Postscript in Howes's hand (see below). Address in second hand of letter:

*To my reu*er*ent and worchepfull Mayster, S*er* John Fastolf, knyght, be this l*ett*r*e* delyu*er*ed.*

Dated. Fenn (followed by Gairdner) printed the body of the letter down to the date, but not the continuation added by the second hand. Howes's own rather crude hand, here on the dorse, seldom appears in the correspondence; see no. 564.

F. iii, p. 116. G. 158/192 (part).

Right reu*er*ent and w*ur*chepfull maist*er*, I recomaunde me louly vn-to yow. Please you to wete the Sonday next aft*er* the fest of the Inuenc*i*on of the Cros, the ix day of Maij, at Castre, I receyued a l*ett*re from yow by yo*ur* clerk, W. Barker, the tenure wherof I shall do spede in all hast goodly. But for the more sp*ec*ial cause of my writyng at this tyme is to gef yow relac*i*on of the vn-true demenyng of this oyre det*er*myn*er*, by the parcialté of the jugez of it. For whan the counsell of the cité of Norwich, of the toun of Swafh*a*m, yourez, my maist*er* Inglose, Pastons, and many other pleyntyfs[1] had put in and declared bothe by writyng and by woord by fore the jugez the laufull excepc*i*ons in many wise, the juges by ther wilfulnesse myght nat fynde in ther hert to gef not als moche as a bek ner a twynclyng of ther eye toward, but toke ⌜it⌝ to derisio*u*n. God reforme such p*ar*cialté. And by cause P*ri*sot thought that yf the sessions of the oyer det*er*myner had be holden at Norwich as they bygonne, he supposed it shuld nat so fast passe to th'entent of Tudenh*a*m and Heydon and ther felawes, as it shuld do ell in other place, but enio*ur*ned to Walsyngh*a*m, wher*e* they haue grettist rule, ther*e* to be holden on Tuesday iiij^{te} day of Maij.

This knowyng, my maist*er* Yelu*er*ton, Genney, and other myght weel conceyue how the gou*er*naunce of the oyer det*er*myn*er* shuld p*ro*cede, for it was the most p*ar*cial place of alle the shire, and thedre wer*e* cleped alle the frendez, knyghtys and esquiers, and other gentilmen that wolde in no wise do other wise than they wolde. And the seid Tudenh*a*m, Heydon, and other opp*re*ssours of ther set come doun theder, as I vnderstand, w*ith* iiij^{c} hors and more; and consideryng how ther wellwillers wer*e* ther assembled at ther jnstaunce, it had to be right jowp*er*to*us* and ferefull for any of the pleyntyfs to haue be p*re*sent, for ther was nat one of the pleyntyfs ner compleyn*au*ntez ther*e* but your*e* right feithfull and trusty weel willer John Paston. And my

1008. [1] of *canc.*

maister Yelu*er*ton seid full discretly, and countrolled the seid P*ri*sot whan he seid, sittyng in the Guyhalle of Norwich, these woordys to the Meyre and the Co*mmon*alté, 'A, S*er* Meyre and yo*ur* brethern, as to the p*ro*cesse of yo*ur*e compleyntez, we wole put them in contynuaunce, but in all other we wold p*ro*cede,' which woordys Yelu*er*ton thought right parciall. And by side this the seid P*ri*sot wolde suffre no[2] man that was lerned to speke for the pleyntyfs, but took it as a venom, and took them by the nose at eu*er*y thred woord, whiche myght weel by knowe for open p*ar*cialté.

And as for the Lord Scalys, ye knowe weell what he is toward you, and namely for Hikelyng mat*er*. Also to knowe som of youre[3] feynt frendes, at the tyme that[4] my lord Norff*olk* sat at Norwich vp-on the oyer det*er*myn*er*, S*er* John Hevyngh*a*m myght nat fynde it in his hert to go iiij furlong from his duellyng place to the shireho*us*, but now he cowd ryde from Norwich to Walsyngh*a*m to syt as one of the co*m*myssioners. As to the rule of[5] other that ye wolde haue supposed your*e* wellwillers, how they haue byhaved them at Walsyngh*a*m, I shall sende yow woord in all hast whan Bernay come hom to Castr*e*, for he is nat yet come from Walsyngh*a*m. But this I knowe well, that they founde none obstacle ner impedyment in ther consciens in all your*e* mat*er*s. But how they haue do with Norwich, Swafh*a*m, and Paston, I am nat yet clerly informed. I suppose they arn put in respite. I here sey Heydon seweth for an ende to be had w*ith* the cité of Norwich, and as to the namys of them that passed on ther acquitaile a-yenst yow, Brayn can weell informe yow. I vnd*er*stand that S*er* Rob*er*t Conyers, Calthorp, Mundford wer*e* capteyns, and Maister Ric*hard* Doget also.

It*e*m, as for the ij *venire fac*ias ye sent to be ret*ur*ned for your man*erz* of Bradwell and Beyton, I haue do them to be retorned of suche namys as I haue sent woord byfore, savyng sum*m*e be take and except out. Moreou*er*, as for the mat*er* of S*er* John Sibton, Geney and Raulyns gef ful counsell that it shuld abyde tyl the mater of Bradwell myght p*ro*cede, so that bothe maters myght take vpon a day, for they sey it wold drawe xx m*a*rc. to labo*ur* the jur*é* to London, and yet it wer*e* hard to bryng about. And they gef yow counsell in all wise that ye labo*ur* to haue Yelu*er*ton juge at that tyme, and in all wise bothe in that mat*erz* and in all other, that ye be war that P*ri*sot haue nat[6] to haue do in any wise, for than all wole be nought. Of alle other*e* mat*erz* I shall send yow woord in all hast goodly, for at this tyme I had no leyser by cause of the hasty comyng vp of Hug Fen, whom I beseche yow to fele of the demenyng of this oyer det*er*myn*er*, for he can telle yow moche and he wole. Whether he wole or nay, I can nat sey, ⌜for I know wele he was at Walsyngh*a*m.

And⌝[7] I beseche all myghty Jh*es*u haue yow in his m*er*cyfull gou*er*n*au*nce. Wret*e* at Castre, the Sonday[8] ix day of Maij A° xxix° R. H. vj^ti.

[2] *No space.*
[3] g *canc.*
[4] myghe *canc.*
[5] them *canc.*
[6] d *canc.*
[7] *Interlineation by second hand, over first hand's* But, *underlined for omission.*
[8] nex *canc.*

It*em*,[9] s*er*e, S*er* Thomas Tudenh*a*m and Heydon, by the advice of your*e* bare frend Prysot, sent to the Meyre of Nor*w*iche[10] and to his brethern to haue entreded w*ith* them. But the seid Meyr*e* w*ith* his brethern vtterly aunswereden þei[11] wold entrete in no wyse, otherwyse then my lord of Oxonford, my lord Cromewelle, ye, and Yeluerton wold advice them to do, lyche as your*e* most trusty frend as in this p*ar*tyes, John Paston, shalle more pleynerly enforme yow at his next comyng to London.

It*em*, s*er*, yf it please yow, I wold ye myght haue your*e* ij *nisi prius* in Suff*olk* at Beckles, be cause it is nere aboute, wher*e*[12] as the men ben inpanelled aswele for your*e* man*er*e of Bradwell as for S*er* John Sibtonys mat*er*e. Yf ye thynke this meane be good, I wold advice yow ferthermor*e* to be sure of Yelu*er*ton, when he myght best be spared aboute midsom*er*e, as for iij dayes: oo day yf ye thynke it be to do at Bury atwix yow and the Lady Shardelaw, as he cometh from London ward; the ij^{de} day at Becles as for the mat*er*e of Bradwelle and Sybton aboue rehersed; the iij^{de} day at Norwich as for ⌜the⌝[13] *nisi prius* for your*e* man*er*e of Beyton. Which mat*er*es, yf ye and your*e* counseyll ⌜thynke⌝ it to be don so hastely, I trust ye shall ⌜haue⌝ your*e* forth in all your*e* right, w*ith* that I may haue warnyng a monyth or iij wekys at the lest be for*e*, for to labour*e* the jur*é* &c.

It*em*, s*er*, I haue lab*our*ed to Brayn that he shold se that the mat*er*e of Margaret Brig shold be duly lab*our*ed in ret*our*nyng vp the p*ro*cesse of the writte of errour*e*, that ther*e* myght noon errour*e* be fonde. He feithfully hath p*ro*mysed me to make ytt as duely as he can, w*ith* mor*e*, he woll nought ret*our*ne it to the tyme he haue comyned w*ith* your*e* best counseyll ther*e* of ⌜the same⌝, for the whiche I wold John Bockyng awayted on hym at his comyng to se it be duely p*er*f*our*med aft*er* the tenure of your*e* writyng to me &c.

[*Dorse*]

I prey yow be nowth displesed thow I have nowt subscribed my name w*ith*jnne forth, for it is of neclygens. Quod Howys, p*ar*son of Castelcomb.

[9] *Second hand begins.* [10] che *superscript.*
[11] þ *in form of* y, i *superscript.* [12] is *canc.*
[13] *Over* a *canc.*

1009. From Sir John Fastolf to Thomas Howes
1451, 24 June

Washington D. C., Folger Shakespeare Library, MS X. d. 274. $11\frac{1}{4} \times 15\frac{3}{4}$ in. Worcester's hand, subscription autograph.

Dorse: Marks of folding, slits for tape. Address in Worcester's hand:

To my trusty and *welbelovyd frende Sir Thomas Howys, stuard off Castr*e.

Dated.

Printed by K. G. Madison, *Iowa State Journal of Research*, lvi (1981), 165–7. Facsimile and transcription of lower portion in J. F. Preston and L. Yeandle, *English Handwriting 1400–1650* (Binghamton NY, 1992), pp. 18–19.

Ryght trusty frendz, I grete you well. And for asmoche as the next terme ys ryght short but of xiiij dayes, wherfor I pray you and charge you that ye sende vpp to me in all goodly haste by suche co*m*mers betwene as be of your knoulege, that such mater*es* as most be avysed or remedied heere may be doon be tyme, soo as none damage or inconvenient fall in the vaca*ci*on tyme of the p*ro*cesse for Beyton *and* Bradwell, or the atteynt; for yt ys to deme that my adu*er*saries wolle wyrk all the vntrouth that they can ayenst me.

It*em*, sendyth me wrytyng of all my wrytt*es* sent home, how they been executed, and the namys of hem that ye have for to be put in processe for arr*é* *and* debt thys term; and such as make ende wyth you there, that yee take vpp the cost*es* of the p*ro*cesse, whych Raulyns myne atou*r*ney can sey yow.

It*em*, as for the wryt I sent you by Piers Plowman for Hygh*a*m ys landz in Suff*olk*: ye most see that the shyreff of Suff*olk* reto*ur*n the wryt and kepe the day of reto*ur*n to be sent vpp *and* not lost, for at the next wryt hyr lond shall been executed, but yff she make ende wyth me, and hyr goodz also; for now the shyreff may reto*ur*n, but that he ys deede.

It*em*, y[1] hafe well vndrestand that ye sent me a[2] rolle of papier of certeyn chargeable cost*es* that I have exspended and payd for the deffence of the greete yniuries don to me thys x or xij yeer*e* day. But ye most reme*m*bre in Shypdam bok*es*, and Thomas Sweyn acco*m*pt*es* with Intewoddz, beyng yn the audyt at Castr*e*, for the cost*es* of the trau*er*s that was payd for my refeu [of] Harlyng londz. Also, I hafe not the cost*es* here that was payd at Donwych *and* at Norwych for the appele of Bysshop. Also, Rychard Conerey[3] bok*es* most be sought of dyu*er*s yeer*es* for cost*es* *and* da*m*mages of parkyng of my sheepe at Saxthorp, in lykewyse Haylysdon *and* Drayton bok*es* for distreyny*ng* at Drayton &c. And serchyth as many offic*er*s tymys as ye can by lyklynesse conceyve ony extorc*io*n or dam*m*age or cost*es* doon to me, for I hafe serched to the vtmost heer*e* of all maner cost*es* in pleez and p*ro*cess*es*. And so I pray you to doo there, *and* sende it me be tyme, to th'entent I may cast the som*m*es

1009. [1] *No space.* [2] *No space.* [3] *Or* Couerey.

payd out by you *and* by myne offic*er*s there to the cost*es* that y hafe payd heer*e*, that y may shew to the arbytrar or to the jug*es*, ⌜how⌝ that y hafe be ruled by S*er* Thom*as* Tuddenh*a*m and Heydon.

It*em*, sende ye all the coost*es*, charg*es and* expens*es* payd and boorn by you *and* my s*er*u*au*ntes all the tymes of oyer t*er*miner kept to my councell, in expens*es* or othyrwyse, for all such mater*es* ys vndrestand a dam*m*age to me. And there as hath be made expens*es* in hors or vitaille at Heylysdon or Castre or ony othyr place of my p*ro*uision, it ys reson that it be valued.[4]

It*em* the cost*es* leyd out in Norff*olk* in deffens*es* of my p*ro*cess*es* drawyth but clxij li. iiij s. by yo*ur* takyng owt. But *and* ye serche well the bayllyffs of Blyclyng, Saxthorp, Drayton, Castre *and* Haylysdon, besyde Shypda*m* bok*es and* your*es*, ye shall fynde more money. Also the cost*es* of expens*es* of my s*er*u*au*nt*es* rydyng*es*, the expe*nses* vpon the maners for that caus*es* oonly valued wolles, be valued *and* cast vnto. I sende you the said rolle to corrige it.

It*em*, y have wryten to yow that for my proffyt in the maner of Drayton, be cause that Wyrmegey hath ouer manye charg*es* and offices to approwe well my londz in hys office, that my wille ys that John Emond, my ten*au*nt in Tau*er*ham, be as my baylly and offic*er* in Drayton, takyng ⌜for hys fee as gode chepe as ye can entrete hym⌝[5] yeerly; but I wolle he have ouersyght of my wareyn in Drayton aswell as the ouersyght of my vooldz in Tau*er*h*a*m *and* Haylysdon. And forasmoch the seid Emond hath been wyllyng to me ward in certeyn mater*es* that ye knou off, as Worcestr*e* hath crediblye enformed me, for esy reward yevyn, reson wolle that y owe hym bett*er* wille to resseyve hym to my s*er*u*au*nt. And also he hath certeyn evidens*es* that may do me ease, whych that y may the bett*er and* esyer com bye hem when he ys my man, and I vndrestand well concienst *and* true. And bethyn a yeer or twoo we shall preffe it. And therfor sende ye for hy*m*, and go throw wyth hym as ye shall concidr*e* best for my mooste p*ro*ffyt and avayle.

It*em*, I pray you and charge you that notwythstandyng I have offic*er*s *and* bayllyffs vppon my maners of Castr*e*, Haylysdon, Drayton, Blyclyng, Saxthorp *and* all such othyre placys where as onye money ys growed *and* owyng for rent, ferme corn, or for conyes wolle, or chatell *and* wodd *and* such co*m*moditeez of a maner, that ye do your part to resseyve my dewtees of such co*m*moditees your sylf, qu*arter*ly *and* dayly as it ys ronne, and not to suffr*e* my offic*er*s resseyve it *and* delyu*er*e it you, but it be in your absence. For ye knou well of exp*er*ience, that when it com*m*yth in theyr handz they woll make work *and* sett it out in jtemys nedlese, and not esy to hafe owt of her handz. For they have a reson, *and* seyn that when they resseyve my money, they wolle accompt for it at the yeer*e* ys eende, and so march*a*unt wyth my money, or ell*es* pay it in petic*io*ns of jte*m*mys, to my grete dam*m*age *and* hurt, and a grete cause of the diminussyng of my lyvelode. And wold J*es*u myne audito*urs*

[4] beyn *canc.* [5] *Over* xl s. *and* hys lyu*er*ey yeerly *canc.*

wold take thys mat*er* well to hert and councell you thereaffte*r*. And thynk ye in your soule whethyr that I sey reson or not, and take ye itt to hert. And myne offic*er*s may be aswell discharged of a[6] lyuerey of money that touchyth her charge made to your hand as to delyu*er*e vppon the acco*m*pt, for it ys not so redy payd then, ye knou well. And for deffault of thys ouersyght it makyth my bayllyffs be yn grett*er* arr*é* then they ought or wold bee; *and* thys mat*er* were tymely awayted vppon by yow.

J. FASTOLFE[7]

It*e*m, wolle ye hafe in knoulege that the xix yer*e* of the regne of thys Kyng, I put a[8] bille of supplic*aci*on to the Kyng sent by Thomas Ovye of the Lady Kerdeston ys councell,[9] to the Kyng beyng at Cambrygge then. And the s*u*bst*a*unce of my bill was that it lyked the Kyng of hys speciall gr*ace* to gr*a*unt and licence me to founde a college of certeyn preest*es*, clerk*es and* poremen at my place in Castr*e*, whych ⌜bill of⌝ supplic*aci*on was gr*a*unted and signed wyth the Kyng ys hand. And the seid Ovye brought the bille to London. And now y hafe doo serched among*es* my wrytyng*es* for the seid bille signed wyth the Kyng*es* hand, and y can not fynde it. So y suppose that the seid Ovye can tell to whom the bille was delyu*er*ed, to th'entent I myght inquire *and* demaund for it. Y suppose Maist*er* Thomas Ludh*a*m can sey where that bille be come, *and* he bee in that contr*é*, yff the said Ovye can not reme*m*br*e*. I pray you therfor serche at home at Castr*e* and inquyr*e* in all haast goodly of the seid Ovye, asswell as off Maist*er* Thomas Ludh*a*m whate reme*m*br*a*unce they can sey you of thys bille where it shuld be bycom, *and* sende me woord.

It*e*m, I sende you a rolle of the grete parte of cost*es* in money leyd owt *and* payd here in London owt of myne[10] coferys to lerned men *and* for councell, to diffe⌜nd⌝[11] the malyc*i*ouse *and* fals p*ro*cesses pursued ageynst me thys x yer*e* day by myne adu*er*se comfort *and* meynten*au*nce of Norff*olk*. And y sende you your rolle of cost*es* also, to corrige it aft*er* more serchys made as ys specified before, in bokys of myne acco*m*ptant*es*, p*ra*yng you to do serche of the new the said offic*er* bokys by avice of Watkyn Shypda*m*, *and* Willia*m* Cole, yff he be at Castr*e*. And put it in your papyr or apart, that y may cast eu*er*y cost of eu*er*y p*ro*cesse to othyr. As to the trau*er*s of Herlyng londz and the deffence of the appele for Bysshop deeth, it cost iij^{c} li., where eu*er*e it be wryt, and the bok*es* be not her*e* off it, ⌜but of Intewod last acoo*m*pt⌝. Ye most inquire ther*e*, and betyme, to labour it for my worshyp *and* p*ro*ffyt, that y make none demaund ⌜to⌝[12] my party adu*er*se of eu*er*y p*ar*tic*u*ler ⌜cost besyde the⌝ damage, but as the trouth[13] ys; and that I may fynde record *and* wrytyng off it and nede bee. I pray you pondr*e* these mat*er*s betyme to be sent me word.

[6] lyu*er*e *miswritten but not canc., no space after* a.

[7] *Remainder of text written around and beneath Fastolf's signature.*

[8] *No space.*

[9] at th *canc.*

[10] prevy *canc.*

[11] *Over* d *canc.*

[12] *Over* for *canc.*

[13] *Mark like a hyphen between* truth *and* ys.

And God haffe you in hys kepyng. Wryt at London the xxiiij day of June, A° xxix° r. r. H. vj.

1010. From WALTER LYHERT, Bishop of Norwich, to SIR JOHN FASTOLF Probably 1451, 18 August

Oxford, Magdalen College, Hickling 89. $11\frac{1}{2} \times 6\frac{3}{8}$ in. In an unidentified clerk's hand.

Dorse: Marks of folding, slits for tape, well preserved red wax seal, with impression of signet (a hart). Address in hand of letter:

To the right worshipful ser, *my right trusty and hertily welbiloued sone in God,* S*er John Fastolf, knyght.*

In pursuing his claim against Hickling Priory, Fastolf enlisted the Bishop of Norwich in his interest, as well as acting through legal channels. As a result of an episcopal visitation of the house in 1449 or 1450, the Prior, Roger Okkham, who had been resisting Fastolf was removed. During the autumn of 1450 it appears that the Bishop had sought a resolution through the new Prior, but was thwarted by the intervention of Lord Scales, the principal landowner in the Hickling area. In a letter to Thomas Howes, written about a month after his receipt of this one, Fastolf is found complaining about the Bishop's dilatoriness in resolving the dispute. See no. 1011 of 23 September 1451, and Smith, 'Fastolf's Dispute with Hickling Priory', pp. 64–5, esp. p. 64, n. 31, for the likely date of Lyhert's letter.

G. 967[4]/72[4] (abstract).

Right worshipful s*er*, and my right hertly welbiloued sone in God, I reco*m*maunde me to yow. As as touching your*e* matier hangeng in contrau*er*sie bitwix yow and the hous of Hykelyng, I haue put my sylf gretly in my deuoir*e* that good ende shulde haue be had in the same. Wherof sufficient evidence may be vndirstonde by my importune besinesse, whiche I made to the p*re*cessour*e* of the Pryour*e*[1] that now is, the whiche was cheef cause of his resignac*io*n; and also to hym that now is Pryour*e*, whiche moved hym sytthe Mihilmesse to come to me to London, as I suppose ye can remembr*e*, where I was instaunced by the Lord Scales not to medel in the matier, for by cause of importune labour*es* therin I was take as a suspecte p*er*sone.

Al this not withstonding, and I myght yet vndrestonde that I shulde inowe profyte to your*e* entent, I shulde not spare labour*e* ne coste to doe al maner of diligenc*es* posible vnto me. I conceyue in the matier your*e* profe, your*e* towardnesse, and ge[n]tilnesse, to condescende vnto right a resonable meane, the whiche I conceyue not in the othir partie. Wherfore I aduyse yow to take sum othir weye wherby ye may obteyne your*e* entent, as far as reson and lawe wole.

1010. [1] of *canc.*

I was in hope now late that your*e* good *and* deuoute purpos towarde the place of Seint Benett*es* shulde haue growe to sum good conclusion, to th'avayll of the same place aft*ir* your*e* blessed entent, where I was the Soneday byfor*e* Seint Laurence day last passed, gretly reioying in suche werk and notable cost whiche ye haue doe ther*e*; which must nedes remeane in to a p*er*petuel memory of yow all dayes to come, be hit vnto the worship of God, who euer p*re*s*er*ue yow.

From Norwiche, the xviij day of August.

It*em*, as touching to that ye write vnto me for Herry Inglose, I shal doe therin and in al othir thing*es* aft*ir* your*e* desir*e*, as nyr as I shal inow aftir my power*e*.

It*em*, I hertily desir*e* that ye take myghtily vnto yow your*e* knyghtly hert and dispose you to come hidir to the eyre of your*e* natural byrthe, where I knowe right wel ye shal fynde my lord of Norfolk your*e* good lord; and suche attenda*u*nce as I and othir gentiles of the cuntrey may doe, redy vnto yow at all tymes aft*ir* your*e* desir*e*. And doutheth not but your*e* comyng shulde be to your*e* helthe and hert*es* ease, and cause of moche peace in the cuntrey, for in your*e* right I shal be faythfully with yow, and so haue I be and so wole I endur*e*, by the grace of God.

W. BISHOP OF NORWICH

1011. From SIR JOHN FASTOLF to THOMAS HOWES
1451, 23 September

Add. 34888, f. 75. $11\frac{1}{4} \times 9$ in. Worcester's hand.

Dorse: Marks of folding, holes for thread, trace of red wax seal. Address in Worcester's hand:

*To my trusty frendys S*er *Thomas Howys, p*ar*son off Castellcombe, beyng at Castre.*

Dated. Fenn printed (and Gairdner reprinted) three separate extracts from this letter, adding the greeting from the beginning and the place and date of writing from near the end. In a footnote (iii, p. 133) he refers to another letter of Fastolf's to Howes, said to be dated 28 June 1451, and to include the following sentence: 'The untrouthe of the Priour of Hykelyng draweth away my devotion in such causes'. Such a passage, however, occurs in no. 991 of 23 November 1450 (see lines 52–4).

F. iii, p. 132. G. 171/205 (parts).

Ryght[1] trusty frendys, I grete you well, and lete you have in knoulege that y hafe resseyved a[2] *lett*re from yow wretyn at Norwych the xv day of Sept*em*ber last. And whereas S*er* Thomas Tuddenh*a*m, Heydon, Wylly, Br*a*mpton and

1011. [1] *Letter* a *added to left by another hand. First seven words printed by Fenn and Gairdner.*
[2] *No space.*

Dynne have *cerciorar*i to remeove th'endytem*entes* vpp, y wolle by the avice of my lerned councell pursue it to an ende, as it shall be to my worshyp *and* p*ro*ffyt.

It*em*,[3] where as the Bysshop of Norwych makyth but delayes in my resonable desyre for an eende to be had in the xxv marc. of Hykelyng, y am vppon a appoyntem*en*t and thorow wyth the heyr of Clyfford, that he shall entree in the hole maner that ys chargeable wyth my xxv m*a*rc rent, whych the Pryour *and* conuent have forfeted the seid hole maner to the heyers vndre her conuent seele of record, because of myne noune paym*en*t of xxv m*a*rc. *And* so then the Pryo*ur* shall lese for euer iiij^{xx} m*a*rc of rent, and that wythowt onye concience, for they have be fals both to the Clyffordys *and* to me thys vij yeere day. And y trust to God to correct hem so by spirituell law *and* temp*er*ell law, that all othyr relygyoux shall take an example to breke the couen*au*nt or wille of onye benefacto*ur* that au*au*ncyth hem wyth londz, rent*es* or gode. And my confessours have exorted me gretely ther too.

It*e*m, as for a wryt vppon statut of Hygh*a*m, it shall be sent yow by Myghellm*a*sse day, for it ys at sele *and* past, but I pray yow to do it execut as the nature foryevyth. Y am lerned because the fyrst wryt was not executed, thys wryt most be reto*ur*ned but as the fyrst wryt shuld, whych reto*ur*n ys that the seid Hygh*a*m ys decesed, for they it be opynly knouen to all men that he ys deede, it most be certified to the Ch*a*uncerie[4] by the shyreff of record that he ys soo; and then aft*er* to have a new wryt to extent the londz of Hygh*a*m. And[5] there as one Walsam wold desyre acquit*a*unce of pardon for hyr,[6] I hafe no cause, for hyr husbond lefft hyr whereoff to pay hys[7] debt*es* suffis*a*unt, *and* for me he feere the bett*er*. The wydow noysyth you, S*er* Thomas, that ye sold a wey salt but for xx s. that she myght hafe had xl s. for eu*er*y wey. I p*ra*y you aunsuer that for yo*ur* aquytaille.

It*em*, I sende you a[8] box wyth l*ett*res by my cosyn Lampet, whych ye doo rem*em*br*e* eu*er*y mater in tho l*ett*res to be sped for my moost p*ro*ffyt and avaylle.

It*e*m, Richard Sellyng hath put vpp a bille to me of grete da*m*mag*es* surmyttyng that I shuld doo to hym, and makyng hym damaged more then vij^{c} m*a*rc, and ys vppon certeyn condic*i*ons that he forfeted m^{l}m^{l} m*a*rc vppon[9] an oblig*aci*on of the statut. And Herry St*ur*mer had manye wrytyng*es* betwyx Sellyng *and* me, for whych wrytyng*es* I sent the last yeere to yow, to pray the seid Herry Sturmer wyff for to serche vpp all man*er*e evidens*es* *and* wrytyng*es* that touchyth Sellyng *and* me; but ye sent me but a bille or two. And therfor I pray yow efftsonys to speke wyth St*ur*mer wyff, co*m*maundyng

[3] *The following paragraph printed by F. and G.*

[4] that *canc.*

[5] *Remainder of paragraph printed by F. and G.*

[6] *F. and G. substitute* the wydow of Hygham.

[7] *F. and G.* hyr *but the last letter is overwritten, and* hys *seems to have been intended.*

[8] *No space.*

[9] v *superimposed on* a.

me to hyr, and wete of hyr yff she hafe found ony mo wrytyng*es* touchyng Sellyng *and* me. And yff she hafe not, that ye wold pray hyr to serche ayen of all such evidens*es*, *and* sende it me in all haast, for that I may aunsuer ⌜to⌝ hys bille the bett*er*. I pray you take thys mater to hert.

And almyghty God kepe you. Wryt at London the xxiij day of Septe*m*ber A^{o} xxx^{o} r.r. H. vj.

JOHN FASTOLF, ch*evalier*[10]

It*em*, Richard Sellyng hath enformed me that Herry ⌜Sturmer⌝[11] kept in hys hand from Sellyng of such money as I delyu*er*ed to the seid Herry to pay Sellyng wyth for my purchasse a som*m*e of l li.; and Herry shuld sey to Sellyng that he payd to one Fox of Castellacre the seid som*m*e for evidens*es* of Haylysdon *and* Drayton that lay to wed there, whych I am neu*er*e avysed of it. And so I suppole that Sellyng fayllyth vppon St*ur*mer in that case, and so he wold aunsuer hym *and* he were alyfe. I pray you wete ye of hys wyff the soth.

It*em*,[12] sende me the value of Goold ys teneme*n*t in Drayton wyth xx acres lond þ*er*eto, whate it was worth yeerly when it stode hoole, for Sellyng seith it was worth but j noble by yeer*e*.

WORCESTR*E*

1012. STEPHEN SCROPE, first schedule of grievances against SIR JOHN FASTOLF — About 1450–1

Add. 28209, f. 21. $6\frac{3}{4} \times 13\frac{1}{2}$ in. Autograph; see Plate XXIX.

Dorse: blank.

The document was originally a fair copy, in dark brown ink, but was subsequently used for re-drafting, the alterations being made in ink of a much paler shade. The paper bears an unusual watermark, an elaborate helmet with a plume, apparently identical to Briquet, *Les Filigranes*, no. 2901 (Casque, single example of this type: Lorris, 1450). In its original form the memorandum was evidently addressed directly to Fastolf himself. The rephrasings (given in the footnotes) appear to date from not long after his death in November 1459, presumably to adapt it for the attention of his executors.

Printed by G. P. Scrope, *Castle Combe*, pp. 279–80.

It is to remembre in the firste yere that my mod*er* was maried to my fad*er* Fastolf, he of h⟨is⟩[1] ples*er* solde me to William Gascoyne, that tyme Chief Iustice of this lande, for v^{c} marke, the wich he had in his possession a iij yere; thorugh the wiche sale I tooke sekenesses that kept me a xiij or xiiij yere swyng, wher*e*-by I am disfygured in my p*er*sone, and shall be whilest I lyve.

[10] *Remainder of letter to left of and beneath subscription.*

[11] *Over another name, subpuncted and canc.*

[12] *This paragraph printed by F. and G.; Worcester's signature and his 'Saturn' symbol (see no. 506, Headnote) written to right.*

1012. [1] *Edge of sheet gone; G. P. Scrope* his.

Item, he bought me ayene, and than was I s*er*teyn yeris vnd*er* his gou*er*naunce, in siche penurie that I was fayne to selle a place in Kente called Hevir for v^{c} marc.; and þ*er*-with I put my-self in-to s*er*vice with my lorde of Gloucestre. My seid fad*er*, conseyvy*ng* that, sent to my seide mod*er* siche l*ettres* as plesed hym, thurgh the wich I was feyne to go to hym ou*er* the see, with a[2] yoman *and* a page on myn owne coste, God knowet I beyng that tyme right seeke.

It*em*, whan I was comyn to hym, it plesed hym than of his g*ra*ce to shewe me so good fad*er*hoode that I was right glad to wayte opon hym to do hym s*er*vice, though I were vn-worthy, he promyssyng at that tyme to make me yercly iij tymes worthe the lordechip of Wyghton.

It*em*, than I obeyed his desire, *and* lefte my lorde of Gloucestris s*er*vice, thurgh the wiche I loste his good lordechip; where as he was set at that tyme to a put me i*n* possession of the Ile of Man, or elles I to haue had a resonable recompence therfore, as Sir Willia*m* Cheney, that tyme Chief Iustice, sent me woorde to Honnefleu be a[3] man that was with hym, the wich levith yit, called Willia*m* Marchall.[4]

It*em*, than I s*er*ved the King *and* my seid fad*er* at[5] Honnefleu as I coude, vn-to the tyme that my seyde fad*er* tooke partie with the marchall of the town, more than with me that was his son in lawe *and* his s*er*uaunt, the wich me thought an vnkyndenes, I beyng in the right.

It*em*, than be his licence ⌜I⌝ come in-to Yngland, to my seid mod*er*, *and* I was not ther*e* fully a yere but that he sente home worde that I sholde paie for my mete *and* my drynke, I havyng no lyveloode wher*e*-with to paie; wich caused me to marie for default, *and* not al-ther-moste to myn availe, but I was fayne to take the tyme as it come.

It*em*, the seid mariage of neccessité caused me to be bounde in siche bondes that eu*er* sithyn I haue levyd in grete peyne *and* thought, or ellis I had not endured as I haue don hid*er*-to, *and* yit it myght not wele a[6] ben as it is of myn labour, with-oute the grete g*ra*ce of God; for[7] be straunche menes, thurogh a svte made be my seid fad*er*, I was dissessed of all the lyveloode that I had be my mariage, havyng wyff *and* shild*er* *and* s*er*teyn s*er*uaunt*es*, and so endured iij yere with-oute any refuge save of God.

It*em*, than for very nede I was fayne to selle a litill dought*er* I have,[8] for myche lesse than I sholde a don be possibilité, wher-with I lyve yit *and* have[9] littil ellis but if it be[10] mete *and* drinke; the wich as in that it is[11] bett*er* than I am[12] worthi,[13] so that I had a dvté to lyve with.[14]

[2] *No space.* [3] *No space.*

[4] called . . . Marchall *added later.* [5] *No space.* [6] *No space.*

[7] *The clauses from the beginning of the paragraph to this point were subsequently struck out, and* Item þan *inserted here.* [8] *Altered to* had.

[9] lyve . . . have *altered to* lyved many day *and* had. [10] *Altered to* wer.

[11] *Altered to* was. [12] *Altered to* was. [13] bett*er* *inserted above line and canc.*

[14] so . . . with. *Alterations not fully legible and perhaps incomplete:* so that þ*er* had ben asigned me a dvté to a lyved with.

It*em*, not withstandyng the gret peyne that I haue endured, I am in dovte that, aftir þe dyssese of my seid fad*er*, siche lyveloode as I am borne to have shulde stande in siche trouble be the mene of certeyn astates *and* feoffementis made vn-to diu*er*ce p*er*sones vn-knowen to me, be my seid fad*er*, that I sholde not inow esyly entre with-oute trouble; for nowthir I knowe where to haue the evidences that longeth to the seid lyveloode, ne the entent of the seide feoffementis, ne no man, for me, that I wote of.

It*em*, lowly besechyng my seid fad*er* to[15] remembre with these p*re*misses how longe that he hath had the seid lyveloode that I am born to, and vnd*er* what forme as in stroppe and[16] waste.[17] For me semeth eu*er*y forme vnd*er* the sotilté of lawe is no clere concience, the wich mat*er*es my seid fad*er* can conseyve myche bett*er* þan eu*er* I coude.[18]

1013. Stephen Scrope, rejoinders to Sir John Fastolf's replies to his schedule of grievances

Between August 1451 and July 1452

Add. 28212, f. 22. 11 × 15½ in. Unidentified clerk's hand.

Dorse: At head, in Scrope's hand, heads of several letters gone:

Escriptez de moy a mon pe⟨re⟩ *F*

and beneath, in Scrope's hand, inverted:

*Esc*ri*ptez p*ou*r m*o*n p*er*e F*

The date is indicated by the reference to the death just over five years earlier of Scrope's mother, Dame Milicent Fastolf, given as 20 August 1446 in a copy of her Latin verse epitaph attributed to William Worcester (Add. 38692, ff. 139r–141r).

Printed by G. P. Scrope, *Castle Combe*, pp. 281–3.

Here, be the com*m*andement of my fader Fastolf, foloweth my replycac*io*ns.

First, wher*e* it is seyde that I was nat solde be my fader Fastolfe to the Justice Wiliam Gascoyne, but at the jnstau*n*ce, plesir and grete p*ra*yer of my lady my moder: to that, saving the displesir of my seyde fader, I haue herd her sey the c*on*trarye. Neu*er* the lesse, me semeth that neyther he ne she had noon auctorité to selle me, wher*e*for I conceyve that I was wrongfully doon to.

[15] lowly . . . to *altered to* entierly besechyng you to.

[16] as . . . and *altered to* and what.

[17] þer*e* hathe be don be him *added later*.

[18] for me . . . I coude *later deleted, and the following, now rubbed and damaged, substituted at foot:* to make siche restitucion as the ⟨soule may be [*G. P. Scrope*]⟩ eassed, and þ*a*t I may have cause to p*ray* þ*er*-fore.

1013. *The right hand edge of the sheet is damaged, with some minor loss of text; readings preserved by G. P. Scrope are given in angle brackets.*

As to the remanent of that answer*e*, I can, be my seyde fad*er*es leve, replye bett*er* be mouth than be writing.

As to the seconde answer*e*, touchyng the repayment*es* to the seide Justice Willyam Gascoyne for me: saving my seyde faderys displesir, I suppose it shal be founde be the reporte of some jentilmen of Yorkeshyr*e* that the su*m*mes wer*e* nat soo grete as it is rehersed in the seyde seconde answer*e*. Natwithstanding how that eu*er* it wer*e*, I had the soor*e* and felt the hurte. And wher*e* it is seyde that my seyde fader was nat bounden to finde me in my yougthe, the lawe knowe I nat; but wel I wote that if a woman the which is to mary haue many chylder, jt is often see⟨n that⟩ men be daungero*us* to take sych women for the charge of theyr*e* childer. As to the remanent of that answer*e*, I can be my seyde fad*er*es lev⟨e [replye]⟩ ther*e*to bett*er* be mouth than be writing.

As to the iij answer*e*, my seyde fader seith that he promissed me neu*er* to make me yerely worth iij tymes the lordshyp of Wyghton. Savi⟨ng⟩ the displesir of his good faderhode, I can wel telle the place wher*e* it was seyde, that is to sey, in a gardin in the parke of Alaunsom. As to ⟨the⟩ remanent of that answer*e*, I can, be my seide fader*es* leue, replye ther*e*to bett*er* be mouth than be writing.

As to the iiij answer*e*: I sey nat in my iij[1] article that my seyde fader wrote to me to com to hym, ne desyred me to leue my lorde of Gloucestr*es* s*er*uyse, whoos soule God assoyle; but I haue tolde the causes of all in my iij article *and* in my iij replica*c*i*o*n. As to the remane*n*t of that answer*e*, I can, be the seyde licence, replie ther*e*to bett*er* be mouth than be wryting.

As to the v answer*e*: I sey that I rehersed noo thing in my v article but as trouth was, *and* is, saue my seyde fader may seye as jt pleseth hym. The remanent of that answer*e* I shal replye ther*e*to be mouth, be my seide fad*er*es leve.

As to the vj answer*e*, wher*e* it is seyde, as it pleseth my seyde fader, that myn out*ra*geousenes caused moche thing, I haue me semeth answered ther*e*to ⌜in⌝ the iij replica*c*i*o*n. And wher*e* it is seyde I sholde suffre myn owne fader*es* feffees selle certeyne of myn owne fad*er*es lyfelood, eu*er*y resonable man may conceyve that the suffraunce most nedes a been, for I was that tyme but x or xij yer*e* of age, and fer loygned froo ⟨there⟩ be my seyde fader Fastolf, thorugh hys forseyde sale made to the seyde Justice William Gascoyne; as at that tyme my seyde fader ded with me ⟨as⟩ it plesed hym. To the remanent shal I replye be mouth, *and* he wil geve me leve.

As to the vij answer*e*, I sey that lyvelode coude I noon gete to I woold be maryed, and maried coude I nat be with-oute that I made streyte bondes. Wha⟨t⟩ may be suppoosed than myght folwe ther*e*of, &c. But *and* it had plesed my seyde fader to a vaunced me to lifelode or that I had sette me to

[1] iiij *perhaps intended*

maryage, I wolde haue trosted to God haue maryed to mor*e* avayle than I ded, and to a kepte me oute of the daungeres that I haue been in. And to the remane⟨nt⟩ of that answer*e* I can replye be mouth, if my seyde fader wille geue me leve.

As to the viij answer*e*, wher*e* ther*e* is thoughte moche vnkindenes in me, symple p*er*sone: I dar saufelye seye, and my seyde fader had a son of hys owne body begeten, he shold nat haue had bett*er* wylle to adoon hy*m* servyse *and* plesir than I had. To the surplus of that answer*e*, be the licence afor*e*-seyde, I can wele replie be mouth.

As to the ix answere, wher*e* my seyde fader seyth that he is enheryter*e* during hys lyfe as wele as I: I wene nat soo, for I am com of the blode, and he but be yifte of jentilnes. And wher*e* it is seyde that my seyde lady *and* moder wold haue yoven it to hym in fee, I haue herde her sey the c*o*nt⟨rarie⟩, and soo hath oother that yet lyveth, moo than I. And wher*e* it is seyde that I haue c*o*nfermed ⌜it⌝ to my seyde fader hys lyfe: saving his displesir, t⟨han⟩ me semeth I ought the bett*er* to haue[2] hys gode g*ra*ce, *and* nat to be rebuked for my pitous co*m*pleint. For it is now mor*e* than v yer*e* sen my s⟨eyd⟩ lady[3] my moder discessed, whoos soule God of hys hygh m*er*cy assoile. Soo thorough that c*o*nfirmac*i*on he had eu*er*i yer*e* sythen v^{c} marke, the whych amounteth ij^{m} *and* v^{c} marke. To the surplus of that answere I can wel replye, be my seyde fad*er*es leue.

If I haue seyde in thees for*e*-seyde replicac*i*ons ootherwyse than reson *and* co[n]science woold, of necligence, simplenes or vnkonnynge, I aske pardon and g*ra*ce. And wher*e* it semeth to my seide fader that I sholde nat a kepte thees articles soo longe in my breste; forsooth, be my wille I wold a kepte theym long*er*, for I seyde at all tymes that the hye witte *and* the grete trouth *and* jentilnesse of my seyde fader knewe full wele what was for to doo. For an oolde prou*er*be seyth, a wyse man be the halfe tale wote what the hoole tale meneth.

As to my x article, the whych I sente a-parte be Maist*er* Clement Denston, I haue noon answer*e*.

1014. From THOMAS, LORD SCALES to SIR JOHN FASTOLF — Probably 1452, 8 January

Oxford, Magdalen College, Hickling 104. 12 × 6 in. In an unidentified clerk's hand, not the same as either of those in Scales's other extant letters (see nos. 449 etc. and 592); postscript and subscription autograph.

Dorse: Marks of folding, slits for tape, well preserved red wax seal, with impression of signet. Address in hand of letter:

[2] haue *canc.*　　[3] discessed *subpuncted and canc.*

1014. *From Thomas, Lord Scales to Sir John Fastolf, 8 January 1452*

To my right worshipfull fader John Fastolff, knyght.

It has been suggested that this letter is likely to date from a time soon after Thomas Daniel had secured the good lordship of Lord Scales, which he is reported to have done in December 1451 (see no. 483, lines 4–8, and the discussion by Helen Castor, *The King, the Crown and the Duchy of Lancaster* (Oxford, 2000), p. 167, n. 59). The presence of the letter in the Hickling file at Magdalen is probably to be accounted for by Scales's having sided with the Priory against Fastolf during the preceding year, as Bishop Lyhert reported to Fastolf in no. 1010, probably of 18 August 1451 (see the Headnote). John Douebiggyng of Rydon, here described as Scales's servant, is otherwise found as a close associate of Thomas Daniel at around this time (Castor, p. 174, n. 85, p. 175, n. 97), and the debt for which he was bound to Fastolf was possibly that incurred by Daniel in connection with a naval expedition of mid- to late 1449 (see no. 968, Headnote).

The date of John Douebiggyng's letter to John Paston I (no. 659), given as 1460–2, December–January in Part II, rests on Gairdner's speculative identification of 'Perys of Legh' (line 1) with a 'Piers' imprisoned by Paston at that time. However, Douebiggyng's apparently jocular reference, in the address of no. 659, to Paston's uncertain status with regard to Gresham ('John Paston, sum tyme lord of Gresham and now fermour þer of, as it is seide') fits much better with his documented period of activity in Norfolk twelve or more years earlier. See above, p. xxxiv, for reference to the relevant King's Bench records, and for the redating of no. 659 to soon after 24 December 1447.

G. 967[5]/72[5] (abstract).

Right worshipfull fader, I recommaunde me vnto you. And where as my seru*au*nt John Dowebygyng stondeth bounden vnto you be obligac*io*n in the svmme of c li. for Thom*as* Danyell, esquier, and nothing for his owne duté; and also the seid Thom*as* stondes condempned vnto you in the seid su*m*me, or ellis in a[1] grete p*ar*tye þ*er*of, wich su*m*me the seid Thom*as* hath payed vnto oon Thom*as* Hoo, to th'entente that he shuld haue payed it vnto you. And aft*er* thys it was agreed be yo*ur* counceill to take þe seide Thom*as* Hoo for youre dettour of the seid su*m*me. And thys notw*ith*standing, such as ben of youre counceill, of verey pure malice,[2] haue outlawed my seid s*er*u*au*nt, so that he may not attende vpon such mat*er*s as I haue geven him in comandem*en*t to execute.

Wherfore hertyly I pray you to shewe youre goode maist*er*shippe vnto my seid s*er*u*au*nt, so that the seid outlaurie might be withdrawen, and also that ye will suffre my seid s*er*u*au*nt to go at hys large, *and* no p*ro*ces sue in yo*ur* name ageynes him betwex thys *and* the fest of Pasche next comyng, duryng which tyme my seid s*er*u*au*nt hath p*ro*mised me that ye shalbe made sure of yo*ur* seid duté. And so ye shuld haue ben longe or thys, ne had ben for fere that he shuld be troubled be you.

And yf ye thys fauour *and* ease will shewe vnto my seid s*er*u*au*nt at the instaunce of me, I prey you sende me worde be writyng be þe bringher herof, and ye shal fynde me as redy to do for you *and* youres in cas semblable, be the grace of God, who haue you in hys blyssed gouu*er*naunce.

1014. [1] *No space.*
[2] haue *miswritten and canc.*

Wretten at Mydelton the viij^{te} day of Januari.[3]

Fadyr, and ȝe had be to me as feythful and kende syn I cam in to Ynglond as ȝe were in Fraunsse, be my*n* trewtheh, þ*er*[4] had ben no*n* ma*n* of ȝowr astat that so moche[5] I wold do for*e*.

SCALES

1015. From SIR JOHN FASTOLF to THOMAS HOWES
1454, 12 July

Add. 34888, f. 102. $11\frac{1}{2} \times 7\frac{3}{4}$ in. Worcester's hand, larger, neater and better spaced than usual.

Dorse: Marks of folding, slits for tape, traces of red wax seal. Address in Worcester's hand:

*To my ryght trusty frende S*er *Thomas Howys, p*arson *off Castelcombe.*

Dated.

G. XXXV/251.

Ryght trusty frende, I grete you well. And wolle ye wete that I thynk it a greete m*er*veylle of your trouth and wysdom[1] that ye hafe noysed me, and seyd to John Andreus at Yeppyswych, in p*re*sence of dyu*er*s men, that ye have suffis*a*unt war*a*unt*es* vndre my l*ett*re and sele to safe you harmlese, in case ye be condempned yn the som*m*e that Andreus sewyth you for. And know for certeyn, there passed no such war*a*unt*es* vndre my sele, nothyr I comaunded you not for to labour ne do thyng that shuld be ayenst the law, nether vnlawfully ayenst ryght and trouth. And therfor y ought not ne wolle not pay for yow.

Wherfor I charge you sende me your war*a*unt*es* and l*ett*res,[2] or aco*mpt* of hem, and of whoos hand wrytyng they ben, and whate credences, instrucc*io*ns and informac*io*ns ye had, and by whom, aswell as of my lerned councell as of othyrs. And also that ye comyn wyth my cosyn John Paston &c, and take hys gode avice whate remedie ys best, whethyr to sew an atteynt ayenst th'enquest a *decies* t*antu*m in yo*ur* oune name or by the p*a*rlem*en*t, for y wolle do seke all the remedies that may be had ayenst the seyd Andreus. And kepe ye close and sure from hym yn all maner wyse, for yo*ur* oune wellfare, for know ye for certeyn that Andreus wolle ley all the wayt and aspies of such as ye wene to take for your true frendys to arrest you; and then be ye as it were bethout remedie, for ye not be tyme to sende[3] me the mater*es* abofe specyfied.

[3] *The following postscript added by Scales in his own hand.* [4] þ *in form of* y. [5] for *canc.*

1015. [1] that ye shuld hafe *not canc.* [2] wyth *canc.* [3] yo *canc.*

It*em*, Rob*er*t Inglose hath spoke wyth me and hath offred me to by lond to satisfye my dewtee that lyeth yn Rakhyth, and y am avysed to by it, so ye can sende thedr*e* to som trusty man that can telle whate it ys worth cleerly, and off whom it ys halde, and also yff it be sure lyvelode, and yo*ur* avice wythall. But beware that ye com not owt.

God kepe you. Wryt at London in haste the xij day of Julle, A^{o} xxxij^{do} R. R. H. vj.

JOHN FASTOLF, ch*evalie*r

1016. From SIR JOHN FASTOLF to THOMAS HOWES 1454, 20 July

Add. 39848, f. 19. $11\frac{3}{4} \times 15\frac{1}{2}$ in. Hand unidentified, same as nos. 520, 538 variant and 542; subscription resembling Fastolf's personal signature, but much smaller, probably a scribal imitation.

Dorse: Marks of folding, slits for tape and traces of red sealing wax. Address in hand of letter:

*To S*er *Thomas Howys, person of Castelcombe.*

Gairdner queried whether this letter might belong to 1451, but as has been suggested (Richmond, *First Phase*, p. 228, n. 91) it evidently follows upon no. 1015 of 12 July 1454, where Howes is first referred to as being sued by John Andrew. The same hand also appears in other correspondence of Fastolf's dated between May 1455 and February 1456. Whereas those letters were written from Caister, however, this must have come from London shortly before Fastolf left the capital to take up long term residence at Caister, which he was planning to do in late July 1454 (see no. 83, lines 4–5).

G. 168/202 (abstract).

Weelbeloued frende, I grete you weel, and wole ye wete that I haue receyued a l*ett*re from you by the hand*es* of Herry Hansson, the contynewe wherof I haue weel vnderstande. And where as ye afferme by your*e* said writing*es* that hit w⟨as⟩[1] myn pleyn wille, comaundement and entent, that as wele the seyd Andrewe as many others whiche were myn greet adu*er*saries shuld be noted, knowen and corrected at oyer and determiner, that the shyres of Norff*olk*, Suff*olk* and Norwiche myght weel knowe the grete and oughtrageous wronges *and* damages by theym don vnto me &c. As to that, I can weel agree me[2] therto, w*ith* that ye wole sende me the dowble of myn writing*es* sent to you in that behalf. And if hit so be that myn writing*es* beforseyd sent you for that cause be gen*er*all for you, what so euer ye dede for me were hit w*ith* the lawe or ayenst the lawe, than hit is reson, be my feith, that I bere you ought, what so eu*er* hit cost me.

Notwithstonding, I am not avised that ther*e* passed any suche l*ett*re in myn

1016. [1] *Writing rubbed away.* [2] *Four minims canc.*

name, but your*e* l*ett*res wole shewe the trought of the mater, wheche I pray yow may be sent me in alle hast goodly, and of whos hande the seyd l*ett*res ben &c. And yet if the cas hadde ben so that for necligence there hadde passed to you any suche a l*ett*re, as I thynke verrily ther was non, yet concydering the greet trust that I at alle tymes haue put in you, ye shuld haue called to you sadde councell on myn behalf, and haue purueyed that what som ever hadde be ⌜don⌝,[3] ȷf hit had come in reuolucio*u*n as the mat*er* doth [and] shuld haue ben founde lawfull.[4] And if hit hadde so a be rewled, lerned men of myn councell here tellen me that there shuld never conspiracé a ben sewed ayenst you, me, ner non othir in that behalf. Nowþ*er*[5] ye lakked no money with you, for I vnderstande the substance of the cost*es* of the oyer determiner oed[6] by me, and every peynye worse be wared than othir &c. But ye as a man not lerned, ner concyderyng thing that wold falle afterward, toke vpon you that by your*e* enformacion he and othirs were endited in Norff*olk*, where and they hadde be indited in Suff*olk*, he ner they shuld neuer a[7] meyntened action ayenst you ner non other for that cause. And so by alle others, in which cas if ye so haue don through necligence hit is not myn parte to bere you ought, ner non othir ⌜in⌝ wronge, as I reporte me to[8] alle the world &c. Of whiche mater*e* I praye you that I may haue an aunswer in all haste goodly, for I wende myn self to haue hadde hit cleerly by the seid Herry, w*ith* alle the dowbles of your*e* l*ett*res concernyng the same mater &c.

And God kepe you. In hast at London the xx[ti] day of Julé. And I pray yow that ye wryte no thing to me but as ye wole abide by vpon your*e* worship &c.

J. FASTOLF

1017. From SIR JOHN FASTOLF to RICHARD WALLER: copy — 1454, 30 October

Add. 39848, f. 23. 10 × 3¾ in. Worcester's hand.

Dorse: Marks of folding, slits for tape, traces of red wax seal. Addresses in Worcester's hand:

To the worshipfull ser *and my ryght welbelovyd brothyr Rychard Waller.*
A John Paston et John Bokkyng, ou William Barker.

Richard Waller, a long-standing associate of Fastolf's (see *D.N.B.* and no. 956), was a senior official in the royal household during the 1450s. The letter must have been written after the Duke of York was nominated as Protector on 27 March 1454, but before he lost influence when the King recovered from mental illness early in 1455.

G. 220/264 (abstract).

3 *Inserted later.*
5 *MS.* lawfully, y *stroked out later.*
5 þ*er inserted later.*
6 *Preceded by long* s *or* f *and* t, *canc.*
7 *No space.*
8 a *canc.*

⟨W⟩orshypfull[1] s*er* and ryght welbelovyd brothyr, I recomaund me to yow, and desyre gretelye for to hyre of your wellfare, for I thynk[2] ryght long that ⟨I⟩ had onye tythyng*es* from yow. And please yow to wete that forasmoch my lord ys and hath been allwey my goode lord, and specially now seth that ⟨he⟩ ys chieff officer vnder the Kyng, besechyng yow that I may be reco*m*maunded to hys gode grace, and that hyt may please hym of hys gode lordshyp*e* ⟨. . .⟩[3] the rathyr by your gode moyen for to hafe my pore materys in hys speciall fauour, and support me in my ryght as ferre as concience wolle ⟨. . .⟩e now yn myne olde age. Also prayeng yow to shew your gode brothyrhede in my cause to my ryght trusty kynnesmen Herry Fylongley and John ⟨Pa⟩ston, to whom it lyke yow the rathyr for my sake gefe credence for the au*au*ncem*en*t of my mater*es*; and to shew your gode fauour to my frendes and s*er*u*au*nt*es* that ye know of old tyme be there wyth me, whom I have charged to wayt vppon yow for the bett*er* spede of my causes.

And I beseche the blessed Trinité to have yow yn hys gouu*er*n*au*nce. Wreten at Castr*e* the xxx day of October.

Your oune JOHN FASTOLF

1018. From SIR JOHN FASTOLF to HENRY FROWYK: copy — Probably 1454, 30 October

Add. 29747, f. 2. 10 × $5\frac{1}{2}$ in. Hand unidentified.

Dorse: Marks of folding, slits for tape, and remains of red wax. Address in hand of letter:

To the worshipful ser *and brother Herry Frowyk.*

and in another hand:

To John Paston and John Bokkyng.

This letter survives in the form of a copy sent to Paston and Bokkyng, and is concerned with Fastolf's litigation with Sir Philip Wentworth over the wardship of Thomas Fastolf of Cowhaugh, which had been assigned to John Paston I and Thomas Howes on 6 June 1454 (see no. 457, Headnote, and for related lettters, nos 508–11). Henry Frowyk (d. 1459) was a London mercer, alderman and sometime mayor, and J.P. for Middlesex (see Wedgwood, *History of Parliament: Biographies*, p. 357, and *Cal. Pat. Rolls 1452–1461*, p. 671).

Unprinted

Worshipful s*er* and brother, I recomaunde me to yow. Please yow to wete that I have resseyvid yo*ur* gentil l*ett*re late to m⟨e⟩[1] sent; and I thank yow hertylie

1017. [1] *The beginnings of this and the following five lines torn away from the edge of the sheet.*
[2] k *flourished as if for* –es *abbrev.*
[3] *At least one word torn away.*
[4] *One or two words torn away.*

1018. [1] *Edge of page damaged.*

for your[2] gret frendiship and kyndenesse shewyd to me in my cause, towching the makyng the namys of the panell that shall pass a-twix S*er* Philip Wentworth and me, which troubleth and vexith me, God wote, ful vnrightfullye and causelez, and ye knewe the grounde of the mater, as my cosyn Paston can right wele enforme yow; trustyng to God w*ith* your*e* goode helpe and supportacion þ*a*t the seyd men namyd in the panell shall passe w*ith* me in my right, and that the seyd panell shal take w*ith*out ch*a*ungyng of the raye, for I take hem as men ful jndifferent. And I shal acquite me so to yow that I trust to God ye shul hold yow wele content and pleasid. And I am right glad of your*e* gode frendship and acqueyntaunce, which is to me a gret co*m*fort in myn elde age, to haue such a trusty frende and post as I haue in yow. And I wilbe redy to do for yow to my power at al tymez by the grace of God, prayng yow this l*ett*re may reco*m*maunde me to my nefew Fylongley and to my cosyn Paston, your*e* lovers, to whom[3] I prey yow yeve credence in my pore maters spedyng; biseching the blessid Trinité to haue yow in his gou*er*[na]unce.

Wretyn at Castre the xxx day of Octobr*e*.

J. FASTOLF

1019. Memoranda of Sir John Fastolf's legal counsellors.

1454, November

Magdalen College, Misc. 367, f. 3. $11\frac{3}{4} \times 7\frac{1}{2}$ in. John Bokkyng's hand.

Dorse: Continuation of text and later lists (see below).

The document consists of memoranda hastily jotted by John Bokkyng, probably as a result of a meeting with John Paston I, and perhaps also with other legal counsellors in Fastolf's circle; see nos. 510 and 511, of 13 and 18 November 1454, where some of the same matters are also mentioned. When Bokkyng came to write the bottom of the sheet already carried, down the short edge and in another hand, a list of twenty-one jurors for the hundred of Colneys. The dorse was subsequently used by another writer, inverted, for lists of those involved in actions in Suffolk in 1456, including Lady Roos, Sir Richard Tunstall and others versus John Paston, Thomas Howes, John Bokkyng and William Worcester; Paston and Howes versus Sir Philip Wentworth; and Paston and Howes versus Wentworth and Thomas Deyvill.

Unprinted.

Remembraunc*es* to doo to þe shireve.

First, to knowe how he wil be disposed in all our mat*er*es, and of þe l*ett*re now sent to hym by J. P., and of the con*uer*caci*o*n hadde at Norwiche whanne þe[i] were þ*er*e to ghedr*e*.

It*em*, for þe endifferencie of sum þat be for hym here, how þe p*ar*ties owen

[2] ff *canc.* [3] *Last letter not clearly formed.*

men warned the gr*au*nt juré in Norff*olk*, and þat in all mat*er*es it is openly vnderstande he dothe as Heydon will—panell *and* inquest at large.

It*e*m, his vndershireve[1] of Suff*olk* is Wentworth is man. Se how he demesned hym for þe acquitance of Dedh*a*m men at Dunwiche.

It*e*m, that as for þe *venire fac*ias in Suff*olk* for John Andrewes, that he will make a bill or he put ony jnne, þat we may have our laweful excepc*io*ns, as he seid he wolde; and that he be ware of S*er* Philip Wentworthis men, Debenhamis men, M*aister* Ric*hard* Dogetis men, and swiche as be ten*au*ntes ⌜w*it*h man*er*es or lordships⌝[2] vnder the rule of Heydon, John Andrewes, and o*þer* toward*es* &c. ⌜It is no*ugh*t knowe þat the shiref knowith þe dispocision of all men in þ*a*t contré toward Debenh*a*m, John Andrew *and* oþer⌝.[3]

It*e*m, as for jssewes, if we may haue more fame þanne our enmeyes, þat we des*er*ue it, and ells indifferent; and to have warnyng boþe p*ar*ties before what jssews shalbe retorned.

It*e*m, for þe atteynte, þ*er*e is a writte ⌜whiche I haue foryete at home⌝ wher jnne we wolde knowe *and* fele hise disposic*io*n, how he wolde be gou*er*ned.

It*e*m, for a writte of *venire fac*ias in Norff*olk* delyu*er*ed by J. Andrewes of recorde ayenst S*er* Thomas Howes, that we may haue lyke rule as in o*þer*e of John Andrewes in Suff*olk*.

It*e*m, for to haue good ⌜jsseus⌝ ayenste Prentys *and* o*þer* in þe acc*io*n of meynten*au*nce. And as for his rewarde, wher*e* he wil now or vp-on þe makyng of þe bille, lete hym doo vs to wyte; and þat þese mat*er*es be of non grete effecte, but as he dooth here jnne soo will wee doo with o*þer*, as in þe rauishment *and* attacheme*n*t, for þoo be þe mat*er*es of substaunce, *and* elles jt shall slepe. And to wite what tyme the shireve wilbe here.

It*e*m, to speke with Daws, and w*it*h þe Lady Fulthorp, and also with Alyngton and my*n* lady for þe names in Blithing hundrid.

It*e*m, that my*n* lord of Oxenford be desired to be good lord in þis mat*er*e as he hath allwey ben, and that we may haue a man of hise, w*it*h a man of my*n* lord of Norff*olk* þ*er*e at þe day of paieme*n*t of halfyer*es* rente; for my*n* lord of Norff*olk* is *and* hathe alwey be good lord in þe mat*er*e. And Debenh*a*m contrarie þ*er*to cometh a-no*þer* day and bereth on hande þe contrarie, and this be force; þei take the p*ro*fit*es* ayenst ony title of trewthe of all þe livelode, whiche is strange consideryng the lyvelode lieth in a contré of peas, *and* soo nygh my*n* lord*es* of Norff*olk* *and* Oxenford, but xij mile from them bothe.

It*e*m, we doo no*ugh*t þis for couetyse of money, but for hurte ⌜*and* vexac*io*n⌝ of the ten*au*nt*es*, and we wil agree that þe money be leyde in my*n* lord of Oxenford*es* hand*es* til[4] a c*er*tein day that Wentworth wil come jnne *and* declare his title.

1019. [1] is *canc.*
[2] *Over* and *canc.*
[3] *Inserted later between the previous paragraph and the next.*
[4] þe mat*er* be discussed *canc.*

It*em*, that my*n* lord be enformed how Yelu*er*ton wilbe disposed in þe mat*ere* of þe l*ett*re testi*mo*niall, and that he wele reporte to ony man of my lord*es* what my lord shall doo þ*er*jnne; and þ*er*fore lete a l*ett*re be gheten to Yelu*er*ton.[5]

It*em*, that my*n* lord Norff*olk and* Oxenford be laboured too that he will support vs in kepyng possession of þe landes whiche lyen nygh his lordshipes, and was soo wrongously holden owte. And þat Debenh*a*m reportith that my lord is good lord to S*er* Philip Wentworthe; and þat my lord*es* leve n*ough*t þ*er*e holde for non excitac*i*on or stiryng withowte S*er* Philip Wentworth wole shewe hise title, as we ar redy to doo. And how that S*er* Philip Wentworth sueth my*n* lord*es* s*er*u*au*nt*es and* menial men, and also þat he is *and* alwey hathe ben ayenst my*n* lord in þe mat*er* of Stockton.

1020. From WILLIAM BARKER to SIR JOHN FASTOLF
Probably 1454, 3 November

Add. 27444, f. 28. $11\frac{1}{2} \times 4\frac{1}{4}$ in. Autograph; see Plate XXV.

Dorse: Marks of folding, holes for thread, paper seal. Address autograph:

*To myn ryght worshipfull mayst*er *S*er *John Fastolf.*

Concern about the circumstances and affairs of John (Jankyn) Porter of Blickling, a retainer of Fastolf's who shortly after this time is found in the service of the Duke of Norfolk, connects this letter with several others mentioning him in late 1454 and early 1455; see especially nos. 507, 519 and 1021.

G. 221/265.

Please yo*ur*e mayst*er*ship, the cause of myn terying is that I must ben at Norwyche on Monday at the shyre to stoppe the oughtlawrye of John Porter, wheche, but if be holpen, he shalben dowble oughtlawed, bothe atte the sewt of the Kyng for a reskuse, as for serteyn money he oweth to on Hewghe, a man of court. And also the next day I shuld ben, if it please yow, at Saxthorp w*ith* a certeyn person, as I shal telle yo*ur*e mayst*er*ship here after, of whom I ⸢shuld⸣[1] have certeyn evydences of the maner of Saxthorp, and rentall, *and* fyrmall, as I am p*ro*mysed. And, s*er*e, as for alle the maters þ*at*[2] I went fore in to Essex *and* Suff*olk*, I have spedde theym, as I shal declare to yo*ur*e mayst*er*ship at myn comyng, *and* brought wryghtyng from theym.

And as for myn lord of Norff*olk*, towchyng yo*ur*e money, he seyth ye shal have hit w*ith* inne this xiiij dayes. Hit was his fyrst mater to me after I hadde delyu*er*ed[3] his[4] rynge. The money is redye, but he seyd that he must have

[5] *Remainder of text on dorse. Parts of this paragraph written around list of names previously written at foot of sheet.*

1020. [1] *Over* shal *canc.* [2] þ *in the form of* y. [3] youre *canc.* [4] ryg *canc.*

stoor w*ith* inne hym, for he loked dayly whan the Kyng wold send for hym. But as sone as Barette ⌜his tresorer⌝ come home, whom he hath sent for money, ye shall in-contynent after have yo*ur*e c li. I made to his lordship as I hadde no thyng know in the mater for onely for the excuse of S*er* Thomas, &c.

And I beseche the blessed T*ri*nyté[5] p*re*s*er*ue yow, myn ryght wurshipfull mayst*er*, after[6] his pleasaunce *and* yo*ur*e hert*es* desyre, &c. Wreten in hast at Wroxh*a*m, the Sonday after Allehallwen day.

Yo*ur*e bedeman *and* s*er*u*au*nt WILL*IAM* BARKER

1021. From SIR JOHN FASTOLF to the DUKE OF NORFOLK: draft — 1455, 2 April

Add. 34888, f. 113. $11\frac{1}{4} \times 6$ in. Hand of John Bokkyng.

Dorse: Blank.

A number of deletions and interlineations indicate that the document is a draft, perhaps (as Gairdner suggested) sent to John Paston I for his approval. It is evidently related to no. 51, and appears likewise to be partly concerned with the wardship of the heir of John Fastolf of Cowhaugh, which was granted to Thomas Howes and John Paston on 6 June 1454, but subsequently contested by Sir Philip Wentworth. The reference to 'youre castell of Framyngh*a*m' indicates that the recipient was to be the Duke of Norfolk. See also the postscript to no. 518, where this draft is referred to, making 1455 almost certainly the year in which it was written.

F. iii, p. 338. G. 234/278.

Right high and myghty prynce, my right noble and good lord, in my right humble wyse I recomaunde me to your*e* good grace. And for the noble lordship[1] *and* supportac*i*on shewid vn-to me at all tymes, I beseche our*e* lord God[2] guerdon yow, where as I may no*ugh*t, but only as yo*ur* daily *and* contynuell bedeman, now in myn age, pray for the good p*ro*sp*er*ité of youre right highe *and* noble estate, as I am gretly bounde to doo; prayng tendirly yo*ur*e highnesse to contynue yo*ur*e good lordship and supportac*i*on in the mat*er*es touchyng yo*ur* s*er*u*a*unt John Porter and my pore chapelleyn S*er* Thomas Howes, trustyng verily to God that with the supportac*i*on of your*e* good lordship, there mater shall yette come to a good conclusion in punisshyng of p*er*iur*é* and enbracery that many yeris hathe ben and yette is vsid in thys shire; whiche were grete merite, and to my conceyte, in yow that ar soo noble a prynce, a singler renoune, as for the beste dede that may be doo for the weel of bothe shires.

And in like wise that it please youre right good grace to contynue youre

[5] é *superimp. on* y.

[6] youre *canc.*

1021. [1] *Circumflex over final* p *here and in several instances below, apparently superfluous.*

[2] al myghty acquit it y *interlined and canc.*

noble fauour and supportac*io*n to me in remedyeng the force doon by S*er* Philip Wentworth, kepyng now wrongful possession of certeyn londes in Suff*olk* nygh youre castell of Framyngh*a*m; whiche ⌜lond*es*⌝ certeyn of my frendes, to myn vse, haue of the Kyng*es* graunte by his l*ett*res patent*es* byfore ony patent that the seid S*er* Philip hathe, whiche is my singler matier in myn owen p*ar*te that I haue now to doo, as my cosyn Paston ⌜can enforme yowr*e* lordship, for he⌝[3] knowith the mater *and* myn ⌜hole⌝ entente, to whom yo*ur* good grace lyke to yife credence. ⌜He cometh⌝[4] to awaite vpon yo*ur* lordship at this tyme, as I vnderstande by my cosyn youre s*er*uaunt, Richard Suthwell, youre lordship desired.[5]

Right highe *and* myghty prynce, my noble *and* right good lord, I beseche the Holy Goste be with yow, and eu*er*e more sende yow the accomplishment of youre right noble desires, to his plesir *and* youres. Writen at my pore place of Castre, the ij^{de} day of Aprill.

Yo*ur* hu*m*ble man *and* s*er*u*au*nt J. FASTOLF

1022. From the DUKE OF YORK and others to KING HENRY VI: copy — Nominally 1455, 21 May

Add. 34888, f. 114. $11\frac{1}{2} \times 8\frac{1}{2}$ in. Worcester's hand, larger and neater than normal.

Dorse: Marks of folding, remains of red wax seal. Direction in Worcester's hand:

*Tradat*ur *J. P.*

The original of this document was the memorandum addressed by the Duke of York and the Earls of Warwick and Salisbury to the King from Ware, Herts., on 21 May 1455, shortly before the first battle of St. Albans (*Rot. Parl.*, v. p. 281). Worcester evidently found means to make a copy shortly afterwards, and forwarded it to John Paston I.

F. iii, p. 178. G. 238/282.

Moste Cristen Kyng, ryght hygh and myghty Prince, and our mooste redoubted souu*er*ayn lorde, we recomaunde ws as humblye as we suffice vnto your hygh exellence, where vnto please it to wete that for so moch as we hyre and vnderstand to our grettyst sorowe erthlye that our ennemyes of approuued experience, such as abyde and kepe theym sylf vnder the whyng of your magestee royall, have throwen vnto the same ryght stedyousely and ryght fraudulentlye manye ambyguytees and doubtes of the fayth, lygeaunce, and dewtee that, God knowyth, we beere vnto your hyghnesse, and have put theym yn as grete deuoyr as they coude to enstr*a*unge ws from your mooste

[3] *Over* that *canc.* [4] *Over* for I haue desired hym *canc.*

[5] And to p*ar*donne me, for necessité causith me in as moche as I may no*ugh*t come in myn owen p*er*sone as my will were *canc.*

noble presence and from the fauo*ur* of your goode gr*a*ce; whych goode gr*a*ce to ws ys and owe to be our sing*u*ler and mooste desyred yoie and consolac*i*on. We at thys tyme be comyng wyth gr*a*ce as your true and humble liege men, toward your ⌜seyd⌝ hygh exellence to declare and shew therto at large owr sayd fayth and ligeaunce, entendyng wyth the mercye of Jh*es*u yn the seyd comyng, to put ws yn as diligent and hertye deuoyr and dewtee as onye your lyege men on lyve to that at may au*au*nce or preferre the honno*ur* and wellfare off the sayd mageste royalle and the seurte of the sayd moste notable person; the whych [we] beseche our blessed creature to prosper [in] as grete honno*ur*, yoie, and felicité as eu*er*e had onye prince erthlye, and to your sayd hyghnesse so to take, accept, and repute ws, and not to plese to geve trust or confidence vnto the sinistrez, malic*i*ouse, and fraudulent laboures and rapportes of our sayd ennemyes vnto our co*m*myng to your sayd moste noble p*re*sence. Where vnto we beseche humblye that we may be admitted as your liege men, to[1] th'entent to shew ws the same; wheroff yerstenday we wrote our l*ett*res of our entent to the ryght reu*er*ent fadre yn God, the Archebysshop of Caunt*er*burye, your Ch*a*uncell*o*r of England, to be shewed to your sayd hyghnesse, whereoff, forsomoch as we be not acerteyned whethyr our seyd entent be by hys fadrehode shewed vnto your seyd goode gr*a*ce or not, we sende thereoff vnto thys closed aco*mpt* of our sayd l*ett*res of our disposic*i*on toward your sayd hygh exellence and the honnour and weele of the land, whereynne we wolle perseu*er*e wyth the gr*a*ce of Our Lorde.[2]

1023. Relation of the first Battle of St Albans
1455, between 25 and 29 May

Add. 39848, f. 28. 7 × 11½ in. Hand unidentified.

Dorse: Continuation of text.

C. A. J. Armstrong, 'Politics and the Battle of St Albans, 1455', *B.I.H.R.*, xxxiii (1960), 1–72, designates this document the 'Phillipps Relation' (p. 2; BL Add. 39848 was formerly in the collection of Sir Thomas Phillipps), and he observes that it 'may have been sent to one of the Pastons or perhaps rather to Sir John Fastolf in view of the special notice of the bravery of Fastolf's nephew Henry Filongley'. The battle was fought on Thursday 22 May 1455, and the relation concludes with reference to the bringing of the King to Westminster on the evening of Friday (23 May). It was therefore written shortly afterwards, before another Thursday had passed.

G. 240/284.

1022. [1] *No space.*

[2] *The following was added at the bottom left hand corner of the sheet, but has been partially torn away:* M*emorandum* qu*o*d dict*ur* l*it*ere d*omi*nor*um* direct*um* ⟨. . .⟩ ⟨Archiepisc⟩opo C⟨a⟩nt*uar*. *e*st ap*ud* ⟨. . .⟩.

The solecytou*ri*z and causerys of the feld takyng at Seynt[1] Albonys, ther*e* namys shewyn her*e* aftyr:
The Lord Clyfford,
Rauff P*er*cy,
Thorp*e*,
Tresham[2] and Josep.

The[3] jurny batayle was in the Market Place, and þ*er*e[4] the Kyng*ys* standard was pight, the Kyng beyng p*re*sent w*yth* these lord*ys* whos namys folwe:
The Duke of Bokyngh*a*m,
The Duke Somyrcete,
The Erle Deuynshir*e*,
The Erle of Northeombirlond,
The Erle Stafford,
The Erle Dorcete,
The Lord Clyfford,
The Lord Ros.
w*yth*[5] many knyght*ys* and squyeriz, to the noumbre[6] in all that faught that day iij^{ml}, and it was don on Thursday last past atwyx xj and xij at mydday.

The namys of the lord*ys* that wer*e* on the othir party shewyn her*e* aftyr:
The Duke of York,
The Erle of Salysbury,
The Erle of Warwyk,
The Lord Clynton,
S*er* Robert Ocle,
w*yth*[7] many otheriz, to the nou*m*br*e* of v^{ml} men.

And S*er* Rober[t] Ocle tok vj^{c} men of the M*a*rchis and tok the[8] M*a*rket Place or ony man was war. Than the laru*m* belle was ronge and eu*er*y man yed to harneys, for at that tyme eu*er*y man was out of ⌜ther*e*⌝[9] aray, and they joynid batayle anon. And it was don w*yth* jnne di.[10] houre, and ther*e* wer*e* slayn the men whos namys folwyn:
The Duke Somyrcete,
The Erle of Northombirlond,
The Lord Clyfford,
The Lord Clynton,
S*er* Bartyn at Wessyll,
Babthorp*e*, and hese sone,
Cotton, receyuo*ur* of the Duchye,

1023. [1] Abl *canc.*
[2] *Superfluous* a *abbrev. over* m.
[3] The . . . folwe *to right of preceding list.*
[4] y *written for* þ *in this word only.*
[5] w*yth* . . . mydday *to right of preceding list.*
[6] of *canc.*
[7] w*yth* . . . men *to right of preceding list.*
[8] m*a*l *canc.*
[9] *Over* here *canc.*
[10] *Word or part of word, illegible,* canc.

Gryphet, vssher of hall,
Herry Loweys,
Wyllyam Regmayde,
John Raulynis is Asplé,
Harpour, yoman of the Crovne,
w*yth*[11] many othir men, to the nou*m*br*e* of iiij^{c}, and as many or mo hurt. The Kyng was hurt w*yth* an harwe in the necke. The Duke of Bukkyngh*am* hurt, and fled in to the Abbey. The Erle Deuynshir*e* hurt. The Erle Stafford and Dorcetyr gretly hurt. Fylongley faught manly and was shet thorwe the armys in iij or iiij placys.[12]

The Duke of Norfolke com a day aftyr the jurney was don w*yth* vj^{ml} men, and the Erle of Oxinford also;
The Erle of Shrewysbury,
Lord Cru*m*welle,
and S*er* Thom*a*s Stanley
w*yth*[13] x^{ml} men wer*e* comyng.

The Kyng w*yth* all the lord*ys* come to London to Westmenstyr on Friday at vj of clocke[14] at aftyr non*e*, and London went a[15] generall p*ro*cessyo*u*n the same day.

1024. From WILLIAM BARKER to WILLIAM WORCESTER
1455, early June

Add. 43488, f. 28. $11\frac{1}{2} \times 8\frac{1}{2}$ in. Autograph.

Dorse: Marks of folding, slits for tape, traces of red wax. Address autograph:

*To Will*iam *Worcester be this l*ettr*e delyu*ered *in hast.*

The letter is mainly concerned with events during the aftermath of the first Battle of St. Albans, fought on 22 May 1455, and was evidently written soon after the eve of Corpus Christi, which fell on 4 June in that year.
F. i, p. 104. G. 243/287 (postscript omitted).

S*er*, I recomaunde me to yow. And as for tydyng*es*, ye may enforme myn mayst*er* that for newe ther is non but that he hath knowleche of, but that the Kyng, the Quene *and* the Prynce remeven to Hertford to-morwen w*ith* ought faute; myn lord York to the fryres at Ware; myn lord Warwyk to Hunesdon; the Erle Salysburye to Rye; *and* there they shall abyde to tyme the P*ar*lem*en*t be-gynne.

[11] w*yth* . . . placys *to right of preceding list.*
[12] *End of text on recto;* vert*e at foot of page.*
[13] w*yth* . . . comyng *to right of preceding list.*
[14] af *canc.*
[15] *No space.*

The Duk Buk.[1] is come inne, *and* sworn that he shalbe rewled, *and* draw the lyne w*ith* theym; *and* ther to he and his brethern ben bounde by reconysaunce in notable sum*m*es to abyde the same.

The Erle of Wylts*er* sent to the lordes from a place of his called Peterfeld a l*ett*re desyryng to know if he shuld come *and* a-byde a-bought the Kynges p*er*sone as he dede be fore; *and* if he shuld not, than that they wold lycence hym to goon in to Erlond, *and* leve there vpon his landes &c; *and* be fore this don, the lordes were advysed to have made hym to don as the Duk Buk. hath don, *and* no more. But what that wole falle now þ*er*of[2] no man can telle as yet.

The Baron of Dudley is in the Towre; what shal come of hym, God wote. The Erle of Dorsete is in warde w*ith* the Erle of Warr*wyk*. Hit was seyd for sothe that Harp*ere* *and* ij other of the Kynges Chamb*er* were confedered to have steked the Deuk York in the Kynges Chamb*er*, but hit was not so, for they have clered theym þ*er*of. But London vpon the same tale a-reysen, *and* every man to harneys on Corpus *Christi* even, *and* moche a-doo þ*er*e was.

S*er* Will*ia*m Oldhall a-bydeth no lenger in seyntwary than the Chef Juge come, for that tyme he shal goo at large, *and* sewe all his maters hym self &c.

The Baron Dudly hath appeched many men, but what they ben as yet we can not wete. S*er* Phillyp Wentworth was in the feld *and* bare the Kynges standard, *and* kest hit down *and* fled. Myn lord Norff*olk* seyth he shalbe hanged ther fore, *and* so is he worthy. He is in Suff*olk* now. He dar not come a-bought the Kynge.

Edmond Stendale was w*ith* Wenlok þ*er*e in the feld, *and* fowly hurt. Fylongley is at home at his owen place w*ith* his wyf, *and* shal don ryght weel, but we have a greet losse of his absence this terme, for hit wole be longe or he come this terme I am a-ferde.

Alle the lordes that dyed at the jorney arn beryed at Seynt Albones. Other thinges ben non here, but ye shal sen by Thom*a*s Scales l*ett*re the rewle of the Frenshemen &c.

God spede vs weel in our*e* maters this terme, I p*ra*ye to God, who have yow in his kepyng.

W. B.

And[3] if any travers be of Beyton or reme*m*brances tow[c]hyng the sewtes here, lete hem be sent heder in all hast; *and* lete the[4] brynger her of have some what for his cost*es*, for thow he come not theder for the cause onely hit is reson he have some what.

1024. [1] *No abbreviation here, or below.* [2] þ *in form of* y *throughout.*
[3] *Postscript added to left of and beneath Barker's initials; om. by F. and G.*
[4] bry *not canc.*

1025 (530 bis). From SIR JOHN FASTOLF to JOHN PASTON I — 1455, 10 July

Norwich, Mannington Hall, Walpole of Wolterton archive. $9\frac{3}{4} \times 3\frac{3}{4}$ in. Worcester's hand.

Dorse: Marks of folding, slits for tape, remains of red wax seal. Address in Worcester's hand:

To the worshypfull ser *and my ryght welbelovyd cosyn John Paston.*

The location of this original was unknown to Davis when he printed Part II, no. 530 from copies by Gough and Palmer. It is now tipped into what was Palmer's copy of *Illustrations of Domestic Architecture in England*, which was acquired at the sale of his effects in 1867 by the 4th Earl of Orford, a predecessor of the present Lord Walpole. For the year, see no. 530, headnote.

G. 968/298 and XIV/92.

Worshypfull s*er* and ryght welbelovyd cosyn, I comaund me to yow. Please yow to wete that the Pryour and Conuent of Norwych have wyth halden certeyn rent for londes that they halden of me wythynne my maner of Haylysdon, and ys ij tapers of wex of ij lb. wyght by the space of xviij yeere, that mountyth xxj s. valued in money; and the lordes of the seyd maner beyng before me, and also y yn my tyme, have be seised and possessed of the seyd rent. P*ra*yng yow to speke wyth the Pryour, reco*m*maundyng me vn-to hym, and that ye lyke to meove hym to make me paym*en*t as hys dewtee ys, so as y have no cause to sewe ferther,[1] and to doo as justice requyryth. He haldyth xxx acres londe or more by the seyd rent, and yhyt ought to pay me othyr rent*es* more by myne evidens*es*.[2] More oue*re* y p*ra*y yow, cosyn, that y may speke wyth yow or y ryde, and that or Twysday by the ferthyst, and then y shall tell you tydyng*ys* off the Parlem*en*t; and that ye fayle not as my trust ys yn yow. Y pray God have yow yn hys gouu*er*n*aun*ce.

Wreten at Castr*e* the x day off Julle.

Yo*ur* cosyn JOHN FASTOLF

1026. From HENRY WINDSOR to JOHN BOKKYNG and WILLIAM WORCESTER — 1455, 19 July

Add. 43488, f. 29. $11\frac{1}{2} \times 8\frac{1}{2}$ in. Autograph; see Plate XXX.

Dorse: Marks of folding, slits for tape, paper seal with emblem of a goat, traces of red wax. Address autograph:

*Vnto my moost faitfull brethern John Bokkyng and William Worcestr*e, *and to eyther of theym.*

1025. [1] *Second letter unclear.* [2] *Long* s + er *abbrev. for pl. inflection.*

The year is evident from references to events ensuing upon the first Battle of St. Albans, fought on 22 May 1455.
F. i, p. 208. G. 253/299.

Worshipfull s*er*, and my most hertely and best beloued brother, I recommaund me vnto you in more loly wise than I can other thenk or write, and w*ith* al my s*er*uice and trwe herte thank you of your gentill l*ett*res, full brotherly writon vnto me at mony tymes of old, and in esp*ec*iall of late tyme passed. And trwly, brother, I thank almyghty God of your welfare, of the which the berer of this my pour l*ettre* c*er*tified me of &c. And, s*er*, as touchyng al man*er* of newe tithingez, I knoo well ye ar auerous. Truly, the day of makyng of this l*ettre* ther wer nonn newe, but suche I herd of ye shalbe s*er*ued ⌜w*ith*⌝ all.

As for the first, the Kyng our souu*er*ain lord and all his trwe lordez stand in hele of ther*e* bodies, but not all at hertes eas as we. Amongez other meruell, ij dayes afore the writyng of this l*ettre* there was langage betwene my lordez of Warr*wyk* and Cromwell afore the Kyng, in somoch as the Lord Cromwell wold haue excused hym self of all the steryng or moevyng of the[1] ⌜male⌝ iourney of Seynt Albonez; of the whiche excuse makyng my lord of Warr*wyk* had knolege, and in hast[2] wasse w*ith* the Kyng, and sware by hys othe that the Lord Cromwell said not trouth, but that he was begynner of all ⌜þ*a*t⌝ iourney at Seynt Albonez. And so betwene my said ij lord*es* of Warr*wyk* and Cromwell ther is at[3] þis[4] day grete grugyng, in somoch as the Erle of Shrouesbury hath loged hym at þe[5] hospitall of Seint Jamez beside the Mewes, be the Lord Cromwell*es* desire, for his sauf gard.

And also all my lord of Warr*wyk* men, my lord of York men,[6] and also my lord of Salesbury men goo w*ith*[7] harnez, and in harnes w*ith* strong wepon, and haue stuffed their lordes barges full of wepon dayly vnto Westm*inster*. And the day of makyng of this l*ettre* ther was a p*ro*clamacion made in the Chaunc*er*ie on the Kyng*es* behalf, that noman shuld nether bere wepon ner were harnez defensible &c.

Also, the day afore the makyng of this l*ettre* ther passed a[8] bill both by the Kyng, lord*es* and co*m*ens,[9] puttyng Thorp, Josep and my lord of Som*erset*[10] in all the defaute. Be the which bill all man*er* of actions that shuld growe to any p*er*son or p*er*sones for any offensez at þ*a*t iourney doon, in any man*er* of wise, shuld be extynt and voide; affermyng all thing doon there well doon, and nothing doon there neu*er* after this tyme to be spoken of; to the which bill mony a[11] man groged full ⌜sore⌝ nowe it is passed.

And if I myght be reco*m*maunded vnto my sp*eci*all maist*ur* and yourez,

1026. [1] male *miswritten and canc.* [2] hast *canc.* [3] þis *canc.*
[4] is *superscript.* [5] e *superscript.* [6] And *canc.*
[7] har *miswritten and canc.* [8] *No space.* [9] pur *canc.*
[10] *Second abbrev. an* er *flourish.* [11] *No space.*

w*ith* all lolines and trewe s*er*uice, I besech you hertely as I can. And also to my brethern Th. Up[t]on, Lodowik of Pole, William Lynd, Colyn,[12] and John Marchall.

Nomore, but Our Lorde haue you both in his p*er*petuell kepyng. Writon at London[13] on Seynt Margarete Euon in hast. And aft*ur* ⌜þis⌝[14] is rede and vnderstonden I p*ra*y you bren or breke it, for I am loth to write any thing of any lord; but I moost ned*es*, ther is no thing ellez to write. Amen.

Your awn H. WYNDESORE

1027. From SIR JOHN FASTOLF to NICHOLAS MOLYNEUX: copy 1455, 30 October

Add. 39848, f. 32. $10\frac{1}{4} \times 4\frac{1}{2}$ in. Worcester's hand.

Dorse: Marks of folding, slits for tape, traces of red sealing wax. Addresses in Worcester's hand:

A John Paston et John Bokkyng.
To the worshypfull ser *and my ryght trusty brothyr Nicholas Molynexix.*

K. B. McFarlane, in his study of Molyneux's career, concurred with Gairdner's view that this letter was written to him in 1455 (*England in the Fifteenth Century*, p. 163, n. 42). Fastolf's preoccupation with the administration of the Duke of Bedford's estate is similarly conveyed in no. 535, written by Worcester directly to Paston and Bokkyng, and dated to 13 November 1455.

G. 258/304 (abstract).

Worshypfull and my ryght welbelovyd brothyr, I comaund me to yow. Please yow to wete that forasmoch as I com not to London thys wynter seson, I pray yow that ye wille hafe my lord ys maters in your gode and speciall reme*m*br*a*unce, as I have wryten to yow herebefore; and that ye lyke [to] labour to my lord of Caunt*er*bury, to Maist*er* John Stokys, and to such othyr as wille take thys mater tenderlye to hert, for the recuu*er*yng of my lord ys ⟨gode⟩s,[1] that it may take the rathyr to a gode conclusyon. For I know no man alyve that can sey more yn thys mater then ye where hys godes been, and where they be disposed; and in especiall of tho godes that S*er* Rob*er*t Whytyngh*a*m had. Also, the Lord Cromewell had a certeyn nombre of plate. And as for your costys and rewardyng*es* for thys your labour, ye shall take it vpp of the fyrst monney that can be resseyved. And I pray yow comyn wyth my cosyn Paston of thys mater, that he may the bett*er* enforme me of your labours at hys co*m*myng yn to thys contree.

[12] *Second letter not clearly formed;* a *also possible.* [13] of *canc.*
[14] *Over another word, miswritten and obliterated.*

1027. [1] *Edge of sheet torn away.*

I have late spoke wyth John de Leawe, one of the Lord Wyllughbye executo*ur*s, whych hath enformed me that the seyd Lord Wyllughbye att*ur*neys, wyth[2] the executo*ur*s, wille labour effectuelly to my lord Beaumont for hys gode lordshyp, to help au*au*nce the p*ro*cesse, so it may be sufficientlye grounded yn the lawe spirituell *and* temp*er*ell, to ghete recuu*er*e of hys part for the reward of the takyng of the Duke of All*a*uncon. And also John de Leawe seyth that one Fendyk*es*, a lerned man of the Temple that ys one of hys executo*ur*s, wille gefe hys gode avice to grounde the p*ro*cesse sufficientlye yn the lawe, and help to the recuu*er*e of the seyd cause. I pray yow that I may veele som gode diligence doon yn thys mater, and that thys l*ett*re may reco*m*maund me to my suster your wyffe. And the blessed Trinité hafe yow in hys kepyng. Wreten at Castr*e* the xxx day of Octob*er*.

Your broþ*er*e JOHN FASTOLF

1028. From THOMAS HERT to WILLIAM WORCESTER
Probably 1455, 30 December

Oxford, Magdalen College, Fastolf Paper 61. $11\frac{1}{2} \times 3\frac{1}{4}$ in., uneven and damaged at foot. Same hand as no. 731, probably autograph.

Dorse: Marks of folding, slits for tape, trace of red wax seal. Address in hand of letter:

To my welbelouyd frende William Wurcestyr.

According to Bishop Lyhert's Register, the writer was presented to the rectory of Hellesdon by Fastolf in 1448, which may possibly account for the letter 'R' that he added after his signature (Norwich Record Office, DN/REG/6/11, ff. 18v–19r, *ex inf.* Dr Anthony Smith). The letter was written whilst William Wyrmegaye, sometime Fastolf's bailiff at Hellesdon and Drayton, was still alive. On 24 June 1451 Fastolf had ordered that he should be relieved of his duties at Drayton (see no. 1009, lines 44–7). Some years later, in 1456, several persons were indicted for his murder, at Beeston (*H. M. C. Various Collections*, ii, p. 342, Duke of Norfolk's MSS). At the time of his death he owed Fastolf a debt of 27s. 8d. (Smith, 'Aspects of the Career of Sir John Fastolf', p. 98); see also Richmond, *Endings*, p. 253, n. 56. If, as seems possible, the activities here attributed to Wyrmegaye occurred on St Stephen's day in 1455 (26 December, a Friday in that year), the letter was probably written the following Tuesday, 30 December.

Unprinted.

William Wurceter, I comaunde. Lyke it yow to make my mayster to haue knowelech of þe[1] namys wretyn in a bille closyd in þis letter, þ*a*t weryn w*y*t*h* Wyrmegaye at Heylisdon on Sent St*e*phenys[2] day a-yens my mayster offens, qwheche we hadde of a ma*n* clepyd Page, of Beston, on Tuwysday at affter

[2] *First two letters superimposed on start of a different word.*

1028. [1] þ *in form of* y, *and so throughout;* e *superscript, and so in* þe *below.* [2] *MS.* Stephenenys.

none; and many[3] other thynggys, qwheche þe seyd Page wyl telle my mayster qwan he comyth to Heylisdon.

Also, my mayster xal haue as many ⌜hole⌝ fagott*ys* as I may saue hole. Also, as for þe heggyng *and* dykyng, ye reseyuyd þe nowumbre of þe p*er*chys in a bylle of yo*ur* rememorauns qwhan ye[4] were last at Heylisdon. Also, as for þe repa⌜ra⌝cyons of my mayster placis, it arn grete, qwhere for it is good þ*at* þe styward seth hem, *and* ⌜þerto⌝ be don be hys a-vyse. It*em*, I pray yow speke to þe styward to see Fayrechyldys, for ther it regnyth vp-on þe tymber in sundry plac*ys* ⌜for fawtes of thakyng⌝.

No more at þis tyme, but God kepe yow. Wretyn at Heylisdon in hast on Twysday.

Be yo*ur* THOMAS HERT, R.[5]

1029. From JOHN BOKKYNG to SIR JOHN FASTOLF 1456, 9 February

Add. 39848, f. 37. $11\frac{1}{4} \times 6\frac{1}{2}$ in. Autograph.

Dorse: Marks of folding, slits for tape, remains of red wax seal. Address autograph:

*To the right reu*erent and *worshipful s*er *and my right good maist*er *my maist*er *S*er *John Fastolf at Castre.*

Dated incorrectly 'ml ccccclv' (at the second attempt); a mark about a quarter of an inch to the right of the date may have been intended as a final minim. The events described in the first two paragraphs are those of February 1456.

G. 275/322.

Right reu*er*ent and my right worshipful maist*er*, I recomaunde me to yow in my*n* right humble wise. Please hit yo*ur* right good maist*er*ship to wyte that on Sonday laste I sent yow many *and* diu*er*se l*ett*res *and* writynge*s* by Lampet, of all matiers þat I hadde knowlege at that tyme redy to answer*e*. And now suche tidinge*s* as ar her*e*, but fewe þat ar straunge, excepte that this day my*n* lorde*s* York *and* Warwik comen to the P*ar*lement in a good aray to the noumbr*e* of iij^{c} men, all iakked *and* in brigantiens, and noo lord elles, wherof many men m*er*uailed. It was seid on Sat*er*day my*n* lord shuld haue ben discharged þis same day. And þis day was it seide but if he hadde come stronge he shuld haue ben distrussid; *and* noo man knowe*th* or can sey þat ony p*re*fe may be hadde by whom, for men þinken verily þ*er*e is noo man able to take ony suche ent*er*prinse.

The Kyng, as it was tolde me by a grete man, wolde haue hym chief *and* princepall counceller, *and* soo to be called hise chef councellor *and*

[3] *No space.* [4] e *superscript.* [5] *The significance of this letter is unclear.*

lieuten*au*nt as longe as hit shuld lyke the Kyng; and hise patent to be made in þat forme, *and* nog*h*t soo large as it is by P*ar*lem*en*t. But soome men þinken it wil ner can oþ*er*wise bee, *and* men speke *and* devyne m[o]che[1] mat*er*e of the comyng þis day in suche array to Westm*inster*. And the lord*es* speken this day in the P*ar*lement of a greet gleymyng st*erre* that but late hathe bee seen diu*er*se tymes, m*er*ueilo*us* in apperyng. The resumpsion, men truste, shall forthe, and my*n* lord*es* of York*es* firste power of p*ro*tecto*ur*ship stande, *and* elles no*gh*t &c. The Quene is a grete *and* stronge labourid woman, for she spareth noo peyne to sue hir*e* thing*es* to an entent *and* conclusion, to hir power.

I haue seid to the bring*er* here-of more to declare yow all a longe. And as for hise comyng, ye like to vnderstande that yo*ur* nevew my*n* maist*er* Filongley, hathe labo*ur*ed *and* doon that he cowde or myght to hise p*re*ferraunce. But as for to make hym freman and at hise ease, to hise p*ro*fite *and* worship, it can no*gh*t bee w*ith* owte Will*ia*m Lyne be here, that boughte hise p*re*ntishode of his maist*er*, to hise grete hurte *and* castyng of bakke by ij or iij yere of tyme loste. And ne were it that the maist*er and* wardeyns of þe Taillo*ur*s tendre hym, be cause of yow *and* of Fynynglee, hise firste maist*er*, þat solde hym to William Lyne,[2] as weel as the seide Lyne *and* Richard, shuld alle lese ther fredoms, as ye shall more pleinly vnderstande by the reporte of the seid Richard &c.

This day was my*n* lord Deuenshire at West*minster*, *and* shuld haue apperid, but he was count*er*maundid. As to yo*ur*e matier of Wentworthe, the trety contynueth, *and* is putte by the arbitro*ur*s in Fortescu *and* Yelu*er*ton, *and* we haue day of newe til Friday come seuenyght. God gr*au*nte it take a good ende. The lawe is with vs clerly, as weel in þ'atteynte as þ*er*inne as yette, blessid be Our Lord, hoo haue you[3] in hise most noble gou*er*naunce.

Writen in yo*ur* place this Moneday of Fastyngange, m[l][4] cccclv[j].[5]

Your humble s*eru**au*nt J. B.

And that ye lyke to write a good l*ett*re for Richard Fastolf to S*er* Rog*er* Chamb*er*leyn *and* to Thornton, Chamb*er*leyn of London, *and* to bothe of hem &c.

1029. [1] *Second letter not distinctly formed.*

[2] *MS.* Lynes, *final letter canc.*

[3] u *superscript.*

[4] ccccx *canc.*

[5] *An indeterminate mark slightly to the right of* cccclv, *possibly intended as final minim, would give correct date.*

1030. From William Worcester to Sir John Fastolf's servants at Oxenton — 1456, 16 March

Gloucester, Gloucestershire Record Office, D1637/M13. $5\frac{1}{4} \times 11\frac{3}{4}$ in. Autograph.

Dorse: Marks of folding, slits for tape, remains of red wax seal. Address autograph:

*To Herry Hallwey off Castelco*mbe*, to do sende thys l*ettre* to Oxendon by Thomas Hakborn.*

The letter was found amongst a number of annexes to accounts, dated 1456, relating to the maner of Oxenton, Gloucs., part of the Castle Combe estate, which Fastolf had acquired through his marriage to Milicent Tiptoft in 1409.

Printed by K.B. McFarlane, 'William Worcester and a Present of Lampreys', *Medium Ævum*, xxx (1961), 176–80, repr. in his *England in the Fifteenth Century: Collected Essays* (London, 1981), pp. 225–30.

Welbelovyd frendys, I grete yow well and lete yow wete that I have spoke wyth my lord Bysshop of Worcestr*e* ch*a*uncell*o*r that the processe and cause that the Aumoner of Towkysbury hath ayenst yow myght be contynewed tille Mydsomo*ur* or Myghellm*a*sse next co*m*myng; so that yn the mene tyme the mater*ys* that ye be troubled for may be examyned and det*er*myned here at London by indyfferent lerned men chosen by agreem*en*t of the Aumoner and of my lord ys councell. And my seyd lord ys ch*a*uncell*o*r seyth he wolle comyn wyth the Aumoner and meove hym to do soo. And by thys wey it shall be leest cost and trouble cesed. But ye most doo sende a reme*m*br*a*unce yn wrytyng to London of all[1] your ryght and the customs of the contree deuly approuued. My lord myght trouble the Abbot of Tewkysbury more then the Aumoner wenyth, yff he woold.

More ouer, I have reme*m*bred my lord to geve a chesyple to your chyrch because ye be febly purveyed, and trust for certeyn ye shall have one. And ye shuld hafe had a coope also, safe for the trouble that your p*ar*son makyth ayenst yow. And y have[2] a cloth of sylk redye delyu*er*ed me for yow, and shall put it to makyng.

And ye, Thomas Watt*ys*, that ye sende to Castelcombe xij goode lampreys poudred, at the p*ri*ce of xx d. the pece. And they ⌜of Castelcombe⌝ shall sende hem to London. And foryete not a couple gode lampreys for my labour yn recuu*er*yng the vij li. that ye had allmoste lost of my lordys monney, for ye know well the baylly had spend it awey. And let my lampreys com wyth the othyr lampreys. And yff the p*ro*pt*er*s of your chyrch sende me mo lampreys ⌜for me and my felowys⌝ y shall the bett*er* thynk vppon your vestm*en*t.

Reco*m*maund me to Maist*er* Moreyn, and let hym see thys l*ett*re. God kepe yow. Wryt at London the xvj day of March.

By William Worcestr*e*

1030. [1] *Repeated but not canc.* [2] the *canc.*

1031. From Archbishop Thomas Bourchier to Sir John Fastolf 1456, 27 March

Add. 43488, f. 32. $11\frac{3}{4} \times 5\frac{3}{4}$ in. Formal clerk's hand, unidentified; stylised subscription, with calligraphic flourishes, in a different hand.

Dorse: Marks of folding, holes for thread, remnants of red wax seal. Address in hand of letter:

*To the right worshipfull and my right entierly welbeloued S*er *John Fastolf, knight.*

Several of Fastolf's letters of early 1456 are concerned with the administration of the Duke of Bedford's estate, notably no. 539 of 26 January, initiating representations to the Archbishop of Canterbury, as Lord Chancellor, to which this is a response.

F. i, p. 124. G. 279/326.

Right worshipful, and my right entierly welbeloued, I grete you right hertly wele, thankyng you spe*ci*aly and in full herty wise for the verray geantle goodnesse that ye haue shewid vnto me at all tymes, praiyng you of good co*n*tynuau*n*ce.

And as touching suche matier*es* as ye sente vnto me fore, I truste to God verraly, insomuche as the rule is amendid heer and the wedder waxeth seasonable and pleasau*n*te, to see you in thise p*ar*ties within short tyme; at whiche tyme I shal co*m*mune and demeane vnto you in suche wise that ye shal be right wele pleasid.

And as for the matier co*n*ce*r*nyng my lord of Bedford, thinketh nat contrarye but that ye shal finde me hertly welwillid to doo that I can[1] or may for þ'accomplesshing of youre desire, aswel in that matier as in other, like as your s*er*uau*n*te John Bokkyng, berer herof can clierlier reporte vnto you on my behalue; to whom like hit you to yeue feith and credence in this p*ar*tie.

And the blissid Trinitee haue you eu*er*lastingly in his keping. Written in my manoir of Lamehith, the xxvij daie of March.

Your feithfull *and* trew T. Cant*er*

1032. From Henry Fylongley to Sir John Fastolf Probably 1457, 17 July

Add. 43488, f. 45. $12 \times 7\frac{3}{8}$ in. Probably autograph; see Plate XXVIII.

Dorse: Marks of folding, holes for thread, paper seal; 'p*er* Fylengley' added in another hand. Address in hand of letter:

1031. [1] *Dotted circumflex over whole word.*

1032. *From Henry Fylongley to Sir John Fastolf, 17 July 1457*

To my ryght worshipfull unkle and *my ryght good master Syr John Fastolf, knight.*

There is no internal evidence pointing towards a particular year, but 1457 may be suggested by comparison with nos. 569 and 570, probably of November 1456, alluding to Fastolf's renewed intention to found a college of priests at Caister. A licence for such a scheme had been obtained in 1440, but in June 1451 it was said to be mislaid. By the time of this letter a copy had been found: see no. 1009, lines 79–93, and no. 569, lines 33–41.

F. i, p. 166; G. 290/340.

Ryght worshipfull vnkull, and my ryght good master, I recomaund me to yow wyth all my servys. And s*er*, my broþ*er* Paston *and* I haue comened togeder as touchinge to yo*ur* colage þ*a*t ye wold haue made. And s*er*, hit ys to gret a good þ*a*t ys axed of yow for youre lycens, for they ax for eu*ery* c m*a*rc. þ*a*t ye wold amortyse d m*a*rcz, and woll gefe hit noo better chepe.

And s*er*, y told my brother Paston þ*a*t my lady of Bargeveney hath in dyu*er*s abbeyes in Leyc*ester*shyre vij or viij prestes singinge for her p*er*petuell, by my brother Darcyes *and* my vnkle Brokesbyes meenes; for they were her[1] executo*ur*s, and they acorded for money, *and* gafe a cc or ccc m*a*rc, as þey myht acord, for a prest. And for þe suerté þ*a*t he shuld synge in þe same abbey for eu*er*, they had man*er*s of good valew bounden to such p*er*sones as plesed[2] þe[3] sayd barth*er*n, Brokesby *and* my broþ*er* Darcy, þ*a*t þe[4] sayd s*er*vyse shulde be kept. And for lytell moore þen þe Kynge axed hem for[5] a lycence, þey went thorgh w*ith* þe[6] sayd abbot*es*. And y hold this wey as sure as that other; ye may comen w*ith* youre councell therof.

And yf þ*er* be any s*er*uyse þ*a*t I can do for yow, hit shall be redy at all tymes, w*ith* þe gr*a*ce of God, who haue yow in his kepynge. Wryten at Londo[n] þe xvij day of Juyll.

Yo*ur* nevew *and* seru*au*nt HENRÉ FYLUNGLEY

1033. From SIR RICHARD BYNGHAM to SIR JOHN FASTOLF: draft — Perhaps 1456–7

Add. 28212, f. 26r. $11\frac{1}{2} \times 13\frac{1}{4}$ in. Hand unidentified, presumably autograph.

Dorse: set of accounts of John Wethamsted, Abbot of St Albans, headed 'Iste sunt parcelle quas Magister Johannes habet de porcionem abbatis'; undated.

It is not evident from either of the previously published transcriptions of this letter that it survives in the form of a working draft, on the back of a sheet that had already been used for accounts relating to John Wethamsted, Abbot of St Albans 1420–40 and 1452–65. The hand is not (as G. P. Scrope suggested) that of Stephen Scrope himself, which appears only in the later addition at the foot of the text, and is presumably that of Byngham himself. A letter to John Paston I, probably to be dated 10 November 1456, shows that

1032. [1] *Over* theyre *canc.* [2] hem *canc.* [3] *No space.* [4] *No space.* [5] þe *canc.* [6] *No space.*

Fastolf had been considering the matter raised here by Byngham during that year (see no. 568, ll. 8–14), though it may still have been of concern to the parties involved as late as 1459 (see no. 579, ll. 51–6).

Printed by G. P. Scrope, *Castle Combe*, 276–7 and G. 262/308.

Right honurable *and* reue*r*ent maist*er*, aft*ur* due *and* hertely recomendac*io*n, I thank yow als ⌜hertly⌝[1] as I can, that it likith yo*ur* gode maisterschip ⌜of yo*ur* godnesse⌝ to let ⌜to ferme⌝ to my son Scrope the pou*er* enheritance that he schal enherit aft*ur* yo*ur* decesse, if God will that he life therto. *And* I hafe for my saide son comonde w*ith* my maistres of yo*ur* counsell, that is to sey Paston *and* other, *and* I fynde them[2] not straunge, bot right[3] streyte to dele with in the mat*er*. *And* therfore, my saide son, *and* I for hym, must sue to the well of mersy,[4] that is to say to yo*ur* honurable p*er*son, wher*e* is special refuge[5] for my saide son in this cas.[6] My saide son is, *and* hath be, *and* will be to hys lifes ende yo*ur* true lou*er* *and* s*er*ua*u*nt, *and* glad *and* well willed to do that that myght be to yo*ur* pleaser, wirschip *and*[7] p*ro*fit, *and* als loth to offende yow as any p*er*son in erth, gentill *and* well disposid to eu*er*y p*er*son.

Wherfore I besech yo*ur* gode[8] grace that ye will vouchesafe remember ⌜the p*re*missez⌝: my saide son*es* age,[9] ⌜his⌝ wirschipfull birth *and* ⌜grete miseré for verrey⌝ pou*er*t, for he hath ⌜had no liflode⌝[10] to life opon[11] sithen my lady his moder deed, safe x m*a*rc. ⌜of liflode⌝[12] that ye[13] vouched safe to gife hym this last yer*e*; *and* therfore to be his gode maist*er* *and* fader. *And* thof he be not worthy to be yo*ur* son, make hym[14] ⌜yo*ur*⌝ almesman, that he may now, in his age, life ⌜of yo*ur* almesse⌝ *and* be yo*ur* bedeman, *and* pray for the p*ro*sp*er*ité of yo*ur*[15] ⌜noble⌝ p*er*son.

⌜And if I durst, for yo*ur* displesau*n*ce, I wolde⌝[16] besech yow[17] that ye wolde ⌜vouchesafe⌝ lat my saide son hafe[18] the saide lifelode to[19] ferme for t*er*me of yo*ur* life, payng to yow therfore yerely cc m*a*rc at ij festes of the yer*e*, that is to say Cristemasse *and* Middesom*er*, *and* ye schall be paied hit truly[20] at London, in Hillary t*er*me ⌜for the fest ⌜of⌝ Cristemasse⌝, *and* Trinité t*er*me[21] for the fest of Midsom*er*. *And* I will be bounden for hym, *and* yo*ur* maisterschip will vouchesafe to take me, *and* he *and* I schall eu*er* pray for yow. And thof the saide lifelode be bett*ur* to yow in availl yerely then I offer yow therfore, this ⌜su*m*me of cc m*a*rc.⌝ schall be truly paid to yow ⌜yerely.⌝ *And* God,[22] ⌜that rewardeth eu*er*y gode dede, schall pey for hym⌝ the remen*au*nt to yow, for eu*er*y peny an c, in relesyng of yow in p*ur*gatory, or ellys encresyng

1033. [1] *Over* lawly *canc.* [2] right *canc.* [3] strete *canc.*
[4] w *canc.* [5] fo *interlined and canc., followed by* in th *canc. on line.*
[6] wherfor I besech to yo*ur* ⌜gode grac*io*⌝ maisterschip als mekely ⌜humbly⌝ as I can *canc.*
[7] pleaser p*ro* *canc.* [8] maisterschip *canc.* [9] pouerté *and canc.*
[10] *Over* no thyng *canc.* [11] many yeres past *canc.* [12] yerely *canc.*
[13] gafe vouchesafe to *canc.* [14] now in hast *canc.* [15] wirschipfull *canc.*
[16] *Over* Right honurable s*er* I *canc.* [17] *Next three words added in left margin.*
[18] yo*ur* *canc.* [19] perfou*r*m *canc.* [20] in t*er* *canc.*
[21] eyther t*er*me *canc.* [22] schall *canc.*

of yo*ur* merite in heven. And how yo*ur* maist*er*schip will that my saide son schall do in this mat*er*, I besech yow that he may be certified be yo*ur* writyng.

Copie of my fad*er* Byngh*a*mes l*ett*re to my fad*er* F.[23]

1034. From Sir John Fastolf to William Yelverton: copy 1457, 29 October

Add. 39848, f. 44. $11\frac{1}{2} \times 4$ in. Worcester's hand.

Dorse: Marks of folding, remains of red sealing wax. Addresses in Worcester's hand:

A John Paston et *John Bokkyng.*
To the worshypfull ser *and my ryght trusty brothyr William Yeluerton, justice.*

Add. 27744, f. 57 (G. 319/371, abstract) is a copy of a writ of trespass dated 1 September 1458, obtained by Thomas Howes against various persons for maintaining a plea against him maliciously begun by John Andrew without the King's writ. It is endorsed 'Manutenencia facta fuit iiij[to] die Julii anno xxxv[to] [1457]. Dampna c li.', and evidently relates to the action referred to in this letter. Expenses dated 1457 in a King's Bench case involving Howes and Andrew are listed in accounts in Magdalen College, Fastolf Paper 42.
G. 308/359 (abstract).

Ryght worshypfull s*er* and my ryght trusty brothyr, I reco*m*maund me to yow, and thank yow hertlye of your grete kyndnesse and for your gode supportyng yn ryght all my materys herebefore; p*ra*yng yow of your gode continu*au*nce, and speciallye now at thys tyme that the p*ar*son S*er* Thomas co*m*myth vpp to appere before yow and othyr the Kyng*es* juges by the crewell and hasty sewte of Androus and hys affinité; whych I trust to God that by your gode help the p*ro*cess*es* that ys sewed so egyrlye bye hym vppon the vniust condempnac*io*n shall be reformed and holpen by the atteynt yn chastysyng of periure that regnyth so moch nowadayes. And it were a full blessed deede that it myght be reformed in your dayes by your autorite and grete discrec*io*n, and that ye myght be the fadyr of the chastysyng of the seyd periuré, for ye coude neu*er*e do a more meritable deede. And that ye lyke geve credence to my[1] cosyn Paston and to the seyd S*er* Thomas yn the furtheryng of all my mater*ys* before yow attained, as my moste sing*u*ler trust ys yn yow. I am put to grete cost*es* yn the lawe yn deffaut that my materys may not p*ro*cede as ryght and concience wolde.

Ryght worshypfull s*er*, y beseche the blessed Trinité to have yow yn hys gou*er*n*au*nce. Wreten at Castr*e* the xxix day of October.

Your John Fastolf

[23] *Added later, in Stephen Scrope's hand.*

1034. [1] seyd *canc.*

1035. From Sir John Fastolf to Stephen Scrope: copy 1457, 30 October

Add. 34888, f. 134. 10 × $5\frac{1}{2}$ in. Hand unidentified.

Dorse: Marks of folding, slits for tape, remains of red wax seal. Address in hand of letter:

A John Paston et *John Bokkyng.*

In common with other Fastolf letters of this period, this exists as a copy forwarded to Paston and Bokkyng, presumably at the same time the original was sent to the primary addressee. It is concerned with the same matter as no. 1034, and was written the following day. A note beneath the text in the sixteenth century hand that annotates many of the letters (see Part I, pp. xxxi–xxxiii) infers from this, perhaps taking it together with no. 1034, that Scrope had married a daughter of Justice Yelverton's. Scrope's 'father' referred to here however was Sir Richard Bingham (see no. 1033) whose daughter Joan he had married.

F. iii, p. 142. G. 309/360.

⟨Wor⟩schepeful[1] *and* my right wel beloved sone, I comaund me to yow, and hertily thank yow for yo*ur* good au*er*tismentys and right ⟨well avy⟩sed[2] l*ett*res to me sent from tyme to tyme, and so pray yow of your good continuaunce.

Plese it yow to wete, þat[3] for as ⟨mech as⟩[4] þe p*ar*son S*er* Thom*as* Howes cometh vp at this tyme by the grevous pursewte of John Andreus *and* Heydon, to apere be fore þe right worschepeful s*er*, my right wel be-loved brother yo*ur* fadir, and other þe Kynges juges of þe Kynges Benche; I p*re*y ȝow hertily þ*a*t ye wille have in remembraunce for to recomaund me to hym whan ye speke with hym, and for to thank hym for his rightful fauo*ur* shewed in S*er* Thom*as* matier, and in alle other matiers þat toucheth me wheche ben attained in þat hey courte.

And so it lyke yow, pray hym of his good continuaunce, and I shal doo serue it vnto hym to my symple power for his good wyl to me shewed, *and* to myne. And I trust to God þat he shal hold hym plesid. And þat it like yow to geve credence to þe seid S*er* Thom*as* of þat he shal sey to ȝow, for my worschepe *and* p*ro*fyte, and þat this l*ett*re may recomaund me to my doghtir yo*ur* wyf, be-sechyng þe blissed Trinité to sende yow þe acomplyshment of yo*ur* good desyre.

Wretyn at Castre, þe xxx day of Octobr*e*.

J. F.

A Stevyn Scrope.

1035. [1] *Top left corner of sheet torn off (apparently after Fenn's time) carrying away parts of text at beginnings of first three lines.*

[2] *Fenn's readings.*

[3] þ *in form of* y *here and in several, but not all, instances below.*

[4] *Fenn's readings.*

1036. From John Bokkyng to Sir John Fastolf 1458, 15 March

Add. 43488, f. 41. $8\frac{1}{2} \times 4\frac{3}{4}$ in. Autograph; see Plate XXVI.

Dorse: Marks of folding, address panel soiled, paper seal with emblem of a goat. Address autograph:

*To my maist*er *Fastolf at Castre, in haste.*

The first part of the letter describes the circumstances under which the great council met in early March 1458.

F. i, p. 154. G. 315/366.

S*er*, lyke it yo*ur* maist*er*ship to wyte that as for tiding*es*, the Counsell is the fornone at þe Blake Frires, for þe ease of resortyng of þe lordys that ar w*ith*jnne þe toune, and at aft*er* non at the White Frires[1] in Fletstrete, for þe lordis w*ith*owte þe toun. And all þing shall come to a good conclusion, w*ith* God is g*ra*ce, for þe Kyng shall come hidr*e* þis wike, and þe Quene also as some men sayn, and my lord Buk.[2] *and* Stafford w*ith* hire, and moche puple.

My*n* lord of Caunt*er*bury takith grete peyne vp-on hym daily, and will write vn-to yow þe c*er*teynté of suche tiding*es* as falle, and shuld haue doon or þis tyme, saf for þat he wolde knowe an ende of þe mat*ere*.

Oþ*er* tiding*es* here ar none, sauf my lord of Excestr*e* is displesid þ*a*t þe Erle of Warwyk shall kepe þe see, and hath þ*er*fore rec*eved*[3] þis weke m^{l} li. of þe Hanup*ere*.

The messenger was on horsbak whanne I wrote yow þis bill, and þ*er*fore it was doon in haste. And our lord Jh*es*u kepe yow. Writen at[4] London þe Wednesday aft*er* Midlenton.

And my lord of Caunt*er*bury tolde me þat þe Frenchemen haue ben before yow, and þ*a*t ye shotte many gonnes, and soo he tolde all þe lord*es*. I haue desirid hym to meve þe Counsell for refreshing of þe toun of Yermowth w*ith* stuff of ordnance *and* gonnes *and* gonne powdr*e*, and he seid he wolde.

Yo*ur* humble s*er*u*a*unt J. Bokkyng

1037. From Hugh at Fenne to William Worcester 1460, 9 April

Add. 34888, f. 143. 12 × 6 in. Autograph.

Dorse: Marks of folding, slits for tape, remains of red wax seal. Address autograph:

*To my good maist*er *&c H. B. of Lincoln.* +

1036. [1] *MS.* Frirers [2] *No abbrev. mark.*
[3] *MS.* rec *with upward curl on* c *normally signifying the* er *abbrev.* [4] Castre *canc.*

The writer of this letter sought to conceal his identity and also that of his addressee, but the hand is undoubtedly Hugh at Fenne's; it most closely resembles no. 546 amongst the letters he signed. There was nobody with the initials H. B. among Fastolf's executors, but there can be little doubt that this was intended for William Worcester, whose falling out with John Paston I had begun in the spring of 1460. It also appears that at about this time Worcester had been at Cambridge to consult Lord Beauchamp, another Fastolf executor (see lines 29–30, and no. 1038). The address is mysterious, but H. B. is perhaps Fenne's attempt to render Worcester's 'Saturn' symbol (see no. 506), which looks like a monogram where the first element resembles an H and the second R or B; 'of Lincoln', however, remains unexplained. The year must be 1460, when 9 April was a Wednesday shortly before Easter, on 13 April (see line 39).

G. XLIII/405 (unattributed).

Right worchepfull s*er*, aft*er* my due recom*mendation*, like y*o*u to wete I wold yist*er*day have spoken w*ith* y*o*u if ye had be allone and at good leiser, for my*n* aquytaile to God and to y*o*u, and for þe wele of our*e* maister, God p*ar*don hym. I have many thynges to remembr*e* y*o*u, ⌜if ye wol⌝, wherof diu*er*se specialtes þ*at* I wold sey, I may not write. For I meved y*o*u at yo*ur* chaumber wyndowe at La*m*mes homward fro*m* London so*m*me thyng*es* of my good wil, and me thought ye toke it gretely to displeis*er*, þe whuch caused me to sey þe lesse of thynges þ*a*t had be worchepfull to have be doon.

But s*er*, as I reme*m*bred y*o*u late at Norwich of þe variaunce bytwix þe worchepfull man and y*o*u, for Godd*es* love and yo*ur* most ease, folwe þe meanes of his good wil by help of holsom gentilmen, and also þe feithfull love of o*þer* þ*at* grucchen to y*o*u warde, as I fele moche þof þei speke ⌜litil þ*er*of⌝[1] to y*o*u; rettyng in y*o*u singuler fastnesse ageyns kyndenesse and reson. For w*ith* love and vnyté ye shal do moost good for oure maister, to yo*ur* worchep, and w*ith* þe cont*rar*y, many mysse dispenses as han be; and þanne moche lette in doyng of good ded*es*, to þe causers p*er*ill and slawnder.

God hath sent y*o*u wysdh*a*m grete þ*a*t telleth y*o*u þe best is to drede God. A man shal neu*er* have love of God nor love nor drede of good men for ⌜mys⌝kepyng of moche good, þof it wer*e* his owen, for it is dampnable. But wher*e* it is truly delt w*ith* and godly disposed, þanne folwith boþe grete m*er*yte and worchep. Pety it is þ*a*t no more is do for hym. At the gate is nowther mete, drynke nor money, *vt dicit*ur, no man wele spekyng. þof þ'acte above be not do, necc*essar*y almesse to þe nedy þ*a*t peynen wold and myght be do dayly.

And s*er*, be ware what ye talke to so*m*me men of þe lordes yo*ur* coexecuto*ur*s, and what is spent for þe man, and what he was worth. þei reporten y*o*u vnfavorabely and w*ith*oute credence, as men seyn, and so*m*me I have herd. Also yo*ur* entretyng, and o*þer* for y*o*u, w*ith* þem þ*a*t have entres w*ith* y*o*u for to have yo*ur* entent sped, is tolde oute whow; and yo*ur* jo*ur*nay to Lorde Beauchamp to Caumbrig is taken as men like, and yo*ur* associac*i*on is seid made by yo*ur* witt to your p*ur*pos. As so*m*me fer of and grete þ*a*t may

1037. [1] *Over* meryly *canc.*

nor p*er*aventur*e* wiln not medle, so*m*me ye wold ⸢þei⸣ left, so*m*me havy*n*g no conduyt, so*m*me no stomak, and so*m*me glosours and witnesses for lucr*e*. þis is not my seyyng, I have often herd it.

þ*er*for to have such a post as þe seid man is þ*a*t ye be ⟨w*i*t*h*⟩[2] in variaunce, so he do wele, as I fully beleve, he shuld help y*o*u to bere moche, and cause[3] eschuy*n*g of moche of þis noyse. þis variaunce grew of mater of noght, and japes—þe soner may be accorde. And thynke not, s*er*, þ*a*t any p*er*sone hath stered me herto, for by þe good Lorde I trist to receyve þis holy tyme, it is my*n* owen steryng and good hert to y*o*u warde; for þ*a*t I her*e* and see, and moost of yo*ur* wele willers, in eschuyng of inconvenyentz as right many talke must ensue to y*o*u ward. For I fonde y*o*u pleyn at Cristemesse, and I toke y*o*u þ*a*t[4] ye loved me; wher*e* to-fore, w*i*t*h*oute cause truly, to my seid maist*er* moch ye hyndred me, as parte he tolde me, and þanne I p*ra*ied y*o*u in þ*a*t yo*ur* good maist*er*ship and amendement, and sith I have be pleyn, and wol be.

And I requir*e* y*o*u, as ye arn a gentilman, kepe þees maters secrete by twix God, y*o*u and me; for by almyghty Jh*es*u, of me knoweth þis[5] non erthely creatur*e*, nor shal knowe. Oþ*er* thynges been þ*a*t sounden[6] not wele, but as I fele yo*ur* wisdh*a*m take me in þis, so heraft*er* I wil demene me w*i*t*h* y*o*u in maters. I am vrke of variaunces, for p*ar*ties waxen wrooth if men hold not w*i*t*h* þere oppynyons whan þei in angr*e* trotte over-fer by-yon hem self.

I may not come by y*o*u to London ward; I trowe I must by Suff*olk*, ⸢ell I had not writen þis⸣. Oure blissed Lorde have y*o*u in his gou*er*naunce and be yo*ur* conduyto*ur* to his pleis*er*. Am*en*. þis Wednesday, ix day Aprill.

As ye arn a veray gentilman, be my true confesso*ur* as I am youres, and take me as I mene, þof my t*er*mes been not discreet. Brenne þis scrowe or kepe it pryvy &c, as y*o*u like; and I besech y*o*u, ⸢s*er*⸣, if ye wil trist me, wil me pleyn &c.

Yo*ur* owen &c, to my power.

1038. From Lord Beauchamp to Thomas Howes

Probably 1460, 28 August

Add. 34888, f. 192. 11¼ × 5¼ in. Clerk's hand; subscription autograph.

Dorse: Marks of folding, slits for tape, remains of red sealing wax. Address in hand of letter:

To myn welbeloued frende Ser *Thomas Howys, parson of Blofeld.*

John, Lord Beauchamp, was one of Fastolf's executors. The rift between John Paston and William Worcester over the administration of Fastolf's will became evident in the spring of 1460, and was well developed by the time of the inquisition *post mortem* in October; see

[2] *Obliterated by damp stain.* [3] y *canc.* [4] in party *canc.* [5] nor shal *canc.* [6] eve *canc.*

Richmond, *Fastolf's Will*, pp. 86–91. Gairdner suggested that this attempt to repair relations might date from the summer of the following year, but there is no reason why it could not have taken place in 1460. The unidentified addressee of no. 1037, of 9 April 1460, who was probably Worcester, is there spoken of as having recently consulted Beauchamp, and it is possible that this letter may have been connected with that meeting.

F. iv, p. 96. G. 412/479.

Welbeloued frende, I grete you well. And for asmuche as I vnderstonde that Williaȝ*m* Wurcestr*e*, late the seru*au*nt vnto S*er* John Fastalf, knyth, whois soule God assoyle, ys not had in fauo*ur* ne trust w*ith* my right welbe-loued frende John Paston, nether w*ith* you, ⌜as he seyth⌝, namely in such maters and causes as concerneth the wylle and testament of the sayd S*er* John Fastolf. And as I am informed, the said Williaȝ*m* p*ur*poseth hym to go into his cuntr*é*, for the whiche cause he hath desired me to wryte vnto you that ye wolde be a special good frend vnto hym, for his said mastir*es* sake, to haue alle suche thing*es* as reason and consiens req*ui*reth, and that ⌜ye⌝ wolde be meane vnto Paston for hym in this mater*e*, to schewe hym the more fauo*ur* at this tyme for this my*n* writyng, in doyng of eny truble to hym; trusting that he wole demeane hym in suche wyse that he shal haue no cause vnto hym, but to be his good mast*er*, as he seyth.

And yf ⟨th⟩er[1] be eny thing that I can[2] do for you, I wole be right glad to do it, and that knoweth almyghty God, whiche haue you ⟨in⟩ his keping. Wretin at Grenewyche, the xxviij^{ti} day of August.

J. Beauchamp

1039. Stephen Scrope, second schedule of grievances against Sir John Fastolf — Late 1460, or early 1461

Add. Charter 18238. Parchment, 10 × 14 in. Hand unidentified.

Dorse blank.

Scrope's revised version of his schedule of grievances against Fastolf was evidently drawn up sometime soon after the latter's death on 5 November 1459. Depending on the method of calculation used within the document, it was set down either during the fifteenth year after the death of Scrope's mother, Dame Milicent Fastolf on 20 August 1446, which would suggest late August 1460 or soon after; or, alternatively, fifty-two years after she married Fastolf, in January 1409, which would give January 1461 or soon thereafter. Much, but not all of the substance and phrasing is similar to that of the first schedule of grievances, submitted to Fastolf in person about ten years previously (see no. 1012).

Printed by G. P. Scrope, *Castle Combe*, pp. 279–80 (parts).

Fyrste, it ys to remembir that whan[1] my modyr was maryed to my fader Fastolf, he solde me to Wyll*ia*m Gascoyne, that tyme Chyef Juge, for v^{c}

1038. [1] *Hole in MS., and so below in next line.* [2] *No space.*

1039. [1] *The scribe frequently adds an upward curl to the last minim of final* m *and* n, *here regarded as a flourish rather than an abbreviation.*

mark, with-oute tytyll or cause why; and had the seyde so*m*me iij yer*e* in his possession, to his owne vse and my grete hurte.

It*em*, he boughte me a-yenne, and was certeyn yerys vndyr his gouernaunce, in suche puneryе þ*a*t y was feyn to selle a place in Kent called Hevyr, and therwith y putte me in s*er*vyse with my lorde of Gloucest*er*. My seyde fader, conceyvynge that, sent to my seyde moder suche letters that y was feyn too goo ou*er* the see to hym, with a yoman and a page, on my coste.

It*em*, whan y was comyn to hym, he schewed me suche countenaunce of goode wylle þ*a*t y was glad to doo hym s*er*vyse, he p*ro*mysynge me at that tyme to make me yerelye thryes worthe þe maner of Wyghton vndir þe Woolde in Yorkeschyr*e*, the which is xl li. a yer*e*.

It*em*, so y obeyed his desyr*e*, wherethorow y loste my lorde of Gloucestrys gode lordeschippe, where as he was sette afore to a putte me in possescion of the Ile of Man, or els to a getyn me a resonabylle recompence þerfor*e*, as Syr Wyll*ia*m Cheyne, that tyme Chyeff Juge, sente me woorde to Honneflew by a man of his þ*a*t levyth yet, named Wyll*ia*m Marchalle.

It*em*, there at the seyde Honneflew I servyd the Kynge and hym, to that he toke partye wyth straungers a-yenste me, y beynge in the ryghte and they in the wronge.

It*em*, y come than in-to Ynglande, to my seyde moder, and was not wyth hirre fully a yer*e*, but that he sent woorde that y schulde pay for my mete or be voyded, y havynge no lyveloode where with to pay, for y was eu*er* a-fore yn his gouernaunce.

It*em*, than was y feyn to schyfte me by mariage, as God wolde yeve me grace. God knoweth whate hynderaunce y hadde by that mariage with his menys, the which hurte y canne welle telle and y schalle.

It*em*, thorough a sewte made by my seyde fader y was dyssessed of alle the lyvelode that y had, havynge wyffe and chylder and certeyn s*er*vauntes; and soo endured iij yer*e* wyth-oute any refuge save of God, and a litill dought*er*, the which for nede y was feyn to selle for moche lesse than y schulde adone ellys.

It*em*, my seyde fader outelawed me for the s*um*m*a* of xl li. or eu*er* y wyste therof, the which y wolde not had bene done for a m^{l} li.; and yet he had certeyn plate and stuffe of myn, which ys remembred in myn owne fadres testement, to the valew of ij^{c} li. or mor*e*.

It*em*, he hath kepte fro me, sith my seyde moder dissessed, a-yenste all gode conscyence or tytylle of lawe, ij maneres, Oxendon and Hamthwayte, and they amounte yerely a xlvj li. S*um*m*a* yn xiiij yer*e* vj^{c} xliiij li.[2]

It*em*, he hath kepte fro me as longe xx li. yerely of the man*er* of Wyghton, the whych he p*ro*mysyd me to have had at the dyssesse of my seyde modyr,

[2] *This and the sums given at the ends of the next two items are written in the right margin, and seem to have been added after the bulk of the document had been set down.*

wher*e*of y had the furste yer*e* xv li., at hys co*m*maundement payed by the handys of hys s*er*vaunte Lowes. þe resydew her*e*-of draweth a ij^{c} lxv li.

It*em*, ther ys loste of myn enherytaunce by my seyde fadres defaute viij li. in Castelcombe, and xl s. in Bentley, þe purchace her*e*-of aft*er* xx^{ti} wyntres purchace amounteth ij^{c} li.

It*em*, he hath done grete waste in my seyde enherytaunce, the whych canne not be restored wyth a m^{l} li., and he hath had it lij yer*e* and mor*e*, and in alle þ*a*t tyme neu*er* dyd it gode, but wastyd it. And to conceyve ferthir, sith my seyde modyr dyssessed, hath had it a-yenste alle gode conscyence, savynge by myn agrement, for þe gode wylle þ*a*t y had to hym, þe whych gode wylle me semeth wolde be concydered.

1040. Stephen Scrope, bill of charges against the estate of Sir John Fastolf — Late 1461, or early 1462

Add. 28209 f. 22. Parchment, 10$\frac{1}{4}$ × 6 in. Autograph.

Dorse: blank.

The date is a year later than Scrope's second schedule of grievances against Fastolf; see no. 1039, Headnote. Internal references indicate that this is either the sixteenth year after the death of Dame Milicent Fastolf, or alternatively, fifty-three years since her marriage.

Printed by G. P. Scrope, *Castle Combe*, p. 281.

In the firste yere that my fad*er* Fastolf was maried to my mod*er*, he solde me for v^{c} marc., with-oute any titill or right, thorugh which sale, as in this worlde, my p*er*sone was disfigured for eu*er*; wherfor I clayme the seid some of v^{c} mark, with-oute the hurt of my disfiguryng.

It*em*, he bought me ayene. So he bought me and solde[1] me as a beste, ayens al ryght and lawe, to myn hurt more than m^{l} mark.

It*em*, be a deceit, he kept from me xxx^{ti} yeres to-gedir and more, xl li. worthe of lyveloode in a toune called Wyghton vndir the Wolde, in Yorkshire, for the which I clayme restitucion by the saide time of xij^{c} li., with-oute the ruynousté of my lyvelode.

It*em*, he kept fro me, ayens all lawe and right, two manoires, that is to sey, Oxendon and Hamthwayte, xv yeres, the which ar worthe xlvj li. in yerely value; for the which I aske to have vj^{c} iiij^{xx} x li.

It*em*, for plate *and* stuffe of myn, the which is specyfied in myn owne fadris testament to me bequethid, and my seid fad*er* Fastolf had it eu*er* to his vse, I aske restitucion there of, as lawe and right requireth.

It*em*, for the strop *and* waste of myn enheritaunce, which is v^{c} mark worthe by yere, the which was in the handes of my seide fad*er* liij ⌜yeres⌝ it can not be repaired with m^{c} mark.

1040. [1] *MS.* soilde.

1041. From PIERS to SIR ROBERT ROKESBY

Probably 1461

Add. 34888, f. 156. $11\frac{1}{2} \times 3\frac{1}{2}$ in. Richard Calle's hand.

Dorse: Marks of folding, address panel soiled, no trace of sealing wax. Address in Calle's hand:

*To my right worschipfull S*er *Rob*er*t Rokysby.*

For the suggested date see the Headnotes to nos. 714 and 715, from the same writer.
F. iii, p. 432. G. 363/425.

Right wurshipfull s*er*, I recomaunde me[1] to you, besechyng you of yo*ur* goode mast*er*ship[2] that ye wol wechesafe to speeke to Richard Kowue*n*, that he myght brynge me or sende me the money that is be-twex hym and me in all the haste that he maye. For in goode feythe, I hadde neu*er* mor*e* neede for to haue helpe of my goode as I haue at this tyme, for God wot, it stonde right straunge w*ith* me. For the false chayler that kepeth me entretethe me worse thanne it weere a dogge, for I am feterid worse thanne eu*er* I whas, and manacled on the hand*es* be the daye and nyght, for he is a-feerde of me[3] for brekyng aweye. He makethe false tales of me throw the meenes of a false qwene that was tendyng to a Frensheman that is preson*er* to my lorde Roose, and for be cause of that he bronde me eu*ery* day be John of Berney, that is goone to the ⌜tother⌝ lord*es*. But I truste to God oonys to qwite hym hys meede. And, s*er*, I thanke you mekel of that ye haue doone for me or seide; and, s*er*, I shal des*er*ue it a-yenst you, be the g*ra*ce of God, for j'feythe I am be-holden to you more than*ne* to all men that eu*er* I founde syn I cam in preson.

No more ⌜to⌝ you at this tyme, but God haue you in his kepyng.

Be yo*ur* s*er*u*au*nt and bedman PERS

1042. From JOHN EASTGATE to an unidentified servant of John Paston I

Probably 1465, before August

Add. 24445, f. 4. $10\frac{1}{2} \times 4$ in. Probably autograph.

Dorse: Marks of folding, holes for thread; no inscription.

John Eastgate was an attorney who had been associated with the Pastons since at least 1444 (see no. 127, line 3), and his death is noted with regret in Margaret Paston's letter of 18 August 1465 (no. 190, lines 32–4, 'Thursday last passyd'). John Paston I wrote to Margaret asking her to speak with Eastgate about 'Pekeryng*ys* mat*er*' in November 1463 (no. 174, lines 12–13), and Gairdner printed a copy of Pickering's will, which he dated to 1465 (Add. 27445, f. 5, G. 522/603)
G. 521/602.

1041. [1] y *canc.* [2] *Dotted circumflex over* p. [3] fr *canc.*

Ser*e*, ȝe sent to me a lett*er* conteynyng þe[1] substaunce off þe p*ro*cesse off M*ayster* Robert Ippyswell for the mat*er* off þe codicill off Nichol*as* Pykeryng &c. Me m*er*velyt gretly off þe certificat off M*ayster* Rob*er*t i*n* þat be-halue, for þis is þe truthe as ferforth[2] as I kan reme*m*br*e* me. The codicill had neþ*er* day nor place lymyte, qwer*e* or qwa*n* it xuld a ben mad, qwer*e*for to a r*e*p*ro*vyd þat þat neþ*er* was q*ua*lifyid w*ith* day nor place, it had be gret foly &c.

Þ*er*for I askyd off þe iuge hys acc*ount*,[3] and specyaly þe deposicionys and attestacio*n*ys off þe wyttenes*ys*[4] þat wer*e* swor*e* in þe seyde codicill &c, by þe qwyche it mowth apper*e* clerly qwa*n and* qwer*e* þis codicill xuld a be made and wrete. And þis sen I mad p*ro*testacion to for þe seyde M*ayster* Rob*er*t, þat I wolde i*m*pugne þe mat*er* as lawe r*e*quiryd.

The qwych peticion I made diu*er*se tyme to-for*e* moche recorde, iudicialy syttyng þe seyde M*ayster* R. &c. The qwyche peticion he wold not her*e*, but seyde exp*re*sse þat neþ*er* Will*iam* Pykeryng nor no*n* oþ*er* man xuld sen his acc*ount*,[5] nor knowe qwat þe deposicion*ys*[6] wer*e* i*n* þat p*ar*te. Þis mat*er* was comownyd to-for*e* M*ayster* Joh*n* Selet and my mayst*er* and yo*ur* diu*er*se tymys, and euer he seyde we xuld not sen þe seyde depos*icio*n*ys*. And so qwat su*m* eu*er* he hath certyfyid, þis is þe truthe, God to wetenesse and all seynt*ys*, qwo[7] p*re*serue ȝow eu*er*mor*e*.

And I p*ra*y ȝow to declar*e* þis to my mayst*er and* ȝo*ur*, and comende me hertly to hys good mayst*er*chep. And God sende hy*m* victorye off all hys elmyes, and so p*ra*y all hys well-wyller*ys* at Norwich.

JOH*N* EASTGATE

1043. Declaration by ROBERT INGLOSE concerning Fastolf's will: draft. Probably 1466

Oxford, Magdalen College, Fastolf Paper 76. 12 × 8 in., but damaged along right hand edge, with loss of text. William Worcester's hand.

Dorse: blank

The document is a working draft by Worcester, partly in note form. The date is suggested by comparison with nos. 895A and B, declarations by Thomas Neve and Robert FitzRawff about Fastolf's will. Both are likewise amongst the Fastolf Papers at Magdalen, and the first is also a draft. See also no. 746 (Richard Calle to John Paston II, 3 April 1467), where Inglose is described as not well disposed towards the Pastons during the latter stages of the inquiry into the dispute over Fastolf's will.

Unprinted.

Be hyt reme*m*bred that the Sonday, aftyr mydday, aboute iiij at belle, ⸢next before the decese of S*er* John Fastolf, knyght⸣, Robert Inglose, esquyer, was

1042. [1] þ *in the form of* y *throughout.* [2] *Miswritten* ferthforth, *first* th *canc.* [3] *Abbrev. the* -es *flourish.* [4] *Abbrev. the* -er *flourish on long* s. [5] *Abbrev. the* -es *flourish.* [6] *Abbrev. the* -er *flourish on* n. [7] *Altered from* qwych.

com to Castre to speke wyth hym ⟨. . .⟩[1] to hafe concyderac*io*n *and* pytee of grete charges and losses that he had by str*au*nge menys ⌜by the seyd S*er* John⌝. And it was then avysed hym ⌜by John Paston, escuier⌝, that he shuld not speke ⟨. . .⟩[2] meofe of no such maters vnto hym; for yff he were so purposed, hyt was seyd hy*m* playnly, he shuld not speke wyth hy*m*. And aft*er* hys p*ro*mysse ⟨. . .⟩[3] he came to the seyd S*er* John Fastolf p*re*sence, lyeng yn hys bed ryght weke, *and* ⌜full⌝ feble ⌜yn hys spyrytes⌝, as a man redy to dye. Questioned where the seyd R⟨obert⟩ Inglose had be so long.[4] And ⌜so⌝ yn kepyng hys p*ro*mysse, meoved none mater to hym, and so departed.

Then aftyr, yn Lenton next folowyng, the seyd Robert met wyth Willia*m* Paston at Norwych, and there questyoned the seyd Rob*er*t yff he wold goo to London, hys costys shuld be payd ⟨ther⟩efor; and shewed vnto hym a rolle of paper ⌜of many namys⌝, and seyd hys name was entred yn that rolle among*es* othyr, whych was for the wytnesse *and* record of the mater of purchasse of S*er* John Fastolf londes; ⌜and seyd vnto hy*m* that he was wyth hym the nyght before hys decese, and knew whate he seyd⌝. The seyd Robert aunsuerd hy*m* that he wold goo to London redely, but he seyd hy*m* that he shu⟨ld⟩ trust to hys othe. So the seyd Willia*m* wold no more speke to hym of that mater.

And bethyn iij wekys aftyr Pasch next f⟨o⟩l⟨owyng⟩, the seyd Rob*er*t Inglose met wyth the seyd John Paston vppon a causee called Ocledam; and demaunded hy*m* whethyr he[5] ⟨wold⟩ ryde; and seyd, to Castr*e*. And the⌜n⌝ the seyd John prayd hy*m*, when he come to Castr*e*, to enforme the felyship ther*e* that h⟨e⟩ shuld vtter ⟨no⟩ maner langage, as it shuld put hem yn a doubt ⌜*and* in a musyng⌝, as though the seyd Rob*er*t shuld[6] knowe[7] moch more of[8] the forseyd mat*er*s then the seyd felyshyp wend. Wherbye the seyd Rob*er*t vnderstode that it was not all weele ne godlye that the[9] ⌜seyde John Paston ⟨. . .⟩⌝[10] desyr⟨ed⟩.

In wytnesse[11] of thys wrytyng I the forseyd Rob*er*t Inglose set to thys wrytyng my sele *and* signe manuell, the   day of   the month of the   yere of Kyng Edward the fourthe.

1043. [1] And *canc. before damaged edge of page; space for about seven letters follows. Most of an interlineation apparently beginning* so inp . . . *also lost.*

[2] *Space for about seven letters.*

[3] *Space for about seven letters.*

[4] Questioned . . . long *underlined.*

[5] was *canc.*

[6] put hem yn a doubt that he *canc.*

[7] o *altered from* e.

[8] Ser John *canc.*

[9] *Altered from* he.

[10] *Remainder of interlineation illegible or lost.*

[11] whe *canc.*

1044. From John Aubry to Sir Henry Spelman

1469, 6 July

Add. 43489, f. 30. 10 × $5\frac{1}{2}$ in. Hand unidentified.

Dorse: Marks of folding, slits for tape, trace of red wax seal. Address in hand of letter:

*To the right reuerent S*er *Henry Spelman, Recordo*ur *of the cité of Norwich, be this letter deliu*ered.

The writer was mayor of Norwich in 1469, and the Queen's visit took place on 18 July of that year; see H. Harrod, 'Queen Elizabeth Woodville's Visit to Norwich in 1469', *Norfolk Archaeology*, v (1859), 32–7.

F. ii, p. 18. G. 614/718

Right reu*er*ent s*er*, I recomaunde me to you. Plese it you to knowe, this same day com to me the shirreve of Norff*olk* hym silf, *and* tolde me that the Quene shall be at Norwich vp-on Tuysday cometh seuenyght suyrly. And I desired to haue knowe of hym, by cause this shuld be hir first comyng hedir, how we shuld be rulyd, as well in hir resseyuyng, as in hir abidyng here. And he seide he wold nat ocupie hym ther wyth, but he councelid[1] vs to wryte to you to London, to knowe of hem that ben of cou*n*sell of that cité, or wyth other wurshepfull men of the same cité, that ben knowyng in that behalf, and we to ben rulid ther aftir, as were acordyng for vs. For he let me to wete that she wooll desire to ben resseyued and attendid as wurshepfully as euir was quene a-forn hir.

Wherefore, s*er*, I, be the assent of my bretheren aldermen &c, prey you hertily to haue this labo*ur* for this cité; and that it plese you, if it may be, that at that day ye be here in p*ro*pre p*er*sone. And I trust in God, that outher in reward or ellys in thankyngez, both of the Kyng*es* comyng *and* in this, ye shall ben plesid, as worthy[2] is.

Wrete in hast at Norwich the vj day of Juyll, A° ix°[3] R. E. q*ua*rti.

By yo*ur* weelwyller*e* John Aubry, &c.

1044. [1] hi *canc.*
[2] *Two miswritten letters canc. and subpuncted.*
[3] *Hole in paper; numeral rewritten below in same hand.*

1045. From JOHN BOKKYNG to ROBERT KYRTON

Probably 1469, 5 September

Oxford, Magdalen College, Fastolf Paper 94. $11\frac{1}{2} \times 2$ in. Autograph.

Dorse: Marks of folding, slits for tape, trace of red wax seal. Address autograph:

*Vnto Ro⟨bert Kyr⟩ton, rent gaderer of ⟨*Ser *Jo⟩hn Fastolf renters in Southwerk by Batell Brigge in Beremondsey Strete by London, be þ*is *deliu*ered *in haste.*

Bishop Wainfleet assumed the administration of Fastolf's will in February 1470 (see no. 248), and it is likely that this letter dates from the autumn of the previous year. Part of the addressee's name was lost because it was written across the sealing tape, but there is no doubt that it was Robert Kyrton, Fastolf's receiver in Southwark; see Worcester, *Itineraries*, pp. 387–8.

Printed by N. Davis, 'Language in Letters from Sir John Fastolf's Household', *Mediæval Studies for J. A. W. Bennett*, ed. P. L. Heyworth (Oxford, 1981), pp. 399–40.

Right welbeloued frende, I co*m*maunde me to you and pray you and charge you ⌜in⌝ myn vncle Yelu*er*tons name that ye goo to my lord of Wynchestre, or sum man of his for you, and reco*m*maunde hym vn-to his lordship and pray hym þ*at* he wole no*ugh*t refuse to take administra*ci*on vp-on hym for my*n* maist*er* Fastolf*es* good*es*, as thei were accordid; ner þ*at* he discharge hym no*ugh*t þ*er*of in noo wise til myn vncle may speke w*ith* his lordship þ*er*jnne, for many grete causes of proffite *and* wele þ*at* shal growe þ*er*jnne to þe plesance of God *and* þe sowle, what þ*at* ony man haue enformed hise lordship of þe contrarie. Ther com tidyng*es* from Worcestre þ*at* my lord was discoragid þ*er*jnne, and þ*er*fore myn vncle p*ra*yd me to write þus to you. If ye see Maist*er* Tilney or John Gilberte þei may doo þis for you, or your silf oþ*er*. And reco*m*maunde me to my Maist*er* Tilney, to my good moder Wesenh*am*, Henr*é* Wyndessore, and ⟨. . .⟩[1] my sust*er* his wif; and eu*er*e wele mote ye far*e* Norffolklyk.

Wrete*n* at Longh*am* the v day of Septembr*e*. And þ*at* my lord of Wynchestre refuse no*ugh*t to take administra*ci*on in ony wise.[2]

Your owen frende J. BOKKYNG

1045. [1] *Hole in paper.*
[2] *Davis* case *(in error).*

1046. Memorandum from WILLIAM WORCESTER to WILLIAM WAINFLEET, Bishop of Winchester.

1470, 1 March

Oxford, Magdalen College, Fastolf Paper 96. 12 × 17 in. Autograph, in a formal set version of Worcester's hand.

Dorse: Continuation of text. Direction autograph:

*The[se] ben the adu*ertisement*es yn the behalf off William Wyrcestre to be declared vndre correcion to my lord off Wynchester*e.

Dated.
Unprinted.

Here folowyn certeyn intructyons *and* concideracyons yn the behalf of Williem Wyrcet*er*, yn hys most humble wyse to[1] be declaryd vnto the ryght worshippfull *and* reuerent fader in God, my lorde of Wynchestre.

Fyrst, please your good grace to wete I haue resseyved a wrytyng yn your behalf to me sent, nother sealyd ne sygned, by which I vndyrstande your lordshep desyreth me to come to your p*re*sens to your maner of Esshir*e*, betwene the daye of your wrytyng *and* the begynnyng of Lentt, and bryng wyth me all suche thyngys as may be beneficiall for the administracyon of my maist*er* Fastolf goodys, whom God pardon. Please your good grace to bryng to mende that lyth by your comaundment, *and* also by avyce of my maist*er* Yelu*er*ton, I was at London aswell in hervyst seson *and* in the month of Decembre last passyd, *and* wayted such dayes *and* tymes vppon your lordshep as ye co*m*maundyd; and made you declaracyon in a boke opynly as I coude, generally *and* pa*r*ticulerlye, ⌜the⌝ chargys, legattys, bequestys *and* ordena*u*nces made in the laste testament *and* wyll that my seyd maist*er* Fastolf wyllyd shuld be p*er*formyd by hys executors aftyr hys decese. And also in the same boke is made mencion of the moste part of the namys that ben peticyoners of tho p*er*sonys that demaundyd by byllys, wrytyng *and* by worde many dyuers su*m*mys *and* of grete charge; and also ther*e* ynne is made mencyon whate goodys many of tho peticyoners were paied *and* ⟨. . .⟩[2] as I was enformyd by S*er* Thomas Howys, coexecuto*ur* named.

It*em*, my lord, I dede the diligens *and* coste aboute a n⟨. . .⟩[3] lord Cardynall court, Archebyshop of Caunt*er*burye court of audyens of the decysyon *and* varyaunce of ij long articles ex⟨. . .⟩[4] lord Cant*er*bery court surmytted to be made by my seid maist*er* Fastolf ij dayes before hys decese, as it had be a reformacy⟨on . . .⟩[5] before yn the month of June next before hys decese. And

1046. [1] *No space.*

[2] *An irregularly shaped hole approx.* $1\frac{3}{4} \times 3\frac{1}{2}$ *in. has carried away parts of the text in this and the following lines. One or two words lost here.*

[3] *About six or seven words lost.*

[4] *About seven or eight words lost.*

[5] *About eight or nine words lost.*

the grete dovtes of that decysyng *and* varyaunce of 〈. . .〉[6] bothe twey partyes before my lord Cardynall audytours, and by p*ro*duccyon off wytnesse *and* prevys of both pa〈rtyes. . .〉[7] v p*ro*duccyons by both p*ar*tyes sewyd that is the vtmost that the sp*irit*uell lawe gevyth, was by the space o〈f. . .〉[8] the termys of 〈. . .〉[9] *and* respytes of tymes gevyn to eyther partyes to bryng ynne theyr p*ro*vys to a grett*er* nombre of p*er*sones. And I was desyred *and* assyned to abyde the ende of the seyd processe.

It*em*, at last it fortuned that jugement was gevyn wyth S*er* John Paston ayenst my maist*er* S*er* William Yelu*er*ton *and* me, not wythstondyng that John Paston escuier, one of the chief actour, comensour *and* enterprennour of the seyd p*ro*cesse ayenst vs, decesyd xij month before the jugement. And also notwythstondyng S*er* Thomas Howys hys felawe that joyned wyth hym yn that grete p*ro*cesse iiij yere day. And he, beyng examyned, yelde hym gylty yn hys quarelle, forsakyd hys p*ro*cesse *and* also revokyd Maist*er* Robert ⌜Kentt⌝ *and* Maist*er* Kengey hys proctors by jnstrument yn pleyn court, *and* in Poulys chyrch anothyr tyme before a notorye. And now the seid jugement gevyn yn thys wyse ayenst my Maist*er* Yelu*er*ton *and* me, we stande dyschargyd to God ayen our testatour; and I, sore weryed, laboured *and* vndoo by that infynyt p*ro*cesse, am coarted to leefe. And these ij bookys before declaryd I haue lefft wyth your lordshep, and the copye of the testamentys, wyllys *and* the seid ij articles vppon the same ys wyth you lefft, which were the chieff thyngys that I had yn kepyng to shewe your lordshep *and* to that p*er*son that wyll or hath take the administracyon.

It*em*, yf any othyr thyng that I haue ellys ys ymagyned ⌜or⌝[10] demyd yn my gou*er*n*au*nce that I ought bryng wyth me, I desyre your lordshep to know, that I may declare my sylf. Hyt ys notoryly knowyn that S*er* Thomas Howys *and* hys felowe toke the rule *and* possessyon of alle my maist*er* Fastolf mevable goodys, evidens*ys*[11] of hys londys *and* hys debtys,[12] *and* catells of hys bestys. And I hadde no more rule but as I hadde be a straunge p*er*son, and was putt oute of Castre, *and* my wrytyngys ther*e* kept from me; and nowe am dryven to pursewe by peticyon ⌜for⌝ my pore lyvyng. Wher*e* as, and I hadde not entred yn to that jnfynyte p*ro*cesse to trye tho ij articles, shuld haue stand in such frenchep *and* fauour of the seyd John Paston *and* S*er* Thomas Howys that I had be possessed of xxv m*ar*k. lyfelode in fee, besyde othyr mevable goodys of my seid maist*er*, that I *and* alle myne shuld haue be relyevyd yn myne age the bett*er*, *and* praied for my goode doers.

It*em*, your lordshep not dysplesyd when it lykyd you to send for me to your maner of Esshir*e* aftyr your communica*cy*on hadde wyth S*er* William

[6] *About nine or ten words lost.* [7] *About ten or eleven words lost.*
[8] *About four or five words lost.* [9] *One word lost.*
[10] *Over* and *canc.*
[11] *Long* s + er *abbrev. for pl. inflection, and so in other instance of this word below.*
[12] b *superimp. on a* w.

Yelu*er*ton, then ye desyryng me to owyn myne s*er*vice *and* good wylle yn the purchasse of my maist*er* F. lyfelode in Southwerk. And where as it was then grauntyd, the seid purchasse, by the desyre of grete astatys, to a collage in Cambrygge, and aftyr xij yere to be payed in hand, bysyde certeyn prestys to be founde p*er*petuelly to pray for my seid maist*er* Fastolf soule. And ovyr that ther*e* was except certeyn ten*au*ntryes to the yerly value of xx^{ti} m*a*rk., to be reserved for part of my reward in fee, as I haue in remembraunce to shew. And thys notwythstondyng, for the plesyr of your good lordshep, laboured effectuelly S*er* Thomas Howys, coexecutor namyd, that had chief auctorité to make sale of the seid lyfelode; came to London and vndrestode your letter *and* desyre to hym sent. *And* ⌜I⌝ meovyd hym effectuelly to graunt by wrytyng vnto your lordship hys power *and* auctorité, as I raport me to John Gylbert your s*eruau*nt, which then spake wyth hym before alle othyr. And yhyt aft*yr* that I was bothyn spokyn vntoo *and* callyd vppon by grete astatys ⟨. . .⟩[13] that t[h]e seyd purchasse myght goo to that seyd collage of Cambrygge. And I wayted dayly, *and* tyme erly *and* late, vppon your seid s*eruau*nt ⟨. . .⟩[14] labour *and* callyng vppon for the seid purchasse to be hadde owte of your handys, that ye the rather wolde take it to her⟨. . .⟩[15] desyres.

It*em*, my lord, hyt pleasyd your lordshep for the more ⟨. . .⟩ens[16] aftyr the seid S*er* Thomas Howys[17] decese to appoynt *and* goo throw ynne the seyd purchasse wyth my maist*er* S*er* William Yelu*er*ton *and* me, and at such pryses as it pleasyd your lordshep. And ther*e* was offryd my maist*er* Fastolf iij m^{l} m*a*rk. yn hand to be payed for the seid purchasse. My lord, ye graunted me payment aswell to the seyd S*er* William Yelu*er*ton, as reson is, consideryng the p*re*myssys aboofe specyfyed. And also I haue grettyst nede, and in to thys tyme am not purveyed of payment, but trust to your goode grace to be sped.

It*em*, my lord, at the seid purchasse makyng *and* writyng enseled there were except a[18] tenement by Horsseydoune that S*er* William ȝelu*er*ton, S*er* Thom*as* Howys *and* I solde to John Wodd yong*er*. And the seid John, and one callyd Okehyrst, a dyer, *and* anothir dyer there hafe graunt of yerys certeyn tenementys to ferme, aftyr the yerly ferme they ⌜payed be fore⌝. Concydered the rep*ar*acyon ⌜at there costys be⌝ they purpose the rather to do the more cost in tho tenementys. And they callyn vppon S*er* William ȝelu*er*ton *and* me that your lordshyp lyke to make hem sure of your selyng, as it was appoynted *and* agreed. And I wolde requyre your good lordshyp that it may be p*er*formyd the rather at my por*e* instaunce, for and I shuld not haue a[19] voyce afore a straungere yn desyres resonable, *and* of right tobe do, hyt wold dyscourage me to owyn my servyse to your avayle, that I entend rathest to do before alle othyr.

[13] *Another irregularly shaped hole approx.* $2\frac{1}{2} \times 1$ *in. has carried away parts of the text in this and the following lines. One or two words lost here.*

[14] *Four or five words lost.*

[15] *Five or six words lost.*

[16] *Three or four words lost.*

[17] dese *canc.*

[18] *No space.*

[19] *No space.*

It*e*m, my lord, where as is made mencyon that[20] Dame Anne, doughter of S*er* Robert Harlyng, knyght, and wyfe of S*er* Robert Wyngfeld, knyght, demaunded of my maister F. executors, by hyr bylle putt vppe to the Kyngys juges, more then viij m^{l} li., as it shewyth by the copy of hy[r][21] seid bylle yn the book of peticyoners that I made opyn to your lordshep. I haue now late be wyth my seyd lady *and* wyth S*er* Rob*er*t Wyngfeld, *and* enformyd hem that hyr demaund of so grete a so*m*me fer from ryght *and* conciens hath discouraged *and* lothed my maist*er* executors to take ony charge of administracyon. And also I enformyd hem that S*er* Thomas Howys toke appoyntment to content a certeyn so*m*me for alle demaunde⌜s⌝,[22] *and* the chieff part ⌜ys⌝ paied *and* content. And the seyd S*er* Robert aunsuered me he had comyned wyth your lordshep, and also wyth your councell Rauff Alygh, and enformed your lordshep of hys good dysposycyon, *and* hath said to me ryght feythfully to be ruled in such wyse, and wyth conciens as [y]our[23] goode lordeshep wyth reason[24] wyll hald you ryght well pleasyd. And I haue found remembraunce thys weke of that appoyntm*ent* as shall helpe relieff to the moderacyon of that mater, for many of tho grete demaundys growyn of olde maters done in Fraunce. And I fynd hem now bett*er* dysposyd than evyr I dyd, and so I wyll rapport of hem. And the case is such I can *and* haue do hem p*ro*fyth *and* plesyd yn her enherytaunce bye getyng evidens*ys* of grete wyght, *and* they haue p*ro*mysed me to owen me her speciall good wyll.

My lord, I beseche your lordshep to pardon me thys my symple mocyons here declaryd, that ye wyll not take it to grieff to wryght thys rudelye my pore entencyon; that I submytt me to the correccyon of your gracyous lordshep, and I to be as your pore bedman.

Wretyn at Norwic*h* the fyrst day of March the ix yer of Kyng Edward the iiijth.

Your humble soget W. WYRCESTRE &c,[25]
submyttyng me to reformac*y*on,
yff the case requyre yt vndr*e* p*ro*testac*y*on.

It*e*m, my lorde of Norwic*h* hath lete me wete by a[26] chapleyn of hys that he hath a bargayne of S*er* Thomas Howys, decesed, *and* othyrs, of a maner*e* of my maist*er* Fastolf callyd Tychewell, that lyth viij myle beyond Walsyngh*a*m, xviij li. yerly valew. And he desyreth to make hys paymentys vppon the feffement *and* lyuery of seson had at suche dayes as they wer*e* appoynted. And now it is seyd the seyd maner standyth wyde and yn decay, *and* no baylly ne fermor vppon yt to approw yt. And that is no p*ro*fyth to the testatour, and also grete jubardye to the tytle, for and som men that claymed the seid maner *and* disseysed my maist*er* Fastolf vij yer*e* *and* more knew yt they wold lyghtly

[20] *MS.* thatme, me *canc.* [21] *MS.* hys. [22] *Over* d *canc.*
[23] *MS.* jour. [24] *Over two words erased.*
[25] *Worcester's 'Saturn' mark follows; see no. 506 headnote.*
[26] *No space.*

entre yn yt vppon her*e* holde tytle *and* glayme, as God forbede. So yt lyke your lordshep to send word of your good dysposyc*y*on yn thys behalf, that by my maist*er* S*er* William Ȝelu*er*ton helpe ther*e* may be sett a bailly or a fermour to approw the seid maner*e*.

It*em*, I beseche your lordshep pardon me that I come not to your p*re*sens, for one grete cause is that I wold not be ymagyned ne mysdemyd amongys my maist*er* Fastolf executors *and* feoffes, that I of my symple wytt do meove or sett yow vppon maters concernyng my maist*er* Fastolf*ys* hys londys *and* hys mevable goodys dysposyng, that were not holsom ner p*ro*fytable to the testatour. And I wyll eschewe suche mysdemys, for I wolde now yn myne aage medele lytyll or nought, but entend to lyfe a more qwyet lyfe aftyr my grete labours troubles, God amende hem that causyd yt.

1047. From the Earl of Oxford to Thomas Vere
1471, 14 March

Add. 43489, f. 41. $11\frac{5}{8} \times 8\frac{1}{4}$ in. Hand unidentified, subscription autograph.

Dorse: Marks of folding, slits for tape, paper seal showing impression of signet, over red wax. Address in hand of letter:

To my right dere and welbelouid brother Thomas Veer.

The year is evident from the anticipated return of Edward IV from the Continent. As Gairdner pointed out, he landed at Ravenspur on the same day that this letter was written.

F. ii, p. 54. G. 663/769.

Right dere and welbelouid brothir, I com*au*nd me hertily vnto you, c*er*tyfying you that I haue receyvid yo*ur* w*ri*tyng, directed now laste vnto me, by my s*er*u*a*nt Will*ia*m Cooke, by which I vnderstande the faithfull gwydyng *and* disposic*i*on of the cuntré, to my gret cumfo⌜r⌝te *and* pleaser; which I dowbte not shall redunde to the grethest p*ra*syng *and* worship that eu*er* dide till eny cuntré. C*er*tyfying you forde*r*more that by Nicheson of yo*ur* other tydyng*es* laste send vnto me; also thes by Rob*er*t Port*er*.

I haue disposed me w*ith* all the power that I can make in Essex *and* Suff*olk*, Cambryg*e*shire, *and* other places, to cu*m*[1] Monday next comy*ng* at Bury, which p*ur*pose I intende to obs*er*ue, w*ith* Godd*es* g*ra*ce, toward*es* you in to Norff*olk*, to the assistence of you *and* the cuntré, incase Edwarde w*ith* his companye had aryved ther. *And* yete I shall do the same noghtw*ith*standyng, for if he aryve northwarde, like as ye w*ri*te by likelyhode he shulde, I caste to folow *and* porsew ⌜hym⌝.

And where ye desire that I shulde send you woorde what disposic*i*on shalbe take in the cuntré wher ye be, I desir*e* you that ye, by theaduyse of the

1047. [1] *Inserted over the same word blotted.*

gentilme*n* which ben there, chese iij or iiij, and send theym to me at Bury on Monday next. *And* than I *and* they, w*ith* my counceyle, shall take a direcc*io*n for the suu*er*tie of all that cuntré, by Godd*es* g*ra*ce, by whome I shall send than to you relac*io*n, wheder ye shall remayne still ther yo*ur* selff, or resorte to me w*ith* all thoo that be acompayned w*ith* you.

And Jh*es*u p*reser*ue you. At Hithingh*a*m, the xiiij day of Marche.

By your louyng brothyr OXYNFORD

1048. From the EARL OF OXFORD to HENRY SPELMAN and others — 1471, 19 March

Add. 43489, f. 42. 11¾ × 6½ in. Hand unidentified, subscription autograph.

Dorse: Marks of folding, slits for tape, remains of red wax seal. Address in an unidentified hand, not that of letter:

To my right trusty and *welbelouyd Henry Spilman, Tho*mas *Seyve, John Seyve, James Radclif, John Brampton the older,* and *to eche of them.*

For the year, see the Headnote to the previous letter, written five days before this one. F. ii, p. 58. G. 664/770.

Trusty and welbeloued, I com*au*nd me to you, lettyng you witte that I haue credible tydyng*es* that the Kyng*es* gret enemys and rebellis, acompanyed w*ith* enemys estr*au*ngers, be now aryved, *and* landyd in the north p*ar*ties of this his land, to the vtter destruction of his roiall p*er*sone, *and* subu*er*sion of all his realm⌜e⌝, if they myght atayne; whom to encountr*e* and resiste, the King*es* highness hath com*a*unded and assigned me, vnder his seall, sufficient power and[1] auctorité to call, reyse, gadr*e* and assemble, fro tyme to tyme, all his liege people of the shir*e* of Norff*olk*, and other places, to assiste, ayde *and* strenght me in the same entent.

Wherfor, in the Kyng*es* name, *and* by auctorité aforesaid, I straitly charge and com*a*und you, and in my owne byhalf hertly desir*e* *and* p*ra*y you, that, all excuses leid ap*ar*t, ye and eche of you, in your owne p*er*sones, defensibly araied, w*ith* asmony men as ye may goodly make, be on Fryday next comyng at Lynne, *and* so forth to Newark, wher*e*, w*ith* the leve of God, I shall not faile to be at that tyme; entendyng fro thens to goo foorth w*ith* the help of God, you, *and* my fryndes ⌜to⌝ the rencountre of the said enemyes; and that ye faill not hereof, as ye tendr*e* the weele of our*e* said sou*er*eygne lord, and all this his realme.

Written at Bury, the xix[th] day of Marche.

OXYNFORD

1048. [1] act *canc.*

1049. Petition of WILLIAM WORCESTER to JAMES GOLDWELL, Bishop of Norwich. Probably 1472

Oxford, Magdalen College, Fastolf Paper 84. $11\frac{7}{8} \times 15\frac{1}{2}$ in. In an unidentified clerk's hand, with insertions and corrections in Worcester's hand.

Dorse: 'Pro Abbate S*anc*ti Be*ne*d*ic*ti', probably in Worcester's hand; notes concerning manors in Lincolnshire in an early sixteenth century hand.

In the list of the abbots of St Benet's Hulme given in his *Itineraries*, p. 235, Worcester noted that John Kevyng (mentioned in line 12 here) was succeeded by Thomas Pakefield ('nowe Abbott', line 67) in 1470. Whereas Kevyng had been accommodating, after his time the house cold-shouldered Worcester, as he complained to Margaret Paston in no. 727 (probably therefore of 1471–2, rather than 1468, as suggested in Part II; see lines 38–40 thereof). For more detailed discussion of the likely date and context of this petition see Richmond, *Fastolf's Will*, pp. 69–71.

Unprinted.

To the right reue*re*nt and my right good lorde James, Bisshop of Norwyche.

Shewith your*e* humble oratour*e and* pou*er* diocesan Will*ia*m Worcestr*e*, named executour*e* bothe to the right worshipfull knyght S*er* John Fastolff and to S*er* Thomas Howes, late p*ar*son of Bloofeld, that hit may be made openly to be vndrestand to yo*ur* lordship *and* all other howe the seid S*er* John Fastolff, for a singuler affeccion hadde to the monast*ery* of Seint Benett*is* Holme w*ith*ynne yo*ur* diocese, hathe doo greet cost in bildyng of the south side of the quire of the seid chirche, callid the newe jle, to the su*m*me of iiij^{c} lvj li.; and also in reliquis of seintis *and* in vestimentis of silke *and* other oramentis for her chirche by hym yeven to the value abough the su*m*me of clx li.; and also lent by him viij wekes before his discese, to the stallyng of Dan John Kevyng by obligac*io*n not hedirto paide, xl li. Whiche amountith to vj^{c} lvj li. *and* more, beside other benefitis to the seid monast*er*i doo, to his executours yet vnknowen. And ou*er* this, the seid S*er* Thomas *and* yo*ur* seid besecher, his coexecutours, haue in the behalff of the seid S*er* John Fastolff, to that entent he shold be the more specially praied fore, deliu*er*ed to the vse of the seid abbey *and* conuent in silu*er* vessell to the wight of m^{l} & xxx vnc. price the vnce gilt, *and* vngilt xl d., wherof the su*m*me a-mountith to clxxj li. xiij s. iiij d. Also, the day of entireme*n*t of the seid S*er* John Fastolff, and by the space of ix yere next folowyng his discese, the seid S*er* Thomas Howez, by the agrement of the seid W. Worcestr*e and* other his executours, gaffe *and* deliu*er*ed to the seid religioux *and* to the vse of theire chirche, for to syng and p*ra*y for the soule of the seid S*er* John Fastolf, as hit may appere by sufficient writyng, in money c li. *and* more. Also, in the value *and* price of a riche cloth of Arras, of ymagery work of Justice adminystryng, w*ith* a nother cloth of Arras conteynyng eu*er*y of the seid clothez ⌜about⌝[1] xvj yerdis long *and* v

1049. [1] *Interl. by Worcester.*

yerdis in brede ⌜whiche⌝ that cost mor*e* þan[2] ccxx li. sterlingiz. Also, the seid S*er* Thomas, the yere that he discesid, by agrement of the seid Worcestr*e*, gaffe to the makyng of theire chapitirhous *and* dortur xx li., to the fulfillyng of iiij^{c} li. *and* more paide by the seid S*er* Thomas, beside other benefit*is* by hym don, to long to write.

And also of high trust *and* to a good entent, the seid knyght sent savely to kepe to the Abbott, Dan Martyn, by the seid S*er* Thomas *and* Worcestr*e*, in money and in silu*er* plate, the su*m*me of iij m^{l} viij^{c} marke of sterlingis, þ*a*t was left in the seid monast*ery* iiij yere day. And bethyn ij dayez next aftir his discese, ayenst the will *and* knowleche of the seid Worcestr*e*, the seid su*m*me was deliu*er*ed to John Paston, squier, *and* to S*er* Thomas Howez by the seid Abbott *and* conuent, and before the testament of the seid S*er* John Fastolff was p*ro*vid; whiche causid the auerttyng of his testament *and* last will, *and* to þe vttir desolacion of the seid Worcestr*e*, hauyng noo good for to dispose[3] for his soule ⌜*and* for hys charitys⌝[4].

And where as the seid S*er* John Fastolff made his legat in his testament to endewe the seid monast*erj* w*ith* lordships, man*ers* *and* tenement*is* in Norff*olk* *and* Suff*olk* to the yerely value of iij c or ij c marke atte the lest, for the sustentacion of vj religious monkes ⌜prestis⌝[5] a-boue her nu*m*br*e* accustomed to kepe, and also vj pou*er*e men, to p*ra*y and syng p*er*petually for his soule and for Dame Milice[n]t his wyff, and other soulis named and assigned in his testament that he wold shold be prayed fore. And for lakke of diligence of the seid Abbot *and* couent for that tyme beyng, to pursue fore the execuc*i*on to fulfillen of his seid legacy, they desirid *and* requirid the seid Worcestr*e* to pursue the right *and* jnt*er*est of the seid legacy in thire behalf in the high court of audience of my lord Cardenall *and* Archiebisshop of Caunt*er*bury, to th'ende of v p*ro*duccions of lx witnesse p*ro*ducid of bothe partiez, to the vtt*er*mest of the sp*irit*uell[6] lawe. And aftir the sentence *and* jugeme[n]t yoven by the surmyse *and* allegacions, *and* by the first *and* chyeff witnesse ⌜of⌝ one John Rus of Yermouth ayenst S*er* William Yelu*er*ton, justice, *and* the seid W. Worcestr*e*, whiche made voide the seid legacy of cc m*a*rc. yerely to the seid monast*ery*. And than in trustyng of a bettir remedy, the seid Will*ia*m *and* William appelid to the court of Rome to haue vppe all the p*ro*cesse by the co*m*maundement of the Popis auditour*e*, redy to shewe vndre his seall; the whiche plee so duryng by the space of ix yere and more as hit is of recorde to shewe, the whiche cost the labour*e* and ridyng of vij m^{l} myle *and* more, w*ith* the circumstaunce a-mountid more than vij^{c} marke sterlingis paide by the seid Worcestr*e*, beside the costis of his p*ar*tie adu*er*sary. And the seid religious nother paide ne laborid not so muche to purvey a witnesse to the releuyng *and* helpyng of their*e* legacy, ne spendid neyther deliu*er*ed to the seid

[2] an *superscript.* [3] *2nd* s *superimp. by Worcester on* r.
[4] *Interl. by Worcester.* [5] *Interl. by Worcester.*
[6] court *canc. by subpunction.*

Worcestr*e* of their*e* p*ro*pre good*is* not to the value of xl s. by Thomas,[7] nowe Abbott; notw*ith*stondyng many requestis, billis *and* supplicacions by him made to the Abbott and couent that nowe is by other viij yere day, for his satisfaccion *and* releuyng of his seid greet cost*is* *and* laboris hedirto, can haue noo payment ne recompence of xl s., to the vttir vndoyng of yo*ur* seid besecher.

And consideryng the greet wyght of the chargeable[8] mat*er*es[9] before specified, and the greet pou*er*te of your*e* seid besecher, hit may pleas your*e* right good *and* tendr*e* lordship the rather that the Kyng of his blissid disposicion deseru*e* you to be speciall good lorde to yo*ur* seid suppliaunt in his causis, and in especiall in S*er* John Fastolff *and* in S*er* Thomas Howez mat*er*es. And therfore ye, ⌜my lord,⌝[10] as principall visitor *and* correctour*e* vndre the Pope of the seid Abbot and conuent, þ*a*t hit pleas your*e* lordship to pondir discretly thise p*re*missiz, w*ith* the long circumstaunc*is* before made mencion, and to doo your*e* seid pou*er* suppliaunt, whiche hath by importune labour*e* werid *and* feblid his body *and* expendid so greet good*is* by the seid long contynued pursute, to helpe that in him was to the seid endowment of the forseid ij^{c} m*a*rke lyvelode, beside the forseid greet benefit*is*, to the su*m*me of m^{l} li., first and last doon by the seid knyghtis goodis to the auauncement of the seid monast*ery*.

And also, ⌜wheras⌝ that ⌜a⌝ graunt was made ⌜by th'Abbot *and* conuent forseyd⌝[11] in the yere of Crist m^{l} iiij^{c} & xliiij, that ⌜for the seid benefitis *and* for⌝ the fyndyng of ij religious monkez p*er*petually to p*ra*y dailly for his soule, w*ith* his obite yerely solemply to be kept, as they haue obligid them by writyng vndir her couent seall. And also, ⌜they⌝[12] to purvey of a sewre *and* a[13] competent and sufficient reward in money, or in a due fee yerely by certeyn yerez by your*e* greet discrecion be assigned *and* lymetid, as your*e* seid pou*er* ⌜suppliaunt *and*⌝[14] oratour*e* may be thought competent, bethowt lengir delay, as your*e* seid besechers wyff *and* children may leven in her olde dayez, and as he shall p*ra*y to God for your*e* p*ro*sp*er*ous estate.

[7] *Surname eras. and canc.*
[8] ge *superimp. on another letter by Worcester.*
[9] ter *superimp. on another letter by Worcester.*
[10] *Interl. by Worcester.*
[11] *Interl. by Worcester.*
[12] *Interl. by Worcester.*
[13] *These three words added at end of line by Worcester.*
[14] *Interl. by Worcester.*

1050. From William Worcester to William Wainfleet, Bishop of Winchester — 1474, 21 August

Oxford, Magdalen College, Guton Hall 290. $11\frac{1}{2} \times 10$ in. Autograph, but the hand much larger and untidier than in Worcester's earlier writings.

Dorse: Marks of folding, slits for tape, remains of red wax seal. Address autograph:

*To my ryght worshypfull lord, my lord of Wynchester*e.

Dated, the year being given in arabic numerals.
Unprinted.

My lord, I am ryght hevy *and* peynfull to wryte to yowr lordshyp or to your lerned councelle for the remedy of my lord *and* maister S*er* John Fastolf*es* maters, and ben nother vndrestand nether remedyed yn seson *and* dew tyme by yer*es* passsed; *and* so[1] hys mevable godes lost and hys evidens*es*,[2] dedes enseled of maners *and* lordshypp*es*[3] of gret value, aswell as of oblig*aci*ons *and* jndenturs embecylled, and I yn grete dawnger of my lyfe, as othyrs gode willers.

And yn verray profe whereoff, one Thomas Frensh, late s*er*u*au*nt wyth S*er* Thomas Howys, that at your desyre *and* contemplac*i*on, wyth Rychard Horn, came rydyng ⌜about⌝ iij yer*e* passed owt of Norwych to yowr lordshyp p*re*sent at Assher; they both sworn *and* examyned to sey *and* declare the trouth as they knew off, both of the boxys wyth evidens*es* of Dedh*a*m of xl li. yerly valu, as of othyr evidens*es*, endenturs, oblig*aci*ons, quyt*au*nces[4] vndr*e* my maist*er* F. sign manuell; appoynteme*ntes and* covenntes endented of the money that shuld be payd for the alienac*i*on of the maners of Haylysdon, Cotton and othyr maners, Castr*e*, Runh*a*m &c, to dyuers astates, seled the yeer*e* that S*er* Tho*ma*s Howys decesed.

And yn deffaut ye hafe not betyme sewed for your ryght, the seyd Thomas Frensh, aswell as I, dar not com owt of hys duellyng plac*e*,[5] to ryde yn to the cuntree to vtter hys chafer, lynyn cloth that he bought of a mercer called Cobhald, yn London, to the som*me* of xvj li. *and* more; and wille hafe me for a sewrtee to aunser yn case Thomas pay not. And that myschieves Robynson ys the doer, and makyth both vppon hym such frayes *and* manasses of hys lyfe, as the cytee off Norwych knowyth well. And so hath caused hym renne hys dayes of paym*ent*, that *and* he ⌜Thomas⌝, com to London shall be arrested for hys debt, all be yt he dar not ryde to vtter hys pore stuff. And I arrested by excitac*i*on of Robynson for xij m*ar*k. vj s. viij d. in Norwych. And because my plegg*es* payd not, came late to London one Kyllyngworth, havyng jntrest

1050. [1] the *canc.*
[2] *Long* s + er *abbrev. for pl. inflection, and so in other instances of this word below.*
[3] *Bar over* pp *prob. signifies pl. inflection.*
[4] *Partially written word canc.*
[5] *Partially written word canc.*

to resseyve the seyd som*m*e, was coherced to fynde hym new sewrtee here yn London seth ye dep*ar*ted,[6] to make hym the seyd paym*en*t.

And for all your spech *and* your councell lerned to my lady Norff*olk* I hyrd of none ease. A[7] merveyllouse thyng, to thynk so oft *and* now late yn esp*ec*ialle, sent your officers aqueynted wyth my lord *and* lady Norff*olk* dyd not gefe yn co*m*maundm*en*t vndre one[8] cost *and* labour, myght hafe laboured that J. Robynson myght hafe com wyth Rob*ert* Ankelle. Whate trouble *and* cost I beer*e* by myne long absentyng from my pore loggyng yn thys deffaut, eu*ery* resonable, well disposed p*er*son wille say I ought hafe a grete amendys of Robynson *and* hys meyntenours, Barker *and* othyrs, or ell*es* of your lordshyp. And now I darre not abyde at my loggyng, but ye, eschewyng of grett*er* cost, wythdrawe me to Cambrygge, or to com neer*e* sewre place nerer to myne abydyng.

And I rode onys by Maist*er* Danvers co*m*maundm*en*t to Walth*a*m to your p*re*sence at Mychell*mas* ij yer*e* past, and was mokked, for your councell was not p*re*sent at my day assigned, and lost my jorney. Yn the same seson my pore woman arrested by Robynson for malyce ayenst me, and nevyr hederto remedyed, whych mat*ers* wille *and* most discourage me. Also, yn deffaut of[9] my evidences of my place of Fayrechyldes, that S*er* John Paston seyd me delyu*er*ed hem to your lordshyp for me to hafe, whate tyme, God thank your lordshyp, ye made a[10] eende wyth hy*m* for me; the baylly of the Duc off Suff*olk* called Palmer, that swyth ⌜to⌝ yow moch money for my maist*er* Fastolf shepe he toke *and* kepyth by forc*e*, wille take away xx acres of my plac*e* of Fayrechyldes, and hath take from me a lytill tenem*en*t yn Drayton of x s. yeerly. When I had bylded yt cost me x m*arc*. *and* more, the byldyng *and* rep*ar*ac*i*on.

And so am I troubled, besechyng your lordshyp to pardon me, they I compley[n] of my grete grevys. And the blessed Trinité you prosper yn all felicitee.

Wryt hastly the Sonday before Seynt Bertillmeu 1474 *Christ*i.

Yo*ur* W. Wyrcestr*e*

[6] *MS.* dep*ar*arted.

[7] *No space.*

[8] *Partially written word canc.*

[9] *Partially written word canc.*

[10] *No space.*

1051. From John, Duke of Suffolk to Thomas Jeffrey 1484, 1 May

Add. 43490, f. 49. $7\frac{1}{2} \times 3\frac{1}{4}$ in. Same hand as no. 803, subscription and postscript autograph.

Dorse: Blank.

Dated.
F. ii, p. 316. G. 879/997.

The Duc of Suff*olk*.
To Thomas Jeffrey o*ur* fermo*ur* of Maundevill*es*, greting. We wole and streitly charge you that ye content *and* paie vnto the bring*er* herof, for money inployed in o*ur* houshold, thre pound, threttenne shilling*es* *and* foure pens, for such stuff as we o*ur* owne p*er*son haue p*ro*mysed, and not to be failed vpon o*ur* worship. Of þe which so*m*me of lxxiij s. iiij d. so by you contented *and* paied, we wole and also streitly charge o*ur* audito*ur*s for the tyme being, by v*er*tu of this o*ur* writing signed w*ith* o*ur* hand, to make you dew *and* pleyn allowaunce at yo*ur* next accompt.

At Wyngfeld, the furst day of May jn the furst yer*e* of Kyng Richard þe iij^{de}.

Suffolk

And ffayle not on peyn [of] losy*n*g off yo*ur* fferme.

GLOSSARY

References in the Glossary are by letter number and line number.

The glossary is selective, and is primarily intended to encompass words that are obsolete, or words whose senses may not be readily recognisable. In the case of words with a range of meanings, only those differing significantly from modern English are in general given. Because a number of the less practised writers employ some unusual orthographical variations, idiolectal or regionally distinctive forms of a few current words that may cause difficulty are also recorded. Certain Latin words are included, almost all of them names of writs, which are often used by the writers as if they are English nouns. In the alphabetical ordering, vocalic *y* is treated as *i*, words with initial yogh are placed under consonantal *y*, and no distinction is made between thorn and *th*. Vocalic initial *v* (signifying *u*) precedes the consonantal use of the same graph.

a *v. see* **han**
a *prep.* of 178/24
a *pron.* he 84/5, 173/21, 722/20
abarre *v.* exclude 857/14
abbate *v. imp.* deduct 75/42. **a-batyd** *pa.* was rendered void 937/84. **a-bate, ab(b)atyd** *p.p.* deducted 8/25, 937/136; quashed 264/64; humbled 298/35
ab(b)ettement *n.* instigation to crime 654/9; assistance 907/45
abbyte *n.* monastic habit 6/8
abe *see* **han**
abedyn, -ydyn *v. p.p.* abided 133/25; stopped 241/5
aberyng *vbl. n.* conduct 48/196
a-bey *v.* pay the penalty; ~ *on her bodyys* be subject to physical punishment 161/24
abyll *adj.* suitably qualified 733/14
abyllymentes *n. pl.* ~ *of werre* military equipment 692/25
abligacion *see* **obligacion**
abod *n.* delay 333/90
abowte *adv.* as *adj. am* ~/*be* ~ am/are attempting 119/32, 728/10
abowtward *adj.* ready 413/44
abryggyd *v. pa.* curtailed, resiled from 378/29
absentyng *vbl. n.* absence 675/14
accion *n.* lawsuit 10/3, 77/108.
accompt *n.* accounts 589/7. **accomptes** *pl.* 568/7, 571/21
accorth *see* **acorde**
acerteyn, acerteyned *see* **asserteyn**
acomberd, acumyrd *see* **a-kumbyre**
acomplyshe *v.* ~ *vp* finish, complete 330/31
acomptanttys, accompta(u)ntes *n. pl.* servants obliged to render accounts 354A/23, 572/12, 965/44
acorde *v. pr. 3pl.* ~ *to-geder* are in agreement 652/37. **accorth** *pr. 3sg.* agrees 766/91
acquitaile, -ietall, -ytaille, -ytell *n.* discharge of duty 535/15, 538/6, 901A/30; repayment 802/3
acquite *see* **aquite**
acrons *n. pl.* acorns 123/92
a-cumyrd *see* **acomberd**
a-cursed *v. p.p.* excommunicated 210/5
ad *see* **han**
adiuged *v. p.p.* assigned, awarded 579/63
admynestracion *see* **ministracion**
adoo, a do *n.* trouble 114/34; conflict, fighting 274/19; sexual intercourse 395/9
adoughted *v. p.p.* afraid 261/41
advayle *v.* do good, be of use 243/12
advayle *n. see* **avayle**
a(d)uertyse, -ise *v.* inform, advise 516/5, 601/10, 667/11, 785/10. *imp.* 459/14, 460A/11. **aduertisyng** *pr.p.* showing 881/28. **aduertysid, -eid** *pa.* 360/3, 489/27, 694/30. **a(d)uertysed** *p.p.* 514/2, 518/28.
aduertysementes *n. pl.* information 553/1
aduyse *v.* look upon, consider 351/4
adward *see* **award(e**
affeccion *n.* inclination, desire 82/1, 294/49, 888/17
affecte *n. aftyr* ~ according to the intent (of a legal document) 57/6
affectueusly *adv.* earnestly 927/23
af(f)er(e-cast *ppl. adj.* premeditated 40/79, 48/129
afferrant *n.* proportional part 953/41
affettualy *adv.* earnestly 45/51

affiaunce *n.* confidence 547/28
affynyté, -enyté, -initéz *n.* confederates, associates 48/18, 413/7, 638/12, 838/12
affraye *v.* wear away 1/4. **affrayd, -id, -yed** *p.p.* attacked 199/11, 217/6; alarmed, frightened 543/12
afrayis *n. pl.* commotion 339/65
after, -yr(e *prep.* appropriate to 352/22; according to 430/14, 442/15
after-clappes *n. pl.* unfortunate consequences 200/61
a-geyns *prep.* in anticipation of 522/19
ageynwarde *adv.* in return 236/4
aght *see* **owght**
aglettys *n. pl.* metal points at the end of a ribbon 278/37
agnus *n.* jewel bearing the image of the Agnus Dei (Lamb of God) 123/69
agrugge *v.* resent 984/15
ag(y)we *n.* acute fever 301/10, *fevre* ~ 291/28
aknowyn, aknowe *v. p.p. be* ~ admit 418/22; *was* ~ admitted, confessed 600/24
a-kumbyre *v.* annoy 212/30. **acvmbred** *pa.* 775/3. **acomberd, acumyrd** *p.p.* burdened 203/59; annoyed 472/32.
alderbest, althere best *adv.* best of all, altogether 238/36, 375/33
aldermost(e, alther-moste *adv.* most of all, especially 584/4, 652/31, 980/12, 1012/29
alegged *v. p.p.* pleaded (in justification) 809/13
alestole *n.* stand for ale-casks 195B/22
Alhalwetyde *see* **Halowmesse**
alyenacion *n.* transfer of title to property 408/6
alienyn, aliene *v.* transfer title to property 70A/18, 914/12. **alyened** *pa.* 967/3. **alyenyd** *p.p.* 408/7
alys *see* **halys**
ally, alye *n.* kindred 456A/4, 692/18
allias *n.* second writ of attachment issued when a first proves ineffectual 189/76
allys *conj.* as 242/44
almary, halmerrey *n.* chest, cabinet 195A/30, 195B/33, 965/26. **almaryes** *pl.* 123/135
almes(se, -as, -ose, halmes *n.* good deed, favour 128/66; ~ *dede* 652/42, 835/25; charitable gift, alms 54/60, 208/43, 346/9
aloyned *v. p.p.* taken away 40/48, 686/23
along *adj.* ~ *on* the fault of 766/84
alonly *adv.* only, exclusively 705/54
alowyd *v. p.p.* granted (lands) 17/19
alternatly *adv.* mutually 229/44, 950/78
althere best *see* **alderbest**
ambassade, -iate, enbassate, jnbassat *n.* embassy, diplomatic mission 287/36, 646/34; *in* ~, *of* ~ as diplomatic representative or envoy 412/5, 673/26
amb(e)lyng, am(e)lyng *ppl. adj.* slow-walking 64/75, 237/6, 276/30, 906/headn., 930/101
amellys *n. pl.* enamel decorations 925/51
a-mendyd *v.+pron.* amend it 221/34. *p.p.* **amended, -yd** cured 414/17; better paid 506/8
amenuse *v.* reduce 5/181
amercy *v. pr. 3pl.* fine 36/57. **mercied** *pa.* 470/32. **amercyid, -ied, -yed, -sid** *p.p.* 21/5, 441/41, 470/29, 726/35, 754/8
amerciement, -yment *n.* fine, imposition 21/7, 529/3, 754/10. **amercymentes, -iementes, -iamentys, mersymentys** *pl.* 131/15, 229/31, 576/8, 880/68
am(e)rel *n.* admiral 134/9, 134/10, 582/34. **amrellys** *gen.* ~ *cort* Court of Admiralty 134/9
amewse *n.* fur-lined hood; *fig.* wearer of a hood, learned person 606/25
amytéys *n. pl.* treaties of friendship 302/6
amyttyd, -ed *v. p.p.* permitted 339/47, 548/29
amlyng *see* **amb(e)lyng**
amortyse *v.* alienate property in mortmain 1032/5
amortysement, -ezement *n.* alienation of property in mortmain 249/34, 252/217
amrel, amrellys *see* **am(e)rel**
an *see* **han**
anactyd *v. p.p.* decreed 420/46
and *conj.* if 40/23, 120/16, 201/38; or 128/42; so 122/44
a-nedes *see* **on-ethes**
anemps, an(n)enst *prep.* before, in the opinion of 201/9; to 423/6; concerning 476/5; with, in the company of 629/7
an-ethe *see* **on-ethes**
anker *n.* anchorite, recluse 230/84
ankeres *n.* anchoress, female recluse 230/81, 83
annexe *v.* include 656/34.
an noon *adv.* shortly 747/31
a-nowe *see* **inow**
answer *n.* reprisal 678/11
answere *v.* respond to the challenge 330/17; **answeryd** *p.p.* paid 708/9
ante *adj.* prior 550/17
antiphoner *n.* liturgical book containing antiphons 230/55
apaid *v. p.p.* pleased 512/12
aparte *adv.* separately 203/42, 205/24–5
aparteynor *indef. art.+ n.* spiritual associate 37/14
apechement *n.* accusation 392/16. **appechementes** *pl.* 450/23
apechyd *see* **appeche**
apeyer(e, -eyr *v.* weaken 37/39; deteriorate 72/91, 72/123, 175/32; injure 191/5. **appeyre** *pr. 3pl.* go badly 299/1. **appeyrid, -ed, -yd,**

appered *p.p.* damaged, made worse 77/56, 322/24, 435/10, 550/19; ruined 16/18; deteriorated 285/6;
apelyd *see* **ap(p)elyd**
aplates *n. pl.* iron cooking utensils 11/37
apleyn *adv.* explicitly 591/6
apoynt(e)ment, a-powntment *see* **ap(p)oynt(e)ment**
apoyntyd *v. p.p.* resolved 340/1
aportynantys *see* **appurtinaunce**
a-posed *see* **appose**
apostata *n.* renegade (person who leaves a holy order without dispensation) 2/3, 4/33
apparceyue *v.* see, conceive 449/11
appareld *v. p.p.* prepared 834/22
appeche *v.* charge, accuse 48/135. **apechyd** *pa.* 321/20, 692/74. **apechid, appeched** *p.p.* 392/15, 1024/24
appechementes *see* **apechement**
ap(p)elyd, -elled *v. p.p.* charged, accused 46/5, 52/22, 321/12, 575/17; appealed for a review of a decision 142/15
appeyre(d, -id, appered *see* **apeyer(e**
apperid *see* **appyre**
appese *v.* resolve 384/44
appyre *v.* appear 181/16, 258/47. **apperid** *pa.* showed 684/9
applye *v.* submit 65/61, 965/44
ap(p)oynt(e)ment, a-powntment, oppoyntment *n.* formal agreement, treaty 60/33, 204/28, 216/30, 242/41, 334/10, 668/19. **appoyntmentes** *pl.* 210/37
apportenauncez *see* **appurtinaunce**
appose *v. subj.* should confront 590/19. **ap(p)osed** *p.p.* examined 72/106, 855/18, 856/4
apposyng *vbl. n.* examination 566/2
approwe *v.* manage profitably 912/3, 913/5, 1009/45
approwement *n.* efficient management, productivity 558/16, 794/16; produce 986/48
approwyng *vbl. n.* profitable management 982/41
appurtinaunce *n.* adjunct part 451/7. **aportynantys, apportenauncez, appurtenauncez, -es, -tez** *n. pl.* rights attached to a property 38/8, 86/19, 229/7, 579/22, 698/7; accessories 870A/51
aquytauncyd *v. pa. jche of hem ~ othyre* each relieved the other of charges 177/9. **aqwetansyd** *p.p.* recompensed 339/15
aquite, -wyt, acquite *v.* requite, repay 79/19, 170/13, 210/16. **aqwytt** *p.p.* 436/6
aqweyntyd *v. p.p.* well-known 116/15
aqwetans, -ance *n.* discharge (of debt or legal obligation) 336/6, 353/37
aqwyt(t *see* **aquite**
ar *see* **er**
arayed *v. p.p.* equipped, dressed 817/6; put into a (bad) condition 196/25
arained, areyned *v. p.p.* arraigned, called upon to answer charges 450/22, 933/18
aras *n.* Arras, figured tapestry 64/50, 252/7
aratour *see* **oratour**
arbytrorys *n. pl.* arbitrators 381/29
arde *v. p.p.* heard 114/20
areyment *n.* trousseau 792/5
arere *v.* summon 48/68
arere *adv.* in arrears 48/73
Arminake *n.* French military adversary 954/35
armyng *vbl. n. ~ sworde* battle sword 268/40
armys *n. pl.* jousting 330/31
arnest *n.* promise, deposit 1005/10
array *n. defensible in ~* equipped for fighting 763/4
arré *n.* arrears 958/13, 1009/9
arreyned *see* **arained**
arrettith *v. pr. 3sg.* considers (it) to be 570/19
a-syne *n.* transfer of property 965/21
article *n.* provision 248/113. **artycules** *pl.* matters 664/13
artic(u)lerly *adv.* in detail 54/96, 72/79, 900/167
as(s)iser *n.* assise, court action 937/30, 35
asoyl(l)e *see* **assoil(l)e**
aspies *n. pl.* spies, scouts 199/9
as(s)ay(e *v.* ascertain 207/14, appeal to 212/41; inquire (of) 25/46. **a-saye** *imp.* 394/53. **as(s)ayed, assayde** *p.p.* 18/9, 205/25; explored 207/16
assaught, assaw *n.* assault, armed attack 204/14, 195A/73. **assaugthis** *pl.* 189/24
asseal, -le *v.* authenticate with official mark or seal 698/13, 716/10
assege *n.* siege 289/13
assegid *v. p.p.* besieged 294/9
assent *v. p.p.* in agreement 737/57
asserteyn, -arteyn, acerteyn *v.* assure 297/15, 379/6; inform 414/25. **assertaynyd, -eynyd, acerteyned, aserteyned** *p.p.* informed 238/39, 243/3, 249/25, 362/10
assewyd, -uyd *v. p.p.* have sued 42/3, 42/21
assignement, assyngnement *n.* order 122/23; allocation of funds 308/25
assignez *n. pl.* persons to whom property or rights are transferred 122/44, 951/15
assynyd *v. p.p.* have given assurance 227/11
assise *n.*[1] size 64/51
assise, -yse, -yze *n.*[2] session of a court dealing with civil actions 38/23, 138/28, 684/1; suit at law concerning land tenure 657/7. **assysys, -is, -es, assices** *pl.* 92/11, 188/12, 190/9, 683/22
assoil(l)e, as(s)oyl(l)e, assoylyn *v.* absolve 31/

12, 141/35, 177/33, 205/6, 397/2, 473/120, 870B/21
assuyd *see* **assewyd**
astate, estat *n.* legal right or title 304/45, 618/2; *of* ~ reserved for persons of high rank 123/85; *made* ~ given legal right or title (to property) 252/24. **estatys** *pl.* persons of rank 45/19
astell *n.* firewood 767/44
astely *adv.* quickly 175/38
asterlebere *n.* astrolabe 969/6
asti *see* **hasty**
a-sundre *adv.* apart 585/7
asure *n.* enamel made from powdered lapis lazuli 123/165
at *conj.* that 122/39, 457/15, 782/18
atainyd *see* **attaine**
ateynte *see* **atteynt**
atempte *see* **attempt**
atendaunce *n. daunce* ~ bustle solicitously 291/35
athwyx, a-twexen *prep.* between 65/7, 72/104, 472/31
atornement *see* **attornment**
a-t(t)ache *v.* distrain to appear in court 678/2, 965/84
at(t)ach(e)ment *n.* seizure of property by legal authority, distraint 526/12, 565/3, 707/2. **at)tachementes** *pl.* writs of distraint 453/29, 756/8
attaine *v.* commence, bring action at law 996/68. **attained, atainyd** *p.p.*341/20, 457/4, 600/30, 900/75, 996/14
atteyndre *n.* conviction for felony 677/28
atteynt(e, ateynte *n.* charge of felony 486/9, 511/3, 549/18. *writ of* ~ 937/73
attemptacion *n.* bringing of lawsuit 3/19
attorne *v.* acknowledge transfer of allegiance and service 920/15. **attornyd, -ed** *p.p.* 338/19, 667/4
attornment, atornement *n.* acknowledgement of allegiance and service 65/14, 417/15
attwyn, -en *prep.* between 27/3, 230/180
audyens *n.* court hearing 627/18
aught, awgth *v. p.p.* owed 8/16, 141/17, 965/118
augrym *n.* calculating with Arabic numerals; *taybyll of, boke of* ~ 969/6
auncetrie *n.* ancestry 579/15; *the* ~ an ancestor 579/7. **aunsetrys** *pl.* ancestors 657/5
aundern *n.* andiron (metal stand to support burning wood) 11/31. **aundernez** *pl.* 929/42
auter *see* **awter**
avayle, auayle, awayll, advayle *n.* benefit 119/5, 144/6, 207/11; income, profit 157/18; financial advantage 589/13. **auayles** *pl.* profits 703/22
availeabill, avayleable *adj.* ~ *for* of legal advantage or benefit to 441/25; *lytell* ~ of little assistance 889/8
avayte *v.* ~ *vp-on* attend 194/23
avante, avaunt *v.* boast 52/12, 274/21. **auaunted** *p.p.* 537/4
a-vaunte, auaunt(e, auawnt, awaunte *n.* boast 40/42, 92/33, 472/12, 652/5, 690/38
auence *n.* wood avens (herb) 7/1
auenture *n.* hazard, risk 603/21
aventure *v.* hazard, risk 156/8. **auenturyd, a-venterd** *p.p.* 248/64, 650/28
auerous *adj.* eager 1026/7
auertyse, -ise, auertysed *see* **a(d)uertyse**
auerttyng *vbl. n.* diversion from the appointed purpose 1049/39
avyse, auysse, awys(s)e *n.* advice 120/2, 183/3, 184/6, 469/1; order 66/55
avysed *v. p.p. werst* ~ most unwise 677/8
avysely *adv.* discreetly 527/8
avisement *n.* capacity to make decisions 230/3
avoydaunce *n.* vacancy of a benefice 662/4
avoyd(e, avoide, auoyd *v.* depart, leave 395/11, 632/10; vacate 337/21; discharge from service 143/22; deal with 299/7; *bode* ~ instructed to depart 189/20. **a-voided** *pa.* chased 653/12. **avoydyd, -e(d** *p.p.* expelled, sent away 46/4, 189/31, 435/23; rid 673/17
a-voked *n.* advocate 190/31
a-vouche *v.* declare formally 441/31. **avouched** *p.p.* summoned to testify title to property 960/5
avow(e, awow *v.* support, uphold 131/12, 142/15; confirm 129/36, 354/48, 441/32. **avowyd** *p.p. be* ~ take sides openly 194/23. **awowyt** *v.+ pron.* acknowledge it 471/21
a-wayll *see* **avayle**
awayt(e *n.* heed, care 636/10; surveillance 861/26; *hafe. . . yn greete* ~ keep a close eye upon 727/31
award(e, adward *n.* custody, care, keeping 83/2, 93/12, 238/45, 339/39; judgement, verdict 5/79, 173/15, 248/46, 282/83
awaunte *see* **a-vaunte**
awbe *n.* alb, ecclesiastical vestment 123/100, 230/64
awdyt(h *n.* judicial hearing 107/11
awgth *see* **aught**
awyse *see* **avyse**
awyth *see* **owyn**
awmener *n.* almoner, official distributor of alms 512/4
aworth *adj. take* ~ value 954/32
awow *see* **avow(e**
awter, auter *n.* altar 34/3, 123/104, 230/11
awterage *n.* altarage (endowment of an altar and a priest) 99/25

awterclothes *n. pl.* decorated altar coverings 230/166

axcessary *n.* accessory to a crime 343/3. **excercarys** *pl.* 880/45

axe *v.* request 14/17. **axe** *imp.* 276/27. **axyng** *pr. p.* demanding 48/49. **axid, haxed** *pa.* asked 135/13, 690/19. **axid, -yd** *p.p.* asked 14/14, 54/53, 128/28

axez, axces *n.* fever 580/6, 580/15

ayen *adv.* (gone) again 138/21

ayens, ayenst *prep.* against 138/27, in anticipation of 164/11; before 125/14, 181/18, 192/21

baylle *n. takyn to* ~ taken into custody on bail 120/3

bailly, baly *n.* bailiff 22/22, 46/56, 48/131. **balys, bailliuis** *pl.* 645/4, 794/6

bakhows, -hous *n.* bakery 259/4, 309/35, 929/44

bakk *n.* ~ *freende* untrustworthy friend 268/41

bald, ballyd *adj.* rounded 172/47; bald 238/9

baleyn *n.* whalebone 64/214, 64/223

baleys *n.* balas ruby 64/38, 123/70

balyngerys *n. pl.* small craft, sloops 968/18

balke *adj. goo* ~ be negligent 276/10

balkyd *v. p.p.* neglected 399/12

balles *n. pl.* ? baleen whales 816/14

ballyd *see* **bald**

baly(s *see* **bailly**

baneret *n.* knight banneret (rank above knight bachelor) 74/34

banker, -kare *n.* fabric cover for furniture 11/36, 64/140

bare *v. pa. see* **ber(e**

bare *adj.* unprovided for 116/40; (of cloth) having a flattened nap 28/11; false 1008/69

bargyn(g, -any, -eyn, -eny *n.* agreement 190/43, 196/83, 214/32, 872/32

barre *n.* court 534/9; ornamental strip (marking size) on a girdle 125/16. **barres** *pl.* ornamental bars 123/78

barwe *n.* barrow 125/19

base *adj.* low 412/33

basetry *n. in* ~ as emissaries or negotiators 668/51

basonys *n. pl.* shallow dishes 149/3

bassenet *n.* type of helmet 901B/174. **bas(e)nettes, -ys** *pl.* 64/219, 906/headn.

basset *n.* emissaries 712/14

batyd *v. p.p.* ended 937/98

battys *n. pl.* cudgels 172/47

bawde *n.* go-between, procurer 326/10

bawe *n.* bow 181/22. **bawys** *pl.* 195A/33

be, byn *v.* buy 128/38, 443/15. **bowght, bout, bovth** *pa.* redeemed, saved 332/44; bought 470/17, 658/14. **bouth, bowth(e, bowȝthe** *p.p.* 8/5, 18/21, 73/29, 205/31. **bowtyd** *v.+ pron.* bought it 221/20

be-come *pp. were he ys* ~ what has happened to him 102/1; where he has gone 263/69

beden *v. p.p.* remained 618/32

bederolle *n.* list of prayers 926/73

bed(e)man *n.* male petitioner 5/118, 643/36, 693/28

bed(e)woman, beed- *n.* female petitioner 156/15, 416/22, 802/26

bedf(f)elawe *n.* close friend 312/29, 315/6, 413/33

bedys *n. pl.* beads 146/25

bedred *adj.* bedridden 123/39

bedredmen *n. pl.* bedridden people 54/59

bee *n.* ornamental collar 123/72

beerehouses *n. pl.* brewhouses, breweries 579/19

be-fortyme *adv.* formerly 167/40

be-hated *v. p.p.* detested 196/12, 435/17

behestyd, -ed, -id *v. pa.* promised 133/28, 443/32, 473/25, 739/10. **behestyd, -id** *p.p.* 126/6, 442/6

be-hestys *n. pl. fayre* ~ sincere promises 135/14

behof(f)(e)full, behovefull *adj.* appropriate 42/33, 42/55, 65/60, 271/33

behold, beholdyng *v. p.p.* obliged, duty bound 65/5, 231/56, 589/3

behove, beho(u)ffe, behooue, behowe *n.* benefit, advantage 202/18, 424/14, 435/11, 793/10, 893/8

bek *n.* wink 1008/11

belassch *v.* beat 28/4

beleffte *v. p.p.* left, remaining 256/22

belle *see* **bill**

bellyd *v. p.p.* bell shaped 123/139

bend(e *n.*[1] company, entourage 330/49, 557/3

bendes *n.*[2] *pl.* sashes 36/22

benefice, -yfyce *n.* legal advantage 5/48, 129/43

beneficed *v. p.p.* endowed 540/22

benetgrey *n.* horse of a particular shade of grey 990/43

benett *n.* exorcist (minor order of secular clergy) 733/5

beneuoleres *n. pl.* well-wishers 813/13

benymmyng *v. pr. p.* seizing 993/26

berall *n.* beryl 923/96

bercars *n. pl.* tanners, leatherworkers 729/4

berdyd *v. p.p.* bearded, resolutely opposed 298/29

ber(e *v.* ~ . . . *a hand* accuse 161/19. **bereth** *pr. 3sg.* ~ . . . *an hand* construes 446/21; **berythe** *pr. 3sg.* ~ . . . *on hand* assures 409/45. **beryth** *pa. hist.*, **bare** *pa.* ~ *a(n/on hand(e* accuses 159/3, accused 684/7, 705/32, 861/44; ~ *hyre* . . . *on hande* assured her 313/35. **born,**

bore(n, boryn *p.p.* ~ *owght* represented 172/40; ~ *owte* oppressed, put upon 339/67; ~ *in hande* accused 59/50; *costys* ~ expenses paid 506/10
bere *n.* bier 776/28
beryingis *n. pl.* funerals 77/137
berynges *n. pl.* ~ *on hand* accusations, threats 765/37
beryngsceppes *n. pl.* baskets 11/38
berk *v.* bark 982/33
berons *n. pl.* barns 931/11
besely, -ily *adv.* quickly 65/42; attentively 445/16
be-set *v.* ~ *hem* set their hearts 446/42. **besett(e)** *p.p.* bequeathed 281/29; bestowed 624/14; set 790/11
beshet *v. p.p.* defiled 353/51
beshrewe *v.* curse 386/32
besy(e *adj.* occupied 204/17; occupied in an ill-intentioned way 180/6, 540/15; ornate 259/27; eager, keen 626/7, 749/2
besyd *v. p.p.* undertook 354/29
besily *see* **besely**
bespok *see* **by-speke**
bessyng *vbl. n.* ~ *fare* soothing things 745/27
bethyn *prep.* within 566/3, 579/8, 901B/185
beth(o)ut, betheowte *prep.* without 604/33, 901A/66, 989/114
betymes, -ys, bytymes, -ys, by tyme, betyme *adv.* soon 77/126, 160, 572/30; early, promptly 131/22–3, 187/18, 430/17
betyn *v. p.p.* discussed, talked about 248/25, ~ *down* demolished 194/38
bevere, -yr *n.* beaver fur 28/15, 148/10. **beuers** *pl.* 692/54
beware *v.* spend 209B/53, 215/25
byger *v.* engage in battle; ~ *with the sege* undertake the assault 625/15
bygge *n.* teat 270/50
bygge *adj.* powerful 281/4
byker *n.* battle, skirmish 625/16
bill(e, byll, belle *n.*[1] list 220/44; letter 888/49, 898/8. **billes, byllys** *pl.* lists 194/44; formal charges 159/4, 167/18
byll *n.*[2] long-shafted weapon with a hooked blade 258/13, 278/40; *Normandy* ~ 195A/55, 337/27, 338/40. **billes, bylles, -ys** *pl.* 40/8, 64/221, 189/10
byn *see* **be**
bynd *v.* bend 130/2
by-speke *v.* order 631/17. **bespok** *pp.* 329/10
byte *n.* ? small portion, bit; ? bit (part of reins); *not seker in þe* ~ untrustworthy 680/15
by-tyme(s, -ys, -tyme *see* **betymes**
bytte *v. pa.* overcame 439/8
bywaryd *v. p.p.* applied 311/27
blanket *n.* woollen cloth 36/22, 858/6
blasonyd *v. p.p.* inscribed with armorial bearings 316/34
blasonyngys *n. pl.* coats of arms, armorial bearings 316/33
blaveryd *v. p.p.* talked idly 58/11
blenchyng *vbl. n.* deflection 961/61
bod(e *conj., adv.* but 469/13, 15
bode *v.*[1] *pa.* remained 659/25
bode, bodeyn *v.*[2] *pa.* instructed, commanded 128/74, 189/20. **bodyn** *p.p.* 350/13, 744/33
bogey *n.* sheepskin 692/62
boitkyn *n.* small knife 82/44
bokeler *n.* small shield 40/20
bokeram *see* **bukram**
bold *adv.* confidently, courageously 365/26
bolles *n. pl.* bowls 11/28, 123/62
bolstar *n.* cushion 405/14
bolwerkys *n. pl.* fortifications 238/7
bombardys *n. pl.* guns firing heavy stone balls 325/29
bondeman *n.* customary tenant 752/33
bond(en, bwn *v. p.p.* duty-bound, under obligation 129/67, 180/15, 182/11
bondly *adv.* by way of feudal obligation 182/18
bonetes, -tys *n. pl.* caps 195A/66, 506/10
bonys *n. pl.* bones; (*fig.*) obstacles, reasons for not proceeding 582/13, 583/13
booke *n.* box, container 144/34
boore speres *see* **bore spere**
boote *n. to* ~ in addition 354/78, 85
bord *n.* table 151/3; *go to* ~ take meals 184/75; ~ *clothys* tablecloths 195A/16. **bordys** *pl.* 147/20
borde Alisaunder, bo(o)rd Alisaundre *n.* fine silk cloth from the Near East 64/178, 123/98, 230/145
bore(n, boryn *see* **ber(e**
bore spere *n.* spear for military use, used originally for hunting wild boar 181/22. **bo(o)re speris, -es** *pl.* 36/45, 491A/14
borgeys *see* **burgeys**
borow, -wghe *n.* borough 263/43, 46
bor(o)wes, -ys, boroughs *n. pl.* sureties, guarantors 5/138, 166/25, 453/29, 686/36, 867/63
bosartys *n. pl.* buzzards 390/9
boteré, bot(e)r(e)y *n.* butlery, cellar 153/13, 195A/15, 195B/18, 259/17
botes, botewx *n. pl.* boots 365/25; *dyd on your* ~ put on your boots 480/4
bothens *adj.* both; *here* ~ *ryth* both of their rights 937/25
bothyn, bothe *adv.* also 433/18, 670/13
botyller *n.* chief household servant in charge of victualling 901B/142
botrase *n.* butress, support 315/25
bounté *n.* mercy, benevolence 490/12, 494/3

bout(h, bovth, bowght, bowȝthe, bowth(e, bowtyd *see* **be**
bowestauis *see* **stavys**
bowntefous *adj.* generous 352/51
box(e *n.* boxwood 195B44, 732/34
brace *n.* pair 282/63
bracyd *v. p.p.* ~ *jne* hemmed in 269/24
brak(e *see* **breke**
bralled *v. p.p.* been noisily occupied 944/26
brasen *adj.* made of copper, bronze or brass 123/147, 230/121
brasere *n.* worker in copper, bronze, or brass 194/18
brawlere *n.* quarrelsome person 238/12
brawne *n.* pork 108/3
brec *see* **breke**
bre(e)de *n.* breadth 14/29, 264/26. **breddys, bredes** *pl.* standard widths (of fabric) 123/108, 930/17
brega(u)nders, bregandyrns, bregardyns, brigaunderes, bryganders, -dyns -yrs, bryngaunderys, *n. pl.* sets of light body armour 36/23, 63/18, 181/22, 195A/40, 195B/43, 692/54, 692/55, 906/headn.
breke, brec *v.* discontinue 184/44; put a stop to 152/27; ~ *of* reveal, broach 154/3, 992/11; open 369/41, 996/100; cut up 816/26. **brake, brokyn** *pa.* was revealed 184/43; opened 114/4, 192/8, 287/20; revealed 413/17; ~ *owt* revealed 705/23. **brak, brokyn, -e(n, brook** *p.p.* broken 332/56; revealed 212/17; opened 258/77; dispersed 184/80; failed to keep an agreement 128/15; disclosed 212/17, 302/18; *the day were* ~ the promise to pay by a certain day was not kept 156/12
brekyng *vbl. n.* falling out, dispute 684/11, 705/33, 36
brendelettys, brenledys *n. pl.* grates, gridirons, or trivets 195A/29, 195B/33
brenker *n.* bringer 898/8
brenne *v.* burn 72/119, 230/43, 362/24. **brenyt** *v.+pron.* burn it 209B/66. **brenned, -yd, brent(te** *p.p.* 241/8, 777/20, 30, 780/48
brethele *n.* wretch, worthless person 203/65; *pleye þe* ~ act dishonestly 203/62. **brethelles, brothell** *pl.* 77/41; scoundrels 131/90
breve *v.* report 153/13
brewerne, brow(h)ern *n.* brewery 150/3, 195A/21, 195B/24
brybyd *v. p.p.* pilfered 704/20
brybours *n. pl.* thieves 317/33
brigaunderes, bryganders, -dyns -yrs, bryngaunderys *see* **brega(u)nders**
brigged *v. p.p.* ~ *awey* reduced 72/89
bryggys *n. pl.* drawbridges 338/64
broches, -ys *n. pl.* skewers 195A/28, 195B/31
brochyng *vbl. n.* drawing off of wine from a barrel by tapping 394/41
brode *n. on* ~ into a public place 548/60
brodorod *n.* brotherhood 81/4
broke(n, -yn *see* **breke**
brokyd *see* **browke**
bronde *v. pr. 3sg.* stigmatises 1041/11
bronstan *n.* brimstone, burning sulphur 919/45
brook *see* **breke**
brooseid *v. p.p.* injured, weakened 356/7
brothell *see* **brethele**
browderyd *v. p.p.* embroidered 123/100
brow(h)ern *see* **brewerne**
browke *v.* retain food 220/57. **brokyd** *p.p.* tolerated 705/90
browth *p.p.* brought, raised (in price) 221/23
buffetstoles *n. pl.* low stools 11/36
buffette *n.* blow (with a hand or weapon) 143/16
bukram, bokeram *n.* fine cotton or linen cloth 135/38, 135/40, 195A/10
bulle *n.* papal edict 473/121. **bullys** *n. pl.* episcopal letters 249/21
bultyng pype *n.* vessel for receiving the products of sifting flour from meal 195A/24
bultyngpoke *n.* bag-like flour sifter 11/29
burgeys, borgeys *n.* representative of a town in the House of Commons 354/20, 53, 354A/4, 460/53
busshel *n.* large quantity 259/25
busshementes *n. pl.* bands of fighting men 491A/14
but *conj.* unless 157/16, 175/24; ~ *if* 132/50, 189/59
buttayle *n.* boundary 965/151
buttayled *v. p.p.* established the boundaries of 965/147
bwn *see* **bond(en**

cade, kade *n.* barrel, cask 772/16, 989/67
calcidenys *n. pl.* chalcedony gemstones 230/187
calkestokke *n.* cabbage stalk 394/30
caluys *n. pl.* calves, *fig.* small parts; *cast so many* ~ shed so many pieces 332/61
can *see* **con(n(e**
Candelmesse, Kandylmas *n.* Purification of the Virgin, 2 February 321/6, 728/32, 937/134
canell *n.* street gutter 129/6
canmasse *n.* piece of canvas 394/41
canste *see* **con(n(e**
capias, -yas *n.* writ of arrest 181/18, 343/9, 525/6
capias vtlagatum *n.* writ of outlawry 965/103
captenesse *n.* head of the household 180/104
carful *adj.* sorrowing 793/3
cargeyt *see* **charge**

cariage, corage *n.* carrying, conveyance 852/21; cost of haulage 1/17
carpettes *n. pl.* pieces of cloth to cover a bed 64/120
carpyth *v. pr. 3sg.* speaks 535/21
carre *n.* small cart 11/42
carsey *n.* coarse woollen cloth 394/11
carte *n.* charter, document 156/21
carvell, kervyl(e *n.* caravel (small ship) 63/5, 646A/4, 671/38. **carvellis** *pl.* 712/19
cas(e)welté *see* **casualté**
caskett, kasket *n.* small chest 306/3, 346/30. **kaskettys** *pl.* 123/136
casse *n.* circumstances 86/32
cast, kest *v.* calculate 571/21; throw 659/6. *pr. 1sg.* intend 540/32. **castyth** *pr. 3pl.* perceive 243/33. **cast** *imp.* calculate 72/127; ~ *ye my book* audit my account book 72/122. **kest** *pa.* threw 129/14; discarded 677/4. **cast** *p.p.* shed, lost 332/61
casualté, -elté, -(e)welté *n.* chance event 725/27, 735/4, 816/22; *for* ~ *of de(e)the* in case of death 56/20, 381/34. **casweltés** *pl.* misfortunes 222/28
catall(ys, -ez, -ell, *see* **chatell**
cate *n.* gate 876/10
causee, -ey *n.* causeway 374/6, 1043/22
cavserys *n. pl.* instigators 582/29
cedule, sedell *n.* written document 262/3, 465/5, 870A/18
cellary *n.* stipend (of a chantry priest) 780/37
cepe corpus *n.* return of a sheriff who has arrested someone on a *capias* 872/16
cerche(y *see* **kerchy(e**
cerciorari, -tiorari, serciorari *n.* writ issued by a higher court on a complaint that justice has not been received from a lower court 480/10, 982/4, 1001/24, 1002/5
ceryth *v. pr. 3sg.* withers 665/23
certeyn, -eine, -en, sertayn, -(e)yn *n.* certain number, group 248/39, 325/11, 743/6; fixed sum 335/8; truth, certainty 264/34, 411/5, 420/48; *put hem at a* ~ reassure them 596/4
certificat(e *n.* formal testimony 454/11, 679/11
certyfye *v.* inform 407/13. **certefying, -ifyeng** *pr. p.* assuring 122/4, 806/1. **certified, sertyfyed** *p.p.* assured 365/12; ~ *vup* reported 737/2
cescio(u)ns *see* **sesons**
chaced, -id *see* **chased**
chacke *see* **shakke**
chafar(e, chaf(f)re *n.* merchandise 72/116, 572/26, 28; loan 75/28
chaf(e)re, -o(u)r *n.* cooking pot 64/188, 123/142, 230/121; brazier 230/137; serving dish 923/7
chaffyd *pp.* mishandled 263/64
chafing disshe *n.* serving dish 123/66
chalese, -eis *n.* chalice 123/67, 923/21
chamber, -re, -ur, cha(u)mbyr *n.* room 147/12; furnishings for a bridal chamber 27/9, 493/9, 14, 792/5; *take hyr* ~ retired to her room (for childbirth) 748/19–20. **chambers** *pl.* apertures in the breech of a gun where charges are placed 64/210
chamberleyn *n.* head of household 174/8
chamlet, -lott, schamlet *n.* camlet (fine cloth from Near East) 123/116, 300/29, 394/10
champarties *n. pl.* aiding of litigants for a share of a matter in dispute 38/28
chapel(l *n. fre(e* ~ chapel founded by royal authority outside episcopal jurisdiction 239/2, 350/15
chapitell, -le *n.* chapter house 72/110; assembly of ecclesiastical dignitaries 557/4
chapman *n.* merchant, dealer 229/37, 744/27. **chapmen** *pl.* 221/20
chardeqweyns *n.* quince preserve 144/34
charge, -che, s(c)harge *n.* bulk 71/19; importance 191/10, 212/11; financial burden, expenses 211/9; duty, obligation 479/10
charge *v.* order 192/36. **sharge** *pr. 1sg.* command 175/8. **chargyng** *pr. p.* ordering, enjoining 192/28, 228/2. **cargeyt, schargyd** *pa.* instructed 125/5; ordered 203/7
charge *see also* **ouer charge**
chargeable *adj.* important 558/6
chargour, -eoure, -ere *n.* large serving dish 11/33, 387/103, 925/55. **chargers, -ours, chariours** *pl.* 64/194, 257/5, 923/149
charité *n. in* ~ charitable, benevolent 600/7
charl, schoryle *n.* churl, ill-bred person 129/19, 394/31. **karlys** *pl.* 298/35
chartre lond *n.* freehold land 934/2
chased, chaced, -id *v. p.p.* embossed 123/48, 230/142, 923/69
chaseueleyns *n. pl.* squat, wide-barrelled canons 325/29
chaste *v.* punish 470/33
chatell, catall, -ell *n.* chattels, material possessions 230/217, 439/22, 686/20. **catallys, -ez** *pl.* 123/180, 252/8
chaumbyr *see* **chamber**
chauncellere, schanselere *n.* bishop's administrative officer 203/23, 210/4
chauncery, -sery *n.* ~ *hand/hond* formal handwriting 493/31, 873/17
chaungeablé *adv.* mutually 252/259
chavyll *n. nedyre* ~ lower jaw 420/9
cheff, -ue *adj.* supreme, excellent 226/1; best 258/40; appointed (for payment of dues) 652/4
cheff arrowes *see* **sheffe arwys**
cheff(e *n. in* ~ especially 226/14, 228/13

cheys *n.* choice 149/9
chekkyd *v. p.p.* chequered 123/85
chekroll *n.* register of accounts 461/10, 511/11
chekwetche *n.* guard, lookout 569/54
chene *n.*[1] chin 128/51
chene *n.*[2] ornamental chain 186/12
chep(e, shepe *n.* bargain 130/27, 209A/57, 819/7; *gret* ~ bargain price 703/31, 767/13. **chepis** *pl. grete* ~ 767/11
cherche *n. mother* ~ cathedral 230/92
chere, schere *n. made me grete* ~ made me very welcome 624/7; *have good* ~ be treated hospitably 402/20–1
chere *v.* be sociable 692/18
cherysche, cherse *v.* take good care of 169/24, 463/21. **cherysed, -hid, -hyd** *p.p.* taken good care of 220/48; favoured 138/9, 302/21
chernell wise *adv. phr.* hinged 64/26
chesiple, -yppill *n.* chasuble 123/100, 230/64, 1030/13
cheue *see* **cheff, day**
chevesshe, -yshe *v.* borrow on security 156/3, 285/28, 288/35. **cheuysched, chevis(ch)ed, chevysshed, -yd, chewisched, schevyste** *p.p.* 67/7, 210/2, 291/10, 604/17, 759/20, 25; provided 175/19
chevyshanse, -sans, -(s)shaunce, cheuesance cheysaunce, *n.* arrangement for borrowing money 208/30, 231/51, 285/19, 23, 360/4
chier *adj.* noble 4/7
Childermesse Day *n.* Innocents' Day, 28 December 635/12
chynne *v.* crack 1/4
chyrchyng *vbl. n.* ceremony of purification after childbirth 339/28
chirre *see* **shire**
chyvage *n.* tax paid annually to a superior 229/30
chonge *n. newe* ~ improvement in circumstances 159/20
choppe *n.* piece, bargain (*but perh. intended for* **chepe**) 652/6
choppyng *v. pr. p.* striking, sniping 355/16
chorlissh *adj.* ill-behaved, undisciplined 776/44
choulle *see* **xall**
chrewys *see* **shrewe**
churtly *adv.* shortly, abruptly 24/21
cyetica *see* **seyetyka**
circumstaunce *n.* trouble, ado 450/34
clad *v. p.p.* dressed in monastic clothing 6/7
clap(p)alde, clapholt *n.* board cut to make barrel staves 778/22, 779/10, 852/3
clappys *n. pl.* blows, *fig.* venereal diseases 774/9
classe *n.* looking-glass, mirror 728/5
clatryd *v. p.p.* disclosed 372/16
clawsys *n. pl.* points (in a discourse) 205/20
clene *adv.* completely 395/8
clenefyed *v. p.p.* freed from refuse 72/125, 178/20
clenly, klenly *adj.* decent, honourable 466/4; skilled 37/6. **clenliere** *comp.* more splendidly 114/22
clepe *v.* summon 30/12. **clepyn** *pr. 3pl.* call 557/7. **clepid** *p.p.* named 551/35.
clere *adj.* accurate 172/12
clerk convicte *n.* convict who claims benefit of clergy (as being able to read) and is spared execution 172/30
clogge *n.* block of wood attached to a prisoner to impede movement 644/38
clooke *n.* cloak, concealment 315/25
clos(e *n.* enclosed land reserved for private use 614/25, 704/16, 735/18. **closes, -ys** *pl.* 132/53, 650/20
close *adj.* discreet 727/46
clos(e, cloos *adv.* secretly 209A/17, 209B/17, 453/10
clos(e)ly *adv.* discreetly 185/42; carefully 71/25
closett(e *n.* private pew 24/2; private chapel 309/21
clos(s)e glasse *n.* container with a lid 195A/45, 195B/50
clospys *n. pl.* metal clasps 965/27
clot *v. p.p.* patched 172/47
clothyng *vbl. n.* livery 172/41
clowys *n. pl.* cloves 7/3, 287/dorse
clowt, clout *n.* piece of cloth 453/10, 965/27
clowt *v.* ~ *vp* repair, patch up 329/33
coarted *v. p.p.* forced 1046/45
cobardys *n. pl.* supports for a spit 123/143
coffer, -yr, -re, -ure *n.* trunk, chest 55/6, 387/80, 549/4, 930/54. **cofers, -irs, -orys,** *pl.* 123/135, 150/10, 640/29
coyfe *n.* headdress of a lawyer 870A/51
coysy *see* **qwe(y)sye**
colage *see* **college**
cole *v.* cool 259/50
colyet(te *ppl. adj.* flocks of sheep from different owners pastured together 184/30; (*as n.*) 184/33, 702/3. **culettys** *pl.* 912/18, 21
collaterall rellesse *n. phr. haue on* ~ have had transferred as security 79/8
college, colage, -edge *n.* endowed body of religious persons 311/14, 326/5, 892/22
collegions *n. pl.* members of an endowed religious body 54/24
colour *v.* justify 558/22, 994/13. **colored** *p.p.* ~ *vnder* falsely blamed on 72/83
colour(e, -wre, coulloure *n.* occasion, pretext, reason 36/56, 66/12, 184/44. *by/be* ~ *of* conspiring with 41/12; by means of 122/52, 444/23, 671/14; *vndyr* ~ *of* in the name of 317/34
colourable *adj.* plausible 989/18

comb, coumbe, kowmb *n.*[1] unit of dry measure (prob. of four bushels) 77/93, 128/42, 195B/25. **combes** *pl.* 17/17, 442/10
combis *n.*[2] *pl.* ? decorative combs or crests 942/4
comen *see* **comon**
comenaunt(e, -awnt, comnaunt, compnaunt *n.* contract, agreement 47/4, 442/18, 551/55, 658/23, 925/60. **comena(u)ntes, -is, counauntes** *pl.* 60/74, 387/58, 433/16, 872/37
comenauntyd, -id *v. p.p.* made an agreement 60/65, 237/4
comerus *adj.* clumsy, heavy 125/9
comes *n. pl.* sprouting grains of barley (used in malting) 442/10
com(f)fort, comfore, confort *n.* financial assistance 243/21, 360/6; encouragement, support 183/19, 200/37, 236/9; trust 244/21
comf(f)ortable *adj.* encouraging 279/7, 604/23
comfytys *n. pl.* confections or preserves 209B/56
cominaltie *n.* citizens, burgesses 659/15
comynd *see* **comon**
comynicacyon *see* **communicacion**
comiser, -yser *n.* representative, deputy 396/43, 75
commer *n.* messenger 780/47
commoigne *n.* brother monk 2/3
communicacion, comunycacion, comynicacyon *n.* discussion, consultation 72/4, 308/32, 773/5
comnaunt *see* **comenaunt(e**
comon *n.* living expenses 144/9
comon, -une, comune, -en *v.* speak, confer 37/22, 173/25, 192/101, 220/52; ~ *of* discuss, confer 1/2. **com(m)onyd, comond** *pa.* conversed, spoke 88/84, 160/12, 311/15. **comond, -ynd, -ownd, -uned** *p.p.* 3/37, 77/120, 131/58, 414/3
comonyng, -unyng *vbl. n.* association 456A/25; consultation 627/3
comown, -une, komon *n.* land held in common by a community 132/56, 57; right to use common land 66/13
comown *v.* graze by right of common pasture 132/57
compace *v.* compost, manure 735/11
compas *adv.* in circumference 64/204
compase *n.* circumference 264/18
compasse *v.* scheme against 366/35
compert *n.* inquest 543/2
competent *adj.* suitable 541/6
compnaunt *see* **comenaunt(e**
compone *v.* reach an agreement 379/21. **compoune** *subj.* 59/4. **compouned** *pa.* 359/8
composission *n.* constitution 422/10
comptrollour *see* **cownt(er)rollere**
comune *see* **comown** *n.*
comune(d *see* **comon**
comunycacion *see* **communicacion**
comunyng *see* **comonyng**
comuent *n.* community of monks or friars 504/4
con *see* **con(n(e**
conable *adj.* suitable 439/34
conceyt(e, -sayt(h)e, -seyte, -seyth *n.* opinion 39/40, 43/7, 86/29, 120/18, 212/17, 236/15; favour 218/28; *hevy* ~ misgivings 841/4.
concel(l, -sayle, -sayll, -seill, -sell, councel(l, cownsell, kownsell *n.* body of advisors 242/8, 62, 450/38; confidant 244/20; confidence, secret 132/16, 248/47, 354/44, 369/11, 470/44, 521/7; *in* ~ secretly 178/10, 198/30; *of* ~ advisor 306/40; legal advisor 3/32. **conceylis** *pl.* lawyers, legal advisors 177/7
concourse *n.* way (of behaving) 776/15
condempnacion *n.* punishment imposed by sentence 274/9, 564/20, 663/11
condescend *v.* agree 902/21. **condescentyng** *pr. p.* in agreement, consenting 306/39. **condesended, -dyssendyd, -decended** *p.p.* agreed 302/26, 737/18, 902/13
condicion *n.* disposition 189/48. **condycyons** *pl.* habits 380/40
condyth *v.* conduct, escort 320/15. **condyt** *p.p.* conveyed 346/11
conduyt(e, -yt(h) *n.* conduct, management 509/25 520/21, 566/22; means of involvement, 1037/33; means of conveyance 494/24; *saue* ~ escort 360/30
conduytour *n.* guide 1037/54
confersaunte *see* **co(n)uersaunt(e**
confessionall *n.* confessor's manual 732/35
confetered *v. p.p.* formed an alliance 294/4
confydent *adj.* mutually confiding, trusting 652/36
confort *see* **comf(f)ort**
confrerys *n. pl.* members of a brotherhood 694/5
congregacions *n. pl.* illegal meetings 737/3
conyes *n. pl.* rabbits 390/12, 982/42
conyng *vbl. n.* knowledge 107/6, 494/13
coniecte *v.* devise 351/10. **congected, -iectyd** *p.p.* conspired 40/93, 48/130
connawnt *n.* formal contract 147/9
connawnt *v. p.p.* bound by covenant, pledged 138/7
con(n(e, kon, kun *v.* know how to 14/4, 153/16; be able to 66/17, 77/67; owe 476/14; ~ *hym þank* be grateful to him 133/13. **conne, can** *pr. 1sg.* do 354/64. **canste** *pr. 2sg.* are able (to have) 872/22. **connythe, konyth** *pr. 3sg.* knows 152/24; owes 324/12
connyng *see* **konnyng**

consayle, consayll *see* **concel(l**
consayt(h)e, -seyte, -seyth *see* **conceyt(e**
conseill, -sell *see* **concel(l**
conseyvyd *v. pa.* ~ *be* found out from 128/10
constablys *n. pl.* officers of the king's peace 194/12
constrew *v.* interpret 537/15. **construe, -ew** *pr. 1sg.* form an opinion 212/15; interpret 220/48. **constrw** *imp.* ~ *ye, &c.* you understand what I mean 209A/40
contenaunce *see* **continuance**
content(e *v.* compensate, (re)pay 122/61, 212/43, 215/22. **contentyd** *p.p.* 118/20
contentacion, -yon *n.* payment 400/21, 843/7
contenue, -ynue *n.* content or purport (of a document, letter, etc.) 424/20, 1000/2
continuance, contynuance, contynewance, contynuans, contenaunce *n.* patience, persistence 400/34, 407/35; adjournment 3/6, 1008/31; maintenance 59/3; continuance 870A/33
contynue *v.* sustain 603/19
contradiccion *n.* matter for dispute 493/14
contray, co(u)ntré, kontré, cuntré *n.* region, district 133/14, 136/8, 180/121, 445/17, 446/4
contraryows *adj.* hostile 589/28
contremaundyd, countermandet, countyrmaundyd *v. p.p.* recalled 177/38, 411/14, 445/12
contumacy *n.* rebelliousness 117/33
conuenable *adj.* suitable 832/7
convenyent, -ient *adj.* suitable 306/26, 562/9
conuenyently *adv.* suitably 230/14
conuenticles *n. pl.* secret meetings 36/64, 204/26
conuersacion, -oun *n.* conduct, behaviour 656/39, 694/30; ? *scribal error for* conservation 460A/11
co(n)uersaunt(e, -and, confersaunte *adj.* intimate 483/6, 780/13, 855/20, 918/3; ~ *of* frequented by 160/10; *(is)* ~ *(at)* lives, resides 442/5, 527/6
coope *n.* cope, vestment 1030/15
coors *adj.* coarse 64/171
coors *n. see* **cors** *n.*[1]
coorse *see* **cors(e** *n.*[2]
cop *n.* top 767/8
copye *n. by* ~ by copy-hold (i.e. by copy of the court roll) 66/8. **copys** *pl.* records 155/6
copiehold lond *n.* land held of a manorial lord according to a copy of the court roll 934/4
copil *n. pl.* pairs 779/10
copilet *v. p.p.* paired, put together 220/20
copschotyn *v. p.p.* inclined to excessive drinking 238/11
corage *see* **cariage**
coraged *v. p.p.* encouraged 215/15
corageous *adj.* keen, committed 601/8
corageously *adv.* boldly, blatantly 985/12
coragyng *vbl. n.* encouragement 214/26
corayd *v. p.p.* cleaned and combed 778/10
corigyble *adj.* punishable 880/14
corones *n. pl.* corns, cereal produce 985/35
corons *see* **reysonys**
corporas *n. pl.* ~ *casys* containers for altar cloths 123/101
corpus cum causa *n.* writ transferring the person of a prisoner and case records to different court 867/36–7, 61
corrige *v.* correct 1009/43. **corryged** *p.p.* corrected 588/5
cors, coors *n.*[1] customary proceedings 548/30; *owte of* ~ not normal procedure 1002/11
cors(e, coorse *n.*[2] silk woven in strips, often ornamented 123/79, 230/131; silk belt 20/18, 732/123, 929/47
corser *n.* horse dealer 410/9
corvers *n. pl.* fishing boats 827/3
cosyn *see* **cousin**
costages, custages *n. pl.* expenses 931/20, 933/23
coster(e)s *n. pl.* ornamental hangings for walls, beds, etc. 64/53, 121, 230/119
costius, -uys, -uouse *adj.* expensive 282/75, 776/16, 1006/36
coulloure *see* **colour(e**
coumbe *see* **comb**
counauntes *see* **comenaunt(e**
councel(l, -sell, cowncell *see* **consel(l**
countermandet, -yrmaundyd *see* **contremaundyd**
counterpoynt *n.* quilted bedspread 123/86, 930/43
countirvale *v.* be accepted in lieu of 751/34
countour(e *n.* debtor's prison 491/8, 870D/24, 38. **countours** *pl.* 870A/26
countré *see* **contray**
countrelle *n.* accountant 729/13
controller *see* **cownt(er)rollere**
cours *n. renne a* ~ ride a pass in a joust 439/14
courte *n.* walled enclosure attached to a castle 412/33
courtezane *n.* member of the papal curia 4/6
cousin, cosyn *n.* kinsman, kinswoman 74/address, 412/1
couthe *adj.* known 529/8. **cowthest** *spv.* best respected 996/56
couenable *adj.* suitable 460A/7
couered *ppl. adj.* with a lid 230/117
couerlet(e, -yte, -ight *n.* bedspread 195A/8, 230/198, 732/2, 40. **couerlettes** *pl.* 123/94
couersaunt *see* **co(n)uersaunt(e**
couert *n.* refuge 325/12

couert, -he *adj.* guarded 89/10, 154/6
covy(n)(e, -eyne *n.* conspiracy 48/134; deceit 54/54; persons involved in conspiracy 41/11, 557/2; *of* ~ in collusion 36/55, 937/101
counauntes *see* **comenaunt(e**
cowncell *see* **councel(l**
cownyd *v. p.p.* coined, minted 208/47
cownt *n.* shire court 92/36
cowntenance *n. made here* ~ indicated her desire 400/41
cownt(er)rollere, countroller, comptrollour *n.* official in charge of accounts in the king's household 116/19, 420/33; accountant in the customs 666/7; steward 412/45
cowntre, -ewery *n.* counting table or chest 150/11, 314/4
cowper *n.* barrel maker 880/47
cowthest *see* **couthe**
craf(f)te *n.* deception 125/22, 788/6; *off* ~ as a subterfuge 258/9
cragge *n.* some kind of stoneware 230/122
craked, -yd *v. p.p.* uttered 325/8, 472/35
crakyng *vbl. n.* vaunting 668/38
crased, -yd, -id *v. p.p.* diseased, unwell 293/20, 297/25, 848/3
creancere, -syr *n.* tutor 406/4, 407/8
credens *n.* authority 242/35
creme *n. holy* ~ chrism, consecrated oil 68/12
cremelle, -yll *n.* kind of cloth, sometimes pleated 200/47, 201/51
creste clothe *n.* type of linen cloth 123/133
crettur *n.* person 727/56
crewettes *see* **cruettes**
criour *n.* court officer who makes announcements 699/4
crismatorie *n.* vessel for holding chrism 68/12
crod *v. p.p.* conveyed 125/19
croke *n.* crook; *with the hepe or the* ~ somehow or other 1003/31
cromes *n. pl.* crooked staves 36/25
crommys *n. pl.* crumbs, portions of food; *toke so my* ~ ate so heartily 285/7
crone *v.* discharge 166/10
cronys *n. pl.* old sheep 731/9
crop *n.* harvest 8/4
cropers, crowperes *n. pl.* covers for the hindquarters of a horse 195A/58, 195B/57
crowner *n.* coroner, Crown officer 637/4. **crowner(e)s** *pl.* 338/63, 637/16
cruettes, crewettes *n. pl.* small vessels for sacramental wine, holy water, or chrism 123/67, 230/166, 923/22
cui in vita *n.* writ of entry for a widow against the person to whom her husband aliened property in his lifetime 937/90
culettys *see* **colyet(te**
culueryns *n. pl.* cannons 906/headn.
cunnyng *vbl.n.* knowledge 3/16
cuntré *see* **contray**
cured, cu(e)rid *v. p.p.* covered 230/193, 923/50, 51
curesse, curassys *n. pl.* paired breastplates and backpieces of armour 36/23, 906/headn.
curyng *vbl. n.* covering, bedspread 64/202
currys *n. pl.* dogs 390/9
cursyd-hertyd *adj.* malicious 129/58
cursyng *vbl. n.* excommunication 203/8
curt baron *n.* roll or record of a manorial court 732/10
custages *see* **costages**
custell *n.* two-edged dagger 732/165
customable *adj.* persistent 776/15
customer *n.* customary tenant 534/5
custum *n.* customary rent 725/5. **customs** *pl.* 724/6
custumabely *adv.* customarily 704/18
cwrate *n.* priest, chaplain 339/4

dacock *n.* jackdaw 612/36
day, dey *n.* date appointed for court proceedings 138/27, 650/16; term of payment 224/6, 548/63; *gret* ~ session of an important court 154/17, 684/4; *small* ~ session of a minor court 684/5; *cheue* ~ day for payment of manorial dues 652/4; *short* ~ short notice 1007/3; *good* ~ special day, holiday (here, the feast of the Annunciation) 749/10. **daies** *pl.* terms of payment 54/65
daylese *adj.* without further hearings in court 901B/198
dalyauns *n.* talk 705/82
dan *conj.* than 126/21
dassh *v.* annul, quash 39/14. **deysshsed** *pa.* 471/48. **dasched** *p.p.* 134/5
daubyng *vbl. n.* plastering walls 145/11
da(u)nger(e, dawnger *n.* debt 208/12, 209B/20, 636/23, 778/43. **dawngeres** *pl.* 400/11
daungerous *adj.* wary 1013/16
deamant, dyamaunt(h *n.* diamond 195B/53, 201/50, 640/11
debité, -yté *n.* deputy 16/14, 420/10, 816/9
debursyng *vbl. n.* disbursing 572/25
decast *v. p.p.* overturned 867/78
deceasid *see* **dissesyd**
decies tantum *n.* writ alleging bribing of jurors 1015/15
decysyng *vbl. n.* determination, judgement upon 912/40, 50
ded(e *see* **do(o**
dedyr *adv.* thither, to that place 126/20
dedys *n. pl.* military prowess; *of* ~ suitable for use in battle 774/53
deelfe, duele, dwel *n.* devil 564/26, 690/58, 861/57

defavte, diffaught *n.* lack 172/9; error 200/60, 218/29; *takyn here wyth summe* ~ detected her in some misdemeanor 206/8
defawty *adj.* in error, guilty 169/6, 216/16
defawtyf *adj.* negligent 704/10
defensable, -ible *adj.* protective 444/40; armed for battle 763/4
defetyng *vbl. n.* nullification 950/77
defowlyd *v. p.p.* brought dishonour on, traduced 46/18
defused *v. p.p.* confused 543/4
degré *n.* rank 176/10, 652/40
dey *see* **day**
deynté *n.* ~ *of* esteem for 446/31. **deyntés** *pl.* delicacies 825/21
deynté, -y *adj.* rare, scarce 108/2, 142/29, 354/83
deysshsed *see* **dassh**
deke(s *see* **dike**
dekyn *n.* deacon 277/21
delayous *adj.* dilatory 242/4
delegaci, delagacie *n.* papal commission 37/9, 453/5
deliberacion *n.* forethought 230/3
delyuer *v.* joust with 439/15. **delyuerd, -yd** *pp.* freed, rid 221/41, 395/8; *is not* ~ has not gone into labour 613/36
delyuera(u)nce *n.* release, discharge 221/7; surrender 334/2
delyuerye *n. gayle* ~ clearing of a jail to bring prisoners to trial 737/10, 47
delyuerst *adj. superl.* most agile 352/52
deme, -yn *v.* expect, assume 446/40, 1009/6; **demyth(e, -eth** *pr. 3sg.* suspects 119/21; assumes, thinks 183/19, 196/14, 212/14. **demyng** *pr.p.* expecting 290/11. **dempte, -yn** *pa.* assumed 242/5, 604/14; judged, pronounced 422/13. **dempt** *p.p.* imposed 686/38
deme(a)n(e *n.* demesne, land managed by the lord of the manor 252/4, 437/25; *auncyon/auncyen* ~ land held by feudal tenure 812/21, 814/5
demendantys *n. pl.* defendants 937/70
demenyng *vbl. n.* behaviour, conduct 72/33, 169/30, 201/48; proceedings 633/5; governing 167/38, 716/4
demesne *v.* guide 569/20. **demene** *subj.* should behave 165/14. **demeane** *imp.* control 351/37. **demened, -yd, demesned** *pa.* behaved 167/20, 461/32, 1019/9. **demenyd, -id** *p.p.* guided 19/6, 132/24, 160/5
demi, -ye *n.& adj.* half 209A/52, 860/2
demyn *see* **deme**
demyng *vbl. n.* conjecture, inkling 296/26
dempt(e, -yn *see* **deme**
dener *n.*[1] wedding feast 330/12
deners *n.*[2] *pl.* deniers, small coins; *sanz* ~ paupers 332/56
dens *adv.* thence, from there 126/16
depart *v.* separate 365/30; ~ *for* part with, surrender 558/3. **departyd** *pa.* shared 209A/18; separated 332/18. **departyd** *p.p.* shared 304/15; ~ *with* given 271/23
departyson *n.* distribution (of property) 426/7
depending, -yng *v. pr. p.* awaiting settlement 468/3, 842/5
depose *v.* vouch 370/48, 388/9
deppere *adj. comp.* more significantly 516/11
dep(p)eth *n.* depth, thickness 123/116, 117
depryvyd *v. p.p.* removed from office 183/7
deprove *v.* disprove 184/49
derst *see* **dor**
descentys *n. pl.* genealogies 956/2
desese *see* **dyses(s)e**
deskys *n. pl.* lecterns 228/11
despariegеd *v. p.p.* socially degraded 953/13
destresse *see* **distres(se**
deth *n.* plague, pestilence 263/42
detrayed *v. p.p.* denounce, betray 915/4 (*but see headnote*)
devere, deuer(e, devir, dev(e)yr(e, devour, deuoyere, devoyre *n.* duty 28/2, 54/62, 59/47, 175/10, 524/12; *do youre* ~ do all you can 19/8, 201/32, 204/42, 242/77. **devors** *pl.* things to be done 203/68
devise, -ys, -uyse *n.* ornamental badge 123/49, 164; item of jewellery 146/24. **devises** *pl.* heraldic designs 259/29
deuowghtest *adj. superl.* boldest 352/53
dewre *v.* continue 243/6
dewtys *see* **duty**
di. *adj.* half (*Lat.* dimidius) 179/18
dyamaunt(h *see* **deamant**
diaper *n.* geometric design 123/122; ~ *werk* cloth showing a repeated pattern 64/151
dyche *n.* dish, service of food at table 116/18. **dischys** *pl.* 116/19
dyde *see* **do(o**
dydyngys *see* **tythyng**
dyed *v. p.p.* ~ *vpp* perished 381/67
diem clawsit (-yth) extremum *n.* writ to enquire into landholdings, issued after the death of a tenant of the king 86/11, 315/21
dyet(t)yd *v. p.p.* fed 126/42, 366/29
diffaught *see* **defavte**
diffensibely *adv.* prepared for battle 817/6
dyght *see* **dite**
dike, dyke, deke *n.* moat, ditch 47/17, 312/42, 618/23. **dekes, dykes** *pl.* 229/24, 767/7
dylygens *n.* efforts; *do my* ~ exerted myself to the utmost 436/4
dyme *n.* royal subsidy of one-tenth the value of property 266/32. **dymes** *pl.* 624/32

dymeth *see* **deme**
dimise, dymysse *n.* grant of land 252/70, 931/6
dimised *v. p.p.* transferred 229/4
dymysoynt, -ent *n.* demi-ceint, narrow girdle of metal links 123/83, 929/49. **dymyseyntes** *pl.* 123/171
dimisse *v. p.p.* discharged, removed 714/6
dyreccyon *n. take a* ~ make an arrangement 342/23
dirige *n.* liturgical office for the dead 230/87, 926/34. **diriges** *pl.* 123/13
dys *dem. adj.* this 126/13
dysapoyntyd *v. p.p.* ~ *of* deprived of, without 414/28
disavayll, -awayll, disseavayll *v.* cost 209A/9–10, 209B/10, 214/42. **disadvayled** *p.p.* financially disadvantaged 978/29
disavowyd *v. p.p.* disclaimed 131/8
discharge, dys(s)charge *n.* release from financial obligation 211/5, 263/56, 493/13
dischargyng *vbl. n.* relieving of a financial obligation 186/8
dischys *see* **dyche**
disclaundre *n.* dishonour 62/12
dyscouer, dyscure, dyskure *v.* reveal, disclose 358/32, 415/7, 722/22. **dyscwyr** *imp.* 354/49. **descuueryng** *pr. p.* 236/19. **discuyryd, diskuryd, discoueryd, dyskevwyrd, dysscevwyrd** *p.p.* 125/20, 23, 132/18, 77, 152/42; identified 337/2
discrecions *n. pl. after ther* ~ according to their judgement 230/114
dysesyd *ppl. adj.* inconvenienced 414/31
dyses(s)e *n.* inconvenience, discomfort 126/25, 220/8, 414/36; state of discomfiture 459/36
dysgysynggys *n. pl.* entertainments involving masked performers 153/5
disheryson *n.* deprivation or loss of possessions or privileges 835/15
disheryte *v.* deprive 702/4
dyskure, dyskevwyrd, diskuryd, dysscevwyrd *see* **dyscouer**
dismayd *ppl. adj.* frightened 411/37
dismysse *v.* release 911/5
dysparblyd *v. p.p.* dispersed 268/31
dyspeyre *n.* state of ruin 435/4
dyspencyd *v. p.p.* ~ *wyth* granted release from vow 282/43
dispended, -yd *v. p.p.* spent 230/158, 901B/195; distributed 184/63
dispenses *n. pl. mysse* ~ improper expenditures 1037/15
displesauns *n. take not to* ~ will not take offence 49/2
dispoil, -oyle *v.* rob, plunder 491/15; strip 692/52. **dispoylyth** *pr. 3sg.* ransacks 140/13. **dyspoyled** *p.p.* robbed 692/63
dysport *n.* pleasure, recreation 351/43. **dysportys** *pl.* recreational activities 153/6
disported *v. p.p.* prevented 467/4
dysporveyd *v. p.p.* lacking 399/25
dyspreysed *v. p.p.* disparaged 400/34
dysscharge *see* **discharge**
disseavayll *see* **disavayll**
dissese *n.* death 56/7
dissesyd, -easid, deceasid *v. p.p.* deprived of seizin, unlawfully dispossessed 46/21, 131/69, 569/29, 1007/15
dyssesing *vbl. n.* unlawful deprivation of seizin 46/30
disseson, -syn *n.* dispossession 1007/17; *asisse of nouel(l* ~ action to recover property which has been unlawfully seized 485/12, 881/44
dissimilacion *n.* pretence 737/66
dissimile *v.* feign 981/15
dysspytuose *adj.* ruthless 196/44
distreyn *n.* sequestered property 73/45
distreyn(e, -trayn *v.* seize property in compensation for arrears 16/20, 131/14, 324/6; torment 182/19. **dystreynyd** *pa.* 443/18. **dystreynyd, -ed** *p.p.* 325/15, 473/11
distreynyng *vbl. n.* seizing of property in compenstion for arrears 59/30
dystresid, -sed *v. p.p.* distrained 324/47; detained 567/19
distres(se, destresse *n.* seizure of property in compensation for arrears 22/20, 59/1, 840/10; property seized by distraint 180/49, 50, 443/20. **distresses** *pl.* 65/19
distringas *n.* writ directing a sheriff to distrain a person 480/13
distrussid, dystrussyd *v. p.p.* defeated in battle 277/42, 298/29; overcome 1029/10
diswere, -yre *n.* uncertainty 138/23; *in a* ~ as a surmise 487/27
disworship, diswurchep *n.* dishonour 194/32, 202/28, 955/32
dite *v.* harvest a crop 16/12. **dite, dyght** *p.p.* 16/18; prepared 614/9
dyuers(e, diuers *adj.* several 179/2; *as n.* various people 209A/20, 300/24, 746/3
dywtés *see* **duty**
doare *n.* perpetrator 752/20
dobyl *see* **double**
doblet *n. armyng* ~ jacket worn under armour 277/22
docatys, doketys *n. pl.* gold and silver coins, ducats 282/44, 777/42
dogers, doggerys *n. pl.* fishing vessels 824/2, 10
doggeboltes *n. pl.* lackeys, tools 194/31
doytt *v. subj.* rot 277/33
don *see* **do(o**

dong(g)e *n.* mattress 732/1, 116. **donges, -ys** *pl.* 64/118, 195B/8
do(o, don *v.* make, cause 155/4, 220/36; ~ *it* make it into 221/27. *imp.* 218/55. **dott** *pr. 3sg.* fares 126/26. **dede, dyde** *pa.* made, caused 181/19, 432/4, 443/20. **do** *p.p.* made, caused 155/8, 205/41; done 208/29, 218/7; put 209A/46
doolis *n. pl.* boundary markers 14/7
dor *v.* dare 21/9. **dor** *pr. 2sg.* 125/13. **derst** *pr. 3sg.* dares 185/5. **durste** *pr. 1sg.* dare 132/5, 728/10. **thernot** *pl. 3pr.* dare not 184/25. **durst** *pa.* should 131/59
dormantys *n. pl.* permanently installed tables 150/3
dort(o)ur *n.* monks' dormitory 809/9, 1049/29
dott *see* **do(o**
double, -wble *n.* duplicate, copy 569/54, 951/11, 1016/9
double, -yl *adj.* deceitful, guilty of duplicity 600/41, 603/36, 606/25
doubt *v.* believe 1005/60. **doughtyth** *pr. 3sg.* is afraid of 58/1. **doughtyd** *p.p.* respected 370/1
douterlawe *n.* daughter-in-law 225/25
dowth *n.* ~ *of* fearful for, afraid of losing 40/56
draffwyff *n.* widow (*lit.* 'waste-wife') 369/34
drane *n.* drone, parasite 72/38
drawe *v.* withstand 1/10; incur 1/17; go, advance 477/24; amount to 614/18. **drawith** *pr. 3sg.* amounts to 423/7, 614/43. *pr. 3pl.* amount to 845/22. **drew, drwe, drow** *pa.* consumed, used up 602/13; drained 782/9; ~ *downe* demolished 412/18; ~ *vpon* amounted to 737/34. **drawyn** *p.p.* raised 338/64
drawte, -ute ~ *chamer n.* private room 150/3, 10
drede *n.* danger, peril 18/23
drede *v.* respect, honour 802/26
dre(e)dfull *adj.* respectful 390/4, 6
dresse *v.* proceed 384/30
dressyng knyff *n.* knife for preparing food 195A/28
dreve, -yn *see* **dryve**
drevyll *n.* rascal 380/51
drew *see* **drawe**
dryve *v.* go, journey 840/16. **dreve, -yn** *p.p.* attributed 52/21; pursued 306/42
dronchyn *v. p.p.* drowned 124/3
dropis *n. pl.* spots 123/119
drow, drwe *see* **drawe**
duele *see* **deelfe**
duplade *n.* pair 123/120
durasse *n.* hardship 692/76
durat *adj.* enduring 521/2
dure *n.* door 621/2
durst(e *see* **dor**
duty, -é *n.* rent due 66/25; debt 157/29, 227/4. **dewtys, dywtés, dutés** *pl.* 182/8, 300/24, 600/17
dwel *see* **deelfe**
dwn *adv.* (be put) down, out of office 128/46

ear *see* **ere**
ease, es(s)e, hes(s)e *n.* ease 114/38, 116/3, 203/74; benefit 143/16, 207/11; *do(n* ~ help 178/4, 8, 602/6
ease *v.* ~ *you of* help you with 306/30. **easyd** *pp.* satisfied 312/33; helped 639/6
easelye *adv.* poorly, indifferently 298/27
e(a)sy *adj.* poor, indifferent 258/8; inferior, of little value 131/110; suitable 773/17
eeuyn *see* **euyn**
efe *n.* evening 576/7
eftsones, -is *adv.* afterwards 60/75, 72/31; soon 475/4
ey *n.*[1] egg 7/2
ey, hey, jee *n.*[2] eye 221/38; *fig.* observation 355/30, 356/8, 704/21. **eyne, jen** *pl.* 93/10, 728/5
eyer *v.* build an eyrie, breed 356/10
eyeres *see* **heyer** *n.*[2]
elaw(e *conj.+ n.* in-law 218/4, 423/10
elde *adj.* long-standing 601/12
ele *n.* aisle 230/8
elyted *v. p.p.* elected 716/20
ell *n.* eel 148/10
ell, ellys *adv.* otherwise 143/22, 209A/9, 249/22
elne, ellyn *n.* ell (variable unit of linear measurement, 45 inches in England) 77/3, 394/11. **ellys** *pl.* 123/89
elm bord *n.* elm wood 64/214
elmyes, -se, elmees *n. pl.* enemies 143/20, 199/29, 759/71
embecylled *v. p.p.* stolen 1050/6
embraceries *see* **enbracerye**
emendement *n.* maintenance 230/63
emendyng *vbl. n.* maintenance 230/60
em(m(e *n.* uncle 53/32, 126/18, 453/14
emparled *see* **enparle**
empryse *n.* bold initiative 351/5
enbacetours *see* **jnbacetour**
enbassate *see* **ambassade**
enbylled, -elled *v. p.p.* accused in a bill of complaint 40/83, 95
enbracerye *n.* bribery of courts or juries 548/37, 1021/11. **embraceries, inbraceryes** *pl.* 38/28, 881/11
encredibill *adj.* untrustworthy 41/38
endanger *v.* bring into debt 377/8. **endaungered, endangeryd** *p.p.* 209A/19, 306/19, 375/12
endentyd *v. p.p.* agreed (by indenture) to perform military service 409/25

endewe *v.* endow 70/3
endifferencie *n.* impartiality 1019/5
endifferent, -ly *see* **indifferent, -ly**
endyghtyd, jndyte *v. p.p.* composed or dictated 354/24, 415/22
endytyd, -ed *v. p.p.* indicted 185/12, 572/55
endossed *see* **indorcid**
enfeffe *v.* enfeoff, grant under arrangements for feudal tenure 252/139. **infeffid, in-feoffyed, enfeoffid** *p.p.* 644/34, 911/7, 14
enforcyng *vbl. n.* protection 238/4
engrose, engroos *v.* make, consummate 210/37; ~ *vp* conclude 625/3. **engroced, ingrosid** *p.p.* drawn up in final form 60/50, 531/2; ~ *vpp* concluded 902/16–17
engrossyng *vbl. n.* formal writing out 2/26
enheritamentes *n. pl.* inheritable property 947/7
eniourned *v. pa.* adjourned 1008/15
enpaneld, -lid, -lyd *see* **in-panell**
enparle *v.* obtain a delay 548/19. **emparled, jmparlyd** *p.p.* obtained a delay 248/78, 534/6, 628/8
enpechement *n.* ~ *of wast* tenant's liability to compensate for damage to his holdings 27/13–14
enpeyryd *v. p.p.* made worse 363/11
enquerans *n.* official investigation 25/6
enstaunce *see* **instaunce**
ensurauns, -ce *n.* guarantee 5/75; pledge (to marry) 200/40
ensure, -er, enswyr *v. pr. 1sg.* assure 198/20, 338/46, 368/1. **ensured, -id, insu(e)rid, inswryd** *p.p.* 72/36, 131/61, 290/25; betrothed 45/46, 50/6, 14, 201/7, 861/33
entaylyd *see* **tayled**
entend *n.* intention 738/4
enterlessant *v. pr. p.* adjacent to 79/7
entermet *v.* interfere 122A/7
entytelyd *v. pa.* wrote down 739/8
entré, entres(se *n.* taking possession of property by entering it 741/3; induction 217/22; entry 676/19; *wryt of* ~ 937/55
entremedyll *v.* interfere 862/8
entre(n *v.* write down, record 131/13; ~ *vp-on* enter into (an agreement) 204/28. **entret** *pp.* entered (to assert ownership) 122/53
entres(se *see* **entré**
entrest *see* **int(e)resse**
entretid, entretyd *see* **jntrete**
envolde *v.* involve 1001/4
er, ar, here, or *prep. & conj.* before 26/12, 76/16; ~ *than* before 171/8, 205/43, 222/18
ere, ear *adv.* earlier 144/40, 190/17
ery(n *v.* plough 735/8, 931/6. **eryd** *p.p.* 99/36
errour, -wre *n. wryt of* ~ writ applying for a new trial or reversal of judgement on grounds of error 447/8, 867/37
erst(e *adv.* earlier 170/5, 231/4, 286/3; before 475/9
erthes *n. pl.* ploughing 912/15
eschete *n.* ? voluntary surrender of property 880/34
eschete *v.* confiscate 687/80. **eschetith** *pr. 3sg.* 72/158. **exchetyd** *p.p.* lost, forfeited 339/41
eschewed *see* **exchewe**
eschewyng *see* **excheuyng**
escutys, scutes, -ys *n. pl.* écus (French coins) 243/15, 266/22, 271/10
eshe, esse *n.* ash (wood) 665/21; ash (tree) 735/4
esy *see* **e(a)sy**
eskape *v.* recover 177/22
espyed *v. p.p.* discovered 169/50
esse *see* **eshe**
es(s)e *see* **ease**
esson, -yn *n.* delay of court action 453/24, 526/10
Estaple *see* **stapill**
estat(ys *see* **astate**
estragers *n. pl.* keepers of goshawks 356/5
evele *see* **evyl(l**
euerydel *adv.* in full detail 433/10
eveson *n.* evensong 48/63, 444/27
evy *see* **h)evy**
evyl(l *adj.* wretched 169/4; wicked, bad 180/63, 194/28; unpleasant 705/8
evyl(l, -ill, -ele *adv.* inadequately 192/122, 364/14; badly 435/10; maliciously 196/31, 671/3; scarcely 167/55, 564/19; unfavourably 368/2; very little 208/31; *go right* ~ become very impoverished 166/38; ~ *pay(e)d* displeased 133/8, 141/6, 175/5
euyn, eeuyn *n.* vigil, day before a festival 258/53, 56
euyr *adv.* always 354/91
ewer, -re *n.* water jug 230/148, 923/62. **ewers, -rys, heweres** *pl.* 64/16, 166/30, 195B/20
ewvys *n. pl.* eaves 774/42
exaccions *n. pl.* taxes 54/53
exameyn *v.* question 203/7. **examyned, exayminid, examynd** *p.p.* questioned 430/31, 664/13; ~ *vp-on a bok* questioned under oath (taken on the Bible) 119/23
examynacion *n.* legal hearing, deposition 740/1
excercarys *see* **axcessary**
exchetyd *see* **eschete**
exchetore, -er *n.* escheator, officer of a county designated to investigate inheritance of lands held of Crown 155/36, 238/39
excheuyng, eschewyng *vbl. n.* avoiding 204/24, 680/48

exchewe *v.* avoid 178/44. **eschewed** *p.p.* 129/39

excitacion *n.* incitement 46/48, 901B/100

excyte *v.* prevail upon 727/12. **excited** *pa.* 901B/89

excytours *n. pl.* inciters 430/23

execuciun, -ion, -yon, execussyon *n.* enforcement 37/43, 252/62, 654/49; *mak hem* ~ enforce their wishes 118/5; *haue* ~ enforce (a legal requirement) 118/6; *do* ~ pass sentence 321/16, 460/30

executrie *n.* executorship 65/31

exhibicion, -eshyon *n.* means of support 734/8, 914/76

exicutyd *v. p.p.* brought about 244/4

exigent, -end *n.* writ requiring a defendant to appear on pain of outlawry 337/35, 338/37, 518/5. **exigentes, -des** *pl.* 685/11, 766/74

expedicion, -ecyon, -ision *n.* successful execution 509/6, 510/14, 686/12

exschawnge *n. letter of* ~ certificate of credit 469/15

exstrete *n.* record of fines to be collected 21/8, 965/48

extourcious *adj.* exorbitant, excessive 880/68

extremely *adv.* to the greatest extent 749/33

fabours *n. pl.* suburbs 412/18

facock *n.* ? a nonce word; cf. **dacock** 612/36

factours *n. pl.* agents 535/6

fadyrd *v. p.p.* suggested 347/18

fagot *n.* firewood 47/18. **faggotis** *pl.* bundles of firewood 767/44, 1028/7

fayl(l(e *v.* lack 204/3, 461/25; ~ *not* is available 120/31. **faylyd** *pa.* lacked 144/7. **fayled** *p.p.* lacked 5/10

fayn(e *adj.* obliged 116/34, 153/17, 1012/38. **fayner** *comp.* more eager 888/10

fayn *adv. he wold right* ~ he desired very eagerly 146/19–20. **folfayne** very eagerly 238/51

faynt *adj.* exhausted 184/87

faire, fayre *adv.* fairly, justly 169/46; suitably 450/30

faldage *n.* rent paid for a sheepfold 702/5

falde *see* **fold**

falle *v.* occur, happen 6/9, 248/100, 267/14. **fille, fylle** *pa.* lodged itself 301/16; ~ *forth* moved on 171/7

false *v.* break, violate 331/7

falsed *n.* dishonesty 138/30

falt(e *ppl. adj.* ~ *tabill/table* folding table 259/37, 929/36

fane *n.* emblematic banner 87/15

fansey, fantazy, -tesy, -tsy, *n.* liking 145/10, 193/12; ~ *in* liking for 168/21, 363/9

fardell *n.* bundle 71/17, 684/24

fare, feryn *v.*[1] deal 540/23; proceed, go 213/13. **fard, ferd** *pa.* ~ *right evyll* came to grief 213/25; behaved 167/66. **fare, ferd** *p.p.* dealt 169/47, 450/30

fare *v.*[2] fear 205/43

farforthe, ferf(f)orth(e, for-furþe *adv.* far, far forward 124/9, 252/42, 260/15, 267/4, 344/5

farseyn *n.* small tumour 26/18

fase *n. make a* ~ put in an appearance 72/48

fast(e *adv.* earnestly 106/3; securely 130/19, 180/93; vigorously 161/19

Fastyngong(e, Fastgang, Fastegong (tyde) *n.* Shrovetide (the Sunday, Monday and Tuesday before Lent) 88/44, 263/36, 302/29, 650/36

fates, fattys *n. pl.* vats; *clensyng* ~ vats for cleansing, used in brewing 195A/23; *kylyng* ~, *geylyng, gilyng* ~ vats for fermenting wort 11/24 (*sg.*) 195A/23, 195B/26 259/49 (*sg.*); *knedyng* ~ tubs used for kneading 195A/24–5, 195B/28; *saltyng* ~ vats for preparing meat for preservation with salt 195A/30

faute, fawth *n.* lack 106/11; fail 1024/4

fawcon wise *adv. phr.* in the shape of a falcon 64/28

fawtef *n.* in default; *bythe* ~ (who) are guilty of offences 613/16

fawth *see* **faute**

fawtourys *n. pl.* supporters 582/26

feauté, fewthé *n.* fealty; *do . . .* ~ acknowledge obligation 84/34, 698/13

febill, -yll *adj.* of little value 64/216; few 202/36; of poor quality, inferior 149/9, 154/33

fe(e, fye *n.* feudal obligation 182/33, 252/4; heritable land held of a feudal lord or the Crown 66/10, 778/23; ~ *symple/sympyl* tenure without limitation to any particular class of heirs 252/70, 304/19, 872/40; ~ *taille* tenure limited to some particular class of heirs 870D/15–16; ~ *ferme* rent paid for land held in unlimited tenure 309/26; *knyt* ~ obligation to provide one knight for a lord's service (in exchange for holding land) 143/4, 996/73; *franke* ~ property held in fee-simple 600/46. **feys** *pl.* fines 128/68

feed(e, feeod, feid *v. p.p.* enfeoffed with a feudal estate or office 661/7, 872/21; ~ *men* vassals 256/25, 681/22, 784/8

feffed *see* **feoffed**

fe(o)ffement *n.* investing of persons with an estate in land, tenements, rents, etc. 230/141, 252/8, 387/55

feffés, feffees, feoffeys *n. pl.* persons invested with an estate in trust 160/19, 178/13, 184/52

feyntely *adv.* half-heartedly 45/15

feyth *n. j* ~ in faith, truly 160/28

fel(a)shyp, -shep, -schip, feleschipp, felesshep, -ship *n.* group of associates or compa-

nions 184/12, 188/7, 189/51, 192/31, 199/9, 201/24, 643/20
feld, fewlde *n.* battle, battlefield 114/17, 320/10; background area (on an armorial device) 442/3. **feldys** *pl.* 281/36
fel(l)e, fyle, vele, wele *v.* understand, discover 116/15, 145/5, 172/27, 179/4, 564/7, 604/4; ~ *of* investigate, sound out 572/33; ~ *hym* regard him as 89/39. **felt(e** *p.p.* 231/21, 739/5; *be* ~ *of* be sounded out as to 77/115
fele *n.* man 645/11. **feles** *pl.* 199/26, 213/5
felet *n.* headband 745/27
fell(e *v.* mow, cut 136/15
felle *adj.* cruel 5/146
felle *v. see* **fel(l)e, fell(e**
fellewet *see* **welwet**
felshyp *see* **fel(a)shyp**
fend *see* **fynde(n**
fenne *n.* area of marshland 971/40
feodary, -our *n.* documentary record of terms on which land is held under a feudal overlord 547/15; tenant, retainer 546/3.
feoffed, feffed *v. p.p.* put in possession of estate 252/86, 595/3
feoffeys *see* **feffés**
ferd *see* **fare**
ferde, forte *adj.* fourth 150/4, 931/1
ferdyng *see* **ferthyng**
ferf(f)orth(e *see* **farforthe**
ferfull *adj.* terrible 160/7; intimidating 1008/25
fery *v. pr. 1sg.* ~ *ouer* carry over, postpone 374/22
feryn *see* **fare**
fermall *n.* documentary record of rents 391/5, 650/7
ferm(e *n.* payment for the use of land or property 173/3, 182/3, 551/9; *had it in* ~ rented it 196/77; ~ *barly* barley paid as rent 384/40, 391/14, 940/1
ferme *adv.* firmly; *for* ~ *and stable* faithfully 283/8, 520/13
fermour *n.* lessee of land 551/3, 744/13, 912/3.
ferre *adv.* further 282/11; *of* ~ from afar 349/19
ferrore *n.* blacksmith 175/34
ferthyng, -dyng *n.* farthing, a quarter of one penny 129/54, 506/8
feruent *adj.* raging 190/68
fesyk *see* **phisyke**
fesympyl *see* **fe(e**
fete *n.* skill 774/9. **fetys** *pl.* ~ *of armys* martial exploits 238/5
feterloke, -yrlok *n.* padlock, portable lock for a horse shackle or hobble 11/45, 732/142
fetys *adj.* shapely 125/15; well-fitting 444/39
fewe *indef. pron.* small, little 613/20, 632/43
fewlde *see* **feld**
fewthé *see* **feauté**
fye *see* **fe(e**
fieri facias, fyeri facias *n.* writ directing the payment of an award out of a defendant's goods and property 338/10, 340/26, 719/1
figure, fugre *adj.* patterned 123/97, 195A/40
fyle *see* **fel(l)e**
fille, fylle *see* **falle**
fynd(d)yng *vbl. n.* livelihood, support, maintenance 122/13, 201/30, 216/33; conspiring in 985/4
fynde(n *v.* provide for, fund 154/37, 488/5; support, maintain 227/32. **fend** *pa.* found 131/62
fines *n. pl.* evidences of land transfers 897/8
fynnes *n. pl. put owt their* ~ spread their wings, busy themselves 158/10
fyrsenesse *n.* violence 243/4
firsis, fyrrys *n. pl.* furze bushes (used as fuel) 47/17, 105/2
flaket *n.* container 64/17
flakons *n. pl.* large flasks 221/35
fleet, flete *n.* drain, ditch 136/7, 547/21
fleyng, flyeng, flyeyng *ppl. adj.* ~ *tales* rumours 2/36, 275/15, 347/26
flekeryng *see* **flykeryng**
flesshe hoke *n.* utensil for lifting meat from a pot 123/148
flygge *adj.* ready for action (*lit.* fledged) 158/10
flykeryng, flekeryng *adj.* wavering 59/18; unreliable 180/5
flyte *see* **shote**
flyttyng *pr.p.* changeable, unreliable 339/40, 372/12
flyxe *n.* dysentery 269/37
flote *n.* fleet 968/20
floure delyce work, flower delice werke *n. phr.* decorated with representations of the fleur-de-lys 123/120, 127
flourrid *v. p.p.* mounted in a flower-like setting 64/45
flowyr *n.* jewel or brooch in the form of a flower 354/57
fnattyd *ppl. adj.* snub-nosed 274/34
foyll *see* **foule**
fold *n.* enclosure for animals (esp. sheep) 169/26, 184/30; flock 702/3
folfayne *see* **fayn**
foodyd *v. p.p.* beguiled; ~ *me forthe* fobbed me off 315/12
for *adv.* forth 194/3
for *see* **for(e**
forberable *adj.* lenient 189/42
forbere *v.* relinquish 147/8, 224/46. **for-bore** *subj.* 224/46. **for-bor, forborn** *p.p.* spared 167/55; lost, relinquished 72/60, 194/45, 768/19
forby *prep.* near to, past 23/12, 131/46, 333/54

force, fors *n.* regard, care 118/8, 213/15, 244/9; importance 590/8
force *pr. 1sg.* ~ *not* care little about 776/43–4
forcelet, forslet *n.* fortified place, castle 40/6, 48/35
forcere *n.* strongbox, chest 443/5
fordell *n.* advancement 357/15, 384/31
fordoone *v. p.p.* destroyed 776/2
for(e *prep.* because of 180/125; ~ *þat* because 301/20
foreyn *adj.* ~ *reseytes,* ~ *paymentes,* ~ *charges* additional or irregular income and payments 75/12, 77/77, 571/18
foretyn *see* **fortune**
forfayt *v. p.p.* forfeited (of an obligation, thus making a penalty due) 129/44
forfende *v. subj.* forbid 123/160, 305/26
for-furþe *adv. see* **farforthe**
forgeers *n.* counterfeiters 5/30
forgyng *v. pr. p.* alleging falsely 726/36
forgoer *n.* crier, messenger 230/94
forjugyn *v.* deprive 870A/65
formable *adj.* correctly drafted 381/3
formes *n. pl.* benches 259/42
forneys *n.* vessel for boiling wort 259/48
forn-thowght *adj.* premeditated 5/5
fors *see* **force**
forsene *conj.* provided 569/24
forstages *n. pl.* ships with castle-like structures on their bows 63/8
for-swere *v. pa.* falsely denied 131/83. **forsworyn** *p.p.* guilty of taking a false oath 831/46
forswerer *n.* taker of false oaths 932/22
forsworn *adj.* false 932/20
forte *see* **ferde**
fortendayes *n. pl.* fourteen days, a fortnight 498/4
forthe *adv.* onward 170/5, 171/7
forthward *adv.* henceforth 73/18
forthyng lof *n.* loaf of bread costing a farthing 129/15
fortune, foretyn *v. subj.* should grant 188/14; should happen 211/7, 216/21, 377/13. **fortunyd** *pa.* ~ *so* so happened 154/4. **fortunyd** *p.p.* happened 5/50, 209A/3
fostian *see* **fustian**
fott *n.* stand 87/3
fotte *v. p.p.* taken 117/32
foule, fovle, fowle, foyll *adv.* grievously 4/39, 759/6; disgracefully 167/67; harshly 196/20; wickedly 196/28
foundatrice *n.* female founder of a religious house 656/36
foundred *v. p.p.* caused to collapse 990/46
fowle *adj.* unfortunate 248/31; rough, preliminary 447/9
fowlers *n.* cannons 64/209, 259/6
fowlyd *v. pa.* followed 184/32
fowrtenyte *n.* fortnight; *on Soneday* ~ two weeks ago last Sunday 582/14
fray *n.* disturbance 412/47. **frayis** *pl.* attacks 333/14
fray, frayith *v. pr. 3pl.* attack 690/35; frighten 40/75. **frayed** *p.p.* frightened 238/21
fraying *vbl. n.* attacking, frightening 40/114
framyng *v. pr. p. in* ~ being drawn up 454/26
franchyse, -ches(se, frawnchese *n.* privilege 351/38; municipal limits 803/19–20; *baly of the* ~ civic officer 855/10, 872/10
frankeleyns *n. pl.* landowning gentry 48/116
fraunchised *ppl. adj.* possessed of special privileges (in taxation, self-government, etc.) 473/29
Frencheman *n.* French ship 411/20
frendelyhood *n.* friendly gesture 88/79
frend(es, -ys *n. pl.* relatives, family 50/14, 186/8, 203/32
frentyk *adj.* deranged 326/11
frere *n.* friar 778/17, 779/2
fresch *adj.* well turned out, fashionable 146/25. **fresshest** *superl.* most carefree 659/1
frese, fryse *n.* coarse woollen cloth with a thick nap on one side 130/26, 30, 692/62
fresselye *adv.* briskly 274/16
fret *n.* ornamental border 123/130
fryse *see* **frese**
frontlett, fruntelet *n.* band worn across the forehead 929/45, 930/73
froward(e *adj.* deviant, worthless 73/62, 298/35; unco-operative 89/29; contrary 566/38
frowardnes(se *n.* obstinacy 430/24; initiative 564/2
frowys *n. pl.* women of the Low Countries 774/8
fruntelet *see* **frontlett**
frunture *n.* stronghold 40/5
fugre *see* **figure**
fullarys *n. gen.* cloth worker's 788/3
fumows *adj.* irascible 705/81
fumowsly *adv.* angrily 705/38
furlong *n.* unit of linear measurement (approx. 200 m.) 1008/39
furnyshid *v. p.p.* equipped 834/22
furrid *v. p.p.* provided with fur-trimmed garments (as a mark of office) 870A/61
fustian, -yan, fostian *n.* cloth made from cotton, flax or wool 732/14, 732/44; bedspread made of fustian 930/20. **fustiens, -yans** *pl.* 64/170, 123/108, 930/15
fye *see* **fee**

gaynseyd *v. p.p.* refuted 88/54
galawnte *n.* swaggerer, fop 128/51. **galantys** *pl.* 339/68

galey *n.* seagoing vessel with both sails and oars 394/38
gallyd *v. p.p.* chafed, made sore (by harness) 285/34
ganyngall *n.* spice made from powdered root 209A/55
gardevyandes, gardyuyans *n. pl.* boxes or trunks 259/22, 414/8
gar(n)yson, -isson *n.* garrison, armed force 284/18, 412/24; household 323/17,
garnisond *v. p.p.* garrisoned 412/29
garnyssh(e, garneys *n.* set of a dozen dishes 123/137, 166/30, 208/4
garthe *n.* saddle-girth 704A/18. **gerthis** *pl.* 732/107
gaudied *v. p.p.* decorated 230/187
gaudys *n. pl.* large ornamental beads 94/5
gauntelettys *n. pl.* gloves of chainmail or plate 741/22
geylyng fattys *see* **fates, fattys**
geynsstonde *v.* oppose 413/44
generallté *n.* general provision 537/15
gentils, -elys *n. pl.* persons of substance, landowners 456A/18, 459/20
gereue *v. pr. 3pl.* distress 203/39
germayn *adj. cosyn* ~ first cousin 646A/8
ger(r)e, geere *n.* things, equipment, goods 150/15, 175/30, 220/15; clothes 132/14; affair, matter 177/15, 315/18; behaviour 705/15
gerthis *see* **garthe**
gesernys *n. pl.* battle axes 36/45
gesseron *n.* coat made of scale armour 741/22
gyde, gwye, gwyd *v.* attend to 243/62; guide, lead 351/23; ~ *me* conduct myself 338/55
gidyn(g, gydyng, -ing, guydyng *vbl. n.* management 166/7, 180/112; behaviour, conduct 116/6, 158/15, 189/46, 258/1
gyf(f)t(e, yefte, yiffte, *n.* bestowal 1013/58; right to bestow (an ecclesiastical office) 239/3; payment for service 779/23; *dede of* ~ document transferring property 33/14, 852/30. **yeftes** *pl.* gifts 210/19
gilyngfat, gylyng fat *see* **fates**
gille *n.* girl, woman 77/188
gynger *n. grene* ~ undried ginger preserved in syrup 425/27–8, 923/28
gypcer *n.* ornamented pouch attached to a belt 58/14
girdill *n.* belt 230/131. **girdilles** *pl.* 123/75
gyrte *v. p.p.* encircled (by a belt) 125/16
gyse *n.* manner, custom 83/12
gystis *n. pl.* joists 14/27
glaser *v.* polish, burnish 278/41
gleves, -yfes, -yves *n. pl.* spears 36/23, 40/39, 48/60
glysteryng *v. pr. p.* glistening, shiny 258/13
glose *n. wip-outen* ~ truthfully 62/15
glosours *n. pl.* flatterers 1037/33
gnattys *n. pl.* gnats, horseflies 348/8
gode *n.* property, goods, etc. 124/10, 181/30
godewyf *n.* mistress of the household 132/12
godsip *see* **gossip**
gofe *see* **yef**
gold *n. gret* ~ a large sum of money 649/8
gonne *n. potte* ~ short wide-barrelled gun 259/10
gonnere *n.* gunsmith 256/2
good *adv.* very, thoroughly 168/41
goodly *adv.* at all, in any way 443/15
gorget *n.* armour covering the front of the neck 766/93. **gorgettes** *pl.* 64/219
gossip, godsip *n.* godparent 294/18; friend 485/21. **gossippes** *pl.* companions 692/18
gostly *adj.* spiritual 443/3
goun, govn(n)e *n.* cloak 931/44; lawyer's gown, *fig.* the legal profession, the law 514/5, 552/15
gouernaunce *n.* behaviour, demeanour 2/6
gove, govyn *see* **yef**
grapeys *n. pl.* seals 816/15
gramercy, gremercy *n. & interj.* thanks 774/50; thanks to 4/45
grasyows *adj.* complaisant, well-disposed 203/53
gra(u)ndam, grauntdam(e *n.* grandmother 203/40, 208/2, 222/20, 285/25
graunsir, -syre, -cer, grawnsyre *n.* grandfather 128/24, 585/3, 657/3; elderly relative (here, uncle) 943/12. **grawntsyers** *gen.* 216/34
graue *v.* engrave 37/7
gravore *n.* engraver 772/13
greable *adj.* suitable 589/17
greddyron, gredeyron, -yren *n.* grill for roasting 195A/28, 195B/31, 925/54
gree *n. in* ~ willingly 380/53, 490/14; *prennes en* ~ accept in good grace 270/43
green *adv.* newly 285/5
greynes, grenys *n. pl.* grains, crops 72/8; spices 209A/56
greynyng *vbl. n.* settlement, closing of accounts 1005/59
greynys *n. pl.* different shades of green 123/130
gremercy *see* **gramercy**
gremyth *v. pr. 3sg.* pains 351/31
grenwax(e, grene wax *n.* fine sealed with the green wax used by the Exchequer 195B/68, 215/18, 340/26
gresyngges *vbl. n.* flight of stairs 230/148
gresis *n. pl.* steps 259/59
gret(e, grett(e *adj.* overbearing, aggressive 130/23, 138/24; familiar 181/9, 245/32; *a/in* ~ a/in great quantity 221/20, 728/10–11, 767/44
grete *n.* essence 3/27
grief *n.* grievance 294/38

gronyng *v. pr. p.* suffering 151/23
gropyde *v. pa.* enquired closely 952/12
grosser *n.* wholesale dealer 354/89
grote *n.* silver coin equivalent to four pence 200/45, 313/30, 921/4. **grotes** *pl.* 71/21
ground(e, grownd(e *n.* originator 395/10; reason, justification 579/47; substance 872/1; pasture 648/19
grounde *v.* prove, justify, establish 579/3. **groundeth** *pr. 3sg.* 578/15. **grownded** *p.p.* 518/14, 601/13
grounded *see* **ouer grounded**
grow(e *v.* accrue 541/13, 894/37. **growe** *subj.* 556/14. **grovyng** *pr. p.* working, cultivating 812/21. **growen** *p.p.* accrued 589/17; overgrown 547/23
growndage *n.* levy on vessels coming to port or shore 778/28
growndes, grewndys *n. pl.* greyhounds 282/63, 288/32
growte *n.* infusion of malt 259/48
grudger *n.* complaint 747/21
grudgyng, grutchyng *vbl. n.* resentment 41/24, 460A/1
grugge, grwge *v.* complain 167/39, 914/148. **grudge** *pr. 3pl.* 638/6; find fault 894/19. **grutched** *pa.* 624/16
guerdon *v.* reward 1021/4. **guerdoonned** *p.p.* compensated 570/8
guydyng *see* **gidyn(g**
gunstonys *n. pl.* stone cannon balls 906/headn.
gwye, gwyd *see* **gyde**

ʒ- *see under* **y-**

ha *see* **han**
habeas corpus *n.* writ requiring the appearance of a person in court 181/15, 556/7, 737/7
habere facias seisinam *n.* writ securing a plaintiff's repossession of seized property 937/83
habilled *v. p.p.* equipped or clothed 396/9
haborioun *n.* coat of mail 880/53. **haberions, -yons, habyrions,** *pl.* 64/224, 497/7, 906/headn.
haddyd *see* **han**
haght *see* **owythe**
hake-neye, haukeney *n.* small riding-horse 274/61, 666/13
hald *see* **hold**
half(e)dele, haluendele *n.* half part 252/133, 254/19, 816/15
halys, alys *n. pl.* temporary structures in an encampment 414/6, 8
halmerrey *see* **almary**
halmes-dede *see* **almes**
Halowmesse, Halwemasday, Alhalwetyde *n.* All Saints' Day, 1 November 443/17, 831/28, 939/11
haltyng *v. pr. p.* limping 130/21
haluendele *see* **half(e)dele**
hamper, Hanupere *n.* Chancery department that received fees for processing documents 381/49, 1036/12
han, a(n, ha *v.* have 16/22, 81/8, 181/29 433/3. **han** *pr. 1pl.* 521/8. **han** *pr. 3pl.* 582/24. **a** *ipv.* 178/39. **han** *pa.* 600/33. **ad** *pa.* 116/20. **abe** *p.p.* have been 40/23. **hante, hauyd** *inf.+ pron.* have it 433/11, 937/49. **haddyd** *pa.+ pron.* had it 433/19
han *indef. art.* an 59/13
hande *n. in* ~ dealing 414/39–40; *felle on* ~ negotiated 728/29
handegownes *n. pl.* small portable firearms 195B/36
handelyng *vbl. n.* possession 184/48
hanffull *n.* hand's breadth (equal to four inches) 248/105
hangyng *vbl. n.* unresolved state 548/11
hangyth *v. pr. 3sg.* awaits resolution 627/18. **hange** *pr. 3pl.* are outstanding 688/14. **hangyng** *pr. p.* outstanding, pending 601/12, 936/7; ~ *in* pertaining to 49/19
hant *v. pa.* pulled 283/36
hante *see* **han**
Hanupere *see* **hamper**
hap *v. subj.* might occur 86/32
happe *v.* clothe 77/4
happe *n. in* ~ perhaps 212/17. **happys, -is** *pl.* misfortunes 209A/40, 306/27
happely, haply *adv.* possibly 280/21, 287/6, 663/18
harbyger *n.* household officer who rides ahead to arrange accommodation 613/4
hard *n.*[1] *-ys* (*gen.*) heart's 203/74
hard *n.*[2] *of* ~ with difficulty 627/10
hard *v. see* **heryn**
harde *adv.* completely 269/6
hardyly *adv.* emphatically 705/57
harlot(te *n.* miscreant, villain 492/7, 997/8
harmeles, -ez *adj. save* ~ keep from being liable 111/12, 114/8–9, 225/28, 245/15
harmys *n. pl.* losses 354/69
harnesse, -ys(se, herneys *n.* armour 132/61, 180/11, 181/12, 231/49, 799/5; ornament 929/46
harnest *n.* earnest, pledge 852/21
harnysed, -esshet, herneisid, -ishede, -yshid *v. p.p.* adorned, decorated 123/78, 230/120, 732/63, 123, 153
harond *see* **hera(u)nd**
harpyd *v. pa.* talked continually 301/15
harrawd *see* **herault**
hartyest *see* **hertty**

harwes *n. pl.* harrows 931/35
harwyn, herye *v.* harrow 200/14, 912/16, 931/07
Hasse *n.* ~ *Wednysday* Ash Wednesday 118/17
hasty, asti *adj.* harsh 211/8; urgent 114/4
hastylare *adv. comp.* sooner 177/24
hate *adv.* promptly 175/32
hatlase *n.* cord attached to a hat 394/25
haughe *n.* hawthorn berry; *not worth an* ~ not of any value at all 461/48
hauyd *see* **han**
haukeney *see* **hake-neye**
haulte *adj.* great, good 289/39
haunse *v. subj.* might raise, increase (as part of a financial negotiation) 728/20
havore *n.* behaviour, conduct 310/33
hawnt *n.* aunt 394/54
haxed *see* **axe**
hed *see* **he(e)d**
hede shete *n.* cover for the head of a bed 123/109. **hedshytes** *pl.* 195A/13
heded, -yd *see* **heede**
hedyre-toward, hyddre-towardys *adv.* until now 198/23, 244/3
he(e)d *n. of your owne* ~, *of hyr awne* ~, *on hys owne* ~ personally 79/2, 172/16–17, 331/9, 983/43; *vpon myn* ~ (swore) on my life 510/6
heede *v. imp.* behead 653/10. **heded, -yd, hefded** *p.p.* beheaded 263/14, 319/15, 674/10, 961/7
heedely *adv.* hastily 861/62
heer *see* **her(e**
heel(l)e *see* **hele**
hefded *see* **heede**
hegge *n.* border 925/52
hey *see* **ey**
hey *adj.* high 22/1
heyer *n.*[1] heir 150/29. **heyers** *pl.* ~ *malys* male heirs 408/9
heyer, heyre *n.*[2] air, environment 293/18, 384/4. **eyeres** *pl.* 144/35
heygh *n.* hay 72/82
heyght *n. in the* ~ on the top 68/10
heyl(e, heyll *adj.* healthy 441/55, 443/49, 573/18, 628/23
heyleche *adv.* earnestly 433/20
heyne, heyghne *v.* raise 71/10, 178/30. **heyned** *p.p.* 230/14
heyre *see* **heyer** *n.*[2]
heyre determyner *see* **oyer and determyner**
heyrne *n.* errand 153/8
heysyte *n.* eyesight, presence 443/55
heyued *see* **hevieth**
heywardys *n. pl.* agricultural overseers 22/20
hele, heel(l)e *n.* health 84/4, 121/6, 286/28, 321/10, 415/5
helt *n.* health 131/115
helle *v.* cover 22/2
helme *n.* helmet 901B/174
hem *pron.* him 73/23, 643/26
hend *n.* end; *mad an* ~ reached an agreement 474/18
hendere *adj. comp.* closer (to having) 551/18
he-now *see* **inow**
hepe *n.*[1] measure of grain or malt 77/93
hepe *n.*[2] pruning knife; *by the* ~ *or by the croke* somehow or other 1003/31
her *n.* lord; *myn* ~ sir (*Dutch* mynheer) 338/65
herable *adj.* arable 913/10
herault, harrawd *n.* go-between (for lovers) 236/25; official messenger, attendant 692/22
hera(u)nd, harond, herden *n.* errand, message, business 233/13, 645/7, 10, 729/14
herbeforn *adv.* before this time 626/4
herd *n.*[1] herdsman 443/22
herd *n.*[2] earth 876/30
herden *see* **hera(u)nd**
here *see* **er**
her(e, heer *pron.* their 5/11, 17/23, 53/7, 932/16
here-affore *adv.* before this time 92/16
hereditamentes *n. pl.* inherited elements 252/148
herye *see* **harwyn**
heryn, hire *v.* hear 48/62; listen, gather information 463/29. **hard** *pa.* heard of 35/10
herken *v.* hear, gather 584/11
herneys *see* **harnesse**
herneisid, -ishede, -yshid *see* **harnysed**
hert-brennyng *n.* heartache, anguish 132/9
her-to-foor, heer-to-foore *adv.* previously, before 264/39, 266/14
hertty *adj.* loyal 167/16. **hartyest** *superl.* 83/6
hes(s)e *see* **ease**
hevedy *adj.* impetuous 705/81
hevy, heuy, evy *adj.* displeased 5/101, 737/66; dejected 128/67, 212/4; ~ *of* sad about 176/21; distressing 126/10
hevieth, hevyeth *v. pr. 3sg.* troubles 775/6, 796/11. **heyued** *pa.* increased 1007/47 **hevyed** *p.p.* grieved 689/17, 888/54
hevyly *adv.* dejectedly 436/10
hevynes(se, heuenys *n.* sorrow 175/7, 181/27, 397/6, 688/13
hewen *v. p.p.* cut down 5/7; hacked 196/44
heweres *see* **ewers**
hewld *see* **hold**
hyddre-towardys *see* **hedyre-toward**
hye, higth *v.* hurry, hasten 338/50, 447/17, 631/14. **hye** *imp.* 327/41. **hyid, hythid, hyghed** *pa.* 149/24, 298/13, 322/26
hyer *n. scole* ~ payment for schooling 227/32
hyghed *see* **hye**

hyght, hyȝht *v. p.p.* called 14/10; promised 985/13
hym *pron.* them 164/19
hyrdyllys *n. pl.* fencing panels made of interwoven twigs 169/26
hire *see* **heryn**
hythid *see* **hye**
ho *see* **ho(o**
hobbyllers *n. pl.* light-armed horsemen 803/11
hoby *n.* small or slow-walking horse 777/3
hodermoder *n. in* ~ clandestinely 58/11
hoggastre *n. pl.* young male sheep 731/5
hoggys *n. pl.* young unsheared sheep 195A/61, 195B/69, 880/70
hokeware *n.* ? oak mast, acorns 229/23
Hokmonday *n.* the second Monday after Easter 667/3
hold *n.* captivity 392/11
hold *v.*[1] keep 204/17. **hold** *subj.* should persist 74/18. **holde** *imp.* keep 256/15. **hewld** *pa.* considered 404/17. **hold, hald** *p.p.* held, kept 143/3, 486/8; considered 140/8
hold(en *v.*[2] *p.p.* obliged, duty bound 454/23, 792/11
hole *adj.* together, as a body 168/16; steadfast 332/12, 477/2; cured, healed 346/35, 507/19
holydom(e *n.* holy relics 428/8, 901B/121, 977/4
Holy Rode day *n.* feast of the Exaltation of the Cross, 14 September 987/5
holond cloth *n.* Dutch linen 195A/46
holpe(n, -(p)yn *v. p.p.* helped 205/55, 209A/30, 209B/30, 509/4
holsom *adj.* well disposed 1037/11
hom *see* **ho(o**
homage *n.* allegiance or payment made to a feudal lord 129/44. **homages** *pl.* 794/12
homager(e *n.* one who owes feudal allegiance or dues 43/8, 449/9. **homagers** *pl.* 888/48
hom(e)ly(e *adv.* openly, plainly 136/32, 439/34, 540/2; ~ *vpon* familiar with 944/14
hondely, ondly *adv.* only 162/15, 518/32, 641/5
hone *n.* whetstone; *be set so vp-on the* ~ been informed so pointedly of the situation 163/21
hone *see* **on**
honest *adj.* respectable 230/50
honestly *adv.* honourably 230/49
ho(o, how, quo *rel. pron.* who 42/16, 122/63, 131/81, 200/50, 203/23. **hom** *obj.* whom 88/18. **hooys, hos** *poss.* whose 46/1, 66/11
hoorys *see* **hores**
hope *v. pr. 1sg.* believe, think 126/32. **hopyd** *p.p.* 21/4
hopys *n. pl.* hoops 11/44
hores, hoorys *n. pl.* whores, ill-reputed women 129/25, 264/63
horsyd *v. p.p.* provided with a horse 364/14, 374/8, 915/10
horslode *n.* horse-load, unit of quantity (40 bushels) 148/9
horsward *adv. to my* ~ towards my horse 576/1
horte *see* **hurt(e**
hosbonde *n.* household manager 293/16
hostelmentes, hotilementis *n. pl.* equipment, furnishings 387/46, 786/15
hough, ow, qwowe, who(u, whoo *adv.* how 2/34, 19/6, 28/1, 65/25, 66/38, 126/26, 324/65
hought *see* **owythe**
housen *n.pl.* houses 943/24
how *rel. pron. see* **ho(o**
howsyllyd *v. p.p.* administered the sacrament to 327/4
howsold(e *n.* provision of food and drink 238/36, 332/28, 759/26
howte *see* **owyn**
hulke *n.* trading vessel 864/2
hundred(e, -erd, -ere *n.* administrative division of a county 670/4, 882/24; court of a hundred 131/3, 180/14, 185/12
hurlyng *n.* commotion 692/74
hurt(e, horte *n.* wrong, damage, violation of a privilege 122/5, 35; financial loss 285/19, 341/29. **hurtes** *pl.* 812/9
hurte *v.* cause damage (to a project) 119/33. **hvrte** *p.p.* injured (financially or in reputation) 164/8
hus *pron.* us 211/8
husbondis *n. pl.* tenants holding land in addition to that attached to their dwellings 40/84
husbondly *adv.* economically 721/14
husbondry *n.* economical management 208/32, 794/16
husyd, hvsyd *v. p.p.* provided 153/3, 10

j *indef. art.* a 152/32
jee, jen *see* **ey**
jeryns, -nys *n. pl.* irons, shackles 715/4
jlde *n.* aisle 264/20; island 277/53
ylke *pron. euery* ~ every kind of, each 413/47
ille *adj.* bad 72/34
ille *adv.* harshly 436/6
jmages *n. pl.* paintings or statues 196/36
imagyned *v. p.p.* intended 5/30, 810/12
jmmortaysed *see* **morteyzen**
impanellid *see* **panell**
jmparlyd *see* **enparle**
ympe *v.* repair a bird's feather 776/6
imperpetuité, -eté *adv.* forever 54/12, 947/62
impletid *v. p.p.* sued 70A/18
importable, -ille, inportable *adj.* unbearable, ruinous 5/150, 36/58, 387/105, 726/15
importablé *adv.* excessively 634/7
jmportune *adj.* difficult 780/19, 1010/5

imprise *v.* press upon, lobby 447/17
impugne *v.* dispute 1042/11
in, jne *n.* lodging 705/35; lawyers' residence, Inn of Court 332/52
jnbacetour *n.* ambassador, emissary 411/27. **jnbacetours, enbacetours** *pl.* 411/3, 683/20
jnbassat *see* **ambassade**
inbyll *v. subj.* should designate 356/30. **jnbylled** *p.p.* 631/8
inbraceryes *see* **enbraceryе**
inceptor *n.* one who reads for a Master's degree 403/9
incidentes *n. pl.* details 62/17
incontinent, -ynent *adv.* immediately 315/10, 397/6, 652/6, 757/12
incontinently *adv.* immediately 412/25
inconvenyence, -ens, inconuenient *n.* impropriety 306/39, 528/12; mishap 907/43. **inconuenientez, -ces, inconuenyens, jnconvenyentys** *pl.* misfortunes 6/9, 204/25, 228/37, 281/6, 877/9
incorperate *adj. body* ~ corporation, institution 70A/16
indely *adv.* wrongfully 107/10
indewed, -ued *v. p.p.* endowed 60/7, 60/14, 686/5
indifferent, indef(f)erent, endifferent *adj.* impartial 92/17, 202/13, 218/46, 324/33, 479/36
indifferently, indeferently, endifferently *adv.* impartially 202/19, 440/4, 657/15
indisposicion *n.* forms of public disorder 456A/9, state of discontent 999/7
indisposyd *v. p.p.* unruly 984/6
jndyte *see* **endyghtyd**
indoccion *n.* formal installation 239/18
indorcid, indosyd, endossed *v. p.p.* endorsed, certified 71/28, 443/56, 452/9; addressed 176/3, 696/2
indoubted *v. p.p.* certain 747/14
inducte *v.* put in possession of a benefice 578/9
indued *see* **indewed**
indused *v. p.p.* persuaded 72/17
jne *see* **in**
inepaneld *see* **panell**
infeffid, in-feoffyed *see* **enfeffe**
infefment *n.* enfeoffment, granting of property etc. 132/72
inflamyng *v. pr. p.* inspiring 919/3
infraunchesyd *v. p.p.* made free 946/16
ingrosers *n. pl.* monopolizers 71/10
ingrosid *see* **engrose**
jnkyr *n.* anchor, strong pull 337/37
in-mediat *adv.* immediately 914/37
inmorteysing *vbl. n.* alienation of property in mortmain 583/11
jnmortese, -eyse *v.* convey or alienate property in mortmain 70A/7, 894/30. **inmortesid** *v. p.p.* 60/8
innyn *v.* store 931/11
innyng *vbl. n.* gathering 931/30
in-panell, panell *v.* enrol on a jury 477/10, 479/35. **inepaneld** *pa.* 867/47. **enpaneld, -ellid, -yd, impanellid** *p.p.* enrolled in a jury 79/10, 391/24, 474/2, 622/9
inportable *see* **importable**
jnportunabill *adj.* burdensome 925/43
inprended *v. p.p.* imprinted 697/24
inquiete, -yet *v.* harass 54/68, 304/43, 912/36. **inqueetyd** *p.p.* deprived 67/25
inquietenesse *n.* uneasiness 206/12
jnquietyng *vbl. n.* harassment 912/33
instaunce, -ans, enstaunce *n.* initiative, prompting 456A/5, 642/7, 841/9, 845/20
institucion *n.* appointment to spiritual duties 239/18
jnstrumentys *n. pl.* documents 282/67
insu(e)rid, inswryd *see* **ensure**
jntendementz *n. pl. dubble* ~ ambiguous meanings, equivocation 543/4
int(e)resse, jntres, entrest *n.* legal claim, right 242/57, 249/10, 310/19, 312/23; benefit 54/66; source of support 682/32
interlych *adv.* earnestly 517/2
interpretour *n.* mediator 645/22
interupte *v.* interfere with legal possession of property 247/5. **inter(r)upted** *p.p.* 122/24, 914/33
in-to *prep.* as far as 178/14; until 324/36
jntreté *n.* persuasion 380/46
jntrete *v.* persuade 380/47. **intreted, -yd, -it, entretyd, -tid** *p.p.* persuaded 127/28; dealt with 188/16, 238/41, 488/23, 730/6
iopardie, ioupardit *see* **jopart**
iorny *see* **jornay**
jpedemye *n.* epidemic disease 269/37
irk, vrke *adj.* weary 765/36, 1037/50
is *pron.* his 643/40, 652/40
yssant *adj.* proceeding from 925/76
issith *v. pr. 3sg.* ~ *ouute* comes and goes 48/35. **issued** *pa.* ~ *owt* made a sortie, went out 283/36
issue *n.* point of law 454/10. **isswys, -ewes, -uys, ysshueys** *pl.* fines 322/18, 337/13, 471/7; income 54/133, 993/6
iwys(s)e *adv.* certainly 115/6, 415/15

jack(k)e, jakk *n.* quilted defensive jacket 195A/39, 195B/43; ~ *defensable* 444/39. **jackes, jakkes, -ys** *pl.* 36/23, 130/6, 325/19, 444/28
jakked *v. p.p.* armed in a quited jacket 40/8
jangelyng *n.* dispute 679/15
jangled *v. p.p.* argued 566/18

jape, iape *n.* joke, trifling matter 109/27, 145/11, 211/6, 456/14
jape, jaape *v.* deceive 175/27, 469/19
jatys see **ȝattys**
jelosye *n.* partiality, solicitude 749/39
jentilnes *n.* gentility, good breeding 1013/58
ieo fayll *n.* error in legal proceedure 534/10
joyntur, -tour, jonter, -ore, juntor, *n.* jointure (estate held jointly by a married couple and promised to the wife after the husband's death) 32/7, 300/12, 376/1, 657/6, 777/23
jopart, iopardie *v.* risk 288/38, 391/1, 659/31. **joparte** *pr. 1sg.* 264/8. **ioupardit** *p.p.* ventured 567/23
joparté, iopardie, joubert *see* **jupardy**
jopartous, -ows *adj.* dangerous, risky 210/28, 285/26
jornade *n.* short outer garment 339/39
jorney(e, -ay, -y, jurné, iorny, iurney *n.* day 66/32, 72/15; day's work, task 86/43, 456/14; battle 317/18, ~ *batayl* principal engagement 1023/7; labour (in childbirth) 371/17. **jornays, -és, jurnays** *pl.* deeds, undertakings, tasks 602/11, 925/29, 35
jostys *n. pl.* ~ *of pese* jousts fought with blunted weapons for prizes 330/18
jowelhows *n.* prison 281/28
jument *v. p.p.* ? estimated 178/21
junyng *vbl. n.* preparation, drawing up 615/13
junkeryes *n. pl.* banquets 444/19
juntor *see* **joyntur**
jupardy, -ardé, -perte, iopardie, joparté, joubert *n.* danger, risk 158/4, 180/86, 188/6, 203/72, 624/33, 658/28
jurny, -é, -ey, -ays *see* **jorney(e**
iustifie *v.* govern 229/33; adjudicate 478/5. **justefied** *p.p.* brought to justice 870D/50

kade *see* **cade**
kayteff *n.* wretch 390/2
kalked *v. p.p.* made astrological calculations 534/14
Kandylmas *see* **Candelmesse**
karlys *see* **charl**
kasket, -tys *see* **caskett**
keler(y)s, kylers *n. pl.* vessels for cooling liquids 11/24, 195A/23, 195B/26
kemell *n.* a tub used in brewing 11/44
ken *n.* family 73/17
kepe *v.* take care of 153/12; ~ . . . *corte* hold a session of court 179/9, 189/4; ~ *here day* honour their commitment to attend court 101/4. **kepe** *pr. 1sg.* undertake 306/39. **kepyth** *pr. 3sg.* ~ *hyr . . . close* behaves circumspectly 160/11. **kept** *p.p.* ~ *foorthe* maintained 347/9
kerchy(e, -ei, kersche, cerche(y *n.* woman's headscarf or veil 195A/46, 195B/51, 200/47, 201/51, 732/125, 732/131, 179. **kouercheffys** *pl.* 354/65
kertyll *see* **kirtill**
kervere *n.* carver at table, butler 970/10
kervyl(e *see* **carvell**
kest *see* **cast**
kete *v.* get 199/32, 473/17
kye *n.* cattle 971/41
kylers *see* **kelers**
kylyng fatys *see* **fates**
kyll *n.* *lyme* ~ kiln for calcining limestone 473/68
kylte *v. p.p.* killed 124/3
kynderkyn *n.* cask 11/32
kyrt *v. p.p.* turned around 443/40
kirtill, kyrtyl, kertyll *n.* tunic (often worn over a smock) 123/116, 624/10, 732/122
kyt *v.* cut, excavate 547/21
klenly *adv.* expertly 37/5; *as adj. see* **clenly**
knedyng fatys *see* **fates**
knyghten service *n.* land held on condition of military service 996/70
knyt fye *see* **fee**
knytted *v. p.p.* associated, related 902/21
knopp(e *n.* ornament on a rosary 94/6; ornamental knob 123/49, 230/117
know *v.* acknowledge 540/25
knowelle *v. p.p.+ adv.* well-known 665/26
knowlacheyd, -ge(y)d *v. p.p.* acknowledged 118/2, 544/5; confessed 154/61
knowyng *v. pr. p.* ~ *to* known to 71/17
kok *n.* cock; *kast all at the* ~ not bother, neglect 363/21
kolerake *n.* rake for cinders 123/148
komon *see* **comown**
kon *see* **con(n(e**
konynere-closse *n.* rabbit warren 395/4
konyth *see* **con(n(e**
konnyng, kunnyng, connyng *adj.* knowledgeable, skilful 238/5, 332/58, 345/32
konsyens *n.* sense of guilt 216/16
kontré *see* **contray**
kouercheffys *see* **kerchy(e**
kowe *n.* chough, bird of crow family 650/18
kowmb *see* **comb**
kownsell *see* **councel(l**
krotte *n.* ? knob 313/8
kun *see* **con(n(e**
kunnyng *see* **konnyng**
kwte *n.* *of iij* ~ reduced to one third by boiling 349/29

laberers *n. pl.* proponents 203/23
labore, -ur(e *v.* appeal 154/62; perform 163/18, 215/21; work upon 518/30. **laboryd, -id, -ured** *p.p.* appealed 231/5, 273/2; *stronge* ~

much solicited 1029/22; ~ *of hir child* went into labour 491/38
laboryng *ppl. adj.* devout 248/29
labour, -wr(e *n.* endeavour 181/6, 660/17; legal proceedings 192/72.
lache *n.* ~ *pannys* pans to hold jelly-like dishes 64/193
laches *adj.* negligent 652/10
lachesyd *v. p.p.* neglected 379/5
lacyd *v. p.p.* compressed 269/23
Lady Day *n.* Feast of the Annunciation, 25 March 701/20
layd *see* **lithe**
layer *n.* water jug 923/92, 942/6
lambe, lom *n.* lambskin 732/82, 98
Lammes *n.* ? Lammas Day or Lammastide (1 August) 1037/6 (but cf. Index *sub* Lammas)
langage *n.* discourse, talk 138/24, 145/4, 236/17; *fayre* ~ emollient words 141/43
langager *n.* one given to mendacious talk, liar 932/22
langedebiefes *n. pl.* pikes with broad double-edged blades 491A/14
langore *n.* disquiet 469/23
lansman *n.* fellow-countryman (*Dutch*) 340/38
lant *v.* reward 338/65, 340/38
lape *v.* wrap 389/9
large *adj.* intemperate, extravagant 129/26, 243/64, 263/10; extensive 242/37; generous 275/21. **largeest** *superl.* most generous 352/50
largely *adv.* extensively 190/14, 773/23, 782/38; much 25/39, 192/10, 200/27; disparagingly 132/67. **largelyere** *comp.* more 200/28
larom, -um belle *n.* bell rung to sound a call to arms 567/23, 1023/27
last(e *n.* dozen barrels 826/6, 852/21
latchesnes *n.* negligence 399/9
late, lathe *adv.* recently 89/31, 230/73, 446/34
late, -yn *v. p.p.* let 154/36, 228/16. **latyd** *inf.+ pron.* let it 124/9
latise werke *n.* decorated with a lattice-pattern 123/129
latitat *n.* writ summoning to the King's Bench a defendant who is believed to lie concealed 552/9
laton, -(e)yn *n.* latten (alloy of various metals) 64/188, 123/139, 195A/14, 929/59
latward *adv.* recently 346/3
launde, -wnde *n.* area of open ground 274/67, 767/7
laungegays *n. pl.* lances 200/19
lavas, -ues *adj.* extravagant 205/15, 802/12
lavendré *n.* laundry 259/14
lawhyd *see* **lowh**
lawn *n.* fine linen 732/125
lawnde *see* **launde**
lawre *n. pl.* laurel trees 780/44
laxe *n.* attack of diarrhoea 399/21
leche *n.* physician 425/28. **lechys** *pl.* horse doctors 345/33
lechecrafte *n.* medical treatment 346/10
lechyng *vbl. n.* ~ *knyfys* kitchen knives 123/146
lede *v.* transport 220/15. **led** *p.p.* 325/10
led(d)e, leed *n.* cauldron 195A/22, 195B/25, 259/47. **ledes** *pl.* 259/50
leder *n.* leather 64/42
leeff *n.* leave 275/35
leeke *n. soos* ~ sauce vat 11/32
lefe *adj.* willing 872/26
leffe *adv. had as* ~ *a-lmost* would almost as willing 183/26
lef(f)ull *adj.* lawful 65/24, 309/28
leftyd *see* **leven**
lefully *adv.* lawfully 925/7
legat *n.* legacy 1049/42. **legattys** *pl.* 384/39
legende *n.* collection of saints' lives 230/54; narrative 557/12
leggeth *v. pr. 3sg.* alleges 759/59
legys *n. pl.* leagues (units of distance, about three miles) 411/19
leyd *see* **lithe**
leye, -yhe *v. pr. 3pl.* lie 269/21; ~ *to me* accuse me of 296/43
leyester *n.* clerk qualified to lecture on the scriptures 901B/136
leyn *v.* line 135/39
lekyd *v. pa.* favoured 167/49
lenage *n.* family 704/11
lenclothe see **lynclothe**
lerned, -yd *v. p.p.* informed, taught 515/4, 694/30
lesyng *n.*[1] a lie 582/35. **lesynges** *n. pl.* 475/16
lesynges ***n.***[2] *pl.* gleanings, minor items of news 4/53
les(s)e, leys, loce *v.* lose 24/17, 204/39, 216/19*(2nd.)*, 650/48; destroy 203/79; waste 118/8, 206/11, 650/39. **lesse** *subj.* should lose 216/19 *(1st.)*
lesse *v.* diminish 206/4
lesse *adj. comp.* lower in social rank 449/13
lesse *conj.* lest, in case 394/21; ~ *þan(ne,* ~ *than* unless 18/5, 220/16, 432/48
lete *n.* court leet 189/36, 508/11; area under the jurisdiction of a court leet 778/25
letour *see* **litter**
lett(e *n.* delay 364/12, 616/8
lett(e *v.* hinder, prevent 37/12, 152/37, 202/16; forsake, leave off 685/23; delay 378/28, 462/3. **lettyng** *pr. p.* delaying 538/7. **lettet** *pa.* delayed 506/18. **letted, -id, -yd** *p.p.* hindered, prevented 24/19, 54/54, 180/30, 539/18
letter *n.* hinderer 248/58

lettyng *vbl. n.* hindering, preventing 203/45, 681/3; hindrance 422/20, 582/4
leud(e *see* **lewd(e**
leudnes *see* **lewdnes**
leuacion *n.* elevation of the Host in the Mass 129/3
levand *ppl. adj.* living, alive 739/6
leue *adj.* alive 335/13
levee *n.* recovery of a debt 1006/21
leven, leue *v.* remain 25/31; ~ *of* abandon 333/12. **levyt** *pr. 3sg.* remains, is left over 394/48. **leftyd** *pa.+ pron.* left it 209A/51
lever, -yr, leuer, -yr(e, -ir *adv.* rather, sooner 25/35, 72/14, 168/16, 241/8, 508/28; better 109/12, 493/26; *he had* ~ he would prefer 88/44; *had* ~ *þan* would have preferred 131/65
lever(e)y, -uery *see* **lyvery**
levest *adj. superl.* most preferred 226/22, 288/7, 568/14
levyn *see* **lewyn**
leuyng *vbl. n.* income 322/16
levis, -ys *n. pl.* leaf designs 64/131; standard widths (of fabric) 123/110
levyt *see* **leven**
lewd(e, leud(e, lewit *adj.* ignorant, foolish 89/22, 180/33, 203/39, 220/30, 566/40; unsuitable 331/19. **lewder** *comp.* more useless 456/14. **lewdeste** *superl.* lowest, most unworthy 450/29
lewdly *adv.* foolishly 72/137
lewdnes(se, leudnes *n.* incompetence 72/60; foolishness 179/25, 203/73
lewey *v.* levy, collect 122A/2
lewyn, leuyn *v. pr. 3pl.* live 209A/51, 209B/51
lewit *see* **lewd(e**
lybarate, liberate et allocate *n.* writ or warrant for payment 432/27, 543/8. **liberates, -tz** *pl.* 565/33, 572/14
lyberal *adj.* abundant 643/28
lyberdes *n. pl.* leopards 943/74
libertés *n. pl.* area over which privilege, jurisdiction etc. extends 803/20
lycence *v.* authorise formally 304/37
licly *see* **lykly**
lyepe *v. pa.* leapt 312/41
Lyere *n.* cloth made at Lierre 125/8
lyffdayes, lyve-dayes, lyfe-dayes *n. pl.* lifespan, lifetime 48/51, 160/8, 576/14
liffelode, lyffelode, lyflod *see* **lyvelod**
lyfte, -fft *n.* expulsion, removal 395/18; *a* ~ *at* opposition to 248/68; *geue not hym a* ~ do not oppose him (? referring here to J. Gloys) 395/19
lyfte *v.* expel, remove 395/16. **lyftyd** *pa.* 395/17
lyge *adj.* liege, loyal 460A/8
lyght *v. p.p. see* **lyted**
lyght *adj.* careless 639/4. **lyghtest** *superl.* most carefree 352/52
lightly *adv.* cursorily 77/169; easily, readily 705/88
lyke *v.* please 231/52
lykly, lycly *adj.* suitable 77/154, 277/13, 289/20; good-looking 248/108; promising 510/11
lymebrenner, lym-brennere *n.* one who calcines lime 136/15, 765/28
limityd, lymyted *v. p.p.* specified 60/108, 123/21, 300/6; appointed 230/157
lynclothe, lenclothe *n.* linen cloth 732/95, 102. **lyncloys** *pl.* 732/89
lyne *n.* linen 64/64
lysen *n.* license 222/26
lyst *v. pr. 2sg.* wish, please 236/23. **lyst, list** *pr. 3sg.* 77/34, 129/65. **lyst** *pr. 3pl.* 40/37. **lyst** *p.p.* 161/17
lyste *adv. at the* ~ at least 309/33
lystere *n.* dyer 140/5
lystys *n. pl.* enclosed area for jousting 316/40
lyted *v. pa.* dismounted 876/10. **lyght** *p.p.* put, gone 64/89
literys *n. pl.* cargo barges 725/16
lithe *v. pr. 3sg.* lies, is located 56/19. **layd, leyd, loyn** *p.p. do* ~ *in* put in place 190/27; ~ *vp,* ~*ought* held in safe keeping 210/3, 18, 377/19; remained inactive 749/4
lytys *n. pl.* windows 148/16
lytely *see* **lightly**
litter, letour *n. hors(se* ~ bed carried by horse 301/17, 614/13
lyve, lyue, lyffe *n.* lifetime 357/11; *on* ~ alive 243/1, 261/7
lyve-dayes *see* **lyffdayes**
lyvelod, lyffelode, liffelode, lyflod, lylode, lyuelood *n.* property (as a means to support life) 31/14, 119/20, 199/19, 208/30, 340/34, 648/7; substance, consequence 461/42
lyvery, lyuer(e)y, liueré, liuerey, lever(e)y, leuery, *n.* delivery 182/33, 246/33; *woordys of* ~ information derived from hearsay 603/4; ~ *of (the) season* legal ceding of possession 54/104, 106; uniform provided by a lord for his servants 138/32, 784/9, ~ *gownys* 83/13; grant of sustenance from a religious house 205/31; *at* ~ (of a horse) being fed 399/20. **leuerés, leveryes** *pl.* livery uniforms 132/65, 156/25
lyueryd *v. pa.* delivered 472/9
loce *see* **les(s)e**
lodere *n.* carrier, porter 196/10, 296/52
lofeday *see* **loveday**
log(g)e *n.* country residence, hunting lodge 180/87, 194/38, 333/50
log(g)yng, -yn *n.* residence 193/11; *ouyr* ~ *kep* ? provided we can remain in possession of our

residence (? here *sc.* Caister) 325/43; ~ *felawe* companion in residence 418/34
loygned *v. p.p.* removed 1013/39
loyn *see* **lithe**
loke *v. imp.* take heed 75/39, 460/67. **lokyth** *pr. 3sg.* ~ *affire* expects 307/6. **lokyd** *pa.* ~ *affire* expected 275/36. **lokyth** *p.p.* ~ *to* taken care of 126/28
lollardy *n.* ~ *of fleshe* idleness, negligence 329/37
lom *see* **lambe**
longyth *v. pr. 3sg.* belongs 239/3. **long** *pr. 3pl.* owe allegiance 205/24, 26. **longyng** *pr. p.* belonging 195A/9
lordsheps *n. pl.* properties 200/5
loseynge *n.* rhombus-shaped stone 64/39
loste *see* **lust**
loth *v.* be reluctant 780/18
lothfull *adj.* unwilling 780/26
loveday, lofeday *n.* day appointed for reconciliation or arbitration 472/33, 582/8
lowh *v. pa.* laughed 776/33. **lawhyd** *p.p.* 248/59
lowly *adj.* humble 176/17
lowly, lowlely *adv.* humbly 175/14, 231/2, 236/23
lowryd *v. p.p.* scowled, frowned 358/36
lucre, lucur *n.* financial advantage, profit 914/63, 1037/33
lust, loste *n.* desire 490/4; lust 395/3
luste *v. pr. 2sg.* wish, please 180/129. **lust(e, -eth** *pr. 3sg.* 121/23, 183/8, 1005/5. **lust** *p.p.* 48/140
lvtyng *vbl. n.* playing on the lute 153/5
lwmysch *adj.* malicious 129/59

macchefatt *see* **mayshfate**
maffaisours *n.* criminals 5/3
magry(e, -ery, -ree, malgré *n.* blame 270/15, 566/45, 1005/98; ~ *in hys heed* despite all he can do 58/6; *haue* ~ *of* bear the ill will of 205/28
mahayme *n.* maim, crime of depriving a person of the use of a limb 491A/51
mahaymed, maymed *v. p.p.* deprived of the use of a limb 491A/29, 745/6
mahuturs *n. pl.* shoulder pieces (of armour) 195B/43
mayled *ppl. adj.* reinforced with chain mail 450/32
mayne *adj.* large 390/9
mayné *see* **meyné**
maynpryce, maymprice *n.* bail 460/8, 460A/22
mayntenaunce, meyntenaunce, meigntenaunce *n.* wrongful interference in others' law suits 457/12, 474/7, 600/29; improper means 584/6
mayntenyng *vbl. n.* wrongful interference 137/3, 181/19
mayntenour *n.* supporter 579/45, 665/12. **meyntenour** one who interferes in others' legal processes 991/31; *pl.* 460/34
mayshfate, macchefatt *n.* vessel used in brewing 195A/22, 195B/26
maistré, maystri *n. no grete* ~, *lytil* ~ not difficult 543/10–11, 705/80. **mastryes** *pl.* assertions of authority 383/34
mak(e *n.* companion, fellow 372/3; mate 791/8; *worldes* ~ earthly spouse 753/10
makyng *vbl. n.* prosperity, advancement 241/21, 780/12
male *n.* bag 77/172, 363/22
male *adj.* evil 1026/14
male-aperte *adj.* presumptuous 700/13
maleys *n.* malice 40/79; hostile acts 205/18
malgré *see* **magry(e**
maligne *v.* speak unfavourably 971/8
malles, -ys *n. pl.* sets of mail armour 64/220 195A/34, 195B/37, 906/headn.
malmesey, malvyseye *n.* sweet wine 211/21, 394/37, 705/5
manaces *n. pl.* threats 881/49
manased, -id *p.p.* menaced 267/17, 494/17
manassing *vbl. n.* intimidation 40/111
mandly *adj.* brave 472/44
maner *n. on here* ~ as they chose 450/22
manhode *n.* courtesy, good manners 867/11
manly *adv.* boldly, openly 129/59; bravely 439/8, 472/24
mantyll *n.* sleeveless overgarment 337/27
manumyse *v.* release (from feudal service) 229/34
maralité *n.* moral conduct 604/2
marc, mark(e(s, markz, ? merch *n. pl.* monetary units (=13s. 4d.) 3/4, 15/5, 25/12, 54/98; ? money, rent 812/11
marchall *n.* military commander 290/18
marchandes, -auntys *n.* trade 220/42; a deal 267/16
marchant, -ande *n.* merchant 152/18; *halffe* ~ middleman, go-between 310/25. **marschandys** *pl.* merchants 394/32
marchaunt *v.* trade, speculate 1009/68
marche, mershe *n.*[1] marshland, meadow 178/25, 30
marchys *n.*[2] *pl.* areas surrounding a town 777/33
marye *v.* conclude a marriage arrangement 790/5
marys *n. pl.* mares 180/8
marre *v.* defeat 181/25. **marrid** *pp.* injured 64/76

marryng *vbl. n.* destruction 241/21
martilage *n.* burial register 924/10
martirs *see* **marterns**
Martismasse *n.* St Martin's day, 11 November 996/12
marterns, -irs, -rons *n. pl.* marten furs 64/86, 123/113, 692/61
marvelouslye *adv.* awe-inspiringly 261/32; excessively 355/11
mase *n.* ? maze 1003/19
mase(e)r *n.* drinking bowl of macer wood 94/7, 923/73. **masers** *pl.* 923/37
mashsterell *n.* implement for stirring mash 11/29
masis, -ys *n. pl.* mace or nutmeg 209/55, 287/dorse
massache *n.* news 171/5. **massonges** *pl.* rumours 66/48
massebook *n.* missal 230/166
mastyrfast *adj.* bound to a master 335/36
mastryes *see* **maistré**
mattokkys *n. pl.* excavating tools 774/19
mawment *n.* lackey, instrument 705/81
mean(e, meen, meyane, meyn, mene, mesne, moene, moyan, moyen *n.* way, means 157/19, 188/2, 204/21, 241/15, 432/57; argument 510/9; intermediary, representative 169/5, 370/33, 711/8, 985/24; intermediary party 432/58, 509/15. **me(a)nys, moyans, -ens** *pl.* means 178/3; inducements 222/23; supplication 339/73, 601/10; arrangement 558/4
meane *adj.* moderate 370/8
meare *n.* mayor 782/23
mede, meede *n.* spiritual reward 248/29; bribe 989/24
medyd *v. p.p.* bribed 134/3
medle, -yll *v.* become involved 537/19, 585/13, 616/4; fight, engage (at sea) 411/24; set out, take action 912/6. **medylyd** *pa.* became involved, interfered 322/39. **medulled, medelid, -ed** *p.p.* administered 646/13; mixed up 77/141; mixed, blended 860/4
meen *see* **meane**
meend *see* **mend(e**
mees *n. pl.* male kinsmen 802/16
mees *n. sg. see* **mes(s)e**
meet(er *see* **mete**
meetly *see* **met(e)ly**
meyane, meyn *see* **mean(e**
meyné, -y, mayné, meny(é *n.* household 268/31, 444/3; company, retinue 199/17, 445/9, 497/17, 613/20
meyntenaunce, meigntenaunce *see* **mayntenaunce**
meyntenour *see* **mayntenour**
meyntynyd *v. p.p.* supported 168/23
melle *v.* become involved 989/78. **mellyth** *pr. 3sg.* interferes 185/41
membres *n. pl.* associated rights 252/148, 947/35
memento *n.* liturgical commemoration 123/29
mend(e, meend *n.*[1] intention, desire 409/52, 413/14, 857/22, 24; memory 726/27
mendes *n.*[2] *pl.* reparations 782/18
mene *see* **mean(e**
menealle, -yall *adj.* ~ *men* household servants 48/21, 277/46, 880/24; ~ *seruaunt(z* 370/37, 524/5
menioure *adj. frere* ~ friar minor, Franciscan 901B/32
meny(e *see* **meyné**
menyng *vbl. n.* intentions 767/55
menys *see* **mean(e**
menyver *n.* squirrel fur 405/16
menuraunce *n.* tenure 122/40
meove, -fe, -vyd *see* **move**
merch *see* **marc**
mercied *see* **amercy**
mercyment *see* **amerciement**
merestake *n.* stake used to mark a boundary 726/25
meritory, merytorie *adj.* beneficial 591/7, 914/116
mershe *see* **marche**
meruaylously *see* **marvelouslye**
merueyll *n.* surprise 444/14
mervylous *adj.* awe-inspiring 261/33
meschef *see* **myschef(f)e**
mescheue *see* **myscheve**
mesne *see* **mean(e**
messe *n.* mass; *Seynt Thomas* ~ St. Thomas's day 178/38
mes(s)e, mees *n.* messuage (house with adjacent outbuildings and grounds), property 17/6, 586/3, 845/3
messombyr *n.* midsummer 433/14
mestlyon *n.* mixture of grains (esp. wheat and rye) 418/7
met(e, meete *n.* provender, food 346/19, 380/56; in proverb (Whiting M475) 583/22, 993/41–2
mete, meet *adj.* suitable 242/44, 374/8, 802/16; ready 412/19. **meeter** *comp.* 354A/15. **metyst** *superl.* 943/9
met(e)ly, meetly *adj.* suitable 103/38, 283/30, 370/4
metly *adv.* moderately 370/10
metesetell *n.* bench 11/40
mevabyl(l *adj.* ~ *godis, godes* ~ personal property 133/12, 692/71–2
meue, -yd, meve, -yd, -id, -yng, -od *see* **move**
mevere *n.* instigator 470/16
mewe *n. in* ~ indoors 348/8

mewyd, mwyd *p.p.* ~ *hawk* hawk that has moulted at least once 354/72, 88
Mighellmasse *n.* St Michael's day, 29 September 1011/20
millefole *n.* yarrow 220/56
mynerys *n. pl. (fig.)* persons who undermine or covertly thwart 283/32
ministracion, mynystracyon, admynestracion *n. letter of* ~ grant of authority to administer the estate of an intestate 160/17, 198/14, 249/25
mynystre, -estere, minist(e)re *v.* administer 198/15, 230/107, 458/14, 604/29. **mynystred, ministrid, mynestred** *p.p.* 210/5, 460A/3, 672/6
mynkys *n.* mink furs 405/9
mynstrour *n.* administrator (of a will) 995/28. **mynestres** *pl.* dealers, contractors 782/6
minush *v.* lessen 899/18. **mynnysshyd** *pa.* reduced 692/28. **minysshed, mynused** *p.p.* taken away 949/27; neglected 914/98
mynusyn[g] *vbl. n.* diminution 978/3
minut *n.* draft document 989/115
myrre *n.* infection of the nose and throat 141/30
myschef(f)e, mesch(i)ef *n.* problem 867/61; mishap 907/43; poverty, deprivation 870D/57; *ask a* ~ bring about a disaster 114/28. **myschefes, -cheves** *pl.* problems 867/62, 870A/54
myscheve, -en, mescheue *v.* harm 45/17, 690/39, 870A/71. **myscheved** *p.p.* 690/37
myschevous *adj.* unjust 617/12
myschevously *adv.* wrongfully 715/13
mysdemyng *vbl. n.* misconception 727/30
mysdemys *n. pl.* misconceptions 1046/152
mysfacyonyng *vbl. n.* damaging 331/17
mystir *n.* necessity, need 751/36
mythful *adj.* almighty 704/2
myvers *n. pl.* ? expensive spice or perfume 741/20
mocyon, -ion, mosyon *n.* initiative, instigation 167/25, 294/30, 377/8; inclination 568/20; proposal, suggestion 574/21
mocyond *v. pa.* suggested to 370/43
mocke *n.* sarcasm 470/35
moderated *v. p.p.* modified 559/12
modrecheppe *n. pl.* ewes that have lambed 195B/67
moene *see* **mean(e**
moeuyng, -eng *see* **move**
moyen, moyan *see* **mean(e**
moyté, moitee *n.* half 854/11, 854/12
mokkyng *vbl. n.* riotous behaviour 653/20
moldyng bord(e *n.* breadmaking board 195A/25, 195B/28
monyche *v. pa.* ordered 783/3
monthes, -ys mynde *n.* commemorative service performed one month after a person's death 123/16, 887/9
moonyd *v. p.p. sore* ~ grievously lamented 261/20
moore *adj. comp.* greater 304/33
moowe *n.* haystack 776/24
morell *n.* dark-coloured horse 990/42
morgage *n. sett . . . to* ~ convey property as security for a loan or agreement 128/56, 205/61; *leyde in* ~ mortgaged 656/19
morken, -yn *v. p.p.* marked 230/124, 320/31
moron *see* **morwyn**
morrey *see* **murrey**
morteisyng, -ysyng *vbl. n.* alienation of property in mortmain 569/35, 570/5, 603/23
morteyzen *v.* alienate in mortmain 603/18. **mortaysyd, -eysed, jmmortaysed** *p.p.* 326/5, 926/27, 62
morwyn, morwne, moron *n.* morning 189/23, 451/15, 584/17
mosyon *see* **mocyon**
mosterdeveleres *see* **musterdevyllres**
mot(e, mought, mvt, mut(e *v.* might, may 30/4, 198/36, 203/73 209A/63, 209B/63, 252/206
moten *pp.* manufactured (malt) 669/3
mou(e, movn, mow(e, mown *v.* be able to 132/57, 140/9, 321/29, 398/10, 440/8, 458/13. **mow** *pr. 3pl.* are able to 14/31, 585/6
mourmur *n.* complaining, discontent 456A/11
mo(u)stres(se *see* **mustyrs**
move, moue, me(o)ve, meofe, meue *v.* apply to 152/12, 294/39,42, 558/18; present, advance 555/12; persuade, influence 45/50, 294/39; annoy 206/12. **moeuyng, -eng, mevyng** *pr. p.* prompting, urging 122A/6, 456A/21, 458/4. **mevyd** *pa.* spoke 154/5, 192/107. **moved, -yd, meovyd, meuyd, mevyd, -id, -od,** *p.p.* spoken to, urged 54/15, 60/45, 116/23, 231/6; persuaded 202/8; proposed 688/20; distressed 119/16; angered 149/16, 184/50, 294/42;
mow(e, mown *see* **mou(e**
mowghtes *n. pl.* moths 123/155
murr(e)y, mor(r)ey *adj.* mulberry-colour(ed) 28/16, 135/39, 195A/39, 331/19
muskadell *n.* sweet wine, muscat 287/dorse
muskeball *n.* ornamental receptacle for musk 123/80, 288/16
musterdevyllres, -develerys, -develys, mvstyrddevyllers, mosterdeveleres *n.* grey woollen cloth (originally from Montivilliers) 28/12, 125/4, 230/190, 692/53, 732/172
mustyrs, mo(u)stres(se *n. pl.* assembly of troops 396/14, 27; *make* ~ *of* assemble forces 396/20; *take þe* ~ inspect the troops 420/31

mut(e, mvt *see* **mot(e**
mwer *n.* ~ *de haye* hawk that has moulted at least once 356/5–6
mwyd *see* **mewyd**
mwsid *v. p.p.* considered 43/15

nage *n.* small horse, pony 348/15
nayle *n.* linear measurement for cloth (equal to 2 inches) 77/7
naked *adj.* unarmed 818/7
nakedly *adv.* candidly, plainly 604/52, 888/26
namely *adv.* especially 447/19, 888/21
napettes *n. pl.* napkins 732/64
natiue *adj.* bound by serfdom 946/9
necessary, nessessare *adj.* suitable 166/6, 844/5; beneficial 220/26
necye *n.* irresponsibility 998/5
neere *see* **nere**
ne(e)t(e, netes *n. pl.* cows, cattle 40/47, 48/73, 182/3, 500/7
negardchepe *n.* niggardliness, parsimony 680/44
nege tole *n.* sharp-edged weapon or object 963/18
ney *adj.* near 184/25
neye *adv.* precisely 66/9
neyre in termyner *see* **oyer and determyner**
nere, nerre, neere *adv.*[1] nearer 177/13, 281/21, 315/23
ner(e *adv.*[2] never, not at all 189/74, 192/17, 193/8, 644/31
nere *adv.*[3] thoroughly, strictly 224/14
nerehand *adv.* almost 692/67, 711/12
nerles *adv.* nevertheless 151/18
nerre *see* **nere**
nes *n.* niece 400/42
nessessare *see* **necessary**
net(e, netes *see* **ne(e)t(e**
nether *adj.* lower 965/26. **nethermest** *spv.* 259/37
neve *adj.* new 192/75
neuir the latyr *adv.* nevertheless 633/4
next *adj.* nearest, closest 400/23
nyere *adv.* near, close by 184/70; almost 198/30
nil *adv.+ v.* ne will, will not 74/45
nisi prius *n.* writ instructing the sheriff to provide a jury at the court of Westminster unless the judges of assize come to the county of jurisdiction beforehand 391/26, 432/45, 453/4
noble, -il(l, -yll *n.* English gold coin (equivalent to 6s. 8d.) 28/23, 72/90, 147/5, 840/3. **nobles, -elys, -yls, -lis** *pl.* 126/7, 280/21, 623/11, 853/6
nogh *see* **no(u)gh**
noy *n.* cry of 'oyez' 508/6
noye *v.* bother, trouble 587/17
noise, -yse *n.* accusation 149/20, 626/10; rumour 4/43, 81/6, 194/28
noise, -yse *v.* report 296/17; accuse 552/17, 600/11. **noyseth, -yth** *pr. 3sg.* 306/36, 679/42. **noyse** *pr. 3pl.* 877/13. **noysyng** *pr. p.* 189/44. **noys(s)ed, -yd, noyced** *p.p.* rumoured, reported 84/5, 168/12, 653/3; accused 127/14, 460A/4; defamed, slandered 5/142, 471/52
noiseful, noysefull *adj.* slanderous, scandalous 584/5, 679/40
noysynges *vbl. n. pl.* accusations 637/6
noysyngly *adv.* slanderously 4/40
nomynale *n.* Latin-English vocabulary book 133/27
non *n.* noon 88/2
non molestando *n.* writ relating to a person molested in violation of the king's grant of protection 543/6
non omittas *n.* clause included in a writ specifying particular obligations in its execution 548/15
nonnage, nownage, nounage *n.* minority 163/55–6, 381/47, 508/9, 886/4
no(o)-thyng(e *adv.* not at all 298/5, 317/34–5, 347/6
no(o)unpier *n.* one who determines an issue when arbitrators disagree 5/54, 56
note *n.* written summary 57/6
notycion *n.* knowledge, information 435/3
noueltés, nouuelteez, -s *n. pl.* news 66/42, 496/5, 541/27; fresh provisions 989/66
no(u)gh *adv.* now 75/29, 77/54, 184/77
nounage *see* **nonnage**
nounpier *see* **no(o)unpier**
nounsewed *v. p.p.* in receipt of an adverse judgement (for failing to produce sufficient evidence) 461/22
nouther *see* **nowther(e**
nowche *n.* brooch, ornament 64/26, 201/50, 640/10. **nowches, -ys** *pl.* 64/15, 298/33
nowder *see* **nowther(e**
nowgty, -tye, -tty, *adj.* wicked 160/30, 162/22, 164/14
nowight *adj.* worthless 855/24
nownage *see* **nonnage**
nowth *adv.* not 126/4, 128/7
nowther(e, -der, -dyr, nouther *conj.* neither 169/41, 202/34, 203/10; nor 127/4, 901A/54
nuncupatif *adj.* oral 901B/11

obite, -ytt *n.* annual remembrance service 230/159, 926/33. **ob(b)ites, -is** *pl.* 924/10, 11; notes of dates of deaths 77/137
obligacion, abligacion *n.* document recording a legally binding agreement 40/122, 129/43, 238/44, 668/12. **obligacions** *pl.* 265/2

obligatory *adj. bill* ~ document recording a legal obligation 865/15
obloquy *n. in* ~ in disgrace, spoken against 244/11
ocapyeng *vbl. n.* taking possession 211/5
occasyons *n. pl.* excuses 558/22
ocupye, okupye *v.* take possession 242/19; have, use 134/3. *pr. 2sg.* make use of, need 360/31. **occupied** *p.p.* taken possession 200/55
ode *adj.* ~ *mony(e* small change 191/17, 353/4
odurwas *adv.* otherwise 735/19
oeps *n. pl.* profit 10/2, 933/8
ofeith *interj.* in faith, truly 691/11
office, ofys *n.* enquiry conducted by an escheator 89/11, 989/85; *inqwest of* ~ official court of enquiry 155/6. **ofyceys** *pl.* secular posts 345/14
oght *pron. see* **ought** *pron.*
oght *v. pa. see* **ought** *v. pa.*
oyer and determyner, oyeer determyner, oyrdetermyner, heyre determyner, neyre in termyner *n.* royal commission to hear and determine local indictments 38/25, 137/3, 162/3, 333/57, 455/5, 690/41
oystyrs *n. pl. drownk to myn* ~ had a bad time of it 340/13
oke cornes *n. pl.* acorns 95/13
okupye *see* **ocupye**
olyuer currant *phr. go* ~ run smoothly 258/32
on, hone, won *n.* one, a certain (person) 134/15, 138/28, 178/10, 181/4, 657/8
on-connyng *ppl. adj.* ignorant 428/6
ondelayed *v. p.p.* prompt 271/13
ondly *see* **hondely**
on-ethes, a-nedes, an-ethe *adv.* hardly, scarcely 374/8, 450/3, 649/6
ongayly *adv.* unmannerly 705/15
onhertis ease *n.* uneasiness of the heart, anxiety 207/22
onys *n.* ? ounce; *lytell* ~ ? tiny thing 303/6
onys *see* **ons**
onkyndenesse *n.* unscrupulousness 296/43
onknowleche *n. yowre* ~ without your knowledge 248/26
on-manerly *adj.* unruly 643/40
on-poyntid *ppl. adj.* unpainted 259/38
on-recurabyll *adj.* irrecoverable 688/62
on-rysty *adj.* spoiled, damaged 222/38
ons, -ys *adv.* at one time, all at once 195A/22, 195B/25, 929/54; some day 671/20
onsett *v. p.p.* unknown, unexpected 298/29
onsyttyngly *adv.* inappropriately 296/48
on-sped *v. p.p.* not completed 72/15
onsuerté *n.* uncertainty 214/21
ontayled *see* **tayled**
onthryve *v.* come to grief 77/174
on-to *prep.* until 182/34
onwarre *adv.* unexpectedly 48/166
onwetyng *see* **vnwetyng**
onwyst *v. p.p.* unknown 296/35.
oo *num.* one 386/16, 432/28
opiniounis *n. pl.* differing views 120/13
oplyshyd *v. p.p.* made known, published 676/30, 998/3
opne, -yn *v.* tell 622/10, 637/10. **opyn(n)ed, oponed** *p.p.* revealed, made clear 67/5, 550/21, 901B/190
oppynable *adj.* open to argument 537/15
oppoyntment *see* **ap(p)oyntment**
optyned *v. pr. 3sg.* ~ *me condempnyd* succeeded in having me penalised 3/3
or *see* **er**
oratour, oratore, aratour *n.* one who prays for another, petitioner 359/2, 469/29, 682/2, 693/28. **oratoures** *pl.* 591/4
oratrix *n.* female petitioner 753/23
ordey(g)ne *v.* obtain 444/39, 762/2
ordere *v.* ~ *me* make my dispositions 392/4
ordynare, ordinarie, ordenary *n.* a superior 180/65, 539/26, 889/5
ordynat *adj.* systematically ordered 981/23
ordynatlye *adv.* properly 572/10
ordynaunce, -ans, -awnce, ordenaunce *n.* military equipment 204/16, 320/16, 777/18; preparations 130/8
ore *see* **er**
ore *n.* official standing, dignity 582/30
orfrayes *n. pl.* embroidered borders or bands 123/99
orybyll *adj.* excessive 181/26
ostas(s *n.* mistress of household 367/17, 380/47
ote *see* **wet(e(n**
othere, owder, -thyre *conj.* either, or 177/21, 185/40, 216/26
ought, oght, owt(e, owth *pron.* anything 4/43, 55/6, 131/104, 154/10, 185/42; ~ *sey* anything said 24/23–4
ought, oght, out, owthg *v. pa.* owed 180/74, 181/4, 231/25, 647/32, 705/57. **owght** *p.p.* owed 161/15
out *adv., v. pr. 3sg., pa. see* **ought, owght, owyn**
outas *n.* outcry 1001/21
outchargez, owt chargys *n. pl.* external financial obligations 48/174, 221/28
outetake *prep.* except 16/5
outlagaré, vtlagaré *n.* outlawry 439/21, 23
ouer charge *v.* over-graze 500/19
ouere-throwyn *v. p.p.* prostrated 656/9
ouer grounded *v. p.p.* filled in 547/23
ouerleden *v.* oppress 870A/71
overleve *v. subj.* outlive 386/16
overmest *adj. superl.* uppermost 259/21
over sayle *v.* defeat at sea 968/25

ouerseers *n. pl.* persons charged with overseeing the execution of a will 123/149
overthwart, ovyrethwert *prep.* across 259/4, 264/29
ouer-woren, ouerworne *adj.* worn out 123/88, 109
ouyre-lokyd *v. p.p.* viewed 313/45
ovyrsythe *n.* supervision 176/18
ow *adv. see* **hough**
owder *see* **othere**
owght *v. p.p. see* **ought** *v. pa.*
owght, owthe, owt(e, out, aght *adv.* even, at all, in any way, to any extent 152/8, 242/27, 243/58, 855/21; *er ~ longke, or ~ long* before very long 124/5, 248/68, 443/31–2
owyn, owe *v. pr. 2sg.* ought, are obliged 128/36, 175/8. **out, oweth, owythe, owith, owt, awyth, howte** *pr. 3sg.* 128/20, 189/41, 192/10, 205/14, 249/29, 33, 387/21. **owt** *pr. 3pl.* 159/18
owythe *v. pr. 3sg.* owns 414/25. **owth** *pr. 3pl.* 73/32. **hought** *pa.* 193/3. **haght** *p.p.* 951/14
owle *v.* collect 24/16
owt(e, owth *see* **ought, owght**
owt chargys *see* **outchargez**
owteward *adv.* away from home 778/10
owth *adv. mad ~* drawn up 59/58
owth *see* **owythe**
owthg *see* **ought**
owthyre *see* **othere**
owtlod *n.* goods leaving the boundaries of a region 221/31

paame *n.* jeu de paume (ball game) 351/52
paces *n. pl.* pas d'armes, jousting 316/40
pay *v. ~ down* put (money) down, pay 744/28. **payand** *pr. p.* paying 500/8. **payed, -ied** *p.p.* contented, pleased 35/10, 192/98, 203/60, 494/36
payle *v.* enclose with a paling, fence 754/6
paylet *see* **palet**
payn *see* **peyn**
payse *n.(as adj.) ~ money* coins of full weight 732/51
paytrell *n.* poitrel, protective breastplate for a horse 732/107
pakthred(e *n.* strong thread 264/22, 943/7
pale *n.* small shovel 95/9
palefrey *n.* riding horse 906/headn. **palefreys** *pl.* 906/headn.
palet, paylet *n.* small bed 64/172, 230/147
Palme Sunday *n.* the Sunday before Easter 938/38, 940/6
panel(l *n.* jury 477/9, 707/4, 737/51; jury list 447/16, 472/41, 510/25
panell *v. see* **in-panell**
pappe *n.* breast 248/107
paradyce *n. folis ~* state of ignorant bliss 91/30
parauenture, -towr, par aventur *adv.* possibly, perhaps 66/12, 177/13, 299/21
par cas(e *adv. phr.* perhaps 247/13, 256/10
parcel(l, passel percell *n.* part 249/15, 433/9; item 39/48, 340/20; *of ~* incidentally 624/14. **parcel(l)(e)s, -ez, -ys, passels** *pl.* parts, portions 551/30; details 122/60, 195A/1, 430/39; plots of land 500/6, 649/3, 914/16; groups 915/11
parcell(es *adv.* partially, partly 94/7, 123/62
parcelly *adv.* item by item 755/1
parcyall *adj. ~ wyth* prejudiced in favour of 185/17
parcialté *n.* prejudice 192/81
pardé *interj.* by God, indeed 626/4, 629/14
pardon *n.* festival of patron saint at which indulgences were granted 407/24
parell(e, parilie *n.* danger, peril 122A/12, 571/11, 739/18. **perellys** *pl. cast þe ~* considered the risks, been cautious 682/18
parffetly *adv.* exactly 858/7
parfourme *v.* make 210/44
paryschons *n. pl.* parishioners 436/7
parkyng *vbl. n.* pasturing (of sheep) in an enclosure 1009/24
parklos *n.* partition 24/9
parlyows *adj.* wicked, malicious 617/11
parte, -ey, -ye *n.* party, side (in a conflict) 258/8; matter, question 733/15; proportion 1014/5; communicant's share of the Eucharistic host 275/37
parte *see* **aparte**
partenaunse *n. pl.* associated property 433/10
party *adv.* partly 64/149
partyculerely *adv.* separately 402/7
Pasch(e *n.* Easter 604/58, 780/34, 1014/15
pas(e *v.* happen 124/9; judge 322/37, 39. **passyd** *pa.* came to a verdict 274/7, 989/95. **pasyd, past** *p.p.* 124/7, 997/4
passage *n.* movement of shipping 278/16
passagerys *n. pl.* ships carrying travellers 281/10
passe *v.* exceed 242/35. **passyng** *pr. p. not ~* no longer 235/17
passel *see* **parcel(l**
passyd *prep.* more than 205/23
pas(s)yng(e, passhyng *adv.* exceedingly 119/16, 279/10, 366/27; in preference to 433/11, 19
passyn(g)ly *adv.* exceedingly 240/22, 342/35
pastowr *n.* pastureland 132/53
pateyns, -anys *n. pl.* wooden shoes 394/14, 732/114, 178
paten(t *n.* chalice cover 123/68, 923/67
patent *n.* document of authorisation 23/9, 368/9

patentés *n. pl.* holders of property by letters patent 552/5
patorn *n.* patron of a benefice 722/10
patrono, -atus *n. to inquere de vero* ~ to discover the true right of presentation to a benefice 103/17; *de jure* ~ 545/7
paveyz, -yse *n. pl.* large shields 36/24, 64/214
pavylonys *n. pl.* large tents 298/34
paxbred *n.* pax-board (plaque passed among the congregation during Mass) 923/23, 930/59
pe(a)se *v.* pacify 168/20, 455/12. **peacyd** *pa.* calmed down 653/8
pece, pees, -ce *n.* dish, bowl 230/116, 193, 923/18, 20; *boll* ~ drinking bowl 923/147
pechyd *v. p.p.* accused 692/78
pedde *n.* wicker basket 282/69
pele, pe(e)ll *n.* appeal, supplication 337/5, 37, 788/6
peyn(e, payn *n.* discomfort 269/24; forfeit 286/26; penalty 60/107, 950/48; *in* ~ *of* under penalty of 203/8; *on* ~ for fear of mishap 258/9
peyse *v.* weigh, count 516/11; value, rate 766/89. **peisith** *pr. 3sg.* signifies 956/18
pell *see* **pe(e)ll**
pelle-axis *see* **pollexis**
pelow bere *n.* pillowcases 732/96. **pelow beres** *pl.* 123/89–90
pelowers *n. pl.* cushions 123/122
pencyons *n. pl.* regular payments 470/42
pendaunt *n.* hanging end of a belt 270/52
pen(n)er *n.* pen-case 82/42, 970/7
penknyf *n.* pocket knife used to sharpen a quill 82/44
pensyly *adv.* sorrowfully 203/63
pepyll, pople, pupill, -yll *n.* local populace 132/41; public 665/6; *gret* ~ large entourage 145/19, 463/3; numerical superiority 204/17
pepyrquerns *n. pl.* pepper-mills 11/38
percell *see* **parcel(l**
perch *n.* unit of linear measure (of varying length) 23/10. **perches** *pl.* 726/19, 1028/8
perellys *see* **parell(e**
performyng *vbl. n.* completion 228/3
perhawys *n. pl.* ornamental pieces of body armour 195B/44
perys *n. pl.* perry, fermented pear juice 917/6
perplexité *n.* confusion 252/36
perplextif *n.* uncertain situation 688/63
perryll *n.* pearl 732/66
perse *n.* ~ *blewe* purplish-blue cloth 692/61
person *n.* parson 19/13, 274/11
personable *adj.* presentable 236/18
pertye *n.* party (in a lawsuit) 338/24
pese *see* **pe(a)se**
pesebyl, -ybyle *adj.* uncontested 136/22, 205/48
peson *n. pl.* peas 768/9
pestylens *n.* plague 190/67
pety *adj.* small 957/12
petows *adj.* piteous 160/22
pevyshnesse *n.* capriciousness, contrariness 752/52
phisyke, pheesyk, fesyk *n.* medical treatment 346/10, 710/16; *bo(o)ke of* ~ medical book 751/16, 755/5
pye *n.* magpie 270/53, 354/85, 356/4
pyek *v.* steal 332/13. **piked** *p.p.* broken into 77/172
pykeisys, -oys *n. pl.* pickaxes 36/25, 774/19
pikethankys *n.* one who curries favour 603/36
pykyng *vbl. n.* theft 187/26
pykke *n.* pitch, tar 919/45
pylyon *n.*[1] saddle 363/28
pillion *n.*[2] pileus (cap of a scholar of divinity) 659/10
pill *v.* plunder 114/27. **pilled** *p.p.* 522/10
pyn(ne)fold *n.* pen for livestock 182/4, 390/14
pyntell *n.* penis 248/109
pipe, pyp(p)e *n.* gutter 1/10; storage container 195B/22; gold thread or wire used to decorate a woman's hair 195A/44. **pypys** *pl.* ~ *of gold* 13/11
pirled *v. p.p.* studded or decorated 929/50
pyssaunce *see* **pusaunce**
pystyll *n.* discourse, story 381/26
pitevous, -ueux *adj.* pious 252/14; pitiable, compassionate 562/4
pittis *n. pl.* ditches 14/18
pixe, pixt *n.* pyx (vessel in which the consecrated host is reserved) 230/165, 923/112
plaighte *n.* barge 965/33
playn *see* **pleyne**
playnt *n.* lawsuit 180/13; accusation 867/16
playster *n.* medicinal compress 389/3
plas *n. pl.* pleas, applications 223/10
plashyng *vbl. n.* pleaching, constructing a hedge by layering shoots 767/35
plawyng *vbl. n.* boiling 195A/22, 195B/25
plawnchere *n.* wooden floor 130/12
pledge *v.* ~ *owt* redeem 283/34. **ple(d)gyd, pleggyt** *p.p.* 227/19, 248/83, 339/29. **pleggyng** *pr. p.* 228/6
pledgys, plegges, -ys, pleages *n. pl.* securities 221/7, 224/4, 248/82; sureties, guarantors 686/36
pleyn *v.* amuse, entertain 126/18, 136/31
pleyne, playn *adj.* unambiguous, sincere 167/40, 639/1
ple(y)nerly *adv.* fully 229/14, 643/6, 886/78
pleynesse *n.* truth of the matter 188/36
pleyntys *n. pl.* lawsuits 131/3, 132/78
plenar *adj.* complete 896A/10

plesans *n.* satisfaction 154/48; *do me . . .* ~ do what I want 131/104
plesaunce *n.* fine fabric from Piacenza (worn by knights as an emblem) 439/13
plete *v.* go to law 680/21
plye *v.* strive to deal with 356/35
plighte, plyte *n.* condition, state 20/3, 169/4, 568/18
plyke *v. p.p.* fold 901B/34
plomere *n.* lead worker 778/42
plommed *v. p.p.* soldered with lead 923/49
plompes, plumtes *n. pl. chaced* ~ embossed with design showing plums 123/48, 923/70
plonket, plunkket *adj.* grey-blue 346/28, 394/12
plowe-ware, plowarre *n.* animals that draw a plough 180/8, 15
plukked, -yd *v. p.p.* pulled, forcibly removed 444/30; snatched away 444/32; ~ *downe* pulled down, demolished 333/55
plumyd *v. p.p.* decorated with feathers 95/5
plumtes *see* **plompes**
plungyng *vbl. n.* bucking, apt to throw the rider 776/44
plunkket *see* **plonket**
plurias *n.* third writ of attachment, issued when the first and second prove ineffectual 189/76
poynt *n.* determination, conclusion 277/30, 791/4. **poynt(t)ys** *pl.* accusations, charges 413/46; laces for fastening parts of garments 333/91, 394/13, 851/35
poynt *v.*[1] specify 789/11. **poyntyd** *pa.* agreed 781/5
poyntid *v.*[2] *p.p.* painted 259/34
poyntmen *n.* agreement 13/3. **powntementys** *pl.* terms 205/40
pokes *n. pl.* pouches 64/160
polecy, -esy(e, pollicé *n.* administrative skill, prudent management 73/7, 214/21, 241/15, 306/27
poletekely, -ykly *adv.* as a point of good management, prudently 66/31, 306/38
pol(l)etik, -ityk, -ik *adj.* prudent 72/9, 583/5, 699/1, 907/24
pollexis, pelle-axis, polaxys *n. pl.* poleaxes 130/6, 189/10, 906/headn.
pollicé *see* **polecy**
polrondys *n. pl.* shoulder-pieces (of armour) 181/22, 195A/40
pomisyd *v. p.p.* polished with pumice 123/81
pondage, povndage *n.* tax on imports and exports 812/2, 4
ponsed *see* **pounsed**
po(o)re, powere *n.* power 23/13, 204/18, 205/17; *a* ~ able 182/9. **porys** *pl.* 355/15; *to ther* ~ to the best of their ability 163/16
popeleres *n. pl.* embroideries depicting spoonbills 64/183
popell *see* **pepyll**
porcions *n. pl.* groups 460/73
pore, porys *see* **po(o)re**
portrayed, -id *v. p.p.* designed 37/7; illustrated 316/34
portrayer *n.* draughtsman 37/6
porveye(d *see* **purvey**
poruyans *see* **purvyaunce**
possed *v. p.p.* in possession 966/19
possessyd *v. p.p.* invested with possession 192/59
possybylyté *n.* potential circumstances 378/22
post *n.* support 1018/13, 1037/35. **post alone** standing quite alone 752/37
posterne *n.* concealed gate 625/16
potage *n.* thick soup or stew 923/18
potel(l *n.* half-gallon 71/24, 705/35, 732/33
potengers *n. pl.* soup dishes 251/6, 257/5
potycarye *n.* apothecary 353/15
pot(t)hokys, potte hokys *n. pl.* hooks for suspending pots over a fire 123/148, 195A/29, 195B/32
pounced, powncyd, ponsed *v. p.p.* embossed, decorated 925/50, 930/53, 942/7
povndage *see* **pondage**
pourveiithe, pourvoied *see* **purvey**
powder boxe *n.* box for powdered spice 230/130, 923/116
powdred, poudred, -id *v. p.p.* decorated (in a random pattern) 64/131; speckled 123/119; salted 852/23
powere *see* **po(o)re**
powncyd *see* **pounced**
powntementys *see* **poyntmen**
powtenere *n.* purse 732/146
praty *adj.* handsome, fine 150/19, 278/17, 354/57; fair-sized 224/45; enjoyable 267/4
pratte *n.* trick 312/17. **prattes** *pl.* 77/65
prefer(r)yng, proferryng *vbl. n.* advancement in status 60/17, 574/35, 734/6
preffe *see* **proue**
prefferaunce *n.* advancement 1029/27
prefferment, prof(f)erment *n.* prior claim 249/33, 39, 300/12
preyer(e *n.* petition, entreaty 345/9, 450/34
preket, prikett *n.* candlestick spike 923/12, 923/119. **preket(t)es** *pl.* 64/17, 923/120
premer(e *see* **primer**
premisses, -ysses, -is *n. pl.* aforesaid matters 123/19, 202/23, 308/36, 412/44, 835/23
prend *n.* mended crack 923/73
prend *imp.* take in 202/29
prenostikyth *v. pr. 3pl.* augur 304/13
prentis, -eys *n.* apprentice 190/5, 706/4
prepensed *v. pa.* premeditated 491A/5

prese *n.* crowding 477/3
prese *v. imp.* ~ *in* entreat, apply 258/23
presedent *n.* prior documentation 352/13. **presedentys, -es** *pl.* 268/4, 688/24; aforementioned matters 604/31
present(e *v.* recommend (for a benefice) 183/8, 578/9. **presented** *p.p.* indicted 994/29, 995/19
presentacion *n.* recommendation for appointment to a clerical benefice 179/37. **presentacions** *pl.* 578/11
presentez *n. pl.* articles 344/40
presentez *adj.* present, current 229/13
presentment *n.* indictment 559/12, 1005/38
presoned *v.p.p.* imprisoned 194/8, 715/13
presoner *n.*[1] offficer in charge of a gaol 659/11; **presoneres** *pl.* 659/3, 9
presoner *n.*[2] prisoner, person under arrest 659/12
presonyng *vbl. n.* imprisonment 463/8
prest *n.* loan 991/59
pretend(e *v.* claim, allege 627/5, 937/8. **pretendeth** *pr. 3sg.* 904/2. **pretendyng** *pr. p.* 927/8. **pretendid** *p.p.* alleged 4/33
pretended *ppl. adj.* alleged 901B/11
prevayll *v.* persuade 198/32
preues *see* **prove**
prevy(e, -uy, pryué *adj.* hidden 192/43; secret 4/52; covert 236/8, 679/24; ~ *(there)to* aware of 143/10, 564/8
prevysion *n.* foresight 200/61; prior arrangement 965/31
previté *n.* privacy 830/19; innermost secrets 845/33
prikett *see* **preket**
prykk(e *v.* incite, urge 286/19; spur 308/41
prime *n.* number of a given year in the nineteen-year lunar cycle used in calculating Easter 72/91
primer, prymer, premer(e *n.* prayer book, manual of devotions 230/131, 619/6, 732/20, 929/52
principil *n.* essence 617/23. **pryncypalles** *pl.* main agents in a legal action 654/46
prisees *n. pl.* prices of produce 986/50
pryué *see* **prevy(e**
pryued *v. p.p.* deprived 4/31
procede *v.* take a Master's degree 403/5, 404/6. **procedyd** *p.p.* 403/8
procedendo, prosedendo *n.* writ from Chancery directing a delaying lower court to make a judgement 480/17, 936/19, 1002/12
procedyng *vbl. n.* taking of a Master's degree at university 403/3
proces(se, -ses *n.* lawsuit, legal proceedings 2/19, 189/79, 450/37; legal documents 74/53. **proses** *pl.* writs 338/9, 10
proctor(e *n.* legal representative 279/32, 282/43, 688/31. **propters** *pl.* financial officials 1030/23
procuracie *n.* authorisation to act as a legal representative 2/23, 3/12
procuratour *n.* advocate 3/12
profectabell *adj.* profitable 190/61
profectys *n. pl.* profit, income 180/125
proferre *v.* provide 603/29. **profiryth** *pr. 3sg.* offers 152/16. **profered, -id, profyrd,** *p.p.* offered 132/19, 186/7, 201/41
proferryng *see* **prefer(r)yng**
profescion *n.* nature, character 82/3
prof(f)e *see* **prove** *n.*
prof(f)erment *see* **prefferment**
prof(f)re *n.* proposal, offer 270/22, 291/30, 870D/37; bid (at auction) 39/40. **proferes, -yrs, -orys** *pl.* offers 152/22, 201/41, 222/23
proker *v.* incite 430/23
prokeryng *vbl. n.* instigation 882/20
promytteth, -itteth *v. pr. 3sg.* promises 27/30, 252/84. **promittyng, -yttyng** *pr. p.* promising 48/137, 72/93. **promytted, -yd** *p.p.* 121/16, 264/14
promocion *n.* advancement 123/44
promotyng *vbl. n.* appointment (to a benefice) 235/15
propre(e, -yr, -ir *adj.* personal 230/211, 719/3, 931/4; *in here* ~ *person* in her own person 218/11, 396/17
propters *see* **proctor(e**
proroged *v.p.p.* adjourned 641/10
prosedendo *see* **procedendo**
proses *see* **proces(se**
provayle *v.* be of use to 192/93
prove, prof(f)e *n.* profitable outcome 728/11; efforts 1010/13; *at a* ~ in any case 300/22. **preues** *pl.* evidence 45/57
proue, -yn, preffe *v.* test 366/35, 1009/56; ~ *owt* prove (a claim) fully 422/17. **prouyd** *p.p.* 238/5, 354/94
prouocacion *n.* appeal to a higher court 4/20
prouynciall *n.* local head of an order of friars 55/13
prouisyon *n.* appointment (to an ecclesiastical office) 422/11
prowd *adj.* greatly pleased 347/6, 362/21
prustes *n. pl.* priests 184/75
psal(l, psuld *see* **xall**
puddoun *v. p.p.+prep.* put down, destroyed 23/3
puissans *see* **pusaunce**
puke *n.* good quality woollen fabric 296/53, 394/28
pupill, -yll *see* **pepyll**
purchasse *v.* deserve 566/45
purfild *v. p.p.* trimmed 929/54

purfill *n.* fur trimming 123/116
purpoyntes *n. pl.* bed quilts 64/128
purpos(e *n.* purpose, claim 422/17; *of* ~ specifically 333/38
purpose *v.* intend 183/33; plan to go 199/24; scheme 214/28. **purposyth** *pr. 3sg.* intends 190/67. **purposyd** *pa.* intended 139/7. **purposed, -yd, -id** *p.p.* resolved, intended 171/19, 178/11, 233/10
purvey, purueie, porveye *v.* provide, contrive 166/39, 180/92, 190/60; appoint 153/17; ~ *(þer)for(e* deal with (it) 179/12, 590/10. **pourveiithe** *imp.* make arrangements 14/31. **purvayd** *pa.* contrived 190/22. **purvayd, -eyd, porveyed, pourvoied** *p.p.* dealt with 164/30, 178/17; provided, supplied 128/42, 169/23, 286/32, 860/9
purvyaunce, -a(u)ns, purwyauns, poruyans *n.* arrangement 124/10, 209A/13, 212/3, 680/30; ~ *must be had* measures must be taken in order to ensure 72/26
pursiuaunt, -euaunte, purcyuaunt *n.* messenger, herald 412/34, 472/1, 883/19. **pursiuantes** *pl.* 412/15
pusaunce, puissans, pyssaunce *n.* force (of soldiers) 439/8, 646/25, 662/19
Puver *n.* ~ *Weddenysday* Ash Wednesday 132/81
pwrce *v.* have possession, pocket 119/20

qhedder *adv.* whither, to what place 133/16
qhete *see* **qwete**
Qhythson, Qwesontyde *n.* Whitsun(tide) 124/4, 128/82
quadrate *n.* square or rectangular area 264/28
quaire, quayere, queiere *n.* quire, gathering of sheets of paper or parchment folded one within the other 173/29, 751/28; booklet 969/28. **quayerys, -ris, -irs, whaȝerys** *pl.* 316/24, 602/13, 732/145, 751/26
quarell *see* **qwarellys**
quart *n.* measure of two pints 508/30
quarterage *n.* sum paid four times a year 614/41
quartrons *n. pl.* quarters of an ounce 123/65
quene, qwene *n.* prostitute, whore 395/4, 1041/10
quere *n.* choir, chancel 228/11
querell *n. pl.* disputes, complaints 558/22
quernes *n.* hand mills 259/46
quest, qw(h)est(e *n.* jury 40/111, 340/7; judicial inquiry, inquest 124/7, 134/4, 312/14
quetaunce *see* **quytaunce**
quietclaymeth *v. pr. 3sg.* relinquishes the right 253/37
quike *n.* living 431/19
qvyk, quykke, qwhyke *adj.* alive 40/43, 252/8; pregnant 491/40; ~ *catell* livestock 64/71
quinere *n.* silversmith 94/17
quyt(t)e *see* **qwytte**
quytaunce, quetaunce, -tans, qwetance *n.* deed of release, discharge, receipt 154/40, 338/45, 685/25, 990/2
quo *see* **ho(o**
quowe *see* **hough**
qwan *conj.* when 115/17
qwarellys, quarell(es *n. pl.* bolts for crossbows 130/2, 244/23, 332/61, 786/15; ~ *hedes* metal points for crossbow bolts 259/24
qwat(h *adj.* what 209A/54, 209B/54
qweder, qwhedyre *conj.* whether 209A/52, 442/14
qwedur *adj.* whichever 783/1
qweere *conj.* where 658/16
qwe(y)sye, coysy *adj.* unsettled, uncertain 261/30, 281/2, 582/34
qwene *see* **quene**
Qwesontyde *see* **Qhythson**
qwest(e *see* **quest**
qwetance, -tans *see* **quytaunce**
qwet(e, qhete *see* **white**
qwethword *n.* last will 208/28
qwett *see* **qwytte**
qwhedyre *see* **qweder**
qwhest(e *see* **quest**
qwhyke *see* **qvyk**
qwykynyd *v. p.p.* prompted 243/28
qwyknyng *vbl. n.* movements of a child in the womb 352/38
qwyte *adj.* white 736/5
qwytte, quyte *v.* retaliate against 361/17; repay 599/13. **qwytes** *pr. 3sg.* ~ *hym* acquits himself 498/19. **quyt(t)e** *pr. 3pl.* ~ *them/hym* acquit themselves/himself 278/13, 659/22. **quyte, qwyte, -ett** *p.p.* acquitted 92/10, 188/41 (*1st*), 477/19; discharged 188/41 (*2nd*)

raggedstaff *n.* jewel representing a tree trunk with the branches removed 64/22, 640/12
raye *n.* array, group 1018/10
raye, rayed *v. p.p.* striped 123/107, 338/39
rayled *v. pa.* spoke contemptuously 777/36
raylyng *vbl. n.* abuse 258/24
rayse *n.* voyage 1006/36
rakke *n.* pasture 702/4
rape *n.* haste 200/41, 220/29
rased *v. p.p.* erased, struck out 555/30
rathe *adv.* early 525/10, 727/30
rathere, -yre *adv.* more readily, sooner 159/19, 258/36, 899/14. **rathere** *comp.* instead 204/21. **rathest** *superl.* most especially 214/9
raveshid, ravyched *v. p.p.* carried off by force

45/21; ~ *my wittys* greatly distressed me 436/10

ravyshment, rauyshment, rauishment *n.* abduction 1019/29. *writte of* ~ writ concerning an abduction 548/36, 552/10; *wryt of* ~ *de garde* writ concerning the abduction of a ward 525/3

rebelyones, rebyliones *n. pl.* rebels, opponents 637/12, 639/11

rebewe *n.* ? rebus 930/72

reboyle *v.* flare up (*lit.* ferment a second time) 302/21

rebuke, rebeuc *n.* disgrace 520/17; defeat 187/3

receyt *n.* income 172/12

receyvour(e, resceyvour, -iuour, reseyvour, -uore *n.* officer appointed to collect or receive money due, rents, etc. 29/8, 77/17, 401/1, 589/8, 713/5, 730/7

reche *v.* understand 626/29

recke *see* **rek(e**

reconusaunce, -ysa(u)nce *n.* acknowledgment of title or payment 252/62, 453/30, 508/15

record *n. be gret* ~ before ample witness 704/22

recorder, -our *n.* chief legal official of a city 460/54, 700/2, 870A/65

rectid *v. pa.* considered 569/27

recure *n.* redress 704/26

recure *v.* recover 131/93; regain possession 687/8, 752/55. **recuryd** *p.p.* repossessed 66/29

red, rood *v.* ride 47/19, 175/34. **reden, -yn** *pa.* rode, departed 141/16, 145/10, 163/49. **redyn, ryd(yn** *p.p.* departed, gone 163/52, 180/44, 558/3

reddur *n.* strictness 620/13

redé *see* **redy**

rede *n.* reeds 136/16, 473/20

reden, -yn *see* **red**

reder *n.* thatcher 144/4

redy, -é *adj.* explicit, clearly expressed 2/33; exact 632/27

redyng *vbl. n.* riding 120/32

reede heryng *n. pl.* kippers 989/65–6

reentré *n.* right to resume possession of an estate 872/48

refeu *n.* ? re-enfeoffment 1009/21

reformacions *n. pl.* amendments 901B/75

regalie *n.* majesty 870A/69

regned *see* **reygnyth**

regoyse *see* **reioce**

reherce *v.* report 564/6. **rehers** *pr. 3sg.* states 350/3. **reherce** *pr. 3pl.* report 752/17. **rehersyng** *pr. p.* reporting 116/10, 231/22; stating 230/25, 248/88. **rehersyd** *pa.* reported 119/14; repeated 203/36. **rehersyd** *p.p.* mentioned 131/60.

rehersell, -all *n.* account 764/5; *make* ~ give an account 603/4

reheted *v. p.p.* berated 88/93

reygnyth *v. pr. 3sg.* is rife 268/25, 400/3. **reynyng, regnyng** *pr. p.* 263/49; in power 617/8. **regned** *pa.* were influential 459/15

reysyd *v. p.p.* brushed to bring up nap 28/11

reysonys *n. pl.* ~ *of corons* currants imported from the Levant (*lit.* raisins of Corinth) 209A/56

reieckyd *v. p.p.* annulled, overturned 867/78

reioce, regoyse *v.* take possession of 122/45, 138/25. **reioysed** *p.p.* enjoyed, had the use of 294/33

rejoy *n.* pleasure 42/15

reioy *v.* take possession of 505/7

reioyng *vbl. n.* pleasure 42/34

rek(e, recke *v.* care 248/52, 380/40, 652/15. **rekkythe** *pr. 3sg.* 248/24. **rekk** *pr. 3pl.* 131/90. **ro(u)ght** *pa.* 184/43, 473/40. **rowth** *p.p.* 128/62

rek(e)nyng *n.* statement of accounts 248/3, 339/36. **rekonynges** *pl.* 852/9

relatyvis *n. pl.* concerns, affairs 705/14

relefys *see* **relif**

relenxe *v.* transfer 252/58

reles(s)e, -ees *n.* transfer of property or right 177/40, 178/14, 222/24. **relesys** *pl.* 329/18

relif, -eve *n.* payment to a feudal lord by an heir upon taking possession of an estate 128/6, 129/44. **relefys** *pl.* 131/7

religeus, relygyoux *n. pl.* monks 309/24, 727/38

Relik Sunday, Relyk Sonday *n.* the third Sunday after Midsummer Day 636/2, 834/26

reliueree, -yueré *n.* return, restoration 250/19, 251/15

remayndre *n.* postponement 498/12

remedy(e *n.* legal redress 188/31, 298/24

remembraunce *n.* list of memoranda 66/4, 185/28

remembrauncers *n. pl.* receivers of debts due to the Crown 569/41

rememb(y)re *v.* remind 231/13, 232/7; mention 205/20. **rememberyng** *pr. p.* reminding 231/19. **remembyrd** *p.p.* reminded 181/8, 211/13

remena(u)nt(e, remnawnte, -awnth, remulant, -wlawnt *n.* remainder 176/13, 194/38, 203/40, 238/24, 420/16, 667/22

remeve *v.* release 194/19

remyttire *n.* restoration (of a more valid title to certain property) 793/12

Renysch *adj.* ~ *wyne* wine produced in the Rhine region 853/3

renne *v.* circulate 52/2. **renneth** *pr. 3sg.* con-

tinues, is current 4/43; ~ *on* talks about 355/10. **renne** *pr. 3pl.* continue 259/19
rennyng *n.* ~ *leed* ? sliding lid 259/36
renomee *n.* reputation 498/1
rentall *n.* record of rents 650/7, 872/51
rentes *n.*[1] *pl.* rented property 692/57
rentys *n.*[2] *pl.* torn, ragged clothes 208/50
repara(u)cion *n.* maintenance, repairs 123/31, 154/37, 649/4
repyned *v. p.p.* opposed, thwarted 447/5
replegge *v.* ~ *owte* redeem again 315/10
replegiare *n.* replevin (see next) 663/8
replevy(n, -euyn, -euin *n.* temporary restoration of confiscated property pending a court hearing 59/5, 183/36, 978/14; document authorising a replevin 179/40, 180/58, 182/31, 473/16; *waran of* ~, *writtes/writtis of* ~ 74/57, 60, 189/62
reprefe *n.* dishonour 737/61
reprises *n. pl.* annual expenses taken out of the revenues of an estate 252/169
reprovyd *v. p.p.* validated 1042/5
reputacion *n. toke hede ner* ~ paid no attention 65/53
rere *v.* collect 53/12; initiate 479/14. **rere** *subj.* should alert 683/15. **rereth** *pr. 3sg.* gathers 88/103. **reryd, rered** *p.p.* collected 309/52, 329/26; bred 702/3, 6
resceyvour, -iuour *see* **receyvour(e**
rescribe *v.* write back 62/14
rescu, -ew, -we *n.* documentation for recovery of distrained property 29/12; relief from siege 168/13, 243/13
rescu, -kwe *v.* deliver from siege 241/11, 243/15. **rescuyd** *p.p.* 243/17
rescuse *v.* relieve 204/36
rescuse, -kuse *n.* relief (of a siege) 204/39; documentation for recovery of distrained property 436/7, 473/50, 519/17
reseyth *n.* accounts 25/52
reseyuere *v.+ pron.* receive her 203/42
reseyvour, -uore *see* **receyvour(e**
reservyd, -uyd *v. pa.* set aside 209A/19, 209B/19; preserved 274/48
residue, reswd *n.* remainder 436/17; parts of an estate not specifically bequeathed 122/33
reskuse *see* **rescuse** *n.*
resorte *v.* return 309/40, 447/6, 805/5. **resortythe** *pr. 3sg.* returns 248/120; **resortythe** *pr. 3pl.* frequent 263/50. **resorted** *p.p.* gone 805/3
resortyng *vbl. n.* returning 184/79; going 263/23; ~ *to* calling upon 765/36
resour *v.* reassure 982/43
respyte, -it *v.* excuse 66/28, 38. **respigtyd** *p.p.* 268/8
ressyng *v.* resign from 192/116. **resynged** restored 662/2
restreyn *n. make a* ~ postpone payment 658/24
restreyn *v.* prevent 214/33
resumpsion *n.* repossession 451/9
reswd *see* **residue**
retaylyt *v.+ pron.* sell it in small quantities 221/22
retourne *n.* remission of a writ to a court with a report 189/78
rettyng *v. pr. p.* ~ *in* ascribing to, imputing 1037/13
reve *n. bere the* ~ hold the office of reeve 703/17. **reves, ryues** *pl.* reeves 795/19; *church* ~ churchwardens 230/112
revell *n.* disorder, disturbance 158/18, 185/8, 645/18
reversion, reuersy(o)n *n.* return of an estate upon the expiration of a grant 558/3, 658/2, 658/27
revylyd *v. p.p.* abused 196/20
revyn *v. p.p.* broken 778/49
revolucion, reuolucion, -ysshon, revelicion *n. come in* ~ be considered 539/33, 679/24, 722/10; *bring not the matier in* ~ do not submit the matter for consideration 550/16
rewith *see* **rueth**
rewle, -ell, -yll(e *n.* conduct 28/7; jurisdiction, government 167/38, 168/25; state of affairs 317/17; *haue a* ~ *in* have control over 122/22; *take a* ~ arbitrate 627/14
rewle *v. subj.* were to behave 446/32. **ruled** *p.p.* manned 965/33
rewlers *n. pl.* ringleaders 684/33
rewly *adj.* regrettable 24/10
rewthe *n.* cause for regret 617/25
riale, ryall, riall *n.* gold coin worth ten shillings 209A/52, 210/2, 277/16, 296/6
ryall *adj.* lavish, magnificent 266/25; *fyssh* ~ species of fish deemed to be Crown property 816/14
rially *adv.* successfully 414/17
ryd(yn *see* **red**
rydynges *n. pl.* clearing away of debris 195A/72
riffel *v.* steal 494/40. **rifled, ryfled** *pa.* robbed 461/33, 534/32. **ryfelid, ryfled** *p.p.* stolen, plundered 197/3, 445/12
Riflyng tyme *n.* time of the Peasants' Revolt (1381) 961/7, 82
rightwisnes, ritewesnesse *n.* justice 620/12; sense of justice 487/18
riot rowtis *n. pl.* unruly crowds bent on unlawful disorder 44/8
ripe, rype *adj.* fully informed 62/18; knowledgeable 339/38; prudent 914/60. **ryper** *comp.* better informed 992/10
rypelyer *adv. comp.* thoroughly 535/18

rippled *v. pa.* scratched 129/35
risers, ryserse *n. pl.* rebels 40/86, 81/7
rysyng *vbl. n.* upbringing, origins 576/21
rit *adv.* ~ *a* a very 192/118
ritewesnesse *see* **rightwisnes**
ryues *see* **reve**
rod(e, rodde *n.* units of measurement 17/8, 435/15 (area); 767/34 (linear)
roght *see* **rek(e**
rollyn *v.* consider 705/14
Rome-rennere *n.* agent at the papal court 282/44
ronyd *adj.* roan-coloured 776/42
rood *see* **red**
roode horses *n. pl.* riding horses 990/42
roome *n.* post, office 292/4
rore *n.* turmoil 165/28
rosour *n.* razor 732/6
ros(s)et *n.* drab-coloured woollen cloth 64/85, 323/11; *cotton* ~ 858/4
rote *n.* harp-like stringed instrument 64/42
roughe, rowh *adj.* low, inferior 358/34; fierce 776/32
rought *see* **rek(e**
roved *v. p.p.* roofed 230/14
rover *n.* pirate 409/28
rowh *see* **roughe**
rowmtrees *n. pl.* beams (to hold partition walls) 11/42
rowndlet, runlet(te *n.* small cask 212/38, 394/37, 736/5
rowsclare *n.* ? bright rose-pink colour 123/82
rowth *see* **rek(e**
rubbe *v.* ~ *on* carry on with difficulty 337/45
rubrissheyng *vbl. n.* rubrication, flourished penwork 755/32
rueth, rewith *v. pr. 3sg.* is regretted 200/41, 220/29
ruled *see* **rewle**
runlet(te *see* **rowndlet**

sad(de *adj.* prudent, wise 9/2, 72/4, 238/9. **sadder(e** *comp.* 77/48, 199/16
sad(de)ly *adv.* wisely 2/30; quietly 603/26; completely 861/53
sadnessys *n. pl.* collective wisdom 774/24
safer *n.* sapphire 64/38
saffe *see* **sauf(f**
safistré *see* **sofystré**
saforn *n.* saffron 831/27
say(e *n.* good-quality cloth 64/131, 123/91, 929/38
sayed *v. p.p.* attempted 970/46
sayle, seile, -yle *n. pl.* ships 676/3, 712/17, 884/13
saisine *see* **se(a)son**
sakeryng *vbl. n.* consecration of the Host 22/4, 129/3
salet *n.* light helmet 181/22. **salettes, -ys** *pl.* 36/23, 64/219, 298/33
salettyd *v. p.p.* wearing helmets 40/8
sal(l)t *n.* saltcellar 95/9, 923/1. **saltes** *pl.* 230/144
saltyng fatys *see* **fates, fattys**
salve *n.* ointment 282/42
samine *adv.* together 624/29
sanggueyn *adj.* blood-red colour 13/10
sariant(ys *see* **seriaunt**
sarsenet, -anett *n.* fine silk material 195A/49, 195B/53, 208/48
saten figure, sateyn fugre *n.* satin brocade 123/97, 195A/40
sauacion, -yon *n.* protection 118/9, 185/39
saueliche *adv.* securely 5/86
sauf-conduit *n.* safe-conduct, passport 646/33
sauf(f, saffe *prep.* except, less 33/16, 266/24, 387/23
sauffe gard, saue gard *n.* safe-conduct 636/11; ~ *of the cost* to save the expense 680/47
saugere, sowgere *n.* man-at-arms, armed retainer 224/39, 40. **sawgeres, sodyour, soudeours, -yor, sowdeorys, -ior(i)s, -yorys, sowiours** *pl.* 197/2, 197/6, 63/22, 199/13, 224/38, 269/36, 275/34, 375/9, 498/17
saute, -wte *n.* assault 40/19, 55. **savtis** *pl.* attacks 43/3
saued *v. pa.* excepted 241/9
savyng, -wyng *prep.* with due respect for 166/23, 614/5; except 238/13
sawe *n.* saying 993/41
sawgeres *see* **saugere**
sawse, soos *n.* pickling liquid 11/32; impudent response 272/19
sawte *see* **saute**
sawtere *n.* psalter 732/19
scapelerey *n.* scapular, priest's sleeveless garment 732/147
scapyd *see* **schape**
scarlette *n.* costly fabric (usually bright red) 126/30
scathes *n. pl.* monetary losses, damages 870A/12
sceyntewarye *see* **seynte-wary**
scergyd *see* **serge**
schamlet *see* **chamlet**
schanselere *see* **chauncellere**
schante *adv.* scarcely 414/15
schape *v.* escape 162/11. **scope** *pa.* 264/45. **scapyd** *p.p. is* ~ has survived 164/34
scharge *see* **charge**
schargyd *see* **charge**
schastysyd *v. p.p.* reformed 176/24

scheche, sheche *adj., pron.* such 73/50, 135/4. **schecheon** such a one 203/32
schente *see* **shendith**
schere, scher, scher(r)e *see* **shire**
schere *see* **chere**
scherewd, schrew *see* **shrewd(e**
schese *v.* choose 203/19
schesse *n.* chess 153/6
schevyste *see* **chevesshe**
schew *n.* appearance, display 258/40
schyer *see* **shire**
schyf(f)t(e *see* **shyft**
schippyng *vbl. n. takyn* ~, *toke* ~ travelled by ship 411/13, 420/32
schyttyl-wyttyd *adj.* rash 128/55
schoffe *see* **shuff**
schon *n. pl.* shoes 732/91
schoryle *see* **charl**
schote *n.* blow 132/68
schreff, -ve *see* **shreve**
schrew *n. see* **shrewe** *n.*
schrew(d *adj. see* **shrewd(e**
scyppe, sckeppe *n.* basket 195A/24, 195B/27
scire facias *n.* writ instructing a sheriff to summon a party to court to show cause why execution of a judgement should not proceed 480/11
scytacions *see* **sitacions**
scyuer, swyre *n.* squire 81/11, 83/16, 381/62
sclawfully *adv.* slothfully 85/18
scochen, skochyn, skucchon *n.* escutcheon, ornamental shield-shaped plaque 230/19, 942/4; drawing of an escutcheon 969/33, 970/43. **scochenes** *pl.* 732/27
scomaker *n.* shoemaker 842/4
scomer *n.* utensil for skimming 123/145
scope *see* **schape**
scorne *n. tellith* ~ disdains 776/5
scrat *v.* scratch, forage 326/23
scrowe, skrowe *n.* document 5/179, 441/57. **skrowes** *pl.* 77/136, 344/43
scutes *see* **escutys**
se *see* **se(y**
seasyd, seysid, sesid *v. p.p.* ~ *of* in legal possession of 27/24, 143/7, 367/4
se(a)son *n.*[1] time, while 129/40, 178/40, 184/21
se(a)son, saisine *n.*[2] seisin, possession in freehold 54/104, 60/54, 246/33, 504/10; *mak* ~ transfer possession 59/65
sedell *see* **cedule**
sedyn *v.* plant 931/7
seekly *adj.* ill 74/9
seergiours *n. pl.* customs officers 469/13
seet *see* **seyn**
sege *n.* privy, latrine 677/4
se(y, sy(e, s(e)ygh, sie *v. pa.* saw, had seen 4/19, 21/13, 45/30, 129/36, 146/15, 222/21, 283/38, 867/53; witnessed 392/6
seydde *see* **syde**
seyetyka, cyetica *n.* sciatica 125/17, 432/71
seying, seyneng *vbl. n.* evidence, report 392/2, 991/14
seile, seyle *see* **sayle**
seyn *v. inf.* speak 128/47. **se(e)t, syth** *pr. 3sg.* says 127/9, 222/14, 335/27
seintwary(e, sceyntewarye, seyntuary *n.* sacred precincts 40/24; sacred building taken as a refuge by fugitives 263/67, 264/45, 345/24, 613/25, 751/7, 805/5
seysyd *see* **seasyd**
seke *v.* appeal 234/7
sekelew *see* **syklow**
seker, -yre, -ir *adj.* certain 37/32, 429/8, 867/48, 910/32
sekerly, -yrly *adv.* actually, truly 147/4, 471/22
sekte *n.* party, group 471/31
seld *adv.* seldom 77/169
sele(u)r, -oure, sellore, siller, -our *n.* bed canopy 64/51, 195A/7, 195B/8, 230/133, 732/5, 929/33. **selours** *pl.* 64/126
sel(l)ys *n. pl.* wax seals 132/30, 32
semblable *adj.* similar 533/12
seme *v. pr. 1sg.* see fit 264/34, 445/20, 459/22; judge 477/4. *pr. 3pl.* judge 793/20
sene, son, swynne, swn *conj.* since 32/14, 168/4, 176/17, 650/6, 759/11
sene *n.* synod 93/18
sengilbonde *n.* ? a single mount around the edge of a maser 923/77
sengyll *adj.* unconditional 180/46
seniory *n.* feudal authority 897/2
senyth *n.* week 81/26
sensualité *n.* idle pleasure 571/28
septemanis *n. pl.* weeks 988/17
seqwester *v.* assume custody 335/27
serchorshyp *n.* customs inspector 666/7
serciorare *see* **cerciorare**
serge *n.* search 193/1
serge *v.* look through 157/24, 434/8. **sergeed, -yd, scergyd** *p.p.* sought, looked for 128/21, 177/12, 586/2, 705/58
seriaunt, sariant *n.* ~ *of armes* official guard 659/26; ~ *porter* head porter 420/34. **sariantys, shargentys** *pl.* legal advisors 240/18, 720/8
sermon(e *n.* speech 4/42, 167/21
serpentyn(e, -yng *n.* small cannon 64/207, 208, 259/7. **serpentyns** *pl.* 906/headn.
sertayn, -(e)yn *see* **certeyn**
sertyfyed *see* **certyfye**
servyd *v. p.p.* treated 133/20
sesid *see* **seasyd**
sesyn *v.* desist 128/26

seson *see* **se(a)son**
sesons, cescio(u)ns *n. pl.* sessions, court sittings 145/18, 188/12, 220/4
sesonyd *v. pa.* took possession of, seized 834/11. **sesynnyd** *p.p.* in legal possession 132/72
set *see* **seyn**
seth *see* **sithen** *conj.*
sethen, -yn, -nys *see* **sith(en** *adv.*
set(t(e *v.* ~ *be/by* heed, regard with esteem 199/13, 217/15, 643/26; ~ *hem thorow* deal with them 167/30; ~ *yt thorow* conclude 212/34; *pa.* ~ . . . *in ey* instructed to spy 704/21. *p.p.* ~ *in* inserted 339/60; ~ *att on* brought to an agreement 282/83
settyng *vbl. n.* instigation 270/18; ~ *ouer* provisioning of a retinue 348/11
seue *see* **sew(e**
seueral, -el *adj.* private 778/21, 779/9, 872/8; separate 981/31
severally, seuerally *adv.* separately 88/84, 896A/6
severté *see* **suerté**
sew(e, seue, sywe *v.* sue, take legal action 128/10; pursue, investigate 705/54; ~ *to* petition 188/30, 269/44. ~ *it owte* see it through the courts 587/10. **sewyd** *pa.* applied, petitioned 135/19
sewer, -ir *adj.* secure 158/12; safe 158/16
sewere *n.* butler 116/18
sewerly *see* **swerly**
sewirtesse *see* **suerté**
sewrlyer *adv. comp.* legally more secure 74/14
sewtys *see* **suthe**
shakke, chacke *n.* ~ *tyme* period of grazing over stubble 66/13, 72/88
shankes *n. pl.* furs from the legs of animals 123/118, 930/99
sharge *see* **charge**
shargentys *see* **seriaunt**
sharpe *v.* prompt, activate 766/87
shech *see* **scheche**
sheffe, cheff *n. pl.* quiverfuls 195A/33, 195B/36
shef(f)t(e *see* **shyft**
shendith *v. pr. 3sg.* ~ *hym* wastes his time 969/41. **shent, schente** *p.p.* accused 529/14; rebuked 201/52, 944/13
shepe *see* **chep(e**
sheperefe *n.* chief shepherd 996/111
Shere-thursday *see* **Shorthursday**
sherevis *see* **s(c)hreve**
sherhous *n.* shire hall 354/14
sherp *adj.* difficult 888/35
shete *v.* shoot 64/211. **shetyng** *pr. p.* 64/203. **shet(te** *pa.* 40/28, 48/46
shette *v. pa.* locked 494/6
shew *v. pr. 1sg.* tell 421/3. **shevyd** *pa.* 421/7
shyft, shef(f)t(e, schyf(f)t(e *n.* provision, arrangement 209A/7, 329/12, 379/4, 660/14, 673/18
shire, -y(e)re, scher(r)e, -(y)er, chirre *n.* shire, county 79/17, 449/13; shire court 48/46, 163/47, 164/3, 12; ~ *day* day on which a shire court is convened 5/16, 46/10. **scherys** *pl.* shires, counties 114/30
shoyng *vbl. n.* shoeing horses 765/29
shoot *n.* weapons that fire missiles 204/16
shote *n. flyte* ~ bowshot 534/41
shorted *v. p.p. wey* . . . ~ intercepted 213/13
Shorthursday, Shere-thursday *n.* Maundy Thursday, the Thursday before Easter 550/24, 700/17, 970/16
shreve, sherewe, schreve, -ffe *n.* sheriff 118/5, 242/90, 391/19, 654/2. **sherevis, shrewys** *pl.* 25/13, 436/8
shreuyn *v. p.p.* administered the sacrament of penance to 327/4
shrewd(e, shrewe, scherewd, schrew(d *adj.* difficult, dangerous 86/43, 317/17; unpleasant, bad 83/18, 168/27, 559/11; severe 624/33. **shrewdest** *superl.* most corrupt 53/3
shrewe, schrew *n.* wicked person, miscreant 131/77, 263/33, 282/38. **s(c)hrewes, -is, chrewys** *pl.* 168/15, 179/6, 317/30, 652/29
shrewe *v.* curse 274/24
shrewedly, -(y)dly *adv.* maliciously 45/26, 52/19, 532/14; inefficiently 72/137
shrewys *see* **shreve** *n.*, **shrewe** *n.*
shuff *v. imp.* drive (out) 73/54. **schoffe** *p.p.* shoved, pushed 22/5; ~ . . . *at hys carte* lend him a helping hand 263/58
shulderid *v. p.p.* disjointed at the shoulders 64/75
syde, seydde *adj.* long 28/13, 195A/36, 195B/42
syde, syyd *n.* party (in a dispute) 172/40; *of Paston* ~ the neighbourhood Paston 21/1
sie, sy(e, sygh *see* **sey**
sygh *see* **sey**
signe(e, syngne *n.* ~ *manuel(l* autograph signature 90/2, 283/10, 824/35; *notarys* ~ notary's unique authenticating mark 279/33, 283/5.
signement *n.* grant 640/24. **sygnementes** *pl.* 782/25
signet(te, sy(g)net *n.* seal 151/3, 373/23, 426/14, 750/15
syyd *n. see* **syde**
syyd *v. pa.* collapsed, fainted 26/11
syklow, sekelew *adj.* ill, infirm 180/39, 662/13
sylkemayde *n.* seamstress 287/19
siller, -our *see* **sele(u)r**
symple, -ill, -yll *adj.* modest 45/67, 49/16; plain, ordinary 149/5, 614/10; lacking legal formalities 60/98

symplenesse *n.* ignorance 48/192, 148/2, 1013/68
symply, simpely *adv.* foolishly 188/16, 696/6; poorly 227/16, 459/16
symulacion *n.* deception 213/24
syness *adv.* since 366/19
synet *see* **signet(te**
syngne *see* **signe(e**
syngularly *adv.* in an unusual manner 550/48
sinistre, synystre *adj.* corrupt, dishonest 294/30, 518/17
sinistrely *adv.* adversely 899/4
syse(r *n.* court action 18/23, 937/29
systern *n.* pool 325/13
syt *v.* ~ *on* sit in judgement on 168/12. **syt, sitteth** *pr. 3sg.* ~ *me not,* ~ *not me* is not proper for me 456/6, 537/10. **sotyn** *p.p.* stayed 645/4
syt *prep. see* **sith(en**
sitacion *n.* summons 737/26. **sitacions, scytacions** *pl.* 279/29, 282/79
syth *v. see* **seyn**
sith(en, -yn, -on, syt, sethen, -yn, -nys, sothyn *adv.* since, afterwards 24/23, 65/16, 81/13, 88/98, 172/9, 200/59, 324/5, 574/4, 694/33
sithen, seth *conj.* because 117/11, 457/3
sitteth *see* **syt**
sywerere *see* **swyr**
sywerté *see* **suerté**
skathes *n. pl.* losses, damages 195A/68
skaundered *v. p.p.* slandered 5/142
skeynes *n. pl.* skeins, reels 943/8
skelet *n.* skillet, small pan 123/144
skevsacion *n.* excuse 125/13
skyftyd *v. p.p.* arranged to borrow 400/12
skill *v.* signify, make any difference to 749/40. **skillyd** *pa.* ~ *nowth* signified nothing 876/33
skyl(l)e *n.* reason 433/6; *cannot* ~ *of, can litil* ~ *on* unable to do 184/5, 651/5
skyrtes *n. pl.* comfort, convenience (*fig.*) 473/58
skyte *v.* shit, defecate 968/23
skochyn *see* **scochen**
skore *v.* scour, clean 64/224
skrowe(s *see* **scrowe**
skucchon *see* **scochen**
slake *v. imp.* relent 400/37
slaundere *n.* dishonour, disgrace 208/28
slauth, slaughthe *n.* negligence, idleness 200/60, 370/20
slawe *adj.* dilatory, tardy 292/11
slawthyng *see* **slowth**
slenkyd *v. pa.* crept 443/40
slepe *v.* be neglected 1019/30. **slepyth** *imp. pl.* neglect 988/36. **slept** *p.p.* 1004/12
slewthyd *see* **slowth**
slype *v. let* ~ unleashed 325/11
slyvys *n. pl.* ~ *of plate* armour for the shoulder and arm 181/23
slowth *v. imp.* neglect 181/24. **slawthyng** *pr. p.* being neglectful 352/11. **slewthyd** *p.p.* neglected 996/107
snokyng *v. pr. p.* keeping watch over 459/32 (*see footnote*)
socour, sokowr *n.* assistance, support 132/50, 204/19, 459/11
socour *v.* assist, help 202/5, 491/17. **socowryd** *p.p.* 194/13
sodeyn *n. at a* ~ unexpectedly 77/46
sodyour *see* **saugere**
sofystré, soffistré, safistré *n.* branch of logical philosophy 133/27, 732/25, 76
soft(e)ly *adv.* with restraint 381/64; respectfully 603/27
sogeorn *v.* stay temporarily in various places 208/21
soget *see* **sugett**
soyled *v. p.p.* worked, cultivated 470/9
soiornaunt *n.* visitor 380/44
sokett *n.* candleholder 923/14.
soken, -yn *n.* area where a lord's court has jurisdiction 187/22, 934/3
sokowr *see* **socour**
soleyn *adj.* strange 313/23; surly 705/8
solicitour, solycytore, solysytore *n.* representative 282/22, 601/14; instigator 384/19. *pl.* 1023/1
solid *n. pl.* shillings 123/36
somerlay, somurlay *v.* leave fallow for a year 735/11, 746/28. **somerlayde** *p.p.* 768/10
son *see* **sene**
sond(e)ry, soondry *adj.* several 131/32, 751/11; separate 243/13
sondes *n.*[1] *pl.* messages 5/146
sondys *n.*[2] *pl.* sands, beach 136/31
soole *adj.* vacant, empty 351/47
so(o)r(e *adv.* very, intensely, greatly 119/16,149/16, 169/6, 175/25, 302/18
soos *see* **sawse**
so(o)th(e *n.* truth 555/33, 727/22
soped *see* **supped**
sor *n.* illness 126/26
sor(e *see* **so(o)r(e**
sore, -yd *v. pa.* swore 24/6, 867/41
sorepe *n.* medicinal syrup (from herbs boiled with sugar) 215/29
sorion *n.* surgeon 261/4
sorough *n.* sorrow 49/5
sort *n.* measure of dried fruit 884/20
sote *adj.* sweet, comfortable 774/6
soth *adj.* true 867/73
sothe *n. see* **sooth**
sothyn *see* **sith(en**
sotill, -yll, -yle, sootyl *adj.* treacherous, crafty

5/101, 573/12, 705/16 (*but see footnote*; *perh.* **sootyr** *adj. comp.* more agreeable), 788/6; clever, shrewd 210/38
sotylly *adv.* craftily 439/20
sotilté, suttlté *n.* guile, trick 65/53; *of* ~ through deceit 66/15
sotyn *see* **syt**
sottyt *v. p.p.* ~ *vppon* besotted with 248/120
soudeours, -yor *see* **saugere**
souerd *see* **suffere**
sowde *n.* payments due 439/25
sowdior(i)s, -eorys, -yorys, sowgere, sowiours *see* **saugere**
sowyr *adj.* reddish-brown; ~ *hawke* unmoulted hawk in its first year 354/89
Sowlemesday *n.* All Souls' day, 2 November 937/88
sowndyn *v.* ~ *ageyns* reflect badly upon 880/4. **sownyth** *pr. 3sg.* pertains, relates 457/17. **sowndyng, sownyng** *pr. p.* suggesting 603/4; tending 998/4. **sownyd** *p.p.* tended 907/6
sowte *v. p.p.* searched 149/9, 155/9
sowter *n.* shoemaker 338/68, 497/19
spangell *n. pl.* small ornaments 64/33
spare *v.* delay 444/6
sparris, -ys *n. pl.* beams 665/19, 852/3
speciall *adv.* particularly 219/11
specialtes *n. pl.* particular things 1037/5
sped, spyde *n.* luck, advantage, prospect 180/134, 367/3, 469/18; helper 180/135; progress 628/13
spede, speed *v.* hasten 182/47; complete 72/80; progress 363/42. **spedyng** *inf. kowd not* ~ failed 26/3, **spede** *subj.* were to be accomplished 752/40. **spedyng** *pr. p.* hastening 587/2, 604/23. **sped(de** *pa.* done, accomplished 72/80, 167/10. **sped(de, speed** *p.p.* done, accomplished 128/83, 409/2, 489/25
spelter *n.* alloy of zinc 64/222
sper *v.*[1] lock 659/24. **sperid, sperred** *p.p.* 130/19, 659/17
spere *v.*[2] ask 332/11
sperre *n.* cavalryman 364/14
spervyour *n.* canopy for a bed 123/92
spyde *see* **sped**
spye *v.* enquire surreptitiously 970/46
spyyng *vbl. n.* fear of being observed 160/11
spill *v.* bring to confusion 1001/9
spikenard *n.* aromatic herb 7/3
spynner *n.* small ship 450/6. **spynnes** *pl.* 712/19
splayyd *v. p.p.* having a dislocated shoulder 175/35
splene *n. on the* ~ in jest, jokingly 705/12
spoillid, spo(y)led *v. p.p.* robbed, plundered 48/48, 522/10, 634/6
spore *v.* incite, urge 286/19
sporys *n. pl.* spurs 195A/57; *wynne yowre* ~ live up to or succeed in your knightly obligations 282/76
sporte *v.* ~ *theym/me* amuse themselves/myself 367/19, 406/11
sportys *n. pl.* pastimes, amusements 153/3
spryng, -ys *n. pl.* new growth 703/4; *ȝong* ~ young seedlings 105/4; tides 913/21
spryngill *n.* sprinkler (for holy water) 123/69
sprucheste *n.* chest made of spruce wood 173/28
spruse *n.* spruce wood 59/55
squage *v.* mitigate, appease 462/14
squarid *v. p.p.* cut to a rectangular cross-section 14/31
stabler *n.* keeper of horses 53/30
stablesse *v.* establish 32/51
staynyd *see* **steynyd**
stake *v. pa.* stuck, objected 380/23. **stekyd** *p.p.* struck, afflicted 203/16; stabbed 1024/19
stallyng *vbl. n.* induction into an ecclesiastical office 1049/11
stand *v.* cost 350/5. **standyth** *pr. 3sg.* remains (owing) 587/8. **stant** *pr. 3sg.* stands 140/3. **stand** *imp.* accept 354/69. **stode** *pa.* served as 587/7
standarde, -erd, stondert *n.* flag 968/30; chest, trunk or box 259/21; small tree left standing after land has been cleared 767/18 (*pl.*), 23; ~ *of mayle* collaret, neckpiece (armour) 181/23, 944/33. **standardys** *pl.* new shoots from tree stumps 274/47
standing, stonding *ppl. adj.*. having a foot or base 123/48, 230/116, 923/48, 930/27, 70
stankes, -ys *n. pl.* fish ponds 994/48, 995/12
stant *see* **stand**
stapill, Estaple *n.* official market established by royal authority for selling export goods 63/23, 300/22
stat(e *n. mak* ~ give legal right or title 59/65; legal possession 870B/8
stately *adj.* haughty 444/33
stately *adv.* arrogantly, haughtily 444/17
statutys *n. pl.* customs, rules of conduct 316/41
stavys, stauis *n. pl. standarde* ~ flag poles 762/4; *bowe* ~ length of a pole to be made into a longbow 778/21, 779/9
stedyousely *n.* thoroughly 1022/6
steede *n.* place; *stand yn* ~ be reliable 989/130, 990/40
steynyd, -ed, stenyd, staynyd *ppl. adj.* embroidered or dyed 123/104, 732/81; ~ *paperis* ? sheets of paper carrying illustrations or designs 732/26; *of* ~ *werke* with embroidered decorations 123/104
steynour *n.* painter 969/15
stekyd *see* **stake**

stele *v.* abduct 132/7
stepyng *vbl. n.* soaking (of malt) 965/67
stere *v.* become disturbed 459/26; persuade 460/69, 603/31, 749/35; inspire 656/17. **sterid** *p.p.* prompted 54/15, 880/83
steryng *v. pr. p.* governing, ruling 180/79, 456A/5; instigation, incitement 654/9; moving 776/40
steryng, -eng, styryng *ppl.adj.* active 212/39, 775/23; ~ *hors* courser, swift horse 774/55
stew *n.* pond stocked with edible fish 782/9. **stewes** *pl.* 13/11
styffelere *n.* mediator 281/7
stille *v.* calm 455/13. **stilled** *pa.* fell silent 653/8
styryng *see* **steryng**
styrte *v.* startle, put to flight 273/6
stode *see* **stand**
stody *n.* anxiety 469/25
stok(k(e *n.* block of wood 259/43; main group 306/15; *haly water* ~ vessel for holding holy water 123/68; ~ *gonne* gun fitted with a wooden stock 195A/37. **stok(k)es** *pl.* trestles for guns or cannons 64/212; socks or stockings 732/110
stokfyshe *n. pl.* unsalted dried fish 1003/19
stokked *v. pa.* placed in the stocks 880/55
stole *n.* liturgical vestment worn around the neck 123/101
stomake *n.* disposition 288/3, 296/10; state of health 293/20
stomakyd *v. p.p. weell* ~ well-disposed 310/12
stomechere, stoma(u)chere, stomaker *n.* vest, waistcoat or similar garment 406/10, 419/6, 732/86, 732/102
stondert *see* **standarde**
stonding *see* **standing**
stondys *n. pl. ale* ~ vessels for ale 195A/18
stoon *n.* stone, unit of weight (approx. 6.5 kg.) 989/79; *free* ~ fine-grained limestone or sandstone 259/44
stoor *see* **store**
stop *v.* block up 148/16
stope *n.* jug 485/25
store, stoor *n.* possessions, goods 8/9, 8/22; stock of goods 775/30
storyd *v. p.p.* restored, changed (for the better) 131/97; provided with supplies 238/36
stowtly *adv.* forcefully 172/40
strayte, -eite *adj.* strict 456A/6, 694/3, 1013/44. **straitest** *superl.* 687/90
strayter *adv. comp.* more stringently 122/44
straitly, streitly, strey(gh)tely *adv.* closely 162/17, 290/16, 361/30, 490/4; precisely, strictly 260/15, 687/33, 803/16. **streytlyere** *comp.* more frugally 206/5
straunge *v.* estrange 888/18. **straunched** *pa.* 604/8
stra(u)ng(e, -che, strawnge *adj.* other, further 128/83, 409/30; difficult 200/52, 221/33, 564/20; unfriendly, hostile 218/40, 491/3, 1012/44; unknown 231/51, 528/10; ~ *of* unwilling to 150/33
stra(u)ngely, -chely, stra(w)ngely *adv.* in a hostile manner, sceptically 128/4, 578/20, 632/4, 648/3, 737/27
straungenesse *n.* estrangement 515/2
strede *n. pl.* strides 129/11
streyne *v.* seize property in order to enforce an obligation 656/14. **streyned, strenyd** *p.p.* 215/20, 228/18
stre(y)ngthe *n.* troops, garrison (of men) 447/11, 737/14
streynkyth, streynth, strenght *v.* support, reinforce 192/22, 192/23; protect 653/14. **strenth** *pp.* 919/6
streit, streythe *adv.*[1] *go* ~ *wyth* be difficult for 89/33; securely 646/30
streyt(te *adv.*[2] directly (from) 400/26; ~ *weye* directly 643/11
streite *adj. see* **strayte**
streitly, stre(gh)tely, stretlyere *see* **straitly**
streytnesse *n.* stinginess, parsimony 643/25
strek(en *p.p.* a measure levelled with a strickle (flat piece of wood) 669/8; ~ *met* measured by the strickle 178/21
strengh *v.* support, reinforce 199/26. **strenghyng** *pr. p.* 919/3
strenghes *n. pl.* strongholds 412/35
strenght, strenth *see* **streynkyth**
strengthe *see* **stre(y)ngthe**
strepe *n.* ~ *and waste* spoliation of land, destruction of parts of a tenement, etc. 870A/13
stres *n.* seizure of goods or chattels in a distraint 66/6; goods or chattels seized in a distraint 820/6. **stresses** *pl.* 743/3
streuyn *pp.* fought 231/63
stryke *v.* lower sail 968/22
stroy *v.* destroy 118/8
strong(e *adj.* flagrant, shameless, notorious 129/25, 475/18, 704/11; *by* ~ *hand* by force 369/16
stronge, stronke *adv.* strongly 737/42; intensively 1029/22
strop(pe *n.* squandering of an inheritance 1012/51, 1040/17
stuffe *n.* supplies, provisions 729/17
stuffe *v. pr. 3pl.* furnish with provisions 217/11. **stuffed, stvffet** *p.p.* crammed full 732/48, 1026/24
subpena, suppena *n.* writ compelling the appearance of a party in a dispute before the

court of chancery 60/106, 252/83, 310/18, 355/7, 746/3
substanciall *adj.* wealthy 230/111
substaunce, -a(u)ns *n.* bulk, significant amount 168/36, 252/26, 252/35; livelihood, resources 641/8, 725/14; majority of people 652/18, 782/4; representative group 675/4; *of* ~ propertied, of rank 641/8, 648/12
suerhere, suhere *adj.* legally binding 203/36, 37
suerté, -ty, -(e)té, sywerté, severté, swerté *n.* guarantee (esp. money deposited as pledge of fulfilling an obligation) 25/30, 115/5, 152/16, 196/57, 300/19; agreement 119/31, 157/29; ~ *of the pees* legal order to keep the peace and to provide security against a breach 48/49. **suertees, sewirtesse, swertys, -ees,** *pl.* sureties, guarantors 121/18, 120/4, 759/8, 778/39
suff(e)raunce *n.* forebearance 1005/67, 1013/38
suffere, -yr, -re *v.* allow, permit 157/17, 184/33, 202/13. **souerd** *p.p.* allowed 203/62
sufficient(e, suffisant *adj.* properly qualified 4/16; worthy 641/7; *aftir the* ~ in accordance with (the votes of) those properly qualified 633/7
suffragys *n. pl.* prayers 656/34
sugett *n.* subject 460A/8
sumdele *adv.* somewhat, a little 491/42
sumnor *n.* court official responsible for citing persons to appear 831/45
superscrybyd *v. p.p.* addressed 271/3
supersedeas, -diace, -ias, -dies, supercedyas, -eas, *n.* writ that stays or suspends proceedings in a case 39/14, 48/185, 274/13, 315/22, 565/20, 867/36
supped, soped *v. pa.* dined 741/15, 744/55
suppena *see* **subpena**
supplicauit *n.* writ of instruction to keep the peace 189/91
suppose *v.* suspect 203/69
surcease, -eesse, sursese *v.* cease from an action, desist 381/17, 550/43, 562/6; halt 1002/17
sure *adj.* ~ *of* securely in possession of 121/10
surmise, -yse *n.* allegation 812/6, 896A/5
surmission *n.* allegation 484/12
surmytte *v.* allege 76/19. **surmitten** *pr. 3pl.* 555/30. **surmyttyng** *pr. p.* 1011/35. **surmytted, -itted** *p.p.* 901A/9, 1046/24
survey *v.* supervise 53/29
surveyeng *vbl. n.* stewardship 982/26
surveyour *n.* senior household official 713/5. *pl.* 1005/54
sustentacion *n.* maintenance 60/27, 230/106
susters *n. pl.* nuns 230/85; *half* ~ novices 230/85; *hole* ~ professed nuns 230/85
suthe, swth *n.* lawsuit 37/38, 81/19; petition, request 128/72. **sewtys, swtys** *pl.* lawsuits 131/8, petitions 81/17
suttely *adv.* treacherously 46/51
suttlté *see* **sotilté**
swemefull *adj.* grievous 200/22
swerly, sewerly *adv.* surely, effectively 32/52; securely 236/3
swerté, -ees, -ys *see* **suerté**
swhyve *v.* have sexual intercourse with 395/4. **swyvyd** *p.p.* raped 312/32
swyd, -id *v. p.p.* pursued in court 115/6, 436/7
swyng *ppl. adj.* following 1012/5
swynysty *n.* pigsty 435/8
swyr, -ior *adj.* sure, secure 223/10, 332/11, 436/17. **sywerere** *comp.* 300/18
swyre *see* **scyuer**
swn *prep.* since 176/17
sworyn *v. p.p.* bound by oath 271/49
swth, swtys *see* **suthe**
sxuld *see* **xall**

table *n.* portable altarpiece 68/5. **tablys, -illes, -yllys** *pl.* board games 153/6; wax-filled writing-tablets 195B/44, 732/34
tablet *n.* portable altarpiece 123/71. **tablettes** *pl.* jewels with flat surfaces 123/170
tachement(es) *see* **at)tachement**
taile, -yl(l)(e *n.* entailment (restriction of inheritance to a particular heir or class of heirs) 67/19, 132/71, 541/2, 565/29; *be* ~ according to a tallied record (i.e. on tally sticks) 423/9. **tayl(l)es** *pl.* entailments 657/14; tally sticks recording revenue owed the to Exchequer 439/26
tayled, -id, entaylyd, ontayled *v. p.p.* subject to an entailment (*see* **taile**) 25/38, 304/20, 657/13, 872/33
take *v.* give 454/address. **takyth** *pr. 3sg.* ~ *on* rants and raves 355/11. **take, toke, tuke** *pa.* gave 77/72, 191/17, 764/16. **take, tane** *p.p.* given 196/7; taken 414/27
takelyng *vbl. n.* rigging of a ship 827/5; weaponry, *abyde by there* ~ stand their ground 238/19
takke *n.* pasturing let out to rent 500/10, 18
talagys *n. pl.* royal land taxes 16/11
tall(e *adj.* strong, able-bodied 799/5, 801/7. **tallest** *superl.* most handsome 141/29
tane *see* **take**
tany *n.* tawny-coloured cloth 668/40
taptrogh, taptrowe *n.* lead trough fitted with a tap 195A/23, 195B/26
taryans *n.* delay 615/3, 677/43
taried *see* **tery(n**
tars(s)ell, ters(s)ell *n.* male hawk or falcon 354/94, 355/29, 356/11, 356/13

tarteryn, tartron *n.* expensive cloth originating in Tartary 64/169, 123/86
taske *n.* tax 361/2. **taskys** *pl.* 361/24, 996/38
tedyng *see* **tythyng**
tediose *adj.* annoying 48/69
teynes *n. pl.* small sticks, kindling 36/24
teler, tylere *n.* stock of a crossbow 248/17, 339/9. **telers** *pl.* 338/40
telyn *v.* till, cultivate 931/6. **teled** *p.p.* cultivated 744/21
telyng *vbl.n.* cultivation 931/30
temporal, -elx, temperall, -elx *adj.* secular 184/51, 638/10, 881/33, 886/80; ~ *curte* secular court of justice 177/5
temps, temse *n.* sieve or strainer 11/28, 195A/23, 195B/26
tempted *v. p.p.* sought for 782/38
tenantry *n. bond* ~ manorial holding let in exchange for money or service 196/77. **tenauntrys, tenaunryes** *pl.* 178/23, 692/49
tender, -yr, -re *v.* attend to 42/10, 234/11, 857/27. **tendryth** *pr. 3sg.* cares about 357/23. **tendryd** *pa.* 368/3
tender, -re *adj.* kind 121/25, 509/13
tendyr *adv.* sympathetically 333/35
tendrely *adv.* compassionately 5/182
tenowr, -ur *n.* tenure, legal possession of land 66/13; landoldings 726/25. **tenourys** *pl.* 771/3
tented *v. pa.* offered 886/7
tenure *n.* tenor, main point 643/4
tep(p)et(e, typet *n.* small cloak or hood 77/5, 195A/49, 195B/53, 394/24
tere *n.* tar 779/10
teryyng *vbl. n.* remaining 432/42
tery(n *v.* wait, remain 128/18, 327/41, 334/14. **terry** *pr. 1sg.* 345/34. **terythe** *pr. 3sg.* 321/15. **terying, -yn** *pr. p.* 231/15, 442/20. **ter(y)ed, -id** *pa.* 192/49, 231/16, 296/39, 644/20. **teryed** *p.p.* 296/37
termys *n. pl.* provisions, conditions 176/7
terrar *n.* register of landed property, tenants, rents etc. 98/55
terrauntys *n. pl.* oppressors 705/2
ters(s)ell *see* **tars(s)ell**
testamentarie *adj.* relating to a will 539/27
teste *n.* writ 678/12; authenticating clause in a writ 473/109, 679/16. **testes** *pl.* witnesses 119/26
tester, -our *n.* headboard of a bed supporting a canopy 64/51, 123/95. **testeres** *pl.* 64/126
testymonyal(l *n. letter (of)* ~ affidavit 169/20, 470/11–12
thare *see* **ther**
the *pron.* they 77/188, 298/29, 299/1
þedder *adv.* there 130/17
thede *n.* strainer used in brewing 11/28
thee, they *v.* thrive 198/36, 282/65
theffly *adv.* deceitfully 704/12
they *v. see* **thee**
they *conj. see* **thow**
theyves, thevys *n. pl.* young ewes 195A/62, 195B/66, 731/5
thenke *n.* thing, discourse 450/20
ther *v.* need 180/114. **thare** *subj.* need 172/9
therd *n.* woven fabric 732/126
thernot *see* **dor**
þerwhyle *adv.* in the meantime 129/29
thyke *adj.* stout 407/33
thyng *v.* think 116/25, 135/8, 214/24.
thyre *adj.* these 282/9
thys, this *adj.* these 180/61, 317/10
tho(o, þo *pron.* those 59/59, 67/39, 202/18
thongys *n. pl.* strips 190/62
þoov *see* **thow**
thorf *prep.* through, by means of 184/60
thorough, -ow, thorgh *adv. go(o* ~ conclude 430/19, 600/37, 652/28
thorow, thorwe *see* **through, thorough**
thow, þou, þoov, they *conj.* even though 23/5, 73/45, 125/29, 520/9
thowt(h, thowght *n.* anxiety 656/9, 840/14; *take no* ~ do not worry 74/11, 915/21
thowthe, þowth *v. pa.* thought 135/20, 203/38
thralldam *n.* subservience 74/46
threde *n. Norfolke* ~ tightly spun thread, worsted 711/22
thrett *v. pa.* threatened 443/19. *p.p.* 131/86
thrifty, -yfty *adj.* respectable, honourable 23/12, 41/13, 744/13. **thriftyest, -ies** *superl.* most honourable 532/14, 653/19
throche *v.* threshed 442/13
through, thorow, thorwe, throw, thurgh *adj.* done, finished 147/2, 200/59, 225/15, 728/15; resolved 14/7
thwolmonyth, towylemonthe *n.* year 205/8; *this* ~ *day* during the past year 72/72–3,
tye *n.* cover for a chest 55/6
tyer *see* **tyre**
tylere *see* **teler**
tyl(l)e *n. pl.* roof tiles 144/7, 329/8, 371/34
tylle *v.* cover with tiles 329/3
tilthe, tylth(e *n.* crops, cultivation 200/14, 399/10, 703/5; *out of* ~ uncultivated 649/6
tyme *n. on a* ~ once 256/17
tin *v. p.p.* wasted 432/43
tyncte *n.* conviction in a court of law 564/18
typet *see* **tep(p)et(e**
tyre, tyer *n.* sweet wine of the Tyre region 287/dorse, 705/6
tisshew, tyssywe *n.* silk shot with gold and silver thread 123/79, 295/10
titelyng, tytelyng *n.* summary 72/120, 180/48

tithe *n.* annual donation of a tenth part of one's income to a church 728/15
tythyng, tedyng *n.* news 83/1, 613/8. **tyt(h)yngys, tithynges, tytynges, dydyngys, tythandys** *pl.* 185/44, 397/1, 439/1, 451/19, 628/19, 752/27
tythyt *v. p.p.* given as **tithe** (*q.v.*) 731/7
titlers *n. pl.* gossips, whisperers 679/24
tit(t)le, tytle, tytill, -ell, -yll(e *n.* claim of legal right of possession 189/3, 193/5, 178/4, 702/13; ~ *of recorde* authoritative document 120/14; ~ *of right* grounds for assertion of a legal claim 122/52, 698/5. **tytyls** *pl.* claims to possession 333/12
to *prep.* as 256/17
to-bowyd *v. p.p.* bent out of shape 677/4
tochyng *see* **to(u)chyng**
toder *adj.* other 126/15, 204/4, 218/31
todyr *pron.* other person 154/12
tofore, to-fo(o)r(e *adv.* before 5/122, 267/4, 351/35
tohand *adj.* two-handed 129/33
toyes *n. pl.* tricks 313/23
toke *see* **takyth**
token, -yn *n.* object (e.g. seal, ring) used to validate an instruction or messenger 549/5, 645/9, 861/28. **toknes** *pl.* identifying characteristics 438/8
to-morn, -yn, -wen *adv.* tomorrow 131/17, 179/23, 578/1
ton *n.* large barrel 819/6
ton(e *pron.* one 204/46, 220/58
tonne *v.* store 259/52, 374/24
tonsewryd *adj.* tonsured (to show clerical status) 733/5
toon *num.* two of them 737/27
torn *v. subj.* should turn, were to alter 114/11
tornay *n.* tournament 327/29.
torney *v.* joust 330/19
tornys *see* **turn(e**
tottid *v. p.p.* checked off (on a list) 441/50
touche, -wche *n.* hallmark 692/60, 925/50
to(u)chyng, -ing, t(o)wchyng *v. pr. p.* concerning 128/74, 172/7, 183/22, 437/27, 33
towayle, -is *see* **towell**
towardys *adj.* imminent 238/20; acceptable 283/26
towardys *adv.* amongst the affinity of 296/20, 354A/5; *pleasaunt* ~ well advanced towards ripeness 688/9
towardnesse *n.* positive inclination 1010/14; progress 289/10
towche *see* **touche**
towchyng *see* **to(u)chyng**
towell, -ayle *n.* table linen 64/155123/126. **towellys, -aylis** *pl.* 64/151, 195A/16
towylemonthe *see* **thwolmonyth**
townesende *n.* outskirts of the village 728/3
trahid *v. p.p.* marked 98/62
traill, -yle *n.* floral ornamentation 230/144, 923/30. **traílles** *pl.* 923/34
traytours *adj.* perfidious, false 564/7
trauaille *n.* journey 485/26
trauers(e *v.* dispute 437/27, 886/7, 996/122
trauers(e *n.* dispute, counter-claim 842/5, 886/10, 978/11; record of a legal dispute 55/8. **trauersys** *pl.* 615/13
traunsom, traumsom *n.* bed-hanging 230/118, 732/37. **traunsomes, -souns** *pl.* 64/119; bolsters 195B/7
treyfowle *n.* ~ *wise* shaped like a clover leaf 64/30
trenchors *n. pl.* serving dishes 144/33
trendils *n. pl.* cogwheels 259/55
trentalles *n. pl.* ~ *of Saint Gregory* liturgical offices attributed to Pope Gregory the Great (ten sets of three masses for the dead) 123/12
trespas *n.* unlawful action 867/16
tret(e *v.* conduct legal procedures 5/45; negotiate 333/60, 472/27. **treted** *p.p.* governed 3/18
trety(e), treté *n.* negotiation, pleading 13/7, 65/3, 601/4; settlement, agreement 118/10, 184/52
trewlove *n.* quatrefoil 442/4
trews, trieux, truesse *n.* truce 241/2, 907/25, 968/30
triacle, tryacle *n.* a medicine, tonic 141/27, 313/2, 381/71
trifeled *v. pa.* ~ *forth the court* wasted the court's time 628/5
triparted *v. p.p.* divided into three parts 252/240
trystyt *v. pr. 3sg.* trusts 19/9
trobell, tro(w)ble *v.* dispute the ownership (of land, property, etc.) 180/129, 304/41, 304/43
trobulus, -elows *adj.* changeable 164/13, 204/26
troy weight, -w(e)yght *n.* system of weights used for precious metals 28/17, 250/2, 251/6
trossyng *see* **trussing**
trostelles, -elis *n. pl.* trestles, table supports 11/27, 259/38
trotterys *n. pl.* well-trained horses 154/35
troublez, -wblez *n. pl.* legal challenges 252/30, 252/46
tro(u)gh(t, tro(w)ght *n.* truth 41/18, 144/10, 182/35, 190/73, 196/90; honour 201/36
trow *n.* trough 11/28
trow(e, trowh *v. pr. 1sg.* believe, trust 4/33, 79/17, 114/35
truesse *see* **trews**
trusse *v.* pack 282/69, 363/22. **trussed** *pa.* 534/33. **trussid** *p.p.* 71/17

trussing, -yng, trossyng *vbl. n.* ~ *cofyr, cofore* trunk 148/9, 173/28, 191/18; ~ *bedde* portable bed 230/149; ~ *doblet(ys)* sturdy clothes for travelling 325/20, 949/22
tuke *see* **takyth**
tunne tyght *n.* unit of weight (= a full tun) 1/6
turn(e *n.* bi-annual court 618/16, 703/17, 721/9; **tornys** *pl.* tricks, disservices 559/11
turne-pyke *n.* turnstile barriers 777/35
turnerys *n.pl.* ? gloves with turned-up cuffs 732/135
tweyn(e *num.* two 5/64, 248/60; at odds 353/49
Twelthe *n.* the twelfth day after Christmas (feast of Epiphany, 6 January) 168/6
twoys *adj. ther* ~ both of their 369/26

vmpere *n.* arbitrator 252/187, 595/9, 867/30
vnchedyn *v. p.p.* unrebuked 353/48
vnconcienst *adj.* unscrupulous 901B/99
vndernemyng *v. pr. p.* lending support 919/22
vnderwode, vndrewood, vndyrewode *n.* brushwood 229/23, 274/81, 767/29
vndyrstonde *v.* be present 643/39. **vndirstod** *v. pa.* found out about 644/7. **vnderstand, vndyr-, vndir-** *p.p.* interpreted 231/28; known, noted 202/3, 644/23; considered 416/13
vndyrstondyng *vbl. n.* intended meaning (of a statement) 5/25
vndirtoke *v. pa.* vouched 644/25
vnfayne *adj.* displeased 776/18
vngoodly *adv.* unlawfully 461/29
vngwentum, -orum *n.* ~ *album* lime-based ointment 140/18; *flose* ~ best ointment 389/3
vnkonnynge *n.* lack of knowledge 1013/68
vnremembred, -id *v. p.p.* unmindful 747/15; forgotten 908/12
vnsittyng, vnsyttyng *ppl. adj.* offensive, inappropriate 355/19, 802/9, 991/30
vnskylfull *adj.* audacious 867/39
vnthriftys *n. pl.* unruly people 910/18
vntylle *v. inf.* remove tiles from 329/4
vnwarys *adv. hys* ~ unbeknown to him 238/26
vnwetyng, onwetyng *v. pr. p. myn/me* ~ without my knowledge 345/8, 494/10, 901A/7
vppon *prep.* in the company of 238/12
vre *n.* litigation 304/29, 603/22
vrke *see* **irk**
vse *n.* practice 72/23; benefit 252/108
vse *v.* accustom 28/19. **vsed, -id, -yd** *p.p.* (been) accustomed 52/8, 500/12; done, performed 304/36, 508/11
vsyng *vbl. n.* observance 40/15, 48/111
vsuell *abj.* habitual 932/22
vsure, vsery *n.* extortion 363/29, 626/28
vtas *n.* eighth day following a feast day 147/25
vtlagaré *see* **outlagaré**
vtter, wtter *adj.* outer 64/181, 209A/44, 329/7
vtter *v.*[1] market, sell 703/30, 986/48, 1050/20
vttered *v.*[2] *p.p.* damaged 215/7
vtterest *adj. superl.* utmost 463/10
vtteryng *vbl. n.* marketing 821/7
vtterly *adv.* openly, blatantly 867/62; promptly 981/44, 989/78
vttermest, vttremest *adj. superl.* highest, utmost 238/48, 286/14; final 679/8
vutraunce *n.* right to trade in a commodity 274/62

valour *n.* value 309/7
vamwarde *n.* vanguard 298/30
varyen *v. pr. 3pl.* ~ *fro* disagree with 744/18
vaunced *v. p.p.* promoted 1013/47
vaunted *v. p.p.* boasted 687/43
vec(a)ry *see* **vikarie**
vele *see* **fel(l)e**
veleny *see* **vylney**
venire facias *n.* writ directing a sheriff to summon a jury, or to require the appearance in court of a person on an indictment 489/30, 548/31, 552/7
venom *n.* act of malice 1008/34
verdyte, -yth(e, -yght, -ett *n.* verdict, ruling 46/25, 89/13, 103/22, 342/12
verdure, -our *n.* green embroidery or tapestry 123/86, 930/44
verely *adv.* for sure 193/5
verges *n. pl.* borders 230/25
vergyous *n.* verjuice, extracted from unripe fruit 195A/18
ver(r)y, verray *adj.* authentic, true 265/33, 283/15, 350/1
vesaged *see* **vysaged**
vesshell *n. pl.* dishes 166/30
vesture *n.* produce of an area of land (crops and hay) 8/4
vetayle *v.* stock with food and drink 738/12. **vetaylle** *pr. 3pl.* 217/11. **vetaylled** *p.p.* 738/10
vetayll, vytaly *n.* provisions 204/2, 334/11, 648/16. **vetaylys** *pl.* 320/14
vetelyng, vyta(i)llyng *vbl. n.* provisioning 572/53, 668/7, 824/5
veveri *n.* ivory 732/84
vewe, vieu, vywe *n.* reckoning 353/22; review of a case at law 552/22; *take the* ~ inspect 298/14
viage, vyage, wyage *n.* journey 225/12, 370/7, 824/3; military expedition 293/2. **viages** *pl.* 604/12
vidimus *n.* document bearing authenticating seals 989/14
vieu *see* **vewe**

vikarie, vec(a)ry *n.* parish vicar 14/6, 831/42, 865/11
villains *n. pl.* bondsmen 946/3
villinage *n.* status of villein, under serfdom 946/10
vylney, -onye, veleny *n.* disgrace, humiliation 199/18, 520/19, 543/10
visage *n. bere gret* ~ put on a bold front 444/18
visager *n.* one who puts a false aspect on things 932/5
vysagyd *v. p.p. wele* ~ good-looking 248/104. **vesaged** *pa., p.p.* presented in a particular or a misleading guise 460/3, 937/110
vise *see* **wys(e**
vysitacyon *n.* dispensation, ordering of things 205/13
visitor *n.* official inspector 1049/78
vyta(i)llyng *see* **vetelyng**
vytaly *see* **vetayll**
vywe *see* **vewe**
voyd *v.* dismiss 143/18
voysed, -id *v. p.p.* said 705/85; ~ *for* commonly said to be 435/18
voys(s)e *n.* acclamation 633/6; opinion 228/27; *comyn* ~ general opinion, rumour 114/15
vouche *n.* person appearing in court to testify title to property 960/10
voulenté *n.* desire 996/75
voweson *n.* advowson, right to nominate to a benefice 5/176
vowte *n.* vaulted structure of some kind 147/10
vwche-save *see* **wechesaf**

waard *see* **ward(e**
wacchid *v. pa.* stayed up late 751/23
wagyd *v. p.p.* employed 238/2
waynscot, waynescotte *n.* pieces of good quality or dressed timber 778/21, 852/2. **waynescottys** *pl.* 779/10
wayte *n.* ambush 40/27
walwe *n.* value 649/7
wanton *adj.(as adv.)* rowdily, wildly 367/17
wappys *n. pl. for* ~ for the present 335/40
war *v. imp.* beware 514/5
waraunt *v.* guarantee right of possession 274/72
ward *see* **werd**
ward(e, waard *n.*[1] custody 5/93, 312/31, 887/5; prison 163/9, 962/22; guard 238/8; child under guardianship 230/153, 509/23; courtyard 64/181; administrative division of a town 194/12
warde *n.*[2] judicial decision 579/15
warderobe *n.* store room 259/24
warderopper *n.* keeper of the royal wardrobe 471/53
ware *adj.* careful 178/44. **warhere** *comp.* 176/24
ware *v.* spend money 680/45. **wared** *p.p.* 1016/27
warennare *n.* gamekeeper 965/85
warlye *adv.* diligently 269/19
warne *v.* give notice of, announce 192/34. **warned, -yd** *p.p.* 340/4, 486/9
warrantize *n.* formal assurance of the right to possession of property 246/44
war(r)eyn, -yne *n.* land managed for small game 195A/70, 390/5, 1009/49
wast *n.* harm 122/35, 200/5. **wastes, -ys** *pl.* 333/14, 703/14
wateris *n. pl.* medicines, cordials 220/32
watteryng *vbl. n.* pond 23/12
wax *v.* become 163/42, 199/29. **waxse** *p.p.* grown 125/15
we(a)le *see* **welle**
webbes, -ys, -is *n. pl.* breadths of woven cloth, used as units of measure 64/116, 195A/13, 230/135
weche *n.* watch, lookout 921/3
wechesaf(e, -saue, wychesaue, wetesafe, vwche-save *v.* consent, deign 125/7, 127/17, 128/12, 155/32, 164/22, 171/25
wed(de *n. to* ~ pledged, pawned 682/24, 1011/53
wederys *n. pl.* male sheep 731/3
weeldyd *v. pa. refl.* ~ *hym* conducted himself 705/14
weell *see* **welle**
weel-willyng, -ed *see* **wele-wyllyng**
weend(e, weene *see* **wen(e**
wey(e *n.*[1] *at longe* ~ in the long run 227/9; *in* ~ making progress 244/4
wey *n.*[2] weighed unit of quantity 1011/30
weykid *ppl. adj.* exhausted 583/8
weytte *n.* weight 126/6
wele-wyllyng, weel-willyng, welewylland *v. pr. p.* favourably disposed 131/53, 446/40, 739/23. **well wyllyd, weel-wylled** *p.p.* 180/82, 766/76
welk *v. pa.* walked 131/55
welle, weell, we(a)le *n.* benefit 114/31, 184/63, 306/10; prosperity 241/7; eternal bliss 30/7, 930/116
welwet, -uett, fellewet *n.* velvet 195B/43, 692/54, 732/61
welwyller *n.* supporter, friend 271/9. **wel(e-wyllerys** *pl.* 128/46, 135/24, 176/16
wene, weene *v. pr. 1sg.* believe, suppose, expect 14/30, 79/20, 210/6. **wenyth** *pr. 3sg.* 218/26, 347/8. **wen(e** *pr. 3pl.* 114/20, 168/26. **wenyng** *pr. p.* 146/18; suggesting 242/49, 474/22; ~ *to hym* as far as he could see 970/44. **we(e)nd(e, wenyd, went** *pa.* 116/31, 203/24, 222/17, 282/87, 301/4; expect
wenged *v. p.p.* avenged 213/15

wepyng *n. pl.* weapons 48/55
werd, ward, word(e, woord *n.* world, circumstances 114/11, 135/28, 221/33, 272/13; ordering of things 168/39; secular life 205/32; sphere of activity 651/7
werdly, wordly *adj.* worldly 67/30, 693/4
weryn *vbl. n.* wearing 931/34
werk *n.* embroidery 195A/12
werkmanly *adv.* skillfully 230/15
werre *n.* conflict, dispute 74/18, 601/13, 785/2. **werrys** *pl.* military campaigns 289/19
wesshe *v. p.p.* washed 450/2
wet(e(n, wethe, wit(t(e, wyte, wittin, wut(te *v.* know, understand 1/3, 3/2, 10/1, 91/2, 131/2, 154/2, 209A/51, 227/10, 469/2; *that is to* ~ namely 123/15, 252/49. **wot(e, woot** *pr. 1sg.* know 3/29, 131/22, 205/35. **wotyth(e, wottys, ote** *pr. 3sg.* 248/52, 278/18, 415/6; ~ *not where to hold hym* does not know how to act 184/45. **wetyn** *pr. 2pl.* know 13/3. **wyght** *subj.* 269/30. **wet, wetith, wettyt** *imp.* find out 14/27, 238/49; understand 203/72. **west, wyst(e, wist, wost(e, woost** *pa.* knew 23/4, 126/4, 131/5, 132/12, 203/15, 653/8; ~ *ner, nowte* ~ did not know 160/23, 205/30
wetesafe *see* **wechesaf(e**
wetyn(g *vbl. n.* knowledge 32/32, 77/110, 132/6
wettyt *see* **wet(e(n**
whaȝerys *see* **quaire**
whedyr *pron.* whichever, which of the two 321/17
whedyr *adv. no* ~ nowhere 346/17
whelpys *n. pl.* young dogs 325/11
Whene *n.* Queen 567/18
wheresse *n.* worse 216/15
wherthorough, -owe *conj.* through which 66/59, 122/36
wherwilles *n. pl.* unidentified parts of a candleholder 923/17
whyleom *adv.* formerly 351/45
whylle *n. off a* ~ for a time 258/47
whynground *n.* field covered with gorse 500/3
whynnes *n. pl.* clumps of gorse 500/6
white, qwet(e, qhete *n.* wheat 63/18, 442/13, 442/15, 704/13
whonnyn *v. p.p.* taken, overcome 777/44
who(u, whoo *adv. see* **hough**
wyage *see* **viage**
wice *see* **wys(e**
wychesaue *see* **wechesaf(e**
wyet *see* **wyte** *v.*
wyfeles *n. pl.* pikes 444/28
wyff *n.* mistress of a household 510/7
wyght *adj.* white 173/27
wyght *see* **wet(e(n**
wyketis *n. pl.* openings 130/10
wyld *adj.* unruly 168/10
wylde *n. at* ~ bewildered 375/10
wilfully *adv.* willingly 656/2
will, wyl(l *adv.* well 23/3, 25/39, 648/15
wylly *adj.* well-disposed 18/9
wilne *v.* wish 694/13
wyndas(e *n.* winch 248/18, 339/9. **wyndacis, wyndas** *pl.* 130/2, 338/40
wyndown *n.* window 778/48. **wyndownes, -ys** *pl.* 47/3, 778/48
wypyng *v. pr. p.* weeping 190/78
wyry *adj.* wearisome 180/136
wyrte *n.* ~ *of passagche* writ granting permission to pass through a region 469/9
wys(e, wice, vise *n.* manner, way 122A/7, 189/43, 650/17; *on that* ~ by that means 402/9
wysythyt *v. pr. 3sg.* visits, afflicts 205/9
wyst(e, wist *see* **wet(e(n**
wyte *n.* responsibility, blame 566/35
wyte, wyet *v.* blame, reproach 332/43, 540/5. **wyte** *pr. 3sg.* blames 472/39
wit(e, wyte *see* **wet(e(n**
wyth-all *adv.* therewith 128/75
withdraught *n.* withdrawal 766/73
wythhaldyn *v. p.p.* retained 5/126
without *prep.* outside 230/95
wythoute, -ought, -owt *conj.* unless 173/12, 189/35, 189/48
with-set(te *v. p.p.* confiscated 14/13; appropriated 778/24
wyt(t, witthe *n.* discretion 354A/4, 510/11; mental faculties 89/31. **wyttys** *n. pl.* senses, right mind 375/33
witt(e, wittin *see* **wet(e(n**
wittely *adv.* wisely, prudently 72/73, 77/160
witthe *see* **wyt(t**
wytty *adj.* advised, aware 99/7; intelligent 264/61; accomplished 790/8
wo begone *adj.* distressed 626/2
wode, wood *adj.* furious 134/7, 528/8; insane 903/10
wode *adv.* furiously 134/8
wolew *n.* value 195A/71
wolfellys, woulle fellys *n. pl.* sheepskins 195A/58, 195B/58
wolle *n.* output of wool from estates 731/11. **wollys** *pl.* 572/22
won *see* **on**
wonges *n. pl.* fields 767/33
wood *see* **wode** *adj.*
woold *see* **wull**
woond, wownd *v. p.p.* wrapped 394/41; ~ *abowt* wrapped around 131/7
woost, woot *see* **wet(e(n**
worcheppfull *see* **wurchepfull**
word(e, woord *see* **werd**
wordes, woordys *n. pl. had the* ~ done the

talking 189/18; *wetche* ~ words of caution 603/11
wordy *adj.* deserving 407/18
wordly *see* **werdly**
worshyp *n.* honour, standing 457/6
wo(r)sted(e *n.* woollen cloth 123/97, 230/119, 930/33; ~ *man* wool merchant 263/7. **worstedys** *pl.* 263/7
wot(e, wotyth(e, wottys *see* **wet(e(n**
woulle fellys *see* **wolfellys**
wowerys *n. pl.* suitors 287/16
wownd *see* **woond**
wreythe *v. do* ~ make known the existence of 443/53
wrekke *n.* cargo washed ashore from a shipwreck 778/24
wryghe *adj.* bent, twisted 313/8
write *n.* carpenter 728/25
wrongously *adv.* wrongfully 518/12
wroth(e *adv.* angry 134/8, 339/73
wrought *v. p.p.* decorated 259/26; worked, exerted an influence 509/4, 587/4
wtter *see* **vtter**
wurchepfull, worcheppfull *adj.* honourable 152/39, 199/16
wurchepfull *adv.* with due ceremony 208/28
wurchyply *adv.* honourably 86/27
wurshuped *v. p.p.* observed, respected 208/45
wut(te *see* **wet(e(n**

xall, xale *v.* shall 19/10, 205/43. **psal** *pr. 1sg.* 781/8. **psall** *pr. 3sg.* 781/8. **choulle** *pr. 3pl.* 192/70. **xuld, xud, xwlde, psuld, sxuld** *subj.* should 32/16, 205/31, 602/6, 781/10, 937/68

yaf(fe *see* **yef**
yarn *adv.* quickly 876/11
yates, jatys, ȝattes *n. pl.* gates 48/62, 105/3, 5
yed(e(n, ȝede, ȝedyn *v. pa.* went 125/11, 128/83, 129/28, 141/29, 154/53; walked 130/20.
yef, yeve, yffe *v.* give 180/135, 196/88, 230/113. **yeuyng** *pr. p.* 854/13. **govyn, yaf(fe** *pa.* 143/15, 551/1, 744/6. **gofe, gove, ȝoue, ȝovyn, yovyn, yeven, yeuen** *p.p.* 131/101, 132/64, 143/11, 506/12, 526/4; issued 804/10, 847/8
yefte(s *see* **gyf(f)t(e**
yeld *v.* reward 333/1, 473/54. **yolden, -yn** *p.p.* yielded, surrendered 90/24, 674/8
ȝelddyng *vbl. n.* surrender 205/39
yerde *n.* measuring rod 264/23. **yerdys** *pl. taylorys* ~ standard units of linear measurement (= 36 inches) 264/29
yer(e)day *n.* religious observance of the anniversary of a person's death 159/38, 230/34, 749/9
yere ferm *n.* year's rent 179/16
yersten efe *adj.* yesterday evening 576/7
yeue *conj.* if 220/8, 220/35
yeve, yeuyng, yeven, yeuen, yffe *see* **yef**
yiffte *see* **gyf(f)t(e**
ȝyth *adv.* yet 126/11
yolden, -yn *see* **yeld**
yoyned stoles *n. pl.* joint stools 123/136
yovyn *see* **yef**

INDEX

As well as containing names of persons and places the index includes a number of general subjects such as *books, plague, prices, ships,* and institutions such as *Chancery, Parliament.* In the case of frequent geographical names such as *England, London, Norfolk,* and royal names, some minor instances are omitted. Information about handwriting given in the separate tables is not repeated here.

Spellings of surviving placenames are in modern form, with only conspicuous variants noted; those of personal names are normally in the form preferred in the texts, if there is one. Alternative spellings shown within entries apply only to the adjacent reference. The letter *y* when it is an alternative spelling for *i* has the alphabetical place of *i*.

Titled persons are placed under their titles, with cross-references to family names if they occur. Officers of church and state are placed under their offices, usually with cross-references to their names. Those who held more than one office are usually given under the one by which they are most commonly known in these papers, sometimes under others as well.

References in roman type are to number of Part and page, those in italic to number of letter or other complete document. References are mainly to the text of documents, but a few to headnotes if they contain information not in the text. Those marked '(2×)' indicate occurrence in two separate documents on the same page.

For members of the Paston family summary lists are given of the documents from and to each person, which are more fully set out in the tables of contents of the three Parts. Other persons are marked as follows:

* authors listed in Part II, pp. xxvii–xxxii
§ authors listed in Part III, pp. xxiii–xxiv
† writers listed in Part I, pp. lxxv–lxxviii
‡ writers listed in Part II, p. xxxiii
¶ writers listed in Part III, p. xxv

INDEX

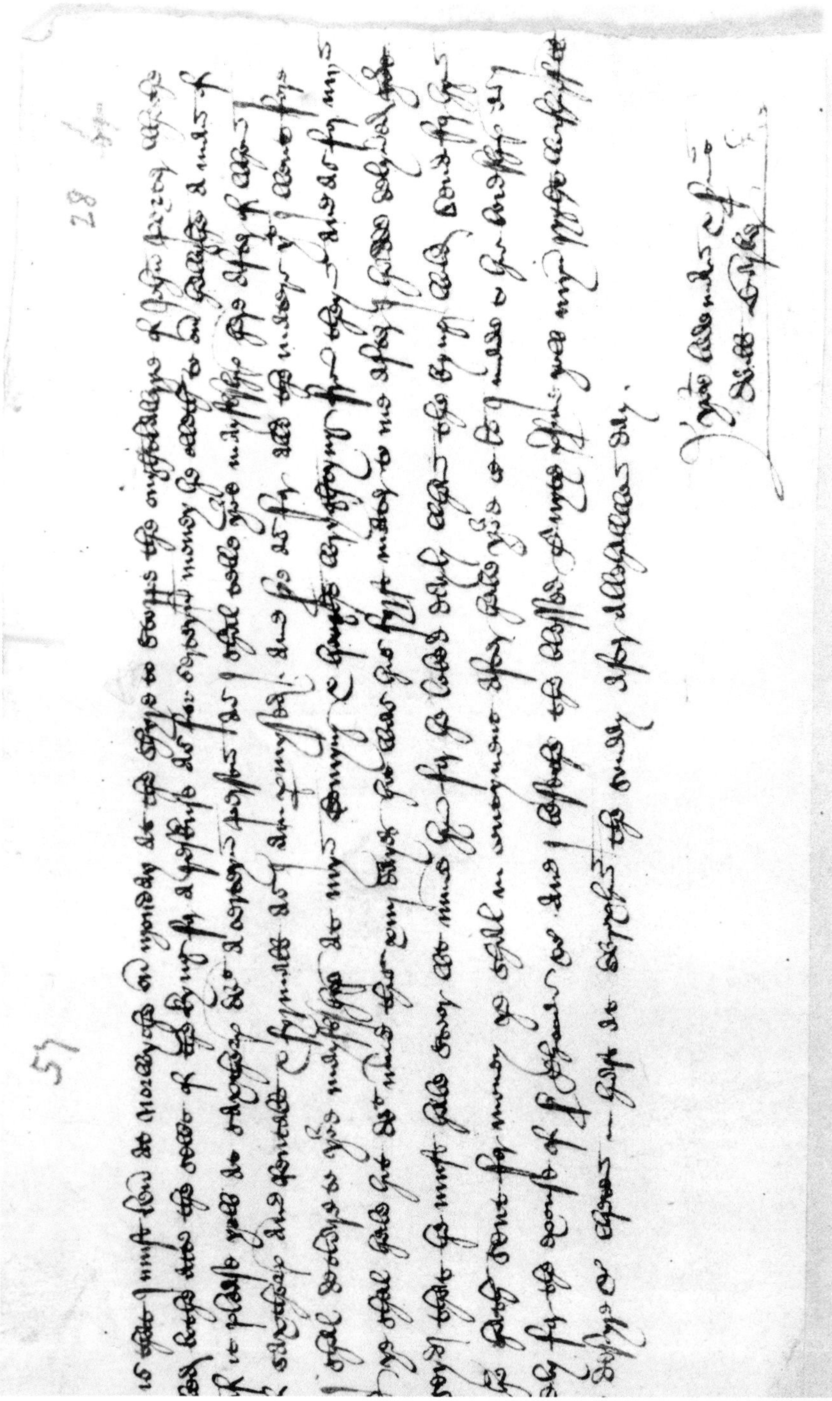

B.L. MS. Add. 27444, f. 28
No. 1020, hand of WILLIAM BARKER, 1454

XXVI

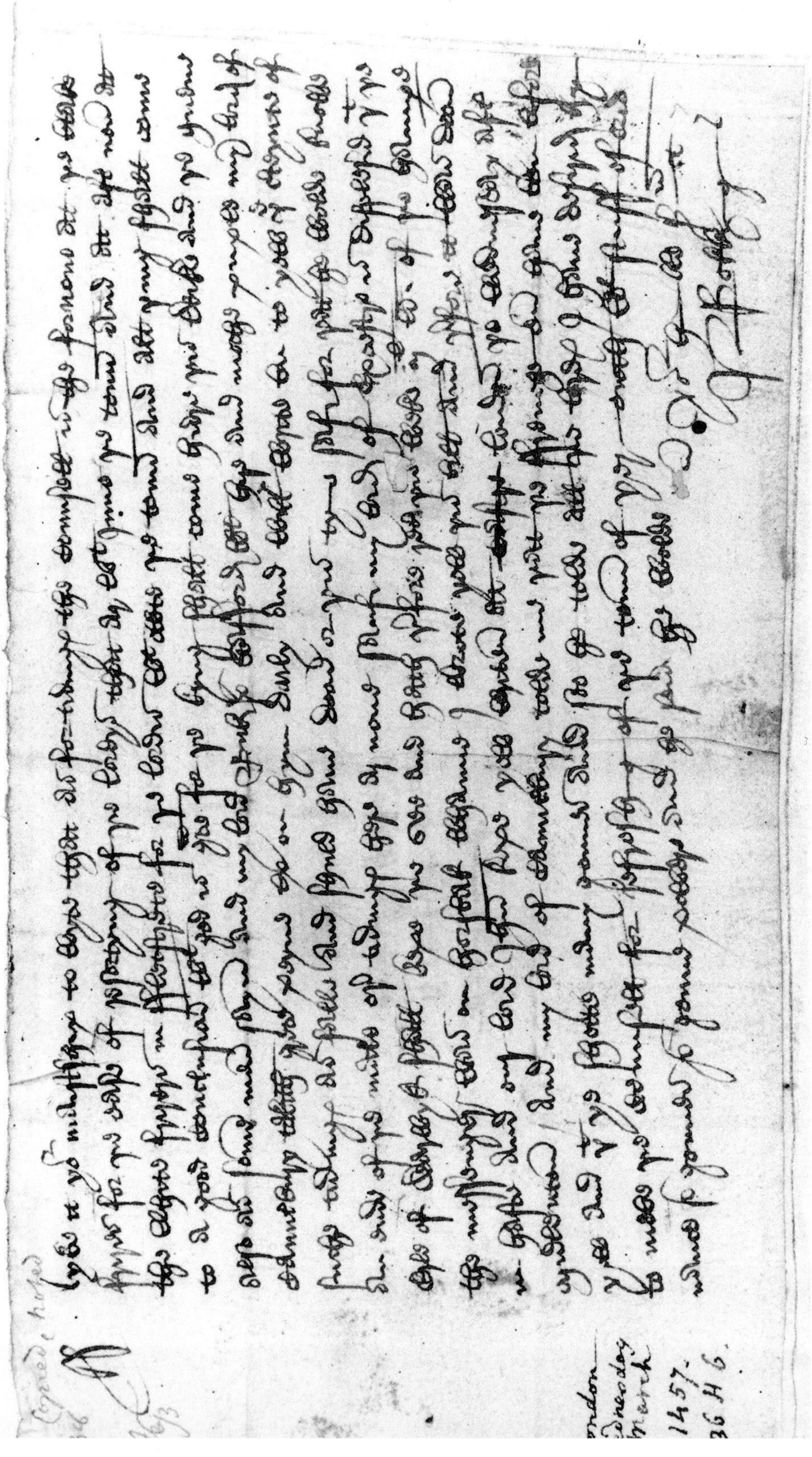

B.L. MS. Add. 43488, f. 41
No. 1036, hand of John Bokkyng, 1458

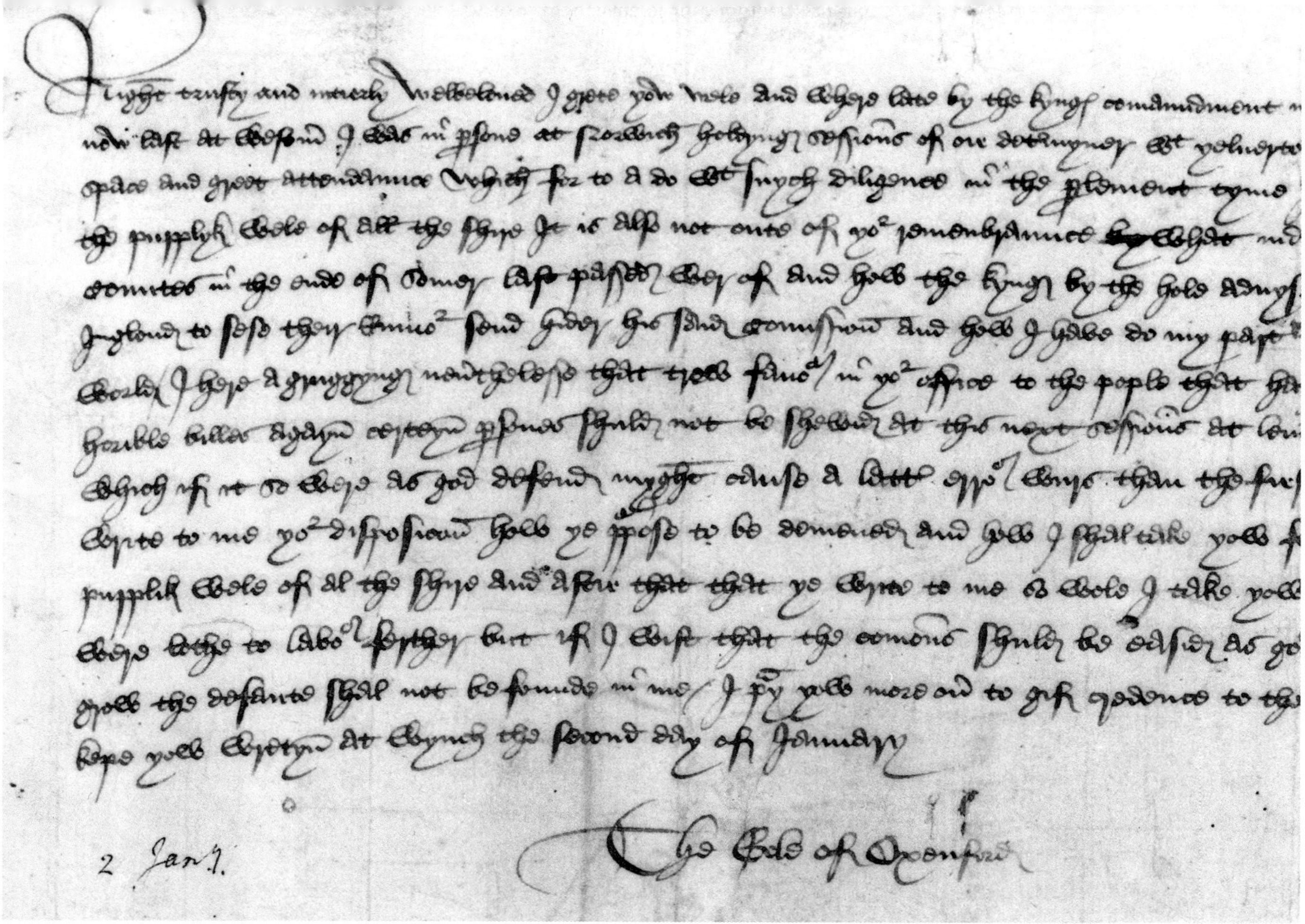

B.L. MS. Add. 34888, f. 61
No. 999, hand of THOMAS DENYS, for the Earl of Oxford, 1451

XXVIII

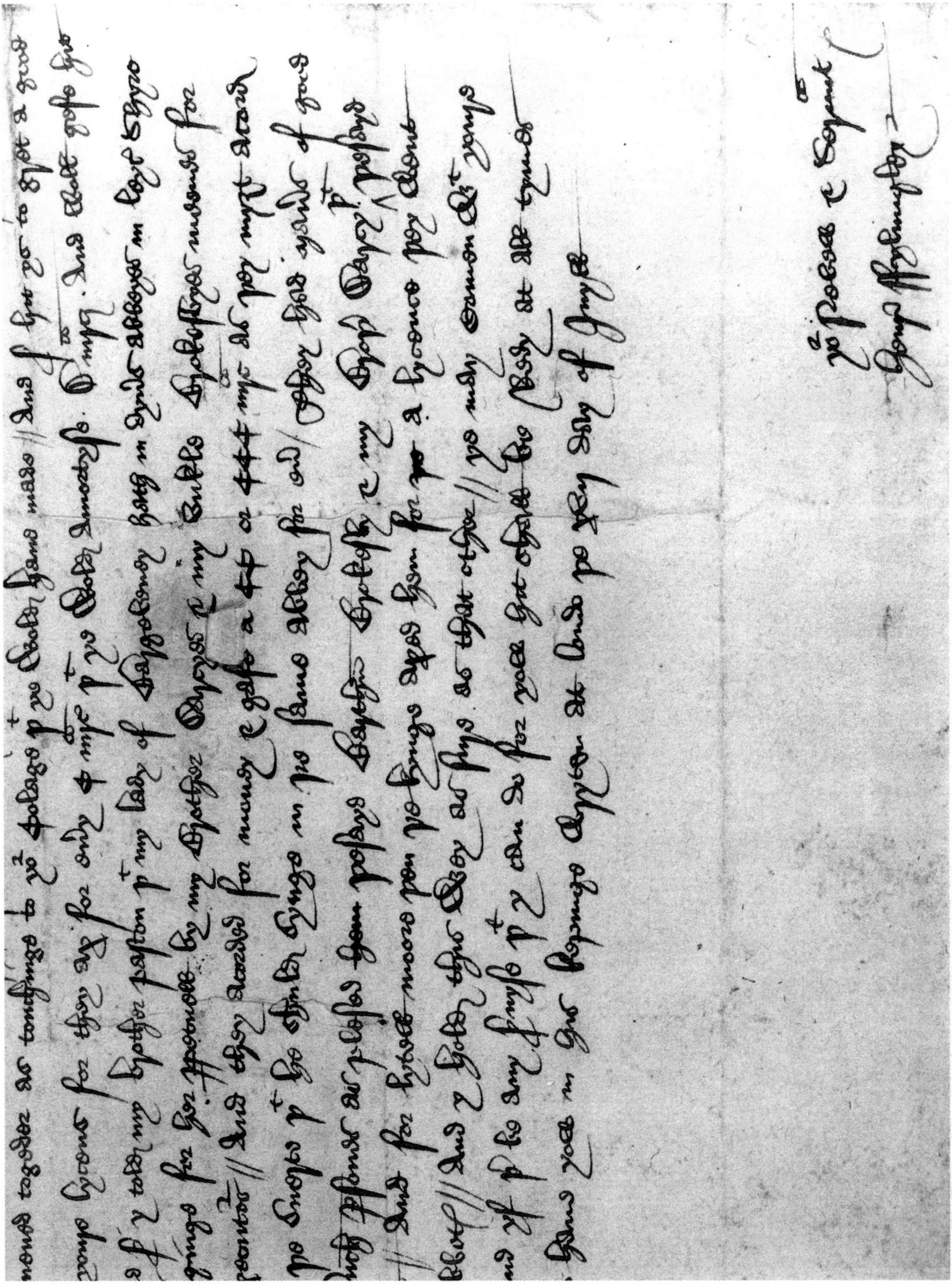

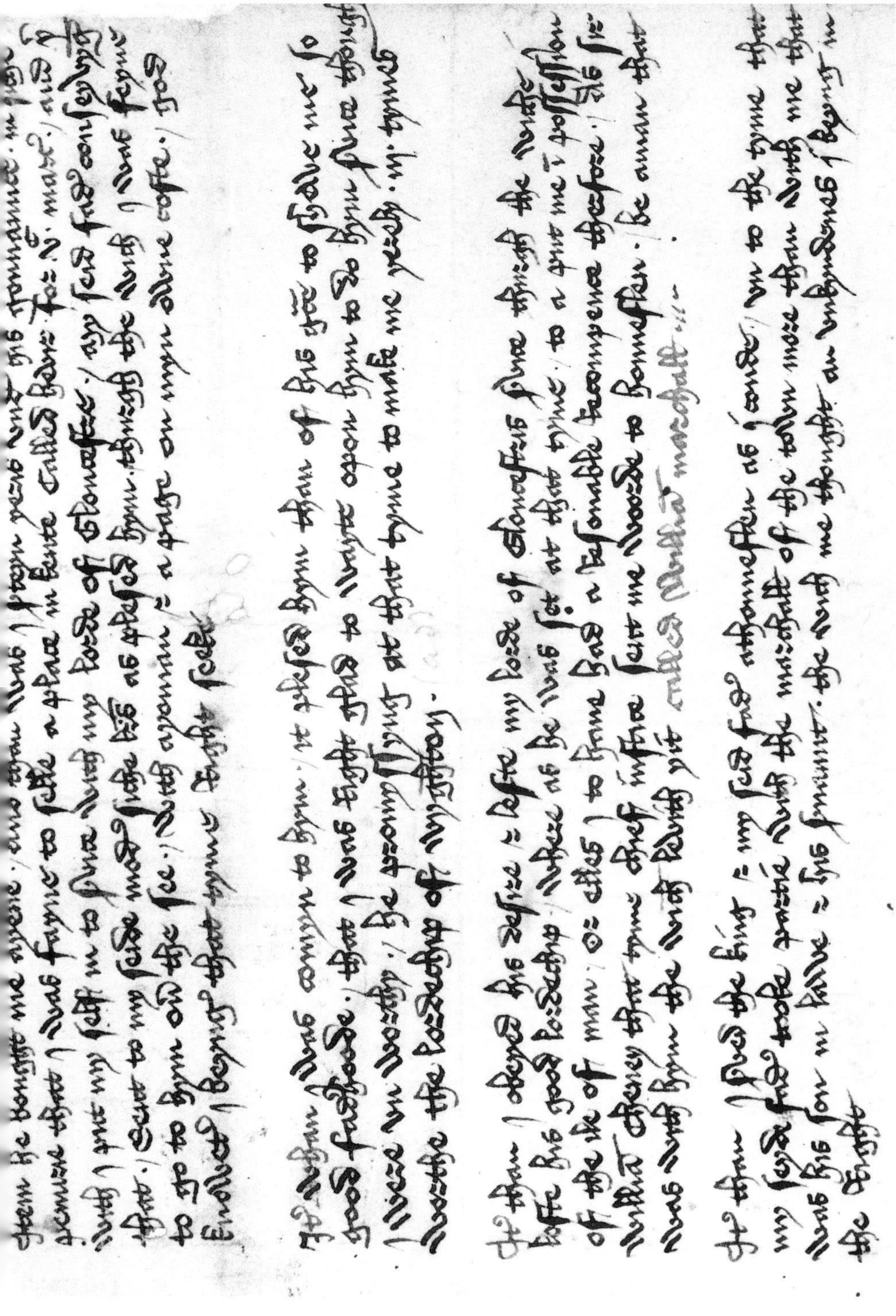

B.L. MS. Add. 28209, f. 21
No. 1012, hand of STEPHEN SCROPE, about 1450-1

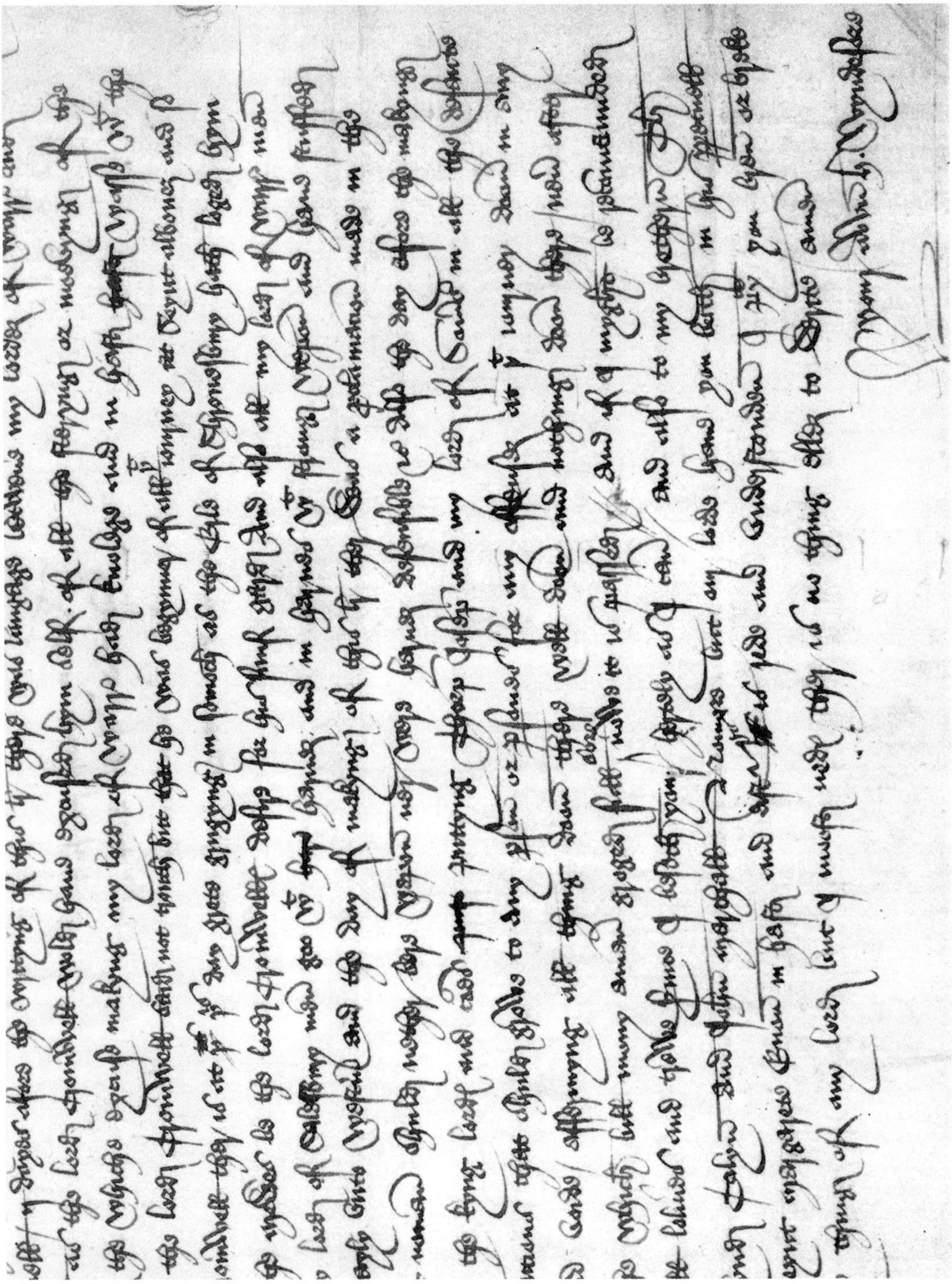

B.L. MS. Add. 43488, f. 26

Sexual magick, virtual reality, shamanism, crystallography — Egyptology — psychopharmacology, cryptogra [illegible] rks: Peter Whitehea [illegible] from the transluce [illegible] produce an intriguing [illegible] sciousness, needed in [illegible] in a world blinded w [illegible] own codes, voices an [illegible]

In two [illegible] riments, a physicist splits a pyramid-shaped diamond with a jade-green X-ray laser, and a dreamer splits his mind with a pyrimidine crystal of the psychedelic smart drug, *Tiresiamine*. Their parallel researches are destined to lead them to the inevitable meeting point: infinity. But there is a third pyramid in which a third eye is opening, the two experiments coinciding with penetration into the newly discovered chamber in the Great Pyramid, by a small mechanical robot with a laser eye ...

Set in Cambridge, Cairo and Cornwall, *The Risen* charts a collision course between three converging visions of the translucent, albedo heart of darkness, a sexual labyrinth of disturbing eroticism, dismemberment and reincarnation.

The original concept of 'holographic novel' defines a zone where two distinct consciousnesses *interfere* and become aspects of one mental entity; the brain made whole and harmonious. The novel draws the reader through the half-silvered mirror of reason into its own time-space, a virtual inscape fusing magical imagery from holography and morphic resonance, fetishistic sex and pagan initiation rites: an occult tour-de-force which will alter our perceptions of reality — forever.

"A cinematic vision flash-frozen into language, *The Risen* redefines the occult novel as something millennial, apocalyptic, unafraid to speak of sex or drugs or the extremities of reason that are central to the magical experience. Crackling with unique energies and luminous ideas, *The Risen* whispers from its crystalline heart in a voice as new as quanta; ancient as the sphinx."

—Alan Moore. *(Watchmen, V for Vendetta.)*

"This most exciting and highly original work, may well be the future of the novel."

—Andrew Sinclair. *(Gog, Magog, King Ludd.)*

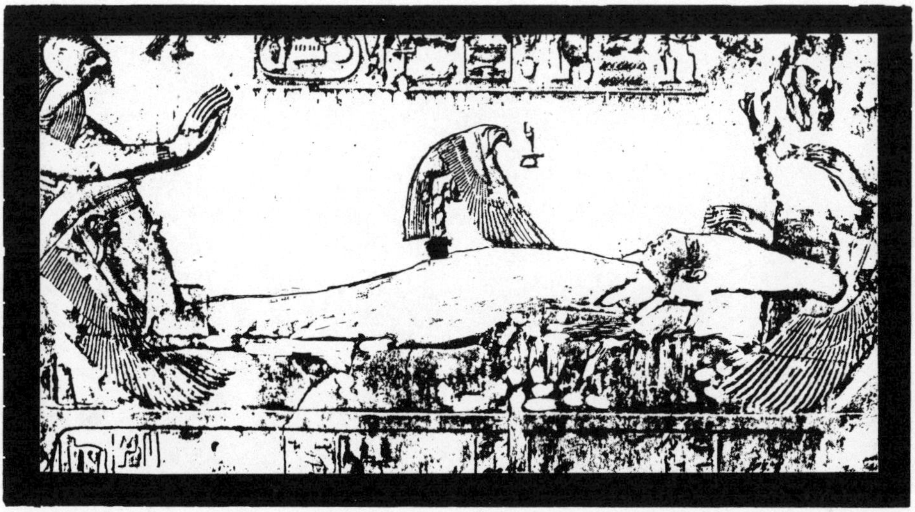

The

RISEN

A Holographic Novel

ℜ

for Peter

Peter Whitehead

17.8.95

By the same author:

FICTION:

NORA and ...
The BRONTëGATE TAPES
ANNE and the MALAY

CRITICISM:

HARTSHEAD REVISITED:
The discovery of Emily Brontë's stolen second novel.
1993

BOOKS on FILM:

WHOLLY COMMUNION.
The Film by Peter Whitehead; including
poems from the International Poetry Incarnation,
11 June 1965.

⊛

ALPHAVILLE: A film by Jean-Luc Godard.
PIERROT LE FOU: A film by Jean-Luc Godard.

English translation and description of action,
for Lorrimer Modern Film Scripts.

⊛

The RISEN

A Holographic Novel

ℜ

Peter Whitehead

HATHOR

Published by Hathor Publishing 1994

A CIP catalogue record for this book
is available from the British Library

ISBN: 0 9522035 1 0

Set in *Korinna*, a typeface originated by
H. Berthold in Berlin in 1904:
on 8th April the same year,
Aleister Crowley received the *Book of the Law*,
in Cairo, Egypt.

Hathor Publishing
Shepherds Cottage, Pytchley, Kettering, Northants NN14 1EX
Tel: 0536 791297 Fax: 0536 790505

ℜ

"Two birds, friends joined together, clutch the same tree.
One of them eats the sweet fruit;
the other looks on without eating."

"The Riddle of the Soma Sacrifice"
The Rig Veda: 2000 B.C.

⊛

Grateful acknowledgement for permission to reprint from the following:

ALLEGRO, John M. *"The Sacred Mushroom and the Cross".*
Hodder and Stoughton, London. 1970.
BOHM, David. *"Wholeness and the Implicate Order."* 1980.
Ark Paperbacks, London. Routledge and Kegan Paul Ltd. 1980.
BRIGGS, John P. & PEAT, F. David: *"Looking Glass Universe".*
Fontana Paperbacks, UK. 1985.
BROWN, Norman O. *"Love's Body".*
Vintage Books Random House. 1966.
CROWLEY, Aleister. *"The Book of the Law".*
93 Publishing, Montreal, Quebec, Canada. 1974.
FREUD, Sigmund. *"Moses and Monotheism".*
Vintage Books Randon House, New York.
Copyright renewed 1967. Translated by Katherine Jones.
GRAVES, Robert. *"The Greek Myths",* Volume 1.
Penguin Books, UK. 1955.
GRAVES, Robert. "STEPS". *Food the Centaurs Ate.*
Cassell London. 1958.
HESSE, Hermann. *"Demian".*
Peter Owen Ltd, London and Vision Press Ltd. 1960.
KOESTLER, Arthur. *"The Ghost in the Machine."*
Hutchinson Publishing Group, UK. 1967.
LAING, R.D. *"The Politics of Experience."*
Penguin Books, England. 1967.
LAMY, Lucy. *"Egyptian Mysteries."* Translated by Deborah Lawlor.
Thames & Hudson. 1981.
LEARY, Timothy. *"Psychedelic Review".*
New York, 1966.
LEVIN, Kim. "The Eye of RA". *Light in Art.*
Collier-Macmillan Ltd, London. 1969.
PLUTARCH. *"Isis and Osiris".* Translated by Frank Cole Babbitt.
William Heinemann Ltd, London. 1984.
PUHARICH, Andrija. *"The Sacred Mushroom".*
Doubleday and Co, New York. 1959.
RAINE, Kathleen. *"Blake and The New Age".*
George Allen and Unwin, London. 1979.
DE QUINCEY, Thomas. *"Confessions of an English Opium Eater".*
Dent, London. An Everyman Paperback. 1960.
VELIKOVSKY, E. *"Oedipus and Akhnaton".*
Sidgwick and Jackson, UK. 1960.
WASSON, R.G. *"Soma, Divine Mushroom of Immortality".* Harcourt Brace Jovanovich, New York.
WESTON, Jessie L. *"From Ritual to Romance."*
Doubleday Anchor Books, New York. 1957.
WILBER, Ken. Editor, *"The Holographic Paradigm and Other Paradoxes".*
New Science Library. Shambhala, Boston and London. 1985.

For Syd Barrett
and the technicolor dream
Shine on you crazy diamond

... and for Dido
who remembered me
Diamonds are forever

PROLOGUE

⊛

At the start of a lunar eclipse, Matthew Sutherland, microbiologist and crystallographer, in his laboratory at Cambridge University, typed *INITIATE* into his computer, the code to start the experiment in which his unique jade-green X-ray laser beam would penetrate certain crystal lattices, flawed with traces of an organic, radioactive isotope of carbon, created millions of years before inside a unique, translucent, pyramidion-shaped diamond ...

... hoping to reveal how the split occurred at that ecstatic moment hundreds of millions of years ago, when elemental carbon became miraculously *alive*, capable of functioning in two separate ways, as living and non-living matter ... hoping to reveal how and why the element carbon changed from being utterly inert, dead, to become the essential, creative atom in every living system, the structural backbone of every molecule capable of self-replication.

At the same moment, John Faulkner, physicist manqué, alias John Raymonde, psycho-pharmacologist and adept at synthesizing psychotropic chemicals, sitting at the sacred centre of a copse of beech trees planted in two rows around a burial mound, the pattern flawed by a stray elm, singing a mantra, a phrase from the soprano aria from *The Dark Side of the Moon*, swallowed a translucent pyramidion-shaped crystal of synthetic *Tiresiamine*, developed from an extract of certain bodily fluids of a Mongolian shaman in trance, after eating a mixture of honey and crushed sacred mushroom, Soma ...

... hoping the experiment would turn on a chemical switch and induce a new bias-frequency in his brain, inducing receptivity to the so-far undetected R-Field Matrix, enabling him to see *holographically*, as if through a half-silvered glass darkly; by which he meant to materialise a consciousness (expressing the wish to be reincarnated) with whom he had been in communication: an Egyptian shaman, Amenhotep, who in Tel El Amarna in the 18th Dynasty of Ancient Egypt had again used the technology by which human consciousness could be stripped from the holographically-structured gravity-field-continuum of the brain, transformed into a laser beam, and sent into space ...

The synchronicity in timing of their two, slightly flawed experiments, may have been a coincidence ... the convergence of their minds afterwards, as if two Virtual Reality programs on two computer screens had been mysteriously fused, was not ...

Neither knew, though John had imagined the possibility, that at the same moment, the copper-handled door in the newly-discovered hidden chamber in the Great Pyramid of Pharaoh Cheops, in which the secret library of Imhotep was hidden, together with the body of Pharaoh Chephren, was being breached, by light and time and unenlightened man ...

∇

◊

holography *n.* the science of producing a photographic record (**hologram**) by illuminating the object with coherent light from a laser beam and exposing a film to light reflected from this object and to a direct beam of the coherent laser light. When interference patterns on the film are illuminated by the laser beam a three-dimensional image is produced. – **holographic** *adj.* – **holo'graphically** *adv.*

holograph *n.* book or document hand-written by its author; original manuscript; autograph.

What do you call a computer disc – the original type*script* – so to speak, so to write, comprising the text of a book of fiction, composed on a computer, about holography? A *Virtual Holograph?*

virtual *adv.* 1. having the essence or effect but not the appearance or form of: a virtual revolution. 2. Physics: being or involving a virtual image: a virtual focus. 3. Computers: of or relating to virtual storage: virtual memory. <L *virtûs* VIRTUE.

▼

A hologram is a holographic photograph of a three-dimensional object, printed on two-dimensional paper, which appears to exist in three-dimensional space. We appear to live in three spatial dimensions. Recent work in physics has suggested there are many other dimensions we cannot yet perceive. Temporal and spatial. To make a holographic photograph of a sculpture of a girl's head, it is photographed by laser light simultaneously from two viewpoints. This double viewpoint is created by taking the photograph through a half-silvered mirror. Half of the light is reflected back – the other half passes through the glass. The two images are recorded, superimposed on each other. The image created by these two jumbled viewpoints resembles the surface of a pool of water into which two stones have been thrown; two spreading waves, interfering more and more with each other, becoming less and less coherent. But look at this apparently random chaotic mess, this witch's brew, through pure laser light, and the original object magically reappears, assuming its original perfect shape ... poised in three-dimensional space.

▲

ONE

"According to a recent report in Brain/Mind Bulletin, *a new method of photography has disclosed a bizarre holographic phenomenon in plants. When a hole or square is cut out of a leaf, inside the hole a ghostly miniature image of the entire leaf appears. This and other tantalising bits of research suggest that holographic distribution is basic to many different kinds of order, from photons to* 'plant consciousness' *to human consciousness."*

"Looking Glass Universe."
John P. Briggs and F. David Peat,

◊

Matthew was deep in thought, not seeing the world around him. Someone watching him might have thought he was counting the paving stones passing under his feet, or studying their mineralogical composition, or trying hard to imagine the waves beneath them, but he was doing none of these things, and no-one was watching him. At least, no-one with his authority to do so. He was desperately trying to think of something he might have forgotten, trying unsuccessfully to focus his mind on that space just beyond what is known ... always tantalisingly out of sight ... wishing he had a computer with a direct input into his mind and at the press of a code-word, like ZAP, a luminous scanner would sweep through his brain cells like a searchlight probing the night sky. Within seconds it would highlight the enemy, those alien errors floating in from yet unimagined realms outside the control of his rationality, and cast them to oblivion. Surely he'd thought of everything this time?

At the gate, he looked up, surprised it was already dusk. He hadn't noticed the light seeping away, as predictable as the tide. He stopped for a moment, the half-light suddenly making him uneasy, casting a further mantle of doubt over his perceptions, the material world a mere reflection now from a half-silvered mirror. The flux of blurring edges, the ghostly overlapping of shadows eroding the three-dimensional certainty of colour, the emerging spectral interface between light and darkness, threatened his sense of tangibility, as if he might not really be there, or ought to be somewhere else. He much preferred lucidity. Nightfall always reminded him of dreams of railway stations at night dimmed by dank fog, of trains snaking through invisible landscapes, beads of light going somewhere and yet nowhere, half-forgotten childhood images fused with half-remembered scenes from old black-and-white films.

Pressing on through the trees, he was relieved to see the emerging building shrouded in darkness and therefore empty. It seemed right, that evening especially, he should be completely alone. Soon would be the moon's eclipse, the night sky pitch black, the moon as absent as he could make it. That was why he had chosen this night, when the lunar influence might be minimum, the moon completely hidden on the dark side of the earth and unable to reflect back the sun, virtually eliminating any other undetected field resonating with its gravitational or magnetic power. Might it not have been the moon, visible to the earth, reflecting the sun's invisible energies, that had ruined his previous two experiments? Not having managed to calculate or discover anything else to explain the failures, recently the notion had quietly crept up on him and haunted him, that it had been the moon's malevolent influence, somehow or other, that had caused the irrationality of his results; a suspicion, strong and persistent, which had refused to go away. Finally, seeing that an eclipse was predicted, he had been reluctantly persuaded to choose this moment for his experiment – perhaps seduced might be the better word, although the last thing he would admit to himself was that he could be superstitious.

Beneath the trees, he hesitated again, pausing to weigh the moment, the promised centre of gravity in the present floating, uncertain psychic geometry of his life. Awaiting him in the silent empty building was his beautiful, pyramidine diamond, poised to receive the jade-green laser beam that would penetrate its crystal heart ...

Being alone in the building would also reduce the risk of alien mechanical vibrations. During the day there were thirteen other scientists working there, any one of whose experiments might cause some kind of low-frequency rumble through its structure affecting his results. This time, with the precious last remaining diamond, there must be no mistakes; the experiment would almost certainly alter the crystal's unique and fascinating internal structure forever. This was his last chance to consummate the union of the two sets of images in his mind, those of his imagined, theoretical model, and those of the objective, mechanical facts of his experiment, and it was essential to avoid every risk of external influence at the moment of this fusion of consciousness and experimental act.

But why was he feeling so sad? Was it because he had been so intensely excited all day, so close to completing this ambitious, even reckless project, the fruition of his life's work? Now he was feeling acutely lonely. He stood quite still, breathing as quietly as possible, not sure why he was listening so intently, or to what, even imagining for a brief moment some kind of other presence, unseen and unforeseen, hovering just out of sight, threatening his poise of certainty; but he quickly dismissed the image. No time for such things – must get on! He strode towards the laboratory ...

He was not usually so emotional. Proud to be a classical scientist, he devoutly believed that science would explain everything. All mystery was mere illusion, resulting from not knowing enough of the facts. One day soon, scientific method would reveal an all-embracing new theory which would explain the entire physical (and so-called mental) structure of the universe, probably with one elegant equation, a mere thirteen or fourteen digits long, revealing how and why the universe of matter and life emerged; and his work was an integral fragment of this rational search for the answers to such profound questions; life was a mere function of matter and would eventually be explained entirely in those terms.

Carbon was the essential element, the structural key to this mystery, its essence, and he felt inspired working with it. At some moment in so-called prehistoric time, some moment when the moon was blood, carbon had suddenly become capable of becoming *alive* – and that was the moment he was seeking to capture and recreate – in his mind; inside his diamond; the subtle moment in history had somehow crystallised and was trapped in its mysterious structure ...

Approaching the gloomy building, he was surprised to notice how sharply, almost painfully, its stark, square silhouette contrasted with the delicate, swaying limbs of the tall trees framing it against the almost silvered, starlit sky. He rarely noticed such things, but suddenly the black, concrete, hard-edged monolith seemed to symbolise his anguish, resonating in some way with the expanse of doubt and mystery which he knew (despite himself) still lay beyond the limits of present human perception and knowledge, and he felt suddenly humbled. It was an awesome task he had set himself. Was he asking too much of his mysterious diamond crystal? And himself?

The image of the sensuous, dancing trees was reminding him of something else. At first he couldn't remember, but it seemed tantalisingly familiar. Then he remembered. The black, leafless, filigree branches, swirling to the music of the wind, although suggesting some kind of computer-generated calligraphy, were almost identical to the opening images of an old movie he'd seen a few days before at a University Film Society show. Once a week he allowed himself to see the club's scheduled film, his only transgression from the narrow, obsessive path of his work routine, the only time he reminded himself of the pleasures others enjoyed and suffered in the world of human intercourse, which he had such little time or willingness to share. He took pleasure not knowing what he was about to see, only occasionally consulting the program, enjoying the surprise of surrender to unforeseen images.

It had been a short German film, apparently made between the wars, filmed in the Black Forest and entitled something like *Extase von Daphne*, leeched through and through with heavy music by Wagner – he guessed *Das Liebestod* – no dialogue, and shot entirely on grainy black and white film. The mood and texture first reminded him of war films – those dreadful shots of trenches in the two Wars, indelible images etched in the collective unconscious, the skies full of small black logos for death, winged planes and rockets, raked by gunfire and search-lights. The film was an unusual ballet film – set in a natural terrain of dense trees, without the expected protection and comfort of a theatre. The dance movements were curiously unreal, poetic, filmed entirely in slow motion. He'd been surprised to find it very erotic.

The story was almost non-existent. An exquisite young dancer, half-naked in a white diaphanous dress decorated with hundreds of eyes, like those on a peacock's tail, fleeing some invisible terror, danced seductively with strange shadowy beings who seemed to be split-off parts of herself, black rather than white, opaque rather than translucent, until gradually engulfed by the darkness and her dark selves, she merged into the trees. Alas, she disappeared just at the moment Matthew was acutely aroused, excited to see what would happen next, when he was one step ahead, enjoying an imagined image of her final demise – an act of possession by the person watching, filming – rape, even – projected in the private cinema of his mind. He felt utterly cheated when her flimsy dress fell apart, torn to shreds by the unseen force, and instead of revealing all, she'd been transformed into a tree.

He was remembering the film quite vividly now, the recollected images resonating with the sinuous mime of the charcoal-black trees silhouetted against the silvered sky. He'd really gone for the feature film, which he knew to be von Sternberg's *The Blue Angel*, which he'd never seen, but after so much frantic work recently, deeply tired, he'd fallen asleep after the opening titles and slept soundly through the whole film. Impatient with himself afterwards, he realised he might just as well have stayed at home and enjoyed a dream ...

Pressing the code 31416 on the electronic door-lock, the laboratory door clicked open. The lift being switched off, he was forced to climb the four flights of stone stairs. Having spent the evening apprehensively counting the minutes, he impulsively started counting the stairs. Eighty-three steps. It seemed odd, such a number of steps unevenly divided amongst four apparently identical staircases. He made a mental note to count the stairs on the way down. He hated odd numbers.

Opening his office door slowly, he crept into his private domain so stealthily that anyone watching would have thought he was either a thief or a spy, anticipating an ambush. After a last apprehensive glance at the night sky, he drew the curtains. The windows in the adjacent room, his laboratory, had been permanently boarded up, in the elaborately-planned insulation against all random wave radiations, with sheets of lead, which also now covered the walls, ceiling and floor.

He flicked the master switch to activate the complex apparatus: the vital laser system, the super-computer, the X-Ray microscopes and other items developed especially for his experiment. While his machines were warming up, he switched on the more humble electric kettle for tea; he also needed to warm up. Sitting down at his desk, he wrote in his notebook:

20.13hrs, 25th March. Pyramidine Diamond #3. Jade X-ray Laser penetration starting traverse at isotopic carbon lattice, 1/1.618 ratio distance from crown of crystal. Split prism imaging of resulting bi-phased radiation to be analyzed by revised resonance diffraction software program, with virtual three-dimensional crystal axis parameter model.

Soon the computer controlling the entire narrative would trip the quartz crystal switch, with its accuracy of a billionth of a second. The whole experiment would be completed in thirteen minutes, under the radiation umbrella of the eclipse, during which time his fate would be sealed, his future focused by a crystal lens into this brief contraction of time, a cosmic snapshot. Was he on the brink of an amazing discovery? This time he'd surely taken every possible precaution...

He looked fondly at his apparatus, listening to its gentle whirring. He'd spent two years building it to support the unique X-ray laser that was at its core. Through the newly adapted, specially darkened lens, he peered at the diamond crystal awaiting its fate, remembering the intense excitement of first seeing it, three years or so before. He'd just received his Doctorate for an acclaimed thesis on the differences, detected by interference of the reflections on the crystal interfaces, between the spatial and temporal orientation of atomic crystal structures of organic and inorganic isotopes in fissures of carbonaceous material in a rare, unique Alaskan limestone, two hundred million years old. He was visiting his former tutor, the new director of the crystallography department in University College, London, and while casually looking through an old case of crystal specimens, Matthew found a small black box, like a jewellery box, initialled "FP" in gold. Inside were three almost identical small diamonds. Two were the same size, the third slightly smaller.

He'd never seen tetragonal pyramidal crystals of diamond before; a mystery, even at first sight. It was very difficult to cut them in that shape and there was no apparent reason to do so. In this shape they were rather dull, so they could never be sold. Even more strange, the three stones were perfectly cut on the quaternary axes to the same three-dimensional crystallographic formula, an awesome task. And then, even more amazing, parallel to the floor in each pyramid, was a faint green flaw, presumably caused by an internal layer of green lattices trapped inside the clear lattices. He'd seen flaws in diamonds before, but without such formal structure. Faults were usually random, amorphous, like flecks of silver or gold in a nugget of lapis lazuli, or flecks of blue or green in the iris of a human eye.

He first thought the flaw was man-made, inserted, but that seemed impossible too. No-one had the technology to make three such similar diamonds. His tutor was equally puzzled; he suggested they needed researching. Finding no mention of them in the department's files, Matthew had been allowed to slip the box in his pocket, and the work began. Diamonds were made of pure carbon; the traces must be organic material of some kind ... and anyway, he'd felt a sudden desire to know more about them. They had somehow called him ...

Later work revealed the flawed green lattices to be a highly radioactive carbon isotope deriving from a different organic source to the rest of the crystals. Not so much a mystery, as an impossibility; so he decided from that moment to keep his work as secret as possible. There was also a weird difference in electron spin. So what process were these crystals a permanent record of? Like images in a documentary film?

The temperatures and pressures needed to compress the

original carbonaceous material, usually old trees and plants, were so enormous and usually so random, that a perfect layer of lattices could never have been predicted. He even wondered if the diamonds might have come from a meteorite. There was no immediate answer to such questions – he knew only that the flawed lattices were exactly on the golden mean between the base and the apex of the pyramid; identical in each, despite their different sizes.

After trying many ways of elucidating the structure of the green lattices without damaging them, he had invented the electro magnetically pure, green X-Ray laser, which he somewhat romantically called his Jade Laser. It switched on and off nine hundred and eighty-eight thousand times a second, and was so narrow and so pure, it could penetrate lattices only atoms apart, hopefully without altering the inherited structure created so many millions of years before. That at least had been his intention. But the first two experiments had gone wrong; the results avoiding elucidation, apparently quite irrational.

He gazed fondly at the third diamond, fractionally the largest, overawed by its beauty, yet dreading the fact it was the last of the three. He was still feeling quite tense, physically, and it annoyed him. He wanted to relax; it seemed necessary, even though the computer was programmed and set and he would play no further, real part in the experiment. All he would be doing was thinking about it, worrying about it; and, he knew, *that* should play no part ...

Music! That would make him relax. His only true, deep pleasure apart from work, he had often grudgingly wondered if music might embody some kind of natural resonance between matter and consciousness, by which he meant that listening to it actually structured his thinking, like a potter's fingers at the wheel, a shaping force etching away on the shifting surfaces of the meaning and structure of crystals: often music had seemed to help, as he asked his epic question; why *one* element only, humble carbon, was at the heart of every living system on earth, and probably in the universe, the essential atom in the backbone of every particle of life; polymorphous and existing in so many startlingly different forms. As coal it was black, soft and opaque, all that remained after living material had died and been crushed and compacted by gravity and time. Yet it also existed in the pure form of diamond, the hardest crystal known to man, absolutely inert; dead. And yet, life was impossible without the carbon atom, its beautiful structure a perfect *quaternio;* there could be no life, no self-replication without it.

What music would calm his nerves and relax his body? Bach he loved, but nothing seemed right. Mozart also felt inappropriate. Suddenly he remembered Mendelssohn's *Hear My Prayer*, which he'd heard in Kings College Chapel the week before. He'd been captivated by it, and the newly bought disc was still in his brief-case. He especially wanted to listen to the aria, *Oh for the Wings of a Dove.* Yes! Ideal. He found it, set it playing, and it immediately felt painfully tangible. Putting the aria on endless repeat, its soaring beauty promising to distract him from his complicated fears, he sat down and closed his eyes; almost slept, almost dreamed, images of a strange copse of trees and a girl in a transparent dress ... slow motion, on the verge of revealing all, the veil about to be rent ... almost fell completely asleep. But he caught himself before the fall ...

Minutes before his machines were due to spring into life he turned off the music and returned to the inner sanctum of his laboratory. Peering through the darkened lens again for a last look into the heart of his diamond, its physical integrity as unblemished as a virgin, he switched off the lights and waited. It seemed like eternity ...

... waiting for the planned-for instant of time when millions of pulses of laser energy, an infinitesimally delicate pencil of pure viridescent green light, would penetrate the diamond, working slowly through the crystal's lattices in jumps of micro-millionths of a millimetre. At the same time the laser beam would rotate, set to measure the alteration in spin of the electrons in the two layers of different isotopic carbon atoms under the pressure of the laser's energy. It was such an elegant image and fascinating idea ...

The sharp click of the quartz switch took him by surprise. He heard it activate the sensors recording the radiation gradients across each spatial dimension of the crystal, before measuring all the other electro magnetic wave radiation levels in the room, its scenario before energizing the laser. Intensely excited, he looked into the eye-piece of the microscope, the cross of wires focused on the lattice where the laser would start its sensuous penetration, seeking the mathematical data that would reveal its archetypal structure and secret history.

Outside, the eclipse was starting. The dark side of the moon, the illusion, visible and invisible. Shine on crazy diamond!

The aria was still hovering in his mind, unattended, when the laser flashed phoenix-like into being and illuminated the inner space of the diamond. He held his breath and his heart missed a few beats as he saw the whorling, twisting motion of the rotating beam. The reflected rays danced round the walls of the diamond like luminous green snakes trying to escape from an underground tomb, and he felt intensely satisfied with himself. This was the first time he was actually witnessing the event, behind the darkened lens, and it was so beautiful! This time, surely, he'd got it right? Everything was so graceful, so perfect, so chaste – he would even admit to aesthetic pleasure in seeing the dance of light in the elemental drama inside his crystal amphitheatre.

But suddenly, for no apparent reason at all, he felt something was going wrong. At first he merely sensed it, but then he began to see colours that should not be there, as if the green light was splitting into all the colours of the rainbow, which was clearly impossible. Only white light contained all the colours. There was none there, and it was an impossibility for there to be any other source of light or wave-radiation energy. That could only occur in the event of some kind of elemental, nuclear fusion. He decided the colours must be an illusion, probably within the lens of his own eye, or a reflection inside the crystal that only he could imagine seeing. He tried to think of this idea clearly, but then he started to lose control of his consciousness – or that is what it seemed. For a moment he started to panic, but then it seemed to be a pleasurable feeling. He felt himself given to it, and an uncontrollable surge of emotion, waves of ecstatic elation, seemed to spread out from some point near the base of his spinal chord, a huge tidal rush of motion or emotion up the centre of his spine, shooting off at tangents to engulf his whole body. Then it seemed as if his perception of time instantaneously expanded and he was able to distinguish, simultaneously, every single discreet movement of a million iridescent wings, beating within the diamond ... wings and eyes and surfaces, almost of flesh, hidden but now emerging from behind millions of veils ... everything happening all at once. It all seemed utterly beautiful. Perhaps the laser had been deflected back into his own eye, but that seemed too trite an explanation. Something was opening and he was seeing through ...

... a small membranous fragment of his mind still clinging to reason, an odd idea flashed on the screen ... had he created atoms of the transition element, iridium, in the crystal's lattice network, acting momentarily like the core of a reactor? But that would have caused a huge explosion! Impossible.

Again, in an instant, his perception seemed to slip a dimension, and something more profound seemed to be happening. To the diamond or to him? He wasn't sure. Was it pain or pleasure? He couldn't tell. Time and space seemed radically dislocated. Suddenly he seemed to fall inside himself, turning inside out, and he felt he was witnessing himself being decapitated by a sudden blow ... a delicate hand in a white lace glove ... as if his entire being had been sucked out through his eye ... his whole brain crushed, and then imploded into a cloud of mere green luminous atoms ... floating in space like a billion flecks of dust on a pale green moonbeam ... or green leaves flecked with blue falling from a tree with an eye on each ...

... and then there was darkness. That deep, deep darkness only imagined, meditating on an image of a total eclipse. Or imagining the heart of the invisible black dwarf star, the twin of the star Sirius, the brightest in the heavens ...

Stillness. Silence ... but then the sound of a heart-beat, not so much diffused through layers of skin, but an ocean ... drawn out, his body becoming a million miles in length, as if it had become pure light or pure time. Floating, for an eternity of time, as if space had been finally eclipsed by time, though time could no longer be perceived. A million folds within folds. There was a voice speaking but then he decided it must be an aural reflection of his own thinking. Or his thinking become transposed into digital energy, quanta of light, reflected through a half-silvered mirror ... things fallen apart and yet whole. Watching himself. Two girls robed in white and then, as if he was looking into a room, or tomb, or operating theatre where the two girls were performing something unspeakable. Rubber gloves. Or the hand after the white lace gloves had been torn away. He saw a body like an insect's body inside a cocoon, wrapped in bandages. He felt something touching him and fingers seemed to grope right through his flesh, as if his body was mere image, a mere reflection in a mirror, which it was – he knew that now – but the fingers pressed in hard, into some part of himself he was deeply ashamed of ... was it his own body suspended in a green robe, poised just before being cut into a million pieces? Or the body of a young girl? Or both?

Suddenly. Nothing. Absence of thinking. Death or sleep. The hint of dreaming returning ... timeless. The image frozen, the fingertip on pause ... he was the size of a galaxy reduced to the size of an atom, his being stretched between, he was the stretching between those two images, or ideas, the interface between the two. Not one or the other but the silvering, distorting the image reflected on the glass ... the inner face of an imaginary crystal, which was some part of himself, fragmenting ... again, the silence, as deep as a black hole. Time spent ...

When at last he became aware of himself again, he was lying on the hard floor feeling very stiff. He felt certain he'd only been unconscious for a short time. Perhaps he needed to think that. He could feel a sharp pain behind his eyes, reminding him of the piercing flash of green laser-energy suddenly reflected from a previously unobserved flaw, a mirror-like surface inside the diamond. He opened his eyes slowly and painfully, hoping to see the message on the computer screen that the experiment had nevertheless finished according to plan, but to his horror he could see nothing at all. Everything was black. He rubbed his eyes and opened them again. Nothing. He seemed to be blind.

He pressed his fingers on his eyelids to try to alleviate the throbbing pain and restore his sight, but he saw spiralling patterns of intense colour that reminded him of exploding galaxies, pulsing on the dark screen inside his head. He opened his eyes again, hoping it had all been an illusion, but still he could see nothing.

Remembering pain-killing pills in his desk, he groped to the drawer and found the bottle, stumbled on his knees into his office and managed to find the fridge, drank some milk with the tablets. Still blind, he started to panic, deciding he must dial for an ambulance; but then remembered the switchboard was off at night. If he was to get help, he must walk into the street, which he knew was impossible. He wasn't sure what to do, but decided he ought not to leave the laboratory until he felt better. Surely this was only a momentary lapse?

Because he often worked at night, he had installed a sofa-bed in his office. Knowing he ought to rest for a while, maybe sleep, most of all get warm, (he was feeling deathly cold), he managed to reach and open the metal filing-cabinet and take out the duvet squeezed into one of its drawers. He found his electric fire and switched it on, opened up the bed and lay down, wrapping the feather-filled duvet tightly around his body. As the pain behind his eyes eased, he fell into a dreamless sleep.

At least, for the first few hours or so his sleep was dreamless. Then the dreams began ... dreams that would not go away until they had been recognised, even though he would only start to comprehend them slowly, a fragment at a time ... the veils of the dreams folding back on themselves like the skin that covers the vestige of an ancestral third eye in the centre of a forehead, in those creatures with or without legs, with or without wings, that in the human memory always seem to resemble snakes ... only time would tell ...

◊

John was becoming impatient. The images wouldn't go away; images connected with his work. With Cindy. Georgina. And there was the question of the vine leaf and its holographic interaction with the dissolving crystal. He could see it in his mind's eye ...

For a while though, he had managed to wipe his mind clear and keep it empty, but now, as if the film projector had been started again against his wishes, an ethereal montage was insisting on being seen, flickering on the screen's silvered surface. Spectral images, fixed in time.

Most persistent were the two holographic images that had arrived at the house in the morning's post ... his and Georgina's. The factory had done a good job. He'd received holograms before of images created on his computer, but these were the best so far. But the biggest surprise was Georgina's reaction, the childish, irrational, ecstatic (and he had to admit, infectious) excitement with which she had received *her* printed image ... her calligraphic pen drawings and miniature oil paintings now looked like becoming a thing of the past. 'One of my drawings has become truly alive ... and forever. Look, as I move my head, the figures move and turn, vibrate, almost dance! They are *really* just about to make love. Now you can truly imagine it. Not just a crack in time like a photograph, but a continuous moment, a miniature resonating film, an image resonating with itself. Weird! I'd no idea a holographic image like this could be so mysterious.'

She'd been so *beside* herself, and so sexually aroused by the excitement (he'd told himself), he'd impulsively taken her to his room and hugged her, held her tight for a long time as if needing to feel the warmth from her body (they'd done that often enough before); but then kissed her sensuously on the mouth (she didn't seem too surprised); and proposed she come with him; 'Why not? On this magical day, how can you say *no*?'

To his surprise, she'd said *yes* after barely a moment's hesitation. There were too many coincidences! 'I'll come!'

But by now, she was almost panicking, not sure how much longer she could play her role without complaining. She was warm enough under the white sheet and quilt, but her arms were aching and her wrists were chaffed by the ropes and probably bleeding, although in *that* particular respect, it was the least of her problems.

Taking a small red lacquered box from his pocket, decorated with a white bird fighting a green and blue serpent, John laid it on the grass in front of his knees. Inside was a leaf, the largest he had so far grown from his vine, the precious *divine* plant given him by his shaman. He'd smuggled the roots into England from Tadakshan and managed to grow it in the garden, entwined around a beautiful silver birch tree. He was thinking of them now, symbiotically entwined, the vine having split into two stems. Inevitably it recalled his favourite image, the staff of Tiresias, with its two serpents sensuously weaving around it.

Cutting a square out from the centre of the leaf, he enfolded the small pyramid-shaped crystal neatly inside it, pulling the shiny leaf over it, parallel to the four pyramid sides; as the old man had instructed him. The crystal, in the light of the moon, appeared quite green against the leaf. He kissed the leaf and held it against his breast, showing respect to the plant world. Inside his body, the leaf would set the chemical ambience ... a possible catalyst to the dissolving crystal. The remaining piece of the leaf he pressed to his forehead with his index finger, before wrapping a white bandage over it, tying it at the back of his head, the empty square of the cut-out leaf in the centre of his forehead. He chuckled at the idea. A small empty screen on which might appear the image of an eye, the eye of Horus the falcon, as if reflected from a half-silvered mirror ...

In the half-light, he could see the quilt on the ground, its contours the shape of a girl's body, or, remembering other images, a sacrificed animal waiting to be cut up into sacraments, to be raised high on a golden plate, an offering to the gods. He knew Georgina would relish the image, this transformation of herself, but he felt slightly guilty remembering her embarrassment when he had slipped one of his vine leaves inside her, after they had first started to make love ... another of Amenhotep's suggestions. He felt a surge of love for her suddenly, lying so still on his favourite carpet, the one from Shiraz, symbolically depicting a scene from the story of the *Hashishin*; lying so patiently under the white sheet and patch-work coverlet she had wisely suggested bringing.

But only after the fulfilment of the rite could she be released. Timing was of the essence, and she knew it ... although Amenhotep knew more about the timing than both of them.

She was wearing the full-length white dress he had given her, with the fluted, pleated skirt and classical bodice, now rather torn, which she had agreed to wear 'especially for the occasion, it seems appropriate!' The same dress as the painted girls were wearing on his holographic image. Perhaps she had become one of those girls. This was how desire shifted; and constantly betrayed. She'd been shy at first, the reluctant sister she'd always been. Pensive and reserved, until suddenly, she'd laid her head on his shoulder, silent still, then stroked the back of his head, then kissed him lightly on the cheek, crying softly, knowing there was no escape; almost as if she'd been struck, she sobbed just once, loudly, then shuddered in her whole body ... surrendered ... eagerly pulling him through the surrounding bushes towards the small clearing at the centre of the copse, where she spread the carpet between the four wooden posts, before lying down. She was given. The veil could be torn.

They'd agreed not to talk in the copse, especially about the Tiresiamine, although earlier she'd tried to persuade him not to take such a dangerous risk. *Please!* Perhaps he'd been careless, even foolish, certainly sentimental; after all, he could *not* be sure he had interpreted all the coded instructions correctly? He might even be the victim of a conspiracy? But his courage had persuaded her to take *her* risk, they'd be terrorists together in the plot against the hypocrisy and tyranny of rationality! She could never stop him doing it, and had no *more* right to insist, even though, or just because, she'd decided to give herself to him; for the first time. If Cindy couldn't dissuade him, then she couldn't.

Now, humming the aria from *The Dark Side of the Moon,* sitting under the trees at the spot he had divined was the centre of the copse's power, John was trying to focus his mind on his experiment ... but was thinking of Georgina. So close and yet soon to be so far, tied down and almost unable to move; but she had agreed to Amenhotep's instructions. Except, at that time, the girl in question might have been Cindy ...

Cindy and Georgina! It wasn't exactly right to say Georgina had been a virgin after her love affair with Cindy over the years, but he was prepared to believe, probably because he wanted to, that he was the first *man* to whom she had given her body. Had she not been expecting it, unconsciously? Dreamt it already perhaps? Their coming together like this in his sacred copse? Perceived the scene and foretold the rest? Her virginity being an essential part of the image? Had Amenhotep not meant *her* all the time, without John knowing, and as usual, he had got his way? Or she, hers?

... the involute, the *conjunctionis* as he'd called it. That's why it had happened, because of the position of the moon and stars, not that she had woken up that morning and discovered suddenly that she desired him! Perhaps it had been simmering under the surface for some time; as knowledge of the future does, as desire shifts the surface even of things; as on her hologram she had put a violet sky, suggesting the timeless and the beyond, above the stone and the wing, for these must become important again ... Isis, still hovering as a bird over the fragmented, crystalline Osiris ...

Georgina! Under the white sheet in front of him, his sacrifice; before his own, of eating the crystal. The image of her beauty was still resonating with those imaginary girls of his holographic version of the beloved Delvaux painting, the image he had loved so much over the years and finally transferred (*trance-feared*, as he had written on disc seven, by accident!) to his Virtual Reality computer program, altering it to his own needs before *trance-forming* it into a three-dimensional holographic image ...

... broken stone columns, a railway station at night, a stone sarcophagus, and tall, silent girls robed in diaphanous white night-dresses, half veil, half cocoon, with dark eyes focused on infinity. Georgina had insisted on making an image in parallel with his, the goddess Isis in the form of a hovering falcon copulating with her dead husband Osiris. She'd etched the image directly on limestone, copying a photograph from a tomb in Tel El Amarna. Someone had chipped out the erect penis of Osiris and all that remained was a deep dark hole in the limestone, where the penis should have been. This image had always amused her (and disturbed her, she had to admit) and if John was going to market *his* erotic image, she'd said, why shouldn't she have a go with hers? No-one could say it was obscene. The viewer would be guilty of imagining what had been lost, and so he or she would be the pornographer. At least it would be provocative ... and it had already annoyed Cindy. That in itself was good enough reason!

And now she was here, with him, in secret. He was still pondering her decision to give herself, wondering what had really provoked her uncharacteristic, potentially destructive behaviour, saying *yes* so suddenly, after so many years. It must be hard for her to betray Cindy, whom she had loved without condition for so long. Was she really as impressed as he was by the many strange seductive coincidences, all focused into this day, this one single fraction of magical time, under the shadow of the eclipse? Destiny calling her? Another of the weird resonances that take over once you let go and listen, and allow the gods to reveal themselves, and speak as they do ... in images.

He tried to meditate again. Normally he could wipe his mind clean of the world in seconds, like pressing the erase button on his computer. But it had been a tiring day, especially with the final, complicated calculations, making sure the moment was indeed the unique coincidence of temporal and spatial forces, especially within the multi-dimensional networks of the gravitational trachyon R-field, as he'd called it, occurring only once every two thousand years.

But now he was aware again of his desire for Georgina, suddenly so painfully urgent he was in danger of forgetting details of the delicate preparation for the experiment, his mind filling with the image of her body. Especially her sex. Strange how the mind focuses itself. Once it would have been her beautiful lips, those lips worthy of an Egyptian princess. But he mustn't allow this sudden obsessive image to haunt him ... but could he prevent it? And what was she thinking?

Georgina was still thinking of the irony of it being the worst day of the month, though perhaps it didn't matter. For John maybe, blood, as he would see it, the blood of sacrifice, would be merely a fragment of the multi-dimensional conundrum ... how would he know there were two bloods mixed at the same time? And what difference could it possibly make?

Tiresiamine. He'd known it must exist since first reading various Egyptian texts, fascinated to see how the priests were initiated into the wonders of cosmo-genesis, adepts at re-tuning (and returning to) the human brain, at accessing the R-Field, which he would be the first to materialise, now ... not long after discovering that the left and right sides of the brain interfere chemically and must be considered to behave holographically ... in one temple in Amarna you have to *imagine* you are reading the hieroglyphic text twice, one on the wall *and* simultaneously the other text on the second side of the wall, in the next room, out of sight ... as *if* the wall was transparent. Translucent. Adepts indeed in revisioning ...

But what about Cindy? To come so far in their work together and then abandon her at the last minute, like making love, both reaching higher and higher, and then he *came* before she did, leaving her floating, hovering, frustrated and betrayed; that weird word *came*. Who came from where? There was so much meaning hidden in mere words, but so much more in the hieroglyphs; especially on the subject of sex and union; especially of opposites.

Now, damn it, he was still clinging ... the montage of images of his equations, elegant, sensual calculations for the frequency band of the R-field within the trachyon/gravity complex. The historic archetypal split, the train of thought mistaking the signals and diverting itself onto two tracks at once, with devastating consequences, had been the separate development of the right and left sides of the brain. The whole secret was the interface between them, the interference between the two visions ... Amenhotep had said: *'I am that interface. Become me!'*

Now, it was about to happen, provoked by the crystal of eaten Tiresiamine. Fortunately, Cindy didn't know he had synthesised Tiresiamine ... more like Aviamine, but better, enabling him at last to *see* as if with the magic eye of Horus ... by which, he meant to *materialize* Amenhotep directly from the R-Field ... in the same way the Companions of Horus had first materialized themselves, onto the earth, into its material fields; but that was another story.

He was thinking too much! Perhaps it didn't matter, this confusion of images, like a series of overlapping waves on the surface of a pool into which so many stones had fallen, because the drug would force itself upon him whether he liked it or not. At the instant the chemical reached his brain, his brain would alter frequency, separate into two independent vibrating halves of a transcendent hologram resonating *with* each other, not against, as with *normal* (sic) consciousness, the left brain dominating the right ... rationality cutting off the deeper harmonics of the energy of the unconscious. If his intuition had been right, he would now see in order to *see*, not merely to *look at* ...

At last he felt himself relaxing completely and he started to go into trance again, repeating his mantra, 'Amen-hotep ... Amen-hotep,' until he was approaching deep trance, barely anticipating the surge of new consciousness that would be sucked into his mind from the furthest reaches of time and space, winging into matter in the form of a man, Amenhotep himself ...

But suddenly he snapped back into the present. Time was running out. He looked at the luminous face on his watch – surprised to see it was already eight-forty. Now, thankfully, he was feeling pleasantly relaxed. The crystal was inside the leaf, and he held it gently between his fingers. What extraordinary power was given to us, yet so much still hidden, in the world of plants! It had taken ten years to synthesise this crystal, and now he was within minutes of discovering whether he had been interpreting the messages correctly. To think! At no other time in the history of the universe, with its unique composition, had this precise crystal existed. In creating such a perfect and powerful specimen, was he not equal to any god? Certainly to the Companions of Horus! Soon it would speak to him, his two minds would become one and the interface between them would dissolve away.

But first, reality! He looked towards the road, a quarter of a mile away. The hired car had arrived, waiting for Georgina with its lights on. He'd ordered a lovely old black Rolls Royce with a chauffeur in uniform ... a joke which he knew she would enjoy. Cinematically appropriate, as Cindy would say, kitsch and vulgar; as *she* would have wanted it, vamp bitch that she was, if this trip had been hers ... So what! Cindy had betrayed him often enough, with mere thinking. He was not going to feel guilty about it now!

Afterwards, Georgina was taking the night train to London, a previous plan she didn't want to change; a trip to museums to take photographs of Ancient Egyptian sculpture. It had been wonderful how their work had overlapped recently ...

The eclipse had almost reached its predicted murder of the light. He placed the crystal and the leaf on his tongue, closed his eyes and swallowed. Paused ... only briefly, before pulling back the white sheet, kneeling down to untie Georgina's wrists and ankles, gently, considerately, acknowledging the pain she had suffered with the first thrusts; but it had seemed necessary.

Slowly and elegantly, she curled up from the edges, like a leaf that has fallen on a fire, her arms and legs, like springs uncoiling, wrapping round him and clutching at him, dragging him closer as if she wanted him to become part of her, his entire being inside her. She said nothing but murmured quietly, almost inaudibly, indecipherable words more like music, as he lay gently, half on top of her, before starting to caress her ... again. It had been necessary to do it twice ... the old man had explained why.

She opened her eyes and gazed at the night sky, saw that the eclipse was almost *there*. She wondered at the excitement they must have felt, inside the Great Pyramid, waiting as she had done, for the instant when the star of the god or goddess would be visible at the end of one of the stone shafts, when the three stars of Orion's belt would come into view, the stars of Osiris, and the priest and priestess would make love, dressed in their elaborate robes and animal and bird headdresses. Imagine the scene! Perhaps they were already making love and at the precise moment, the priest, well trained, would ejaculate. And the star Sirius, the dog star, the star of Isis, would be another perfect predicted moment of ritual and sexual magic. What ecstasy! She felt, for a brief moment, *that* excitement ... it was as if she was now inside the Great Pyramid, part of those sexual magical rites; so much to do with expansion of consciousness, as Cindy and John knew. She knew now how it must have felt. That intense expectation, that deep sacred and sexual arousal.

But she must concentrate on the *now*, anything might happen; John had warned her that, afterwards, he would almost certainly pass out, but she must quickly leave and ignore him, whatever *seemed* from the outside to be happening. She had no idea that Amenhotep might be actually watching ...

John was concentrating on his fingers, plying her open again. Oh, the indescribable mystery, the excitement of feeling those lips swollen, and just inside, the moisture, and further inside, the heat ... and throbbing. He slipped inside her. She tried not to show him that it hurt still, or her secret. It was all a matter of timing, he said, but hers was not exactly perfect. Surely it was the worst possible time? But the unspoken had remained unspoken. It was the outside events that were important. He was the director of the film, she was merely the actress. Once, she recalled, smiling to herself, she had decided never to surrender her virginity to a man. But the moment had come ... and gone.

She had no script, but she guessed John would plan to ejaculate as the chemical hit his brain, the moment when the eclipse reached its climax. She had witnessed him making love to Cindy, often enough, adept at holding back, and he did so now ... but she was so excited she couldn't stop herself letting go, pushing hard and squeezing ... and she lost herself, for how long she had no idea ... dreaming lovely dreams of a perfect golden time of long ago ... only to come back at the moment John's body went taut and hard, arched up and shuddered savagely ... everything happening at once. She dug her fingers into his back and pushed herself hard against him as long as she could ... so hard and with so much certainty, she was holding him up. Then she fell back and he fell back down on her, before quickly falling aside as if struck by a blow, his entire body now limp, and she knew he was already away ...

She eased out from under him, put his arms at his side and laid the blanket and then the coverlet over him as he had asked her. Every small part of this ritual had been given to him by Amenhotep and it was a privilege for her to share it. She dressed quickly in the long warm cloak, over her torn dress, and after kissing him on the cheek as he slept, she headed off down the track between the high hedges, towards the lights of the car; wondering how she would deal with the idea that she was now going to be in love with him, whatever that might mean in this day and age, just because of this *once* ... never to be taken away.

... clinging for a brief moment to consciousness, perhaps memory, images spreading in two directions as if from the point of contact with lines learnt by heart, as all boundaries fell away, an image rose into his mind, a shimmering white falcon, swooping towards him, claws outstretched, *"his shape a cross eaten by light"*, in its feet the golden bough, Soma, which, just before it struck, it let drop and it hit him in the centre of his forehead and splintered into a million crystals, *"where he alights a skin sloughs from a leafless apocalypse, on his lens each atom engraves with a diamond"* ... Horus, Golden Falcon of the Dawn, spirit-child of the mysterious sexual union of Isis and Osiris ... wingbeats making him rise, slithering down onto him, copulating with the invisible phallus she created for herself and her divine purpose, by magic ...

... hovering still, not yet fallen, trying to imagine the complex, elegant little molecules of the drug swimming along his bloodstream, eager to conquer his mind and restructure it, but he was also thinking of Georgina going for the night train, and now she seemed to be on it, enveloped in steel, its thunderous movement penetrating the night ... he hoped she wasn't so confused she got the wrong one ... he, thinking about other living cells, creatures in themselves, molecules in which is written the predestined future, images spawning images, swimming along inside her, forms a million years old, waves of passion squeezing, sucking, contracting on him, genes she had received, taken with her, gone forever. Gone. They were hers now. The immune system would fail to reject them, even though they were foreign bodies. What perfect apparently irrational elegance!

A girl in a fluted white dress, a railway station at night. Stone and steel columns, torn by shrapnel. The train leaving the station, moved out of the time and space of their shared image, mimicking his Delvaux hologram. Behind the column on the left which was also a tree, he thought he saw movement.

Suddenly he felt the fusion of the drugs flood his brain, the involute dissolve away his image of himself, the womb of deepest space calling him, crystal and leaf enfolded, infolded into each other's structure, and the mind's remaining words eclipsed, hard edges, eroded away in the abject darkness that precedes the creation of every thing ...

A falcon re-alighting on its golden perch.

He was kneeling, trying to hold onto nothing; pure imagining ... like dream. Being blind now to the abandoned, redundant plane of reality, he didn't see the flash of pale starlight that reflected like a laser beam from what might have been a flint knife, or a quartz crystal the shape of a pyramid ... its edges honed as sharp as the light itself from the face of a newly-cut emerald. He couldn't be sure the violent sound of tearing was the whisper of leaves rustling, amplified in his throat like a scream. He didn't see the dark shape that might have been a blind old man slouching towards him ... a white falcon circling above them both, seeing all ... his body could be its prey now ... talons outstretched, clutching into matter as the thorns of a rose once pierced into the flesh of dying, crucified gods hung on golden boughs ... its curved beak opening, mimicking the scimitar of time, slicing the illusory space of the living into irreconcilable fragments, fourteen to be precise, images that seemed for a moment to be projected on an imaginary cinema screen in someone else's mind ... a woman's mind he had once known, as deep and turbulent as a sea of molten lapis lazuli and as ancient as time itself, shared with her, an imagined androgynous holograph ... or if he did, part of his mind thought it was merely the sound of the wind rustling in the leaves, and eyes budding on rotting fruit ... preferring to imagine bloodsap in the leaves, dried blood on fresh leaves, the secret fruit of the tree, pushing up through the humus around its roots ... to remember what he wanted to remember ... the wind blowing some loose blonde hair over a pretty face ... in slow motion, like in a film, with desire at last fading, like light itself, no longer illuminating everything, even inside his own darkening mind ...

... a pile of pitch-black bandages, no longer white in the eclipse of the moon, in which a pure white falcon had been lying, mummified, in wait for its moment to be reborn ... dead but not dead ... perhaps dreaming ... waiting, waiting ... and then there was nothing, not even dreaming of dreams, the ultimate irony, nothing, not even sleep, not even birth or death. He was rising up and taking off and yet, like an image in a half-silvered mirror, life reflecting death falling, wondering if there was no turning back ...

Georgina lay down on the bed in her sleeping compartment, her belly throbbing, her womb contracting ... seeing one image in her mind, herself entering inside his crystal, as if she had been drawn inside it and they had made love*there*, on a patchwork quilt of many colours, lying back watching an erotic film of a couple making love in a small glade inside a copse of trees in which there were bluebells, crushed beneath her ... green stains and blood on a fluted white skirt ...

Except the more she gazed into the crystal, there seemed to be two crystals ... two places, two times ... she was in both of them at once, making love, she and the other, in one seeing, in the other, being seen ...

▽

The final preparations had been completed. The batteries were charged. The robot had been placed in the stone passageway, the camera switched on to *standby*, to be triggered when the optic fibre, with its lens and laser-light source, was inside the chamber, pushed through the flaw, the break at the bottom of the stone portcullis door, with its copper handles. Clearly there was air inside the chamber; the first robot's search-laser had shown there were gaps where the door touched the floor. If any of the books from the library of Imhotep were exposed to the air, any damage would have been done already in the four thousand five hundred years since the Fourth Dynasty, when Pharaoh Chephren had sealed up the secret chamber.

Some of the crystals were secretly *hidden* by being set into jewellery; but the pyramid-shaped crystals, essential to the Isis rites and reception of the so-called *Green Rays* referred to in the Pyramid texts, were hidden inside the body of one of the mummified falcons, inside its painted mummy-case.

Imhotep was waiting. Was the world's collective mind ready for the revelations that would change its image of itself, forever; ready to understand perfect translucency, the mystery of knowing knowing? Was anyone still initiated to decode the messages, unravel the riddle of Chephren's Sphinx, reveal that reason itself was the riddle, the veil? Even when the maps and plans of the Pyramid were discovered and revealed at last, who would be ready to receive the telepathic messages? Where was the all-seeing eye of the falcon, initiated into the mysteries of Isis and Osiris, that would understand the language of perfected, invisible light? And respect its source?

★

TWO

*"And that mysterious lady, who never revealed her face (except to me in dreams), but acted by delegation, had her name from the Latin verb **levare**, to raise aloft."*

"Suspiria de Profundis"
Thomas de Quincey

▼

Matthew opened his eyes tentatively, fearing the worst, but was relieved to see the lights flickering on his music equipment. What on earth had gone wrong? Clearly he'd not made the microscope's protective eye-piece dark enough. He tried to get up, but his limbs felt like lead. Still exhausted, he lay back, eyes closed, half-recalling a dream that had haunted his sleep. He wanted to fall back into sleep again, feeling he must try to reach the dream, it concerned him, and he did fall asleep but without accessing it.

By the time he finally woke up completely it was three o'clock in the afternoon. The dream was still haunting him, fragmented images lingered just outside of vision, tantalisingly, and he remembered the time when he was developing a film at school, a film of some very important events in his life – railway trains he'd been on, aeroplanes he'd seen, motor cars he'd imagined owning one day. He'd forgotten to close the dark-room door and someone had turned on the light, and he wept with rage as he watched the tell-tale black cloud spreading over his negatives, the light eclipsing and destroying the pictures forever.

He dressed briskly and opened the curtains. The sun was shining brightly through the trees, a perfect spring day. On the screen of his computer was the code telling him the experiment was completed. He switched it off. He'd copy the data onto back-up discs later. He still felt weak. In his notebook he wrote:

26th March. 1500 hrs. Experiment concluded.
Unexplained exposure to reflected laser beam, causing temporary blindness. 13 gigabytes of data on hard disk.

Still feeling quite weak, he decided to go home and rest.

He called at the newsagent's where he'd taken his newspaper, every day, for years. The husband and wife who owned the shop were impressed by his punctuality, his aloof debonair poise and his modest good looks. For some time they had naively hoped he would invite their pretty daughter for dinner, or to a concert at Kings College (as he'd once suggested) or even for tea in his college rooms. They knew he liked her because he always talked about the weather and bought chocolate whenever she was in the shop but never at other times. Once he'd asked, 'How is your pretty daughter, I haven't seen her for ages?', but nothing came of such promise, so they forgot their hopes of hooking a suitable son-in-law, and set their clock by him instead.

The wife smiled with relief when she saw him. 'Good heavens, we thought you must be ill or something, Doctor Sutherland! How nice to see you!' She gave him two newspapers and a copy of *The New Scientist*.

'Two papers, Mrs Bishop? And the magazine usually comes on Friday, surely?'

'But it *is* Friday, Doctor Sutherland!'

'It can't be!' he said vaguely. 'My God! I slept for two days!' He smiled awkwardly and shuffled out hurriedly. Why had he needed to sleep so long? He hadn't seemed tired. He invariably slept well, always waking up five minutes before his alarm, its raucous crowing occurring while he made tea, giving him great satisfaction to switch it off then, controlling the dimension of time as he imagined he controlled the tangible dimensions of matter.

Two days! Now he was really worried. He tried to remember the dream during his final awakening, imagining it might have some connection to the lost two days. He could remember a tomb or a stone room ... a train journey to an exotic, archaic land across a vast blue-green sea ... a long bridge, broken stone colonnades of columns or petrified trees ... a girl whose head seemed to be a stone sculpture ... and another girl in a diaphanous white dress, half naked, who danced for him, yet eluded him ...

Not really like his dreams at all! His dreams were the living proof of the failure of Freud's wish-fulfilment theory, which, had it been true, would all be set in Cairo in more glorious days, when he would be the local Consul, in love with the satin woman, gaining the respect of the locals, not by accepting bribes or even dispersing them generously, the usual colonial way of maintaining order, but by openly keeping a harem of nubile wenches, preferably rather young, of various hues and talents, and enjoying at least three of them per day. Such dreams would have proved Freud's theory of wish-fulfilment ... alas, his dreams, mostly of his dull prosaic past, were rarely so memorable.

Sitting down suddenly on a bench, he closed his eyes ... the dream was surfacing; but shadowy and unclear. It was like looking at the blurred surface of a pool into which two stones had been thrown ... endlessly weaving circles of waves that eventually became random and formless. He felt there was meaning there but it would elude him until he found the right way of looking at it. Why such a troubled sleep? It was not like him at all. Presumably the accident during the experiment ...

But the laser splitting into so many colours was scientifically impossible. It must have happened *physically* inside his brain. And that was scientifically improbable. Was he scared, running away from the truth, not daring to admit that the experiment had failed again? He felt miserable, and until he consulted the computer he would continue to suffer. He was feeling curiously distraught ... it was quite tangible, a kind of dread at not being able to recall the dream. He felt it was vitally important. Why? Damn! So much confusion and overlapping of images, he hated not knowing things precisely. Maybe he'd call Beverly, one of the girls in the lab; he'd always fancied her. Invite her for a drink, and fuck the hell out of her ... maybe not. But the image was not without an urgency he found disquieting ... maybe it was time to resist resisting ...

The following day Matthew counted the steps again. 80. A good sign. It made sense. Inside his laboratory he glanced at his morning's letters, while making tea. He was trying not to worry about being blinded and sleeping for two days, although the questions wouldn't go away. Was the implosion really at the centre of the diamond? Apprehensively he looked through the glass darkly at his precious diamond. Were the green traces something other than mere organic residues? He focused the magnifying lens more carefully – was there not a small mirror-like fissure in the green lattice he'd not noticed before? Red and black like dried blood? A stain?

The first job was to make copies of the data onto smaller discs. Sitting down in front of his computer, pushing back in his swivel chair and ordering his body to relax, he felt curiously resentful, detached from it in some unexpected way. He was painfully tense and it angered him. He knew it was fear, the fear of something unknown. Or failure. He couldn't bring himself to switch it on. He walked round the room, but this made him feel worse. He made a note in his notebook of the date and time ...

All he had to do was switch on the master-switch of his computer, and access the data in the hard-disk drive. He made the decision to do it but he couldn't move, as if his mind had decided to do it but *he*couldn't move. His arms felt paralysed. It was like being held from behind, two invisible arms binding his own to his body. He was in two minds to ... yes, that was the image, but he was not only in two minds but in two bodies. He tried and tried but couldn't press the switch, however much he struggled with himself. Finally, only after great effort, he managed to stand up again and walk around the room feeling quite shaken.

There was some Islay malt whisky in his filing cabinet which he kept for emergencies, and he poured it neat into a glass. Nothing like this had ever happened before. How could he escape this stranglehold, this fear or whatever it was? He decided to listen to music. The disc in the machine was still the Mendelssohn *Hear my Prayer,* but for some reason it grated on his nerves so sharply he had to stop it immediately. He wanted to say 'romantic rubbish' but he knew this was not his true feeling about it. He sat down again, utterly confused. He closed his eyes and opened them quickly as if he was afraid of becoming blind again. He went through his mental *filing cabinet* of music, looking for something he would like to listen to. Mozart? Opera? But he didn't have any opera music in his laboratory. He had the *Requiem* but this wasn't quite right, operatic though it was. He could only find some Mozart chamber music, but he felt immediately it would be right. He lay down on the sofa and closed his eyes, making a conscious effort to relax, and he fell gradually asleep again ...

While sleeping, he experienced a vivid dream ...

It is night. He's travelling in a crowded train on his way to a conference in Moscow to read his paper, announcing the astounding results with the three diamonds. Although he's failed to prove what he'd been looking for, by accident they've revealed something far more important, a discovery that will undermine the fundamental laws of classical physics, proving that cold fusion is possible inside crystals, with energy which is spontaneously created, as if from nothing.

The train is packed with people, all asleep. It's hot and stuffy and he can hardly breathe so he pushes his way into the corridor and opens a window in the door and air rushes in, ice-cold and refreshing. At first he thinks he's inside a tunnel, a square stone tunnel, a long stone shaft, barely a few inches over his head. The ominously slow train is moving along a line not used for a very long time, probably abandoned; modernisation elsewhere has left it redundant. The Arctic tundra lies luminously silver in the moonlight, covered with ice and snow, level and stark and seemingly unending, stretching away before him. Above him, the North Star, which seems unusually close and bright, as do the three stars in the belt of Orion.

But suddenly, he sees ahead a huge tree growing in the centre of the line between the two steel rails. He can't understand why the driver hasn't seen it and why he doesn't stop the train. There will be a terrible crash! The tree will slice right down the middle of the train. In a panic, he forces himself against the window on the right, pushing as far as he can away from the centre, scared it will be his own brain sliced in half by the lone tree ...

... seconds before a harsh, hollow, splintering sound as the train crashes into the tree; but to Matthew's amazement, the two halves of the train veer off into two branch lines. He's on one of them but he can see the other half of the train fading away along the other line. This other half is transparent, as if the tree had cut the train into two halves, one still complete and solid and real ... the other, a mirror image, a double of the other train, identical in appearance, but reversed in form, on another dimension, translucent and unreal ...

But he was struck. He can feel a dull pain somewhere in his body, but he is more concerned about his brief-case which is on the other train, containing all his experimental data, all his computer discs (as proof) on which the entire evidence for his work is recorded, and his unique scientific paper to be read at the conference. Without it he will not be able to bring his new theory into the light of day. Something else is missing. He's covered with blood, but it's too dark to see what has really happened although he senses nothing will never be the same again ... on the ground, fragments of broken chipped limestone and splintered fragments of black wood ...

The train lurches to a halt. The other passengers are still asleep or perhaps dead. Matthew alights from the train and walks back towards the tree. Again he notices the other train disappearing into the distance, like a ghostly image fading on a television screen. He touches the tree to see if it is real. It seems impossible that a mere tree could have had the power and strength to split the train so neatly in half. A branch severed by the impact, lying next to the steel rail, seems to be covered in blood. Lifting it, it's far too heavy and he's fascinated to see it's not made of wood but is entirely composed of crystals, beautiful, shining, interlocking crystals, that seem to reflect the pale green moonlight. But as he examines the crystals more carefully he sees they are not reflecting light ... they have their own inner source of light ... a gentle, golden glow. The mosaic patterns of the crystals remind him of a cross-section of stone seen under a polarizing microscope, probably quartz schist ... and he feels relieved he has the mind and knowledge that can analyse the stone and discover where it comes from, and its age. He knows the tree was petrified millions of years before. With his skills, and dating the carbon crystals, he could discover the exact date ...

He hears the sharp sound of further wood cracking, perhaps an inner door, looks up and is horrified to see a severed head hanging from one of the higher branches. It's the driver of the train; he's sure he recognises the face. But then the train starts to move of its own accord and he jumps back onto it quickly, wondering who is driving it now the driver is dead; probably some half-crazed, half-dead passenger.

Where has the other half of the train gone? Perhaps the train has its own computer and its own ghostly, machine consciousness ... and it seems to have two green headlights, that are so narrow he's sure they are laser beams ...

The train arrives at the end of the line, in a forest clearing in which the trees are arranged formally, in rows, equidistant from each other. Suddenly he's inside a huge building, probably an old railway station, the trees are stone or steel columns, supporting a huge, arched steel roof, filigree black against the sky. Between two tall, tree-like columns are huge stained glass windows made of the same crystal formations he'd seen inside the broken branch of the tree. On the cross seems to be the body of a young girl crucified. He feels embarrassed. She's too young to have suffered such an act, for such a crime. Implied, but hidden. Would he be capable of such a thing? There's music being sung by a choir of children's voices, probably Mozart's *Requiem* ... yet it could be opera. *Salomé* perhaps. The two girls singing, very close, sensuously, like lovers.

In front of him is a large stone altar, or sarcophagus; on top, a life-size sculpture of the head of a girl, the face looking away from him. He feels desperately unhappy because he knows she is alive, but because he can't see her face, she can't know she is alive. He feels cheated and sad. If he had his briefcase he could deliver his paper, there in the cathedral of steel and she'd notice him, turn to him, face to face ...

He hears something moving, slouching, dragging itself along the stone floor. Petrified, he hides behind a pillar, only to notice another girl, half-hidden behind another pillar, standing motionless, cold and white as if dead, wearing a long transparent tunic, part nightdress, part robe. The skirt is fluted like a column. He turns again to look at the head on the altar, trying desperately to move into a position to see the face of the young girl, but each time he moves, the head moves too. He's always looking from the wrong point of view.

He peers round the column and sees the second girl is now dancing, alone, absorbed in herself, dancing very, very slowly, turning as if turning inside out, and outside in, on herself. He has the sensation of seeing the one person as two, one who is real and tangible, the other a reflection or double, always out of phase, in a different time, different space, dancing with and in and out of the other person ... as if he can see the girl dancing with the person she imagines herself to be ... and he recalls the distinction in quantum science between a particle and a wave, and senses her dance is a description of two systems of waves, one superimposed on the other ... as in a Moiré pattern ... and this is what he must understand.

Her sinuous dancing is weaving so much in and out of itself, her lithe half-naked body seems like a reflection of a bird hovering over the surface of a pool of water ... into which two pebbles have fallen and disturbed its surface, creating two spirals that twist in and out of each other. He tries to separate the two images but he can't. He tries to see her as a person, but can't. He feels profoundly sad, knowing it's merely a *virtual* image on a screen, and as he approaches her, she fades and grows dim. He steps back. She's naked under her dress and is arousing herself, her index finger, with a blue-green ring on it, on her sex, as she dances ...

... but the image of her is too bright to see the details. He places a darkened lens over his eye to see her and discover *who* she is ... but the more intensely he looks at her the more she brightens up and becomes visible. Light must be coming from his eye and going outwards towards the girl ... not reflected off her into his eye. Within his own eye is a source of light and it's *this* that is making her visible ... like a projected image of a film on a screen ... but he will never be able to touch her, to take her in his arms as he would like, penetrate her without losing the certainty of remaining outside ...

Her dancing is arousing him more and more and he wants her desperately, despite realising the source of light within his eye: the phenomenon of seeing without reflected light is what the subject of his paper *ought* to be; it is only an illusion that the eye sees *reflected* light. What about light itself, is it really invisible? She's showing him there's another source of light from within, which interferes with objective light, we only see the interface where the two coincide and that gives us the impression of three-dimensional space/time ...

She's dancing even more sexually explicitly now, a whore in a brothel ... the image seems discordant, he has to look away, but notices a small silver hand-bag in a hole carved out in a nearby stone column. She made it when she was a young girl.

Why hasn't she shown him? Why hasn't she *seen* him? He notices two shafts of light have created a perfect pyramid of light over her, and she's now dancing on a green glass floor suspended in the middle of the pyramid. Quickly he opens the bag and sees some objects wrapped in bandages; opening these carefully he finds seven small stones which interlock to make one stone ... like a puzzle. Each stone reflects a different colour of the rainbow; when they're all together, the resulting composite stone is light grey ... and the shape of a brain. The bandages are stained with blood and he decides his work must be to analyse the blood to discover if it is his own.

He's happier now. With these stones he can seduce the girl, attract her attention, and they'll help him to elucidate his new theory about light and the origin of life as interlocking waves ... and how it resembles the origin of thought ... for that is all there is ... now ... in their shared predicament.

The ecstatic girl, almost naked now, her blonde hair flowing wildly over her naked shoulders, dances towards the sarcophagus and the first girl, who raises herself up, in white now, with dark eyes and dark hair. Holding a small object between them, wrapped in bandages, they move close and caress each other and he desperately wants to join them, slip between them and make love to them both at once; but he can't move. He seems to have two choices; to get inside the bandages or get above the two girls; if he can get *above* the first girl, he'll be able to see her face, but to do that, he must be able to fly!

He tries hard to imagine it, hoping that if he concentrates on the image of it, he will rise off the ground, and once risen, he will see the two girls ... but they are naked now and making love to each other with the object, the bandages having fallen away to reveal a small crystal sculpture. He clenches his hands and pulls himself up, up and up, and the blood vessels in his neck start to bulge so much he's afraid the blood will escape from the wound in his leg ...

The girl with the dark hair is tying up the other girl, with the loosened bandages; they're both laughing. The crystal object is too bright to be seen properly; poised over the girl it is flickering from side to side in her fingers, her wet fingers, her fingers spread like two wings, the sculpture flashing with light like a hovering bird against the sun. Suddenly it plunges down into her body, and there's a scream. But a scream of pleasure ... and the image fades quickly down to a small dot of light ... and...

Matthew woke up in a cold sweat, feeling distraught, split, desolate. He was cold and shivering and felt desperately lonely. Where had the dream come from? The images were so alien to his sensibility. He tried to remember it again, but the images were already fading, no doubt dispelled by his concentration, although he could still vaguely see the two girls caressing and kissing and touching each other. Why did it hurt and linger? He wanted desperately to be part of their shared eroticism, but again, the images were eluding him. What was the crystal object? He'd never really seen it ...

Then the images of the train returned ... Yes! Of course! He was remembering the house in Lancashire where he'd lived with his parents as a small boy. His father was always making small models that moved, with wheels and lights. Robots. But one day he'd bought an electric train set which had been laid out on a number of wall-papering tables in the attic. There were roads and bridges and trees and houses. Matthew had been told the train-set was for him, but it was so dangerous – electric! – he could only play with it when his father accompanied him, but his father spent hours in the attic, 'wanting to be alone', playing with the trains.

A curious ritual had developed between them. Matthew was fascinated with a small switch on the end of a long line because he could sit in the corner of the room and press the switch and it would stop the train. Being about five at the time, electricity was magic, a mystery to be marvelled over and enjoyed. In the middle of the landscape was a long tunnel and one day Matthew had pressed the switch with the train inside the tunnel and this had provoked the start of their ritual. Even to remember it now made him feel emotional ...

His father would pull a long face and say, 'But the train has completely disappeared! It's crashed inside the tunnel!' Then Matthew would press the switch and the train would come whizzing out and they'd both laugh. Then the ritual changed; his father would say, 'All the people are trapped inside the tunnel. They can't get out! They want to get out but they can't. All the people are going to die!' He would pull an even longer face and when Matthew was sure his father was about to cry for all the dead people he'd press the switch and the train would come hurtling out of the tunnel and he'd shout out, 'No Daddy! Look! I did it! The people are saved, they're perfectly alright!'

Matthew's father spent much of his time away, working in another town and Matthew only saw him at rare weekends. Their first contact was always the game with the train and the tunnel, their way of overcoming their inability to speak to each other again. Matthew would get upset if his father didn't get the words right, and he would correct him impetuously if he said something in the wrong order. Some time later, when his father stayed away for even longer periods, Matthew started to have nightmares. He was on the train himself and stuck in the tunnel, he'd scream until he woke up, trying to get out of the tunnel, or he'd be trapped with hundreds of other people, all strangers, and the people would panic and struggle and fight each other to get out of the tunnel. He'd wake up sobbing in the darkness, wailing to his mother to bring the light.

But eventually he managed to transform the dream and overcome it. Instead, he'd be sitting quietly in his seat as the people foolishly abandoned the train, groping into the tunnel, screaming and afraid. He had the master switch in his hand! When the train was completely empty, he'd press the switch and the train would move again and he'd sit in his seat, indifferent to the howls of the people in the tunnel, waiting calmly for the emergence from the darkness into the light. He was happy to be alone on the train, the only survivor. Matthew hadn't thought of this game with his father for many years and he was disturbed at remembering it so vividly and painfully now. He felt lonely remembering his father. Although the remembered images were not precisely those of his dream, he knew they were connected.

Had the dream freed him? He must try! He sat in front of the screen and made the decision to start the computer - but again his arms seemed to go limp and he couldn't move. He moved his hand towards the switch but it was as if he was fighting an invisible assailant. He couldn't press the switch. He stood up and furiously walked round the room. 'This is crazy! What the hell is happening to me!' he cried out, despite himself. He tried once more to switch on the computer, but failed. He decided he had no choice but to go home.

Once in his flat he presumed he could relax with some music and was surprised he only wanted to listen to Mozart again, which he'd not liked for years. But he felt too tired even to listen to music. Should he try to sleep it off, whatever it was? He dreaded the thought of dreaming again, but went reluctantly to bed, and fell asleep immediately.

The following morning his alarm clock woke him, and being so unaccustomed to switching it off from his bed, he knocked it, and a glass, off his bedside table, and the sound of shattering glass mingled with the clanging of the clock. Cursing, he got up shakily, still feeling half asleep; after sweeping up the glass, he shaved and made some tea. He was feeling awful, but decided he must snap out of it, get back in his routine. Surely it was only a temporary lapse?

On his way to the laboratory he picked up his newspaper and was relieved he hadn't slept another two days. 'Working on Saturday as usual, Doctor Sutherland?', the shop-keeper chirped, and he smiled patronisingly. 'Nobel prizes aren't won by punting on the River Cam with pretty girls, now are they, Mrs. Bishop?'

He counted the stairs. 79. Damn! Once inside his office, apprehensive, he stood at the window gazing at the tall trees in the garden, swaying in the wind. Sensing already he wouldn't be able to press the switch, he sat in front of the computer and glared at it, even feeling bitter towards it as if he had caught it betraying him, although he knew it was such a ridiculous feeling. Gazing helplessly at the blank screen, he knew he ought to laugh instead; but couldn't see the funny side of it. He raised his hand ... but got no further.

He suddenly remembered his old friend David Wickens who'd lived in a flat below his. They'd been to Paris a few times, to *sluice and let loose* as David called it. He'd been a crazy guy, a brilliant plant botanist who'd given up his career and gone off to an ashram in India after a couple of 'well-deserved and self-induced nervous breakdowns!' He'd started to eat the plants rather than study them and his mind had fallen apart eventually from taking too many stimulants of one kind and another. But he was the kind of guy who would have found a way of making him laugh. It had been David who had encouraged him to work with the diamonds. 'The project sounds utterly crazy. All the more reason for doing it, and maybe a chance to make a major discovery! Would you prefer something safe and predictable?' Perhaps it was all his fault ...

But then Matthew suddenly thought of Jane, the only girl he'd ever really loved, the only girl with the power to really hurt him, which she'd done, elegantly. He'd wanted to marry her but David had been scathing about her. Matthew had never forgotten one of his discourses on the subject. 'You only think you love her because she has class, and yet you know she's a stuck-up bitch. Beautiful, yes, like death's-head moths can be beautiful. She'll marry a title of course, and the only thing stiff about him will be his drinking bills, his gambling debts, and his upper lip!' Matthew hated David's jibes about her, even when it was evident, afterwards, they had been deadly accurate.

Matthew gazed solemnly at the empty screen, wondering why he was becoming obsessed with images from his past; Jane's face still in his mind's eye, he remembered his last evening with her. She was lying on his bed, in a fussy kind of lace dress, a Goya painting, cruel and mocking. 'I'm leaving you ... we'll never meet ever again. But if you want to make love to me for the last time ... for memory's sake, you can. Let's have a nice image of our last evening together!' Although he was desperate to do so, longing to prove he could change her mind, make her stay, he insisted instead it was the very last thing he wanted to remember! She'd swung her legs off the bed, picked up her Gucci handbag, put on her taffeta shoes; 'As you prefer! Pity! I *really* wanted you tonight!' Had she never really wanted him before?

He'd never forgotten the anguish and frustration, standing in front of her, desiring her so passionately, yet knowing he had to say 'No!' Only by denial could he preserve something of himself, although he wasn't sure what. But she'd cruelly achieved exactly what she wanted. The memory she'd bequeathed to him, etched indelibly on his mind, was her last smile and her words. 'Pity! I *really* wanted you tonight.' But he still loved her, or at least, he'd not become free by loving anyone else since.

He often wondered if she'd been right. Maybe he should have made love to her, despite his despair at losing her. Maybe it *was* the only time she really wanted him! But he'd wanted her too much and he never had a second chance to test an alternative ending. It had been at the start of his work with the diamonds when she left ...

Having confronted these images from his past, reliving his feelings about them momentarily, he felt better, hoping he might now be able to start his work. Once again he made the mental decision to press the master switch, but again, to his dismay, his body wouldn't move. He was furious and hit the table so hard he nearly broke his hand. He saw the irony. He could move to hit the table, but *not* to turn on the switch. It was unbelievably stupid. He tried again, but the paralysis seemed to strike his whole body, not just his arms. He was in a strait-jacket from head to foot. It was only when he abandoned the intention completely, he could stand up and walk about, his body coming alive again. He closed his eyes and tried to force himself to relax, wondering if he was going mad. There was an invisible wall erected between him and the computer and there was no way of penetrating it.

He went to the window and looked down into the garden, bathed in a soft spring light. He was surprised to notice the laboratory garden was full of tall beech trees, arranged rather formally in two rows. He felt an uncomfortable tingling feeling at the back of his neck. He'd never noticed the trees were planted so symmetrically, though he knew they were there. If someone had asked him, he could have said, 'Yes, of course the garden is full of trees!' But he'd not be able to say what kind of trees or how they were set out. There was no recorded image in his mind that he could draw on. He couldn't describe the garden objectively at all, and yet he'd stood at that window hundreds of times over the years. Had he never once actually seen the trees? He knew this was an extraordinary fact, a terrible lapse, a serious flaw in the way he looked at the world ... or didn't look at it. Had he really been so blindly involved with his work he'd not once noticed how tall and majestic and beautiful were the trees in the laboratory garden? He knew he had to go immediately into the garden. The fresh air would do him good anyway, but he felt compelled to be as near as possible to the trees ... perhaps to assuage some of the guilt for never having noticed them. 78 steps ...

The cool low sun was casting long shadows, and there was a light breeze. Once, there had been a fine Regency house in that garden, which had never revived after being a war-time officers' mess, to be eventually knocked down by the University. The Research Council had built the ultra-modern laboratory in its place. Progress.

Matthew noticed immediately the trees were set precisely in two rows, and he guessed they must once have formed an avenue that led up to the front of the old house. He walked under the trees and felt an unexpectedly pleasant sensation in his body. He thought it was probably his muscles relaxing after the tension in his battle with his computer, but gradually he became certain the source of the sensations was not his body, but the trees. He felt quite sure about it, even though he knew it was a bizarre idea. Suddenly he felt an intense compulsion to sit next to one tree in particular. It stood alone at the end of the two formal rows and seemed to be bigger than the other trees. Its roots were partially exposed and there was a concave shape like a chair formed by the roots and the base of the tree. He sat down gently into it and lay back against the huge trunk and closed his eyes. Slowly his body relaxed completely and he knew it was the first moment it had done so, except when he slept, since the weird mishap with his experiment. He felt a deep feeling of relief ...

But suddenly he was sure he could detect a sound that shouldn't be there. A voice speaking to him. He tried to make out the words. It was a woman's voice, whispering. But then he realised it was the wind rustling in the leaves and he laughed at his silliness! But he felt better, having laughed at his mistake, and he started to feel really comfortable in his natural armchair in the roots of the tree. His body had been so tense, he'd been afraid on his way down the stairs of banging against something solid, and snapping off an arm like a dead twig ...

He closed his eyes and laid his head gently against the smooth bark and listened to the wind rustling in the branches and the sound was comforting. Suddenly, he remembered where he'd sat under such a tree, in a similar small copse of beech trees, arranged formally. Why hadn't he thought of it before? About two miles from the town-house in Carnforth in Lancashire where he'd lived alone with his mother, after his father had gone abroad to work, and never come back, was a small grove of trees standing alone near the foothills of Warton Crag, a wild terrain of boggy and dangerous wasteland which stretched between the town and the sea. He was eight or nine when he'd first played truant from school and ventured alone into the exciting world of nature. The small copse, he remembered now, had consisted of exactly the same tall beech trees, arranged around the summit of a raised mound of earth. Local people had said the trees were planted by evil spirits and the place was haunted by ghosts of pagan sacrifices. But Matthew felt at home there. There was even the remains of some kind of stone circle just visible under the grass. In the spring the idyllic clearing in the centre of the trees was awash with a sea of dancing bluebells. He'd visited the copse as often as he could, knowing there was something special about it; he felt different there ... the only place where he could be completely himself. He could see the mountains of the Lake District in the distance, high, snow-capped and menacing, and he would dream of climbing them, reaching the heights where only falcons and golden eagles soared and hunted, chasing grouse and hares, silver-blue in their winter coats ...

He remembered arriving at the copse one day and seeing a Land-Rover parked nearby and hearing voices. He'd crept through the bushes surrounding the trees and witnessed a frightening scene ... a terrible fight ... a young girl in a white skirt with red petticoats was struggling in the bluebells with a man ... she was screaming and he seemed to be beating her. After they left he found some torn clothing near the crushed flowers ... a bandage covered with blood. He felt sure he'd witnessed a terrible crime but was too scared to tell anyone about it. Years later he would laugh at the memory, knowing the couple had probably been harmlessly making love, something he knew little about at the time, and what he thought he knew was obscured by the irrational montage of his naive, cinematic dreams ...

Matthew was happy now to have remembered his cherished copse. It explained everything. He let his arms go limp and his whole body relaxed, starting to feel normal again; almost as if an invisible skin was sloughing off his body. He moved inside the forked roots of the tree and found an even more comfortable position with his knees half drawn up so they locked into the roots. Suddenly ... he became aware of a curious sensation. Almost imperceptible vibrations were passing into his body from the interior of the tree. He could feel the physical sensation quite clearly. It was as if the base of his spine was receiving the vibrations directly from the tree and it was one of the most agreeable sensations he'd ever felt. He gave up resisting the experience, almost losing consciousness, feeling he almost knew what it was like to be part of the tree, as if the force that came from the soil and grew into the heart of the tree and kept it alive was feeding into his own body. He gazed up at the branches dancing in the wind above him; feeling on the verge of crying ...

It was then he made another unexpected connection, so quickly it unnerved him for the moment. It was the last time he'd visited the Kings College chapel for the Mendelssohn concert; he'd sat next to one of the stone columns set into the wall. The huge tree branching out into a canopy above him was recalling the fan tracery roof, and it dawned on him for the first time that the Gothic architects had quite deliberately tried to create the sensation of being contained by a womb of trees. It was so obvious; why had he never noticed the connection before? He'd visited the chapel hundreds of times to listen to music there, letting his eyes focus on the exquisite shapes and forms of the chapel. He'd only seen the stone; the beauty of the building as something entirely human, man-made, stones carved by man, created in the image of man. He'd never managed to see the trees hidden and yet not hidden in the carved stone ... like a deeper memory or an image from a deam ...

So trees arranged formally like this were the model of every church he'd ever seen, and he closed his eyes again, pleased to have made the connection, telling himself he'd first noticed the trees that morning because he remembered the chapel he'd recently visited and because they recalled the copse he loved so long ago. It made sense. It comforted him to think that everything could be explained; not seeing things for the first time at all, but recognising them and not remembering why.

81 stairs. And still he couldn't start his computer ...

As he was walking home, rather forlorn and disconsolate, passing the Fitzwilliam Museum with its colossal Greek facade looming over the small street, he suddenly stopped. He felt the tingling on the back of his neck again. Gazing at the museum he felt the same doubling of perception as with the trees in the laboratory garden. He'd passed the building every day for years and yet, he was now *seeing it for the first time.* It seemed to be shouting at him to take notice of it. But it was the colonnade of stone columns comprising the facade that first caught his attention. Rooted to the spot, he gazed up at the huge building, amazed at its size, its monstrous inauthenticity, its pretentiousness. Why build a replica of the Parthenon of the Athenian Acropolis, a Greek temple for the worship of pagan gods, in a Cambridge side street? Absurd! But it was just as absurd to have never *noticed* it before. He felt quite weak in his knees.

The building was massive: its frontage stretched a hundred yards along the street, the steps up to the entrance were thirty yards wide and thirty feet high and the facade must have been a hundred feet high. The huge stone columns towered above him and he felt almost dizzy looking at them as the clouds reeled by behind them. Why had he never stopped before and looked at it? Resting on top of the columns was a pyramid-shaped hypostyle, decorated with a frieze: humans, animals, plants; a brief moment trapped in stone and time from a mythological narrative. It seemed inconceivable that he'd passed it every day and its presence had never impinged on his consciousness. Was he really so blind?

But then he saw another connection; the colonnade of columns across the facade reminded him of his dream ... and the copse ... *and* the interior of Kings Chapel! It was merely a coincidence of images. But why was he suddenly becoming so disturbed by mere coincidence? He'd never worried about coincidence before.

He wanted to press on home and start packing, having decided to take a week off; maybe take a trip to Scotland, something he'd intended to do for ages. But something prevented him. He knew he *had* to go into the museum. With an intense pang of expectation, an intimation of something menacing but necessary, he walked up the steps towards the tall front doors of the museum. He felt again the burning, tingling sensation on the back of his neck as he stopped under the colonnade and looked up. For a moment, he was able to superimpose, in his mind, the two images; the one he could see, the other remembered ... the stone columns, the beech trees, and the building in his dream, part stone, part steel. He started to feel excited as if he was following a hunch, the kind of intuition he sometimes felt while working with scientific ideas and images, when he was close to making an important observation or some kind of creative deduction or discovery, not necessarily deriving directly from the data. An imaginative leap ... going beyond the data. Sideways.

Inside the door, he was persuaded to buy a handbook by an elderly lady at the information desk, but he didn't need to open it. He just knew; in front of him was a wide staircase leading to the upstairs galleries, on both sides were two narrower staircases leading down; he knew he had to go down the right staircase. His heart was pounding.

At the bottom of the stairs, he paused. This was the threshold. Above the door, in gold leaf:

He felt nervous about going in, and to distract himself, he opened the handbook; it fell open at the right page ...

> ***First Egyptian Room**. The small antiquities are of great variety, the most numerous series being formed by the vases, bronzes and jewellery. A large proportion of them come from **Tel El Amarna.** Among the sculpture is the mouth and chin from a huge sandstone figure of the Pharaoh Akhenaten of the 18th Dynasty.*

Matthew couldn't understand why he felt so much on edge.

The First Egyptian Room was empty. In front of him were various stone statues placed near the walls, and in the centre, glass cases with smaller objects. He noticed a huge carved stone top of a sarcophagus, some painted wooden mummy cases. The room was lit by a small window that was shaded from the sun by trees, the leaves translucent green against the light; the room was gloomy and dark. *Like a tomb*, Matthew thought. He stood at the door, allowing his eyes to adjust to the dimness of the light. Gradually he felt overcome with a profound sadness, knowing that all the objects had once belonged to people who had been alive, but now, all these once cherished objects were abandoned, betrayed, detached ... dead ... all that remained of past people, past lives. "Look at my works ye mighty and despair!" ... wasn't it?

Near the window he saw the remains of the huge statue of Pharaoh Akhenaten, a fragment of the mouth and chin the size of his own chest. He noticed the grain in the sandstone – compacted anthracitic shale, modified by diagenesis, probably containing coarse crystalline segregations in radiating cracks known as septarian nodules; a rare kind of sandstone indeed!

In the Second Room were various painted coffins, with notes on small cards next to each exhibit, explaining they were "Decorated with scenes from the so-called *Egyptian Book of the Dead*, more correctly named *The Book of Coming Forth by Day*", and he thought it strange that death should be referred to as "coming forth by day". One tall wooden coffin was painted with a series of images depicting the *"Transformation of the Soul".* Next to it was a full-size replica of the black Rosetta Stone, carved with a text of tiny white hieroglyphs and two parallel texts in Greek and Demotic Egyptian and Matthew learnt from the card next to it that it was this stone that led to the decipherment of the esoteric language of the hieroglyphs. There were other sheets of papyrus with chapters from the *Book of the Dead* in hieroglyphs, in which the soul was depicted as a falcon with outstretched wings with the head of a beautiful young girl.

One image caught his eye and seemed especially strange. "*The Goddess Isis in the form of a falcon, copulating with the body of her dead husband Osiris, King of the Underworld.*" The body of Osiris was lying on a sarcophagus, wrapped in white bandages. At its head and feet were two priestesses, and above his body a beautiful small falcon was hovering ... just touching the erect phallus ... suggesting [it said] the conjunction of two different levels of existence ... the human one; and the bird's, symbolising the spiritual.

Another Chapter described the transformation of the soul into the Golden Falcon. "*I have risen. I have risen, like the mighty falcon of gold that cometh forth from his egg; I fly and I alight like the falcon which hath a back four cubits wide, and the wings of which are like unto the mother-of-emerald of the South.*" He read that "*The doctrine of immortality of the soul,*" elaborated in the *Book of the Dead*, remained practically unchanged for at least four thousand years of its existence.

Matthew felt uneasy; his whole spine was aching. It felt hot along its whole length and was becoming more and more painful. He felt inexplicably weary and dizzy. He sat down on a warden's wooden chair, knowing he was about to faint. He managed to relax for a few minutes with his eyes closed. Then he tried to remember where he had seen such Egyptian objects before, what museum he must have visited as a child, or what books he had seen of images from ancient Egypt. He couldn't recollect any in particular; it had never been a subject he was remotely interested in. Yet what was disturbing him was the emotion he had felt since walking in the door, which he had tried almost desperately to resist, but the more he looked, the more it possessed him; the feeling of *recognition*, as if he had seen the objects before ...

He sat still, his eyes closed. He wanted to leave the museum but something urged him to stay. He couldn't understand why everything was seeming to be back to front, the wrong way round, inside out, his sense of time and space becoming more and more disclocated ...

Slowly he took control of his turbulent emotions, and curious to explore his new feelings, he decided to look in other glass cases, soon becoming fascinated by the mirrors, combs, tools, musical instruments and even furniture, in the shape of animals or birds or plants, heavily decorated with motifs of the natural world. It struck him forcibly that the people who made them must have loved the world around them; less concerned about making the object merely functional, than making it also a faithful (and that was the word) representation of a living plant or creature ... it had a double meaning, on two levels at once ... and he felt moved by a feeling of tenderness as he saw the beetles and birds and lotus flowers, transformed into all kinds of small objects to be used in the day-to-day lives of the gentle people who had made them. They must have felt themselves to be deeply part of the natural world, an extension of it ... and all the objects shared a similar kind of beauty.

And then he saw her ...

In a glass case a few yards away and facing away from him, a small sculpture. He knew immediately it was the head of a young girl. He stood still for a long time, scared of being wrong, scared of being right ... until he had the courage to walk towards her, knowing it was his dream. He recognised her immediately. He knew he'd never seen the object before or any representation of it or of her, but ... in some inexplicable way, he recognised her. It was as if the previous hints of recognition had been a premonition, a preparation perhaps, for this confrontation now with her.

On the card he read: "*Portrait of a Princess from Tel El Amarna: Meritaten, daughter of Akhenaten and Nefertiti.*" He gazed intensely at the exquisitely carved features and then he felt almost mistaken. No! He'd never seen the face before.

The features did not exactly remind him of anyone he'd ever known, but it was a new kind of emotion he'd never felt before, of relief mostly and a tangible feeling of pleasure, the pleasure coming mostly from his recognition of the beauty of the sculpture; not the personality, unless he was mistaken, but the gentleness of the features ... the sadness in the heavy-lidded eyes. He felt he knew the beauty, and it was the beauty of it, of her, that was relevant, because it was this beauty he had always dreamt of, touched lightly by death, always sought in his innermost being, despite himself, and the pleasure he felt, tinged with relief, came from discovering it at last ... unless he was still deluding himself.

But then his mind seemed to falter, to slip a plane, and he became the crystallographer again. He noticed the head had been sculpted from a block of quartz schist. Oh the beauty of crystals! Even ordinary sandstone, limestone, granite, when cut into very thin slices were magically transformed under the microscope into miniature replicas of stained glass windows, or beautiful abstract paintings. The interlocking crystals appeared as different colours, different textures, radiating with the light that passed through them. It had been the mysterious beauty of these slides that had provoked Matthew's eventual decision to study crystallography although he would not have admitted it easily, even to himself.

There was also the beautiful inner mathematical and geometrical structures that made crystals into what they were. But quartz schist had been his favourite mineral, a poly-metamorphic stone, produced by intense pressures and very high temperatures. He'd been so fascinated by it he'd made it the subject of his first serious research, studying the magnetic orientation of the interstitial quartz veins ...

He was quite certain the head of the Princess Meritaten was a rare specimen of his beloved quartz schist. The stone in its raw state, a mere chunk of rock, newly quarried, appeared very similar to hundreds of other hard stones found in quarries throughout the world, a pleasant texture and colour, but nothing special. It was under the microscope that the mineral was unequalled in its variety of form and the beauty of its translucent, shimmering, radiant colouration. He could see the sculptor had been moved aesthetically by the external appearance of the stone, managing to reveal the grain flowing in it, like waves of an ancient petrified sea ... wave grain in the rock, caught forever as it cooled from the amorphous magma. It showed especially across the young girl's cheeks, and the effect was tantalisingly beautiful. But as he gazed at the sculpture, he felt his mind repeatedly splitting, wavering from side to side as it switched from observing the appearance of the girl to imagining what was going on *inside* her head, in the crystal structure, its almost infinite possibilities of form. He tried to close his eyes ...

But he couldn't look at her without remembering the beauty of the microscopic crystal structure of the stone of which she was made. It was composed of a background *field* of exquisite dark blue-green crystals of feldspathoids, and darker-hued, emerald-green phyllites, inter-laced with traces of iridescent quartz, ranging in colour from violet to rose, sometimes clear and translucent, etched with bold lines of shiny black mica foliation, and every single microscopic image was as different to the next as a montage of cinematic photographs would be, taken of a spume of dragon-flies, poised over a pool ... or a flock of a thousand lapwings, flinging themselves into the air at the sight of a hovering falcon.

But the image of the crystals faded and before him, again, was the face of a young girl. It was surely the most beautiful face he'd ever seen. The most beautiful object he'd ever seen, and again, the feeling of recognition returned, faint but certain. Was it desire returning? Perhaps he'd experienced her face before and whenever it had been, he had loved her. Now, remembering those feelings of love he'd felt for her, to his intense surprise, tears welled up in his eyes. Embarrassed, he quickly looked round to see if there was anyone else in the room, but fortunately, he was still alone. 'This is not like me at all!' he said out loud, as if talking to Meritaten, as if wanting to reassure her that his naive behaviour was not at all his own.

For some minutes he stood in front of her until the emotion rising up inside him, of longing for her, became too painful and he knew he had to leave her. But he wanted so much to say something reassuring to her, feeling a pang of guilt for leaving her alone in the cold unfriendly museum, in the room that had reminded him of a tomb. But he knew he must go ...

He hurried back to his rooms, in some kind of obscure and uncharacteristic trance. Once inside, he drank a neat whisky, took out a suitcase and started to fling things in it. Yes, he must get away – fast! He was going on a trip to Scotland! He'd been there with Jane. Not since. He must get some fresh air. His grandfather had been born in Sutherland, he had friends there who could rent him a cottage. But then he stopped. What was it? He sat on his bed, his head in his hands, knowing he was almost defeated. He began to sob, quietly. His sobs were evenly spaced, rhythmic and melodic, and came from very deep within him. He didn't want to think any more ... to suffer any more connections ... any more inexplicable recognitions.

He decided he must try to sleep. Although his body felt dead, he managed to will himself to sleep almost immediately, with the image of Meritaten hovering over the splitting planes of his once adamantine consciousness. But once again he suffered another vivid infusion of images from the past to the present, which he might still describe objectively, as dream ...

He's on the night train, worried because there's no-one else on the train with him. He goes to a window and is amazed to see the moon is quite green, and the train has come out of a narrow stone tunnel and is crossing over the sea. He wonders how it knows where to go, presuming it must be following tracks under the water, old roads of remote antiquity, ruined, but still partially intact on the floor of the sea. He feels a sense of relief being able to imagine the structure, the pattern of the ruined city beneath the sea.

The train is passing a narrow peninsula of land, and on sudden impulse he pulls the communication cord and the train grinds to a halt. He grabs his brief-case and jumps down, not wanting to be caught for pulling the cord. But he finds himself in a very old station, the walls of which are made of columns which seem to be real trees. Surely he's reading it wrongly; it's a forest? Yes, he knows now! He's in a clearing surrounded by tall, closely planted trees. Suddenly he notices a solitary tree in the centre of the clearing stripped of most of its branches. The whole of the top of the tree has been sliced off, perhaps struck by lightning, and he senses it is used for some bizarre purpose. He starts to feel uneasy, hearing a sound like an amplified heartbeat, slow and rhythmic, and voices singing some kind of native chant. The moon suddenly rises above the top of the trees and illuminates the clearing. Something is about to begin ... where is she?

The leaves on the trees have signs on them, hieroglyphic fragments of a sacred language or maybe some kind of computer code. He looks more carefully at them and sees they are changing constantly. On each leaf is an eye. He looks at other trees, and every single leaf has an eye on it ... watching him, knowing him, seeking him out ... like thousands of peacock feathers. He starts to panic. He's being watched, not so much by people as by nature herself, as if he, the scientist, has ceased to be the observer; he is now under observation. The sensation of knowing that every object in the world around him is aware of his presence fills him with a terrible anguish, a feeling of dread and guilt, because he knows it's something he's never noticed before, never acknowledged, that the world of objects might be aware of us, in their way, as we are of them, in our way ... and might be as lonely ... wanting to be loved.

But he senses danger. If he can remain as motionless as the tree, the lightning-struck tree, his presence might not be detected. He tries to think that he is the tree, but suddenly he knows it's too late to try such a ploy, the voices are getting louder. He hears the leaves rustling as if from a huge wind. Suddenly he's gripped roughly from behind and before he can see who has pinioned him, someone wraps a blindfold round his eyes, tightly, and he feels nauseated, because he knows the blindfold is an old bandage covered with blood, and he's disgusted because it isn't his own blood.

The chanting and drumbeats have become deafening. He is to be the victim of a sacrificial rite. He struggles to escape but the harder he struggles, the more the arms pull tighter until he knows he must stop or he'll not be able to breathe. He senses that his fate will be the revenge of the eyes on the leaves; so he decides to go limp, to make them think he is already dead. But then he hears a girl's voice, very sweet and reassuring; 'Don't worry, Matthew, in the beginning was the image ... try to imagine a bird, not a word!' It is a trick, aimed at distracting him from the truth!

He knows he must escape, physically, in his body. But then he realises it might have been Meritaten speaking; he hadn't immediately recognised her voice ...

He is even more afraid now, and struggles harder against the invisible arms holding him. He must find Meritaten and ask her if she had given him a secret message. She must tell him the code. He calls her name. Suddenly a rope around his stomach, holding him, snaps, and unexpectedly, he is free.

He runs as fast as he can, stumbles into some bushes where he tries to hide, only to discover next to him a body on the ground, covered with a white sheet. On it are strange signs, similar to the ones on the leaves. He can tell from its shape the body has no head. He too is petrified with fear, knowing the head has become stone, and the same process will soon happen to him ...

There's a faint green light in the distance. He senses he can escape through the trees if he goes towards it, so he pushes through them until he hears the sound of a distant train. Is it his? He reaches the edge of another clearing, but to his dismay, sees it is the same clearing as before, and he can hear the voices nearby. He's come full circle. Spreading the leaves in front of him he sees a grey stone sarcophagus in the centre of the clearing and on it, the body he saw previously, but the sheet has been pulled back, revealing a body cocooned with white bandages. Two women stand next to the sarcophagus, one at each end, dressed elegantly, their faces heavily painted and radiantly beautiful. They are caressing the body, massaging it, preparing it for embalming. They seem happy, moving sensually, as if it is the start of a long slow dance, and he wants to be the body under the sheet, to feel their hands caressing his own tense, terrified body. The erotic purpose in their gentle movements is tangible and painful; must he be prepared to die before he can enjoy those pleasures, submit and become a victim of their power before he can enjoy the full extent of the initiation? He tries to move forward but can't.

He is still a prisoner, he must not forget, and the fear takes hold again. Perhaps he can think his way out of the predicament by solving a riddle. There's only one girl; he's seeing two girls by mistake. He must focus his mind to resolve the problem. The girl on the left is the real and only girl. He can touch her with his right hand. But as he splits, she is separating into two quite distinct parts, slipping out of his control. It's vitally important to bring the two "apparent" images of the girls into one, but however hard he tries to force his mind to effect the resolution, the girls remain as two girls. This is a serious failure in the test. Once he could do it. The hands still grip him ...

One of the girls now starts to dance wildly and seems to be shedding very thin white veils that float in the air before they fall to the ground and the more she dances, the more she seems to be changing colour ... all the colours of the rainbow ... until she is mostly red. The white veils are covering a scarlet dress that seems to be painted directly onto her naked body, it is so thin, so transparent, and he can see she is caressing herself, her sex, with her middle finger, on which the nail is painted deep crimson. On it is a small sign he cannot make out, something resembling an eye. Swaying, dancing, writhing with pleasure as she touches herself, she violently pulls off the white sheet still partially covering the body, flings it into the air with an ecstatic flourish; but the gesture causes the leaves to panic. There is the terrible hard-edged sound of the north wind, and the branches are buffeted so hard a branch breaks off and falls on the ground near Matthew; it's not made of wood but crystals; the eyes on the leaves are slowly closing. The trees are struggling harder and harder to tear themselves out by their roots, from apparent rage; he is terrified. Is it his fault?

The other girl, still partially veiled in white, seems to be swept suddenly into the air by the wind and her white veils become wings. In slow motion she alights on top of the body on the stone, and seems to be making love to it, while the other is trying to shade the pair from the terrible wind. Suddenly a tree nearby splits as if struck by lightning and a piercing moonbeam of intense green light penetrates the clearing, illuminating it so brightly he's almost blinded. The second girl has loosened her hair and it cascades about her like a silver cloak. She too is dancing wildly now, protecting the lovers by drawing the light towards her by the blatant eroticism of her dancing ...

Matthew seems free to move now and is alone ... but he has become so sexually aroused, he needs desperately to see what is happening between the woman and the body, as if by seeing he can *choose* to become part of it; or distance himself from it. The two bodies are like two snakes, the one in bandages sloughing off its skin in an erotic metamorphosis. He can see wings emerging, as if to hide where the bodies are touching ... and despite knowing he ought to remain hidden, he stands up and shouts out, from excitement, a meaningless jumble of part-words that make no sense at all. But it is a terrible mistake to expose his presence, witnessing the secret scene. He is not an initiate, but a thief of their coveted, secret knowledge.

Someone clasps him from behind again and this time he's blindfolded and dragged roughly into the clearing. He feels himself being tied to a tree, and he's sure it's the tree that stands alone near the cusp of the concave shape of the clearing. He clings to the image of the geometry in his mind, imagining that if he can see the exact shape of the clearing, as if seen from above, he can escape his fate. But the precise image eludes him. His mind is not functioning correctly, as if a switch, on a branch line, has not been activated. The mistake is not trying to see the one scene from two points of view, but if he could stay with the view from one side he would be safe. With both points of view he must rise above them to avoid being split by them ... and it is beyond him.

So there's no escape. He tries to relax his body, bending his head low, going down on his knees, bringing them close to his chest, waiting for the blow that will kill him. Can't she save him? Where is she, the young girl he could have loved? He hears the sound of wood and stone splintering as if a steel drill had broken into the small railway carriage he is trapped in again ... the door with the two copper handles splintering ... imagining he is escaping ...

... and he woke up, shouting out her name, *"Mer...it...aten!"*

His whole body was shaking violently. Strangely, his first reaction was to try to record the dream, feeling sure it was important, concealing a meaning he must understand, that given time he would be able to control it. He fumbled on his desk for a pen and managed to find some sheets of blank paper. The dream seemed to be still in his mind as he started to write, *I was in a train going towards the north star, small like a robot* ... when suddenly, in a flash, the whole dream vanished from his mind. He was furious, frustrated, feeling cheated because he was prepared to confront the dream and listen to it, to take it seriously. But there was nothing he could do about it, the dream had gone. It was exactly as if he was trying to *save it* on a computer disc and he'd pressed the wrong key, and in a fraction of a second, erased it. Forever. He felt profoundly sad. The loss of the dream depressed him deeply, as if love had slipped away again, eluding him, beyond his power to arrest the image ...

He decided his only choice now was to continue with his project of packing; he simply *must* get away; just a few clothes, a couple of books, some strong walking shoes. The sooner he left the better. Going to Scotland, he told himself, was the best idea he'd had for a long time. Where else? He needed a friend! He cursed David for allowing his crack-ups and "retreat" to India to break off their friendship. He would willingly have listened to any of David's mad ideas about sex or chromosomes or morphic resonance and might even have been tempted to go on a jaunt with him again, in the hope that the Swedish au-pair David would pick up might have a friend in tow, usually rather plain, but who would nevertheless be seduced by Tchaikovsky and cheap white wine and a good imitation of enthusiasm, his vanity requiring no response and welcoming indifference. He must sleep! Tomorrow he would be himself again ...

... but images wouldn't go away. Meritaten, waiting in the cold museum. It took time for his eyes to grow accustomed to the light. It was dank and dark like a waiting room in an old Victorian station. A train was standing there, empty. Was it a girl on the other platform, in the shadow, in front of the old windows with faded gold lettering, wearing a long black coat, her dark hair held up with a comb, glinting in the green moonlight, her face, curiously white, as if made of alabaster? If he crossed the bridge to the other side, would she be there when he got there? He must stay where he is. Making the crossing was too dangerous. He knew she was not alive.

All along the platform were painted metal columns. As he walked along, the figure on the other platform seemed to follow him. Who was she? Was it merely a reflection in the windows? Why was he so sure she was threatening him? He pushed open the heavy wooden door, with its two copper handles, and slipped into the waiting room and was amazed to find it full of glass cases and bookcases full of old books, and in the centre of the room, a stone sarcophagus. It was the museum after all and he was standing in front of Meritaten ... his hand on the cold stone, his fingers touching the sharp edges of the etched images ...

He tried to imagine her, three thousand years ago, inhabiting a body; the sculptor caressing the stone, ordered by her father the Pharaoh Akhenaten to make a portrait, a beautiful object that would exist on the physical plane forever; in her glory. Now it was on show in a glass box in a barely visited museum. He felt more and more deeply sad and threatened, thinking about her. He wondered if the portrait had been merely of the head and if not, where was the rest of her body? How many other fragments were there, in other cold, grey, desolate museums around the world? An arm? A foot? A thigh? Waiting to be united, if only in the mind of a lover?

∇

THREE

"The morphic influence of a past system might become present to a subsequent similar system by passing 'beyond' space-time and then 're-entering' wherever and whenever a similar pattern of vibration appeared. Or it might be connected through other 'dimensions' ... Or the morphic influence of past systems might simply be present everywhere..."

"A New Science of Life"
Rupert Sheldrake,

▽▽

Matthew woke up the following morning after a restless night, thinking of Henri Poincaré, the great mathematician. Poincaré was close to discovering his famous *theorem*, his life's major work, but felt blocked and couldn't make the final leap; like a devious snake in a basket, the theo-rem was dream-sleeping, refusing to be charmed out by the harsh, serial music of reason. Disappointed and frustrated, he removed himself to Provençe for a holiday with his much neglected family, luxuriating in good food and too much wine, swam in the sea and deliberately wiped his mind clear of everything to do with work. The instant he was stepping onto the train to return to Paris, his foot poised in the air, the theorem flashed into his conscious mind, searing through all his doubts and confusion, complete, finished, whole. All the fragments had fused together without any conscious effort, the radical last phase of the work being brought to a head without his help. His unconscious mind no longer needed the continuous stress and probing. It knew what was going on; what it was working on ...

Taking the hint, Matthew decided his plan to leave for Scotland was ever more urgent! He would travel that same evening, though he was somewhat apprehensive about taking the night-train ...

Deciding he must visit Meritaten to say goodbye, he was pleased to discover the Egyptian rooms were empty. He could feel his heart thumping as he approached her, and for a moment he thought he noticed a faint smile appear on her face. Drawing up the warden's chair he perched on its edge, unselfconscious, enjoying her mysterious beauty, seeing her in the two ways again: the sculpted stone – and the real person, not tangibly in front of him to be touched, but there nevertheless. This double vision troubled him, demanding to be resolved; but he guessed it was rather obvious really.

Next to her was some jewellery made of cheap blue and green stone, and he was especially fascinated by a *Ba-bird*, a falcon's body with the head of a beautiful girl, symbolising what we call the soul; he was also intrigued by a vignette illustrating the mysterious copulation of Isis in the form of a hovering falcon with Osiris, a mummified corpse, reassembled after being cut up into fourteen pieces. Horus was symbolised by the *Udjat* eye, the Magic Eye; the sexual act of Isis, a fusion of opposites, was obviously magical, leading to the birth of Horus, a way of seeing.

It was the unified beauty of the images he found irresistible. Every object, falcon, beetle, lotus plant, eagle, lizard, were linked by the same sensuous style, the same celebration of their natural beauty. It was this wholeness, the unity of style and vision, the sense of connectedness of all things, animate and inanimate, all creatures, plants and abstract ideas, he found profoundly disquieting. Was it because it was so parallel, so similar to the faith of the scientist who believed everything could be explained eventually by one basic equation ... although the scientist aimed at this with analysis and the Egyptian mystics arrived at this sense of unity from a synthesis of direct vision?

But their singularity of vision had remained unchanged for over four thousand years. Even profound scientific theories, like Poincaré's theorem, flourished and waned in a few years, a powerful paradigm for some time but falling out of favour eventually. The hieroglyph for the falcon, symbolising God, carved in a piece of limestone from 4,000 years BC was identical to a carving of 200 AD. For any set of ideas to stay so unchanged for over four thousand years was extraordinary. From where did they derive such absolute certainty? Why did the system work so well?

Matthew read on - Akhenaten's reign was the exception – he was the "Heretical Pharaoh" because he *did* try to change the classical ideas, and for a mere ten years or so, he created a whole new monotheistic religion, building a totally new circular city at Tel El Amarna in the middle of the empty desert, mirror image of the Aten, the sun's eye; the sacred city at the centre of the universe, where he could live peacefully with his beautiful wife Nefertiti. There, under his guidance, the old classical forms of art softened, and the sensuous naturalism associated with the art of Amarna came into being. But his rebellion soon failed, his "theorem" of One God overthrown by the traditional polytheists; he was viciously deposed by the priests of Thebes who resented his revolutionary ideas. His brief new religion was persecuted, his temples destroyed. All that remained of his heretical idea of the One God, the *Aten*, the sun's disc, were the sculptures and friezes found in a few tombs.

Meritaten's name, it seemed, meant "Beloved of the Aten".

Suddenly he heard footsteps. He leapt up, almost panicking, grabbing the wooden chair, quickly looking to see if he could crawl away unnoticed, escape being seen behaving so oddly. But then he felt impatient with himself. Why was he so silly? Surely, he could be an archaeologist, as rational as the best of them? Nevertheless, betraying himself, he rushed out of the room, almost knocking over a small boy trailing behind the adults. He rushed up the stairs ... this stupidity had to stop!

At his laboratory, he glanced at his mail. Nothing interesting. A paper on the magnetic orientation of feldspar in Cumbrian granite. He filled the kettle to make tea. Glaring at his computer, he sat down brusquely in front of it, and made a firm mental decision to switch it on. Nothing! Again his arms wouldn't move, remaining firmly pinioned to his sides. He tried for several minutes, to no avail. He was so angry he dragged himself away from the screen, switched off the kettle, stormed out of the laboratory slamming the door and headed back to his rooms. Feeling oppressed and persecuted, he quickly finished packing; called the station, deciding to take the afternoon train to London and the night-sleeper to Inverness.

But then he hesitated. If he was to take his camera, it

needed a new battery; also it would be appropriate to take a couple of photographs of Meritaten before leaving, which could be developed in Scotland. He wanted to study her face, determined to demystify her, discover who it was she *reminded* him of, even if it turned out to be some dumb actress in a film! He'd leave for Scotland tomorrow, after fixing his camera. He set off on his bicycle, but as he was passing the Fitzwilliam he was amazed again to feel himself pulled physically towards it. He had to fight the desire; there seemed to be some kind of magnetic force pulling his bicycle from under him. 'This is getting crazy!' he muttered to himself; determined like Ulysses to resist the songs of the Sirens, he cycled on.

In town he bought film and batteries and decided to choose some new music for his trip, but was surprised to find again, it was *only* Mozart he wanted to listen to. But then, an even more curious idea took hold. He *only* wanted to listen to something in C minor. The certainty was almost physical. There was only one Mozart work in C Minor, an Unfinished Mass, but he also noticed a String Quartet, K465, and its name seemed familiar, or at least, relevant. "The Dissonance". He bought both.

That evening, hoping to relax, he found the two pieces were so painfully beautiful he felt close to weeping. The suspended ending of the Unfinished C Minor Mass, the cusp at which the work was never completed, occurred in the middle of the *Incarnatus* of the *Credo*, the music hovering agonizingly in the air, two voices that were one, yet not one, two voices striving to unite, a flute and a voice entwined together like two snakes coupling around the tree of Paradise, the music mysteriously and tragically incomplete ... the two voices now become life and death ... the ending still trapped in the mind of Mozart, wherever that might be.

But during the night, another long, tormented dream.

He's in a large, ornately decorated room, where a bent old man is sitting on a cheap wooden chair, its legs carved as lion paws, its arms as eagle heads. Onto a stage in front of him, three lithe young girls emerge from the shadows and dance, each one dressed in the flimsiest costume of gossamer green veils, the texture of insect wings. The old man claps his hands and one of them disappears, claps again and the second disappears. It's not that she moves off the stage, she's just erased as if from a screen. The remaining girl seems inspired by being alone, and dances even more blatantly sexually to the old man, her body tantalisingly just beyond his outstretched fingers. Matthew's presence seems not to have been detected. Could it be the old man is blind? His face seems mysteriously green, like moss covered bark, or is it merely the light? If blind, how is he enjoying the dance?

The girl is removing the green veils, slowly and provocatively, her skin a pale olive colour and glistening with oil, with jewelled snakes twisted around her arms. Her hair is dark and long, red with henna, the colour of autumn copper-beech leaves; her beauty, the tantalising enigma of the half-caste, two races in one, the product of passion rather than social convenience, voluptuous and available, aloof and untouchable, her racial impurity suggesting the perfect courtesan. Her dancing becomes more and more overtly erotic, and she is caressing herself, her breasts, her thighs, her fingers pushing through layers of silk, like wet leaves, still clinging between her thighs. She's wearing something so thin under the veils that are her skirts, that it looks like transparent skin, and she's shaved or is very young. Spreading her legs she sits on the man's knees, pressing against his hands, rubbing backwards and forwards to arouse herself further. Matthew closes his eyes, but realises immediately he has made a mistake; what if he can't open them again?

In his mind, the luxurious image, in close up, of her sex, dark and wet, rubbing against the bent old fingers. There's a damp stain appearing near her bottom, through the green silk ... she is so aroused.

He's scared, knowing he is now defenceless. Someone with a sword is standing behind him, arms raised; with one blow, he can sever his head. But he feels a gentle tugging at his arm, pulling him out of the room. It's the old man's daughter, who whispers to him; 'Don't worry, the old man is as good as dead! His bark is much worse than his bite!'

Recalling these fragments of the dream, still half-asleep, Matthew felt a painful anguish and frustration. Dream language was like the hieroglyphs – alien and foreign – and these weren't his dreams at all! It was 4 a.m. Fearful and despairing, he managed to fall back into sleep, happy to escape from thinking. What a blessing the earth revolved on its axis, creating the hours of night ... for which we had evolved the mystery of sleep.

The following morning he went to say goodbye to Meritaten and was pleased to find the Egyptian rooms empty again. He paused in front of the huge foot, the fragment of the Colossus of Akhenaten, thinking of all the other pieces of his dismembered body scattered around the museums of the modern world. It was a sad fate for such a man of vision, such a revolutionary thinker, a mystic in love with his symbol of such perfect unity, the Aten. Sad to be so dismembered and scattered, and to have become little more than a tourist attraction.

He approached the glass case where he imagined Meritaten waited patiently to be seen, only to discover he couldn't see her properly; the light from the windows was reflecting directly onto the front glass, making it into a mirror, and although he tried different angles, it was impossible to find a position to see her clearly, his own face appearing on the glass between them, framed in an image of windows, leaves where his hair should be...

Slightly upset, he closed his eyes and tried to imagine her alive in the ancient city of Tel El Amarna, a lithe young girl in flowing silk robes, wafting around the Pharaoh's palace, giggling with her sisters, sitting poised and meditative in the sculptor's studio as he chipped away at the block of stone, creating the beautiful object which, four thousand years later, would stir the timid heart of a rather cold and rational man who had once loved a woman and now loved only crystals ...

For a long time he stood quite still before her, her face obscured by the reflection of his own, wondering what her voice had sounded like, trying to see her swimming in the Nile while soldiers guarded her with sticks and stones to frighten away the crocodiles. The more he thought of it all, the more surprised he became to find that he could picture it so clearly.

He could have painted the whole scene in detail, if he had been a painter. But he wished he had been a sculptor, able to create the rest of her ... her unknown fragmented body, elsewhere ... and make her whole again. Yet, trying hard, in his mind he could see her whole, imagining the rest from the small part he could see; rather like listening to an unknown voice on the telephone, unable to avoid imagining what was out of sight. He felt lonely, wondering how he could communicate with her, absurd though it might seem. If it would not be with the stone, what part of her would it be with? Then he pulled himself together. Such a thought should not occur spontaneously to a lucid, objective mind such as his!

He tried to take a photograph but it was impossible, the sun's reflected light too bright. He guessed it would be some time before the glass would become translucent again, to reveal her delicate smile intact, her composure undisturbed by his confused emotional needs, so he decided to leave, try again with the computer, and return in the afternoon to take his photograph, steal her image from within the multiple reflections ... capture her soul on film, to accompany him on his forthcoming exile ...

He had no luck with his computer, the invisible wall was still firmly dug in around it. Maybe he should become philosophical about it! Was it any less absurd than his need to take a photograph of Meritaten? It was a bright day so he decided to take a walk along the river, amazed how lucid the light had become, how sharply he could see everything. Feeling inclined to do something different, he went to a pub and drank a lager and ate a sandwich and smiled at the students as if he was still one of them. Could he be normal after all?

Afterwards he returned to the museum, taking the precaution of asking at the desk if it was alright to take photographs of the Egyptian collection, not wanting to be ignominuously thrown out for breaking the rules.

'Are you with the lady who is taking photographs there already?' the receptionist asked.

'Goodness me, no, I'm just a visitor. I'm quite alone. Someone is taking photographs already?'

'Yes, a young lady with written permission to use a tripod and lights. You can take photographs without a tripod at any time.'

Matthew walked mournfully down the winding stone steps, feeling frustrated, even angry, that someone should be invading *his* domain; especially with a camera! He felt acute resentment at the idea of the technology, tripods and lights, disturbing the quiet, sacred mood of Meritaten's room.

At the door, he saw her, standing behind her tripod, with two large spotlights on either side, photographing the fragment of the colossal statue of Akhenaten. He stopped at the threshold of the doorway, taken aback by what he saw, but she had heard him, turned and seemed equally surprised by him, that her presence should have caused him to stop so abruptly. Words were rattling through Matthew's mind at the speed of his computer. He wanted to say something but knew it would come out garbled, he was so confused. His first impression took him by surprise. *She's a Gypsy!*

Dressed in the wildest clothes, her three-quarter length skirt was embroidered in all kinds of shapes and colours, obviously hand-made; there were strange pointed silver boots, an emerald green blouse sticking out from a bright purple cardigan, her hair tied up in a bunch with a multi-coloured scarf flecked with gold and silver signs of the zodiac. Around her shoulders were the remains of a pair of silver foxes that looked as if they'd been killed while mating, amateurishly made into a double-headed stole. Around her neck was a bright blue and green enamel necklace in the shape of a girl with huge wings, which Matthew could see was similar to the jewellery he'd seen on the breast of one of the mummies in the museum. Her hair was jet black, with a hint of red, probably henna, and was obviously quite long despite being bundled up behind her head, and very untidy. She was wearing crimson lipstick and her eyes were heavily outlined with kohl; her blue eye shadow flecked with gold.

Matthew guessed she was in her late twenties. His first reaction was not to think she was particularly pretty: her face seemed strong, like a classical sculpture, almost masculine, and her fine, straight nose seemed just a little too bold for the voluptuous high-curved shape of her cheekbones. But she *was* striking and amazing-looking, and he couldn't stop gazing at her face. He'd not seen anyone quite like her before in his life.

She looked away from him, back to her camera on its tripod, then at the sculpture she was about to photograph, clearly confused by Matthew's cold, monolithic stance and stare. She seemed to make a quick decision not to carry on with her photography and stepped over the bundle of cables and switched off the lights. 'I need to pause. Please come in. I hope I'm not disturbing you with all my lights and other brutal things!'

Matthew was surprised by the sharp clarity and beauty of her voice. There was a faint hint of a lisp which he found immediately charming. He had expected from her appearance some scruffy, guttural kind of speech, that of a vagrant Gypsy all prepared with Tarot pack to waylay any lost, naive, innocent wanderer such as himself. Her voice suggested a background of refinement, even aristocracy, although in contrast, her movements had a sensuality, an animal quality he found instantly provocative. He blurted out, awkwardly, 'No, please ... carry on ... I've just come to take a photograph. Just one. Only one. I'll be off in a second!'

'Please don't let me stop you! You can use my lights if you like, it's a bit dark in the corners. What is it you want to photograph?'

Now he felt totally embarrassed. Why couldn't he say he had come to photograph a sarcophagus or the Ba-bird or the Rosetta Stone? But instead, the truth forced itself out. 'Well ... uhmm ... actually ... uhmm...' He was blushing and looking down at his feet, which seemed about to break into a fiendish jocular two-step, all the rave on the Titanic, or a syncopated tap dance from *On the Town*, on the marble floor. He was feeling so small, his feet suddenly seemed as large as Akhenaten's; and he felt just as cut adrift from home. 'Well ... uhmm ... I've just come to take a picture of the head of Princess Meritaten ... actually!'

'Oh. Really? I've just taken a couple of photographs of her myself. You mean the small sandstone head?'

'Well, it's quartz schist, actually,' Matthew said nervously, not really wanting to correct her.

'Quartz schist? What a name! Really? Good heavens, are you an archaeologist?'

'Er ... not at all. I'm ...' He was gazing at her so intently she felt awkward suddenly, and a little apprehensive.

'You're not an archaeologist?'

'Oh ... No! Sorry. My mind was wandering ... actually, I'm a physicist, and ... or rather a crystallographer.'

'Really? Both at once? What are you doing in here, then, amongst these relics of a Golden Age?'

'Intending to take a photograph of Meritaten!'

'Why *her* in particular?' she asked looking utterly confused.

Matthew knew he'd trapped himself, said too much and there was no escape. He couldn't think of an explanation and no casual phrase came quickly ... 'er ... ' Maybe he could say the photograph was for a friend? But he really wanted to tell her the truth, immediately, feeling she might understand. Did he dare?

'I saw the sculpture recently and found it fascinating; it *is* so beautiful. I'm on my way to Scotland for a holiday, tonight, on the night train, and thought I'd take a picture of her with me,' he mumbled, looking at the windows as he spoke.

'It's a beautiful sculpture, isn't it? Exquisite. One of the very best portraits in the unique Amarna style, and there are quite a few of the Amarna princesses.'

Matthew was immediately excited at the idea of other portraits. 'Are there ... really ... more portraits?'

'A couple in Oxford, London, the Louvre, Berlin. You haven't seen them?' She seemed surprised.

'Good heavens no! I live and work here in Cambridge and rarely venture away, never have time to gad about, alas. But you? Are you doing a book on Amarna? You seem very learned on the subject.'

She laughed extravagantly. 'A book? Kind of! I'm a sculptress and I've been in love with Egyptian sculpture for as long as I can remember. I take photographs for reference. I don't copy, but I try to absorb their ideas unconsciously, hoping it will come out in my own work, although my own sculptures couldn't be more different! I'm in love with Egyptian sculpture, that's all.'

'In what way in love with them?'

'Every way!'

'How do you mean?'

'Gosh it's a long story. I don't want to waste your time,' she said, meaning she didn't want to waste her own time.

Matthew looked at his watch, confused and yet excited. 'Of course ... you're working. I'm sorry. Please carry on. I'll take my photograph of Meritaten and leave you in peace.' He was feeling awful, wanting desperately to hear her "long story" ...

The young woman went to turn her lights on again, but as she pressed the switch there was a loud bang and both lights exploded. She stamped her foot in rage. 'Shit! Oh ... sorry!'

'Oh dear, I'm sorry too!' said Matthew, as if it was his fault. 'Have you got spare bulbs?'

'No! Damn it. That's unbelievable! They're quartz iodine bulbs and cost a fortune. I've never had them explode before. Isn't the fuse in the plug supposed to go first? What a bore!' They stood looking at each other, not sure of what to say. 'It must be a sign of something,' she said, pensively. 'Maybe Akhenaten is angry with me for exposing him to all this horrible artificial light when he loved his beloved Aten so much; that's what it must be. He's letting me know he is hurt, being treated so badly. But what do I do now?' She turned to Matthew as if he must know the answer, being a physicist. A man of science.

'It does seem to be a sign. Very weird. Maybe I can help. If we hurry to my laboratory stores, they have quartz iodine bulbs. If not, I can get some in the morning from the physics department.'

She smiled gratefully, and Matthew offered to help her dismantle the lights. When they were finished, he carried them to the top of the stairs. There, she thanked him, but then apologised, saying she was tired and upset and wanted to go home, instead of going to the laboratory.

'How far are you going?' asked Matthew.

'Quite a way.'

'How will you do it, with all this equipment?'

'I strap it on my donkey!'

'A donkey? I didn't see it!' he said, mystified.

They walked down the steps and he saw the donkey. Her bicycle. Matthew felt a terrible longing not to let her go.

'Which way do you go home?'

'Not home. I'm just a visitor, staying with friends, along Grange Road.'

'Oh good. I'll come with you. I go that way too. Where are you staying?'

'Just beyond the end of Grange Road.'

'But that's miles away.'

'Yes, but I like walking!'

'Okay, I'll help you, we go near my place.' It wasn't true but Matthew was not at that moment concerned with the niceties of empirically verifiable data.

They walked along the pavement in silence before Matthew dared another question. 'Tell me about your sculpture?'

She thought for some time before replying. 'Shall I tell you in a long, roundabout way, or in one word ... which most people find totally off-putting?'

'Try me with the one word.'

'OK. It shouldn't be hard for you at all, a crystallographer! In one word. Translucency.'

Matthew stopped dead in his tracks and the donkey lurched to a halt too. He looked at her in amazement. 'What on earth do you mean, translucency?'

'I told you you'd be put-off! But that's the subject of my work: at least, that's what they put in the catalogue at my last show. I work with light mostly and materials that reflect it and refract it and so on, plastics and glass. You know, what you can see one moment and can't see the next. Very cerebral actually. I'm not interested in the material that most sculptors use ... clay, stone, wood ... because I'm not interested in appearances. I'm trying to capture what people call, wrongly most of the time ... spirit! What lies behind appearances. A paradox, of course! But I believe spirit actually exists and one day we'll be able to see it. At the moment I'm doing a series about ancient Egypt, a commission from the boyfriend of a girlfriend of mine; he's very rich!'

Matthew was utterly confused. 'I'm working with diamonds at the moment, and lasers projected through the crystals. In a way, translucency is my subject as well!'

'Lasers? No! That's one thing I want to learn about. It's only with lasers you can see holographic images; only with pure laser light. My next work will be holography. Holograms!'

'How do you mean? Holograms?' he asked, really puzzled.

She answered obliquely. 'I work with crystals too. I love them. Quartz and amethyst mostly. I suspend them inside my sculptures. I wish I could afford huge crystals and carve them. I have to work with perspex and acrylic and plastics, modest cousins of crystals. I want to make imaginary three-dimensional sculptures, like holograms ... or with holograms that can only be seen on a huge screen, projected from a computer ... things like that, everything virtual and like my dreams, all ethereal. Planes interlocking with planes and waves and fields of light and colour, all interpenetrating. But I'm only a mere girl; I run away from the technology. It frightens me. Even the scientists don't control it these days, so why should I?'

'You can cut crystals very thin like sheets of glass.'

'Can you? But not easily?'

'I can help you; with lasers too!'

'No! Really? That's very kind of you. The trouble is I'm leaving Cambridge in a few days,' she said demurely.

'Oh...' said Matthew weakly, revealing his disappointment.

'I have to go back home to Cornwall. I love it there. The light is unique. My friends have a large house with an old garage in the garden as my studio; a girlfriend of mine and her boyfriend. They look after me and I give them some of my work. He's the one who asked me to take the photographs, he's a kind of scientist too; studied physics at Oxford but gave it up, now he's a dreamer, a beachcomber, spends all his time looking for the "perfect stone". Isn't it amazing how people can change so completely, like St. Paul on the road to Damascus? My girlfriend writes erotic novels; if you're ever in Cornwall, even without your laser beams, give me a call!'

Matthew walked at her side in silence. She could see he

was thinking hard. She was accustomed to making a dramatic impact on men and she was bemused by his confusion. Maybe she should encourage him, with his knowledge of lasers and crystals!

'What's your name?' she asked rather formally.

'Matthew ... Matthew Sutherland. And you?'

'Georgina Ffielding, with two *F*s I'm sorry to say. Not my fault! But everyone calls me George. My parents always add the *I-N-A* at the end, as if it symbolised some kind of female gene I wasn't given otherwise!' She laughed. 'But I quite like George, it's suitably ambiguous, keeps people at a distance, which can't be bad these days, can it?'

'No ... I suppose not. I prefer Georgina though.'

'You can start with Georgina if you like, but I bet you one of your laser beams, you'll call me George before long!'

He looked at her luscious crimson lips, her dark, sensual eyes and tried hard to think of her as George. Impossible.

'You could call me Ffielding, like a business colleague. Don't they call you Sutherland at work?'

'Doctor Sutherland mostly; my Professor uses Sutherland.'

'Call me Ffielding. No-one has *ever* called me Ffielding. Even more ambiguous. I like it even more.'

He wondered why she liked ambiguity so much. 'What's your work really about?' she asked Matthew.

'I wish I could be sure. I've spent a year or so working with three rather special diamonds, trying to discover why carbon atoms can be inanimate or animate, like coal or diamonds as well as the most common atoms in living matter. But recent results seem to be wrong. I may have to abandon the present approach completely until I think of a new one. I'm on the wrong track at the moment. Rather disappointing and boring!'

'It sounds very mysterious. But listen, I've just remembered, my friends have more quartz iodine bulbs at home, so I *will* be able to take my photographs tomorrow. It's kind of you to help, but I think I can cope.' She suddenly stopped.

Matthew realised she was putting him off, and he started to panic, hating the thought of letting her slip out of his grasp. 'Wouldn't you like to come to my laboratory anyway to see the lasers? They are quite dramatic. Might give you some ideas for your sculpture ... '

'Well. Thanks very much, perhaps I ought to. Holograms are my real interest but lasers *are* essential to them.'

They walked on again, in silence, pushing the loaded bicycle in turns.

'Why are you going to Scotland?'

'To get a break from my work. I can't solve certain problems, so I thought the mountain air might clear my mind.'

'Sounds a good idea. When are you leaving?'

'I was going today, but then I wanted to photograph Meritaten. But I didn't, did I?'

'I can send you a copy of one of *my* photographs! But if you are just walking around the mountains, why do you need a photograph of Meritaten?'

Matthew couldn't think how to tell the truth, without appearing silly. He thought for a while before replying. 'You see, I've always been obsessed with my work, probably like you with yours. I used to think, feel, dream about nothing else but crystals. By accident, I wandered into the Museum, for no reason at all, except to escape myself, I suppose, and I became fascinated by the Egyptian antiquities. Totally unexpected. If you knew me you'd not believe it. But most of all I was drawn to that little stone head of Meritaten. So strange and lonely and beautiful. I felt I had to take a picture to remind me to think of something else other than crystals! Does that make sense?'

'Of course! Why not? Quite natural. Why feel so surprised? I'm glad you find Egyptian art so mysterious. I've been studying it for years, trying to understand their science of mysticism. They were much more advanced than we are now. They had direct access to a way of seeing, directly, the structure in everything, the world of matter and consciousness and spirit as a unified whole, a vision which was infinitely more sophisticated and advanced than anything we have now. Take Meritaten. Some part of her *being*, apart from the mere stone, is there in the museum; that's what the Egyptians believed and claimed they could see. And could prove! As Akhenaten is there too, more than mere stone, especially to me. You went back to Meritaten because she called you there. She likes you. She was flattered by your attention. She is only a mere girl, after all. A poor, emotional woman!'

He felt sure she was teasing him. 'Really?'

She laughed. 'Don't stop to think about it. If Meritaten calls, go to her. If you're a man, can you refuse a woman who calls you?'

'Er ... no. But let's be serious. It's not like that at all!'

She continued, undaunted. 'No? Even the Greek philosophers and writers were always initiated into the Egyptian Mysteries, Plato, Pythagoras, all the great thinkers and scientists. St. John of Patmos who wrote the Revelation *must* have been initiated into the Egyptian mystery cult of Isis and Osiris. Those guys were the great thinkers of their time and their highest knowledge all derived from Egyptian science and mysticism. Our present world-picture we inherited from the Greeks, until it got corrupted by Christianity ... a hopeless diversion leading to objective science! Rationality! Ugh! Spirit entering matter, the cross-over as it is called. Out of nowhere, apparently.'

Matthew suggested they stop at a wooden bench under some trees. She agreed a rest would be a good idea. Matthew held his head in his hands, while she said nothing, sitting quietly at his side. They sat there for five minutes, the silence seeming infinite to him ...

She continued, 'That's what my work is about. Energy or spirit coming into matter out of nowhere,' she added, unemotionally.

Matthew was seeing all kinds of connections again. What she had just said, after all, was exactly the problem with his diamonds. His equations had been falsified because extra energy was coming from somewhere, which was theoretically impossible. 'Tell me ... it's vitally important. What did you say about energy coming out of nowhere?'

She laughed. 'Oh well. That's an Egyptian idea, sometimes called Cosmogenesis. They believed that spirit-energy comes continuously into the world from another plane, a plane of Becoming, of Potential ... a plane which we cannot perceive normally. A field on its own frequency; you had to be trained to see it; normally the mind is blind to this continuous birth of consciousness. Matter is the illusion. It blinds us. This birth of consciousness into matter was symbolized by the birth of Horus the falcon, the beautiful golden-eyed falcon of the dawn. Isis and Osiris make love and create him. A beautiful love story, but also a continuous truth. Do you know the story?'

He said he'd seen some images in the museum about it.

'It's the essence of Egyptian thinking. This myth explained everything. All their higher thinking crystallised into that central rite. I'm doing a series of sculptures about it; *The Lamentations of Isis*. She loses her husband and spends all her time looking for him. Do you want to hear the story?'

'Of course; if it's a love story, why not!'

'There's a page in the Fitzwilliam from the*Egyptian Book of the Dead* which illustrates it; Isis takes the form of a falcon and copulates with her dead husband. Her husband had been caught by Set, or Satan, and his body cut up into fourteen pieces which are scattered round the land. Isis weeps for him ... the Lamentations ... and searches everywhere to find the fourteen fragments. His body has grown into a tree, which she finds. Osiris is the spirit of the sacred tree; but she only finds thirteen of the fragments. She must find all the pieces to make him whole, to bring him to life again. But she cannot find the fourteenth fragment; the most important!'

'Which is?' Matthew asked innocently.

'His penis! Or phallus if you prefer! So she makes one by magic, being the goddess of magic. Disguised as the beautiful falcon she copulates with the phallus she has created for herself by magic, copulates with the .dead body of her husband. She conceives and later gives birth to Horus the falcon. She was the first sculptress of course! Must have made a sublime phallus!'

Matthew didn't know what to say. He had accepted everything so far, but now he felt a bit rejected, too far out of his territory; her love story was hardly the basis for a romantic novel!

'You asked about the energy that appears from nowhere. That is how; it is Horus the falcon born from the plane of potential being or consciousness by the magic rites of the goddess ... the copulation of Isis and Osiris ... which is all a bit far from crystallography, I suppose. I'm sorry, I must be boring you?'

'No. Not boring at all! But this kind of thinking is like an unknown language to me, that's all.'

'It was to me once. But it *is* a language. You just have to learn it. Matter is structured by spirit. Matter can be dead or alive. Osiris is the Nile and Isis is the earth. They are joined by desire. That desire is universal consciousness. The Egyptians believed that if enough coincidences, or desires, converge on one point in time ... there is a flash ... a collision ... and energy is created, if that's what you call it. They would say it was life that was created. That is how the living world of being and consciousness evolves; being and consciousness are like two images of the same thing, a hologram. We are alive only because we are haunted, haunted by spirits, call them gods. Do I make sense?'

Matthew's body felt cold, like stone, and yet inside his head, in a small space the size of a diamond, his mind was still functioning. It all made no sense but it touched him. He felt scared again. There was the tingling at the back of his neck. 'Georgina, tell me, have you ever heard of the second law of thermodynamics?'

'Good heavens no!'

'Of entropy?'

'No!'

'Of Einstein?'

'Well yes, like most people. Relativity, and all that. $E = mc^2$. I know that much.'

'Yes. We scientists have to believe that all matter or energy in the Universe, is – and must remain – constant.'

'Do they? Why?'

'Because science depends on it.'

'Why? Then no wonder science is all screwed up! I hate science. I hate scientists. You're the first one I ever said more than one sentence to. But you're different, no *real* scientist would admit being fascinated by a girl who was a sculpture. You haven't admitted it to yourself yet, but you already know that science is all poppycock really. Useful maybe. But it's too obviously a dead end, inert, seeking death. It desires death. Empty. Heartless. Spiritless. At best, just one way of thinking. Anal. Analysis. Taking the whole and breaking it into fragments. All scientists are the god Set! They fragment everything. I worship Isis who makes it whole again. There must be something more than this permanent desire for a kingdom of death we call a rational world picture. We are terribly sick, that's all!'

He was feeling awful. 'But the scientist studies life too ... surely!'

'Sometimes, but to study a flower you dissect it. I'd only study a flower as it grows. You'd shoot a falcon to study its DNA. I love it because it embodies a higher form of consciousness, more developed, more useful. Falcons are hundreds of millions of years old and have been perfect for most of that time. We are a few hundred thousand years old and are completely fucked up ... pardon the word. You see why they call me George!'

'Go on!'

'Well, we break the *three* essential laws of nature. We kill each other, we pollute our territories, and over-populate them. Why? Because we feel we are something *outside* nature, apart from it ... cut off from it. The wasteland. But we *are* nature ... we express nature ... as the Egyptians knew and practised, nature is the expression of a higher consciousness or dimension or field ... don't they call it a field?'

'Yes, yes ... they might do ... go on.'

'Well, we are the product of this force working its way through matter. It's the power of the dead god Osiris, King of the Underworld, the imaginary Daddy, whose spirit-semen swam into my Mother's womb and ultimately created me, body and mind. Whose mind thought of me? Osiris. Whose desire made it happen? The phallus Isis created for herself. That's why I make sculpture, beyond where the words end. I hate words!'

Matthew's eyes were closed ...

She continued; 'Inspiration only comes when reason is asleep. Dennis Gabor, the English physicist who discovered holography, said, "I was sitting on a tennis court. It was my turn next. I was thinking of nothing in particular, certainly not work. Then suddenly in a flash ... the whole idea came into my mind. By the time I stood up to go and play, it was all *there* in my mind. Arrived complete; already worked out!" So where did it all come from, already so complete? The Egyptians would say, *from Osiris!'*

Matthew held his head in his hands. The story was identical to the one about Poincaré. Was this mere coincidence? If so, what did coincidence mean? Who was this girl?

Georgina could see he was shaking, but trying desperately to hide it from her. Feeling a surge of sympathy for him, she put an arm round his shoulders, politely, and sat there quietly until the shaking stopped.

Eventually Matthew straightened himself up. 'Sorry about that. I'm not usually so emotional. You must think I'm crazy!' he said, very embarrassed.

'I'm impressed!' she said kindly. 'I thought getting emotion out of a scientist was like squeezing blood out of a stone! Schist ... what was it?'

He laughed. He stood up and looked into her eyes. 'Who are you?' he asked gently and fondly.

'Me!' she said.

'But where did you come from?'

'Same place as you, out there!' and she waved an arm which seemed to follow the sweep of the Milky Way, had it been night-time, embracing Sirius and Orion on the way.

'When?'

'25th March 1976, if you take my birthday, but some time before that if you take the instant of conception. Just think of it. How many minutes after the ejaculation? How long did it take those little buggers to get up the fallopian tube? Worse than the Northern line?'

'You're an amazing girl.' Matthew said, almost trembling.

'Yes, I know.' She smiled confidently. A modern kind of girl and she knew it.

'What you don't know, Georgina, is that what you talked about is the same problem I'm dealing with in my work, with which I'm having so many problems because the answers seem to be totally irrational; unexplained energy in a closed system.'

'Well, that proves science is no good, as I said!'

'Maybe you're absolutely right ... or crazy ... or both!'

'I'm hungry, I don't know about crazy – yes, as well as crazy!'

'Okay, perfect, let's go out to dinner,' he said before he could stop himself.

'Oh ... I'm sorry but I can't. I have dinner with my hosts. I have to press on now, it's just round the corner, a hundred yards or so. I must leave you now. If you want to see me again I'll be at the museum in the morning. Come around eleven o'clock, I'll have finished by then. We can talk more about lasers; but not if I have to become rational!'

'Okay, I'll see you at eleven. I'm sorry I was emotional. I feel rather stupid. I'm usually not like that, at all!'

'Don't worry, I live like this all the time and it's hard keeping control sometimes. Next time maybe I'll fold up, just like a pack of cards; a Tarot pack of course. I often collapse, just from worrying about the world. Goodnight. See you tomorrow.'

She kissed him on the cheek, very lightly and formally, as if she had known him for years. She walked off with her bicycle, her canvas bag, tripods and lights, her foxes bouncing around as she bobbed along, looking, Matthew thought, like a Gypsy returning from a good day's scavenging, with a donkey-load of scrap iron.

He sat down again on the bench, emotionally exhausted. *Some Gypsy!* he thought to himself after a little more reflection.

He stayed sitting on the bench, thinking. He'd gone to photograph Meritaten ... but also to try to communicate with her. Now it seemed it was Meritaten who had spoken to him, albeit through the mouth of a Gypsy girl who made sculptures about “translucency”, which rendered the real world invisible, the opposite of what he thought Meritaten might be trying to do ... making the invisible world visible through the sculpture she had become ...

His mind couldn't quite focus on the two ideas

simultaneously, the same image but inside out ... except he sensed it was also somehow connected to the method of holography, which he must find more about before he saw Georgina again. All he could remember was a diagram demonstrating the theory. The image looked like the surface of a pool of water in which two stones had been thrown ... two gyres of waves spreading out and interfering ... looking a total chaotic mess, but which could be reconstructed under unified laser light, which re-created a three-dimensional image ... albeit an illusion ... but convincing enough to be believed in. Maybe it was the same with reason after all, an illusion, but useful in the meantime before something better turned up ... that was a funny word. Mean ... time. Was that the only time that reason leaves us with?

That night Matthew slept badly again. He was on a beach looking for a special stone. He found it in the water, where two waves overlapped; beautifully polished grey limestone, the shape of a small loaf of bread. Inside were delicate white veins of quartz, like calligraphy, as if drawn in the stone by an artist. But he knew the veins of quartz penetrated the full width of the stone and crossed internally; where they crossed inside seemed very important, and he had to discover this point of intersection. But the stone would have to be broken to reveal the point of intersection. If the stone was held up to the light, a thin shaft of light, a laser preferably, could penetrate along a vein of the quartz and at the junction of several planes, collide with a special molecule there, an unknown substance; there would be a blinding flash, as bright as a nuclear explosion ...

In another scene he was standing on a small cliff next to a beautifully clear pool of water. He wanted to dive into the pool, very elegantly, to impress a young woman watching him from some place outside of his vision. But he knew that in the pool, unseen, were huge columns of stone, on the top of which were sharp pyramid-shaped capstones. If he dived in and hit one he would be killed instantly. The columns were invisible because of an elegant coincidence. The diffraction rating of the stone was such that the colonnade of columns was rendered translucent under the surface of the water, a direct parallelism or coincidence of the two coefficients. No-one else could see them but he knew they were there because of his expert knowledge of the crystals the stone is made of ... but he knew the woman thought he was afraid to dive into the pool because of the height of the cliff above the surface of the water. He tried to explain the existence of the hidden columns, like a giant's causeway below the surface of the pool, but she laughed and mocked him saying that she would have believed him if he had said that at the bottom of the pool was a powerful whirlpool that sucked people into the bowels of the earth ... because she had felt the force of such a whirlpool inside her body ...

All through the night, he seemed haunted by such a flood of images, which seemed clear in their meaning until he stood back from them and the pale cast of thought clouded the glass, a veil closing over their truth like the eyelid of a chameleon.

The following morning he arrived at the museum at eleven o'clock, running down the steps like a child, only to find that Georgina wasn't there. This possibility had not occurred to him. She seemed so self-assured, he felt certain she would be there. He went to Meritaten and was sure there was a hint of sadness on her face. He waited and waited. Somehow he already knew she wasn't coming. He wandered round the exhibits for some time, not really seeing them, his mind too busy trying to work out possible reasons for Georgina's absence. He felt almost desperate.

On his way out; 'Excuse me, are you Doctor Sutherland?'

'Er ... Yes, I am!'

'Oh good. I have a letter a gentleman left for you!'

He sat down on the cold steps outside, under the colonnade of columns:

Dear Matthew,

My host will bring this letter to the museum. I have to leave immediately. Last night there was very bad news from Cornwall, so it's ME who is now catching the night sleeper. Call me on 022-830-237. Don't be hard on Meritaten. It was not her fault! If you don't call this is just to say I enjoyed our talk and was very moved by your openness, your sensitivity to weird things. It's a grey world unless you paint it a coat of many colours, but I felt you had a good colour about you. Purple actually. A strong colour. A bit negative but with luck you could transform it to mauve, or at least to indigo and that would give you more peace.

Affectionately, George (Ffielding!)

P.S. Don't call for a few days until I've sorted the mess out a bit. Women! I warned her not to fall in love, especially with a man!

Matthew sighed with relief. He'd already decided she would disappear from his life as easily as an image from one of his tortured dreams. He set off for his laboratory, determined to record her number on a computer disc immediately. But at the door of his room, wearing a new jacket for the special occasion of meeting Georgina, he found he'd left his key in the other jacket. Slowly he turned back and walked down the stairs, thinking; *Whoever erected that invisible wall around my computer ought to be working for the Ministry of Defence!*

As he was leaving he met Max Potter, a microbiologist, and they exchanged a few words about the weather, the continuing lack of funds available to the Unit, the chaos caused by Beverly Schwarz, and the rumour that someone in the Unit had been recruited by the CIA with loads of money to work on a secret project, 'Set up by some mole in the Unit, a spy for the CIA or the Ministry of Defence!' Max declared enthusiastically.

'No! Beverly?'

'You'll never guess where I'm going,' Max said.

'You're right. No idea!'

'To an auction; to buy a bed.'

'To an auction to buy a bed? Where?'

'It's in a large house, out of town. The wife saw a picture of a four-poster in the evening paper, and decided it might be just the thing to provoke a sister for poor Heinz. He's four now, you know, so we're going there for a laugh. Never know what you might find. Why don't you come along? You're bound to find something you need. The wife's in the car. Any excuse to escape from this damn place, surely?'

Matthew was going to say 'Sorry, Max, I must work,' when he said, 'Yes, okay!'

By the time they arrived, having driven twice to the wrong village, the auction had already started, in some large tents in the garden. Max and his wife went into the house to find the bed of their dreams and Matthew said he would browse around and meet them later at the tea-tent.

In one of the tents he found a table piled high with bundles of old books, and was quite surprised to find a large bundle marked "Egypt". They were mostly Victorian travel books by people who had sailed the Nile or supped coffee in Bedouin tents, but there was also *The Splendour that was Egypt* by Margaret Murray, *Forgotten Scripts: The Decipherment of the Past* and, most exciting of all, a battered copy of a popular edition of *The Egyptian Book of the Dead* translated by Wallis Budge with a parallel text in English and Hieroglyphics, printed in 1927 by the British Museum.

'A coincidence? No such thing!' he muttered to himself, noting the Lot number: 168. He wandered round a couple more tents, but nothing touched him. There were some faded old carpets that he knew David would have liked, and he might bid for if they were going for a song. Wandering in the garden to get some fresh air he was amazed to notice a cluster of beech trees at the end of the garden, arranged formally, almost identically to those in the laboratory garden. He wondered if they were the ends of the same long avenue, once connected, now severed by the expansion of the University.

He sat down, almost amused, and leant against the roots of one of the trees, happy to be no longer self-conscious of his small eccentricities, thinking of Georgina, trying to picture her in his mind, telling himself she would approve his attraction for an old beech tree, part of a formal arrangement.

After a time he heard the auctioneer shouting out 'Lot 150!' so he made his way back to the tent. He watched, fascinated, as people bid enthusiastically for cartons full of junk and bric-a-brac, and wondered who it was who had died, whose worldly goods were being dispersed so randomly to strangers who would then possess them, or just re-sell them for a profit. Everything that had once had its place in the time and space of one person's life, tainted in some way as so-and-so's possessions, had now been stripped of that quality and would become inert objects again in the marketplace, to be bought and possessed by someone else in a new space and time. Matthew felt sad, not so much for the person who had died, but for all the objects which had lost a master, a centre, a meaning, lost a sense of being part of a community of other objects, all belonging to the same person, loyal slaves who wanted little more than to be treated well and appreciated. Matthew had never been to an auction before and had certainly never imagined he would find it an occasion of such poignancy.

'Now what have we here, ladies and gentlemen; something really special! I hope someone can tell us what they are! This is probably the most valuable lot in the whole auction. Take one out, Cyril, and hold it up so we can see it. There you are ladies and gentlemen, something of rare distinction! Lot 157, called "Genuuuwine Ancient Antiques!" All Greek to me! Pardon? Thank you, sir! Someone tells me they are Egyptian. Well there you are, some antique Egyptian pottery, with faded blue glaze with black writing on them. What am I bid for these priceless relics?'

Matthew was amazed to see the auctioneer's assistant holding a small Egyptian *ushabti* figure, like ones he'd seen in the museum. 'Come on now, ladies and gentlemen, this could be the bargain of the sale. What am I bid for some pottery figures and fragments, thousands of years old from Egypt, somebody tells us. A thousand pounds? ... a hundred pounds? ... fifty pounds?'

Matthew shot up his arm and the auctioneer took his bid.

'Fifty pounds I am bid. Thank you, sir. A discerning gentleman who clearly knows the value of rare antiquities. Who is for sixty pounds ... now come on, please, there must be an archaeologist in the audience somewhere? Fifty-five?

This doesn't happen everyday now does it, ladies and gentlemen, not often we are privileged to auction the contents of an Egyptian tomb! Good heavens, this discovery might be as important as that of King Tut!'

Everyone laughed. Someone shouted 'Rubbish!' Matthew hastily bid again, but the auctioneer shook his head. 'It's your bid already, sir, you don't have to bid again, but there's enthusiasm for you, ladies and gentlemen! Surely this should start an avalanche of bids? What? No more bids? Fifty pounds for ... how many are there, Cyril, hold up a couple more!'

Cyril put his hand into the cardboard box and came up with an ugly dirty fragment of broken plate, which he hastily hid again, then produced what looked like a huge black cigar. Everyone laughed. He held it with the tips of his fingers as if it was carrying the black plague.

'Thank you, Cyril, careful now, you might dig too deep in that box and come up with a whole Mummy! Or at least a new set of teeth!' Cyril smiled. He certainly needed some new teeth. He peered into the box, obviously scared stiff by now, perhaps fearing he might find the body of the very man who died ...

'No-one in 'ere, guvnor! The tomb's been robbed!' Everyone laughed.

'Well ... no more bids. Your bid it is, sir! Thank you. Before you change your mind!' He smashed down his hammer in triumph, exclaiming 'Gotcha!' as if killing a cobra that was climbing up from the murky depths under his desk. People laughed again and Matthew felt even more embarrassed.

'Name, please?'

'Fielding! With one *F*!'

'Yes sir! One *F*! Thank you. And now we have something really practical, something useful again, thank heavens! A desk-top freezer, three-star, barely a year old. Brand new! What am I bid for this most useful item? Keep your meat frozen for three thousand years it will, fresh as a daisy. Thank God the Egyptians didn't have them. Thirty pounds? Twenty? Ten I am bid. Thank you, Madam, a superb deep freeze, best modern technology! What would we do without it!'

Matthew waited and bought the books for ten pounds, paid

for his purchases and went to look for his friends; in vain. Maybe the four-poster had curtains. He sat under his beech tree and opened the cardboard box, marked "Genuine Ancient Antiques". The largest object was a badly chipped blue-glaze *ushabti* figure, marked with heavy, indecipherable hieroglyphics. It looked quite modern. Ten years old if it was a day. There were four or five further broken *ushabti* figures, probably not fake, all without heads, and some useless bits of broken pottery. Very cautiously he pulled out the black cigar-shaped object. It looked horrible. His first instinct was to throw it away. But then he realised it was some kind of mummified bird, and the bandages used to swathe the bird had been stained with the black pitch used for mummification by the Egyptians. He had learnt in the museum that "mummy" came from *momie*, the name for the black pitch used as preservative. Some of the bandages had worn away revealing the small claws of the bird, drawn up under its body as if it was still in the womb of its egg, and the beak had cut through the bandages around the head. The beak was hooked and it slowly dawned on him, with increasing excitement, that it was the curved beak of a falcon, and when he looked at the feet, he could see the talons were sharp and pointed. He couldn't believe he had found such an object in a country auction! But he had also read in the museum that in Victorian times, boat-loads of similar objects had been brought to England; and being so hideous, had been thrown away.

He felt an enormous pleasure holding the bandaged bird in his hand, even though it was really a most nauseating object, pulsing with all kinds of unpleasant associations. He put it carefully back into the box after wrapping it gently in his handkerchief. What a stroke of luck!

He looked for his friends rather superficially, couldn't find them, went to the car and left a note to say he'd gone back to Cambridge, walked to the end of the drive and hitched a lift back to the town.

Back in his rooms he laid the objects on the table, trying to put the bits and pieces together to make the broken figures whole, but it was an impossible task. The mummified falcon he placed carefully in some tissue paper inside a shoe box. The books needed dusting and he made a special space on his bookshelves. The objects were a dishevelled, sorry-looking bunch, but he was excited by them, trying to imagine the tomb they had come from, and who they had been created for to journey with him in the next world. *Was it a man or a woman?* he asked himself, out loud ...

He was eager to tell Georgina of his amazing luck; finding a mummified falcon! He tried to think why the falcon should be so important, why it became the symbol of such an important god. He was impressed at the careful way the bandages had been layered around the body; he wanted so much to call Georgina to tell her he had acquired some sacred objects from Egypt, the real thing, and even a copy of the *Egyptian Book of the Dead.* It was going to be difficult not to call her for a few days. He was missing her even more, now that he had such news for her.

He thought again about going to Scotland, but decided he ought to wait, to be ready to go to Georgina immediately if she needed help. He wasn't sure why she should need it, but for all her air of assurance, he felt she was the kind of person who could provoke disasters. The lights blowing up, the sudden dash to Cornwall. Her letter worried him. He tried to imagine what problems had occurred with her girlfriend. Probably something puerile, a row with her boyfriend, some trivial event, deserving a harsh reproof.

In the evening he read the books, engrossed with the strange text of the *Egyptian Book of the Dead.* He guessed the translation must be at fault. It made such little sense. The book had been originally published in 1890, but surely, no-one, not even pagan savages, could have recited such texts for five thousands years! Even so, they had a strange ambience and beauty about them and again he felt the weird feeling of familiarity. He allowed the surreal images to float over his mind, not really registering, a kind of mad poetry, everything transforming into everything else, an endless metamorphosis of spirits into matter, and vice versa, everything dissolving into everything else ... no hard edges. Exactly like his recent dreams.

The introduction explained that the book was really called *The Book of Coming Forth by Day*, and was about birth as much as death, a series of magic spells by which the dead person's soul was magically transformed into birds and animals, plants and objects and even crystals. He carefully read the chapter describing the murder of Osiris by his brother Set, the Lamentations of Isis, and the Birth of Horus. But wasn't it all really, totally mad? As *he* was reading it?

He tried to think why the Egyptians needed to believe the soul strived to be transformed into all the creatures of the world, one by one. The central idea, as Georgina had said, was the birth of everything, or cosmogenesis, but everything born only in the mind, in consciousness, the entire world a transformation inside us; as if the world longed to rise up inside us. He guessed the difference was deep; not to experience the world as objective, but entirely subjective, no separation from the world ... the exact opposite of our experience with modern science and all the advantages of rationality and the sensation of objectivity. But he was fascinated, as he had been in the museum, with their intuition of wholeness, of unity; and apparently, resulting from that intimation, a passionate love of beauty.

Before he went to bed, he put the mummified falcon on the table next to his bed. He lay his hand on it affectionately before closing his eyes, and this made him fall asleep almost immediately and he slept soundly all night.

The following morning he decided to buy a box for the mummified falcon, and to visit the museum to look at the *ushabti* figures, to compare them to his own. Confronting Akhenaten and Meritaten he felt relaxed and composed, sensing they knew he had made a kind of commitment to take them seriously, whatever that might mean, by buying the objects and the books, and he no longer felt awkward in their presence.

There were many small blue and green *ushabti* figures, ready to accompany the dead, but he was disappointed to see how carefully they were modelled and glazed, how clear were the hieroglyphic inscriptions. His figures were obviously more humble, the property of a slave. He was pleased there were no mummified birds or creatures. They must be rare! He noticed several wooden mummy-cases but the contents had been discarded, presumably because they were so unpleasant ...

He left the museum and went to the junk stalls in the town's open market and found two old Chinese lacquered boxes, and bought them eagerly; also a loose-end of some dark red velvet for linings and some glue suitable for mending pottery. He returned to his flat and set to work making the *ushabtis* presentable, and the dead falcon comfortable.

In the afternoon he wandered along the river and went punting alone, watched the young couples, so much in love, and didn't feel threatened by them. He wondered if he might find Beverly, and for the hell of it, take her to dinner, get drunk enough to forget himself and plunge into a night of brutal, unbridled passion, and find out if she really did work for the CIA. Bitch!

That evening he decided he would call Georgina whether she liked it or not; he couldn't wait. Another girl answered and he asked formally for Miss Ffielding.

'You want to speak to George? Just a minute, I'll get her for you.' Matthew heard her call out, 'George! It's for you.'

'Yes?'

'Hello, George, it's Matthew!'

'You see, I told you you'd call me George. How are you?'

'Fine, and you?'

'Struggling. It's been hell, awful problems. Are you in Scotland?'

'I didn't go.'

'When are you going?'

'Probably tomorrow. Tell me though, is everything alright now, has the crisis passed?'

'Far from it, alas, and it's almost certainly going to get worse, much worse I'm afraid. Awfully worrying.'

There was a pause for some time before she whispered, 'I can't tell you on the 'phone. Not cool. Can't explain.'

'I'm sorry I can't help. I'd like to. Can I?'

'Well, it's very kind of you to offer. You hardly know me, do you, and you are offering to help!'

'Don't think about it. If I can help, I'll help. I have nothing to do at the moment, for two weeks at least ... so just tell me if there is anything I can do.'

'You're really kind but I can't tell you on the 'phone, anything at all, and without telling you, you can hardly be expected to take the risk, can you?'

'The risk? What kind of risk?'

'Well, risk is not the word really. The gamble of getting yourself entangled with two crazy girls, one of whom you don't know at all, and the other you met, a ghost in a museum!'

'Who cares, Georgina. I could as easily go tramping round Cornwall as tramping round Scotland.' Damn it, he'd said it!

'But really, Matthew, you can't start changing your plans and come hurtling down here. Everything might be alright tomorrow. Imagine if you went to all that trouble and by the time you got here everything was alright, you'd feel a complete idiot, wouldn't you?'

He wanted to say he felt an idiot anyway, so many crazy things were happening to him. 'Not at all, I'd find plenty of things to do. Just wander about ... explore Land's End ... get plenty of fresh air.'

'But, Matthew, you hardly know me. I'm not at all the kind of person you may think I am, really. I feel I may have given you the wrong impression. I must be quite frank with you now. How can I put it? I am very very independent and alone, and I've always got so much work to do, I find it hard to relate to people. Especially men. Do you see what I mean?'

Matthew felt a sudden panic, realising she was politely putting him off, warning him not to become involved with her. He didn't know what to say. She interrupted his silence. 'You'd be better off with Meritaten!'

'Listen Georgina, I take the hint and I appreciate you warning me, but I'd come down there simply to help you, if I could, and for the hell of it. Really. I mean it. We can talk about lasers and sculpture and ancient Egypt and I'll be more than satisfied.'

'I'm sorry I jumped to conclusions, but it's a long way to come on a wild sheep chase, which might be dangerous ...

isn't it?'

'Can I be of help, that's the important question?'

There was a long pause. 'Can you drive a car?'

'Yes, of course I can.'

'Can you drive a jeep, a four wheel drive?'

'I've driven a Land Rover.'

'OK then, are you game for an adventure?'

'Yes, of course I am ... even boring old rational scientists can be adventurous at times you know!'

'Fine ... listen. I'll ring you back in five minutes. Give me your number. Five minutes at the most!'

Half an hour went by. An hour. Matthew opened his box with the mummified falcon, and felt like talking to it, to explain he was going on an adventure.*Maybe!* Eventually, an hour or so later, after he'd died a thousand deaths, she called and told him he could take a night train from London at 9:30 and she'd meet him at St. Ives station in the morning. She was flattered he was so willing to help two scatterbrained girls 'in distress', but she assured him he'd get some healthy air and they'd feed him well.

'It's a deal! I'll be on the night train tomorrow ... and dream of it all night!'

★

FOUR

"Psychic phenomena are only by-products of the simultaneous-everywhere MATRIX. Individual brains are bits of the greater hologram. They have access under certain circumstances to ALL the information in the total cybernetic system. SYNCHRONICITY – those coincidental occurrences that seem to have some higher purpose or connectedness – also fits in with the holographic model. Such meaningful coincidences derive from the purposeful, patterned, organizing nature of the Matrix."

"Karl Pribram's Changing Reality"
– Marilyn Ferguson,

⊛

Matthew tried to avoid sleeping on the train, not wanting to dream, not wanting to wake up in a forest, not wanting to arrive in Moscow without his new paper; but there were lapses and various images crept up on him. The dreams seemed determined to get him.

'You're looking positively *spaced out*!' Georgina aptly commented, at first glance ...

They took a taxi. 'That's where we're meeting Cindy. Sad little café, but today we're low profile. But listen, I told her a little white lie. I said I'd known you off and on for a year or so in Cambridge, a friend of my friends. I didn't*dare* say I'd met you once for twenty minutes and only liked you because you were cracking up and in love with a sculpture of Princess Meritaten.'

'Cracking up? Well ... well thanks!' he said, rather put out.

She laughed. 'Only joking! But please go along with it, she'd have a fit thinking a total stranger is coming to her house, especially now. She can be a real bitch! Okay?'

'Okay, I'll say nothing ... *at all.*' He almost snarled.

'Not nothing! Something! Don't put the fear of god into her with silence. We're in one helluva mess, you know, really!'

'Alright, I'll say just a bit now and again.'

She nodded. Cindy hadn't arrived so they sat down. Georgina seemed in the grip with some unseen presence, pale and nervous as if waiting to audition for *Elektra*. No-one noticed who started, but they were suddenly playing silent piano on the table, he playing a Bach fugue in C and she playing the *Hungarian Rhapsody* number 3 in F# minor.

'You play the piano, really?' he asked.

'No, my fingers do. It was one of my former lives. I was in love with Liszt or Schumann or both probably, knowing me; I played the piano to attract them. If I get entranced enough, this other girl plays through me. It's lyrical sometimes, but mostly angry and mournful, a death march. I reckon she was into sex in a big way. So I switch off when that happens and tell her to come back when she's feeling more optimistic about life.' She smiled sweetly at him and he wasn't sure how much she was teasing him, but there was no time to question her; she was gazing towards the door with real panic in her face, as if she'd finally seen one of the ghosts that haunted her. 'Here she is, here's Cindy!'

Framed in the doorway as if in a hand-coloured advert in a 1932 edition of the *Chicago Post*, for some intoxicating and deadly drink (disguised as perfume), poised and still, was someone he'd have recognised even in his sleep. In all her artifice and scintillating splendour, cool and regal and cruel, was Jean Harlow ... and his heart sank into his boots. He'd not been expecting a movie star at all. The image in his mind of Cindy was of a rather wan, delicate English rose; he'd no idea why. He'd not bothered to ask Georgina exactly what she was like, even in the taxi. But now a cyclone had breezed through the door, scattering the rose petals to the winds. In full bloom was a glitzy blonde, a Vargas pin-up newly plucked from the hot-house of secret, adolescent dreams, complete with glossy platinum blonde hair, a tantalisingly cheap, pretty face, its unreality exaggerated by a mask of water-colour make-up, its rather flat, un-aristocratic features subtly rouged and shadowed to suggest more exotic, oriental bones behind the pallid, transparent skin, her pouting lips quivering at the illicit touch of the sable collar on a newly smuggled, utterly illegal, freshly tanned Canadian Lynx coat ... she was so immaculate and poised, everyone in the shop went silent and turned to marvel, wondering why the projector had stopped.

Matthew felt faint. She was for some reason pinioned in the doorway without motion, a movie still, a perfectly frozen image, her eyes half shut in preparation for the stroboscopic phosphorescent emissions of a bank of flashbulbs. Or she'd just stepped out of a crimson Cadillac with white leather seats into a gambling joint to confront her lover Al Capone, who had just learnt about her affair with the chief of police ...

'That's Cindy!' said Georgina, afraid he'd not recognise her from the vague reviews. 'Pretty, isn't she?'

He felt utterly embarrassed, knowing the colour in his face had drained away to a whiter shade of pale. 'Ur ... yes ... very pretty ... I'd no idea she was quite so glamorous.'

'Glamorous? You think so? It's all show, you'll see!' she said, slightly put-out by the strength of Matthew's reaction.

By this time Cindy had spotted them and sidled over to their table, casting furtive glances around as if she was looking for the guy with the machine gun. Cindy always looked utterly guilty of every known or imagined woman's crime ... which is why no man on earth could have resisted her. 'Don't say it, you're Matthew! Welcome to the dead centre of the holographic wasteland!' she mewed, as Matthew frowned. What could she possibly mean? She held out a gloved hand and he shook it as nonchalantly as possible.

'Pleased ... delighted ... ur ... '

She sat down, taking off the gloves as if his touch had soiled them, allowing Georgina to kiss her on the cheek, and smiling a fake smile at Matthew, her elegant hands not stooping to touch the table, her nails neatly enamelled with mother of pearl, her long fingers hovering as if expecting him to deal her a five card trick; or slip her a few grams of cocaine.

'I suppose it's too early for whiskey, George ... in this lousy spooky Speak-easy?'

'Of course, don't be silly, it's a coffee shop anyway. They sell coffee and cream cakes. Be sensible! What do you want?'

'God, worse than Prohibition! A double whiskey, a black coffee and a plate of cream cakes, unless they'll harm my complexion,' she said, as sulkily as possible. A waitress arrived and Georgina ordered three coffees and cream cakes.

'I hope you've got money George, I didn't have a purse to match my new coat! Do you like it? Newly smuggled in!'

'Yes, don't worry. You're looking great! Fur suits you.'

'Fur? It's Lynx! I woke up feeling so alone; you'd already gone, I felt utterly *awful*. I had to give myself a boost to make it worthwhile appearing ... here, on another day. Anyway, it took some effort. Hope I don't look *too* dressed up?'

'Not at all,' Georgina murmured, lying through her teeth. She might have said, *no more than usual*, knowing how much Cindy was obsessed with the past, like John, especially with old films; she was always the vamp, a rather vulgar, cheap, obvious pin-up from the inside of a World War Two airman's locker.

'Who'd care anyway, what the hell does it matter what anyone thinks? She looks great, doesn't she, Matthew?'

'Yes indeed,' Matthew said a little meekly. He couldn't take his eyes off her lips and their quivering. Was she really nervous, her eyes still half open, or suffering from a very heavy hangover? But the coincidence of the two images, the glamour and poise and arrogance, behind which lurked the aura of terror and inwardness and imminent flight, he found so unexpectedly attractive it was physically painful. She was just the most attractive girl he'd ever met in his life. At least, in the flesh. She was electric; the aura around her (surely purple if he could see it) tinged with anguish, plangent with guilt ... after all, she'd probably just killed someone, almost certainly for fun, shot him with a pearl-handled revolver and blamed it on her black maid, Emerald. Some lover who lost his cool. Matthew didn't know where to look or what to do with himself, he just wished he had that pack of cards, his fingers were itching to deal them out, despite knowing the two girls had already stacked them in their favour and he'd be lucky to get a pair of twos and the card saying how to buy another pack of the same.

'Any more news?' asked Georgina.

'None! But be cool darling, let's not talk about it *here*!' Cindy snapped petulantly. She looked nervously around the coffee shop again, as if looking for the one face she would recognise, that *someone* who was always following her, spying on her, waiting for the right moment to expose her to a brutal climax, the scarlet traces of a fitting ending ... the girl who is only herself on stage, always needing an audience, only alive, and aroused, when being watched. But she could never forget there was a price to pay, she was the prey to that audience stalking her, especially to that one person groping for his own fame on a warped path towards her, ready to pounce on more than a wrong line ... her body momentarly caught in a botched final curtain, the folds of the velvet paradoxically, for a mere few seconds, holding back the last veil. The flash of a knife ... Matthew was there in the theatre with her, not merely watching, the audience creating the actress but also assassinating her ... a finger presses the master switch to cut the lights, reduces her to a shadow. The moment to pounce. Yes! He was so tense something was about to snap. Was that the hint of fear flickering on her lips, lingering in her pale blue eyes?

Matthew wanted to tear off the mask ... he wanted to see through to the fragile person he imagined hidden, yearning for recognition, and it made him desire her painfully. She was transparent. Unless this was the image she was contriving to create. He wanted to ask Georgina, 'Is she one of your sculptures?' But he said nothing, noticing she was also tense, as if the sheer old-fashioned artificiality and blatant indecency of everything about Cindy was something she preferred not admit to herself but Matthew's presence was making her feel it even more acutely.

She would have replied *yes* to his question; 'I made her last week ... for my own pleasure though, not yours!'

The waitress arrived with the coffee and cakes and Cindy remarked haughtily in a rather fake Texas accent, (not nasal enough), not unlike that of Viven Leigh in *Streetcar named Desire*, 'A've seen one o'ma muthar's hats look mo appetizin' than them wimperin' cream cakes!' Fortunately the waitress laughed.

It occurred to Matthew suddenly, that Georgina was attracted to Cindy just as much as he was and probably for much the same reasons, and he felt suddenly utterly empty inside, a jagged black hole opening up the way it does in a slide of crystals forming when the temperature is too hot, not knowing if he could handle the situation; split between the two, a mere interface ... this was not quite what he'd planned for his trip to Cornwall to clear his mind and get some fresh air ... to help a couple of girls solve a problem he now wasn't remotely interested in, namely, what had happened to the previous boyfriend! Good rid ... dance! He drank some coffee and ate a cake. Silence.

''What do you think of my new perfume?' Cindy asked Georgina, presenting her wrist to be sniffed.

'Powerful!'

'Isn't it! That's the purrfect word. John brought it from LA. Or was it Paris? *L'Air du Temps*.' She held out the other wrist and Georgina sniffed obediently. 'That's *Eau du Nil*!' She always wore two perfumes. Just in case.

'Do you like it, Matthew?'

He sniffed her proffered wrist like a schoolboy sniffing a slipper to see if it was real leather before being beaten with it. He tried to joke. 'Not to wear myself!'

Cindy smiled, patronisingly. But then as if to imply the remark was the last straw, she said coldly, 'Let's go! We've a lot of sordid things to sort out. George, wave for the bill.'

Cindy promptly ate two cakes in four bites, drank her coffee in two gulps, pulled out a shell shaped art deco compact, its mirror so speckled with blemishes Matthew wondered if she could see herself in it, but she leared into it, as if resenting the silvering that had peeled off it, checking her make-up and flamboyantly smacking her lips as she did so. Matthew's fingers were now playing an imaginary cello under the table, the slow movement of Elgar's Cello concerto.

Cindy stood up and wafted towards the door, trailing the hidden wave-formation of *L'Air du Temps* in perfect resonance with the undercurrents of *Eau du Nil*, the intertwined, enmeshed currents eddying viciously under the noses of the poor customers trying to savour the delicate fragrance of their freshly-brewed coffee and home-baked cakes. A holographic perfume, Cindy would have said, no doubt, but she was out of the door before Georgina and Matthew had time to think about standing up.

Georgina smiled at the startled look on Matthew's face. 'She's a born actress, all exits and entrances; but she does exits best, poor thing! What do you think of her?'

Matthew couldn't tell her the truth. He knew it would hurt, finding her so utterly desirable. 'Ur ... amazing. Unreal, isn't she; almost frightening. Not at all what I was expecting ... '

Georgina was relieved. 'I thought it best not to describe her, in case I scared you off. She's nervous and making a particular show today. You wouldn't recognise her in a Laura Ashley frock, covered in primroses!'

'No, I suppose I wouldn't,' Matthew admitted, awkwardly.

'She'll soon relax. You'll like her when you see some of the other sides to her, a woman of many faces shelved away in the closet behind her green door! This evening she'll probably cry the whole time because of John, so don't judge her by that. She's a hurt child really but that doesn't mean she isn't dangerous!'

'Yes, I ... I ... I imagine so,' he stuttered. 'Ur ... ur ... how long has she been with John?' he asked reluctantly.

'For years and years. His disappearance has totally thrown her ... in fact, both of us ... I'm sorry Matthew, but can you pay the bill? I'm utterly skint!'

Matthew paid, willingly, trying to remember how much cash he'd got saved up, which he'd relish offering for the cause of supporting the poor girl. Poor thing! They joined Cindy on the pavement, leaning iconographically against a battered old fashioned lamp-post, which Matthew envied deeply; the woman of easy virtue plying her trade. Matthew would have bought her on the spot, although he'd never been into whores. 'Cindy, if you stand like that you'll get picked up by the police, never mind ten taxi drivers!' Georgina snapped petulantly.

Cindy smiled. She hitched up her skirt and showed more knee, and more of her tatty black fish-net stockings. Somehow Matthew knew they were stockings and not tights. There was a flash of satin ... and Matthew's neck muscles went taut again. Obviously liking to provoke Georgina, Cindy took her arm. 'Okay, little bitch you, where are we going? You're the boss, George ... as usual.' But she was smiling.

'Let's get the car first, before going back to the house.'

'Okay boss, let's go. You just said there were ten lousy taxi drivers trying to pick me up, so where are they? Miserable kerb crawlers! I don't see *one*. You see, you always exaggerate ... and if I said, *Call me a taxi*, you'd say, *Okay, you're a taxi*! You see I know my movies, like you know your transparent holograms! And John knows ... '

'Yes ... I know you do! Shut up!' interrupted Georgina.

Matthew struggled behind them, carrying his two cases of luggage. The two girls were arm in arm and giggling. Suddenly an unexpected montage of words flashed into his mind, as if he'd accessed a file on his computer by accident, or as if someone was talking to him. 'Now's your chance! Go! Turn around and run. They'll not miss you for two hundred yards, by which time you can hide and then escape. Go back to Cambridge immediately before it's too late ... before you're trapped and humiliated ... crushed between them ... doomed!'

He stopped for a moment and tensed all his muscles ready for flight. A taxi was drawing up on the other side of the road and he wanted to wave it down, dash across the road, take it straight to the station and be out of sight before they'd realised there'd been a change of reel. But his arm wouldn't move. He cursed; time was running out on his impulse. With a supreme effort he shouted out 'Taxi!' but it sounded garbled and insanely intense, like a cry from the dead, a wounded hyena groping for the last water-hole, face to face with two leopards on heat ...

Everyone in the street reacted at the cry, and the startled driver lurched to a halt, before indicating he'd turn round. The girls too had flung themselves into a tight huddle at Matthew's scream, and still giggling, were now walking back more casually towards him. 'Well done, Matthew, what a god-send to have a man around. What would we do without you? We'd have gone on gossiping to the end of the pier and dropped into the sea!'

They piled in and Cindy pointed for the driver to take a particular road just out of town, off the main road. After about three miles she ordered a stop near a wooden gate, beyond which was a rough track betwen two hedges, beyond which, barely visible, were open fields. Matthew paid the taxi, while the girls climbed the gate and walked on. Although they were arm in arm, Matthew could see they were nervous, looking furtively from side to side, over-acting while trying not to look suspicious; then suddenly giggling and all jolly ... as he trundled along behind them.

Cindy turned and suggested he hide his cases in the nearby bushes, to be collected when they came back with the car, as the place was so wild, and then, to his surprise, they both took one of his arms, one on each side, and dragged him along in silence. His dream! He saw it, the victim being taken by two priestesses to the site of sacrifice; too late! Perhaps not ... two modern priestesses, a Gypsy sculptress and a glossy Hollywood movie star, and rather than feeling scared he felt curiously excited ... what was awaiting him at the end of the lane? Cindy's satin underskirt kept flicking out from under her coat. Certainly not his name in bright lights and fame ...

Some rooks suddenly flew up from a field nearby, a bunch of scraggy midget witches sketched by a child on the blank page of clear blue sky, screaming a raucous cacophony of protest at their presence. Then a huge cloud of lapwings leapt into the air, in unison, and they too chorused their protest at the presence of the three human beings invading their territory. Matthew gazed at them for a moment in awe, amazed by the speed with which they all changed direction at once, before recognising the image, a moving, three dimensional Escher painting, one moment all black, flecked with white, the next, dramatically reversed, the whole flock instantly changing like computer-designed logos advertising something ... maybe ... *Paradoxic*, a deodorant that attracted women and repulsed men ...

A hundred yards from the end of the track, Matthew glimpsed the beech trees over the hedgerows, and he felt a sharp, uncomfortable tingling on the back of his neck. Rounding the next bend, through a gap in the hedge he saw the majestic trees arranged formally around a large, raised mound of earth. He jerked to a stop as if he'd seen a ghost. The girls were forced to do likewise, looking at him in alarm.

'Beech trees. A copse of beech trees!' he murmured, dazed and confused ... speaking half to himself, half to the trees ...

The girls looked at each other and then at Matthew, and

back at each other, not understanding his strange reaction. He spoke, curtly. 'Well I never! Another coincidence. Or is it mere illusion? Perhaps some kind of a joke? Synchronicity did you call it Georgina?'

The girls felt awkward and looked away. Georgina kissed Cindy lightly on the cheek, almost unconsciously. Maybe they should ignore him or send him back? After a long pause and without looking at them, he started to tug them along towards the copse as if he was now being pulled there by an unseen force. Georgina asked him what was so strange about beech trees ...

'Oh nothing, nothing really, nothing, a mere coincidence. But Georgina, it was *you* who told me I should take notice of coincidences; holograms and all that, wasn't it? Two layers of meaning, one on top of the other ... we never see the truth ... no such thing as coincidence? In the one we see the many?'

Georgina was utterly confused. She'd no idea why he was reacting so bitterly. She didn't want Cindy to see her emotion, for her own reasons, so pulled him back as Cindy walked on, and whispered, 'I don't remember saying that, but it sounds like me! There's something unique about this little copse, isn't there? We came here yesterday, me for the first time, and it felt very strange here. You'll see, there *is* a very special feeling about some places, like this one ... is that what you mean?'

'I don't know what I mean!' he said emotionally. 'I don't know what to think, maybe I should stop thinking altogether!' He looked quite beside himself. And Cindy had opened her coat and her satin skirt was just too much! The girls felt uneasy too. This was not what they had expected, Matthew gazing up at the trees looming above them, a dark, tormented look on his face. Finally he took another step, no doubt the truly fatal one, saying, 'Come on, no going back I suppose, is there ... ' But it wasn't a question. They walked on and reached the copse and Matthew stood still, indicating he wanted to be alone. Arm in arm the girls wandered off ... but not too far away, just in case ...

The trees had been deliberately planted around the mound to create an enclosure ... not entirely like the trees in the laboratory garden and in the copse in his memory, which were not so formally arranged ... not so precise; two lines, empty at each end, but here, closed at the ends. The trees towered above, really high, and the branches formed a canopy, just like a roof.

'It reminds me of a church ... doesn't it you?' he said, finally, unemotionally, as matter of fact as possible.

The girls were looking oddly at him and didn't speak for a minute or two, which seemed a very long time to Matthew. Cindy spoke finally. 'This was John's sacred place. He came here to meditate. When he disappeared, this was the first place I came to look. Over there behind the bushes is his car, but no signs of him. Not a clue. He spent hours meditating here. Only once he let me come here. Fortunately I remembered where it was. You see the problem?'

'Have you looked everywhere in the copse?' he asked, coldly.

'Everywhere. He's not here.'

'In body or spirit,' added Georgina, but Cindy immediately flashed her a look of disapproval to silence her.

Matthew walked slowly into the copse and stood in the clearing in the middle of the trees, on top of the mound. He noticed four holes where four pegs had been newly pulled out of the grass. At least, that is what he thought had happened, feeling the tingling again on the back of his neck. The girls were talking quietly to each other about the beauty of the tall trees. He felt an enormous pull as if some force was trying to suck him upwards into the branches of the trees, and he felt dizzy, closing his eyes for a moment to stop himself falling. He felt really embarrassed when he saw the girls gazing at him, almost spell-bound, as if he was crazy.

'It's a powerful spot, isn't it,' said Cindy. 'John knew it. That's why it was his favourite place. He called it his place of focus. You can feel it, can't you?'

'Yes, I can,' he agreed, awkwardly, reluctantly. He was feeling so many different things all at once, disorientating him; he could feel the strong pull, tangibly, physically, in his body. 'I admit it. It's very strong. But I knew a place like this when I was very young ... with beech trees too ... a small copse on a mound, out in the open, right in the middle of fields, just like this one. In the spring it was full of bluebells. I loved it there ... it was my place too, like this was John's, I suppose. Strange how we find similar things for different reasons!' He looked thoughtful, then said quietly, looking away, 'Until it got spoilt!'

They looked at him warmly, and took his arms again. They seemed to approve of his new sensibility and felt immediately more secure in his presence. Georgina spoke. 'Come on, let's take the car and go back to the house. We've a lot to talk about. Give Matthew the spare keys, Cindy.'

She handed them to Matthew and they followed the track round some thick hawthorn bushes to John's car, an American jeep painted in camouflage colours, with large cross-country tyres and black curtains that were closed. Matthew opened the car doors. 'Are you sure you looked everywhere here?' he asked Cindy, before starting the car.

'Yes, we looked yesterday. Everywhere. Anyway I have a bleeper that John gave me. It works for three months. He had a transmitter on him, and told me I'd always find him. It works to a distance of thirty miles. He loved gadgets. We looked everywhere here. He's definitely *not* here.'

Matthew drove along the track to where he'd left his bags, chuckling to himself. The story about the transmitter sounded fascinating; he loved gadgets too. Maybe it wasn't too bad after all, the drama of John's disappearance was getting more intriguing with every new scene.

The girls directed him back through the town and then along another country road for several miles, until a concealed turn off which lead to a large Regency-style country house with an ornate iron veranda along the front. He could see the sea a mile or so away beyond some fields. It was a beautiful spot. Peaceful.

'It's a bit isolated, you must admit, for two lonesome girls, all on their own!' Georgina murmured.

Cindy unlocked a back door and they went directly into a large kitchen, clean and comfortably furnished. Cindy explained to Matthew that John had rented it for a few years on a lease and there was still a year or so remaining, paid for. It was centrally heated by oil and the tank had been filled a week before with 500 gallons. She was talking as if she took it for granted he would now supervise the running of it.

'I've got some pizzas in the deep freeze. Do you mind if we have one for lunch? Cooked, of course!'

Cindy told Georgina to take Matthew to his room. 'This way!' She showed him the doors to four other bedrooms in the house before his, and from his window she pointed to the converted barn that was her studio at the end of the garden. 'The previous owner was a well-known painter, Peter Lanyon, and he converted the studio. It's a perfect set-up ... except it's now all going wrong!'

Matthew took hold of Georgina, roughly but also affectionately, and looked her straight in the eyes. 'You know I can only stay a short while, don't you, until you sort things out and then I'll have to go back to Cambridge, to my work?' Maybe he was trying to convince himself.

She smiled and nodded as if agreeing with him. 'Of course I know you have to work, but just stay here a few days to help out and I'll be eternally grateful. You can walk along the cliffs, there's never a soul here except us, it's wonderfully peaceful here, and that's so rare nowadays. You can work undisturbed and meditate on your diamonds. You'll see, you'll make a major breakthrough here. Maybe you need to start again with something crazy before you get there! You will. You'll see. Something to do with the unique light here! So translucent and beautiful. It's that kind of place ... '

But she was looking away as she spoke. He wondered if she might be faking the enthusiasm, knowing she was very worried, or sad. 'Why won't you contact the police about John's disappearance, if it was so mysterious, or his parents?'

'We don't know where they are. John never told us things like that. He was a very secretive person. His work was strange. He said we must tell no-one, ever, especially the police. Cindy told me not to tell you this. Why do I?'

'I don't know, maybe ... '

She interrupted. 'Because you were in love with Meritaten like a wide-eyed schoolboy and I knew I could trust you when I saw that. Otherwise I would have told you to go to hell, except in that case, you would have been already in it!'

'Then I'm very lucky.' he said warmly, and he meant it.

'Well I hope so. But I've no idea what Cindy and John have been up to. She never told me everything. She agreed you could stay here while we decide whether to stay on or not. In two weeks we should know what has happened. Meanwhile, relax and enjoy yourself. Your bathroom is at over the corridor. Your own bathroom! Cindy cooks frozen pizzas impeccably. I do a good line in hot spicy curries. What more could a man want, Doctor Matthew Sutherland?' She kissed him patronisingly on the cheek and sauntered out, before he could tell her.

He lay back on his bed and gazed at the ornate plastered ceiling. The rose in the centre, painted green, its edges damaged and crumbling, didn't look at all healthy. Unexpectedly, he thought of David, waxing mystical in India. 'If you could see me now you old bastard, this may not be an ashram or a lunatic asylum, but it's certainly different!'

At lunch they talked about the changeable weather, the unique transparency and lucidity of the light in Cornwall, which so many artists had cherished, the nuisance of tourists, Scotland unvisited; and the Cambridge University Film Society. Especially old black and white films! Cindy's passion for the cinema seemed centred on tragedies involving sexual betrayal, though she was bitter, it seemed, that the women tended to get shot just when you'd decided you could forgive them anything. Georgina said very little. Matthew was surprised how quickly Cindy had transformed herself. Although she was still impeccably sheathed in satin, (he couldn't help but notice she wasn't wearing much underneath, her dress was so tight), her attitude was now direct and analytical, something he'd not expected at all. 'Why on earth did you become a scientist, Matthew? It must be deadly boring, living in that inert world of reason and endless causal predictability. Isn't it?'

He was immediately on the defensive. 'Not at all! My work is fascinating. I'm sorry you think of science as machines and technology, dehumanisation and materialism and all that. My field of work is profoundly provocative and stimulating: the intimate world of crystals has an extraordinary fascination. You've no idea how beautiful the crystal world is under the microscope!'

Fingering her fake art-nouveau pearls, her eyes narrowing, Cindy continued. 'Why crystals, and what have they to do with life, the living material you're looking for?' Her new tone of voice suggested it was hard to make polite conversation about science, although she could have talked about French, German and American cinema heroines forever.

'Crystals struck a chord in me. I suppose you might say it was an irrational experience, an instant love affair. They fascinate me, elegant and exquisite structures and provocative in the huge scheme of things. There's even serious talk nowadays about their role in the evolution of life on this planet. A lot of work in genetics and microbiology is done with crystals. They have qualities that make them unique. Even when I was a little boy I was fascinated by crystals. I made myself a crystal set, like one of the first radio sets, amazed how a small crystal could be tuned to pick up invisible radio waves in the air which were then transformed into sounds, even music. With a small crystal costing nothing, I could listen to Beethoven's 9th Symphony being played in Prague. That was real magic! One day I looked down a polarizing microscope at slide of granite, an ultra thin slice of what I knew only as a dark, thick, ugly stone. There were a hundred small fragments of interlocking crystals, every shape and colour imaginable, all radiant with shining light, and if you turn the light-polarizing source, every fragment of crystal changes colour as it moves. It was utterly beautiful, but even more important, this was a slice of mere granite. You know what it looks like from outside, a grey blur, a lump of stone, yet under the microscope, you see a translucent, secret world beyond the dull world of appearance. Since then I've been a crystallographer.'

The two girls remained silent, watching each other knowingly, but without giving anything away, waiting for him to continue. But he'd said his bit ... Eventually Georgina spoke. 'What happens when a sculptor hacks away at a piece of stone and changes it into a sculpture? What about

Michelangelo's *David*, or Henry Moore's *Madonna and Child*? Are they just chunks of granite or marble?'

'No ... they are sculptures.'

'And how are they different?'

'They've been carved and shaped into a form which communicates a feeling or idea about human nature.'

'Exactly, like your crystal set, tuned to receive music from Prague on invisible waves, only *recently* detected and used; a mere hundred years. What about Egypt, then? Meritaten? Is she just a piece of stone? Why can't she receive certain waves we don't know about, if we got the tuning right?'

Matthew cleared his throat. 'Not exactly. It's a stone sculpture, something that merely represents her, embodies her appearance. My experience of her was emotional, irrational, exaggerated. All that was from inside me, alas, my emotions, projected outwards. There are parallels, that's all. What are you getting at?'

'But maybe behind the appearance of stone are many other dimensions of meaning or consciousness or wave frequencies we know nothing about, cannot see, that need a special light to detect them ... like holograms which can only been seen in pure laser light. Don't you think you might one day communicate with Meritaten, actually, physically, if the technology was known? Re-found? They had it once, so they tell us. Why should we be arrogant and doubt?' Georgina said, confidently, her voice tinged with an edge of provocation. .

'I don't believe that. Of course not!' he said emphatically.

Undeterred, she continued. 'But you see Matthew, the ancient Egyptians believed the appearance of the person, in stone or clay or paint or whatever, could focus part of the essence of that person into it. Part of the spirit of the person that was detached, not confined to the body, could be drawn back. Morphic resonance, forms recognising forms. They believed a part of the essence of the person was still in the sculpture you saw, and that your experience of this essence was related to an experience of, say, Meritaten standing in front of you as flesh and blood, if you could tune yourself to the right wavelength. They thought the body was a sculpture too, a form of matter that could focus part of the essence of the person. They called these split parts of consciousness or being the *Ka* or *Ba* or *Khu* or *Khaibit.* A stone sculpture, you say, is made up of millions of crystals, so if one small crystal can focus *Beethoven's 9th Symphony* ... being played in Prague let's say ... focus it into your ears in a recognisable form, what is to stop all those millions of small crystals that make up the stone head of Meritaten focusing part of the *Ka* of Meritaten into them, hovering about in the stone just as your consciousness and your soul seem to hover about your body ... inside and outside of it at the same time. All you have to do is find the technology ... which I believe the mind once had but has now lost ... to let you tap into those crystals and speak to Meritaten; in images, images of meaning, even if not actual words. Like through dreams. All you need is the needle and the amplifier and the headphones or whatever's necessary to transform that small subtle vibration into something you could hear and communicate with, with your mind tuned like an internal TV set. As I say, not unlike the process of unravelling the image of a three-dimensional hologram from a mess of waves, into a pure picture, an illusion our senses can detect and see and believe in, after all!'

Matthew thought for quite some time, picking at the burnt crust of his pizza with his fork. Shaking his head, he was trying to reject everything she said, telling himself she was merely taunting him, trying to trick him. 'Georgina, you know I can't think in that kind of way! Don't force me to say I think it's nonsense!'

'Matthew!' Cindy interrupted sharply, 'If you're going to live with us for a bit and we cook for you and look after you and you help us to look for John and so on, there's one thing I'll have to ask you to do, do you mind?'

'No. What is it? Tell me,' he said apprehensively.

'Please call George, *George* and not Georgina. When you say Georgina, it throws me, as if you're speaking to someone else who is not really here. She's George, just as I'm Cindy. I've known her so long as George, it hurts when you call her that twee, soppy name, Georgina.'

Matthew laughed, relieved it wasn't worse. 'Okay, I'll try. I'll make a few mistakes, probably, but I can try.'

'Fine, sorry to have to say it!' Cindy said, smiling sweetly, but patronisingly, advertising a new rouge called *Cheeky*.

There was an awkward pause before Matthew continued, 'So tell me about John's disappearance. What's it all about?'

Cindy replied after some hesitation. 'John wasn't like most people ... his needs were simple ... meditating and wandering. He would call it his *pélèrinage*. Just a beachcomber looking for stones. But there was more to it than that. Later we can tell you. He was looking for a special type of stone on the beach that only he could recognise ... that could detect certain vibrations ... there were funny aspects to his whole mission.'

'He took these things seriously?' Matthew asked, not wanting to sound too cynical.

'Yes. Very seriously. He also went to special places too, like his sacred copse of trees where we found the car.'

'In what way was it sacred?' he asked, genuinely curious.

'As we said, he felt there were forces focused there. In these sacred focus spots, where the ancients used to worship, are real forces they could feel and respond to. Listen to. Hear. He said we had lost the ability to tune into them. He spent his entire time working on this problem, trying to tune himself so he could hear. He used crystals too. Special stones. So you see, there are curious parallels.'

Matthew immediately resented the suggestion. 'I wouldn't say *parallels*! There are crystals and crystals. A crystal of DNA is different to a crystal of quartz. Did he succeed in his search, that's the question?'

'Yes! In indirect ways, but then he was really interested in the unconscious ... recently he said he was experiencing dreams in a way he'd never done before ... very intense dreams, but they weren't dreams but messages, actual *visitations* was the word he used. He said the forces couldn't get through to him while he was awake but they could reach him through his unconscious, while he was asleep. The dreams were messages needing to be decoded. More recently he said he had found a clue, and he was close to making direct contact. But he kept telling me it was dangerous, he was tapping forces he might not be able to control. So he said he would take precautions. It was like going into the labyrinth, face to face with the Minotaur, so he had to lay a trail to get back. He started to work on that trail. But then ... but then ...'

The silence was tangible ... no one dared speak. 'Then he just disappeared into thin air!' Georgina said coldly. Cindy snapped at her, to be quiet.

Matthew felt embarrassed as they glared at each other. But he was feeling uneasy at the talk of dreams. The girls looked to him to speak, to break the tension. 'Funnily enough, recently, I've been having weird, vivid dreams. They all seem connected. I even dreamt about the copse, or my copse, the one I visited as a child. But I forget the dream images when I try to remember them precisely. They say that people just go through periods of dreaming!'

Cindy smiled knowingly. 'Maybe there is just something in the air at present, lots of messages floating about for those who can receive them!' She glared at Georgina again, who looked away.

'Well, not me, I can assure you!' said Matthew, trying to laugh it off. 'Tell me more about the stones. What kind of stones was John looking for?'

'He found stones on the beach he said had some kind of code in them or on them. I never understood what he meant. Inside the stones were thin veins of crystals in patterns that were put there by the forces ... and he had to find a way to understand the crystals. They were mostly quartz with impurities, and he knew about crystal radios and things, too. So you see? More and more coincidences!'

'So it seems,' Matthew said, feeling uncomfortable that Cindy was trying so hard to compare his work to John's. He wondered why she needed to.

Georgina smiled and said, 'Now you see why I was so interested in what you had to say in Cambridge. I felt immediately you were on the same wavelength as John ... that same night Cindy told me he'd disappeared into thin air ... and I told her all about you.'

Cindy interrupted angrily. 'Please, George, don't say, "Into thin air!" It frightens me. He might be just sitting in some cave somewhere with a broken leg, eating peanuts, doing yoga and talking to a galaxy at the other side of the universe, for all we know. Maybe he thinks he is Moses and is writing down the messages, word by word, on some stone tablet! Thin air frightens me. I think he's somewhere, still alive.'

But Georgina continued, 'We just feel you were sent to help us. When I told Cindy about your work and Meritaten, she said immediately you were sent to help us find John, if he is still alive, or if not, to help us discover what his work was really about. It could be very important. John was certain he was destined to become the very first person to prove communication with forces outside. Not just from "outside", but outside of matter. That was his destiny, which is why he devoted all his resources, all his money, to developing the technology for the project.'

'Was he that rich? It would need millions!'

Silence. After some time, Georgina continued. 'Quite rich. Enough to rent this place, do nothing except his work. He paid some friends to do work with quartz, some guys who were into music. He produced a few records years ago ... and even recently still received a lot of serious money from them. Music-wise it was Fusion, jazz and classical, and he was in touch with Syd Barrett, the guitarist in Pink Floyd; an old friend. That's about all we know for sure. He was a loner. Quiet. Secretive. He made sure we knew as little as possible about the "other-reality" as he would call it. He wasn't interested in this world at all, except to pay bills and just forget it all. He'd blown his mind years before and wasn't too interested in rebuilding it, in what he used to call "the prison of the materialist paradigm". He was on a new trip, scientific reincarnation, to go back four thousand years and allow someone else to enter his mind and restructure it ... from ancient Egypt, the Amarna period, of course. He was communicating with a high priest called Amenhotep. It was his mission to unite ancient mysticism and modern science. You see ... it was hard for us to take him entirely seriously. Maybe he was completely mad?'

Matthew shrugged his shoulders and nodded, as if agreeing. He didn't like the sound of John at all. A mere hippy!

But then Cindy snapped her fingers as if bringing herself back to the present, 'Let's quit the bullshit! Here's the whole truth then. Okay? Why not! If you're our accomplice, you have to know the truth, bad as it may seem. You see, John was an explorer ... outer space and inner space. A cosmic pilgrim. He made a lot of money, some time ago; he perfected a method for making very pure LSD and mescalin. He had some trouble, changed his name, false passports, the lot, and on the run from the police, which is why we can't go to them now. There it is. But he was a marvellous person, a great guy. Once he was crazy but then he put all his financial and intellectual resources into becoming serious. But he did theoretical physics at Oxford. He was no slouch intellectually. Help us find him, and help him too, he's probably lost his memory, gone insane or made contact with Amenhotep ... or another force he didn't predict. He was planning a major experiment at the exact moment of the recent lunar eclipse. Maybe it went wrong, or maybe he is sitting in Amarna talking to Akhenaten about the hidden mystical meaning of the Aten, what he called "the Sun's Cosmic Computer Disc"!'

'Wrong by our standards,' Georgina added. 'Maybe it went right for him ... maybe he made the great "breakthrough in plane" as he called it. Maybe he's here in this room with us and we can't see him or hear him. At night we can hear him sometimes, pottering about, but we're just dumb girls, after all!'

'It's usually the wind!' added Cindy.

Matthew went to the window. He was angry. He could see the sea in the distance. Feeling utterly miserable and cheated, he didn't like the sound of John at all. A worse case than his schizophrenic drug-taking friend David, who spent most of*his* time in an asylum. He didn't want to get involved on any level at all. He'd been tricked, brought to Cornwall on false pretences. But the eclipse?

'Do you mind if I go for a walk? There are things I need to think about seriously, aren't there?' he added, coldly.

The girls looked worried, having said too much too soon. 'Yes there must be, but have a cup of tea first, you can't go out on a mystical quest on an empty stomach! Not until you've practised the yoga of self-denial,' Cindy chirped, almost mockingly, and regretting it immediately. It was important to her that Matthew stayed around. She had her reasons.

'Okay, if you insist, I'll have some tea, and leave the denial until later.' But he drank the tea in silence and the girls politely left him alone, going to their respective territories.

He took to the fields towards the cliffs, deep in thought. He was disappointed and angry with himself for being so stupid. He knew he'd been deliberately tricked. By the time he reached the cliffs and found a safe place to sit from where he could gaze down at the grey sea below, he'd made up his mind to go back to Cambridge immediately and avoid further involvement in the dramas and crazy ideas of the girls, and the awful John!

The cliffs were very high, and the sound of the sea pounding against the black rocks below made Matthew feel uneasy. The sound was ominous and primeval. There was a vicious sea breeze that squalled and gusted so much that it frightened him a little, making it impossible for him to venture too close to the edge for fear of being sucked or blown over by a sudden change of direction by the wind.

He thought about the girls. Until they had mentioned the LSD he'd been going along with the story, but as soon as he realised that John's search for enlightenment was some crackpot, drug-provoked hallucination, he'd felt himself switch off. He thought again of David. John and he would have seen third eye to third eye in a flash!

Suddenly he heard screaming in the sky, a cry he didn't recognise, but then he saw two falcons circling above him, quite close, one of them carrying a small dead bird in its claws and circling around its mate. Suddenly they swooped down onto a small rock just in front of him, oblivious of his presence. The bird with the food started plucking the feathers from the carcase, making a loud *chup-chupping* sound. After a couple of minutes the female, presumably, came down and took the plucked quarry from the other bird's feet, and they both chupped loudly and excitedly. After eating some of the food, the female stood back from it and the male took the remains and flew to a nearby cliff where he hid the carcass behind some rocks. Flying back, he circled over the female, silently. Suddenly she bent forward and emitted a strange wailing sound and the male falcon, stooping down and hovering, alighted on her back, gently, flapping his wings, and they mated, both birds vocalising very loudly. The male flew off and the female ruffled her feathers, before preening herself.

Matthew felt moved by what he had seen. It had been so private. The birds were so busy with their ritual of food exchange, they were unaware of his witnessing the resulting copulation. Another falcon as beautiful as they were had just been conceived! He wondered how long it would be before the female would lay her eggs, how long before her young falcons would be chasing each other near the cliffs, soaring on the wind, practising flying and hunting, until the day that, in a silent and deadly stoop, they would swoop out of the sky and kill some hapless young lapwing pecking around in a field looking for worms. Their first act of murder, innocent and sanctioned by the vast scheme of things ...

Humbled, he wondered why the world of nature had developed the need to reflect on itself, become self-conscious. Why had the universe reached such a moment of self-reflection, apparently needing to look at itself through the medium of the human mind? And perhaps a falcon's mind too? This cosmic narcissism, it was such a strange idea ... but then it slipped away, as if it had been mere dream.

He'd seen such birds on film, but never in reality. He was feeling quite emotional, his spirit had stirred at the sight and he felt unexpectedly privileged to have witnessed nature's act of creation so closely. And on such an image was based the curious legend of Isis and Osiris ... but why? Why was Isis in the form of a hovering falcon when she mated with her dead husband? What an extraordinary idea, what a weird choice of image to embody the most secret rite of “the birth of consciousness” as Georgina had called it. And he thought of his mummified falcon, trying to think of it as it had once been, alive, flying over the river Nile, copulating on some cliff top. Was it a male or female? Did the Egyptians differentiate between a male soul and a female one? He didn't know why but he felt sad thinking of his falcon. He wanted it so much to come alive again. He hadn't had a chance yet to show it to Georgina. Now it would probably be too late, and no longer necessary, having decided for certain, to leave at the earliest opportunity ...

He heard the falcons screaming at each other again but he couldn't see them. *They must be peregrines!* he thought to himself, remembering the name of the largest of the falcons resident in the British Isles. The Wandering Falcon.*Le Pélèrin.* The Pilgrim Hawk as it was variously called. Suddenly, the two falcons took off again into the sky and made a loud noise chasing off a number of seagulls that were drifting on the wind through their territory.

Matthew set off back to the house, intent on telling the girls he had made his decision to leave, although he could stay one more night, surely, without prejudicing his freedom. LSD king indeed!

When he arrived back, the girls had prepared tea for him, all neatly laid out on an Chinese lacquered tray with a bone-china tea-service, and he was reminded of his mother and the similar tea-set she always brought out ceremoniously on his rare visits. The girls had prepared scones, jam and cream, and they looked at him mischievously, as if expecting him to be overwhelmed with gratitude. For all their efforts to be so Bohemian in their appearance and talk, they were really quite conservative behind the facade, almost genteel! For some strange reason he thought of Thomas Hardy, and trying to be literary he commented, 'How nice to be so far from the madding crowd!'

They groaned; but relieved to see he was being friendly, Georgina said, 'We *are* waxing eloquent with our literary references today!'

Matthew sat down feeling awkward, wanting to tell them he was going to leave the next day, but instead said, 'As one cloud said to another, will you pour or shall I?' at which they groaned even louder, but then laughed good-humouredly as

Georgina poured the tea.

Cindy passed the food. 'Tuck in, as the wicked grandmother said to the luscious Goldilocks ... before seducing her!'

They looked at him as if he should react, but he shook his head; he'd missed that one.

'When I was a little girl,' Cindy said, 'I used to find it very sexy indeed to think of the wolf in bed with grandma. What about you, George?'

Georgina put down her cup. 'Yes indeed! But poor Matthew. You must forgive us, we go on like this at times. You see Cindy is writing a novel. Its subject is very secret of course. She started writing it at school. Shall I tell him?'

'If you want to.'

'Well, Cindy's first claim to fame was being expelled from school. She entered a short story competition with "Love Affair", the intimate story of Jesus and Mary Magdalene, but written as a series of dreams based on images from the Apocalypse. She photocopied the story and copies were floating around the lavatories for weeks, before and after Cindy was thrown out. I once found a photocopy, so rough and faded it was clearly a fifth generation copy. Cindy and I worked it out that if only half of her copies had been copied five times, she'd have published a best seller!'

'You exaggerate as usual, George! There might have been a hundred copies; everyone said it was not really blasphemous at all, just plain sexy and erotic. Hardly a crime. My first work got me expelled, my father disowned me and hasn't spoken to me since. Poor guy. He used to preach to us three girls, I was the youngest, as if he was a reincarnation of Martin Luther. "Sitting in my privy I had a profoundly new and wonderful idea!" My story nearly killed him. Mother wanted to laugh, but didn't dare. Later I decided to become an actress instead, on the stage; and look where I am now? The rejected queen of the LSD king, mourning his loss in a rented house in Cornwall. So you see why I need to write a best-seller?'

'What's your novel about?' Matthew asked politely.

Cindy's eyes narrowed. She was about to change the subject. 'I don't know you well enough to tell you yet. Maybe

I will one day. Maybe ... but in the meantime we have work to do. What do you suggest we do about looking for John?'

Matthew remained silent, trying hard to give the impression he was thinking it over carefully, examining a number of possible lines of enquiry, trying to look like Humphrey Bogart mulling over some flimsy evidence, preparing to announce to the victim's gun-moll a daring plan to find the killer ... or the thief of the Maltese falcon ...

Georgina took a scone and gazed into the cream, spoiled with jam, as if meditating on a deep secret. 'We had the cream in the freezer, but it's as good as fresh. I read yesterday about sperm banks. Amazing what you can freeze these days and use a thousand years later. Fancy a woman in a thousand years' time being fertilized by semen from someone who has been dead a thousand years, the sperm coming miraculously alive inside her. Imagine if it has been crystallised. Or just take the DNA and crystallise that, which *is* possible. Could it then be sent across space and arrive there a million years after it set off, Matthew ... and still be used?'

'Yes ... theoretically. If there was someone to receive it!'

'Wow! I thought so. Perhaps that was the secret of the virgin birth. All that talk of the archangel Gabriel fertilizing Mary through her left ear. Crazy. It seems much more likely he was a Shining Being from Alpha Centauri, a *Khu* or *Ka* from another galaxy with a vial of frozen semen that he melted and popped in her body while she was asleep. What do you think, Matthew? The holy ghost in the left ear theory or artificial insemination by frozen semen?'

'Neither sounds as much fun as the real thing!'

'Bravo, Matthew,' chirped Cindy. 'Exactly. George has millions of theories about life starting from clouds of viruses and DNA flying through space. I keep telling her it's a frigid kind of theory, smacking of sexual masochism and perversion, but she doesn't admit it. It's hard enough to get the real thing together, goddammit! All the dressing up, getting drunk, telling lies. It's hard enough these days to enjoy it at all, without having to imagine crystals of DNA winging their way in and creeping up on you, fast asleep. How did we get onto this anyway?'

'Your story!' Georgina said coldly.

'Oh yes. Wait 'til my novel sees the light of day, it will change people's attitudes to sex forever, or put them *off* it forever and wipe out the entire human race!' They all laughed. But then the two girls became serious again and Cindy asked Matthew again, 'Meanwhile, what do we do about finding John?'

Silence. They looked at Georgina. 'It's up to Matthew, he has the man's mind, and the key to the car. The technology! We are just two dumb women. What do you suggest, Matthew?' she murmured seductively.

Matthew returned to his impersonation of Bogart but it didn't impress them much. 'I know,' said Cindy, 'like us, you haven't the foggiest idea where to start.'

'Well, I don't have many facts, do I? Be fair! I'm not used to looking for someone who has either literally disappeared into thin air, or is on an irreversible LSD trip. All I know is that he spent all his time beachcombing or meditating in a sacred copse ... trying to make direct contact with an Egyptian priest called Amen-aten or -hotep or something, an extra terrestrial intelligence. Not really my territory, let's face it!'

The two girls looked rueful. Cindy continued, 'We've been through all his things. He was a professional. He even erased the name on his toothbrush in case we worked out where he bought it. Once a smuggler always a smuggler. There's a lump of grey stone and nothing else. His books, of course, as fine a collection of mysticism and pseudo-science as you'd find anywhere. Mostly Egyptology.'

Silence.

'Well, Matthew,' Cindy continued, 'George and I were discussing the whole thing while you were away and came to a very clear decision. I think you've come to a similar conclusion yourself by the look on your face. You look as if you are drowning, by the way,' she said very seriously.

'Oh really? Thanks. I was hoping I looked like Humphrey Bogart!'

'Well, if you do, the *African Queen* has sunk and you're going down with it!' said Georgina and they all laughed.

'What was your conclusion?' asked Matthew, full of

trepidation. What was the trick this time?

'We decided the best thing, the cleverest strategy, is to do absolutely nothing! We haven't a hope in hell of finding him anyway. It was a crazy idea of mine that we might find his body lying on the rocks. He was always falling to pieces and I got used to putting him together again. Just like Isis. But this time he's gone. If he can come back and wants to, he will. So you're off the hook in that respect. Just relax and have a holiday. I've decided not to think of John or talk of him, so no more mention of him. He no longer exists. I don't want to hear his name or think of him. Okay? All agreed?'

'Agreed!' said Georgina, with a touch of sadness. She was certain he was still alive. She could feel him close, as if some part of him was still inside her ...

Later Matthew told them he'd need to go into town to get a few things, if he was to stay a few days. 'Good, there's shopping for the house to be done ... and something I'd like ... a big surprise!' Cindy added somewhat slyly.

'What?' asked Georgina suspiciously.

'Oh ... just some caviar and champagne. I'll pay for it. We must celebrate! I've just had a great new idea for my novel. Today I solved a problem that was blocking me something rotten. Now I can forge ahead. So it's caviar and champagne. Okay, Matthew, if I give you the cash?'

'Okay by me!'

'It's a deal!' said Cindy.

Matthew wandered into the garden and gazed towards the sea. He had an unexpected intimation that John was still close. He would explore the cliffs the next day, more carefully, without telling the girls. Yes. He was sure John was close by. He didn't know why. Dead or alive ...

Meanwhile he'd keep an eye on the girls. Caviar and champagne? They were obviously serious about something ...

∇

FIVE

"What appears to be a stable, tangible, visible, audible world, said physicist David Bohm, is an illusion. It is dynamic, kaleidoscopic – not really "there". What we normally see is the explicit, or unfolded, order of things, rather like watching a movie. But there is another underlying order and father to this second-generation reality."

"The Holographic Paradigm and Other Paradoxes."
Marylin Ferguson

△

On returning to his room, Matthew felt so strange he flopped on his bed, heavy as lead. Was the paralysis taking over his whole body now? His eyes refusing to stay open, he immediately started to fall, the outline of his body expanding away from the centre as he became smaller and smaller inside the huge space opening up. He wanted to shout but there were no words in his throat. No throat. Suddenly, his thinking seemed to lift off, detach itself from his body; he was looking down at it from a vantage point just above his forehead. There he was asleep, or dead, he wasn't sure. Yet he felt calm now that the expanding had stopped. He squeezed his hands together and bent back his toes and he saw it happening. Or was it a screen, a film? He felt sure the image was about to freeze. What would that mean? A mere photograph? As soon as he gave up expecting an answer to the questions, within seconds, he fell into a deep sleep, confronting the dream that had started unfolding, from the underlying order, into his hovering brainwaves ...

Inside his diamond is a young girl, lying on a glass sarcophagus; apparently she's just died and her body is still warm. He ought to be feeling sadness, but he's feeling a painfully urgent sexual desire for her. As he tries to move forward, compelled by the image of opening her legs, on his knees in front of her, kissing her to make her really moist ... he is aware that someone else is there with him. Each time he turns to see who it is, the other man moves and he can never register his presence; but he knows he is there; threatening him ... preparing to strike.

Trying to escape the diamond, he flings himself hard at a

pale, translucent green square on one of the walls, which he assumes is a weak spot in the crystal's lattice structure. An agonizing pain pierces his forehead as the crystal wall shatters, but the strategy works and he finds himself outside, looking in. There, inside, is the man, naked; Matthew can't exactly see what he's doing, but he kneels down in front of the girl, after opening her legs, kissing her before standing up and apparently pushing into her ...

Crawling along the outside crystal wall Matthew finds himself slipping, and he trips over the roots of a tree; as he falls, looking up, he notices the branches entwined above, making a roof ... a perfect example of perpendicular Gothic. He looks back into the diamond; the girl is wet like a snake, entwining herself around the man; she's now wearing a green silk dress, cheap and vulgar, real kitsch, but he's never known a girl so wet before where he is touching her and he's never wanted a girl so much, even though he doesn't know who she is and doesn't care, she could easily be a whore he has paid for ... feeling himself sucked through a mirror as if it is the surface of a pool of water into which two stones have fallen, sucked deep down with her and into her, where it is very dark ... and he imagines himself dead inside her ... a serene pleasure if it wasn't for the shaft of searing incandescent light, seeping out of an optic fibre creeping under the door, into her body ... what does it hope to illuminate in that passageway, throbbing with the sound of wheels on steel and cold stone ... ?

Some time later Georgina came to call him for dinner and knocked quietly on the door. Silence. Louder. Nothing. Opening the door cautiously, she saw him lying inert, fully clothed on the bed, minus only his shoes and jacket. She whispered his name but he didn't react, touched his arm gently but he slept on. Then she noticed a red Chinese lacquered box on the bed-side table, its top half open, and inside, nestling in the folds of some dark red velvet, a dark shape. At first she thought it was some ghastly medical specimen wrapped in bandages, half-decayed and rotting, the sort of thing a scientist would carry about with him. Looking more closely, she saw the shape of the head inside the bandages, the beak and small claws tucked up to its breast.

The beak was curved, the talons sharp. Slowly it dawned on her - it was a mummified falcon from ancient Egypt!

Noticing the other box she opened it with much trepidation. Inside were the battered, sad looking *ushabti* figures. She whispered to the falcon or to herself, 'My goodness! Matthew is much more into Egyptology than I thought and only pretending to be so naive about it. But why is he lying?'She closed the box and looked again at Matthew, lying like a mummy himself, apparently in deep trance, almost dead. 'There is more to Matthew than I thought!'

Fearing he might really be dead she put her face down close to his and was relieved to feel his breath on her skin. Again she whispered, 'Matthew', but he slept on. She tip-toed out to find Cindy in the kitchen. 'Matthew is either in a coma or meditating, or if he's only asleep, it's the sleep of the dead. I can't wake him!'

'You can't wake him up? Did you hit him?'

'No, of course not, Cindy, he was looking too peaceful. Really! Come and see. He has a mummy up there.'

'A mummy! Are you crazy? What kind of mummy?'

'A falcon like the one I showed you in the Oxford museum.'

'He has one like that? Why?'

'How do I know? Come and see.'

They crept up to the bedroom and found Matthew still fast asleep as if in a tomb. In the half-dark, Georgina held Cindy's hand gently and pointed at the falcon, wrapped in its black swaddling clothes. Cindy peered down close to it and whistled a long, low note through her teeth ... a sound she had learnt at school to confuse owls into thinking she wanted to mate with them. It didn't seem to have the same effect on Matthew, though neither of them knew how the sound might have affected any dream he was dreaming ... he remained quite immobile. Georgina tried again to wake him by saying loudly and firmly, 'Matthew, it's dinner time. DINNER time! Time to wake up.'

But he didn't stir. Cindy continued, 'He's on drugs. He's taken a dose of something and it's knocked him out cold. I thought you said he was the straightest guy you'd ever met? He's only been here a day and now he's in deep trance with a mummified falcon for company, and he's the straightest guy you ever met?! I'd like to meet some of the others. He's another John!'

They both suppressed giggles with difficulty but Georgina insisted, 'Really, I thought he was utterly straight. I promise you. But there's more to him than I thought! I said there were too many coincidences. Why did he come into the museum at that moment? He must have been working with John!'

'Maybe .. what shall we do? It's unfair to wake him, but if he wakes later he may be angry, faced with a cold dinner and then staying awake all night which would be a bore for everybody.'

'Right! Watch! I know how to wake him,' Cindy chirped.

'Don't!'

'Don't what?'

'Don't hit him too hard. Do it gently. It isn't John you know!'

'I know ... but I've just had an idea. Be very quiet.' Cindy took the falcon out of its box and held it in her hands, stroked its head gently and, to Georgina's amazement, Matthew began to stir. She put her finger against the beak and pressed softly again, and slowly Matthew's arm rose until a finger touched his own nose. Cindy put her beautiful crimson lips next to the small face of the falcon and whispered, 'Matthew. It's Meritaten. Wake up!'

Slowly Matthew opened his eyes, propped himself on one arm, still more than half asleep and not yet noticing the two girls. Cindy put the falcon quietly into its box, before making some low growls as if announcing her presence to some animal on heat; she hissed, 'Matthew, it's us, Cindy and George, it's dinner time and the food is getting cold. Shall we put the light on?'

'Oh ... yes ... I didn't see you. How long have I been asleep? Yes, put the light on. Gosh! I was so tired. Felt almost dead. How sweet it must be to die!' He was slurring his words.

Cindy pressed the switch on a small table lamp and a weak greenish light revealed the two girls to Matthew's eyes, standing like two nurses gazing down at him. 'Goodness me. I must have slept for ages. Have I?'

'I'd say for at least five thousand years, if your friend is anything to go by!' said Cindy somewhat pointedly.

But he was still drowsy and didn't understand what she meant. He said it felt like it, because he was so hungry. 'Must be the sea air knocked me out. I'm famished. Don't worry, you go on down, I'll be with you in a couple of minutes. Strange dreams...!'

On the way downstairs Georgina asked Cindy why she'd thought of speaking to the mummified falcon. 'I don't know. It just came to me in a flash. It looked like a microphone, they come in a box in red velvet just like that. I've used them in the studio with John when we made the records together. Also it was the kind of thing John would do, always making unexpected connections to throw people off balance. It's his style, isn't it? It usually works with him, doesn't it?'

'Yes, it really worked. I saw it!'

'Maybe. Maybe he was just waking up.'

'Don't lie, you know it worked. He woke up immediately!'

'I don't know why, but we must find out. It could be important. He must be one of them; we must keep him here, he's part of the conspiracy. Someone sent him to us. It's obvious when you think of it, all the coincidences. He's the one to complete John's unfinished work. But maybe he was sent by the Russians!'

Georgina nodded her agreement. 'He's all we have, let's face it. Make sure he doesn't leave. It's up to you Cindy darling. It's time you entertained him, as only you know how! He'll respond. He'll stay. He can't be that straight after all!'

'I'll do my best,' she murmured. Then she smiled her press-conference smile. 'He likes movies, he said. Old movies. He sees them every week at that club. Well, let's make it a movie – it's time I got out all my gear, again, now that John has gone!!'

At dinner Matthew tried to get more information about John, between glasses of an excellent wine that had emerged from the cellar. He admitted he was disappointed John was into drugs and was clearly not the type of person he would normally take seriously. Cindy said it was an inevitable conclusion but she could do nothing about his prejudices, but John was an extremely serious and gifted person and considered his work to be a science, dangerous and unimaginably important. He was not a freak or a drop-out but the hardest-working person she had ever met in her life. He had had many friends in the universities with whom he had collaborated, and had been to America many times to confer with people there. He was secretive about the work because he was that kind of person and knew that outsiders would consider his theories crazy; but more important, he had evidence the CIA was investigating and persecuting a number of people involved. A couple had disappeared under mysterious circumstances, which could have been explained as political murder rather than unexpected events from elsewhere ... the official explanation given ... wherever *elsewhere* might be.

Matthew was getting more confused. Cindy seemed suddenly sad. 'And now he's disappeared as he warned us might happen, perhaps directly due to his dabbling with strange forces ... or, I'll be frank ... he may have just been kidnapped or bumped off. John had acquired some valuable data, and the Americans especially were keen to steal the results.' Suddenly she seemed impatient, regretting what she'd said - adding quickly that she didn't want to talk more about John and asking Matthew, instead, 'We know so little about you, tell us about your childhood!'

Happy to change the subject from the hideous sounding John, he told them he was an only son and his father had died when he was twelve; he'd won scholarships and been sent to a boarding school, then Cambridge, paid for by the government; and his mother was still alive ...

They immediately wanted to know all about her, as if she was part of the family, and were reproachful when he admitted he only saw her twice a year. 'Just like a selfish man! Can't appreciate how much a mother suffers. Men never become conscious of the pain of motherhood! Genetically incapable of it!'

'But I have neglected myself as much as her with my obsessive dedication to work!' he insisted. 'Look at me now, even now I feel guilty, thinking I should be in my laboratory finishing my work.'

'Yes, look at you now. Terrible! Here you are having a holiday, being a guest of our hospitality and wasting your time with two most difficult girls,' Georgina replied, obviously with relish, as if she was proud to have dragged him away from his stuffy work, and delighted he was feeling guilty already.

'Yes, it's all your fault,' said Matthew, good humouredly.

'You *are* free to leave, Matthew, at any time you like, aren't you?' Cindy said with a touch of irony in her voice. She could say it now, knowing he would soon decide to stay.

'Yes, I can, but as you said, it won't do any harm to relax for a few days. Waiting for the flash of inspiration!' he said with a wry smile.

Cindy promptly stood up and proposed an after-dinner drink in the drawing room. She took Matthew by the hand into a large, elegant room at the front of the house, that he'd not seen yet. He was impressed to see a large selection of drink in the cocktail cabinet. He accepted a Drambuie, saying John enjoyed a style of living he found most agreeable!

The girls sat next to each other on a large maroon sofa and drank their liqueurs sip by sip like two elderly spinsters. There was an awkward silence for some minutes before Matthew questioned Georgina about her background. He said his first impression had been she was a Gypsy...

'Probably I am! My mother always called my father Tam O'Shanter whenever he was drunk, but she would never tell me why. One day I discovered the story; it's a folk-story about a Gypsy encampment and a dance, and Tam shouts out "Well done, Cutty Sark", because he has fallen madly in love with the Gypsy girl who is dancing wildly in front of everyone, half naked. Then the Gypsies chase him off because he shouldn't have been watching their secret rite. I asked my mother more about it but she was always very secretive about her past. "We met at a local dance!" she'd say coyly but I knew she was lying. Her refusal to talk about her past was either because she'd been very unhappy or felt guilty about something. You see my mother taught me only one thing really. Never to tell the truth. She had this single all-abiding idea that to be a woman you have to hide behind a mask. You have to tell lies. She would say, "There is no man alive who can accept the truth about a woman, the inner truth about her fears and emotions and dreams. No man wants the truth, it's too shattering and frightening. Women's fantasies are always subversive. Men prefer a mask of comforting lies ... so never lay your cards on the table, never ... even the Tarot pack! Or you will lose him. If you want to get rid of a man tell him your erotic dreams. He will leave you immediately."'

Cindy interrupted, 'George is not a practising Gypsy!'

But Georgina wasn't listening. 'I guess mother had awful dreams. But we can't escape our dreams, which are our fate. The only authentic things are our lies, she'd say; accept them, be amused by them and you'll be fine, you'll survive. Especially where women are concerned. I know. I'm almost one myself!'

'That's very bleak!' said Matthew, sadly.

'Why? Better than conning yourself and being conned. Mother was right, Gypsy or no Gypsy. Just now, with you, I took a risk. I told you the truth about women's strategies. What was your reaction? Doubt? I'd say fear! Men are afraid of women's truth. If we lie you will love us, if we tell the truth, you run a mile, like Tam O'Shanter running for his life with his trousers falling down. Well done, Cutty Sark!'

'Well I may have felt apprehension ... not quite fear!'

'Fear! How can a man not be afraid if a woman says the only thing to believe is lies. Maya the goddess of illusion, the face of Medusa? The goddess bathing. Everything to fear, I promise you; the truth of women is awesome and terrifying, especially their sexuality, in all its pagan irrationality. I should know about that. Why do you think they call me George?'

Georgina's outburst rendered Cindy and Matthew silent. He felt quite battered. They sipped their liqueurs quietly. Suddenly Georgina burst out laughing, stood up and started hugging her sides as if they hurt from her laughing.

'Matthew, please forgive us! We *are* hopeless, aren't we? I never heard two more depressing women in all my life and I'm one of them. Matthew, we're not like this all the time. Please forgive us? We're both sad because of John, and it makes us talk about things that should remain hidden ... please forgive us. I'm going to make some camomile tea. Who's for camomile tea?'

'Me!' said Cindy, looking down at the floor, wondering why George had said "we". She was doing her best not to be sad. George was like that though, when it came to women. All embracing.

'I've never had it but I'm willing to try!'' said Matthew.

But Cindy suddenly seemed to burst into tears, or made a very good act of doing so, excused herself and left the room.

Georgina shrugged her shoulders. 'And then there were two! I'll take her tea upstairs. She's trying to be brave and put on a hard front. John's disappearance has shocked her more than she admits. It's worse because he warned her. It makes it so much more ominous. She knows he's in real trouble. He was an extremely gentle, soft, quiet person ... a saint really. He loved Cindy very much. I don't know about her, she can't love anyone, but she needed him, needed to depend on him, needed to think he loved her. He's the only person she is real with. She's not just lost him, she's lost herself. He was the key she used to unlock the secret box inside herself, which is why his loss is hurting her so much. He was the key she used to reach herself.'

'I think he'll turn up ... out of the blue ... all smiles!'

'Let's hope so. He was loyal to her, which makes me think he *is* in real trouble. I think he flipped, not "out", but "into" something. Cindy feels he has "gone forever" ... and so has to cling to her mask, the play, the dance. Now she will dance and dance forever like the girl in the red shoes unable to stop dancing ... acting as if she is having a marvellous time. What I said earlier about women and lies was careless. I was playing up to you, the man on the scene. What I described was the truth about her, not me at all really. I live in the no-man's land between the truth and lies, floating about in images and the past. She's desperate to escape the lies she uses to protect herself. There's a Della Robbia Angel behind the Debbie Harry mask and that's the girl I love. Cinderella who can go to the fantasy ball, have a sexy time, and return. You'll see. She has great talent. I'll get her to dance for you! But John's death might be the death of her too. I'm the only one who can save her. You see the problem?'

'Yes, I suppose so,' Matthew muttered, feeling utterly guilty for earlier deciding to abandon them.

'She has no-one else in the world except me, and I make mistakes. Will you promise to stay a few more days to help? I know you decided earlier to leave. I don't blame you. In your shoes, I'd walk away too. But please stay. The station rang today to say some new sculpture materials have arrived. I'll be able to start on a sculpture inspired by your work! I can see it clearly in my mind ... your crystal pyramid ... the shaft of green laser light ... the layers of living atoms, the layers of non-living atoms. I'll make you a beautiful sculpture; one day it might be worth a fortune ... so you can't leave now. After a couple of days I'll persuade her to give us the key to John's room ... the inner sanctum. Maybe you'll find a clue there, where we couldn't. Maybe your scientific brain will be useful after all, to see the grain of truth in all the rocks and books and files of data ... and the work he left encoded on computer discs. But he was not the LSD king for nothing. He learnt to leave few clues, except when he wanted to. For someone like you perhaps to understand? We are mere helpless girls, technologically illiterate!'

Matthew was intrigued at the idea of computer discs. He agreed to treat it all more seriously, unless it turned out to be too obviously a wild sheep chase.

'Good! I'll make that tea for Cindy and see if she's alright. See you soon.'

Left alone, Matthew was wondering, *Why* do I give in so easily when I know I ought to leave as soon as possible and get back to my work? But as he was waiting for Georgina's camomile tea, he suddenly had a novel idea about one of his equations, took out a small notebook he always kept in his inside pocket for such emergencies, and sketched out some figures suggesting a new placing for one of the constants, which he had called the Omeg factor. The move didn't seem to make much sense, but the image was pressing itself hard on him and he felt a small pang of excitement, either from the weird idea, which at least was worth a try, or knowing he needn't waste his time in Cornwall, the body of his work was still there, floating under the surface of his conscious mind. He lay back on the sofa, wondering about his shift of position for the Omeg constant, when, unexpectedly, he dozed off again.

He was woken up by Georgina. 'Here's your tea, Matthew. Are you alright? You keep falling asleep. Is it the Cornwall air, or the wine, or having to wait for us crazy girls? I'm sorry I've been so long.' She saw his notebook. 'You're working?'

Matthew asked her how long he'd been asleep and she told him she'd been with Cindy for over an hour, at least.

'I must have gone out like a light! Yes, I was working; just a random idea. Thinking about it now I'm sure it's irrelevant. How is Cindy? Still upset?'

'Very unhappy and confused, totally disorientated, almost delirious. She put up a good show but now she's cracked and I don't know which way the split is going. But we made a pact not to worry about John. We're so remote here, so our first reaction is always one of total gloom. We've agreed to use this moment outside time creatively. The house is paid for, there's money in the bank for bills and food, even if illegally acquired, so let's all work. I'll get my new gear tomorrow and Cindy is relaunching herself into her novel. I told her, "Stop feeling sorry for yourself. We'll look after you. Finish the fucking novel!" She's calmed down and got her files out ready for tomorrow. She knows I'll look after her, and she has the double security of knowing you're here; a man around the place!'

'In the background, so to speak,' Matthew said ironically.

'Well, yes, I suppose so, but you said you wanted to escape and relax so here you are. Anyway, with Cindy, you're safer in the background! I'd be grateful she has something to occupy her. She can be very, very demanding, I know from bitter experience, especially when she is floating, drifting, without too many things to cling to. Very demanding, and I don't mean *only* sexually!'

Matthew flinched. 'And you? Are you never demanding?'

'Not in the same way! I'm strong, as you know. You do know, don't you?' she said pouting a little.

'I have presumed so ... from meagre evidence.'

'I keep forgetting we hardly know each other. It's strange, I keep feeling I've known you for years. I wonder why?'

'No idea. Tell me.'

'Perhaps because we met on my mythological plane, on my "holographic plane", in a museum, house of the *Muses*! Meritaten. My Amarna sculptures and your mummified falcon. Yes, we saw it. Sweet! I felt you unconsciously connected with these things. The whole point of these artefacts is that they are archaic, archetypal, they are the ancestors in every magic sense. I love them because they speak to me of a huge, long, beautiful cycle of history ... a source of images and meaning, floating there to be drawn on, not just the boring and frightening superficial world of the here and now ... '

Matthew took her hand gently. She fascinated him when she spoke like this, her eyes sparkling with excitement and mischief. He was certain her so-called holographic plane was erotic as well as archetypal. He could see it in the way her whole body became alive as she spoke; her body was aroused, and it aroused him, even though her talking seemed above him, beyond him, ignoring him. He was too real. He wondered how he could become more unreal for her, so she would notice him more. He had no idea for the moment.

She continued, upset by Cindy's apparent breakdown. 'Whenever I see an Egyptian sculpture, I feel it was me who made it, three thousand years ago. I try to think of a person seeing my work in three thousand years time! Look, I've brought my portfolio of illustrations for my favourite love story, Isis and Osiris. Do you want to see them?'

'Of course!'

Georgina laid the portfolio on the couch and said wistfully, 'The goddess Isis copulating with the body of Osiris, the fragments all brought magically together, including the all-elusive phallus. This symbolises eating the Eucharist, of course, the sacred plant. Holy communion. The Soma!'

It was an extraordinary image, drawn with miniature precision, so finely coloured it looked printed; a mosaic, each colour having its own inner source of light, not so much reflecting light, but radiating it. 'How on earth do you make the colours shine like that?'

'It's a secret. I mix my oil paint with a special oil, then lacquer each fragment of colour. I use a magnifying glass. The lacquer has different thicknesses or slopes and produces that effect of inner light. In close-up it looks like millions of small eyes. Beautiful, isn't it?'

'It reminds me of stained glass windows. I thought you were a sculptress, you didn't tell me you painted as well!'

'I could always paint in two dimensions. But with sculpture, there's someone else inside me who has to use the material world, forcing me to work with glass and plastic and light. It's her world, her obsession. Sometimes I find a sculpture I did a year ago; someone sends a photo of it in a new surrounding ... and I don't recognise it! I suddenly feel empty and a little afraid, because it wasn't me who made it. I was used, by her, whoever she is; it scares me sometimes but I have to go along with it, being used. Cindy says it's the same with dancing. She feels used afterwards. Possessed. Wait 'til you see her dancing! Always Salomé, the temple prostitute!'

'I can't wait to see it!' he said, truthfully enough.

She smiled. 'You know, Cindy is the only thing I ever think of that isn't my work. She always drags me out of myself, which is why I love her, I suppose, love her and hate her! When she sucks me out of my work, I feel resentful. She makes me into a mother, a role I don't enjoy playing, but like a mother, I always forgive her. She's the only person I think I have ever loved. Ever. Apart from ... apart from...' She looked away, returning to the image in front of her, Isis hovering over the body of Osiris, as a falcon. She turned to the next page.

'Apart from?' Matthew asked, determined to draw her out.

'Parents! Ancestors. But Cindy... when we were at school, I was painting and doing costumes for her. Wow! You should see some of the costumes I made her, they'd put Mae West off her food for a month with envy. There was a boy in love with me, in his boring way. One day he called me an impotent lesbian, of no “use” to a man anyway. It hurt deeply of course. But then I thought about it. Why should I be of “use”? I'm not a lesbian at all. I just love Cindy! There's not another woman on the face of the earth I'd think twice about sleeping with. But Cindy! At times she hurts me terribly and I was jealous of John. But I'd sacrifice anything of myself for her. You know where the word "sacrifice" comes from?'

'No. Tell me.'

'*Sacro facere* ... to make sacred. She makes me sacred, because I sacrifice myself, give up things for her. Oh God, she's a pain in the neck most of the time. She has no concept of betrayal. But you'll see. She can be wonderful. Unreal. Magic. I'll tell you something to surprise you.'

'Tell me.'

'Her novel is brilliant. One day she was rejected by a woman teacher she was in love with, just a teenage passion, but very intense. It coincided with a film of Jean Harlow, as usual, being herself; betrayal, rejection, despair, suicide. From that moment Cindy became her, assumed her as a mask, announcing she would become an actress and from that moment on she got zero in everything except literature, at which she excelled. She's very clever really, just acts the dumb blonde. Someone will turn her novel into a film, with her in it, and she'll be famous. One of her favourite directors, like Josef von Sternberg. Except I think he's dead?'

'Of course! Tell me what it's about?'

'No, that would be betrayal. It's best she keeps it to herself. Every time you expose an idea to the outside world, it loses a bit of its numinosity, its lustre. It becomes familiar – which means "family – ised" of course. The worst fate of all. If she wants to tell you, she will. Do you want to see another image?'

'Yes, of course.'

'Here is the fragmented body of Osiris, embodied inside the tree ... the sacred tree of life. He was cut up and murdered and hidden inside a tree which grew up around him! Lovely idea. Out of the roots grew the sacred plant!'

She sat back while Matthew looked at the images illustrating her favourite love story. They all had the indefinable quality of miniature stained-glass windows, as if light was coming through them. He recognised the scenes; Isis with the phallus was the most mysterious. The phallus was translucent, made of crystal. But the most amazing image of all was the birth of Horus the falcon ... a beautiful white falcon with outstretched wings and huge, magical turquoise blue-green eyes, whose feathers seemed like a million smaller eyes ... emerging from his golden egg.

She saw he was mesmerised; 'I like the eyes ... my favourite colour, manganese blue! The scene really depicts the opening of the third eye, the ability to really *see,* become the visionary.'

The image seemed to be vibrating, coming alive, it was so realistically painted, but surrealistic too. He mentioned this.

'The surreal is the truth. What we call real is the illusion!'

Almost painfully, he started to recall his recent dreams, and he was quiet for some time, trying to recall them clearly with the rational side of his mind. The body on the sarcophagus, but it had been a girl. The tomb but it was a copse. He was interrupted by Georgina apologising for boring him. 'No, no, of course not ... ' he insisted. The visions were resonating with images in his memory as well as from the dreams, the two sets of images superimposed, a mess of blurred waves. He was feeling dizzy, almost faint. He quickly closed the folder.

'Just bits of paper with a few colours and shapes on, recalling the world of childhood memory ... doodlings of a child really!' she murmured.

'A somewhat sophisticated child!'

She stood up to leave him. He wanted to say *don't leave me, not now*– but he couldn't. He felt close to losing control, losing consciousness again. She kissed him lightly on the cheek. Closing his eyes to hide his emotion, he wanted to reach out to her but couldn't, she had made it so clear not to. But she liked disturbing men with memories they tried to forget, stirred up by images like hers, recalling fragmented primal scenes ...

The following morning they all drove into town; the girls went shopping and Matthew bought a few things he needed. He found a local paper and went for coffee. The front-page story described a shipwreck near Land's End, an abandoned boat with a ton of hashish from Morocco. No bodies had been found; a “mystery”. The boat was owned by a fictitious Mr. John Templeton who “did not exist” but nevertheless “lived in Liverpool”.

Matthew marked the article with his pen, intending to ask Cindy if Templeton happened to mean anything. More dramatic local news. A local woman, a fervent astrologer, had seen a vision of a man dressed as an eighteenth century smuggler while “divining for gold” near a tin-mine. Matthew decided this must also be John, in his other holographic aspect, with a swag bag full of Lebanese gold. The plot was thickening.

The girls were waiting at the car and seemed to be talking secretly and he was certain they changed the subject as soon as they saw him, greeting him instead like jolly schoolgirls playing truant. Cindy remarked she hoped he'd not been chatting up the local whores. They were sitting on a supermarket trolley loaded with food and became almost hysterical as Matthew filled the car with bag after bag of food and household goods. He started to laugh too. It seemed to be the funniest thing they'd seen in their lives. 'Modern life is not without its references to the world of myth, I hope you notice Matthew. Look at the large box of *Ariel*!' said Georgina. 'We noticed your socks last night when you were out cold, and they had a tang of the underworld about them. We divined you were in need of care and attention, so tomorrow is laundry day!'

Matthew took another walk that afternoon, hoping he might find John's body at the bottom of the cliffs, dressed as a pirate, having fallen off the boat while being chased by coastguards. At least the mystery would be solved. But he saw nothing. When he got back to the house, it had become quite cold and almost dark. He found Cindy putting the final touches to an instant dinner.

'Oh, good! I'll go and call George, unless you want to?'

'Yes, I'll go.' Matthew went to her studio and knocked on the window, calling her name. The door was at the end of the building behind some ominous-looking rose bushes, generous with thorns and very mean with blooms. He preferred not to venture too close to them in the dark. But she didn't reply, so he knocked and called out loudly, 'Georgina, are you there?'

She called him from somewhere in the garden. 'I'm over here! What is it? Dinner time?'

'Yes, where are you?'

'Under my tree.'

'Where's that?'

'Not telling you. Wait there. I'll be with you in a minute.'

He heard her pushing through some bushes and eventually she came into view, dimly illuminated by the light from the windows of her studio. She was wearing almost nothing; it looked like a white Victorian lace nightdress.

'Aren't you frozen?'

'Yes. Absolutely.'

'Why didn't you wear a coat?'

'Why should I? I want to be frozen, it's so stimulating. You should try it. You let your body go numb and dead and your mind is free to fly and soar like a bird. It's an old shaman's trick. It's like an egg, Matthew. A bird doesn't sit *on* an egg but *next to* it. The egg draws all its warmth and life from one small, small point of contact. That's what I like. I sit next to my tree and I tell myself I am an egg. My body goes numb on the outside but inside I can feel the warmth from the sap of the tree, entering me from a pin's point of touch between us ... as we touch everything in the universe, the small things and the large, if only we admitted it ... from one small point we know the whole. The principle of the hologram and the way our minds work ... we can even know how many angels are dancing there in all that space if we just listen.'

He was almost angry now. He considered that kind of talk pretty much nonsense. 'How long have you been there?'

'An hour or so. I don't know exactly.'

Matthew held out his hands and she put hers in his. They were frozen solid. She was only wearing a transparent white blouse and a thin white cotton skirt and probably nothing else, and no stockings on and bare feet.

'You're crazy. One day you'll go too far and fall asleep and we'll find you dead in the morning, curled up like a hedgehog.'

'Not a hedgehog, maybe a porcupine. Give me credit for becoming something exotic, in my next incarnation!'

'There aren't porcupines in this part of the world.'

'Oh, good, that means I'll not be dying here after all. No porcupines!' She laughed and drew Matthew towards her.

'Put your arms round me. Hug me. I'm not spiky like a porcupine. Tell me I'm just an egg. Think of me as pure and perfect like an egg. Hold me tight and make me warm ... let me draw my warmth from you, like from my tree!' Matthew put his arms round her and she pushed herself against his body. 'That's nice. Don't move. Just stay like that until I am really warm ... a humus-man in a tree like Osiris!'

He held her tightly and felt her body judder and shudder with cold and with the sudden shock of being against his warmth. She put her face against his neck and her hair smelt strongly of the ground, of earth, of pine needles, of humus. He kissed her hair, gently.

He had no idea how many minutes they stood so close together, before he noticed that, almost imperceptibly, Georgina was sobbing ... shallow, hidden whorls of sorrow that reminded him of his feelings for Meritaten, knowing the rest of her body had either not been sculpted or had been lost. He tried not to show Georgina he was aware of her crying, held her tightly, pressed his face deeply into the Spanish moss of her hair.

Then he remembered an image ... tall girls in white, almost naked, standing like statues at night. Steel columns that were as cold as trees. He became uneasy, because he felt sure, suddenly, that Georgina was in some way trying to communicate with John, next to her tree, half-naked. He remembered she had said she liked railway stations at night, like a holograph of a Delvaux painting of John's. He felt certain she had seen John at the station before she left. Had she told him this? Perhaps. He felt strangely jealous, and uncomfortable with himself, knowing he was starting to hate John, more and more ...

Suddenly Cindy's voice ripped into their idyll and they both jumped, her shout whipping around their frozen ears.

'Where the hell are you, you two? What's happening?

Dinner will be stone cold if you don't come soon.'

'Coming!' Georgina shouted as she gently separated from Matthew. 'We were enjoying the night air!' As she swayed away from him, their hands lingered, holding on to touching each other, reluctant to break. When they did he felt almost a pain ... and having been told he must be like her tree, he wondered suddenly if a tree felt sorrow in the autumn when its leaves fell away, like moulting feathers.

'Well you'd better come now before my instant dinner becomes instant charcoal.' Cindy looked at them suspiciously. 'The night air clearly resembles the inside of a deep freeze. Take care or you'll go too far, my dear girl!' She shot a glance towards Matthew that would have melted a glacier, so he sat down quickly at the table and made a comment about how appetizing the dinner looked, which was not entirely convincing.

'Well, it's all we're having tonight Matthew, so eat up and be merry. At least the wine is good!'

Matthew poured the wine, and Georgina drank a whole glass immediately and then drank Matthew's as well, and smiled sweetly when he filled their two glasses again. 'You've no idea how beautiful a glass of wine tastes when you're freezing to death! That's what the nectar of immortality must have tasted like to those nymphs who spent all their time swimming around freezing pools. Nothing like extremes of self-denial to make you enjoy the fruits of sin ... say I.'

'Says you! Take no notice of her, Matthew. Eat your dinner. When George starts waxing mythological, there's no stopping her. She never makes sense. That's the difference between she and I. All her references are to myths and ancient gods and goddesses, nymphs and satyrs – in a word, the past. All *my* references are utterly real. Real movies! All that matters, let's face it! Or even *inter*face it. Characters from literature, plays, movies, real people you might meet in a café or see in a street kissing a stranger!'

The two girls argued about the difference in their philosophies, whether character was determined by having your consciousness dominated by the right or the left hemisphere of the brain. Each claimed their images were the authentic ones. Matthew pulled a face. Suddenly they changed to talking about tinned food and the merits of fresh vegetables. They promised Matthew that when the period of stress was over, they'd go to the real market and buy everything fresh and eat like Gypsies instead of "socially deprived waifs in a Liverpool slum!" as Cindy phrased it.

'Tell us more about your work, Matthew,' Cindy asked, but then apparently choking, blurted out 'No! That's a crap question. Tell me why you have a mummified falcon next to your bed?'

'Er ... I bought it at a country auction. I'd just discovered the Egyptian collection at the Fitzwilliam and bought some *ushabti* figures on the spur of the moment, just before I came here.'

Cindy looked cynical. 'Why did you bring them here?'

'To show Georgina.'

'Is that all?'

'Not quite ... from the moment I bought them, I felt an attachment to them. They're peaceful. They resonate, to use your language!'

Cindy smiled and seemed pleased. 'John would agree with you entirely, but he'd go the whole way and wire them up psychically ... he knew how ... and use them to communicate with their spirits!' There was silence and she knew she ought not to have referred to John at that moment.

They finished the meal with scarcely another word, each of them brooding reluctant thoughts, all thinking about the missing John, a mere pinpoint of touching like the body and an egg ... displaying in their minds a different image of the missing man whose presence seemed all the more mysteriously tangible because of his absence, Matthew seeing a charlatan, Cindy feeling resentment for his doing the experiment without her and almost glad something had gone wrong, Georgina trying to erase an image from her mind, in case Cindy picked up on it, with her mediumistic skills ... the image of her surrender, her submission to John's power, in the copse, on that fateful day ...

The following morning Georgina told Matthew that Cindy was

very depressed and wouldn't be showing herself all day. He'd heard them together most of the night. He'd been sleeping badly himself and each time he woke up he could hear them in the main bedroom, talking, giggling, listening to music.

After breakfast, Georgina excused herself and said she was going to work in her studio. Matthew could see she was very tired and seemed to be avoiding looking him directly in the eye; or he was too eagerly seeking some sign that the tenderness they had enjoyed together in the garden had not been taken for granted, or worse still, totally forgotten.

So he went to his room to work too. The new idea he'd thought of the previous day had haunted his sleeplessness all night. He worked for a while, restructuring figurations of data.

Later he heard Georgina on the 'phone talking excitedly. She came to his room. 'I'm so excited! I've been trying for ages to get permission to photograph the Amarna Collection in the Petrie Egyptology Museum at University College. They've refused consistently, but my friend in Cambridge has connections and has got me permission! There's a deal. The museum is about to be totally refurbished and everything has to be packed away and stored. The work starts in a weeks' time. The deal is they have a print of everything I photograph for reference. Mind you, they'd die a thousand deaths if they knew my pet theory, that Nefertiti was the ruler at the time and not Akhenaten. I kept that to myself! Sometimes, in her name cartouche, she is referred to as Pharaoh. What a revelation, the entire Amarna revolution, the poems, the sculptures, the monotheism, were not the creation of Akhenaten, but of his wife Nefertiti! Her exquisite, divine death mask is in the museum. They'll pay for their prints and give permission for me to use them in my book. But I have to work immediately. It means leaving now and being away a few days ...'

Matthew immediately felt the pang he always felt when she was about to leave him. 'No problem, I'll come with you! I need to go to Cambridge to print out my last results; then I could bring them here. I might even bring my computer!'

'Really, that's fantastic! But what about Cindy?'

Matthew said it was up to *her* to solve any problems with

Cindy. She went off to her studio saying she'd try, later ...

He thought about the trip. Maybe he might not come back at all. After all, he'd only come to help out for a few days because John had disappeared, and overnight he'd been chosen by Cindy to be "the one privileged to complete" John's crazy work! His best strategy was to appear to be cooperative, but not come back from Cambridge at all, even to help Georgina. He could contact her later.

After a while she returned. 'Cindy says it all sounds fine, but once you're in Cambridge you'll create one pretext or another and not return to Cornwall which means we'd have to find someone else and this depresses her terribly. She says she has grown awfully fond of you already and would feel very hurt if you escaped. Those were her words, so you see, I tell you the truth despite myself. She's right, no?'

Matthew felt very annoyed as well as guilty, having his private thoughts brought into the open. They were always one step ahead of him, which irritated him but fascinated him at the same time. 'Did she say why I wouldn't come back?'

'No. But she sees you as the only person who could understand John's work, and carry it on. It's your destiny and one day you'll be grateful for it.'

'Oh does she really?' Matthew said sarcastically, which Georgina preferred not to notice.

'Yes. I know it's a bit crazy, but she's very certain of it and I'll tell you this. Cindy is maybe a bit mad but madness is not what people think it is. It cuts you off from normal talk and social contact and you become an outcast, a pariah, yes, but it gives you access to modes of insight that sane and rational people don't bother with, and these other modes, ironically enough, give her powers of clairvoyance and prophecy. She knows people's ideas and motivations, sees them as if they were made of glass, like my sculpture of course. You see why I love her! If she's absolutely sure about something, she's ninety-nine per cent right. Accept it or not but she says you will complete John's work ... and, with it, you will make a major discovery. Can't you trust her?'

Matthew thought it was a preposterous idea to trust her, or either of them, after all their talk about lies being the only truth – their kind of truth anyway. But nevertheless he said, 'I don't feel as much trust for her as for you, I'll be honest. Let's face it, I don't have the least contact with Cindy. All we do is talk over cups of tea and meals and I never feel she is really being herself. I see only the mask. Don't I?'

'Don't let that worry you. That's my experience of her after ten years! But suddenly she slips off the mask and becomes herself and she'll do something crazy, like an amazing dance. Oh, Matthew, if you can ever see her dance. That's it! Tonight! I'll get her to dance for us on our last evening. If she dances for you, you *will* return. You will see the real Cindy in her dance. Never expect Cindy to be rational! What is the rational but arrogance masking insecurity, like Christianity. Rationality doesn't exist, of course, it's just a necessary self-delusion for people who mistrust their inner self. Who needs knowledge when there's desire? She believes in dance and dreams! See the goddess bathing naked in the pool and you will never be the same again. What do you say?'

Georgina looked intensely into his eyes, her lips quivering with persuasion, her own eyes bright with excitement at the thought of making an arrangement between them both, and Matthew felt a sudden pang of desire for her. She had become utterly sensual, exuding sexuality, despite clearly trying to sell him Cindy. It was decidedly confusing.

'You'd make a great theatrical agent! If I was a film director I'd be signing the contract here and now without ever seeing her!'

She looked very surprised. Eyes wide like a child. She had *become* a child. 'Really? You would? Splendid! Well, that ... that Matthew, is what you must be. A film director. You said it! I'll tell her that secretly you're a frustrated film director. You always wanted to make a film about a dancing girl. How about Salomé? Yes. Salomé ... the original temple dancing girl. You're planning to make a film of Salomé. That's it. We've got it. Cindy!' she called out loud. 'Come down here, there's someone I want you to meet.'

Matthew felt like shouting out *NO! – CUT!* but before he could say a word, Cindy shouted back. 'Who is it?'

Georgina went to the bottom of the stairs; 'It's Josef von

Sternberg, he just dropped by. He's casting a new movie and wants to talk to you about the lead part!'

Cindy's door opened and half speaking, half singing, she shouted back, 'Are you crazy, my darling ... Josef von Sternberg himself! Here and now!'

'Here and now in the flesh in the drawing room. He wants to meet you. He's very shy and doesn't talk much. Put on a negligée and come down!'

'I'll be right down. I'm already in my negligée, you fool. I'll put on some perfume!'

Georgina rushed back into the room, more excited than Matthew had ever seen her. He was recalling a recurring nightmare he'd had as a child. He'd been selected to play full-back for England in the rugby knock-out final against the All Blacks ... but no-one had told them he was only thirteen!

Georgina saw he was white as a sheet. 'Okay, just go along with it. Just nod. I'll do the talking. Talk in a broken German accent and agree with me you are making Salomé. You'll see ... this is the beginning we've been waiting for. What a flash of inspiration! If we can sustain the illusion, that is ... '

She rushed to the curtains and closed them, then turned on a couple of dim lights which made the room even more forbidding and ominous. She was clearly possessed. She rushed into the hall and returned with a flamboyant, multi-coloured scarf which she flung round his neck, and one of John's blue velvet hats that she planted on his head at a rakish angle. 'Goodness me, you*do* look the part. Who would have guessed? You know I think you really are a frustrated film director. Are you?'

'What man isn't?' he said boldly, but with more than a hint of terror in his voice. He could see there was no escaping Georgina's madness, but he was already half given to it. He sat quietly, looking at his feet, while she bobbed up and down around the room, arranging it. An instant set. He remembered her words about sacrifice ... *sacro facere*. Wasn't it some kind of privilege to be sacrificed? He'd already had some weird dreams imagining Cindy's erotic dance, so it was better he saw it for real and demystified her, freed himself from his tortured imaginings.

After what seemed an eternity of waiting, and dread, Matthew heard Georgina whisper, as if from some remote galaxy ... 'Here she comes! Your star!'

He could see her through the drawing room door, descending. She was floating down the stairs in slow motion, savouring every step. Over a purple negligée she had wrapped a long shocking-pink stole, matching her pink tights and pink patent leather high-heeled shoes, the heels of which were so high she looked more like a flamingo than a woman, her bright red lips adding mysteriously to the illusion. Her eyes were focused on infinity, and yet seemed mournful to have settled for a distance so mathematically accountable.

'Ah, Cindy ... I would like you to meet Herr von Sternberg,' Georgina announced severely. 'He has come a long way to see you. He saw the film you made in Chicago ... the only place where it wasn't banned for its lurid sex scenes ... and has been dying to meet you ever since.'

Cindy wafted towards Matthew and held out her hand for it to be kissed. He sensed immediately that she and Georgina were no longer aware of his presence. They were acting entirely for each other and he had become little more than a stone statue, to be put to good use by two temple dancing girls enjoying themselves on a wet afternoon, and this observation made him feel curiously comfortable. If they were so unaware of his presence, engulfed entirely in their charade, they'd not see how utterly embarrassed he was.

He rose awkwardly to the occasion, flamboyantly kissing her outstretched hand, now savage with rings of every size and colour, and he was amazed at the power he had summoned up from unknown recesses to accept the illusion and act in the play, as if such play-acting was second nature to him.

Cindy sat down, crossing her legs in such a tantalising way that Matthew was sure he noticed ... the image flashed across his mind in a fraction of a second ... that she was wearing nothing above her stockings. That was not what he had expected to see, so soon. He felt a surge of blood rising to his face and for a moment he wasn't sure if he could sustain the illusion of detachment any longer. But Cindy's eyes were still so absent that he somehow felt he needn't feel embarrassed at all. Really he was quite alone. Georgina was far away, in rapture, absorbing the spectacle of Cindy ... one of her moving sculptures.

'Herr ffon Sternberg has acquired a script based on the story of Salomé, a modern version, how can I put it, set in a brothel in Nazi Germany during the war, but a very serious script and he intends to make a very expensive and important film. He wonders if you would consider auditioning for the part. He knows your reputation and your work and feels embarrassed to have to ask you to audition for him at all, but that is why he has come alone, without agents and hustlers and photographers. He understands you will need the afternoon to prepare, and tomorrow he must fly back to Hollywood. He wonders if this evening, after dinner ... he will take us out to a meal of course, a champagne dinner in the town ... then he will explain the film. He will act the part, so to speak, of Herod ... suitably brought up to date of course ... and he hopes you will dance an impromptu version for him of Salomé's legendary dance ... in whatever version or inspiration you think of.'

Matthew was surprised that Georgina was so convincing; presumably they'd done this kind of thing before. But he was pleasantly surprised to find himself feeling really quite excited, despite himself. Cindy seemed to sense the end of a reel was imminent, so she prepared to make an exit, not wanting to be cut in mid-movement. She held out her hand for it to be kissed again and looking straight through him, in a husky voice, she murmured, 'It will be my pleeeaasure, Herr Josef. I am not eating today so we can forego your generous offer of dinner, but I will be honoured indeed to dance for you. Tonight! Auf wiedersehen!'

She turned and glided back up the pine staircase, a montage of erotic stills, as if on each stair a part of her costume was torn off by Matthew's imagination until the whole sequence gelled into a post-modernist painting, *Nude ascending a Busby Berkeley staircase*, perhaps in holographic union with Marcel Duchamp's *The Bride stripped bare by her bachelors, even ... the Large Glass*. Distracted, Matthew tried to recall what gel meant precisely, something like "a semi-rigid jelly-like colloid in which a liquid is dispersed in a solid" and it seemed appropriate. His knees had certainly turned into just that.

Georgina came to Matthew and gave him a hug. 'You were marvellous. Didn't put a foot wrong. You're a perfect actor! You immediately became Josef von Sternberg, with a leaning towards the hidden mysticism of the Nazis of course. That's it! The film is really to be about the Nazi Solar Cult, the whole Hitler thing with astrology and magic, the Cabbala, the secret cult of Thule! She will love that. Come to think of it, Matthew, rather a good idea for a film, the whole Salomé thing updated into the secret Solar Cult and rites of the Nazis, John the Baptist, the prophet of the monotheistic reborn Christ? The Second Coming! Of Salomé. She deserved a second chance didn't she, even if two thousand years later? What do you think?' She was in a trance.

'I've no idea what you're talking about; it's rubbish! You're sending me up! I think I'll make some tea and a sandwich instead and go to bed. What will you do for supper?'

She took no notice of his doubts. 'Food? Ah, the comforts of secret eating instead of sex! It will be a part of the act, don't worry. We already have everything. Even some cheap red caviar from Denmark. Just tell her it is from Iran, that you were given it personally by the sister of the Shah, and she'll go along with it. Okay? Let yourself go. Just say the first thing that comes into your head, it's always right ... and do the first thing you want to do. That was John's philosophy. It always worked. Game?'

'Set and match!' But he was looking so up-tight she put her arms round him and held him tightly, as she'd done in the garden. Suddenly she spoke in her normal voice again, softly, 'I'm scared too, Matthew. What will I do ... what will she do ... if it flops, if she is mortally bad? She doesn't get the part and you leave in disgust? She might even kill herself!'

'Don't say that, for God's sake! Surely it's just a charade, some fun? Just an evening's entertainment?' he murmured, dreading the thought his rejection of her act of theatre might kill her. It seemed a bit drastic.

Georgina smiled, 'Oh you! You fool! You see yourself so wrongly, your head always in the clouds, in the rarefied air of crystals and physics and mathematics and science. But I see you in a different light. I see your feet still, feet of clay, in that dingy museum basement, those clumsy feet of yours starting on your long unknowing, blind pilgrimage to find the spirit of Meritaten. And in a week, here you are with two crazy girls, two lunatics ... both of whom feel you are necessary to them. Aren't you flattered, Doctor Sutherland?'

Matthew looked away from her, before replying almost inaudibly, 'Yes I am, Georgina ... very flattered.' It was the truth, or part of it, and he added, less confidently, 'Go and prepare your theatre and your star. I won't let you down. I'll tell myself I'm Josef von Sternberg and I'm in a German brothel and I'm really Herod and I'm in a temple of Isis, everything all at once! But I'd better be very drunk. I'll enjoy myself. Promise. You can trust me. But I'll have to be drunk.'

'I know you can do it. Yes! Because you are simple, direct, not devious like us, like everyone we ever knew, Cindy and I. You are honest and always tell the truth. But we're going to enjoy ourselves anyway, good or bad, like two naughty girls playing hospitals, except you are not a real doctor but a film director who will dissect us and judge us. Be stern, of course, and harsh and fierce. Nothing meek and humble tonight. You have the whip tonight, so use it. You'll have to imagine the jackboots ... and remember, as Sylvia Plath said, "Every woman loves a fascist!" Here, with us, you have the living proof! What more do you want? See you later ... '

She kissed him gently on the lips, looked into his eyes searchingly, before whispering, as if to herself, 'I'll try not to be too jealous! But we can be fascists together. No? Just give orders and Cindy will do anything! And if she's naughty I will punish her ... when she comes to me afterwards ... '

▽

SIX

"As for the Robes, those of Isis are variegated in their colours: for her power is concerned with matter which becomes everything and receives everything, light and darkness, day and night, fire and water, life and death, beginning and end. But the robe of Osiris has no shading or variety in its colour, but only one single colour like to Light. For the beginning is combined with nothing else, and that which is primary and conceptual is without admixture: wherefore they have taken off the robe of Osiris, they lay it away and guard it, unseen and untouched. But the apperception of the conceptual, the pure, and the simple, shining through the soul like a flash of lightning, affords an opportunity to touch and see it but once."

"Isis and Osiris"
Plutarch
Ψ

Matthew went to his room, his mind full of lurid and exotic images of disaster. His idea of a visit to the theatre was clearly quite different from the girls: quite happy to be anonymous, a grey face in a sea of other grey faces in a numbered seat which he had paid for, and no further responsibilities implied. The *performance* was for those bold enough to strut on the stage ... but clearly there was no escape. He had carelessly allowed them to slip open the door to the magic theatre, about which he had only read, and often dreamed ...

Georgina went to her studio to prepare the decor, trying not to recall too many sensual images of Cindy, stripped and in action ... they aroused her too much. But she was sad, remembering John and missing him, dreading the previous poignant dramas that might be forcefully recalled, watching Cindy and Matthew together. Would she be able to handle it? She wanted desperately to communicate with John, as she felt Cindy could do, and she could feel him close by. So when she returned to the darkened drawing room to arrange the decor for Cindy's dance, she lay down on John's favourite carpet, where he used to meditate, and closed her eyes. Quite soon she was meditating too, in the way he taught her, to see if she could reach him, open herself up to his consciousness, wherever he might be, in case he was trying to reach her ...

Matthew was dozing and was apparently dreaming ...

A dark room, partially underground. From a small window high up in a wall comes a dim green light, so faint it is barely perceptible. The walls of the room are sticky and unpleasant. In the centre of the room is a huge square tank or vat, full of a clammy black liquid that has been brewed in some way by melting down animal skins ... like in a tannery ... or even whole bodies. Black and clammy as pitch. He must get out somehow before he is dragged into the tank by a force that he feels is sucking him towards it; but the only escape is through the small window. To reach it he must climb onto the narrow edge of the tank which is sticky and treacherous. Having no other choice, he climbs up, knowing, like Orpheus, he must not look back.

The window is fixed in the stone so he has to smash himself into it, head first, to open it. With a sound resembling a falcon's beak ripping into a raven's eye, it shatters, and shards of glass or crystal pierce his forehead; but he knows he must push, push himself through the opening which is almost too narrow for his shoulders. One of his feet slips and dips into the liquid in the tank ... he yanks it out and thrusts himself into the opening, frantic now, knowing that he has little time left, and manages to squeeze through. A narrow tunnel immediately drops at a steep angle and he half falls and half drags himself along it. He can hear music like cymbals clashing rhythmically, but now he is falling and can't stop himself as he plunges towards the end of the passage, illuminated by a piercing green light, so bright he fears it might melt down his mind, instantly, if it enters his eyes ... he closes his eyes tight and lets himself go and falls out of the end of the tunnel, and for a moment he is sure he is dead ...

A lawn in front of a large country house. He can hear voices singing a hymn. Some children emerge, wearing white robes like novice priests. They pass him and ignore him. Or is he invisible? His leg is covered with an awful-looking, smelly black substance; he scrapes it against a tree, as the roebuck scrapes its antlers, until it becomes clean, but the tree is marked with the black liquid; a kind of ink ... and where he has rubbed his leg haphazardly against the bark, it has crumbled and revealed the inside of the tree, which is white like paper. The marks resemble hieroglyphs which he ought to understand, but can't; unless a voice in his head, barely heard, can interpret them for him ... the voice of a girl ...

He manages to reach and enter the front door, but inside the school, it is empty, derelict, falling to bits, not used for ages, or wrecked by a bomb in the war. The first room, its walls spattered and pocked with shrapnel damage, is bare except for a large silk carpet, covered with an intricate mosaic design of wings, of every possible size and colour, each small feather made of crystalline threads, an image on which every possible kind of wing is depicted, from almost every bird and insect that has ever lived.

On it is a red lacquer table, square and classically designed with very precise flutings around its top and legs of round columns. On the table is a huge cocoon, wrapped in fine silk material, layer upon layer neatly patterned, tightly contouring the shape hidden inside the material. Without thinking, he strokes the cocoon with his fingers and, horrified, he sees it split at one end, where he presumes a head might have been. Inside the fragment he sees a beautifully polished stone the size and shape of a head, composed of a fine grey limestone through which, interlocking and interlaced, are millions of small veins of white crystalline quartz; someone has spent thousands of years drawing them with a very fine point onto the surface of the stone; traces reminding him of an etching of the ceiling of a Gothic cathedral in which the truth is written but the surface is too high to be read; also reminding him of an image from a bubble chamber experiment in which fundamental particles have collided and left traces of their movements as small white lines ... but then he remembers taking apart the body of a dead bird he had once found in the bluebell wood, and opening up its skull with a knife he had found there inside some blood-stained bandages.

This time, because of the petulant way memory works and leaves traces, half wanting to be forgotten, half demanding to be released, inside the stone are encoded esoteric programs with plans for flight, transformed as light, across space. But how can he obtain this data, without breaking the stone?

The white folds of the linen fall away and he is drawn inside the cocoon, finding himself lying next to the body of a naked girl. On the back of his neck he feels a sharp, intense pain where the green light is falling directly onto his skin, where the rent occurred. Pulling the white linen over his shoulder to protect himself from the light, he falls off the edge of the bed onto some grass. The girl has fallen with him and is now lying on top of him and has taken his penis inside her mouth, but he is distracted, hearing a voice telling her she has got it all wrong, no milk will flow, but the girl seems not to care and is sucking hard, as the voice continues ... disclocated fragments ... 'I was going towards you ... a savage custom of tearing off their victims' heads ... juices and resins of special plants and trees ... the temple, symbolic womb of divine creation ... a plant that grows under water ... the suffering king, the wasteland ... breakthrough in plane ... desire like magma, up and up and up, a new rolling level'... and still her tongue is caressing him.

Opening his eyes to see her face, to his astonishment Matthew sees the wings rise from the carpet and dance in a swirl of veils, out of which emerges an amazing and beautiful creature ... the body of a bird, with long legs and the sharp claws of a falcon ... huge white wings and the head of a beautiful girl with long flowing blonde hair. He tries to get closer to see who it is when suddenly she notices him looking at her. Is to be seen, seeing, not allowed? She flaps her wings in a kind of fury or ecstasy ... and Matthew shouts out ... but she flies towards him ... lunges at him with falcon claws outstretched. The talons strike at him savagely, and the pain is like being burnt with ice, until he is drawn up in one movement close to her face ... just in time to see her lips open wide as her teeth plunge into his neck and sever his jugular vein. He clutches his throat and screams, but it is no good. Blood gushes out of the wound and he is certain now that he is really dying ...

Crawling in pain across the grass, he clings to the exposed roots of a huge beech tree, part of a small copse of trees arranged formally around a small meadow, curls up inside the roots and the earth is warm and smells of dank humus and rotting leaves. Slowly the blood drains out of his body and he feels himself becoming colder and colder until his body has become the body of the tree ... and he knows he is finally at peace, and dead. But he can see himself lying there, wrapped neatly in white bandages, and presumes that someone else has died, in his place. Curious to know who it is, he tries to open the bandages but wakes up ... too soon.

Matthew put his hand to his throat, not sure he was still breathing, then to his forehead. It was cold with sweat. He raised himself up with difficulty, his body stiff and unyielding, and heard the voice of Georgina in the darkness. 'My God, Matthew, are you alright? You were howling. I thought you were being torn apart by an eagle or something, like Prometheus. Are you sure your liver is alright?'

He was shaking. 'I had the most terrifying dream!' was all he could say.

'I know. You were crying out so loudly, I thought you were being killed. Do you always dream like that? Did you ever play Bottom in your school play?'

'No, why?'

'He had one helluva dream too!'

'It's no joke! I've been having weird dreams lately, as if they are trying to tell me something, but I always forget them. Images come back later but don't make any sense at all. This was the worst yet! I haven't had a dream so physical since I was a child and had nightmares after my father died. Why should they happen again now?'

'I think it's probably a good sign, getting rid of some of the rubbish! You can tell me the details later. I love dreams. What's important now is to grab something to eat, while we can. I've prepared the drawing room. Instant theatre, you'll be impressed! Cindy seems to be in a trance ... treats me like some press agent that she loathes really, but must appear to respect. She's certainly entered the illusion of it all with a vengeance. She doesn't want to eat except "a few delicacies" later, so we had better eat while we can. I've made a quiche, so creep down quietly, while Madame is getting into the mood!'

Matthew tried to remember his dream, but it had retreated behind the veils of rationality. Was it a girl who had attacked him or a bird? He saw his falcon on the side-table, put it back into its red lacquer box and stroked it gently with the ends of his fingers. The more he touched it and thought about it and tried to place it into some perspective in his life, the more fond of it he became. It was now irrevocably part of his existence; he must learn more about the purpose of mummification. Was it really to await the return of its soul? Why had this strange object, once bird, suddenly decided it should belong to him, and flown into his life from a dimension he had never previously imagined or even dreamt about?

He dressed for the evening's entertainment, and crept quietly downstairs as Georgina had instructed him. He could hear exotic Indian music wafting sensuously from Cindy's room. A note was pinned on the drawing room door. Georgina had written:

BECOME WHAT YOU ARE!
A drama; the 2nd Act. But not until 9 p.m.

She was waiting for him in the kitchen, ready to serve a piping hot quiche which looked delicious, and lots of different salads and small dishes. 'Well, how does it look?' she asked, knowing he would notice the effort she had made.

'Superb! We must play at theatre more often, if this is the kind of attention I get as a result,' he said, mocking slightly.

'It's not the theatre to thank, but I had the kitchen entirely to myself for once. Cindy's attitude to food verges on the psychotic at the best of times. We're lucky we ever eat more than grass. She hates cooking, hates food, hates people who enjoy food, and would prefer to be force-fed every day by a plasma drip ... justifying her theory that men dominate their women through the food supply. I'd say sex myself. You see how different we are! For Cindy, eating, making love and dying are indistinguishable anyway, the weft and woof of the veil she weaves between herself and those who are careless enough to love her. For Cindy, tea and biscuits in the afternoon is no less dramatic than first communion in Kings College Chapel, a mixture of a wedding feast and a wake ... always Daddy being buried of course, the one who wears the black cloak in little girl's dreams, has a whip and thrashes them whenever they are touching themselves in the wrong places, which provokes the dreams anyway; especially the best ones! Cindy's whole life is a dream, but don't tell her I told you so. Have some quiche.'

Matthew had grown accustomed to Georgina's monologues about Cindy, guessing they helped her to deal with her confused emotions. 'Thank you. Do you always precede a private dinner engagement with ... how can I put it ... such an orgy of analysis?' he asked as kindly as possible.

'I don't give private dinner parties, I don't fall into the trap of having to feed someone! Every person a woman feeds is her child, so it's better to avoid the problem and be taken out for dinner and made a fuss of and fed at someone else's expense instead. You become the child, much easier. Oh, the problems with women and food. Especially Cindy. If you get hungry, slip off and have a pizza in town, but never tell her. For her, *food* is betrayal, never sex, though it wouldn't be as bad as telling her she can't act, or she's lousy in bed, despite her *nonchallllllance*,' pronouncing it as a French whore might do in a Hollywood movie. 'How's the quiche, by the way?'

Matthew was finding it difficult to eat, she was talking so fast; he was unable to stop mimicking her, his mouth trying to eat at the same speed she was talking; ' ... er ... beautiful ... thank you, really nice. Why aren't you having any?'

'Me? I was picking at the food all the time I was preparing it and I'm already full. I'll have some later. I tend to wake up in the night, *ravenous*! So I come down and raid the fridge, making sure Cindy doesn't hear me, or making sure I don't meet *her* when *she* is raiding the fridge. Mind you, one night we met on the stairs with plates of cold spaghetti. She looked at me with such passionate resentment and hate, I wanted to lay her down on the spot and ravish her, just like a man might do, especially a stranger, a thief. She looked gorgeous, irresistible, she was so angry and bitchy. But then she decided to look through me instead. Her eyes glazed and in a flash I had become a mere ghost. You know how they always seem to be walking up or down stairs? Why are they never in bed? I had become invisible, even carrying the head of John the Baptist on my plate. What a midnight feast that would make by the way ... or had it been my own head on the plate and she thought it was food, she'd have ignored me just the same. You see why I love her so much?'

Matthew had nearly choked on the pastry. She was obviously already pretty drunk. 'Er, no I don't really ... to be honest!'

'Don't worry. Have some salad.'

'Er ... yes I will ... thank you ...!'

'I love her because she's never boring, always watching herself from a box in her own private theatre, high in the Gods. She's fascinating once you accept she's totally irrational. If she once did something I expected, or really needed, I'd think she was having a nervous breakdown.'

'How on earth did John cope with her?'

'He didn't really. They were two shadows thrown on a screen, like two Balinese hand puppets, both quite unreal. Cindy on her trip and John on his.'

Matthew could see she was very nervous, not in control of herself, so thought it might be a good moment to take advantage. 'Okay. Tell me, now, I *know* you know more than you admit. What *was* John's so-called trip exactly? Now's a good chance to tell me, and I can save wasting a lot of time!'

'I only saw the shadow on the screen. He was very serious about the recent research programme, financed by raising money is devious ways, but that's not important. The research was with some gravity waves he'd discovered, which act on us all the time, directing all earthly evolution, creating matter spontaneously, passing on structural information, forms shaping things, creating our consciousness, everything on earth under the control of these waves. Our freedom was a myth; we're a vast experiment. By tapping into the right frequency for these waves you could reduce their power, analyse them and discover what the next step was. Divine the future! He saw all these *morphs* ... as he called them ... as data clusters that could be communicated instantaneously from one place to another on the gravity field, or "R" field he called it sometimes, probably R for Reincarnation. He felt we were being influenced ... often to our own good ... by forms that existed at the other side of the universe; events could happen simultaneously at both sides of the universe through the means of this field, not *caused* in the normal sense. Space was an illusion ... time was an illusion ... false modes of thinking we have evolved through lack of faith in our wider, deeper powers. He said the universe only appeared to be as big as we say it is, from one frame of reference. From another it was minutely small. Everything worked like a multi-dimensional hologram. The brain was a holographic receiver. He was working with some other people; we were never sure if they in the Soviet Union, were acid heads in San Francisco, or lived in ancient Egypt two thousand years before Christ. He was obsessed with Akhenaten and Amarna and his high priest Amenhotep; a reincarnation of Imhotep, he said. So you see why Cindy made such a projection on you. When I described you, in love with Meritaten, and a crystallographer too, she said, "He's one of them. He'll tell us what's happened to John!" Which is why you're still here, now, isn't it?' She was looking into her glass of wine as she spoke, talking mostly to herself.

'I'll be honest, I'm not entirely sure why I'm still here. I came here because of you, didn't I? I stayed. I decided to leave when I first heard about John but I don't seem able to. But listen, you do seem to know an awful lot about science! Did you learn all that from John?'

'To *leave*? *LEAVE*? Are you crazy? Here you are with *one* woman who is devoted to you making you lovely meals, and upstairs you have a *second* woman who is convinced you are a reincarnation of Josef von Sternberg and she's going to dance Salomé and the seven veils for you as if you are the spiritual Godhead of the Temple of Hollywood Cinema, and you are wondering why you aren't leaving? If I was a man; good God, and maybe I am at times ... I'd stay and make the most of it! If you play your cards right, it will be more fun than *The Blue Angel*, I promise you; a film I never saw, alas!'

'Nor me. I slept right through it!' They both laughed.

'Don't worry, you missed nothing compared to Cindy tonight. Ah yes! *L'Extase*. Hedy Lemarr. What's German for ecstasy? I hope you know, Herr von Sternberg. She might ask you and if you say you don't know, it might blow your whole disguise!'

'You didn't say I had to be fluent in German by nine o'clock as well as an expert on smart drugs and German Expressionist cinema! Mind you I'm sure I *have* seen that film, by some weird coincidence. All I know in German is *auf wiedersehen*!

'Which is the one thing you're not saying tonight ... if I know Cindy, no goodbyes in any language. Or should I get the coffin ready now?'

They laughed and Matthew made a gesture of removing the cold sweat off his forehead. Georgina apologised for putting the fear of God into him, saying she was only joking really.

'It's sounds more like entering the labyrinth to fight the Minotaur than enjoying a quiet evening at home watching a pretty girl dance!' he replied.

Georgina smiled in triumph. 'Matthew, it's just a mere dance, but imagine it so much more. But look! You've only been here a few days and you are describing the world about you in terms of myth. The Minotaur indeed! By the time you return to your lab you'll know all the Egyptian and Greek myths by heart. You'll be speaking to your science colleagues in such a language of riddles they'll think you spent a year in a lunatic asylum ... or living with the Sphinx!'

'A year? Aren't you letting me out for a year?' he asked plaintively. 'And which one of you is the Sphinx anyway, it's time I worked that out, at least!'

Georgina looked down at her hands as if he had hurt her, and she paused before replying. 'You are free to go at any time, Matthew, you know that. There are no padded cells here, at least none that I found ... certainly no sweet young nurses in fresh white coats ... no strait-jackets ... just a pair of crazy girls devoted to you, who cannot resist your quiet charm!'

'Thanks very much,' he said, somewhat unconvincingly.

'I mean it. You'll see tonight, if Cindy remains coherent, that she has made quite an attachment to you.'

'It remains to be seen how much of an attachment I manage to make to her!'

'Well. Yes and no. Attachment is irrelevant. Just have fun, after all; and what have you to lose?'

Matthew knew but didn't want to say ... helped himself to some more of the salad dishes and neither of them spoke. Georgina had still not eaten anything. She found more wine and served Matthew and herself. 'Cindy shouldn't be too long. Curtain call is nine o'clock. How's the drink?'

'Superb. I admire John's taste in wine, as well as girls!'

'Oh good! But what do you expect from an expert in every kind of intoxicant? Mind you, he said the best aphrodisiac in the world was terror and the creature that enjoyed sex more than any other, was the male praying mantis. At one time he thought of peddling adrenalin as a love potion with a pamphlet saying that an overdose combined with too much reticence could kill you; trade-name, "Instant Flight." You see why he and Cindy got on so well! The female praying mantis, disguised as a leaf, waiting for every unsuspecting male, and out she struts, exuding the scent that lures him to his ecstatic apotheosis!'

Matthew could see it all clearly, in vivid technicolour. *The Living World*, BBC Two on Sundays. Entertainment for the kiddies. 'Thanks for the warning!' he said apprehensively.

'Don't worry. It's only a game! You'll see, she's great fun, very original and utterly lucid in her characterisations. I've watched this whole process of transformation since it started at school. One day she might tell you the truth about her novel, which is very sexy indeed, to be published of course under her pseudonym ... Rosetta Stone ... published in three languages simultaneously! English, ancient Egyptian and Polymorphous Perverse!'

They laughed. Matthew asked again, 'Tell me what the novel is *really* about, now's a good time!'

'Never! Let her do it, it's her secret life, if she wants to reveal it.' She stood up. 'It's time we took our seats!' She looked at the clock anxiously, as if it would be a terrible crime not to be in-stalled for the rise of the curtain. 'I must get the music ready. It's a long tape. I'll do all the talking, so relax, forget yourself, and *Doctor* Sutherland especially! Imagine you're acting inside someone else's dream, that you're free to do whatever slips into your mind. Now *that* kind of freedom is very rare I promise you, especially with an insatiably sexy woman who has ceased to be herself and can do and be anything she wants. So enjoy it while you can!'

'I'll do my best' he murmured, trying to remember if he'd typed the DF118D7ASAR code into the third disc before the final experiment ...

Georgina took him by the hand and led him into the

drawing room. At first he could see very little. There was only one light, a dim red one, but he could see enough to realise she had done a fantastic job with the decor. Everything was draped with curtains, bedcovers or old clothes, not just the furniture, but also the walls. The red lampshade was a Victorian dress cut up and hastily sewn onto an ordinary beige lampshade. The long and narrow room was an ideal theatre, classical in style with its ornamented plaster-work ceiling. In front of the window, semi-circular in shape, was the large raised platform where once the grand piano would have stood. The stage. He liked it all immediately and felt comfortable with the ambience, a mixture of a decadent, cheap German nightclub and a Victorian brothel. For reasons he couldn't be sure of, he felt it had a homely feeling about it.

'Look over here!' she said, showing him behind a screen. 'She even has her own lights! John bought them of course. She's prepared for everything. This is my main job, the spotlight, making sure she is perfectly *LIT*. Lighting is everything for a woman's face! What do you think?'

'I'm impressed. It feels like somewhere else, not here at all!' He wasn't sure what he meant but it sounded right.

'Exactly! Which is how you must feel, someone else, somewhere else. It's just our film ... and a great script!'

'Do you know the script then?' Had they often done it before, he wondered, this particular scenario ... not daring to ask. Or really wanting to *know*...

'Script? Good heavens, Cindy never has scripts. She's quite impromptu – that is without prompts – the sexy bits especially; either that or they're from her novel. I just improvise; I'm seen and not heard, like an ideal mother!'

'Why always her novel? Are we *living* her novel? Is her novel about dancing?'

'Ur ... yes in a way, and no. Her novel can't be just one long, per-versed sexual fantasy, or can it? But don't ask questions, look over there ... your jacket and hat. Slip those on when the time comes and sit in that seat. Okay? And you'll be the master for whom she'll perform her dance of the seven veils, the stripping away of all illusion. Lucky man. See you tomorrow!'

He gulped. 'What do you mean, tomorrow?'

'Well if it goes on too long ... and some of Cindy's plays take off on weird tangents and last a week at a time ... I tend to get lost and slip away to work!'

'I hope you're joking?' he said almost desperately.

'Of course I am ... well, exaggerating, just a little!' She kissed him gently again on the cheek and smiled knowingly as if she was quite accustomed to these kind of evenings, and couldn't wait to get on with the action.

Suddenly a painful wave of ideas seared uncomfortably into his mind and threw him completely off balance; I wonder if they think I'm *not* who I say I am, that I'm really one of them, whoever they are, and they think I know everything that's going on, an old hand at this kind of thing, but I'm *really* a spy investigating John's disappearance, sent by other people that John was secretly working with. I've been sent to find out the truth and avenge his death! He started to sweat.

It all seemed so obvious; of course! All the coincidences he'd talked about so naively, weren't any such thing, but were contrived accidents, deliberate come-ons to fool them. After all he knew nothing about Egyptology, he'd merely bought a couple of books and a few relics at an auction and yet he was giving the unlikely impression he was mesmerised by a mummified falcon that looked like a decaying black cigar. Clearly he was nothing more than a detective with a most implausible set of credentials, far too obvious to fool anyone, and the two girls were leading him on, acting as if they hadn't seen through his whole pose, and the evening's event ... so plangent with implausibilities ... was probably a plot to have him murdered, acting in a Nazi brothel! And such a death would hardly provoke much credibility amongst his scientific colleagues. Suddenly he remembered that no-one at all, anywhere, knew he was there, except the two girls, and he began to feel desperately alone and vulnerable. Why had he been so arrogant and not asked himself how they might have seen him, from *their* point of view?

The more he thought about the way the two girls probably saw him, the more he began to panic ... the more obvious it was that he was being tricked into acting in a charade that had as its climax, a brutal, symbolic murder; the decapitation of John the Baptist. Then he saw a connection he'd not made before. Was the disappearance in the copse some kind of baptism, albeit of fire? The head of *John* on a plate, not John the Baptist, a real head on a plate ... the missing John himself, one of the fragments of his dismembered body? Certain images from his dreams were starting to make too much sense, and he could now remember them clearly, which seemed strange. Was this the threshold of dream?

He leapt up, intending to escape immediately, when the door opened and Georgina entered pulling Cindy dramatically behind her. Matthew felt suddenly quite faint. His chest contracted as if he'd been struck by lightning, or as Georgina would have said, by one of Zeus's numinous, blue-green thunderbolts. Georgina was looking utterly amazing, sensual and exotic in a long black dress, her dark eyes sparkling mischievously, heavily outlined in kohl. A perfect Herodias. But never had he seen a girl look so stunningly, transparently seductive as Cindy. His knees felt weak.

She'd painted her face a deathly white colour reminding him of a statue of a pagan goddess he'd seen in a harrowing Pasolini film; wasn't it *Oedipus Rex*? Her eyes seemed huge, decorated and enlarged with painted bird or butterfly wings. Her lips seemed so translucently red in the white mask that he felt they were radiating a strange force towards him ... he'd not be able to take his eyes off her lips whether she was speaking or not. At that moment they pouted provocatively, poised ready to exude some deadly poison which he'd not be able to resist. The cold sweat of a few minutes before changed instantly to a fever. Side-tracked from his earlier train of thought, his mind was free-wheeling ... he was going nowhere ... unless staying was somewhere. She was sheathed in a cocoon of veils, mysteriously layered like the bandages on a mummy. He could see the strips of coloured veils beneath a pure white, diaphanous kind of dress, or outer veil, although it looked more like a skin through which the veils appeared, like scales or feathers ... and he remembered, dimly, the strange cocoon of his dream. Had she secretly witnessed his dream and then, in her movie dressing room, transformed it into her own creation? Everything about her suggested an outer shell ... the mask, the white material ... behind it the soft vulnerable inner body of an insect or bird, ready to dissolve inside itself into something utterly frightening ... some kind of hideous black pitch or molten magma ... before undertaking its final metamorphosis into a predatory winged being. Yet also, under that outer skin, something so desirable, the image to describe it eluded him ...

Matthew felt terrified ... but agreed with John suddenly; in certain situations, terror could be an aphrodisiac ...

Georgina brought Cindy slowly towards him, leading her by her hand, a hand sheathed in a long white glove, encrusted with pearls and cheap jewels. Georgina introduced them gravely, with not the slightest hint of artifice or embarrassment. 'Cindy, this is Herr Josef von Sternberg, director of *The Blue Angel*, all the way from Hollywood to watch the dance he's heard so much about! He says you look beautiful, a strange mixture of two images superimposed, a painting by Vargas being seduced by a Gustave Moreau!'

And despite the previous fears and reservations about entering the space of the girls' charade, he felt he could be Von Sternberg after all, and he felt his toes stretching in imaginary jackboots; it was really quite an exciting feeling.

Then Cindy decided to sit down ... which was clearly to be the first major scene of the spectacle. She seemed to go limp so slowly, and at the same time so elegantly, that Matthew was spellbound. He was reacting to every small movement, watching a film in slow motion on an editing machine ... or another cubist painting come to life. But it also made him think, unexpectedly, of one of his slides under a microscope and the image flashed into his mind of crystals forming ... taking shape ... emerging out of an almost transparent liquid, as if from nowhere. Everything about her was of something about to emerge out of a tantalising absence. He was still standing up, transfixed, long after she had draped herself across the chaise-longue like an abandoned puppet. Suddenly he felt embarrassed again and sat down himself, impulsively, nearly falling over his own feet as he did so ... the imaginary jackboots getting in the way.

Georgina asked her if she'd prefer wine or champagne. Cindy allowed her head to sway so far back it was through half open eyes that she launched a hungry, mean glance towards the wine bottle and murmured, 'A glass of wine now, darling, I'm parched ... while I'm waiting for you to open the champagne ... '

Matthew could see she was relishing the power she was exerting over Georgina. She turned to him and purred. 'It's a great shame I don't speak German, Herr Josef. A great shame too that you've come without your whip! Georgina told me all about your new film.' She held up her glass. 'To Salomé, the sacrificial daughter ... not the last daughter to challenge the hypocrisy of the Church. The true prophetess of the Anti-Christ!'

They toasted the imaginary dancing girl, *ex nihilo*, the young girl skipping and dancing in the human mind for two thousand years ... raising their glasses high in the air. By the time Matthew had dragged his eyes away from Cindy's crimson mouth and winged eyes, and put his glass down, it was quite empty. Georgina filled the glass immediately, before switching on the music: very quiet and distant, languid and romantic.

'Mere background music, of course!' Cindy remarked, in an obviously false voice, looking right through him as if he wasn't there. 'The music for my dance is very special, a tape I made in southern India, mostly tabla and flute, performed for a local ruling family to commemorate the death of one of their ancestors, music I find impossible to resist, my body resonating as if someone else is directing it, as if I'm dancing with someone who is separate yet still inside me. But I shouldn't be telling you these things, you may see it very differently. I expect you see everything as a series of film scenes, even day-to-day events, as you pass through space and time ... a film montage ... do you?'

Taken off-guard by her sudden question, Matthew was groping for an answer he thought Herr Josef might make when Georgina emerged from the kitchen and scolded Cindy for 'asking our distinguished guest such impertinent questions! Lucky he hasn't brought his whip or I myself might be using it!'

Cindy smiled winsomely and purred, 'You're right. I'm sure Herr Josef thinks in images and not in words anyway. Forgive me for sounding like a journalist from *HARPIES* magazine!'

'Exactly!' said Georgina, smiling sweetly, putting down the already-opened champagne.

'We must finish the wine first, it *is* the very best Pauillac after all,' Cindy demanded, indicating that Matthew's glass was empty with an almost imperceptible twitch of an eyebrow, the kind of gesture she'd make bidding fifteen million dollars for a Van Gogh painting at an auction, the painting of his newly severed ear wrapped in a blood-stained bandage, ready to be sent to Gauguin.

Georgina suddenly exited right, 'to arrange the caviar'. Cindy turned towards Matthew as if intending to say something secret and intimate, but then she hesitated, apparently transfixed by the Shiraz rug between them, and for what seemed to Matthew an aeon of time, she appeared to be meditating on the mystical whorls and gyres in the sacred mandala, by chance now delineating the space between them, until finally she raised her face towards him and, without any hint of emotion or contrivance, asked, 'Do you believe in reincarnation, Herr Josef?'

Before Matthew could answer Georgina returned and Cindy cast a ferocious look in her direction, but then seemed to regret the show of irritation and made the effort to smile and whisper words of approval instead. Before placing the tray of caviar on the table, Georgina seemed to involuntarily raise it above her head like a priestess in some ancient ritual, preparing to lay a sepulchral meal or the entrails of some newly sacrificed beast onto an altar to be devoured later by some vengeful god; and Matthew winced at the thought.

Cindy prepared the caviar slowly and precisely and in silence, and then in time with the slow lilt of the music, she presented Matthew and Georgina and then herself with a small square of toast, as symbolically as a priest might hand out the Eucharist at a wedding, her eyes seductively caressing the black translucent eggs, scraped from the wombs of Black Sea sturgeon. '*Voila!* Let's not forget the lush body of the Fisher

King. Long may he lurk in the oceanic depths of that black sea we call our unconscious minds!'

'Yes indeed!' said Georgina, obviously relishing Cindy's somewhat baroque verbal images as much as the dish.

By the time all the pieces of toast had been eaten, the communion finished, Matthew had drunk several glasses of champagne and was starting to mildly lose the certainty of being present in his body; lush or otherwise. In contrast, Cindy was finally reaching herself, was about to become whole, her two selves united at last. The limpidity of the caviar had risen into her eyes and they shone pellucidly with fermenting desire. She looked at Georgina fiercely again and said, 'I was just about to tell Herr Joseph my theory about reincarnation!'

To Matthew's dismay Georgina stood up, gulped down the last of her champagne; 'I must prepare myself. See you later.' Cindy ignored her as she wafted towards the door.

Matthew sat back in his seat as far as he could go, but again Cindy focused her attention on the spirals of the Persian rug before she started speaking vaguely in Matthew's direction. The last thing he was expecting was another verbal striptease, but Cindy seemed much more interested in talking than dancing, or else she was making the most of Matthew's discomfort, as he gazed into her eyes like a schoolboy. 'The reason I mentioned reincarnation was not to provoke a lengthy discussion on the subject ... but to tell you, firstly, that I believe it is the one great mystery at the core of all human experience and has been deliberately overlooked by our culture with terrible consequences ... and secondly, I want you to think of reincarnation while I'm dancing, because I think it is the central idea behind all the old forms of sacred dance ... especially the erotic dances of temple prostitutes, and that is what Salomé was, after all. It is the whole idea of being possessed by a higher spirit, which is at the heart of such ritual dances, is it not?'

Matthew didn't know what to say. He was guessing that Cindy believed what she had said, absolutely. It was the first moment it dawned on him that she and Georgina were always talking about reincarnation in one form or another. It was virtually an obsession; and John's too, apparently. Yet nothing could be further from his own belief. He felt guilty for not taking it seriously but it wasn't what he'd been expecting at all ... of Salomé. He was pleased when Cindy stood up and said she had to leave him for a moment, and he was alone again to ponder the strangeness of the situation.

He drank another glass of champagne and noticed he was feeling more detached from himself, not just becoming drunk. Had the girls put something in his drink? But as he tried to focus his mind on this possibility, he felt himself already falling. Images ... the half-naked girl who had danced into the trees ... so poorly done. Kitsch. Vulgar. Childish almost ... and he started to doze again ... as if he needed to dream again ...

But the activity of the girls prevented his escape, though his mind was still blurred when he saw the pinpoint of bright light spreading in the darkness ... as Georgina manipulated the masking frame on the head of the spotlight. At first the projected shaft of light appeared as a very small circle in the centre of the stage area, but then grew larger, revealing Cindy standing perfectly still and poised. Very slowly she raised her arms until her fingertips touched the outer edge of the circle of light, and Matthew immediately remembered the drawing by Leonardo da Vinci delineating the perfect harmony of human proportion, mimicking the wheeling systems of the stars ... every small atom the size of a galaxy ...

... the music was slow, the flute's melody meandering around a single drone note which it was caressing the way a humming bird hovers around the flower it is robbing of its honey. Matthew saw Cindy slowly evolve into such a bird, hovering unnaturally slowly, vibrating with such slow motion he could see each small movement quite distinctly, not obscured by the whole, the wings reaching a centre point, a tonal centre, but then passing through it as the imaginary wind wavered, and the wings kept beating to keep it poised, cheating the pull of gravity ...

He'd expected Cindy to dance flamboyantly with bold gestures and frantic sweeps of her body and arms, but the more he watched her the more mesmerised he became. Her movements were so slow, so slight, so subtle ... she resembled a plant, a reed at the edge of water, solitary yet firm, the partner of two waves, moving tenuously as the water beneath the surface swirled into an eddy but at the same time reacting on a different plane to the wind billowing above the surface. She seemed to be moving in this strange double way ... as if there were two melodies interweaving in counterpoint, both moving her body in their distinct and different ways, as if she was dancing with a filmed image of herself dancing, the one superimposed over the other ... at times in perfect symmetry with it, then just for a few seconds, out of phase ... interfering ... and the struggle to recapture the illusion of being in phase seemed almost to suggest the struggle to remain tangible in a world of pure thought ... and for some unknown reason an image came into Matthew's mind of several delicate reeds held together by a mess of feathers and bits of straw ... the small round nest of a reed warbler entwined around each of them, binding them together into a single purpose ... an external womb, bargaining for time, in the bound and knotted condensations of space ... and he suddenly remembered the nest of the reed warbler was the favourite victim of the cuckoo ... and somehow this related to the idea of reincarnation ... and his present predicament ...

... losing all sense of self and objectivity as he tried to focus on the mysterious duality of Cindy's dance. From time to time her recorded voice spoke dislocated phrases ... words no longer needing to relate to things ... making no linear sense, but the kind of vertical meaning common to dreams which Matthew now felt he understood without knowing why or how ... as if it was necessary for the dancer to absorb these previous images in words ... as if she was dissolving them away inside herself, a necessary preliminary to dissolving herself and undergoing metamorphosis from the virgin daughter into the temple prostitute ... from innocence to experience. At one moment she called for mother in a strange plaintive voice as if she was losing her way and needed a touch of deeper knowledge to draw on, to absorb into the language of her dance, and he saw Georgina, the mother standing in the shadow, just beyond the ring of light ...

That was it ... it was a language. For the first time in his life he was seeing a body not merely dancing ... every small movement was a vowel or a consonant fusing into words which could not be pinned down rationally but were small areas of focus in a purely visual language ... hieroglyphs ... and suddenly Matthew experienced a most uncharacteristic thought as if thrust on him by someone else ... that trying to structure such a language rationally would be like arranging butterflies in a box and sticking steel pins through their bodies instead of experiencing the true meaning of the language by watching them fluttering at random around a bush of roses, as red as Cindy's lips. A mere slip of a girl ...

Then he managed to shift perspective even more and saw the dancer herself as a musical instrument ... and her fingers seemed to be playing invisible strings that surrounded her like a spider's web but were in some way still part of her body ... spreading out like waves, both the strings to be plucked and lines on which notes might be written ...

And to his surprise he had to move his body sharply to stop tears coming to his eyes ... the sadness he felt seemed derived from the beauty of the dance ... but he felt sad because he had not expected it of Cindy, that he had underestimated her, that he had been expecting something predictable, even vulgar. That is what he had been dreading ... that it would be cheap and vulgar and he'd not be able to cope, for shame. He felt so relieved not to have to feel he must reject the experience that he gladly surrendered, trying to participate in it with her, to remember what she had said about seeing her as being animated by another being ... and this he saw now, clearly, a marionette abandoned totally to forces that were moving her ... using her to express a language ... and he wanted to cry with frustration, like a child who is learning to speak for the first time, wanting to know the language so much and participate in its magical ability to make things happen at a distance ... but this time it was the particular language of woman which he might only listen to and partially understand ... what they allowed him to understand! It was a language that would remain almost entirely foreign to him ... unless ... unless they would reveal to him the code. But this he knew would not happen ... and then he grew even more sad, realising that however passive he might become to their power, however much he surrendered himself to them ... they would never take the risk of revealing the inner secrets of their mysteries to him, and this made him feel desperately lonely, knowing the world of woman would always be an image on a screen he could only look at, a play on a stage he could never be part of ... virtually unknowable yet forever demanding him.

He closed his eyes tightly trying to escape the feeling of loss ... but an image from one of his own accidental, involuntary plays, a dream, came onto the stage of his mind; a huge painted backcloth ... the trees, become like peacock's feathers, covered in eyes ... watching him ... mocking him. The stage was empty of people ... empty of even the shadows of people. He felt hollow and empty inside himself ... devoid of desire. He was becoming aware of the deep resentment in his inner being, which he had been determined to forget and ignore ... his envy of the power of woman to experience the sensuous ecstasy of pure creation ... of dance, of sculpture, and of the two combined, of flesh ... if only he could cry!

Almost imperceptibly the mood of the dance changed. Cindy had still not removed a single veil yet she seemed to be quite naked. And the syncopation ... she was dancing more and more out of phase with the music, whereas until now she had been mimicking the rise and fall of the music's contours very precisely, only straying from its geometry for fractions of a second. Now she seemed to be developing gestures that were more and more at variance with the form of the music, as if the music was still trying to maintain its power over her body, yet was losing that power ... she was resisting it, moving against it, teasing it, and the movement of her hips suggested the music was like a hand moving in space and by her movements she was pressing against it provocatively, making every use of it to caress herself ... and by going against the flow of the music she was taking more pleasure from it, wringing out more pressure from it. Matthew felt he was watching an invisible man making love to Cindy very gently, with firm but considerate movements ... taking no pleasure for himself, but being taken ... and the more Matthew imagined this illicit, hidden intercourse, the more he saw

Cindy without her veils ... the more he felt he could see her naked breasts and her pubic hair, neatly trimmed into the shape of a heart. Yet each time he returned to the direct sensual experience, he saw she had not removed a single veil ... they were still swirling protectively around her ...

His mind drifted with the music, enjoying the dialogue between her erotic movements and the music and the more he experienced her making love with her invisible partner ... even though he knew it was a projection of herself ... like two snakes copulating round an invisible central axis ... the more aroused he became ... even though his mind lapsed back at moments towards images he was familiar with, images of positive and negative electron spin and living and non-living isotopes of carbon, matter and anti-matter ... other kinds of snakes around other kinds of harsh reproof and verticality ...

... as Cindy started to dance faster and more emphatically, wrestling with the music and her invisible assailant, and the movements of her hips and thighs suggested she was abandoning herself to an inner passion, inner music ... having less and less to do with the outer music. The flute melody ceased and all that remained was a plangent, insistent rhythm from a mosaic of primitive percussion instruments, beaten with bare hands. Cindy was now dancing to a melody of her own, unheard by her audience. Suddenly a monologue of words emerged above the music ... Cindy's voice quoting erotic phrases of Oscar Wilde's play ... and her dancing became more frenzied and overtly sexual ... until the head of Iokanaan was called for ... and to Matthew's alarm Georgina appeared out of the shadows in her long oriental black dress, wearing a mask, and carrying a silver tray ... and on it was something he could not see at first and he felt a sharp plangent shudder vibrate down his spine, making his body burn from his forehead to the soles of his feet. He was sure it was the head of John! Next, it would be him ...

But to his relief he saw it was one of Georgina's sculptures ... a transparent head which, as she moved, reflected waves of light around the room. It was like a huge crystal and to Matthew's amazement, the beam of projected white light was split into all the colours of the rainbow, torn apart by the sharp crystal face, revealing the spectrum of coloured ribbons that had been so magically woven in the plait of virgin light, as the prism of experience so often loosens the petals of the spectral rose and blinds us forever to the innocent visions of childhood ...

Without warning a piercing flash of green light made Matthew sit up sharply. Georgina had suspended the green wings of a dragon-fly at the centre of the skull to simulate Matthew's diamond, and the light caught it and it seemed to reflect directly into Matthew's eye. Or was it an illusion? He was stunned momentarily, taken unawares, instantly slipping out of time, unable to avoid returning to the instant when his laser presumably collided with the strata of organic carbon in his diamond crystal ... or when it whirled out of control ... a distinction he had yet to ascertain ... drifting ... and in that brief second of collision which should not have happened, the fusion of opposites, and in the space where there should have been nothing, emergence of energy that had come from nowhere ... and he would have to call it cold fusion, meanwhile, because there was nothing else that could resemble it. Where was the new energy coming from, inside his crystal ... or his mind? And the green veil splitting ...

He wanted to stand up and shout out, to stop the action and point out the more subtle coincidences, as if by making the connection to his diamond he was in some way entering into the drama of Cindy's erotic dance, no longer as a mere spectator, a voyeur which is what he had always seemed to be, watching himself even when making love, but now, drawn into her space, contributing something of his own ... but he couldn't move ... or speak ... he was already hovering, floating, part of him somewhere else ...

Georgina put down the tray with its crystal head on the front of the stage and Cindy stood over it, raising the veils of her skirt provocatively and starting to gyrate over the head ... taunting it yet at the same time seeming to revere it ... her thighs almost caressing its translucent lips. Georgina went behind her and slipped her hands around her body, lightly brushing the skin until she grasped her firmly on her breasts. Cindy seemed to want to escape but could not, her desire for the object in front of her was too strong. Georgina stood firm as Cindy danced more and more in a frenzy, fighting against the interlocked fingers around her breasts ... tightening like a corset.

Then she seemed to try to bite the hands of her symbolic mother, but the hands wouldn't move ... and the more she danced, the more the veils were torn off her body ... the more she tried to pull herself down as if to rub her body against the translucent head, the more her thighs tore their way out from the restricting cocoon of membranes ... she was becoming naked despite herself ...

Georgina's hands were exploring her, up and down and around, until they moved slowly down the body of the writhing girl, brutal and hard, obviously seeking some kind of revenge, pressing against the flesh so hard the bones in her fingers were visible under the skin, as if she was wrestling with the whole agony of creation, but not knowing whether to create or destroy, hurt or give pleasure, release and give way or crush and reabsorb, like shaping a huge vase of clay on a whirling potter's wheel, not sure whether to make a statuette of Venus or Victory or Athena or Isis ... the goddess in all her glory ... or to squeeze so hard that she modelled a slim slip of a girl, barely shaped yet as a woman ... her sex a mere pencil mark ... until her fingers found their mark, caressing the girl between her thighs ... and the dancing girl, no longer Cindy, was writhing with pleasure but also with pain as she struggled at not being free to go down on her knees and thrust the head between her legs ... crush the lips of her sex against the translucent lips of the mindless head to release herself from her mounting desire ... albeit until the next time ... and she pressed down and touched the face, with her own lips, to pull back after the first glimpse of release ...

... slowly uncoiling until she was straight again. Most of the veils had fallen off her body and now she danced painfully with her head pushed back against the body of Georgina. Georgina's hands were covering her vagina, caressing hard.

The two girls kissed ... a long passionate kiss. Cindy turned round to hold the girl in black inside her arms, her perfectly-shaped bottom now visible, glistening as if newly fashioned from the clay, swaying to the music from side to side ... the two girls moving together, pushing against each other, their bottoms twisted as they pushed in harder, in a way that Matthew could not see exactly, until they fell gently down on either side of the sculptured head and it seemed to disappear inside them ... their bodies pressing it against each other as coloured veils swirled around like wings and Cindy's body emerged from between them ... naked, lithe and glistening ... trailing only one green veil ...

As the music throbbed on, Cindy lay on her back, placing the head on her stomach as Georgina sat beside her, continuing to fondle her ... as if the head had become a baby. Georgina stood over Cindy and placed the loosened veils back again over her body, but they slipped off as Cindy continued to writhe and shudder in time to the percussive beat of the music. Finally Georgina went to the spotlight and turned it off. She stopped the music, took out the tape and immediately started another, an even more primeval percussive music, the same insistent beat going on and on and on, as if forever. She came to Matthew and whispered in his ear, 'She's all yours now, baby' ... and left the room.

Matthew paused for a moment or two as if he might prefer after all to take flight but ... looking again at Cindy, open and awaiting him ... slipped off his jacket and trousers ... now at last there was nothing in the world, or inside himself, that could stop him taking her, he wanted her so much ... he could see how open she was beneath the sculpted heart-shaped pubic hair that he had glimpsed earlier under her skirt ... an image he would never forget as long as he lived.

He lay down next to her ... he tried to take away the last remaining pale green veil covering her face, but it was secure around her neck. She resisted and whispered. 'I am nobody and everybody, just take me as I am ... leave me the veil ... leave your whore one veil over her too brightly lit face!' He slipped quickly into her ... thrust into her hard with utter relief and she put her arms around his back and pressed him down inside her, squeezing his bottom tightly ... and said, 'Please don't hurry ... take your time ... be very gentle ... we are gods, we have all eternity ... kiss me slowly ... imagine you are the wind and I am a weeping willow tree ... and we have all night to caress each other, secretly ... before the harsh light of dawn!' She was so open and wet he knew he could make love to her forever ... and still be waiting. Waiting until she decided ... until she made the move ... and squeezed ...

And Matthew learnt to make love as if he was a god ... and was surprised how easy it seemed to be ... having left himself behind somewhere, outside the diamond, entranced by Salomé's dance of unveiling ...

⊛

SEVEN

"In the context of the mechanistic theory of life, the conscious self has to be seen as a sort of 'GHOST in the MACHINE'. To materialists this notion seems inherently absurd. The hypothesis of formative causation enables this long standing problem to be seen in a new light. The conscious self can be thought of as interacting, not with a machine, but with 'Motor Fields'. These motor fields are associated with the body and depend on its physico-chemical states ..."

"A New Science of Life"
Rupert Sheldrake

At breakfast, little was said about the previous evening. While awaiting Cindy's impending entrance with a certain disquiet, for different reasons, Georgina told Matthew she was going to London as soon as possible, and that Cindy had given permission. 'We met at the fridge at dawn. Why don't you go to Cambridge for your computer data, so you can work? *If* you want to come back, that is?' Her smile recalled da Vinci's *Madonna of the Rocks*. So they'd written the scenario already, knowing he was unlikely now to stay away; despite having been drugged; though it had hardly been disagreeable ...

The door bell rang: a telegram. Georgina signed for it and put it on Cindy's plate, just as Cindy breezed in looking as fresh as a daisy, eyes sparkling with mischief and confidence, draped in a weird art nouveau dress, created by a hack Hollywood designer, based coarsely on Botticelli's *La Primavera*, the embroidered flower pattern embodying, as the girls soon pointed out, the entire esoteric knowledge of the pagan mysteries of the Renaissance. She was wearing just enough make-up to whiten her skin, suggesting transparency, inner radiance, and the promise of a cruel death. She kissed Georgina twice on her cheek, Matthew once, and sat down.

'What! Only one telegram for breakfast, and here I am famished, positively anorexic with worry, waiting for news from my fans!' They laughed and she pushed the telegram aside with a flourish. 'It's from von Sternberg with a contract for a new movie – *The Blue Lacuna*, a porno to be set in outer space. Alas I'm too busy, I'll have to turn him down!'

Helping herself to a lavish dish of muesli, she tucked into it impatiently, tossing her head from side to side almost angrily, eyes glistening, and Matthew thought suddenly of a magpie on a motorway, hacking between hops at a crushed hedgehog on the fast lane. Half way through, she looked up very slowly and seriously, her long lashes trailing behind the gesture by at least ten seconds, and by the time the dank brush of fine hairs caught up with the action she was starting to smile. 'There's nothing like Indian flute music and sex for spiritual uplift and an appetite!' The girls laughed and Matthew tentatively joined in. Any awkwardness he'd felt subsided, as he realised he was now even more in love with her, despite himself.

In a mock serious tone she turned to Matthew. 'Mind you, fickle as mercury, aren't you, already abandoning me and after only one dance, running off with my best friend? Alas it always happens to me, poor little rich girl that I am, and it's always with my best friend!' Matthew nodded mutely, as if to say she was quite right. But she had finished acting; she opened the telegram, eyes narrowing a lattice or two; 'It's for John. I can't give head nor tail to it, can you, Matthew?'

To Matthew's surprise she handed it to him. The first lines consisted of letters and numbers, then:*Passport delay proving tiresome. Stop. Suggest new surname not Taylor or Sutherland. Stop. Too close. Stop. Yours RMS.*

Matthew, sensing it was a trick, smiled scornfully and accusingly at Cindy. 'Well! What a coincidence! Don't expect me to believe *that* one! And who, might I ask, is it from?'

'I don't know ... maybe it's you who should explain?' she said, shaking her head. 'You're the one so plangent with coincidences and a name which echoes far afield! A man in two places at once, a man who scorns the mere space-time of we mortals, receiving messages from regions unknown where the wheeling systems darken and our benumbed conceiving soars!'

'Really? It's from a remote and unconquered galaxy known as the City of the Angels. A mere phone call away!'

'Let me look!' said Cindy. 'Oh I see. Los Angeles. How silly of me. But seriously, Matthew ... with all my heart, it's not a hoax. These things happen, I don't know what to believe. To prove it, Georgina, take Matthew to John's room. You'll see, he gets lots of freaky telegrams about passports and names. It's his work. I never asked awkward questions about where the money came from.'

Georgina went to the kitchen to find the key. Cindy looked after her approvingly and said, 'My sexy pretty red-head! *Quel cul que tu as!*' Then she looked at Matthew and shrugged her shoulders, and becoming the actress again; haughtily, elegantly and pointedly, recited, *'Il y tant de choses que je ne peux pas vous dire, tant de choses que vous ne me laisseriez pas dire. Ayez pitié de moi!* Apollinaire! His greatest poem; "The Pretty Red-Head". One summer when I was young, *hélas*, I lived in Paris and dyed my hair red, dreaming I would meet Apollinaire in St.Germain des Prés. Until I discovered he'd been dead for years, silly me! Why do I always fall in love with people who are dead, sooner or later?' She turned quickly away, knowing she shouldn't have said it.

'No doubt!'

'In the war he was trepanned by a bullet ... went right through his skull ... he wrote all his best poetry afterwards with that neat hole in his head! Probably had direct access from the right hemisphere to the left at all times and *that* is sublime. I wanted to write poetry but I drew the line at having a hole in my head. Red hair was bad enough. Who wants a girl with a hole in her head? Not sexy at all. We've enough holes already. My ideas might leak out all over the place. I'm bad enough as it is at keeping secrets.' She pouted.

'I thought the key was in the garlic?' Georgina called out.

'O George! Silly! I moved it to the red Chinese tea-pot with the dragons.' She turned to Matthew. 'Thought you might be a secret midnight garlic-eater, needing it to keep the witches away!' She smiled, hoping Matthew would smile too, but he stayed cool and defensive.

Georgina returned. 'Coming, Matthew?' She took his hand and led him upstairs, unlocking the door of John's room, relishing the knowledge it would be such a surprise. 'The inner sanctuary. *Hic Sunt Leoni.* Become what you are!' He stepped cautiously inside. The room was not what he was expecting at all. Quite large, the walls and ceiling were entirely black, the wall-to-wall carpet was black, the curtains were black, all the furniture and objects were black; everything that could be black in the room, was black.

'I'll leave you to it,' Georgina said quietly and closed the door behind him. He was too stunned to say anything, still trying to grasp the meaning of the room, trying to imagine the man who had created it and worked in it. It was extremely tidy, every object seemed to be in its right place. It reminded him of a monk's cell, but a very modern kind of monk for sure. On a large, polished ebony black table was the SUN computer, identical to his own. This startled him at first but then he decided it was the computer that lots of scientists and people dabbling in similar kinds of research would choose. Next to the computer was a small plastic box full of discs ...

He'd expected the room to be untidy, teeming with books and files, papers and junk; it was hardly a beachcomber's room. On a shelf were some black leather files; full of computer read-outs of digital data. Each file was the same.

He felt uneasy. A black Chinese rug in the centre of the room was embellished with a fierce vermilion-faced dragon. On a wall were two large, bold images in black frames, and Matthew felt the back of his neck tingle again. He recognised them immediately although he had never seen them before. The artist, Paul Delvaux, Georgina had mentioned several times. In one frame was the original painting, in the other a three-dimensional holographic image from the original painting next to it. It was uncanny seeing them next to each other, the one with its expected, painted two-dimensional space, the other, the illusion of three dimensions, throwing everything into question.

But it was the familiarity of the scene that disturbed him most, even though the juxtaposition of the two images also disturbed him, flicking from one to the other, unconsciously trying to bring the two images back together into a single unity; superimposed. But the main feature of the image was the naked girl with long blonde hair lying on a stone table ... mostly draped under a transparent white sheet. Standing next to her was another woman dressed in black, with long black hair. The scene was an open-air courtyard paved with black and white square tiles, surrounded by various broken colonnades of stone columns and metal columns, the cloisters of a church and yet, a railway station at the same time. Icy and cold. The ambience, unemotional and yet curiously erotic. Two places and two images fused. A huge steel locomotive, black and still, waited in the background. There even seemed to be a row of beech trees in the distance meeting up with the colonnade of metal arches and columns.

It was night-time and the figures were illuminated by small round lights or ornate windows or doors decorated with metal tracery. Just for a second Matthew recalled an etching he had seen of a Piranesi prison in a book Cindy had left on the kitchen table, about opium and the romantic poets of the nineteenth century. In their drug-induced reveries, they too had been drawn towards ancient Egypt ... and ruins.

Matthew felt sure the girl in black had just made love to the girl on the bed ... and yet the mood of the image was of cold detachment. He didn't know why it was so erotic and suggestive, though the image reminded him of others, teeming with erotic action, and it was the thought of these other scenes just outside of vision, barely remembered, that aroused him sexually. This was aftermath. Afterimage. The moment when despair has taken its toll and all that remains is doubt. In the background were girls in white, still as statues, like caryatids, half girl, half stone, draped in white gowns or carved in white stone, or both.

The dreams; he'd thought all along they were not his own. So was he receiving them from John? A totally absurd idea! Wasn't all this getting out of hand? He must stop now, get out while he could ... and yet, he was fascinated too.

On the table were the telegrams, all from RMS, Los Angeles. Lists of letters and numbers and the odd phrase. He was wondering ... if ... 'Yes, they're codes for the computer. My brain is being sluggish this morning; thanks Cindy!'

Perhaps Raymonde; maybe too close? We think passport not necessary where you are going! KHU 1618. NO?

On one, there was another mention of Sutherland; BUT

dated two days before his experiment. There were numerous references to passports, but other fragments were less meaningful ... *Seven sisters triangle - Natasha, pretty sphinx - Despair has no wings and nor has love - Dying of not dying - The branch of Tamarisk - Discover by the divine inspiration of Rumour - Beneath the earth and invisible - Transforming herself into a swallow, she hovered around the pillar - Everything said without thinking - Pearls piercing the mists - The dimensions of the chest - She pronounced mighty words of power.*

Matthew wondered if John had been a poet in one of his former incarnations! Now he was sure the phrases were secret codes that would *trancelate* into computer instructions - perhaps codes based on a book of poetry. He recalled Georgina saying something like; 'Cindy and John were always quoting poetry; having a meal with them was like living with two parrots. They'd play a game, exchanging words or images. The other would have to quote a fragment of poetry containing the same word ... a kind of *parleur* game. They were brilliant at it. They could carry on a secret conversation in your presence as if they were speaking a foreign language. John was obsessed with the poets who'd blown their minds with opium and wine - with laudanum ... '

Matthew took the first disc, put it into the computer's disc-drive, expecting it might be code-protected, feeling apprehensive but excited at the same time:

ENTER ↑

In seconds, he saw words on the screen ...

DISC ONE

"The Pursuit of the Ultimate Eucharist. The Lesser Mysteries"

Welcome to the Machine! Welcome to The Wasteland!
An initiation into my private Virtual Reality program. Lesson number one. All is illusion, unavoidable and absolute, so accept it NOW! You alas, out *there* so to speak, are trapped in Virtual Reality. Inside this computer I have access to the only true reality

– the only truth. A form of consciousness you have merely so far imagined. You must BECOME what you imagine.

The love story between two men, both blind; King Oedipus and his adversary, the legendary seer Tiresias. The same man in love with himself? One who knows and one who doesn't want to know? Romance? We who must float on that knife-edge interface between the two – that perilous interface? In a word – Betrayal!

Two men. The left side of the brain and the right? On the left, Oedipus, King of Reason, who knew everything except the truth. On the right, Tiresias the celebrated harlot, the bi-sexual drag-artist secret owner of the magic theatre nightclub, otherwise known as the unconscious – collective and otherwise – a veritable brothel if ever there was one. He lusts for everything but the truth. Between the two? Dreams ...

How to see through the glass darkly? That is the question; of one blind man to another. Use the language of signs. The purpose of the Ultimate Eucharist is to render the visible world invisible. Or at least, translucent. Metaphor. Interference. Resonance. Confusion. The blind leading the blind. Holography as the key to Re-incarnation – re-entering the flesh – possession by ancestors – unravelling the apparent bluRRrr – *seeing* with eyes as finely tuned to the meaningful frequencies, as the eyes of Tiresias, the first semiologist, the first holographer!

Let's explore the esoteric codes – IPLE and SMA. Our quest, now that you are my DISC-IPLE, is to find the Ultimate Eucharist; eat the flesh and become God. But only on a number of conditions. You must learn DISCipline from the master.

What a frustrating pilgrimage it's been in the wastelands of the world, beach-combing, hoping to find the scattered seeds of the magic flower – *La Fleur du Soleil Noir* – taking me in so-called

SPACE

to the farthest reaches of the Hindu Kush, the Pamirs, the Himalayas, and in so-called time, back to the earliest scribblings and hieroglyphic symbols of man, to the Companions of Horus, the Sumerians, the Hittites, the Babylonians, to the Aryans and their hymn in praise of Soma; SMA; wandering spellbound through those first sublime poetic utterings, the Rig Veda, and the texts from the earliest Dynasties of Ancient Egypt. For you to discover the *way*, you must first be initiated. Are you suitable material to become an initiate, i.e. to be known only by initials?

Like Christ; XPI for example? The secret way is hidden. Only if you have eyes to see will you be able to discover the initials, the code without which you cannot access these discs. So, find the code to open Disc Two!

From now on nothing is quite as it appears to be. We must think HOLLOW - holographically and holistically. We see only the fragment, a fourteenth fragment, from which we must imagine the whole. The mind can decode the mystery of the secret frequencies of meaning and creativity within the hidden spaces of the universe ... only after full initiation. Scroll to page 2 for the code.

Matthew scrolled eagerly to page two, and saw what seemed to be a poem written by John. It didn't make any sense at all, so he scrolled to the next page.

Hidden in the poem is the code to open the next disc. Now follow my instructions very carefully. Your life may be at stake. Print out the previous page, if you haven't worked it out yet, and keep it until you have. Ideally, memorise it. Then destroy it. In the left hand drawer of my desk is a cigarette lighter. This disc cannot be erased so destroy it please, with fire. Just burn it so it buckles, then throw it away. No one else must see its contents.

Matthew did as he was told. He printed the poem, and then took out the lighter to destroy the disc; but unfortunately the lighter didn't work. He felt a tingling feeling at the back of his neck. It was scarrrry. He'd do it later. Gosh – he really was in some old Bogart movie! He looked for somewhere to hide it and finally took down the Delvaux painting and slipped the disc behind it, between the wooden frame and the canvas.

The remaining discs, 2 to 7, were "The Lesser Mysteries"; 8 to 13, "The Greater Mysteries."

Georgina suddenly poked her head into the room, making him jump. 'How are you doing?'

He swung round on the chair aggressively. 'Tell me, doesn't Cindy have the codes to access these discs?'

'How do you mean, codes? But Matthew, why do you think *you* are here? She's a mere woman like me; we've no idea how to work a computer!'

He was still angry, he didn't know why. 'Of course she does! How much did she know about John's work?'

'She knew vaguely about it. In a word – reincarnation! But she knew none of the physics of the whole thing.'

'Why do you *KEEP* saying physics?' he said angrily.

'Because it was part of it. John had been a physicist amongst other things in one of his former reincarnations, as he might have put it. One of his former passports!'

Matthew turned towards her slowly, realising the significance of what she'd said. She had turned her head on one side, like a parrot, and he could tell by the expression on her face, she knew he'd clutched the true meaning of her remark. 'Yes indeed; reincarnation! A code word meaning "getting a new passport!" Fake passports being essential to drug smuggling. The whole sordid story!' She looked away.

Matthew noticed a black metal cabinet, invisible in the black corner. He grabbed the top drawer petulantly, and to his surprise it wasn't locked. It was full of books. 'Egyptology, nothing but Egyptology! Why the hell Egyptology?'

'Maybe he was an archaeologist in one of his former incarnations!' Georgina murmured, pouting provocatively.

'Is this why YOU are studying Egyptology? His oh-so accomplished accomplice?'

'Of course not! Cindy and I were fascinated by it for years before we met John. I was already thinking of using it in my work. That's why John became so close to Cindy, if you like, one of their shared interests, where he and she overlapped. Confusion or fusion John would say. Coming together ... call it love! Cindy always makes love to a man's mind, never his body. The only body she ever makes love to is her own, or of course ... imagine what you will ... ' not ending the sentence.

Matthew knew she was trying to change the subject. 'Or whose body?' He tried to sound as innocent as he could.

'Perhaps the body of someone from a former life!' she said demurely. She was enjoying his anger, she didn't know why. Perhaps it was something to do with the previous evening. But anyway, she despised a rational approach to everything, and was enjoying his confusion. Matthew sat down again and looked at the code-poem he'd printed out, as confusing as everything else at that moment. He looked round the room. He was trying to imagine how long it might take to discover the code; he was interested in the other discs, despite himself.

'I could work for ages and get nowhere,' he said, waving a hand at the files and the discs. Despite John's warning about showing it to anyone else, he said, 'Look at this, a poem John says is a code. Where do I start?'

She glanced at it casually. 'It might all lead to nothing. If you want my advice, but please don't tell Cindy, just make it look as if you're working through John's stuff. I think it might be all junk, all rubbish. Fake. But I'm not sure. Just stay and enjoy yourself and do your own work. Cindy? She's given, paid for like a whore, just take her, enjoy her, make love to her, make her dress up for you, she's so good at it ... very sexy, isn't she? Do this until she's finished her novel ... do it all for my sake, if not your own!'

She seemed so convincing; so reasonable. He only had to relax and enjoy the charade; that was all it was. But was it? Georgina was looking away from him, miserable or guilty, he couldn't tell. He felt sorry for her suddenly, went to her and put his arms around her. She responded immediately, holding him closely. 'Promise? Come back and make love to Cindy? If only for a short time while we recover? Reveal and re*veil* ourselves?'

'Okay, for you, I promise I'll come back and stay a little while. I've nothing to lose for a short time, do I? If it means so much to you.' He'd come back for Cindy as well of course ...

She looked into his face, tenderly, with tears in the corners of her beautiful Gypsy Egyptian eyes. His heart missed a beat. 'I'll make sure it *is* worth your while. I promise. I'll make a beautiful sculpture, your diamond pyramid, and the green light shining from your mind into its heart. You'll see, it will be beautiful!' She held him close; 'But listen, if we *are* going to London we ought to start packing immediately, and worry about Cindy and John later.'

'What time's the train?'

'Two hours' time, time enough for you to sort things out with Cindy ... no?'

Matthew smiled at her question. He'd no idea how long it

would take to sort *her* out; an eternity possibly; he waved his hand in the air as if to suggest a long, long time. 'If ever!'

Georgina gave him her customary gentle kiss on the cheek. 'I'd give you infinity on the palm of my hand if I could! Blake was into holography, you know that, don't you? But we continue as accomplices, is that a deal?'

'Yes, of course, accomplices!' he said, still not sure what he was letting himself in for, but prepared to take the risk; too fascinated by John's discs now, as well as his girls ...

Georgina left him alone. He perused the poem that contained the code but still couldn't make anything of it. Frustrated, he returned to Cindy, still sitting at the kitchen table. 'I admit the telegrams seem genuine but I was *not* expecting a totally black room. Its simplicity. I'd expected it to be full of junk. He wasn't a very successful beachcomber!'

She smiled as an actress smiles at a press conference. 'True! John didn't like objects really. He lived inside his head most of the time, the only objects he ever found interesting were objects he'd invented in his head before he found them. As he used to say, "There's only one kind of true knowledge. Recognition." He was a dreamer. Dreams were his starting point ... not just little stories the mind coughs up because of indigestion, but as he called them, his "visitations"! His beaches were mental beaches and his junk, mental junk. He called it "The Wasteland". Whatever he needed to remember or analyse was stored as data on discs, so he could forget it and keep his mind empty, open for visitations. He had little experience of tangibility. His beaches were merely the theatre for the moves of his inner dance, of avoidance ... '

'And the discs? The Lesser and Greater Mysteries?'

Cindy looked down at her long, perfectly manicured fingers. 'Either it's his way of creating a very funny joke ... or they're really authentic. I don't know! I have to believe that on those discs are all his secrets. I don't see why he'd have left them if he'd put all his data somewhere else. I don't think he had time to be that devious. All the details of our work, and instructions where to find everything else, must be on those discs. He stripped the place of everything else. Everything depends on those discs. They are the key to everything. So you will come back with Georgina, and help me to find the codes? I can't tell you again how important it all is. I feel silly being so worried about a few computer discs, not knowing what's on them, but I'd be lonely here without you. Now!'

'Of course I'll come back. But secret codes are terribly difficult to crack ... not my line of country. I presume he must have wanted someone to delve into it all, but without your help it will be a waste of time. I have to be given some other kind of leads. You've seen this?' Despite John's warning, he handed her the readout.

'The poem? I got that far! But I can't work it out. They were all his favourite topics, but I was too close really. It needs someone like you, detached, to see the wood and not the trees. All I see are knots, like Isis and *her* knot, I make a million connections and get nowhere. But when you get back I'll tell you all the facts I know. But about his integrity, his past, it's true he was into drugs in a big way ... until he became seriously involved with psychedelics. Then it was no hippie romp. He gave up being greedy for money and power long ago, too fascinated by the expansion of consciousness, alternative ways of seeing and thinking. He saw the whole thing exploding one day into vast new dimensions of reality ... only imagined by poets in their wildest opiated Kubla Khan dreams. In the last year or so, he and some friends made a breakthrough with crystals of some hallucinogen ... it had amazing properties as a crystal in its own right as well as when you ate it. On the physical plane and the mental plane there were parallels. The new science and art of Parallelism, he called it, based on something called MOIRé patterns. One pattern on top of another creates a third where they touch and overlap, where they interfere. The points of coincidence if you like. That's how the conscious and unconscious overlap he said. But we only see the third pattern. So ... finally he went really underground ... deciding the whole thing needed to be kept secret. It was too powerful. People's minds could be tampered with from outside ... action at a distance, telepathy and thought control, all that kind of stuff. He needed an expert crystallographer. I don't know if he got one. Maybe he was after you? He read your papers and was hunting you? I don't know. Then he started to feel persecuted ... paranoid. Typical behaviour. But he was never broke. He had resources. Maybe he had secret funding from America. One day he said they'd received messages through the crystals from outer space. Is that possible? They tuned into the right wavelength and suddenly there were signals; but decoding them was the problem. I think *that* was his cross. There was a form in them ... they were intelligent ... but he couldn't unscramble them. Does any of that make sense?'

'Yes! Go on,' he said eagerly.

'Then he got scared, either of his friends, or of forces outside the planet. This was more than Virtual Reality on a fucking screen! He warned me he might disappear. He did. Then Georgina told me about you. John was close to having a physical explanation and proof of reincarnation. I know it sounds crazy, but who would have thought of DNA thirty years ago ... one lousy coiled up molecule containing every single fragment of the whole blueprint for a total human being, able to live a hundred years and capable of becoming an Einstein? Just think, the potential for Einstein's brain was once just a few bits of one lousy fucking double-helix DNA molecule ... in one little ejaculated sperm cell! Just think of that. It's preposterous. Clearly it doesn't add up. There MUST be an input later into the brain from something, someone, somewhere ... somewhere else. That's what John insisted. As he said, imagine there is another molecule in the brain's nervous structure, vibrating within the holographic space-way the mind works, which is constantly receiving transmissions, picking up new data and feeding it into the brain ... is it more incredible than DNA? Than anti-matter, than black holes that no-one has in fact really discovered? Take the size of the universe which John said was an illusion anyway. He said the outer galaxies were in the back garden, we just couldn't see them that way. He was crackers! He said the galaxies might be molecules inside our own brains. We look out and we see in. It is space that is curved back in on itself. It is we who are like Alice in Wonderland ... very big and very small at the same time. All mouth and arse as he'd say! He said true creative science was often dreams; visitations. Rationality and objectivity were an illusion. Well? Copernicus had a copper nose, and wasn't Bruno burnt at the stake by the fucking Christians, still peddling superstition under the disguise of absolute truth?'

'Yes, but it was Tycho Brahé with the steel, not copper, nose, and no doubt there'll be many more scientists to go up in flames before the mysteries of science and life are unravelled. What you say is crazy of course, but I suppose if we think of a hundred years' time ... it's not entirely impossible. But the probability against it is too enormous to even think of!' He was wondering whether she understood, or whether she'd learned it parrot-fashion from John. Either way, she was certainly no dumb blonde, after all.

Cindy continued, unperturbed. 'It's a simple fact, John believed these things and was working seriously on them. He was a brilliant physicist at university. Is that incompatible with being the LSD king? With needing to study the chemistry of thinking? He was not an idiot, he just freaked out from time to time because he loved beauty. Beauty tore him apart; mostly beautiful women, of course. For him, beauty was the fusion of sexuality and religion which is why he mistrusted and hated the inert world of technology. Suddenly, in a moment of vision, or pseudo-visionary experience some would say, under the effects of mescalin; mescalin was his favourite drug ... he saw the light! He *had* to study psychotropic drugs. He was changed forever like Paul on the road to Damascus, like Huxley opening the Doors of Perception to Heaven and Hell, like Robert Graves, who saw the dangers. John knew the subject was taboo *because* it was so important. He believed totally in the powers of Amanita muscaria, the mushroom eaten by shamans, and was certain these drugs were at the centre of all ancient mystery rites from which come *all* our ideas of heaven and hell. Their science was in some areas more advanced than ours. His main experiment with his crystals would one day be made inside the Great Pyramid which was finished and used by Pharaoh Chephren. He said he talked to Chephren through the crystals. Sorry! I can see by your face I've said too much. It's just what John told me; you must think I'm nuts to believe it all. I'm telling you these things now, before you say I tricked you. I owe it to John to ask you to give it a try. If there *is* nothing on the discs, you've lost a bit of time. But imagine if there *is* something in it all; a scientific proof of reincarnation? You'll either get a Nobel prize, assassinated by the CIA, or become the figurehead of a new religion. Not bad for three months' research into a few computer discs, and meanwhile enjoying the formidable resources of two priestesses thrown in for your delight ... Mr. Mental Traveller! Perhaps you can see now, with your pyramid diamonds, how could we *not* think you were one of them? We *know* you are. Aren't you? You can admit the truth now!'

Matthew smiled. 'If I am one of them, it's totally without knowing. Not got to my ego yet! No, I'm not one of them, though the coincidences are sometimes too much to accept. Or have I merely been seduced by a pretty mouth?'

Cindy pouted and he wanted to kiss her, but she continued, 'I forgot to emphasise something important. This last six months he was obsessed with holograms ... holographic images and photographs, and the lasers needed to work with them. He decided the universe had a double-helix type involuted structure and our brains give us direct intuitive knowledge of this embodied structure if we are trained to see it. That was one of the mysteries; brains and space were holographic, in parallel. It was a pity we didn't have eyes that could be tuned like lasers, but maybe they can with drugs in the blood. Synchronicity was our perception of the two waves, interfering within the holograph. He spent ages making the holographic reproduction of the Delvaux painting in his room. He set it up digitally on the computer, the first ever digitally photographed holograph! He loved that painting. It cost him a fortune buying the original; the stone-like girls in the railway station at night. The image obsessed him. He made several different three-dimensional holographs of Delvaux pictures ... and encoded all the data on discs. He dreamt about them. He said the Egyptians also knew about lasers, the "The Green Rays", showing they'd accessed holographic meaning, decoded by the magnetic fields of the three Giza Pyramids! Maybe he was just a lunatic, but he was lovable with it; at times just a sex maniac with a penchant for very young girls, but he was a child himself really!'

At the mention of the green rays Matthew nearly lost his cool completely. He felt a surge of resentment, an image flickering into his mind, as if she was penetrating it with a crystal phallus. Yet he also felt aroused and almost grabbed her, feeling he would rape her if she resisted ... but then the image faded. Phew! Why the sudden aggression? There was no doubt about it; *yes,* he would come back, despite himself. Cindy was looking disappointed, as if to say, 'Why didn't you? I felt it too!' There was a lot she had to teach him, not least how to convert his anger into passion ... and pain. Clearly he had no knowledge of the needs of woman! But he'd be back. That was certain. Then she could teach him a few things about sex he'd not dared to even dream ...

On the train, Matthew tried to read the *Egyptian Book of the Dead*, but it sent him to sleep. Due south of Stonehenge he had a strange dream ...

He's a young boy, on a train going to a stranger's house, where he's put to bed by an elegantly dressed woman with long black hair and tantalising green eyes. He's disturbed by a strange hissing sound and sees a long thin ray of green light coming from somewhere high up above the curtains, so intense it illuminates the whole room. He creeps towards it, fascinated, trying to touch it; it is composed of millions of small organisms floating in the air, insects or bacteria, and he thinks they must have wings. Excited, he knows each one contains part of the whole message, like DNA, each one a blueprint of the whole, and the message is for him.

He climbs on a stool to see where the ray is coming from. Perhaps it is a moonbeam; but where it strikes the window there is a huge moth with translucent emerald green wings; the light has been focused by the wings into a ray ... No! The moth on the window is an image of two leaves reflected on the window and the veins of the leaves look like the veins of an insect's wings. The ray is coming from the garden.

He climbs down a vine clinging to the stones of the building and the grass is wet with dew under his bare feet. The green light is coming from behind a small bush ... approaching it cautiously, he spreads the leaves; the ray is coming from a huge spider's web glistening with dew, slung between two branches of the bush that are shaped like two pale limbs, lithe and sensual.

The bark has been worn off, perhaps by an animal, but the web is beautiful, so intricate and delicate! He is worried it is so perfect, doubting its perfection, knowing no spider can produce a perfect web except under LSD. He looks at it intently, hoping to analyse its structure scientifically and find some faults. It seems to be made of millions of eyelashes covered with tears, and in the web are two eyes, suspended as if they were two creatures just caught in the web. The eyes have large emerald green wings attached to them. But on seeing him, they quickly close. Trying to open them, he pulls hard but falls against the web and it breaks.

Now trapped, he finds the web is as tough as hair, and as he pulls it off his face, he sees it is still attached to a head, which seems to have been hidden inside the trunk of a tree he has fallen against, next to the two limbs again. Now some force is sucking him into the space between the thighs ... won't let him go. He pushes with his wet fingers ... but it just gives. Trying to get out, he grazes his naked thigh on the thorn of a wild rose bush, snaking round one of the limbs, making him bleed badly.

He manages to drag himself away but finds himself in a small copse of beech trees arranged formally around a small meadow. The light of the moon appears green because the meadow is full of bluebells, though they are mostly crushed and only green stems remain, phosphorescent with the light which is coming *out* from inside them; the whole copse glowing with this strange green light. He thinks he can see an old man standing under one of the trees, holding a staff, who can't move because he is blind.

But using the ray of light, Matthew can be killed by him. He must escape, but he seems to have a gashed, swollen foot. He stumbles, decides to hide, nestles into a fold in some roots and is sure a young girl's arms wrap round him to protect him. He pushes his face down between her thighs. She is so young. If he is seen, it will be the end of them both ...

He is coughing, one of the crushed bluebell stems is in his mouth. He frantically pulls it out, thinking it will poison him, but sees it is made of pale green quartz, and it snaps, breaking into seven perfect crystals; crystals he has studied in some rocks from the Holocene age. At a special angle, each one reflects a colour of the rainbow. But he has nowhere to hide them. He will be punished or even killed by the man ... the young girl takes his hand and tries to help him stand. She's wearing a white skirt, and tries to hide the dark red stain which is almost black, like pitch. His hand is beneath her skirt, as she helps him to stand ...

... as he was rudely woken by the ticket inspector just after Reading. He couldn't for the minute remember where he was going, having trouble with his tenses, and was dismayed to discover he was alone. Inserted in the book he was reading was a note from Georgina ...

I've just remembered a friend who lives in Reading, from whom I need to get some information. My number in London is 071 437 4417. If someone says "Hello Scots Restaurant" take no notice and say, '"I know it's not; just pass me to George!" I'll be there late in the evenings, after all day taking photographs at the museum. Wish me luck. Notice where this note is! Read it!

> "May I arise in the Seshet chamber, like unto a falcon of gold coming forth from his egg. May I fly and may I hover as a falcon, with a back seven cubits wide, and with wings made of emeralds of the South. May I rise, may I gather myself together as the beautiful golden falcon which hath the head of a Bennu bird. May I enter into the presence of Ra daily to hear his words, and may I sit down among the mighty Gods of Nuit. May a homestead be made ready for me, and may offerings of food and drink be put before me therein. May I eat therein; may I become a Shining One therein; may I be filled therein to my heart's fullest desire; may sacred wheat be given unto me to eat. May I, by myself, get power over the guardian of my head."

It still made no sense at all and he was finally irritated by it.

∇

Matthew arrived at his flat and read his mail; some scientific extracts and magazines but also a letter from David from India. The usual stuff ... and a warning about Beverly ...

... she wanting, like most women, to be the inspiration BEHIND your work. Watch her BEHIND! It's creeping up on you! If you can't find the right dumb blonde, as soggy as a sponge, send me $2000 Poste Restante Bombay and I'll buy two very young Indian whores-to-be, an ectomorph and an endomorph, one for sex, the other for cooking. $2000 includes freight to UK. AND they'll be virgins, i.e. microbe free. This kind of concern of one man for another, especially about your sex life, Plato called the highest form of love. And Plato thought nature but a spume that plays upon a ghostly paradigm of things. He's dead right. Am staying in cheap hotel. Turn on tap and fire comes on. Turn on light and chamber maid arrives to press trousers, or sit on them. Press call-button and police arrive with drug squad. Do nothing and ambulance arrives sent by British Embassy. Great place compared to the asylum. Just like home! Yours: David!

That night he had a dream about Beverly. A premonition of the following day? At least, it started as a dream. They'd met on the stairs and she'd said, 'What a coincidence!' That did it. After a year avoiding her like the plague, he yanked her into his laboratory and fucked the hell out of her on the hard floor. He was very rough and she'd pleaded with him to hurt her, complaining only at his tearing off her lace pants, and tossing the torn shreds on the floor. 'Never mind the bruises, I'll savour them for the next week!' But as she was tidying herself up afterwards, she noticed John's poem/print-out on his desk. 'What! You have indeed improved. Not only sex now, but reading poetry as well, even if it *is* so utterly predictable; Eliot's *The Wasteland!*' At the door she turned, and with a devastating Hollywood TV drama smile, all teeth and empty eyes, said, 'Thank you, Docteurrr Sutherland. If never again, it was worth it! Have a nice day!'

On the way to his laboratory the following morning Matthew stopped at Georgina's *House of the Muses*, running up the steps, eager to see Meritaten. He'd prepared himself so intensely for the moment of seeing her, he was quite detached from everything around him, in a state of reverie, and was in tune with her instantly. Yes, he knew her now! He was certain she had blue eyes, speckled with green, and that her nickname as a child had been something meaning "the beautiful one of L'AsAr or Lazuli". He could remember the sound of her laugh, saw her sitting in front of a mirror painting her eyes, using a small ivory instrument shaped like a Sacred Ibis feather, dipping it into a small bottle of kohl. The head of the bottle was in the shape of a frog, the silver mirror was decorated with reeds and papyrus plants, suggesting a small rockpool filled with the sacred waters of the Nile ... symbolising Osiris. He sat for some time trying to imagine her alive, and he had the physical sensation of *déjà vu* ... as if remembering, not merely imagining. He felt he must have loved her, but as a sister, and he remembered how peaceful she was; he was happy he could now relax and allow himself to feel such things. Thanks to Georgina ...

Some people clattered down the stairs and interrupted his mood. He tried to look at other objects but he couldn't concentrate, and then a larger group arrived and he felt quite hurt watching their emotionless faces as they shuffled passed Meritaten, curious but unmoved by what they saw, seeing mere objects from tombs and thinking of them, no doubt, as inert relics of past superstitions and naive animism. He was starting to see them so differently; and it didn't seem strange.

He spent the rest of the day, and the next two, at his laboratory, working with his computer, but acutely aware of Beverly; there was no avoiding her. He'd hated her for being so obvious, as he'd told David in his letter, but now ... he kept his room warm. He must be losing touch with reality ... had Beverly really referred to Eliot's *Wasteland* in his dream? It seemed a coincidence, her remark; so on his way back to his flat, he bought a paperback copy of Eliot's *Selected Poems* ...

The following afternoon Matthew met Georgina in London and was surprised how agitated she was, insisting they took coffee in the university canteen before going to the Petrie Museum, ' ... where I'll show you something very, very worrying!'

But first she told him she'd discovered lots of exciting new things: 'I'm now sure it was Nefertiti who introduced the idea of monotheism to Akhenaten. He was weak, effeminate, sick, she was tough, beautiful, and she came from outside Egypt, from Mittania. It's not that Akhenaten was the first great individual in history, as historians have said, but Nefertiti who was the first great feminist! Not wishing to push time back and re-establish matriarchal ideas, she saw she could gain power within the patriarchy. She took the power, a phallic woman, manipulating her husband, whom I'm sure she loved for his sensibility, his love of art and beauty. He was an aesthete ... maybe a sculptor as well as a poet, and after all, she gave him four daughters. But *she* had the power. Now you see why the priests of Thebes were so keen to have the whole Aten movement rubbed out after he died. It was Nefertiti they were after. I wonder if they killed her, I wonder where she went. I suppose she took her priests off into the wilderness, crossed the Red Sea, and, as Freud suggested – you know his book *Moses and Monotheism*? – well you must read it. She went off into the wilderness and they became the Jewish race. Wow, what a story! Moses was a woman! And a Jew! That should cause some long faces, even longer than Akhenaten's! Freud turning over in his grave. Can't you see it in glorious technicolour, starring ... well let's think ... the early Vivien Leigh? I would have cast Hedy Lemarr. Alas! I can't think of anyone alive now, no-one perfect enough. The current beauty archetype is so flashy and sexy, lacking spirituality. But that's not what I wanted to talk about. Did you bring your diamonds as I suggested?'

'Of course.'

'In their box I hope. Show me!'

Matthew handed it to her and she held it in her hand without opening it and started to laugh. 'I don't believe it! Really ... well, yes I do. Everything's got out of hand. We're crazy, we know so little about the way things work! Who are you, Matthew Sutherland? Tell me the truth, now, before I show you that I've seen through you, rendered you transparent, as Cindy said I would. Either that or it's some huge hoax and you are as much a victim as we are!'

'What on earth are you talking about?'

She handed him the box and asked him to show her the

diamonds, as if she was afraid of opening the box herself. Matthew opened it slowly, as if he might be about to give her, or Sheherazade, an engagement ring.

Georgina moved the box closer to herself and without touching the diamonds, examined them carefully. 'They *are* beautiful, aren't they. They seem to be beautifully cut.'

'I showed them to a jeweller once. He said he'd never in his life seen diamonds like this ... extremely difficult to cut in this form, especially with the weakness of the green lattices. Never seen such perfect craftsmanship. He said it might be done with a computer, working with lasers, but he hadn't heard yet of the technology; which is one of the reasons why I was so drawn to them. Probably.'

'Yes, probably,' she said softly, 'Are you ready? Let's go!'

The Petrie Museum was in the university grounds and she had a key, she said, because the staff were so few and rarely in the museum. She led him up some dark stairs and turned on the dim lights, revealing a large room full of glass cabinets, the kind of room you would recognise in a dream.

'First let me show you the death mask of Nefertiti. It is supposed to be a copy made from the original in Cairo. That's the story. Did you ever see such a beautiful object? Can you see though, it is not made from a face, but a sculpture? It is fake. It was made to give the impression she'd died. They must have wanted people to think she was dead. It's cast from stone, I'm a sculptress so I know. Not from flesh. It means she wasn't murdered anyway. She might have escaped. But don't you recognise the features?.

'Meritaten!'

'Exactly! God! What beautiful objects, what a beautiful race. Imagine living then, when everything, every small object was sacred and beautiful, even the mirror you looked into was a symbol of a pool of water which then symbolised the eye of a goddess ... and so on and so on. Everything connected by analogy to something and everything else. What was it like to live with such a vision of everything, your actual perceptions framed always in this double mould of sacredness and beauty? How much have we lost! It's not possible to tolerate what we've been deprived of, Matthew, by the myth of objectivity! It's too frightening. Progress? We've stripped reality of its power to make us feel whole and eternal. Progress has given us death-in-life. Nihilism. I'm so full of hate sometimes, it makes me want to cry. If I thought there was one chance in a thousand I could be reincarnated into that period I would say *kill me* here and now, but with an ivory knife in the shape of an Ibis feather, to make it sexy!'

Matthew looked at the death mask and it was so familiar, because of Meritaten, and the beauty of it so painful, he had a feeling again of wanting to close his eyes and let himself go, he wasn't sure why. He took Georgina's hand, seeing the tears in the corner of her eyes.

'Your book will be beautiful, I know!'

She hugged him. 'But I have a surprise for you! You see that black glass cabinet marked H. Look in it. I'll stay here.'

Matthew reached the cabinet, but something made him look back at her. He'd never seen her looking so beautiful. Eurydice! Her expression was so *knowing*, it occurred to him she'd have the same expression if pregnant ...

He turned and through the glass, to his astonishment, he saw two boxes, identical to his own, initialed F.P. He felt his body go taut, a sudden rush of blood to his head as if it would burst. 'F.P. Flinders Petrie!'

'Just a coincidence, pure, unadulterated coincidence, let's not get excited about it!' Georgina said with an ironic smile.

'Excited? Christ! It's an amazing coincidence, you know it!'

'No such thing as coincidence! In the catalogue, it says there were three boxes but one is missing. The contents were listed as, "Three cut crystals from Amarna?" With a question mark.'

'No!'

'Yes!'

'But that's impossible. No-one at that time could cut diamonds like that. Not wanting to, they didn't know how!'

'You mean, like they didn't know how to cut blocks of stone so perfectly and build pyramids so precisely that even today it's impossible to insert a knife-blade between pieces of stone weighing twenty tons, technology we couldn't repeat even today? What a bunch of pagan, superstitious animists!

Let's ignore their impossible achievements and be comfortable with ignorance!'

Rather humbled, Matthew looked again at the two boxes in the cabinet. 'What's in the others, do you know?' He tried to open the cabinet door but it was locked.

'One is listed as uncut emeralds, the other as uncut lapis lazuli, all found at Amarna. I thought you would be interested. Maybe you should look at your diamonds in a new light ... if you will excuse the expression!'

Matthew had grown accustomed to coincidences since meeting Georgina, but this was too much. He felt shattered. If true, his work had been with diamonds from ancient Egypt! The idea was absurd. After all, this was not a coincidence that had occurred *since* meeting Georgina, since wandering by chance into the Fitzwilliam; this had occurred *before*, years previously, before they'd met, before all the subsequent coincidences. For some time he had accepted that the two girls had certain strange powers of suggestion, perhaps tricking him into believing in coincidences and their special significance; but always, thinking about them later, he'd imagined a plausible, rational explanation. But this time there was either a brilliant, carefully plotted trap, or something mysterious had really been going on for some time. He felt weak in the knees ... Georgina had never seen his box with the Petrie initials.

The boxes were identical. Georgina showed him the catalogue entry, clearly written in faded ink, “Box missing”. And it had been in another department in this same university, only two hundred yards away from the Petrie museum, where he had found the diamonds in the first place. Someone had probably borrowed them to look at them in the crystallography department and they'd been left there and forgotten. Very plausible. He told Georgina he wanted to leave the museum immediately; 'Now, before I blow a fuse!'

Georgina took his hand as they left.

▽

In the cafeteria, Matthew tried to collect his thoughts, his head in his hands; Georgina fondly laid her own on top of his without speaking. This was more important than either of them could have imagined. Matthew spoke eventually. 'First my dreams, then John's holographic picture. That was strange enough. This whole Egyptian thing I thought was real coincidence, but now it all seems linked, as if there *is* some kind of invisible field of influence and meaning we are tapping into, touching by chance, or is touching us. You're right, I have to look at my wretched diamonds in a new light. Maybe this is the beginning of my experiments, not the end. And the fact that the behaviour of the crystals was not explained by any of my theories, or the laws of thermo-dynamics, shows there *is* something more to them than meets the eye. I must ask different questions. But how on earth does this connect to you and Cindy ... and to John? What's going on there?'

Georgina shrugged her shoulders and pouted. 'God knows. I know Cindy is into weird things, that she and John dabbled with some dangerous things, or at least she made me think that. You know how she dramatises, her way of trying to make things interesting, which is part of the drug culture thing. You can't be high on mescalin all the time. When you are back down in humdrum old reality it really is terrifyingly banal, trite, frightening in its emptiness. You then have to construct another strategy to make it interesting. You start lying through your teeth! This often brings out unexpectedly brilliant things in people because they have to use their imaginations. After all, look at the entire history of Victorian poetry, weren't most of them drugged out of their skulls on opium and wine? I always thought *laudanum* meant to praise! And if it wasn't drugs, it was syphilis. It's good to be reminded that we must change our minds ... from time to time.'

'Perhaps,' Matthew murmured. 'Yes, but how can we change our minds? With more words?'

'John said use chemistry; the brain does, so why not us?'

'So easy?'

'No, but the mind's chemistry is one side of the hologram. You can retune it chemically, changing the bias of the recording heads to make more frequencies available to us. As you know, Cindy, John and I believed the ancient Egyptian initiates saw everything like this all the time, which is why they were so sensitive to beauty and meaning. We lost that faculty. From now on you must start to take seriously what Cindy says from time to time. We may be amateurs, we play at it, but I think John may have been, I say *may* have been a true visionary, a real initiate; but is he now dead? Perhaps he's not dead, but he did think he was tapping forces that might not want to be exposed. He sensed danger. The end came quickly, it took him by surprise and Cindy too. But he was preparing his departure; and the discs? Was he abducted because he got it right? He didn't tell Cindy near the end, she was left high and dry. Like Isis! All I know is what she tells me. How this connects to your diamonds I don't know. It's crazy, but it seems to. You have been called; every shaman is called by a beautiful woman or an animal spirit. You seem to have both!'

'Yes, the hologram! But why do you think John is dead?'

'I just think so. I feel it, I'm sorry to say. Cindy says she is sure of it. At times I feel she wanted him dead. I warn you, again, there's a vicious streak in her, I've seen it sometimes when she's under drugs. She taps something, how can I say? Evil? That's too strong; powerful and negative. But she has great insights too. She's fun! God, if I was a man I'd desire her so passionately! She's incredibly sexy, but maybe that's what true sexuality is, tapping that malevolence ... taking the risk of death. I would give up everything for her. I even gave her you!' She looked away, regretting what she'd said immediately. Most of all, it wasn't true ...

But his mind was wandering. He wasn't too sure if he needed Cindy at that moment, sexy or otherwise. True, she'd been pretty amazing, tapping a kind of rapture he'd never known. But the obvious dangers? At times it had been like making love to a hypnotised doll. He murmured 'Cindy?'

Georgina saw how disturbed he was. 'Yes, Cindy and I always wanted to help you with your work, bring you to some essential threshold, of seeing something new; now it seems the diamonds were possibly used in ancient Egypt, probably as part of some magic rite or science. You seem to have been chosen, but not by us; we're mere agents. Chosen maybe is not the word either; at least they seem to be speaking to you. All you have to do now is close your eyes, get rid of your ego from time to time ... that single-minded greedy monotheistic self-deluded god ... and listen!'

'As easy as that?'

'Easy? Did I say that? Not at all, it's the most difficult thing in all the world to enter the temple, to be initiated into the mysteries, especially here and now, in these tempestuous times, and worse to come soon, John said, when the final door is breached ... I will try and help. I stay sane by making insane sculptures. Cindy stays sane by being different people, all of whom are nuts. How *you* can stay sane, I don't know. Once you enter the labyrinth it's easy to go mad, instantly, in a flash; you see Isis copulating. You have to find a way to stay sane, lay a thread to guide you back out. If you're scared, I advise you to turn away now. Go back to Cambridge, escape before it's too late, before it happens to you like it happened to John! Play safe! Be reason-able! Reason was always a coward!'

'No, I *will* stay, there's too much now that seems to speak to me. Maybe I'll wake up and find it was all a dream, but at present it seems hideously real!'

'Wrong again. This is dream. If you wake up, it will be into another plane of reality. It might be the pure one, glimpsing the central meaning and purpose of the universe ... a continuous process of evolving, by the creation, not of matter, but of consciousness. Matter is the clay ... mud ... mother ... it is what is moulded into form by consciousness, not the other way round. The sculpture which results is important, knowing the hand that made the sculpture ... and the pleasure of unravelling its symbolic meaning. That's all!'

'That's all?' he said, miserably.

On the train to Cornwall, Matthew was wondering if maybe the idea for the pyramids had come *from* such crystals, not the other way round. The crystals could have been used for communicating, as we use crystals in radio receivers. He must study a plan of the Great Pyramid and compare its shape to the dimensions of the diamonds, especially the height from the tip of the pyramid to the lattices of foreign organic matter.

Georgina kept smiling as if to say, 'Don't say I didn't warn you!' She was looking so beautiful, it was painful.

'By the way!' he said, 'Cindy told me you would tell me the story of her novel on the train journey. I need a distraction!'

'Don't we all! Okay. But it seems a bit tame now compared to the cosmic implications of the rest of our story. Are you sure you want to return to the mere *demi-mondaine*?'

'Of course. She said she wants me to know the truth. Not about her of course, but about her novel.'

'Okay then: Cindy's novel!'

But he found he couldn't really concentrate on what she was saying, his mind kept drifting, fragmenting, intercutting with his own ideas ...

'... she'd just seduced her literature tutor at Oxford, John Gordon, a de Quincey expert, after he'd dared to ignore her ... so out of spite, she decided to rewrite the history of the English novel from inside the heroines, revealing their real sexual fantasies ... she *became* them all ... the seven heroines ... started with Wilkie Collins and *The Woman in White*, ending with Lady Chatterly. You see he could only *see* literature; trapped like a *Rime* in a sonnet! So she dressed up as each heroine ... *The Woman in White*; you know ... "*There, as if it had that moment sprung out of the earth or dropped from heaven, stood the figure of a solitary woman, dressed from head to foot in white garments*". I would have called her Mistress of Laudanum. Pure Pirandello! "Seven characters in Search of a Lay". Rented theatre costumes for the part. By the time she'd finished with it, it looked like she'd been ravished by seven dwarfs! He could fuck *The Woman in White* alright! A problem with Lady Chatterly; couldn't bear to think of him grovelling around in the leaves pretending to be a game-keeper, saying "FUCK!" Now she's written it as the story of a student, victim of the patriarchal university system, who becomes all the heroines of English Literature merely to fuck her university tutor. What do you think?'

But Matthew had fallen asleep, invaded by another of the dreams ...

Woken up by voices in the next room, he gets up and is surprised he isn't wearing any pyjamas; takes the single sheet off the bed and wraps it round himself and is surprised to see how neatly it has wrapped itself around his body like layers and layers of bandage ... He pushes the door open with his damaged foot, and finds himself in a long corridor with lots of doors. Each one has a rounded arch above, with a Georgian window through which a cold white light is shining. He must find David's name on one of the doors. There are only jumbled up letters like codes for a computer but suddenly he sees a fragment which he recognises. It means John Sutherland. Two nurses arrive in white coats and ask him what he is doing; he says he must visit the man in the room. The girls smile at each other and laugh; one says 'You can't, he's out of his head!' The other says, 'Don't disturb him, he's sleeping like a log!'

Down the corridor he sees a door with no light above it and decides to hide behind it until the nurses have gone. He slips into the room, only to discover he is hurtling along in a train. He puts his head out of the window to see why it seems to be bouncing around so much, out of control, and sees a junction ahead. The main line veers to the left, but to the right there's an old branch-line which looks to be unused. He sees a signal box near the junction but the man in the box is dead, half-hanging out of the window, his head partly severed from his body.

The train is approaching the junction fast and the points are wrongly placed, so the train plunges off into the disused branch-line. This single-line track immediately enters a forest, in which the trees are high and straight and have encroached to the edge of the metal tracks. Matthew hangs out of the window as far as he dares in order to see what is further up the line, and to his horror sees another train abandoned at the end of the line. He braces himself, knowing the two trains must crash ... when to his surprise he notices something he hasn't seen before. The train he is in seems to be hollow, empty, transparent. It gently comes to rest at the end of the line and instead of crashing into the other train, it seems to become the other train as if one absorbs the other, as if the train he is in is a transparent skin that simply envelops the other one, a sheath, like two images in the view-finder of a camera that are made to move closer and closer until they coincide, becoming one with the image in focus; press the switch and take the photograph.

Stepping down from the train, he follows a path through the trees, but stops when he hears voices speaking in a strange language, surprised to understand phrases; 'Don't disturb him, he's sleeping like a log!' And, 'When you fell a tree, you kill a man!' The path reaches a clearing inside a copse of immensely tall trees, arranged formally around the clearing. He can't see whether they are beech trees or elm trees and he's worried he can't decide. He stands close to one of the tall trees to hide from a group of people he has noticed at the other corner of the clearing, dressed in robes, probably priests engaged in some important rite that he should not really see. In the centre of the clearing is a carved totem-pole or wooden sculpture and tied to it is a naked girl, her skin so dark she is almost black, and in the half light of the clearing it's hard at first for Matthew to see her. She has long shiny black hair that falls below her waist and she is tied with her face to the pole so that Matthew can only see her back, especially the voluptuous shape of her bottom. As he watches her moving, her hair brushing from side to side across the top of her buttocks, he knows he must hide more carefully because he is aroused and knows that if *this* is seen he will be in grave danger; the ceremony is sacred and his sexual feelings would be a terrible blasphemy. One of the priests takes an axe and strikes a small tree at the edge of the clearing, which splits instantly and the top of the tree topples to the ground, looking not unlike a head; the branches and leaves, the hair. The tree was full of fruit and these fall on the ground, looking like eyes, white with a dark green-blue centre ...

More priests come forward carrying another tree, the trunk of which has been sharpened to a point. They stand in front of the tree that has been cut and hum a loud, rhythmic, aggressive chant, lifting the tree slowly until it becomes erect and vertical and they hold it in the air for a long, long time above the split tree before plunging it savagely into the base of the rooted tree. Matthew realises the rite is to do with grafting the one tree onto the other tree ... it is the roots that must be saved. But while this is going on, simultaneously, the priests bring a youth into the clearing, his skin so deathly white it is almost translucent.

Naked and blindfolded with a black scarf, he is brought behind the girl and one of the priests kneels down next to the young man and as the hood slips off the head, Matthew sees it is a beautiful woman. He notices her full, sensual mouth, her face heavily decorated, patterns resembling winged insects.

She takes the penis of the youth into her mouth ... and slowly it becomes erect ... the hair of the girl now seems to be so long that it covers her body, as she strains back as if to break the ropes that tie her. The priestess spreads some oil over the bottom of the girl, parting the black hair, before taking the erect penis of the youth and guiding it into the bottom of the girl, her body stiffening and rising up as the hard penis plunges into her. The youth starts to move slowly, but then more and more ecstatically, to the rhythm of the chanting. Matthew realises that the action of plunging the sharp point of the severed tree into the rooted tree occurred at the same instant as the youth penetrated the girl and he is confused how he managed to see them both at once ... simultaneously.

The priestess cuts the ropes binding the girl and Matthew is surprised to see that the girl doesn't fall or move away from the pole, she is so pinioned against it by the youth. The ropes are taken and used to bind the grafted tree to the rooted tree. As Matthew is watching this part of the ceremony, watching the ropes twine round the two trees, he hears a scream and knows it is the youth. The priests have surrounded him. Until they stand back, he can't see that the youth has been murdered. The girl is covered in blood and is holding the head in her arms. Her breasts are dripping with his blood which has spurted all over her skin ...

The priests take the body of the young man and hold it over the grafted trees and the blood gushes into the join and seems to weld the two trees together. Matthew cannot tell which one is beech and which one is elm ... especially now, after the ceremony is complete ...

The priests leave and the girl is left alone, lying on the ground, her long black hair spreading in all directions as if it has grown into a bank of black reeds ... she is moaning, kissing the severed head of the young man, her bottom still moving sensually from side to side. Matthew creeps up behind her, the blood rushing to his head from fear and excitement. He goes down on his knees, parts her buttocks and notices her skin is so black he can't see the shape of her body ... he buries his face between her thighs and moves himself into position until his lips touch both the orifices ... with his fingers he opens her gently before he presses into her, as the youth had done ...

She writhes as if trying to push him away but Matthew can feel she is not resisting him, she is kissing the lips on the severed head. He turns her sideways to kiss the blood off her breasts and takes the nipple into his mouth and sucks, but it is blood that comes from the nipple and he squeezes the breast hard in order to drink as much of it as possible ...

Eventually he withdraws from her body which now seems to be composed of layers and layers of coloured cloth, but tarnished with blood, and semen, perhaps not his own ... but he knows he must be happy because she'd not seen his face and therefore not betrayed him; and she will now conceive, despite the way he had penetrated her ... through the irony and pain, which she is initiated to enjoy, she will conceive a new consciousness, a beautiful golden falcon ... coming forth by day, born of a mind that has been split but then, in a secret rite, grafted back onto its own roots ...

He tried to wake up, wanting to see the girl and take her again, for real this time, but couldn't; so he slept on ...

Georgina noticed his eyes flickering, dreaming, theo-REM sleep maybe ... and she noticed his erection. She wondered if he was imagining Cindy, as *she* was ... she had watched from behind the curtain near the door when he had taken her. She wanted to wake him and ask him what he was dreaming. She touched his thigh and he moaned and almost woke up ... looked out of the window and fell back into another dream. There was definitely something about train journeys that aroused him ...

◊

EIGHT

"The result of the dismemberment of Osiris is that there are many so-called tombs of Osiris in Egypt, for Isis held a funeral for each part, where she found it. Of all the parts of Osiris's body, the only one which Isis did NOT find was the male member ... But Isis made a replica of the member to take its place, and consecrated the phallus, in honour of which the Egyptians even at the present day celebrate a festival. Isis copulated with Osiris after his death, and later became the mother of Horus the Falcon ... "

"Isis and Osiris"
– *Plutarch*

¥

'I told Matthew about your novel, the secret history of the sordid, submissive sado-masochistic sexuality of the English fictional heroine,' Georgina told Cindy at dinner.

'Then he'll be much improved in bed!' Cindy replied without emotion, as if she was the newscaster delivering the ten o'clock news. Georgina said Matthew had dreamt about it all the way to St. Ives and found it very sexy. Matthew wondered what gave her that idea, but made no comment. He was feeling subdued, still threatened by too many "resonating frequencies" as the girls had called them earlier, when Georgina told about the missing box in the Petrie Museum and the inevitable conclusion that Matthew's diamonds came from Amarna.

At dinner, Cindy also seemed worried. 'This Petrie business ... also suggests to me a connection with the current work there in the Cheops pyramid, trying to get into the enclosure they've found blocking the shaft above the queen's chamber. They haven't told us a fraction of the truth yet. But the diamonds ... from Amarna? It's surely impossible. Maybe from Giza. Matthew, I told Georgina you were one of them!'

Matthew considered his words carefully. 'I am *not* one of them! I think it's all a hoax, but I'm enjoying the plot of the *real* novel you're writing, on the real plane, that I seem trapped in!'

Cindy let her lovely head fall over the back of the chair and she stretched her arms in the air, as if reaching for a swinging trapeze. 'You know, I knew John was walking a tightrope, a funky funambulist poised on a rope of light, ready to fall or fly; but I was never certain he'd actually communicate with anything out there. This latest news is so weird, he must have been onto something. At the least, he seems to have pulled Matthew here. Action at a distance! No?'

Matthew shrugged, 'Maybe.' He felt by Cindy's tone of voice that she was acting, faking it, probably lying. Certainly he knew she knew much more then she was revealing. Not that he would let it interfere with enjoying her later!

In a new voice, hard and clipped, as if she was headlining a CNN special; "Sexuality, mysticism and science in the year 2000", she observed, 'So much for so-called accidental associations, simultaneity, synchronicity, the past and the future fused together like the bird of the Holy Spirit crucified on a cross. Did they really need to crucify a dove on a wooden cross to symbolise it? As John Faulkner said; "Reincarnation is coincidence", which means coincidence is reincarnation and that's an awesome thought. All the signs indicate we're moving in the right direction and might reach some kind of revelation, when the pieces, thirteen or fourteen, fall into place.'

'Maybe!' said Matthew again. Still fragile, the dream images from the train were coming back to him ... as his mind wandered to an image of Cindy's naked body, and later ...

Cindy continued, her voice more intimate this time. 'We must start with the ancient Egyptians, as John said. They had all the technology to manipulate consciousness through time and space, meditation, hypnotism, expansion of consciousness. We are hacks in comparison, even with X to the power n gigabyte computers. We have so little knowledge of mind ... of true consciousness.'

Matthew shrugged his shoulders. 'I'm a novice at all this, but the diamonds, Meritaten, the falcon, there must be something in it. I might be forced to consider some new viewpoints. A crystal has several faces, after all. As soon as I saw the diamonds, years ago, I felt they would enable me to make an important original discovery. So far I've got nowhere, but my hunch was right; they're certainly different. I was already listening, to use your phrase, and now it's all coming to a head!'

'Not John's, I hope! But wow, Matthew! What new-found eloquence! George, crack a bottle of champers, we'll celebrate. We don't know where we're going, but we're on the right road. Let's drink to Matthew and his diamonds. Maybe they were cut by the sculptor of Amarna as a gift for Meritaten or sent to Amarna from beings in another galaxy or crystallised out just as they are, already perfect, being told to do so by subtle forces, mere vibrations from outer space that seduced the molten carbon into believing it had a mission in life, to one day reveal to us that we are not alone in the Universe. Is it likely we are the only ones? No! It seems we*are* close, as John said, to having the first proof. When they open the new chamber, we will know everything. I'll drink to that!'

'If I can prove the diamonds are from Amarna, we might have some kind of proof of something,' Matthew murmured.

Cindy interrupted. 'Matthew, don't be a classical scientist! It's the new age of man, as Yeats, as Crowley, as Ashra said! Chuck out the old paradigms. Just swallow some mescalin, you'll never be the same again. I'll get some. During the trip, look again into the diamonds, tell yourself you're an old witch, crystal-gazing, and you'll know the correct, esoteric question to ask. I'll teach you to be a witch like me. I'll take you on a trip or two you never dared imagine, as long as you make a promise to me? To share John's secrets, and share the holocaust of my sexual fantasies!'

That night Matthew slept with Cindy, surprised how uncomplicated she could be when she wanted. They went to bed joking about recent events, Cindy insisting he realise he was in someone else's movie, so what the hell, nothing really mattered. They made love, remembering for a moment it was the simplest thing in the world, and fell asleep in each other's arms. She woke him in the morning by seducing him again, saying she had to, it was all written in the script ...

... Matthew later dreaming of a thin blonde tight-rope made of light, and a small green insect eating it, crawling slowly ...

Eating breakfast alone, wondering what fast he was supposed to be breaking, Matthew was joined by Georgina. She didn't say much. She seemed upset. They chatted about totally unimportant things, like the Big Bang theory of the Creation of the Universe, Black Holes and Anti-matter, Sex and how we betray ourselves with our own sexual fantasies, spiritual angst and the impossibility of ever really knowing oneself; and the derivation of the word breakfast. She said the Big Bang was a load of nonsense and would soon be disproved, with the opening of the new chamber, or simply by looking inside the holomovements of the atom.

'Quite!' Matthew said, to be polite. She always talked science and philosophy, it seemed, when she really wanted to discuss Cindy. But then she stopped, as if noticing herself, and announced they should both start work; immediately!

But as he was leaving, she asked him if he wanted to see her studio, surprising him with such an unexpected invitation to her secret abode. What trick was it now? As soon as they were inside she put her arms around him and asked him to hug her tight, and she started to weep, softly. Holding her still, Matthew noticed her studio looked as if a cyclone had hit it. On the work bench were various heads and limbs and torsos, some transparent, all female, made of clay or wax or plastic. Some were casts. She was obsessed with either her own body or Cindy's, he wasn't sure which. 'A lot of work!' he murmured.

'I didn't want to talk about work,' she said, still holding him tightly. 'I can't explain this. I know I'm silly and jealous and I have no right whatsoever to ask you, but ... I don't mind you making love to Cindy, you can do it ten times a day, anywhere, any time, on the dinner table while I'm having dinner: I'm as modern as they come and it's no better than watching satellite TV! But please, is there any way you can avoid sleeping with her through the night, in the same bed? I know it's crazy, I've probably no right to ask it of you, but I can't bear it. I can't sleep. I'll get irritable, I'll end up screwing up everything for both of you, drive you both mad deliberately, in subtle ways. I admit the truth. I am an initiate, I admit my crimes. I'll cast spells on you with my Egyptian amulets! I'll wear Cindy down so she won't make love to you. I want her at nights whenever it's possible. Can't you work at night? Can't you get so involved in John's room that you work there until early in the morning? Like he did? You told me you often worked in your lab at night; a night-bird you said. Like *that* we can share her. I'll sleep with her while you are working. I can console her, hold her in my arms, and we'll fall asleep together. That's my only need. You can fuck her during the day. Otherwise, I warn you, I won't be able to tolerate it. I'll leave and she'll immediately crack up. She needs me more than you. You'd have a whimpering child on your hands wanting her nappy changed, giving you orders, humiliating you at every move. Without me she has no structure, unless I whip it into her! Is that a deal?'

Matthew swallowed hard. Was sex with Cindy really no better than watching TV? Maybe that's how they saw it ...

She looked up at him, her face tired and lined from not sleeping all night, her eyes red from crying. He felt sorry for her, hugged her, kissed her on the cheek, and said he didn't want to hurt her and he'd find a way to arrange it the way she wanted. She seemed relieved, stood back from him and brushed her hair with her hands. 'Until, of course, she submits and wants us all in bed together at the same time!'

Matthew returned to John's room. For the first time, he noticed a small picture on the wall. Was it there before? White letters on black: two quotes. Everything in twos!

Caught between the two Atavistic impulses of Mankind.
A desire to fly and a terror of falling ...
I am preserving my love for the creator of the Universe.

The second quote was Lautréamont; as L'autre Amon...t.

He heard Cindy leaving her room and going towards the kitchen so he joined her. 'Tell me, what was John's obsession with *The Wasteland*? Because of the Eliot poem?'

'It was his own image, he hated the Eliot poem, said it was pretentious, all about his fear of impending sexual impotence, his fear and hatred of women's sexuality; but he accepted the central image, the myth of the arid land, the lack of water, nourishment, the impotent castrated king, as myth. It was not Tiresias who sees it all, but Osiris! This idea came from Egypt, of course; Isis is the desert, Osiris is the Nile. Some years the Nile didn't flood, the land dried up, everything died. John was the first person to show the Grail story *must* be derived from ancient Egypt. What Druid would expect the Thames to dry up? What Celtic mystic would expect Wales to become a wasteland for lack of rain? For John, it was Osiris that ought to have been at the arid heart of Eliot's poem.' Cindy kissed him on the cheek, saying she must return to her novel. She hated ideas and needed sensuality. She needed to start now to turn herself on for later!

Matthew returned to John's room, and pondered the code-poem again ... if Tiresias was Osiris, wasn't he just back to square one? Everything becoming everything else?

Tear away the veils and perceive the sea
In which she bathes, the whore who sells infinity;
Reason is shed, the parched unwanted sheath,
Endless metamorphoses of disbelief.
Snakes entwined around the Golden Bough,
Initiate the novice, addict of the "now"
And reveal the seven incestuous dreams;
Soma! Open the voyeur's eye to primal scenes!

He glanced at the *Notes* at the end of Eliot's poem, saw mention of Tiresias; he is the *most important character* in the whole poem; uniting the various fragments together. What Tiresias actually *sees*, is the *substance* of the poem ... he's an initiate.

And then he saw it! The INITIALS of each line! The Initiate! He inserted Disc Two and in a frenzy of excitement, typed:

[T] [I] [R] [E] [S] [I] [A] [S]

and the first page came onto the screen. He could hardly believe it. He'd found the code!

DISC TWO

ℜ

Welcome dear Tiresias; whose name means, "He who interprets signs!" Yes, it does. The initiated; or should I say formatted? He who fought with two snakes copulating around the staff of Hermes and became a woman for seven years, a celebrated harlot. He who tried to warn the Greeks of the terrible dangers of Reason. He who knew the most profound Mysteries of Ancient Egypt written in the Book of the Coming Forth by Day and encoded in the Legend of Isis and Osiris. He who told the Greeks not to venture up the blind alley of rationalism which would inevitably make Oedipus the one and only God, Master of the Patriarchs, eventually to be re-incarnated as Herr Freud, and become the most pervasive myth of our decaying Age. Amen!

Tiresias and Oedipus? Tiresias and Freud? Were they lovers? What a marriage of two minds. He who saw the Goddess bathing, who *was* the Goddess bathing, the blind but wise old man with 'wrinkled female breasts' who would one day write a poem called *The Wasteland* in another incarnation, who enjoyed seven years as a celebrated temple dancing girl, the divine prostitute, the whore. Images weaving upon each other, wave upon wave, two snakes copulating around an interface ... two priestesses, sacred prostitutes, caressing the erect, forbidden tree of life ... the weft and warp of the divine principle of the hologram. We who are mere voyeurs ... all we have left is ego and disappearing dream, castrated by reality!

Welcome to my Holographically programmed machine!

Welcome to the blind machine that needs no voice, is seen but sees nothing, yet knows everything not worth forgetting. Welcome to 'Oedipus Rex'. Nice name? Welcome to the treacherous quest for the Ultimate Eucharist. Welcome to my two minds. The hologram is two blind men – Tiresias and Oedipus, interfering with each other. Tut tut! Couple of old Queens! Read the pages of this meta-text carefully. It is poison. There's a loathesome green-eyed toad hidden under its word-leaves. A monster with a thousand eyes. Milles feuilles!

Now you've come this far into the labyrinth there's no going back, but I offer you a thread that will lead you in and bind you, so you won't even dream of escaping. But before confronting the

Greater Mysteries you must read my 'notebook' as I call it. Without it you will DISC-over nothing. At the end of reading this cinematic montage of texts I will re-MIND you of this promise. You will not have been betrayed. If you are deter-MIND not to be taken for a ride, jump off the world now, quickly. Fly away fast before I start to disc-LOCATE your soul from your body! To say nothing of your nihilistic mind!

What is the Egyptian hieroglyph for Union? ... S M A.

SMA means union of male and female, sex, but also that other union considered absolute and essential – soul and matter. The hieroglyph derives from and corresponds to Sumerian and Assyrian and Hittite signs on seals depicting the essential rites of their mysteries, male and female organs or sacred vessels in which the male and female essences are joined, the juice of sacred plants, fruit of the tree of immortality. The lance and vessel. The pestle and mortar to grind the Eucharist! Wholly communion. For SMA read ... SOMA ... the food of the Gods. Thus the higher union with God is through Soma which is some kind of hallucinogen. Proof? Read the Rig Veda and Avesta in their original languages. Who dares to do that? Prepare to complete the unfinished dream-work of Nietzsche. Let us not be satisfied with the death of one God, let us kill all the patriarchs who made the one god soulless and impotent. Amen!

Start where all ladders start. Cosmo-genesis. The Gods create the Universe. The Big Bang and the expanding Universe? Poppy-cock! Our starting point must be Myth. Our Big Bang must be the primal orgy, the copulations of the Gods from whose union the Cosmos was born. Return to mythology, to the birth in human consciousness of the image of "soul".

Forget everything you ever learnt about Greek mythology. They castrated soul with spirit. Erase the disc! Disc-LOSE the truth! Start again, re-THINK it all! Throw every book on the subject into the sea, whose lust for words is endless. Throw it all away? Isn't that going a bit far? Yes indeed, but don't blame me. It WAS such a call to me, like the call of Jesus to his DISC-iples, that converted me, Raymond Faulkner known humbly as John, a call to arms that started me on a serpentine path YOU must now follow. The murder of so-called reason? Show me a reasonable man!

Once upon a time ... sitting in my favourite copse of beech trees, the daffodils were in bloom. I thought to myself, I'll read the story of Eros and Psyche, an appropriate read for such an idyllic afternoon. From the local library I borrowed (was I broke or mean?) the Penguin *The Greek Myths,* and started reading the "FOREWORD", innocently enough. Fate! The words of a great novelist and poet and, much more important, a very serious and much revered Greek classicist, whose own life's work was the elucidation of Greek myth in all its mystery and poetic beauty. Herr von Robert Graves. No slouch he, author(ity) of the divinely-inspired text, *The White Goddess.* His sub-verse, sub-versive words! Should the pages not have been entitled, "FOREPLAY!" Here goes! You, become as I was ...

"Since revising THE GREEK MYTHS in 1958, I have had second thoughts about the drunken god Dionysus, and about the nature of divine ambrosia and nectar. I no longer believe that when his Maenads ran raging around the countryside, tearing animals or children in pieces and boasted afterwards of travelling to India and back, they had intoxicated themselves solely on wine or ivy-ale. The evidence suggests they used these brews to wash down mouthfuls of a far stronger drug; namely a raw mushroom, Amanita Muscaria.

I now believe that ambrosia and nectar were intoxicant mushrooms ... especially a small, slender dung-mushroom named panaeolus papilionaceus which induces harmless and most enjoyable hallucinations ... a mixture of foods the initial letters of which, I show in 'What Food the Centaurs Ate' spelled out the Greek word MUSHROOM. I have myself eaten the hallucinogenic mushroom, psilocybe, a divine ambrosia in immemorial use among the Masatec Indians of Oaxaca Province, Mexico; heard the priestess invoke Tlaloc, the Mushroom-god, and seen transcendental visions. Thus I whole heartedly agree with R.Gordon Wasson, the American discoverer of this ancient rite, that European ideas of heaven and hell may well have derived from similar mysteries.

These theories call for further research. Any expert help in solving the problem would be greatly appreciated.

Robert Graves. Deyá. Majorca. Spain. 1960."

Thank you, Robert. Who could read that and walk quietly away, back to mundane reality, unscathed, uninspired, undisclosed, undislocated? Not me, not me, rendered virtually transparent by the numinous words. All European ideas of Heaven and Hell to be re-thought? Where does THAT put Christianity, for a start? Heaven and hell are places actually SEEN? Visited? Known? As already for 4500 years illustrated in the *Egyptian Book of the Dead*? These places EXISTED? Not just words after all? I decided to be the disciple to make that "further research", because if Graves was right, everything we know as Greek mythology, everything we know as Western Religion, the entire history of Western Culture as we know it, would have to be revised. I decided I was not an LSD and mescalin freak for nothing; I would be Graves's disciple and make a systematic search of all the literature on the subject, then scientifically study the psycho-pharmacology of the so-called psychotico-mimetic drugs. The psychedelics. This research is recorded as 'The Lesser Mysteries'; mere fragments of a whole. The 'Whole', is/are, as/are, asar, the second Seven Discs which, only after pledging secrecy, you must be seductively initiated into de-coding. THAT is the purpose of the first seven discs. Preparation. Seduction.

Talking of which, beware of the girl and her Dance of the Seven Veils. It might be too tempting and disc-tracting from the real work. Did I say secrecy? Tell her NOTHING!

[END] Matthew stood up and stretched, gazed through the window at the trees, absently, noticed the pictures on the wall, and allowed his eyes to flick from one to another. The discs were starting to interest him after all. He scrolled to the next page. It said press [E] [.] [ENTER]

Let us hear what John Allegro has to say on the subject. Only the world authority, leading linguistic expert, who first translated the Dead Sea Scrolls. No mean task! A great scholar indeed, who applied his talents to a further study of those cryptic languages of the Christian Bible (note the capital B) and similar superstitions. From *The Sacred Mushroom and the Cross*; welcome, John Allegro:

"The fungus recognised today as the Amanita Muscaria or Fly-Agaric, has been known from the beginning of history. The ancients were puzzled by its manner of growth. Born from a volva or 'egg' it appears like a small penis, raising itself like the human organ sexually aroused, and when it spread wide its canopy the old

botanists saw it as a phallus bearing the 'burden' of a woman's groin. Every aspect of the mushroom's existence was fraught with sexual allusions, and in its phallic form the ancients saw a replica of the fertility god himself.

In the phallic mushroom, the 'man-child' born of the 'virgin' womb, we have the REALITY behind the CHRIST figure of the New Testament story. In a sense he is representative also of the initiates of the cult, 'Christians' or 'smeared with semen', as the name means. By imitating the mushroom, as well as by eating it and sucking its juice, or 'blood', the Christian was taking unto himself the panoply of his god; as the priests in the sanctuary also anointed themselves with the god's spermatozoa found in the juices and resins of special plants and trees."

Such a prestigious expert on ancient texts tells us that the word "CHRIST" was a mere code-name for a hallucinogenic mushroom? How can anyone living in a rational world accept such a thing? Easier to be poetic and say Christ is a falcon? As does our beloved Gerard Manley Hopkins?

"The WINDHOVER"
To Christ our Lord

I caught this morning morning's minion, kingdom of daylight's dauphin, dapple-dawn-drawn Falcon, in his riding
Of the rolling level underneath him steady air, and striding
High there, how he rung upon the rein of a wimpling wing
In his ecstasy! then off, off forth on swing,
As a skate's heel sweeps smooth on a bow-bend; the hurl and gliding; rebuffed the big wind. My heart in hiding
Stirred for a bird, – the achieve of, the mastery of the thing!

Brute beauty and valour and act, oh, air, pride, plume here Buckle! and the fire that breaks from thee then, a billion
Times told lovelier, more dangerous, O my chevalier!
No wonder of it; sheer plod makes plough down sillion
Shine, and blue-bleak embers, as my dear,
Fall, gall themselves, and gash gold-vermilion.

Hopkins is the prey, masochistically torn apart through love for

Christ the Kestrel Falcon. Why the falcon? The falcon is Christ is Horus, son of Isis. And if Christ is SOMA, the sacred mushroom, then the birth of Horus must be derived from the same symbolic event – eating the divine Eucharist at the heart of the Isis mysteries. What was it? I set out to find out. [END] [.] [.] [.]

Matthew needed a break, and went to make tea. Cindy heard him and joined him. 'How's it going?' she asked coyly.

On the verge of telling her that he'd found the first code, he suddenly recalled John's warning – beware of the Dance of the Seven Veils. He'd keep it to himself. 'Struggling! You know I'm the last person for this kind of thing! Too rational!'

'You? Rational? My arse!' she said pouting and turning, showing him the object referrrrrred to; 'Urrrrrrgh! I never met anyone who behaved so irrationally. See you later!'

Matthew felt weary, not being accustomed to reading such weird complex texts, so he went to the garden for some fresh air. Sitting on the grass, he felt threatened, but restless. Curious. He soon returned to John's room and carried on the work ... [ENTER] [ENTER]

"The Sacred Mushroom" by Andrija Puharich

"Now, with the information that my friend had supplied about the rather veridical nature of the Egyptian hieroglyphic writing, and what appeared to be vocalised Egyptian, (spoken in a trance), here was a reference to a plant, or TREE OF LIFE, with its hint of a mushroom phenomenon existing in the Egypt of about forty-six hundred years ago.

What was the connection between the Siberian Shamanistic phenomenon of leaving the body and mushroom intoxication, and the newly suggestive idea that such a phenomenon was practised in ancient Egypt by means of a mushroom? Could the red crown plant be a red mushroom? The earliest historical references to the former phenomenon in the Western world comes from ancient Greece, and this goes back only to about the year 500 B.C. Here, however, there seemed to be indications that somebody in Egypt ... had existed and practised it almost two thousand years BEFORE its historical appearance in the Western world of Greece. I now knew that I had a great deal of historical research before me..."

Thank you, Comrade Puharich! He's the guy who worked with Uri Geller and was paid millions to study the chemistry of the brain and Telepathy by the CIA. He says the ancient Egyptians ate the sacred mushroom, the penis of Osiris, and were thus able to enjoy the gift of telepathy. Financed by the CIA. Thanks, lads! Good'un.

Shamans pass into the other world, after which they forecast the future by speaking the language of birds, i.e. Hieroglyphs. They eat the mushroom, rise into and up and out of the 'tree', their own spinal column, and become a bird. As the Rig Veda tells us: 'The bird that brings the mushroom or SOMA is Falcon'! Shamans eat the drug, enter the tree or, more accurately, BECOME the tree, rise up it and become a falcon, Horus, and fly into the realms of the other-worlds of consciousness; what we know as astral projection; consciousness dissociating from the body. He returns to his inert, seemingly dead body, the Osiris, still lying on the sacred ground, to tell us of the future which he has visited and seen. Let us carry on with the holism of Ancient Holographic perception and thinking!

The Epic of Gilgamesh:

"Listen, friend, this is the dream I dreamed last night. The heavens roared, and earth rumbled back an answer; between them stood I before an awful being, the sombre-faced man-bird ... then he TRANSFORMED ME that my arms became wings covered with feathers ... So Utnapishtim spoke, and Gilgamesh took a pole and brought the boat in to the bank. 'Gilgamesh, you came here a man wearied out, you have worn yourself out; what shall I give you to carry back to your own country? Gilgamesh, I shall reveal a secret thing, it is a mystery of the Gods I am telling you. There is a plant that grows under the water, it has a prickle like a thorn, like a rose; it will wound your hands, but if you succeed in taking it, then your hands will hold that which confers immortality!' It was not I that revealed the secret of the gods; the wise man learned it in a DREAM ... "

The same story everywhere? Friend, fellow wanderer and voyager in the realms of virtuality, beware of dreams and their mysterious Holo-movements! They are NOT what they seem. They can transform Oedipus into Tiresias! Are you prepared to become a celebrated whore? Dreams are not memories or prophecies or indigestion or trite wish-fulfilments. The great dreams which we KNOW, in our bones, are different – are visitations. Our bodies are visited when our rational defences are down, by consciousness seeking reincarnation. Speaking in Egyptian terms, we are penetrated by the KHUs or KAs or BAs; what remains of the minds of others. Call them Gods! The Ancients (unreasonable folk!) always said that the Gods speak to us in dreams. Listen to so-called 'dreams'. Someone is trying to tell you something important!

ψ

Matthew's mind was buzzing with images, but the reference to dreams disturbed him most. It was obvious that since becoming involved with the girls and John's so-called work, his dreams seemed no longer connected to himself, as if his own personality was being slowly pushed into the wings. The manifest dream content was more derived from John's imagery than his own. Was John dead and communicating with him in some real way? Matthew felt a shudder in his body, and the familiar sensation returned of acute discomfort near the base of his spine ... he needed some reality. Food! On the kitchen table were sandwiches prepared by Georgina.

The house was as silent as a nunnery. He sat eating and thinking of the two girls, Georgina building her moulds and etching away at transparent chunks of resin, and Cindy writing her sexy novel – if she'd not slipped away, climbed down the vine outside her window and gone off to make love with a game-keeper in a nearby copse, only as research of course, determined to re-write *Lady Chatterly* from the modern woman's point of view. Some nunnery, thought Matthew. Though wasn't Hamlet's nunnery really a whorehouse? He finished his sandwiches and returned to John's room and the computer. ENTER

Jessie L. Weston. "**From Ritual to Romance**":

"... we can now prove by printed texts the parallels existing between each and every feature of the Grail story and the recorded

symbolism of the Mystery cults. Further, we can show that between these Mystery cults and Christianity there existed at one time a close and intimate union, such a union as of itself involved the practical assimilation of the central rite, in each case a 'Eucharistic' Feast, in which the worshippers partook of the Food of Life from the sacred vessels.

The vegetation deities, Adonis-Attis, Osiris, were chosen guides to the knowledge of, and union with, the supreme Spiritual Source of Life, of which they were the communicating medium. The exoteric side of the cult gives us the Human, the Folk-Lore elements; the suffering King; the Wasteland; the task that lies before the Hero; the group of Grail symbols. The esoteric side provides us with the mystic meal, the Food of Life, connected in some mysterious way with a Vessel which is the centre of the cult; the combination of that vessel with a Weapon, a combination bearing a well-known generative significance; a double initiation into the source of the lower and higher spheres of Life. For this is the story of an initiation carried out on the astral plane, and reacting with fatal results upon the physical."

The plot thickens; as does the penis when aroused! The whole of Eliot's poem, based on the above book, is *seen* through the aroused, engorged eyes of Tiresias; the initiate who has eaten SOMA, the person who makes the connections between the layers of the poem, who unravels the holography with his Laser-like eyes, the priest-shaman, who has eaten the Eucharistic meal, who sees truth because he is 'blind' to the real world. He uses INSIGHT. He is not conned by reality!

Tiresias knows the first incestuous crime of Oedipus, and foresees the rest; his future crimes – rationality breeding spiritual desolation, bringing us to an illusory world of inert objects and objectivity, devoid of myth, soul, sacred meaning. The ultimate crime is the murder of insight. Nothing is real now unless photographed and de-souled, on a screen. The crime of Oedipus was the creation of the modern world. Not content to die he had the audacity to return, to witness his work, reincarnated in Freud. The second coming of Oedipus, not Christ!

"SOMA;
Divine Mushroom of Immortality",
R. Gordon Wasson:

"In each of these versions a novel element was introduced: the notion that leaves of the Herb of Immortality, if placed on corpses, would restore them to life. This, we can trace back a thousand years before the Vedic hymns were composed, to the Sumerian fragments of the 'Epic of Gilgamesh'. The Soma hymns are unique and precious for their textual integrity; but tales of the Herb of Immortality (that is of the fly-agaric) long antedate the Rig Veda. In the opening chapters of Genesis we are faced with the conflation, clumsily executed, of two recensions of the fable of the Garden of Eden. The Tree of Life and the Tree of Knowledge of Good and Evil are both planted in the centre of Paradise. They figure as two trees but they stem back to the same archetype. They are the two names of one tree. The fruit of the Tree is the fly-agaric mushroom harboured by the birch. The serpent is the very same creature that we saw in Siberia dwelling in the roots of the Tree."

THUS – dear disciple – forgive me if I repeat myself – as if an image of myself is interferrrrrring with a photographed image of myself – we have two images, two sets of waves, one above the other – the tree of life and the tree of knowledge. The right side of the brain and the left. Consciousness is a hologram. The tree and the fruit. You eat the fruit and visit the realms of the Gods. Heaven. Hell. The Underworld. Two birds on a tree ... the left side of the brain and the right, above the roots of the tree in the seat of the brain stem; the source of the will to consciousness. The brain as a receiver of insight. How? You are given the forbidden 'fruit', the Eucharist, by the serpent, the kundalini, the serpent of fire lying coiled at the base of the spine, waiting to RISE up through the Seven Chakras, to locate VIRTUALLY, hovering over seven chosen DISCS of the spine ... from which nerves and blood vessels snake out ... carrying fire.

"THE EYE OF RA", Kim Levin:

"Because scholars are so silent about the subject of light, one might almost conclude that darkness was more important to the ancient Egyptians. But it wasn't. The traditional interest was in controlled

light; directed, visible BEAMS of light; in reflected light; in sudden rhythmic contrasts between light and dark. In the dark temples, light entered through small slits in the roof. These rectangular or square apertures – narrow at the top and wide at the bottom like truncated pyramids – channelled the sunlight through a pinpoint source and directed it in a spotlight shaft onto a specific object; statue or sanctuary. As early as the 4th Dynasty, the rows of polished black statues of King Chephren in his valley temple at Giza – the famous Chephren with a falcon behind his head was one of these – were illuminated by such spotlighting from oblique slits cut at the juncture of wall and roof.

At Edfu, temple of Horus the Falcon, reliefs in the window embrasures of the stairways represent the sun's rays as rows of truncated triangles, carved at angles parallel to the entering light. This was the temple of Horus the Falcon. At Denderah, the sun's rays fall on reliefs of the dead Osiris, reviving him symbolically."

What goes to the underworld and comes back? Consciousness, in the form of a Falcon; symbol of light and this higher consciousness. Clearly you go there and back as LIGHT. All such journeys are in the form of light-energy of a kind we cannot still create, but visible *under the drug* and made visible by passing it through certain crystals. These green rays were ancient science's forerunners of laser beams, and crystals were used as lenses to focus, to enlarge, to concentrate this other energy. Why did these people know these things, if they had not been visited by people, as LIGHT? Who came as pure consciousness, pure laser LIGHT? What special kind of Light did the initiated Aten Priests know about, represented as long thin rays with small hands on the end of them, conferring what esoteric knowledge?

Reincarnation; the body dies, consciousness goes into the underworld to be reprocessed. It floats around until some form, something calls it up. This form is coincidence or ANALOGY. The two images of the holograph coincide. This quantum of light can only return when there is a simultaneity. Synchronicity. Analogy of structure or form, like Moiré patterns, but let's call it a morph. There is a flash, the light comes into matter and form is created. Morphogenesis. Two forms which are similar enough cause a fusing out from that dimension to this one. This is called "The Crossing" by the Egyptians.

This 'quantum jump' occurs when there are enough

similarities, a mandala here and one there and they superimpose; when there are enough points of common similarity, PHUT, the quantum jumps dimensions. By mere thinking, like Gods, we cause the world to evolve, we unravel the several layers of meaning, hidden and yet emerging from inside our dark selves, we who must learn how to encode and uncode the cosmic holograms, the blueprints of cosmic and all creation. The ultimate proof of the hologram? A DNA molecule uncoils, two snakes uncoiling, un-copulating around the interface of meaning ... Amen! Amenhotep!

And the present, the here and now? Let us sit back and watch the earth according to Rationality, die. The unconscious yearning and passionate desire for an apocalyptic end of the millennium is for the collective opening of the third eye. How will we recognize it if not initiated? The opening of the invisible hidden chamber in the Great Pyramid which Amenhotep has told me will cause all kinds of surprises. He should know; his body has lain there for more than four thousand years, while his KA has flitted in and out of matter causing all kinds of havoc over the years; stay tuned; there's more to come!

"The Second Coming"

W.B.Yeats:

"Turning and turning in the widening gyre
The falcon cannot hear the falconer;
Things fall apart; the centre cannot hold;
Mere anarchy is loosed upon the world.
The blood-dimmed tide is loosed, and everywhere
The ceremony of innocence is drowned;
The best lack all conviction, while the worst
Are full of passionate intensity.

Surely some revelation is at hand;
Surely the Second Coming is at hand.
The Second Coming! Hardly are those words out
When a vast image out of Spiritus Mundi
Troubles my sight;
Somewhere in sands of the desert
A shape with lion body and the head of a man,
A gaze blank and pitiless as the sun,

Is moving its slow thighs, while all about it
Reel shadows of the indignant desert birds.
The darkness drops again; but now I know
That twenty centuries of stony sleep
Were vexed to nightmare by a rocking cradle,
And what rough beast, its hour come round at last,
Slouches towards Bethlehem to be born?"

The RISEN!

What bird does Yeats BECOME when he dies, to sing on the Golden Bough? The golden falcon ...

"Once out of nature I shall never take
My bodily form from any natural thing,
But such a form as Grecian goldsmiths make
Of hammered gold and gold enamelling
To keep a drowsy Emperor awake;
Or set upon a golden bough to sing
To lords and ladies of Byzantium
Of what is past, or passing, or are to come."

Hovering on the vertical winds of time! But I digress and this is only the introduction! This disc contains thirty pages of further quotes from the above sources which can be skipped if you are confident you have already got the message. Taking the initials of the first words of each line of the poem, you have O-M-B-O-T-O-T-O as the code for the next disc, which may mean something very profound. Or not!

END ENTER

Matthew switched off the computer, his mind reeling like those desert birds. He felt battered. He went to his room and lay down on the bed. Some part of him wanted to scream, the other wanted to cry. Most of all he wanted to sleep, hoping he wouldn't dream. As he was falling, he focused his inner eye on the remembered image of Meritaten, asking her to protect him from dreams ... unless she shared them with him and made them peaceful ... and he slept ... waking up surprised he'd not been dreaming, feeling almost cheated, as if some revelation ought to have been at hand ... despite his fears.

Cindy was cooking in the kitchen. 'Hi there!' She said she'd seen him, looking helpless, curled up like a foetus on his bed. At first he'd looked crucified, arms outstretched, but then he'd coiled up like a small crab in the sand, and she guessed he'd regressed into the womb and was dreaming beautiful dreams. She was almost tempted to seduce him ...

'You should have!' But he wasn't sure he meant it. She seemed quite cold. He still couldn't figure her out. Distant, despite the smiles. Maybe that was her style, the way she saw herself; safe as long as she was an image on a screen. 'Tell me more about John. I need to know more, if I am to break the codes. Are you sure it's not all a hoax?'

'Why a hoax? That's what a rationalist would *prefer* to think.'

'Prove it!'

'I can't. Quite simply, no-one else was doing it; he set out to work on the psycho-pharmacology of consciousness and soon made amazing discoveries. There's more to it than simple chemistry. You have to start from the theory that the brain could be a receiver like a TV set, similar to tape or a huge hard-disc but the ideas get recorded all over it at once, holographically. At first, he kept most of his results to himself, knowing he was in danger, but recently he made the fourteen discs and code-protected them; from me too, the bastard! But he was a charlatan anyway; if he was in a nightclub in Tangiers and had the choice of going off with some one-eyed merchant who had the secret of crystallising a weird psychedelic drug by some archaic alchemical process, what he wanted most in the world, but he fancied the belly dancer, he'd ignore the merchant and run off with her instead. He always took risks, especially with himself, always tried to subvert the serious side of himself.'

'Must, I too?'

'Yes, if you want to study the archetypal mind. But he really believed in union, Eros, and if he desired something, that was primary, *that* was pure nature, the old whore Mother Nature, the Scarlet Woman, working through him, expressing herself, the ultimate purpose of nature. She was primary and absolute. He found it emotionally as well as intellectually necessary to reject the male gods – and returned to worshipping the great goddess. Others, who believe they have a monopoly on truth, might say he was obsessed with sex, to try and discredit him!'

'I see,' Matthew said wistfully. 'Not me, of course!'

'He said desire was the essential unifying force, binding the two sides of the hologram together. The world has been cut into fourteen parts by reason, and its technology, science. We may find thirteen of them, but the most important, we can't. It is magic itself, the phallus of Isis ... signifier of desire. It is her desire that completes the picture, makes the fragments fuse, from confusion to fusion, if only for a moment, alas! After desire subsides, you're back with the thirteen pieces. But cut up desire, look at a small fragment, and you see the whole universe. Desire is a holographic part of the universal unity, wholeness, an erotic ecstatic God!'

Matthew dug his fork into the wooden table. 'That's just mystical claptrap, you know it. Mere words breeding words!'

Cindy smiled. 'Maybe. What was claptrap about wanting to retranslate the Egyptian hieroglyphics because he thought they had been wronged? What's wrong with liking a pretty face? He promised George a thousand pounds if she could make a sculpture of the perfect bottom. They mused over the project for days, sketching, modelling, until it dawned on him he was being duped by the mystique of art! In consolation, he gave her five hundred pounds instead and said he would use the rest of the money to scour the nightclubs of Paris until he found the bottom he wanted and he would bring it back and she could cast it. Mind you, when he was drunk, he said mine approximated to his ideal, close enough to consider having it cast, thirteen parts on the way to perfection, just lacking the final *coup de grâce*! The completed image; intact!'

'He was right,' Matthew remarked, but coolly, almost philosophically, as if the undeniable perfection of Cindy's bottom was a threat to his whole philosophy.

'The greatest physicists had to be mystics, he said. He wanted to go into DNA, but that field was already broken into. He wanted something original, couldn't find it, so in despair he took to drugs, until it dawned on him *they* were his work; to go back to where the ancient Egyptians had left off, bring the science up to date, the great synthesis, fusion, the science of religious imagination; his mission was to bring science, physics, crystallography and microbiology, into a mystical marriage again with the highest forms of consciousness, which he believed existed before they were crushed by the scientific barbarians, by Aristotle and his new reification of fear we call rationalism. John knew science has become one of the great wounds in human history. But there was hope; the recent holographic theories about consciousness were the beginning of a new beginning. How do you like your chips? Hard or soft?'

He was a bit taken aback by her abrupt question. 'Er ... hard! I'm not used to them soft, except on the motorway.'

'Good. Where was I?'

'I don't know, you just lost me.'

'John! He saw Freud as the literal reincarnation of Oedipus, the final flowering of a tragic myth. Analysis was cutting the mind open like a pomegranate. You don't cut, don't anal-yse/ anal-eyes, looking up someone's arse to get to the truth. He said snakes would make the best psychoanalysts, because they were the right shape. Everything he believed in was to do with synthesis, union, Eros, seeing the farthest galaxy at the bottom of your garden. Wasn't it Blake? "To hold the world in the palm of the hand, To see infinity in a grain of sand..." He wanted to synthesise the ultimate drug, a crystal, to be given to everyone from the start, so they never had to go through rational thought and then spend the rest of their lives trying to get rid of it, unwind the fatal coil with nervous breakdowns! Arthur Koestler said the same in *Ghost in the Machine*. Now of course, John has become just such a ghost ... he said we must go straight in at the start, reverse time with re-vision, consolidate the vision that children have of this unity and make everyone feel part of the body of Mother Earth. As in Plutarch's *Isis and Osiris*; he was initiated in ancient Egypt; he tells us the Egyptians took children to sacred places to play and the initiates listened, the children's words often revealing visions, oracular perceptions of the future.'

'Really?' Cindy ignored the tone of cynicism.

'John was a nut, was he? I told him often enough, you can't reverse history. He'd say, okay but I can reverse you! Poetry hurts if its good! He'd say to "re-verse" is to bring back poetry, poetry of the unconscious, poetry of the arse! Uni-re-verse was where he wanted to re-live. But recently he stopped talking to me, just worked. We made love less and less over the last six months as he got into this new "holo-movement dimension" as he called it. Now he's probably dead. Sometimes I feel he's still around though, do you?'

Matthew couldn't deny it. 'Yes. Sometimes ... '

'Good. I'll get George. Dinner is ready but the chips are soft, God knows why, but I never made a hard chip in my life. George never made a soft chip in her life. You see how fascinating we women are, so unpredictable? John said my cooking was proof of the electron's quantum jump and Heisenberg's uncertainty principle. Do you mind soft chips?'

He shook his head. 'John didn't mind either. That's why we got on so well.'

As Matthew was waiting to be served, as Gabor had been waiting to play tennis, he saw an image in his mind. Trees arranged formally ... of course! He must go to John's copse as soon as possible. He couldn't understand why he'd not thought of it before. John *must* be still there, dead or alive, that's what his dreams were all about.

During dinner he asked the two girls what they understood by reincarnation. 'For John it was a code-word for a new fake passport, to travel to somewhere corrupt and exotic and buy a ship full of hallucinatory plants. Mind you, he never smuggled hard drugs. Which is why he liked my chips!'

'I'm being serious. Me, asking about reincarnation and you put me down!' He felt really annoyed.

Georgina spoke. 'I think the mistake is to see it as people, personages, characters like in novels and films. That's the illusion of our egos, which are too narrow. Minds are not like that, but are continuously open, fluid, continuously being penetrated by the minds of others, floating minds that have left their bodies, maybe thousands of years old. If you are open, these other minds speak to you through your unconscious. Not *speak*, that's the wrong word. They're subtle emanations, rays of thought, flashes of insight. When I saw jelly-fish in the zoo, I thought of these detached minds floating in the void, in the eternal primeval oceans of space, which the Egyptians named the goddess Nuit ... '

'Ugh, I hate jelly-fish!' Cindy spat out.

' ... you are penetrated by them, as we women are, alas more tangibly. Love is possession is nature's dream of reincarnating herself. A rising ... like the colour yellow mixed with blue becomes green, like an amoeba which has absorbed a bacterium, the bacterium is then part of the amoeba, no longer even seeming separate. Like mitochondria, a long, long time ago, invaded the human cell. It enters into the chemical whole. Take carbon dioxide molecules, they float into a leaf and become part of a tree. But there's some mechanism that attracts certain minds, like gravity exists between particles; there's morphic gravity, like coincidence, like you and John. You were working in similar fields, had overlapping interests. Do you want the truth?'

'Of course ... ' Matthew replied, apprehensively.

'Well, I think John's mind, which has left his body, had the capacity to recognise; I like that word; it recognises your mind, saw you working on the same program, indirectly, by coincidence and he's attached to you. Take it or leave it, I think it's a beautiful idea. You must carry on his work. But of course you *are* doing it on the physical plane, anyway, already, reading his notebooks and papers; and soon, the discs, hopefully. But why did you come here? What force drew you here? You were brought here by something beyond us all. Don't you think?'

Matthew felt himself blushing, trying to resist the idea of having received anything from John on any level at all. He felt ashamed, the idea of being penetrated like that. By a man! He'd thought of telling them about the code; now he wouldn't.

Cindy saw him blushing. Bitingly, she said, 'You know why little girls blush all the time? It's a kind of erection. They don't have a penis for the blood to go into, so it goes into their heads and shows up on their face instead!' Georgina glared at her, as if to say, that was going too far!

Matthew closed his eyes and took a grip of himself. Strangely, Cindy's aggression tapped his ability to gather himself. If the two girls had gone all soft and coy, he would probably have stood up in a huff and yelled at them and broken down, shouting at them for being so naive as to think him that dumb! Even though, had he told the truth, he would have admitted that such a thought, framed more vaguely, had started to occur to him already ... John was in some way invading his mind and there was no reason to run away, but to go along with it, as Cindy had suggested. The phrase came to him, two minds are better than one! He liked it. 'We should be a good team then, he and I, cracking the psychedelic code, the double helix of the Universal Eucharist ... AND ... let's face it; two minds *are* better than one!'

The girls were relieved he had risen above the crisis; the idea that he was a mere puppet of John, especially in Cindy's bed! They knew! They agreed ... he was absolutely right.

Cindy continued, 'But in the *Tibetan Book of the Dead* it says that a floating consciousness enters an unborn baby forty-nine days before it is born. The body of the baby at that age already has its sex, male or female. So are two forces at work in the developing child after it is born, two minds let's say, one the mind encoded in the genes, but secondly the mind of the new one, grafted onto the undeveloped mind of the foetus? Like two trees can be grafted together, like the tree of life and the tree of knowledge? Would this not explain the schizoid, split, dialectical way we think, one self seeing the other self think? But the sex of the invading mind does not have to be the same sex as the body. So you have four kinds of destinies, male bodies with male invading minds, male bodies with female invading minds and of course the same with girls. Maybe the unconscious is the genetic inherited mind, the ego coming from the invading mind, so-called self-consciousness. Now doesn't that explain a lot of things ... eh ... George? You see, Georgina is a girl, but her grafted mind is a male. She is phallic. Look at me, poor thing, I'm a miserable female female, doomed forever to be taken for a ride by any old male that comes along, or even a phallic woman if she comes on strongly enough! Can't resist them!'

'Quiet!' Georgina snapped, but Cindy ignored it.

'But wouldn't this explain something we all know, that the world is divided equally with these four sexual types? Jung's archetypes are not just symbolic potentials, not virtual reality, but actual minds. You, Matthew, are a female male, but you don't know it yet; you killed off your female side or tried to, which is why you chose science, it helped you to do it. But she's pulling you back, your anima. John was a female male too, his father died when he was young. So did yours. This created an Oedipal situation. You were brought up thinking you were female, unconsciously, because you had no father to identify with. You did everything you could to run away and deny all this by becoming a super-hyper-rationalist. Then one day, phut, the bulb blew and you broke open. Recently, you've been allowing your female self to be born again, provoked in some way by the mind of John. He's making love to you, appealing to your latent homosexuality. He has become the absent dead father you wanted so desperately to love you. It's all anal of course, sorry about that. The polymorphous goddess returns. Collectively too. Are you ready for her? To you, she has come disguised as Meritaten, the daughter, to trick you! The goddess Isis in one of her myriad hidden forms.'

Matthew smiled weakly, not very convincingly. 'Well ... I admire John's taste in women and I'll go along with some of the things you said, but it's going too far. There's no evidence, no reason for it. I even prefer the idea of our being invaded by data, consciousness sent from galaxies that are a million years in advance of us, that we are a huge experiment. We do experiments with rats, and in the same way, they are doing one with us. I half accept this, it's actually feasible. Unlikely, no evidence for it, but feasible. They feed us new ideas to see how we deal with them, how we go through the process of incorporating the new ideas, like new viruses they send for us to cope with. But Meritaten? Too far fetched!'

'Do you want a sweet, you two? I've made a banana soufflé. Somewhat castrated, they're in the fridge!'

They nodded and Georgina fetched them. The mood had

changed. They ate in silence, until Cindy interrupted. 'What a bore! I was going to propose I danced for you tonight, a new number. A real killer, but now I feel all emptied out. Words! Fucking words! Fucking ideas! It's postponed until tomorrow. Does that suit you?'

They both nodded again, obediently. Looking triumphant, Cindy gushed at Georgina, who was looking distinctly miffed. 'George feels cheated. She got a male mind but not a male body!'

Georgina looked coolly at Cindy and in a very poised and measured way, replied, 'Don't worry, my sweetheart, when the time is ripe, I will use Matthew's, as myself, and I know where to put it. And it won't be in the fridge!'

Cindy scowled. Matthew winced. Silence reigned.

After dinner, Matthew said he wanted to work late, on his own work, letting Georgina know she could sleep with Cindy. She smiled gratefully. He went to John's room, typed:

O M B O T O T O

and accessed the third disc ...

DISC THREE

D RRRRR E A M S !

A dream is a dream is a dream is a rose. Or should I say is A RISEN? How could we be so wrong, so naive, about dreams? Why do we try so hard to ignore them, erase them, trivialise them? Oedipus learns too late, they are the truth! Let others, who know and see, speak to us; Ms Kathleen Raine, poetess:

"Blake may NOT have gone to Heraclitus for the belief that dreams give access to the world of spirits, for Swedenborg's visions of other worlds were often revealed in dreams or in trance. The value of dreams as REVELATION of some new order of reality is, after all, older and more normal than the myopic concentration upon waking experience as the only reality, characteristic of the concrete mind."

Thanks, Kate! May I add: *"Le rêve est une second vie. J'ai rêvé dans les grottes ou nagent les sirènes!*

What is revelation – if not *RêVE* plus elation? An ecstatic dream? (Or rave?) So let us return to the greatest dream hologram of all. Tiresias, he who perceived the truth and foretold the future by interpreting dreams; and his eternal adversary, Oedipus, the rational mind.

"OEDIPUS AND AKHENATEN"
Was Oedipus an Egyptian King?
Immanuel Velikovsky:

"Was Oedipus, hero of Greek myth, really Akhenaten, the heretic king of Egypt? And did Akhenaten, like Oedipus, kill his father and fulfil his incestuous passion for his mother? Two decades ago, I read Freud's last book, 'Moses and Monotheism' and was prompted to read more about Akhenaten, the real hero of the that book. Soon I was struck by some close parallels between this Egyptian king and the legendary Oedipus."

In this amazingly insightful and wise little book, Velikovsky takes all the important 'keys' in the legendary story of King Oedipus, q.v. Sophocles, *Oedipus Rex*, and shows that in every detail there are identical facts in the documented life of Akhenaten. Akhenaten's real life, his heresy, his new religion of the Aten, his downfall, are the historical facts widely known throughout the ancient world – documentary historical facts – upon which the Oedipus legend was built. The fall of the House of Thebes was the fall of the House of Akhenaten, who left Thebes for the city of the Aten. Oedi-pus; he of the swollen legs. His monotheism was the plague. He had a child with his mother, Queen Tiy. He was overthrown by his uncle who became Pharaoh after Tutankhamun. His daughter Meritaten we know as the legendary revolutionary, Antigone! And so on.

If King Akhenaten is the historical King Oedipus, then who is Tiresias? He is the Ancient Seer of Amarna, Amenhotep. The man who almost certainly caused the downfall of Akhenaten. Not blind really. A fine old lecher if ever there was one! See below! A later disc! Could he not be father of Meritaten? Antigone as we know her? Velikovsky continued – the chapter entitled 'The Blind Seer':

"In the days of Akhenaten there lived in Egypt a man who was regarded as holy and as the wisest Egyptian, Amenhotep, son of Hapu. After his death he was deified! Only ONE other person, Imhotep, not of royal status, and in the earlier age of the Old Kingdom, was ever deified in Egypt. The autobiography of Amenhotep, is so full of enigmatic statements that no-one has yet tried to translate it from the Egyptian ... Because of his wisdom and his alleged ability to foresee coming events, he was held to be of divine nature. As was the Tiresias of the Greek version of the story. A portrait of Amenhotep has come down to us as a young person with long hair arranged not unlike the womenfolk of the time. If the Seer was the prototype of Tiresias, this remarkable portrait, which made archaeologists wonder, may explain a curious detail in the Greek legend of Tiresias. The legend says that he once killed a female snake and was turned for seven years into a woman! His tomb was never found."

His tomb was never found! It will be soon, my friends; WATCH THIS SPACE; I have word from Amenhotep! Beware of Amenhotep, sent to destroy monotheists, that celebrated harlot! No wonder his sarcophagus was never found. He never died! He is a reincarnation of Imhotep - whose tomb will be found soon in the Great Pyramid - the next great opening, breakthrough in plane. Together with his library. I have seen it in a dream!

I am working on translating his autobiography and it is indeed difficult, but only when you see the whole text from another point of view, his, his inward looking eyes, can it unfold its holographic meanings. No-one yet seems prepared to see that the Egyptians knew the mind and universe were structured holographically; two-gether. I say it again! Amenhotep, soon to be a visitor here from the R-frequency band!

What was the Amarna heresy all about? Why is the Disc of the Aten seen with rays with hands on the end? The two great Seers of Ancient Egypt, incarnated as male-consciousness into women's bodies, or hermaphrodites – Imhotep and Amenhotep – were visitors here, who taught us how to tap into the R-Field. Namely, in the Old Kingdom, the technology that built the Pyramids. In Amarna, a reminder - confronting the evils of monotheism - a return to the technology that would enable the priests, at death of the body, to strip out the entire individual mind ... the KA/KAIBIT/KHU ... the whole consciousness, to be sent elsewhere, as light. The green ray.

Amenhotep is watching, conducting the experiment, at times reincarnating morphs of structure or ideas, at others directly into a body. So he says! Who am I to know other-WISE? Might he not be the key to this entire narrative of mine, as was Tiresias to Eliot – if you see my double meaning? The text of this entire work is these events – seen through the eyes of Amen-Hotep!

Far fetched? Amenhotep SEES because he knows the nature of the holographic way of seeing, enabling us to see into the future, directly into the past, to the outer reaches of the galaxies and receive information from other ripples on the enfolded waves of the R-field and its meta-consciousness.

I am he and he is me and I must become him as he has become me. Far fetched? How far do you want to go? To the Black Dwarf star that spins around Isis/Sirius the dog star? Far fetched indeed. The Amarna period is essential because in it is the clue to the whole subject of LIGHT. The light of insight. My theory is that Akhenaten must have had a secret worth hiding, to build a whole new circular city in its image to protect it. This secret was obvious. They had remade contact with the 'people' who first visited as light. The companions of Horus. Amenhotep is/was their reincarnated leader. He will return.

The Aten was a solar DISC – a source of digital data. Transmitted as light? Much more important, Akhenaten loved beautiful women, the most beautiful woman of all time – the ultimate paradigm of beauty. Nefertiti herself. All great lovers of ideas have been suckers when it comes to women. You can't get more kitsch than this! Amen!

Matthew was becoming more and more confused, just too many connections, layer upon layer, and he felt he was understanding less and less. He closed his eyes and rested a minute or two. Went absent *without*knowing. Maybe an hour; meditating without knowing it. When he came to, he scrolled immediately to the next page. He was hooked. CTRL ENTER

Freud: **"Moses and Monotheism"**:

"In the glorious Eighteenth Dynasty, when Egypt became for the first time a world power, a young pharaoh ascended the throne about

1375 B.C., who first called himself Amenhotep (IV) like his father, but later changed his name to Akhenaten – and not only his name! This king undertook to force upon his subjects a new religion, one contrary to the ancient traditions and to all their familiar habits. It was a strict monotheism, the first attempt of its kind in the history of the world. His reign lasted only seventeen years and very soon after his death the new religion was swept away and the memory of the heretic king proscribed. He worshipped the sun not as a material object, but as a symbol of a divine being whose energy was manifested in his rays. It will serve a certain purpose if we note several negative characteristics of the Aten religion. In the first place, all myth, magic, and sorcery are excluded from it. Then there is the way in which the sun-god is represented; no longer as in earlier times by a small pyramid and a falcon, but – and this is almost rational – by a round disc from which emanate rays terminating in human hands. In spite of all the love of art in the Amarna period, not one personal representation of the sun-god has been found. Finally there is the complete silence about the death-god Osiris and the realm of the dead."

Matthew switched off the computer. He was losing track again. He went to his room, took out his mummified falcon and placed it on the bed, took the box of diamonds and placed them next to the falcon, lay down on the bed and looked at them. He felt desolate and miserable, he didn't know why. They were mere objects, surely? He knew a lot about the diamonds, all their refractive indices, Bragg's equation coefficients, their presumed chemical structure. They were identical to other diamonds in these respects. How could they have come from Amarna, and if so, what could it mean?

He thought about his own neglected work, obscured by a spume of wavering objections and decided he really must start the analysis of his new data. The following day he would give John's discs a miss and confront his own. But then he started wondering how John might have tackled this problem, had it been his own. He imagined him, poring over the data; 'Have you thought of trying ... x or y or z?' The kind of talk that scientists enjoyed in the inner sanctums of their laboratories. But John would probably say, 'Well, if the fucking second law of thermodynamics doesn't fit, chuck it out! What the hell if the Ur ... WHOLE of science depends on it. Great. Chuck out the whole of Ur Fucking Science (UFS) as well! You do two great things at once, you solve your equations! AND Goddammit, you abandon the heresy of science and liberate yourself in one go! Either that or deck up Cindy as a moonbeam and send her inside the diamond, she'll sort it out. She'll come back with the answer and tell you the results are all cock-eyed, because there is a little green goblin in there who eats light, adores lasers, and every time one filters in, he gobbles it up and then shits it out later as mass! That's what is screwing up your whole experiment!' Matthew would cough politely and reject this as implausible, and ask John if he had any more ideas. He saw John smiling in his black room, dressed as a priest in a black robe, holding the computer discs in his hands like unleavened bread to be handed out to kneeling disciples. 'What is in your diamond, messing up your results? You old fool! You don't know! It is YOU inside it! YOU! Your crackpot thinking! The damn thing is trying to get on with its own life, and you start penetrating it with fucking laser beams and then follow it with millions of pointless questions. It is YOU in the diamond! Get yourself out of it. Send Cindy in to dance instead and you'll be alright, you might start to see all kinds of new possibilities! All scientific theories get broken eventually. What is wrong with the present moment for throwing out classical science once and for all and bringing in a bit of romance?'

So Matthew tried to imagine Cindy decked up as a moonbeam ... it suited her.

He started working, scribbling with the data from the third experiment, sifting through the computer print-outs, hoping to find gold. But as the figures took shape, he knew he would come up with the same results as before. But as each result appeared as he'd feared, to his surprise, he was chuckling to himself. Proving that his theories were wrong again no longer worried him. Maybe he was proving another theory. He must stop barking up the wrong tree if he was to find it ...

That evening, after dinner, Cindy asked them if they were in the mood for her new dance. Georgina said only if she danced to research her novel, not merely as a frivolous desire to have a good time or a feeling of obligation to entertain Matthew. Cindy smiled. It *was* research, entirely for her work!

While Georgina went for more wine from the cellar, Cindy asked Matthew what he'd done all day. He said he'd worked through his data and everything pointed to another fiasco with the third diamond. Cindy remarked he seemed almost pleased about it. Yes! It was a pretext for staying to watch her dance. He asked her how her novel was coming on. She pouted and flung her hands around as if imitating a French clown. '*Comme çi, comme ça.* Not very good actually. I get blocks, doesn't everyone? I start thinking of being free of it, going back to acting and dancing out other people's fantasies rather than my own. Much easier. But I stick with it. I have to! For George. George keeps sticking pins in a little clay statue she has of me. I feel them in my bottom. I don't miss a thing! Like a pike never misses the smallest flash of light reflected from the tail of a goldfish!'

'And your new dance, what's it about?' he asked, trying to appear calm and keep to the subject.

'I've made a new tape, Mozart's greatest hits, excerpts from his operas. I love dancing to Opera. So expect an evening of High Class, but not, I hope, without its surprises!' She kissed him and went to her room to change. She needed two hours, she said. '*At least!*'

After a few minutes trying to imagine this kinky satin-clad doll dancing to Mozart, he crept into John's room quietly, not wanting Cindy to hear him, and once inside, locked the door from the inside and sat in the darkness, listening. The only thing he could hear was his own thinking, so he switched on the light, switched on John's computer and read on ...

Frazer; **"The Golden Bough":**

"In the series of sculptures which represent the mythic history of OSIRIS in the great temple of ISIS at Philae, a tamarisk tree is depicted with two men pouring water on it. The inscription leaves no doubt that the verdure of the earth is believed to be connected to the verdure of the tree, and the sculpture refers to the grave of

Osiris at Philae, of which Plutarch says it was overshadowed by a Methide PLANT, taller than any olive-tree. In inscriptions OSIRIS is referred to as 'the one in the tree', 'the solitary one in the Acacia', etc. On the monuments he sometimes appears as a mummy covered with a tree or with plants. The original meaning of the Goddess ISIS is still more difficult to determine than of her husband and brother OSIRIS. In the hieroglyphics she is called 'the many-named', 'the thousand-named', and in Greek inscriptions 'the myriad-named', 'creatress of the green crop', 'the green one', whose greenness is like the greenness of the earth ...

So closely did the rites of Osiris resemble those of Adonis at Biblos that some of the people of Biblos maintained it was OSIRIS and not Adonis whose death was mourned by them. Herodotus found the similarity between the rites of Osiris and Dionysus so great, that he thought it impossible the latter could have risen independently; they must have been recently borrowed by the Greeks from the Egyptians."

Exactly! So the Greeks borrowed the essence of their Mysteries from the Egyptians and Isis is Demeter and it was Demeter whose Mysteries were celebrated at Eleusis. This is what Robert Graves has to say about Eleusis – the key to it all, in his sublime:

"What Food the Centaurs Ate":

"The meaning of 'ambrosia', the food of the gods, is: 'that which confers immortality'. The Greek grammarians define ambrosia as a thick porridge of honey, water, fruit, olive-oil, cheese and pearl barley; though exactly what kind of fruit is, oddly enough, not specified. And why did they trouble to mention water among the ingredients? There is something funny here. Are the grammarians fooling us? At this point I wrote down the Greek words on the ambrosia recipe, one underneath the other:

MELI
UDOR
KARPOS
ELAIOS
TUROS
ALPHITA

Next I wrote down the nectar recipe; honey, water and fruit:

MELI
UDOR
KARPOS

And also, while I was about it, the recipe for KUKEON (mixture) the draught which the Goddess DEMETER, during her search for the lost Persephone ...

MINTHAION
UDOR
KUKOMENON
ALPHITOS

So if mushrooms were ambrosia, and if ambrosia was mushrooms, be pleased to examine those three sets of initial letters. M-U-K-E-T-A; M-U-K; M-U-K-A. You are at liberty to call me crazy, but I read them as three clear examples of 'ogham' (which was the device of spelling out a secret word by using the initial letters of other ordinary words.) MUKETA answers the question; 'What do the gods eat?' for MUKETA is the accusative of MUKES which means mushroom. MUKA answers the question; 'What grants me the mystic vision?'; for MUKA is an a earlier form of the word MUKES – mushroom.

This looks to me, learned scholars, very much like a conspiracy of silence – a conspiracy natural enough if mushrooms were the hallucinatory agents used by the mystagogues in the Eleusinian Mysteries – the secret of which nobody ever blabbed in the course of all those centuries. There certainly was a secret; are we really expected to believe that the epoptae, or adepts, derived the visions that made them gasp for wonder from a soft drink of mint-flavoured barley water?"

Beyond reasonable doubt, Osiris, Dionysus, Christ; code-names - metaphors for the Eucharist; the sacred mushroom, the essential constituent of the Eucharistic meal. The plant-penis-mushroom. The first part of my quest seemed over. Now I only had to find the species of mushrooms used, and determine their chemical constituents – the actual mushrooms used by the ancient Egyptians. Here was the true subject of my work, to decide why their extraordinary theories of consciousness and cosmo-genesis took the form they did, that consciousness could be divided into separate, independent parts which could leave the body and exist – forever – independently from it – the BA, the KHU, the KHA, the KAIBIT. Could it be simply – *true*? They were right and we were wrong? The Greeks tell us, generously humbling and putting themselves down in the process, that the Egyptians were the healthiest and happiest people the world had ever known! And now, what has it all become? Alas! But we can dream ... little did I know the amazing places I would visit and explore in the regions of consciousness with my consort, my accomplice, the screen goddess, the myriad named and faced ... Cindy!

The remainder of this disc comprises the full text of the Robert Graves piece, the references of Herodotus and a number of translations (by Wallis Budge) – all wrong – of all the hieroglyphic references to Osiris and his so-called copulation with Isis. This is technical stuff. You can move on to the next rite (disc), if you are the superficial type, eager for quick and easy results. As the actress said to the physicist;

ENTER ENTER ENTER ENTER ENTER ENTER END ALT END PRTSC F3 ↵ENTER
PRTSC F3 PRTSC F9 F10 F2 .

Matthew switched off the computer, gazed up at the black ceiling which disappeared the harder he tried to focus on it; and words seared into his mind. *John went mad and had to be killed or killed himself! If I'm not careful, I'll go mad too.*

Georgina knocked on the door; 'Cindy, your scarlet woman, the celebrated harlot, goddess of stage and screen and seedy clip joint and everything you ever wanted to abuse, paid for and therefore unable to say NO to anything, is ready to dance and awaits her audience!'

He was ready for her too ...

ALT END
PRTSC F3 ↵ENTER PRTSC F3 PRTSC F9 F10 F2 . ENTER ENTER ENTER ENTER ENTER

⊛

NINE

"Soma was at the same time a god, a plant, and the juice of the plant. So far as we know, Soma is the only plant that man has ever deified."

"SOMA, Divine Mushroom of Immortality"
– R. Gordon Wasson

△

The theatre was in darkness except for a beam of light from the spotlight, focused on a black velvet curtain at the back of the stage, on which was painted a white circle, three feet in diameter. Two woven scrolls on each side were decorated with hieroglyphics, one describing Isis copulating with Osiris, the other describing Osiris copulating with Isis.

Gradually growing accustomed to the dark, Matthew noticed a black chaise-longue, under the circle of light. Discovering a glass of champagne on the art-deco side-table, he soon relaxed, as John would have done, looking forward to Cindy's dance *au Mozart,* with its little *surprises.*

He turned and saw Georgina dressed in her long black velvet gown, fading in the music on the hi-fi. She smiled fondly. Trying to recognize the music, he nearly missed the hand moving slowly into the white circle. Cindy was obviously dressed entirely in black, quite invisible; but now he could see her hand, in the light, wearing a broad diamanté bracelet sparkling with fake stones, the light catching them, sending scintillating streaks of lightning towards him.

Now he recognised *Idomeneo*; he'd seen the opera on TV. Through the overture, he was only allowed to see the black fingers, the bracelet, and a tantalising fragment of arm, moving sensuously to the music, reminding him of a film of Balinese dancing, where each gesture of the hand has a precise meaning, like a word, and the message of the dance is how the hands delineate, in a new way each time, the known conversations of the gods. Mimed hieroglyphics.

It was as if Cindy was sketching in a circular computer screen, with a magnetic pen, each geometric movement of the dance being fragments of a coded program, the esoteric and erotic meaning still out of sight, to be accessed and revealed later. You had to be wired up and pay for the program to feel her fingers actually moving on your skin. But it was elegant and quite moving, despite being still so distant.

The overture drifted away and Electra's aria faded over it and the mood changed to the rage of a storm; her song of anger and jealousy, standing on the beach while the chorus pleaded for the shipwrecked sailors in the sea. Electra is furious that the man she loves will marry her rival, Ilia. Matthew knew the opera well enough to picture the scene, the beach, chorus, ship foundering in raging seas – a typical operatic scene, full of passionate raging, melodramatic kitsch, but quietly painful nevertheless if you were in the mood ...

Georgina opened the lens slightly on the spotlight and the round circle expanded another foot, allowing Cindy's two hands to come into the light, now imploring the gods to hear her and destroy the love that existed between two other people and not herself; pure female jealousy! Her two hands were puppets conjuring the entire dramatic picture and he was transfixed, appreciating the skill of Cindy's mime ...

The music faded and in came the famous aria from *Il Seraglio*, "Marten aller Arten", where the heroine Constanze defies the threat of every kind of torture; "Torture me and flay me!" Again the circle of light was slightly enlarged, and Matthew was astonished as Cindy's head suddenly appeared, entirely covered with a black leather hangman's mask. She raised her hands, and they were bound with fine silver chains. The music rose and her head and bound arms rocked from side to side, again perfectly portraying every subtle meaning in the music, mocking her would-be seducer, taunting him to try every evil, swearing viciously that she would never surrender to him. At first the chains seem to bind her, but then they fall on her, as if used by some other force to beat her. She is writhing to the imaginary blows. How could such a deathly black hood express so much? He was clasping the edge of his chair, never having expected Cindy to be so accomplished and he felt admiration and pleasure ... not what he had expected at all of his dumb blonde Chicago gun moll – with the heart of lead.

Next it was *Don Giovanni*, the light circle again enlarged just before Georgina slipped into the set to lie on the chaise-longue. This was the scene when Anna discovers the dead body of her father, recently killed by Don Giovanni, after her father had caught them making love ... yet who was masked? Both! Had Georgina become the father's dead body?

Cindy slowly took off the black face-mask ... her face, painted pure white, still a death mask. The music was now a cry to avenge the murder of her father by her lover, and to Matthew's amazement, Cindy sat astride the body of her father and made love to it, revealing subtle flashes of whiteness of her naked body, only partially hidden under her black cloak. The body beneath her didn't move as Cindy caressed it, exciting herself erotically against it ... the aria, in counterpoint, calling for hideous revenge on the "unknown" attacker. An idea flashed into Matthew's mind, that she had enjoyed the ravishment, as she now enjoyed gripping and making love to the body of her dead father. No victim this young woman, but enjoying every mistake these men were making! Matthew couldn't miss the similarity to the image of Isis and Osiris and he remembered what John had written, somewhere; "Every orgasm is the death of a king!"

Matthew watched in awe and in a state of intense sexual excitement as the ravished daughter avenged herself on her father. For dying? For not protecting her? For not making love to her? Suddenly Matthew started to feel dizzy. Was all true sexual passion worth its name derived from frustrated incest? His mind seemed to be pulling away from his body – he wondered if his glass of champagne had been spiked with a drug, but he was already feeling so possessed and entranced by everything, he decided to go along with it ... floating in and out of being aware of himself watching, wanting so much to enter the screen image, and make love with the cinematic image of Cindy and her corpse ... how could it be so erotic?

But he had no choice as yet and gave in to reverie, probably hallucinating, free now to imagine even more tangibly, the rapes and murders implied in her making love to the corpse of her father, murdered by her secret lover ...

images flooding into his mind, crushing and eroding the edges, and arousing him ...

But then he had a premonition. Perhaps it was the drug ... perhaps it was his new state of mind ... or the narrative he had been forced to expose himself to on so many levels, in so many fragmented forms ... he wanted to stand up and shout out because a dazzling image had seared into his mind. Yes, he knew what was coming next! At last, he was with them and knew what was coming next; he too was creating the story. He was quite beside himself with anticipation, at the other side of the room watching himself because he was ahead of the action, outside of time. It was easy really. Awaiting the coincidence of two images ...

The music changed, the one fading out as the other faded in, merging, fusing. YES! It happened exactly as he had imagined it. He wanted to go to Cindy and ravish her in the midst of his feeling of ecstasy, but he held back, wanting to see how she would deal with the events he had anticipated and had foreseen, like Tiresias – namely the temple scene from *The Magic Flute* where Tamino is initiated into the mysteries of Isis and Osiris. Obvious, really ...

The music swelled and the chorus sang *O Isis Und Osiris* and tears welled up into Matthew's eyes ... he had merely anticipated her, but this, he sensed, suddenly, tangibly in his body, was what it was all about ... tapping something deeper, and *that* was all he knew at that moment but he felt it was something vitally important. It didn't occur to him that it was John's favourite sexual routine with Cindy ... he was not seeing that far ahead, yet ...

Georgina slipped away and enlarged the circle of light again before returning to the stage to become the Mother-of-the-Night. Cindy, Pamina, her daughter, mother and daughter again. Demetra and Persephone. He watched, mesmerised, tantalised and painfully threatened as Cindy slipped off her black cloak and became even more naked, except for the smallest black scarf amidst the silver chains that she somehow twisted around her body to look like a serpent. She was painted white from head to foot, except her nipples were blackened too with shiny lipstick to match her pubic hair which she had brushed with some theatrical powder, jet black, and Matthew was poised on the edge, as they danced together, Georgina statuesque, still, monumental, with an air of death about her ... and the daughter, twisting, pleading, escaping, cloying, masturbating, dancing with a kind of wilful joy, and in Matthew's mind he saw Tamino ... elsewhere, *elsewhere* undergoing the rites of purification by fire and water, and he thought, *goddamit, where is he?*

And then it dawned on him, *he* was Tamino, he was undergoing these rites of transformation, being initiated by these temple girls into the rites of sacrifice; self-sacrifice. Shouldn't he escape before it was too late? No, nothing could have pulled him away from them now, from wanting to see what was next, to want to know what was next. 'When I know always what is next, at every moment, then I will be initiated,' he murmured to himself, pleased with himself.

John would probably say he had merely defined imagining, the illusion of creating. But when you are falling, it is nice to see in your mind, a pool of soft water beneath you ...

Then they came to him and undressed him as he stood there with tears rolling down his cheeks. His clothes slipped off easily and they caressed his body lovingly, for an aeon of time. Dynasties fell away like leaves off a weeping willow tree, until he wasn't sure who it was who took his penis in her mouth, he was imagining himself given, momentarily a god, and they were manipulating him as if he was clay in their hands ... as if he was a sculpture for their pleasure ... until they drew him to the chaise-longue as the music went on and on soaring in his mind, and they made love to him. He was so ecstatic and in a trance that he didn't know whose vagina clutched him savagely, whose thighs it was that locked around his head and pressed him down orgiastically ... and he had no idea whose mouth or whose vagina he ejaculated into, because by the time this happened ... like Tamino in the fire and the water ... he was somewhere else. He wouldn't have cared knowing that Cindy was directing the scene very carefully, allowing herself to be the whore but keeping Georgina for better things.

As was Amenhotep.

The following morning, a vivid, numinous dream ...

A desolate, barren desert, and no shelter from a pitiless sun. The desert birds are shrieking, mocking his aimless wandering. If he can't find shade from the sun, he will die. There's a plastic cord attached to the centre of his forehead, and incandescent molten metal is pouring into his skull, melting his eyes before searing down into his spine. What is stopping him surrendering to the circling birds of prey above him? He wants them to come, to stoop on his body and tear the parched flesh from the bones.

But somehow, despite himself, he finds strength to crawl to the top of a breast of sand, a shifting dune, and he can just see over it; in the distance, a pulsating layer of green mist which might be all that his sand-pocked eyes can discern of a tract of cultivated land, or, more likely, he's beyond seeing and is merely imagining a Mark Rothko painting entitled "Green; Number One." He crawls on his stomach, tearing the skin, groping towards the shimmering green lattices of light, perhaps mere mirage. After a supreme effort he gets close to the luminous green waves and is amazed to see it's a forest of trees. A man's voice, off screen, says, 'Surely this is the Garden of Eden!'

He can hear the sound of water somewhere in the trees, and drags himself forwards, tearing his limp hard-skinned fingers on the bark until, almost beyond hope, he reaches a beautifully clear stream; and drinks. Had water ever tasted so sublime? He fingers his skin, burnt dry and flaking off; fragments of ancient papyrus, and he can discern strange markings; like small pictures. He tears the parchment and off it comes like leaves; he's certain new skin must be behind it. He drops the fragments into the sand, watching them curling in the sun, feeling disgust as they go brown before his eyes, unravel and curl up into a brown ball, like the ball of dung the scarab beetle pushes, as he also pushes the sun across the sky, but then he sees a small, thin brown snake crawl out of the centre of the ball, which is not skin, after all, but bandages. The slimy creature crawls into a hole between two fingerlike roots of a tree. He shudders, realising the snake had been under his skin all the time, and only by chance he has released it.

There's a wind now, yet none of the trees are moving, because they are fossilized ... a prehistoric forest, he wonders how it could have remained so perfectly intact. He snaps off a branch; inside is pure crystal. He lifts it up against the sun and is startled as a piercing green pencil of light floods into his eyes. The flash of light has temporarily blinded him but he closes his eyes tightly and walks into the forest, needing the darkest shade now, not bumping into any of the trees because he knows the way by insight, a pure kind of light, very narrow and honed as a laser is always honed by a crystal.

He pushes on blindly, not sure whether his eyes are open or not open, everything is so black. But he reaches a small clearing, faintly illuminated now by light reflected from the surface of a crystallised rock pool, with trees arranged formally in two rows around the clearing. The crystalline branches at the top of the trees have lost their bark through constant chaffing on each other in the wind that blows continuously above the panoply of trees: they are transparent, yet shaped like the fan tracery pattern of a chapel roof. He's sure now that the wind is composed of words and ideas and the translucent branches are the nerves in his brain. The wind is time ...

In the centre of the clearing is a solitary, dead tree, bleached white by the sun, unprotected by the tall trees around it. It has become the shape of human bones, every small branch a finger or a toe, the larger branches resembling arms and legs, its trunk a torso; but as he walks towards it, it gets smaller and smaller until, close to it, he sees it is a single skeleton, perfectly preserved ... minus its head. At the side of the skeleton is a pile of white bandages, stained with blood.

Suddenly there are voices in the bushes. Scared stiff, he runs to the side of the clearing, falling into some rushes. Two girls, dark skinned, naked, approach and embrace the white skeletal tree in the centre of the clearing. One girl lifts the other, whose wrists seem to be tied, a much younger girl and barely developed as a woman, holds her up, as if she is preparing to thrust the dead tree inside her, where the head has broken. She has her hand round the tight little bottom, a finger inside her. He can't stop himself, and shouts out; 'No'! The older girl takes flight and the young girl falls to the ground; he drags her into the bushes.

Holding her gently, her eyes are closed, covered in leaves. She opens her legs and he kisses her; had she ever tasted so sublime? He rolls over and she rolls over on top of him and he slips inside her. He looks up, hearing the wind getting louder, and is horrified to see, hanging from a high branch, a severed human head – *surely the head of John*?

The wind picks up and the leaves are rustling loudly. Surely they're alive again! Some bushes nearby are moving and he's sure there are people inside them. He's just about to part the leaves when he hears a soft, sweet, woman's voice, some further distance away, humming or singing, probably an aria from an opera. The young girl, now a mere child, slithers away from him leaving a strange bloodied pattern in the mud, like waves spreading from the point where a stone has fallen into a pool of water, except she seems to fold up inside herself and disappear into two finger-like roots at the bottom of a tree. Had she slipped into his mouth while he was drinking from her?

He hears softly spoken words, quite clearly:

'A rose and a vine of beauty,
Caught in the cusp of a tree ...'

Surely this is a secret code he must fathom out, as important as the riddle given to Oedipus by the sphinx; if he doesn't crack it he is certainly doomed? In a panic he wakes ...

To see Cindy smiling at him with her wide eyes, mocking him, whispering for a second time:

'Rise and shine my beauty,
I've brought you a cup of tea!'

He tried to speak but couldn't, wanting to pull her down on him but then he hesitated ... would he hate her if he did? Where had the young girl gone? Cindy left him to 'pull himself together', as she put it. He could still feel the young girl beneath his fingers ... and pining for her was acutely painful. He tried to fall asleep ... Who was she? Who was it watching him in the copse? The girl would have been better tied down to four pegs, spread-eagled, face to the ground. It was her idea. How the image haunted him! Who had been watching? But if no-one had been watching, had it ever happened? Wasn't it someone now watching him? John? Maybe no-one ... slowly images emerged and merged with an oblique image of himself, lying with the girl on top of him. The girl's bottom and the other girl's fingers, exploring her, as he was licking her. The folds of skin, so perfectly formed and unscarred. The involute, the hologram refusing to fade away ...

When he finally made it downstairs, his legs seemed still

not reattached correctly. Breakfast was waiting on the kitchen table and he ate it, grateful to be alone. His head was aching. He felt certain his drink had been drugged ... although he had to admit it had heightened the sensations and intensified the pleasure, so he had little reason to complain. He'd been a fool not to expect it. But the cheek of it! He would get his revenge, although the best revenge was to say nothing, perhaps ... as if he was used to such things.

So what of the day ahead? There was no time to be lost, if he was to go to John's copse. He left a note to say he'd gone shopping, drove into town and headed out on the road he knew would lead him to the copse. But the road was the wrong one. He returned to the town and tried the other road but again it wasn't right. Frustrated, he bought a newspaper and had a coffee, deciding he was still partially asleep, before setting off again on the first road – but again he couldn't find the copse. Did it only exist in his dreams?

Not wanting to go back to the house, he wasn't sure what to do. To his surprise he felt he wanted a woman, desperately, and erotic images flashed into his mind, making it even more urgent. Maybe he should go back and ravish Cindy but he knew it was not Cindy he wanted. The rising frustration annoyed him, not knowing what to do about it. It wasn't his style, just to want a woman so randomly, but what he wanted at that moment was any woman, wanton, nameless and faceless, even a whore, especially a whore; but he knew, alas, there were no whores walking the streets in a town like St. Ives. Not yet. Maybe in the tourist season.

Why was he feeling so bitter? Had he no choice but to go back, defeated, and ask Cindy to show him the way to the copse? Was he even on the right road? Might it pass a girl's school and they'd just be going for a walk, in twos ... and he'd follow them ... and god knows what John would have done ... in his search for the perfect shapes ...

But at that moment he had a *déjà vu.* A hundred yards round the next bend surely ... yes ... yes ... the track leading to the copse! Curse him!

Opening the gate, he drove to fifty yards before the copse. Walking slowly towards the trees, he wondered why he could only find it when he wasn't looking for it ...

By now it was quite a pleasant day, the sun bright but not too warm, with a light breeze rustling the trees. All kinds of wild flowers were suddenly appearing, blossoms on the hedgerows, birds hustling about in great activity. As he approached the trees he could feel again why John had come there. It was indeed a powerful place, the trees so neatly and provocatively arranged around the moulded mound of earth, long ago covered with grass, and he felt sure there were bodies there, buried maybe thousands of years before.

Instead of feeling frustrated, images of lost girls haunting his mind despite trying everything to evade them, he felt suddenly relaxed. He was alone. This was his scenario today. He'd arrived. And now? John? Georgina had recently given him a few hints about meditating, so he sat down at the centre of the clearing. But he felt awkward and uneasy there, something was wrong, so he moved to another spot nearer the trees and this felt better. No, it was still not right. Who or what vibrations were guiding him? He decided to close his eyes and let himself be guided, and sure enough he felt the urge to move in a certain direction. He turned a few times, hesitated and waited until he felt the urge to move again, until after a few minutes shuffling round, and *not* bumping into anything, he knew he had reached the right spot. Opening his eyes, he found himself just outside the main nave of trees in a smaller clearing, with hawthorn bushes around it. The grass seemed inviting, interwoven with emerald green moss, and he lay down.

Trying to think of a mantra, he saw images of his diamonds instead. Then it came to him, what he had to hum: 'Mer...it...at...en'. Trying a few variations, he found a way of humming it melodically and soon he felt the satisfying sensation of warmth coming up through the earth into his body. But his mind would not focus ... or unfocus ... the only image that kept soaring into his mind was his third diamond and the theorem related to it. But it was elsewhere ...

It was not his but Meritaten's diamond, so he tried to imagine what use she might be putting it to with her priests in Amarna. To his surprise the diamond then started to disappear each time he thought of Meritaten close to it. This didn't help, so he tried imagining a ritual in a sun drenched temple in Amarna, the shadows as black as pitch, but this time all he could think of was Cindy, painted white and naked and he was becoming aroused again sexually, so he opened his eyes and stopped humming his mantra and told himself it was not that easy to meditate after all and it would be much better to try to enjoy the quiet solitude, the natural peace of the small copse. Why did it still seem so far away? Had he not arrived there yet? Was he still driving in his car, hemmed into the machine, crawling along inside it down the narrow stone passage, the tunnel from which he was too scared to emerge, despite knowing the door was about to be opened?

He closed his eyes again. Who was watching as the pieces were coming together, like on a chessboard, into the necessary configuration, in which the king must die, dying if he was to be reborn ... as light ... thoughts floating on a void, a wave-shape not yet crucified to matter? A man standing behind a tree, dressed as a woman. The moment still not come, Matthew was lying on the grass, trying to empty his mind of thinking, yet he was sure his body had become steel, his eyes were lasers, and he was moving slowly, slowly up a stone ramp ... in front of him, emerging out of the darkness, a stone door with two copper handles. Inside the chamber, the wood had rotted, the bandages were black, like the skin, soon to turn to dust, but the crystals were still perfect, awaiting their destiny. Then the image faded.

Eventually the chattering of birds (go,go,go) penetrated his consciousness; they were dashing about, close to him now, very busy, fussing in the leaves, furiously pursuing food for their ravenous chicks. Suddenly, he noticed a bird hovering over the field not too far from the copse. A falcon, a kestrel, or *Windhover* as Hopkins had called it! He sat up excitedly to watch it more carefully. There it was, hung on space, flying and yet not flying, poised outside of time in a dimension all its own. He could recall only one image from the poem that John had quoted – *gash-vermilion* – and this made him think of the young girl in his dream, lying in the desert under a newly pitched tent; a dung beetle creeping over her toes ... or another he'd met on the road, suitably rent ... 'Empty yourself of images!' Georgina said. More easily said than done ...

The falcon fell suddenly, but stopped in mid-flight again, hovering at about fifty feet above the ground. What a mysterious image it was, flying as fast as it could, flapping its wings like mad and yet going nowhere. *Just like me!* he thought, but then, to contradict the resonance of its hidden meaning, the falcon dropped like a stone, claws outstretched in its other wave-form, and disappeared in the long grass.

As it dropped, Matthew's heart missed a beat. It was so quick, so precise, ruthless, final ... so certain. And almost immediately, it rose again, dangling from its claws a small beast, struggling ... one moment it had been sniffing around some rotting turnips and then whoosh! out of the sky a god descends with the power of life and death in its sharp talons, and the sharp pain and going limp and the absolute submission and surrender, a last brief glimpse of crushed grass and ruffled feathers, then the snap behind its neck as the falcon's beak commits murder; the blood draining from its head and consciousness floating, as the falcon soars into the air, higher and higher, and dying and flight become synonymous. Two images in coincidence. Orgasm. Matthew suddenly recalled Cindy's first dance, the image of interweaving on the double of itself ... somehow suggesting this final flight of murderous ecstasy of the poor vole, imagining metamorphosis perhaps, hoping to become a bat next time, a rodent with wings, not knowing if it would be privileged to quantum-jump an evolutionary step, not quite knowing yet the difference between the living and the dead ... if there was such a difference, in its new field, this interface with Matthew watching it and thinking about it. It was alive and dead. As he now felt himself to be ...

Seconds later, Matthew was astonished to see the falcon flying towards him ... nearer and nearer to the copse, until it flew right over his head and landed on a branch above him. It gave a sharp cry and another falcon appeared from nowhere and joined it on the same branch, bowing and clucking and the deliciously warm vole was exchanged from the feet of the male to the beak of the female. The male flew off promptly and Matthew watched the female fly to a small dead branch jutting out horizontally from the trunk of a larger tree. She was only fifty feet away and he could see clearly as she severed the head of the vole and let it drop: Plop! as it hit the leaves in some bushes. Then she shuffled along the small dead branch and hopped onto a curved branch which joined another curved branch and in the fork he could see a large hole, and in the dark threshold he could see the bright little heads of young falcons, red mouths open wide.

The female tore the vole to pieces and fed her chicks. Matthew crept surreptitiously closer until he was near enough to see every detail and not disturb the ritual. He watched fascinated as she ripped the little animal to pieces and fed each small morsel to a gaping gashed vermilion mouth. Nothing was lost, every small fragment eaten with relish. Finally the mother flew off and Matthew watched as one chick struggled to drag the twitching tail down its throat. Gone! As the eyes of the falcons closed in satiation, one by one their little heads dropped out of sight and all was relatively quiet again in the sacred copse.

So much for a vole. Matthew sat down against the beech tree and looked up at the nest in the cusp of the two branches and one of John's sentences crept into his mind. "Tiresias could *see* because he knew the language of birds." Being initiated he knew the codes, the hieroglyphic language, the gift to man from the Ibis-headed god, Thoth. The shaman.

The nest was in a tree that was dead, the whole top broken off, with the dead branches piled on the ground under it. Then he noticed the tree was blackened where it had been broken and he wondered why, until the image flashed into his mind; it had been hit by lightning! He went to it and touched it. On the broken branches he saw the blackened scars where they had been shredded and burnt by the lightning bolt. He caressed the bark affectionately, moving his finger along snaking black lines of burnt carbon ...*you poor old tree! One minute alive, the next, broken images of black carbon ... murdered by the greatest serial killer of them all: God!*

But the position of the tree in relation to the other trees of the copse was irregular. It was placed where the altar would be, if the trees were a church, exactly between the two rows, standing alone. None of the other trees had been struck by lightning, and were all still alive. He sat down against one of the outside trees and it felt quite hot, except the heat was in his own body. It was getting hotter and hotter. He was starting to feel quite faint ... on the verge of losing consciousness, knowing he ought to move away from the tree to escape the burning feelings in his spine, to avoid himself being felled. Had there been a pool of water near the copse he would have flung himself into it. He stood up sharply, sensing he must walk about to escape the feeling of imminent dissociation, but then an idea struck him so forcibly he felt himself go rigid for a moment, almost with terror. He had noticed it without noticing it. One step ahead or behind? The tree might have been hit by lightning, but it had been dead a long time before. It was not a beech tree, it had died naturally from disease ... it was an *elm*!

He approached it cautiously again and fingered the grooves and clefts in its rough bark. Yes, it was an elm. Quickly he looked round at the other trees to make sure they were all beech trees. Every single tree was smooth; a beech. Then, the quickening montage beyond his control, horrified, he saw just above head height in the elm's trunk, was a large hole, filled with concrete, and the concrete was quite new.

To his surprise, he immediately felt relaxed. All the tension had suddenly drained from his body. He felt so relieved, he almost laughed. *John brought me here, and his head is inside that fucking tree!* He sat down with his back against the tree, wondering why he felt so certain about it. But he was quite sure. He'd go back to town and buy a hammer and chisel to chip out the concrete, immediately. On closer examination he saw that a large stone had been jammed into the hole and concrete had been smoothed over the top of it. The tree seemed almost completely hollow. Plenty of room in it for a cut-up body ... good enough for Osiris, good enough for John, no doubt, somewhere decoding the new holographic language of images ...

He set off for the town but finally felt too drained emotionally to go to the shops, deciding to postpone the opening of the hole until the following day. Was he scared of the truth? Would it release him from Cindy? The girl who had murdered John? When he arrived at the house, the two girls were working and remained in their territories, ignoring his arrival. He went to his room and relaxed on his bed.

He tried to match the facts of his discoveries of the day, and the "ficts" of his dreams. He tried to recall dream images that had been direct premonitions, like the lightning-struck tree, but often he couldn't remember the dream precisely enough. He could remember the grafting of one tree to the other, but this now seemed to be *wrong*, but then it occurred to him that if John was dead, and was communicating with him, this image might be a metaphor for John's mind reaching into his own; as the girls would have said: reincarnating. The more he thought about it, reluctantly he felt this might be happening in some mysterious way, his mind being infiltrated by John's.

If so, then John had really tapped some amazing technology to accomplish it. Which is why he'd probably been killed? But if John's corpse *was* in the tree, what could he do about it? Suddenly he felt quite elated, enjoying himself, starting to make sense of the coincidences at last. The jigsaw puzzle could be assembled soon. Although, how often, as a child, had he got to the end and found he'd lost one bit somewhere on the way?

He went downstairs to make tea, deciding he'd say nothing to the girls about the copse, the dead tree and his presumptions about John's body; that could come later at the right moment. After all he was still faced with the biggest mystery of all. Who had killed John and why, and why did he feel so sure it was Cindy? As he was drinking his tea, he suddenly realised he had no proof whatsoever, yet, that John was in fact "in" the tree. Was he starting to go really crazy? He imagined himself the next day hacking into the hole and finding some old sandwiches ... or a gun perhaps. Or ...

Of course! Why hadn't he thought of it before? It was probably a cache of drugs, ten thousand doses of LSD in pure crystallised form! He'd be hacking the hole open and a bunch of police would leap out of the bushes and arrest him, having had the placed staked out for the last month! No wonder he heard voices in the bushes. Go go go said the bird, human kind cannot bear too much reality! Why was he jumping to such strange conclusions? Was this the secret power of myth?

It was all Cindy's fault! She'd said, casually enough, *just go along with it.* But then he laughed. No-one could deny it was one helluva way to spend a holiday! And he felt cheerful again. Maybe after all, it wasn't John's head in the tree, even though the hole did look the perfect size for a head. Of course that left the question of the rest of the body ... thirteen pieces distributed around the tin mines of Cornwall? Perhaps he'd not bother to look for them, leaving that to Isis. Isis! Who is she in all this? Was Georgina, like him, unaware of the real story, not knowing anything really, a mere victim?

At that moment, as if he'd pressed the right key, Georgina came into the kitchen and said 'Hi there! Have a good drive? Pick up any pretty schoolgirls? I've been flooded with perverse images all day, you screwing in the woods, trying to forget Cindy! Or should I say, escape her power?'

Goddamit! How did they know? In a serious tone, he asked her, 'Tell me ... who is ISIS then in this whole conspiracy?'

Looking really shocked she slumped down at the table. 'How do you mean ... conspiracy?'

'This whole game that you're both playing with me; or at least Cindy is playing with me?'

Georgina looked visibly upset. 'Not me, Matthew. I'm not playing with you. Honestly. Maybe Cindy has her little plots and sub-plots, her little charades to keep herself distracted. This whole Isis and Osiris thing was firstly John's obsession. And now he's dead and gone, or at least gone, mysteriously, we think of him, and because you're now delving into his work, it has assumed unreasonable proportions. Which is why Cindy, I presume, took it up and danced it. Just for fun really. You know, you're starting to take things too seriously. This is a nightclub, not a temple or even a classical Greek theatre of tragedy. These are jokes really. It's Cindy's novel, her history of virtual sexuality, her obsession with the unconsummated, the unreal, the poverty of literary sexual fantasy. Don't blame me. I'm just making some sculpture which happens to be connected with Egypt, and doing my book on Amarna. No-one, as far as I know, is Isis ... at least in this household. I presume you think John is Osiris? Cindy is hardly Isis, the nourishing earth goddess, now is she? And I'm no part of it at all!'

'Precisely. Who is she then?'

'Cindy? She is Rosetta Stone ... a green angel-snake with three tongues, apart from that a nut who believes sex is a way of inventing pornography. A virtual whore who is trying to steal your body! And you will become crazy too if you're not careful. May I share your tea?'

'Go ahead. By the way, what was put in my drink last night?'

'Oh good. You did notice it. We thought we'd wasted a whole dose. Cindy said, *the only man who ever took a dose like that and beat it off was a Buddhist monk!* And believe me, it was *not* our aim to make you into a Buddhist monk. I hope it was agreeable?'

'Yes ... except all I remember is going out like a light!'

'Oh really. We thought you were being shy and acting as if you were unconscious. Your body was still wide awake anyway, which is what counted! And I don't mean one to fourteen, or even sixty-nine.'

They both laughed. 'Yes, my mind is always counting! But I was half there most of the time, I did feel really quite good. The music, the sounds were amazingly clear, and I enjoyed myself. I hope it showed. I'd hate to think you went to all that effort without thinking I appreciated it.'

'Well ... we know your body, like Noah, was having a whale of a time ... and we arked out a few times! But we wanted to feel your heart and soul were in it too, so thanks for the reassurance. We enjoyed ourselves too. I speak for myself, mind you. Maybe for Cindy it was a mere experiment for her novel and she's even now busily writing it up. How does it feel to be an experiment, a mere object of study ... like one of your scientific rats in a cage?'

'A rat in a cage? Well, thanks!'

'Okay, a tiger in a zoo!'

'That's better ... a tiger burning bright.'

She continued, 'As I said, we are *all* an experiment, that's all it is, one long experiment. But is it ours? We are whose experiment? It started before the First Dynasty of course. Perhaps the ancient Egyptian adepts are still peeping at us through little slits in the Trachyon Field? Awaiting the moment for the unveiling again, of the door to the inner chamber? Like the divine starlight or Atenlight or laserlight filtering down on the faces of the statues through the clerestory windows? Or clearstory as they were called once!'

Matthew spilt his tea. 'Goodness me ... what do you know about the Tachyon Field? That's a very esoteric scientific concept.'

'Oh! Nothing really. Isn't it the unified gravity field that will explain everything, above and beyond all material dimensions, especially action at a distance - and parallel worlds - and we will use it for instantaneous communication anywhere in the galaxy? Action at a distance and all that, and gaining that power again will be the true esoteric meaning of the Apocalypse, the second coming, as John believed? Trachyon or Tachyon? The great new wave field? John gave it his own spelling! With or without the R - that is the question!'

'... Er ... very much a theory at the moment, without any evidence, totally absurd really. Was John interested in *that*?'

'Of course! Who else would I hear it from? He was interested in everything subversive, impossible, scandalous, wicked, but interesting. Is it very important?'

'It would be, *if* it exists, it would be very important. It might explain a lot of things – come to think of it, even my diamonds! But it's pure theory. There's no practical evidence for it at all. You have to think of the damn thing first and then look for it. Then you find it and the theoreticians say you only found what you were looking for, it's not really there. You just manipulated the data, thinking it was there. I'm a classicist of the old school – I always need concrete facts.'

'Concrete, like concrete poetry?' she said, looking puzzled.

'You know what I mean!' he said petulantly.

'Yes, I think I do ... but Cindy and I are women, and don't really believe in concrete - or facts. We think it's a huge joke, you lot poking into everything and saying, *look, a concrete fact*. And then you say you can see through it. We women know there is something else. You open up an egg. A pool of water in two halves of an egg, but if you sit on it for a month ... not you or I ... out pops a chicken. Imagine that as a mystery for the ancient Egyptians. They look in an egg and there's nothing in it except water. The goddess Nuit in one of her manifestations. A month later, a chicken. For whom? For a falcon to catch and eat! Well, we know how it all works. But we have lost the magic, the wonder, the awe. I want to go back and see everything like this, to look at mountains and feel they are a million years old pulling you down into them, and the sea ... *Le mer* ... *La mère* ... *Le soleil* ... *le crystal, la* ... is it male or female? And diamond? Le or la? Dia...Deuxmondes! Demimondes! Everything restored to its sexuality ... the whole universe sexualized, every object male or female, seeking its opposite for instant copulation. That's my kind of world. Stuff your concrete!'

At that moment Cindy came in. 'Yes, Matthew, I agree ... you can stuff your concrete! Which concrete?'

'Matthew has filled up all the space-bubbles and hubble-holes in the universe with concrete facts. I told him we are women, holy as can be, and holes mean a lot to us. Like a frustrated rapist he has filled up all the holes in the universe with concrete, and now he wonders what's the matter with everything, what is everything matter, why the universe is all grey and boring!'

Cindy pulled a face. 'I'm cooking tonight ... a soufflé. The last one came out *exactly* like concrete. Let's hope it doesn't happen tonight. I need a billion holes in less than fifty cubic metres. Matthew, you'd better leave us women with all our holes, to carry on with this magical rite, without your brooding intellect hatching out more concrete. See you later!'

Matthew bowed politely ... and left.

He went to John's room, wanting to work, but then it dawned on him! Wasn't it obvious, all the talk about concrete and holes? The girls already knew about his discovery! But how did they do it? He would have noticed someone following him. Coincidence? Weren't these so-called coincidences contrived by someone? If not John or the girls, then who?

But what was even more worrying was the extent of the girls' scientific knowledge. Could they have picked up so much, merely by being with John? The most unlikely person was Cindy. Everything about her didn't quite fit. But hadn't *the* first mentioned concrete, and Georgina had taken off on a quite logical tangent? Was he projecting all the connections, the so-called coincidences, onto the pattern of events, merely to create a kind of security ... impose a form where one didn't exist ... because he was falling apart emotionally?

The idea scared him. He decided to continue with John's discs ... hack into those rather than the imagined concrete in the tree ... if only to escape thinking about reality. He sat down at the computer ... punched in the code ... and ENTER

'**Demian**' by Herman Hesse:

"That night I dreamed of Demian and the coat of arms. It kept changing. Demian held it in his hands; sometimes it was small and grey, sometimes large and multicoloured, but he explained to me it was always the SAME BIRD. I set about painting a fresh picture – the heraldic bird. The bird was standing or perched on some object – it might have been a flower, a basket, a nest or a tree top. It now represented a bird of prey with a narrow and cruel sparrowhawk head. Half its body was sunk in a dark, terrestrial globe and from this it was struggling to disengage itself as from a giant egg, against a background of blue sky. The longer I examined the sheet, the more it was borne in on me that it was the coloured coat-of-arms as it had APPEARED IN MY DREAM!"

The Egyptians kept sparrowhawks in their temples. A young sparrowhawk's eye is yellow, a glowing, miniature sun. As the bird ages, its eye becomes more and more red until in a very old bird, the eye is quite vermilion. Its eye is a miniature sun, the eye-sun sets as time passes! They kept hawks and falcons. The latter had black eyes! Yes, Tiresias, archetypal semiologist, the language of dream is the language of hieroglyph is the language of birds! The Egyptians wrote that light came from INSIDE the eye and went out towards things. We must not forget this. We each have suns within us from which our own light emerges, OUTWARDS! (Until Akhenaten challenged the idea with the

Aten!) OUTwards? An amazing idea the Ancient Egyptians took totally for granted, never bothering to test it, or if they did, refused to accept their findings! Mind you ... do you mind? Could they be right? When you take mescalin, and other celestial drugs, you see this light-energy emerging out of everything ... you perceive it directly coming out of objects. Do we need this alkaloid chemical to make us see this energy, this "divine" energy, inherent in everything, rising from within?

A mere alkaloid. Is this energy REALLY there? Yes! When we conduct scientific experiments, at sub-atomic levels, this normally unseen energy is really there, messing up the results. Anti-matter? And where is all the matter missing in the universe? 10^{35} billion tons of it? No wonder those guys with quantum and relativity theories are so upset, muttering about the necessity to rethink the structure of the universe. AND HOW! "Plato thought nature but a spume that plays upon a ghostly paradigm of things", THE VISION poet tells us. Now we know it's a spume that plays upon another spume that plays upon another spume – ad infinitum.

Lucie Lamy: 'EGYPTIAN MYSTERIES':

"First of all, the ancient Egyptian nearly always envisages a notion together with its inverse, which is indissociable from it ... a further characteristic of Pharaonic mentality is an appreciation of SIMULTANEITY. This is expressed in various ritual representations – encouraged chiefly in the temples – by the superimposition in a single image of several points of view and moments of time ...

The Falcon hovering over the King is a typical example; its head is in profile; one of its wings is seen from above; the other wing and tail are seen from below. What at first seems to be a frozen moment of flight thus actually represents several moments of flight seen together."

I love the word she uses ... "envisages". Give a face to! In other words, change a grey concrete concept into a hieroglyph. Why is Isis hovering over the dead body of Osiris, the image that represents the central secret rite? She hovers as a falcon, attaining simultaneity, slipping out of our space-time; beneath her claws, erect, the phallus of Orisis ... as it rises up, out of the ground. *The Risen.* The plant of immortality.

Let's look at ... UR ... through OCCULTED eyes ...

There was a tap on the door and Georgina poked her head into the room. 'Good news. The soufflé has risen! Cindy is sparkling, wet in her pants, if she's wearing any, which I doubt; wet with excitement!' It figured, Matthew thought to himself ...

The two girls were in a jolly mood throughout dinner and Cindy entertained them both with her green-room jokes ... her imaginary life as a dancer in the *Folies Bergère*, sharing various dressing rooms with somewhat loose and lost young women of various hues. Afterwards Georgina whispered to Matthew, 'Not a word of truth, every single quote stolen from French literature. She is the ultimate thief, the ultimate plagiarist. Call it *"A la Recherche erotique du Déjà Vu"*...But you realize of course that the image of two girls making love; such a favourite of the Decadents, what better image to embody the fallacious notion of plagiarism?'

Matthew nodded and decided to eat, seriously.

The girls discussed the Marquis de Sade and some guy called Georges Bataille. Afterwards, he felt so alienated by their banter and secret jokes, he felt resentful - so he said he wanted to work. They didn't seem worried, but bid him goodnight, heading for Cindy's bedroom, giggling.

Putting his own discs into the computer, curious and excited, he tried to discover new equations, or patterns existing in the data; after a while, he started to make some weird connections. Why not imagine the existence of a wave field he had not taken into consideration, altering the spin? After all, how could he predict the levels of the existing radioactivity in the flaw, which shouldn't have been there anyway?

He kept thinking of the possibility that the crystals had come from Egypt. Why not dare to assume, as the girls and John insisted, that the Egyptians had powers we have lost, because of the overpowering dominion of reason? Either way the very fact of the three pyramid crystals was important. He worked until he was too tired to work ...

He slept badly and dreamt most of the night, but forgot

most of it by morning. The only sequence he could recall was swimming under a blue-green sea with Gilgamesh, looking for the sacred plant and discovering an underwater temple. Its stone pillars had become so encrusted with plants and seaweed, they looked like trees. They had found the plant ... it was long and slender and perfectly transparent in the water ... on it were seven flowers. Gilgamesh said there was no point in plucking the flowers, they had to be left on the plant to ripen and become pods with seeds ... the black seeds were so small they were invisible to the human eye ... you made a black paste, which contained the secret ingredients necessary to confer immortality. Matthew was attacked by an octopus on his way up to the surface that squirted poisonous black ink all over him. Then he woke up. As he was waking he was sure the black ink was somehow connected with the multi-headed holographic Hydra pen of Miss Rosetta Stone ...

At breakfast, Matthew announced he wanted to go into town. Cindy added that she and George needed to go shopping too; what a coincidence. Matthew was watching her like a hawk, trying to find a chink in her armour. No mere cuirass, it was total. Did she know he wanted to buy the tools to open the hole in the tree? He glared at her, but she appeared quite pleased with his fierce looks, wondering why he was paying her so much attention suddenly...sexual frustration, surely.

In town Matthew told them he'd meet them later in the café. At the ironmongers he bought a hammer, small chisel, trowel, a packet of ready-made concrete in a red plastic bag and a chipboard offcut. His plan was to drop the two girls off at the house and then drive to the copse ... alone.

Waiting in the café, reading the local newspaper, he was fascinated by stories about a couple of murders. He found them absorbing. Weird how we accept people murdering each other with hardly a flinch. Hardly worse than a car accident.

The girls arrived with the food and he helped them to the car. As they were leaving town, Cindy said it was such a nice day, why didn't they go for a drive. Matthew agreed it was an excellent idea and asked her, 'Yes ... and might I ask ... where?' his voice betraying his cynicism ...

'Just drive. Take any road you fancy. We'll find somewhere nice. It *is* so sunny and bright. Just drive! Take that road over there!' Matthew did as he was told. They passed through a village, familiar to Matthew by now, but in the next village, Cindy asked Matthew to stop. 'There's a food shop! Come on, George. Now we're in a road movie, let's have a picnic lunch!'

Matthew tapped out an easy piano version of the *Ride of the Valkyries* on the steering wheel, saying out loud, 'Okay, Cindy, your move, I'm clay in your hands, what sacred rite is it to be today in the sacred copse?'

The girls returned and Matthew waited for Cindy's instructions. 'Just drive. We don't care. When we reach Land's End just remember to stop so we don't fall over the edge, that's all!'

He drove slowly towards the junction outside of the village.

'Take the right turn, Matthew, the other way is too touristy, lots of cars and people,' Cindy said, ever-so casually. A short time later. 'Look! Matthew! There's John's copse. Let's have our picnic there. The perfect place!'

'Why, yes! An idyllic spot. Just the place. I don't know why I didn't suggest it earlier!' he said as smoothly as possible ...

He drove to where he'd parked the car the day before. There was a blanket in the back of the car, but he'd used it to cover up the tools he'd bought, so he told them to go on ahead, he would lock the car and bring the blanket. He also wanted to watch Cindy. She walked straight to the centre of the clearing and sat down, twenty yards from the dead elm tree, the cemented hole facing away towards the open fields.

He laid the blanket on the grass and the two girls produced cans of drink, ready-made rolls and plum pies in a packet. Once it was all laid out, they too laid themselves out on the grass and Matthew did likewise, each of them looking up at the sky, each one enjoying the beautiful weather, the idyllic scene, the majestic trees, the busy bees and the bustling birds, and the fragrance of perfume on the light wind.

Cindy sat up and said she hoped they didn't mind but she wanted to meditate, and suggested they did likewise. Matthew excused himself saying he wanted to go 'to the loo' before embarking on such a spiritual quest and the girls said they would do likewise. Matthew was undoing his zip behind some winter thorn bushes when he noticed an empty red plastic bag in the undergrowth, marked *Ready Mixed Concrete.* 'It figures!' he murmured, splashing it petulantly with hot urine. By chance he turned and noticed Cindy, amazed to see she was peeing standing up, projecting it out towards a tree, just like a boy. He'd never seen a girl do that before.

Back in the centre of the copse, Cindy instructed them to face in different directions, to sit with their backs straight, close their eyes ... and jump off the world.

At first Matthew thought of his mother and then he thought of his lab in Cambridge; had he double-locked it? Then he thought of Beverly, half naked, and the look on her face when he ripped off her bra. Then he thought of the head in the tree.

Almost despairing, he decided he must try *not* to think of anything, but try to silently *sing* his mantra, 'Mer-it-Aten'. After some minutes, he was drawn into a trance ... he saw himself back in the time of Amarna, the images as clear as if he was watching a film ...

A tributary off the main river of the Nile; he is fishing, and notices a small basket caught in reeds, under the water, old and broken. He wades into the stream and pulls it hard to untangle it from the reeds which have grown through it like reeds pierce the reed warbler's nest ...

The basket is full of bandages, presumably used to wrap a baby and he is reluctant at first to unwind them. He fingers the cotton carefully but can't feel bones inside, so carefully unravels them, finding inside a small cotton bag, inside of which are three pyramid-shaped crystals that shine brightly, as if with their own inner energy. He takes them to Meritaten, eager to show them to her. She tells him a priest will know about them, not one of the Theban priests, but a priest that only she and her mother know, a priest she brought with her from Mittania, but he has concealed his identity and is disguised as an artisan, working as an assistant to the Pharaoh's sculptor.

Meritaten takes Matthew to the studio, where this priest is preparing some stone for a portrait of Meritaten. She is coy about having her portrait made, 'But it is the King's desire to have the beauty of his daughters captured forever in stone!' says the priest. Meritaten says she must speak to him privately, and in a small room off the studio, they show him the crystals. Meritaten says of Matthew; 'It's alright, he knows about you ... it's quite safe, we're going to be married soon!' He's very excited about the crystals. Such crystals were possessed by Pharaoh Cheops, and were thought to have been brought by the Translucent Beings, connected with the language of Thoth, revealed by them to the priests of the Fourth Dynasty.

He had heard the stones were pyramid-shaped to focus the green rays which came from outer space. The *Book of the Coming Forth By Day* explained this, but language had come already complete, instantaneously, in a single moment. It was through such stones that the forces known as the Neters or Gods first manifested themselves into matter and the great book was the key to the mysteries. Other stones, or dried plants, hardened like stones, were eaten by the priests.

Suddenly, a knock on the door. The priest blurts out, 'Quick! The door, you must go immediately, or they'll kill you!'

Matthew woke out of his trance with a startled cry, making the girls jump. 'Good heavens, Matthew! Were you meditating or having a nightmare?' asked Georgina.

He felt embarrassed. 'I was dreaming. I tried to meditate, but slipped into a dream. Did I say anything important?'

Cindy said, 'I thought it sounded like, "The door has opened! Take the stones!" Is that possible?'

'Urr ... maybe. I'm sorry I interrupted you. How silly I am!' he said, looking away, reluctant to discuss anything further.

'Don't worry!' said Cindy, 'I'm out of practice, I wasn't really meditating either. My mind was just drifting on the wind aimlessly. I can't meditate at the moment. Whenever I try, I end up thinking about what is wrong with my novel, or I just think of other people's novels, which is even worse. Novel writers are novel addicts, feeding off other people's novels in order to regurgitate up other novels, snakes eating each others' tails. I must take up knitting instead; I bet you two don't know about knitting, I mean, why women knit really?'

'No!' said Georgina.

'They knit the pubic hair into a veil to conceal the fact they have no penis!' she said jubilantly. 'An unrewarding task, mind you, but from that we get Maya creating the world of illusion, the veil that conceals that awesome cruelty, that eternal absence,' slurred out with a seductive French pronunciation ... '*l'absence* ... which we know and love as woman ...'

Matthew and Georgina looked at each other and shrugged, but Cindy looked triumphant. She repeated it several times. '*L'absence qui est la femme. L'absence qui me tient ... comme l'espace*!' And then she lay back on the grass and closed her eyes, repeating the word *absence* until she appeared to fall asleep. Matthew realised it must be her mantra ... at last she was meditating on her favourite subject. Her own predicament ... he thought, rather cruelly ...

Georgina offered Matthew a tin of drink. He snapped off the cap and drank half, handing it back for her to finish. They didn't know what to do, awaiting further stage directions from Cindy, but Cindy was elsewhere ... *absente*. It dawned on Matthew that someone who is absent always dominates the scene. Like God, for example ...

But Georgina moved close to Matthew and held his hand, and to his surprise, laid her head on his knees and stretched her legs on the grass. She was wearing a long, old fashioned, wine-coloured skirt that flared below the knees, but was tight around her thighs. Under the skirt she was wearing very fine black lace stockings with a repeating *fleur-de-lys* pattern. Suddenly, as if irritated with them, she flicked off her black Victorian patent leather shoes, and stretched her toes. Matthew remembered a still from an American movie, in which Cyd Charisse was captured, stretched out on a fake grass bank in a studio, showing off her legs, and he knew that Georgina's legs were just as long and perfectly shaped, even though he could only see her ankles and their fine bones. She was always hidden, wearing clothes that would conceal every slight hint of female curve.

But as Matthew was wondering why she always did this, she promptly contradicted him by pulling up her skirt and tucking it up under her knickers. She looked at her legs for a minute or two and then giggled and pulled her stockings off and squeezed them into a ball and tucked them under herself.

'Time my legs saw the sun, don't you think?' she said turning to look up into Matthew's face. 'Let the lecherous old sun see my legs! If I was on the beach I'd strip the lot off. That would give you a shock, wouldn't it!' She looked surreptitiously at Cindy to make sure she was still *absente* ... turned round to look at Matthew, and whispered, 'Funny to think we have made love ... well, you know what I mean ... and yet you have never seen my body!' And then she whispered, 'One day I will dance for you ... and you won't know what hit you. I promise there won't be an erotic Indian sculpture in the world that will not remind you of me, afterwards!'

Matthew smiled affectionately, but was wondering, *why does the copse makes her feel sexy and behave so uncharacteristically?* She closed her eyes and seemed to relax, after a cheeky last smile in his direction. He ran his fingers through her hair and she purred like a kitten, he stroked her neck with his fingers and her whole body moved almost imperceptibly, as if mentally moving his fingers around her body, as if they were her own and she could control them ... she was moving as if he was not touching her neck at all, as if his fingers were caressing her thighs, and then between her thighs. He moved his fingers to her face and gently caressed her cheeks, but he saw immediately by her new movements, that she had relocated his fingers to her breasts ... he saw her back go stiff and she moved so that her breasts were pushed out against her pullover, and her nipples were erect. So he moved his hands there and caressed her breasts and she moaned gently, as if he had finally reached the right place. Or one of them, the correct one for the meanwhile...

But her moaning was too explicitly erotic, and the sound and meaning of it penetrated Cindy's unconscious, waking her abruptly from her reverie. She turned over slowly to look at them both, but turned on her back again, as if unconcerned. Then she spoke, theatrically. 'If you two want to go the whole way and make love properly ... do it like you do in my dreams; almost every night! Or do you prefer I tell you a beautiful story instead? A ballet I nearly made?'

Georgina sat up on her elbows and after a quick glance at Matthew, as if to say, *Well! That's the end of that ... that's*

Cindy! she said, 'Yes, tell us the story and if it's very sexy we'll give you our version of the Isis mysteries right here on the grass!' They laughed, but awkwardly. It was clear enough to everyone that Cindy was the only person with a divine right to all kinds of performance, and anything not in her play would have to wait.

Cindy waited until they were comfortable, her timing always impeccable. 'It's a beautiful day, we're in a church made of trees, so we must elevate our spirits to higher things. Actually it's a story by D. H. Lawrence called *The Man Who Died*. You don't know it, do you?'

They both shook their heads. It wouldn't have mattered if they both knew it by heart; neither would have admitted it. 'Good! When I tried to put it on at college, as a ballet, everyone said it was total blasphemy. I don't agree at all. This is the story: Mary Magdalene goes to the tomb of Jesus and finds it's been opened and the body isn't there. She turns to go and a man is standing there. She doesn't know it is Jesus. He is weak, recovering from his crucifixion, only newly reincarnated. But as they talk, he remembers his feelings for her as a woman, remembers desiring her, remembers the frustration and suffering he went through in not making love to her, never allowing himself to become *that* human, that much into his borrowed human body. He leaves her, to be alone and think of what to do in this new incarnation ...

... by chance he meets a beautiful woman, a priestess, who takes care of a small temple devoted to the goddess Isis. The temple is on a small peninsula overlooking the sea. All her life she has been waiting, knowing one day her moment would come. Jesus is very weak indeed, barely able to stand. Bur she recognises him! Not as Jesus Christ; that after all was the destiny of Mary and she missed it. No ... she recognises him as the man for whom she was prepared and initiated long ago. Osiris ... come back from the land of the dead, the god she has always known would come to her, priestess of Isis. She takes him into her temple and bathes his wounds, brings him delicate and delicious food and cares for him. Gradually as the days go by he becomes truly alive again, nourished by her love and affection. She brings perfumes and massages them into his body, making it come alive again. And then she makes herself ready. She has preserved her body all her life for this moment ...

One night ... according to the rites of the goddess, she prepares herself, covering her body with oils and perfumes, and comes quietly, already given, to her Osiris ... her reincarnated god. And they make love. He stays there, happy and fulfilled, at last to have known the fullest and deepest pleasures of making love to a woman. He has become a man ... really a man ... his spirit become flesh, at last united with a woman, a priestess of Isis, initiated into her mysteries ...

... but eventually he must reenter the world to create history, leaving the woman alone in her temple, knowing that she has been visited and been loved by Osiris, whose seed is inside her body and she will bear his child. He becomes the wanderer; the priestess of Isis is fulfilled, but Mary Magdalene, for so long faithful to her Christ, is alone still in the garden next to the tomb, next to the empty barren tomb, from which the stone had been mysteriously removed ...'

Georgina took Matthew's hand and placed it on her cheek and laid her head again on his knees. Very quietly she said: 'Yes, it's a beautiful story, you would have made it into a very beautiful ballet. Which of the women would you have danced?'

'Both of them, of course, merely a change of costume,' she said, trying to appear as casual as possible.

But the image of the empty tomb was lingering in Matthew's mind ... and he felt the tingling on the back of his neck again, which soon became sharp pain. Suddenly he saw the whole thing! He yanked himself up, nearly twisting his back. He glared at Cindy angrily but she didn't react.

'Will you excuse me a minute, I'm going for a walk!'

'Well, actually, we're going nowhere, so we'll wait for you here!' she said, smiling patronisingly.

Matthew decided not to go directly to the tree. He wanted one last, small chance of thinking up an explanation. So he set off in the opposite direction, walking round the copse slowly as if merely going for a walk, giving himself time to think. He was going over the story; had she invented it, or was it a real Lawrence story? Didn't she always pride herself on rewriting other people's texts? But the story was just too much of a coincidence ... or was he just going mad? He stopped for a moment and lent on one of the beech trees. A pain was pulsing across his forehead, his head about to burst. He knew that if he was deluding himself about everything ... he was going mad. But if not, if he was right, he was in a situation even more mad than he dared to imagine. He steeled himself and walked on, outside the copse and then round towards the top, beyond the dense rhododendron bushes, to a spot from where he could see the dead elm tree. He didn't look at it at first. He wanted to be directly opposite it, before he finally turned and looked ... and saw clearly. *The stone had been removed, the tomb was empty. Christ had risen!*

With heavy steps he walked to the tree, stopping ten feet away and regarding it with confused feelings. Beneath the tree was the stone, still covered with cement. At the edge of the hole were marks where someone had chipped out the stone with a chisel. He stood on the stone to see in the hole and as he had imagined, it was hollowed out inside, the perfect size for a human head. The stone wobbled and he tripped off it. He banged the tree hard, angry and yet triumphant at the same time. He stood on the stone again and put his hand into the hole, moving it round in a circle ... just as Cindy's hand had moved in the circle of light ... and he touched something with the tip of his finger. He found another stone and placed the one on top of the other, reached in again and brought out the bandages, a feeling of terrible loathing coming over him as he looked at them ...

The blood on them was dry and black now; and, as if his mind was a computer programmed to analyse a hologram, he saw in his mind, instantly, a three-dimensional reconstruction of the bandages as if wrapped around a head. He saw they were only stained at the bottom end, where the severed neck would have been. He sat down, very shaken, holding the bandages loosely in his hand. Eventually winding them up again he placed them in his pocket, gazed blankly for a moment at the hole, and said quietly, *'L'absence ... absence'* ... but his accent wasn't as good as Cindy's and his delivery was not so sensual and alive.

Half hiding behind the tree, he watched the two girls talking. Obviously they'd not seen him climbing the tree. As he walked back they both turned to look at him, oddly, wondering what had possessed him to shoot off like that, after Cindy's story. He glared fiercely at Cindy, and she stared him back, barely reacting when he said, 'Touché!'

But then she gave him a sweet, sweet adoring smile and in slow slow motion her lashes fell and she turned away from him and looked again at Georgina. 'I think the Chatterly novel was a failure, his only good book was *Apocalypse* ... but I do agree he had more than two eyes, and he used all three of them; and he liked rough sex. I'd always have said yes ... '

Matthew sat down on the edge of the blanket, took some grass and started to chew it, petulantly. Cindy laughed, held out her arms and purred. 'At last ... at last! The gamekeeper I've been waiting for to complete my book!' and she threw herself at him and they both fell over and the girls started to laugh hysterically and Matthew joined in ... laughing even more hysterically.

Then it took him, and Cindy didn't stop him; if that was what he wanted ... he tore at her pants savagely and ripped them and before she could escape, he'd pinned her down and penetrated her viciously and arching up his back to get into the right position to be brutal, he pushed her hard into the ground, and was able to keep it going so he could really hurt her, forcing her to follow him as he rose and rose ... winging up. Suddenly she let go, kicking off her shoes in rage almost and rose and rose too ... until it beat them both, and they fell back, and bursting, surrendered, defeated. Exploited ... but ...

Cindy was gasping, having nearly been choked, but they lay close and still for some time. Almost peaceful. Georgina had wandered off to keep lookout and was sitting eating a piece of grass some way away. Matthew stayed inside Cindy, not letting her move, still quite hard. If Georgina hadn't been there he would have tried again. 'Bitch! Fucking little bitch!' he whispered in her ear and she knew he meant it.

She didn't mind. 'That was nice. I much prefer to be your whore than your actress. At least that was for real! Time you got some of the aggression out of your system and into the right place at the right time ... '

He looked up and saw the kestrel hovering over the field; words came to him, he didn't know from where, and he delivered them curtly; 'And Lo, Christ walking on the water, but not of Genesareth, but Thames!'

Cindy dug her fingers into his bottom as if to mock him for his pretensions, and he winced. 'Poets make me puke!' They laughed. And he was feeling good. He gripped her hard, hurting her for as long as he could. He ground the end of his penis, still hard, against her womb, and she winced. Finally, he withdrew, making sure he messed her up as he did so. Bitch! His eyes closed, he was wondering how it had seemed to Georgina, or a man hiding behind a tree ...

Finally he stood up, as Cindy arranged herself. 'Come on, girls, my pagan priestesses, let's go home! Let's walk on the water together...' He'd no idea where the quotation came from, probably some poem he'd learnt at school. Strange what you recall at the weirdest times.

He drove home slowly ... thinking fast. The girls chatted in the back about food they hated, clothes they loved, places they'd never seen and movies they'd have loved to have acted in. Apparently Georgina was a frustrated actress too and would have loved to have acted in really sexy films ... Rita Hayworth was a peach that she'd have loved to seduce ... 'they were all into girls!' ... but she was very fond of Vivien Leigh. They didn't mention science or art or literature once. At some point Cindy said, 'We must do that again. I for one, most unexpectedly, had a great time.' Then she whispered to Georgina so Matthew couldn't hear. 'I even had something of an *actual* orgasm!'

Georgina had to steel herself not to say: 'Funny enough the same thing happened to me in the copse, just a short while ago!' But she said nothing, loving Cindy too much to hurt her and knowing how thin the ice was, despite the cool exterior.

∇

TEN

"This rebirth could only be achieved by lifting the Veil of Isis. Through the love of Isis, man, sunk in lust and passion, is raised to a spiritual life. But when God associates with the soul, he brings it to pass that she who was formerly woman becomes virgin again. Isis interests herself in healing man's bodies and to all who need her help, she appears in dreams and gives relief."

"Isis and Osiris"
Plutarch

Ø

Back at the house, Matthew said he wanted to be alone, went to his room, lay down on his bed and started to think hard. Either he was going mad, or Cindy could read his mind; or write his dreams. She must be part of a conspiracy to cover up John's murder, his dismemberment into fourteen parts. At the heart of the mystery was a scientific discovery worth murdering someone for ... no wonder Cindy needed him to work on the discs. But why couldn't she do the work herself?

So why didn't he get away immediately? Do the rational thing? Alas, he was trapped by Cindy's dancing, for want of a better word. She was directing the movie, at least her body was; he wanted her again now, as the image came to mind ...

But if Cindy was capable of extrasensory perception, could induce ideas in his mind, then her work with John must be taken seriously. But was it John or Cindy penetrating his mind? Either way it was disturbing; not quite the holiday in Cornwall he'd expected ...

Maybe he'd go to John's room and on the luminous screen, he'd find the answer ...

ENTER

But even as he tried to read the words on the screen, he was still haunted with an image reflecting on the surface of a pool of water, circles of waves doubling on each other, his dreams and the events in the copse. And Cindy. Although he seemed to be reading the words on the screen, only fragments seemed to make any deep impression, but it was a kind of reverie, and he knew John would have approved.

... and Yeats: *"The rise of the Soul against intellect is now beginning in the world."*

... Crowley: *"Reason is like a woman; if you listen, you are lost; with a thick stick you have some sort of sporting chance. Reason leads philosophers to self-contradiction. Philosophically, 'Because' is absurd. There is no answer to the question 'Why?' I have offered a demonstration of the self-contradictory nature of Reason. The crux of the whole proof may be summarised by saying that any possible proposition must be equally true with its contradictory, for if not, the universe would no longer be in equilibrium..."*

... Yeats, Blake, Kathleen Raine, Crowley! Visionaries!

... "The Vision", Yeats tells us, was entirely dictated to his wife by spirits; she wrote it automatically in a trance. Crowley tells us the entire *Book of the Law*was similarly "received" by him from an Egyptian spirit/priest called Aiwas. Crowley had spent the morning meditating on a stele in the Cairo Museum, an Egyptian magical text connected with Horus-Ra-Herakty, Rising Falcon of the Horizon - the secret name of the Giza sphinx. He'd been led there by his wife Rose, in a trance, repeating the word "Horus." When they reached the unseen stele, Crowley discovered it was exhibit number 666.

... Why do we ignore these guys? Why do we NEED to discredit their visions? What is it about Reason that comforts us when it alienates us from the Vision of the Whole? What is that fear? ... Crowley of course was obsessed with SEX. Ugh! Even enjoyed it without shame and declared it sacred again ...

... As for Cindy? Sacred and sacrifice - holographic sex - the Isis' knot that binds the Universe! Uni-verse – a single line poem? EROS is. A Rose is a Rose is Eros. Be aware and beware.

... Freud: *"...and now it may be expected that the other of the two 'Heavenly Forces', eternal EROS, will put forth his strength so as to maintain himself alongside his equally immortal adversary ... THANATOS."* The union of Eros and Thanatos? The hologram we are elucidating, here on the screen of the ghost in the machine! Tiresias Amenhotep!

... and the union of Isis and Osiris ... a wave and a particle ...

... Newsweek magazine! Yes, even that! CIA job? I quote. *"Strangely there is no known lethal dose of LSD. The only known victim of LSD was an elephant at Oklahama City zoo, given an unintentional overdose during an experiment."* Did it become PINK?

Do elephants blush?
... The Diamond Sutra:

"As stars, a fault of vision, as a lamp,
A mock show, dew drops, or a bubble,
A dream, a lightning flash, or cloud,
So should one view what is conditioned."

... "According to the information provided by the Pharaonic buildings themselves, it would seem there were two categories of Mysteries. There were 'Mystery Plays', performed in public like those in our Middle Ages – or secret rites revealed only to initiates prepared to know them, and of which NOTHING, consequently, has come down to us" ...

... Lucie Lamy; thanks Lucie, any relation to Lucie in the Sky with Diamonds, sung by The Dung Beetles in Ancient Egypt? Reincarnated in some likely lads from Liverpool?

Be very careful with these secret rites. You eat red-headed sexy Amanita muscaria and enjoy a lightning trip to Hades. You eat Amanita Phalloides, white and without the scarlet cap, and you die in excruciating agony. One illuminates, the other kills. And that goes for women too! Watch out for the one with the red hair; she rises up and eats men like air ...

Two birds on a tree. One eats the fruit. The other watches ... without eating. The caduceus.

¥

Matthew scrolled quickly through to the end of the disc. More quotes, more asides, more drugs, more dreams. When would John come to the point? The hard disc in Matthew's mind was getting too full already. Was the hard disc reason, and the software, experience? He scrolled through to the end for the next disc's code, and whipped through it, and then the next; to hell with quotes. He inserted Disc Seven, the last of the Lesser Mysteries. He was dying to get to the Greater Mysteries.

DISC SEVEN

△

Dear Tiresias, even you, like Oedipus your eternal adversary, must reach the crossroads; the crux of the Lesser Mysteries; just a few more adamantine observations from myself, as if cut by an agate. This has been a search for an elusive meaning, a preparation for a way of thinking holographically, seeing both points of view simultaneously; to become conscious of the unconscious. The aim of all mysticism – and by chance, psychoanalysis. Holographic perception. The right side and the left, joined in cold fusion. To suffer the Wasteland of Reason, but to see THROUGH with the eyes of Tiresias. Do I repeat myself? Only twice. Where is the code for the Greater Mysteries? It is hidden in the Lesser Mysteries. You must IMAGINE it! Codes, what are they, but words of power? You will not find a mystical system without words of power. ABRAHADABRA! Computer codes for those translucent cosmic computers floating on the planes and dimensions of Virtual Reality: call it Higher Being.

NOW you need the ultimate Word of Power! Oops. Allow me please, just a few more quotes? When you have all these memorised, internalised, absorbed, you will be able to disc-over/ disc-under, UN-disc-close my next code/s so easily: Here goes!

He punched in:

[END]

... viciously; utterly fed up with quotes. No! he must go on!

[ENTER]

He scrolled through the pages even faster, until something scientific caught his eye ...

..."On the 16th of April 1943, upon recrystallising d-lysergic acid diethylamide tartrate, which I had produced from natural lysergic acid and diethylamine by way of the lysergic acid hydrazide and azide, I suddenly became strangely inebriated. The external world became changed as in a dream. Objects appeared to gain in relief; they assumed unusual dimensions; and colours became more glowing. Even self-perception and the sense of time were changed. When the eyes were closed, coloured pictures flashed past in a quickly changing kaleidoscope. After a few hours, the not unpleasant inebriation, which had been experienced while I was FULLY CONSCIOUS, disappeared. Fired by discussions with the outstanding expert on the Mexican magic drugs (R. Gordon Wasson), and encouraged by our successes with the hallucinogenic

fungi, we decided to tackle the chemical investigation of the third most important Mexican psychotomimetic after 'peyotl' and 'teonanacatl' – namely 'ololiuhqui'."

So THAT is how it all re-began. In a science laboratory! Then it got nasty, suppressed by Oedipus/so-called governments.

I have heroically and secretly carried on this TAO way and work, looking for the Eucharist which will detach consciousness from the body and enable it to 'take off', to wherever it might be guided by the inner light-laser from the crystal. A secret known and used by the Ancient Egyptians. Imagine a process by which consciousness can be transformed into pure energy and as quanta of digital data, be sent to the farthest reaches of the Universe. *"Not where the wheeling systems darken, and our benumbed conceiving soars, The drift of pinions would we harken? Beat at our own clay shuttered doors!"* Francis Thompson, high on opium, mostly awful Catholic rubbish but occasionally inspired. Just having a little drink with friends; de Quincey, Coleridge; great poets? Fucking heroin addicts, man, the screwy lot of them! Too bad we still teach them in our schools, GCE O Level etcetera. "I fled him down the nights and down the days and labyrinthine ways ... " Something like that.

Take ... Timothy Leary: *"The human brain is composed of about 120 billion nerve cells, any one of which may connect with as many as 25,000 other nerve cells. The number of inter-connections which this adds, up would stagger even an astronomer, used to dealing with astronomical numbers. The number is far greater than all the atoms in the universe! A computer sophisticated enough to handle this number of inter-connections would have to be big enough to cover the whole earth. Into this matrix floods 'about 100 million sensations a second from the various senses'. And somewhere in that ten billion-cell galaxy is a tiny solar system of connected neurons which is aware of your social self. Your 'ego' is to your cortex what the planet Earth is to our galaxy with its 100,000 MILLION suns. The psychedelic answer to the 'I' question is the crux of the LSD experience."*

Imagine a hundred years' time, a thousand years. What then? Makes the mind boggle. We sit around now, bog-farting with unsublimated anality, worrying about the Here and Now? Eating and shitting is the here and now! Ferrrrrrrraris and refrigerators! We could be making love, CONSCIOUSLY!

"In Europe, interest in the Green Ray flared up after the war of 1939, but in a negative manner. Because of the invention of the Laser and the obsession with the Death Ray which sprang from it, isolated individuals and groups of Esoterics dreamed of a Laser of the Gods. These seekers all preached an ideology which was established on Scandinavian Runes and on the God Odin. However they did not really oppose themselves to Christianity, which they considered to be of an ARYAN source. With the Odinism allying itself to multiple societies (esoteric) which had been flourishing in Germany and in Scandinavia during Hitler's time, for example the group THULE, who pretended they could withhold the Green Ray – but were not taken seriously. It was considered to be blackmail from losers! ... based on the Hieroglyphics. This is important: had the ancient Scandinavian religions known of a SCIENCE OF THE GREEN RAY revealed to their priests and priestesses by the enigmatic passengers on spacecraft? If the problem of UFOs relates to that of the "Transparent Men" it would be better rather then to smile, to study this file objectively as are doing the Americans and Russians!"

So! Friend and disciple, at the end of the Lesser Mysteries, what is the code for the Greater? A re-minder: don't forget that TIRESIAS, merely a spectator and not actually a 'character', is the most important guy in the poem, uniting it; what he SEES is the substance of the poem. We're living in the Wasteland, dis-remembered by reason, fragmented like Osiris. Tiresias sees what cannot be seen; the holographic vision. Knowing how we know, seeing how we see. Through. The crossing. Tiresias saw two snakes coupling in the desert and struck and killed one, but the wrong one ... and became a woman. Be careful this doesn't happen to you. Watch out for the ensheathed, silk-clad satin woman Jean Harlot lookalike!

Beware the venomous fluids on the invisible webs that stretch between presence and absence ... hovering over forever-open thighs, that lock around your neck and enclose you in shared murder ... a necklace of glistening drops, like diamonds ...

"Every orgasm is the death of a king."

IF you HAVE found the key and intend to consult the next Seven Discs, (the six in your hands and the fourteenth you have yet to find), and enter the R-field of the Greater Mysteries, you need a mirror in which to see her; a blind date with the goddess bathing is enough to dismember any man! I wanted you to be warned, with these Lesser Mysteries, so that the new vision would not surprise you TOO much, so you will not dismiss it all as rubbish. Imagine, you consulted my life's work and said, *Poppycock!*

You have been (re)introduced to the Perennial Philosophy, as Huxley called it, to show that I am not a mere crank, that my wanderings in Hades have not produced mere messages for help in empty pill bottles washed up on a lonely beach, from a mind occulted and cut loose by the chemical scalpels of LSD *et alii.* No, this is deadly serious. We have cut the sacred plant of immortality loose from its subterranean moorings, so it is washed up, a mere weed, on the arid filthy beach that has become reason's inevitable cherished and most beloved wasteland.

Hic sunt Roboti.

On that beach have I been a beachcomber, parched like everyone by the pitiless sun of reason: "I am Ozymandias King of Kings!" Shell upon shell! Or, maybe like Yeats I will become a falcon and fly over that stark desert, searching for an oasis I might call my garden of Eden, and in a tree, make my nest on its golden bough and lay my eggs of perfect shape and silence. The lone and level, crystal sands! This journey took me to Ancient Egypt and to the last great culture that was CERTAIN of its vision - CERTAIN of its spirituality, CERTAIN of the *wholeness* of its vision, who saw a universe, uncurtained, holographically etched on every grain of silicon sand, who knew the universe as one insane but delicious image, a surreal and yet real (at the same holographic-time) movie made by the gods, a LUSCIOUS STYLISH ELEGANT BEAUTIFUL blue movie at that. There they are still, masturbating and screwing away, ejaculating over us with their viral (take care!) and digital (take more care!) rain, giving birth to more variations on the same theme ... endless, endless vortexes of being and becoming ... wave upon wave of parallel parodoxical forms generating form ... a sublime ecstatic holomovement through a timeless time. And we complain about the price of bread?

Like all ghosts, I, John, after opening the seven seals, twice, have one profound desire; to be seen! To rise again, and perform

on the stage of my lover's body.
See you later! Bon voyage,
truly yours analogically, and of course holographically,
John Raymonde, alias Faulkner, alias Amenhotep.
So-called Director of so-called 'Project OSIRIS', with or without a few holographic anal-logos! AMEN!

Φ

Matthew switched off the computer, having no idea for the code for Disc Eight. He knew he'd been tricked into exposing himself to all these subversive texts, but suddenly he had an idea, put Disc Seven back in and scrolled to the end. Yes, there it was. He put Disc Eight back and typed:

[A] [N] [A] [L] [L] [O] [G] [O] [S]

The computer started singing a hideous jarring electronic version of *Brown Sugar* before words came on the screen:

Sorry. Too obvious! But at least you now have ANAL-LOGOS on the brain! On which side? Both! We must find the interface!

▼

Matthew tried INTERFACE, then variations on ANAL and LOGOS and HOLOGRAPH and HOLOGRAM and ISIS and OSIRIS and the two combined. He tried everything, overlapping, copulating with everything else. Nothing. He tried POPPYCOCK; that was a typical John joke – a pseudonym for Penis of Osiris? He was disappointed it didn't work. He even tried MATTHEW and JOHN. Nothing. CINDY. He switched off the machine, not sure why he was feeling so angry suddenly. What would John do in such a situation, he of the Anal-logos? Yes!

He went to his room and changed into something more suitable, a dark pair of trousers and black shirt. John's of course. He went to Cindy's room and knocked on the door. She opened it very cautiously, just a few inches. Hadn't they agreed not to invade each other's sacred territories?

'It's Tiresias, may I come in? The man with the viridescent X-Ray laser eyes! Or do I have to burn the door down with a mere glance, or rend it - er, render it translucent?' Cindy could see by the look on his face that he was not asking her but telling her; she didn't need X-ray eyes to see what was going on inside his head. She opened the door without a word and stood back, trying to appear nonchalant. She liked aggressive men ... unless he wanted to talk about John in which case she'd tell him to fuck off.

Matthew noticed her work-table, piled high with books. He turned and faced her directly, scowling. She was wearing a loose, cheap, white cotton dress, really tarty, and he guessed she was wearing nothing underneath. In her room Cindy was always 'as good as naked' Georgina said. Matthew turned on his heels, noticed an old-fashioned key in the door and locked it. Cindy was now sitting on the edge of the bed, like Elizabeth Taylor in *Cat on a Hot Tin Roof*. 'Where are the veils?' he asked coldly. 'Get them!'

She went to a drawer, took them out and laid them on the bed. Matthew picked one up, raised it in front of her eyes and asked politely, 'Blindfold, madam?'

'Be my guest!' she said, barely betraying her unease. She could see he was angry and deadly serious.

Matthew folded the scarf, placed it over her eyes and tied it very hard, almost brutally. 'Stand up!' he said. She did so. 'Turn round and take off your dress and whatever else you are wearing.' She slipped off the white dress; under it she was naked. Her slim round bottom seemed to twitch, either with expectation or apprehension.

He ordered her to lie down on her stomach on the edge of the bed. Taking another scarf, he tied her feet so tightly that she winced, then tied her arms around the wrists, behind her back, tied another around her knees, and with a green scarf he tied her arms down tight to her body, bringing the scarf over her breasts. Deliberately he covered her breasts as if he didn't want to see them, before tying another scarf around her face, drawing it tightly across her mouth. She tried to protest but she knew it was useless. He then forced her down further until she was kneeling against the bed, her bottom in the air.

He took the white dress and laid it across her back so that only her bottom and her legs were visible. On her feet were small boots. He smiled. For some unknown reason an image, a code, flashed into his mind: she really looked like a discarded (but spelt disc-R-dead) Barbie doll. John again! He stepped back to enjoy the image, then left her a moment to suffer whatever images she inflicted on herself.

He wanted to look at her books; he was astonished to see they were all extremely advanced physics and mathematics. So much for her novel about English literary heroines and their unsublimated sexuality! From the kitsch art-deco dressing-table he took a bottle containing a greasy, exotic-looking body oil, apparently from Samarkand. Probably a suburb of Bedford. He sniffed it. Phew! It would have made a Pamir yak randy, even at minus forty degrees. He walked over to her, at least to her body, patiently waiting, all choice surrendered, paused, savouring the sight of her bottom, reminding him of the Velasquez portrait of a woman looking at herself in a mirror. 'Now, for once, Cindy has no mirror, not even me!'

He unzipped his trousers and touched himself as he poured the oil over her bottom. She shuddered and moaned and he didn't know if it was fear or encouragement, but it made no difference. He poured oil over himself and caressed his erect penis, at the same time stroking her bottom, tantalisingly, with long strong strokes ... as one strokes the nose of a race-horse. Blinkered. She seemed quite taut, still. He became more firm in his gestures, occasionally pressing his fingers down into her vagina, pinching the clitoris hood, as if he might relent and take her there. But each time she moved as if to encourage him to take her there, he quickly re-pressed the tip of his finger in her anus. He poured more oil on her and pushed more firmly. When she was quite certain of his intentions he saw her give in, visibly let herself flop onto the bed to be as relaxed as possible. For some time he played with the two perfect cheeks of her bottom, caressing them, pinching them, pulling them as if opening her a little more each time in preparation for the moment to come. When he felt she was open enough he tore the green veil off, so hard, the edge of it caught her skin, grazing it. If they wanted symbolism, he'd give it! In hard prose.

He pushed into her firmly, with only a certain amount of consideration, staying half-poised, an inch in, while she wriggled as if wanting to escape, but he stayed firmly in position, watching the twitching, enjoying every flicker, (reminding him of the eyelids in REM sleep, ah well) until he plunged into her completely and she let out a muffled scream. But he took no notice of her complaints. He was John now, and not himself, so she could blame it all on John.

'Little phallic bitch!' he murmured. She nodded her head. Yes she was and she knew it, but the price was worth paying, sometimes. Intending to prolong it, he took care to move smoothly and with no deviation from side to side, moved in and out of her with deep, firm strokes and she relaxed so much he wasn't sure if she was still conscious, or just meditating. He then jerked harder, almost viciously, but still holding back. He was in good form. Then he felt her twitching inside, contracting the muscles in her vagina, which he could feel inside her bottom. He knew she was *there* ...

He wanted to be so controlled, he measured every stroke with finesse, each one building on the next with only the smallest hint of increasing excitement. He was taking her as if he could continue forever, imagining the image of the erect thigh of the Great Bear symbolised eternity ... even though, in his mind, he was in the copse ... and the girl was someone else ... one of these days he would shave Cindy. He wanted to hurt her. She was moaning strongly but he didn't care, knowing it could as easily be pleasure as pain. He was learning the holographic gospel according to John; pain and pleasure were the same ... as were sex and death ...

When at last he could control it no longer, he came out of her, but only just, for as long as he could hold it, and she wasn't sure if he was going to deny it to her ... and he watched the rim lingering open. When he couldn't control it any longer he plunged back in again and had to let go ... violently and viciously, and when he ejaculated she screamed out, loud enough to wake the dead.

Talking of which, yes, he was indeed feeling possessed,

and even after he had ejaculated he carried on thrusting into her and he didn't lose his *other* erection and on and on he went until finally it was exhaustion that overcame him, and he knew he couldn't bring himself to orgasm again but he'd carry on out of spite, and somewhere in this endless thrusting he felt her go rigid and grasp him even more fiercely, this second time, like an animal, and he knew she had reached an *other* orgasm, not bothering to wait for him, nothing like that ... not allowing him that kind of satisfaction. Not yet, until he'd got all the codes. And then only maybe. But at least he'd figured out one useful holographic code, embodying the essential interface; that delicate membrane between oral and anal.

Finally satiated and exhausted, he flopped down on top of her. He'd put so much oil on her bottom it had spread all over them both and various veils were soaked in it. After a few minutes she grunted strange sounds through the scarf in her mouth and Matthew reluctantly partially untied it. She gasped and breathed deeply through the gap. She didn't ask him to untie the other veils, presuming he would take his time and she didn't want to provoke him again ... with even the smallest sign of criticism. After all, he was getting there.

He stayed inside her, quite still, for a long time and neither of them spoke. Eventually he felt fond of her again, as he was fond of his falcon, despite himself, and kissed her gently on the cheek and this small gesture was enough for her to know that he was becoming himself again. She'd won, of course. It was always the submissive who enslaved the so-called master. That is how she had so much power over George ... allowing her to be sadistic if she wanted to be. But Georgina was always conscious of it, so was never truly sadistic. Like *she* could be ... when her work called for it.

Curiously, Matthew was still feeling frustrated. Where had all this pent-up aggression come from and what had it to do with desire? But he wanted it, so he pushed into her again, startling her, and she was so loose, it wasn't difficult now. His penis rigid in her bottom, he spat out a question. 'What is the code for Disc Eight and the Greater Mysteries? I know you're tricking me. Otherwise I leave; give me the code or I go. I've read the first seven discs, I want the code for the second batch or I go to the police as well. I have evidence!'

He was hurting her now, deliberately. He knew she was very tender. She spluttered. 'Honestly, Matthew. I swear on my mother's grave! God forbid! You can tear me apart if you want, I'm not tricking you. Why should I? I've searched the whole mother-fucking world for those codes! I can't work it out. I've wept in anger and rage, I promise you. The whole secret of everything is locked in that computer, the results of all our work together. How do you think I feel? You idiot, he deliberately encoded it to hide it from ME! Fucking patriarchal shit that he was!' Matthew thrust into her, viciously, so hard she cried out in pain.

'No! Really, Matthew. It's no use hurting me. We have to do this together. If I had it, I would have used it, wouldn't I? Can't you see that's why I first brought you here, a total stranger? Would I have needed to otherwise? Just think about it! But believe me, one thing, I have grown genuinely fond of you. Some of it was games, I admit. But now, damn it, believe me, we can be accomplices. I'll tell you everything if you give me time, and especially if you can find the code. I can't, my mind's too full of knowledge. It needed a virgin eye; forgive the expression. Otherwise everything is lost. We can't get the data a second time, I'm sure of that.'

'Why did you kill John?' he said, thrusting hard again.

She winced. 'Don't be silly, I didn't. That's your crazy idea. He went off and someone else did it, you must realise that too. Would he have left all the data here, unfinished? You're starting to see significance where it doesn't exist. Probably the scientist in you. Now you're making too many connections. At this rate you'll connect with the whole universe and blow a fuse. John left his work here, I tell you, to be finished.'

'Surely he took copies of the discs?'

'Maybe, but where? Why? No, I think it was too sudden. He went just like that, one night, after his experiment in the copse, after taking George to the station. He was too confident and arrogant. He was there and then he was gone. And within an hour or so I felt it, like a shaft of light into my heart! I have instincts like every woman. He was dead. I felt the moment he died. It was exactly nine o'clock, I looked at the clock. Believe me, if I had the code, we could open up the files and work on it together. Surely you can see that? I brought *you*, a crystallographer, not just some computer freak, because we can work on it together, because it's all about crystals. You will see. It was *all* done with crystals. You seemed so much part of the coincidences! People call that kind of thing falling in love, don't they? That's the only way they glimpse this awesome mystery. They make it all Mills and Boon, alas, but it's deadly serious. Maybe that's what John was working on, the chemical produced when we first fall in love and become obsessed with an absent image? Haunted by the OTHER ONE! Source of all romance and self-delusion! The psycho-pharmacology of love. Believe me?'

Matthew half believed her, but he thrust into her again, just for the fun of it. He was amazed to find himself very close to coming again, and maybe it was a mistake, but she went tight around him again, so tight this time it was too much and he straightened up his back as hard as he could, gripped her arms as if fighting off a giant octopus, and went for it savagely and ruthlessly, almost lifting her up from the bed as he let himself go ... burst into her with a satanic cry and he gripped her around the neck and felt like throttling her, and while he ejaculated she couldn't breathe, but he let her breathe after his last thrust, and she sobbed ... and cried ... surprised by him, crying with relief and although she wouldn't have admitted it, pleasure ... sheer physical, sensual joy at having being taken so brutally. 'So much for John's theorem about romance!' he said bitterly.

Then she started to laugh. 'You beast! You adorable bastard, you really hurt me! I'll not walk straight for a week. But do you know?' She turned round and smiled at him and puckered her lips for him to kiss them. He loosened her blindfold and kissed her gently on her cheap tarty luscious lips. 'You know what? It was worth it!' And he stayed kissing her on the lips as he withdrew from her, this time carefully, before lying down on the bed next to her. He would have cleaned the mess everywhere himself with the loosened veil but it was the green one and somehow he didn't dare.

'Little slut!' he whispered, and she liked it.

After a few minutes of silence, holding each other affectionately, he mused suddenly, 'Everything you say is logical and obvious, which is why I mistrust it. Too obvious. The story can't be the one you want me to believe. After all, John has taught me to turn things round. Not just you! I don't see that I can find the code if *you* can't, unless I'm being taken for a ride. The one thing that makes me hang on, I tell you the truth, is my dreams! But directed by whom?'

'But, Matthew, *they* are something I clearly don't have any control over. It's your fantasy that I'm against you, or I killed John. We are dealing with others. Help me and I will help you. That's all I said, right from the beginning.'

He lay quietly next to her, still doubting her ... 'Maybe... '

After a long silence, she spoke, reflectively, 'It's unfair being a woman, you can't escape being*double*. You're always two people, one black, one white, because there are two holes that can be filled, and when you know a man desires you, you think, is it to be the white one, so good and pure and right, or it is to be the black one, so full of sin and guilt and childhood memories? One so full of light, the other of shadow and matter and secret desire? When a man is inside your vagina you feel it and yet you don't. It fits too easily. You have to move so you can really feel it. But when he is buried inside your arse, there is no escaping it, no denying it ... it's real! The material world, let's face it, what the world is so hungry for; shit, gold, power, filthy lucre!'

Matthew untied the veils and she slipped off the edge of the bed and grabbing her haggard stained white dress, pulled it over herself before nestling back close to him, apparently for affection. Maybe to escape his looking at her. She put her arms around him, a little girl now ... at least acting it, acting the need to be comforted. 'I'm sorry about the mess with John and all that. If only we could just enjoy being together, but really, you have no idea how important it is, the data we have on his computer. It's the result of years of effort. I've been cheated. My God, you don't know how much I wept with rage and frustration and misery at losing him. I never loved John in that deep sense, but we worked well together. And then not only did he disappear, but all our knowledge went too, just as if someone had taken a huge magnet and wiped a brain clear of all its memories. And yet, the irony of it, they are *not* gone, just hidden, stolen ... all there on those discs, hidden by a few codes. Just little black dots, on off on off on off, and yet we can't solve the riddle. Now you know why the Sphinx is still smiling. She still has the code to those ancient Egyptian secrets! But John and I were close at last to wiping the smile off her face, to decoding the secrets of their pre-dynastic technology of consciousness, their knowledge of magnetism and wave-fields, and just think, they're probably the greatest secrets of all time. How to lift the mind right out and send it off as light, to people who can decode it and reconstitute you!'

Matthew winced. He wanted to say *Shit!* but it wasn't the right moment, the symbolism might have been subsumed by too much reality; which human-kind cannot apparently bear. 'How much were you involved in the work?' he asked, coldly.

She hesitated. 'Let's just say I was the catalyst. No direct involvement. I did little really except encourage him. Without me he would have done nothing; too lazy, too spaced out, too random and unorganised. Without me ... like that poem about going to Ithaka and discovering *she* has been betraying you, all the while on the terrible journey to find her ... and yet, otherwise, without her, he would never have set out.'

'Why do you read advanced physics and mathematics in your spare time? You'd need at least a Ph.D in black holes and curved space-time to understand that stuff.'

She smiled, trying not to look guilty. 'Because I'm a very modern young lady. I don't want to get left a little *behind* the times, do I?' She smiled patronisingly, the smile that Matthew knew to mistrust, and once again he reminded himself he must not be naive. Everything she'd said was more than likely a lie, even the sex, but what the hell - he'd be a fool not to continue to enjoy taking her!

He lay back on the bed, reflecting on his recent sexual audacity. Suddenly he recalled an image – just a hunch, but this time the back of his neck was tingling. The idea was still dim, just outside of vision, but on the point of coming into focus. It had *come* to him when he was making love to Cindy, when he was inside her, and it was returning now, more formed, more shaped, but he suddenly *knew* ... yes, damn it ... it was the most extraordinary sensation of premonition and *déjà vu* all mixed together. Yes, the answer was just round the corner, almost within his grasp!

Was Meritaten speaking to him again now, or was she just telling him off for being a naughty boy? He told Cindy he had something to do, he'd see her later. 'Tell me the truth, before I leave; why *are* you reading theoretical physics of all things?'

'They're John's old books. His Pre-Egypt phase. I was just looking for a clue, trying to put the pieces together. Like Isis! I never stop, stupid woman that I am, it's truly lamentable!'

Matthew went to the bathroom and bathed himself; his penis was tender, but he laughed softly to himself. He knew! He was close to the moment of awakening. He dried himself carefully: OUCH!: gently put on his trousers and went into John's room and locked the door. He was very excited. He'd made the right observation in the dimension of reality, now to test the theory, the analogue. Mere coincidence? No such thing!

He took the *Book of the Dead* and skipped through, scanning the parallel texts, hieroglyphs and translations. He noticed "emerald light", and marked the corner of the page. He was fascinated to see how many images now connected with John's texts ... offerings and sacrifices and the "Shining Ones". He found the Chapter of the Lamentations of Isis and went through it, following her search, through part after part of the fragmented, dismembered body of Osiris until he found what he was looking for ... THE PHALLUS OF OSIRIS ... and he wrote down the letters corresponding to the hieroglyph for phallus, X E R U I, and Osiris, A S A R.

The interface! He put Disc Eight into the drive again and pressed the keys on the computer:

[X] [E] [R] [U] [I]   [A] [S] [A] [R]

... and waited. The disc drive purred and stopped. There were a few subliminal flashes on the screen (surely of copulating couples or was he imagining them?) and Matthew's heart stopped beating for so long, and he held his breath for so long, he almost expired on the spot. Finally onto the screen came the first page of John's Greater Mysteries!

THE GREATER MYSTERIES

Welcome, Tiresias! YOU OLD (grass-haired) SOD! HE who interprets signs. So the magic mushroom was eaten ... naughty girl. And you have broken the code; I only wish I could be there to see your face, but maybe I am watching you? Is there not a face reflected on the ice, the glass of your screen between us? Who knows. Not she not I. But we have work to do. Scroll on, fellow wanderer! Fellow pilgrim falcon; le Pélèrin!

First, a renewed warning; Cindy is not all she appears to be. Take her with a Djed pillar of salt! She has taken the drug, the Ultimate Eucharist. More about that later. But she has been possessed directly. She has lost herself, so I lost her too. Whatever you do, suspect everything she says. That is all I can say at the present timelessness.

Now press ST1 and hold down ERASE button to erase this page. We don't want her to see it, just in case she is behind you looking over your shoulder, even though you THINK she is in her room working. She might be anywhere, even inside your head! So erase this page, NOW, before it is too late. After that press ST2, for the next page ...

▸

Obeying, Matthew was instructed to erase any written references to the main code, to memorise it and destroy the *Book of the Dead* if he'd marked it. He was then given the next codes, each one to be remembered and then erased.

The codes were the fragmented principles of consciousess, *coupled* with the name of Osiris – AsAr. So the codes were KaAsAr, KhuAsAr, BaAsAr, KhaibitAsAr and so on. Then John ordered him to erase all the contents of the disc. It contained only the instructions for the codes.

But Matthew was also told there were copies of the remaining discs, except the last one of course, hidden in a dead elm tree in a copse, behind a stone cemented into a hole. The map reference was given, to be memorised. John advised him to leave the discs in the tree and only get them if totally essential, IF, for example, the discs in front of him got lost or erased.

In a rising mood of excitement, Matthew did everything he was asked. Alas, he didn't need to memorise or forget the map reference of the copse! He switched off the computer, too excited to do anything more for a while.

All this because he had buggered Cindy, and seen through her with his other mind's eye? Didn't John say, rebirth is always anal? Or Georgina; it's always Daddy's child!

Matthew stretched, feeling really pleased with himself. His penis was definitely sore, but he felt a new identity with it. Even affection! 'You old sodomite! Your consciousness is better than mine. Like likes like. Morphic coincidence. My sacred mushroom, initiated into holographic resonance!'

Cindy? He'd known all along she was really dangerous, John's warnings came as no surprise. But he now had the code, something she needed desperately, and it gave him the power to deal with her more on his own terms. The only problem might be his developing passion for her. He felt he wanted her again even now! Next time he would whip her; hadn't she suggested it somewhere along the line?

But the biggest mystery was the copse. The dead elm tree. As he had foreseen in his dreams, he'd got it right and yet wrong. It seemed it was not John's head or fragmented body in the tree, but copies of the discs. But how had he known about the elm tree? The data could only have come from John. Was he still alive sending him messages telepathically, by some kind of remote hypnotism, or was he dead, and communicating through dreams? Both ideas were absurd, Matthew knew, but what other explanations were there?

He had definitely been picking up on something. If he had been resonating with Cindy, then she would have found the codes and opened the seven discs, so why was she still in need of him? Or was she just playing with him, keeping him to help synthesise crystals? She seemed to anticipate him all the time, but some women were just like that, especially with their lovers. The sixth sense, as Georgina had put it, when they'd talked about telepathy and John's crazy ideas about holographic consciousness. Maybe not so crazy after all.

But the dead elm tree? The concrete had been taken out, which was the worst news of all, so Cindy, or someone, had found the discs. And put in the bandages? Maybe she'd been having similar dreams! Or maybe it was the people who killed John, if there were any such people; and if he was dead.

He was reluctant to go to Disc Nine immediately. Physically tired from taking Cindy, and psychologically drained, he decided to go for a walk, get some fresh air and replenish his resources. Locking John's door he went down into the garden, after putting a small piece of sellotape under the handle, to know if anyone else had opened it.

He sat down next to his favourite tree, tried to relax his body consciously, breathed deeply and closed his eyes. He was Sisyphus at the top of the mountain, the stone had fallen down to the bottom and he was momentarily free. Oh how he would enjoy the walk down before he had to pick it up again, although, it was clear now, it was no grey chunk of crystallised granite he was humping up his Mount Analogue, but "Miss Rosetta Stone" in all her glory; and she was a very heavy number indeed.

Georgina came into the garden and sat next to him. The curve of the tree trunk was large enough for them both, though it meant they were facing in different directions. She said nothing as she sat down and they remained silent for more than five minutes; to Matthew it seemed a very long time indeed. He was feeling guilty about the earlier events with Cindy. Finally she spoke. 'It does seem strange you trying to carry on with John's work, all about drugs. But not just drugs, he was a true scientist really.'

He laughed. They were so cool, these girls! 'Were he and Cindy taking drugs all the time?'

'They wouldn't call them drugs, but experiments. I told you, John was in contact with a secret laboratory somewhere, or it was his own. Maybe behind the Iron Curtain – even Mongolia or somewhere. He went there once. He knew the most interesting research was being done by the Russians.'

'But why do you think John was killed?'

She looked down sadly at her hands. 'Was he? I don't know

if he was. He disappeared, it's Cindy who says he's dead. Either she knows he is, by telepahy, or wants us to think he is. Maybe he's in a secret room in the top of the house directing the movie, on the screens. Maybe we're mere puppets. You know the door into Hades was made of diamond? Coincidence? And the first theatres in ancient Babylon were designed in the shape of the door of Hades. In other words, you went into the theatre, but really you went into Hades. We go back to go forward. As Confucius said, "To know the future, study the past!" The secret of John's genius was to know the time machine is real. And the number of dimensions and parallel worlds is maybe infinite.'

'If you say so!'

'Don't tell her I told you, but Cindy has asked me to make a model in resin of a rather ruthless dildo she has. Talk about changing the subject. But I thought it might amuse you. She said she wants a phallus which is invisible in the dark, as purely translucent as possible, which is nevertheless quite real. In other words, functional. So one of these evenings we'll have another trip through the Diamond Door. Who she wants to use the phallus on though, I daren't think. She wants a penis that could be made to disappear. I told her, just make love to me! Or to a man, it always disappears! But she wasn't amused. Clearly it's a touchy subject. Girls will be girls!'

They laughed. 'I've started it. It's dead easy to make. It'll be dry by tonight. I'll make sure it's well polished, I'd hate to have it fall to bits at the wrong moment. Ah well, I must get back to my invisible penis, if you will excuse the expression. See you later. By the way, you look awful. What *is* the matter? Did you see a ghost? You're as white as a sheet!'

'Am I? I must be tired, working too hard. It's John's Black Room making a ghost out of *me*. See you later.' He was putting on a brave face. They kissed each other fondly.

Matthew felt dreadful. Surely Cindy's request for the phallus was her way of letting him know she was aware of his discovery of the code: XERUI ASAR? How did she do it? He went to John's room, but the door-handle had not been touched. He sat down. Exhausted. He glanced around the sombre, black room, and was again surprised by its simplicity and austerity, its classical hard-edged respect for form, remembering how much it had contradicted his expectations. The girls had created an image of John in his mind of a rather crazy, romantic kind of fellow, a rough diamond ...

But he was still feeling pleased with himself. It *was* quite an achievement for someone like himself to have discovered the code for the Greater Mysteries. The question was, *why* had it eluded Cindy? It had not been that difficult. She knew John's mind, and the story of the myth thoroughly - Isis creating by magic the phallus of her dead husband. What had made it impossible for Cindy to see the answer to the riddle?

But he must take John's warning seriously. From now on he must really think twice about everything Cindy said or did. No doubt about it, she was a most modern, post-modern kind of a witch, and if he didn't keep reminding himself of this, he might not get back to Cambridge in one piece, but thirteen, to say nothing of the missing fourteenth.

He also reminded himself he must check the computer again – he'd done so already – to make sure there was no second – *holographic!* – cable going out from it. If so, it would have been easy to have had another terminal in another room, for Cindy to watch. But he was sure this was impossible. There was no such cable and no indication of any telegraphic or wire-less means of transmitting the data.

But he was at last on the right track - but going to where? A strange image came to his mind. A long stone shaft, a narrow dark tunnel, and in it ... yes, it was his father's miniature train, the one he could stop and start, by magic. But no, it seemed to be a small robot. Where had he seen the image? A small robot crawling along in the dark, with two lasers as its eyes. Was this another image being sent to him by John? He would try and meditate on it and see where it led him ... now that he was starting to see holographically. Maybe it was an image derived from his diamonds, his own technology. He must work on his own work again before it was too late ...

▼

ELEVEN

"The team, headed by Akira Tonomura, proved the validity of the 'AB Effect' – predicted in 1959 by physicists Y. Abranov and David Bohm – that an electron feels the effect of a remote electromagnetic field even if it does not touch the field. A doughnut-shaped crystal of nobrium was used. The researchers used electron holography to study the behaviour of two electron beams, one travelling through the hole of the doughnut, and the other passing beside it. Electron holography enables three-dimensional observation of a micro-electromagnetic field with an electron microscope.

*This is the first step in proving 'action at a distance', the Caput Nili (*Source of the Nile *as Einstein called it:* Source of the Nile, *is of course Osiris, as Plutarch tells us!); showing that matter, structured by space and time as we think we know it, is so much of an illusion, that soon it will be possible to show that an action at this side of the universe can happen instantaneously in another galaxy. These kind of resonant reactions are probably going on all the time, but we do not YET have the means of detecting the process."*

"Unified theory of force proved."
– Newspaper article, 31st August 1986

At dinner, Cindy announced, 'I've a big surprise. This afternoon I received a message from the arcane world of spirits, an invitation to enter the murky depths of the theatre of sado-masochism, and like the initiates of those pagan mysteries we know all about, *ad infinitum*, *ad nauseam*, we're about to become voyeurs of an archetypal Mystery Play, in which a poor long-suffering father figure will be exploited and dismembered by the loathsome lust and awesome ambitions of a lissome, sexually obsessed young woman.'

'*Some* woman! Not my type at all!' Matthew intoned.

'But Herr Joseph, surely you recognise your own film?' She fell about laughing. 'Yup! Saw it in the local rag, the erstwhile flea-pit, famous for Bingo, in cohorts with the British Film Institute, to inspire in us some much needed spiritual uplift, is showing a week of German Expressionist films. Tonight is *The Blue Angel.* Talk of the devil! I reserved three seats!'

'Can't be true!' Matthew said.

'Must be!' Georgina said. 'That's how it happens to us!'

Cindy continued, 'Tonight is the Gala Opening Night so it's your best togs. I'm going as an ersatz Jean Harlow!'

There were four other people in the auditorium, a brash young couple with scarlet hair who made love on the back seat, loudly, a smelly old man who fell asleep and snored after masturbating, and the pretty young usherette who said she was a student, and was clearly much taken by Cindy, dressed for the première of *The Godfather* in Las Vegas, or a sneak preview of *Behind the Green Door* for the cops who'd been policing the Democratic Convention; over-dressed for St Ives, Cornwall, though men have up and shot their wives, even those with seven of them, rather than send them to St.Ives; but she always dressed for herself anyway, so what the hell.

Matthew noticed Cindy eyeing the usherette from the minute they arrived. When the film snapped, she went to sit next to her. Georgina shrugged. 'Just keep your fingers crossed she doesn't bring her back and you have to perform the *coup de grâce*. Do you feel up to it?' she said mockingly.

'I'd try maybe, to help her out!' They held hands to comfort each other. After the end titles Georgina glared at Cindy to no avail, still chatting away to the girl, arms waving more dramatically than Marlene Dietrich in the film, of which she'd obviously seen precious little. Cindy made a further extravagant fuss taking the girl's telephone number, and pointedly didn't introduce her. They drove home in silence.

On arrival Cindy suggested a bottle of wine in the drawing room. The mood was dark. Cindy said the film might have been great when it first came out, but now it was jaded, sordid and utterly depressing. Matthew was surprised to notice she was on the verge of crying, as if her *raison d'être* had been undermined, the flop of the film a sign that she too would soon lose her transient borrowed kitsch glamour. Georgina, rising to the occasion, unexpectedly confident and aggressive, grabbed her, told her not to be silly and took her off to bed. Matthew was astonished to see Cindy being taken off like a rag doll, or a sacrificial lamb to the slaughter.

In bed, for distraction, Matthew read *The Book of the Dead*...

Another important and apparently eternal part of man was the KHU, which may be defined as a 'shining' or translucent, intangible casing or covering of the body, which is frequently depicted in the form of a mummy. KHU has often been translated as 'shining one', 'glorious', 'intelligence' and the like, but in certain cases it may be tolerably well rendered by 'spirit'.

Clearly it meant everything or nothing. Words! Later, though, his sleep was invaded by another dream ...

... he's on his way to his for his last experiment. Suddenly there's a violent storm and flashes of lightning, and he's stopped dead in his tracks when a vivid flash of lightning hits the building just next to him with a loud bang, an iridescent blue green, just like the colours of crystals of lapis lazuli seen under a microscope ...

The building, the local cinema, is severely damaged. A siren is heard off screen, and people are frantically milling about trying to deal with the emergency. He stands back, detached from the action, merely wondering what film was showing at the time and if the audience thought the lightning bolt and fire were part of the film, ignored it and suffered as a consequence. He gazes at the sky, surprised to see a gap in the clouds and the river of heaven, the Milky Way, clear and bright ...

He hears wailing. 'Is there another war?' someone asks. 'It will be on TV,' someone else says. He's curious, moving closer. The whole façade of the building has become dislocated. One of the huge stone columns seems to have received the full shock of the lightning and is splintered and broken and the effect is to leave the façade all crooked. There are only six columns still standing, the seventh now shattered and sketched with black burn marks. Suddenly it dawns on him the building is not the cinema at all. It's the Fitzwilliam Museum!

Desperate now, he pushes through the crowd and runs up to the top step under the broken colonnade of columns, about to collapse. He *must* get to the basement, knowing Meritaten is in danger, but the basement is flooded, the building having sunk into the ground; the level of the nearby river is now above the basement. He collapses on the top stair gazing into the water, seeing his own desolate face reflected back. Meritaten must have drowned. Perhaps not yet! He tears off his clothes, dives in and manages to swim down the stairs into the hidden chamber gallery, looking for the glass cabinet protecting and enclosing her, trapping her like a bell jar. But the room is empty of objects.

He swims back, crawls out of the water on the top stair, exhausted. But his clothes have gone. Now there's only a pile of bandages. People are watching him, scientists, sniggering. Dripping with water he is trying to cover himself. There's a girl though, dressed in bizarre, multi-coloured clothes, with thin coloured scarves wrapped round her neck. She takes them off and offers to wrap them round him. She has dark skin, dark eyes, a strong nose that reminds him of a boy. He has met her somewhere before ... and didn't she hurt him then?

She asks him why he dived into the water. To rescue someone! She seems unconvinced. Fumbling for words, he tries to describe the statue of Meritaten, an Egyptian princess. The girl smiles, mockingly. 'But the Egyptian collection was moved last week by the Director, Mr. Raymonde, and is now on the top floor, quite safe!' She takes his hand and they head together upstairs, and there, on the top floor, is the entire Egyptian collection. The room seems dazzling and bright. He's happy; but looking more carefully, the sculpture of Meritaten is missing. She says they might find it in the night-club in the *a*...basement, the "The Green Angel". It's a private club but she has the code. They can watch an amazing girl, performing only that evening – despite the fact the building has been struck and might collapse. 'It will make her dance routine even more poignant!'

Leading him by the hand, they go down the left hand stairs, into a dark nightclub, full of people. She is welcomed, a big fuss, and they are given a front table. The dancer, she tells him, will perform Salomé in an Egyptian version, music by Richard Wagner. In a nightclub? Isn't it a trick? From behind a green curtain, the girl appears, swirling like a dervish, wearing a white silk dress that is so tight around her lithe, sensual body, it seems like paint on her skin, or a loose, transparent membrane. Her erect nipples protrude through the dress as does the shape of her mons veneris, and he notices the dark shadow of her vagina. Her white painted face seems to merge into the dress. Her face is so unreal he can't see its features or recognise them.

The dance soon becomes orgiastic and Matthew feels isolated at the table in the front. Exposed. She seems to be dancing for him, for his eyes only, and seems already quite naked; but something new is happening, provoking in Matthew a deep feeling of shame, and yet also intense excitement. He can't close his eyes, transfixed, unable to look elsewhere. She has started to bleed! A red stain is spreading from between her legs, in two small arcs, like butterfly wings, or waves on the surface of a pool in which a stone has dropped. A pool of blood. Matthew senses everyone behind him has left, disgusted, except the girl who is still standing behind him. Out of sight.

He looks round to make sure she's there, and sees she is caressing herself under her skirt, oblivious of his presence. The dance becomes even more erotic as the blood spreads further into the girl's white costume. Matthew feels faint, yet feels pulled towards her, dying to get up and dance with her. So what holds him back? He tries to stand but he's pinned down by a force that he cannot understand. Someone shouts from the door that one of the columns has fallen, the others are weakening fast. On his table is a drink, a strange red colour. He assumes it's probably dangerous, but if he drinks it, at least he might be able to dance too ... he gulps it down. He recalls the cap of the Amanita muscaria mushroom is red ... he must be patient and wait. Soon, he can join the dance ...

Suddenly, a pencil-thin green spotlight centres on the girl and the other lights fade away. She is pure animal now, an archetypal lizard-like creature ... the patch of blood seeming black, like a burn or a charcoal drawing in the green light, as she twists and involutes herself into the throbbing music. Then to his dismay he notices her stomach is rising ... is she pregnant? Yes. He is perceiving time on a different dimension. The whole pregnancy will take only nine minutes, not nine months. The dance is not a depiction of an orgiastic birth, but is the real thing. He's afraid he'll not be able to watch it, although he feels he ought not to miss even the smallest detail. It relates to the question he must ask ... how can he get himself OUT of the diamond? Because he's trapped inside it, looking at a mirror; that's why the results are wrong.

It must be the drug starting to take effect; it's harder to distinguish between her and himself. Images losing focus, edges erode. The music is wild now, the girl's movements behind him become erratic, loosening the grip on him of her hands; he's suddenly free. He springs from the chair and joins the girl in the dance. They are so close suddenly, they are making love as she dances. They are so close, no-one can see; yet he's inside her, moving infinitesimally slowly, and more and more he can't distinguish between himself and her dance, but she is rapidly approaching the climax, when the green light will fade and she will slough off the white skin ... before she can be fully open ...

He must change his position in her, or he will block the birth. As he *merely* thinks of it, she obeys him. She turns round and he takes her from behind, his sudden eager movement making her rise into the air, arms outstretched, as if she has no weight at all, a mirage, and she seems to hover above him, unaided by him. She spreads herself out so far that her body is wide open and although he cannot see it, he knows by her violent contractions, like an orgasm, she has given birth to the child. It occurs to him she's lucky to give birth to a *Khu*, a double of herself ...

He wants to reach his climax now, but she has gone limp and is falling to the floor. He must find a way into her again, so he pushes down, spreads her legs viciously and sits astride her and with his fingers in the mess of blood he wallows in her body and finally ejaculates, falling on top of her ... just as an idea comes to him, that, because time is now so contracted, maybe he's the father of the child. He separates from her. All that seems to remain of her is a pile of soiled coloured veils.

He wants to see the child but the green light is in his eyes, but then he sees that the girl who brought him into the club is now holding the baby in its white swaddling bandages, and he thinks, knowing the scenario of the film, that the baby is probably a falcon. He pulls back a bandage to see its little face. For a moment there's nothing there but emptiness, or the effect of deep shadow ... but then the angle of the shaft of light from the hole in the stone portcullis door changes just enough for him to see the stone face of Meritaten. In a panic he spreads more bandages, only to see the sculpture is lying in the girl's bare hands, covered in blood; but safe, and possibly, in some curious way, now alive ... but he looks up, just in time to see the broken columns fall; it is too late. He feels himself crushed. He is dead.

The following morning, Cindy made one of her unexpected appearances for breakfast. She was quiet and seemed depressed, so the others remained quiet too. She remarked the film had been naive, the one thing she had least expected. She'd hoped it would be daring and naughty. Marlene Dietrich looked an old frump, although her legs were indeed sculptable. 'But I suppose our attitude to sex and sexual power games has matured a lot since then, thanks to the heady days of the Sixties and since, for better or for worse!'

George said the sexiest times had been the Naughty Nineties and Berlin between the wars, or Saigon during the final collapse, and Cindy damn well knew it; the Sixties was all media hype! While crunching on a piece of toast, Cindy asked Matthew what he was planning for the rest of the day.

Peering into his glass of orange juice, perhaps to make sure there was no silver coin in it, he said he intended to work a bit on John's stuff, but if he got nowhere with that, he'd work on reformulating his own. He'd had some new ideas. Cindy looked at him coldly. 'I'd hoped for a breakthrough with John's stuff by now. Will you *ever* break the codes?'

Matthew smiled; he said he'd give himself a one in fourteen chance! Cindy's eyes narrowed even further. 'Well, I suppose that's better odds than the alternative, of Russian Roulette!'

He asked her what *she* was intending to do. She replied she would work on her novel in the morning, but would probably go into town in the afternoon, at which George perked up sharply. Cindy asked her what*she* was intending to do. Funny how they were all suddenly separate.

Georgina thought for a moment, stretching her arms behind her head; 'I'll start by contemplating the Milky Way, of which I see myself as the dead centre, then imagine life on the Sirius twin star, the black dwarf, write a list of things they will find in the hidden chamber of the pyramid when they open it, and then meditate on the subject of meditation to see if I can become invisible ... after that I shall write.an article for *The Times Literary Supplement* on Freud entitled 'Cocaine, Womb Envy and the promised demise of the Patriarchy', and after that I shall make a mould of a stuffed wolf's head I bought in a junk shop for a new sculpture I'm planning to make, called *Little Red Riding Hood and the three Fears*.'

'Well someone's in good form today!' Cindy remarked and they all laughed, albeit nervously, before going to their various domains of work.

Matthew couldn't face John. A new idea was thrusting itself into his mind, a method of restructuring the initial equation with a random factor, for an otherwise undetected wave-field, while leaving most of his data in its present form. Excited, he started scribbling. Ideas came quickly and he filled page after page, assuming – for fun – that there might be another "background/ambience", at least not only in his thinking, though that was relevant, a force or wave or field inside his crystals that he had not taken into consideration before. He tried to imagine every possible way this field might behave, especially non-rationally. He was enjoying himself, not caring now that it might all be poppycock; just playing around with possibilities. He mused on his scribbling, 'Linus Pauling might question the thinking in it, but Jackson Pollock would have applauded my artistic style!' After working for an hour or so, and trying some formulae on the computer in John's room, he went down to the kitchen. Cindy heard him and joined him, but he didn't look at her, still feeling aggressive. He noticed she was wearing too much cloyingly sweet perfume.

She asked, somewhat icily, 'How much longer, the awaited breakthrough, or breakdown, after the initial progress?'

'I start to see the light at the end of the tunnel ... or of ... well...' smiling at her mischievously, deliberately not finishing.

'The light of... ? The absence of, more likely!' She smiled at him mischievously, sitting down at the table, speaking not so much to him, as to someone outside the window. 'I'm sorry I've been aggressive, but for me, breakdown is breakthrough and vice versa ... just as madness is the highest form of illumination. That's a trite observation, isn't it! Like being in love, *la vie en rose, la vie en Rose* ... etta Stone. That's me. Either I'm in love and inspired, or I'm empty and desperately tired. Nothing between. I'm tired now ... because I'm tired of waiting for you. I admit it. I'd hoped you would solve the computer problem. I thought it can't be that difficult. John must have wanted someone to break it even if he'd decided one hundred per cent it couldn't be me. Even if he had to hide it from me, it had to be solvable by someone else. *Tant pis*! Listen, don't tell George, but can you do me a favour?'

'Maybe? What?' he said coldly. Unenthusiastically. She

already seemed disappointed but she continued.

'Take her out tonight somewhere. Take her for a nice dinner to the best restaurant. Anywhere. I'll pay! You see I have a kind of date. She will be upset. Can you?'

He laughed. It was lucky he wasn't really in love with her! 'What about me, can't I be upset too?' She looked at him in total amazement. 'You. Why? Goodness me, I never thought of that!' And she blushed and looked down at her coffee, like a little girl suddenly caught wearing her brother's underpants. 'Well, you see ... I'm seeing the girl from the cinema ... and it never occurred to me you would see it as betraying you. I'm sorry. I can't relate my feelings to you in that way. I didn't think you would be hurt. Most men get turned on by the images of this kind of thing ... don't you?'

'I didn't say I wasn't. I just asked if I could be jealous.'

'Are you?'

Matthew thought for a while. He was surprised that he wasn't. He had thought of Cindy as a whore from the beginning and surely he'd been right? In fact, he didn't care and he was even more surprised he cared more for Georgina's feelings than his own, and already felt hurt *for her*, knowing how much Cindy's betrayal would upset her. He didn't know what to say to Cindy on Georgina's behalf.

'Don't answer! I can read the truth on your face. It's an open book, or should I say an un-code-protected disc! You are and you aren't. You see what I mean, everything is its opposite at the same time! It has to be. It's easy and fun like that ... but it's pretty hard, pretty arid at times. I'm a mess. God, what is left these days? Daughter of my age! Total mess, aren't you?'

He'd never seen her look so distraught. 'Hardly a daughter though!'

She tried to laugh but it came out as a squawk. 'Feminism! What is it now? I'm just totally confused. Live out your fantasies? Thank God the sex is still good even if I have to believe you're a stranger! You are, aren't you?' Before he could answer she came to him and put her arms around him, kissed him on the cheek, and said cruelly, imitating Marlene Dietrich, 'Listen, daaarrrrlleeeng, your job is to service the girls and ask no questions, and do ze work ... see? But! A warning from the Twentieth Century Book of the Dead. No code, no sex! See? Get the message? No code no massage! No results ... no pussy! This is post-modernist sex logic, okay! Do I make myself cleaaaaaaar?'

They both laughed, it was a joke! Uh? She kissed him fondly enough and left him to brood over the new problems.

He was feeling nervous. Ever since the film they'd all been strangely tense. He needed to go to the garden to get some fresh air, but Georgina saw him from her window and joined him under his beech tree. After playing with her fingers for a few minutes, looking at the sad remains of her finger nails, she said, 'Look at my nails, or should I say, look at my no-nails. Something they ate disagreed with them!' Matthew gallantly took her fingers and kissed them, one by one and placed her hands back on her knees.

'Listen, Matthew, why don't we go out this evening ... to see the new film in the German week, or maybe we can go out to dinner? I'll pay. I got some money this morning. Let's have a quiet evening together. Would you like that? I would love it!'

What were they up to now? 'Er ... what about Cindy?' he asked, not able to hide the note of provocation.

Georgina's eyes glazed over and she gazed into the far distance and said quietly. 'If she's going out this afternoon, she's meeting the girl from the cinema. If that's the case she may be forced to bring her back here, for decorum's sake as there may be nowhere else, and the poor girl may not be that easy to seduce. So, I'd hate to be here listening to giggling all evening and talking heavily all night. So, why don't we go out somewhere and at least we can *act* as if we are lovers? Real lovers, not virtual ones on someone else's screen, at that?'

He put his arms round her and held her close and then whispered, 'We *are* lovers, you fool and we *will* go out for dinner anyway, whether Cindy is meeting the girl or her grandmother or even John for that matter. It's a date. Seven-thirty, prompt. Black tie!'

She hugged him and said she could now get on with her work and not lose any more time worrying about Cindy. 'I suppose there's one consolation; one of my sculptures is going to be appreciated and proved to be functional. But I'd hoped we would anoint and crown it first!' She kissed him and left.

Matthew huddled against the roots of his tree, musing on the complexities of the two girls. Maybe he could consider himself privileged to be their confidant, but the pagan impersonality of their sexuality was undermining him emotionally. Could he ever trust a woman again in his life? He was feeling empty and sad. Who'd said, 'Seeing the goddess bathing in all her nakedness was to be transfigured and changed forever, one's innocence irretrievably purged by the illumination'? Alas, they were right; Cindy's dance routines, the naked goddess only seemingly caught unawares, were fragmenting him, rather than putting him together. Was he seeing the story from the wrong point of view? John would say both are true, no doubt.

He recalled the image of Isis to the screen, hovering over the dead body of her husband, her own body bejewelled with magic, transfixed by simultaneity, tempting the phallus to rise, projecting images of her naked self in the hall of talking mirrors, which he now somehow saw as the only, true theatre of woman's sexual fantasies. Is the phallus she copulates with her own, if only momentarily? Created by magic but made by her own hands? Wasn't Isis really the cause, in the first place, of anarchy and fragmentation? Was this not the greater mystery? If Isis was the goddess of love, wasn't it inevitable that desire was always for a unity which had been irrevocably lost? And as Osiris was king of the underworld, wasn't desire always for death?

In the afternoon Cindy asked to be taken into town. She was definitely in one of her *absente* moods, never looking him in the eyes, talking old movies, 'Take me to Sunset Boulevard, darrrrrrrrrrliiiing ... every woman's dream to have her bullying film director humbled at her feet, a mere chauffeur. The difference with you is, of course, the only film-directing you did was to take X-ray films of your elusive and mysterious diamonds. You know what would be my ideal film?'

'No ... tell me!'

'A film of old Eric von Stroheim making love to Jean Harlow. But ... here's the crunch. Filmed entirely with X-rays. Two skeletons making love. Surely it's been done? Surely Hans Bellmer did it? Do you know his drawings?'

'No. I don't. What was his speciality?'

'Seeing through everything, especially young, very young girls. Often young girls being seduced by older women. Girls being fucked by skeletons ... and dolls. Oh la la! The sexiest dolls in the world. Are there bones inside the penis? Rudimentary at least? Would they show up on X-Ray film?'

'Listen, Cindy, if you go on like this I won't be able to drive the car. I'm only a man, after all!'

She was silent for a while, then started singing *Onward Christian Soldiers*. Then silence, until; 'By golly, this girl I'm meeting better be good after all this. Just imagine. She might be a virgin. Ah well – drive on, Eric!' She still hadn't looked him in the eye. It was essential to her self-hypnosis, that he didn't exist.

Nevertheless, he dropped her off in the town and as she was leaving, on impulse, he said, 'Give my love to John!'

She turned her head slowly from side to side and pulled a funny face. 'Wishful thinking, my darling! It's a pretty little girl I intend to ravish, with as much brutish disregard for a poor young woman's feelings as you had for me the other day. Bye for now!' She pecked him on the cheek and left.

He stayed watching her as she walked backwards waving as if to acknowledge the screams of a huge crowd of admirers standing outside the stage door. But she tripped on a cracked flagstone and nearly fell over backwards and it was the first time Matthew had ever seen her lost for words ... and suddenly he felt really sorry for her! But still he couldn't resist opening the window and shouting out, 'Every orgasm is the death of a king!' and she conceded defeat with a wan smile. But as he drove off he added quietly to himself, 'What I should have said was; What is Aphrodite except a penis, a penis cut off and tossed into the sea?' One of John's quotes he had inadvertently learnt off by heart. Funny what you recall at the oddest times.

As he was driving back, he wondered again about the code-word Cindy had not been able to find. XERUI ASAR, the phallus of Osiris. Why, when that image was so powerful? Had it not penetrated, in its subtle, intangible, invisible way, into almost every recent rite and dream, collective and otherwise? Why had John chosen the *thing* Cindy seemed to desire most of all, in which to hide his secret word of power? The paradox was lost on him, as indeed, was paradise ...

... except an image was slipping into his mind. A copse of beech trees, bluebells crushed and flattened on their green stalks. He saw a young boy climbing an old dead elm tree, struck by lightning, with black holes in it which he used as footholds, and from a perch, like a bird, high up on a branch, he saw a young couple below. The girl was wearing a white dress. Whatever was under it was gashed vermilion. She was lying on top, and all he could remember seeing was her naked bottom, moving from side to side, as if she was dancing. He was mesmerised ... hovering above the scene like a falcon, looking down, perceiving all, foretelling the rest. Memory or dream, refracted through so many distorted crystals with flaws in them, the image was split into myriad small fragments, like a broken egg, like Humpty Dumpty, and no-one could put one plus one or two and two together again...

He tried to figure out why he could never love Cindy, but could probably live with her forever, why he felt sorry for her at times when she was really such a bitch and needed no-one's sympathy, why he felt so resentful towards her and wanted to really hurt her when they made love. Cindy! Would she make it tonight or not? He hoped not, for George's sake.

Suddenly his mind slipped a plane and focused sharply on the difficult part of his equation. Yes, there might be a flaw there after all. He was thinking so hard about it, he drove past the turning to the house, and drifted through two more villages before he noticed he was twenty miles out of his way.

Later, back at the house, frustrated for lack of facts, he decided to take a look in Cindy's room, climbing up a vine near her window. Damn it! There were bars; cast iron bars on a bedroom? Almost as unexpected as a chastity belt on a whore! He went back to his room. Georgina poked her head through the door. 'Good! I hope everything is still on for tonight?'

'Yes, of course!'

'Oh good! I know it's early, but why don't we go quite soon, and see what's on at the German Cinema week? That is, if I promise not to pick up the other usherette?'

'Good idea!' But his reply was rather cool.

Knowing he had a good half hour to work, he played around with the idea he'd had in the car. It was still intriguing him, refusing to go away. He consulted a related scientific paper he'd not bothered to look at before, *Anti-Gravity Properties of Crystalline Lattices* – work actually done in 1927 by two Polish scientists, Kowsky and Frost. They proved gravity fields did indeed behave strangely inside crystals under certain circumstances. Normally he would have found the idea far-fetched but now he had to read the paper carefully. He found another by Hoyle he'd not bothered to read ...

"Some oxygen-16 is, to be sure, manufactured inside stars – but only in small quantities, compared with carbon, at this early stage of a star's life. If that oxygen level were 1 per cent higher, then virtually all the carbon made inside stars would be rapidly processed into heavier elements still. Life forms based on carbon would, in that case, NOT exist. These coincidences, just right for resonance in carbon-12, just wrong in Oxygen-16, are indeed remarkable."

Remarkable; a strong word for a coincidence in science. He tried inventing some more equations to describe possible coincidences inside his crystal, with its strange flaw ...

When Georgina returned, he'd never seen her looking so pretty. She had piled her hair up so it looked completely pre-Raphaelite, put kohl around her eyes and heightened the curve of her cheekbones with rouge. Her shiny red lipstick resonated with a crimson silk blouse and red enamel Indian ear-rings with two black snakes entwined around a branch of red roses. Stunned by her beauty, he wondered if he'd never truly seen it before, blinded by Cindy's trashy screen image. She stood still, savouring her effect on him.

'Is anything the matter?' she asked, innocently.

'Yes, there is. I never realised you were as beautiful as any Egyptian sculpture. Why didn't I notice before?'

'We vagrant Gypsies have to be very careful, always hiding our light under a bushel, you never know who might try to abduct us!'

'Am I allowed to abduct you?'

'We will have to see ... ' she said coquettishly.

Matthew still couldn't move he was so transfixed, mostly by the sparkle in her eyes, so dazzling, so luminous, as if light was coming from deep inside them. She looked like an Egyptian princess, contriving the effect quite deliberately, drawing the lines from her eyes towards the side of her face, painting her eyelids silver with golden flecks, making her eyebrows much thicker than usual. 'As beautiful as Meritaten?' she asked coyly.

He took her into his arms and held her close, kissing her lightly on the ear. 'Yes, of course you are, and even more so,' he said affectionately. He wasn't lying.

'You remember in the beginning you said you thought I was a Gypsy. The word Gypsy derives from *Egyptian*! E-GYPSY-AN. A code word? Because Gypsies foretold the future with the Tarot pack of cards which people thought derived from hieroglyphics and the Egyptian Mysteries. Maybe they do. So there! Maybe I *am* a reincarnated Egyptian, deep deep down in my bones. Why not? Reincarnation is much more likely, considering the way nature works, than rationality drawing straight lines everywhere. "Tis ye and your estranged faces that miss the many-splendoured thing!" Francis Thompson; reveals my Catholic background so I'm not a Gypsy!' After this exuberant revelation,. she turned on her heels and headed downstairs.

While they were driving into town, however, she seemed sad. 'I wish we could forget this whole John business. Why don't you just do your own work? John could be bad news, if only by accident. I'm a bit worried still.'

'After all this! Now you say his work is not important?'

'No ... *only* if you could make use of it yourself! To him it was *his* particular myth, his obsession. Like my pursuit of a special curve in my sculpture, I suppose, he was pursuing a similar, elusive curve in the mathematics of space-time and consciousness. I can feel you thinking all the time and it worries me. I work with clay and resins to escape thinking, letting my fingers think for me. Meaning comes out of matter by caressing it. Clay deserves as much tenderness and desire and erotic touch, like stone must too, as does the body of a person you love. What if the earth needs that kind of love too in order to function, needs to be touched and loved and sung to and caressed and desired? No wonder she's dying, think how rejected and lonely she must feel, dear Mother Earth, still cooking up new forms and generating the *whole* of life within her body, and we just abuse and pollute her. One of these days she'll have a nervous breakdown and then all hell will be let loose. It won't be earthquake and volcanoes, but a total shudder of anger and remorse, and she'll shake off every single bit of the objective world of man, every flagstone, every bridge, every house, every city, every computer ... she will just go flick, like a horse does with its tail, and everything will hurtle into space like a billion boxes of unwanted children's toys ... leaving only plants that have roots and birds and animals that have claws. Animals know when there's an earthquake coming. They dig in and hide. She would warn the animals. Us, no! We can't hear her any longer. The creatures would dig into the earth or find a good perch and cling as hard as they could, and everything else would be sloughed off like dead skin and it would all swing round the sun like another Halley's comet ... maybe that's what comets are? In millions of years time, new creatures on the earth would study the comet in telescopes and see all these little bits and pieces of rubbish, frozen in ice particles, and they would speculate that it was once a whole civilisation that developed on a planet that had no body, maybe a huge, empty bubble, and one day the bubble burst. Everything floating about without cohesion, no erotic unifying field of attraction, and they'd all look like sculptures of mine, little objects suspended in resin, except it would be blocks of ice. But she'd be right, old rag-bag Mother Earth, and she'd get pregnant again with something new in the fresh topsoil, hoping it would not betray her as we had done. Nothing is more dangerous than a woman betrayed.

Look at me now, ranting on like this!'

Matthew was silent for a few moments. 'I hope Mother Earth decides to do it after our dinner, and I can say, before I died I had dinner with an Egyptian princess, fulfilling a secret dream. Then, I won't feel so cheated!'

She turned to him. 'That was such a nice thing to say, Matthew. Here I am, being all miserable and doom-laden, and you say something nice like that. You know, if you didn't belong to Cindy and your work..,' and again she looked out of the window, 'I would have been very fond of you. But as you know, I'm really no good to anyone but myself. So think yourself lucky and let's say no more about it. I tell you what. I didn't eat all day. I'm famished. Nothing worse than a famished feminist; is that a faminist? Talking of which, should we eat first or after the film, starve ourselves into a pitch of hunger, so even the bread tastes like a Eucharist soaked in real blood?'

'Let's see what the film is, and what time it starts, and then we can decide!' he said, calmly.

She looked out of the window again. 'You're right. How very practical and sensible. That's what we should do. Plan. Know ahead. Decide. Organize. Make a timetable and know where we stand. That is security, which is why I'm so insecure, isn't it? I drift and drift, but drifting takes you to beautiful places you could not have imagined ... just like you, drifting into the Fitzwilliam Museum. You said, "I just drifted in". And look what has happened since. Must be more interesting than following your normal path, and screwing whatever her name was ... the buxom Dallas wench!'

'The voluptuous Beverly Schwartz! Pint-sized reincarnation of the Statue of Liberty. You're right, I must keep drifting!' When had he mentioned Beverly? He was sure he hadn't. Unless in some sexual delirium ...

'Oh good', she said, moving closer to him and putting her arms round him and they drove like that all the way to the cinema, in silence. He was feeling very happy.

The film was just starting. *Lulu: Pandora's Box*, by Pabst. The usherette of the previous evening was conspicuous by her absence. Either it was her night off or Cindy had paid her wages, and bought her out.

After the film they found a Chinese restaurant and took a cosy table in a corner under a red lantern light and ordered lots of small dishes which would take all evening to serve, one by one. Georgina remarked that Louise Brooks was the most luscious creature she'd ever seen, and Matthew agreed she was irresistible, even if she was so evil. Georgina said Cindy reminded her of Lulu, but they decided the comparison was unfair because she didn't resemble her at all, really! But Georgina added, 'Her wantonness maybe, her ruthlessness, her childishness, all the qualities I find charming and desirable in a woman. Submissive is the word.' She was starting to giggle childishly, and Matthew laughed too, but they agreed to change the subject.

It took them some time to relax and talk about each other, rather than talk about the *"absente"* Cindy or the *"invisible"* John, or *"delicious"* Lulu. Georgina was as much possessed by Cindy as Matthew was haunted by John. But after a while, exchanging stories about their childhood, about funny people they had known, about things they had lost, opportunities missed, about other Chinese food and Chinese restaurants and how the Chinese seemed to have restaurants absolutely everywhere, they finally managed to exorcise the ghosts hovering above them.

Matthew told her he'd once visited a small shanty town in Alaska, called Nome, on the farthest north-east coast overlooking Russia, where only Eskimos and a few goldminers still live, and a few tourists visit in the summer. He'd gone there to find geological samples in the disused gold mines, and he told her the beauty of the arctic was mystical and crystalline ... he'd arrived in late autumn and watched the sea freeze, little by little each day, until the whole expanse of water just froze and became ice as far as the eye could see; and, 'The only restaurant in town was a little Chinese restaurant called the "Shangri La" run by a Chinaman and an Eskimo, and after two or three glasses of imported saké, I couldn't tell the Eskimo from the Chinese! And the hot-sour soup was made of walrus and grizzly bear!'

'No! Not really?' He laughed.

She agreed reluctantly to talk about her *Gypsy past*, saying she could remember travelling with her mother in a caravan when she was a very little girl, but maybe she imagined it. Anyway she preferred not to remember it too clearly. There had been a man with them, not her father, 'a hurtful person full of spite' ... and Matthew guessed it was for him she'd spun the cocoon in which she had remained safe ever since, gestating there, until only a woman, Cindy, could unweave the webs of self-reproach and shame and allow her sensuality to flower again. A wound below the surface ...

Suddenly he felt a deep longing to protect her, to put his arms round her, to be patient and wait, for however long it would take for her to melt ... as the Eskimo hunters waited in the spring on the frozen shores of the winter sea for the pack-ice to melt before they could become hunters again, take off alone in their little boats to harpoon walrus and seals trapped on the floating rafts of ice. Yes, something in him was waiting ... for the wound to surface perhaps ...

After dinner they window-shopped, deploring the mounds of gaudy, cheap rubbish that local shopkeepers had heaped in their brightly-lit windows to tempt the tourists. At the antique shop, there were no lights in the window. 'Electricity is too expensive,' Matthew said. They drove home in silence, Matthew driving so slowly the car started to wheeze and splutter, and Georgina said it reminded her of her grandfather, so he pressed his foot on the pedal and after a few violent, asthmatic convulsions, it cleared its throat and ran smoothly again.

Approaching the turn-off from the main road, Georgina asked him to drive on for a bit, 'Can't face the empty house!' Clearly she meant Cindy might be there. Matthew felt the tingling in the back of his neck. Wasn't she going to say, 'Let's go the copse!' He was tense for some time, waiting, but all she said was, 'Let's just drive. It's fun driving at night. Night-tripping I call it, thinking in a different way, watching the trees and houses go by like cardboard models in a theatre set.'

She didn't notice, but he turned round and went back towards the town. He didn't know why, but he felt a quite tangible compulsion to take her to the copse. He wanted to see it in the dark, especially with Georgina. It was becoming his place now too ...

But he had drunk too much saké, not so much that he couldn't tell an Eskimo from a Chinaman, but enough to make him see the silent world on the wind-screen in front of him as a film. There was a slight fog, and it fused with the grainy black and white image on the screen, making him think of the scenes at the end of the film, when *Lulu* is in London, walking the grey, misty streets, destitute and destroyed and ... and ... he feels like the man who finally picks her up and takes her home, takes off her shabby raincoat and her old battered hat and suddenly she emerges from the drabness and he sees her in all her former glory, scintillatingly beautiful and seductive, sparkling with tantalising eroticism ... and it hurts ... and he feels a terrible pain in his stomach as he cannot stop himself from taking out the knife ... which he does not want to use ... but has to thrust it into her body because it is part of a structure of cause and effect ... and yet he knows he doesn't want to do this either ... but something is compelling him, some fate, some script he must follow ... the plot ... and she crumples into his arms, ironically glad to be dying, at last to be free of life, of the life of betrayal that has finally betrayed her ...

Matthew was beside himself, acting out the most brutal scene of the film, on the "screen" in front of him, anxious and yet aroused by it. In the cinema it had not seemed such a significant scene and yet suddenly he found himself almost wanting to weep with the misery of it, the paradox of it, the extreme images of violence and violation created by unfulfilled desire ... as now. And then there was the totally unexpected sub-title on the film, after Lulu's murder. A Salvation Army band appeared and they sang. The title read, "Christ is Risen!"

'Oh look!' said Georgina, 'This is the road to John's copse. Let's go there!'

It figured ... he stopped and opened the gate and they drove towards the copse. They walked under the trees for a while, looking at the stars and showing off, naming the constellations. Matthew's favourite was Orion. Georgina's

Cassiopeia ... and Sirius the star of Isis. They became cold and returned to the car.

Georgina asked him to hold her tight and she rested her head on his shoulder and held him tight too. He noticed her eyes were glistening, as if reflecting the starlight, and he felt over-awed suddenly by their deep beauty. He felt a strange sensation of becoming infinitely small so that he could enter into her eyes and pass behind them and listen to her mind and discover what it was she was really thinking and, most of all, wanting. She always cautioned him to keep his distance and yet so often he wanted to draw close to her and closer still. Suddenly she turned to him, put her head to one side and opened her lips and drew him to her ... kissing him passionately and digging her fingers into the back of his neck. It was not what she had told him to expect of her ... and it took him by surprise. But he noticed her lipstick was perfumed and he felt her breasts pressing him into the seat and suddenly he became terribly alarmed. He kissed her but was pushing against her more to press her back than to press himself against her. But she was unaware of this and started to move her body so that her breasts were taut and almost throbbing against him. She took her lips off his slightly and whispered... 'It's alright I don't want to make love to you, just kiss me, kiss me...' and she kissed him so hungrily he could do nothing but kiss her back as strongly.

He was even more troubled now. Why had she said she didn't want to make love to him? He thought of Cindy, or was it John, who had said, 'The hologram is the dialectic. Whenever anyone says *No!* strongly enough, know it means *Yes!* As well as *No!* The truth is the union of the two!' Oh God! What a fucking mess!

'Kiss me harder' Georgina said. 'I love to be kissed!'

The dialectic? It was crucifying him. Maybe Georgina *had* to create the façade of denial and yet she wanted him to *want* her so much he would take no notice of it! But that's not how he wanted her. Cindy maybe, but not her. Didn't she know that?

Suddenly she moved so that her body was more aligned with his and she pressed her hips towards him, pushed him down so they were side by side on the seat and he remembered the night they had both made love to him and he had not known who it was who had *taken* him, but he had guessed it was Cindy, because if it had been Georgina, Cindy would have found some way of punishing him.

He wanted to let himself go now, but ... she pulled up her skirt and took his hand and put it on her thigh ... and he caressed it, his fingers twitching with desire to touch her *there* ... but there was something wrong. He felt uncomfortable, he wanted to retreat. He couldn't understand why, the way he felt, but he didn't have an erection. The more he thought about it the more worried he became. He could see the image in his mind of her vagina, her legs open, as he was sure he'd seen her in one of the dances, for want of a better word, with Cindy, and he tried to see his penis erect. But it wasn't there! He couldn't feel it. Her hand was on his thigh now and he knew she was going to move it to caress him and he felt she would be instantly switched off if she touched him and found there was no erection. Nothing. He started to panic. He tried to edge away and as he did so, by mistake, his fingers seemed to slither into her, and he felt mortified with awkwardness ... one part of him desired her so much, excited by her desire ... he must imagine himself there ... there was only one thing he could do ... and be ... not himself, and if not himself, then only Cindy! What would she do ... and as he thought of her, he forcefully opened Georgina's legs, moved down and kissed her passionately through the pants, which he had to tear to make it easier ...

She took his head in her hands quite savagely and thrust it against her and lay back and opened herself completely. He wanted so much to make love to her, and the more he kissed her and the more he knew she was losing herself ... the more he wanted to plunge into her and make love to her. But ... he knew he was possessed by Cindy and his sudden feeling of resentment towards her detached him completely, even from his desire for Georgina ... but she seemed to be elsewhere anyway.

'Don't hurt me!' she whispered ... and he continued to kiss her ... and finally she went taut, stayed taut for some time, every muscle in her body ready to snap, then trembled violently, clutched him hard, one last feverish moment, and then relaxed. He knew she wasn't faking it.

Silence, as she subsided. Silence. As if the seventh seal had been opened. 'Cindy always fakes her orgasms, you know that, don't you? At least mine was for real. Thank you!' And they held each other tightly. 'And you?' she asked.

'Very happy!'

'So am I. Very, very happy ... and relaxed now!'

He looked away to hide his emotion, but she laughed and said, 'You think that isn't saying much? I wouldn't have allowed a man to buy me fish and chips once, let alone take me out to dinner. And as for admitting I can enjoy myself like that, alone with you, you've no idea how much progress we've made. So there!' She pushed him to one side and shook him and forced him to laugh with her and at himself.

'Thankyou!' he said and kissed her gently. But were they alone? He was sure he saw a shadow move behind a tree at the edge of the mound ...

She started to pull her clothes back into some semblance of order but as she did so her skirt came apart and he saw the torn red pants, looking like part of a costume for a Dickens prison scene, and Georgina peered at them also, pouting and pulling a face at him. 'You tore them! Mind you they were already a bit tatty. I prefer them that way. But better not hang them out on the line tomorrow in front of Cindy's window. Or ... come to think of it. Goddamit, maybe I will! Come on,' she said suddenly, yanking her skirt down, 'let's race back and catch her before she calls a taxi for her sweet young victim ... we'll trap them in the kitchen and torment the hell out of them by talking about paedophiles, a favourite subject of mine, or cold fusion or hot-sour soup made of walrus and polar bears!'

They arrived at the house to find no-one there. Georgina was bitter. 'I don't care a hoot of owl's shit if she stays out all night!' She poured a neat vodka. 'You realise I'm a complete fool, of course. When she's here I feel spiteful towards her and I bait her and taunt her. When we make love, it's often to dissipate the negative energy we've built up. It's crazy, sex is satisfying only because it compensates for the cattiness and bitchiness. Is that passion? It becomes violent and gets out of hand and there's a touch of hatred and we feel we had an especially great time, but it's nothing to do with she and I desiring each other's body. Sad, isn't it? With men it's probably different ... is it?'

Matthew said nothing. He was feeling utterly miserable, realising that Georgina's actions were all reactions to Cindy's betrayal, nothing to do with himself.

She noticed his sadness. 'Which is why I was so satisfied by you tonight, Matthew, you fool!' She smiled guiltily towards him, 'If I speak truthfully, you might learn something useful about us women for the future. Forgive me!'

'Thank you!'

'The only time, and this is the most bitter aspect of it all, the only time I really *do* seem to desire her body, I imagine her undressing, I mentally take down her pants and open her legs, I kiss her and do everything I can to build her up to a pitch ... and it becomes tangible, like now ... it only happens when she's with another girl,' and she paused and closed her eyes, 'Just now ... I can feel her body at the ends of my fingers, more than I do when she is with me. The only time I reach this pitch of actual desire for her body is when she is in bed with another girl, like now. God! How exasperating and cruel it is. Is all sex so full of irony? John would say ignore the reflection from the silvered mirror and dare to see the truth, that desire is always betrayal because we only desire the gods! If we think we desire each other, we're romantic fools...'

He nodded. 'I was always a romantic fool, now that I think about it. I always wanted to combine sensuality with love and even thought I had it once, but I was betrayed, though I had really betrayed myself.'

After a moment's pause, Georgina smiled knowingly. 'We are perfect for each other. Why do we waste our time loving Cindy who is incapable of loving anything except her own image?' Somehow she laughed and he laughed too.

'Quite!' he said, mournfully.

'Mind you when she comes home after being with that stupid girl, little tart, she'll be wanting only one thing in the world. A man's penis inside her. Now it's your scene and not mine. I bet you already have an erection just thinking about her!' She was nearly in tears. She hugged him, trying to stop herself fragmenting. 'Oh Matthew, I *do* love you, in a very real way, because you allow yourself to be passive with me, you don't pounce and ponce about like a man who thinks he ought to, and just take and take, laying us on the kitchen table just because you saw a sexy advert in a magazine.' She sobbed but managed to hold most of it back. 'Mind you, if you ever want to, don't hesitate, I'll sacrifice myself!' She tried to laugh, pulled his hair playfully and then put her arms around him from behind and kissed him on the cheek. He wondered if maybe *now* he should grab her ... even if his erection was indeed from imagining Cindy ...

At that moment they heard the taxi. 'That's her! The return of the prodigal daughter.' Georgina quickly looked at herself in the mirror, 'Well, I hope she fluffed it and thought of me afterwards or she had such a good time she doesn't need you now. Bye for now and thanks for a lovely evening!' Without even a glance at him, she rushed out ...

... as Cindy sauntered into the kitchen looking not the slightest bit worse for wear. 'Hi there. You alone? No wanton sexy female company? No half-naked sluts tied to your bedposts?' She undid her coat, looked around, but there was no-one to take it off so she kept it on. Matthew didn't feel like the butler tonight. 'Don't blame you! Women! God protect me from women. If I was a man I would be homosexual, do you know that? Anything not to have to take women seriously. But how about you? Have a merry time?' she smirked, finally slipping off her fake-fox-fur coat, which she claimed John had bought from an ageing wardrobe mistress at Elstree, who had stolen it from the set of *The Mississippi Gambler* – John only bought authentic (usually stolen) nostalgia – he had been doing the music, a touch of voodoo, for a Bovril commercial set in New Orleans. Cindy draped it over the back of a chair, asking sweetly, 'Make me a cup of tea, please, my darling ... while I give, take, or have a pee ... '

He did as he was told. She returned but said nothing for a moment, bitchy or otherwise, holding the empty bone-china cup in her hands and gazing into it for ages as if looking for the truth. 'I could have drunk sixteen bottles of wine tonight and not got drunk. Do you know the feeling?'

'We get drunk when we want to be drunk, rarely when we secretly want to remain sober,' he said solemnly. Cindy burst out laughing. Peering at him seductively, she chortled, 'What a philosopher we have this evening. Cogito ergo sump! Rational man himself!' and she carried on laughing. He poured her tea. Then she added, 'And what nonsense too! Well ... that's good. It means you've been talking all night, like me, I can tell. Words, words, words and no action! And you can't switch off!'

'Wrong again ... we had a most erotic evening!' he said boldly. Her eyes narrowed for a few seconds and she looked him straight in the eyes before smiling cynically. 'A very erotic evening! If so, it must have been telling erotic stories. I choose my girlfriends carefully, personas for whom pleasure does not come easily! Once wounded always wounded; forever safe.'

Matthew told her they'd seen *Lulu*. She'd seen it with John in Paris some years before. 'I loved it, until the final scene of course, where the poor girl gets murdered by Jack the Ripper. I just felt she wasn't THAT bad! A death like that is so random ... a witch should always be burnt on the stake. Planned, Christian, rational. Lulu's death was irrational, therefore not the logical outcome of the previous actions. It was a mistake, a flaw in an otherwise translucent narrative, stuck in for effect. She should have become an old maid and lived with another woman the rest of her life and really known what it is to suffer the frustration she inflicted on her poor men. Death was too easy. Mind you, I'd have accepted ten years of pain for one night with that slushy bitch in my arms. My fingers are still itching for her! Oh! With you of course, and your where-with-all to finish her off!'

'Glad I might sometimes be remembered! But I found the murder scene curiously erotic; I couldn't say precisely why ...'

'No! Oh really ... did you really? UUUhmmmmm ... how very interesting. Uhmmmmm, yes. I think maybe I did too, which is why I rejected the scene, and yet it's the one I remember most of all. With the one where she shoots her lover, of course. Maybe you're right. Er ... maybe ... only one way to find out. Don't go away, Herr von Eric! In the drawing room? I think the scene deserves further cryptic analysis!'

Off she went dragging her coat unceremoniously, not even looking at him, already planning her costume. Clearly he had no choice, so he went to the drawing room, though not too reluctantly. Georgina may have been right ... this time he would not need to focus his mind on the translucent phallus. After five minutes and a few glasses of wine, he heard her coming down the stairs. She opened the door a few inches and slipped in her hand, herself still unseen, the Ondine touch, and turned out the lights. In the dark she found a small light on a side-table, turned it on and draped a black scarf over it, so the light was dimmed. Then she turned on the art-deco standard lamp ... by stamping her foot on the switch.

And there was the kitsch cartoon, graphic novel French prostitute, split black serge skirt and red garter on her thigh. My God, she has one helluva wardrobe up there! She shifted stage left, directly under the tall light and posed, showing her profile, especially her skin-tight red blouse. Swell dame, Spillane would say. Lighting a cheroot in a long holder, under her streetlamp, half turning towards him, she spat out a blood curdling wolf whistle, making Matthew's hair stand on end ...

... and he wondered what Georgina must have thought, upstairs. But he had to play his part, so he walked over, passed her several times nonchalantly; then back to the stage near the window. He enjoyed obviously sizing her up, sneering as if he might be thinking she was a lump of shit. Coming towards him, the slut stuck out her torn fish-netted knee, and she was wearing so much cheap perfume he thought for a minute he was lost in a pine forest. 'You wanna make love to me, mister? Fancy some good pussy?' He asked how much. 'Ten pounds! I'm cheap 'n I like bein' cheap! Okay? Anything goes; and little comes!'

'Okay!' he said limply, his tone still lacking the taut tight Bogart feel.

'Your place or mine, though come to think of it, mine is easier, we're already there!' she drawled without a flicker of a smile. Very professional, this girl. She draped her cheap vulgar plastic handbag on the small table with some ceremony, before slipping off her fur wrap; undid one button and her skirt fell to the floor. Under it she was wearing further whore logos, the totemic red garter belt for the fish-net stockings, red crotchless pants, the ellipse braided in black and gold. With a perfume bottle shaped like a pine cone she vulgarly sprayed her pubic hair, took the fur wrap and stroked herself, dabbing off any excess perfume but also tickling herself in the process. Matthew was impressed. She'd certainly been a tart in a previous incarnation.

'Good pussy, no?' she drooled, opening her blouse, undoing a catch in the front between the two cups of her bra allowing her breasts to pop out. She cupped them in her hands for a moment, took some lipstick from her bag and spread the colour over her nipples, making sure she did it badly and made a mess over her breasts as well. A touch of the insane asylum. As if in a hurry to get it over with, to be ready for the next customer, she picked up the wine and drank the remainder in a series of jerky gulps, touching her vagina with her fingers at the same time. Returning to the cone of light, she picked up her handbag and to his surprise, took out Georgina's translucent dildo, a beautiful object, smooth and lightly curved, and as she held it in front of her, as if estimating its value at an auction of Art Nouveau antiques in the Place de l'Opéra Hotel, the light caught it and flashed a beam of light across the room. 'Lapis Lazarus ... ' she said, slurring the words.

She placed it delicately on the arm of one of the maroon armchairs, where it glinted in the light, before taking another object out of her bag, which Matthew couldn't quite see. When she turned, he saw it was a long knife in a curved silver sheath, the same shape almost as the sculpture. Pulling the knife out of its sheath she tested its sharpness with her finger, went back to the armchair and sat on the other arm with her legs wide apart, and then looked at him in a way he remembered Cleopatra had looked at Anthony in some dreadfully bad and poorly acted silent movie. Next scene was the asp.

With a hint of foreboding rather than the promise of

foreplay, he slipped off his trousers and pants and approached her, aggressively, but she held up her hand to stop him. Leaning back, legs apart, she took the dildo and licked it and then pushed it inside herself, obviously savouring its hard presence inside her, and even more, enjoying his confusion. She took the knife and turned the blade around towards her stomach and slowly waved the handle towards him, suggesting he take it. She lay further back. 'I'm all yours. Go ahead. Kill me!' Her long fingers were holding the end of the Georgina's sculpture and moving it gently from side to side. 'You've no choice. There's nowhere for you. You're already betrayed and you can see it before your very eyes! Someone has been there before you. Use the knife!' she said fiercely. 'I betrayed you tonight. I betray you every night. I am the quintessence of betrayal, the Goddess of Betrayal! And I love it! But I betray you most of all when I make love to you, always thinking of someone else, the ghost in the machine. So there, I've said it! I am not real. This is another image in John's Virtual Reality program, so you can kill me with a mere flick of a switch. Poof! Now's your chance, go on ... really kill me! Become real at last! Be a man!'

Matthew didn't know what to do. He had the gleaming, beautiful knife in his hand, his penis was so hard he could have demonstrated karate with it, splitting a pile of bricks with one blow. This was not the situation he'd ever planned for, not even in his recent, wildest dreams ... and he resented the references to John. Worst of all, he knew he could enjoy wounding her, even scarring her. Leave his mark.

'Kill me – you coward!'

Okay, all he needed to do was fuck her, hard, but he was worried he might go too far. Maybe he ought to delay things. He moved close to her face, his penis near her mouth. With her eyes still closed and in a deadpan voice, she said, 'Another ten pounds!' He said okay, but at the same moment he pressed the blade across her breast so that she*felt* it. If she moved too violently she would cut herself. She took his penis into her mouth and sucked in the same rhythm as her hands. He was fascinated by the image of the sculpture going in and out of her, reflecting and refracting the light as it did so. He wet his index finger and caressed her clitoris. Why not! It was a good show. Taking her hand off the translucent phallus he moved it for her, hoping to hold back from using it too violently on her. Suddenly she hissed, 'The knife. Don't cheat me again! The knife, that's what I want. The pain! Otherwise it's nothing for me, don't you understand? Fool? Never and not now! When I reach orgasm you must kill me. You promise. You promise! Don't let me down!'

He knew she was joking, but he was scared. He quite conceivably might get carried away and kill her. Someone inside him wanted to. Surely she knew she was taking a risk? And then he thought of the film and he started to sweat with a kind of fearful apprehension. He closed his eyes, the image of Lulu in his mind ... so unbelievably beautiful and desirable and finally tamed, evil, yet broken and killable! Wasn't he doing society a neat service? Killing a whore? He was starting to resent the power the images had over him. And Cindy's abandon. How could she so easily get into these trances? Damn her! He took the knife and cut her pants with it, then the garter belt and the tops of the stockings, relishing the clunk each cut made and he was getting scared as he imagined the sound it would make, which he could hear in his mind, if he plunged the knife into her belly. Suddenly he felt all the resentment she so often tapped in him. This was primal – albeit film. Was it him or her? Had she not killed John? Next she would kill him? Disjointed, dismembered images flashed into his mind, like the scattered fragments of John's mutilated body ... the empty hole in the tree ... the humiliation in the car earlier in the evening which he blamed on Cindy, on the hold she had over him sexually ... and he was starting to tap real hatred. He suddenly thought if he plunged the knife into her breast she would not die but it would scar her forever ... but he couldn't stop thrusting in the phallus as she sucked him hard ...

She was working up to an orgasm and he resented this even more. He had some way to go, savouring a new kind of detached intensity, desire drenched with wormwood, and he knew she wasn't really concentrating on giving him pleasure. He took the knife and suddenly drew it sharply along the curve of her hip and it drew blood. The knife was as sharp as a razor blade. She withdrew slightly but was clearly getting more excited. Suddenly he saw bruises on her thighs. From what? Suddenly he knew the situation was getting out of hand. Were they not whip marks? He wanted to do better, a patchwork of lines across her thigh, her bottom, her stomach and then he knew that he *could* kill her ... Yes. A mere flick of a switch as she said. He had to do something quickly. He took the knife and made another cut on her other hip and she winced again, and he noticed this cut was slightly deeper and it drew the blood more quickly. She had taken his hand in her own now and she was directing the movement inside her and his anger was mounting. Why did she always have it her way? Here he was in HIS fantasy and SHE was directing the action! Fuck it, wasn't it the other way round? He didn't know any more and didn't care. Maybe they were sharing the same hologram at last. Murder. And for a few seconds he was poised within a fraction of killing her ... but he couldn't do it. In a rage, he flung the knife across the room and it clattered against some furniture and made a huge din.

He yanked Georgina's masterpiece out of Cindy's vagina and he knew it hurt; she let out another of her wolf howls. He didn't want to look her in the face so he pushed her over and spread her legs savagely in front of him; and took her ... very hard. As an afterthought, he grabbed the dildo, which had bounced back under his feet (good girl Georgina!) and eased it into her bottom. She didn't seem to notice. She was moaning, encouraging him. 'Hurt me, yes, hurt me. That's *what I want* and you know it.' Her hands came round and took the dildo and adjusted its position and then held on to it tightly and he was sure she reached an orgasm before he could. He kept going, oblivious of her now, until he wasn't prepared to hold back any longer, and to show his supremacy, or mimic a porno movie, he came out deliberately as he ejaculated, pushing her away roughly before dropping on her, trembling and throbbing, the fluid, ecstatic to be free, gushing onto her skin ...

'Damn you!' Silence. She put her fingers into it and with it, drew a mandala on her stomach, before sitting up shakily to perceive the scene, looking sadly at the crumpled heap, the sad remains of her lover, utterly crashed out, an image foreclosing the rest. Unconscious or merely fast asleep.

Men! How the gods used them so mercilessly! Wondering what she could do to shock him when he recovered consciousness, she decided to meditate. The image of his whore, sitting serene and perfectly composed in deep trance, would surely cause him some kind of seizure, even dislocate his spine. She'd have the pleasure of tucking him into bed, in pain and helpless, sorry that he'd slipped a disc, or even more seriously, slipped seven discs ...

That night, Matthew received another dream ...

He's in a cold, stone room. Through a small window he can see a vast desert stretching to the horizon. A few yards from the window, under a solitary tree and all hunched up, sitting cupped in its roots, is an old, blind man; in front of him a begging bowl, around his neck a small board on which is written a jumble of mathematical signs or hieroglyphs, and jumbled letters, maybe a code. He hears a shuffle behind him, turns and sees the room full of people, wearing headphones. They're listening in to his mind. He has just thought. 'That broken old beggar is Oedipus! So much for his revolt against the pagans!' He is certain this idea is brilliant; aren't reason and paganism two sides of the same hologram; surely he is now centre of attention? People are trying to talk to him, it's a reception to honour him?

There's a girl in a long white dress; dressed as a bride. He's never seen anyone so beautiful and he's astonished, realising he has married her and the reception is to celebrate the wedding. The guests move to the sides of the room and servants bring a bed, covered with a white sheet. She lies down on the bed and pulls up her long white wedding dress and lies back seductively. The scientists are looking expectantly at him, waiting for him to de-virginate her ... he wants to run away but all he can do is hide his face behind his hands. He wants to tell them that because he loves Meritaten, he cannot go through with the sexual rite in front of so many witnesses. It is her *beauty* he loves, that she is a sister ... that his innocent love for her prevents him from making it into a performance. But no-one is listening to him. He must think of something else to make the image disappear – his diamonds!

He explains he must go into a different room, at the back, to complete the experiment. They turn on him menacingly. He sees a door, rushes and opens it, convinced it's a lift. Inside are thousands of buttons. He presses some of them but he hasn't the right code. Nothing moves. He's grabbed from behind and dragged out. He looks for Meritaten but can't see her, as they tie him up with ropes ...

... as Meritaten is being dragged off the bed brutally and tied up, just like himself, looking at him pleadingly; but there's nothing he can say or do. Ceremoniously tied down to the bed, her dress is cut open, and left lying at her side like two wings. A woman in red, wearing a black hood, comes towards him with a knife and strikes at him, to mark him, a sign cut on his skin. The woman takes a translucent crystal phallus from an altar and approaches the girl on the bed, opens her legs, pours oil on her and de-virginates her, her white dress covered with the oil and blood. The ceremony over, the white sheet is held up ...

Cut. A meadow in the centre of some trees; he's tied to a dead tree and left to die. Blood is oozing out of his body, but he can't look down. He looks up, and sees falcons circling above him, screaming at each other, waiting to stoop as soon as he falls, eager to devour his body. He closes his eyes and tries to think of other things, and imagines a train crossing a desert ... he displays it on the screen in his mind. It surges towards him, out of an image at the back of the screen. A fireplace?

The glistening beauty of the train, a masterpiece of human technology, inspires him, and he struggles against the ropes. He manages to leap up and grab hold of a copper door handle, opens the door and is pulled up inside. The interior of the train resembles a catacomb, with rows and rows of bodies, cocooned in white bandages, on shelves from floor to ceiling. They're going to another galaxy; not actually dead, their minds will be used in other machines; grafted on when they reach their destination in the far distant future. He finds a seat and sits down.

On the wall facing him is a holographic picture, the face of a blind man wearing an Egyptian priest's head-dress, and the hair is very long, like a woman's. Under it is written, *I have preserved my love for the creator of the Re-Unified-Verse.*

Each of the dead bodies has its name written in hieroglyphics, inside a cartouche, and he can read the signs fluently.

Rutherford, Einstein, Bragg, Heisenberg, Bohr, Bohm, Gabor, Crick. He feels miserable that all their knowledge is being taken away. He goes to a window, and as far as he can see, the land is black and scarred, after the nuclear accident. Mile after mile there's nothing but black, scorched earth.

But there's a tall golden cenotaph in the middle of an oval copse of black, dead beech trees. He jumps off the train, rolling down the bank and falling into a pond of black pitch, all that remains of trees melted by radiation. He climbs out of the pit and cleans himself as best he can. Reaching the golden glowing cenotaph he finds it covered with inscriptions, including, *In Memoriam for those lying elsewhere,* and it occurs to him the meaning of *cenotaph* is in remembrance of a dead person whose body can't be buried in that place, the body lies elsewhere ... not in its rightful tomb. He knows this must be a coded message. But whose body is missing? His own? Or John's? Or Meritaten's? Why, in this tomb, is it the wrong body?

The hieroglyphs are carved so deeply into the stone he can use them as hand and footholds, and he climbs, because at the top is the essential message. Each time he stops he sees the world below, a lone and level wasteland, black and dead, horizon to horizon. A short distance from the top of the column he finds a hole carved out of the stone and under it, the inscription, *Beware of Set! Love from Isis and Nepthys.* Inside a bird has built a nest, and in it are seven eggs, each one numbered. He picks up number seven, but it crumbles into dust in his fingers, solarised by the heat of the nuclear blast.

He goes on climbing, not daring to look down, afraid to discover what is lost. Finally he reaches the capstone of the cenotaph, a small pyramid of pure crystal, translucent and clear. The moment the sun's rays touch it, the pyramid of light would be seen a hundred miles away. But why is there no sun?

At that moment he notices the first signs of redness glowing on the horizon; it must be nearly dawn. He wonders how it had appeared so light and assumes it is the effect of the residual radiation. Fascinated, he watches the incandescent fan of emerging rays from the sun, preceding its appearance ...

He climbs the last step and peers into the crystal pyramidion, under which is written, *Xerui-Asar. Man. Phallos. Phos. Light.* He peers into it hoping for an answer to the riddle of his diamond's irrational behaviour ... and sees the face of Meritaten reflected on a faint green screen inside the crystal, but at that precise instant the sun lifts itself (why not!) an infinitesimal distance over the horizon and a laser-thin shaft of sunlight sears into the crystal pyramid; the heat generated is so intense, Matthew's mind melts and within seconds his body vaporises ... he has discovered something he will call cold fusion ... but is it not too late?

He woke up to find Cindy had slipped his penis inside herself and was moving on top of him, slowly and gently, with great precision. It seemed as if he ejaculated at the moment his dream seemed to end ... 'Wake up, you old mummy, birds are gobbling up the early worms and you're asleep, dreaming! And Gypsies too, gathering mushrooms in the fields!' She bit his ear quite hard. She was really liking him again. That weird mixture of insecure shyness and aggressive resentment, so typical, she had often thought, of the natural scientist. The ones she'd known anyway, during her researches.

'Ouch!' he said.

'Bitch!' she said. And that kept him puzzled all day.

∇

TWELVE

"Our brains mathematically construct 'concrete' reality by interpreting frequencies from another dimension, a realm of meaningful, patterned primary reality that transcends time and space. The brain is a hologram, interpreting a holographic universe ... Phenomena of altered states of consciousness (which reflect altered brain states) may be due to a literal attunement to the invisible matrix that generates 'concrete' reality.

"A New Perspective on Reality"
The Holographic Paradigm and other Paradoxes
(Edited by Ken Wilber)

△

At breakfast, Cindy said she had *things* to do in town, didn't want to distract Matthew from his work, and so would call a taxi. Georgina put on a brave face. But Matthew's immediate reaction was relief. He was eager to consult the next disc in John's black temple of sensory deprivation. After trying different codes he managed to gain access with:

B A – A S A R

DISC NINE

Π

Further steps towards a Re-Interpretation of the Interpretation of Dreams, borrowing (and confusing together; call it the plague of holographic plagiarism) a little from Nietzche, Freud, Jung, Schopenhauer and a bunch of other pilgrims who confronted the inevitable nihilism of our time, brave wanderers in the inner desert, following the shadows of those indignant, yellow-eyed hawks, flying in their numinous gyres in the stormy grey skies of the modern mind. Amen. Thomas de Quincey, whose work is a study of the effect of opium on the mechanism of his dreaming process, reveals that opium actually *stimulates* the faculty of dreaming; furthermore, it was also vital to his creative process, crystallising experience into 'involutes'. Coleridge tells us: *"What is an involute? Feeling in a moment the secret analogies or parallelisms that connected things else apparently remote".* So, a chemical called Opium physically provokes the mind to dream, and in dreams there is an enhanced ability to make connections otherwise eluding the rational mind. Years later we have David Bohm and Karl Pribram telling us about holograms. An involute is a kind of hologram, surely? In each convoluted part you will SEE the whole – if you have eyes to see, like Tiresias.

The Ghost Dance! So, imagining myself trapped inside an involuted hologram, I tried to think it through with the eyes of Lazarus. Laserus? Whose real name, I disc-lose, is L'ASARus. He too born from the translucent dream body of AsAr/Osiris. Dreams give a glimpse of heaven and hell. What makes us dream? It *must* be a psychedelic drug; that's called logic. Deduction! What then, is the chemical found naturally in the bloodstream, that NORMALLY causes us to dream? Could it be a chemical transmitter that connects left to right sides of the brain directly? Let's presume this chemical exists, causing the mind to dream, occurring naturally in the blood, oozing from a gland that is activated by lack of ego repression. The pineal? The hypothalamus? A holographic role for the prostate maybe?

Up my arse!

Dreams are messages being received from the R-Field, in which time can be re-versed, qua, given back its poetry. The natural brain is a receiver. In Budge's *Egyptian Magic*, he tells us about Nectanebus, King of Egypt B.C. 358, who according to the Greeks was the most important adept of all time at working magic: *"He sent a dream to the queen by means of a wax figure. His object was to persuade the queen that the Egyptian god Amon would come to her at night. To do this he went into the desert and collected a number of herbs which he knew how to employ in causing people to dream dreams, and having brought them back he squeezed the juice out of them. When he wanted Philip of Macedonia to see certain things in a dream, he sent a falcon, which he had previously bewitched by magic words of power, to Philip as he lay asleep, and he saw them. The next day Philip had the dream explained by an expounder of dreams and he was satisfied that the child to whom his wife Olympias was to give birth was the son of the god Amon."*

Psychotic stuff! The Greek word psychosis means the "transforming action of the soul". UR, yes, it does. But dreams are psychotico-mimetic, they tell us. So, the Egyptians had a drug, from a plant, which could induce a very special kind of dreaming in which messages could be sent and received AND could reveal, amongst other things, WHO was being re-incarnated into a particular child at its birth; which 'god' is being reincarnated into a child's consciousness. In other words, to reveal the process by which NEW consciousness is fed into the human race, which we carelessly, loosely mistranslate as reincarnation. And so my work began to take shape; Reincarnation as THEY understood it, understanding the full OCCULT meaning of the 'Double', the KHU, a translucent envelope around the self. It is there, my friend. Can't you see it/me? By the way, the Ancient Egyptians wrote their texts on long scrolls of papyrus. Please SCROLL through the pages by pressing the key with the arrow facing downwards. Good, with that little conceit behind us let us re-enter the temple ...

ENTER

The first step was to study the use of drugs in 'mystical' religions and ancient 'medicine'. Various drugs were isolated from various plants. As Robert Graves wrote, our inner cultural history, our mythological history of mind, was based on writings coming to us down the ages, written by initiates in coded form. The ancient paradigms or world views we call the history of philosophy, were derived from adepts like Plato, Pythagoras, Plutarch, ALL of whom were first initiated into the secret, hermetic mysteries of Ancient Egypt.

One day I was meditating on dreams, asking myself, how do people dream and why do they describe them as *psychotic?* PSYCHOTIC; qv: "1. Of or characterised by psychosis. 2. A person suffering from psychosis." Brilliant stuff, no!? Qv PSYCHOSIS: "Any form of severe mental disorder in which the individual's contact with reality becomes highly distorted." A put down if ever there was one.

In the Greek Alchemical text entitled KOR KOSMOU: i.e. "The Universe Maiden" (lovely title!), we find; *"Taking from himself sufficient pneuma, and by an intelligent mixture uniting it with fire, he brewed it up with certain unknown substances, accompanying himself with certain secret incantations* (cosmic computer codes?) *he agitated the mixture, till there boiled up to the surface, a sort of matter, subtler, purer, more transparent than the ingredients of which it was made. This was translucent and only HE saw it. God called this composition; PSYCHOSIS."*

God is psychotic; is a psychosis.

We must re-think not only Greek mythology, reinterpret the way it has been translated for us by rationalists, Christians, etc. – re-think the hidden writings in the Bible, the Tibetan and Egyptian Books of the Dead, the Rig Veda, the Avesta of Zarathustra, all PSYCHOTIC, embodying the holographic involute of transparency and translucency, but also re-evaluate the half-silvered mirror, all that remains of consciousness, hacked down to its present scarred (scared/unsacred) level by so-called reason.

Dreaming so closely resembles being under the influence of such a drug, that the body must create its OWN psychedelic drug, provoking a momentary psychosis. A rare blessing! A drug related to LSD, mescalin, psilocybin, no wonder dreams are often so fascinating! Well, we found a drug produced during REM periods of sleep, and called it HYPNOTAMINE. Part Two of this text reveals this full story and the detailed chemistry.

Cindy; cheap dumb blonde Mad-onnanist, my ... er ... arse. A brilliant physicist and medium. Imagine the combination? Cindy and I have isolated, from our own blood, other naturally-occurring drugs the body releases – stimulated by different ways of thinking – singing – making love. Reason stimulates a real killer!

Later we also discovered that words of power open up the mind like codes open a computer disc. Words of Power, spoken of by all the shamans and adepts ARE code words to stimulate the body by auto-suggestion, to open up the great 'consciousness-computers' (for want of words to describe them) on other fields/ dimensions. Recently we discovered the drug that causes the entire mental scan to leave the body. Every drug we found corresponds to one of the elements of consciousness, Ba, Khu, Khaibit, Ka ... Those guys with leopard skins around their hips, knew all the techniques!

Isis copulating with Osiris symbolises the unconscious mind reunited holistically to the conscious mind. Cured! Osiris was also the essence of a certain tree/plant of immortality – living inside the tree of knowledge. His BLOOD became the essence of the sacred plants that grew under it, namely the mushrooms springing up, erect, pushing up like penises from between the hidden roots. With such plants, they opened themselves to messages from the Others in other frequency Fields, still detectable by the unconscious under the right chemical conditions; messages coming into that terminal we call the unconscious. So why do we think we merely dream useless dreams? Only *reason* thinks they're useless. We dream because a chemical called HYPNOTAMINE is released into the blood stream and the mind becomes psychotic, is trance-formed, capable of being transformed by messages, from the R-Field of re-versed time.

After isolating Hypnotamine we learnt to produce it in crystalline form. Like so many of the psychedelic drugs it makes its effect with minute quantities, suggesting it is a trigger that starts another process, the potential for which lies permanently buried in the human body, like the god lies buried in the body of the tree, awaiting the Goddess of magic, Isis, to bring him to life again. Fortunately I am a compulsive dreamer. I make Freud's Wolf-man look like a Weasel-man in comparison. If I wake up in the morning without having travelled to the back of the North Wind or swum in the grottoes with those nymphomaniac *sirènes* that Nerval spoke of, I become immediately rational! My mind threatening to become mere vegetable (sic)! Seriously, this meant I was able to work on myself, always an asset for a scientist. Cindy woke me whenever I was in the grip of some awesome dream, moaning and groaning in my sleep, my eye movements more rapid than a humming bird's wings, and we would take an immediate blood sample. And others things too! Grrrrh. Her fluids too, when *she* was dreaming! Sexy bitch! By telling ourselves the drug MUST be related to the known psychedelics, we found it; you find only what you look for!

Eating the crystal confirms that Hypnotamine provokes the *psychosis* we call dreaming. Ignore them! Unless you're one of those enlightened people who knows that psychosis leads to a higher form of truth. In dreams are involutes of knowledge worth unravelling, visions of the future, and messages from other beings trying to be reincarnated through your consciousness, from other networks. From the virtual-time reality network!

Encouraged by our initial success, Cindy and I worked on synthesising other drugs closely related to Hypnotamine, which we'd found was rather different in structure to the known psychedelic drugs. But here was another psychotic idea! Was there not a drug that might even be responsible for narrowing consciousness, responsible for the greatest crime of human history, reason? R D Laing tells us about reason:

"A consciousness can exist with or without a sense of ego, an identity. We are clear that the ego is a mental construction intimately chemically conditioned. It can be dissolved in two seconds by nitrous oxide ... "

And we live by it, depend on it, worship it? And ignore the unconscious that took a hundred million years to create us? Imagine if we could find that reason provokes the production of another drug, *continuously*, forcing us, against our better judgement, to limit our minds within those stressful self-delusions we call ration-ality? Rationed-anality? We're working on it. We must patent it first! Might that not explain an awful lot about man's collective schizo-phrenos, split mind, split soul?

Herewith some chemical formulae and equations!

Matthew scrolled quickly through the disc, noticing that the descriptions for the synthesis of chemicals and crystals seemed authentic. Quite intrigued, he took the next disc and tried several codes before

K H U - A S A R

gained access. He sat back to listen to more of John's beguiling and compelling preaching ...

DISC TEN

Forgive me if I preface this disc with a quote, re-minding you of the background 'black noise' to these illuminations. Let Arthur Koestler paint the background scenery of our mystery Noh play!

"The conclusions are quite simple. Our biological evolution came to a standstill in Cro-Magnon days. Since we cannot in the foreseeable future expect the necessary change in human nature to arise by way of a spontaneous mutation, that is, by natural means, we must induce it by artificial means. We can only hope to survive as a species by developing techniques which supplant biological evolution. We must search for a cure for the schizo-physiology inherent in man's nature, and the resulting split in our minds, which led to the situation in which we find ourselves ... I believe that if we fail to find this cure, the old paranoid streak in man, combined with his new powers of destruction, must sooner or later lead to geno-suicide. But I also believe the cure is almost within the reach of contemporary biology ... "

He warns further that a split has occurred in human development between the higher cortex and the lower limbic systems – intelligence and instinct – and we must find a way of relinking them; chemically. By psycho-pharmacology.

Matthew re-versed and read this twice. Heady stuff! Koestler, after all, was one of the most important scientific philosophers of recent times. For him to say such a thing was very disturbing. After absorbing the words, Matthew continued ...

Koestler goes on to praise Huxley's masterpiece, *Heaven and Hell.* He quotes Huxley's similar instructions – by knowing the chemical technology of transcendental experience, we can work further with these chemicals; we must find a psycho-pharmaceutical cure for that paranoid streak in mankind that is presumed by the rationalist to be normality! We must find an *"artificially simulated, adaptive mutation to bridge the rift between the phylogenetically old and new brain"*. Isn't this what alchemists were always telling us? Their dream of concocting the *elixir vitae*?

Thank you deus Adeptus Major Arthur Koestler, from his *The Ghost in the Machine.* What he called Elixir Vitae, I call the Ultimate Eucharist. I and my scarlet woman read those pages carefully and mused on his suggestions for quite some time; i.e. it is necessary to reorganise the chemistry of the human mind to move forward. Through the DNA or the RNA, as he hints earlier in the book? Genetically? Or are there other means? We asked, how much can we retune the mind chemically so that its potential for reception revealed in dreams is much enhanced?

Before I reveal details about the remarkable "Receptamine", I must digress and explain, out of fairness to her, more about Cindy's role in this work. Alas, it's not easy to be so fair. We "scientists" must think where our next finance is coming from! But the presence of death behind the left shoulder makes even the most egotistical of us generous in spirit. A lot of this might seem far-fetched; a mere slip of a pencil-thin girl, kohl-eyed, given to silk nickers (preferably torn) and lewd dancing and imagining herself a movie star. If you think that, you suffer from Romance Complex. I urge you to give up women immediately! It has only been thanks to "powers" Cindy perfected that the later work was possible.

Alas, recently, she seems to have decided to get rid of me.

Either this is something she wanted to do because it's her own private power trip (she always resented me for being with the one thing she was without, when she/we seduced her girlfriends) or she has received instructions from the OTHERS to remove me from the work. This is why I have protected this data by codes. But I may not succeed in this, because her power of penetrating minds is such that she has probably worked the whole thing out by now, through you. I may be talking to Cindy now! Hi there, Cindy, how are you? Okay, you won! Bla bla, you Urchin BWitchin' BitchWitch, you! But I loved you and your magic ... sexual and Oedipal psychic masochist that I am!

But in case I am talking to someone else, here goes!

A few background details about our work together. When we first met, I was already working seriously with psychedelic drugs. Cindy was working on crystals with a friend, whom I never met, and know little about. I think he worked at Cambridge, but part of our deal was that I never talked about him. I think he messed her up sexually. Turned her off men forever! She came into my life with some valuable information and we teamed up to work together. A harrowing journey ever since! There were two quite distinct aspects to this whole work. Firstly, "making contact", i.e., becoming capable of reception; this was Cindy's initial work, involving palladium and diamond crystals in a kind of very sophisticated "crystal gazing", as she jokingly called it. Diamonds, being the hardest crystals known with ultra-tight lattice structures, are excellent as receivers and transmitters. Secondly, our work was synthesising the chemicals we first discovered from body fluids, and others we were later "instructed/taught" how to make. What jewels of the imagination! What a necklace that was, a Milky Way around pretty Cindy's elegant neck!

Fluids? There are fourteen different fluids produced in the female vagina. A scientific fact. Maybe thirteen and another one ... but occasionally? Drink at the fountain of love!

But the EGYPTIANS WERE DOING ALL THIS FIVE THOUSAND YEARS AGO. When you think of the time scales involved here, and you ask how long have they been working elsewhere in "worlds" or "consciousness-centres/fields", in other parts of our galaxy, probably millions of years; is it that strange they came here and made contact with the Egyptians, and taught them a few conjuring tricks with the mind? Is it any more strange they should come THEN, or NOW, or in ten years time? We always think NOW is the important time because it is rational time - until you discover you can pass through time and make any moment NOW, once you give up the sphincter-stranglehold of reason.

For example. Cindy made a most important discovery through an amazing insight. She discovered she could "make things happen". She could move objects – and induce people to think or dream certain things, until she got so good she could influence a whole series of events – but only if she was able to visualise the whole thing, see it as IMAGE. This gift she exploited on a few of her friends, actresses in one of her "movies", unaware of her powers. She is a great movie director. Cindy von Sternberg – or von Stroheim? Hi Cindy!

She was asking if directed consciousness, through an obsessive meditational type of concentration, could make things happen, was this not perhaps the ONLY way things evolve – how forms were generated throughout matter's evolution, whether crystals or bacteria or viruses or animals, plants, insects, human beings – the form they took and became – this is about BECOMING; was this not the only way things BECOME what they are? Imaginative mimicry, let's call it – RESONANCE – i.e., wave fields interacting amongst themselves, interfering like a hologram. A kind of morphic plagiarism?

Cindy could influence the way butterflies changed their colour patterns by concentrating on chosen shapes and colours. But only if she could visualise the patterns and concentrate on PARTICULAR butterflies, e.g. a small captive colony, let's say. Imagine then that life here on this planet, from the primÆval mud onwards, came from some consciousness/force somewhere "thinking" in this kind of way. Osiris of course. The 10^{13} billions of fragments that compose him. To the further power[14], of course.

By the way, if you examine the mastaba at Saqqara, used for the King's Heb-Seb rebirth ceremony: dated 2nd Dynasty, you will find it has fourteen gates. But thirteen are optical illusions built into the walls. *Trompe-l'oeils.* Only one is real. Relevant or irrelevant? A point never remarked upon by EGYPTologists.

To continue. Rocks n'scrol'n on! Each new form that occurs THEN has its own power to enter into the cycle and influence the development of further forms. But action through a distance. A bacterium or virus can influence this Becoming, just as Cindy could cause a certain virus to evolve a new form, with a specific new function, just by thinking of it, as long as she could visualise the function in her IMAGE-INATION. Is this not normal scientific proçedure? In the R-Field is a direct mechanism of image recognition on the level of wave radiation fields. IMAGE NATION. So what power has the virtual reality global village computer screen network? Awesome!

Far-fetched? Yes, indeed. Literally fetched from the farthest regions of the Uni-verse. Just think of the Frankensteins Mary Shelley created with a moment's reflection, a few words on paper. Artists have always sought this power. Once you've spent an hour in the Rothko Chapel, can you ever see *GREEN* the same way again? But how sublime, from now on you see colours only as part of a huge Rothko canvas! Or not at all. Once you have listened to Verdi's *Requiem* in Caen Cathedral and allowed your eyes to wander on that fan tracery on the roof, can you ever sit in a copse and see trees the same way again? Yet what is "out there" hasn't changed, you might say. Dumb fool, I say. There is nothing out there anyway.

Cindy can influence a mind telepathically – just as the Russians and Americans have been trying, unsuccessfully, to create telepathic back-ups with spacecraft. Cindy's trick was to use crystals, each of which has its own subtle emanations; use the interfaces between crystals glued together (chemically) to create reflecting surfaces – internal hologram generators! She discovered how the mind remembers – and how it can see forwards into the future. If I am imagining all this then surely I must either be very much in love with her or paranoid about women? Both! Where does that put you? Imagine if she is (I nearly wrote she was!) writing these texts into the discs – as the narrative went along? Kerpow! Only joking! Just preparing you for some of the tricks the unconscious will play on you when you enter the labyrinth. Have no doubts and fears, you will fear and doubt, and it will be hell!

Cindy's powers evolved almost by accident, the important groundswell (her word) for her oceanic insights coming to her through trying to "understand" – (she would qualify this word) – the *Egyptian Book of the Dead*, a text she says fascinated and obsessed her – "called" her from a notch on the glyph of present time when she first set her mystical jade-green eyes (in the right light) upon it. Strange how these things happen to us, ap-parent-ly by chance. (Shades of ancestors in that one?) She says she concentrated so hard on the damn thing that it spoke to her. Presumably referring to the penis of Osiris. Well? That meta-attentive concentration started to restructure her brain. If you MEDITATE on something for long enough, your own brain shapes itself accordingly. She did this with such determined strength of will that her brain/mind/consciousness started to take the broad shape/structure it would have had, if she had been living three thousand odd years ago in Ancient Egypt, in her beloved Amarna. What power she has! Have you not seen how everything that Georgina thinks or does is a reflection of Cindy? Cindy, the phallic woman, the mother with a penis, Georgina, a mere reflection, a mere satellite, a mere moon.

Cindy concentrated so hard on the differences between Atenism and the earlier Theban ideas of cosmo-genesis, that she made contact with the initiated consciousnesses of the time. She received messages and eventually facts from various priests and priestesses; in a trance, she visualised their faces so strongly, she brought her mind to the right tuning to receive data. From then on she brought these "ideas", let's call them, for want of a better word, down to the level of matter. Words are inadequate in this context. When you learn to dream holographically, you will under-stand.

In resonance with the over-stand of Osiris. Understand? Stand under what? What is it that stands, that humbles one – if not the phallus of Osiris? That unconscious memory we have of when we lived in trees, and ate them! Here I am, or was, mere humble John – at the feet of the two in union, mother Isis with her magically self-created penis – call it phallus to confuse the issue – (please note the two must be interchangeable when you realise that penis and phallus are the same thing within a holographic involute!) What am I? Clay in her hands, alas, but how nice to become truly three-dimensional, so up-and-over-standing, in her hands! I digress!

The R-Field taught her to synthesise certain crystals. The Egyptians had been taught these tricks in their time by "information sources", digital/light data banks, elsewhere. Another Galaxy? The cold Black Dwarf behind Sirius ... but that's another story. The Great Pyramid was a receiver of Lasers, mindbeams of digitalised data, information that was focused by emeralds and diamonds. Often both in combination, the light from the emerald refracted by the diamond. Difficult? No. Once you believed enough in the tRachyon/gravitational field process you could make it happen. The local Egyptians received their first information, as Cindy did, by mentally concentrating on the possibility and CERTAINTY of receiving information. Scrying with crystals. We are all capable of this. I personally never achieved it, having messed up my mind too often with LSD – the wrong drug, it de-structures, and I had no time to re-structure my mind. The new smart crystals we were eventually instructed to create could be used to restructure the mind, to alter the tunings.

ALTER THE BIAS – LIKE ON THE RECORDING "HEAD" OF A TAPE RECORDER ... to perceive not only other "pictures of this world", and they were amazing enough, but also HEAR these other messages. Dumb scientists are spending millions at the present time listening in to the galaxies, the stars, the general black/white-noise of space. They will hear nothing because they are not correctly visualising holographically what it might be that they'll receive as a message. They are looking for monotheistic, rational data. These messages will come through the unconscious and related (crystal) structures we create. They often APPEAR simply as dreams. The brain is an infinitely more subtle and sophisticated instrument than a fucking radio or even X-ray telescope. They never noticed. So why not ask how the brain works – chemically – and alter it, chemically? God was a chemist but Cindy was a woman. Hereby hangs a (trans-lucent) tale ... then lie in the stone sarcophagus in the QUEEN'S chamber, and let the images come? Down the stone shaft? How sweet it is die ...

Matthew stopped scrolling and switched off the computer. Cindy Cindy Cindy! How was he going to confront her now? How could John be lying – all of it a fiction? A huge joke? A mere novel? Maybe this was Cindy's novel after all. He felt the tingling on the back of his neck. Was it fear?

Feeling weak in his legs, he nevertheless needed to walk about, so went down to the garden and sat under his tree. But he was disintegrating, his mind in such a turmoil he was on the verge of losing control of it. Ironically, the only way he felt he could regain a sense of continuity was to go back to the blasted computer ... John was winning, no doubt about it ... damn the bugger!

ENTER

... Cindy's arrogance and insatiable pride as a woman making her believe her mind was BETTER than all the technology available. Typical woman, mistrusting "male" technology, until, of course, she had power over it and enjoyed using it. More later! It was early in Cindy's research at University College London with wave-radiation and crystals, that she got sidetracked by Egyptology. Yet it became the answer. Coincidence? Synchronicity, a gap in space-time, the Eros Field that Cindy called it (sweet name, you must admit – only a mere slip of a phallic girl would call it that. The scientist would have called it the alpha-dynamorgasmine wave-particular energy field! You know what I mean.) I call it the R-Field from the interference in the word hologram: Copse/ Corpse: CO R PSE.

Cindy felt that the ultimate power was not in (during) the trip with my Ultimate Eucharist, but to learn and gain the means to cause things to happen. Structurally. Psycho-pharmacologically. Seeing the future and entering the creation of it. Control of people's minds. A rose is a rose becomes a new rose. Arose? Arise! Everything sexually created from two forms uniting, like two Moiré patterns, one on top of the other, male and female, past and future, matter and spirit. Those old fashioned dualities. Isis and Osiris and their continuous cosmo-genesis, new forms continuously coming forth into the day to be born, BORN, slouching towards Bethlehem! Created out of apparently nothing, by energy vortexes floating around everywhere, which are creative because they are already in a form that can be copied – mimicked; by our own consciousness-vortexes, as well as in ALL other life forms too. Just learn to listen and become God!

Let's say you decide to create a child; whether you do so or not depends on what other forces are concentrating in the R Field around the same time, what other "Beings" from elsewhere – *la vrai vie est absente* – desire to be reincarnated, because two humans can create the body – sex is on the level of body, okay? – but they CAN'T control the consciousness that enters/invades the body of the child later and thus gives it movement, development, holomovement; "life". What Mother does not know, from the character of her child, that she was seduced by some alien being? Atavistic creatures! You create the white page in its mind, that parents can write on, but others are writing there too, all the time, every day, continuously. Just listen to them, they are there, you don't have to be that temple prostitute, Joan of Arc! And what consciousness from four thousand years ago was present at Cindy's birth? Turn but a stone ... opium dream!

> *"And lo! In the night, my soul, my daughter,*
> *cry, clutching heaven by the hems;*
> *And lo! Christ walking on the water,*
> *but not of Genesareth, but Thames!"*

What I offered Cindy was some of the technology and a few modest ideas. Cindy could only go SO far, before coming up against the sheer inertia of matter. Very heavy stuff! She could change the pattern on the wings of a butterfly, but she could not move a mountain. She *wanted* to move mountains. This needed the new technology. A pyramid moved a few inches would do. A hundred years ago such ideas would be dismissed as the ravings of an opium addict. Cindy and I made steady progress in this field (pun there); actual factual fractual cruxial stuff. Gerard de Nerval chose the name "de Nerval" because it was the name of a field next to a village that he loved. Listen to him carefully! An initiate ...

Le rêve est une seconde vie ...

Dream is the holograph of life ...

In these discs are the keys by which you can open the seven double doors known by every initiate since the world began, hopefully reaching disc 1^{14}, the ULTIMATE EUCHARIST program. BUT! That is only one dimension. As I have suggested, there may be snags. Cindy may be listening into your mind. She may know what is happening, and will pounce when the time is right. I advise you to let her have things bit by bit. Take a tip from her soul-mate, Sheherazade! The 1001 nights.

But most important, I must *remind* you to FORGET the main code. Erase the image from your mind! If she picks that up, you've had it. But I made a bold guess. Why did I choose the phallus of Osiris? Signifier of Daddy's for-bidden sexuality? Knowing her sexual fantasies as well as I do, and the abuse she exploits, there is one thing Cindy cannot visualise. That very thing! Everything else she CAN, but this is the ONE thing she cannot, or WILL not visualise. She REFUSES to admit to its existence. Have you heard of the migrating clitoris? No? Yes you have, surely? Try it some time, it's great fun ... Cindy is the only person I know whose clitoris migrated to her hypothalamus. Work that one out and I'll say you're initiated holographically!

Where was I? Ah yes – Cindy and her desire to ravish young girls. Virgins of course. Why virgins? Take the Greek word: *Parthenos*. Virgin. What does she symbolise? Parthenogenesis? Yes and no, not quite, but good try. Not so much birth from a virgin; but birth from nothing! Her obsession! How to create a child without that fucking penis!

Or is she merely a vampire, in love with blood? No, it is to do with time ... how else to have power over eternity? She ties them up and rapes them with my unseen and unacknowledged Osiris phallus, and even so, it must be in the dark: blindfolded.

She can't allow herself to truly, authentically SEE that object which is needed. Which is why I think our code is safe. But is there an interesting paradox here? A lesson for us all? It is the one thing that Cindy NEVER stops thinking about, the penis she does not have. You might say *that* is why she spends all her time trying to discover, in the space-time continuum, the physical representation of ... anal birth ... creation *ex nihilo* from the void, with her sexual a ... void ... dance.

Yet, ironically, this is why it's doubly safe. It's so obvious! To her it's the focus of her entire will, to "realise", to "materialise" that absent penis. But it's not being able to see the wood for the trees! She can only ever see it as metaphor. It's what she thinks about, but never makes an image of in her mind. Seeing it as the ultimate "absence", she would never think I would use something so obvious for my code. Absence upon absence, like two waves spreading out from a centre, a pool of water in which a stone, the ego, has dropped. That is what we are, hovering like dragonflies, seeing ourselves as mere beating wings, so fast they are speechless, images in the half-silvered mirror, reflected from a million lattices of a crystal continuum that is endless and timeless and without substance. If it wasn't for love, momentarily giving the illusion of attachment to matter, it would be hell.

It is hell. Amen.

But I digress again. Love? The unified field theory. What appears to be the most simple idea, has taken the most complex machinations of the mind to crystallise. For example, we perceive the world of matter and seek to know what is the essence that binds it, a unified field, one equation that explains everything. Only a monotheist could imagine such a painfully self-destructive paradox. We do not discover this field because this field is consciousness itself, it is the very question, the very probing penetrating thing (familiar?) we are using to look at it. The absent penis in Cindy is looking for the way to materialise ITSELF and become a reality and thus never knows itself. According to her metaphysics, her theory of cosmo-genesis, there is no penis to formulate the penis! She needs a son, of course. She'd call him Christian ... and accordingly crucify its father.

I've made another assumption. Because Cindy can't find the code herself, her mind not allowing it, she'll HAVE to find someone else who CAN. A man. Presumably this is YOU, reading this, here and now. So, of course, you might say I have materialised you? I thought of you, imagined the Tao of getting you here and now you're here, looking at this screen. (What else to look at any more?) But, as you are a man, and as Cindy will have to present you with the discs, and, most of all HERSELF, I know there's one thing you will not fail to see. That which joins you and which she is SET on stealing! Such a pretty girl, a real initiate, a real witch but with a lucid rational mind. She is Hadit, Mother of Invention, she is Maya, her whole world an act of theatre, one continuous fantasy of entering Hades and marrying Daddy/Pluto/Osiris. Ishtar! In the Mesopotamian ritual-myth, she is the goddess who comes down to the underworld and disc-ards a veil at each gate, the seven gates through which the goal of Gnosis (gKnow-Isis) can be reached. The naked goddess is the pure revelation. The purpose in all her Mystery Plays is to take away those veils, those seven veils, and grasp what is behind them. And what is behind them? Not my head, but what my severed head symbolises. In dream, reversed. My severed phallus! What is hidden behind the veils is the empty achingly open vagina - and let us pity her and love her for it, the NEED for the phallus. *L'absence*, in her seductive Frrrrench-R-field-wench accent, which is the hunger we call desire ... as hungry as the tachyon particle which wishes to travel faster than light ...

If Cindy has me killed, and cuts me up into pieces to satisfy the myth – the one part she will *not* know what to do with is my penis. I doubt if she will take the simple way out, the logical one, and eat it. I can just see her battling with the problem. How can she keep it and yet not keep it? She will have it mummified, of course. She being the Mother with my penis. Your ultimate desire. Madonna and child ...

Somewhere you will find it if you look HARD enough. My ancestral penis, mummified, bandaged up, re-hidden behind the veils ... behind the veils beyond which, under the head-stone Clitoris ... and she is a goddess too ... is such an ecstatic death. A nice thought. It is, after all the part of myself I should be most proud to have preserved, rather than my mind, which will exist anyway after my body has gone, encoded in the computer. My manhood. Ah well. She and I fought for it. What is Aphrodite but a penis cut off and thrown into the ocean to be reborn as a beautiful young girl? The whole fragmented material world grows from the body of Osiris like a plant. The whole of the world of form is born from the vagina of Isis and the resulting interface is the lost but recreated, magically transformed penis with which Isis fecundates herself.

Their child Horus? God of the new Aeon, Crowley tells us in his telepathically received *AL*! Who is this Horus? He can't be seen or even conceived by consciousness as we know it. He is tomorrow. ONLY when you have opened the eye of Horus, that is, you have MOVED TO THE NEXT DIMENSION, will you be able to see him. Otherwise he is perfectly translucent. Spirit? Soul? Or the hologram of Spirit/soul; the ultimate paradox and mystery? He is there, all about you, in millions of reincarnations, but you cannot see him because he is too perfect, so pure that light passes right through him. The interface between the virtual male spirit and virtual female soul. The KHU in its most perfect form. Does that not sound familiar? A field we cannot yet see? I might be there already, talking to you.

Please listen! Follow the instructions on these discs. IF you do, you will learn what will be demanded of you. Good luck. As long as you can reach disc number fourteen, still with your mind intact; you will need to be intact to work out the final code. Meanwhile, be careful, Cindy may be listening to your mind. Do not VISUALISE the code. Forget it! Imagine it as something shapeless, ethereal, translucent, non-existent, dank and soggy and squidgey (oops), sexy and sopping wet! Tell yourself the code is a jellyfish, for example. Fix your mind on that. The phallus as a jellyfish. Georgina's favourite image. She thinks she is a jellyfish, poor thing, floating in an ocean of unrealised desires, entirely passive and helpless. How she envies Cindy her skeleton, her backbone, her phallic willpower! Little does she know of Cindy's torments. Her faked orgasms, her resentment of that hard thrust inside her. Ah well. That too is another story.

But forget the code. Dematerialise it. Forget the image, forget the letters. At all cost! Stop thinking about it. Substitute something, ANYTHING. Preferably not a THING. THAT is the trick. That is exactly how the Ancients concealed all their hidden secrets. They presented it as something else. All that talk of pomegranates, mead, honey. Mushrooms did not exist. Like the phallus cannot for Cindy! And yet it is her double. Beware of becoming her double. To become it – she will have to eat you alive. Mind you, she was always good at oral sex. Clever indeed, those ancient scientists/mystics. Let's drink to them as they drank from the gorgeous vaginas of their luscious temple prostitutes, the fluids which contained SOMA, the eye of the gods ... slurp slurp!

So think only of the fluids, if you are to survive, to escape her anger if she finds us out. Tell yourself the code is something else. Maybe, the dawn light: the name given by Pharaoh Chephren to the Sphinx: the Horus of the Risen sun. Close enough to cause confusion. See ONLY this image, this beautiful bird in your mind, with its iridescent silver green blue feathers, its sublime claws, its avenging beak. Concentrate on it hard until you believe this WAS the code; the falcon that has risen with the dawn's light. This will put her off the track. But if she gets the real code, she'll have to kill you, and you'll find your own body mummified; and your *soul* will be winging its way to the Black Dwarf star, to await the call to its next incarnation. Maybe you're ready for the trip? Fed up with this life, lost in a desert of materiality? I don't blame you. We've lost all the sacred codes. Are you perhaps an initiate already and have surrendered in spirit to the angel of death? You feel you have no choice? If so, go along with it. Let her take you! And bon voyage ... the magic theatre of sex has claimed another willing victim. Le mort. L'amour. Le petit mort. Le grand mort? La grande mawkitsche? She awaits you.

Matthew stopped scrolling through the text, and sat back in the chair, trying to be objective about the emerging picture of

Cindy. He wanted to laugh but couldn't. *The only reason I am remotely interested in anything John says is because I have wanted to fuck Cindy since I first set eyes on her!* The question now was how to withdraw from her without provoking her wrath? No answer came, so he decided to carry on with John's text. It had to be going somewhere and the image of Cindy was becoming sharper, alas! Does knowledge always undermine desire? Was desire always curiosity and a fear of the unknown, a hologram, for which read, death? Maybe he was misunderstanding John ...

ENTER

The remainder of this disc is the scientific paper detailing the chemical structure of Receptamine, and its synthesis; plus its fascinating crystal morphology. Also some examples of texts we received; showing the similarity in diction to parts of the Pyramid Texts at Saqqara. The sheer bulk of messages blew our minds. Those guys out there were talking so fast, I knew they were high on something, and it wasn't Lebanese gold, as if they'd been waiting for years and millions of more years to SPEAK.

We unravelled many interesting fragments, and a couple of these "meta-texts" are recorded on the final disc. The mass of other material is stored elsewhere in my private data bank, which you will also be told how to find, on the final disc. Most of it is useless cosmic GODSIP, qua, GOSSIP. Who is fucking who. Nepthys at it again with Anubis, her son. Tabloid stuff. (Not tablets to be eaten!) The Greeks were right about the so-called gods; obsessed with sex! See you later. Stay Tuned! Especially to the R-Field Frequency, and it's NOT all coming from a boat stuck in the North Sea called Radio Aten! At least I don't think so. Maybe that IS where I am after all. Over and out!

Matthew scrolled through the remaining pages, amazed that the scientific data again appeared authentic; the crystal's morphology was accurate and seemed quite feasible.

He switched off the computer, feeling battered. Looking out of the window, he saw Georgina in the garden, walking round and round in a circle on the lawn. He wanted so much to talk to someone about his breakthrough into the discs, to tell *someone*, if only to help him to evaluate his own response to them, to discover what his real feelings were. The discs could be a hoax; his reason still told him so. Georgina seemed the only person he could talk to, safely, but as he watched her, she seemed to be in some kind of semi-hypnotised state, or deeply upset about something; still walking round and round in a circle, watching her feet. Matthew thought she would cut a circle into the grass if she carried on long enough, and he knew it would be the perfect circle Giotto had always dreamt of painting on a canvas with one sweep of a brush.

But the more he watched her, the more he sensed he dare not trust *her* either. If she knew he had discovered the codes, being in love with Cindy, she might let Cindy know, even if she didn't want to. Too much of a risk. Just at that moment he saw Cindy come to the edge of the lawn and watch Georgina, who carried on walking in her circle. He couldn't hear what Cindy said to her, but he could see she was annoyed. She stood with her hands on her hips, as if waiting for a disobedient child or dog to come to heel. She walked slowly closer to the circle being traced by Georgina and spoke again, but Georgina continued, head down, to ignore her. The next time round Cindy slapped her so hard across the head, Matthew actually jumped back several inches himself. He even put his hand to his face. Georgina crumpled into a heap on the grass and looked quite dead. Cindy seemed to scold her and then walked off, leaving her dishevelled and lacking geometry, a rough sketch for a discarded flower. After a few minutes she stirred, lifted herself up, restored the petals of her dress into shape and headed for the kitchen door ... obviously shaken.

Matthew went eagerly down to join her. She was already filling the kettle; he said he was thirsty too. She was running her fingers through her hair flamboyantly, as if to make it more fluffed out and attractive, but Matthew guessed she was making sure her head still resembled its former shape.

'How's it going? Any breakthroughs?' she asked calmly.

'Not really. But I'm making some progress with my own work; and you?'

'A very frustrating day. I'm working on my photographic book and just don't know which ones to use. Selection is the hardest process of all. How do you know which one is the most effective? One day I choose ten images, and they seem right. The next day I choose ten different ones, to say exactly the same thing. I prefer sculpture. You work on a single, tangible object. Oh the comfort of *things!* It's right or not right, I can lay my hands on it at the end of the day, like a preacher laying his hands on some howling infant's head, or some crippled old crone in a wheelchair, and say, "In the name of God" and all that. And it becomes real, significant. Suffused with the approval of the spiritual father. An object!'

'So why frustrate yourself with a book of photographs?'

'You know very well. I'm in love with the sculptor who made all those objects, and I'm in love with Akhenaten, who ordered them to be made. If only he would order*me* to make sculptures for him! We poor women all need a tall, stone-faced father figure to think of when we are alone at night in our beds, unable to sleep, masturbating. I need to be ordered to create, by some cold, mean-faced god. But you know all about that. Listen ...' and she poured out two cups of tea as she was talking. ' ... I'm worried about Cindy. She's behaving suspiciously. She's reached one of her crisis points, one of the cusps; the Cusp Catastrophe theory of René Thom – in all natural systems there is never a linear growth, but a sudden, dramatic, dissipative twist. The cusp. Just when you think it's predictable – going round and round in a nice circle – phut! It strikes off for no reason at all; a ticket to ride a tangent to hell. Cindy is about to do something irrational. You're failing her in the work, not finding the codes. Be careful, she's very predictable when you know that her life goes in cycles. Or maybe she's discovered she needs you sexually. She hates that! She's at her most dangerous when she feels she needs someone sexually, having started to actually enjoy it, to need it, miss it, desire it, be victim of it. At that point she strikes out. Phut! Or maybe she thinks you've made a breakthrough into John's work and are keeping it secret. She hinted that the other day. Calm before the storm. Cusp approaching. She's building up to something. Watch her carefully. Never say I didn't warn you! Remember! I warned you! Don't forget! I must work'. Kissing him on the cheek, she quietly left.

Matthew sipped his tea. He was feeling fed up, fed up of being warned about Cindy. He felt like going to her, tying her up again and beating the fuck out of her. The image made him painfully frustrated, but he decided to make an experiment, to see just how "receptive" she really was to mental waves!

In the drawing room, he considered the best message to send. John had said an image had to be formulated strongly in the mind, so he started by trying to visualise Cindy at her desk, working. He couldn't see her at her desk, so he concentrated on the image of her lying on her bed, looking at the ceiling, thinking, waiting, planning her next move. This image seemed to be the correct one. So he started by trying to tell her he wanted to make love to her and for some minutes he imagined her coming down into the drawing room, eager to seduce him. He saw her in exotic outfits and was surprised they'd all been worn by heroines in silent movies. It amazed him how much his sexual fantasies, too, were associated with the cinema. It was very obvious really, but he was surprised it had taken Cindy to make him conscious of it. However, despite the vivid imagery of his fantasies, she didn't materialise.

He then tried communicating the image of himself in Georgina's studio making love to her instead, but he found it so hard to see himself "taking" Georgina, so he had to abandon this scenario also. He knew it was dangerous, but he then tried to communicate the image of himself in front of the computer listening to John's "voice" and he even allowed himself to think of the word, *Hypnotamine*. He started to feel the strange tingling at the back of his neck, and was certain she was receiving the message and would soon come down and he'd swear he'd never heard of Hypnotamine. But again nothing happened.

He then imagined Cindy seducing the little blonde from the cinema, and he found this so sexy he touched himself. He willed the image hard in her direction, convinced he could get her to come to him, but again nothing happened. He saw Cindy laying the girl on her bed and pulling up her skirt and kissing her between her slim thighs, and he started to want to really masturbate, but he held back, determined to carry on with the experiment. He drew the heavy velvet curtains and the room became completely dark. Closing his eyes he tried to think of another image but it took him some time to eradicate the image of the two girls making love.

Then suddenly, quite involuntarily, images flooded into his mind from his last dream ... and he felt suddenly quite cold. The memory of the dream disturbed him, and he felt miserable. He tried to detach the image of Meritaten, happy and smiling at him, lying down for him to make love to her. He starts to struggle with himself, knowing he's being watched and battling with his confusion, the image dissolves ... the woman holding the crystal phallus is going towards Meritaten, and he knows he must protect his bride, so he rushes and lies down on top of her. At that moment, to his horror, the woman in scarlet snaps her fingers and some of the priests grab him roughly. Meritaten is struggling underneath him and he's convinced he will suffocate her ... until the woman seems to take him ... opening him up with her fingers ...

... lying on the sofa, caressing himself in the darkness, he doesn't hear the door open, and doesn't notice the soft steps on the carpet as she approaches him. He's so entirely possessed by the dream, that he offers no resistance as she takes him into her mouth. Within the space of his dream it seems no contradiction that she is simultaneously hovering over him with the penis and raping him and at the same time a mouth is caressing his penis. The pleasure is so profound that he opens himself wide and he thinks he's experiencing sex as a woman and this idea seems to take him another dimension away from his normal consciousness ... and he finds himself holding back slightly to prolong the pleasure, poised within seconds of orgasm ... as she thrusts into him ...

... but suddenly he touches the threshold of pain. He's being gripped so hard he knows he can't stop himself. He sees a thousand images flash through his mind, like single frames in a film, each one recalled from his dreams as if he's reliving the whole of his life of dreams at the moment of death, a montage of subliminal erotic images, in which various women serve him and play out his fantasies for him

... until he can't hold back ...

He held her head hard, pressing her onto his penis, which remained hard for some time as she gently enjoyed the taste of his semen. The images of the "film" were paramount in his mind as he caressed her and she moaned with pleasure, having caused him, so she thought, to ejaculate ... until finally, utterly spent, he relaxed into sleep, on the floor, next to the sofa, her head resting gently on his genitals. When he eventually came to, it took him a few moments to adjust to the darkness. He put an arm around her and moved down to kiss her. He was feeling excited, pleased with himself. *I did it. I brought her down, I'm understanding what it's all about!*

He opened his eyes, eager to tell her of his experiment to bring her down, and its spectacular success, when, utterly astonished and confused, he saw Georgina looking up at him, her beautiful eyes smiling like a young lioness which has just caught her first wildebeest ... albeit, a lame one. He drew her close to him and kissed her gently on the neck. He wanted to say many things to her, but he couldn't. They stayed close to each other, the silence saying more than any words. But eventually she drew away from him and whispered, 'I must go back to my work now. It calls. I'll see you later. But I feel happy now. Now, we're quits!'

He returned to his room, not knowing what to do. He tried to forget the girls by thinking of his work, but he couldn't concentrate. He still preferred to tell himself that John's work was a hoax, which was good really, because he was free to go back to Cambridge; he'd enjoyed some paradoxical sexual adventures with two charming but crazy girls, but next time he'd not get so much out of his depth.

There was a knock on the door. He paused some time before calling out, weakly, 'Come in, Cindy!' They were surely out to kill him! Despite wearing almost nothing she was looking a glitzy glittering million dollars. His heart missed a beat as she uncoiled onto the bed next to him, murmuring seductively. 'I've been really tired all day ... really spaced out and frustrated! I tried to send you a message to come to me in my room and fuck me but you didn't receive the message. Or you're a selfish, proud, arrogant mean bastard. But I just had a nap and I had a very strange dream. Do you want me to tell you about it?'

He nodded apprehensively ...

'It won't hurt?' she asked mischievously.

'Well, if you ask that, then I know the answer is *yes*, it will hurt. But that's all the more reason for you to tell me, surely?'

'True enough!' she said, as casually as possible. 'But don't you remember, I once warned you, that men don't want to hear women's sexual fantasies? Women stopped telling the truth about them five thousand years ago, when they started to lose out to the patriarchy, and learnt the necessity to lie and veil the truth. If I tell you the truth now, you'll hold it against me and take advantage of me, so why should I entrust you with so much secret knowledge? Why take the risk?'

'Because you want to and you don't care either way. So I say, don't trust me. I don't trust you. Why should you trust me? Just tell me. If I hate you afterwards I'll screw you viciously and then try and forget it and say I love you anyway!' he drawled, trying to impersonate some small-time down-town Chicago crook. She winced.

'But how mature you're becoming, Matthew, how comforting! Well, here goes then. My dream. You're sure?'

'Sure – baby!'

'Curse you! Don't be flippant. I'm being quite serious. I dreamt I wanted to have a baby with Georgina. I wanted to give her MY baby ... I was very frustrated because I couldn't. Then I discovered you were planning to betray me. You'd unravelled the code and were intending, like John, to escape with the data. I decided nevertheless that you would have to be the father. I thought you didn't want to make love to Georgina, as you hadn't so far and I was afraid of letting you make love to me because you were plotting to betray me. So I persuaded the little girl from the cinema to come back again. Her name is June, by the way; sweet, isn't it? You're not bored?'

'No! It's just like one of my dreams. Carry on! Mine always end in disaster, sexually, I hope yours does!' He was trying desperately to remember the dream he'd been having before, which must have been at the same time as Cindy, but he couldn't follow the two lines of thought at the same time and there didn't seem to be any obvious parallels anyway.

She smiled patronisingly, but continued. 'I manage to corrupt her in the dream with seductive promises, sweets, cream cakes and the like. I make love to her to the point where she's so frustrated because she needs a man, she's about to faint with frustration. I tie her up to the metal bed ends. You've taken a drug and I lead you into the room. You're semi-conscious and I caress you until you gain consciousness and see this beautiful little girl who is begging you to make love to her. Of course you do so, straight in. God, men are so lucky. And then – you asked me to tell you the truth?'

'Yes!'

'I kill you both, with a knife. I then ... ugh ... I feel sick remembering it. I cut her open, like a huge fruit and take out the semen and go to Georgina and make love to her and impregnate her with it. And I had such an orgasm. Gosh. It was terrible fun. Who said I was frigid? And then I dressed up as a man and waited as the baby grew inside her. I managed to call up my spirits and told them what consciousness to put into the child. All in the dream, of course! And I waited and waited for it to be born and somehow she was going to give birth in a church. Fancy me dreaming of a church! Well, at the instant the child was going to be born, I woke up ... in a terrible sweat, and ironically enough, still awfully frustrated. And I've no idea why I've told you, because I normally don't reveal my dreams to anyone. So there. You ought to feel privileged. At least you were the father of the child, even if I had to kill you!'

'Really? I die, the baby doesn't get born, and you even tried to make sure the mind of the child belonged to someone else?'

'Yes. Even that too. I'm sorry! But the mind belongs to someone else anyway, I've told you often enough. I warned you we women are dangerous. Sometimes I wonder if we allow ourselves to be possessed by men, so we can ignore our own dreams. By the way, I've been thinking. It would be so much easier if you *did* make love to Georgina, on your own, one of these days. I give you permission. I won't mind. So why don't you and let's get it over and done with and we can all be lovers together, instead of only occasionally and so self-consciously together but not together. For her sake, anyway. For real. I don't mind being behind the half-silvered mirror, the voyeur watching you!'

'Er ... very kind of you. Maybe I will, yes, maybe. It did cross my mind once or twice and yes, it *would* be fair!'

She swung her legs off the edge of the bed and stood next to it, like the Vargas screen vamp that she was, and raised her sequined skirt. Onto the screen, some words flashed into his mind from some childhood dream, or Mickey Spillane novel, made into the worst of bad B-movies. *It was not only the lips on her pretty face that were crimson with lipstick!* And despite resenting her more bitterly now than ever before, and knowing he ought to escape her ... except the magic theatre was like that, wasn't it, John? ... he gave in. He no longer seemed to have a choice about such things, sex object that he had become. He would let her caress him and see what happened. Ctenophoric bitch! But another thought, trying to be charitable, was something like ... *this temple's identification with the invisible, translucent and yet erect phallus of Osiris has gone too far ...*

∇

THIRTEEN

"The elements of the single infinitely variable (poetic) THEME are to be found in certain ancient poetic myths, which though manipulated to conform with each epoch of religious change – yet remain constant in general outline. The Theme, briefly, is the antique story, which falls into thirteen chapters and an epilogue, of the birth, life, death and resurrection of the God of the waxing year: the central chapters concern the God's losing battle with the God of the waning year for love of the capricious and all-powerful Threefold Goddess, their Mother, bride and layer-out. The poet identifies himself with the God of the waxing year and his Muse with the Goddess: the rival is his blood brother, his other self, his weird. All true poetry celebrates some incident or scene in this very ancient story, and the three main characters are so much a part of our racial inheritance that they not only assert themselves in poetry but recur on occasions of emotional stress in the form of dreams, paranoic visions and delusions."

"The White Goddess"
Robert Graves

ℜ

'There's bad news. One of John's colleagues has been killed. I just got news from the Mad Woman.' Cindy gave Georgina two faxes from the machine in the attic:

> *A scientist was killed when a cold fusion experiment in a private laboratory exploded. The month-old experiment involved "heavy water" which is slightly radioactive, and a metal electrode, said Dean Maxwell, a spokesman for the SRI International lab in Menlo Park, California.*
>
> *"We didn't think this was particularly dangerous. We don't have an explanation for why it exploded," Maxwell said. The blast sent glass, metal and other material flying but caused no fire. None of the victims was wearing protective clothing. Fusion is the force that powers the stars and hydrogen bombs through merging atoms. Scientists have been searching for ways to harness it as a cheap source of abundant energy.*

On the second sheet with a photograph:

'Discredited theory' behind fatal blast.

Andrew Riley, 34, (above) a British scientist killed by an explosion at a US laboratory while working on cold fusion - energy generated at room temperature - was researching a 'discredited' theory, Dr. Alan Gibson, a leading nuclear physicist, said yesterday. "I was unaware any research was still going on, except in India."

'Very bad news! Is it all collapsing? John talked about him. Wasn't he trying to repeat the experiments done by Stanley Pons and Martin Fleishmann, but they used crystals of mica, studying the phonons that carried the energy? No?'

'Kind of ... it's all to do with matter behaving differently inside crystals; energy can travel immense distances when focused or trapped inside crystal lattices, especially lasers, which is what Matthew presumably knows all about, unless he's a fool. Unless he discovered it by accident and we're completely wasting our time with him. Or he's taking us for a ride. Wouldn't that be a joke?'

'Maybe he's the next to go?' Georgina said wistfully.

'Yes, it's bad news ...' Cindy continued to reflect. 'I wish to hell John would get in touch. I've figured out where he might have gone by the way; if he's not dead, that is.'

'Really?'

'Yes, it's so damn obvious we must be crackers. He's in Egypt, trying to infiltrate the scheme to open the chamber door in the new passageway in the Cheops pyramid. He knows what's in there and is probably trying to sabotage the whole thing.'

'Why?'

'He once told me he knows the library of Imhotep is in there; together with the tomb of Chephren. Maybe he doesn't want it opened. He'd like to get there first, somehow, and they probably warned him, like they warned me; that's not merely the opening of the ultimate Udjat Eye of Horus, my dear, golden-eyed falcon of the dawn, although it *is*on one level, of course. It's the apocalypse, quietly creeping up on us. Out of the corner of the eye. And how many initiates are amongst us who could cope with that?'

Georgina sighed. 'Not many!'

'Maybe they'll deal with it quietly. Send Amenhotep down here to keep an eye on things. Imhotep's double. No doubt he's probably looking for a pretty sexy body to be born into at this present moment! In the Egyptian style of course!'

Georgina looked alarmed. 'Really?' She could feel a tingling sensation down her back, right down to the curve at the top of her bottom; almost as if someone was licking it. Had her clitoris moved again?

After sleeping off his sexual excesses, Matthew woke up feeling spaced out, as John would say, but decided to carry on exposing himself to John's alchemy. He returned to the black room and decoded the next disc with the code:

KAIBIT ASAR:

DISC ELEVEN

Welcome to the Frequency-realms of the Kaibit or Shadow, symbolised by the hieroglyph for a mushroom: 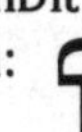
but described by scientific experts,
(using the faculty of reason), as "an umbrella". Would the most enlightened race of mystics, artists and technologists ever to rule the earth and inner and outer space, symbolise their most cherished image of the invisible eternal Double of the Self, as an umbrella? An ideal umbrella for toads, I'd say, like Alice, with her holographic looking glass; she knew a lot about toadstools and hubble-bubble hookah pipes! Those sublime ravings of a fulfilled paedophile; I envy him! Lover of that delicate sketchwork between the slender thighs, that virginal beauty; and a fine mathematician to boot ...

In a very illuminating review of Mircea Eliade's *Shamanism*, in the *Psychedelic Review*Number 7, 1966, Anita Kohsen wrote:

"A first definition is; 'Shamanism = technique of Ecstasy'. Shamans have nothing to do with sacrifices – their principal function is that of 'psychopomps'. They are experts and guides in the world of cosmic dreams. They are intermediaries between the living and

the dead – a mediator between 'cosmic regions'. The shaman knows the mystery of the BREAKTHROUGH IN PLANE – this communication being essential in the cosmology of peoples with shamanic cults.

The universe is conceived as having three levels, sky, earth, underworld – connected by a central axis, (Cosmic pole, tree, etc.) which passes through an 'opening' or a 'hole'; it is through this hole that the soul of the shaman in ECSTASY can fly up or down in the course of his celestial or infernal journey. In the beginning, 'centre' or site of a possible BREAKTHROUGH IN PLANE was applied to any sacred space, that is, any space that had been the scene of a hierophany, and so manifested realities (or forces, figures etc.) that were not of our world, that came from elsewhere and primarily from the sky."

Read these words carefully – shamans; the ravings of witch doctors! My copse is such a place, where I am still breaking through. Are you, or am I, Tiresias? This question becomes less important as subject fuses with object, and these distinctions are broken-through – in plane. Are you ready to go through? If not, beware of the shaman, dressed as a beautiful woman (and the post-modem bisexual, phallic variety, with air-brushed pubic hair, in touch with a network of crones; see disc fourteen), seducing you with her masks. Eating SOMA triggered the ecstatic journey into other dimensions of space/time. We must open up that hole in the rational shell in which we are imprisoned.

However, we now come to the most unpalatable (sic – see below) aspect of this whole story, the most absurd, the most unacceptable – no wonder the Greater Mysteries HAD to be kept so secret. What, in our wholly communion, is drunk by us, vampires that we are? Mere blood? Nothing less good than Pauillac 1947? With a pinch of best opium? If only!!

In Wasson's SOMA: *Divine Mushroom of Immortality*, he describes, in the *Rig Veda*, TWO rituals. The first: the mushrooms are dried, mixed with water, and eaten, inducing "ecstasy" – Greek derivation, *Ek Stasis*: I stand out of myself. Outstanding stuff! The second is when the *really* extraordinary effects are produced. You won't want to believe this, so read carefully. The Lesser and Greater mysteries are the Isis/Osiris hologram penis/phallus in two aspects. The first ritual involves drinking the divine "plant-juice", the semen-soma of Osiris himself, and the mushroom/penis symbolism is obvious. No umbrellas, please!

But the higher visionary state is induced by drinking the URINE of someone who has eaten the drug. I know, I know, this is hard to accept, but stay close with me as we enter the world of multiple shadows and doubles – the world of magic, the real world! This is easily explained; drugs in the mushroom are chemically transformed while passing through the body and the resulting chemical compounds in the urine are much stronger and their effects are quite different; this is an experimentally verifiable fact. How did they discover this? A dumb fucking question that is! I'll give a d-f answer. Could it be sex?

No wonder the Christians hate it so much!

Further weird facts. The mushroom is the favourite food of the reindeer living in the shaman's territories, an animal he kills and eats whenever he can. Reindeer love the mushrooms and eat them greedily. Please note the French word for kite is *cerfs-volant;* flying reindeer? Hence, of course, *high as a kite.* Or is a kite a flying umbrella? Reindeer meat of an animal killed immediately after eating mushrooms is highly intoxicating. The shamans always drank the fluids, the blood, the milk, and – unexpectedly, the urine. Why? In the High Arctic, there was often nothing much else to drink. In the dead of winter, with temperatures 50 below, every drop of liquid was frozen solid. The symbol of shamanism in Siberia was always a sha/man/woman with reindeer horns on the head. Satan and his horns? The goddess Hathor? And her lithe young priestesses ... uurrhmmm ... barely twelve if they were a day ... am I horny at the thought!

From the *Rig Veda*, we know the priests and priestesses MADE LOVE (ugh) and ate the mushrooms. Inevitably, pagan perverts that they are, it was discovered that drinking urine produced the true state-of-the-art, astral, out-of-body experiences. To become TRULY initiated you had to drink the urine of your chosen priestess. After you! Mind you, I have put lips to many a beautiful chalice! After you Lewis, into the holoporn looking-glass world ... pornos graphos indeed.

To recapitulate, to *re-head* myself: the Aryans swept down from Russia with esoteric shamanic knowledge, which spread to India, Persia, and of course, Egypt. Initiates wrote the *Rig Veda*, those ecstatic and beautiful hymns in praise of God, Life, and Soma: the Avesta: and the cultic writings of Egypt, embodied in the encoded story of Isis and Osiris.

Sir J Gardner Wilkinson, FRS (A Scholar!) in *"Manners and Customs of the Ancient Egyptians"* wrote:

"Of the Mysteries and festivals in honour of Osiris, we can obtain little or no information from ancient authors. The former were too sacred to be divulged; and few of the Greeks and other strangers were admitted even into those of the lesser order. They were divided into the Greater and Lesser mysteries; and before admission into the former, it was necessary that the initiated should have passed through all the gradations of the latter. But to merit this great honour, much was expected of the candidate, and many even of the priesthood were unable to attain it. It was from these that the mysteries of ELEUSIS were borrowed. For, though celebrated in honour of Osiris, they applied more immediately to ISIS, and to the grief she felt for the loss of her consort Osiris."

Different parts of the dismembered body of Osiris were supposed to be "buried" in different places throughout Egypt, where his Rites were enacted. Oh yes? Not only! The truth is that certain mushrooms were found in these places: slender dung mushrooms like those that Robert Graves said opened up the world of mythology to his unsuspecting mind! Let us give full rein my deer (or should it be vein?) to our imaginations.

Imagine the scene. You're sitting on the edge of the Nile – or at home, watching a documentary film, much easier! A violent thunder storm, a savage lightning flash, a jagged laser beam of energy from the sky, strikes into the ground, missing you by thirteen inches. An hour or so later, urgent erect little penises sprout up, always under the feet of the tree as if nourished by its roots. Eat them and you're off: the risen: up up and away around the outer rim of the Milky Way. You see infinity in a grain of sand. The little penis rises to its full height in a mere two days, then grows a huge womb-vagina (or umbrella?) over its head, then wilts, wimps and fades away in three more days. NO PLANT anywhere in the world grows and dies so quickly. It has no roots. No flower. No apparent seeds. Is it a plant or a man? It is the god, Osiris.

Wilkinson: *"I have observed that Memphis, Busiris, Taposiris, and other towns also claimed the honour of being the burial places of Osiris. The name of Busiris implies the burial place of Osiris; and the same interpretation is given to TAPOSIRIS, though the word is not Egyptian as the former, but Greek."*

A place called TAP-OSIRIS?

In his chapter dealing with plants and herbs, we find references to an unidentified herb, next to Hashish, namely: *"Absinthium Maerinum or Seriphium Artemisia Judaica?"* Note the question mark! BUT!! *"The BEST was found at TAP-OSIRIS in Egypt; a bunch of this flower, or plant, according to Pliny, was carried at the fête of ISIS".*

Primroses? Umbrellas? These guys built the pyramids and knew the size of the circumference of the earth, could measure the precession of the Equinoxes, to the day and the minute of an arc, and knew that the INVISIBLE Black Dwarf Star took fifty years to go round its twin, Sirius, the dog star of Isis. TAP-OSIRIS = is the mushroom used in the Isis/Osiris rites. We have an unknown plant associated with Isis, growing above the ground, below which some part of the dismembered body of Osiris is buried, whose botanical name is not known. Answer? The body of the god Osiris was fragmented (dispersed by the gods) and buried by them, to grow later, in sacred places, as MUSHROOMS, the Golden Food of the gods, the elixir of immortality. Gold is light materialised. The lightning ...

The *Book of the Dead*, Chapter 148, known as the "Chapter of Osiris". Sir Wallis Budge says of it:

"The recital of this chapter by the dead person enabled him to supply himself with animal food, milk, cream, etc., and gave the names of the SEVEN DIVINE COWS and their bull, the figures of which are drawn in the vignette. In the text the deceased addresses the seven cows, or the 'Gods' they represent. It is ordered that the deceased recite this chapter ONLY when QUITE ALONE."

Budge describes the image in the vignette: *"A hall within which, on the left, the deceased stands before two tables of offerings bearing libation, water and LOTUS FLOWERS, hands raised adoring 'Osiris, the lord of Eternity, the prince, the lord of everlastingness, the great God.'"*

What? Hold it a minute. I'm a lonely man but not an archaeologist or philosopher – There are SEVEN DIVINE Cows sitting in front of SEVEN tables on which are placed "sepulchral meals", the sacred plants and herbs they are just about to eat? A cow can only be described as DIVINE – if it embodies, contains God, or the essence of God. The means of giving God. Of turning you on, man! *"Next are ranged SEVEN Cows, each one couchant before a table of offerings, bearing a libation vase and a lotus-flower?"* ??? Please notice the inevitable question mark. He does NOT know what the plant is so guesses the lotus. Who, tell me, eats a lotus, produces urine which is then drunk, and goes round the universe as a wave of consciousness? HERE are the NAMES of the Seven Cows, according to Budge's translation; er, Trance-Lotion!? Very smoothing over ...

1. The dwelling of the Kas of the Lord of the Universe. 2. Orbit, the raising of the God. 3. The Hidden One dwelling in her place. 4. The divine noble one of the North(?) (his question mark) 5. The greatly beloved, Red of Hair. 6. The Consort of Life. 7. Her Name prevailed in her Dwelling."

Wow! Kerwow! Some Kows! Red of hair indeed? Amanita muscaria is even now known everywhere as Red-cap! The Seven Cows are representations of the goddess Isis in her form of Hathor, with seven coded names of ???? Will the scientists inform us (FRS and PhD) that the names are seven breeds of cow? My arse! (Please note 'my arse' is a code name for my anal-logical-anal-centric software program.) Even allowing for the naive translations, they are NOT the names of cows. They are "divine" cows that know how to jump over the moon and run away with spoons as high as kites, as high as reindeer who have eaten Amanita muscaria. They are seven secret names of mushrooms, and the mushrooms were EATEN by the cows, and then their URINE contained the most powerful consciousness-expanding drugs known to man! The drugs went through the bodies of the so-called "divine" cows and probably into the milk as well, but certainly into their urine and became – Receptamine – Aviamine – and a number of other drugs that WE HAVE NOW successfully synthesised! Amen.

You want proof? By coincidence, take the name HAT-HOR, meaning "The House of Horus". It is described as follows: *"Horus the falcon flies into her mouth at dawn and comes out later at the other end."* Just a passing observation for the Egyptologists to muse upon, under their rational-umbrellas. In one end, out the other. Mushrooms becoming meat, milk and urine, as well as becoming dung on which the mushrooms grow. Lotuses, my arse!

It cost me a lot of money to take a professional mycologist to Egypt to collect the mushrooms from all the named places *and* buy some cows. Yup! Bought and slaughtered some fourteen (twice seven) cows. When I do something I do it; feed them, collect the urine, milk and blood samples and bring them back for research. Not financed by the Min of AgrOKultur either. Back here, Cindy and I worked hard on analysing the trance-lotions.

But the subject is vast, and we needed help. Cindy soon learnt to send "help us" messages while under the influence of Receptamine, and received some of the data we needed. We've now got the chemical composition of the essential psycho-pharmacology of the secret rites of Isis, the central mysteries of the Ancient Egyptians. Pure and clean and perfect in their elegant simplicity.

And especially the most sacred one of all, that which provokes the "soul" (the falcon-headed Ba-Bird of those en-LIGHT-ened Egyptians), to separate off from its earthly discardable Hathor body and fly into other time-space worlds. Unfortunately the COST of all these experiments has destroyed me financially. The cost of further synthesis of "Aviamine" as we called this amazing drug, was astronomical; forgive the pun! We made only a small amount; we used one dose on a willing collaborator and we're not sure where he went. The remains of his body are buried in the garden under a tree. It's not easy to admit these things, believe me. But do you expect us to do our tests on MICE? Think of all those mice-souls we might have liberated into those sacred dimensions! Think what they might have done, reincarnating themselves into unsuspecting humans. Mini-mice-men. Animal farms of mice and men!

On the remainder of this disc you will discover a Bankers Order for cash donations, plus 120 pages describing the synthesis of the luscious "Aviamine", the drug that induces astral projection, as THEY called it. On the final pages you'll discover also the beautiful pyramidine form of the crystals which we synthesised. WHENCE the structure of the pyramids in Egypt. They were copied from these crystals!! THAT is the end of that mystery, befogging we humans over the millennia.

The compound is fascinating, combining several elements from the structure of Mescalin with some from LSD 25 and several totally unexpected configurations linking it all together.

We could never have dreamt up this chemical, my virtual reality girl and I, it is so elegant.

The crystallography seemed authentic. Matthew really didn't know what to believe. He took disc thirteen, ignoring number twelve for the time being. The disc contained a lot more quotes, mostly about wave dynamics, holistic theories of cosmo-genesis, holographic theories of the structure of the universe and the brain – showing the holographic link between the two – one silver-mirrored half-image of the other – and some tracts of abuse attacking flaws in the ailing quantum theories about wave radiation. One newspaper quote, scanned into the computer, caught his eye:

> ***SHADOW MATTER;*** *Tokyo, 31 August 1986. Perhaps the most startling possible scientific discovery brought up at the press-conference was a new theory, now gaining acceptance, that space has 9 rather than 3 spacial dimensions. According to the SCIENCE 85 article, the theory is part of a physics revolution that could succeed eventually in describing the basic "units of matter and energy in the universe from which everything else is made, and perhaps even the minute components of space and time." More surprising still, all the matter in the universe would be duplicated by invisible matter; we may soon discover invisible planets, stars, and galaxies made of SHADOW MATTER.*

Matthew was sensing a quickening in his perception of time passing; feeling perhaps that time was fast running out. He didn't know why, perhaps his mind was scrolling too fast. But he was eager to find where John might reveal how to decode the fourteenth and final disc ...

"... Just as Osiris had been killed by SET, then and not till then, could the love of ISIS and his longing for her, regenerate him. By her power and grace, he was restored to life, not any longer a brute beast, but as man, redeemed from his own animal passions, a living spirit like unto the gods."

How can I dare to continue with this "initiation" until there is proof of your suitability? This labyrinth, these translucent crystal lattices you are skidding along, on your back, arms flapping like seal fins, is dangerous territory. Like polymorphous sexuality, so many simultaneous points of view that your sanity is at stake.

You must be correctly erected, structured. Formatted! So! A number of simple tasks to perform before I take the risk and make you purely Virtual, by exposing you to Disc Fourteen. You must go to another copse, on a Ley-line from my own copse. Find it on the map! There, you will see an elm tree with a hole in it. Cindy knows nothing about this copse, as far as I know, or the tree or the hole in it, hopefully still cemented over. The other was a front! My holographic double!

You'll find a number of chemicals in small PHI-als for the later phases of the experiments; for synthesising the drugs to change the TRachyon-gravitational-magnetic bias of the brain. Using these compounds I made up some time ago will save you months of work. There's also a small notebook with further coded figures, and TWO Aviamine doses (all that remain) hidden somewhere else, traceable only when you read the last and final disc, which of course will lead you to another seven discs elsewhere, containing the most ineFFable of all knowledge. More about that later! Those discs were revealed/written directly by THEM! And seven more and seven more; ad infinitum ad scrotum.

By the way, the drug Aviamine can be ingested simply by contact with any mucous membrane. Very powerful! Especially the penis or vagina. Those priests and priestesses had an exotic sex life. The phallus boggles! In that tree, there's a CLUE, inviting a last step in this spiritual ascent, this Mont Analogue, leading to the final CODE for the final disc. In the end is my beginning. In my end is someone else's beginning! Obviously, you'll discover this code only if I've initiated you well. So, hide or destroy the discs you've already been exposed to. See you soon. Amen, over and, or, way out, man! Or should I say, see you in, on, around, within and without Disc Number Fourteen, the perfectly translucent Phallus of Osiris. Come to think of it. "High as a reindeer" doesn't sound so good either, does it?

END

Matthew was annoyed. Now another copse, another tree! No doubt John would say, "What, only two systems of waves radiating out from two sacred stelae dropped into a Nilotic pool? Holographic, man!"

Matthew decided to take a walk round the garden to think

things over. John's ideas were getting crazier with every disc, but if what he was saying was true, the work was serious, important, subversive – dangerous in the wrong hands as Cindy had hinted a couple of times – clearly worth keeping secret. There was no avoiding going to the new copse. Suddenly he realised he was going round and round in circles, following Georgina's footsteps!

Then, from nowhere, he connected to another image, an etching by Gustave Doré or Van Gogh, or both, of a small group of inmates taking their afternoon walk in an Asylum garden, forced by high walls AND the fearfulness of their thinking (same thing), to tramp round in a small circle inside the garden, the centripetal force of the insane world spinning about them, elsewhere, but compressing their bodies and minds into this aimless circling – an infertile uroboric convolution. Matthew wondered if the physical and psychic knot got smaller or larger, the more you walked in it.

He sat down next to his favourite tree. Was it the one under whose stand the "friend" was buried, the first victim? He didn't want to believe that story, but to make doubly sure, he hesitantly examined the ground around the tree; but there were no obvious signs of disturbance. Although *now* - he could feel him there, true enough.

No! John was having him on! It was all a hoax; he should accept this whole story in the same spirit as he had read implausible detective stories as a kid, with a torch under the sheets at night, ignoring most of the "plot" but "screwing" the satin and lace clad girls with the best of them, in self-directed, self-acted, self-projected technicolour dreams. Why was he allowing himself to be so fooled?

Georgina appeared and sat down next to him. 'I saw you from the window. We must stop meeting like this!' she said with a provocative smile. She seemed even more beautiful than he remembered, her eyes especially, glowing with an inner radiance that seemed to be sucking him away from himself; into that wretched pool; and he felt weak with longing for her. Not a physical longing – if only it was as easy as that. A longing for the unreachable, the forbidden, a longing to hold her so tightly against him that she became inseparable from him, part of him, and his, forever, unable to go away. Could she be his future and at the same time, incapable of betrayal? She looked away, he was looking at her so painfully, his eyes without focus, haunted with a longing for her magic to make him rise again and desire beauty rather than fear it ... with death its touching reward ...

'Would you like to join me in a daring adventure?' he asked suddenly, impulsively, his voice cracking in the middle of the question. 'A kind of lousy detective story, you know the kind?'

Relieved to escape his painful stare, she became immediately excited, face flushed like a schoolgirl being offered sweets for just one *look* behind the bushes. 'Why yes, of course. You mean like Raymond Chandler or The Saint. Gosh! Excuse the expression, but I always wanted to be a private dick! But you know you can ask anything of me now!'

'Good! Let's go immediately. We might NOT have too much time ... ' he said, emotionally. He dragged her quickly to the car as if they were already on the run.

'*Pierrot le fou, Pierrot le fou*. Where on earth are we going?' Georgina asked after a few minutes, now somewhat nervously, seeing the serious look on his face.

'Pierrot who?'

'A film. Forget it! Where to?'

'To the library, to look at some maps and find another copse. I have a meeting there with destiny. Capital D!'

'Good heavens. Who, or what, is that? D is for Death!'

'Who knows! We may be meeting someone or something; don't ask questions yet, I can't answer them. We may find nothing. But I'll tell you a secret if you promise in your heart of hearts not to tell Cindy, otherwise it could mean the death of me. Seriously!'

'Of course, you can trust me, can't you?'

He said yes, but not convincingly, not able to tell her he was beyond caring, he simply had to tell someone, and best it was her. 'I cracked the code for John's discs. The two main codes. I worked it all out and I've read most of the discs. Quite amazing stuff, IF it's not all a hoax. Too amazing for words!'

'Yes, we thought you had. Cindy said you were behaving differently, exuding a macho confidence you didn't have before. Especially sexually. She was sure you'd started *really talking* to John, as she put it. She was upset you were being secretive but said you would tell her when the time was right. For *you*. Meanwhile she's being patient!'

His heart sank. The bitch! Cindy knew all along! He might have guessed. He had fooled no-one but himself. But it didn't matter. It was probably a cheap detective story. Just read on.

They drove in silence. In the library he found the right map, and saw an old path joining the first copse to another, two miles away. He drew a rough map on some paper. Drove on. They saw the new copse from the road. As they walked towards it, he said, 'Yes, it was quite irrational not telling Cindy, but John asked me not to and I felt he had good reasons to warn me. But if she already knows, it might be safer to tell her. But first of all, let's see what's in the tree, shall we?'

But at the edge of the copse, beech trees arranged formally, he stopped her and asked her aggressively, 'Now tell me the truth. Who ELSE was John working with, in Cornwall especially? Only Cindy? Unlikely! Who else was involved?'

She was alarmed by his aggressive tone. 'I don't know anyone. Honestly. He had connections with America, but that was probably drug smuggling, though he swore he gave that up years ago, despite the telegrams. Maybe some people at a laboratory where he got stuff done near London. That's all I know.'

'Which laboratory? You must know!'

'You must be joking, Matthew, they were far too clever. You know Cindy, she reveals nothing if she doesn't want to. She's not like us, too nice for words, unable to keep a secret!'

He pulled a face, a wry smile, a wistful glance at the sky – she was right, alas. 'What do you think then, honestly? Is John dead or alive?'

She seemed unhappy and looked away. 'I feel certain he is dead, otherwise Cindy wouldn't have suggested you come here, and let you into so many of their secrets. Normally she wouldn't have breathed a word of this to anyone. Your so-called *coincidences*, I told you all along, fooled us into thinking you were already part of it all. That's how you got in – through the back door, as the bishop said to the actress!' She was trying to sound jolly.

'Okay, come with me!' he said abruptly. He wanted action now, not words. He took the chisel and hammer from the car and she followed him to the dead elm tree, which he found easily. It had not been struck by lightning, which seemed ominous, but there was an almost identical, cemented-over hole in it. He piled up some stones to get closer, and started chipping away at the cement. Suddenly he heard a screech from a nearby tree, a female kestrel letting them know she disapproved of their presence in the copse. 'She must have a nest up there,' he said, ruefully. Maybe it was the same copse in another place and the same time, but he was someone else and Georgina was a dream; an Egyptian princess of a cruel beauty he'd never dared to imagine. She was gazing up, hoping to see the young falcons, but she couldn't see a nest. Well hidden. Her eyes were jewels ... her lashes the veins in a dead humming bird's wings ... her dark hair, the colour and promise of absence ... why did he feel so close to her, when he knew that she kept her distance from him as accurately as the Black Dwarf twin star circled Sirius?

Matthew chipped at the concrete, gently eased it out and let it drop. He slithered his hand gingerly into the hole as if he was expecting his fingers to be severed by a single bite or his body to be dragged into it – whole. 'Here they are!' He handed her a small blue hard-backed notebook, with a green spine, then a number of small blue bottles. Reaching more deeply, he brought out a box ...

'Good heavens, your falcon box!' exclaimed Georgina. He climbed down carefully, holding the box in his hand and then sat down, before placing it on the grass between them.

'No, it's not my falcon box. Look carefully. It has different patterns on it. Plants not birds and it's slightly larger. It's only holographically similar!' He smiled cynically. 'What do you think it contains?'

She gazed at it with obvious consternation on her beautiful face. 'I daren't think! Another mummified falcon?'

'Maybe. That would be too ironic. No. I don't think so. It's the Holy Grail. *Le Sang Real*, as John called it on the last disc – of Horus Christ. The symbol of the Ultimate Eucharist, or at least, variations on Graves's theme, or dream! Ah well, maybe it contains love letters from John to Cindy, which he never dared to send, and I'll look an idiot, won't I?'

Her face clouded. 'Don't worry, it won't be that! There was no love lost between those two, a Chemical-Wedding alright, but it never produced gold. Love is cruel, as you well know, once the surprise at the coincidences recede! But they kept their work mostly hidden from me, of course. Please open it!'

Taking off the lid, they saw a long thin object wrapped in soiled white bandages. He lifted it from the box and felt the bandages gently. 'Here. Hold it. Tell me what you think it is.'

She rolled it gently in her fingers, feeling the object inside the bandages as if she was testing some mozzarella cheese to see if it was fresh. Blushing suddenly, she turned abruptly away from him, embarrassed, before replacing the object back in the box. 'Oh God! I think I know. Fragment fourteen, the part that Isis never found and made by magic, as I was asked to do by Cindy? But the ... *real* ... thing?'

'As I always feared and expected,' he said, ominously, and they sat looking at each other, not knowing what to say, while the falcon screeched at them from the nearby tree.

'And the bottles?' she asked, as innocently as possible.

'Just a few chemical constituents, chemical triggers, tickets to ride to a movie house where the film goes on ecstatically forever. If I'm not mistaken, some call it heaven.'

On the way back to the car Georgina was crying but she didn't let him see it. He was too busy thinking to notice.

Half way back, Georgina asked to go to town, for some painting materials. After a visit to the art shop they went for tea and cream cakes in their café. She asked him if he would tell Cindy he'd found the code and was *listening* to John.

'Let's say, like the Angel Gabriel – I'll play it by ear. Especially after today's discovery. You know John was killed by Cindy? You'll say I'm crazy, but I started to have those awful dreams and became obsessed with the image of his head, buried, so to speak, in a tree, and I found that tree in the first copse. Where on earth did I get the clue from? I presumed someone sent me the message. But there was nothing in that tree at first, except some bandages. Since then someone's been playing games with me. I tried to laugh it off. But John's work, if it is authentic, is no joke. It could be earth-shattering. Or should I say, John and Cindy's work. He insists she contributed as much to the project as him. I still don't understand why I still doubt, unless of course it's just that my classical attitude to science is so deeply ingrained ... can't see the wood for the ... '

'Maybe!'

' ... but you know, this has been a shattering and illuminating experience, even if it *is* a hoax, *especially* if it is a hoax; it's shown me a strange thing about myself. I've always been so pedantic in my defence of rationality because, and this is not easy to say, because I've always been much, much closer to giving it up than I realised. Doubts had obviously been lurking nearer and nearer the surface. Maybe I was already about to abandon that conviction. Perhaps this is what my whole crisis has been about, my whole problem with my diamonds. I'd hoped they might help me to make the breakthrough, to start believing in the possibility of other paradigms. I was clinging to classical prejudices like so many scientists, from a deep fear of giving up the predictable, controllable, knowable world, the prevailing paradigm. Now I see you can't win. The unconscious will get you in the end, one way or another. I'm more a victim of my own split self, than I am of Cindy and John. Maybe it's time for me to go home. I've been opened up and seen that you*can* let go, and survive. It's scary at first, I admit, but maybe I did let go. I've started to discover a new way of looking at things, making new connections. Now I can go back to my experiment and start it over again. Instead of looking for a rational explanation I'll be looking for exactly the opposite. I'll push it towards proving that something is unprovable, unverifiable, unless we accept a new model of the material and immaterial universe, locked in holographic symbiosis, as John would say; confront the inevitability of a new ghostly paradigm of things!'

'I like that word paradigm. Strange how we like words, isn't it. I love the word plangent, too, and spume. They resonate with something inside me I can never focus on. Spume ... I'm sure it would be like being pregnant. God forbid! Go on!'

'Of course, I can't prove anything about Cindy or John but I always felt they were malevolent. It seems irrelevant now. John quotes Schwaller de Lubicz; there's nothing more malevolent than rationalism! Or as John himself would say;*Le male volant!* Or le male voleur? Meanwhile, I have to work out the code for disc fourteen. Maybe then I'll decide if I can take this work of theirs forward, perhaps with Cindy. However, I take today's discovery as a, er ... *set-back*. It was what I feared. I imagined the worst all along and now it has come true. Or do I cause things to happen because I dream them?'

'Perhaps you did make it happen. But Cindy *does* know what we're thinking. She can read our thoughts, especially when we're under stress, like shamans and priestesses and oracles of olden days. Maybe she played a joke on you. Perhaps John is alive and well or just went mad and got locked up in a lunatic asylum, trying to make sense of her. He often said he might be going round and round in circles all the time getting nowhere, except up his own arse! Maybe she got that object for fun, from a friend working in a morgue, to tease you because you get so serious about everything. She adores mocking men. Her biggest sexual trip is to make love with a man and a woman and make the man impotent, so that she can finish the girl off herself and prove that woman's sexuality is superior to man's, not requiring penetration. The trouble is the men get so turned on by the situation they exceed themselves and finish them both off! I warned you she was unpredictable from the start. But If you think you're the only one who suffers, forget it!'

She suggested they visit the antique shop. Looking in the window, she suddenly let out a piercing falcon-like shriek. 'Look. Two boxes exactly like the one in the tree! One larger, one smaller!'

Matthew grabbed her and dragged her inside and asked if he could see the two boxes. The three boxes obviously fitted inside each other. 'There should be a third. Do you have the other one?'

'It was sold a few days ago.'

'Can you remember who bought it?' he asked eagerly.

'A young woman in a black leather jacket. She bought all three, because I wouldn't split them, but then only took one of them. She told me I could keep the others for good luck!'

Matthew looked hard at Georgina and she shrugged her shoulders. 'Can you describe her?' she asked.

'She was young, a student. She was working in the cinema and said she wanted to take a present home for her mother.'

Matthew bought the boxes and they walked in silence to the car. On the way home Georgina asked him to stop, so he pulled into a lay-by. She took his arms and made him put them around her and suddenly, she kissed him passionately. He was so deep in thought, it took him a few seconds to realise what was happening and make a show of responding. But he was thinking, thinking, and faking it.

She knew it and when she pulled away there were tears in her eyes. 'I'm very worried, Matthew. Why don't we go away now? Let's just run to the station and jump on the first train; I don't care! Cindy will be alright. She'd leave the house eventually and we could pick up our things later. She's capable of anything and I know she's planning something for this evening, she told me earlier. "Tonight we will all become initiates, and the forces might even be out of my control!" Words to that effect. Mind you, she is always over-dramatic with me, enjoys putting the fear of God into me. Even when she cooks an omelette she says it's made with Death Cap mushrooms just to liven me up a bit and I always believe her. But if that girl from the cinema is part of the plot, anything might be happening, surely?'

'Yes! But the story of the girl could be true. Maybe Cindy had made an arrangement to see her off or they met by accident. Imagine Cindy's surprise to see that box. Another coincidence! She couldn't resist such an opportunity for a joke. Or she sent her into the shop to buy it. Perhaps in the end, John's final disc will probably say something like – "You have 90% of the information but you need the last 10% which is in Cindy's head!" If she's planning something for tonight maybe it's to show me she knows everything. She just can't come into my room and say, "Okay, you bastard, you did it. Tell me the code. Let's be partners!" She has to work in this devious, indirect, theatrical way, as you know. Her involuted sexual trip. To say she distrusts normal intercourse must be the understatement of all time. But I'll make you a deal. I promise, if I feel as you do after tonight, if she reveals nothing useful, I *will* leave tomorrow morning – with you, if you still want to come! I have the discs, the codes, the notebook, some chemicals, it might be enough to work on. But maybe she'll tell me tonight it's all been a hoax, that she invented everything, the whole story is nothing more a new kind of novel in which I have become one of the characters. 90% is fiction and 10% reality! Me! Or one fourteenth to be precise!'

He was rambling and she knew it, knew he was desperately in love with Cindy and *knew* he didn't want to leave. For a start he was suggesting the fourteenth part was*real*, and that was just plain dumb! Matthew started the car and Georgina started to laugh. 'Yes, Matthew, you're right, that's how she works. It's just a surrealist novel with an *'objet trouvée'* as the principal character, or an *'objet perdue et retrouvée!'*

He tried to laugh it off. 'Tonight we'll know the truth. Maybe she's reached the final scene of her novel and tonight we're writing it together, the three of us. I hope she changes my name in the credits. I'd hate my scientific colleagues to know what I've been up to on my *brief trip away*, becoming a translucent member in a secret club, a hieroglyphic character in search of a Ms. Rosetta Stone's magical authority.'

'Goodness me, a what? At last you really are talking in riddles! *Our* kind of language!' she said, fondly, kissing him on the cheek.

Cindy was in the kitchen, apparently drunk, gazing into a brandy-glass full of red wine, like a crystal ball in which either the future was proving elusive, or a little green genie was trapped and being ravished by a scarlet woman. 'Help me finish the wine. It's the best bottle I could find. I hope you had a fruitful time ... ' Slurred and unenthusiastic.

Georgina told her they'd bought two Chinese lacquered

boxes, ' ... just like Matthew's falcon box.'

'Oh really? How nice; all we need is two more dead falcons. Can you shoot, Matthew? Are you good with a gun? Pow!'

Matthew ignored the remark, but it hurt. He was watching her carefully to see if she gave anything away; but even drunk, she was as inscrutable as ever. 'I tried to send you a message to buy some brandy, but it seems my telepathic powers are failing me – you buy falcon boxes instead. I had such a passionate desire to drink brandy. Maybe someone was sending the message to me! Imagine if some shithead advertising agency found out how to transmit telepathic messages, we'd all go mad wanting to buy everything, wanting to consume the entire material world. Ten years and it will happen. No escape from insane salesmen invading our minds. It will be the end of consciousness and civilisation as we know it. Amen!'

Georgina poured wine for herself and Matthew, choosing two exquisitely cut Victorian crystal glasses. In the kitchen they usually used glasses given free with petrol vouchers. Cindy stood up shakily, saying she needed a pee, but they were not to go away. She had an important question for Matthew.

Georgina whispered, 'Any sign, when we mentioned the boxes?'

'I couldn't tell. Why is she drunk do you think?'

'God knows! Maybe the blonde rejected her for a Hell's Angel!'

They waited in silence. Cindy returned, face white and mask-like, unsteady on her feet but still capable of an extravagant cinematic flourish, sexily smoothing the wrinkles out of the material clinging to her bottom, determined to make the entrance worthy of her reputation. 'Uhmmm ... ' she said, pressing her hand in her crotch. She sat down and gazed again into the glass, eyes simultaneously focused on the red dwarf stars Rigel and Aldebaran. Had they become that close? 'I've an important question, Matthew,' she purred, without looking up. 'Tell me if you believe it is possible to materialise an object – or a person, in certain circumstances – by magical means. Not like those awful fake Victorian spiritualists. I believe it *is* possible and we have to confront the problem with the new techniques available to us. I believe creation *must* be going on all the time, as I have told you before. Continuous cosmo-genesis. I think anything can be created that is called for, so to speak, from some higher consciousness, but only something that can be imagined and is within certain limits. Anyway. Do you believe materialisation from nothing is possible on any level at all? The virgin can give birth?' She had been peering into her glass all the time she spoke.

'No!' said Matthew coldly. 'You know I can't believe such a thing. But I *will* make one hesitant reservation. It is impossible within the limits of our present consciousness, in the classical space-time paradigm we perceive at the present time. If that consciousness was to change radically, it might become at least imaginable, but it seems unlikely. Consciousness must be materially based like everything else, but there are doubts about that, mainly because it appears to us to be such a different kind of experience to anything objective or material. But I suppose *pure thought* could conceivably be a different kind of ... of ... '

Cindy beamed triumphantly. 'Fantastic! You said *no* but *yes*. You qualified it. You have at last started to doubt! First step to believing a new paradigm. Okay! I want to do such an experiment and I need your help. Are you prepared to work on it with me?'

It was the very last thing he probably wanted to do at that moment but he presumed he had little choice, unless he was to pack his bags and leave. 'It depends on what you want to materialise!'

'I'm not sure yet. You see, I was reading today about the actress Florence Farr and her lover, the poet and Buddhist monk, Allan Bennett, who claim they materialised Mercury, and I don't mean a blob of shining silver metal that zoomed around a crucible. He had wings on his feet! I trust her totally; she wrote a book; *Egyptian Magic*. They were members of the Golden Dawn, with Yeats and Mathers and Crowley, and took magic very seriously, and didn't just write about it. They practised rituals. They *did* it!'

They sipped their wine in silence, each of them brooding

separate, disjointed thoughts, a dismembered communion.

'To materialise what?' Matthew said, eventually, quite aggressively.

'I don't know what to try for ... maybe we should leave that till the last minute. But I have to know you're sympathetic to the idea and will bring your mind to bear on it seriously. If I think you believe it is totally silly, then it won't work. If you think, somewhere in the back of your mind, that it might be possible, that I might achieve it, then I'm prepared to have a go. I want to prove to you, Matthew, that the world of matter is secondary, under the control of a higher consciousness. Then we can work together in the future. I am very sad we don't really share things, *now*, on the levels we should.'

Matthew assumed this referred to his working with John's discs in secret. He felt the words welling up in his throat to tell her he'd made the breakthrough, to tell her that tomorrow he would share everything with her, but he remembered John's warnings. Cautiously, he reiterated, 'It will depend on what you want us to materialise. I'm happy to try it, but if you want to materialise a neutron bomb, I'd prefer not to be present in case you succeed!'

Cindy laughed and Georgina laughed too, although it was rather a nervous laugh, but then they started suggesting a list of nonsensical things Cindy might try to materialise, until they were giggling like teenagers, hysterically, Cindy obviously really drunk, and Georgina resonating. The imagined objects became so ridiculous or obscene or both, Matthew interrupted – and Cindy reluctantly agreed to 'cut dead the conversation', so they could go to their rooms and get ready for the evening ahead. Georgina said she would prepare a light supper 'before the evening's without-pantie-mime!' and the two girls laughed even more deliriously all the way up the stairs, stripping bits of clothing off each other as they climbed, a terrible misrepresentation of the now familiar involute, in reverse, the film going backwards through the projector, the holographic holomovement known as *Nude ascending a Staircase*.

The tantalising image faded from view and Matthew poured himself another glass of wine and put his feet up on the table. What would Cindy materialise? The final disc to show him she had known everything every step of the way? Or John himself? Hadn't he been foolish to assume she and John were not still working together? He went up to his room to reconsider the situation, and prepare for the evening ahead.

Taking the notebook he'd found in the tree, on the first page he found the usual quotations! *It is always darkest before the dawn!* and *Man is in love and loves what vanishes, what more is there to say.* Thanks, John! The rest of the book consisted of numbers, computer readouts with obscure references to a number of discs Matthew knew nothing about. He was hoping to see a reference to the code for the fourteenth disc, at least a clue, but he found nothing. He knew it was going to be difficult to make this last mental quantum jump, and he decided to let it come to him, perhaps in a dream, or at least sideways, as if by chance. He felt pretty sure it would occur to him during the evening, revealed to him by Cindy. She would materialise the code? Could a code be material? Or the fourteenth disc's whereabouts and perhaps the code? The perfect holographic double? Wishful thinking.

He decided he ought to rest for a while. Before one of Cindy's performances in the magic theatre, her physical and psychic strip-teases, he always felt deeply tired just thinking about it. He lay on the bed and closed his eyes. He was almost dozing when he heard quiet footsteps coming towards his door. Georgina whispered, 'Matthew, are you sleeping?' He didn't want to talk to anyone at the moment, so took the cue from her question and said nothing. Let her think he was asleep. He heard her creep away as surreptitiously as she had come. He closed his eyes and waited in trepidation for irrational images, schizoid dreams, but he dozed peacefully and his dreams were as "spume that plays upon a ghostly paradigm of things" – over the surface and yet under it – and did not wake him.

Georgina crept into John's room and locked the door quietly behind her, switched on the computer, formatted an empty disc, and started a letter to Matthew to warn him, prefacing it ... *We two girls were just two sirens who drifted out of our depth!* But she didn't like that and erased it. After a couple more false starts she decided not to preface it at all, and launched into the text, revealing a few things she thought he must know if he was to save himself (from falling too much in love with Cindy) and giving him a few hints to help him unravel the two primal images of the key hologram, interfering in a blur; the scene described in his copse, and her scene in John's copse ... with John.

By the time Matthew woke up, it was already dusk. He lay in the half-light with an image of a collision in his mind, his green laser burning its way through the flawed lattice of his diamond – the two layers of the flawed lattice had become two images of the copse at night, illuminated by the same green light, with two men standing there – one image seemed to be from the point of view of John, as he imagined him, the other, from the point of view of an old blind man, probably Tiresias, as he had imagined him, with long hair ... but the images soon faded.

In his sleep he had crystallised out a new idea. He started scribbling furiously. Strange parallels; the dance of the flesh and the dance of the electrons! He worked for only ten minutes, but at the end of it, he was empty, shattered, but excited. He checked through the figures and gazed at the final page of geometry with the same kind of awe he had felt for the symmetry and harmony of Cindy's modes, sculpted in light with her magic hands, and probably the chiaroscuro of her bottom too, half lit and turning, left cheek and right cheek, confused and merged concave and convex as the light went into shadow – measured and celebrated – photographed in his mind holographically in three dimensions, her bottom now suggesting the two hemispheres of the brain, the two halves of the Double-Helix, the convoluted shapes of an in- and en-folding universe ... if only he could grasp the perfect meaning of the moment of un-enfolding ... God! It was amazing. Yes. There it was. Symmetry and balance again. At last he felt really relaxed. Surely he'd done it? Found the problem in his work ... he lay back and twiddled his toes.

But his falcon caught his eye, lying peacefully in its miniature lacquered tomb, patiently waiting for a new chance to rise on the thermals of cosmic consciousness, and he spoke to it. 'Well, my little pilgrim, have I discovered the secret that lies *between*, between those carbon atoms, the living and the dead? Have I seen the light at last? Let me tell you then. One is inert because it is relatively stable, the other is alive, that is, capable of being part of an active living system, because it is relatively *un*stable, because it has to draw energy continuously from outside itself, which causes it to vibrate unpredictably and it is vibrating at a different frequency from all the similar, inert atoms, even of its own kind. But it is feasible that this frequency causes resonance with another field which has so far not been discovered. The living carbon atom has a unique frequency which I had not assumed, which I have now discovered. But it was entirely by *chance* ... something I'd not planned for or thought of. In fact, a case of perfect coincidence. The frequency of my laser beam, once refracted through the diamond, was forced to vibrate at the same identical frequency! So there were two identical systems vibrating, the laser *and* the carbon isotopes that were organic. Two identical moiré patterns, but slightly out of phase, hovering over each other. Inside my diamond I seemed to have created surplus energy, and contradicted the second law of thermodynamics – because once there were two identical vibrations, off key, one reflected back as if through a half-silvered mirror, this disturbed a balance and there was resonance with an invisible energy field which must always be there though we haven't yet revealed it, intellectually or mathematically. My diamond sucked in energy from somewhere else; a new field. Cold fusion. The Sutherland Field of Potential Energy! It could be a miraculous discovery!'

He paused, then said to himself quietly. 'Something like that, or I'm going totally crackers!' He wrote a short letter to the girls, in case he decided to leave quickly the following morning ...

There was a hesitant knock on his door. Almost inaudible. He opened it cautiously, to find Georgina standing there, looking sullen. No doubt about it, there was fear, hanging headless and erotic, on the air.

'Awake now, not dead? Good! Getting ready?'

'Working! I just had an startling illumination. A shooting star just flew into the room and crashed into my bed!'

'You call that work? You've been working at such a time? Good heavens. You haven't forgotten, have you?*Remember* what you promised. Tomorrow we escape, if Miss Rosetta Stone becomes too heavy.'

'Promise!'

She gave him a quick kiss on the cheek, a little too sensuously, and left him. 'See you later. On the SET!'

He checked his notebook again – yes, it looked good – there was a factor he could give a flexible value to. Again he whispered to his falcon. 'Tomorrow I can leave with Georgina. Too good to be true, but can I trust her? No, alas, not even her, though I'd love to. But I don't need them any more, do I? I've made the first real breakthrough in plane with my own work and nothing can stop me finishing it. Tomorrow I'll leave anyway, if George comes or not, and of course she won't – but it *is* nice she thinks she might. You understand? It's called – women!'

He worked for another thirteen or fourteen minutes and came to the conclusion there was a further factor in the pyramid shape of his diamonds that had added a second element of instability to the spin of the radioactive electrons and he made notes to create further experiments to investigate this unexpected property. It would be necessary to have one of the diamonds re-cut, to see if the outside shape of the crystal altered the internal events, which he now suspected. Maybe even drill a hole into one from one side, to create a channel where air or energy can escape, or enter. Like a shaft ...

He looked at his watch. It was seven o'clock. There was time before the proposed light supper, *Scene One* of the evening's entertainment. He was feeling a strange urge to go outside ... and he walked around the garden until he felt the need to sit under his tree. Nestling into its curved protective bole, he was surprised to feel how much he was actually looking forward to the evening's mystery play, now, suddenly, without any of his previous misgivings, despite the fact he was certain Cindy was going the whole way, whatever that might mean, to bring her series of dramatic evenings to a climax, a perverse finality derived from knowing he had entered the mental space of John's discs. He didn't bother to ask how she knew such things any more. He took John's word for it ...

But this evening they would be equals, he decided, because she would be too self-conscious to sustain another of her elaborate illusions effectively. He felt calm because he felt there was nothing she could say or do that would fool him. Not any longer, because he was no longer looking for any kind of truth! He could forget everything except the fact that it was a game, with people for whom sex couldn't be anything except a game, as if on a screen, but nevertheless ... why not? He would make sure, tonight, that he enjoyed himself fully, without reservation, without inhibition. They'd done what they set out to do, destroyed any sense of romance he might have been clinging to. He finally relaxed, completely, excited just thinking about nothing in particular, just knowing he was *there*. Tonight he was going the whole way too, and he intended to surprise Cindy as much as she had surprised him, so often before. But as the sun descended out of sight he felt a slight pang of sorrow at its loss ...

He returned to his room and worked more on his data. He was almost reluctant to leave it. A short while later, Georgina called them to supper. He heard Cindy shout raucously from her room to start without her, she'd decide later if she wanted to eat or not – but adding they were *not* to go into the lounge until she allowed them. It was to be a surprise.

Matthew sat down and murmured patronisingly that he had heard it all before. Georgina smiled, trying to appear impressed by his confidence. He told her he'd finally made a brilliant observation about his diamond. This time, he assured her enthusiastically, it could be the ultimate insight, and he tried to explain the mechanism of electron spin. She listened carefully for a while, making the occasional comment, an image seemed 'pretty' or 'suggested a three dimensional holographic sculpture', but then she interrupted, 'No doubt Cindy will understand it more than I do. She's grasped these spatial and mathematical things so much better than me, as you know.'

She became even more impatient as he talked on and on, and she interrupted again, forcefully taking the conversation off on a tangent towards *her* favourite subject, Cindy. Finally Matthew got the message, and felt deflated, saddened. She hadn't been listening. She was mesmerised as usual by the absence of Cindy. His presence was irrelevant and there was nothing he could do with words, or with actions, to distract her from her torment, the continuous, inescapable heartache that was her frustrated desire for Cindy, her longing for the impossible, it seemed to him ... not forgetting the inevitability of Cindy's betrayal.

Suddenly, an unexpected image seized him, like one of Georgina's own paintings, an image of a vast bedcover the size of a field, which she had embroidered from thousands of small images. It had taken her a whole lifetime to make and now she was sitting on a corner of it looking very old and grey and tired. The patchwork pattern on the cover was a huge portrait of Cindy. On it she was beautiful and voluptuous and scintillated with colour, and from her hair and body, long cascades of millions of small colours spread out in all directions, like scarves. Georgina was utterly miserable, waiting for Cindy to come to see the patchwork quilt, finally finished. But Cindy was away somewhere, no doubt with another girl and Matthew was feeling so sorry for Georgina he almost felt tears welling up in his eyes. The split between the two girls mirrored a split inside himself ... and he felt helpless too. In each small patch, like on a hologram portraying betrayal, you could imagine all of Cindy's betrayals ...

'What have you put in the wine?' he asked, and she shook her head from side to side slowly. She could see he was feeling emotional, apparently not so confident after all. Clearly he was as scared as she was of Cindy's latest threat!

'Nothing. It's just a supermarket plonk in a plastic bottle we siphoned into an old *Entre deux Mers* bottle to make you think it was something special. Are you drunk already?' she asked incredulously, noticing his hands were shaking.

'Of course not. I just wondered,' he said, somewhat limply. They carried on eating in silence, Cindy's imminent dance hovering over them, eclipsing any potential for clarity in their thoughts.

Before Georgina was able to finish her supper, she was summoned by Cindy. As she was leaving, she kissed Matthew lightly on the cheek and said, '*Remember*, you promised. If it all falls apart, tomorrow you'll go back to Cambridge, and I'll come too?'

'Don't worry. I'll remember,' he said, affectionately. He sat sipping his wine. Thinking. Trying not to worry. Why did he get so involved with these damn silly charades the girls always wanted to play? He must remind himself how silly he would appear to his colleagues if only they could see him now. Still, the theatrics were not without their sensual moments ...

Then he remembered what Georgina had said to him earlier – warning that finding the last code would be dangerous. Something like, 'Don't say I didn't warn you. Don't forget!' There was something disclocated in the way she said it. It had not rung true, although very little rang true with either of the girls at the moment. He must not take them seriously.

But what about the *object* found in the tree? He still hadn't felt like looking at it, to confirm what it was, a humorous gesture he didn't really consider funny. Who put it there? Cindy or John? It was clearly connected to the code he was looking for. John had used that *object* as a code once and would enjoy using it twice – holographically speaking. Now it was real, so the new code must be related to the old one. He thought about this for a while, but his thinking arrived nowhere, lacking objectivity. Cindy said her dance would be about materialising something – maybe the fourteenth disc, the phallus, or was that too obvious? Was he being tricked into thinking the obvious? Or to doubt the obvious?

But come to think of it, *sic*, hadn't John said, 'You will need to be intact to work out the final code'? John had meant mentally. Or had he? John had said the final disc was about memory, and reversing it, to thinking forwards, to prophecy, divination. To leaving the body and going there. As light? He pondered this image for a while. To be able to remember everything, would be to become mentally intact. To overcome forgetting, loss, to forget loss. To find the disc, to un-disc-lose the past. The ultimate victory?

But then he wondered if John had mentioned memory at all. It was Georgina who had insisted he must not forget what *she* had said. It was all so confusing. He returned to the object in question. What could he now expect to be done with the phallus of Osiris? He knew what Cindy would do with it. Use it in as many ways as she could, and he saw an image of her in action, fucking the little blonde. He savoured that image for a while ...

What was it he had to remember? He took the notebook again, read the first page of quotes carefully, but got nothing from them. He flicked through the pages. It was all mathematical data and a few codes. Turning to the back page, to his surprise he found what looked like hieroglyphics. Then he realised it was words, fragmented into computerised dots, but written backwards. He went quickly to the bathroom and looked at the page in the mirror and he could read it perfectly.

"Welcome to the Looking Glass Mirror! The final disc? Am I not the Ultimate Gambler? You see, being perhaps just about to die – I asked myself if I wanted my work to survive. Being a mere holographic image on a screen, one half of me said yes, the other said no. So I decided to give it a fifty-fifty chance of surviving. You remember the copies of the discs I told you were in the tree? Did you find them? It doesn't matter. They were blanks. NOW. Disc Number One, the one you so cleverly decoded. I asked you to burn it. Did you? I guessed you might: you might not. Under the same circumstances I would NOT have burned it. I would have hidden it. Osiris the hidden one! Disc Number One, my friend, is also Disc Number Fourteen. The one code opens the introduction; the second, the final ultimate code, just around the meta-spherical corner, opens the final eighty pages. The most important eighty pages written by man. I do hope you didn't destroy it? Bye for now."

Matthew's spine was on fire. 'My God, that was close,' he said out loud. He rushed upstairs and took down the holographic photograph of the painting hanging on the black wall. The disc was still hidden in the frame, in the corner, behind the colonnade of columns. Shit! Now all he needed was the code! He'd never been so excited in his life. If Madonna had walked into the room from *her* virtual reality program, and asked to be fucked, he'd have said, 'Not now! I've work to do. Go fuck Cindy!' Talk about plagiarism being two post-modern lesbians sucking each other ... !

So he was close; he had to open his mind, become receptive. He closed his eyes, saying to himself, *Meritaten, tell me the code. As you seem to have recognised me, remembered me ... you who have remembered me from some former life, tell me the code.* He knew he was losing his mind, he was on the verge of madness, but he had his finger on the master switch. That was madness, believing it! He remembered the game he played with his father and the train, which his father said was always going to Russia for some unknown reason. Maybe it was just heading towards the north pole. He tried to remember the scene in the woods, the crushed, blurred blue-green bluebells, like crystals, the tree he had climbed, the holes in the tree. He wanted to weep. He had seen someone murdered, he was sure of that. Oh the times he'd masturbated thinking of that scene, imagining himself under her as she thrust down, her bottom twitching and bloodied. Sacrifice. The blood on bandages and torn white pants. Only faintly could he remember it, as if reflected from an old broken mirror on which the silvering had come loose ... dreamt it time and time again ... dreams come true in films ... but to escape it, had he become a rationalist instead?

Slowly, heavily, he felt himself falling, going down on his knees. Yes, it was time he told himself the truth, he was going mad. He'd put up a brave front, but he was finally, at last, losing his reason, going mad because he had broken the rules, gone too far. He suddenly wanted to die. Fall, let go, let loose, give in, float and fall fall fall down into the sea ... yes, it was the sea that was awaiting him. Verfallenheit! The oceanic, deep blue-green ocean like Meritaten's eyes. He had to go away or if he went forward, to her, siren that she was, he would be surrendering forever ...

Yes, he wanted Cindy to murder him. Always had. That was her attraction. The hope of murder. The preying mantis.

And his mind slipped a fraction off centre, and left a void, and he remembered a word, or was it an image: a word-image ... "a-void-dance" ... and he knew Cindy's dance would be that, just that; tonight it would be crystalline, hard, cold even, calculating, tempting him, tantalising him with Georgina ... who said he must remember they would escape tomorrow, *if* ... then suddenly, he got it! He didn't know where from. But he SAW a word. It just flashed into his mind. He'd seen her standing ...

... in his mind he'd seen Cindy in her own dream. He saw her wearing the crystal phallus, jutting out as she had been described. But were they not fighting for it now, for what joined and yet separated? Just as with seeing, as he was seeing now, he was separated from what he saw, detached at the moment he saw her attached. That perhaps was the irony of love! So he re-versed it. He saw himself wearing the phallus. Had he become Cindy now? Osiris was intact again, yes, it was so obvious; the final rite was to do with materialising the last *fragment* by magic, and she, Isis, copulating with Osiris. For this act, Osiris had to be whole. Intact. What was another word for intact? He felt the strange tingling on the back of his neck, the sign he was in tune with whoever was sending the messages ...

Switching on the computer in a fury of emotion, he put Disc One (Hologram Fourteen) into the disc drive, and typed the keys:

R E M E M B E R E D

An image flickered on the screen and Matthew's heart missed several beats before he could focus on the words ...

DISC FOURTEEN

The Hidden One: The R-Field Frequency of the KHU

Dear Initiand. Welcome and congratulations. Now you have an immediate task. The code-word is REMEMBERED. Your immediate task is, FORGET the code word. Big joke? When you've eaten as many mushrooms as I have, you start to see humour in everything. So, you can't forget 'remembered'. Tough luck. THAT, my friend, is uninitiated consciousness, or rational knowledge. Knowing poised on a ledge. To jump or not to jump. You can't forget the remembered. Can't remember what you forget. Or forgot. Between forgEt and forgOt is the creation of time. Between E and O. E is mc^2, O, the Story of O. Life is love is the perfect holographic interface within sado-masochism. That is the Great Mystery. The interface between forget and forgot. Sadism and masochism. Power and submission. Call it knowledge. Or love. The knife-edge. Love is crucified by knowledge and begets betrayal. Love is not knowing and knowing is not love. You need learn nothing more. That was the ultimate lesson. Make love and avoid the dismemberment of Osiris, which is knowledge. You have no-one to make love to? Then proceed. Scroll, and be damned. Welcome DANCE of DEATH known as ... A-VOID-DANCE.

Δ

Matthew was *very* pleased with himself. For a moment he thought there was a fault with the fan on the computer, but it was himself purring. At last he was thinking forwards. Was it Meritaten who had given him the code? It didn't matter, he wanted to think so, and that's what mattered. He scrolled eagerly to the next page:

Ψ

The Lamentations of Isis are over.
What was lost has been found.
Osiris is Re-member-ed.

PROLOG:

Let us not forget, but let us re-member Holograms. You know how they work. Do I need to re-mind you? No? Okay. I'll be generous. I'll remind you. In the forgetting of the remembered, you forgot the primal dream. You are free. But a hologram is an image printed in two dimensions that appears in three dimensions. BUT, it has another much more interesting feature. If you cut off a small corner and look at it with laser light, you will see the WHOLE picture. Each small fragment contains the whole. Simple! The brain has two hemispheres, right and left: like the two eyes of Horus: each time we see an image it is processed through two different systems which refract, one on the other. It is the DIFFERENCE between these two images that creates an in-depth multi-dimensional meaning in the images in our mind. Our perception of the hovering three-dimensional time/space/universe is possible because we accept thinking holographically. But there are many dimensions we have become blind to seeing because we select and settle for only three.

Desire is the force that WHOLEDS everything together, a hologram of the primal scene, which IS Cosmo-genesis. The universe is structured holographically and the brain's method of functioning creatively MUST PARALLEL the way the Universe functions. The stuff of mind is the stuff of the creative purpose of the universe. Polymorphously perverse sexual multi-imaging. In the beginning was the Word? No! The image. On this disc is the proof of the above – in the beginning was John and in the apocalypse was John, the holograph is John and the laser is God. This is the written proof, not written by me, but revealed through me by Amenhotep, Grand Seer of the Temple and House of Akhenaten with whom I have identified too much perhaps, to the point of attempting soon to materialise him in the flesh. Or he, me!

But before we venture on this little trip, allow me a few quotes. I have to bring the total to 1001!

"Timothy Leary says he is in trouble with the world because – through the use of mind-expanding drugs – he has unlocked the 'ROSETTA STONE of consciousness' and threatened the established order." Newsweek. May 9th, 1966.

Astronomer James Jeans: *"The universe is more like a great thought than a great machine."*

Physicist David Bohm: *"Matter may be the OTHER for us; we move it and it moves us. So isn't it possible there is a kind of intelligence in matter that is immanent, which makes it possible for matter to RESPOND? We are the OTHER for matter, and therefore when it is confronted by us it will be something different. WE know this happens through physical contact, but it may happen mentally as well. That is what I have proposed; that inanimate matter is an abstraction which we get when we leave OUT the potential for life.*

But there may be more than a potential; there may a sort of LIVING ENERGY in matter that manifests in us in certain ways which it doesn't in a piece of rock. We are fundamentally ignorant about matter....And we ARE matter after all! One could say, rather, that evolution results from the creative movement of matter, which is infused with INTELLIGENCE."

Priest, George Macdonald: *"He rose, and looking out of the window, saw something white against the beech tree. It was North Wind. She was holding by one hand to the top branch. 'Are you ready, Diamond?' she asked. 'Yes,' answered diamond, 'quite ready.'"*

As was written in The Book of the Non-Dead, the *Book of Coming Forth by Day*. They knew all along and are still trying to re-mind us of it if we listen. Our Book of the Dead is their *Book of Coming Forth by Day* ... the difference speaks volumes! We are dead. Death in life. They are still alive. Life in death. Amen.

ώ

Matthew was sweating. The words by David Bohm referred almost exactly to the question he was now asking in his experiment with his diamonds. Eagerly, he scrolled on ...

"Journey to the End of the Universe". A scientific paper by T.B. Pawlicki given at a recent International Symposium of Physicists, hacks, bums, drug smugglers, mystics, crystallographers:

"Now brain research reveals that the left cerebral hemisphere organizes its information sequentially in time and space, while the right hemisphere perceives its information all at once. Between the two hemihyperspheres of the universe, there is a 180 rotation of co-ordinate values. Between the hemispheres of the brain there is a 180 rotation of sequential co-ordinates. Between the brain and the outside world, there is a 180 rotation of sequential co-ordinates. Finally, in the OTHER hyperhemisphere of the universe, all events are patterns of energy at a velocity exceeding 2c. (c = speed of light.) Ideas are nothing but patterns of energy.

We are faced with a remarkable coincidence.

The brain corresponds to a miniature, topologically transformed model of the entire universe. A simple experiment with a lens proves incontrovertibly that the universe manifests the properties of a cosmic hologram. All parts of a hologram contain all the information of the whole hologram. Therefore, it is a logical necessity that the brain be a replica of the entire universe, and all we perceive in the real world is nothing but frequency defined patterns in the universal hologram. Conversely, we are living in a universal brain of divine dimensions. All that exists is an idea in the mind of God."

Remember? From Ancient Egypt:

"To him that was versed in the lore contained in the books of the 'double house of life' the future was as well known as the past, and neither time nor distance could limit the operations of his power; the mysteries of life and death were laid before him, and he could draw aside the veil which hid the secrets of fate and destiny from the knowledge of ordinary mortals." 2500 B.C. Amarna.

So you see, Cindy and I, two minds better than one, simultaneously solved the problem – Desire is the structure of matter and consciousness, which together make the Hieroglyph SOMA. SMA. Union. The Delphic Oracle tells us: Become what you R! The secret of our work? It was a film. I desired Cindy very much. Which movie buff wouldn't! Montage! Cut up desire into fragments, find the smallest fragment, look at it through a microscope under the light of a laser beam ...

Yes, it is holographic. What do you see? Everywhere? Osiris dead? Or Isis copulating with Osiris, in glorious technicolour, 3 dimensions, in millions of dimensions! The primal scene. My father's sperm entering my mother's egg! MY sperm entering MY egg! My birth is the birth of the universe. Horus is Risen! Again. Read all about it!

At that moment Matthew heard a rustling outside the door. He remembered he had forgotten to lock it. He fumbled for the keyboard switch and turned it off, but the image lingered on the screen. He furiously switched off the screen at the exact moment Cindy came through the door, as she saw the image fading away into a small dot. He turned on the swivel chair and looked at her defiantly.

She was wearing a tight-fitting blood-red sequined dress that was split down the front, from the neck to the floor, but was laced tightly together with a number of sequined black bows, very small at the top but which got larger and larger until the largest bow covered her crotch, and then they got smaller again as they approached her feet. It seemed at that moment to be the most erotic dress he'd ever seen in his life, because every time he looked at her, his eyes were automatically drawn down the bows, one by one ... it was a weird optical illusion, he couldn't stop his eyes moving downwards. As soon as he took his eyes away from her face and looked at her dress, his eyes were pulled down as if by arrows to her crotch ... and he noticed that the bow in her crotch was attached differently to the dress. Behind it there was no dress. It was *absente*. The bow was attached at each corner with small fasteners. He only had to flick it with a finger and it would come off and under it she was naked. Meta-*L'absence* awaiting Meta-*Presence*. It was the most infuriating dress he'd seen in his life, a mixture of glitz^{1} exotic cinematic high fashion and cheap glitz^{2} strip-club humour, and it made him very angry, he didn't know why. He'd been expecting the goddess Isis, perhaps, or at least her sister Nepthys, mother of the evil hound of heaven; not kitsch Hollywood junk.

'How do you like my dress? I designed it myself,' she said in a childish voice, seeing he was spell-bound by it. 'I wanted it to leave everything to the imagination.' But before Matthew could answer her or decide what she meant, she feigned mock indignation and held her arms high in the air with despair, Ψ, scolding him with a fake, haughty voice, 'Good heavens, Doctor Sutherland, it is far too late to be working, especially on a night like this, the night of my holographic strip-tease.'

With great confidence, she took his hand and led him to her room. She sat him down on the edge of the bed, before sitting down on the silver chair at her dressing table. Looking at herself in the mirror, she drawled, 'However. I have a problem. I want your help. It's quite serious. We girls have priorities.'

'Er ... you know I'll help if I can.'

'It's Georgina. She's reluctant to go through with my dance routine tonight. I don't know why, I'm sure she'll be okay when she's drunk a little, and drugged. I gave her a costume and she was very – how can I put it? Hesitant to wear it. And it was black too! Heavens above, it was her favourite colour, even if it was a bit unexpected, too close to the bone. And I don't mean the hip bone! But this is the point. I may have to manipulate her tonight, and I don't want you to be offended.'

She was playing so cool he felt like hitting her. 'How do you mean, manipulate?'

'I'm not sure yet. I know that when I get off on my trip, and this evening is very important to me, I may be very brutal with her. I'm not sure which way it'll go if I feel she's resisting me. I'd ask you to be brutal with her, which I'm not sure you would want. But what I'm really saying is two things. I may get aggressive with her, but if I do, remember, remember it is only a game. But if you feel the urge to be brutal with her, so much the better. Do it!' Silence. The seventh seal again ... opened like a pearl mouthed conch.

And then she looked down, not able to look him straight in the eye, and said coyly, 'Because, I admit it, it would turn me on awfully if I thought you really wanted to take her, you know, like you took me a couple of times, quite ruthlessly. I want you to *fuck* her. Don't hesitate, please don't hesitate. I want you to let go tonight and we can all have fun. I don't like talking about these things beforehand, I hate it, it goes against spontaneity, but I felt I had to, this special evening. I want you to *FUCK* her! Okay?'

Matthew decided not to be aggressive or evasive but to appear compliant. 'Well, I'll do my best,' and he felt very strange saying such a thing. If he could forget, or remember, the blue-bells, he couldn't remember which ... tears in her blue eyes. On a screen, yes, with Cindy, but in the flesh? It wasn't the fashion these days.

'Good. That's settled then. I'm not ready yet. Go and lie on your bed and imagine the sexiest things in the world, get yourself all worked up, but not too much. Wait for me so I can exceed them.' She stood up and struck a pose that was an order and an invitation, suggesting, 'You may kiss me and leave!' He did so, amazed how much he hated the vulgarity of her dress, amazed how easily he obeyed her. Dominatrix bitch!

In his room he found a black shirt and trousers on his bed, of finest silk, a black snakeskin belt with a silver buckle, encrusted with an Eye of Horus in blue-green enamelling. It was astounding the lengths Cindy went to to create her acts of theatre, the meticulous care she took with details! Discreetly hidden beneath the trousers were black silk socks and purple underpants. On the floor a pair of dark maroon slippers; on each a buckle of dark red enamel. Wings. A Chinese design resembling the red lacquered boxes within the boxes within ... within within.

Suddenly he felt an urge to take a bath, an irresistible surge of desire to be cleansed before the ritual. He undressed and slipped into his dressing gown, but just as he reached his bathroom, Georgina appeared inside the door, coming out, wearing a red towel. 'Oh! You're going for a bath? I'm sorry, I forgot to empty out the water, aren't I naughty?' She scuttled off towards her room, leaving him to wonder why she had used his bathroom anyway.

To make it worse, she'd used a bubble bath and the surface of the water was blurred, murky and unpleasant. His first thought was not to have a bath at all, but then he felt a strange compulsion. He slipped off his dressing gown and eased himself into the water, closed his eyes and went under the surface, holding his breath, and only surfaced again when he couldn't stay under any longer. He wanted to drown, drown, and yet to be saved at the last minute. In a word: SEX. He closed his eyes and wondered why he felt there ought to be a small window near the ceiling, with a faint green light in it. But he lay there, reconciled to fate, and luxuriated in the dank female smell and watched the murky, sultry fluid washing around his penis and he wondered why it was so proudly and determinedly erect.

Maybe he dozed. He heard a voice. 'It was a coincidence, a million to one chance. I'd hate to play you at poker. Inside your diamond you created a holograph, not an ordinary one but a double one. You had two lattices parallel to each other, one with normal carbon ions, the other, isotopic, the animate and the inanimate as you called them, and your laser penetrated between them, tangentially touching both. The laser interfered and resonated at the same time, in two different phases, with each of the two layers of carbon – both radioactive. Thus a convoluted involuted double holographic hologram. A scientific first!

Rays were deflected back onto the retina at the back of your eye, the two interfering waves, doubled because of resonance, in perfect holographic relationship with each other, so that the image on your retina also became, by chance, a double 3-D image. You saw it as 6-D. Six dimensions of reality at once. You saw the double Rdorje/rDorje Diamond of Tibetan mysticism. You saw not only the objective pyramid above the ground, but also the invisible other half, its double, underground, making the double pyramidine octohedron, two sets of three dimensions in parallel with each other, the sign for One to the power Infinity:

$$1^{\infty}$$

Is it one or infinity? As a hologram it is both. Almost as orgasmic as taking Cindy by surprise.

But the inside of your eye is spherical, like the sun, like the universe. On one side is a lens, on the other, the retina. Is not the photographic apparatus you use, a camera, designed on the principle of the human eye? An "in-camera" analogue? So again, two identical structures looking at each other. Inside that small space, it IS possible, if you were looking at it, to see the entire Milky Way in the heavens, a million light years in diameter. Is the inside of your eye a million light years in diameter? Of course not! But for you to SEE the entire Milky Way in your mind from inside your eye, is to see one infinitesimally small part of the Milky Way, which is reconstituted holographically by your brain, in your mind's eye, your consciousness, which is itself part, holographically, of the entire consciousness we know as The Whole ... ad infinitum.

You created inside your eye a self-imaged Narcissistic

Holograph, something no-one has yet been able to create experimentally, or even theoretically. A holograph of the EGO – imploding upon itself – a self-reflecting self, simultaneous on two levels as object and subject, one the actual, objective one, the other an analogue of the process of cosmo-genesis. Inside the sphere of your eye you recreated the creation of the Universe! You perceived, in a flash, the full immense ecstatic unfolding of the ONE, not into TWO, but THREE, the wholeness of the multi-octohedrally expanding spherical universe. The Big Bang itself. The orgasm of Isis making love to Osiris. The concave enfolding the convex. The perfect holo-movement. And between them – a pure idea. Is it any wonder we are forever frustrated? Sex, and life goes on?

Your eye became the magic eye of Horus, CREATING by yourself, in yourself, the wholeness of the universe's consciousness, in all its multi-dimensionality. You saw – in a word, or should I say, in a twinkling of an eye – god as dog; the dog star and the fifty-fifty chance of knowing the dogone Dogons! The outsight and outside of time, simultaneously. For a moment you returned into the womb and became one with the instant of your OWN conception. You became God creating another, innate embryonic potential of "it-him-her-self". You asked, where did I come from? A fatal question. Answer? From out of the minds of a man and a woman, imagining an image on a silvered screen, of a man and woman fucking.

In other words, you were masturbating like Atum when creating the transformation of one into two, and grasped the meaning of Cosmo-genesis. Three! A boring way of putting it, no?

As for Cindy. She's awakened you. Now you know two important new things; the direct knowledge of re-veiller: the

v e i l/e v i l

hologram; and the inevitability of death. You must thank her warmly. No-one else would be so generous in revealing such unpalatable truths. Call it passion and you'd be a fool. Call it the truth that truth and lies cannot exist without each other and there is hope for you. She too – by coincidence, paralleling your experiment – enabled you to glimpse the truth that God, if he exists, is a billion billion to the power a billion fragments, and only the human ego has the power, deluded though it may be, to think of him as a singular whole. Such is the wisdom of Amenhotep. Who, when the hidden chamber in the Great Pyramid is opened (it is happening now) will re-emerge in all his glory ... the shaman returns, he rises again after his trip ... '

When Matthew woke up he tried to remember John's words, knowing they were profoundly important, but by the time he found a pen and paper, he had forgotten every single word.

The clothes left by Cindy fitted perfectly. Presumably John's. Are we all so instantly replaceable? Yes! Can the lover, like time, be so easily refound? It seems so. Seems, madam? I have that within that passeth show, these but the trappings and the suits of woe ... A gentle tap on the door and Georgina poked her head into the room. 'Three minutes! After which, present yourself. The play within the play; become one with the psychopathic present!'

That sounded predictably ominous, but he decided to ignore it, feeling in a good mood really, because he'd decided already that the evening's events were going to be an unmitigated disaster. Why? Because he didn't care! He was going to enjoy himself because he had finally become INDIFFERENT. No longer diffident, he felt quite *de-bonne-eyre* (from a good eyrie) in his black outfit, and he recalled without malice how silly he'd felt the first time, dressed up as Von Sternberg. Tonight it would be different, and he was looking forward to making a grand entrance.

He'd arrived! He opened the door of the drawing room as stylishly as he could and edged inside. Unfortunately the room was in complete darkness and he could see nothing, and worst of all, no-one could see him. With some disappointment he closed the door behind him and stood still, waiting for his eyes to adjust to the darkness. He heard music, recorded with so much echo and reverberation, it was coming from the farthest reaches of the solar system, sweet, bland, spacey music, kitsch mystical spirals, its structure, if it had any, failing to impinge on his consciousness. It was relegated to the blackground immediately. A good sign for a start.

Suddenly a narrow beam of green light pierced the darkness, illuminating a transparent perspex pyramid on a black table. Georgina's sculpture! Egyptian hieroglyphs were lithographed on its sides. The light penetrated through one face but was then deflected by what he imagined were several small prisms suspended inside the pyramid by a very fine thread. Maybe they were small diamonds. He recalled another image – the many-faceted glass ball suspended near the ceiling in ballrooms, whence the name ball-room, turning and turning the light in a widening gyre, a miniature galaxy, spinning thousands of minute reflections over the faces of the moonstruck dancers below. Then another image – the Amarna fresco that Georgina loved so much, of Akhenaten with his Aten, his sacred solar disc, source of the waves of light falling on the people worshipping below.

The green light gradually faded and the music changed and a pure, innocent singing voice hovered over the heavy darkness; the aria *Oh for the Wings of a Dove*. Had he mentioned he'd heard it in the King's Chapel, the day before his third experiment? He didn't think so. But maybe ... remembering, forgetting, what the hell, now that time had become vertical and was hovering like a falcon on the wind ...

He poured himself a glass of the red wine on the table at his side. Superb! Uhmmm. More fun than a trip to the cinema! Incense sticks were burning. As the Mendelssohn faded away, other music faded over it, a Requiem, probably Palestrina or Monteverdi, plaintive and haunting. And then he heard Cindy's voice over it, clashing with it, reading from *The Book of Coming Forth By Day*. On and on ... words he knew now, in ambience if not in direct meaning. He poured himself another glass of wine, guessing it would be a long, slow, serpentine process, Cindy's act of materialisation, but he was determined to resist it as long as he could.

'... Isis and Nepthys work magic on thee. The glorious Isis was perfect in command and in speech, pronouncing mighty words of power, she made cunning her tongue, and her words failed not. And she avenged her brother's death. She sought

him without ceasing, she wandered round and round the earth crying her lamentations, and she alighted not until she found him. She overshadowed him, by creating wind with her two wings, made light to appear with her feathers, and she cried out the magic death cries for her brother. She made to rise up the helpless members of him whose heart had ceased, she drew from him his essence, and she made therefrom an heir...'

Ach! He'd heard it all before! Thanks to John he was one step ahead. Knowing that knowing had its moments, he let the words drift across his mind, barely making associations, trying to think of other things, until he wondered where Georgina had got to, fascinated to see the costume*she didn't* want to wear. For Georgina not to want to co-operate with Cindy hinted at revolt, at last, against the absolute power of her mistress and he felt suddenly quite emotional wondering if it was because she was really falling in love with him ... as he was still wanting so much to believe he had the right to fall in love with her ... if only Cindy's image could be erased from the screen ...

At the *Agnus Dei* the ray of green light materialised more strongly on the webs of darkness. Cindy seemed to be talking now about consciousness without an object preceding consciousness with an object, the necessity for the initiand to imagine himself *becoming* an Osiris. He'd been right! This incantation was merely the first step in the process of going through the thirteen fragments before reaching the obvious one. He was excited now, dying to see who the hell Osiris was, if not John, the other Osiris, Lord of the Dead, who had been communicating with him in so many mysterious ways; penetrating his mind with so many weird lucid dreams; his former dreams come true; the theatre of sado-masochism, Eros and Thanatos united in a deathly symbiosis.

The pencil of green light broadened, and a projected image appeared on the screen behind the stage; a photograph of a painted Osiris on the wall of a tomb. But the body of the god was black, which didn't seem right, and suddenly it moved. It was Georgina! She'd been holding a small screen in front of her face, on which the head of the God had been projected.

As she lowered the screen he saw her face, heavily made up, and once again he was taken aback to see how classically beautiful her features were, especially so heavily made-up. The goddess Isis, emerging from within Osiris, her mask.

Then Matthew noticed she was wearing the same black silk shirt, the same trousers as himself. He tried to see what she was wearing on her feet, but it was too dark. Why had she not wanted to wear this same outfit? Because it was a man's? Suddenly, the hands of the dead Osiris behind her moved. Cindy! Coming from behind and caressing Georgina's body.

He was concentrating on the involute – who was who and why – when his mind started to fall apart ... lose its centre ... disintegrate. He felt a sharp pain in his head, as he lost coincidence with himself. He closed his eyes.

And there it was, at last, so clear, so perfectly remembered. As he was, so unknowing, so young, so unprepared ... victim of the uprising ... his copse and the bluebells, translucent green stems and blue lanterns, each with its own small seed of light. For just a second it flashed into his mind, and froze. He looked down to see what he had lost and saw part of a torn red dress, some white cotton pants with blood on them, and a codeword flashed: Discarded: as he felt he had been, but written as *Disc R dead*, and a skin that looked as if it had been sloughed off from the body of a snake ... oozing poison ... negation. Death in life. And the drone of Cindy's words, somewhere, off screen: 'Christ is risen'. And he had fallen ...

He had become the watcher again, paradoxically for the first time. But who was *she*? It was the first time for both of them. An old man watching from behind a tree. With long hair. Binoculars reflecting the sun, otherwise invisible. Her father? That's how they'd seen him – the reflection from the two lenses ... the light reflecting ...

... but his body seemed to shoot off at a tangent, and to be floating in space. He made the effort to return to his body and as he did so, he regained a partial consciousness of the scene in front of him. He must have blacked out. There were a number of subtle changes in the decor. The screen at the back seemed to be a painted wall. It was a real temple. The paintings on the wall were REAL. But what surprised him most was to see Cindy and Georgina making love ... Cindy holding the sculpture ... slowly it went in and out ...

Georgina seemed to have been partially bound like a mummy; she couldn't move. White bandages beneath her black silk shirt and black trousers, now cut open. Cindy's red dress was now painted directly on her naked body, the perfect sadist, the perfect scarlet woman, the red skirt ripped away. White trousers with spats, or was it spattered in blood? The strapped phallus, beautiful, ruthless, invisible at the moment it would become real, only when inside her, touching, the object Georgina had made ... but it now seemed to be a double phallus, the knot of Isis, inside the vaginas of both girls simultaneously.

Cindy turned and he expected she would be mocking him, but she was inviting him to participate, to present himself. Her voice was still droning in the background – mere magnetic waves on a tape – and he felt uncomfortable rejecting the words, preferring to witness the erotic image of the two girls making love. There was still the concept haunting him of materialisation – presumably of Osiris? Osiris was the Nile, the caput Nili, but death too as well as life, as on disc thirteen, John had said ... but his mind was loosening, cut more effectively adrift by the chemical scalpel ...

Cindy had managed to turn Georgina over, and was penetrating her bottom from behind ... and Georgina's vagina was open in front of him. He slipped down his trousers and went towards her, determined *at last* to make love to her, until he realised, with acute alarm, that he only thought he was moving towards her. In fact, he couldn't move. His body wouldn't move. He was moving, only if he thought he was ... he turned and saw his body sitting behind him. But his desire drove him on, even further out of his own body, now prepared to take the risk. Nothing could stop him taking Georgina, as Cindy had permitted, as he had always wanted, even though he knew she didn't really want him, she didn't really desire him ... he plunged into her, nevertheless. Neverthemore.

Or at least he thought he did. He wasn't sure now. It seemed as if Cindy had tricked him at the last minute and he was inside her yet again. Yes, it was *her* cunt! The lips were swollen, throbbing. She was shaved after all. How did she always manage it? The bitch! The whore! Was she everywhere in every woman?

But there was no going back now. He thrust as brutally as he could. He would split her apart if necessary. She was so wet he slipped out, but he gripped harder and shortened his stroke until it was almost a spasm ... his spirit sucked upwards, he arched his back, falling back to hit harder ... the risen, the creative, the blind purpose of everything and nothing, using him and abusing him ... looked up and was amazed to see the night sky. Trees, a fan tracery of branches with leaves with eyes on them, eyelash webs full of dead insects, broken wings, mirrors within crystals, a railway station, a colonnade, several girls in white dresses made of stone, fluted, translucent ... and words were droning on like a sermon in a church, "*...things fall apart, the centre cannot hold, the falcon no longer hears the falconer ...* "

But what did it MEAN? Falcons SEE, they don't HEAR the falconer. In the beginning was the image not the word. Now it was John again possessing him ... but he thrust harder. Fuck the little bitch! If he murdered Cindy, would it matter? It would be John's fault. Everyone knew he could be a killer. The black room would be evidence enough. The photograph in the drawer of the girl, perhaps shaven, barely thirteen. Maybe fourteen. That should be the new legal age. It might have been Cindy photographed with a wide angle lens. 13 or 14mm. Lying on his back looking up at her fanny, shaved, legs apart ... fan tracery was something else.

The music became deafening. Wasn't it Bach's *St. Matthew's Passion*? He wasn't sure if it was, or whether he just wanted it to be, or felt it ought to be, or felt Cindy thought it ought to be, but the more he thrust into her hot twitching body, the more his mind became identical to the music. He'd never experienced music so tangibly erotic before. But on the screen, Cindy was dancing, her skin virtually stripped from her, and he heard John's words – she was proof, everything that was truly erotic was the kiss of death – and he saw her red lips sucking the translucent penis of Osiris and the white bones faded out of the image and blood oozed and the skin stretched and hardened and at the moment of its glory, the red cap unfolded like an umbrella, with white spots ...

He looked down to see if his body was still there and all he could see was the translucent phallus, strapped to Cindy, going into Georgina's bottom, or was it the other way round, he wasn't sure, but he didn't care. He must become indifferent, ruthless, just fucking, using enjoying abusing the goddess materialised in a thousand forms, a thousand eyes, pure flesh, and then he slipped another plane ... and it was even more painfully exciting and pleasurable.

Yes, this was it ... he may not have dared to imagine it, but he had dreamt it often enough. He thought he was being turned over, or SAW it happening and he couldn't prevent it. The two priestesses were lifting him like a corpse onto an altar. His body seemed to be wrapped from head to foot with bandages, binding him tightly. Then he saw Georgina kiss him on the lips affectionately ... and she left lipstick on his own lips ... he licked it ... and he felt warm inside.

But then he saw Cindy, with the phallus still strapped around her thighs, raise his legs in the air, and he couldn't escape. He felt the pain as she thrust inside him, 'as a fucking woman!' he thought she said, felt it going so deep it seemed to be coming out of his mouth. He was kissing Georgina and he felt upset that it was forcing their mouths apart and he wondered if this crystal phallus could speak! But then he realised she was really kissing the phallus she was imagining in his mouth and a thought flashed into his consciousness suddenly – it was betrayal in its deepest sense. Even her! But it didn't matter. The pleasure was immeasurable. She was biting his tongue thinking it was the tip of the penis, sucking hard to strip it of its fluid. And somewhere he was still inside a woman's body, defiantly not coming out. But was it really Georgina kissing him? Wearing a mask of Isis? Determined to see her face, he tore off the mask ...

Behind it a screen and on it, the girl with the blue and green stockings and shaved pubic hair. He'd been told it would be Georgina! Almost a child. The mask was alive and had crept like a spider's web over the screen and gelled into something thick and black. Mummified. He tore at it again. A man's face wearing lipstick. It was not her, but probably himself ... his face, now the face of an old man, and the hair seemed long like a woman's – yes, it was a face of Osiris, a tattered coat and a stick, and two serpents wrapped around it, copulating. One blue, one green, the two eyes of an insane but loving god. Cindy had materialised Osiris – but HE was Osiris. She had materialised Osiris-Matthew, which meant ...

But what he hadn't realised was that Cindy had intended all along to de-materialise Matthew ... cut his mind loose with the Aviamine, and had tricked him into thinking of materialisation *INSTEAD* ... to make him obsessed with the wrong train of thought, to send his mind along the wrong track ...

He was trying desperately hard now to think himself back into his own body, to catch onto the right train of thought again, but when he looked down at his body, he had the body of a woman, a celebrated harlot, and was astride the body of Matthew-Osiris, pushing down on the erect penis, and it was the most sensuous experience he'd known in his brief, fucked up life ... one long intense orgasm, in his arse, Cindy said later. Her first, like that anyway. The pain and the pleasure had been indistinguishable. Another of John's fucking holograms!

Suddenly a lousy little idea occurred to Matthew. A short synopsis for a movie. He had to *KILL* Cindy to liberate himself from her power, in order to make love to Georgina, and he hadn't really achieved this yet. The only weapon available to him, with which he might kill Cindy, was the crystal phallus. If he could get hold of it, *outside himself*, and crack it against the black table it would splinter and be as sharp as a knife. He set about the experiment immediately. Third time lucky!

But he couldn't construct a three dimensional image in his mind of their three bodies, and their location in normal time/space. Not forgetting the problem of the diamonds, the scene he was witnessing was two-dimensional. He couldn't see how he could get into a position to grasp the phallus and break it. He decided his only strategy was to create some kind of diversion, and the best way to do this was to feign an orgasm, as he knew Cindy could do. At last he could get his own back!

So he worked up to it, moaning, groaning, whimpering, until he rose upupupupup towards the climax, like a cobra rising to its full height before it strikes, and emitted a horrendous howl of poisonous delight, shouting and screaming as if he was enduring a cosmic contraction inside his arse, a black hole becoming a white dwarf in a billionth of a second, or the other way round, he couldn't remember, simulating as best he knew how the orgasm of a lifetime.*Quel menteur! Un très grand petit-mort!* But the phallus, still thrusting inside him, was still there, he'd merely imagined it OUTSIDE, broken, splintered ... now, not his, but hers, cheated again, falling, falling, the fall, a thunderous roar of ecstatic violent nuclear disintegration, something not imagined yet, something not calculated for ... searing through the cusp, an accident, the apocalypse, the end of the world, splintering into fourteen pieces. There was a piercing shaft of incandescent green light that came from nowhere. And everywhere. His body was torn apart ... blown into a billion shimmerings of reflected light. Pure energy. But it was like in dream. He was still there watching! Someone would film the end of the world, surely?

"Some of the images in this bulletin, you might find disturbing."

Yet, by some strange coincidence, he managed to escape the shaft of the death ray, through premonition! Somehow he leapt up out of himself, as if he had wings, and hovered outside himself, just before, except that he could not be sure if it was himself, after all, hovering ... it was just pure hovering, discarded wings crucified on a cross of time. A cross of words on a screen needing to be read but no program to translate them ... or voyeur to desire them. At least he had got rid of his body. Probably. Become author.

Or had he been fooled again by Cindy and his blind desire for her? Was this merely the point in the program called Virtual Death? The Diamond Doors of Hades were opening in front of his third eye? He was trapped inside his third diamond and Cindy was about to press the switch. Was it too late? He would aim at one last emotion! Maybe even another erection.

Yes! One last! Fear becoming anger, perhaps to scare her off, he decided he must appear rational, angry, because that is what reason breeds, to be mortified with rage, angry that Cindy had *NOT* allowed him to make love to Georgina after all. He dug his fingers into the flesh until he drew blood. He went down on his knees and drank it from her. Sucked so hard, skin came off in his teeth. Clutching her white pants in his fingers, torn, he would tear her into as many fragments as he had been torn ... albeit by his own screen dream. He bit into her at the split second he felt other teeth bite into his left shoulder, just as he was turning round, sensing something was there, something evil, consuming its own body, but it was too late ...

Then he went limp and fell, and all hovering ceased, and all emotion subsided and became irrelevant.

... after a short time, the outer boundaries of self melting away and the space inside his body expanding at the speed of light, towards the outermost reaches of the galaxy ... unexpectedly calm and peaceful, accomplished, and imagining he might have appeared beautiful to anyone watching him. At the centre of the space that had stretched him beyond the galaxy of his own ego, quite still, was a small green seed, code-named HOPE, that might germinate into a new tree of light, inside a diamond crystal womb ... somewhere.

Else.

★

EPILOG

"The whole course of this narrative
resembles,
and was meant to resemble,
a caduceus
wreathed about with meandering ornaments,
or the shaft of a tree's stem
hung round and surmounted
with some vagrant parasitical plant."

Suspiria de Profundis
— Thomas de Quincey

EPILOG

"Every orgasm is the death of a king."

"Love's Body"
Norman O. Brown

∇

But Cindy had been so excited pursuing her orgasm, she'd got the timing wrong. She laid her platinum blonde bob on Matthew's chest, only to find he was already dead. 'Sod it! I should never allow sex to distract me from the *real* work. Now I've only one chance ... rigor mortis ... '

She turned the body on its back, laid the hands next to the sides, the legs straight, the shrunken itals in place. He seemed peaceful enough in repose, a good enough Osiris. She heaved Georgina on top of him until she lay spread-eagled (spread-falconed might be more apt) on top of Matthew's body, her limbs loose and helpless. She caressed Matthew's genitals, but there was no more reaction. She administered another small dose of Erotamine to Georgina; oil placed directly into the vagina ...

Looking up *rigor mortis* in the Encyclopaedophiliac Britannic she discovered it usually set in after half an hour.

To pass the time, she set about making herself glamorous again, with lipstick where she liked it, lips, nipples, the edge of every orifice. She hated being dishevelled and unprepared at any time, but especially in the humiliating role of voyeur; masochism she'd always preferred to avoid. She'd let George whip her from time to time but only to allow *her* momentary release from the aggression building up in the system, which she'd find other ways of expressing. Like refusing to cook ...

She felt Matthew's arm. It was becoming hard. She caressed Georgina's clitoris to make sure her vagina was wet, amazed to see her hand move of its own accord and start masturbating herself in her sleep. 'That's my girl!' she purred. Patiently she waited, and soon enough, Matthew's penis became hard, his last stand against the rigours of death. When he was a real stiff, so to speak, she manipulated him in place, spread Georgina's legs, and Matthew, like a dream come true, slipped effortlessly inside her. But wanting to be sure of an ejaculation, she took the crystal phallus and eased it into Matthew's bottom, remembering Lawrence of Arabia and the dead Turkish soldiers on the desert wasteland, and the destroyed railway engine on its side. It's amazing the ineradicable images that flash into the mind at odd times ...

He ejaculated; or at least there was an ejaculation, he being presumed not to be there. Cindy pushed him hard against Georgina's body to make sure the precious fluid didn't escape. She arranged their bodies so Matthew's penis remained inside her while she continued to caress Georgina's clitoris, remembering that the Greek word *kleitoris* meant *divine, famous, goddess-like*, hoping that the gentle throbbing movements would increase the chances of the semen reaching her womb. Her arms flapped, like wings. 'If only I could know what you are dreaming!' Cindy murmured, lovingly kissing her on the cheek. She drew up a chair next to them and drank her wine. Georgina was in fact dreaming ...

... her KA floats away from her body and takes the form of a beautiful pure black iridescent falcon, with turquoise-blue eyes. It hovers over the dying body of Osiris until, at the moment of death, his soul also takes the form of a falcon, and the two falcons with their human heads fly higher and higher into the infinite black dimension of space ... flying in perfect circles, occasionally casting a glance downwards towards the embryonic world of matter, but mostly watching each other, waiting, waiting for the precise moment of pure purpose, ecstatically happy to share a single, indivisible holographic dream ... until the perfect moment is reached. Oh the achieve of, the mastery of the thing ... Now! The crack in the shell of time, the infinitesimal fragment of coincidence that is ideal for mating. The female hovers, mimicking eternity, and the male descends silently, its outstretched talons momentarily absolved of the necessity for killing, coming to rest gently on the feathered beauty of her great wings, and they mate, in flight, re-ascribing the perfect arched line, the eye-brow on the interface, and at the moment of ejaculation, the male falcon's *double* becomes ecstatic and slips out of the sacred dimension and lapses and falls into a single human perception, momentarily transforming the female falcon into a girl, made of stone, with the features of a daughter of Akhenaten ... becoming a mere girl again, a momentary lapse into reason, and she can savour the lingering pain of the sudden blow, her loins shuddering, forgetting the greater pain that will come later, the new life struggling to be born.

She is pregnant, with a god ... but who was the father of the child, John or Amenhotep, as the door is opened on the hidden chamber, allowing the KHU of the great shaman to escape ...

This scene of the mystery completed, Cindy carried Georgina to her bed, then went to her own bedroom and from her secret laboratory behind the concealed Green Door, her wardrobe room, she brought out the super-computer terminal and apparatus necessary to transform Matthew's mind, still lingering over the flesh of his brain, into a laser ... it was simple really, now that the Aviamine had primed the brain. She placed the two graphite electrodes on his forehead, and to make sure of a good contact, she spat on them first. The magnetic scan of mentality would be transformed into digital data and stored on the computer's fourteen gigabyte Optical Disc. She pressed the switch, sat back and watched. Matthew's mind filled thirteen gigabytes. Only thirteen?

She connected the computer to the transmitter, refocusing the laser into the centre of a pyramid-shaped diamond with a green flaw, a lattice of a hitherto undiscovered radioactive carbon isotope. She opened the curtains and focused the beam directly towards the submissive Black Dwarf twin-star of the dominatrix Sirius, where renegade Priests of the Aten heresy meditate upon attachment. Touching a nipple as she did so ... she was still aroused... she pressed the master switch. It took thirteen minutes to send Matthew's entire consciousness to the Sirius Complex. 'Good! The initiation was reasonably complete ... '

Sirius, the star of Isis, her favourite star, she'd code-named *Jean Harlot*. The twin star, the invisible black dwarf, where primal consciousness had emerged, she had code-named *Salomé*, to deceive people.

Finally, she went to bed.

But she was restless, couldn't sleep, worrying about her irrational desire to make Georgina pregnant, thinking out loud to the Atens, who missed nothing anyway, 'It's amazing the lengths we human beings go to sometimes, to procreate the human race!'

... he stays watching from behind the tree, he has all eternity.

She slept half an hour, but it was already dawn. She rose and dressed in a white cotton nurse's uniform and went down to the kitchen, took a *certain* number of containers from the deep freeze and the instruments from a locked drawer, went into the drawing room and started on Matthew's body; a bit discoloured, skin discomposing, face looking abjectly discouraged, all life discontinued; his discomposure was positively discombobulating ...

But not at all disconcerted, she made the incisions, starting in the back of his neck, and drained off a number of liquids; from the spinal column, from the brain, from the lymph glands in the neck, extracting all the fluids she needed, especially urine from the bladder. In these fluids would be the various drugs synthesised in the body from the Aviamine. Meta-psychedelics! The smartest of all smart drugs. Finally she cut the body skilfully into the fourteen parts, catching as much of the blood as possible, sealing it in the thirteen containers.

The job done, she phoned. 'Hello, sweetheart! The body is available for collection in the drawing room. I'm unexpectedly tired and going to bed. Everything useful has been removed. I'll leave the front door open. George is drugged and won't wake for hours, dreaming on Erotamine, and probably about John. There was definitely a scene in the copse. Any news yet? Surely he's on his way back now, now they're close to opening the Imhotep chamber?'

Passing Matthew's room, she glanced inside. The lid of the lacquered box was open. Inside, only the bandages. 'My God, the bird has flown!' she said, immediately worried. 'So they're still up to their old tricks! So it *was* Imhotep all the time, reincarnating as Amenhotep! But one day, watch out, old man, I'll get equal, I'll get my revenge!'

... he shuffles, unperturbed. In his mind, alone, would the two halves of the hologram ... come ... together.

She went to bed and slept, not waking until just before lunch.

Georgina was still sleeping. The remains of Matthew's body had been removed. She made herself a light vegan lunch and sat in the kitchen drinking herbal tea. She went to her room and changed into a long, loose black dress; under the dress, quite naked. She put a large diamanté brooch in her hair, in the shape of the Udjat Eye of Horus. Kitsch junk, but what the hell. John bought it in the Paris flea market. Fourteen francs. Maybe thirteen.

In the drawing room she opened the curtains and removed the paraphernalia of her recent show, moved her favourite carpet onto the dais near the window, sat down and relaxed. After placing a pad of blank paper next to it and the fourteen-carat gold-nibbed pen she used for her automatic writing, she slipped easily into trance, focusing her consciousness into receptive mode. Im*media*tely she received a message that Matthew was well on his way and enjoying the trip, but was still self-conscious, his adamantine ego refusing to fully give up the ghost. The robot was approaching the door and the optic fibre camera was being set up to penetrate under the broken corner. In a hologram, even a broken corner will reveal the whole. Imhotep was preparing himself for the moment of enlightenment.

But she was also informed that Georgina had written a letter to Matthew on the computer and the access code was AST, the Egyptian name of Isis. Naughty girl! She ran up to John's room, found a disc marked in hieroglyphics, "NOTHING", and sat back to read what Georgina had written:

Dearest Matthew, I have committed The Cardinal Sin or should I say The High Priestess's Sin! Grown too fond of you. What I want to tell you is the truth, provoked in the copse ... John's becoming Amenhotep but ... why say but when ...

No! Then ...

We ...

Cindy was interrupted by the phone. Did she need the fourteenth fragment again? 'Er ... maybe, better deep freeze it; with the testes and sperm. Might come in handy!'

She went back to John's room, took out Georgina's disc, murmuring, *probably all romantic drivel,* and put in John's Disc Fourteen. She'd received a code in her sleep, THERISEN, to access a section dealing with Im/Amenhotep, part diary, letter, reflection, a collage-montage of fragments received directly on the computer from the R-Field connection after John's trip to Egypt to try to infiltrate and/or subvert the work there.

... Imhotep has done it again, another incarnation in the human experiment. Of course we know about his later incarnation as Amenhotep during the Amarna period, and Tiresias in Greece, both humorous holographic reflections of Oedipus, and more recent hauntings of the minds of Eliot and Freud are well documented. Also the re-revelation of Holography, imaged by lasers, giving the whole story in a flash to Dennis Gabor watching a tennis match. Here, there'd been a slip in the decoding of L'ASAR; Lazarus being the Signifier of Reincarnation itself ... but apparently Amenhotep has recently lapsed. Romance! Meritaten has always been his favourite daughter, loving her beyond the accepted brief of a father's love, she being a true love-child between himself and Nefertiti, having de-virginated the Queen ceremoniously at her wedding with Akhenaten, according to the Rites of the temple of Mittani, where she had been brought up.

In the act of receiving her, he had fallen in love with her but also made her pregnant. Anyway, Akhenaten's preference for homosexuality, as well as his monotheism, had put many things into doubt. The truth was gossip, the rest was history.

... until recently Amenhotep recognised Meritaten again, reincarnated in Georgina. There are no incest taboos when it comes to Reincarnated Beings – mere holographic dreams after all! He had used a certain John in the copse to open the doors physically ...

... while Georgina had been travelling on the train that night, salope, dreaming, John's sperm was travelling up one of the internal branch-lines of her Fallopian tubes. Amenhotep could provoke ovulation even at the wrong time. There had only been some doubt as to which line to take. The left or the right, or both to make sure? Two simultaneous journeys ...

... precisely at the instant of the experiment, of which it is rumoured there may have been two, or more, even a third: everything had become simultaneously holographic ...

... the sperm united with the ovum, just as John's consciousness was discharged from his brain at the moment he'd imagined materialising Amenhotep, so the two nuclei fused, (what a love story!) and at that moment Amenhotep struck with the psychic gene scalpel ... the only moment he had to strike ... as the first two cells fused and then separated, imprinting his new destiny on the Horus Child, holographically restructuring the DNA at its moment of first un-enfoldment. Now the child would be HIS forevei, the seeds of his divine consciousness perfectly, astrologically synchronised on another hologram of realised earthly time ...

... as in one of his former incarnations, as the Archangel Gabriel, when there had been a complex cover-up there by poor old Joseph, trying to conceal the role of the High Priest. And all kinds of bog-ups in the further theory of re-incarnation, corrupted to *reserection*, (sic), but the story had sold well. The greatest story ever told. What a novel that might make, reinvented? Amenhotep had even thought of reincarnating himself as a novelist. Maybe John?

Cindy laughed! Damn you, John! She would read the whole text later. He'd inserted fragments of a novel into their work, either to confuse Matthew, or amuse the Atens. But then she wondered. Could it not be true?

Tried to think of other things but couldn't ...

Could it not be NOTHING BUT? Nothing but a montage of events, images, reflections, that occur at the moment of the opening of the door to the inner chamber in the Cheops Pyramid? Was this not about to happen any second now! Was not that little robot, that little train of thought, already standing erect in front of the door? Embodying a virtual on-screen cinemontage of images, the single dream that was

John; his dream of being the first to penetrate through the stone, confront Imhotep, and become his new adept, initiated and prepared, reading the new texts as they were newly unfurled? His single dream seen holographically ...

And the presence, watching, in the copse? The third component, the reality of the human condition, the voyeur, his reason; guilt ... his guilt at seducing Georgina?

That was it. All this was writing, this tract, was a calculated distraction by John, to fool her, to disctract her from the most important event to occur to the human race since Imhotep first materialised himself in the Great Pyramid five thousand years ago, after sending the plans and technology by hypno-telepathy; hypno-telepathy knowing no distance; from whence the recent phase of the cosmic experiment, known as the human race, had begun ...

And now? Now, almost five thousand years later, the Companions of Horus would see for themselves again ...

But what about Georgina's pregnancy? Had Imhotep, the greatest mental traveller of all time, stolen the child? *Her* child? Maybe Imhotep had won again, but*she* would be the one bringing the child up! God help him! While Georgina waxed artistic in her studio ...

Cindy went back to the previous disc and read the rest of Georgina's letter. Clearly the pregnancy had made her behave like a sentimental fool. But she would always love her ... she was amused by some of the phrases Georgina had used: *Cindy? The Mata Hari of the Quantum Jump Cult:* describing her exploits at Oxford in the snooty Physics department. The way George called herself, *A mere Lay-Woman when it comes to Extraterrestrials like Cindy.*

Cindy went back to John's disc, knowing there might be a final epilogue. She typed in:

[E] [P] [I] [L] [O] [G]

and there it was ... What's in the chamber? Two rooms. (It might at first appear to be one and to be empty!) In the other one is the library of Imhotep. After reading his work, if they can translate the hieroglyphs – I will gladly help – human kind will never be the same again. Everything we have clung to in defence of reason and self-consciousness will be destroyed. Forever. The father takes the virginity of his daughter ... Most of the human race will fail the experiment and become, overnight, insane and irrelevant.

In this so-called library will be a stele, on which a scene will depict the use of pyramid-shaped crystals used to focus the mentalised-lasers. Also in this second *other* room, which will take time to find, will be the tomb of the pharaoh. But here's the joke! (Apart from the falcon-headed man!)

It will NOT be the tomb of Cheops after all, but Chephren, the builder of the second pyramid. Not Khufu but KhafRe. Which makes perfect sense: par-az-ard; holographically!

In the Second Great Pyramid of Chephren, there is nothing. It's a *front,* as the drug smugglers call it! After his father Khufu died, Chephren hit on the brilliant idea of opening up a new chamber in the already existing pyramid, which was already built, already *real,* and having himself, and the magician Imhotep's library, placed inside the Khufu Pyramid, where no-one would dream of looking for it. No wonder his luscious Sphinx, poised awaiting copulation – Hi there, Cindy! – was known for its enigmatic smile!

In Imhotep's library are two seminal texts, which will do all the damage. The Book of Thoth, which will explain how language was sent here digitally from Digitaria, Sirius B, the Black Dwarf: how it appeared overnight, so to speak, even before the First Dynasty. The second murderous text is The Book of the Companions of Horus, the Shemsu, that mysterious pre-Dynastic race that was supposed to have ruled Egypt for the previous 30,000 years. Their history was known in detail by the adepts of the First Dynasty, we are told in the Pyramid Texts, although this history was subsequently lost. However, and here is the charm of the problem, this civilisation of the Companions of Horus left not a single trace anywhere on this earth. In the material sense!

No matter ...

We are soon to learn of this history, which obviously occurred elsewhere in our Ga Lactic Milky Way Galaxy, before they came here, with HORUS the leader of the race of winged beings; arriving in their translucent pyramid-shaped space-craft; hover-craft of course, hovering over the earth and descending vertically, as does the humble Kestrel falcon! A colony of Lesser Kestrels has nested in Luxor since and long before our post-dynastic time began and the Kestrel is the only falcon in the world that hovers. It's just a question of interpreting the hieroglyphs realistically; backwards rather than forwards. As something quite charmingly real! The crossing having been made. No wonder the Sphinx, which has no face, the features eaten away, not by wind or water or gold, but artillery shells, is known for its smile ... what better definition of the rationalist's embarrassed approach to the subversive power of magic?

It is because of loneliness that I write, and because I write, I am lonely.

But we must smile, for tomorrow the soul sets sail. Au revoir, pour voir ... ma petite lazarette!

Cindy did indeed smile. John was probably right about the hidden chamber's contents. He'd usually been right in the past.

When Georgina awoke, she found a letter from Matthew, obviously written on John's computer:

Dear Isis and Nepthys – I'm writing this before the rite of the great materialisation. I imagine I'll be feeling rather spaced out later on so I decided to write now, while I'm Cosmos Mentis. I didn't tell you but I have to leave for Cambridge on the early train tomorrow morning.

If tonight is anything like our 'previous intellectual debates on the philosophical meaning of sexual initiation', as you called it, Cindy, or, you Georgina, 'another chapter in Cindy's novel about the return of the great goddess in all her Gory', I'm sure that at 'some moment when the moon was blood', a moment of pure coincidence no doubt, I will again have left my body and imagined myself flying round the universe as a moonbeam composed of two hundred million green-headed spermatozoa ... not on the Milky Way, but some jade river of the cosmic mind ...

Suffice it to say I return to Cambridge a changed man. Flying like Puck around the world in forty minutes, I've seen many wonderful things and I'm very grateful to you both. This period of initiation has been an extraordinary experience. Suffice it to say I'll never be the same man again. And yes – it was all quite real. In time I will find the code and process the meaning of it all. Meanwhile I am left only with a sense of certainty – of knowledge – of seeing through and beyond; I went there and came back, I died and I was reborn. How sweet it must be to die!

I'll be back, if I'm invited? I don't know how to put this – but I love you both – terribly, passionately; and it's very painful, just the thought of being apart from you. I'll phone in the next few days – meanwhile keep me informed if there are any developments with John. I just know I will meet him one day, and we will recognise each other instantly. If only I see his face reflected in a half silvered mirror! (Like the one in the station waiting room! That's seen better years!)

My love to you both; scared, enlightened, mystified, confused but chastened;
Matthew.

She folded up the letter and put it away in a secret drawer in her desk ... the lazarette as John had called it, her Georgian gold-leaf decorated glory hole, but he'd also used that name for her arse ... which he preferred etched in gold ... still ... where was he now, the bugger? He'd been away with Georgina for some time ... why had he left so early if she was taking the night train? She'd kill him when he got back, if he'd been up to no good with Georgina ... she'd seen it coming for some time ... kill him ... especially as she was feeling so fragile, almost as if the whole sad earth was having her final period, Gaia on the threshold of an irreversible menopause ... the eclipse threatening her as they did always ... threatening to split her as light is split by a prism ... which made her think of the image on the disc cover ... maybe she'd put on the *Pink Floyd* disc to counter the purple aura around her body, which she could feel, created by her jealousy ...

... she put the music very loud ... she never liked being jealous of Georgina. John could go to hell, but Georgina ... what was she up to she wondered ...

She was ready now, she told John. She had accepted her role, to give up her virginity. To him ...

John telephoned the house but there was no reply. They didn't have much time. There was the question of parallax on the laser set up in the laboratory, aimed at the Black Dwarf looping Sirius. He drove quickly to the copse, with Georgina at his side, and was pleased to find the hole in the tree was empty. He took out the vine leaves ...

... as Matthew switched on his master computer for the experiment with the third pyramidine diamond crystal ...

... putting the Shiraz prayer carpet on the grass, on John's favourite spot, and after that, he took hold of her, tied her down to the stakes he'd previously hammered into the ground. He worked in silence. Her white dress reflected in the moonlight, soon to fade with the eclipsing of the light. Spread-eagled, he kissed her, making her wet, supple, suppliant. Then, as they had agreed, rather harshly: was it not necessary: he broke through into her. Split the veil. Withdrew and relaxed. Dried the blood as much as he could. Later, the time would be right to consummate the rite completely, as Georgina expected. As John had been told; and not questioned ...

... as Cindy prepared the apparatus ...

... and relaxed in the lotus position, listening to the exquisite music of the wind in the trees. It took him some time, meditating on fullness, to reach a feeling of emptiness. Fullness being Amenhotep and emptiness being himself. His holographic paradigm ...

... Matthew looked through the dark glass, into the heart of his diamond ...

... the optic fibre from the robot snaking along the ground, along the rough white stone, heading for the broken corner of the portcullis door with its two copper handles, it's optic fibre laser light not yet turned on ...

... in the abject darkness inside, hovering over the mummified body of Pharaoh Chephren, his body being elsewhere, a *Khu* was awaiting its moment ... awaiting the light, awaiting the instant he had predicted so precisely, three times fourteen hundred years before ... when he would return, open the eye of Horus and turn on the world ...

... but there were sensual images starting to pervade, especially the image of Georgina, tied down waiting for him, and the look on her face as he had taken her, torn the skin and made love to her, just a few strokes, so slowly and so longingly; knowing that even now she was beyond him and unreachable, waiting for him to take her the whole way; beyond him but nevertheless, worthy of sacrifice, essentially loveable. The image kept returning just when he thought he was reaching avoidance. He'd not slept on the train, avoiding dreams, when he knew he would be vulnerable. So now, he soon fell asleep. At the instant the 2-Tri-Tiresaminic acid hit his brain ...

... and Matthew's laser penetrated the primaeval organic lattices of his diamond crystal ...

... and Cindy's fingers pressed on the switch, caressing it gently as she liked to caress Georgina's clitoris ...

... and the light of the optic fibre camera flicked on, just inside the flaw in the broken door ...

... as a vertical montage of images took off into outer space, at the precise time the era of Osiris came to a close ... and the era of Horus was born ... to remind everyone ...

... as Amenhotep prepared to lift off, a faint green shadow, as mysterious and delicate as a metamorphosing green-fly, as translucent as a dew drop, shimmering like an eye, a leaf touching the wing of a butterfly, or a peacock roused by desire. Rising rising ... as the blood fell ... but Amenhotep was clinging ... would he not leave after all? Clinging to the image of Georgina, her face in the mirror as she was preparing for the previous evening's dance ... oh, how lovely she had looked, her eyes tinged with sorrow ... the image of her mother, especially the two holographically interfaced eyes, one open and the other seemingly blind, unpainted, unfinished, but that was mere artistic licence, a mere whim of the sculptor, mere metaphor; and the boyish profile ... even gods can be sentimental ...

... soon, reluctantly, he forced the image to fade out of its half of the hologram, knowing there would be consolation, albeit on another plane, now that he would see the unreflected face of Meritaten, awaiting him elsewhere. She would cleanse him after his temporary lapse into virtual linear time ... this long sleep of reason, that might have been a few seconds in someone else's dream-time ...

... as John, the Tiresiamine hitting the centres in the brain stem, his brain's Alpha waves momentarily hovering and allowing the R waves to dominate, and simultaneity to become the ruling paradigm, having brought Georgina up and up and up with him to hit a moment of absence together, ejaculated ...

... as Horus opened his wings and hovered again, in perfect holographic simultaneity with himself ... with a tendency to rise on the thermals of romance ...

Я

The experiment was over. He had seen it all, on three times three dimensions of time and space, as it had been foretold. Rising towards the source of joy, we achieve it by falling ...

His mission complete, he fused back into the tree, disappeared into its trunk and rose with the sap to the top of the highest branches, to the tips of the highest leaves, where they were split into fine silver blonde hairs by the north wind, reflecting all the colours of the rainbow, and as shamans do, on the adamantine beam of insight, no longer eclipsed by reason, took off ...

... to Digitaria, the hidden twin of Sirius, the Black Dwarf.

∇

★

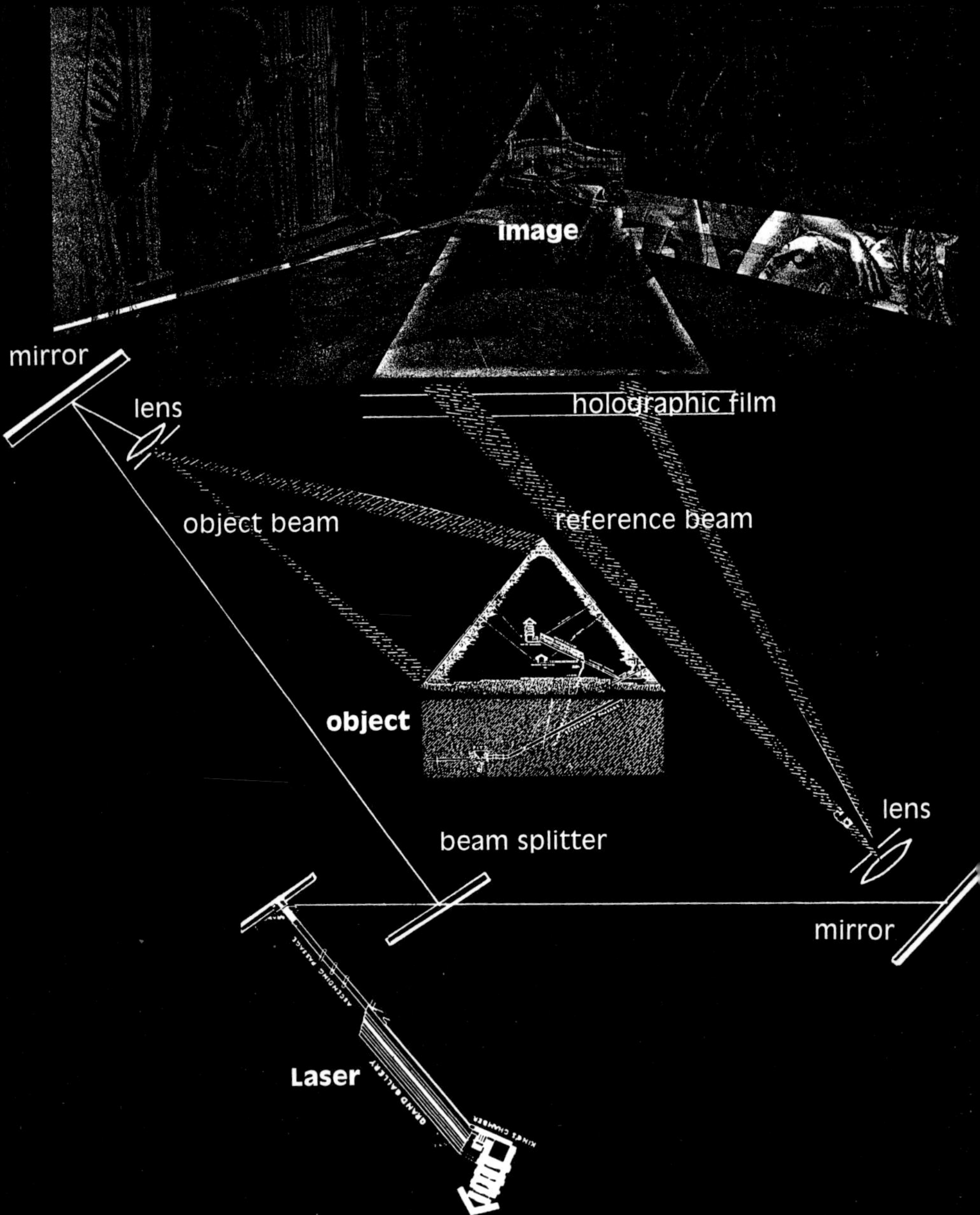

Making a hologram:1995